SAINT THOMAS AQUINAS

SUMMA THEOLOGIAE
SUPPLEMENTUM, 69-99

Translated by Fr. Laurence Shapcote, OP

SUMMA THEOLOGIAE

Volume 22
Latin/English Edition of the Works of St. Thomas Aquinas

Aquinas Institute, Inc.
Green Bay, Wisconsin
2017

This printing was funded in part by donations made in memory of:
Marcus Berquist, Rose Johanna Trumbull, John and Mary Deignan,
Thomas and Eleanor Sullivan, Ann C. Arcidi, and Fr. John T. Feeney and his sister Mary

This printing was also made possible by donations from Kevin Bergdorf, Patricia Lynch,
and John Mortensen; and by donations made in honor of Fr. Brian McMaster,
Dr. Brian Cutter, and in gratitude to the Very Rev. Romanus Cessario, OP, STM

Published with the ecclesiastical approval of
The Most Reverend David L. Ricken, DD, JCL
Bishop of Green Bay
Given on July 16, 2017

Thomas Aquinas, St., 1225?–1274
Summa Theologiae Supplementum, 69-99 / Saint Thomas Aquinas; edited by The Aquinas Institute;
translated by Fr. Laurence Shapcote, OP
p. 432 cm.
ISBN 978-1-62340-021-7

1. Thomas, Aquinas, Saint, 1225?–1274 — Summa theologiae — Supplementum — 69-99. 2. Catholic Church — Doctrines
— Early works to 1800. 3. Theology, Doctrinal — Early works to 1800. I. Title. II. Series

BX1749.T512 2015
230´.2--dc23   2015947392

Notes on the Text

Latin Text of St. Thomas
The Latin text used in this volume is based on the Leonine Edition, transcribed and revised by The Aquinas Institute.

English Translation of St. Thomas
The English translation of the Summa Theologiae was prepared by Fr. Laurence Shapcote, op (1864-1947), of the English Dominican Province. It has been edited and revised by The Aquinas Institute.

The Aquinas Institute requests your assistance in the continued perfection of these texts.
If you discover any errors, please send us a note by email: editor@theaquinasinstitute.org

DEDICATED WITH LOVE TO
OUR LADY OF MT. CARMEL

Contents

SUMMA THEOLOGIAE
SUPPLEMENTUM, 69-99

QUESTION 69

THE PLACE OF SOULS AFTER DEATH

Post hoc agendum est de his quae spectant ad tractatum resurrectionis. Postquam enim dictum est de sacramentis, quibus homo liberatur a morte culpae, consequenter dicendum est de resurrectione, per quam homo liberatur a morte poenae.

Circa tractatum autem resurrectionis tria consideranda sunt: scilicet praecedentia resurrectionem, concomitantia, et sequentia. Et ideo primo dicendum est de his quae, pro parte quamvis non ex toto, resurrectionem praecedunt; secundo, de ipsa resurrectione et circumstantibus eam; tertio, de his quae eam sequuntur.

Praecedentium autem resurrectionem prima consideratio est de receptaculis animarum post mortem eis assignatis; secundo, de qualitate, et poena animarum separatarum eis ab igne inflicta; tertio, de suffragiis quibus animae defunctorum a vivis adiuvantur; quarto, de orationibus sanctorum in patria existentium; quinto, de signis iudicium generale praecedentibus; sexto, de igne ultimae conflagrationis mundi, qui faciem Iudicis praecedet.

Circa primum quaeruntur septem.

Primo: utrum animabus post mortem receptacula assignentur.

Secundo: utrum statim post mortem ad ipsa animae deducantur.

Tertio: utrum de ipsis locis egredi valeant.

Quarto: utrum limbus inferni sit idem quod sinus Abrahae.

Quinto: utrum limbus sit idem quod infernus damnatorum.

Sexto: utrum limbus puerorum sit idem quod limbus Patrum.

Septimo: utrum tot receptacula debeant distingui.

In sequence to the foregoing we must treat of matters concerning the state of resurrection: for after speaking of the sacraments whereby man is delivered from the death of sin, we must next speak of the resurrection whereby man is delivered from the death of punishment.

The treatise on the resurrection offers a threefold consideration: namely, the things that precede, those that accompany, and those that follow the resurrection. Consequently, we must speak: (1) Of those things which partly, though not wholly, precede the resurrection; (2) Of the resurrection itself and its circumstances; (3) Of the things which follow it.

Among the things which precede the resurrection we must consider: (1) The places appointed for the reception of bodies after death; (2) The quality of separated souls, and the punishment inflicted on them by fire; (3) The suffrages whereby the souls of the departed are assisted by the living; (4) The prayers of the saints in heaven; (5) The signs preceding the general judgment; (6) The fire of the world's final conflagration, which will precede the appearance of the Judge.

Under the first head there are seven points of inquiry:

(1) Whether any places are appointed to receive souls after death?

(2) Whether souls are conveyed there immediately after death?

(3) Whether they are able to leave those places?

(4) Whether the limbo of hell is the same as Abraham's bosom?

(5) Whether limbo is the same as the hell of the damned?

(6) Whether the limbo of the patriarchs is the same as the limbo of children?

(7) Whether so many places should be distinguished?

Article 1

Whether Places Are Appointed to Receive Souls after Death?

AD PRIMUM SIC PROCEDITUR. Videtur quod animabus post mortem receptacula non assignentur. Sicut enim dicit Boetius, in libro *de Hebdonad, communis animi conceptio est apud sapientes incorporalia in loco non esse.* Cui concordat quod Augustinus dicit, XII *super Genesis ad litteram: Cito quidem responderi potest ad corporalia loca animam non ferri nisi Cum aliquo corpore.* Sed

OBJECTION 1: It would seem that places are not appointed to receive souls after death. For as Boethius says (*Hebdonads*): *wise men are agreed that incorporeal things are not in a place,* and this agrees with the words of Augustine (*On the Literal Meaning of Genesis* 12.32): *we can answer without hesitation that the soul is not conveyed to corporeal places except with a body, or that it is not conveyed*

1

anima separata a corpore non habet aliquod corpus: sicut ibidem Augustinus dicit. Ergo ridiculum est animabus separatis aliqua receptacula assignare.

PRAETEREA, omne quod habet locum determinatum, magis convenit cum illo loco quam cum alio. Sed animae separatae, sicut etiam quaelibet aliae spirituales substantiae, indifferenter se habent ad omnia loca: non enim potest dici quod cum aliquibus corporibus conveniant et cum aliis differant, cum ab omnibus conditionibus corporalibus penitus sint remotae. Ergo eis receptacula determinata non sunt assignanda.

PRAETEREA, animabus separatis non assignatur aliquid post mortem nisi quod cedat in poenam vel in praemium. Sed corporalis locus non potest eis esse in poenam vel in praemium: cum a corporibus nihil recipiant. Ergo non sunt eis assignanda certa receptacula.

SED CONTRA: Caelum empyreum est locus corporalis. Et tamen ipsum *factum mox sanctis angelis est repletum*, ut Beda dicit. Cum ergo angeli sint incorporei, sicut et animae separatae, videtur etiam quod animabus separatis sint certa receptacula assignanda. Ergo, etc.

PRAETEREA, hoc patet per id quod Gregorius dicit, in IV *Dialog.*, scilicet animas post mortem ad diversa loca corporalia esse deductas: ut patet de Paschasio, quem Germanus, Capuanus episcopus, in balneis invenit; et de anima Theodorici regis, quam dicit ad gehennam esse deductam. Ergo animae post mortem habent certa receptacula.

RESPONDEO dicendum quod, quamvis substantiae spirituales secundum esse suum a corpore non dependeant, corporalia tamen a Deo mediantibus spiritualibus gubernantur: ut dicit Augustinus, in III *de Trinitate*, et Gregorius, in IV *Dialog.* Et ideo est quaedam convenientia spiritualium substantiarum ad corporales substantias per congruentiam quandam, ut scilicet dignioribus substantiis digniora corpora adaptentur. Unde etiam philosophi secundum ordinem mobilium posuerunt ordinem substantiarum separatarum. Quamvis autem animabus post mortem non assignentur aliqua corpora quorum sint formae vel determinati motores, determinantur tamen eis quaedam corporalia loca per congruentiam quandam secundum gradum dignitatis earum, in quibus sint quasi in loco, eo modo quo incorporalia in loco esse possunt, secundum quod magis accedent ad primam substantiam, cui locus superior per congruentiam deputatur, scilicet Deum, cuius sedem caelum Scriptura esse denuntiat. Et ideo animas quae sunt in participatione perfecta divinitatis, in caelo esse ponimus: animas vero quae a participatione huiusmodi, impediuntur loco contrario dicimus deputari.

locally. Now the soul separated from the body is without a body, as Augustine says in the same place (*On the Literal Meaning of Genesis* 12.32). Therefore, it is absurd to assign any places for the reception of souls.

OBJ. 2: Further, whatever has a definite place has more in common with that place than with any other. Now separated souls, like certain other spiritual substances, are indifferent to all places; for it cannot be said that they agree with certain bodies, and differ from others, since they are utterly removed from all corporeal conditions. Therefore, places should not be assigned for their reception.

OBJ. 3: Further, nothing is assigned to separated souls after death except what conduces to their punishment or to their reward. But a corporeal place cannot conduce to their punishment or reward, since they receive nothing from bodies. Therefore, definite places should not be assigned to receive them.

ON THE CONTRARY, The empyrean heaven is a corporeal place, and yet *as soon as it was made it was filled with the holy angels*, as Bede says (*Hexaemeron*). Since, then, angels, even as separated souls, are incorporeal, it would seem that some place should also be assigned to receive separated souls.

FURTHER, This appears from Gregory's statement (*Dialogues* 4) that souls after death are conveyed to various corporeal places, as in the case of Paschasius whom Germanus, Bishop of Capua, found at the baths, and of the soul of King Theodoric, which he asserts to have been conveyed to hell. Therefore, after death souls have certain places for their reception.

I ANSWER THAT, Although spiritual substances do not depend on a body in respect of their being, nevertheless the corporeal world is governed by God by means of the spiritual world, as asserted by Augustine (*On the Trinity* 3.4) and Gregory (*Dialogues* 4.6). Hence it is that there is a certain fittingness by way of congruity of spiritual substances to corporeal substances, in that the more noble bodies are adapted to the more noble substances: wherefore also the philosophers held that the order of separate substances is according to the order of movables. And though after death souls have no bodies assigned to them of which they are the forms or determinate motors, nevertheless certain corporeal places are appointed to them by way of congruity in reference to their degree of nobility (in which they are as though in a place, after the manner in which incorporeal things can be in a place), according as they more or less approach to the first substance (to which the highest place it fittingly assigned), namely God, whose throne the Scriptures proclaim heaven to be. Wherefore we hold that those souls that have a perfect share of divinity are in heaven, and that those souls that are deprived of that share are assigned to a contrary place.

2

AD PRIMUM ergo dicendum quod incorporalia non sunt in loco modo aliquo nobis noto et consueto, secundum quod dicimus corpora proprie in loco esse. Sunt tamen in loco modo substantiis spiritualibus convenienti, qui nobis plene manifestus esse non potest.

AD SECUNDUM dicendum quod duplex est convenientia vel similitudo. Una quae est per participationem eiusdem qualitatis: sicut calida ad invicem conveniunt. Et talis convenientia incorporalium ad loca corporalia esse non potest. Alia per quandam proportionalitatem: secundum quam in Scripturis metaphorae corporalium ad spiritualia transferuntur, ut cum dicitur Deus esse *sol*, quia est principium vitae spiritualis sicut sol vitae corporalis. Et secundum hanc convenientiam quaedam animae quibusdam locis magis conveniunt: sicut animae spiritualiter illuminatae cum corporibus luminosis; animae vero obtenebratae per culpam cum locis tenebrosis.

AD TERTIUM dicendum quod anima separata directe nihil recipit a locis corporalibus per modum quo corpora recipiunt, quae conservantur a suis locis: sed ipsae animae, ex hoc quod cognoscunt se talibus locis deputari, sibi gaudium ingerunt vel maerorem. Et sic locus cedit eis in poenam vel praemium.

REPLY OBJ. 1: Incorporeal things are not in place after a manner known and familiar to us, in which way we say that bodies are properly in place; but they are in place after a manner befitting spiritual substances, a manner that cannot be fully manifest to us.

REPLY OBJ. 2: Things have something in common with or a likeness to one another in two ways. First, by sharing a same quality: thus hot things have something in common. Incorporeal things can have nothing in common with corporeal things in this way. Second, by a kind of proportionateness, by reason of which the Scriptures apply the corporeal world to the spiritual metaphorically. Thus the Scriptures speak of God as the *sun*, because he is the principle of spiritual life, as the sun is of corporeal life. In this way certain souls have more in common with certain places: for instance, souls that are spiritually enlightened, with luminous bodies, and souls that are plunged in darkness by sin, with dark places.

REPLY OBJ. 3: The separated soul receives nothing directly from corporeal places in the same way as bodies which are maintained by their respective places: yet these same souls, through knowing themselves to be appointed to such places, gather joy or sorrow therefrom; and thus their place conduces to their punishment or reward.

Article 2

Whether Souls Are Conveyed to Heaven or Hell Immediately after Death?

AD SECUNDUM SIC PROCEDITUR. Videtur quod statim post mortem nullae animae deducantur ad caelos vel ad infernum. Quia super illud Psalmi [36, 10], *adhuc pusillum et non erit peccator*, dicit Glossa quod *sancti liberantur in fine mundi: post hanc tamen vitam non ibi eris ubi erunt sancti, quibus dicetur; venite benedicti Patris mei*. Sed illi sancti erunt in caelo. Ergo sancti post hanc vitam non statim ascendunt ad caelum.

PRAETEREA, Augustinus dicit, in *Enchiridion*, quod *tempus inter hominis mortem et ultimam resurrectionem interpositum animas abditis receptaculis continet, sicut unaquaeque digna est requie vel aerumna*. Sed haec abdita receptacula non possunt intelligi caelum et infernus: quia in illis etiam post resurrectionem ultimam cum corporibus erunt; unde pro nihilo distingueret tempus ante resurrectionem et post resurrectionem. Ergo non erunt nec in inferno nec in paradiso usque ad diem iudicii.

PRAETEREA, maior est gloria animae quam corporum. Sed simul omnibus redditur gloria corporum, ut sit maior laetitia singulorum ex communi gaudio: ut patet Heb. 11, super illud [v. 40], *Deo pro nobis aliquid melius providente*, etc.; dicit Glossa: *ut in communi gaudio om-*

OBJECTION 1: It would seem that no souls are conveyed to heaven or hell immediately after death. For a Gloss on Psalm 36:10: *yet a little while and the wicked shall not be*, says that *the saints are delivered at the end of life; yet after this life they will not yet be where the saints will be when it is said to them, "Come ye blessed of my Father."* Now those saints will be in heaven. Therefore, after this life the saints do not immediately ascend to heaven.

OBJ. 2: Further, Augustine says (*Handbook on Faith, Hope, and Charity* 109) that *the time which lies between man's death and the final resurrection holds the souls in secret receptacles according as each one is worthy of rest or of suffering*. Now these secret abodes cannot denote heaven and hell, since also after the final resurrection the souls will be there together with their bodies: so that he would have no reason to distinguish between the time before and the time after the resurrection. Therefore, they will be neither in hell nor in heaven until the day of judgment.

OBJ. 3: Further, the glory of the soul is greater than that of bodies. Now the glory of the body is awarded to all at the same time, so that each one may have the greater joy in the common rejoicing of all, as on Hebrews 11:40: *God providing some better thing for us*, a Gloss says, *that the common*

3

nium maius fieret gaudium singulorum. Ergo multo fortius gloria animarum debet differri usque ad finem, ut simul omnibus reddatur.

PRAETEREA, poena et praemium quae per sententiam iudicii redduntur, iudicium praecedere non debent. Sed ignis inferni et gaudium paradisi dabuntur omnibus per sententiam iudicantis Christi, scilicet in ultimo iudicio, ut patet Matth. 25, [31 sqq.]. Ergo ante diem iudicii nullus ascendit in caelum vel descendit ad inferos.

SED CONTRA: Est quod dicitur II Cor. 5, [1]: *si terrena nostra habitatio dissolvatur, domum habemus non manufactam conservatam in caelis.* Ergo, dissoluta carne, homo habet mansionem quae ei in caelis fuerat conservata.

PRAETEREA, Philipp. 1, [23] dicit Apostolus: *cupio dissolvi et esse cum Christo.* Ex quo sic arguit Gregorius, in IV *Dialog.: qui ergo Christum in caelo esse non dubitat, nec Pauli animam in caelo esse negat.* Sed non est negandum Christum esse in caelo: cum sit articulus fidei. Ergo nec est dubitandum animas sanctorum ad caelos ferri. Quod etiam aliquae animae ad infernum descendunt statim post mortem, patet Luc. 16, [22]: *mortuus est autem dives, et sepultus est in inferno.*

RESPONDEO dicendum quod, sicut in corporibus est gravitas vel levitas, qua feruntur ad suum locum, qui est finis motus ipsorum; ita etiam est in animabus meritum vel demeritum, quibus perveniunt animae ad praemium vel poenam, quae sunt fines actionum ipsarum. Unde, sicut corpus per gravitatem vel levitatem statim fertur in locum suum nisi prohibeatur, ita statim animae, soluto vinculo carnis, per quod in statu viae detinebantur, praemium consequuntur vel poenam, nisi aliquid impediat: sicut interdum impedit consecutionem praemii veniale peccatum, quod prius purgari oportet, ex quo sequitur quod praemium differatur. Et quia locus deputatur animabus secundum congruentiam praemii vel poenae, statim ut anima absolvitur a corpore, vel in infernum immergitur; vel ad caelum evolat, nisi impediatur aliquo reatu, quo oporteat evolationem differri, ut prius anima purgetur.

Et huic veritati auctoritates Scripturae canonicae manifeste attestantur, et documenta sanctorum patrum. Unde contrarium pro haeresi est habendum: ut patet IV *Dialog.,* et in libro *de Ecclesiasticis Dogmatibus.*

AD PRIMUM ergo dicendum quod Glossa seipsam exponit. Quod enim dicit, *nondum eris ubi erunt sancti* etc., statim exponit subdens: *idest, non habebis geminam stolam, quam habebunt sancti in resurrectione.*

AD SECUNDUM dicendum quod inter illa abdita receptacula de quibus Augustinus loquitur, etiam sunt computandi et infernus et paradisus, in quibus animae

joy may make each one rejoice the more. Much more, therefore, ought the glory of souls to be deferred until the end, so as to be awarded to all at the same time.

OBJ. 4: Further, punishment and reward, being pronounced by the sentence of the judge, should not precede the judgment. Now, the fire of hell and the joys of heaven will be awarded to all by the sentence of Christ judging them, namely, at the last judgment, according to Matthew 25:31. Therefore, no one will go up to heaven or down to hell before the day of judgment.

ON THE CONTRARY, 2 Corinthians 5:1 says: *if our earthly house of this habitation be dissolved, we have a house not made with hands, but reserved in heaven.* Therefore, after the body's dissolution the soul has an abode which had been reserved for it in heaven.

FURTHER, The Apostle says: *I desire to be dissolved and to be with Christ* (Phil 1:23). From these words Gregory argues as follows (*Dialogues* 4.25): *if there is no doubt that Christ is in heaven, it cannot be denied that Paul's soul is in heaven likewise.* Now it cannot be denied that Christ is in heaven, since this is an article of faith. Therefore, neither is it to be denied that the souls of the saints are borne to heaven. That also some souls go down to hell immediately after death is evident from Luke 16:22: *the rich man died, and he was buried in hell.*

I ANSWER THAT, Even as in bodies there is gravity or levity whereby they are borne to their own place, which is the end of their movement, so in souls there is merit or demerit whereby they reach their reward or punishment, which are the ends of their deeds. Wherefore just as a body is conveyed at once to its place by its gravity or levity, unless there be an obstacle, so too the soul, the bonds of the flesh being broken by which it was detained in the state of the way, receives at once its reward or punishment, unless there be an obstacle. Thus sometimes venial sin, through needing first of all to be cleansed, is an obstacle to the receiving of the reward; the result being that the reward is delayed. And since a place is assigned to souls in keeping with their reward or punishment, as soon as the soul is set free from the body it is either plunged into hell or soars to heaven, unless it be held back by some debt, for which its flight must be delayed until the soul is first of all cleansed.

This truth is attested by the manifest authority of the canonical Scriptures and the doctrine of the holy fathers; wherefore the contrary must be judged heretical as stated in *Dialogues* 4.25, and in *Book of Ecclesiastical Dogmas* 44.

REPLY OBJ. 1: The Gloss explains itself: for it expounds the words, *they will not yet be where the saints will be,* etc., by saying immediately afterwards: *that is to say, they will not have the double stole which the saints will have at the resurrection.*

REPLY OBJ. 2: Among the secret abodes of which Augustine speaks, we must also reckon hell and heaven, where some souls are detained before the resurrection. The rea-

aliquae ante resurrectionem continentur. Sed ideo distinguitur tempus ante resurrectionem et post, quia ante resurrectionem sunt ibi sine corpore, post autem erunt cum corpore: et quia in aliquibus receptaculis nunc sunt animae in quibus post resurrectionem non erunt.

Ad tertium dicendum quod homines secundum corpora habent quandam continuitatem ad invicem: quia secundum ea est verum quod dicitur Act. 17, [26], quod *Deus ex uno fecit omnium hominum genus.* Sed animas *singillatim finxit.* Unde non est tanta congruentia ut omnes homines simul glorificentur in anima, sicut quod simul glorificentur in corpore.

Et praeterea gloria corporis non est ita essentialis sicut gloria animae. Unde maius detrimentum esset sanctis si gloria animae differretur, quam de hoc quod gloria corporis differatur. Nec posset hoc detrimentum gloriae recompensari per ampliationem gaudii singulorum de gaudio communi.

Ad quartum dicendum quod eandem obiectionem Gregorius, in IV *Dialog.*, proponit et solvit. *Si,* inquit, *nunc in caelo sunt animae sanctorum, quid est quod in die iudicii pro iustitiae suae retributione recipiunt?* Et respondet: *hoc eis nimirum crescit in iudicio, quod nunc animae sola Singulari retributione laetantur; postmodum vero etiam corporum beatitudine perfruentur, ut in ipsa quoque carne gaudeant, in qua dolores pro Domino cruciatusque pertulerunt.* Et eodem modo dicendum est de damnatis.

son why a distinction is drawn between the time before and the time after the resurrection is because before the resurrection they are there without the body, whereas afterwards they are with the body, and because in certain places there are souls now which will not be there after the resurrection.

Reply Obj. 3: There is a kind of continuity among men as regards the body, because in respect of it is verified the saying, *God has made of one all mankind* (Acts 17:24, 26): whereas he has fashioned souls *independently of one another.* Consequently, it is not so fitting that all men should be glorified together in the soul as that they should be glorified together in the body.

Moreover, the glory of the body is not so essential as the glory of the soul; wherefore it would be more derogatory to the saints if the glory of the soul were delayed, than that the glory of the body be deferred: nor could this detriment to their glory be compensated on account of the joy of each one being increased by the common joy.

Reply Obj. 4: Gregory proposes and solves this very difficulty (*Dialogues* 4.25): if then, he says, *the souls of the just are in heaven now, what will they receive in reward for their justice on the judgment day?* And he answers: *surely it will be a gain to them at the judgment, that whereas now they enjoy only the happiness of the soul, afterwards they will enjoy also that of the body, so as to rejoice also in the flesh wherein they bore sorrow and torments for the Lord.* The same is to be said in reference to the damned.

Article 3

Whether the Souls Who Are in Heaven or Hell Are Able to Leave?

Ad tertium sic proceditur. Videtur quod animae in paradiso vel in inferno existentes egredi non valeant. Augustinus enim dicit, in libro *de Cura pro mortuis agenda*: *si rebus viventium uterentur animae mortuorum, ut de aliis taceam, meipsum pia mater nulla nocte des er er et, quae terra marique secuta est ut mecum viveret*; et ex hoc concludit quod animae defunctorum rebus viventium non intersunt. Sed interesse possent si de suis receptaculis exirent. Ergo de suis receptaculis non exeunt.

Praeterea, in Psalmo [26, 4] dicitur: *ut inhabitem in domo Domini omnibus diebus vitae meae.* Et Iob 7, [9]: *qui descendit ad inferos, non ascendet.* Ergo tam boni quam mali a suis receptaculis non exeunt.

Praeterea, receptacula, ut dictum est, animabus post mortem dantur in praemium vel in poenam. Sed post mortem neque praemia sanctorum minuuntur neque poenae damnatorum. Ergo non exeunt de suis receptaculis.

Objection 1: It would seem that the souls in heaven or hell are unable to leave. For Augustine says (*On the Care of the Dead* 13): *if the souls of the dead took any part in the affairs of the living, to say nothing of others, there is myself whom not for a single night would my loving mother fail to visit since she followed me by land and sea in order to abide with me*: and from this he concludes that the souls of the departed do not mingle in the affairs of the living. But they would be able to do so if they were to leave their abode. Therefore, they do not go forth from their abode.

Obj. 2: Further, Psalm 26:4 says: *that I may dwell in the house of the Lord all the days of my life*, and Job 7:9: *he that shall go down to hell shall not come up.* Therefore, neither the good nor the wicked quit their abode.

Obj. 3: Further, as stated above (A. 2), abodes are awarded to souls after death as a reward or punishment. Now after death neither the rewards of the saints nor the punishments of the damned are increased. Therefore, they do not quit their abodes.

SED CONTRA: Est quod dicit Hieronymus, contra Vigilantium, sic eum alloquens: *Ais enim vel in sinu Abrahae, vel in loco refrigerii, vel subter aram Dei, animas Apostolorum et martyrum consedisse, nec posse suis tumulis, cum voluerint, adesse praesentes. Et ita tu Deo leges ponis, tu Apostolis vincula iniicies, ut usque ad diem iudicii teneantur custodia, nec sint cum Domino suo, de quibus scriptum est, Sequuntur Agnum quocumque ierit. Et si Agnus ubique est, ergo ei hi qui cum eo sunt, ubique esse credendi sunt.* Ridiculum ergo est dicere quod animae mortuorum a suis receptaculis non recedant.

PRAETEREA, Hieronymus ibidem arguit sic: *cum diabolus et daemones vagentur orbe toto, et celeritate nimia Ubique praesentes sint, martyres post effusionem sanguinis ara operientur inclusi, et inde exire non poterunt?* Ex quo potest concludi non solum de bonis, sed etiam de malis, quod sua receptacula quandoque exeant: cum non habeant maiorem damnationem quam daemones, qui ubique discurrunt.

PRAETEREA, idem probari potest per Gregorium, in IV *Dialog.*, ubi narrat de multis mortuis qui vivis apparuerunt.

RESPONDEO dicendum quod aliquem exire de inferno vel de paradiso potest intelligi dupliciter. Uno modo, ita quod simpliciter inde exeat, ut iam locus eius non sit paradisus vel infernus. Et sic nullus inferno vel paradiso finaliter deputatus inde exire potest, ut infra dicetur.

Alio modo potest intelligi ut exeat ad tempus. Et in hoc distinguendum est quid eis conveniat secundum legem naturae, et quid eis conveniat secundum ordinem divinae providentiae: quia, ut dicit Augustinus, in libro de Cura pro mortuis agenda, *alii sunt humanarum limites rerum, alia divinarum signa virtutum; alia sunt quae naturaliter, alia quae mirabiliter fiunt.*

Secundum ergo naturalem cursum, animae separatae, propriis receptaculis deputatae, a conversatione viventium penitus segregantur. Non enim secundum cursum naturae homines in mortali carne viventes substantiis separatis immediate iunguntur, cum omnis eorum cognitio a sensu oriatur: nec propter aliud a suis receptaculis eas conveniret exire nisi ut rebus viventium interessent.

Sed secundum dispositionem divinae providentiae, aliquando animae separatae, a suis receptaculis egressae, conspectibus hominum praesentantur: sicut Augustinus, in libro praedicto, narrat de Felice martyre, qui civibus Nolanis visibiliter apparuit cum a barbaris oppugnarentur. Et hoc etiam credi potest quod aliquando de damnatis contingat, quod, ad eruditionem hominum et terrorem, permittuntur viventibus apparere; aut etiam ad suffragia expetenda, quantum ad illos qui in purgatorio detinentur; ut per multa quae in IV *Dialog.* narrantur,

ON THE CONTRARY, Jerome writing against Vigilantius addresses him thus: *for you say that the souls of the apostles and martyrs have taken up their abode either in Abraham's bosom or in the place of refreshment, or under the altar of God, and that they are unable to visit their graves when they will. Would you then lay down the law for God? Would you put the apostles in chains, imprison them until the day of judgment, and forbid them to be with their Lord, them of whom it is written, "They follow the Lamb wheresoever he goes?" And if the Lamb is everywhere, therefore we must believe that those also who are with him are everywhere.* Therefore, it is absurd to say that the souls of the departed do not leave their abode.

FURTHER, Jerome argues as follows: *since the devil and the demons wander throughout the whole world, and are everywhere present with wondrous speed, why should the martyrs, after shedding their blood, be imprisoned and unable to go forth?* Hence we may infer that not only the good sometimes leave their abode, but also the wicked, since their damnation does not exceed that of the demons who wander about everywhere.

FURTHER, The same conclusion may be gathered from Gregory (*Dialogues* 4), where he relates many cases of the dead having appeared to the living.

I ANSWER THAT, There are two ways of understanding a person to leave hell or heaven. First, that he goes from thence simply, so that heaven or hell be no longer his place: and in this way no one who is finally consigned to hell or heaven can leave, as we shall state further on (Q. 71, A. 5).

Second, they may be understood to go forth for a time: and here we must distinguish what befits them according to the order of nature, and what according to the order of divine providence; for as Augustine says (*On the Care of the Dead* 16): *human affairs have their limits other than have the wonders of the divine power; nature's works differ from those which are done miraculously.*

Consequently, according to the natural course, the separated souls consigned to their respective abodes are utterly cut off from communication with the living. For according to the course of nature, men living in mortal bodies are not immediately united to separate substances, since their entire knowledge arises from the senses: nor would it be fitting for them to leave their abode for any purpose other than to take part in the affairs of the living.

Nevertheless, according to the disposition of divine providence, separated souls sometimes come forth from their abode and appear to men, as Augustine, in the book quoted above, relates of the martyr Felix who appeared visibly to the people of Nola when they were besieged by the barbarians. It is also credible that this may occur sometimes to the damned, and that for man's instruction and intimidation they be permitted to appear to the living; or again in order to seek our suffrages, as to those who are detained in purgatory, as evidenced by many instances related in the

patet. Sed hoc interest inter sanctos et damnatos, quod sancti, cum voluerint, apparere possunt viventibus: non autem damnati. Sicut enim sancti viventes in carne per donum gratiae gratis datae accipiunt ut sanitates et signa perficiant, quae non nisi divina virtute mirabiliter fiunt, quae quidem signa ab aliis hoc dono carentibus perfici non possunt; ita etiam non est inconveniens ut ex virtute gloriae aliqua potentia animabus sanctorum detur per quam possint mirabiliter apparere viventibus cum volunt; quod alii non possunt, nisi interdum permissi.

AD PRIMUM ergo dicendum quod Augustinus, ut per sequentia patet, loquitur secundum communem cursum naturae. Nec tamen sequitur quod, etiam si mortui possunt ut volunt viventibus apparere, toties appareant quoties apparent in carne viventes. Quia separati a carne vel omnino conformantur divinae voluntati, ita quod non liceat eis nisi quod secundum divinam dispositionem congruere intuenter; vel ita sunt poenis oppressi ut de sua miseria magis doleant quam curent aliis apparere.

AD SECUNDUM dicendum quod auctoritates illae loquuntur quantum ad hoc quod nullus de paradiso vel inferno egreditur simpliciter: et non quod non egrediatur ad tempus.

AD TERTIUM dicendum quod, sicut ex dictis 11) patet, secundum hoc locus animae cedit in poenam vel praemium, quod anima afficitur ex hoc quod tali loco deputatur vel gaudendo vel dolendo. Hoc autem gaudium, sive hic dolor, de hoc quod talibus locis deputatur, manet in anima etiam quando extra loca praedicta fuerit: sicut pontifici, cui datur pro honore ut in cathedra sedeat in ecclesia, non minuitur gloria quando a cathedra recedit, quia, etsi actu ibi non sedeat, locus tamen ille sibi deputatus est.

Ad ea etiam quae contra obiiciuntur, respondere oportet.

AD QUORUM PRIMUM dicendum quod Hieronymus loquitur de Apostolis et martyribus secundum hoc quod eis accrescit ex potestate gloriae, et non secundum quod eis congruit ex debito naturae. Quod autem dicit eos *ubique esse*, non est intelligendum quasi simul sint in pluribus locis aut ubique: sed quia esse possunt ubi volunt.

AD SECUNDUM dicendum quod non est simile de daemonibus et angelis, et animabus sanctorum et damnatorum. Angeli enim boni et mali hoc officium sortiuntur ut hominibus praesint, vel ad custodiam vel ad exercitium. Quod de animabus hominum non potest dici: sed tantum secundum potestatem gloriae animabus sanctorum hoc congruit quod possint esse ubi voluerint. Et hoc est quod Hieronymus intendit.

AD TERTIUM dicendum quod, quamvis aliquando animae sanctorum vel damnatorum praesentialiter ad-

fourth book of the *Dialogues*. There is, however, this difference between the saints and the damned, that the saints can appear when they will to the living, but not the damned; for even as the saints while living in the flesh are able by the gifts of gratuitous grace to heal and work wonders, which can only be done miraculously by the divine power, and cannot be done by those who lack this gift, so it is not unfitting for the souls of the saints to be endowed with a power in virtue of their glory, so that they are able to appear wondrously to the living when they will: while others are unable to do so unless they be sometimes permitted.

REPLY OBJ. 1: Augustine, as may be gathered from what he says afterwards, is speaking according to the common course of nature. And yet it does not follow, although the dead be able to appear to the living as they will, that they appear as often as when living in the flesh: because when they are separated from the flesh, they are either wholly conformed to the divine will, so that they may do nothing but what they see to be agreeable with the divine disposition, or else they are so overwhelmed by their punishments that their grief for their unhappiness surpasses their desire to appear to others.

REPLY OBJ. 2: The authorities quoted speak in the sense that no one comes forth from heaven or hell simply, and do not imply that one may not come forth for a time.

REPLY OBJ. 3: As stated above (A. 1) the soul's place conduces to its punishment or reward insofar as the soul, through being consigned to that place, is affected either by joy or by grief. Now this joy or grief at being consigned to such a place remains in the soul even when it is outside that place. Thus a bishop who is given the honor of sitting on a throne in the church incurs no dishonor when he leaves the throne, for though he does not sit there actually, the place remains assigned to him.

We must also reply to the arguments in the contrary sense.

REPLY OBJ. 4: Jerome is speaking of the apostles and martyrs in reference to that which they gain from their power of glory, and not to that which befits them as due to them by nature. And when he says that they *are everywhere*, he does not mean that they are in several places or everywhere at once, but that they can be wherever they will.

REPLY OBJ. 5: There is no parity between demons and angels on the one hand and the souls of the saints and of the damned on the other. For the good or bad angels have allotted to them the office of presiding over men, to watch over them or to try them; but this cannot be said of the souls of men. Nevertheless, according to the power of glory, it is fitting to the souls of the saints that they can be where they will; and this is what Jerome means to say.

REPLY OBJ. 6: Although the souls of the saints or of the damned are sometimes actually present where they appear,

sint ubi apparent, non tamen credendum est hoc semper accidere. Aliquando enim huiusmodi apparitiones fiunt, vel in dormiendo vel in vigilando, operatione bonorum vel malorum spirituum, ad instructionem vel deceptionem viventium. Sicut etiam vivi homines aliquando aliis apparent et eis multa dicunt in somniis, cum tamen constet eos non esse praesentes: sicut Augustinus per multa exempla probat in libro *de Cura pro mortuis agenda*.

we are not to believe that this is always so: for sometimes these apparitions occur to persons whether asleep or awake by the activity of good or wicked angels in order to instruct or deceive the living. Thus sometimes even the living appear to others and tell them many things in their sleep; and yet it is clear that they are not present, as Augustine proves from many instances (*On the Care of the Dead* 11–12).

Article 4

Whether the Limbo of Hell Is the Same as Abraham's Bosom?

AD QUARTUM SIC PROCEDITUR. Videtur quod limbus inferni non sit idem quod sinus Abrahae. Sicut enim dicit Augustinus, XII *super Genesis ad litteram: nondum inveni inferos alicubi in bono posuisse Scripturam*. Sed sinus Abrahae in bono accipitur: ut ibidem subiungit Augustinus, sic dicens: *non in bono accipiendum sinum Abrahae, et illam requiem quo ab angelis pius pauper allatus est, nescio utrum quisquam possit audire*. Ergo sinus Abrahae non est idem quod limbus inferni.

PRAETEREA, in inferno existentes non vident Deum. Sed in sinu Abrahae videtur Deus: ut patet per Augustinum, IX libro *Confess.*, qui, loquens de Nebridio, dicit: *quidquid illic est quod sinus Abrahae vocatur, ibi Nebridius meus vivit*; et infra: *iam non ponit aurem ad os meum, sed spirituale os ad fontem tuum, et bibit quantum potest sapientiam pro aviditate sua, sine fine felix*. Ergo sinus Abrahae non est idem quod limbus inferni.

PRAETEREA, Ecclesia non orat pro aliquo ut ad infernum deducatur. Orat autem ut angeli animam defuncti *in sinum Abrahae* ferant. Ergo videtur quod sinus Abrahae non sit idem quod limbus.

SED CONTRA: Sinus Abrahae dicitur ubi mendicus Lazarus ductus est. Sed ductus est ad infernum: quia, ut dicit Glossa, Iob 30, super illud [v. 23], Ubi constituta est domus omni viventi: *infernus domus erat omnium viventium ante Christi adventum*. Ergo sinus Abrahae est idem quod limbus.

PRAETEREA, Genes. 42, [38] dicit Iacob filiis suis: *deducetis canos meos cum dolore ad inferos*. Ergo Iacob sciebat in morte sua se ad inferos transferendum. Ergo et, eadem ratione, Abraham ad inferos translatus fuit post mortem. Et ita sinus Abrahae videtur esse aliqua pars inferni.

RESPONDEO dicendum quod animae hominum post mortem ad quietem pervenire non possunt nisi merito fidei: quia *accedentem ad Deum oportet credere*, Heb. 11, [6]. Primum autem exemplum credendi hominibus in

OBJECTION 1: It would seem that the limbo of hell is not the same as Abraham's bosom. For Augustine says, *I have not yet found Scripture mentioning hell in a favorable sense* (*On the Literal Meaning of Genesis* 33). Now Abraham's bosom is taken in a favorable sense, as Augustine goes on to say: *surely no one would be allowed to give an unfavorable signification to Abraham's bosom and the place of rest to which the godly poor man was carried by the angels* (*On the Literal Meaning of Genesis* 33). Therefore, Abraham's bosom is not the same as the limbo of hell.

OBJ. 2: Further, those who are in hell see not God. Yet God is seen by those who are in Abraham's bosom, as may be gathered from Augustine (*Confessions* 9.3) who, speaking of Nebridius, says: *whatever that be, which is signified by that bosom, there lives my Nebridius*, and further on: *now he does not lay his ear to my mouth, but his spiritual mouth unto Thy fountain, and drinks as much as he can receive wisdom in proportion to his thirst, endlessly happy*. Therefore, Abraham's bosom is not the same as the limbo of hell.

OBJ. 3: Further, the Church prays not that a man be taken to hell: and yet she prays that the angels may carry the departed soul *to Abraham's bosom*. Therefore, it would seem that Abraham's bosom is not the same as limbo.

ON THE CONTRARY, The place where the beggar Lazarus was taken is called Abraham's bosom. Now he was taken to hell, for as a Gloss on Job 30:25: *where a house is appointed for every one that lives*, says, *hell was the house of all the living until the coming of Christ* (St. Gregory, *Morals on Job* 20). Therefore, Abraham's bosom is the same as limbo.

FURTHER, Jacob said to his sons: *you will bring down my grey hairs with sorrow to hell* (Gen 44:38): wherefore Jacob knew that he would be taken to hell after his death. Therefore, Abraham likewise was taken to hell after his death; and consequently Abraham's bosom would seem to be a part of hell.

I ANSWER THAT, After death men's souls cannot find rest save by the merit of faith, because *he that comes to God must believe* (Heb 11:6). Now the first example of faith was given to men in the person of Abraham, who was the first to

Abraham datur, qui primo se a coetu infidelium segregavit, et speciale *signum fidei accepit*. Et ideo *requies illa quae hominibus post mortem datur, sinus Abrahae dicitur*: ut patet per Augustinum, XII *super Genesis ad litteram*.

Sed animae sanctorum post mortem non omni tempore eandem quietem habuerunt. Quia post Christi adventum habent plenam quietem, divina visione perfruentes. Sed ante Christi adventum habebant quietem per immunitatem poenae, sed non habebant quietem desiderii per consecutionem finis. Et ideo status sanctorum ante Christi adventum potest considerari, et secundum id quod habebat de requie, et sic dicitur *sinus Abrahae*: potest etiam considerari quantum ad id quod eis deerat de requie, et sic dicitur *limbus inferni*.

Limbus ergo inferni et sinus Abrahae fuerunt ante Christi adventum unum per accidens, et non per se. Et ideo nihil prohibet post Christi adventum esse sinum Abrahae omnino diversum a limbo: quia ea quae sunt per accidens, separari contingit.

Ad primum ergo dicendum quod quantum ad id quod habebat de bono, status sanctorum patrum *sinus Abrahae* dicebatur. Sed quantum ad id quod habebat de defectu, dicebatur infernus. Et sic nec sinus Abrahae in malum accipitur, nec infernus in bonum, quamvis quodammodo sint unum.

Ad secundum dicandum quod, sicut requies sanctorum patrum ante Christi adventum dicebatur sinus Abrahae, ita et post Christi adventum: sed diversimode. Quia enim ante Christi adventum sanctorum requies habebat defectum requiei adiunctum, dicebatur idem infernus et sinus Abrahae, inquantum ibi non videbatur Deus. Sed quia post Christi adventum sanctorum requies est completa, cum Deum videant, talis requies dicitur sinus Abrahae, et nullo modo infernus. Et ad hunc sinum Abrahae Ecclesia orat fideles perduci.

Unde patet responsio ad tertium. Et sic etiam intelligenda est quaedam glossa quae habetur Luc. 16, super illud [v. 22], *factum est ut moreretur mendicus* etc., quae sic dicit: *sinus Abrahae est requies beatorum pauperum, quorum est regnum caelorum*.

sever himself from the body of unbelievers, and to receive a special *sign of faith*: for which reason *the place of rest given to men after death is called Abraham's bosom*, as Augustine declares (*On the Literal Meaning of Genesis* 12).

But the souls of the saints have not at all times had the same rest after death; because since Christ's coming they have had complete rest through enjoying the vision of God, whereas before Christ's coming they had rest through being exempt from punishment, but their desire was not set at rest by their attaining their end. Consequently, the state of the saints before Christ's coming may be considered both as regards the rest it afforded, and thus it is called *Abraham's bosom*, and as regards its lack of rest, and thus it is called the *limbo of hell*.

Accordingly, before Christ's coming the limbo of hell and Abraham's bosom were one place accidentally and not essentially: and consequently, nothing prevents Abraham's bosom from remaining after Christ's coming and from being altogether distinct from limbo, since things that are one accidentally may be parted from one another.

Reply Obj. 1: The state of the holy fathers as regards what was good in it was called *Abraham's bosom*, but as regards its deficiencies it was called hell. Accordingly, neither is Abraham's bosom taken in an unfavorable sense nor hell in a favorable sense, although in a way they are one.

Reply Obj. 2: The place of rest of the holy fathers was called Abraham's bosom before as well as after Christ's coming, but in different ways. For since before Christ's coming the saints' rest had a lack of rest attached to it, it was called both hell and Abraham's bosom, wherefore God was not seen there. But since after the coming of Christ the saints' rest is complete through their seeing God, this rest is called Abraham's bosom, but not hell by any means. It is to this bosom of Abraham that the Church prays for the faithful to be brought.

Hence the reply to the third objection is evident: and the same meaning applies to a Gloss on Luke 16:22: *it came to pass that the beggar died*, which says, *Abraham's bosom is the rest of the blessed poor, whose is the kingdom of heaven*.

Article 5

Whether Limbo Is the Same as the Hell of the Damned?

Ad quintum sic proceditur. Videtur quod limbus sit idem quod infernus damnatorum. Christus enim dicitur infernum *momordisse*, non absorbuisse, quia aliquos inde extraxit, non autem omnes. Non autem diceretur momordisse infernum si illi quos liberavit non

Objection 1: It would seem that the limbo of hell is the same as the hell of the damned. For Christ is said *to have bitten* hell, but not to have swallowed it, because he took some from it but not all. Now he would not be said *to have bitten* hell if those whom he set free were not part of the

fuissent pars multitudinis in inferno contentae. Ergo, cum illi quos liberavit in limbo inferni continerentur, iidem continebantur in limbo et inferno. Ergo limbus vel est idem quod infernus, vel pars inferni.

Praeterea, Christus dicitur in Symbolo *descendisse ad infernum*. Sed non descendit nisi ad limbum patrum. Ergo limbus patrum est idem quod infernus.

Praeterea, Iob 17, [16] dicitur: *in profundissimum inferni descendent omnia mea*. Sed Iob, cum esset vir sanctus et iustus, ad limbum descendit. Ergo limbus est idem quod profundissimum inferni.

Sed contra: *in inferno nulla est redemptio*. Sed a limbo sancti fuerunt redempti. Ergo limbus non est idem quod infernus.

Praeterea, Augustinus dicit, XII *super Genesis ad litteram*: *quomodo illam requiem, quam Lazarus accepit, apud inferos esse credamus, non video*. Sed anima Lazari ad limbum descendit. Ergo limbus non est idem quod infernus.

Respondeo dicendum quod receptacula animarum post mortem dupliciter distingui possunt: aut secundum situm; aut secundum locorum qualitatem, prout scilicet in aliquibus locis poenas vel praemia recipiunt animae. Si ergo consideretur limbus patrum et infernus secundum locorum qualitatem praedictam, sic non est dubium quod distinguuntur. Tum quia in inferno est poena sensibilis, quae non erat in limbo patrum. Tum etiam quia in inferno est poena aeterna: sed in limbo patrum detinebantur sancti temporaliter tantum.

Sed si considerentur quantum ad situm loci, sic probabile est quod idem locus, vel quasi continuus, sit infernus et limbus: ita tamen quod quaedam superior: pars inferni limbus patrum dicatur. Existentes enim in inferno secundum diversitatem culpae diversam sortiuntur et poenam. Et ideo secundum quod gravioribus peccatis etiam irretiuntur damnati, secundum hoc obscuriorem locum et profundiorem obtinent in inferno. Unde et sancti patres, in quibus minimum erat de ratione culpae, supremum et minus tenebrosum locum habuerunt omnibus puniendis.

Ad primum ergo dicendum quod secundum hoc quod infernus et limbus sunt idem quantum ad situm, dicitur Christus *infernum momordisse*, et in infernum *descendisse*, quando patres a limbo eripuit suo descensu.

Et per hoc patet solutio ad secundum.

Ad tertium dicendum quod Iob non descendit in infernum damnatorum, sed in limbum patrum. Qui quidem dicitur *profundissimus locus*, non quidem respectu locorum poenalium, sed in comparatione ad alia loca, secundum quod sub eodem includitur omnis locus poenarum.

Vel dicendum, sicut Augustinus solvit, XII *super Genesis ad litteram*, de Iacob, sic dicens: *illud quod dicit*

multitude shut up in hell. Therefore, since those whom he set free were shut up in hell, the same were shut up in limbo and in hell. Therefore, limbo is either the same as hell, or is a part of hell.

Obj. 2: Further, in the Creed, Christ is said to have *descended into hell*. But he did not descend save to the limbo of the fathers. Therefore, the limbo of the fathers is the same as hell.

Obj. 3: Further, it is written: *all that I have shall go down into the deepest hell* (Job 17:16). Now since Job was a holy and just man, he went down to limbo. Therefore, limbo is the same as the deepest hell.

On the contrary, *In hell there is no redemption* (Office of the Dead, Resp. vii). But the saints were redeemed from limbo. Therefore, limbo is not the same as hell.

Further, Augustine says (*On the Literal Meaning of Genesis* 12): *I do not see how we can believe that the rest which Lazarus received was in hell*. Now the soul of Lazarus went down into limbo. Therefore, limbo is not the same as hell.

I answer that, The abodes of souls after death may be distinguished in two ways: either as to their situation, or as to the quality of the places, inasmuch as souls are punished or rewarded in certain places. Accordingly, if we consider the limbo of the fathers and hell in respect of the aforesaid quality of the places, there is no doubt that they are distinct, both because in hell there is sensible punishment, which was not in the limbo of the fathers, and because in hell there is eternal punishment, whereas the saints were detained but temporally in the limbo of the fathers.

On the other hand, if we consider them as to the situation of the place, it is probable that hell and limbo are the same place, or that they are continuous, as it were, yet so that some higher part of hell be called the limbo of the fathers. For those who are in hell receive diverse punishments according to the diversity of their guilt, so that those who are condemned are consigned to darker and deeper parts of hell according as they have been guilty of graver sins. And consequently, the holy fathers in whom there was the least amount of sin were consigned to a higher and less dark part than all those who were condemned to punishment.

Reply Obj. 1: When Christ, by his descent, delivered the fathers from limbo, he is said *to have bitten hell* and *to have descended* into hell insofar as hell and limbo are the same as to situation.

This suffices for the reply to the second objection.

Reply Obj. 3: Job descended not to the hell of the damned, but to the limbo of the fathers. The latter is called the *deepest place* not in reference to the places of punishment, but in comparison with other places, as including all penal places under one head.

Or we may reply with Augustine (*On the Literal Meaning of Genesis* 12), who says of Jacob: *when Jacob said to his*

Iacob ad filios suos, Deducetis senectutem meam cum tristitia ad inferos: videtur hoc magis timuisse, ne nimia tristitia sic perturbaretur ut ad requiem beatorum non iret, sed ad inferos peccatorum. Et similiter potest exponi verbum Iob, eadem ratione, ut sit verbum magis timentis quam asserentis.

sons, *"You will bring down my grey hairs with sorrow to hell,"* he seems to have feared most lest he should be troubled with so great a sorrow as to obtain, not the rest of good men, but the hell of sinners. The saying of Job may be expounded in the same way, as being the utterance of one in fear, rather than an assertion.

Article 6

Whether the Limbo of Children Is the Same as the Limbo of the Fathers?

AD SEXTUM SIC PROCEDITUR. Videtur quod limbus puerorum sit idem quod limbus patrum. Poena enim debet respondere culpae. Sed pro eadem culpa detinebantur in limbo patres et pueri, scilicet pro culpa originali. Ergo idem debet esse utrorumque locus poenae.

PRAETEREA, Augustinus dicit, in *Enchirid. mitissima est poena puerorum, qui cum solo originali decedunt.* Sed nulla est poena mitior ea quam sancti patres habebant. Ergo idem est locus poenae utrorumque.

SED CONTRA, sicut actuali peccato debetur poena temporalis in purgatorio et aeterna in inferno, ita et originali peccato debebatur poena temporalis in limbo patrum, et aeterna in limbo puerorum. Si ergo infernus et purgatorium non sunt idem, videtur quod nec limbus puerorum et limbus patrum sint idem.

Utrum autem infernus et purgatorii locus sint idem, quaesitum est supra dist. 21.

RESPONDEO dicendum quod limbus patrum et limbus puerorum absque dubio differunt secundum qualitatem praemii vel poenae: pueris enim non adest spes beatae vitae, quae patribus in limbo aderat, in quibus etiam lumen fidei et gratiae refulgebat. Sed quantum ad situm probabiliter creditur utrorumque locus idem fuisse: nisi quod requies beatorum adhuc erat in superiori loco quam limbus puerorum, sicut de limbo et inferno dictum est.

AD PRIMUM ergo dicendum quod ad culpam originalem non eodem modo se habebant patres et pueri. In patribus enim originalis culpa expiata est secundum quod erat infectiva personae, remanebat tamen impedimentum ex parte naturae, pro qua nondum erat satisfactum plenarie. Sed in pueris est impedimentum et ex parte personae et ex parte naturae. Et ideo pueris et patribus: diversa receptacula assignantur.

AD SECUNDUM dicendum quod Augustinus loquitur de poenis quae debentur alicui ratione personae suae, inter quos mitissimam poenam habent qui solo origina-

OBJECTION 1: It would seem that the limbo of children is the same as the limbo of the fathers. For punishment should correspond to sin. Now the fathers were detained in limbo for the same sin as children, namely, for original sin. Therefore, the place of punishment should be the same for both.

OBJ. 2: Further, Augustine says (*Handbook on Faith, Hope, and Charity* 93): *the punishment of children who die in none but original sin is most lenient.* But no punishment is more lenient than that of the holy fathers. Therefore, the place of punishment is the same for both.

ON THE CONTRARY, Even as temporal punishment in purgatory and eternal punishment in hell are due to actual sin, so temporal punishment in the limbo of the fathers and eternal punishment in the limbo of the children were due to original sin. If, therefore, hell and purgatory be not the same, it would seem that neither are the limbo of children and the limbo of the fathers the same.

Whether the place of hell and purgatory are the same is answered above (A. 5).

I ANSWER THAT, The limbo of the fathers and the limbo of children, without any doubt, differ as to the quality of punishment or reward. For children have no hope of the blessed life, as the fathers in limbo had, in whom, moreover, shone forth the light of faith and grace. But as regards their situation, there is reason to believe that the place of both is the same; except that the limbo of the fathers is placed higher than the limbo of children, just as we have stated in reference to limbo and hell (A. 5).

REPLY OBJ. 1: The fathers did not stand in the same relation to original sin as children. For in the fathers original sin was expiated insofar as it infected the person, while there remained an obstacle on the part of nature, on account of which their satisfaction was not yet complete. On the other hand, in children there is an obstacle both on the part of the person and on the part of nature: and for this reason different abodes are appointed to the fathers and to children.

REPLY OBJ. 2: Augustine is speaking of punishments due to some one by reason of his person. Of these the most lenient are due to those who are burdened with none but

li peccato gravantur. Sed adhuc est mitior poena eorum quos non impedit a perceptione gloriae defectus personae, sed solum defectus naturae: ut ipsa dilatio gloriae quaedam poena dicatur.

original sin. But lighter still is the punishment due to those who are debarred from the reception of glory by no personal defect but only by a defect of nature, so that this very delay of glory is called a kind of punishment.

Article 7

Whether So Many Abodes Should Be Distinguished?

AD SEPTIMUM SIC PROCEDITUR. Videtur quod non debeant tot receptacula distingui. Sicut enim receptacula debentur animabus pro peccato post mortem, ita et pro merito. Sed ratione meriti non debetur nisi unum tantum receptaculum, scilicet paradisus. Ergo nec ratione peccatorum debetur nisi unum receptaculum.

PRAETEREA, receptacula assignantur animabus post mortem ratione meritorum vel demeritorum. Sed unus est locus in quo merentur vel demerentur. Ergo unum tantum receptaculum deberet eis assignari post mortem.

PRAETEREA, loca poenalia debent respondere ipsis culpis. Sed non sunt nisi tria genera culparum: scilicet originalis, venialis et mortalis. Ergo non debent esse nisi tria receptacula poenalia.

SED CONTRA: Videtur quod debeant esse multo plura quam assignentur. Aer enim iste caliginosus est daemonum carcer, ut patet II Petri 2, [4]. Nec tamen computatur inter quinque receptacula quae a quibusdam assignantur. Ergo sunt plura receptacula quam quinque.

PRAETEREA, alius est paradisus terrestris, et alius paradisus caelestis. Sed quidam post statum huius vitae ad paradisum terrestrem sunt translati: sicut de Henoch et de Elia dicitur. Cum ergo paradisus terrestris inter quinque receptacula non computetur, videtur quod sint plura quam quinque.

PRAETEREA, cuilibet statui peccantium debet aliquis locus poenalis respondere. Sed si ponatur aliquis in originali decedere cum solo veniali peccato, nullum receptaculorum assignatorum ei competeret. Constat enim quod in paradiso non esset: cum gratia careret. Et eadem ratione nec in limbo patrum. Similiter etiam nec in limbo puerorum: cum in ipso non sit poena sensibilis, quae tali debetur ratione venialis peccati. Similiter nec in purgatorio: quia ibi non est nisi poena temporalis, huic autem debetur poena perpetua. Similiter autem nec in inferno damnatorum: quia mortali peccato caret. Ergo Oportet sextum receptaculum assignare.

PRAETEREA, diversae sunt quantitates praemiorum et poenarum secundum differentias culparum et meritorum. Sed infiniti sunt gradus meritorum et culparum.

OBJECTION 1: It would seem that we should not distinguish so many abodes. For after death, just as abodes are due to souls on account of sin, so are they due on account of merit. Now there is only one abode due on account of merit, namely paradise. Therefore, neither should there be more than one abode due on account of sin.

OBJ. 2: Further, abodes are appointed to souls after death on account of merits or demerits. Now there is one place where they merit or demerit. Therefore, only one abode should be assigned to them after death.

OBJ. 3: Further, the places of punishment should correspond to the sins. Now there are only three kinds of sin: original, venial, and mortal. Therefore, there should only be three penal abodes.

OBJ. 4: On the other hand, it would seem that there should be many more than those assigned. For this darkened air is the prison house of the demons (2 Pet 2:17), and yet it is not reckoned among the five abodes which are mentioned by certain authors. Therefore, there are more than five abodes.

OBJ. 5: Further, the earthly paradise is distinct from the heavenly paradise. Now some were borne away to the earthly paradise after this state of life, as is related of Enoch and Elijah. Since, then, the earthly paradise is not counted among the five abodes, it would seem that there are more than five.

OBJ. 6: Further, some penal place should correspond to each state of sinners. Now if we suppose a person to die in original sin who has committed only venial sins, none of the assigned abodes will be befitting to him. For it is clear that he would not be in heaven, since he would be without grace, and for the same reason neither would he be in the limbo of the fathers; nor again would he be in the limbo of children, since there is no sensible punishment there, which is due to such a person by reason of venial sin; nor would he be in purgatory, where there is none but temporal punishment, whereas everlasting punishment is due to him; nor would he be in the hell of the damned, since he is not guilty of actual mortal sin. Therefore, a sixth abode should be assigned.

OBJ. 7: Further, rewards and punishments vary in quantity according to the differences of sins and merits. Now the degrees of merit and sin are infinite. Therefore, we

Ergo infinita debent distingui receptacula, in quibus puniantur vel praemientur post mortem.

PRAETEREA, animae quandoque puniuntur in locis in quibus peccaverunt: ut per Gregorium patet, IV *Dialog.* Sed peccaverunt in loco iri quo nos habitamus. Ergo hic locus debet computari inter receptacula: et praecipue cum aliqui in hoc mundo pro peccatis suis puniantur, ut supra Magister dixit.

PRAETEREA, sicut aliqui in gratia decedentes habent aliqua pro quibus digni sunt poena, ita aliqui in peccato mortali decedentes habent aliqua bona pro quibus essent digni praemio. Sed decedentibus in gratia cum peccatis venialibus assignatur aliquod receptaculum in quo puniuntur antequam praemia consequantur, scilicet purgatorium. Ergo, eadem ratione, e converso debet esse de illis qui in mortali decedunt cum aliquibus bonis operibus.

PRAETEREA, sicut patres retardabantur a plena gloria animae ante Christi adventum, ita et nunc a gloria corporis. Ergo, sicut distinguitur receptaculum sanctorum ante Christi adventum ab eo in quo nunc recipiuntur, ita debet receptaculum nunc distingui ab eo in quo recipientur post resurrectionem.

RESPONDEO dicendum quod receptacula animarum distinguuntur secundum diversos status garum. Anima autem coniuncta mortali corpori habet statum merendi: sed exuta corpore est in statu recipiendi pro meritis bonum vel malum. Ergo post mortem vel est in. statu recipiendi finale praemium, vel est in statu quo impeditur ab illo. Si autem est in statu recipiendi finalem retributionem, hoc est dupliciter: vel quantum ad bonum, et sic est paradisus; vel quantum ad malum, et sic ratione actualis culpae est infernus, ratione autem originalis est limbus puerorum. Si vero est in statu quo impeditur a finali retributione consequenda, vel hoc est propter defectum personae, et sic est purgatorium, in quo detinentur animae ne statim praemia consequantur, propter peccata quae commiserunt; vel propter defectum naturae, et sic est limbus patrum, in quo detinebantur patres a consecutione gloriae propter reatum humanae naturae, quae nondum poterat expiari.

AD PRIMUM ergo dicendum quod *bonum contingit uno modo, sed malum multifarie*: ut patet per Dionysium, 4 cap. *de Div. Nom.*, et per Philosophum, in II *Ethic.* Et propter hoc non est inconveniens si locus beatae retributionis est unus, loca vero poenarum sunt plura.

AD SECUNDUM dicendum quod status merendi et demerendi est unus status: cum eiusdem sit posse mereri et demereri. Et ideo convenienter debetur omnibus unus

should distinguish an infinite number of abodes, in which souls are punished or rewarded after death.

OBJ. 8: Further, souls are sometimes punished in the places where they sinned, as Gregory states (*Dialogues* 4.55). But they sinned in the place which we inhabit. Therefore, this place should be reckoned among the abodes, especially since some are punished for their sins in this world, as the Master said above (*Sentences* IV, D. 21).

OBJ. 9: Further, just as some die in a state of grace and have some venial sins for which they deserve punishment, so some die in mortal sin and have some good for which they would deserve a reward. Now to those who die in grace with venial sins, an abode is assigned (namely, purgatory) where they are punished before they receive their reward. Therefore, on the other hand, there should be equally an abode for those who die in mortal sin together with some good works.

OBJECTION 1: Further, just as the fathers were delayed from obtaining full glory of the soul before Christ's coming, so are they now detained from receiving the glory of the body. Therefore, as we distinguish an abode of the saints before the coming of Christ from the one where they are received now, so ought we to distinguish the one in which they are received now from the one where they will be received after the resurrection.

I ANSWER THAT, The abodes of souls are distinguished according to the souls' various states. Now the soul united to a mortal body is in the state of meriting, while the soul separated from the body is in the state of receiving good or evil for its merits; so that after death it is either in the state of receiving its final reward, or in the state of being hindered from receiving it. If it is in the state of receiving its final retribution, this happens in two ways: either as to good, and then it is paradise; or as to evil, and thus as regards actual sin it is hell, and as regards original sin it is the limbo of children. On the other hand, if it be in the state where it is hindered from receiving its final reward, this is either on account of a defect of the person, and thus we have purgatory, where souls are detained from receiving their reward at once on account of the sins they have committed, or else it is on account of a defect of nature, and thus we have the limbo of the fathers, where the fathers were detained from obtaining glory on account of the guilt of human nature, which could not yet be expiated.

REPLY OBJ. 1: *Good happens in one way, but evil in many ways*, according to Dionysius (*On the Divine Names* 4) and the Philosopher (*Ethics* 2.6): wherefore it is not unfitting if there be one place of blissful reward and several places of punishment.

REPLY OBJ. 2: The state of meriting and demeriting is one state, since the same person is able to merit and demerit; wherefore it is fitting that one place should be as-

locus. Sed eorum qui recipiuiit pro meritis, sunt status diversi. Et ideo non est simile.

AD TERTIUM dicendum quod pro culpa originali potest aliquis puniri dupliciter, ut ex dictis patet: vel ratione personae, vel ratione naturae tantum. Et ideo illi culpae respondet duplex limbus.

AD QUARTUM dicendum quod aer iste caliginosus non assignatur daemonibus quasi locus in quo recipiant retributionem pro meritis, sed quasi competens officio eorum inquantum deputantur nobis ad exercitium. Et ideo inter receptacula de quibus nunc agitur, non computatur: primo enim eis deputatur ignis inferni, ut patet Matth. 25, [41].

AD QUINTUM dicendum quod paradisus terrestris pertinet magis ad statum viatoris quam ad statum recipientis pro meritis. Et ideo inter receptacula de quibus nunc agitur, non computatur.

AD SEXTUM dicendum quod illa positio est impossibilis. Si tamen esset possibilis, talis in inferno puniretur in aeternum. Quod enim veniale peccatum in purgatorio temporaliter puniatur, accidit ei inquantum gratiam habet adiunctam. Unde, si adiungitur mortali, quod est sine gratia, poena aeterna in inferno punietur. Et quia iste qui cum originali peccato decedit, habet veniale sine gratia, non est inconveniens si ponitur aeternaliter puniri.

AD SEPTIMUM dicendum quod diversitas graduum in poenis vel praemiis non diversificat statum, secundum cuius diversitatem receptacula distinguuntur. Et ideo ratio non sequitur.

AD OCTAVUM dicendum quod hoc quod animae separatae aliquando in loco nostrae habitationis puniuntur, non est propter hoc quod locus iste sit proprius locus poenarum: sed hoc fit ad nostram instructionem, ut, eorum poenas videntes, retrahamur a culpis.

Quod autem animae existentes in carne hic puniuntur pro peccatis, non pertinet ad propositum. Quia talis poena non trahit hominem extra statum merentis vel demerentis: nunc autem agimus de receptaculis quae debentur animae post statum meriti vel demeriti.

AD NONUM dicendum quod malum non potest esse purum absque commixtione boni, sicut bonum summum est absque omni commixtione mali. Et ideo illi qui ad beatitudinem, quae summum bonum est, transferendi sunt, debent etiam ab omni malo purgari. Et propter hoc oportet esse locum in quo tales purgentur, si hinc non omnino purgati exeant. Sed illi qui in inferno detruduntur, non erunt immunes ab omni bono. Et ideo non est simile: quia ibi in inferno existentes praemium bonorum suorum recipere possunt inquantum bona praeterita eis valent ad mitigationem poenae.

signed to all. But of those who receive according to their merits there are various states, and consequently the comparison fails.

REPLY OBJ. 3: One may be punished in two ways for original sin, as stated above: either in reference to the person or in reference to nature only. Consequently, there is a twofold limbo corresponding to that sin.

REPLY OBJ. 4: This darkened air is assigned to the demons not as the place where they receive retribution for their merits, but as a place befitting their office, insofar as they are appointed to try us. Hence it is not reckoned among the abodes of which we are treating now: since the fire of hell is assigned to them in the first place (Matt 25).

REPLY OBJ. 5: The earthly paradise belongs to the state of the wayfarer rather than to the state of those who receive for their merits; and consequently it is not reckoned among the abodes whereof we are treating now.

REPLY OBJ. 6: This supposition is impossible. If, however, it were possible, such a one would be punished in hell eternally: for it is accidental to venial sin that it be punished temporally in purgatory, through its having grace annexed to it: wherefore if it be annexed to a mortal sin, which is without grace, it will be punished eternally in hell. And since this one who dies in original sin has a venial sin without grace, it is not unfitting to suppose that he be punished eternally.

REPLY OBJ. 7: Diversity of degrees in punishments or rewards does not diversify the state, and it is according to the diversity of state that we distinguish various abodes. Hence the argument does not follow.

REPLY OBJ. 8: Although separated souls are sometimes punished in the place where we dwell, it does not follow that this is their proper place of punishment: but this is done for our instruction, that seeing their punishment we may be deterred from sin.

That souls while yet in the flesh are punished here for their sins has nothing to do with the question, because a punishment of this kind does not place a man outside the state of meriting or demeriting: whereas we are treating now of the abodes to which souls are assigned after the state of merit or demerit.

REPLY OBJ. 9: It is impossible for evil to be pure without the admixture of good in the same way that the supreme good is without any admixture of evil. Consequently, those who are to be conveyed to beatitude, which is a supreme good, must be cleansed of all evil. Therefore, there must be a place where such persons are cleansed if they go hence without being perfectly clean. But those who will be thrust into hell will not be free from all good: and consequently the comparison fails, since those who are in hell can receive the reward of their goods, insofar as their past goods avail for the mitigation of their punishment.

Ad decimum dicendum quod in gloria animae consistit praemium essentiale: sed gloria corporis, cum redundet ex anima, tota consistit in anima quasi originaliter. Et ideo carentia gloriae animae diversificat statum, non autem carentia gloriae corporis. Et propter hoc etiam idem locus, scilicet caelum empyreum, debetur animabus sanctis exutis a corpore, et coniunctis corporibus gloriosis. Non autem idem locus debetur animabus patrum ante perceptionem gloriae animae, et post perceptionem ipsius.

Reply Obj. 10: The essential reward consists in the glory of the soul, but the body's glory, since it overflows from the soul, is entirely founded, as it were, on the soul: and consequently lack of the soul's glory causes a difference of state, whereas lack of the body's glory does not. For this reason, too, the same place, namely, the empyrean, is assigned to the holy souls separated from their bodies and united to glorious bodies: whereas the same place was not assigned to the souls of the fathers both before and after the glorification of souls.

QUESTION 70

THE SEPARATED SOUL'S QUALITY AND PUNISHMENT BY MATERIAL FIRE

Deinde considerandum est de qualitate animae exeuntis a corpore, et poena ei ab igne corporeo inflicta.

Circa quod quaeruntur tria.

Primo: utrum in. anima separata remaneant potentiae sensitivae.

Secundo: utrum remaneant in ea actus dictarum potentiarum.

Tertio: utrum anima separata possit pati ab igne corporeo.

We must next consider the general quality of the soul after leaving the body, and the punishment inflicted on it by material fire.

Under this head there are three points of inquiry:

(1) Whether the sensitive powers remain in the separated soul?

(2) Whether the acts of the aforesaid powers remain in the soul?

(3) Whether the separated soul can suffer from a material fire?

Article 1

Whether the Sensitive Powers Remain in the Separated Soul?

AD PRIMUM SIC PROCEDITUR. Videtur quod in anima separata remaneant potentiae sensitivae. Augustinus enim, in libro *de Spiritu et anima*, sic dicit: *recedit anima a corpore secum trahens omnia: sensum scilicet, imaginationem, rationem, intellectum, intelligentiam, concupiscibilitatem et irascibilitatem*. Sed sensus et imaginatio, et vis irascibilis et concupiscibilis, sunt vires sensitivae. Ergo in anima separata vires sensitivae remanent.

PRAETEREA, Augustinus dicit, in libro *de Ecclesiasticis dogmat*. 2: *solum hominem credimus animam habere substantivam, quae exuta a corpore vivit, et sensus suos atque ingenia vivaciter tenet*. Ergo anima exuta a corpore vivit et habet potentias sensitivas.

PRAETEREA, potentiae animae vel essentialiter ei insunt, ut quidam dicunt: vel ad minus sunt naturales proprietates ipsius. Sed id quod essentialiter inest alicui, non potest ab eo separari: neque subiectum aliquod deseritur a naturalibus proprietatibus. Ergo impossibile est quod anima separata a corpore aliquas potentias amittat.

PRAETEREA, non est totum integrum cui aliqua partium deest. Sed potentiae animae dicuntur partes ipsius. Si ergo potentias aliquas post mortem anima amittit, non erit anima integra post mortem. Quod est inconveniens.

PRAETEREA, potentiae animae magis cooperantur ad meritum quam etiam corpus: cum corpus sit solum instrumentum actus, potentiae vero principia agendi. Sed necesse est ut simul corpus praemietur cum anima propter hoc quod cooperabatur in merito. Ergo multo fortius est necesse quod potentiae animae simul praemientur cum ipsa. Ergo anima separata eas non amittit.

OBJECTION 1: It would seem that the sensitive powers remain in the sensitive soul. For Augustine says: *the soul withdraws from the body taking all with itself, sense and imagination, reason, understanding and intelligence, the concupiscible and irascible powers* (Alcher of Clairvaux, *The Spirit and the Soul* 15). Now sense, imagination, concupiscible and irascible are sensitive powers. Therefore, the sensitive powers remain in the separated soul.

OBJ. 2: Further, Augustine says (Gennadius, *Book of Ecclesiastical Dogmas* 16): *we believe that man alone has a substantial soul, which lives though separated from the body, and clings keenly to its senses and wits*. Therefore, the soul retains its senses after being separated from the body.

OBJ. 3: Further, the soul's powers are either its essential parts as some maintain, or at least are its natural properties. Now that which is in a thing essentially cannot be separated from it, nor is a subject severed from its natural properties. Therefore, it is impossible for the soul to lose any of its powers after being separated from the body.

OBJ. 4: Further, a whole is not entire if one of its parts be lacking. Now the soul's powers are called its parts. Therefore, if the soul lose any of its powers after death, it will not be entire after death: and this is unfitting.

OBJ. 5: Further, the soul's powers cooperate in merit more even than the body, since the body is a mere instrument of action, while the powers are principles of action. Now the body must of necessity be rewarded together with the soul, since it cooperated in merit. Much more, therefore, is it necessary that the powers of the soul be rewarded together with it. Therefore, the separated soul does not lose them.

Praeterea, si anima, cum separatur a corpore, potentiam sensitivam amittit, oportet quod illa potentia in nihilum cedat: non enim potest dici quod in materia aliqua resolvatur, cum non habeat materiam partem sui. Sed id quod omnino in nihilum cedit, non reiteratur idem numero. Ergo anima non habebit in resurrectione eandem numero potentiam sensitivam. Sed, secundum Philosophum, sicut se habet anima ad corpus, ita se habent potentiae animae ad partes corporis, ut visus ad oculum. Si autem non est eadem anima quae redibit ad corpus, non esset idem homo. Ergo, eadem ratione, non esset idem oculus numero si non habeat eandem numero potentiam visivam. Et, simili ratione, nec aliqua alia pars eadem numero resurgeret. Et per consequens nec totus homo idem numero erit. Non ergo potest esse quod anima separata potentias sensitivas amittat.

Praeterea, si potentiae sensitivae corrumperentur corrupto corpore, oporteret quod, debilitato corpore, debilitarentur. Hoc autem non contingit: quia, ut dicitur in I de Anima, si senex accipiat oculum iuvenis, videbit utique sicut iuvenis. Ergo nec, corrupto corpore, sensitivae potentiae corrumpentur.

Sed contra: Est quod Augustinus, in libro de Ecclesiasticis Dogmat., dicit: *duabus substantiis homo constat, anima tantum et carne, anima cum ratione sua, et carne cum sensibus suis.* Potentiae ergo sensitivae ad carnem pertinent. Ergo, corrupta carne, non manent potentiae sensitivae in anima.

Praeterea, Philosophus, in XII *Metaphys.*, de separatione animae loquens, sic dicit: *si aptem aliquid remanet in postremo, quaerendum est de hoc. In quibusdam enim non est impossibile. Verbi gratia, si anima est talis dispositionis, non tota, sed intellectus. Tota enim forte impossibile.* Ex hoc videtur quod anima tota a corpore non separetur, sed solum potentiae animae intellectivae: non enim sensitivae vel vegetativae.

Praeterea, in II de Anima Philosophus dicit, de intellectu loquens: *hoc solum contingit separari ut perpetuum a corruptibili. Reliquae autem partes animae manifestum est ex his quod non separabiles sunt, ut quidam dicunt.* Ergo potentiae sensitivae non manent in anima separata.

Respondeo dicendum quod circa hoc est multiplex opinio. Quidam enim, aestimantes potentias omnes esse in anima ad modum quo color est in corpore, dicunt quod anima a corpore separata omnes potentias suas secum trahit. Si enim aliqua ei deesset, oporteret animam transmutatam esse secundum naturales proprietates: quae, subiecto manente, variari non possunt.

Sed dicta aestimatio falsa est. Cum enim potentia sit secundum quam potentes dicimur aliquid agere vel pa-

Obj. 6: Further, if the soul after separation from the body loses its sensitive power, that power would have to result in nothing. For it cannot be said that it is dissolved into some matter, since it has no matter as a part of itself. Now that which entirely comes to naught is not restored in identity; wherefore at the resurrection the soul will not have the same identical sensitive powers. Now, according to the Philosopher (*On the Soul* 2.1), as the soul is to the body, so are the soul's powers to the parts of the body; for instance, the sight to the eye. But if it were not identically the same soul that returns to the body, it would not be identically the same man. Therefore, for the same reason it would not be identically the same eye if the visual power were not identically the same; and in like manner no other part would rise again in identity, and consequently neither would the whole man be identically the same. Therefore, it is impossible for the separated soul to lose its sensitive powers.

Obj. 7: Further, if the sensitive powers were to be corrupted when the body is corrupted, it would follow that they are weakened when the body is weakened. Yet this is not the case, for according to *On the Soul* 1, *if an old man were given the eye of a young man, he would, without doubt, see as well as a young man.* Therefore, neither are the sensitive powers corrupted when the body is corrupted.

On the contrary, Augustine says: *of two substances alone does man consist, soul and body: the soul with its reason, and the body with its senses* (Gennadius, *Book of Ecclesiastical Dogmas* 19). Therefore, the sensitive powers belong to the body: and consequently when the body is corrupted the sensitive powers remain not in the soul.

Further, The Philosopher, speaking of the separation of the soul, expresses himself thus: *if, however, anything remain at last, we must ask what this is: because in certain subjects it is not impossible, for instance, if the soul be of such a disposition, not the whole soul but the intellect; for as regards the whole soul this is probably impossible* (*Metaphysics* 11.3). Hence it seems that the whole soul is not separated from the body, but only the intellective powers of the soul, and consequently not the sensitive or vegetative powers.

Further, The Philosopher, speaking of the intellect, says: *this alone is ever separated, as the everlasting from the corruptible: for it is hereby clear that the remaining parts are not separable as some maintain* (*On the Soul* 2.2). Therefore, the sensitive powers do not remain in the separated soul.

I answer that, There are many opinions on this question. For some, holding the view that all the powers are in the soul in the same way as color is in a body, hold that the soul separated from the body takes all its powers away with it: because, if it lacked any one of them, it would follow that the soul is changed in its natural properties, since these cannot change so long as their subject remains.

But the aforesaid view is false, for since a power is so called because it enables us to do or suffer something, and

ti; eiusdem autem sit agere et posse agere: oportet quod eiusdem sit potentia sicut subiecti quod est agens vel patiens. Unde Philosophus, in principio, *de Somno et Vigilia*, dicit quod *cuius est potentia, eius est actio*. Videmus autem manifeste quasdam operationes, quarum potentiae animae sunt principia, non esse animae, proprie loquendo, sed coniuncti, quia non explentur nisi mediante corpore: ut est videre, audire, et huiusmodi.

Unde oportet quod istae potentiae sint coniuncti sicut subiecti; animae autem sicut principii influentis, sicut forma est principium proprietatum compositi. Quaedam vero operationes exercentur ab anima sine organo corporali: ut intelligere, considerare et velle. Unde, cum hae actiones sint animae propriae, et potentiae quae sunt harum principia, non solum erunt animae ut principii, sed ut subiecti. Quia ergo, manente proprio subiecto, manere oportet et proprias passiones, et corrupto eo corrumpi; necesse est illas potentias quae in suis actionibus non utuntur organo corporali, remanere in anima separata; illas autem quae utuntur, corrumpi corpore corrupto. Et huiusmodi sunt potentiae omnes quae pertinent ad animam sensibilem et vegetabilem.

Et propter hoc quidam in potentiis animae sensibilibus distinguunt. Dicunt enim has esse duplices: quasdam quae sunt actus organorum, quae sunt ab anima effluxae in corpus, et hae cum corpore corrumpuntur; quasdam vero originales harum, quae sunt in anima, quia per eas anima corpus sensificat ad videndum et audiendum et huiusmodi, et hae originales potentiae manent in anima separata.

Sed hoc non videtur convenienter dici. Anima enim per suam essentiam, non mediantibus aliquibus aliis potentiis, est origo illarum potentiarum quae sunt actus organorum: sicut et forma quaelibet, ex hoc ipso quod per essentiam suam materiam informat, est origo proprietatum quae compositum naturaliter consequuntur. Si enim oporteret in anima ponere alias potentias, quibus mediantibus potentiae quae organa perficiunt ab essentia animae effluerent, eadem ratione oporteret ponere alias potentias quibus mediantibus ab essentia animae effluerent illae mediae potentiae: et sic in infinitum. Si enim statur alicubi, melius est ut in primo stetur.

Unde alii dicunt quod potentiae sensitivae, et alias similes, non manent in anima separata nisi secundum quid, scilicet ut in radice, per modum scilicet quod principiata sunt in principiis suis: in anima enim separata manet efficacia influendi iterum huiusmodi potentias si corpori uniatur. Nec oportet hanc efficaciam esse aliquid

since to do and to be able to do belong to the same subject, it follows that the subject of a power is the same as that which is agent or patient. Hence the Philosopher says in the beginning of *On Sleep and Waking* that *where we find power there we find action*. Now it is evident that certain operations of which the soul's powers are the principles do not belong to the soul properly speaking, but to the soul as united to the body, because they are not performed except through the medium of the body—such as to see, to hear, and so forth.

Hence it follows that such powers belong to the united soul and body as their subject, but to the soul as their inflowing principle, just as the form is the principle of the properties of a composite being. Some operations, however, are performed by the soul without a bodily organ—for instance, to understand, to consider, to will: wherefore, since these actions are proper to the soul, the powers that are the principles thereof belong to the soul not only as their principle but also as their subject. Therefore, since so long as the proper subject remains, its proper passions must also remain, and when it is corrupted they also must be corrupted, it follows that these powers which use no bodily organ for their actions must remain in the separated soul, while those which use a bodily organ must be corrupted when the body is corrupted: and such are all the powers belonging to the sensitive and the vegetative soul.

On this account some draw a distinction in the sensitive powers of the soul: for they say that they are of two kinds—some, being acts of organs and emanating from the soul into the body, are corrupted with the body; others, from which the former originate, are in the soul, because by them the soul sensitizes the body for seeing, hearing, and so on; and these primary powers remain in the separated soul.

But this statement seems unreasonable: because the soul, by its essence and not through the medium of certain other powers, is the origin of those powers which are the acts of organs, even as any form, from the very fact that by its essence it informs its matter, is the origin of the properties which result naturally in the composite. For were it necessary to suppose other powers in the soul by means of which the powers that perfect the organs may flow from the essence of the soul, for the same reason it would be necessary to suppose other powers by means of which these mean powers flow from the essence of the soul, and so on to infinity. If we have to stop, it is better to do so at the first step.

Hence others say that the sensitive and other like powers do not remain in the separated soul except in a restricted sense, namely, in the root, in the same way as a result is in its principle: because there remains in the separated soul the ability to produce these powers if it should be reunited to the body. Nor is it necessary for this ability to

19

superadditum essentiae animae, ut dictum est. Et haec opinio videtur magis rationabilis.

Ad primum ergo dicendum quod verbum illud Augustini intelligendum est quod anima secum trahit quasdam illarum potentiarum in actu, scilicet intelligentiam et intellectum; quasdam vero radicaliter, ut dictum est.

Ad secundum dicendum quod sensus quos anima secum trahit, non sunt isti exteriores, sed interiores, qui scilicet ad partem intellectivam pertinent: quia intellectus interdum sensus appellatur, ut patet per Basilium, *super Proverbia*, et per Philosophum, in VI *Ethic.* Vel, si intelligit de sensibus exterioribus, dicendum sicut ad primum.

Ad tertium dicendum quod, sicut iam patet ex dictis, potentiae sensitivae non comparantur ad animam sicut naturales passiones ad subiectum, sed sicut ad originem. Unde ratio non procedit.

Ad quartum dicendum quod potentiae animae dicuntur partes eius potentiales. Talium autem totorum ista est natura, quia tota virtus totius consistit in una partium perfecte, in aliis autem partialiter: sicut in anima virtus animae perfecte consistit in parte intellectiva, in aliis autem partialiter. Unde, cum in anima separata remaneant vires intellectivae partis, integra remanebit, non diminuta, quamvis sensitivae potentiae actu non remaneant: sicut nec potentia regis manet diminuta mortuo praeposito, qui eius potentiam participabat.

Ad quintum dicendum quod corpus cooperatur ad meritum quasi pars essentialis hominis qui meretur. Sic autem non cooperantur potentiae sensitivae: cum sint de genere accidentium. Et ideo non est simile.

Ad sextum dicendum quod potentiae animae sensitivae non dicuntur, esse actus organorum quasi formae essentiales ipsorum, nisi ratione animae cuius sunt: sed sunt actus ipsorum sicut perficientes ea ad proprias operationes, sicut calor est actus ignis perficiens ipsum ad calefaciendum. Unde, sicut ignis idem numero remaneret etiam si alius numero in eo calor esset, sicut patet de frigore aquae, quod non redit idem numero postquam fuerit calefacta, aqua nihilominus eadem numero manente; ita et organa erunt eadem numero, quamvis potentiae eaedem numero non sint.

Ad septimum dicendum quod Philosophus ibi loquitur de huiusmodi potentiis secundum quod radicaliter in anima consistunt: quod patet ex hoc quod dicit quod *senium non est in patiendo aliquid animam, sed id in quo est*, scilicet corpus. Sic enim propter corpus neque debilitantur nec corrumpuntur animae virtutes.

be anything in addition to the essence of the soul, as stated above. This opinion appears to be the more reasonable.

Reply Obj. 1: This saying of Augustine is to be understood as meaning that the soul takes away with it some of those powers actually, namely, understanding and intelligence, and some radically, as stated above.

Reply Obj. 2: The senses which the soul takes away with it are not these external senses, but the internal, those, namely, which pertain to the intellective part, for the intellect is sometimes called sense, as Basil states in his commentary on the Proverbs, and again the Philosopher (*Ethics* 6.11). If, however, he means the external senses, we must reply as above to the first objection.

Reply Obj. 3: As stated above, the sensitive powers are related to the soul, not as natural passions to their subject, but as compared to their origin: wherefore the conclusion does not follow.

Reply Obj. 4: The powers of the soul are not called its integral but its potential parts. Now the nature of such wholes is that the entire virtue of the whole is found perfectly in one of the parts, but partially in the others; thus in the soul, the soul's virtue is found perfectly in the intellective part, but partially in the others. Wherefore, as the powers of the intellective part remain in the separated soul, the latter will remain entire and undiminished, although the sensitive powers do not remain actually: as neither is the king's power decreased by the death of a mayor who shared his authority.

Reply Obj. 5: The body cooperates in merit as an essential part of the man who merits. The sensitive powers, however, do not cooperate thus, since they are of the genus of accidents. Hence the comparison fails.

Reply Obj. 6: The powers of the sensitive soul are said to be acts of the organs not as though they were the essential forms of those organs, except in reference to the soul whose powers they are. But they are the acts of the organs by perfecting them for their proper operations, as heat is the act of fire by perfecting it for the purpose of heating. Wherefore, just as a fire would remain the same in number, although another individual heat were in it (even so the cold of water that has been heated returns not the same in number, although the water remains the same in number), so the organs will be the same in number, although the powers be not the same in number.

Reply Obj. 7: The Philosopher is speaking there of these powers as being rooted in the soul. This is clear from his saying that *old age is an affection not of the soul, but of that in which the soul is*, namely, the body. For in this way the powers of the soul are neither weakened nor corrupted on account of the body.

Article 2

Whether the Acts of the Sensitive Powers Remain in the Separated Soul?

Ad secundum sic proceditur. Videtur quod in anima separata remaneant etiam actus sensitivarum potentiarum. Dicit enim Augustinus, in libro *de Spiritu et anima*: *anima recedens a corpore ex his*, scilicet imaginatione, concupiscibilitate, irascibilitate, *secundum merita afficitur ad delectationem sive dolorem.* Sed imaginatio et concupiscibilis et irascibilis sunt potentiae sensitivae. Ergo secundum sensitivas potentias anima separata afficietur. Et ita secundum eas in aliquo actu erit.

Praeterea, Augustinus, *super Genesis ad litteram,* lib. XII, dicit quod *corpus non sentit, sed anima per corpus*; et infra: *quaedam autem anima non per corpus, sed sine corpore sentit*, ut est timor et huiusmodi. Sed id quod animae sine corpore convenit, potest inesse animae a corpore separatae. Ergo tunc actu anima sentire poterit.

Praeterea, inspicere similitudines corporum sicut in somno accidit, ad visionem imaginariam pertinet, quae est in parte sensitiva. Sed huiusmodi similitudines corporum inspicere sicut in somnis accidit, convenit animae separatae. Unde Augustinus, XII *super Genesis ad litteram,* sic dicit: *Neque enim video cur habeat anima similitudinem corporis sui, cum, iacente sine sensu corpore, nondum tamen penitus mortuo, videt talia qualia multi ex illa subductione vivis redditi narraverunt, et non habeat cum perfecta morte penitus de corpore exierit.* Non enim potest hoc intelligi quod anima similitudinem corporis habeat, nisi secundum quod eam inspicit. Unde praemisit de iacentibus sine sensu quod *gerunt quandam similitudinem corporis sui, per quam possunt ad loca corporalia ferri, et talia, qualia vident, similitudinibus sensuum experiri.* Ergo anima separata potest exire in actum potentiarum sensitivarum.

Praeterea, memoria est potentia sensitivae partis: ut probatur in libro *de Memoria et Reminiscentia.* Sed animae separatae actu memorabuntur eorum quae in hoc mundo gesserunt: unde et diviti epuloni dicitur, Luc. 16, [25]: *recordare quia recepisti bona in vita tua.* Ergo anima separata exibit in actum potentiae sensitivae.

Praeterea, secundum Philosophum, in III *de Anima,* irascibilis et concupiscibilis sunt in parte sensitiva. Sed in irascibili et concupiscibili sunt gaudium et tristitia, amor et odium, timor et spes, et huiusmodi affectiones, quas secundum fidem nostram ponimus in animabus separatis. Ergo animae separatae non carebunt actibus potentiarum sensitivarum.

Sed contra: Id quod est commune animae et corpori, non potest remanere in anima separata. Sed omnes

Objection 1: It would seem that the acts of the sensitive powers remain in the separated soul. For Augustine says (*The Spirit and the Soul* 15): *when the soul leaves the body it derives pleasure or sorrow through being affected with these* (namely, the imagination, the concupiscible, and the irascible faculties) *according to its merits.* But the imagination, the concupiscible, and the irascible are sensitive powers. Therefore, the separated soul will be affected as regards the sensitive powers, and consequently will be in some act by reason of them.

Obj. 2: Further, Augustine says (*On the Literal Meaning of Genesis* 12) that *the body feels not, but the soul through the body,* and further on: *the soul feels certain things, not through the body but without the body.* Now that which befits the soul without the body can be in the soul separated from the body. Therefore, the soul will then be able to feel actually.

Obj. 3: Further, to see images of bodies, as occurs in sleep, belongs to imaginary vision, which is in the sensitive part. Now it happens that the separated soul sees images of bodies in the same way as when we sleep. Thus Augustine says (*On the Literal Meaning of Genesis* 12): *for I see not why the soul has an image of its own body when, the body lying senseless, yet not quite dead, it sees some things which many have related after returning to life from this suspended animation and yet has it not when it has left the body through death having taken place.* For it is unintelligible that the soul should have an image of its body, except insofar as it sees that image: wherefore he said before of those who lie senseless that *they have a certain image of their own body by which they are able to be borne to corporeal places and by means of sensible images to take cognizance of such things as they see.* Therefore, the separated soul can exercise the acts of the sensitive powers.

Obj. 4: Further, the memory is a power of the sensitive part, as proved in *On Memory and Recollection* 1. Now separated souls will actually remember the things they did in this world; thus it is said to the rich glutton: *remember that you did receive good things in your lifetime* (Luke 16:25). Therefore, the separated soul will exercise the act of a sensitive power.

Obj. 5: Further, according to the Philosopher (*On the Soul* 3.9) the irascible and concupiscible are in the sensitive part. But joy and sorrow, love and hatred, fear and hope, and similar emotions which, according to our faith, we hold to be in separated souls, are in the irascible and concupiscible. Therefore, separated souls will not be deprived of the acts of the sensitive powers.

On the contrary, That which is common to soul and body cannot remain in the separated soul. Now all the op-

operationes potentiarum sensitivarum sunt communes animae et corpori: quod patet ex hoc quod nulla potentia sensitiva aliquem actum habet nisi per organum corporale. Ergo anima separata carebit actibus sensitivarum potentiarum.

Praeterea, Philosophus dicit, in I *de Anima*, quod, *corrupto corpore, anima neque reminiscitur neque amat.* Et eadem ratio est de omnibus aliis actibus sensitivarum potentiarum. Ergo non procedit anima separata in aliquem actum alicuius potentiae sensitivae.

Respondeo dicendum quod quidam distinguunt duplices actus sensitivarum potentiarum: quosdam exteriores, quos per corpus exercet, et hi non remanent in anima separata; quosdam vero intrinsecos, quos anima per seipsam exercet, et hi erunt in anima separata. Haec autem positio descendere videtur ab opinione Platonis, qui posuit animam corpori coniungi sicut quandam substantiam perfectam in nullo a corpore dependentem, sed solum sicut motorem mobili: quod patet ex trans-corporatione quam ponebat. Quia autem secundum ipsum nihil movebat nisi motum; et, ne abiretur in infinitum, dicebat quod primum movens movet seipsum: posuit quod anima erat seipsam movens, et secundum hoc erat duplex motus animae: unus quo movebatur a seipsa; alius quo movebatur corpus ab ea. Et sic anima habebat actum qui est videre, primo in seipsa, secundum quod movebat seipsam; et secundo in organo corporali, secundum quod movebat corpus.

Hanc autem positionem Philosophus destruit, in I *de Anima*, ostendens quod anima non movet seipsam, et quod nullo modo movetur secundum istas operationes quae sunt videre, sentire et huiusmodi, sed quod istae operationes sunt motus coniuncti tantum. Unde oportet dicere quod actus sensitivarum potentiarum nullo modo maneant in anima separata, nisi forte sicut in radice remota.

Ad primum ergo dicendum quod liber ille negatur a quibusdam fuisse Augustini: dicitur enim fuisse cuiusdam Cisterciensis, qui eum ex dictis Augustini compilavit, et quaedam de suo addidit. Unde quod ibi scribitur, pro auctoritate habendum non est.

Si tamen auctoritas debeat sustineri, dicendum quod non debet intelligi quod anima separata ex imaginatione et aliis huiusmodi potentiis afficiatur quasi ipsa affectio sit actus potentiarum praedictarum: sed quia ex his quae anima per imaginationem et alias huiusmodi potentias commisit in corpore, in futuro afficietur, vel in bonum vel in malum; ut sic imaginatio et huiusmodi potentiae non intelligantur elicere illam affectionem, sed elicuisse in corpore meritum affectionis illius.

Ad secundum dicendum quod anima dicitur sentire per corpus, non quasi actus sentiendi sit animae se-

erations of the sensitive powers are common to the soul and body: and this is evident from the fact that no sensitive power exercises an act except through a bodily organ. Therefore, the separated soul will be deprived of the acts of the sensitive powers.

Further, The Philosopher says (*On the Soul* 1.4), that *when the body is corrupted, the soul neither remembers nor loves,* and the same applies to all the acts of the sensitive powers. Therefore, the separated soul does not exercise the act of any sensitive power.

I answer that, Some distinguish two kinds of acts in the sensitive powers: external acts which the soul exercises through the body, and these do not remain in the separated soul; and internal acts which the soul performs by itself, and these will be in the separated soul. This statement would seem to have originated from the opinion of Plato, who held that the soul is united to the body as a perfect substance in no way dependant on the body, and merely as a mover is united to the thing moved. This is an evident consequence of transmigration which he held. And, since according to him nothing is in motion except what is moved, and lest he should go on indefinitely, he said that the first mover moves itself, and he maintained that the soul is the cause of its own movement. Accordingly, there would be a twofold movement of the soul, one by which it moves itself, and another whereby the body is moved by the soul: so that this act 'to see' is first of all in the soul itself as moving itself, and second in the bodily organ insofar as the soul moves the body.

This opinion is refuted by the Philosopher (*On the Soul* 1.3) who proves that the soul does not move itself, and that it is in no way moved in respect of such operations as seeing, feeling, and the like, but that such operations are movements of the composite only. We must therefore conclude that the acts of the sensitive powers in no way remain in the separated soul, except perhaps as in their remote origin.

Reply Obj. 1: Some deny that this book is Augustine's: for it is ascribed to a Cistercian who compiled it from Augustine's works and added things of his own. Hence we are not to take what is written there as having authority.

If, however, its authority should be maintained, it must be said that the meaning is that the separated soul is affected with imagination and other like powers, not as though such affection were the act of the aforesaid powers, but in the sense that the soul will be affected in the future life for good or ill according to the things which it committed in the body through the imagination and other like powers: so that the imagination and such powers are not supposed to elicit that affection, but to have elicited in the body the merit of that affection.

Reply Obj. 2: The soul is said to feel through the body, not as though the act of feeling belonged to the soul by it-

cundum se: sed quia est totius coniuncti ratione animae, eo modo loquendi quo dicimus quod calor calefaciat.

Quod autem subiungitur, quod quaedam anima sentit sine corpore, ut timorem et huiusmodi, intelligendum est sine exterioris corporis motu, qui accidit in actibus sensuum propriorum: non enim timor et huiusmodi passiones sine motu corporali contingunt. Vel potest dici quod Augustinus loquitur secundum opinionem Platonicorum, qui hoc ponebant, ut dictum est.

AD TERTIUM dicendum quod Augustinus ibi inquirendo loquitur, non determinando: sicut fere per totum illum librum. Patet enim quod non est similis ratio de anima dormientis, et de anima separata. Anima enim dormientis utitur organo imaginationis, in qua corporales similitudines imprimuntur: quod de anima separata dici non potest.

Vel dicendum quod similitudines rerum sunt in anima et quantum ad potentiam sensitivam, et imaginativam, et intellectivam, secundum maiorem et minorem abstractionem a materia et a materialibus conditionibus. Tenet ergo similitudo Augustini quantum ad hoc quod, sicut similitudines rerum corporalium sunt in anima somniantis vel excessum mentis patientis imaginabiliter, ita sunt in anima separata intellectualiter: non autem quod in anima separata sint imaginabiliter.

AD QUARTUM, dicendum quod, sicut in I Libro dictum est, memoria dupliciter sumitur. Quandoque prout est potentia sensitivae partis, secundum quod concernit praeteritum tempus. Et hoc modo actus memoriae in anima separata non erit. Unde dicit Philosophus, in I *de Anima*, quod, *hoc corrupta*, scilicet corpore, *anima non reminiscitur*. Alio modo accipitur memoria prout est pars imaginis, ad intellectivam partem pertinens: secundum scilicet quod ab omni differentia temporis abstrahit, cum non sit tantum praeteritorum, sed etiam praesentium et futurorum, ut Augustinus dicit. Et secundum hanc memoriam anima separata memorabitur.

AD QUINTUM dicendum quod amor, gaudium et tristitia, et huiusmodi, dupliciter accipiuntur. Quandoque quidem secundum quod sunt passiones appetitivae sensibilis. Et sic non erunt in anima separata: hoc enim modo non explentur sine determinato motu cordis. Alio modo secundum quod surit actus voluntatis, quae est in parte intellectiva. Et hoc modo erunt in anima separata: sicut et delectationem, quae quodam modo est passio partis sensitivae, secundum alium modum accipiendi ponit Philosophus in Deo, dicens, in VII *Ethic.*, quod *Deus una simplici delectatione gaudet*.

self, but as belonging to the whole composite by reason of the soul, just as we say that heat heats.

That which is added—namely, that the soul feels some things without the body, such as fear and so forth—means that it feels such things without the outward movement of the body that takes place in the acts of the proper senses: since fear and like passions do not occur without any bodily movement. It may also be replied that Augustine is speaking according to the opinion of the Platonists who maintained this, as stated above.

REPLY OBJ. 3: Augustine speaks there, as nearly throughout that book, as one inquiring and not deciding. For it is clear that there is no comparison between the soul of a sleeper and the separated soul: since the soul of the sleeper uses the organ of imagination wherein corporeal images are impressed; which cannot be said of the separated soul.

Or we may reply that images of things are in the soul both as to the sensitive, imaginative, and intellective powers, with greater or lesser abstraction from matter and material conditions. Wherefore Augustine's comparison holds in this respect that just as the images of corporeal things are in the soul of the dreamer, or of one who is carried out of his mind, imaginatively, so are they in the separated soul intellectively: but not that they are in the separated soul imaginatively.

REPLY OBJ. 4: As stated in the first book (*Sentences* I, D. 3, qu. 4), memory has a twofold signification. Sometimes it means a power of the sensitive part, insofar as its gaze extends over past time; and in this way the act of the memory will not be in the separated soul. Wherefore the Philosopher says (*On the Soul* 1.4) that *when this*, namely, the body, *is corrupted, the soul remembers not*. In another way, memory is used to designate that part of the imagination which pertains to the intellective faculty, namely, insofar as it abstracts from all differences of time, since it regards not only the past but also the present and the future, as Augustine says (*On the Trinity* 14.11). Taking memory in this sense, the separated soul will remember.

REPLY OBJ. 5: Love, joy, sorrow, and the like have a twofold signification. Sometimes they denote passions of the sensitive appetite, and thus they will not be in the separated soul, because in this way they are not exercised without a definite movement of the heart. The other way is according as they are acts of the will, which is in the intellective part, and in this way they will exist in the separated soul, as will delight, which is in some way a passion of the sensitive part. According to the other mode of taking it, the Philosopher posits it of God, saying in *Ethics* 7 that *God rejoices by one simple operation*.

Article 3

Whether the Separated Soul Can Suffer From a Bodily Fire?

AD TERTIUM SIC PROCEDITUR. Videtur quod anima separata pati non possit ab igne corporeo. Augustinus enim, XII *super Genesis ad litteram*, dicit: *non sunt corporalia, sed corporalibus similia, quibus animae corporibus exutae afficiuntur, seu bene seu male.* Ergo anima separata igne corporeo non punitur.

PRAETEREA, Augustinus, in eodem libro, dicit quod *agens semper est nobilius patiente.* Sed impossibile est aliquod corpus esse nobilius anima separata. Ergo non potest ab aliquo corpore pati.

PRAETEREA, secundum Philosophum, in I *de Generatione*, et secundum Boetium, in libro *de Duabus naturis*, illa solum agunt et patiuntur ad invicem quae in materia communicant. Sed anima et ignis corporeus non communicant in materia: quia spiritualium et corporalium non est materia communis. Unde non possunt ad invicem transmutari, ut Boetius in eodem libro dicit; ergo anima separata ab igne non patitur.

PRAETEREA, omne quod patitur recipit aliquid ab agente. Si ergo anima patiatur ab igne corporeo, aliquid ab eo recipiet. Sed omne quod recipitur in aliquo, est in eo per modum recipientis. Ergo quod recipitur ab igne in anima, non est in eo materialiter, sed spiritualiter. Sed formae rerum in anima spiritualiter existentes sunt perfectiones ipsius. Ergo, etsi patiatur ab igne corporeo, hoc non erit in eius poenam, sed magis in eius perfectionem.

SI DICATUR QUOD *hoc ipso anima punitur ab igne quod ignem videt*, ut videtur dicere Gregorius, IV *Dialog.*: contra. Si videt anima ignem inferni, non potest videre nisi visione intellectuali: cum non habeat organa quibus visio sensitiva vel imaginaria perficitur. Sed visio intellectualis non videtur quod possit esse causa tristitiae: *delectationi enim quae est in considerando, non est tristitia contrarium*, secundum Philosophum. Ergo ex tali visione anima non punitur.

SI DICATUR QUOD anima patitur ab igne corporeo eo quod tenetur ab eo, sicut nunc tenetur a corpore dum vivit in corpore: contra. Anima, dum in corpore vivit, tenetur a corpore inquantum ex ea et corpore fit unum sicut ex materia et forma fit unum. Sed anima non erit forma illius ignis corporei. Ergo supra dicto modo non poterit ab illo igne teneri.

PRAETEREA, omne agens corporeum agit per contactum. Sed non potest esse aliquis contactus ignis cor-

OBJECTION 1: It would seem that the separated soul cannot suffer from a bodily fire. For Augustine says (*On the Literal Meaning of Genesis* 12): *the things that affect the soul well or ill after its separation from the body are not corporeal, but resemble corporeal things.* Therefore, the separated soul is not punished with a bodily fire.

OBJ. 2: Further, Augustine says that *the agent is always more excellent than the patient* (*On the Literal Meaning of Genesis* 12). But it is impossible for any body to be more excellent than the separated soul. Therefore, it cannot suffer from a body.

OBJ. 3: Further, according to the Philosopher (*On Generation and Corruption* 1) and Boethius (*On the Person and the Two Natures*) only those things that agree in matter are active and passive in relation to one another. But the soul and corporeal fire do not agree in matter, since there is no matter common to spiritual and corporeal things: wherefore they cannot be changed into one another, as Boethius says (*On the Person and the Two Natures*). Therefore, the separated soul does not suffer from a bodily fire.

OBJ. 4: Further, whatsoever is patient receives something from the agent. Therefore, if the soul should suffer from the bodily fire, it will receive something from it. Now whatsoever is received in a thing is received according to the mode of the recipient. Therefore, that which is received in the soul from the fire is in it not materially, but spiritually. Now the forms of things existing spiritually in the soul are its perfections. Therefore, though it be granted that the soul suffer from the bodily fire, this will not conduce to its punishment, but rather to its perfection.

OBJ. 5: Further, *if it be said that the soul is punished merely by seeing the fire*, as Gregory would seem to say (*Dialogues* 4.29), to the contrary. If the soul sees the fire of hell, it cannot see it save by intellectual vision, since it has not the organs by which sensitive or imaginative vision is effected. But it would seem impossible for intellectual vision to be the cause of sorrow, since *there is no sorrow contrary to the pleasure of considering*, according to the Philosopher (*Topics* 1.13). Therefore, the soul is not punished by that vision.

OBJ. 6: Further, if it be said that the soul suffers from the corporeal fire through being held thereby, even as now it is held by the body while living in the body; to the contrary. The soul, while living in the body, is held by the body insofar as there results one thing from the soul and the body, as from form and matter. But the soul will not be the form of that corporeal fire. Therefore, it cannot be held by the fire in the manner aforesaid.

OBJ. 7: Further, every bodily agent acts by contact. But a corporeal fire cannot be in contact with the soul, since con-

porei et animae: quia contactus solum fit inter corpora quae habent ultima simul. Ergo anima ab igne corporeo non patitur.

Praeterea, agens organicum, non agit in remota nisi per hoc quod agit in media: unde per determinatam distantiam agere potest proportionatam suae virtuti. Sed animae, vel ad minus daemones, de quibus est eadem ratio, quandoque sunt extra locum inferni; quandoque etiam in hoc mundo hominibus apparent. Nec tamen sunt a poena immunes: sicut enim gloria sanctorum nunquam interrumpitur, ita nec poena damnatorum. Nec tamen videmus quod omnia intermedia ab igne inferni patiantur. Nec iterum est credibile aliquid corporeum de natura elementi esse tantae virtutis ut ad tantam distantiam actionem suam diffundat. Ergo non videtur quod poenas quas animae damnatorum sustinent, ab igne corporeo patiantur.

Sed contra: Eadem ratio est in animabus separatis et daemonibus quod ab igne corporeo pati possint. Sed daemones ab eo patiuntur: cum puniantur ab illo igne in quem corpora damnatorum proiicientur post resurrectionem, quem oportet esse corporeum; et hoc patet per sententiam Domini, Matth. 25, [41]: *ite, maledicti, in ignem aeternum, qui paratus est diabolo et angelis eius.* Ergo et animae separatae ab igne corporeo pati possunt.

Praeterea, poena debet respondere culpae. Sed anima per culpam se corpori subiecit per pravam concupiscentiam. Ergo iustum est ut in poenam rei corporeae subiiciatur per passionem.

Praeterea, maior est unio formae ad materiam quam agentis ad patiens. Sed diversitas naturae spiritualis et corporalis non impedit quin anima sit forma corporis. Ergo nec impedit quin possit a corpore pati.

Respondeo dicendum quod, supposito ex praedictis quod ignis inferni non sit metaphorice dictus, nec ignis imaginarius, sed verus ignis corporeus, oportet dicere quod anima ab igne corporeo patietur: cum Dominus ignem illum diabolo et angelis eius paratum esse dicat, Matth. 25, [41], qui sunt incorporei sicut illa. Sed quomodo pati possit, multipliciter assignatur.

Quidam enim dixerunt quod hoc ipsum quod est ignem videre, sit animam ab igne pati. Unde Gregorius, in IV *Dialog.*, dicit: *ignem eo ipso patitur anima quo videt.*

Sed illud non videtur sufficere. Quia quodlibet visum, ex hoc quod videtur, est perfectio videntis. Unde non potest in eius poenam cedere inquantum est visum. Sed quandoque est punitivum vel contristans per accidens, inquantum scilicet apprehenditur ut nocivum. Unde oportet quod, praeter hoc quod anima ignem illum

tact is only between corporeal things whose bounds come together. Therefore, the soul does not suffer from that fire.

Obj. 8: Further, an organic agent does not act on a remote object except through acting on the intermediate objects; wherefore it is able to act at a fixed distance in proportion to its power. But souls, or at least the demons to whom this equally applies, are sometimes outside the place of hell, since sometimes they appear to men even in this world: and yet they are not then free from punishment, for just as the glory of the saints is never interrupted, so neither is the punishment of the damned. And yet we do not find that all the intermediate things suffer from the fire of hell: nor again is it credible that any corporeal thing of an elemental nature has such a power that its action can reach to such a distance. Therefore, it does not seem that the pains suffered by the souls of the damned are inflicted by a corporeal fire.

On the contrary, The possibility of suffering from a corporeal fire is equally consistent with separated souls and with demons. Now demons suffer from it, since they are punished by that fire into which the bodies of the damned will be cast after the resurrection, and which must be corporeal fire. This is evident from the words of our Lord, *depart from me, you cursed, into everlasting fire, which was prepared for the devil* (Matt 25:41). Therefore, separated souls also can suffer from that fire.

Further, Punishment should correspond to sin. Now in sinning the soul subjected itself to the body by sinful concupiscence. Therefore, it is just that it should be punished by being made subject to a bodily thing, through suffering therefrom.

Further, There is greater union between form and matter than between agent and patient. Now the diversity of spiritual and corporeal nature does not hinder the soul from being the form of the body. Therefore, neither is it an obstacle to its suffering from a body.

I answer that, Given that the fire of hell is not so called metaphorically, nor an imaginary fire, but a real corporeal fire, we must say that the soul will suffer punishment from a corporeal fire, since our Lord said (Matt 25:41) that this fire was prepared for the devil and his angels, who are incorporeal even as the soul. But how it is that they can thus suffer is explained in many ways.

For some have said that the mere fact that the soul sees the fire makes the soul suffer from the fire: wherefore Gregory (*Dialogues* 4.29) says: *the soul suffers from the fire by merely seeing it.*

But this does not seem sufficient, because whatever is seen, from the fact that it is seen, is a perfection of the one seeing; wherefore it cannot conduce to his punishment insofar as it is seen. Sometimes, however, it is of a penal or unpleasant nature accidentally, that is, insofar as it is apprehended as something hurtful. Consequently, besides the

videt, sit aliqua comparatio animae ad ignem secundum quam ignis animae noceat.

Unde alii dixerunt quod, quamvis ignis corporeus non possit animam exurere, tamen anima apprehendit ipsum ut nocivum sibi, et ad talem apprehensionem afficitur timore et dolore: ut in eis impleatur id quod dicitur: *trepidaverunt timore ubi non erat timor.* Unde Gregorius, in IV *Dialog.,* dicit quod, *quia anima cremari se conspicit, crematur.*

Sed hoc iterum non videtur sufficere. Quia secundum hoc passio animae ab igne non esset secundum rei veritatem, sed secundum apparentiam tantum. Quamvis enim possit esse vera passio tristitiae vel doloris ex aliqua falsa imaginatione, ut Augustinus dicit, XII *super Genesis ad literam.*; tamen non potest dici quod secundum illam passionem vere patiatur a re, sed a similitudine rei quam conspicit. Et iterum iste modus passionis magis recederet a reali passione quam ille qui ponitur per imaginarias visiones: eum ille dicatur per veras imagines rerum esse, quas anima secum defert; iste autem per falsas conceptiones, quas anima errans fingit. Et iterum non est probabile quod animae separatae, vel daemones, qui subtilitate ingenii pollent, putarent ignem corporeum sibi nocere posse, si ab eo nullatenus gravarentur.

Unde alii dicunt quod oportet ponere animam etiam realiter ab igne corporeo pati. Unde et Gregorius, in IV *Dialog.,* dicit: *colligere ex dictis Evangelicis possumus quod incendium anima non solum videndo, sed etiam experiendo, patiatur.* Sed hoc tali modo fieri ponunt. Dicunt enim quod ignis ille corporeus considerari potest dupliciter. Uno modo, secundum quod est res quaedam corporea. Et hoc modo non habet quod in animam agere possit. Alio modo, secundum quod est instrumentum divinae iustitiae vindicantis: hoc enim divinale iustitiae ordo exigit, ut anima quae peccando se rebus corporalibus subdidit, eis etiam in poenam subdatur. Instrumentum autem non solum agit virtute propriae naturae, sed etiam in virtute principalis agentis. Et ita non est inconveniens si ignis ille, cum agat in vi spiritualis agentis, in spiritum agat hominis vel daemonis; per modum etiam quo de sacramentis dictum est quod animam sanctificant.

Sed istud etiam non videtur sufficere. Quia omne instrumentum in id circa quod instrumentaliter operatur, habet propriam actionem sibi connaturalem, et non solum illam actionem secundum quam agit in virtute principalis agentis: immo exercendo primam actionem oportet quod efficiat hanc secundam, sicut aqua lavando corpus in baptismo sanctificat animam, et serra secando lignum perducit ad formam domus. Unde oportet

fact that the soul sees the fire, there must be some relation of the soul to the fire according to which the fire is hurtful to the soul.

Hence others have said that although a corporeal fire cannot burn the soul, the soul nevertheless apprehends it as hurtful to itself, and in consequence of this apprehension is seized with fear and sorrow, in fulfillment of Psalm 13:5: *they have trembled for fear, where there was no fear.* Hence Gregory says (*Dialogues* 4.29) that *the soul burns through seeing itself aflame.*

But this, again, seems insufficient, because in this case the soul would suffer from the fire not in reality, but only in apprehension: for although a real passion of sorrow or pain may result from a false imagination, as Augustine observes (*On the Literal Meaning of Genesis* 12), it cannot be said in relation to that passion that one really suffers from the thing, but from the image of the thing that is present to one's fancy. Moreover, this kind of suffering would be more unlike real suffering than that which results from imaginary vision, since the latter is stated to result from real images of things, which images the soul carries about with it, whereas the former results from false fancies which the erring soul imagines: and furthermore, it is not probable that separated souls or demons, who are endowed with keen intelligence, would think it possible for a corporeal fire to hurt them, if they were in no way distressed by it.

Hence others say that it is necessary to admit that the soul suffers even really from the corporeal fire. Wherefore Gregory says (*Dialogues* 4.29): *we can gather from the words of the Gospel that the soul suffers from the fire not only by seeing it, but also by feeling it.* They explain the possibility of this as follows. They say that this corporeal fire can be considered in two ways. First, as a corporeal thing, and thus it has not the power to act on the soul. Second, as the instrument of the vengeance of divine justice. For the order of divine justice demands that the soul which by sinning subjected itself to corporeal things should be subjected to them also in punishment. Now an instrument acts not only in virtue of its own nature, but also in virtue of the principal agent: wherefore it is not unreasonable if that fire, seeing that it acts in virtue of a spiritual agent, should act on the spirit of a man or demon, in the same way as we have explained the sanctification of the soul by the sacraments (III, Q. 62, A. 1, 4).

But, again, this does not seem to suffice, since every instrument, in acting on that on which it is used instrumentally, has its own connatural action besides the action whereby it acts in virtue of the principal agent: in fact, it is by fulfilling the former that it effects the latter action, even as in baptism it is by washing the body that water sanctifies the soul, and the saw by cutting wood produces the shape of a house. Hence we must allow the fire to exercise on the

dare igni aliquam actionem in animam quae sit ei connaturalis, ad hoc quod sit instrumentum divinae iustitiae peccata vindicantis.

Et ideo dicendum quod corpus in spiritum naturaliter agere non potest nec ei aliquo modo obesse vel ipsum gravare, nisi secundum quod aliquo modo corpori unitur: sic enim invenimus quod *corpus quod corrumpitur, aggravat animam*, Sap. 9, [15]. Spiritus autem corpori unitur dupliciter. Uno modo, ut forma materiae, ut ex eis fiat unum simpliciter. Et sic spiritus unitus corpori et vivificat corpus, et a corpore aliqualiter aggravatur. Sic autem spiritus hominis vel daemonis igni corporeo non unitur. Alio modo, sicut movens mobili; vel sicut locatum loco, eo modo quo incorporalia sunt in loco. Et secundum hoc spiritus incorporei creati loco definiuntur, ita in uno loco existentes quod non in alio. Quamvis autem res corporea ex sua natura habeat quod spiritum incorporeum loco definiat, non tamen ex sua natura habet quod spiritum incorporeum loco definitum detineat, ut ita alligetur illi loco quod ad alia divertere non possit: cum spiritus non sit ita in loco naturaliter quod loco subdatur. Sed hoc superadditur igni corporeo inquantum est instrumentum divinae iustitiae vindicantis, quod sic detinet spiritum. Et ita efficitur ei poenalis, retardans eum ab executione propriae voluntatis, ne scilicet possit operari ubi vult et secundum quod vult.

Et hunc modum ponit Gregorius, in IV *Dialog.* Exponens enim quomodo anima incendium experiendo patiatur, sic dicit: *cum veritas peccatorem divitem damnatum in igne perhibeat, quisnam sapiens reproborum animas teneri ignibus neget?* Et hoc etiam Iulianus dicit, ut in littera Magister dicit: *si viventis hominis incorporeus spiritus tenetur in corpore, cur etiam, non post mortem corporeo igne teneatur?* Augustinus etiam, XXI *de Civ. Dei*, dicit quod, *sicut anima in hominis conditione iungitur corpori ut dans ei vitam, quamvis illud sit spirituale et hoc corporale, et ex illa coniunctione vehementer concipit amorem ad corpus; sic ligatur igni ut accipiens ab eo poenam, et ex illa coniunctione concipit horrorem.*

Oportet ergo omnes praedictos modos in unum colligere, ut perfecte videatur quomodo anima ab igne corporeo patiatur: ut scilicet dicamus quod ignis ex natura sua habet quod spiritus incorporeus ei coniungi possit ut loco locatum; sed inquantum est instrumentum divinae iustitiae, habet ut ipsum quodammodo retineat alligatum; et in hoc veraciter ignis ille est spiritui nocivus; et sic anima, ignem ut sibi nocivum videns, ab igne cruciatur. Unde Gregorius, in IV *Dialog.*, omnia ista per ordinem tangit, ut ex praemissis eius auctoritatibus patet.

soul an action connatural to the fire, in order that it may be the instrument of divine justice in the punishment of sin.

For this reason we must say that a body cannot naturally act on a spirit, nor in any way be hurtful or distressful to it, except insofar as the latter is in some way united to a body: for thus we observe that *the corruptible body is a load upon the soul* (Wis 9:15). Now a spirit is united to a body in two ways. In one way as form to matter, so that from their union there results one thing simply: and the spirit that is thus united to a body both quickens the body and is somewhat burdened by the body; but it is not thus that the spirit of man or demon is united to the corporeal fire. In another way, as the mover is united to the things moved, or as a thing placed is united to place, even as incorporeal things are in a place. In this way created incorporeal spirits are confined to a place, being in one place in such a way as not to be in another. Now, although of its nature a corporeal thing is able to confine an incorporeal spirit to a place, it is not able of its nature to detain an incorporeal spirit in the place to which it is confined, and so to tie it to that place that it be unable to seek another, since a spirit is not by nature in a place so as to be subject to place. But the corporeal fire is enabled as the instrument of the vengeance of divine justice to detain a spirit in this way; and thus it has a penal effect on it, by hindering it from fulfilling its own will, that is, by hindering it from acting where it will and as it will.

This way is asserted by Gregory (*Dialogues* 4.29). For in explaining how the soul can suffer from that fire by feeling it, he expresses himself as follows: *since truth declares the rich sinner to be condemned to fire, will any wise man deny that the souls of the wicked are imprisoned in flames?* Julian says the same as quoted by the Master (*Sentences* IV, D. 44): *if the incorporeal spirit of a living man is held by the body, why shall it not be held after death by a corporeal fire?* and Augustine says (*The City of God* 21.10) that *just as, although the soul is spiritual and the body corporeal, man is so fashioned that the soul is united to the body as giving it life, and on account of this union conceives a great love for its body, so it is chained to the fire as receiving punishment therefrom, and from this union conceives a loathing.*

Accordingly, we must unite all the aforesaid modes together, in order to understand perfectly how the soul suffers from a corporeal fire: so as to say that the fire of its nature is able to have an incorporeal spirit united to it as a thing placed is united to a place; that as the instrument of divine justice it is enabled to detain it (enchained as it were), and in this respect this fire is really hurtful to the spirit, and thus the soul, seeing the fire as something hurtful to it, is tormented by the fire. Hence Gregory (*Dialogues* 4.29) mentions all these in order, as may be seen from the above quotations.

Ad primum ergo dicendum quod Augustinus loquitur inquirendo. Unde etiam alium modum ponit determinando, in libro *de Civitate Dei*, ut ex dictis patet.

Vel dicendum quod Augustinus intelligit quod ea quibus anima proxime afficitur ad dolorem vel tristitiam, sunt spiritualia: non enim affligeretur nisi ignem ut nocivum sibi apprehenderet. Ignis ergo apprehensus est proximum affligens: sed ignis corporeus extra animam existens est affligens remotum.

Ad secundum dicendum quod, quamvis anima simpliciter sit igne nobilior, ignis tamen est anima nobilior inquantum est instrumentum divinae iustitiae.

Ad tertium dicendum quod Philosophus et Boetius loquuntur de actione illa per quam patiens transmutatur in naturam agentis. Talis autem non est actio ignis in animam. Et propter hoc ratio non concludit.

Ad quartum dicendum quod ignis agit iri animam non per modum influentis, sed per modum detinentis, ut ex dictis patet. Et ideo ratio non est ad propositum.

Ad quintum dicendum quod in visione intellectuali non est tristitia ex hoc ipso quod aliquid videatur: cum illud quod videtur, nullo modo intellectui possit esse contrarium inquantum videtur. In sensu autem hoc quod videtur, ex ipsa actione quam agit in visum ut videatur, potest esse corruptivum visus per accidens, inquantum corrumpit harmoniam organi. Sed tamen visio intellectualis potest esse contrinstans inquantum id quod videtur apprehenditur ut nocivum: non quasi noceat eo ipso quod videtur, sed alio quocumque modo. Et sic anima videndo ignem affligitur.

Ad sextum dicendum quod non est simile quantum ad omnia, sed quantum ad aliquid, ut ex dictis patet.

Ad septimum dicendum quod, quamvis non sit tactus corporalis inter animam et corpus, tamen est inter ea aliquis tactus spiritualis: sicut etiam motor caeli, cum sit spiritualis, spirituali tactu tangit caelum ipsum movens, per modum quo dicitur *contristans tangere*, sicut dicitur in I *de Generatione*. Et huiusmodi modus sufficit ad actionem.

Ad octavum dicendum quod spiritus damnati nunquam sunt extra infernum nisi ex dispensatione divina, vel ad instructionem vel ad exercitium electorum. Ubicumque autem extra infernum sint, semper tamen vident ignem inferni ut eis in poenam praeparatum. Unde, cum ista visio sit immediate affligens, ut dictum est, ubicumque sunt, ab igne inferni affliguntur: sicut et captivi extra carcerem existentes quodammodo a carcere affliguntur, dum vident se ad carcerem damnatos. Unde, sicut gloria electorum in nullo minuitur, nec quantum ad praemium essentiale nec quantum ad accidentale, si aliquando extra caelum empyreum sint, quod quodammodo in eorum gloriam cedit; ita etiam in nullo minuitur

Reply Obj. 1: Augustine speaks there as one inquiring: wherefore he expresses himself otherwise when deciding the point, as quoted above (*The City of God* 21).

Or we may reply that Augustine means to say that the things which are the proximate occasion of the soul's pain or sorrow are spiritual, since it would not be distressed unless it apprehended the fire as hurtful to it: wherefore the fire as apprehended is the proximate cause of its distress, whereas the corporeal fire which exists outside the soul is the remote cause of its distress.

Reply Obj. 2: Although the soul is simply more excellent than the fire, the fire is relatively more excellent than the soul, that is, insofar as it is the instrument of divine justice.

Reply Obj. 3: The Philosopher and Boethius are speaking of the action whereby the patient is changed into the nature of the agent. Such is not the action of the fire on the soul: and consequently the argument is not conclusive.

Reply Obj. 4: By acting on the soul the fire bestows nothing on it but detains it, as stated above. Hence the argument is not to the point.

Reply Obj. 5: In intellectual vision, sorrow is not caused by the fact that something is seen, since the thing seen as such can in no way be contrary to the intellect. But in the sensible vision, the thing seen, by its very action on the sight so as to be seen, there may be accidentally something corruptive of the sight insofar as it destroys the harmony of the organ. Nevertheless, intellectual vision may cause sorrow, insofar as the thing seen is apprehended as hurtful: not that it hurts through being seen, but in some other way entirely. It is thus that the soul is distressed in seeing the fire.

Reply Obj. 6: The comparison does not hold in every respect, but it does in some, as explained above.

Reply Obj. 7: Although there is no bodily contact between the soul and body, there is a certain spiritual contact between them (even as the mover of the heaven, being spiritual, touches the heaven when it moves it, with a spiritual contact) in the same way as a *painful object* is said *to touch*, as stated in *On Generation and Corruption* I. This mode of contact is sufficient for action.

Reply Obj. 8: The souls of the damned are never outside hell except by divine permission, either for the instruction or for the trial of the elect. And wherever they are outside hell they nevertheless always see the fire thereof as prepared for their punishment. Wherefore, since this vision is the immediate cause of their distress, as stated above, wherever they are, they suffer from hell-fire. Even so prisoners, though outside the prison, suffer somewhat from the prison, seeing themselves condemned to it. Hence, just as the glory of the elect is not diminished, neither as to the essential nor as to the accidental reward, if they happen to be outside the empyrean (in fact, this somewhat conduces to their glory) so the punishment of the damned is in

poena damnatorum si extra infernum ex divina dispensatione ponantur ad tempus. Et hoc est quod Glossa dicit, super illud Iac. 3, [6], *inflammat rotam nativitatis nostrae* etc.: *diabolus, ubicumque sit, sive sub aere sive sub terra, secum trahit tormenta suarum flammarum.* Obiectio autem procedit ac si ignis corporeus affligeret immediate spiritus sicut affligit corpora.

no way diminished if by God's permission they happen to be outside hell for a time. A Gloss on James 3:6: *inflameth the wheel of our nativity*, is in agreement with this, for it is worded thus: *the devil, wherever he is, whether in the air or under the earth, drags with him the torments of his flames.* But the objection argues as though the corporeal fire tortured the spirit immediately in the same way as it torments bodies.

QUESTION 71

THE SUFFRAGES FOR THE DEAD

Deinde considerandum est de suffragiis mortuorum.
Et circa hoc quaeruntur quatuordecim.

Primo: utrum suffragia quae per unum fiunt, alii prodesse possint.

Secundo: utrum mortui iuvari possint ex operibus vivorum.

Tertio: utrum suffragia per peccatores facta mortuis prosint.

Quarto: utrum suffragia pro mortuis facta facientibus prosint.

Quinto: utrum suffragia existentibus in inferno prosint.

Sexto: utrum prosint existentibus in purgatorio.

Septimo: utrum valeant pueris existentibus in limbo.

Octavo: utrum aliquo modo prosint existentibus in patria.

Nono: utrum oratio Ecclesiae, et Sacrificium Altaris, et eleemosyna, prosint defunctis.

Decimo: utrum indulgentiae quas Ecclesia facit, eis prosint.

Undecimo: utrum cultus exequiarum eis prbsint.

Duodecimo: utrum suffragia magis prosint ei pro quo fiunt quam aliis.

Decimotertio: utrum suffragia pro multis facta valeant tantum singulis ac si pro unoquoque singulariter fierent.

Decimoquarto: utrum valeant tantum communia suffragia illis pro quibus specialia non fiunt, quantum illis pro quibus fiunt valent specialia et communia simul.

We must now consider the suffrages for the dead.
Under this head there are fourteen points of inquiry:

(1) Whether suffrages performed by one person can profit others?

(2) Whether the dead can be assisted by the works of the living?

(3) Whether the suffrages of sinners profit the dead?

(4) Whether suffrages for the dead profit those who perform them?

(5) Whether suffrages profit those who are in hell?

(6) Whether they profit those who are in purgatory?

(7) Whether they avail the children in limbo?

(8) Whether in any way they profit those who are heaven?

(9) Whether the prayer of the Church, the Sacrament of the Altar, and almsgiving profit the departed?

(10) Whether indulgences granted by the Church profit them?

(11) Whether the burial service profits the departed?

(12) Whether suffrages for one dead person profit that person more than others?

(13) Whether suffrages for many avail each one as much as if they were offered for each individual?

(14) Whether general suffrages avail those for whom special suffrages are not offered, as much as special and general suffrages together avail those for whom they are offered?

Article 1

Whether the Suffrages of One Person Can Profit Others?

AD PRIMUM SIC PROCEDITUR. Videtur quod suffragia per unum facta alii prodesse non possint. Galat. 6, [8]: *quae enim seminaverit homo, haec et metet.* Sed si unus ex suffragiis alterius consequeretur fructum, meteret ab aliis seminata. Ergo ex suffragiis aliorum nullus fructum consequitur.

PRAETEREA, ad iustitiam Dei pertinet ut unicuique tribuatur pro meritis: unde Psalmus [61, 13]: *tu reddes unicuique secundum opera sua.* Sed iustitiam Dei defi-

OBJECTION 1: It would seem that the suffrages of one person cannot profit others. For it is written: *what things a man shall sow, those also shall he reap* (Gal 6:8). Now if one person reaped fruit from the suffrages of another, he would reap from another's sowing. Therefore, a person receives no fruit from the suffrages of others.

OBJ. 2: Further, it belongs to God's justice that each one should receive according to his merits, wherefore the psalm says: *you will render to every man according to his works*

31

cere est impossibile. Ergo impossibile est quod unus ex operibus alterius iuvetur.

Praeterea, secundum eandem rationem est aliquod opus meritorium et laudabile: quia, scilicet, inquantum est voluntarium. Sed ex opere unius non laudatur alter. Ergo nec opus unius potest esse alteri meritorium.

Praeterea, ad iustitiam divinam pertinet similiter bona reddere pro bonis, et mala pro malis. Sed nullus punitur pro malis alterius, immo, ut dicitur Ezech. 18, [20], *anima quae peccaverit, ipsa morietur*. Ergo nec unus iuvatur pro bono alterius.

Sed contra: Est quod dicitur in Psalmo [118, 63]: *particeps ego sum omnium timentium te*, etc.

Praeterea, omnes fideles per caritatem uniti sunt *unius corporis Ecclesiae membra*. Sed unum membrum iuvatur per alterum. Ergo unus homo potest ex alterius meritis iuvari.

Respondeo dicendum quod actus noster ad duo valere potest: primo, ad aliquem statum acquirendum, sicut per opus meritorium homo acquirit statum beatitudinis; secundo, ad aliquid consequens statum, sicut homo per aliquem actum meretur aliquod praemium accidentale, vel dimissionem poenae. Ad utrumque autem horum actus noster dupliciter valere potest: uno modo, per viam meriti; alio modo, per viam orationis. Et est differentia inter istas duas vias, quia meritum innititur iustitiae; sed orans impetrat petitum ex sola liberalitate eius qui oratur.

Dicendum ergo quod opus unius nullo modo potest alteri valere ad statum consequendum per viam meriti, ut scilicet ex his quae ego facio, aliquis mereatur vitam aeternam. Quia sors gloriae redditur secundum mensuram accipientis: unusquisque autem ex actu suo disponitur, et non ex alieno; et dico dispositione dignitatis ad praemium. Sed per viam orationis etiam quantum ad statum consequendum opus unius alteri, dum est in via, valere potest: sicut quod unus homo impetrat alteri primam gratiam. Cum enim impetratio orationis sit secundum liberalitatem Dei, qui oratur, ad omnia illa impetratio orationis se potest extendere quae potestati divinae subsunt ordinate.

Sed quantum ad aliquid quod est consequens vel accessorium ad statum, opus unius potest valere alteri non solum per viam orationis, sed etiam per viam meriti. Quod quidem dupliciter contingit. Vel propter communicantiam in radice operis, quae est caritas in operibus meritoriis. Et ideo omnes qui sibi invicem caritate connectuntur, aliquod emolumentum ex mutuis operibus reportant: tamen secundum mensuram status uniuscuiusque; quia etiam in patria unusquisque gaudebit de bonis alterius. Et inde est quod articulus fidei ponitur *sanctorum communio*. Alio modo, ex intentione facien-

(Ps 61:13). Now it is impossible for God's justice to fail. Therefore, it is impossible for one man to be assisted by the works of another.

Obj. 3: Further, a work is meritorious on the same count as it is praiseworthy, namely, inasmuch as it is voluntary. Now one man is not praised for the work of another. Therefore, neither can the work of one man be meritorious and fruitful for another.

Obj. 4: Further, it belongs to divine justice to repay good for good in the same way as evil for evil. But no man is punished for the evildoings of another; indeed, according to Ezekiel 18:4, *the soul that sins, the same shall die*. Therefore, neither does one person profit by another's good.

On the contrary, It is written: *I am a partaker with all them that fear thee* (Ps 118:63).

Further, All the faithful united together by charity are *members of the one body of the Church*. Now one member is assisted by another. Therefore, one man can be assisted by the merits of another.

I answer that, Our actions can avail for two purposes. First, for acquiring a certain state; thus by a meritorious work a man obtains the state of bliss. Second, for something consequent upon a state; thus by some work a man merits an accidental reward or a rebate of punishment. And for both these purposes our actions may avail in two ways: first, by way of merit; second, by way of prayer: the difference being that merit relies on justice, and prayer on mercy, since he who prays obtains his petition from the mere liberality of the one he prays.

Accordingly, we must say that the work of one person can in no way avail another for acquiring a state by way of merit (that is, so that a man be able to merit eternal life by the works which I do) because the share of glory is awarded according to the measure of the recipient, and each one is disposed by his own and not by another's actions—disposed, that is to say, by being worthy of reward. By way of prayer, however, the work of one may profit another while he is a wayfarer, even for acquiring a state; for instance, one man may obtain the first grace for another: and since the impetration of prayer depends on the liberality of God whom we pray, it may extend to whatever is ordinately subject to the divine power.

On the other hand, as regards that which is consequent upon or accessory to a state, the work of one may avail another, not only by way of prayer but even by way of merit: and this happens in two ways. First, on account of their communion in the root of the work, which root is charity in meritorious works. Wherefore all who are united together by charity acquire some benefit from one another's works, although according to the measure of each one's state, since even in heaven each one will rejoice in the goods of others. Hence it is that the *communion of saints* is laid down as an article of faith. Second, through the intention of the doer

tis, qui aliqua opera specialiter ad hoc, facit ut talibus prosint. Unde ista opera quodammodo efficiuntur eorum pro quibus fiunt, quasi eis a faciente collata. Unde possunt eis valere vel ad impletionem satisfactionis; vel ad quidquid huiusmodi quod statum non mutat.

Ad primum ergo dicendum quod messio illa est perceptio vitae aeternae: sicut habetur Ioan. 4, [36]: *et qui metit fructum congregat in vitam aeternam.* Sors autem vitae aeternae non datur alicui nisi pro propriis operibus: quia, etsi aliquis alteri impetret ut ad vitam aeternam perveniat, nunquam tamen hoc fit nisi mediantibus operibus propriis; dum scilicet precibus alicuius gratia alicui datur, per quam meretur vitam aeternam.

Ad secundum dicendum quod opus quod pro aliquo fit, efficitur eius pro quo fit. Et similiter opus quod est eius qui mecum est unum, quodammodo est et meum. Unde non est contra divinam iustitiam si unus fructum percipit de operibus factis ab eo qui est unum secum in caritate, vel ab operibus pro se factis. Hoc etiam secundum humanam iustitiam contingit, ut satisfactio unius pro alio accipiatur.

Ad tertium dicendum quod laus non datur alicui nisi secundum ordinem eius ad actum: unde laus est *ad aliquid,* ut dicitur in I *Ethic.* Et quia ex opere alterius nullus efficitur vel ostenditur bene dispositus vel male ad aliquid, inde est quod nullus laudatur ex operibus alterius: nisi per accidens, secundum quod ipse est aliquo modo operum illorum causa, consilium vel auxilium praebendo, seu inducendo, vel quocumque alio modo. Sed opus est meritorium alicui non solum considerata eius dispositione, sed etiam quantum ad aliquid consequens dispositionem vel statum eius, ut ex dictis patet.

Ad quartum dicendum quod auferre alicui quod sibi debetur, hoc directe iustitiae repugnat. Sed dare aliquid alicui quod ei non debetur, hoc non est iustitiae contrarium, sed metas iustitiae excedit: est enim liberalitatis. Non autem posset aliquis laedi ex malis alterius nisi aliquid ei de suo subtraheretur. Et ideo non ita convenit quod aliquis puniatur pro peccatis alterius, sicut quod emolumentum percipiat ex bonis alterius.

who does certain works specially for the purpose that they may profit such persons: so that those works become somewhat the works of those for whom they are done, as though they were bestowed on them by the doer. Therefore, they can avail them either for the fulfillment of satisfaction or for some similar purpose that does not change their state.

Reply Obj. 1: This reaping is the receiving of eternal life, as stated, *and he that reaps gathers fruit unto life everlasting* (John 4:36). Now a share of eternal life is not given to a man save for his own works, for although we may impetrate for another that he obtain life, this never happens except by means of his own works, namely, when, at the prayers of one, another is given the grace whereby he merits eternal life.

Reply Obj. 2: The work that is done for another becomes his for whom it is done: and in like manner the work done by a man who is one with me is somewhat mine. Hence it is not contrary to divine justice if a man receives the fruit of the works done by a man who is one with him in charity, or of works done for him. This also happens according to human justice, so that the satisfaction offered by one is accepted in lieu of another's.

Reply Obj. 3: Praise is not given to a person save according to his relation to an act, wherefore praise is *in relation to something* (Ethics 1.12). And since no man is made or shown to be well- or ill-disposed to something by another's deed, it follows that no man is praised for another's deeds save accidentally, insofar as he is somewhat the cause of those deeds by giving counsel, assistance, inducement, or by any other means. On the other hand, a work is meritorious to a person not only by reason of his disposition, but also in view of something consequent upon his disposition or state, as evidenced by what has been said.

Reply Obj. 4: It is directly contrary to justice to take away from a person that which is his due: but to give a person what is not his due is not contrary to justice, but surpasses the bounds of justice, for it is liberality. Now a person cannot be hurt by the ills of another, unless he be deprived of something of his own. Consequently, it is not becoming that one should be punished for another's sins as it is that one should acquire some advantage from deeds of another.

Article 2

Whether the Dead Can Be Assisted by the Works of the Living?

Ad secundum sic proceditur. Videtur quod mortui non possint iuvari ex operibus vivorum. Primo, per hoc quod dicit Apostolus, II Cor. 5, [10]: *omnes nos manifestari oportet ante tribunal Christi, ut recipiat unusquisque propria corporis quae gessit.* Ergo ex his quae

Objection 1: It would seem that the dead cannot be assisted by the works of the living. First, because the Apostle says: *we must all be manifested before the judgment seat of Christ, that every one may receive the proper things of the body, according as he has done* (2 Cor 5:10). Therefore, noth-

post mortem hominis geruntur, quanto extra corpus erit, nihil ei accrescere poterit ex aliquibus operibus.

PRAETEREA, hoc idem videtur ex hoc quod habetur Apoc. 14, [13]: *beati mortui qui in Domino moriuntur: opera enim illorum sequuntur illos.*

PRAETEREA, proficere ex opere aliquo est solum in via existentis. Sed homines post mortem iam non sunt viatores; quia de eis hoc intelligitur quod legitur Iob 19, [8]: *semitam meam circumsepsit, et transire non possum.* Ergo mortui de suffragiis alicuius iuvari non possunt.

PRAETEREA, nullus iuvatur ex opere alterius nisi sit aliqua vitae communicatio inter eos. Sed nulla communicatio est mortuorum ad vivos, secundum Philosophum, in I *Ethic.* Ergo suffragia vivorum non prosunt mortuis.

SED CONTRA: Est quod habetur II Machab. 12, [46]: *sancta et salubris est cogitatio pro defunctis exorare, ut a peccatis solvantur.* Sed hoc esset inutile nisi eos iuvaret. Ergo suffragia vivorum mortuis prosunt.

PRAETEREA, Augustinus dicit, in libro *de Cura pro mortuis agenda*: *non parva est universae Ecclesiae, quae in hac consuetudine claret, auctoritas, ut in precibus sacerdotis, quae Domino Deo ad eius altare funduntur, locum suum habeat etiam commendatio mortuorum.* Quae quidem consuetudo ab ipsis Apostolis inchoavit: ut dicit Damascenus, in quodam sermone de Suffragiis Mortuorum, sic dicens: *mysteriorum conscii discipuli Salvatoris et sacri Apostoli in tremendis et vivificis mysteriis memoriam fieri eorum qui fideliter dormierunt, sanxerunt.* Quod etiam per Dionysium patet, in ult. cap. *Eccles. Hier.*, ubi ritum commemorat quo in primitiva Ecclesia pro mortuis orabatur; ubi etiam Dionysius asserit suffragia vivorum mortuis prodesse. Ergo hoc indubitanter credendum est.

RESPONDEO dicendum quod caritas, quae est vinculum Ecclesiae membra uniens, non solum ad vivos se extendit, sed etiam ad mortuos qui in caritate decedunt: caritas enim vita corporis non finitur, I Cor. 13, [8]: *caritas nunquam excidit*: Similiter etiam mortui in memoriis hominum, viventium vivunt: et ideo intentio viventium ad eos dirigi potest. Et sic suffragia vivorum mortuis dupliciter prosunt, sicut et vivis: et propter caritatis unionem; et propter intentionem ad eos directam.

Non tamen sic eis valere credenda sunt vivorum suffragia ut status eorum mutetur de miseria ad felicitatem vel e converso. Sed valet ad diminutionem poenae, vel aliquid huiusmodi quod statum mortui non transmutat.

AD PRIMUM ergo dicendum quod homo, dum in corpore vixit, meruit ut haec ei valerent post mortem. Et

ing can accrue to a man from the works of others which are done after his death and when he is no longer in the body.

OBJ. 2: Further, this also seems to follow from the words of Revelation 14:13, *blessed are the dead who die in the Lord, for their works follow them.*

OBJ. 3: Further, it belongs only to one who is on the way to advance on account of some deed. Now, after death men are no longer wayfarers, because to them the words of Job 19:8 refer: *he has hedged my path round about, and I cannot pass.* Therefore, the dead cannot be assisted by a person's suffrages.

OBJ. 4: Further, no one is assisted by the deed of another unless there be some community of life between them. Now there is no community between the dead and the living, as the Philosopher says (*Ethics* 1.11). Therefore, the suffrages of the living do not profit the dead.

ON THE CONTRARY, It is written in 2 Maccabees 12:46: *it is a holy and wholesome thought to pray for the dead that they may be loosed from sins.* But this would not be profitable unless it were a help to them. Therefore, the suffrages of the living profit the dead.

FURTHER, Augustine says (*On the Care of the Dead* 1): *of no small weight is the authority of the Church whereby she clearly approves of the custom in which a commendation of the dead has a place in the prayers which the priests pour forth to the Lord God at his altar.* This custom was established by the apostles themselves, according to the Damascene in a sermon on suffrages for the dead, where he expresses himself thus: *realizing the nature of the mysteries, the disciples of the Savior and his holy apostles sanctioned a commemoration of those who had died in the faith, being made in the awe-inspiring and life-giving mysteries.* This is also confirmed by the authority of Dionysius (*On the Ecclesiastical Hierarchies*), where he mentions the rite of the early Church in praying for the dead, and, moreover, asserts that the suffrages of the living profit the dead. Therefore, we must believe this without any doubt.

I ANSWER THAT, Charity, which is the bond uniting the members of the Church, extends not only to the living, but also to the dead who die in charity. For charity, which is the life of the soul even as the soul is the life of the body, has no end: *charity never falls away* (1 Cor 12:8). Moreover, the dead live in the memory of the living: wherefore the intention of the living can be directed to them. Hence the suffrages of the living profit the dead in two ways even as they profit the living, both on account of the bond of charity and on account of the intention being directed to them.

Nevertheless, we must not believe that the suffrages of the living profit them so as to change their state from unhappiness to happiness or vice versa; but they avail for the diminution of punishment, or something of the kind, that involves no change in the state of the dead.

REPLY OBJ. 1: Man, while living in the body, merited that such things should avail him after death. Wherefore if

ideo, si post hanc vitam eis iuvatur, nihilominus hoc procedit ex his quae in corpore gessit.

Vel dicendum, secundum Ioannem Damascenum, in sermone praedicto, quod hoc est intelligendum quantum ad retributionem quae fiet in finali iudicio, quae erit aeternae gloriae vel aeternae miseriae, in qua quilibet recipiet solum, secundum quod ipse in corpore gessit. Interim, autem iuvari possunt vivorum suffragiis.

AD SECUNDUM dicendum quod auctoritas illa expresse loquitur de sequela aeternae retributionis: quod patet ex hoc quod praemittitur, *beati mortui*, etc.

Vel dicendum quod opera pro eis. facta sunt etiam quodammodo eorum, ut dictum est.

AD TERTIUM dicendum quod, quamvis animae post mortem non sint simpliciter in statu viae, sed quantum ad aliquid adhuc sunt in statu viae: inquantum scilicet eorum progressus adhuc retardatur ab ultima retributione. Et ideo simpliciter eorum via est circumsepta, ut non possint ulterius per aliqua opera transmutari secundum statum felicitatis et miseriae. Sed quantum ad hoc non est circumsepta, quin, quantum ad hoc quod detinentur ab ultima retributione, possint ab aliis iuvari: quia secundum hoc adhuc sunt in via.

AD QUARTUM dicendum quod, quamvis communicatio civilium operum, de qua Philosophus loquitur, non possit esse mortuorum ad vivos, quia mortui extra vitam civilem sunt; potest tamen eorum communicatio esse quantum ad opera vitae spiritualis, quae est per caritatem ad Deum, *cui mortuorum spiritus vivunt.*

he is assisted thereby after this life, this is, nevertheless, the result of the things he has done in the body.

Or we may reply, according to John Damascene in the sermon quoted above, that these words refer to the retribution which will be made at the final judgment of eternal glory or eternal unhappiness: for then each one will receive only according as he himself has done in the body. Meanwhile, however, he can be assisted by the suffrages of the living.

REPLY OBJ. 2: The words quoted refer expressly to the sequel of eternal retribution as is clear from the opening words: *blessed are the dead*, etc.

Or we may reply that deeds done on their behalf are somewhat their own, as stated above.

REPLY OBJ. 3: Although, strictly speaking, after death souls are not in the state of the way, yet in a certain respect they are still on the way insofar as they are delayed awhile in their advance towards their final award. Wherefore, strictly speaking, their way is hedged in round about, so that they can no more be changed by any works in respect of the state of happiness or unhappiness. Yet their way is not so hedged around that they cannot be helped by others in the matter of their being delayed from receiving their final award, because in this respect they are still wayfarers.

REPLY OBJ. 4: Although the communion of civic deeds whereof the Philosopher speaks is impossible between the dead and the living, because the dead are outside civic life, the communication of the spiritual life is possible between them, for that life is founded on charity towards God, *to whom the spirits of the dead live.*

Article 3

Whether Suffrages Performed by Sinners Profit the Dead?

AD TERTIUM SIC PROCEDITUR. Videtur quod suffragia per peccatores facta mortuis non prosint. Quia, ut dicitur Ioan. 9, [31], *peccatores Deus non audit*. Sed, si orationes eorum prodessent illis pro quibus orant, a Deo exaudirentur. Ergo suffragia per eos facta mortuis non prosunt.

PRAETEREA, Gregorius, in *Pastorali*, dicit quod, *cum is qui displicet ad interpellandum mittitur, irati animus ad deteriora provocatur*. Sed quilibet peccator Deo displicet. Ergo per peccatorum suffragia Deus ad misericordiam non flectitur. Et ideo talia suffragia non prosunt.

PRAETEREA, opus alicuius magis videtur esse fructuosum facienti quam alteri. Sed peccator per opera nihil meretur sibi. Ergo multo minus potest alteri mereri.

OBJECTION 1: It would seem that suffrages performed by sinners do not profit the dead. For John 9:31 says, *God does not hear sinners*. Now if their prayers were to profit those for whom they pray, they would be heard by God. Therefore, the suffrages performed by them do not profit the dead.

OBJ. 2: Further, Gregory says (*Book of Pastoral Rule*) that when an offensive person is sent to intercede, the wrath of the angered party is provoked to harsher measures. Now every sinner is offensive to God. Therefore, God is not inclined to mercy by the suffrages of sinners, and consequently their suffrages are of no avail.

OBJ. 3: Further, a person's deed would seem to be more fruitful to the doer than to another. But a sinner merits nothing for himself by his deeds. Much less, therefore, can he merit for another.

PRAETEREA, omne opus meritorium oportet esse vivificatum, idest *caritate informatum*. Sed opera per peccatores facta sunt mortua. Ergo non possunt per ea mortui iuvari pro quibus fiunt.

SED CONTRA: Est quod nullus potest scire de altero pro certo utrum sit in statu culpae vel gratiae. Si ergo tantum illa suffragia prodessent quae fiunt per eos qui sunt in gratia, non posset homo scire per quos suffragia conquireret suis defunctis. Et ita multi a suffragiis procurandis retraherentur.

PRAETEREA, sicut Augustinus dicit, in littera, secundum hoc iuvatur aliquis mortuus ex suffragiis, secundum quod, dum viveret, meruit ut iuvaretur post mortem. Ergo valor suffragiorum mensuratur secundum conditionem eius pro quo fiunt. Non ergo differt utrum per bonos vel malos fiant.

RESPONDEO dicendum quod in suffragiis quae per malos fiunt, duo possunt considerari. Primo, ipsum opus operatum: sicut Sacrificium Altaris. Et quia nostra sacramenta ex seipsis efficaciam habent absque opere operantis, quam aequaliter explent per quoscumque fiant, quantum ad hoc suffragia per malos facta defunctis prosunt.

Alio modo, quantum ad opus operans. Et sic distinguendum est. Quia operatio peccatoris suffragia facientis potest uno modo considerari prout: est eius. Et sic nullo modo meritoria esse potest nec sibi nec alii. Alio modo, inquantum est alterius. Quod dupliciter contingit. Uno modo, inquantum peccator suffragia faciens gerit personam totius Ecclesiae: sicut sacerdos dum dicit in ecclesia exequias, mortuorum. Et quia ille intelligitur facere cuius nomine vel vice fit, ut patet per Dionysium, in 13 cap. *Cael. Hier.*, inde est quod suffragia, talis sacerdotis, quamvis sit peccator, defunctis prosunt. Alio modo, quando agit ut instrumentum alterius. Opus enim instrumenti est magis principalis agentis. Unde, quamvis ille qui agit ut instrumentum alterius, non sit in statu merendi, actio tamen eius potest esse meritoria ratione principalis agentis: sicut si servus in peccato existens quodcumque opus misericordiae facit ex praecepto domini sui caritatem habentis. Unde, si aliquis in caritate decedens praecipiat sibi suffragia fieri, vel alius praecipiat caritatem habens, illa suffragia valent defuncto, quamvis illi per quos fiunt in peccato existant. Magis tamen valerent si essent in caritate: quia tunc ex duabus partibus opera illa meritoria essent.

AD PRIMUM ergo dicendum quod oratio per peccatorem facta quandoque non est peccatoris, sed alterius, Et ideo secundum hoc digna est ut a Deo exaudiatur.

OBJ. 4: Further, every meritorious work must be a living work, that is to say, *informed by charity*. Now works done by sinners are dead. Therefore, the dead for whom they are done cannot be assisted thereby.

OBJ. 5: On the contrary, no man can know for certain whether another man be in a state of sin or of grace. If, therefore, only those suffrages were profitable that are done by those who are in a state of grace, a man could not know of whom to ask suffrages for his dead, and consequently many would be deterred from obtaining suffrages.

OBJ. 6: Further, according to Augustine (*Handbook on Faith, Hope, and Charity* 109), as quoted in the text (*Sentences* IV, D. 45), the dead are assisted by suffrages according as while living they merited to be assisted after death. Therefore, the worth of suffrages is measured according to the disposition of the person for whom they are performed. Therefore, it would appear that it differs not whether they be performed by good or by wicked persons.

I ANSWER THAT, Two things may be considered in the suffrages performed by the wicked. First, the deed done, for instance, the Sacrifice of the Altar. And since our sacraments have their efficacy from themselves independently of the deed of the doer, and are equally efficacious by whomsoever they are performed, in this respect the suffrages of the wicked profit the departed.

Second, we may consider the deed of the doer, and then we must draw a distinction, because the deed of a sinner who offers suffrage may be considered in one way insofar as it is his own deed, and thus it can in no way be meritorious either to himself or to another; in another way, insofar as it is another's deed, and this happens in two ways. First, when the sinner, offering suffrages, represents the whole Church: for instance, a priest when he performs the burial service in church. And since one in whose name or in whose stead a thing is done is understood to do it himself, as Dionysius asserts (*On the Heavenly Hierarchies* 13), it follows that the suffrages of that priest, albeit a sinner, profit the departed. Second, when he acts as the instrument of another: for the work of the instrument belongs more to the principal agent. Wherefore, although he who acts as the instrument of another be not in a state of merit, his act may be meritorious on account of the principal agent: for instance, if a servant, being in sin, do any work of mercy at the command of his master who has charity. Hence, if a person dying in charity command suffrages to be offered for him, or if some other person having charity prescribe them, those suffrages avail for the departed, even though the persons by whom they are performed be in sin. Nevertheless, they would avail more if those persons were in charity, because then those works would be meritorious on two counts.

REPLY OBJ. 1: The prayer offered by a sinner is sometimes not his but another's, and consequently in this respect is worthy to be heard by God.

Tamen etiam quandoque Deus peccatores audit, quando scilicet peccatores petunt aliquid Deo acceptum. Non enim solis iustis, sed etiam peccatoribus Deus bona sua providet, ut patet Matth. 5, [45]: non autem ex eorum meritis, sed ex sua clementia. Et ideo Ioan. 9, super illud [31], *Deus peccatores non audit*, Glossa dicit quod loquitur ut *inunctus*, non sicut plene videns.

Ad secundum dicendum quod, quamvis ex parte eius qui displicet oratio peccatoris non sit accepta, tamen ratione alterius, cuius vice vel imperio agitur, potest esse Deo accepta.

Ad tertium dicendum quod hoc quod peccator faciens huiusmodi suffragia nullum reportat commodum, contingit ex hoc quod non est capax talis profectus, propter propriam indispositionem. Et tamen alii, qui non est indispositus, aliquo modo valere potest, ut dictum est.

Ad quartum dicendum quod, quamvis opus peccatoris non sit vivum inquantum est eius, potest tamen esse vivum inquantum est alterius, ut dictum est.

Sed quia rationes quae sunt in oppositum videntur concludere quod non differat utrum quis suffragia procuret per bonos vel per malos, ideo etiam ad eas est respondendum.

Ad quintum ergo dicendum quod, quamvis aliquis pro certo scire non possit de altero an sit in statu salutis, potest tamen probabiliter aestimare de his quae exterius de homine videt: *ex fructu* enim *suo arbor cognoscitur*, ut dicitur Matth. 7, [16 sqq.].

Ad sextum dicendum quod ad hoc quod suffragium alteri valeat, requiritur et ex parte eius pro quo fit capacitas huius valoris: et hanc homo acquisivit per opera propria quae gessit in vita; et sic Augustinus loquitur. Requiritur nihilominus qualitas operis quod prodesse debet. Et haec non pendet ex eo pro quo fit, sed magis ex eo qui facit, vel exequendo vel imperando.

Nevertheless, God sometimes hears sinners, namely, when they ask for something acceptable to God. For God dispenses his goods not only to the righteous but also to sinners (Matt 5:45), not indeed on account of their merits, but of his loving kindness. Hence a Gloss on John 9:31: *God does not hear sinners*, says that he speaks as one *unanointed* and as not seeing clearly.

Reply Obj. 2: Although the sinner's prayer is not acceptable insofar as he is offensive, it may be acceptable to God on account of another in whose stead or at whose command he offers the prayer.

Reply Obj. 3: The reason why the sinner who performs these suffrages gains nothing thereby is because he is not capable of profiting by reason of his own indisposition. Nevertheless, as stated above, it may in some way profit another who is disposed.

Reply Obj. 4: Although the sinner's deed is not living insofar as it is his own, it may be living insofar as it is another's, as stated above.

Since, however, the arguments in the contrary sense would seem to show that it matters not whether one obtain suffrages from good or from evil persons, we must reply to them also.

Reply Obj. 5: Although one cannot know for certain about another whether he be in the state of salvation, one may infer it with probability from what one sees outwardly of a man: for *a tree is known by its fruit* (Matt 7:16).

Reply Obj. 6: In order that a suffrage avail another, it is requisite that the one for whom it is performed be capable of availing by it: and a man has become capable of this by his own works which he did in his life-time. This is what Augustine means to say. Nevertheless, those works must be such that they can profit him, and this depends not on the person for whom the suffrage is performed, but rather on the one who offers the suffrages, whether by performing them or by commanding them.

Article 4

Whether Suffrages Offered by the Living for the Dead Profit Those Who Offer Them?

Ad quartum sic proceditur. Videtur quod suffragia quae a vivis pro mortuis fiunt, facientibus non prosint. Quia si aliquis pro altero debitum solveret, secundum humanam iustitiam ipse a debito proprio non absolveretur. Ergo per hoc quod aliquis suffragia faciens debitum solvit pro illo pro quo facit, ex hoc a debito proprio non absolvitur.

Praeterea, unusquisque quod facit, facere debet meliori modo quo potest. Sed melius est iuvare duos

Objection 1: It would seem that suffrages offered by the living for the dead do not profit those who offer them. For, according to human justice, a man is not absolved from his own debt if he pay a debt for another man. Therefore, a man is not absolved from his own debt for the reason that by offering suffrages he has paid the debt of the one for whom he offered them.

Obj. 2: Further, whatever a man does, he should do it as best he can. Now it is better to assist two than one. There-

quam unum. Si ergo qui per suffragia debitum mortui solvit, a proprio debito liberatur, videtur quod nunquam debet aliquis pro seipso satisfacere, sed semper pro alio.

Praeterea, si satisfactio alicuius pro alio satisfacientis aequaliter prodesset sibi ut ei pro quo satisfacit, eadem ratione aequaliter valebit et tertio, si pro eodem satisfaciat simul; et similiter quarto, et sic deinceps. Ergo unus una satisfactione posset pro omnibus satisfacere. Quod est absurdum.

Sed contra: Est quod dicitur in Psalmo [34, 13]: *oratio mea in sinu meo convertetur.* Ergo, eadem ratione, et suffragia quae pro aliis fiunt, satisfacientibus prosunt.

Praeterea, Damascenus dicit, in Sermone *de His qui in fide dormierunt*: *quemadmodum unguento vel alio oleo sancto circumlinire volens infirmum, primo ille,* scilicet liniens, *participat unctionem, deinde sic perungit laborantem; sic et quicumque pro proximi salute agonizat, primum sibi prodest, deinde proximo.* Et sic habetur propositum.

Respondeo dicendum quod opus suffragii quod pro altero fit, potest considerari dupliciter. Uno modo, ut est expiativum poenae per modum cuiusdam recompensationis, quae in satisfactione attenditur. Et hoc modo opus suffragii, quod computatur quasi eius pro quo fit, ita absolvit eum a debito poenae quod non absolvit facientem a debito poenae propriae. Quia in tali recompensatione consideratur aequalitas iustitiae. Opus autem illud satisfactorium ita potest adaequari uni reatui quod alteri non adaequetur: reatus enim duorum peccatorum maiorem satisfactionem requirunt quam reatus unius.

Alio modo potest considerari inquantum est meritorium vitae aeternae, quod habet inquantum procedit ex radice caritatis. Et secundum hoc non solum prodest ei pro quo fit, sed facienti magis.

Et per hoc patet solutio ad obiecta. Primae enim rationes procedebant de opere suffragii secundum quod est satisfactorium; sed aliae secundum quod est meritorium.

fore, if one who by suffrages has paid the debt of a dead person is freed from his own debt, it would seem that one ought never to satisfy for oneself, but always for another.

Obj. 3: Further, if the satisfaction of one who satisfies for another profits him equally with the one for whom he satisfies, it will likewise equally profit a third person if he satisfy for him at the same time, and likewise a fourth and so on. Therefore, he might satisfy for all by one work of satisfaction; which is absurd.

On the contrary, It is written: *my prayer shall be turned into my bosom* (Ps 34:13). Therefore, in like manner, suffrages that are offered for others profit those who satisfy.

Further, The Damascene says in the sermon *On Those Who Fell Asleep in the Faith*: *just as when about to anoint a sick man with the ointment or other holy oil, first of all he,* namely, the anointer, *shares in the anointing and thus proceeds to anoint the patient, so whoever strives for his neighbor's salvation first of all profits himself and afterwards his neighbor.* And thus the question at issue is answered.

I answer that, The work of suffrage that is done for another may be considered in two ways. First, as expiating punishment by way of compensation, which is a condition of satisfaction: and in this way the work of suffrage that is counted as belonging to the person for whom it is done, while absolving him from the debt of punishment, does not absolve the performer from his own debt of punishment, because in this compensation we have to consider the equality of justice: and this work of satisfaction can be equal to the one debt without being equal to the other, for the debts of two sinners require a greater satisfaction than the debt of one.

Second, it may be considered as meriting eternal life, and this it has as proceeding from its root, which is charity: and in this way it profits not only the person for whom it is done, but also and still more the doer.

This suffices for the replies to the objections: for the first considered the work of suffrage as a work of satisfaction, while the others consider it as meritorious.

Article 5

Whether Suffrages Profit Those Who Are in Hell?

Ad quintum sic proceditur. Videtur quod suffragia prosint existentibus in inferno, per hoc quod habetur II Machab. 12, [40], *ubi dicitur quod invenerunt sub tunicis interfectorum de donariis idolorum, a quibus lex prohibet Iudaeos;* et tamen post [v. 43] *subditur quod Iudas duodecim millia drachmas argenti misit Ierosolymam offerri pro peccatis eorum.* Constat autem illos peccasse mortaliter, contra legem agentes; et ita in peccato mor-

Objection 1: It would seem that suffrages profit those who are in hell. For it is written: *they found under the coats of the slain some of the tokens of the idols which the law forbids to the Jews* (2 Macc 12:40), and yet we read further on that Judas *sent twelve thousand drachmas of silver to Jerusalem to be offered for the sins of the dead* (2 Macc. 12:43). Now it is clear that they sinned mortally through acting against the law, and consequently that they died in mortal sin, and

tali decessisse; et sic ad inferos esse translatos. Ergo distentibus in inferno suffragia prosunt.

PRAETEREA, in littera habetur ex verbis Augustini quod *quibus valent* suffragia, *vel ad hoc prosunt ut sit plena remissio, vel ad hoc ut tolerabilior sit eorum damnatio.* Sed soli illi qui in inferno sunt, damnati esse dicuntur. Ergo etiam existentibus in inferno suffragia prosunt.

PRAETEREA, Dionysius, ult. cap. *Eccles. Hier.*, dicit: *si hic iustorum orationes et secundum hanc vitam, quanto magis post mortem in illis qui digni sunt sacris orationibus operantur tantummodo:* ex quo potest accipi quod suffragia magis prosunt mortuis quam etiam vivis. Sed vivis prosunt etiam in peccato mortali existentibus: cum quotidie oret Ecclesia pro peccatoribus ut convertantur ad Deum. Ergo etiam mortuis in peccato mortali suffragia valent.

PRAETEREA, in *Vitis Patrum* legitur, quod etiam Damascenus in Sermone suo refert, quod Macarius, inventa in via calvaria cuiusdam defuncti, oratione praemissa, quaesivit cuius caput fuisset; et caput respondit quod fuerat sacerdotis gentilis, qui in inferno erat damnatus; et tamen confessus est oratione Macarii se et alios iuvari. Ergo suffragia Ecclesiae etiam in inferno existentibus prosunt.

PRAETEREA, Damascenus, in eodem Sermone, narrat quod Gregorius, pro Traiano orationem fundens, audivit vocem sibi divinitus illatam: *vocem tuam audivi, et veniam Traiano do.* Cuius rei, ut Damascenus dicit in dicto Sermone, *testis est oriens omnis et occidens.* Sed constat Traianum in inferno fuisse, quia *multorum martyrum necem amaram instituit,* ut ibidem Damascenus dicit. Ergo suffragia Ecclesiae valent etiam in inferno existentibus.

SED CONTRA: Est quod dicit Dionysius, 7 cap. *Eccles. Hier.*: *summus sacerdos pro immundis non orat: quia in hoc averteretur a divino ordine.* Et commentator ibidem dicit quod *peccatoribus non orat remissionem: quia non audiretur pro illis.* Ergo suffragia existentibus in inferno non valent.

PRAETEREA, Gregorius dicit, in XXXIV lib. *Moral.*: *eadem causa est cur non oretur tunc,* scilicet post diem iudicii, *pro hominibus aeterno igne damnatis, quae nunc causa est ut non oretur pro diabolo et angelis eius aeterno supplicio deputatis. Quae etiam nunc causa est ut sancti non orent pro hominibus infidelibus impiisque defunctis: quia de eis utique quos aeterno damnatos supplicio iam noverint, ante illum Iudicis iusti conspectum orationis suae meritum cassari refugiunt.* Ergo suffragia in inferno positis non valent.

PRAETEREA, in littera habetur ex verbis Augustini: *qui sine fide operante per dilectionem, eiusque sacramentis, de corpore exeunt, frustra illis a suis huiusmodi officia*

were taken to hell. Therefore, suffrages profit those who are in hell.

OBJ. 2: Further, the text (*Sentences* IV, D. 45) quotes the saying of Augustine (*Handbook on Faith, Hope, and Charity* 110) that *those whom suffrages profit gain either entire forgiveness, or at least an abatement of their damnation.* Now only those who are in hell are said to be damned. Therefore, suffrages profit even those who are in hell.

OBJ. 3: Further, Dionysius says (*On the Ecclesiastical Hierarchies*): *if here the prayers of the righteous avail those who are alive, how much more do they, after death, profit those alone who are worthy of their holy prayers?* Hence we may gather that suffrages are more profitable to the dead than to the living. Now they profit the living even though they be in mortal sin, for the Church prays daily for sinners that they be converted to God. Therefore, suffrages avail also for the dead who are in mortal sin.

OBJ. 4: Further, in the *Lives of the Fathers* (3.172; 6.3) we read, and the Damascene relates in his sermon *On Those Who Have Fallen Asleep in Faith,* Macarius discovered the skull of a dead man on the road, and that after praying he asked whose head it was, and the head replied that it had belonged to a pagan priest who was condemned to hell; and yet he confessed that he and others were assisted by the prayers of Macarius. Therefore, the suffrages of the Church profit even those who are in hell.

OBJ. 5: Further, the Damascene in the same sermon relates that Gregory, while praying for Trajan, heard a voice from heaven saying to him: *I have heard thy voice, and I pardon Trajan*: and of this fact the Damascene adds in the same sermon, *the whole East and West are witnesses.* Yet it is clear that Trajan was in hell, since *he put many martyrs to a cruel death.* Therefore, the suffrages of the Church avail even for those who are in hell.

ON THE CONTRARY, Dionysius says, *the high priest prays not for the unclean, because by so doing he would act counter to the divine order,* and consequently he says that he prays not that sinners be forgiven, because his prayer for them would not be heard (*On the Ecclesiastical Hierarchies* 7). Therefore, suffrages avail not those who are in hell.

FURTHER, Gregory says (*Morals on Job* 34.19): *The reason is the same why people damned to eternal fire will not be prayed for then* (namely, after the judgment day) *and why we do not now pray for the devil and his angels damned to eternal suffering; which is also the reason that the saints do not pray now for wicked and unbelieving dead men: since for those at any rate whom they know to be damned to eternal torment, they shun that the merit of their prayer should be brought to naught in the sight of the just Judge.* Therefore, suffrages do not avail those in hell.

FURTHER, The text (*Sentences* IV, D. 45) quotes the words of Augustine: *if a man depart this life without the faith that works by charity and its sacraments, in vain do his*

impenduntur. Sed omnes damnati sunt huiusmodi. Ergo eis suffragia non prosunt.

RESPONDEO dicendum quod circa damnatos in inferno fuit duplex opinio. Quidam enim dixerunt in hoc distinguendum esse dupliciter. Uno modo, quantum ad tempus: dicentes quod post diem iudicii nullus in inferno existens aliquo suffragio iuvatur; sed ante diem iudicii aliqui iuvantur suffragiis Ecclesiae. Alio modo distinguebat quantum ad personas in inferno detentas. Inter quos aliquos dicebant esse valde malos, qui scilicet sine fide et sacramentis Ecclesiae decesserunt: et talibus, quia de Ecclesia non fuerunt nec *merito* nec *numero*, suffragia Ecclesiae prodesse non possunt. Alii vero sunt non valde mali, qui scilicet de Ecclesia fuerunt numero, et fidem habentes, et sacramentis imbuti, et aliqua opera de genere bonorum facientes. Et talibus suffragia Ecclesiae prodesse debent.

Sed occurrebat eis quaedam dubitatio eos perturbans. Quia scilicet videbatur ex hoc sequi, cum poena inferni sit finita secundum intensionem, quamvis duratione infinita existat, quod, multiplicatis suffragiis, poena illa totaliter auferetur: quod est error Origenis. Et ideo hoc inconveniens evadere multipliciter voluerunt.

Praepositinus enim dixit quod tantum possunt suffragia pro damnatis multiplicari quod a tota poena redduntur immunes, non quidem simpliciter, ut Origenes posuit, sed ad tempus, scilicet usque ad diem iudicii: tunc enim animae, iterato corporibus, coniunctae, in poenas inferni sine spe veniae retrudentur.

Sed ista opinio videtur divinae providentiae repugnare, quae nihil in rebus inordinatum relinquit. Culpa autem non potest ordinari nisi per poenam. Unde non potest esse ut poena tollatur nisi prius culpa expietur. Et ideo, cum culpa continue maneat iri damnatis, eorum poena nullatenus interrumpetur.

Et ideo Porretani alium modum invenerunt, dicentes quod hoc modo proceditur in diminutione poenarum per suffragia sicut proceditur in divisione linearum; quae, cum sint finitae, tamen in infinitum dividi possunt, et nunquam per divisionem consumuntur, dum fit subtractio non secundum eandem quantitatem, sed secundum eandem proportionem; velut si primo auferatur pars quarta totius, et secundo pars quarta illius quartae, et iterum quarta illius quartae, et sic deinceps in infinitum. Et similiter dicunt quod per primum suffragium diminuitur aliquota pars poenae, et per secundum pars aliqua remanentis secundum eandem proportionem.

Sed iste modus multipliciter defectivus invenitur. Primo, quia infinita divisio, quae congruit continuae quantitati, non videtur posse ad quantitatem spiritua-

friends have recourse to such acts of kindness (On the Words of the Apostle 32). Now all the damned come under that head. Therefore, suffrages profit them not.

I ANSWER THAT, There have been three opinions about the damned. For some have said that a twofold distinction must be made in this matter. First, as to time; for they said that after the judgment day no one in hell will be assisted by any suffrage, but that before the judgment day some are assisted by the suffrages of the Church. Second, they made a distinction among those who are detained in hell. Some of these, they said, are very bad, namely, those who have died without faith and the sacraments, and these, since they were not of the Church, neither *by grace* nor *by name* can the suffrages of the Church avail (Cf. *Decretals*); while others are not very bad, namely, those who belonged to the Church as actual members, who had the faith, frequented the sacraments and performed works generically good, and for these the suffrages of the Church ought to avail.

Yet they were confronted with a difficulty which troubled them, for it would seem to follow from this (since the punishment of hell is finite in intensity, although infinite in duration) that a multiplicity of suffrages would take away that punishment altogether, which is the error of Origen (*On First Principles* 1; cf. Gregory, *Morals on Job* 34): and consequently endeavored in various ways to avoid this difficulty.

Praepositivus said that suffrages for the damned can be so multiplied that they are entirely freed from punishment, not absolutely as Origen maintained, but for a time, namely, till the judgment day: for their souls will be reunited to their bodies, and will be cast back into the punishments of hell without hope of pardon.

But this opinion seems incompatible with divine providence, which leaves nothing inordinate in the world. For guilt cannot be restored to order save by punishment. Wherefore it is impossible for punishment to cease unless first of all guilt be expiated: so that, as guilt remains forever in the damned, their punishment will in no way be interrupted.

For this reason the followers of Gilbert de la Porree devised another explanation. These said that the process in the diminution of punishments by suffrages is as the process in dividing a line, which though finite, is indefinitely divisible, and is never destroyed by division, if it be diminished not by equal but by proportionate quantities: for instance, if we begin by taking away a quarter of the whole, and second, a quarter of that quarter, and then a quarter of this second quarter, and so on indefinitely. In like manner, they say by the first suffrage a certain proportion of the punishment is taken away, and by the second an equally proportionate part of the remainder.

But this explanation is in many ways defective. First, because it seems that indefinite division, which is applicable to continuous quantity, cannot be transferred to spiritual

lem transferri. Secundo, quia non est aliqua ratio quare secundum suffragium minus de poena diminuat quam primum, si sit aequalis valoris. Tertio, quia poena diminui non potest nisi diminuatur et culpa: sicut nec auferri nisi ea ablata. Quarto, quia in divisione lineae tandem pervenitur ad hoc quod non est sensibile: corpus enim sensibile non est in infinitum divisibile. Et sic sequeretur quod post multa suffragia poena remanens propter sui parvitatem non sentiretur, et non esset poena.

Et ideo alii alium invenerunt modum: Antissiodorensis enim dixit quod suffragia prosunt damnatis non quidem per diminutionem poenae vel per interruptionem, sed per confortationem patientis: sicut si homo portaret grave onus, et facies sua perfunderetur aqua; sic enim confortaretur ad melius portandum, cum tamen onus suum in nullo levius fieret.

Sed hoc iterum esse non potest. Quia aliquis plus vel minus aeterno igne gravatur, ut Gregorius dicit, secundum meritum culpae. Et inde est quod eodem igne quidam plus, quidam minus cruciantur. Unde, cum culpa damnati immutata remaneat, non potest esse quod levius poenam ferat.

Est nihilominus et praedicta opinio et praesumptuosa, utpote sanctorum dictis contraria; et vana, nulla auctoritate fulcita; et nihilominus irrationalis. Tum quia damnati in inferno sunt extra vinculum caritatis, secundum quam opera vivorum continuantur defunctis. Tum quia totaliter ad viae terminum pervenerunt, recipientes ultimam pro rueritis retributionem, sicut et sancti qui sunt in patria. Quod enim adhuc restat de poena vel gloria corporis, hoc eis rationem viatoris non praebet: cum gloria essentialiter et radicaliter existat in anima, et similiter miseria damnatorum. Et ideo non potest eorum poena diminui, sicut nec gloria sanctorum, augeri quantum ad praemium essentiale.

Sed tamen modus qui a quibusdam ponitur quod suffragia prosunt damnatis, posset aliquo modo sustineri: ut si dicatur quod non prosunt neque quantum ad diminutionem poenae vel interruptionem, vel quantum ad diminutionem sensus poenae; sed quia ex huiusmodi suffragiis eis aliqua materia doloris subtrahitur, quae eis esse posset si ita se abiectos conspicerent quod pro eis nullam curam haberent; quae materia doloris subtrahitur dum suffragia pro eis fiunt.

Sed illud etiam non potest esse secundum legem communem. Quia, ut Augustinus dicit, in libro *de Cura pro mortuis agenda*, quod praecipue de damnatis verum est: *ibi sunt spiritus defunctorum ubi non vident quaecumque aguntur aut eveniunt in ista vita hominibus*. Et ita non cognoscunt quando pro eis suffragia fiunt: nisi

quantity; second, because there is no reason why the second suffrage, if it be of equal worth, should diminish the punishment less than the first; third, because punishment cannot be diminished unless guilt be diminished, even as it cannot be done away with unless the guilt be done away with; fourth, because in the division of a line we come at length to something which is not sensible, for a sensible body is not indefinitely divisible: and thus it would follow that after many suffrages the remaining punishment would be so little as not to be felt, and thus would no longer be a punishment.

Hence others found another explanation. For Antissiodorensis (*Sentences* 4.14) said that suffrages profit the damned not by diminishing or interrupting their punishment, but by fortifying the person punished: even as a man who is carrying a heavy load might bathe his face in water, for thus he would be enabled to carry it better, and yet his load would be none the lighter.

But this again is impossible, because according to Gregory (*Morals on Job* 9) a man suffers more or less from the eternal fire according as his guilt deserves; and consequently some suffer more, some less, from the same fire. Therefore, since the guilt of the damned remains unchanged, it cannot be that he suffers less punishment.

Moreover, the aforesaid opinion is presumptuous, as being in opposition to the statements of holy men, and groundless, as being based on no authority. It is also unreasonable. First, because the damned in hell are cut off from the bond of charity in virtue of which the departed are in touch with the works of the living. Second, because they have entirely come to the end of life, and have received the final award for their merits, even as the saints who are in heaven. For the remaining punishment or glory of the body does not make them to be wayfarers, since glory essentially and radically resides in the soul. It is the same with the unhappiness of the damned, wherefore their punishment cannot be diminished as neither can the glory of the saints be increased as to the essential reward.

However, we may admit, in a certain measure, the manner in which suffrages profit the damned, according to some, if it be said that they profit neither by diminishing nor interrupting their punishment, nor again by diminishing their sense of punishment, but by withdrawing from the damned some matter of grief, which matter they might have if they knew themselves to be so outcast as to be a care to no one; and this matter of grief is withdrawn from them when suffrages are offered for them.

Yet even this is impossible according to the general law, because as Augustine says—and this applies especially to the damned—*the spirits of the departed are where they see nothing of what men do or of what happens to them in this life* (*On the Care of the Dead* 13), and consequently they know not when suffrages are offered for them, unless this relief be

supra communem legem hoc remedium divinitus datur aliquibus damnatorum. Quod est verbum omnino incertum.

Unde tutius est simpliciter dicere quod suffragia non prosunt damnatis, nec pro eis Ecclesia orare intendit, sicut ex inductis auctoritatibus apparet.

Ad primum ergo dicendum quod donaria idolorum non fuerunt inventa apud illos mortuos ut ex eis signum accipi posset quod in reverentiam idolorum eis deferrent; sed ea acceperunt ut victores, quia eis iure belli debebantur. Et tamen per avaritiam venialiter peccaverunt. Unde non fuerunt in inferno damnati. Et sic suffragia eis prodesse poterant.

Vel dicendum, secundum quosdam, quod in ipsa pugna, videntes sibi periculum imminere, de peccato poenituerunt: secundum illud Psalmi [77, 34]: *cum occideret eos, quaerebant eum.* Et hoc probabiliter potest aestimari. Et ideo pro eis fuit oblatio facta.

Ad secundum dicendum quod in verbis illis damnatio large accipitur pro quacumque punitione. Et sic includit etiam poenam purgatorii, quae quandoque totaliter per suffragia expiatur, quandoque autem non, sed diminuitur.

Ad tertium dicendum quod quantum ad hoc magis acceptatur suffragium pro mortuo quam pro vivo, quia magis indiget: cum non possit sibi auxiliari sicut vivus. Sed quantum ad hoc vivus est melioris conditionis, quia potest transferri de statu culpae mortalis in statum gratiae, quod de mortuis dici non potest. Et ideo non est eadem causa orandi pro mortuis et pro vivis.

Ad quartum dicendum quod illud adiutorium non erat quod poena eorum diminueretur, sed in hoc solo, ut ibidem dicitur, quod, eo orante, concedebatur eis ut mutuo se viderent: et in hoc aliquod gaudium, non verum sed phantasticum, habebant, dum implebatur hoc quod desiderabant. Sicut et daemones gaudere dicuntur dum homines ad peccatum pertrahunt, quamvis per hoc eorum poena nullatenus minuatur: sicut non minuitur angelorum gaudium per hoc quod malis nostris compati dicuntur.

Ad quintum dicendum quod de facto Traiani hoc modo potest probabiliter aestimari: quod precibus beati Gregorii ad vitam fuerit revocatus, et ita gratiam consecutus sit, per quam remissionem peccatorum habuit, et per consequens immunitatem a poena; sicut etiam apparet in omnibus illis qui fuerunt miraculose a mortuis suscitati, quorum plures constat idololatras et damnatos fuisse. De omnibus enim similiter dici oportet quod non erant in inferno finaliter deputati, sed secundum praesentem iustitiam propriorum meritorum. Secundum autem superiores causas, quibus praevidebantur ad vitam revocandi, erat aliter de eis disponendum.

Vel dicendum, secundum quosdam, quod anima Traiani non fuit simpliciter a reatu poenae aeternae ab-

granted from above to some of the damned in spite of the general law. This, however, is a matter of great uncertainty.

Thus it is safer to say simply that suffrages do not profit the damned, nor does the Church intend to pray for them, as appears from the authors quoted above.

Reply Obj. 1: The tokens to the idols were not found on those dead so that they might be taken as a sign that they were carried off in reverence to the idols: but they took them as conquerors because they were due to them by right of war. They sinned venially, however, by covetousness, and consequently they were not damned in hell, and thus suffrages could profit them.

Or we may say, according to some, that in the midst of fighting, seeing they were in danger, they repented of their sin, according to Psalm 77:34, *when he slew them, then they sought him*: and this is a probable opinion. Wherefore the offering was made for them.

Reply Obj. 2: In these words damnation is taken in a broad sense for any kind of punishment, so as to include also the punishment of purgatory which is sometimes entirely expiated by suffrages, and sometimes not entirely, but diminished.

Reply Obj. 3: Suffrage for a dead person is more acceptable than for a living person, as regards his being in greater want, since he cannot help himself as a living person can. But a living person is better off in that he can be taken from the state of mortal sin to the state of grace, which cannot be said of the dead. Hence there is not the same reason for praying for the dead as for the living.

Reply Obj. 4: This assistance did not consist in a diminishment of their punishment, but in this alone (as stated in the same place) that when he prayed they were permitted to see one another, and in this they had a certain joy, not real but imaginary, in the fulfillment of their desire. Even so the demons are said to rejoice when they draw men into sin, although this in no way diminishes their punishment, as neither is the joy of the angels diminished by the fact that they take pity on our ills.

Reply Obj. 5: Concerning the incident of Trajan it may be supposed with probability that he was recalled to life at the prayers of blessed Gregory, and thus obtained the grace whereby he received the pardon of his sins and in consequence was freed from punishment. The same applies to all those who were miraculously raised from the dead, many of whom were evidently idolaters and damned. For we must say likewise of all such persons that they were consigned to hell, not finally, but as was actually due to their own merits according to justice: and that according to higher causes, in view of which it was foreseen that they would be recalled to life, they were to be disposed of otherwise.

Or we may say with some that Trajan's soul was not simply freed from the debt of eternal punishment, but that

soluta, sed eius poena fuit suspensa ad tempus, scilicet usque ad diem iudicii. Nec tamen oportet quod hoc fiat communiter per suffragia: quia alia sunt quae lege communi accidunt, et alia quae singulariter ex privilegio aliquibus conceduntur; sicut *alii sunt humanarum limites rerum, alia divinarum signa virtutum*, ut Augustinus dicit, in libro *de Cura pro mortuis agenda*.

his punishment was suspended for a time, that is, until the judgment day. Nor does it follow that this is the general result of suffrages, because things happen differently in accordance with the general law from that which is permitted in particular cases and by privilege. Even so *the bounds of human affairs differ from those of the miracles of the divine power*, as Augustine says (*On the Care of the Dead* 16).

Article 6

Whether Suffrages Profit Those Who Are in Purgatory?

AD SEXTUM SIC PROCEDITUR. Videtur quod nec etiam existentibus in purgatorio. Quia purgatorium pars quaedam inferni est. Sed *in inferno nulla est redemptio*: Et Psalmus [6, 6] dicit: *in inferno autem quis confitebitur tibi?* Ergo suffragia his qui sunt in purgatorio non prosunt.

PRAETEREA, poena purgatorii est poena finita. Si ergo per suffragia aliquid de poena dimittitur, tantum poterunt multiplicari suffragia quod tota tolletur. Et ita peccatum remanebit totaliter impunitum. Quod videtur divinae iustiae repugnare.

PRAETEREA, ad hoc animae in purgatorio detinentur ut, ibi purgatae, purae ad regnum perveniant. Sed nihil potest purgari nisi aliquid circa ipsum fiat. Ergo suffragia facta per vivos poenam purgatorii non diminuunt.

PRAETEREA, si suffragia existentibus in purgatorio valerent, maxime ea viderentur valere quae sunt ad imperium eorum facta. Sed haec non semper valent. Sicut si aliquis decedens disponat tot suffragia pro se fieri, quae, si facta essent, sufficerent ad totam poenam abolendam: posito ergo quod huiusmodi suffragia differantur quousque ille poenam evaserit, illa suffragia nihil ei proderunt: non enim potest dici quod ei prosint antequam fiant; postquam autem sunt facta, eis non indiget, quia iam poenas evasit. Ergo suffragia existentibus in purgatorio non valent.

SED CONTRA: Est quod dicitur in littera ex verbis Augustini, quod suffragia prosunt his qui sunt mediocriter boni vel mali. Sed tales sunt qui in purgatorio detinentur. Ergo, etc.

PRAETEREA, Dionysius dicit, 7 cap. *Eccles. Hier.*, quod *divinus sacerdos, pro mortuis orans, pro illis orat qui sancte vixerunt et tamen aliquas maculas habuerunt ex infirmitate humana contractas*. Sed tales in purgatorio detinentur. Ergo, etc.

OBJECTION 1: It would seem that suffrages do not profit even those who are in purgatory. For purgatory is a part of hell. Now *there is no redemption in hell* (*Office of the Dead*, Resp. vii), and it is written, *who shall confess to thee in hell?* (Ps 6:6). Therefore, suffrages do not profit those who are in purgatory.

OBJ. 2: Further, the punishment of purgatory is finite. Therefore, if some of the punishment is abated by suffrages, it would be possible to have such a great number of suffrages that the punishment would be entirely remitted, and consequently the sin entirely unpunished: and this would seem incompatible with divine justice.

OBJ. 3: Further, souls are in purgatory in order that they may be purified there, and being pure may come to the kingdom. Now nothing can be purified unless something be done to it. Therefore, suffrages offered by the living do not diminish the punishment of purgatory.

OBJ. 4: Further, if suffrages availed those who are in purgatory, those especially would seem to avail them which are offered at their behest. Yet these do not always avail: for instance, if a person, before dying, were to provide for so many suffrages to be offered for him that if they were offered they would suffice for the remission of his entire punishment. Now, supposing these suffrages to be delayed until he is released from punishment, they will profit him nothing. For it cannot be said that they profit him before they are discharged; and after they are fulfilled, he no longer needs them, since he is already released. Therefore, suffrages do not avail those who are in purgatory.

ON THE CONTRARY, As quoted in the text (*Sentences* IV, D. 45), Augustine says (*Handbook on Faith, Hope, and Charity* 110): suffrages profit those who are not very good or not very bad. Now such are those who are detained in purgatory. Therefore, etc.

FURTHER, Dionysius says (*On the Ecclesiastical Hierarchies* 7) that the *divine priest, in praying for the departed, prays for those who lived a holy life and yet contracted certain stains through human frailty*. Now such persons are detained in purgatory. Therefore, etc.

Respondeo dicendum quod poena purgatorii est in supplementum satisfactionis quae non fuerat plene in corpore consummata. Et ideo, quia, sicut ex dictis patet, opera unius possunt valere alteri ad satisfactionem, sive vivis sive mortuis, non est dubium quin suffragia per vivos facta existentibus in purgatorio prosint.

Ad primum ergo dicendum quod auctoritas illa loquitur de inferno damnatorum, in quo *nulla est redemptio* quantum ad illos qui sunt finaliter tali poenae deputati.

Vel dicendum, secundum Damascenum, in *Sermone de Dormientibus*, quod huiusmodi auctoritates sunt exponendae secundum causas inferiores, idest secundum exigentiam meritorum eorum qui poenis deputantur. Sed secundum divinam misericordiam, quae vincit humana merita, ad preces iustorum aliquando aliter disponitur quam sententia praedictarum auctoritatum contineat. *Deus autem mutat sententiam, sed non consilium*, ut dicit Gregorius. Unde et Damascenus ponit ad hoc exempla de Ninivitis, Achab et Ezechia, in quibus apparet quod sententia contra eos lata divinitus fuit per divinam misericordiam commutata.

Ad secundum dicendum quod non est inconveniens si, multiplicatis suffragiis, poena existentium in purgatorio annihiletur. Non enim sequitur quod peccata remaneant impunita: quia poena unius pro altero suscepta alteri computatur.

Ad tertium dicendum quod purgatio animae per poenas purgatorii non est aliud quam expiatio reatus impedientis a perceptione gloriae. Et quia per poenam quam unus sustinet pro alio, potest reatus alterius expiari, ut dictum est, non est inconveniens si per unius satisfactionem alius purgetur.

Ad quartum dicendum quod suffragia ex duobus valent: scilicet ex opere operante, et ex opere operato. Et dico opus operatum non solum Ecclesiae sacramentum, sed effectum accidentem ex operatione: sicut ex collatione eleemosynarum consequitur pauperum relevatio, et eorum oratio pro defuncto ad Deum. Similiter opus operans potest accipi vel ex parte principalis agendis; vel ex parte exequentis.

Dico ergo quod, quam cito moriens disponit aliena suffragia sibi fieri, praemium suffragiorum plene consequitur, ante etiam quam fiant, quantum ad efficaciam suffragii quae erat ex opere operante principalis agentis. Sed quantum ad efficaciam suffragiorum quae est ex opere operato, vel ex opere operante exequentis, non consequitur fructum antequam suffragia fiant. Et si prius contingat ipsum a poena purgari, quantum ad hoc fraudabitur suffragiorum fructu: quod redundabit in illos,

I answer that, The punishment of purgatory is intended to supplement the satisfaction which was not fully completed in the body. Consequently, since, as stated above (A. 1–2; Q. 13, A. 2), the works of one person can avail for another's satisfaction, whether the latter be living or dead, the suffrages of the living without any doubt profit those who are in purgatory.

Reply Obj. 1: The words quoted refer to those who are in the hell of the damned, where there *is no redemption* for those who are finally consigned to that punishment.

We may also reply with Damascene that such statements are to be explained with reference to the lower causes, that is, according to the demands of the merits of those who are consigned to those punishments. But according to the divine mercy, which transcends human merits, it happens otherwise through the prayers of the righteous than is implied by the expressions quoted in the aforesaid authorities. *Now God changes his sentence but not his counsel*, as Gregory says (*Morals on Job* 20): wherefore the Damascene quotes as instances of this the Ninevites, Ahab, and Hezekiah, in whom it is apparent that the sentence pronounced against them by God was commuted by the divine mercy (Cf. I, Q. 19, A. 7).

Reply Obj. 2: It is not unreasonable that the punishment of those who are in purgatory be entirely done away with by the multiplicity of suffrages. But it does not follow that the sins remain unpunished, because the punishment of one undertaken in lieu of another is credited to that other.

Reply Obj. 3: The purifying of the soul by the punishment of purgatory is nothing else than the expiation of the guilt that hinders it from obtaining glory. And since, as stated above (Q. 13, A. 2), the guilt of one person can bc cxpiated by the punishment which another undergoes in his stead, it is not unreasonable that one person be purified by another satisfying for him.

Reply Obj. 4: Suffrages avail on two counts, namely, the action of the agent and the action done. By action done I mean not only the sacrament of the Church, but the effect incidental to that action—thus from the giving of alms there follow the relief of the poor and their prayer to God for the deceased. In like manner, the action of the agent may be considered in relation either to the principal agent or to the executor.

I say, then, that the dying person, as soon as he provides for certain suffrages to be offered for him, receives the full merit of those suffrages, even before they are discharged, as regards the efficacy of the suffrages that results from the action as proceeding from the principal agent. But as regards the efficacy of the suffrages arising from the action done or from the action as proceeding from the executor, he does not receive the fruit before the suffrages are discharged. And if, before this, he happens to be released from

quorum culpa defraudatur. Non enim est inconveniens quod aliquis defraudetur per culpam alterius in temporalibus, poena autem purgatorii temporalis est: quamvis quantum ad aeternam retributionem nullus defraudari possit nisi per propriam culpam.

his punishment, he will in this respect be deprived of the fruit of the suffrages, and this will fall back upon those by whose fault he was then defrauded. For it is not unreasonable that a person be defrauded in temporal matters by another's fault—and the punishment of purgatory is temporal—although as regards the eternal retribution none can be defrauded save by his own fault.

Article 7

Whether Suffrages Avail the Children Who Are in Limbo?

Ad septimum sic proceditur. Videtur quod suffragia valeant pueris in limbo existentibus. Quia illi, non detinentur nisi pro peccato alieno. Ergo maxime decens est ut ipsi iuventur suffragiis alienis.

Praeterea, in littera habetur ex verbis Augustini quod suffragia Ecclesiae *pro non valde malis propitiationes sunt.* Sed pueri non computantur inter valde malos: cum sit *mitissima eorum poena.* Ergo suffragia Ecclesiae eos iuvant.

Sed contra est quod habetur in littera ab Augustino, quod *suffragia non prosunt illis qui sine fide operante per dilectionem hinc exierunt.* Ergo suffragia eis non prosunt.

Respondeo dicendum quod pueri non baptizati non detinentur in limbo nisi quia deficiunt a statu gratiae. Unde, cum per opera vivorum mortuorum status mutari non possit, maxime quantum ad meritum essentialis praemii vel poenae, suffragia vivorum pueris existentibus in limbo prodesse non possunt.

Ad primum ergo dicendum quod, quamvis peccatum originale sit huiusmodi quod pro eo possit aliquis ab alio iuvari, tamen animae puerorum in limbo existentes sunt in tali statu quod iuvari non possunt: quia post hanc vitam non est tempus gratiam acquirendi.

Ad secundum dicendum quod Augustinus loquitur de non valde malis qui tamen baptizati sunt. Quod patet ex hoc quod praemittitur: *cum ergo sacrificia, sive altaris sive quarumcumque eleemosynarum, pro baptizatis omnibus offeruntur,* etc.

Objection 1: It would seem that suffrages avail the children who are in limbo. For they are not detained there except for another's sin. Therefore, it is most becoming that they should be assisted by the suffrages of others.

Obj. 2: Further, in the text (*Sentences* IV, D. 45) the words of Augustine (*Handbook on Faith, Hope, and Charity* 110) are quoted: the suffrages of the Church *obtain forgiveness for those who are not very bad.* Now children are not reckoned among those who are very bad, since *their punishment is very light.* Therefore, the suffrages of the Church avail them.

On the contrary, The text (*Sentences* IV, D. 45) quotes Augustine as saying (*On the Words of the Apostle* 32) that *suffrages avail not those who have departed hence without the faith that works by love.* Now the children departed thus. Therefore, suffrages avail them not.

I answer that, Unbaptized children are not detained in limbo save because they lack the state of grace. Hence, since the state of the dead cannot be changed by the works of the living, especially as regards the merit of the essential reward or punishment, the suffrages of the living cannot profit the children in limbo.

Reply Obj. 1: Although original sin is such that one person can be assisted by another on its account, nevertheless the souls of the children in limbo are in such a state that they cannot be assisted, because after this life there is no time for obtaining grace.

Reply Obj. 2: Augustine is speaking of those who are not very bad, but have been baptized. This is clear from what precedes: *since these sacrifices, whether of the altar or of any alms whatsoever are offered for those who have been baptized,* etc.

Article 8

Whether Suffrages Profit the Saints in Heaven?

AD OCTAVUM SIC PROCEDITUR. Videtur quod aliquo modo prosint sanctis existentibus in patria: per hoc quod habetur in collecta Missae: *sicut Sanctis tuis prosunt ad gloriam*, scilicet sacramenta, *ita nobis proficiant ad medelam*. Sed inter alia suffragia praecipuum est Sacramentum Altaris. Ergo suffragia prosunt his qui sunt in patria.

PRAETEREA, sacramenta efficiunt quod figurant. Sed tertia pars hostiae, scilicet in calicem Missa, significat eos qui beatam vitam in patria ducunt. Ergo suffragia Ecclesiae prosunt etiam existentibus in patria.

PRAETEREA, sancti non solum gaudent de propriis bonis, sed etiam de bonis aliorum: unde Luc. 15, [10] dicitur: *gaudium est angelis Dei super uno peccatore poenitentiam agente*. Ergo ex bonis operibus viventium sanctorum qui sunt in patria gaudium crescit. Et ita etiam eis nostra suffragia prosunt.

PRAETEREA, Damascenus dicit, in *Sermone de Dormientibus*, inducens verba Chrysostomi: *si enim gentiles, inquit, cum his qui abierunt sua comburunt, quanto magis te fidelem mittere convenit cum fideli ipsius propria: non ut favilla fiant et haec velut illa; sed ut maiorem hinc circumponas gloriam; et, si quidem peccator fuerit qui mortuus est, ut peccamina solvas; si autem iustus, ut appositio fiat mercedis et retributionis*. Et sic idem quod prius.

SED CONTRA: Est quod in littera habetur ex verbis Augustini: *iniuria est in Ecclesia pro martyre orare, cuius nos debemus orationibus commendari*.

PRAETEREA, eius est iuvari cuius est indigere. Sed sancti in patria sunt absque omni indigentia. Ergo per suffragia Ecclesiae non iuvantur.

RESPONDEO dicendum quod suffragium de sui ratione importat quandam auxiliationem. Quae non competit ei qui defectum non patitur: nulli enim iuvari competit nisi in eo quo indigens est. Unde, cum sancti qui sunt in patria sint ab omni indigentia immunes, inebriati ab ubertate Domus Dei, eis iuvari per suffragia non competit.

AD PRIMUM ergo, dicendum quod huiusmodi locutiones non sunt sic intelligendae quasi sancti in gloria proficiant quantum ad se quod eorum festa recolimus: sed quia nobis proficit, qui eorum gloriam solemnius celebramus. Sicut ex hoc quod Deum cognoscimus vel laudamus, et sic quodammodo eius gloria in nobis crescit, nihil Deo, sed nobis accrescit.

OBJECTION 1: It would seem that in some way suffrages profit the saints in heaven on account of the words of the Collect in the Mass: *even as they* (i.e., the sacraments) *avail thy saints unto glory, so may they profit us unto healing* (Postcommunion, Feast of St. Andrew, Apostle). Now foremost among all suffrages is the Sacrifice of the Altar. Therefore, suffrages profit the saints in heaven.

OBJ. 2: Further, the sacraments cause what they signify. Now the third part of the host, namely, that which is dropped into the chalice, signifies those who lead a happy life in heaven. Therefore, the suffrages of the Church profit those who are in heaven.

OBJ. 3: Further, the saints rejoice in heaven not only in their own goods, but also in the goods of others; hence it is written: *there is joy before the angels of God upon one sinner doing penance* (Luke 15:10). Therefore, the joy of the saints in heaven increases on account of the good works of the living: and consequently our suffrages also profit them.

OBJ. 4: Further, the Damascene says, quoting the words of Chrysostom: *for if the heathens, he says, burn the dead together with what has belonged to them, how much more should you, a believer, send forth a believer together with what has belonged to him, not that they also may be brought to ashes like him, but that you may surround him with greater glory by so doing; and if he be a sinner who has died, that you may loose him from his sins, and if he be righteous, that you may add to his merit and reward*. And thus the same conclusion follows.

ON THE CONTRARY, As quoted in the text (*Sentences* IV, D.15), Augustine says (*On the Words of the Apostle* 17): *it is insulting to pray for a martyr in church, since we ought to commend ourselves to his prayers*.

FURTHER, To be assisted belongs to one who is in need. But the saints in heaven are without any need whatever. Therefore, they are not assisted by the suffrages of the Church.

I ANSWER THAT, Suffrage by its very nature implies the giving of some assistance, which does not apply to one who suffers no default: since no one is competent to be assisted except he who is in need. Hence, as the saints in heaven are free from all need, being inebriated with the plenty of God's house (Ps 35:10), they are not competent to be assisted by suffrages.

REPLY OBJ. 1: Such expressions do not mean that the saints receive an increase of glory in themselves through our observing their feasts, but that we profit thereby in celebrating their glory with greater solemnity. Thus, through our knowing or praising God, and through his glory thus increasing somewhat in us, there accrues something, not to God, but to us.

Ad secundum dicendum quod, quamvis sacramenta *efficiant quod figurant*, non tamen illum effectum suum ponunt circa omne id quod figurant: alias, cum figurent Christum, in ipso Christo aliquid efficerent, quod est absurdum. Sed efficiunt circa suscipientem sacramentum ex virtute eius quod per sacramentum significatur. Et sic non sequitur quod sacrificia, pro fidelibus defunctis oblata sanctis prosint: sed quia ex meritis sanctorum, quae recoluntur vel significantur in sacramento, prosunt aliis, pro quibus offeruntur.

Ad tertium dicendum quod, quamvis sancti qui sunt in patria de bonis nostris omnibus gaudeant, non tamen sequitur quod, multiplicatis nostris gaudiis, eorum gaudium augmentetur formaliter, sed materialiter tantum. Quia omnis passio formaliter augetur secundum rationem obiecti sui. Ratio autem gaudendi in sanctis de quibuscumque gaudent, est ipse Deus. De quo non possunt magis et minus gaudere: quia sic essentiale eorum praemium variaretur, quod consistit in hoc quod de Deo gaudent. Unde ex hoc quod bona multiplicantur de quibus gaudendi ratio eis Deus est, non semper sequitur quod intensius gaudeant, sed quod de pluribus gaudeant. Et ideo non sequitur quod operibus nostris iuventur.

Ad quartum dicendum quod non est intelligendum quod fiat appositio mercedis vel retributionis illi beato per suffragia ab aliquo facta, sed facienti.

Vel dicendum quod ex suffragiis potest appositio mercedis fieri beato defuncto, inquantum de suffragiis sibi faciendis adhuc vivens disposuit, quod ei meritorium fuit.

Reply Obj. 2: Although the sacraments *cause what thy signify*, they do not produce this effect in respect of everything that they signify: else, since they signify Christ, they would produce something in Christ (which is absurd). But they produce their effect on the recipient of the sacrament in virtue of that which is signified by the sacrament. Thus it does not follow that the sacrifices offered for the faithful departed profit the saints, but that by the merits of the saints which we commemorate, or which are signified in the sacrament, they profit others for whom they are offered.

Reply Obj. 3: Although the saints in heaven rejoice in all our goods, it does not follow that if our joys be increased their joy is also increased formally, but only materially, because every passion is increased formally in respect of the formal aspect of its object. Now the formal aspect of the saints' joy, no matter what they rejoice in, is God himself, in whom they cannot rejoice more and less, for otherwise their essential reward, consisting of their joy in God, would vary. Hence from the fact that the goods are multiplied wherein they rejoice with God as the formal aspect of their joy, it does not follow that their joy is intensified, but that they rejoice in more things. Consequently, it does not follow that they are assisted by our works.

Reply Obj. 4: The sense is not that an increase of merit or reward accrues to the saint from the suffrages offered by a person, but that this accrues to the offerer.

Or we may reply that the blessed departed may derive a reward from suffrages through having provided for suffrage to be offered for himself while living, and this was meritorious for him.

Article 9

Whether Only the Prayers of the Church, the Sacrifice of the Altar, and Alms Profit the Departed?

Ad nonum sic proceditur. Videtur quod non solum orationibus Ecclesiae, et Sacrificio Altaris, et eleemosynis animae defunctorum iuventur, vel quod eis iuventur praecipue. Poena enim debt per poenam recompensari. Sed ieiunium magis est poenale quam eleemosyna vel oratio. Ergo ieiunium magis prodesset in suffragiis quam aliquod praedictorum.

Praeterea, Gregorius istis tribus connumerat ieiunium: ut habetur causa XIII, qu.: *animae defunctorum quatuor modis solvuntur: aut oblationibus sacerdotum; aut orationibus sanctorum; aut eleemosynis carorum; aut ieiunio cognatorum.* Ergo insufficienter connumerantur hic, ab Augustino, tria praedicta.

Praeterea, baptismus est potissimum sacramentorum, maxime quantum ad effectum. Ergo baptismus vel

Objection 1: It would seem that the souls of the departed are not assisted only by the prayers of the Church, the Sacrifice of the Altar, and alms, or that they are not assisted by them chiefly. For punishment should compensate for punishment. Now fasting is more penal than almsgiving or prayer. Therefore, fasting profits more as suffrage than any of the above.

Obj. 2: Further, Gregory reckons fasting together with these three, as stated in the *Decretals: the souls of the departed are released in four ways, either by the offerings of priests, or the alms of their friends, or the prayers of the saints, or the fasting of their kinsfolk.* Therefore, the three mentioned above are insufficiently reckoned by Augustine (*On the Care of the Dead* 18).

Obj. 3: Further, baptism is the greatest of the sacraments, especially as regards its effect. Therefore, baptism

alia sacramenta deberent vel similiter vel magis prodesse defunctis sicut Sacramentum Altaris.

PRAETEREA, hoc videtur ex hoc quod habetur, I Cor. 15, [29]: *si omnino mortui non resurgunt ut quid etiam baptizantur pro illis?* Ergo etiam baptismus valet ad suffragia defunctorum.

PRAETEREA, in diversis missis est idem Sacrificium Altaris. Si ergo sacrificium computatur inter suffragia et non Missa, videtur quod tantundem valeat quaecumque Missa pro defuncto dicatur, sive de Beata Virgine, sive de Spiritu Sancto, vel quaecumque alia. Quod videtur esse contra Ecclesiae ordinationem, quae specialem Missam pro defunctis instituit.

PRAETEREA, Damascenus, in *Sermone de Dormientibus*, docet *ceras et oleum*, et huiusmodi, pro defunctis offerri. Ergo non solum oblatio Sacrificii Altaris, sed etiam aliae oblationes debent inter suffragia mortuorum computari.

RESPONDEO dicendum quod suffragia vivorum prosunt defunctis secundum quod uniuntur viventibus caritate; et secundum quod intentio viventis refertur in mortuos. Et ideo illa opera praecipue nata sunt mortuis suffragari quae maxime ad communicationem caritatis pertinent, vel ad directionem intentionis ad alterum. Ad caritatem autem Sacramentum Eucharistiae praecipue pertinet: cum sit sacramentum ecclesiasticae unionis, continens illum in quo tota Ecclesia unitur et consolidatur, scilicet Christum. Unde Eucharistia est quasi quaedam caritatis origo sive vinculum. Sed inter caritatis effectus est praecipuum eleemosynarum opus. Et ideo ista duo ex parte caritatis praecipue mortuis suffragantur: scilicet sacrificium Ecclesiae et eleemosynae. Sed ex parte intentionis directae in mortuos, praecipue valet oratio: quia oratio, secundum suam rationem, non solum dicit respectum ad orantem, sicut et cetera opera, sed directius ad illud pro quo oratur. Et ideo tria ponuntur quasi praecipua mortuorum subsidia: quamvis quaecumque alia bona ex caritate fiant pro defunctis, eis valere credenda sint.

AD PRIMUM ergo dicendum quod in eo qui satisfacit pro altero, magis est considerandum, ad hoc quod effectus satisfactionis ad alterum perveniat, illud quo satisfactio unius transit in alterum, quam etiam satisfactionis poena: quamvis ipsa poena magis expiet reatum satisfacientis, inquantum est quaedam medicina. Et ideo tria praedicta magis valent defunctis quam ieiunium.

AD SECUNDUM dicendum quod etiam ieiunium prodesse potest defunctis ratione caritatis: et intentionis in defunctos directae. Sed tamen ieiunium in sui ratione non continet aliquid quod ad caritatem vel directionem intentionis pertineat, sed haec sunt ei quasi extrinseca.

and other sacraments ought to be offered for the departed equally with or more than the Sacrament of the Altar.

OBJ. 4: Further, this would seem to follow from the words, *if the dead rise not again at all, why are they then baptized for them?* (1 Cor 15:29). Therefore, baptism avails as suffrage for the dead.

OBJ. 5: Further, in different Masses there is the same Sacrifice of the Altar. If, therefore, sacrifice, and not the Mass, be reckoned among the suffrages, it would seem that the effect would be the same whatever Mass be said for a deceased person, whether in honor of the Blessed Virgin or of the Holy Spirit, or any other. Yet this seems contrary to the ordinance of the Church, which has appointed a special Mass for the dead.

OBJ. 6: Further, Damascene teaches that *candles and oil* should be offered for the dead. Therefore, not only the offering of the Sacrifice of the Altar, but also other offerings should be reckoned among suffrages for the dead.

I ANSWER THAT, The suffrages of the living profit the dead insofar as the latter are united to the living in charity, and insofar as the intention of the living is directed to the dead. And therefore the works that are especially of a nature to assist the dead are those that pertain the most to the communication of charity, or to the directing of one's intention to another. Now the sacrament of the Eucharist preeminently belongs to charity, since it is the sacrament of ecclesiastical unity inasmuch as it contains him in whom the whole Church is united and incorporated, namely Christ. Thus the Eucharist is like the origin and bond of charity. Again, chief among the effects of charity is the work of almsgiving: wherefore on the part of charity these two, namely, the sacrifice of the Church and almsgiving, are the chief suffrages for the dead. But on the part of the intention directed to the dead the chief suffrage is prayer, because prayer by its very nature implies relation not only to the person who prays, even as other works do, but more directly still to that which we pray for. Hence these three are reckoned the principal means of aiding the dead, although we must allow that any other goods whatsoever that are done out of charity for the dead are profitable to them.

REPLY OBJ. 1: When one person satisfies for another, the point to consider in order that the effect of his satisfaction reach the other is the thing whereby the satisfaction of one passes to another, rather than even the punishment undergone by way of satisfaction; although the punishment expiates more the guilt of the one who satisfies, insofar as it is a kind of medicine. And consequently the three aforesaid are more profitable to the departed than fasting.

REPLY OBJ. 2: It is true that fasting can profit the departed by reason of charity, and on account of the intention being directed to the departed. Nevertheless, fasting does not by its nature contain anything pertaining to charity or to the directing of the intention, and these things are extrin-

Et ideo Augustinus non posuit, sed Gregorius posuit ieiunium inter suffragia mortuorum.

AD TERTIUM dicendum quod baptismus est quaedam spiritualis regeneratio. Unde, sicut per generationem non acquiritur esse nisi generato, ita baptismus non habet efficaciam nisi in eo qui baptizatur, quantum est ex opere operato: quamvis ex opere operante, vel baptizantis vel baptizati, possit aliis prodesse, sicut et cetera opera meritoria. Sed Eucharistia est signum ecclesiasticae unionis. Et ideo ex ipso opere operato eius efficacia in alterum transire potest. Quod non contingit de aliis sacramentis.

AD QUARTUM dicendum quod Glossa istam auctoritatem dupliciter exponit. Uno modo, sic: *si mortui non resurgunt, nec Christus resurrexit. Ut quid etiam baptizantur pro illis? idest, peccatis: cum ipsa non dimittantur si Christus non resurrexit. Quia in baptismo non solum Christi Passio, sed resurrectio operatur, quae est nostrae spiritualis resurrectionis quodammodo causa.*

Alio modo sic: *fuerunt quidam imperiti qui baptizabantur pro his qui de hac vita sine baptismo discesserant, putantes illis prodesse. Et secundum hoc, Apostolus non loquitur nisi secundum errorem aliquorum in verbis illis.*

AD QUINTUM dicendum quod in officio Missae non solum est sacrificium, sed etiam sunt ibi orationes. Et ideo Missae suffragium continet duo horum quae hic Augustinus enumerat, scilicet orationem et sacrificium. Ex parte igitur sacrificii oblati Missa aequaliter prodest defuncto de quocumque dicatur: et hoc est praecipuum quod fit in Missa. Sed ex parte orationum magis prodest illa in qua sunt orationes ad hoc determinatae. Sed tamen iste defectus recompensari potest per maiorem devotionem vel eius qui dicit Missam, vel eius qui facit dici; vel iterum per intercessionem sancti cuius suffragium in Missa imploratur.

AD SEXTUM dicendum quod huiusmodi oblatio candelarum vel olei possunt prodesse defuncto inquantum sunt eleemosynae quaedam: dantur enim ad cultum Ecclesiae, vel etiam in usum fidelium.

sic thereto as it were, and for this reason Augustine did not reckon, while Gregory did reckon, fasting among the suffrages for the dead.

REPLY OBJ. 3: Baptism is a spiritual regeneration, wherefore just as by generation being does not accrue save to the object generated, so baptism produces its effect only in the person baptized as regards the deed done: and yet as regards the deed of the doer (whether of the baptizer or of the baptized) it may profit others even as other meritorious works. On the other hand, the Eucharist is the sign of ecclesiastical unity, wherefore by reason of the deed done its effect can pass to another, which is not the case with the other sacraments.

REPLY OBJ. 4: According to a Gloss this passage, *if the dead rise not again, nor did Christ rise again, why are they baptized for them?* (1 Cor 15:29) may be expounded in two ways. First, thus: *that is, for sins, since they are not pardoned if Christ rose not again, because in baptism not only Christ's Passion but also his resurrection operates, for the latter is in a sense the cause of our spiritual resurrection.*

Second, thus: *there have been some misguided persons who were baptized for those who had departed this life without baptism, thinking that this would profit them: and according to this explanation the Apostle is speaking, in the above words, merely according to the opinion of certain persons.*

REPLY OBJ. 5: In the office of the Mass there is not only a sacrifice but also prayers. Hence the suffrage of the Mass contains two of the things mentioned by Augustine (*On the Care of the Dead* 18), namely, prayer and sacrifice. As regards the sacrifice offered, the Mass profits equally all the departed, no matter in whose honor it be said: and this is the principal thing done in the Mass. But as regards the prayers, that Mass is most profitable in which the prayers are appointed for this purpose. Nevertheless, this defect may be supplied by the greater devotion either of the one who says Mass, or of the one who orders the Mass to be said, or again, by the intercession of the saint whose suffrage is besought in the Mass.

REPLY OBJ. 6: This offering of candles or oil may profit the departed insofar as they are a kind of alms: for they are given for the worship of the Church or for the use of the faithful.

Article 10

Whether the Indulgences of the Church Profit the Dead?

AD DECIMUM SIC PROCEDITUR. Videtur quod indulgentiae quas Ecclesia facit, etiam mortuis prosint. Primo, per consuetudinem Ecclesiae, quae facit praedicari crucem ut aliquis indulgentiam habeat pro se et duobus vel tribus, et quandoque etiam decem animabus,

OBJECTION 1: It would seem that the indulgences granted by the Church profit even the dead. First, on account of the custom of the Church, who orders the preaching of a crusade in order that some one may gain an indulgence for himself and for two or three and sometimes even

tam vivorum quam mortuorum. Quod esset deceptio nisi mortuis prodessent. Ergo indulgentiae mortuis prosunt.

Praeterea, meritum totius Ecclesiae est efficacius quam meritum unius personae. Sed meritum personale suffragatur defunctis: ut patet in largitione eleemosynarum. Ergo multo fortius meritum Ecclesiae, cui indulgentiae innituntur.

Praeterea, indulgentiae prosunt illis qui sunt de foro Ecclesiae. Sed illi qui sunt in purgatorio, sunt de foro Ecclesiae: alias Ecclesiae suffragia non prodessent illis. Ergo videtur quod indulgentiae defunctis prosint.

Sed contra: Est quod ad hoc quod indulgentiae alicui valeant, requiritur causa conveniens pro qua indulgentiae dantur. Sed talis causa non potest esse ex parte defuncti: quia non potest facere aliquid quod sit in utilitatem Ecclesiae, pro qua causa praecipue indulgentiae dantur. Ergo videtur quod indulgentiae defunctis non prosint.

Praeterea, indulgentiae determinantur secundum arbitrium eas facientis. Si ergo indulgentiae defunctis prodesse possent, esset in potestate facientis indulgentiam ut defunctum omnino liberaret a poena. Quod videtur absurdum.

Respondeo dicendum quod indulgentia alicui prodesse potest dupliciter: uno modo, principaliter; alio modo, secundario. Principaliter quidem prodest ei qui indulgentiam accipit, scilicet qui facit hoc pro quo indulgentia datur, ut qui visitat limina alicuius sancti. Unde, cum mortui non possint facere aliquid horum pro quibus indulgentiae dantur, eis directe indulgentiae valere non possunt.

Secundario autem et indirecte prosunt ei pro quo aliquis facit illud quod est indulgentiae causa. Quod quandoque contingere potest, quandoque autem non potest, secundum diversam indulgentiae formam. Si enim sit talis indulgentiae forma, *quicumque facit hoc vel illud, habebit tantum de indulgentia*, ille qui hoc facit non potest fructum indulgentiae in alium transferre: quia eius non est applicare ad aliquid intentionem Ecclesiae, per quam communicantur communia suffragia, ex quibus indulgentiae valent. Si autem indulgentia sub hac forma fiat, *quicumque fecerit hoc vel illud, ipse et pater eius, vel quicumque ei adiunctus, in purgatorio detentus, tantum de indulgentia habebit*, talis indulgentia non solum vivo, sed etiam mortuo proderit. Non enim est aliqua ratio quare Ecclesia transferre possit communia merita, quibus indulgentiae innituntur, in vivos, et non in mortuos.

Nec tamen sequitur quod praelatus Ecclesiae possit pro suo arbitrio animas a purgatorio liberare. Quia ad

ten souls, both of the living and of the dead. But this would amount to a deception unless they profited the dead. Therefore, indulgences profit the dead.

Obj. 2: Further, the merit of the whole Church is more efficacious than that of one person. Now personal merit serves as a suffrage for the departed: for instance, in the case of almsgiving. Much more, therefore, does the merit of the Church whereon indulgences are founded.

Obj. 3: Further, the indulgences of the Church profit those who are members of the Church. Now those who are in purgatory are members of the Church, else the suffrages of the Church would not profit them. Therefore, it would seem that indulgences profit the departed.

On the contrary, In order that indulgences may avail a person, there must be a fitting cause for granting the indulgence (Cf. Q. 25, A. 2). Now there can be no such cause on the part of the dead, since they can do nothing that is of profit to the Church, and it is for such a cause that indulgences are chiefly granted. Therefore, seemingly, indulgences profit not the dead.

Further, Indulgences are regulated according to the decision of the party who grants them. If, therefore, indulgences could avail the dead, it would be in the power of the party granting them to release a deceased person entirely from punishment: which appears absurd.

I answer that, An indulgence may profit a person in two ways: in one way, principally; in another, secondarily. It profits principally the person who avails himself of an indulgence, who, namely, does that for which the indulgence is granted; for instance, one who visits the shrine of some saint. Hence, since the dead can do none of those things for which indulgences are granted, indulgences cannot avail them directly.

However, they profit secondarily and indirectly the person for whom one does that which is the cause of the indulgence. This is sometimes feasible and sometimes not, according to the different forms of indulgence. For if the form of indulgence be such as this: *whosoever does this or that shall gain so much indulgence*, he who does this cannot transfer the fruit of the indulgence to another, because it is not in his power to apply to a particular person the intention of the Church who dispenses the common suffrages whence indulgences derive their value, as stated above (Q. 27). If, however, the indulgence be granted in this form: *whosoever does this or that, he, his father, or any other person connected with him and detained in purgatory, will gain so much indulgence*, an indulgence of this kind will avail not only a living but also a deceased person. For there is no reason why the Church is able to transfer the common merits, on which indulgences are based, to the living and not to the dead.

Nor does it follow that a prelate of the Church can release souls from purgatory however he desires, since for in-

hoc ut indulgentiae valeant, requiritur causa conveniens indulgentias faciendi, ut supra dictum est.

dulgences to avail there must be a fitting cause for granting them, as stated above (Q. 26, A. 3).

Article 11

Whether the Burial Service Profits the Dead?

Ad tertium sic proceditur. Videtur quod cultus exequiarum defuncto prosit. Damascenus enim, in Sermone de Dormientibus, inducit verba Athanasii sic dicentis: *licet in aera qui in pietate consummatus est, depositus fuerit, ne renuas oleum et ceras, Deum invocans, in sepulcro accendere. Accepta enim ista sunt Deo, et multam ab eo recipientia retributionem.* Sed huiusmodi pertinent ad cultum exequiarum. Ergo cultus exequiarum prodest defunctis.

Praeterea, sicut Augustinus dicit, I lib. *de Civ. Dei*, *antiquorum iustorum funera officiosa pietate curata sunt, et exequiae celebratae, et sepulcra provisa: ipsique, cum viverent, de sepeliendis vel transferendis suis corporibus filiis mandaverunt.* Sed hoc non fecissent nisi sepultura et huiusmodi aliquid mortuis conferrent. Ergo huiusmodi aliquid prosunt defunctis.

Praeterea, nullus facit eleemosynam circa aliquem nisi ei proficiat. Sed sepelire mortuos computatur inter opera eleemosynarum: unde, ut Augustinus dicit, in I *de Civ. Dei*, *Tobias sepeliendo mortuos Deum promeruisse, teste angelo, commendatur.* Ergo huiusmodi sepulturae cultus mortuis prodest.

Praeterea, inconveniens est dicere quod frustretur devotio fidelium. Sed aliqui ex devotione in locis aliquibus religiosis sepeliri disponunt. Ergo sepulturae cultus prodest defunctis.

Praeterea, Deus pronior est ad miserendum quam ad condemnandum. Sed aliquibus nocet in locis sanctis sepultura, si indigni sunt: unde dicit Gregorius: *quos peccata gravia deprimunt, ad maiorem damnationis cumulum potius quam ad solutionem, eorum corpora in ecclesiis ponuntur.* Ergo multo amplius dicendum est quod sepulturae cultus prosit bonis.

Sed contra: Est quod Augustinus dicit, in libro *de Cura pro mortuis agenda: corpori humano quidquid impenditur, non est praesidium vitae aeternae, sed humanitatis officium.*

Praeterea, Gregorius dicit, in IV *Dialog.: curatio funeris, conditio sepulturae, pompa exequiarum, magis sunt vivorum solatia quam subsidia defunctorum.*

Praeterea, Dominus dicit, Matth. 10, [28]: *nolite timere eos qui corpus occidunt, et post hoc non habent amplius quid faciant.* Sed post mortem sanctorum corpora

Objection 1: It would seem that the burial service profits the dead. For Damascene quotes Athanasius as saying, *even though he who has departed in godliness be taken up to heaven, do not hesitate to call upon God and to burn oil and candles at his tomb; for such things are pleasing to God and receive a great reward from him.* Now the like pertain to the burial service. Therefore, the burial service profits the dead.

Obj. 2: Further, according to Augustine (*On the Care of the Dead* 3), *in olden times the funerals of just men were cared for with dutiful piety, their obsequies celebrated, their graves provided, and themselves while living charged their children touching the burial or even the translation of their bodies.* But they would not have done this unless the tomb and things of this kind conferred something on the dead. Therefore, the like profit the dead somewhat.

Obj. 3: Further, no one does a work of mercy on some one's behalf unless it profit him. Now burying the dead is reckoned among the works of mercy; hence Augustine says (*On the Care of the Dead* 3): *Tobias, as attested by the angel, is declared to have found favor with God by burying the dead.* Therefore, such burial observances profit the dead.

Obj. 4: Further, it is unbecoming to assert that the devotion of the faithful is fruitless. Now some, out of devotion, arrange for their burial in some religious locality. Therefore, the burial service profits the dead.

Obj. 5: Further, God is more inclined to pity than to condemn. Now burial in a sacred place is hurtful to some if they be unworthy; wherefore Gregory says (*Dialogues* 4): *if those who are burdened with grievous sins are buried in the church, this will lead to their more severe condemnation rather than to their release.* Much more, therefore, should we say that the burial service profits the good.

On the contrary, Augustine says (*On the Care of the Dead* 3): *whatever service is done the body is no aid to salvation, but an office of humanity.*

Further, Augustine says (*On the Care of the Dead* 3; *The City of God* 1): *the funereal equipment, the disposition of the grace, the solemnity of the obsequies are a comfort to the living rather than a help to the dead.*

Further, Our Lord said: *be not afraid of them who kill the body, and after that have no more that they can do* (Luke 12:4). Now after death the bodies of the saints can

possunt a sepultura prohiberi: sicut in Ecclesiastica historia legitur esse factum de quibusdam martyribus Lugduni Galliae. Ergo non nocet defunctis si eorum corpora inhumata remaneant. Ergo nec cultus sepulturae prodest.

Respondeo dicendum quod sepultura adinventa est et propter vivos et propter mortuos. Propter vivos quidem, ne eorum oculi ex turpitudine cadaverum offendantur, et corpora fetoribus inficiantur: et hoc quantum ad corpus. Sed spiritualiter etiam prodest vivis, inquantum per hoc adstruitur resurrectionis fides. Sed mortuis prosunt ad hoc quod inspicientes sepulcra memoriam retinent defunctorum, et pro defunctis orant. Unde et *monumentum* a memoria nomen accepit: dicitur enim monumentum quasi *monens mentem*, ut dicit Augustinus, in I *de Civ. Dei*, et in libro *de Cura pro mortuis agenda*. Paganorum tamen error fuit quod ad hoc sepultura mortuo prosit ut eius anima quietem accipiat: non enim credebant animas prius quietem posse accipere quam corpus sepulturae daretur. Quod omnino ridiculum est et absurdum.

Sed quod ulterius sepultura in loco sacrato mortuo prodest, non quidem est ex ipso opere operato, sed magis ex opere operante: dum scilicet vel ipse defunctus vel alius, corpus tumulari in loco sacro disponeris, patrocinio alicuius sancti eum committit, cuius precibus per hoc credendus est adiuvari; et etiam patrocinio eorum qui loco sacro deserviunt, qui pro tumulatis apud se frequentius et specialius orant.

Sed illa quae ad ornatum sepulturae adhibentur, prosunt quidem vivis, inquantum sunt *vivorum solatia*: sed possunt etiam defunctis prodesse, non quidem per se, sed per accidens; inquantum scilicet per huiusmodi homines excitantur ad compatiendum, et per consequens ad orandum; vel inquantum ex sumptibus sepulturae vel pauperes fructum capiunt, vel ecclesia decoratur; sic enim sepultura inter ceteras eleemosynas computatur.

Ad primum ergo dicendum quod oleum et cera ad sepulcra defunctorum prolata per accidens defuncto prosunt: vel inquantum ecclesiae offeruntur, sive pauperibus dantur; vel inquantum huiusmodi in Dei reverentiam fiunt. Unde et verbis praemissis subiungitur: *oleum enim et cera holocaustum.*

Ad secundum dicendum quod ideo sancti patres de suis corporibus tumulandis curaverunt, ut ostenderent *corpora mortuorum ad Dei providentiam pertinere: non quod mortuis corporibus aliquis sensus insit, sed propter fidem resurrectionis adstruendam*; ut patet per Augustinum, in I *de Civ. Dei*. Unde etiam voluerunt in terra promissionis sepeliri, ubi credebant Christum nasciturum et moriturum, cuius resurrectio nostrae resurrectionis est causa.

be hindered from being buried, as we read of having been done to certain martyrs at Lyons in Gaul (Eusebius, *Ecclesiastical Histories* 5.1). Therefore, the dead take no harm if their bodies remain unburied: and consequently the burial service does not profit them.

I answer that, We have recourse to burial for the sake of both the living and the dead. For the sake of the living, lest their eyes be revolted by the disfigurement of the corpse, and their bodies be infected by the stench, and this as regards the body. But it profits the living also spiritually inasmuch as our belief in the resurrection is confirmed thereby. It profits the dead insofar as one bears the dead in mind and prays for them through looking on their burial place, wherefore a *monument* takes its name from remembrance, for a monument is something that *recalls the mind*, as Augustine observes (*The City of God* 1; *On the Care of the Dead* 4). It was, however, a pagan error that burial was profitable to the dead by procuring rest for his soul: for they believed that the soul could not be at rest until the body was buried, which is altogether ridiculous and absurd.

That, moreover, burial in a sacred place profits the dead does not result from the action done, but rather from the action itself of the doer: when, to wit, the dead person himself, or another, arranges for his body to be buried in a sacred place, and commends him to the patronage of some saint, by whose prayers we must believe that he is assisted, as well as to the suffrages of those who serve the holy place, and pray more frequently and more specially for those who are buried in their midst.

But such things as are done for the display of the obsequies are profitable as being *a consolation of the living*; and yet they can also profit the dead, not directly but indirectly, insofar as men are aroused to pity thereby and consequently to pray, or insofar as the outlay on the burial brings either assistance to the poor or adornment to the church: for it is in this sense that the burial of the dead is reckoned among the works of mercy.

Reply Obj. 1: By bringing oil and candles to the tombs of the dead we profit them indirectly, either as offering them to the Church and as giving them to the poor, or as doing this in reverence of God. Hence, after the words quoted we read: *for oil and candles are a holocaust.*

Reply Obj. 2: The fathers of old arranged for the burial of their bodies, so as to show that *the bodies of the dead are the object of divine providence, not that there is any feeling in a dead body, but in order to confirm the belief in the resurrection*, as Augustine says (*The City of God* 1.13). Hence also they wished to be buried in the land of promise, where they believed Christ's birth and death would take place, whose resurrection is the cause of our rising again.

Ad tertium dicendum quod, quia caro est pars naturae hominis, naturaliter homo ad carnem suam afficitur: secundum illud Ephes. 5, [29]: *nemo carnem suam unquam odio habuit.* Unde secundum istum naturalem affectum inest viventi quaedam sollicitudo quid etiam post mortem de eius corpore sit futurum; doleretque si aliquid indignum suo corpori evenire praesentiret. Et ideo illi qui hominem diligunt, ex hoc quod affectui eius quem diligunt conformantur, circa eius carnem curam humanitatis impendunt. Ut enim dicit Augustinus, in I *de Civ. Dei, si paterna vestis et anulus, ac si quid huiusmodi, tanto carius sunt posteris quanto erga parentes maior affectus, nullo modo ipsa spernenda sunt corpora, quae utique multo familiarius atque coniunctius quam quaelibet indumenta gestamus.* Unde et inquantum affectui hominis satisfacit sepeliens eius corpus, cum ipse in hoc sibi satisfacere non potest, eleemosynam ei facere dicitur.

Ad quartum dicendum quod fidelium devotio, ut Augustinus dicit, in libro *de Cura pro mortuis agenda,* suis caris in locis sacris providens sepulturam, in hoc non frustratur, quod defunctum suum suffragio sanctorum committit, ut dictum est.

Ad quintum dicendum quod sepultura in loco sacro impio defuncto non nocet nisi quatenus hanc sepulturam, sibi indignam, propter humanam gloriam procuravit.

Reply Obj. 3: Since flesh is a part of man's nature, man has a natural affection for his flesh, according to Ephesians 5:29: *no man ever hated his own flesh.* Hence in accordance with this natural affection a man has during life a certain solicitude for what will become of his body after death: and he would grieve if he had a presentiment that something untoward would happen to his body. Consequently, those who love a man, through being conformed to the one they love in his affection for himself, treat his body with loving care. For, as Augustine says (*The City of God* 1.13): *if a father's garment and ring and other things of the sort are the more dear to those whom they leave behind the greater their affection is towards their parents, in no way are the bodies themselves to be spurned, which truly we wear in more familiar and close conjunction than anything else we put on.* Therefore, inasmuch as it satisfies a someone's affections when he buries a man's body, since he himself cannot satisfy them in this matter, it is said to be an act of almsgiving to him.

Reply Obj. 4: As Augustine says (*On the Care of the Dead* 4), the devotion of the faithful is not fruitless when they arrange for their friends to be buried in holy places, since by so doing they commend their dead to the suffrages of the saints, as stated above.

Reply Obj. 5: The wicked man dead takes no harm by being buried in a holy place, except insofar as he rendered such a burial place unfitting for him by reason of human glory.

Article 12

Whether Suffrages Offered for One Deceased Person Profit the Person for Whom They Are Offered More than Others?

Ad duodecimum sic proceditur. Videtur quod suffragia quae fiunt pro uno defuncto, non magis proficiunt ei pro quo fiunt quam aliis. Lumen enim spirituale magis est communicabile quam corporale lumen. Sed lumen corporale, sicut candelae, quamvis accendatur pro uno, tamen aequaliter omnibus prodest qui simul commorantur, quamvis pro eis candela non accendatur. Ergo, cum suffragia sint quaedam spiritualia lumina, quamvis pro uno specialiter fiant, non magis valent ei quam aliis existentibus in purgatorio.

Praeterea, sicut in littera dicitur, secundum hoc suffragia mortuis prosunt, quia, *dum viverent hic, sibi ut postea possent prodesse meruerunt.* Sed aliqui magis meruerunt ut suffragia sibi prodessent quam illi pro quibus fiunt. Ergo eis magis prosunt: alias eorum meritum frustraretur.

Objection 1: It would seem that suffrages offered for one deceased person are not more profitable to the one for whom they are offered than to others. For spiritual light is more communicable than a material light. Now a material light, like that of a candle, though kindled for one person only, avails equally all those who are gathered together, though the candle be not lit for them. Therefore, since suffrages are a kind of spiritual light, though they be offered for one person in particular they do not avail him any more than the others who are in purgatory.

Obj. 2: Further, as stated in the text (*Sentences* IV, D. 45), suffrages avail the dead *insofar as during this life they merited that they might avail them afterwards* (St. Augustine, *Handbook on Faith, Hope, and Charity* 110). Now some merited that suffrages might avail them more than those for whom they are offered. Therefore, they profit more by those suffrages, else their merits would be rendered unavailing.

Praeterea, pro pauperibus non fiunt tot suffragia sicut pro divitibus. Si ergo suffragia facta pro aliquibus eis magis quam aliis valerent, pauperes essent deterioris conditionis. Quod est contra sententiam Domini, Luc. 6, [20]: *beati pauperes, quoniam vestrum est regnum Dei.*

Sed contra: Iustitia humana exemplatur a iustitia divina. Sed iustitia humana, si aliquis debitum pro aliquo solvit, eum solum absolvit. Ergo, cum ille qui suffragia facit quodammodo solvat debitum eius pro quo facit, ei soli proderit.

Praeterea, sicut homo faciens suffragia quodammodo satisfacit pro mortuo, ita etiam interdum aliquis pro vivo satisfacere potest. Sed quando aliquis satisfacit pro vivo, satisfactio illa non computatur nisi illi pro quo facta est. Ergo et suffragia faciens ei soli prodest pro quo facit.

Respondeo dicendum quod circa hoc fuit duplex opinio. Quidam enim, ut Praepositinus, dixerunt quod suffragia pro uno aliquo facta non magis prosunt ei pro quo fiunt, sed eis qui sunt magis digni. Et ponebant exemplum de candela quae accenditur pro aliquo divite, quae non minus prodest eis qui cum ipso sunt quam ipsi diviti, et forte magis, si habent oculos clariores: et etiam de lectione, quae non magis prodest ei pro quo legitur quam aliis qui simul cum eo audiunt, sed forte aliis magis, qui sunt sensu capaciores. Et si eis obiiceretur quod secundum hoc ordinatio Ecclesiae esset vana, quae pro aliquibus specialiter orationes instituit: dicebant quod hoc Ecclesia fecit ad excitandam devotionem fidelium, qui promptiores sunt ad facienda specialia suffragia quam communia, et ferventius etiam pro suis propinquis orant quam pro extraneis.

Alii e contra dixerunt quod suffragia magis valent eis pro quibus fiunt.

Utraque autem opinio secundum aliquid veritatem habet. Valor enim suffragiorum pensari potest ex duobus. Valent enim uno modo ex virtute caritatis, quae facit omnia bona communia. Et secundum hoc magis valent ei qui magis caritate est plenus, quamvis pro eo specialiter non fiant. Et sic valor suffragiorum attenditur magis secundum quandam interiorem consolationem, secundum quod unus in caritate existens de bonis alterius delectatur post mortem, quam ad diminutionem poenae: post mortem enim non est locus acquirendi gratiam vel augendi, ad quod nobis in vita valent opera aliorum ex virtute caritatis.

Alio modo valent suffragia ex hoc quod per intentionem unius alteri applicantur. Et sic satisfactio unius alteri computatur. Et hoc modo non est dubium quod magis valent ei pro quo fiunt. Immo sic ei soli valent. Satisfactio enim proprie ad remissionem poenae ordinatur. Unde, quantum ad dimissionem poenae, praecipue valet suf-

Obj. 3: Further, the poor have not so many suffrages given them as the rich. Therefore, if the suffrages offered for certain people profit them alone, or profit them more than others, the poor would be worse off: yet this is contrary to our Lord's saying: *blessed are the poor, for yours is the kingdom of God* (Luke 6:20).

On the contrary, Human justice is copied from divine justice. But if a person pay another's debt, human justice releases the latter alone. Therefore, since he who offers suffrages for another pays the debt, in a sense, of the person for whom he offers them, they profit this person alone.

Further, Just as a man by offering suffrages satisfies somewhat for a deceased person, so, too, sometimes a person can satisfy for a living person. Now where one satisfies for a living person the satisfaction counts only for the person for whom it is offered. Therefore, one also who offers suffrages profits him alone for whom he offers them.

I answer that, There have been two opinions on this question. Some, like Praepositivus, have said that suffrages offered for one particular person do avail chiefly not the person for whom they are offered, but those who are most worthy. And they instanced a candle which is lit for a rich man and profits those who are with him no less than the rich man himself, and perhaps even more, if they have keener sight. They also gave the instance of a lesson which profits the person to whom it is given no more than others who listen with him, but perhaps profits these others more, if they be more intelligent. And if it were pointed out to them that in this case the Church's ordinance in appointing certain special prayers for certain persons is futile, they said that the Church did this to excite the devotion of the faithful, who are more inclined to offer special than common suffrages, and pray more fervently for their kinsfolk than for strangers.

Others, on the contrary, said that suffrages avail more those for whom they are offered.

Now both opinions have a certain amount of truth: for the value of suffrages may be gauged from two sources. For their value is derived in the first place from the virtue of charity, which makes all goods common, and in this respect they avail more the person who is more full of charity, although they are not offered specially for him. In this way the value of suffrages regards more a certain inward consolation by reason of which one who is in charity rejoices in the goods of another after death in respect of the diminution of punishment; for after death there is no possibility of obtaining or increasing grace, whereas during life the works of others avail for this purpose by the virtue of charity.

In the second place, suffrages derive their value from being applied to another person by one's intention. In this way the satisfaction of one person counts for another, and there can be no doubt that thus they avail more the person for whom they are offered: in fact, they avail him alone in this way, because satisfaction, properly speaking, is directed to

fragium ei pro quo fit. Et secundum hoc secunda opinio plus habet de veritate quam prima.

Ad primum ergo dicendum quod suffragia prosunt per modum luminis inquantum a mortuis acceptantur, et ex hoc quandam consolationem accipiunt; et tanto maiorem quanto maiori caritate sunt praediti. Sed inquantum suffragia sunt quaedam satisfactio per intentionem facientis translata in alterum, non sunt similia lumini, sed magis solutioni alicuius debiti. Non autem est necesse ut, si debitum pro uno solvitur, quod ex hoc debitum aliorum solvatur.

Ad secundum dicendum quod illud meritum est conditionale quo sibi meruerunt. Hoc enim modo sibi meruerunt, ut sibi prodessent si pro eis fierent. Quod nihil aliud fuit quam facere se habiles ad recipiendum. Unde patet quod non directe meruerunt illud iuvamen suffragiorum, sed per merita praecedentia se habilitaverunt ut fructum suffragiorum susciperent. Et ideo non sequitur quod meritum eorum frustretur.

Ad tertium dicendum quod nihil prohibet divites quantum ad aliquid esse melioris conditionis quam pauperes: sicut quantum ad expiationem poenae. Sed hoc quasi nihil est comparatum possessioni regni caelorum, in qua pauperes melioris conditionis esse ostenduntur per auctoritatem inductam.

the remission of punishment. Consequently, as regards the remission of punishment, suffrages avail chiefly the person for whom they are offered, and accordingly there is more truth in the second opinion than in the first.

Reply Obj. 1: Suffrages avail after the manner of a light insofar as they reach the dead who thereby receive a certain amount of consolation: and this is all the greater according as they are endowed with a greater charity. But insofar as suffrages are a satisfaction applied to another by the intention of the offerer, they do not resemble a light, but rather the payment of a debt: and it does not follow, if one person's debt be paid, that the debt of others is paid likewise.

Reply Obj. 2: Such a merit is conditional, for in this way they merited that suffrages would profit them if offered for them, and this was merely to render themselves fit recipients of those suffrages. It is therefore clear that they did not directly merit the assistance of those suffrages, but made themselves fit by their preceding merits to receive the fruit of suffrages. Hence it does not follow that their merit is rendered unavailing.

Reply Obj. 3: Nothing hinders the rich from being in some respects better off than the poor, for instance, as regards the expiation of their punishment. But this is as nothing in comparison with the kingdom of heaven, where the poor are shown to be better off by the authority quoted.

Article 13

Whether Suffrages Offered for Several Are of as Much Value to Each One as If They Had Been Offered for Each in Particular?

Ad decimumtertium sic proceditur. Videtur quod suffragia facta pro multis tantundem valeant singulis ac si pro unoquoque specialiter fierent. Videmus enim quod ex lectione quae uni legitur, nihil ei deperit si simul et alii legatur. Ergo et, eadem ratione, nihil deperit ei pro quo fit suffragium, si ei aliquis connumeretur. Et ita, si pro pluribus fiat, tantum valet singulis ac si pro unoquoque singulariter fieret.

Praeterea, secundum communem usum Ecclesiae videmus quod, cum Missa pro aliquo defuncto dicitur, simul etiam illic orationes adiunguntur pro aliis defunctis. Hoc autem non fieret si ex hoc defunctus pro quo Missa dicitur, aliquod detrimentum reportaret. Ergo idem quod prius.

Praeterea, suffragia, praecipue orationum, innituntur divinae virtuti. Sed apud Deum, sicut non differt iuvare per multos vel per paucos, ita non differt iuvare multos vel paucos. Ergo, quantum iuvaretur unus ex una

Objection 1: It would seem that suffrages offered for several are of as much value to each one as if they had been offered for each in particular. For it is clear that if one person receives a lesson, he loses nothing if others receive the lesson with him. Therefore, in like manner, a person for whom a suffrage is offered loses nothing if some one else is reckoned together with him: and consequently if it be offered for several, it is of as much value to each one as if it were offered for each in particular.

Obj. 2: Further, it is to be observed that, according to the common practice of the Church, when Mass is said for one deceased person, other prayers are added for other deceased persons. Now this would not be done, if the dead person for whom the Mass is said were to lose something thereby. Therefore, the same conclusion follows as above.

Obj. 3: Further, suffrages, especially of prayers, rely on the divine power. But with God, just as it makes no difference whether he helps by means of many or by means of a few, so it differs not whether he assists many or a few. There-

oratione si pro eo tantum fieret, tantum iuvabuntur singuli multorum si eadem oratio pro multis fiat.

SED CONTRA: Melius est plures iuvare quam unum. Si ergo suffragium pro multis factum valeret singulis tantum ac si pro uno tantum fieret, videtur quod Ecclesia non debuit instituisse ut pro aliquo singulariter fieret Missa vel oratio, sed quod semper diceretur pro omnibus fidelibus defunctis. Quod patet esse falsum.

PRAETEREA, suffragium habet finitam efficaciam. Ergo, distributum in multos, minus prodest singulis quam prodesset si fieret pro uno tantum.

RESPONDEO dicendum quod, si valor suffragiorum consideretur secundum quod valent ex virtute caritatis unientis membra Ecclesiae, suffragia pro multis facta tantum singulis prosunt ac si pro uno tantum fierent. Quia caritas non minuitur si dividatur effectus in multos: immo magis augetur. Et similiter etiam gaudium, quanto pluribus est commune, fit maius, ut dicit Augustinus, VIII *Confessiones*. Et sic de uno bono facto non minus laetantur multi in purgatorio quam unus.

Si autem consideretur valor suffragiorum inquantum sunt satisfactiones quaedam per intentionem facientis translatae in mortuos, tunc magis valet suffragium alicui quod pro eo singulariter fit, quam quod fit pro eo communiter et multis aliis: sic enim effectus suffragii dividitur ex divina iustitia inter eos pro quibus suffragia fiunt.

Unde patet quod haec quaestio dependet ex prima. Et ex hoc etiam patet quare institutum sit ut suffragia specialia in Ecclesia fiant.

AD PRIMUM ergo dicendum quod suffragia, ut sunt satisfactiones quaedam, non prosunt per modum actionis, sicut doctrina prodest, quae, sicut et omnis alia actio, effectum habet secundum dispositionem recipientis: sed valet per modum solutionis debiti, ut dictum est. Et ideo non est simile.

AD SECUNDUM dicendum quod, quia suffragia pro uno facta aliquo modo etiam aliis prosunt, ut ex dictis patet, ideo, cum pro uno missa dicitur, non est inconveniens ut pro aliis etiam orationes fiant. Non enim ad hoc dicuntur aliae orationes ut satisfactio unius suffragii determinetur ad alios principaliter: sed ut illis oratio pro eis specialiter fusa prosit.

AD TERTIUM dicendum quod oratio consideratur et ex parte orantis, et ex parte eius qui oratur: et ex utroque eius effectus dependet. Et ideo, quamvis divinae virtuti non sit magis difficile absolvere multos quam unum, tamen huiusmodi orantis oratio non ita est satisfactoria pro multis sicut pro uno.

fore, if the one same prayer be said for many, each one of them will receive as much assistance as one person would if that same prayer were said for him alone.

ON THE CONTRARY, It is better to assist many than one. If, therefore, a suffrage offered for several is of as much value to each one as if it were offered for one alone, it would seem that the Church ought not to have appointed a Mass and prayer to be said for one person in particular, but that Mass ought always to be said for all the faithful departed: and this is evidently false.

FURTHER, A suffrage has a finite efficiency. Therefore, if it be divided among many, it avails less for each one than if it were offered for one only.

I ANSWER THAT, If the value of suffrages be considered according as it is derived from the virtue of charity uniting the members of the Church together, suffrages offered for several persons avail each one as much as if they were offered for one alone, because charity is not diminished if its effect be divided among many; in fact, it is increased; and in like manner joy increases through being shared by many, as Augustine says (*Confessions* 8).

Consequently, many in purgatory rejoice in one good deed no less than one does. On the other hand, if we consider the value of suffrages inasmuch as they are a kind of satisfaction applied to the dead by the intention of the person offering them, then the suffrage for some person in particular avails him more than that which is offered for him in common with many others; for in this case the effect of the suffrages is divided in virtue of divine justice among those for whom the suffrages are offered.

Hence it is evident that this question depends on the first; and, moreover, it is made clear why special suffrages are appointed to be offered in the Church.

REPLY OBJ. 1: Suffrages considered as works of satisfaction do not profit after the manner of an action as teaching does; for teaching, like any other action, produces its effect according to the disposition of the recipient. But they profit after the manner of the payment of a debt, as stated above (A. 12); and so the comparison fails.

REPLY OBJ. 2: Since suffrages offered for one person avail others in a certain way, as stated (A. 1), it follows that when Mass is said for one person, it is not unfitting for prayers to be said for others also. For these prayers are said not that the satisfaction offered by one suffrage be applied to those others chiefly, but that the prayer offered for them in particular may profit them also.

REPLY OBJ. 3: Prayer may be considered both on the part of the one who prays, and on the part of the person prayed: and its effect depends on both. Consequently, though it is no more difficult to the divine power to absolve many than to absolve one, nevertheless the prayer of one who prays thus is not as satisfactory for many as for one.

Article 14

Whether General Suffrages Avail Those for Whom Special Suffrages Are Not Offered as Much as Special Suffrages Avail Those for Whom They Are Offered in Addition to General Suffrages?

AD DECIMUMQUARTUM SIC PROCEDITUR. Videtur quod tantum valeant communia suffragia illis pro quibus specialia non fiunt, quantum illis pro quibus fiunt valent specialia et communia simul. Unicuique enim secundum propria merita reddetur in futuro. Sed ille pro quo non fiunt suffragia, meruit ut tantum iuvaretur post mortem quantum et ille pro quo fiunt specialia. Ergo tantum iuvabitur per communia quantum et ille per specialia et communia.

PRAETEREA, inter Ecclesiae suffragia praecipuum est Eucharistia. Sed Eucharistia, cum contineat totum Christum, habet quodammodo efficaciam infinitam. Ergo una oblatio Eucharistiae, quae communiter pro omnibus fit, valet ad plenam liberationem eorum qui sunt in purgatorio. Et ita tantum iuvant communia suffragia sola quantum iuvant specialia et communia simul.

SED CONTRA est quod duo bona uno sunt magis eligenda. Ergo suffragia speciali et communia magis prosunt ei pro quo fiunt quam communia tantum.

RESPONDEO dicendum quod huius etiam solutio dependet ex solutione primae quaestionis. Si enim suffragia pro uno specialiter facta indifferenter omnibus valeant, tunc omnia suffragia sunt communia. Et ideo tantum iuvabitur ille pro quo non fiunt specialia, quantum ille pro quo fiunt, si sit aequaliter dignus. Si autem suffragia pro aliquo facta non indifferenter omnibus prosint, sed eis maxime pro quibus fiunt, tunc non est dubium quod suffragia communia et specialia simul plus valent alicui quam communia tantum.

Et ideo Magister duas opiniones in littera tangit. Unam, dum dicit quod aequaliter prosunt diviti communia et specialia, et pauperi communia tantum: quamvis enim ex pluribus iuvetur unus quam alter, non tamen plus iuvatur. Aliam autem tangit cum dicit quod ille pro quo fiunt specialia, consequitur *velociorem absolutionem, sed non pleniorem*: quia uterque finaliter ab omni poena liberabitur.

AD PRIMUM ergo dicendum quod iuvamen suffragiorum non cadit directe sub merito et simpliciter, sed quasi sub conditione. Et ideo ratio non sequitur.

AD SECUNDUM dicendum quod, quamvis virtus Christi, qui continetur sub Sacramento Eucharistiae, sit infinita, tamen determinatus est effectus ad quem illud sacramentum ordinatur. Unde non oportet quod per

OBJECTION 1: It would seem that general suffrages avail those for whom special suffrages are not offered, as much as special suffrages avail those for whom they are offered in addition to general suffrages. For in the life to come each one will be rewarded according to his merits. Now a person for whom no suffrages are offered merited to be assisted after death as much as one for whom special suffrages are offered. Therefore, the former will be assisted by general suffrages as much as the latter by special and general suffrages.

OBJ. 3: Further, the Eucharist is the chief of the suffrages of the Church. Now the Eucharist, since it contains Christ whole, has infinite efficacy, so to speak. Therefore, one offering of the Eucharist for all in general is of sufficient value to release all who are in purgatory: and consequently general suffrages alone afford as much assistance as special and general suffrages together.

ON THE CONTRARY, Two goods are more eligible than one. Therefore, special suffrages, together with general suffrages, are more profitable to the person for whom they are offered than general suffrages alone.

I ANSWER THAT, The reply to this question depends on that which is given to the twelfth inquiry (A. 12): for if the suffrages offered for one person in particular avail indifferently for all, then all suffrages are common; and consequently one for whom the special suffrages are not offered will be assisted as much as the one for whom they are offered, if he be equally worthy. On the other hand, if the suffrages offered for a person do not profit all indifferently, but those chiefly for whom they are offered, then there is no doubt that general and special suffrages together avail a person more than general suffrages alone.

Hence the Master, in the text (*Sentences* IV, D. 45), mentions two opinions: one, when he says that a rich man derives from general, together with special suffrages, an equal profit to that which a poor man derives from special suffrages alone; for although the one receives assistance from more sources than the other, he does not receive a greater assistance. The other opinion he mentions when he says that a person for whom special suffrages are offered obtains *a more speedy but not a more complete release*, because each will be finally released from all punishment.

REPLY OBJ. 1: As stated above (A. 12) the assistance derived from suffrages is not directly and simply an object of merit, but conditionally as it were: hence the argument does not follow.

REPLY OBJ. 2: Although the power of Christ, who is contained in the Sacrament of the Eucharist, is infinite, yet there is a definite effect to which that sacrament is directed. Hence it does not follow that the whole punishment of

unum Altaris Sacrificium tota poena eorum qui sunt in purgatorio expietur: sicut etiam nec per unum sacrificium quod aliquis offert, liberatur a tota satisfactione debita pro peccatis. Unde et quandoque plures missae in satisfactione unius peccati iniunguntur.

Credibile tamen est quod per divinam misericordiam, Si aliquid de specialibus suffragiis supersit his pro quibus fiunt, ut scilicet eis non indigeant, aliis dispensetur pro quibus non fiunt, si eis indigeant: ut patet per Damascenum, in Sermone de Dormientibus, sic dicentem: *Deus, tanquam iustus, commetietur impotenti possibilitatem; tanquam sapiens, defectuum commutationem negotiabitur.* Quae quidem negotiatio attenditur secundum quod id quod deest uni, alteri supplet.

those who are in purgatory is expiated by one Sacrifice of the Altar: even so, by the one sacrifice which a man offers, he is not released from the whole satisfaction due for his sins. Hence sometimes several Masses are enjoined in satisfaction for one sin.

Nevertheless, if anything from special suffrages be left over for those for whom they are offered (for instance, if they need them not) we may well believe that by God's mercy this is granted to others for whom those suffrages are not offered, if they need them: as affirmed by Damascene who says: *God is as wise as he is just; justly he measures possibility to the impotent, and wisely he manages the commuting of defects.* And this exchange is effected when what is lacking to one is supplied by another.

QUESTION 72

PRAYERS WITH REGARD TO THE SAINTS IN HEAVEN

Deinde considerandum est de oratione sanctorum qui sunt in patria.

Et circa hoc quaeruntur tria.

Primo: utrum sancti orationes nostras cognoscant.

Secundo: utrum eos interpellare debeamus ad orandum pro nobis.

Tertio: utrum orationes eorum pro nobis fusae semper exaudiantur.

Nam utrum sancti orent pro nobis, dictum est qu. 83 Secundae Partis.

We must now consider prayer with regard to the saints in heaven.

Under this head there are three points of inquiry:

(1) Whether the saints have knowledge of our prayers?

(2) Whether we should beseech them to pray for us?

(3) Whether the prayers they pour forth for us are always granted?

Now, whether the saints pray for us was answered above (II-II, Q. 83, A. 11).

Article 1

Whether the Saints Have Knowledge of Our Prayers?

AD PRIMUM SIC PROCEDITUR. Videtur quod sancti orationes nostras non cognoscant. Isaiae 63, [16], *Pater noster es, et Abraham nescivit nos, et Israel ignoravit nos,* Glossa Augustini dicit quod *mortui sancti nesciunt quid agant vivi, etiam eorum filii.* Et sumitur ab Augustino de Cura pro mortuis agenda, ubi hanc auctoritatem inducit. Et sunt haec verba Augustini ibidem: *si tanti Patriarchae quid erga populum ab eis procreatum ageretur ignoraverunt, quomodo mortui vivorum rebus atque actibus cognoscendis adiuvandisque miscentur?* Ergo sancti orationes nostras cognoscere non possunt.

PRAETEREA, IV Reg. 22, [20] dicitur ad Iosiam regem: *idcirco* (scilicet *quia flevisti coram me* [19]) *colligam te ad patres tuos, ut non videant oculi tui mala omnia quae sum inducturus in locum istum.* Sed in hoc nullo modo per mortem Iosiae subventum fuisset si post mortem quid genti suae eveniret cognosceret. Ergo sancti mortui actus nostros non cognoscunt. Et ita non intelligunt nostras orationes.

PRAETEREA, quanto aliquis est in caritate perfectior, tanto magis proximo in periculis subvenit. Sed sancti in carne viventes proximis, et maxime sibi coniunctis, in periculis et consulunt et auxiliantur manifeste. Cum ergo post mortem sint multo maioris caritatis, si facta nostra cognoscerent, multo amplius suis caris sibi coniunctis consulerent et auxiliarentur in necessitatibus. Quod facere non videntur. Ergo non videtur quod actus nostros et orationes nostras cognoscant.

OBJECTION 1: It would seem that the saints have no knowledge of our prayers. For a Gloss on Isaiah 62:13: *you are our father and Abraham has not known us, and Israel has been ignorant of us,* says that *the dead saints know not what the living, even their own children, are doing.* This is taken from Augustine (*On the Care of the Dead* 13), where he quotes the aforesaid authority, and the following are his words: *if such great men as the patriarchs knew not what was happening to the people begotten of them, how can the dead occupy themselves in watching and helping the affairs and actions of the living?* Therefore, the saints cannot be cognizant of our prayers.

OBJ. 2: Further, the following words are addressed to King Josiah: *therefore* (i.e., *because thou hast wept before me*), *I will gather you to your fathers that your eyes may not see* (2 Kgs 22:20). But Josiah would have gained no such advantage from his death if he were to know after death what was happening to his people. Therefore, the saints after death know not our actions, and thus they are not cognizant of our prayers.

OBJ. 3: Further, the more perfect a man is in charity, the more he succors his neighbor when the latter is in danger. Now the saints, in this life, watch over their neighbor, especially their kinsfolk, when these are in danger and manifestly assist them. Since, then, after death their charity would be much greater if they were cognizant of our deeds, much more would they watch over their friends and kindred and assist them in their needs: and yet, seemingly, they do not. Therefore, it would seem that our deeds and prayers are not known to them.

59

PRAETEREA, sicut sancti post mortem vident Verbum, ita et angeli, de quibus dicitur, Matth. 18, [10]: *angeli eorum semper vident faciem Patris mei.* Sed angeli Verbum videntes non propter hoc omnia cognoscunt: cum a nescientia minores a superioribus purgentur, ut patet per Dionysium, in 7 cap. *Cael. Hier.* Ergo nec sancti, quamvis Verbum videant, in eo nostras orationes cognoscunt, et alia quae circa nos aguntur.

PRAETEREA, solus Deus est *inspector cordium.* Sed oratio praecipue in corde consistit. Ergo solius Dei est orationes cognoscere. Non ergo sancti nostras orationes cognoscunt.

SED CONTRA: Super illud Iob 14, [21], *sive nobiles fuerint filii eius sive ignobiles, non intelliget,* dicit Gregorius, XII lib. *Moral.: Hoc de animabus sanctis sentiendum non est. Quia quae intus omnipotentis Dei claritatem vident, nullo modo credendum est quod sit foris aliquid quod ignorent.* Ergo ipsi orationes nostras cognoscunt.

PRAETEREA, Gregorius, in II *Dialog.: animae videnti Creatorem angusta est omnis creatura. Quantumlibet enim de luce Creatoris aspexerit, breve fit ei omne quod creatum est.* Sed hoc. maxime impedire videretur quod animae sanctorum orationes et alia quae circa nos aguntur cognoscant, quia a nobis distant. Cum ergo distantia illa non impediat, ut ex praedicta auctoritate patet, videtur quod animae sanctorum cognoscant orationes nostras et ea quae hic aguntur.

PRAETEREA, si ea quae circa nos aguntur non cognoscerent, nec pro nobis orarent: quia defectus nostros ignorarent. Sed hic est error Vigilantii: ut Hieronymus dicit, in Epistola contra eum. Ergo sancti ea quae circa nos aguntur cognoscunt.

RESPONDEO dicendum quod divina essentia est sufficiens medium cognoscendi omnia: quod patet ex hoc quod Deus videndo suam essentiam omnia intuetur. Non tamen sequitur quod quicumque essentiam Dei vident, omnia cognoscant, sed solum qui essentiam comprehendit: sicut nec in principio aliquo cognito consequens est omnia cognosci quae ex principio consequuntur, nisi tota virtus principii comprehendatur. Unde, cum animae sanctorum divinam essentiam non comprehendant, non est consequeris ut omnia cognoscant quae per essentiam divinam cognosci possunt. Unde etiam de quibusdam inferiores angeli a superioribus edocentur, quamvis omnes essentiam divinam videant.

Sed unusquisque beatus tantum de aliis rebus necessarium est ut in essentia divina videat, quantum perfectio beatitudinis requirit. Hoc autem ad perfectionem beatitudinis requiritur ut homo *habeat quidquid velit, nec aliquid inordinate velit.* Hoc autem recta voluntate

OBJ. 4: Further, even as the saints after death see the Word, so do the angels, of whom it is stated that *their angels in heaven always see the face of my Father* (Matt 18:10). Yet the angels through seeing the Word do not therefore know all things, since the lower angels are cleansed from their lack of knowledge by the higher angels, as Dionysius declares (*On the Heavenly Hierarchies* 7). Therefore, although the saints see the Word, they do not see in it our prayers and other things that happen in regard to us.

OBJ. 5: Further, God alone is the *searcher of hearts.* Now prayer is seated chiefly in the heart. Therefore, it belongs to God alone to know our prayers. Therefore, our prayers are unknown to the saints.

ON THE CONTRARY, Gregory, commenting on Job 14:21: *whether his children come to honor or dishonor, he shall not understand,* says, *this does not apply to the souls of the saints, for since they have an insight of Almighty God's glory we must in no way believe that anything outside that glory is unknown to them* (*Morals on Job* 12). Therefore, they are cognizant of our prayers.

FURTHER, Gregory says (*Dialogues* 2): *all creatures are little to the soul that sees God: because however little it sees of the Creator's light, every created thing appears foreshortened to it.* Now apparently the chief obstacle to the souls of the saints being cognizant of our prayers and other happenings in our regard is that they are far removed from us. Since, then, distance does not prevent these things, as appears from the authority quoted, it would seem that the souls of the saints are cognizant of our prayers and of what happens here below.

FURTHER, Unless they were aware of what happens in our regard they would not pray for us, since they would be ignorant of our needs. But this is the error of Vigilantius, as Jerome asserts in his letter against him. Therefore, the saints are cognizant of what happens in our regard.

I ANSWER THAT, The divine essence is a sufficient medium for knowing all things, and this is evident from the fact that God, by seeing his essence, sees all things. But it does not follow that whoever sees God's essence knows all things, but only those who comprehend the essence of God: even as the knowledge of a principle does not involve the knowledge of all that follows from that principle unless the whole virtue of the principle be comprehended. Wherefore, since the souls of the saints do not comprehend the divine essence, it does not follow that they know all that can be known by the divine essence—for which reason the lower angels are taught concerning certain matters by the higher angels, though they all see the essence of God.

But each of the blessed must see in the divine essence as many other things as the perfection of his happiness requires. For the perfection of a man's happiness requires him *to have whatever he will, and to will nothing amiss*: and each one wills with a right will, to know what concerns himself.

quilibet vult, ut ea quae ad ipsum pertinent cognoscat. Unde cum nulla rectitudo sanctis desit, volunt cognoscere ea quae ad eos pertinent. Et ideo oportet quod illa in Verbo cognoscant. Hoc autem ad eorum gloriam pertinet, quod auxilium indigentibus praestent ad salutem: sic enim Dei cooperatores efficiuntur, *quo nihil est divinius*, ut ait Dionysius, 3 cap. *Cael. Hier.* Unde patet quod sancti habent cognitionem eorum quae ad hoc requiruntur. Et sic manifestum est quod in Verbo cognoscunt vota et orationes et devotiones hominum qui ad eorum auxilium confugiunt.

AD PRIMUM ergo dicendum quod verbum Augustini intelligendum est de cognitione naturali animarum separatarum, quae quidem cognitio in sanctis viris non est obtenebrata, sicut est in peccatoribus. Non autem loquitur de cognitione quae est in Verbo, quam constat Abraham, eo tempore quo haec dicta sunt per Isaiam, non habuisse: cum ante Christi Passionem nullus ad visionem Dei pervenerit.

AD SECUNDUM dicendum quod sancti, licet post hanc vitam cognoscant ea quae hic geruntur, non tamen credendum est quod afficiantur doloribus, cognitis adversitatibus eorum quos in hoc saeculo dilexerunt. Ita enim repleti sunt gaudio beatitudinis quod dolor in eis locum non invenit. Unde, etsi cognoscant suorum infortunia post mortem, nihilominus dolori eorum consulitur si ante huiusmodi infortunia. de hoc saeculo subtrahantur. Sed forte animae non glorificatae dolorem aliquem sentirent si incommoda carorum suorum perciperent. Et quia anima Iosiae non statim glorificata fuit a corpore egressa, quantum ad hoc ex hac ratione Augustinus concludere nititur quod animae mortuorum cognitionem non habeant de factis viventium.

AD TERTIUM dicendum quod animae sanctorum habent voluntatem plenarie conformem divinae voluntati etiam in volito. Et ideo, quamvis affectum caritatis ad proximum retineant, non tamen eis aliter auxilium ferunt quam secundum divinam iustitiam vident esse dispositum. Et tamen credendum est quod multum proximos iuvant, pro eis apud Deum intercedendo.

AD QUARTUM dicendum quod, quamvis videntes Verbum non sit necessarium in Verbo omnia videre, vident tamen ea quae ad perfectionem pertinent beatitudinis eorum, ut dictum est.

AD QUINTUM dicendum quod cogitationes cordium solus Deus per seipsum novit: sed tamen alii cognoscere possunt quatenus eis revelatur, vel per visionem Verbi vel quocumque alio modo.

Hence, since no rectitude is lacking to the saints, they wish to know what concerns themselves, and consequently it follows that they know it in the Word. Now it pertains to their glory that they assist the needy for their salvation: for thus they become God's cooperators, *than which nothing is more divine*, as Dionysius declares (*On the Heavenly Hierarchies* 3). Wherefore it is evident that the saints are cognizant of such things as are required for this purpose; and so it is manifest that they know in the Word the vows, devotions, and prayers of those who have recourse to their assistance.

REPLY OBJ. 1: The saying of Augustine is to be understood as referring to the natural knowledge of separated souls, which knowledge is devoid of obscurity in holy men. But he is not speaking of their knowledge in the Word, for it is clear that when Isaiah said this, Abraham had no such knowledge, since no one had come to the vision of God before Christ's Passion.

REPLY OBJ. 2: Although the saints, after this life, know what happens here below, we must not believe that they grieve through knowing the woes of those whom they loved in this world: for they are so filled with heavenly joy, that sorrow finds no place in them. Wherefore if after death they know the woes of their friends, their grief is forestalled by their removal from this world before their woes occur. Perhaps, however, the non-glorified souls would grieve somewhat if they were aware of the distress of their dear ones: and since the soul of Josiah was not glorified as soon as it went out from his body, it is in this respect that Augustine uses this argument to show that the souls of the dead have no knowledge of the deeds of the living.

REPLY OBJ. 3: The souls of the saints have their will fully conformed to the divine will even as regards the things willed, and consequently, although they retain the love of charity towards their neighbor, they do not aid him otherwise than they see to be in conformity with the disposition of divine justice. Nevertheless, it is to be believed that they help their neighbor very much by interceding for him to God.

REPLY OBJ. 4: Although it does not follow that those who see the Word see all things in the Word, they see those things that pertain to the perfection of their happiness, as stated above.

REPLY OBJ. 5: God alone of himself knows the thoughts of the heart: yet others know them insofar as these are revealed to them, either by their vision of the Word or by any other means.

Article 2

Whether We Ought to Call Upon the Saints to Pray for Us?

AD SECUNDUM SIC PROCEDITUR. Videtur quod non debeamus sanctos interpellare ad orandum pro nobis. Nullus enim amicos alicuius interpellat ad orandum pro se nisi quatenus credit apud eos facilius gratiam obtinere. Sed Deus est in infinitum magis misericors quolibet, sancto: et sic voluntas eius facilius inclinatur ad nos exaudiendum quam voluntas alicuius sancti. Ergo videtur superfluum constituere mediatores inter nos et Deum, ut ipsi pro nobis, intercedant.

PRAETEREA, si eos ad orandum pro nobis interpellare debemus, hoc non est nisi quia scimus eorum orationem esse Deo acceptam. Sed quanto est aliquis sanctior inter sanctos, tanto eius oratio est magis Deo accepta. Ergo semper deberemus superiores pro nobis intercessores constituere ad Deum, et nunquam minores.

PRAETEREA, Christus, etiam secundum quod homo, dicitur *Sanctus Sanctorum*: et ei, secundum quod homo, orare competit. Sed nunquam Christum ad orandum pro nobis interpellamus. Ergo nec alios sanctos interpellare debemus.

PRAETEREA, quicumque rogatus ab aliquo ut pro eo intercedat, preces ipsius ei repraesentat apud quem pro eo intercedit. Sed superfluum est ei repraesentare aliquid cui omnia sunt praesentia. Ergo superfluum est quod sanctos intercessores constituamus pro nobis ad Deum.

PRAETEREA, illud est superfluum quod fit propter aliquid quod sine eo eodem modo fieret vel non fieret. Sed similiter sancti orarent pro nobis vel non orarent, sive nos oremus eos sive non oremus: quia, si sumus digni ut pro nobis orent, etiam, nobis eos non orantibus, pro nobis orarent; si autem sumus indigni, etiam si petamus, pro nobis non orant. Ergo interpellare eos ad orandum pro nobis videtur omnino superfluum.

SED CONTRA: Est quod dicitur Iob 5, [1]: *voca, si est qui tibi respondeat, et ad aliquem sanctorum convertere. Vocare autem nostrum*, ut Gregorius dicit ibidem, *est humili Deum prece deposcere.* Ergo, cum volumus Deum orare, debemus ad sanctos converti, ut pro nobis Deum orent.

PRAETEREA, sancti qui sunt in patria magis sunt accepti Deo quam in statu viae. Sed sanctos qui sunt in via constituere debemus intercessores pro nobis ad Deum: exemplo Apostoli, qui dicebat, Rom. 15, [30]: *obsecro vos, fratres, per Dominum nostrum Iesum Christum et per caritatem Spiritus Sancti, ut adiuvetis me in orationibus vestris pro me ad Deum.* Ergo nos multo fortius petere debemus a sanctis qui sunt in patria, ut nos iuvent orationibus suis ad Deum.

OBJECTION 1: It would seem that we ought not to call upon the saints to pray for us. For no man asks anyone's friends to pray for him, except insofar as he believes he will more easily find favor with them. But God is infinitely more merciful than any saint, and consequently his will is more easily inclined to give us a gracious hearing than the will of a saint. Therefore, it would seem unnecessary to make the saints mediators between us and God that they may intercede for us.

OBJ. 2: Further, if we ought to beseech them to pray for us, this is only because we know their prayer to be acceptable to God. Now among the saints the holier a man is, the more is his prayer acceptable to God. Therefore, we ought always to bespeak the greater saints to intercede for us with God, and never the lesser ones.

OBJ. 3: Further, Christ, even as man, is called the *Holy of Holies*, and, as man, he is competent to pray. Yet we never call upon Christ to pray for us. Therefore, neither should we ask the other saints to do so.

OBJ. 4: Further, whenever one person intercedes for another at the latter's request, he presents his petition to the one with whom he intercedes for him. Now it is unnecessary to present anything to one to whom all things are present. Therefore, it is unnecessary to make the saints our intercessors with God.

OBJ. 5: Further, it is unnecessary to do a thing if, without doing it, the purpose for which it is done would be achieved in the same way, or else not achieved at all. Now the saints would pray for us just the same, or would not pray for us at all, whether we pray to them or not: for if we be worthy of their prayers, they would pray for us even though we prayed not to them, while if we be unworthy, they pray not for us even though we ask them to. Therefore, it seems altogether unnecessary to call on them to pray for us.

ON THE CONTRARY, Job 5:1 says: *call, if there be any that will answer you, and turn to some of the saints* (Job 5:1). Now, as Gregory says (*Morals on Job* 5.30) on this passage, *we call upon God when we beseech him in humble prayer.* Therefore, when we wish to pray God, we should turn to the saints, that they may pray God for us.

FURTHER, The saints who are in heaven are more acceptable to God than those who are on the way. Now we should make the saints who are on the way our intercessors with God, after the example of the Apostle, who said: *I beseech you, brethren, through our Lord Jesus Christ, and by the charity of the Holy Spirit, that you help me in your prayers for me to God* (Rom 15:30). Much more, therefore, should we ask the saints who are in heaven to help us by their prayers to God.

Praeterea, ad hoc est communis consuetudo Ecclesiae, quae in litaniis sanctorum orationem petit.

Respondeo dicendum quod *iste ordo est divinitus institutus in rebus*, secundum Dionysium, *ut per media ultima reducantur in Deum*. Unde, cum sancti qui sunt in patria sint Deo propinquissimi, hoc divinae legis ordo requirit, ut nos, qui manentes in corpore peregrinamur a Domino, in eum per sanctos medios reducamur. Quod quidem contingit dum per eos divina bonitas in nos suum effectum infundit. Et quia reditus noster in Deum respondere debet processui bonitatum ipsius ad nos, sicut mediantibus sanctorum suffragiis Dei beneficia in nos deveniunt, ita oportet nos in Deum reduci, ut iterato beneficia eius sumamus, mediantibus sanctis. Et inde est quod eos. intercessores pro nobis, ad Deum constituimus, et quasi mediatores, dum ab eis petimus quod pro nobis orent.

Ad primum ergo dicendum quod, sicut non est propter defectum divinae potentiae quod mediantibus secundis causis agentibus operatur, sed est ad complementum ordinis universi, et ut eius bonitas multiplicius diffundatur in reis, dum res ab eo non solum suscipiunt bonitates proprias, sed insuper quod aliis causa bonitatis existant; ita etiam non est propter defectum misericordiae ipsius quod oporteat eius clementiam per orationes sanctorum pulsare, sed est ad hoc ut ordo praedictus conservetur in rebus.

Ad secundum dicendum quod, quamvis sancti superiores sint magis Deo accepti quam inferiores, utile tamen est etiam minores sanctos interdum orare. Et hoc propter quinque rationes. Primo, ex hoc quod quandoque aliquis habet maiorem devotionem ad minorem sanctum quam ad maiorem. Ex devotione autem maxime dependet orationis effectus. Secundo, propter fastidium tollendum. Quia assiduitas unius rei fastidium parit. Per hoc autem quod diversos sanctos oramus, quasi in singulis novus fervor devotionis excitatur. Tertio, quia quibusdam sanctis datum est in aliquibus specialibus, causis praecipue patrocinari: sicut sancto Antonio ad *ignem infernalem*. Quarto, ut omnibus honor debitus exhibeatur a nobis. Quinto, quia plurium orationibus quandoque impetratur quod unius oratione non impetratur.

Ad tertium dicendum quod oratio est actus quidam. Actus autem sunt particularium suppositorum. Et ideo, si diceremus, *Christe, ora pro nobis*, nisi aliquid adderetur, videremur hoc ad personam Christi referre. Et ita videretur esse consonum vel errori Nestorii, qui distinxit in Christo personam Filii hominis a persona Filii Dei; vel errori Arii, qui posuit personam Filii minorem Patre. Unde, ad hos errores evitandos, Ecclesia non dicit,

Further, An additional argument is provided by the common custom of the Church which asks for the prayers of the saints in the Litany.

I answer that, According to Dionysius (*On the Ecclesiastical Hierarchies* 5) the order established by God among things is that *the last should be led to God by those that are midway between*. Wherefore, since the saints who are in heaven are nearest to God, the order of the divine law requires that we, who, while we remain in the body, are pilgrims from the Lord, should be brought back to God by the saints who are between us and him: and this happens when the divine goodness pours forth its effect into us through them. And since our return to God should correspond to the outflow of his benefits upon us, just as the divine favors reach us by means of the saints' intercession, so should we, by their means, be brought back to God, that we may receive his favors again. Hence it is that we make them our intercessors with God, and our mediators, as it were, when we ask them to pray for us.

Reply Obj. 1: It is not on account of any defect in God's power that he works by means of second causes, but it is for the perfection of the order of the universe, and the more manifold outpouring of his goodness on things, through his bestowing on them not only the goodness which is proper to them, but also the faculty of causing goodness in others. Even so it is not through any defect in his mercy that we need to bespeak his clemency through the prayers of the saints, but to the end that the aforesaid order in things be observed.

Reply Obj. 2: Although the greater saints are more acceptable to God than the lesser, it is sometimes profitable to pray to the lesser; and this for five reasons. First, because sometimes one has greater devotion for a lesser saint than for a greater, and the effect of prayer depends very much on one's devotion. Second, in order to avoid tediousness, for continual attention to one thing makes a person weary; whereas by praying to different saints, the fervor of our devotion is aroused anew, as it were. Third, because it is granted to some saints to exercise their patronage in certain special cases, for instance, to Saint Anthony against the *fire of hell*. Fourth, that due honor be given by us to all. Fifth, because the prayers of several sometimes obtain that which would not have been obtained by the prayers of one.

Reply Obj. 3: Prayer is an act, and acts belong to particular supposita. Hence, were we to say: *Christ, pray for us*, except we added something, this would seem to refer to Christ's person, and consequently to agree with the error either of Nestorius, who distinguished in Christ the person of the Son of Man from the person of the Son of God, or of Arius, who asserted that the person of the Son is less than the Father. Wherefore to avoid these errors the Church says

Christe, ora pro nobis: sed, *Christe, audi nos*, vel, *miserere nobis*.

AD QUARTUM dicendum quod, sicut infra dicitur, non dicuntur sancti preces nostras Deo repraesentare quasi ei incognita manifestent: sed quia eas exaudiri a Deo petunt: vel divinam consulunt veritatem de eis, quid scilicet secundum eius providentiam fieri debeat.

AD QUINTUM dicendum quod ex hoc ipso aliquis efficitur dignus ut sanctus aliquis pro eo oret, quod ad ipsum in sua necessitate cum pura devotione recurrit. Et ita non est superfluum quod sanctos oremus.

not: *Christ, pray for us*, but *Christ, hear us* or *have mercy on us*.

REPLY OBJ. 4: As we shall state further on (A. 3) the saints are said to present our prayers to God, not as though they revealed things unknown to him, but because they ask God to grant those prayers a gracious hearing, or because they seek the divine truth about them, namely, what ought to be done according to his providence.

REPLY OBJ. 5: A person is rendered worthy of a saint's prayers for him by the very fact that in his need he has recourse to him with pure devotion. Hence it is not unnecessary to pray to the saints.

Article 3

Whether the Prayers Which the Saints Pour Forth to God for Us Are Always Granted?

AD TERTIUM SIC PROCEDITUR. Videtur quod orationes sanctorum pro nobis ad Deum fusae non semper exaudiantur. Si enim exaudirentur, maxime exaudirentur sancti de his quae ad eos pertinent. Sed de his non exaudiuntur: unde dicitur Apoc. 6, [10–11], quod martyribus petentibus vindictam de his qui sunt : super terram, *dictum est ut requiescerent modicum tempus adhuc, donec impleretur numerus fratrum suorum*. Ergo multo minus exaudiuntur de his quae ad alios pertinent.

PRAETEREA, Ierem. 15, [1] dicitur: *si steterit Moyses et Samuel coram me, non est anima mea ad populum istum*. Ergo sancti non semper exaudiuntur cum pro, nobis orant ad Deum.

PRAETEREA, sancti in patria *aequales angelis Dei* commemorantur, ut patet Matth. 22, [30]. Sed angeli non semper exaudiuntur in suis orationibus quas fundunt ad Deum: quod patet ex hoc quod habetur Dan. 10, [12–13], ubi dicitur: *ego veni propter sermones tuos: princeps autem regni Persarum restitit mihi viginti et uno diebus*. Non autem venerat in adiutorium Danielis angelus qui loquebatur nisi a Deo liberationem petendo. Et tamen est impedita orationis eius impletio. Ergo nec etiam alii sancti pro nobis orantes apud Deum semper exaudiuntur.

PRAETEREA, quicumque oratione impetrat aliquid, quodammodo meretur illud. Sed sancti qui sunt in patria non sunt in statu merendi. Ergo non possunt suis orationibus aliquid impetrare nobis apud Deum.

PRAETEREA, sancti per omnia conformant voluntatem suam voluntati Dei. Ergo non volunt nisi quod sciunt Deum velle. Sed nullus orat nisi quod vult. Ergo non orant nisi pro eo quod sciunt Deum velle. Sed hoc quod Deus vult, fieret etiam eis non orantibus. Ergo eo-

OBJECTION 1: It would seem that the prayers which the saints pour forth to God for us are not always granted. For if they were always granted, the saints would be heard especially in regard to matters concerning themselves. But they are not heard in reference to these things; wherefore it is stated in Revelation that on the martyrs beseeching vengeance on them that dwell on earth, *it was said to them that they should rest for a little while till the number of their brethren should be filled up* (Rev 6:11). Much less, therefore, are they heard in reference to matters concerning others.

OBJ. 2: Further, it is written: *if Moses and Samuel shall stand before me, my soul is not towards this people* (Jer 15:1). Therefore, the saints are not always heard when they pray God for us.

OBJ. 3: Further, the saints in heaven are stated to be *equal to the angels of God* (Matt 22:30). But the angels are not always heard in the prayers which they offer up to God. This is evident from Daniel, where it is written: *I am come for your words: but the prince of the kingdom of the Persians resisted me for twenty-one days* (10:12–13). But the angel who spoke had not come to Daniel's aid except by asking of God to be set free; and yet the fulfillment of his prayer was hindered. Therefore, neither are other saints always heard by God when they pray for us.

OBJ. 4: Further, whoever obtains something by prayer merits it in a sense. But the saints in heaven are not in the state of meriting. Therefore, they cannot obtain anything for us from God by their prayers.

OBJ. 5: Further, the saints in all things conform their will to the will of God. Therefore, they will nothing but what they know God to will. But no one prays save for what he wills. Therefore, they do not pray save for what they know God to will. Now that which God wills would be done even

rum orationes non sunt efficaces ad aliquid impetrandum.

Praeterea, orationes totius caelestis curiae, si aliquid impetrare possunt, efficaciores essent quam omnia praesentis Ecclesiae suffragia. Sed, multiplicatis praesentis Ecclesiae suffragiis factis pro aliquo in purgatorio existente, totaliter absolveretur a poena. Cum ergo sancti qui sunt in patria eadem oratione orent pro illis qui sunt in purgatorio sicut et pro nobis, si nobis aliquid impetrant, illos qui sunt in purgatorio totaliter orationes eorum a poena absolverent. Quod falsum est: quia sic suffragia Ecclesiae pro defunctis facta superfluae essent.

Sed contra: Est quod habetur II Machab. [15, 14]: *hic est qui multum orat pro populo et pro universa sancta civitate, Ieremias, propheta Dei. Et quod eius oratio sit exaudita, patet per hoc quod sequitur [v. 15–16], quod extendit Ieremias dexteram et dedit Iudae gladium, dicens: accipe sanctum gladium, munus a Deo, etc.*

Praeterea, Hieronymus, in *Epistola contra Vigilantium: dicis in libello tuo quod, dum vivimus; mutuo pro nobis orare possumus. Et hoc postea improbat, dicens sic: si Apostoli et martyres adhuc in corpore constituti possunt orare pro ceteris, quando pro se adhuc debent esse solliciti quanta magis post coronas, victorias et triumphos!*

Praeterea, ad hoc est consuetudo Ecclesiae, quae frequenter petit ut sanctorum orationibus adiuvetur.

Respondeo dicendum quod sancti dupliciter dicuntur orare pro nobis. Uno modo, oratione expressa: dum votis suis aures divinae clementiae pro nobis pulsant. Alio modo, quasi oratione interpretativa: scilicet per eorum merita, quae, in conspectu eius existentia, non solum eis cedunt ad gloriam, sed sunt nobis etiam suffragia et orationes quaedam; sicut etiam sanguis Christi pro nobis dicitur veniam petere. Utroque autem, modo sanctorum orationes sunt, quantum est in ipsis, efficaces ad impetrandum quod petunt. Sed ex parte nostra potest esse defectus, quod non consequamur fructum orationum ipsorum secundum quod pro nobis orare dicuntur ex hoc quod merita eorum nobis proficiunt. Sed secundum quod orant pro nobis votis suis aliquid nobis postulando, semper exaudiuntur: quia non volunt nisi quod Deus vult, nec petunt nisi quod volunt fieri. Quod autem Deus simpliciter vult, impletur: nisi loquamur de voluntate antecedente, secundum quam *vult omnes homines salvos fieri*, quae non semper impletur. Unde nec est mirum si etiam quod sancti volunt per hunc modum voluntatis, interdum non impletur.

Ad primum ergo dicendum quod illa oratio martyrum non est aliud quam eorum desiderium de obtinenda stola corporis et societate sanctorum qui salvandi sunt,

without their praying for it. Therefore, their prayers are not efficacious for obtaining anything.

Obj. 6: Further, the prayers of the whole heavenly court, if they could obtain anything, would be more efficacious than all the petitions of the Church here below. Now, if the suffrages of the Church here below for some one in purgatory were to be multiplied, he would be wholly delivered from punishment. Since, then, the saints in heaven pray for those who are in purgatory on the same account as for us, if they obtain anything for us, their prayers would deliver entirely from punishment those who are in purgatory. But this is not true, because then the Church's suffrages for the dead would be unnecessary.

On the contrary, It is written: *this is he that prays much for the people, and for all the holy city, Jeremiah the prophet of God* (2 Macc 15:14): and that his prayer was granted is clear from what follows: *Jeremiah stretched forth his right hand, and gave to Judas a sword of gold, saying,"Take this holy sword, a gift from God"* (2 Macc 15:15).

Further, Jerome says (*Epistle against Vigilantius*): *you say in your pamphlets that while we live, we can pray for one another, but that when we are dead no one's prayer for another will be heard*: and afterwards he refutes this in the following words: *if the apostles and martyrs while yet in the body can pray for others, while they are still solicitous for themselves, how much more can they do so when the crown, the victory, the triumph is already theirs!*

Further, This is confirmed by the custom of the Church, which often asks to be assisted by the prayers of the saints.

I answer that, The saints are said to pray for us in two ways. First, by express prayer, when by their prayers they seek a hearing of the divine clemency on our behalf: second, by interpretive prayer, namely, by their merits which, being known to God, avail not only them unto glory, but also us as suffrages and prayers, even as the shedding of Christ's blood is said to ask pardon for us. In both ways the saints' prayers, considered in themselves, avail to obtain what they ask, yet on our part they may fail so that we obtain not the fruit of their prayers, insofar as they are said to pray for us by reason of their merits availing on our behalf. But insofar as they pray for us by asking something for us in their prayers, their prayers are always granted, since they will only what God wills, nor do they ask save for what they will to be done; and what God wills is always fulfilled—unless we speak of his antecedent will, whereby *he wishes all men to be saved*. For this will is not always fulfilled; thus no wonder if that also which the saints will according to this kind of will be not fulfilled sometimes.

Reply Obj. 1: This prayer of the martyrs is merely their desire to obtain the robe of the body and the fellowship of those who will be saved, and their consent to God's justice

et consensus quo consentiunt divinae iustitiae punienti malos. Unde Apoc. 6, super illud [v. 10], *usquequo, Domine* etc., dicit Glossa: *desiderant gaudium maius et consortium sanctorum, et iustitiae Dei consentiunt.*

AD SECUNDUM dicendum quod Dominus loquitur ibi de Moyse et Samuele secundum statum quo fuerunt in hac vita. *Ipsi enim leguntur, pro populo orantes, irae Dei restitisse,* ut Interlinearis dicit. Et tamen, si in illo tempore fuissent, non potuissent orationibus Deum placare ad populum, propter populi illius malitiam. Et hic est intellectus litterae.

AD TERTIUM dicendum quod ista pugna bonorum angelorum non intelligitur ex hoc quod apud Deum contrarias orationes funderent: sed quia contraria merita ex diversis partibus ad divinum examen referebant, divinam sententiam expectantes. Et hoc est quod Gregorius dicit, XVII *Moral.* 7, exponens praedicta verba Danielis: *sublimes spiritus gentibus principantes nequaquam pro iniuste agentibus decertant, sed eorum facta recte iudicantes examinant. Cumque uniuscuiusque gentis vel culpa vel iustitia ad supernae curiae solium ducitur, eiusdem gentis prae positus vel obtinuisse in certamine, vel non obtinuisse perhibetur. Quorum tamen omnium una victoria est super se Opificis voluntas summa. Quam dum semper aspiciunt, quod obtinere non valent, nequaquam volunt.* Unde nec petunt. Ex quo etiam patet quod orationes eorum semper exaudiuntur.

AD QUARTUM dicendum quod, licet sancti non sint in statu merendi sibi postquam sunt in patria, sunt tamen in statu merendi aliis, vel potius ex merito praecedenti alios iuvandi: hoc enim apud Deum viventes meruerunt, ut orationes eorum exaudirentur post mortem.

Vel dicendum quod oratio ex alio meretur et ex alio impetrat. Meritum enim consistit in quadam adaequatione actus ad finem propter quem est, qui ei quasi merces redditur. Sed orationis impetratio innititur liberalitati eius qui rogatur: impetrat enim aliquis quandoque ex liberalitate eius qui rogatur, quod tamen ipse non meruit. Et ita, quamvis sancti non sint in statu merendi, tamen non sequitur quod non sint in statu impetrandi.

AD QUINTUM dicendum quod, sicut ex auctoritate Gregorii inducta patet, sancti vel angeli non volunt nisi quod in divina voluntate conspiciunt; et etiam nihil aliud petunt. Nec tamen oratio eorum est infructuosa: quia, sicut dicit Augustinus, in libro *de Praedest. Sanctorum,* orationes sanctorum praedestinatis prosunt, quia forte praeordinatum est ut intercedentium orationibus salventur. Et ita etiam Deus vult ut orationibus sanctorum impleatur illud quod sancti vident eum velle.

in punishing the wicked. Hence a Gloss on Revelation 6:11: *how long, O Lord,* says, *they desire an increase of joy and the fellowship of the saints, and they consent to God's justice.*

REPLY OBJ. 2: The Lord speaks there of Moses and Samuel according to their state in this life. For we read that *they withstood God's anger by praying for the people.* And yet even if they had been living at the time in question, they would have been unable to placate God towards the people by their prayers, on account of the wickedness of this same people: and it is thus that we are to understand this passage.

REPLY OBJ. 3: This dispute among the good angels does not mean that they offered contradictory prayers to God, but that they submitted contrary merits on various sides to the divine inquiry, with a view of God's pronouncing sentence thereon. This, in fact, is what Gregory says (*Morals on Job* 17) in explanation of the aforesaid words of Daniel: *The lofty spirits that are set over the nations never fight in behalf of those that act unjustly, but they justly judge and try their deeds. And when the guilt or innocence of any particular nation is brought into the debate of the court above, the ruling spirit of that nation is said to have won or lost in the conflict. Yet the supreme will of their Maker is victorious over all, for since they have it ever before their eyes, they will not what they are unable to obtain,* wherefore neither do they seek for it. And consequently it is clear that their prayers are always heard.

REPLY OBJ. 4: Although the saints are not in a state to merit for themselves once they are in heaven, they are in a state to merit for others, or rather to assist others by reason of their previous merit: for while living they merited that their prayers should be heard after their death.

Or we may reply that prayer is meritorious on one count, and impetratory on another. For merit consists in a certain equation of the act to the end for which it is intended, and which is given to it as its reward; while the impetration of a prayer depends on the liberality of the person supplicated. Hence prayer sometimes, through the liberality of the person supplicated, obtains that which was not merited either by the suppliant, or by the person supplicated for: and so, although the saints are not in the state of meriting, it does not follow that they are not in the state of impetrating.

REPLY OBJ. 5: As appears from the authority of Gregory quoted above (ad 3), the saints and angels will nothing but what they see to be in the divine will: and so neither do they pray for anything else. Nor is their prayer fruitless, since as Augustine says (*On the Predestination of the Saints* 22): the prayers of the saints profit the predestinate, because it is perhaps preordained that they shall be saved through the prayers of those who intercede for them: and consequently God also wills that what the saints see him to will shall be fulfilled through their prayers.

Ad sextum dicendum quod suffragia Ecclesiae pro defunctis sunt quasi quaedam satisfactiones viventium vice mortuorum; et secundum hoc mortuos a poena absolvunt quam non solverunt. Sed sancti qui sunt in patria non sunt in statu satisfaciendi. Et ideo non est simile de eorum orationibus et de suffragiis Ecclesiae.

Reply Obj. 6: The suffrages of the Church for the dead are as so many satisfactions of the living in lieu of the dead: and accordingly they free the dead from the punishment which the latter have not paid. But the saints in heaven are not in the state of making satisfaction; and consequently the parallel fails between their prayers and the suffrages of the Church.

QUESTION 73

THE SIGNS THAT WILL PRECEDE THE JUDGMENT

Deinde considerandum est de signis quae iudicium praecedunt.

Circa quod quaeruntur tria.

Primo: utrum adventum Domini ad iudicium aliqua signa praecedant.

Secundo: utrum secundum rei veritatem sol et luna obscurari tunc debeant.

Tertio: utrum virtutes caelorum, Domino veniente, moveantur.

We must next consider the signs that will precede the judgment.

Under this head there are three points of inquiry:

(1) Whether any signs will precede the Lord's coming to judgment?

(2) Whether in very truth the sun and moon will be darkened?

(3) Whether the powers of the heavens will be moved when the Lord shall come?

Article 1

Whether Any Signs Will Precede the Lord's Coming to Judgment?

Ad primum sic proceditur. Videtur quod adventum Domini ad iudicium non praecedent aliqua signa. Quia I Thessal. 5, [3]: *cum dixerint, Pax et securitas, repentinus eis superveniet interitus.* Sed non esset pax et securitas si homines per signa praecedentia terrerentur. Ergo signa non praecedent illum adventum.

Praeterea, signa ad manifestationem requiruntur. Sed adventus eius debet esse occultus: unde I Thessal. 5, [2]: *dies Domini, sicut fur, ita in nocte veniet.* Ergo signa non debent ipsum praecedere.

Praeterea, tempus primi adventus fuit praecognitum a prophetis: quod non est de secundo adventu. Sed primum adventum Christi non praecesserunt aliqua huiusmodi signa. Ergo nec secundum praecedent.

Sed contra: Est quod dicitur Luc. 21, [25]: *erunt signa in sole et luna et stellis.*

Praeterea, Hieronymus ponit quindecim signa praecedentia iudicium: dicens quod primo die maria omnia exaltabuntur quindecim cubitis super montes. Secundo, omnia aequora prosternentur in profundum, ita ut vix videri poterunt. Tertio, redigentur in statum antiquum. Quarto, belluae omnes, et alia quae moventur in aquis, congregabuntur et levabuntur super pelagus, more contentionis invicem mugientes. Quinto, omnia volatilia caeli congregabuntur in campis, invicem plorante, non gustantes nec bibentes. Sexto, flumina ignea surgent contra faciem firmamenti, ab occasu solis usque ad ortum corruentia. Septimo, omnia sidera errantia et fixa ex se spargent igneas comas sicut cometae. Octavo, erit magnus terrae motus, ut omnia animalia prosternantur. Nono, omnes lapides parvi et magni dividentur in qua-

Objection 1: It would seem that the Lord's coming to judgment will not be preceded by any signs. For it is written: *when they shall say, "Peace and security," then shall sudden destruction come upon them* (1 Thess 5:3). Now there would be no peace and security if men were terrified by previous signs. Therefore, signs will not precede that coming.

Obj. 2: Further, signs are ordained for the manifestation of something. But his coming is to be hidden, wherefore it is written: *the day of the Lord shall come as a thief in the night* (1 Thess 5:2). Therefore, signs ought not to precede it.

Obj. 3: Further, the time of his first coming was foreknown by the prophets, which does not apply to his second coming. Now no such signs preceded the first coming of Christ. Therefore, neither will they precede the second.

On the contrary, It is written: *there shall be signs in the sun, and in the moon, and in the stars* (Luke 21:25).

Further, Jerome mentions fifteen signs preceding the judgment. He says that on the first day all the seas will rise fifteen cubits above the mountains; in the second day all the waters will be plunged into the depths, so that scarcely will they be visible; on the third day they will be restored to their previous condition; on the fourth day all the great fishes and other things that move in the waters will gather together and, raising their heads above the sea, roar at one another contentiously; on the fifth day, all the birds of the air will gather together in the fields, wailing to one another, with neither eating nor drinking; on the sixth day, rivers of fire will arise towards the firmament, rushing together from the west to the east; on the seventh day, all the stars, both planets and fixed stars, will throw out fiery tails like comets; on the eighth day, there will be a great earthquake, and all

tuor partes, unaquaque aliam collidente. Decimo, omnes plantae sanguineum fluent rorem. Undecimo, omnes montes et colles et aedificia in pulverem redigentur. Duodecimo, omnia animalia venient ad campos de silvis et montibus, rugientia et nihil gustantia. Decimotertio, omnia sepulcra ab ortu solis usque ad occasum patebunt cadaveribus ad resurgendum. Decimoquarto, omnes homines de habitaculis suis recedent, non intelligentes neque loquentes, sed discurrentes. Decimoquinto, omnes morientur, et resurgent cum mortuis longe, ante defunctis.

RESPONDEO dicendum quod Christus ad iudicandum venieris in forma gloriosa apparebit, propter auctoritatern quae iudici debetur. Ad dignitatem autem iudiciariae potestatis pertinet habere aliqua indicia quae ad reverentiam et subiectionem inducant. Et ideo adventum Christi ad iudicium venientes multa signa praecedent, ut corda hominum in subiectionem venturi iudicis adducantur, et ad iudicium praeparentur huiusmodi signis praemoniti.

Quae autem sint ista signa, de facili sciri non potest. Signa enim quae in Evangeliis leguntur, ut Augustinus dicit, ad Hesychium de Fine Mundi, non solum pertinent ad adventum Christi ad iudicium, sed etiam ad tempus destructionis Ierusalem, et ad adventum quo Christus continue Ecclesiam suam visitat. Ita quod forte, si diligenter advertatur, nullum eorum invenitur ad futurum adventum pertinere, ut ipse dicit: quia signa quae in Evangeliis tanguntur, sicut pugnae et terrores et huiusmodi, a principio humani generis fuerunt; nisi forte dicatur quod tunc temporis magis invalescent. Sed secundum quam mensuram crescentia vicinum adventum denuntient, incertum est.

Signa vero quae Hieronymus ponit, non asserit, sed in annalibus Hebraeorum se ea scripta reperisse dicit. Quae etiam valde parum verisimilitudinis habent.

AD PRIMUM ergo dicendum, secundum Augustinum, in libro ad Hesychium praedicto, quod circa finem mundi erit persecutio malorum contra bonos: unde simul aliqui timebunt, scilicet boni; et aliqui securi erunt, scilicet mali. Quod autem dicitur, *cum dixerint, Pax et securitas*, etc., ad malos referendum est, qui signa futuri iudicii parvipendent. Ad bonos vero pertinet quod dicitur Luc. 21,. [26]: *arescentibus hominibus*, etc.

Vel potest dici quod omnia illa signa quae circa iudicium erunt, infra tempus iudicii computantur, ut sic dies iudicii omnia illa contineat. Unde quamvis ex signis apparentibus circa diem iudicii, homines terreantur, ante tamen quam signa illa apparere incipiant, in pace et se-

animals will be laid low; on the ninth day, all the plants will be bedewed as it were with blood; on the tenth day, all stones, little and great, will be divided into four parts dashing against one another; on the eleventh day, all hills and mountains and buildings will be reduced to dust; on the twelfth day, all animals will come from forest and mountain to the fields, roaring and tasting of nothing; on the thirteenth day, all graves from east to west will open to allow the bodies to rise again; on the fourteenth day, all men will leave their abode, neither understanding nor speaking, but rushing hither and thither like madmen; on the fifteenth day, all will die and will rise again with those who died long before.

I ANSWER THAT, When Christ shall come to judge he will appear in the form of glory, on account of the authority necessary to a judge. Now it pertains to the dignity of judicial power to have certain signs that induce people to reverence and subjection: and consequently many signs will precede the advent of Christ when he shall come to judgment, in order that the hearts of men be brought to subjection to the coming judge, and be prepared for the judgment, being forewarned by those signs.

But it is not easy to know what these signs may be: for the signs of which we read in the gospels, as Augustine says, writing to Hesychius about the end of the world (Epistle LXXX), refer not only to Christ's coming to judgment, but also to the time of the sack of Jerusalem, and to the coming of Christ in ceaselessly visiting his Church. So that, perhaps, if we consider them carefully, we shall find that none of them refers to the coming advent, as he remarks, because these signs that are mentioned in the Gospels, such as wars, fears, and so forth, have been from the beginning of the human race—unless perhaps we say that at that time they will be more prevalent, although it is uncertain in what degree this increase will foretell the imminence of the advent.

The signs mentioned by Jerome are not asserted by him; he merely says that he found them written in the annals of the Hebrews: and, indeed, they contain very little likelihood.

REPLY OBJ. 1: According to Augustine (*Epistle to Hesychius* 80) towards the end of the world there will be a general persecution of the good by the wicked: so that at the same time some will fear, namely, the good, and some will be secure, namely, the wicked. The words: *when they shall say, "Peace and security,"* refer to the wicked, who will pay little heed to the signs of the coming judgment: while the words, *men withering away*, etc. (Luke 21:26), should be referred to the good.

We may also reply that all these signs that will happen about the time of the judgment are reckoned to occur within the time occupied by the judgment, so that the judgment day contains them all. Wherefore, although men be terrified by the signs appearing about the judgment day,

curitate impii se esse credent, post mortem Antichristi non statim videntes mundum consummari, ut prius existimabant.

AD SECUNDUM dicendum quod dies Domini dicitur *sicut fur* venire, quia ignoratur determinatum tempus, quod per signa illa cognosci non poterit. Quamvis etiam sub die iudicii comprehendi possint omnia illa manifestissima quae immediate praecedent, ut dictum est.

AD TERTIUM dicendum quod in primo adventu Christus venit occultus: quamvis determinatum tempus esset prius praecognitum a prophetis. Et ideo non oportebat huiusmodi signa in primo adventu apparere, sicut apparebunt in secundo adventu, in quo manifestus veniet: quamvis determinatum tempus sit occultum.

yet before those signs begin to appear the wicked will think themselves to be in peace and security after the death of Antichrist and before the coming of Christ, seeing that the world is not at once destroyed, as they thought hitherto.

REPLY OBJ. 2: The day of the Lord is said to come *as a thief*, because the exact time is not known, since it will not be possible to know it from those signs: although, as we have already said, all these most manifest signs which will precede the judgment immediately may be comprised under the judgment day.

REPLY OBJ. 3: At his first advent Christ came secretly, although the appointed time was known beforehand by the prophets. Hence there was no need for such signs to appear at his first coming as will appear at his second advent, when he will come openly, although the appointed time is hidden.

Article 2

Whether Toward the Time of the Judgment the Sun and Moon Will Be Darkened in Very Truth?

AD SECUNDUM SIC PROCEDITUR. Videtur quod circa iudicium secundum rei veritatem sol et luna obscurentur. Quia, ut dicit Rabanus, *super Matth.*, *nihil prohibet intelligere tunc temporis veraciter solem et lunam, cum sideribus ceteris, suo lumine privari: quo modo de sole constat factum esse tempore Dominicae Passionis.*

PRAETEREA, lux corporum caelestium ad generationem inferiorum corporum ordinatur: quia per eam influunt in haec inferiora, et non solum per motum, ut dicit Averroes, in libro *de Substantia Orbis.* Sed tunc generatio cessabit. Ergo nec lux in caelestibus corporibus remanebit.

PRAETEREA, inferiora corpora purgabuntur, ut quibusdam videtur, a qualitatibus quibus agunt. Corpus autem caeleste non solum agit per motum, sed per lumen, ut dictum est. Ergo, sicut motus caeli cessabit, ita lumen corporum caelestium.

SED CONTRA: Est quod, secundum astrologos, sol et luna simul eclipsim pati non possunt. Sed illa obscuratio solis et lunae simul esse dicitur, Domino ad iudicium veniente. Ergo non erit obscuratio secundum rei veritatem, per modum eclipsis naturalis.

PRAETEREA, non congruit idem esse causam defectus alicuius rei et augmenti. Sed, veniente Domino, lux luminarium promittitur augenda: unde Isaiae 30, [26], *erit lux lunae sicut lux solis, et lux solis septempliciter.* Ergo non est conveniens quod, veniente Domino, lux illorum corporum cesset.

RESPONDEO dicendum quod, si loquamur de sole et luna quantum ad ipsum momentum adventus Chri-

OBJECTION 1: It would seem that towards the time of the judgment the sun and moon will be darkened in very truth. For, as Rabanus says, commenting on Matthew 24, *nothing hinders us from gathering that the sun, moon, and stars will then be deprived of their light, as we know happened to the sun at the time of our Lord's Passion.*

OBJ. 2: Further, the light of the heavenly bodies is directed to the generation of inferior bodies, because by its means and not only by their movement they act upon this lower world, as Averroes says (*On the Substance of the Sphere*). But generation will cease then. Therefore, neither will light remain in the heavenly bodies.

OBJ. 3: Further, according to some, the inferior bodies will be cleansed of the qualities by which they act. Now heavenly bodies act not only by movement, but also by light, as stated above (Obj. 2). Therefore, as the movement of heaven will cease, so will the light of the heavenly bodies.

ON THE CONTRARY, According to astronomers, the sun and moon cannot be eclipsed at the same time. But this darkening of the sun and moon is stated to be simultaneous, when the Lord shall come to judgment. Therefore, the darkening will not be in very truth due to a natural eclipse.

FURTHER, It is not seemly for the same to be the cause of a thing's failing and increasing. Now when our Lord shall come, the light of the luminaries will increase according to Isaiah 30:26, *the light of the moon shall be as the light of the sun, and the light of the sun shall be sevenfold.* Therefore, it is unfitting for the light of these bodies to cease when our Lord comes.

I ANSWER THAT, If we speak of the sun and moon in respect of the very moment of Christ's coming, it is not credi-

sti, sic non est credibile quod obscurentur sui luminis privatione: quia totus mundus innovabitur, Christo veniente et sanctis resurgentibus, ut dictum est. Si autem loquamur de eis secundum tempus propinquum ante iudicium, sic esse poterit quod sol et luna et alia caeli luminaria sui luminis privatione obscurabuntur, vel diversis temporibus vel simul, divina virtute faciente ad hominum terrorem.

AD PRIMUM ergo dicendum quod Rabanus loquitur quantum ad tempus iudicium praecedens.

AD SECUNDUM dicendum quod lux est in corporibus caelestibus non solum ad causandum generationem in istis inferioribus, sed etiam ad eorum perfectionem et decorem. Unde non oportet quod, cessante generatione, lux corporum caelestium cesset, sed magis augeatur.

AD TERTIUM dicendum quod non videtur esse probabile quod qualitates elementares ab elementis removeantur, quamvis quidam hoc posuerint. Si tamen removerentur, non est simile de eis et de luce: eo quod qualitates elementares habent ad invicem contrarietatem, unde agunt corrumpendo; lux autem non est principium actionis per viam contrarietatis, sed per viam principii regulantis contraria et ad concordiam reducentis. Nec est etiam simile de motu corporum, caelestium. Motus enim est *actus imperfecti*. Unde et tolli debet quando tolletur imperfectio. Quod de luce non potest dici.

ble that they will be darkened through being bereft of their light, since when Christ comes and the saints rise again the whole world will be renewed, as we shall state further on (Q. 74). If, however, we speak of them in respect of the time immediately preceding the judgment, it is possible that by the divine power the sun, moon, and other luminaries of the heavens will be darkened, either at various times or all together, in order to inspire men with fear.

REPLY OBJ. 1: Rabanus is speaking of the time preceding the judgment.

REPLY OBJ. 2: Light is in the heavenly bodies not only for the purpose of causing generation in these lower bodies, but also for their own perfection and beauty. Hence it does not follow that where generation ceases, the light of the heavenly bodies will cease, but rather that it will increase.

REPLY OBJ. 3: It does not seem probable that the elemental qualities will be removed from the elements, although some have asserted this. If, however, they be removed, there would still be no parallel between them and light, since the elemental qualities are contrary to one another, so that their action is corruptive: whereas light is a principle of action not by way of contrariety, but by way of a principle regulating contraries and bringing them back to harmony. Nor is there a parallel with the movement of heavenly bodies, for movement is the *act of that which is imperfect*, wherefore it must cease when the imperfection ceases: whereas this cannot be said of light.

Article 3

Whether the Virtues of Heaven Will Be Moved When Our Lord Shall Come?

AD TERTIUM SIC PROCEDITUR. Videtur quod Virtutes caelorum, Domino veniente, non commoveantur. Virtutes enim caelorum dici non possunt nisi angeli beati. Sed immutabilitas est de ratione beatitudinis. Ergo moveri non poterunt.

PRAETEREA, admirationis causa est ignorantia, ut patet in principio *Metaphysicae*. Sed, sicut ab angelis longe abest timor, ita et ignorantia: quia, ut dicit Gregorius, *quid est quod non videant qui videntem omnia vident?* Ergo non poterunt per admirationem moveri, ut in littera dicitur.

PRAETEREA, omnes angeli divino iudicio adstabunt: unde Apoc. 7, [11], *omnes angeli stabunt in circuitu throni.* Sed Virtutes nominant unum specialem ordinem in angelis. Ergo non potius de eis dici debuit quod moveantur quam de aliis angelis.

SED CONTRA: Est quod dicitur Iob 26, [11]: *columnae caeli pavent adventum eius.* Sed *columnae caeli* non pos-

OBJECTION 1: It would seem that the Virtues of heaven will not be moved when our Lord shall come. For the Virtues of heaven can denote only the blessed angels. Now immobility is essential to blessedness. Therefore, it will be impossible for them to be moved.

OBJ. 2: Further, ignorance is the cause of wonder (*Metaphysics* 1.2). Now ignorance, like fear, is far from the angels, for as Gregory says (*Dialogues* 4.33; *Morals on Job* 2.3), *what do they not see, who see him who sees all.* Therefore, it will be impossible for them to be moved with wonder, as stated in the text (*Sentences* IV, D. 48).

OBJ. 3: Further, all the angels will be present at the divine judgment; wherefore it is stated: *all the angels stood round about the throne* (Rev 7:11). Now the Virtues denote one particular order of angels. Therefore, it should not be said of them rather than of others that they are moved.

ON THE CONTRARY, It is written: *the pillars of heaven tremble, and dread at his beck* (Job 26:11). Now *the pillars*

sunt intelligi nisi Virtutes caelorum. Ergo virtutes caelorum commovebuntur.

PRAETEREA, Matth. 24, [29] dicitur: *stellae cadent de caelo, et Virtutes caelorum movebuntur.*

RESPONDEO dicendum quod virtutes in angelis dicuntur dupliciter: ut patet per Dionysium, 11 cap. *Cael. Hier.* Quandoque enim nomen *Virtutum* uni ordini appropriatur, qui secundum ipsum est medius mediae hierarchiae; secundum vero Gregorium est supremus infimae hierarchiae. Alio modo accipitur communiter pro omnibus caelestibus spiritibus. Et utroque modo potest accipi in proposito.

In littera enim exponitur prout accipitur secundo modo, scilicet pro omnibus angelis. Et tunc dicuntur moveri propter admirationem novitatis quae in inundo erit, sicut in littera dicitur.

Potest etiam exponi prout *Virtutes* est proprium nomen ordinis. Et tunc ordo ille dicitur moveri prae aliis ratione effectus. Quia illi ordini, secundum Gregorium, attribuitur miracula facere, quae maxime circa illud tempus fient. Vel quia ordo ille, cum sit de media hierarchia, secundum Dionysium, non habet potentiam limitatam. Unde oportet quod eius ministerium sit circa causas universales. Unde proprium officium Virtutum esse videtur corpora caelestia movere, quae sunt causa eorum quae in natura inferiori aguntur. Et hoc etiam ipsum nomen sonat, quia *Virtutes caelorum* dicuntur. Tunc ergo movebuntur, quia ab effectu suo cessabunt, ulterius corpora caelestia non moventes: sicut nec angeli qui sunt ad custodiam hominum deputati, ulterius custodiae officio vacabunt.

AD PRIMUM ergo dicendum quod mutatio illa non variat aliquid quod ad eorum statum pertineat: sed refertur vel ad effectus eorum, qui immutari possunt sine eorum mutatione; vel ad novam rerum considerationem, quam prius secundum species concreatas videre non potuerant. Hanc autem vicissitudinem cogitationum ab eis beatitudo non tollit. Unde dicit Augustinus quod *Deus movet creaturam spiritualem per tempora.*

AD SECUNDUM dicendum quod admiratio solet esse de his quae nostram conditionem excedunt vel facultatem. Et secundum hoc Virtutes caelorum admirabuntur divinam virtutem talia facientem, inquantum ab eius imitatione et comprehensione deficiunt: per quem modum dixit Agnes quod *eius pulcritudinem sol et luna mirantur.* Et sic non ponitur in angelo ignorantia, sed tollitur Dei comprehensio.

AD TERTIUM patet responsio ex dictis.

of heaven can denote only the Virtues of heaven. Therefore, the Virtues of heaven will be moved.

FURTHER, It is written: *the stars shall fall from heaven, and the Virtues of heaven shall be moved* (Matt 24:29).

I ANSWER THAT, Virtue is twofold as applied to the angels, as Dionysius states (*On the Heavenly Hierarchies* 11). For sometimes the name of 'Virtues' is appropriated to one order, which according to him is the middle order of the middle hierarchy, but according to Gregory (*Homilies on the Gospels* 34) is the highest order of the lowest hierarchy. In another sense it is employed to denote all the angels: and the question at issue may be taken either way.

For in the text (*Sentences* IV, D. 48) it is explained according to the second way, so as to denote all the angels: and then they are said to be moved through wonder at the renewing of the world, as stated in the text.

It can also be explained in reference to 'Virtue' as the name of a particular order; and then that order is said to be moved more than the others by reason of the effect, since according to Gregory (*Homilies on the Gospels* 34) we ascribe to that order the working of miracles which especially will be worked about that time: or again, because that order—since, according to Dionysius (*On the Heavenly Hierarchies* 11), it belongs to the middle hierarchy—is not limited in its power, wherefore its ministry must regard universal causes. Consequently, the proper office of the Virtues is seemingly to move the heavenly bodies which are the cause of what happens in nature here below. And again the very name denotes this, since they are called the *Virtues of heaven*. Accordingly, they will be moved then, because they will no more produce their effect, by ceasing to move the heavenly bodies: even as the angels who are appointed to watch over men will no longer fulfill the office of guardians.

REPLY OBJ. 1: This movement changes nothing pertaining to their state; but refers either to their effects which may vary without any change on their part, or to some new consideration of things which hitherto they were unable to see by means of their concreated species, which change of thought is not taken from them by their state of blessedness. Hence Augustine says (*On the Literal Meaning of Genesis* 8.20) that *God moves the spiritual creature through time.*

REPLY OBJ. 2: Wonder is wont to be about things surpassing our knowledge or ability: and accordingly the Virtues of heaven will wonder at the divine power doing such things, insofar as they fail to do or comprehend them. In this sense the blessed Agnes said that the *sun and moon wonder at his beauty*: and this does not imply ignorance in the angels, but removes the comprehension of God from them.

THE REPLY to the third objection is clear from what has been said.

QUESTION 74

Deinde considerandum est de igne ultimae conflagrationis mundi.

    Circa quod quaeruntur novem.

    Primo: utrum aliqua mundi purgatio sit futura.

    Secundo: utrum per ignem sit futura.

    Tertio: utrum ille ignis sit eiusdem speciei cum igne elementari.

    Quarto: utrum ignis ille sit caelos superiores purgaturus.

    Quinto: utrum ille ignis sit alia elementa consumpturus.

    Sexto: utrum omnia elementa sit purgaturus.

    Septimo: utrum ille ignis praecedat iudicium vel sequatur.

    Octavo: utrum per illum ignem consumendi sint homines.

    Nono: utrum per eum involvendi sint reprobi.

We must now consider the fire of the final conflagration.

Under this head there are nine points of inquiry:

(1) Whether any cleansing of the world is to take place?

(2) Whether it will be effected by fire?

(3) Whether that fire is of the same species as elemental fire?

(4) Whether that fire will cleanse also the higher heavens?

(5) Whether that fire will consume the other elements?

(6) Whether it will cleanse all the elements?

(7) Whether that fire precedes or follows the judgment?

(8) Whether men are to be consumed by that fire?

(9) Whether the wicked will be involved in it?

Article 1

Whether the World Is to Be Cleansed?

AD PRIMUM SIC PROCEDITUR. Videtur quod nulla mundi purgatio sit futura. Non enim purgatione indiget nisi quod est immundum. Sed creaturae Dei non sunt immundae: unde dicitur Act. 10, [15]: *quod Deus mundavit, tu ne commune dixeris*, idest immundum. Ergo creaturae mundi non purgabuntur.

PRAETEREA, purgatio secundum divinam iustitiam ordinatur ad auferendum immunditiam culpae: sicut patet de purgatione post mortem. Sed in elementis huius mundi nulla potest esse culpae infectio. Ergo videtur quod purgatione non indigeant.

PRAETEREA, unumquodque dicitur purgari quando separatur quod est extraneum ab ipso inducens in eo ignobilitatem: separatio enim eius quod nobilitatem inducit, non dicitur purgatio, sed magis diminutio. Sed hoc ad perfectionem et nobilitatem elementorum pertinet quod aliquid extraneae naturae est eis admixtum: quia forma corporis mixti est nobilior quam forma simplicis. Ergo videtur quod elementa huius mundi nullo modo convenienter purgari possint.

SED CONTRA: Omnis innovatio fit per aliquam purgationem. Sed elementa innovabuntur: unde Apoc. 21,

OBJECTION 1: It would seem that there is not to be any cleansing of the world. For only that which is unclean needs cleansing. Now God's creatures are not unclean, wherefore it is written: *that which God has cleansed, do not you call common* (Acts 10:15), that is, unclean. Therefore, the creatures of the world shall not be cleansed.

OBJ. 2: Further, according to divine justice, cleansing is directed to the removal of the uncleanness of sin, as instanced in the cleansing after death. But there can be no stain of sin in the elements of this world. Therefore, seemingly, they need not to be cleansed.

OBJ. 3: Further, a thing is said to be cleansed when any foreign matter that depreciates it is removed from it: for the removal of that which ennobles a thing is not called a cleansing, but rather a diminishing. Now it pertains to the perfection and nobility of the elements that something of a foreign nature is mingled with them, since the form of a mixed body is more noble than the form of a simple body. Therefore, it would seem in no way fitting that the elements of this world can possibly be cleansed.

ON THE CONTRARY, All renewal is effected by some kind of cleansing. But the elements will be renewed; hence

[1], *vidi caelum novum et terram novam: primum enim caelum et prima terra abiit.* Ergo elementa purgabuntur.

Praeterea, I Cor. 7, super illud [v. 31], *praeterit figura huius mundi*, dicit Glossa: *pulchritudo huius mundi mundanorum ignium conflagratione peribit.* Et sic idem quod prius.

Respondeo dicendum quod, quia mundus aliquo modo propter hominem factus est, oportet quod, quando homo per corpus glorificabitur, etiam alia mundi corpora ad meliorem statum mutentur, ut sit et locus convenientior et aspectus delectabilior. Ad hoc autem quod homo gloriam corporis consequatur, oportet prius removeri ea quae gloriae opponuntur. Quae sunt duo, scilicet corruptio, et infectio culpae: quia, ut dicitur I Cor. 15, [50], *corruptio incorruptelam non possidebit*; et a civitate gloriae omnes immundi *foris* erunt, Apoc. [22, 15]2). Et similiter etiam oportet elementa mundi purgari a contrariis dispositionibus antequam in novitate gloriae adducantur, proportionaliter ei quod de homine dictum est.

Quamvis autem res corporalis subiectum infectionis culpae proprie esse non possit, tamen ex culpa quaedam incongruitas in rebus corporalibus corruptis relinquitur ad hoc quod spiritualibus ditentur: et inde videmus quod loca in quibus aliqua crimina sunt commissa, non reputantur idonea ad aliqua sacra exercenda in eis, nisi purgatione quadam praemissa. Et secundum hoc, ex peccatis hominum quandam inidoneitatem ad gloriae susceptionem pars mundi recipit quae in usum nostrum cedit. Unde quantum ad hoc mundatione indiget. Similiter etiam circa medium locum, propter elementorum contactum, multae sunt corruptiones et generationes, et alterationes elementorum, quae puritati eorum derogant. Et ideo ab his oportet elementa purgari, ad hoc quod decenter suscipiant novitatem gloriae.

Ad primum ergo dicendum quod, cum dicitur omnis creatura Dei esse munda, hoc intelligendum est quia non habet in substantia sua alicuius malitiae commixtionem: sicut ponebant Manichaei, dicentes bonum et malum esse duas substantias alicubi divisas et alicubi commixtas. Non autem removetur quin aliqua creatura habeat permixtionem naturae extraneae: quae etiam natura in se bona est, sed perfectioni huiusmodi creaturae repugnat. Similiter non removetur ex hoc quin malum alicui creaturae accidat: quamvis non sit permixtum ei quasi pars substantiae ipsius.

Ad secundum dicendum quod, quamvis elementa corporea subiectum culpae esse non possint, tamen ex culpa in eis commissa aliquam ineptitudinem possunt consequi ad perfectionem gloriae suscipiendam.

Ad tertium dicendum quod forma mixti et forma elementi possunt dupliciter considerari. Aut quantum ad

it is written: *I saw a new heaven and a new earth: for the first heaven and the first earth was gone* (Rev 21:1). Therefore, the elements shall be cleansed.

Further, A Gloss on 1 Corinthians 7:31: *the fashion of this earth is passing away*, says, *the beauty of this world will perish in the burning of worldly flames* (St. Augustine, *The City of God* 20.16). Therefore, the same conclusion follows.

I answer that, Since the world was, in a way, made for man's sake, it follows that when man shall be glorified in the body, the other bodies of the world shall also be changed to a better state, so that it is rendered a more fitting place for him and more pleasant to look upon. Now in order that man obtain the glory of the body, it is first of all necessary that those things to be removed which are opposed to glory. There are two, namely, the corruption and the stain of sin—because, according to 1 Corinthians 15:50, *neither shall corruption possess incorruption*, and all the unclean shall be *without* the city of glory (Rev 22:15). And similarly, the elements require to be cleansed from the contrary dispositions before they be brought to the newness of glory, proportionately to what we have said with regard to man.

Now, although, properly speaking, a corporeal thing cannot be the subject of the stain of sin, nevertheless, on account of sin corporeal things contract a certain unfittingness for being appointed to spiritual purposes; and for this reason we find that places where crimes have been committed are reckoned unfit for the performance of sacred actions unless they be cleansed beforehand. Accordingly, that part of the world which is given to our use contracts from men's sins a certain unfitness for being glorified, wherefore in this respect it needs to be cleansed. In like manner, with regard to the intervening space, on account of the contact of the elements, there are many corruptions, generations and alterations of the elements which diminish their purity: wherefore the elements need to be cleansed from these also, so that they be fit to receive the newness of glory.

Reply Obj. 1: When it is asserted that every creature of God is clean we are to understand this as meaning that its substance contains no alloy of evil, as the Manichees maintained, saying that evil and good are two substances in some places severed from one another, in others mingled together. But it does not exclude a creature from having an admixture of a foreign nature which in itself is also good, but is inconsistent with the perfection of that creature. Nor does this prevent evil from being accidental to a creature, although not mingled with it as part of its substance.

Reply Obj. 2: Although corporeal elements cannot be the subject of sin, nevertheless from the sin that is committed in them they contract a certain unfitness for receiving the perfection of glory.

Reply Obj. 3: The form of a mixed body and the form of an element may be considered in two ways: either as re-

perfectionem speciei: et sic corpus mixtum nobilius est. Aut quantum ad perpetuitatem durationis. Et sic corpus simplex nobilius est: quia non habet in seipso unde corrumpatur, nisi eius corruptio fiat ab aliquo exteriori; corpus autem mixtum in seipso habet causam corruptionis suae, scilicet compositionem contrariorum. Et ideo corpus simplex, etsi sit corruptibile secundum partem, est tamen incorruptibile secundum totum: quod de mixto dici non potest. Et quia incorruptio est de perfectione gloriae, perfectio corporis simplicis magis convenit perfectioni gloriae quam perfectio corporis mixti: nisi etiam corpus mixtum in se habeat aliquod incorruptionis principium, sicut humanum, cuius forma est incorruptibilis. Nihilominus tamen, quamvis aliquo modo corpus mixtum sit nobilius quam simplex, nobilius tamen esse habet corpus simplex secundum se existens quam existens in mixto: quia in mixto sunt corpora simplicia quodammodo in potentia; in seipsis autem existentia sunt in ultima sui perfectione.

gards the perfection of the species, and thus a mixed body is more perfect; or as regards their continual endurance, and thus the simple body is more noble, because it has not in itself the cause of corruption, unless it be corrupted by something extrinsic, whereas a mixed body has in itself the cause of its corruption, namely, the composition of contraries. Wherefore a simple body, although it be corruptible in part, is incorruptible as a whole, which cannot be said of a mixed body. And since incorruption belongs to the perfection of glory, it follows that the perfection of a simple body is more in keeping with the perfection of glory than the perfection of a mixed body, unless the mixed body has also in itself some principle of incorruption, as the human body has, the form of which is incorruptible. Nevertheless, although a mixed body is somewhat more noble than a simple body, a simple body that exists by itself has a more noble being than if it exist in a mixed body, because in a mixed body simple bodies are somewhat in potentiality, whereas, existing by themselves, they are in their ultimate perfection.

Article 2

Whether the Cleansing of the World Will Be Effected by Fire?

Ad secundum sic proceditur. Videtur quod haec purgatio non sit futura per ignem. Ignis enim, cum sit pars mundi, purgatione indiget, sicut et aliae partes. Sed non debet esse idem purgans et purgatum. Ergo videtur quod ignis non purgabit.

Praeterea, sicut ignis habet virtutem purgativam, ita et aqua. Cum ergo non omnia sint purgabilia per ignem, sed quaedam necesse sit aqua purgari, sicut etiam vetus lex distinguit; videtur quod ignis non purget ad minus universaliter.

Praeterea, purgatio ad hoc videtur pertinere ut partes mundi ab invicem segregatae puriores reddantur. Sed segregatio partium mundi ab invicem in mundi initio sola virtute divina facta est: quia ex hac opus distinctionis determinatur. Unde et Anaxagoras segregationem posuit actum intellectus moventis omnia. Ergo videtur quod in fine mundi purgatio fiat immediate a Deo, et non per ignem.

Sed contra: Est quod in Psalmo [49, 3] dicitur: *ignis in conspectu eius exardebit, et in circuitu eius tempestas valida*: et postea [v. 4] sequitur de iudicio, *advocabit caelum desursum et terram discernere populum suum*. Ergo videtur quod ultima purgatio mundi sit futura per ignem.

Objection 1: It would seem that this cleansing will not be effected by fire. For since fire is a part of the world, it needs to be cleansed like the other parts. Now, the same thing should not be both cleanser and cleansed. Therefore, it would seem that the cleansing will not be by fire.

Obj. 2: Further, just as fire has a cleansing virtue, so has water. Since, then, all things are not capable of being cleansed by fire, and some need to be cleansed by water—which distinction is, moreover, observed by the old law—it would seem that fire will not at any rate cleanse all things.

Obj. 3: Further, this cleansing would seem to consist in purifying the parts of the world by separating them from one another. Now the separation of the parts of the world from one another at the world's beginning was effected by God's power alone, for the work of distinction was carried out by that power: wherefore Anaxagoras asserted that the separation was effected by the act of the intellect which moves all things (cf. Aristotle, *Physics* 8.9). Therefore, it would seem that at the end of the world the cleansing will be done immediately by God, and not by fire.

On the contrary, It is written: *a fire shall burn before him, and a mighty tempest shall be around him* (Ps 49:3); and afterwards in reference to the judgment: *he shall call heaven from above, and the earth to judge his people* (Ps 49:4). Therefore, it would seem that the final cleansing of the world will be through fire.

PRAETEREA, II Petr. [3, 12] dicitur: *caeli ardentes solventur, et elementa ignis ardore tabescent.* Ergo illa purgatio per ignem fiet.

RESPONDEO dicendum quod ilia mundi purgatio removebit a mundo infectionem ex culpa relictam, et impuritatem commixtionis, et erit dispositio ad gloriae perfectionem. Et ideo quantum ad haec tria convenientissime fiet per ignem purgatio. Primo, quia ignis, cum sit nobilissimum elementorum, habet naturales proprietates similiores proprietatibus gloriae: ut maxime patet de luce. Secundo, quia ignis non ita recipit commixtionem extranei, propter efficaciam virtutis activae, sicut alia elementa. Tertio, quia sphaera ignis est remota a nostra habitatione, nec ita communis est nobis usus ignis sicut terrae, aquae et aeris. Unde non ita inficitur. Et praeter hoc, habet magnam efficaciam ad purgandum et ad dividendum subtiliando.

AD PRIMUM ergo dicendum quod ignis non venit in usum nostrum prout est in materia propria, sic enim remotus est a nobis: sed solum prout est in materia aliena. Et quoad hoc, poterit per ignem in sua puritate existentem purgari iste ignis quantum ad hoc quod habet de extraneo adiunctum.

AD SECUNDUM dicendum quod purgatio mundi quae facta est per diluvium, non respiciebat nisi infectionem peccati. Praecipue autem tunc regnabat peccatum concupiscentiae. Et ideo convenienter per contrarium purgatio facta fuit, scilicet per aquam. Sed secunda purgatio respicit et infectionem culpae et commixtionis impuritatem. Et quantum ad utrumque convenit magis, quod fiat per ignem quam per aquam. Aqua enim non habet vim disgregandi, sed magis aggregandi. Unde per aquam naturalis impuritas elementorum tolli non posset sicut per ignem. Similiter etiam circa finem mundi regnabit vitium tepiditatis, quasi mundo iam senescente: quia, ut dicitur Matth. 24, [12], *tunc refrigescet caritas multorum.* Unde tunc convenienter purgatio per ignem fiet.

Nec est aliquid quod igne purgari non possit aliquo modo. Sed quaedam sunt quae sine sui corruptione per ignem non possunt purgari: sicut panni et vasa lignea et huiusmodi. Et alia lex praecipit purgari per aquam. Quae tamen finaliter omnia corrumpentur per ignem.

AD TERTIUM dicendum quod per opus distinctionis sunt rebus diversae formae collatae, quibus ad invicem distinguuntur. Et ideo hoc fieri non potuit nisi per eum qui est auctor naturae. Sed per finalem purgationem reducentur res ad puritatem in qua conditae fuerunt. Et in hoc poterit natura creata exhibere ministerium Creatori.

FURTHER, It is written: *the heavens, being on fire, will be dissolved, and the elements shall melt with the burning heat* (2 Pet 3:12). Therefore, this cleansing will be effected by fire.

I ANSWER THAT, As stated above (A. 1) this cleansing of the world will remove from it the stain contracted from sin, and the impurity resulting from mixture, and will be a disposition to the perfection of glory; and consequently in this threefold respect it will be most fitting for it to be effected by fire. First, because since fire is the most noble of the elements, its natural properties are more like the properties of glory, and this is especially clear in regard to light. Second, because fire, on account of the efficacy of its active virtue, is not as susceptible as the other elements to the admixture of a foreign matter. Third, because the sphere of fire is far removed from our abode; nor are we so familiar with the use of fire as with that of earth, water, and air, so that it is not so liable to depreciation. Moreover, it is most efficacious in cleansing and in separating by a process of rarefaction.

REPLY OBJ. 1: Fire is not employed by us in its proper matter (since thus it is far removed from us), but only in a foreign matter: and in this respect it will be possible for the world to be cleansed by fire as existing in its pure state. But insofar as it has an admixture of some foreign matter it will be possible for it to be cleansed; and thus it will be cleanser and cleansed under different aspects. And this is not unreasonable.

REPLY OBJ. 2: The first cleansing of the world by the deluge regarded only the stain of sin. Now, the sin which was most prevalent then was the sin of concupiscence, and consequently it was fitting that the cleansing should be by means of its contrary, namely water. But the second cleansing regards both the stain of sin and the impurity of mixture, and in respect of both it is more fitting for it to be effected by fire than by water. For the power of water tends to unite rather than to separate; wherefore the natural impurity of the elements could not be removed by water as by fire. Moreover, at the end of the world the prevalent sin will be that of tepidity, as though the world were already growing old, because then, according to Matthew 24:12, *the charity of many shall grow cold*, and consequently the cleansing will then be fittingly effected by fire.

Nor is there any thing that cannot in some way be cleansed by fire: some things, however, cannot be cleansed by fire without being destroyed themselves, such as cloths and wooden vessels. These the law ordered to be cleansed with water, yet all these things will be finally destroyed by fire.

REPLY OBJ. 3: By the work of distinction things received different forms whereby they are distinct from one another: and consequently this could only be done by him who is the author of nature. But by the final cleansing, things will be restored to the purity wherein they were created, wherefore created nature will be able to minister to its

Et propter hoc ministerium creaturae committitur, quia hoc ad eius nobilitatem cedit.

Creator to this effect; and for this reason is a creature employed as a minister, because it is ennobled thereby.

Article 3

Whether the Fire Whereby the World Will Be Cleansed Will Be of the Same Species With Elemental Fire?

AD TERTIUM SIC PROCEDITUR. Videtur quod ille ignis non sit eiusdem speciei cum igne elementari. Nihil enim seipsum consumit. Sed *ille ignis quatuor elementa consumet*: ut dicit Glossa, II Petr. [3, 10]. Ergo ignis ille non erit eiusdem speciei cum igne elementari.

PRAETEREA, sicut virtus manifestatur per operationem, ita natura per virtutem. Sed ille ignis habebit aliam virtutem ab igne qui est elementum: quia scilicet purgabit universum, quod ignis iste facere non potest. Ergo non erit eiusdem speciei cum isto.

PRAETEREA, ea quae sunt eiusdem speciei in corporibus naturalibus, habent eundem motum. Sed ille ignis habebit alium motum quam ignis elementum: quia circumquaque movebitur, ut totum purgare possit. Ergo ignis ille non est eiusdem speciei cum isto.

SED CONTRA: Est quod Augustinus dicit, XX *de Civ. Dei*, et habetur in Glossa, I Cor. 7, [31], quod *figura huius mundi mundanorum ignium conflagratione peribit*. Ergo igniis ille erit de natura ignis qui nunc est in hoc mundo.

PRAETEREA, sicut futura purgatio erit per ignem, ita praecedens fuit per aquam: et utraque ad invicem comparantur, II Petr., [5 sqq.]. Sed in prima purgatione fuit aqua eiusdem speciei cum aqua elementari. Ergo et similiter erit in secunda purgatione ignis eiusdem speciei cum igne elementari.

RESPONDEO dicendum quod circa hoc inveniuntur tres opiniones. Quidam enim dicunt quod elementum quod est in sphaera sua, descendet ad purgationem mundi. Modum autem descensionis ponunt per multiplicationem. Ignis enim, undique apposito combustibili, augmentatur. Et hoc praecipue tunc fiet, quando virtus ignis exaltabitur super omnia alia elementa.

Sed contra hoc esse videtur quod ignis ille non tantum descendet, sed etiam a Sanctis ascendere perhibetur: ut patet II Petr. 3, [10], ubi videtur quod *tantum ascendet iudicii ignis quantum aquae diluvii*; ex quo videtur quod ille ignis sit circa locum medium generationis.

Et propter hoc alii dicunt quod ignis ille generabitur circa locum terrae ex congregatione radiorum caelestium corporum: sicut videmus quod congregantur in speculo comburente. Tunc autem loco speculorum erunt nubes concavae, ad quas fiet radiorum reverberatio.

OBJECTION 1: It would seem that the fire in question is not of the same species as elemental fire. For nothing consumes itself. But *that fire will consume the four elements*, according to a Gloss on 2 Peter 3:12. Therefore, that fire will not be of the same species as elemental fire.

OBJ. 2: Further, as power is made known by operation, so is nature made known by power. Now that fire will have a different power from the fire which is an element: because it will cleanse the universe, whereas this fire cannot do that. Therefore, it will not be of the same species as this.

OBJ. 3: Further, in natural bodies those that are of the same species have the same movement. But that fire will have a different movement from the fire that is an element, because it will move in all directions so as to cleanse the whole. Therefore, it is not of the same species.

ON THE CONTRARY, Augustine says (*The City of God* 20.16), and his words are contained in a Gloss on 1 Corinthians 7:31, that *the fashion of this world will perish in the burning of worldly flames*. Therefore, that fire will be of the same nature as the fire which is now in the world.

FURTHER, Just as the future cleansing is to be by fire, so was the past cleansing by water: and they are both compared to one another in 2 Peter 3:5. Now, in the first cleansing the water was of the same species with elemental water. Therefore, in like manner the fire of the second cleansing will be of the same species with elemental fire.

I ANSWER THAT, We meet with three opinions on this question. For some say that the element of fire which is in its own sphere will come down to cleanse the world: and they explain this descent by way of multiplication, because the fire will spread through finding combustible matter on all sides. And this will result all the more then, since the virtue of the fire will be raised over all the elements.

Against this, however, would seem to be not only the fact that this fire will come down, but also the statement of the saints that it will rise up; thus 2 Peter 3:10 says that *the fire of the judgment will rise as high as the waters of the deluge*; whence it would seem to follow that this fire is situated towards the middle of the place of generation.

Hence others say that this fire will be generated towards the intervening space through the focusing together of the rays of the heavenly bodies, just as we see them focused together in a burning-glass; for at that time in lieu of glasses there will be concave clouds on which the rays will strike.

Sed hoc etiam non videtur conveniens. Quia, cum effectus corporum caelestium sequantur determinatos situs et aspectus eorum, si ex virtute corporum caelestium ignis ille generaretur, esset notum tempus illius purgationis considerantibus motus astrorum. Quod auctoritati Scripturae repugnat.

Et ideo alii dicunt, sequentes Augustinum, quod, *sicut mundanarum aquarum inundatione factum est diluvium, ita mundanorum ignium conflagratione figura huius mundi peribit*, ut dicitur XX *de Civ. Dei* 7. Ista autem conflagratio nihil aliud est quam congregatio omnium causarum inferiorum et superiorum quae ex natura sua habent virtutem igniendi; quae quidem congregatio non naturali cursu rerum, sed virtute divina fiet; et ex omnibus istis causis sic congregatis generabitur ignis qui faciem huius mundi exuret.

Si autem hae opiniones directe considerentur, inveniuntur diversificari quantum ad causam generationis illius ignis, et non quantum ad speciem eius. Ignis enim generatus a sole vel ab inferiori calefaciente, est eiusdem speciei cum igne qui est in sua sphaera, nisi inquantum admiscetur ei de materia aliena. Quod quidem tunc oportebit: quia ignis non potest aliquid purgare nisi secundum quod alterum efficitur materia eius aliquo modo. Unde simpliciter concedendum est quod ignis ille erit eiusdem speciei cum isto.

AD PRIMUM ergo dicendum quod ignis ille, quamvis sit eiusdem speciei cum igne qui apud nos est, non tamen est idem numero. Videmus autem quod duorum ignium eiusdem speciei unus alterum destruit, maior scilicet minorem, consumendo materiam eius. Et similiter etiam ille ignis ignem qui apud nos est, consumere poterit.

AD SECUNDUM dicendum quod, sicut operatio quae procedit a virtute est virtutis indicium, ita et virtus est indicium essentiae vel naturae quae procedit a principiis essentialibus rei. Operatio autem quae non procedit ex virtute rei operantis, non indicat virtutem ipsius: sicut patet in instrumentis. Actio enim instrumenti magis manifestat virtutem moventis quam virtutem instrumenti: quia virtutem agentis manifestat ut primum operationis principium; virtutem autem instrumenti non manifestat nisi quatenus est susceptivum influentiae principalis agentis secundum quod movetur ab eo. Similiter etiam virtus quae non procedit ex principiis essentialibus rei, non manifestat naturam eius nisi quantum ad susceptibilitatem: sicut virtus qua aqua calefacta potest calefacere, non manifestat naturam eius nisi quantum ad calefactibilitatem. Et ideo nihil prohibet quin aqua habens hanc virtutem sit eiusdem speciei cum aqua non habente virtutem istam. Similiter non est inconveniens, quod ignis ille, qui habebit vim purgandi faciem mundi, sit eiusdem speciei cum igne qui est apud nos: cum vis calefactiva non oriatur in ipso ex principiis essentialibus,

But this again does not seem probable: for since the effects of heavenly bodies depend on certain fixed positions and aspects, if this fire resulted from the virtue of the heavenly bodies, the time of this cleansing would be known to those who observe the movements of the stars, and this is contrary to the authority of Scripture.

Consequently others, following Augustine, say that *just as the deluge resulted from an outpouring of the waters of the world, so the fashion of this world will perish by a burning of worldly flames* (*The City of God* 20.16). This burning is nothing else but the assembly of all those lower and higher causes that by their nature have a kindling virtue: and this assembly will take place not in the ordinary course of things, but by the divine power: and from all these causes thus assembled the fire that will burn the surface of this world will result.

But if we consider aright these opinions, we shall find that they differ as to the cause producing this fire and not as to its species. For fire, whether produced by the sun or by some lower heating cause, is of the same species as fire in its own sphere, except insofar as the former has some admixture of foreign matter. And this will of necessity be the case then, since fire cannot cleanse a thing unless this become its matter in some way. Hence we must grant that the fire in question is simply of the same species as ours.

REPLY OBJ. 1: The fire in question, although of the same species as ours, is not the same in number. Now we see that of two fires of the same species, one destroys the other, namely, the greater destroys the lesser by consuming its matter. In like manner, that fire will be able to destroy our fire.

REPLY OBJ. 2: Just as an operation that proceeds from the virtue of a thing is an indication of that virtue, so is its virtue an indication of its essence or nature if it proceed from the essential principles of the thing. But an operation that does not proceed from the virtue of the operator does not indicate its virtue. This appears in instruments: for the action of an instrument shows forth the virtue of the mover rather than that of the instrument, since it shows forth the virtue of the agent insofar as the latter is the first principle of the action, whereas it does not show forth the virtue of the instrument except insofar as it is susceptive of the influence of the principal agent as moving that instrument. In like manner, a virtue that does not proceed from the essential principles of a thing does not indicate the nature of that thing except in the point of susceptibility. Thus the virtue whereby hot water can heat is no indication of the nature of water except in the point of its being receptive of heat. Consequently, nothing prevents water that has this virtue from being of the same species as water that has it not. In like manner, it is not unreasonable that this fire, which will have the power to cleanse the surface of the world, will be

sed ex divina operatione; sive dicatur quod illa virtus sit aliqua qualitas absoluta, sicut calor in aqua calefacta; sive sit intentio quaedam, sicut de instrumentalis virtute in prima distinctione dictum est. Et hoc probabilius est: quia ignis ille non aget nisi ut instrumentum divinae virtutis.

AD TERTIUM dicendum quod ignis ex propria natura non fertur nisi sursum: sed inquantum sequitur materiam quam requirit extra propriam sphaeram existens, sic sequitur materiae combustibilis situm. Et per modum istum non est inconveniens quod vel in circuitu vel in deorsum moveatur: et praecipue secundum quod agit ut instrumentum divinae virtutis.

of the same species as the fire to which we are used, since the heating power therein arises not from its essential principles but from the divine power or operation: whether we say that this power is an absolute quality, such as heat in hot water, or a kind of intention as we have ascribed to instrumental virtue. The latter is more probable since that fire will not act save as the instrument of the divine power.

REPLY OBJ. 3: Of its own nature fire tends only upwards; but in so far as it pursues its matter, which it requires when it is outside its own sphere, it follows the site of combustible matter. Accordingly, it is not unreasonable for it to take a circular or a downward course, especially insofar as it acts as the instrument of the divine power.

Article 4

Whether That Fire Will Cleanse Also the Higher Heavens?

AD QUARTUM SIC PROCEDITUR. Videtur quod ignis ille purgabit etiam caelos superiores. Quia in Psalmo [101, 26–27] dicitur: *opera manuum tuarum sunt caeli: ipsi peribunt, tu autem permanes.* Sed etiam superiores caeli sunt opera manuum Dei. Ergo et ipsi in finali mundi conflagratione peribunt.

PRAETEREA, II Petr. 3, [12] dicitur: *caeli ardentes solventur, et elementa ignis ardore tabescent.* Caeli autem qui ab elementis distinguuntur, sunt caeli superiores, quibus fixa sunt sidera. Ergo videtur etiam quod illi per ignem illum purgabuntur.

PRAETEREA, ignis ille ad hoc erit ut removeat a corporibus indispositionem ad perfectionem gloriae. Sed in caelo superiori invenitur indispositio et ex parte culpae, quia diabolus ibi peccavit; et ex parte naturalis defectus, quia Rom. 8, super illud [v. 22], *scimus quod omnis creatura ingemiscit et parturit usque adhuc,* dicit Glossa: *omnia elementa cum labore explent officia sua: sicut sol et luna non sine labore statuta implent sibi spatia.* Ergo etiam caeli purgabuntur per ignem illum.

SED CONTRA: Est quod *corpora caelestia peregrinae impressionis receptiva non sunt.*

PRAETEREA, super illud II Thessal. 1, [8], *in flamma ignis dantis vindictam,* dicit Glossa: *ignis erit in mundo, qui. praecedet eum, tantum spatium aeris occupans quantum occupavit aqua in diluvio.* Sed aqua diluvii non ascendit usque ad superiores caelos, sed solum *quindecim cubitis super altitudinem montium,* ut habetur Genes., [20]. Ergo caeli superiores illo igne non purgabuntur.

RESPONDEO dicendum quod purgatio mundi ad hoc erit ut removeatur a corporibus dispositio contraria per-

OBJECTION 1: It would seem that that fire will cleanse also the higher heavens. For it is written: *the heavens are the works of your hands: they shall perish but you remain* (Ps 101:26–27). Now the higher heavens also are the work of God's hands. Therefore, they also shall perish in the final burning of the world.

OBJ. 2: Further, it is written: *The heavens, being on fire, shall be dissolved, and the elements shall melt with the burning heat of fire* (2 Pet 3:12). Now the heavens that are distinct from the elements are the higher heavens, in which the stars are fixed. Therefore, it would seem that they also will be cleansed by that fire.

OBJ. 3: Further, the purpose of that fire will be to remove from bodies their indisposition to the perfection of glory. Now in the higher heaven we find this indisposition both as regards guilt, since the devil sinned there, and as regards natural deficiency, since a Gloss on Romans 8:22: *we know that every creature groans and is in labor even until now,* says, *all the elements fulfill their duty with labor: even as it is not without labor that the sun and moon travel their appointed course.* Therefore, the higher heavens also will be cleansed by that fire.

ON THE CONTRARY, *The heavenly bodies are not receptive of impressions from without.*

FURTHER, A Gloss on 2 Thessalonians 1:8: *in a flame of fire giving vengeance,* says, *there will be in the world a fire that shall precede him, and shall rise in the air to the same height as did the waters of the deluge.* But the waters of the deluge did not rise to the height of the higher heavens but only *15 cubits higher than the mountain summits* (Gen 7:20). Therefore, the higher heavens will not be cleansed by that fire.

I ANSWER THAT, The cleansing of the world will be for the purpose of removing from bodies the disposition con-

fectioni gloriae, quae quidem perfectio est ultima rerum consummatio. Et haec quidem dispositio in omnibus corporibus invenitur, sed diversimode in diversis. In quibusdam enim invenitur indispositio secundum aliquid inhaerens substantiae eorum: sicut in istis corporibus inferioribus, quae per mutuam mixtionem decidunt a propria puritate. In quibusdam vero corporibus invenitur indispositio non per aliquid substantiae eorum inhaerens: sicut in corporibus caelestibus, in quibus nihil invenitur repugnans ultimae perfectioni universi nisi motus, qui est via ad perfectionem; nec motus quilibet, sed locales tantum, qui non variat aliquid quod sit intrinsecum rei, ut substantiam aut quantitatem aut qualitatem sed solum locum, qui est extra rem. Et ideo a substantia caeli superioris non oportet quod aliquid removeatur, sed oportet quod motus eius quietetur. Quietatio autem motus localis non fit per actionem alicuius contrarii agentis, sed per hoc quod motor desistit a movendo. Et ideo caelestia corpora nec per ignem nec per alicuius creaturae actionem purgabuntur, sed ipsa eorum quietatio, sola voluntate divina accidens, eis loco purgationis erit.

AD PRIMUM ergo dicendum quod, sicut Augustinus dicit, XX *de Civ. Dei*, verba illa Psalmi sunt intelligenda de *caelis aereis*, qui purgabuntur per ignem ultimae conflagrationis.

Vel dicendum quod, si etiam de superioribus caelis intelligatur, tunc dicuntur perire quantum ad motum, quo nunc continue moventur.

AD SECUNDUM dicendum quod Petrus se exponit de quibus caelis intelligat. Praemiserat enim [v. 5 sqq.] ante verba inducta quod *caeli prius et terra per aquam perierant qui nunc sunt eodem verbo repositi, igni reservati in diem iudicii*. Ergo illi caeli per ignem purgabuntur qui prius per aquam diluvii sunt purgati, scilicet caeli aerei.

AD TERTIUM dicendum quod ille labor et illa servitus creaturae quae corporibus caelestibus secundum Ambrosium attribuitur, nihil est aliud quam vicissitudo motus, ratione cuius tempori subiiciuntur, et defectus ultimae consummationis, quae finaliter in eis erit. Ex culpa etiam daemonum caelum empyreum infectionem non contraxit; quia peccando statim de caelo expulsi sunt.

trary to the perfection of glory, and this perfection is the final consummation of the universe. This disposition is to be found in all bodies, but differently in different bodies. For in some this indisposition regards something inherent to their substance: as in these lower bodies which, by being mixed together, fall away from their own purity. In others this indisposition does not regard something inherent to their substance, as in the heavenly bodies, wherein nothing is to be found contrary to the final perfection of the universe except movement, which is the way to perfection, and this not any kind of movement, but only local movement, which changes nothing intrinsic to a thing, such as its substance, quantity, or quality, but only its place, which is extrinsic to it. Consequently, there is no need to take anything away from the substance of the higher heavens, but only to set its movement at rest. Now local movement is brought to rest not by the action of a counter agent, but by the mover ceasing to move; and therefore the heavenly bodies will not be cleansed, neither by fire nor by the action of any creature, but in lieu of being cleansed they will be set at rest by God's will alone.

REPLY OBJ. 1: As Augustine says (*The City of God* 20.18, 20.24): those words of the psalm refer to the *aerial heavens* which will be cleansed by the fire of the final conflagration.

Or we may reply that if they refer also to the higher heavens, these are said to perish as regards their movement whereby now they are moved without cessation.

REPLY OBJ. 2: Peter explains himself to which heavens he refers. For before the words quoted, he had said: *the heavens first, and the earth through water perished, which now by the same word are kept in store, reserved unto fire unto the day of judgment* (2 Pet 5:5–7). Therefore, the heavens to be cleansed are those which before were cleansed by the waters of the deluge, namely, the aerial heavens.

REPLY OBJ. 3: This labor and service of the creature that Ambrose ascribes to the heavenly bodies is nothing else than the successive movements whereby they are subject to time, and the lack of that final consummation which they will attain in the end. Nor did the empyrean heaven contract any stain from the sin of the demons, because they were expelled from that heaven as soon as they sinned.

Article 5

Whether That Fire Will Consume the Other Elements?

AD QUINTUM SIC PROCEDITUR. Videtur quod ignis ille alia elementa consumet. Quia, ut dicit Glossa Bedae, II Petr. [3, 10], *elementa quatuor, quibus mundus consistit, ille maximus ignis absumet. Nec cuncta in tantum consumet ut non sint: sed duo ex toto consumet, duo vero*

OBJECTION 1: It would seem that the fire in question will consume the other elements. For a Gloss of Bede on 2 Peter 3:12 says: *this exceeding great fire will engulf the four elements whereof the world consists: yet it will not so engulf all things that they will cease to be, but it will consume two of*

in meliorem restituet faciem. Ergo videtur quod ad minus duo elementa per ignem illum destruenda sint totaliter.

PRAETEREA, Apoc. 21, [1]: *primum caelum et prima terra abiit, et mare iani non est.* Sed per caelum aer intelligitur, ut Augustinus dicit. Mare autem est *aquarum congregatio.* Ergo videtur quod illa tria elementa totaliter destruentur.

PRAETEREA, ignis non purgat nisi secundum hoc quod alia efficiuntur materia eius. Si ergo ignis purgat alia elementa, oportet quod eius materia efficiantur. Ergo oportet quod in naturam ignis transeant. Et sic a natura sua corrumpentur.

PRAETEREA, forma ignis est nobilissima formarum ad quam perduci possit elementaris materia. Sed per illam purgationem omnia in nobilissimum statum mutabuntur. Ergo alia elementa in ignem totaliter convertentur.

SED CONTRA: Est quod dicitur I Cor. 7, super illud [v. 31], *praeterit figura huius mundi: pulchritudo, non substantia praeterit.* Sed ipsa substantia elementorum pertinet ad perfectionem mundi. Ergo elementa non consumentur secundum suam substantiam.

PRAETEREA, illa finalis purgatio, quae fiet per ignem, respondebit primae purgationi, quae facta est per aquam. Sed illa non corrupit elementorum substantiam. Ergo nec illa quae fiet per ignem corrumpet.

RESPONDEO dicendum quod circa hanc quaestionem est multiplex opinio. Quidam enim dicunt quod omnia elementa manebunt quantum ad materiam, omnia autem mutabuntur quantum ad imperfectionem; sed duo eorum retinebunt propriam formam substantialem, scilicet aer et terra; in duobus vero, scilicet in igne et aqua, nori remanebit forma substantialis eorum, sed mutabuntur ad formam caeli; et sic tria elementa, scilicet ignis, aer et aqua, caelum dicentur; quamvis aer retineat formam substantialem eandem quam nunc habet, quia nunc etiam caelum dicitur. Unde etiam Apoc. 21, [1] non fit mentio nisi de caelo et terra: *vidi*, inquit, *caelum novum et terram novam.*

Sed haec opinio est omnino absurda. Repugnat enim et philosophiae, secundum quam poni non potest quod corpora inferiora sint in potentia ad formam caeli, cum nec materiam habeant communem, nec contrarietatem ad invicem; et etiam theologiae, quia secundum hanc propositionem non salvabitur perfectio universi cum integritate suarum partium, duobus elementis sublatis. Unde per hoc quod dicit *caelum*, intelligitur quintum corpus; omnia vero elementa intelliguntur per terram, sicut in Psalmo [148, 7–8]: *laudate Dominum de terra, et sequitur, ignis, grando, nix, glacies,* etc.

them entirely, and will restore two of them to a better fashion. Therefore, it would seem that at least two of the elements are to be entirely destroyed by that fire.

OBJ. 2: Further, it is written: *the first heaven and the first earth have passed away and the sea is no more* (Rev 21:1). Now the heaven here denotes the air, as Augustine states (*The City of God* 20.18); and the sea denotes the *gathering together of the waters.* Therefore, it would seem that these three elements will be wholly destroyed.

OBJ. 3: Further, fire does not cleanse except insofar as other things are made to be its matter. If, then, fire cleanses the other elements, they must become its matter. Therefore, they must pass into its nature, and consequently be voided of their own nature.

OBJ. 4: Further, the form of fire is the most noble of the forms to which elemental matter can attain. Now all things will be brought to the most noble state by this cleansing. Therefore, the other elements will be wholly transformed into fire.

ON THE CONTRARY, A Gloss on 1 Corinthians 7:31: *the fashion of this world passes away*, says, *the beauty, not the substance, passes.* But the very substance of the elements belongs to the perfection of the world. Therefore, the elements will not be consumed as to their substance.

FURTHER, This final cleansing that will be effected by fire will correspond to the first cleansing, which was effected by water. Now the latter did not corrupt the substance of the elements. Therefore, neither will the former which will be the work of fire.

I ANSWER THAT, There are many opinions on this question. For some say that all the elements will remain as to their matter, while all will be changed as regards their imperfection; but that two of them will retain their respective substantial form, namely, air and earth, while two of them, namely, fire and water, will not retain their substantial form but will be changed to the form of heaven. In this way three elements, namely, air, fire, and water, will be called 'heaven'; although air will retain the same substantial form as it has now, since even now it is called 'heaven'. Wherefore only heaven and earth are mentioned: *I saw*, says he, *a new heaven and a new earth* (Rev 21:1).

But this opinion is altogether absurd: for it is opposed both to philosophy—which holds it impossible for the lower bodies to be in potentiality to the form of heaven, since they have neither a common matter, nor mutual contrariety—and to theology, since according to this opinion the perfection of the universe with the integrity of its parts will not be assured on account of two of the elements being destroyed. Consequently, 'heaven' is taken to denote the fifth body, while all the elements are designated by earth, as expressed in Psalm 148:7–8, *praise the Lord from the earth* and afterwards, *fire, hail, snow, ice.*

Et ideo alii dicunt quod omnia elementa manebunt secundum substantiam, sed qualitates activae et passivae ab eis removebuntur. Sicut etiam ponunt quod in corpore mixto elementa salvantur secundum suas formas substantiales sine hoc quod proprias qualitates habeant: cum sint in medium reductae, et medium neutrum extremorum est. Et huic etiam videtur consonare quod, Augustinus dicit, XX *de Civ. Dei* 4: *Illa conflagratione mundana elementorum corruptibilium qualitates quae corporibus nostris congruebant, ardendo penitus interibunt, atque ipsa substantia eas qualitates habebit quae corporibus immortalibus mirabili mutatione conveniant.*

Sed illud non videtur probabile, cum qualitates propriae elementorum sint effectus formarum substantialium, quod, formis substantialibus manentibus, qualitates praedictae possunt mutari, nisi per actionem violentam ad tempus: sicut in aqua calefacta videmus quod ex vi suae speciei frigiditatem recuperat, quam per actionem ignis amisit, dummodo species aquae remaneat. Et praeterea ipsae qualitates elementares sunt de perfectione secunda elementorum, sicut propriae passiones eorum: nec est probabile quod in illa finali consummatione aliquid perfectionis naturalis ab elementis tollatur.

Et ideo videtur dicendum quod manebunt elementa quantum ad substantiam et qualitates eorum proprias, sed purgabuntur ab infectione quam ex peccatis hominum contraxerunt, et ab impuritate quae per actionem et passionem mutuam in eis accidit: quia iam, cessante motu primi mobilis, in inferioribus elementis mutua actio et passio esse non poterit. Et hoc Augustinus appellat *qualitates corruptibilium elementorum*, scilicet innaturales dispositiones eorum, secundum quas corruptioni appropinquant.

Ad primum ergo dicendum quod ignis ille dicitur quatuor elementa absumere, inquantum ea aliquo modo purgabit. Quod autem sequitur, *duo ex toto consumet*, non est intelligendum quod duo elementa secundum substantiam destruantur: sed quia duo magis removebuntur a proprietate quam nunc habent. Quae quidem duo a quibusdam dicuntur esse ignis et aqua, quae maxime excedunt in qualitatibus activis, scilicet calore et frigore, quae sunt maxime corruptionis principia in aliis corporibus. Et quia tunc non erit actio ignis et aquae, quae sunt maxime activa, maxime immutari videbuntur a virtute quam nunc habent. Alii vero dicunt haec duo esse aerem et aquam, propter varios motus istorum duorum elementorum, quos consequuntur ex motu corporum caelestium. Et quia isti motus non erunt, sicut fluxus et refluxus maris et commotiones ventorum et hu-

Hence others say that all the elements will remain as to their substance, but that their active and passive qualities will be taken from them: even as they say too that in a mixed body the elements retain their substantial form without having their proper qualities, since these are reduced to a mean, and a mean is neither of the extremes. And seemingly the following words of Augustine (*The City of God* xx, 16) would seem in agreement with this: *in this conflagration of the world the qualities of the corruptible elements that were befitting our corruptible bodies will entirely perish by fire: and the substance itself will have those qualities that become an immortal body.*

However, this does not seem probable, for since the proper qualities of the elements are the effects of their substantial form, it seems impossible, as long as the substantial forms remain, for the aforesaid qualities to be changed, except for a time by some violent action: thus in hot water we see that by virtue of its species it returns to the cold temperature which it had lost by the action of fire, provided the species of water remain. Moreover, these same elemental qualities belong to the second perfection of the elements as being their proper passions: nor is it probable that in this final consummation the elements will lose anything of their natural perfection.

Wherefore it would seem that the reply to this question should be that the elements will remain as to their substance and proper qualities, but that they will be cleansed both from the stain which they contracted from the sins of men, and from the impurity resulting in them through their mutual action and passion: because when once the movement of the first movable body ceases, mutual action and passion will be impossible in the lower elements: and this is what Augustine calls the *qualities of corruptible elements*, namely, their unnatural dispositions by reason of which they come near to corruption.

Reply Obj. 1: That fire is said to engulf the four elements insofar as in some way it will cleanse them. But when it is said further that *it will consume two entirely*, this does not mean that two of the elements are to be destroyed as to their substance, but that two will be more changed from the property which they have now. Some say that these two are fire and water, which excel the others in their active qualities, namely, heat and cold, which are the chief principles of corruption in other bodies; and since then there will be no action of fire and water which surpass the others in activity, they would seem especially to be changed from the virtue which they have now. Others, however, say that these two are air and water, on account of the various movements of these two elements, which movements they derive from the movement of the heavenly bodies. And since these movements will cease (such as the ebb and flow of the sea, and

iusmodi, ideo ista elementa maxime mutabuntur a proprietate quam nunc habent.

AD SECUNDUM dicendum quod, sicut dicit Augustinus XX *de Civ. Dei*, cum dicitur, *et mare iam non est*, per mare potest intelligi praesens saeculum, de quo supra parum ante dixerat, *mare dedit mortuos suos*. Si tamen ad mare ad litteram referamus, tunc est dicendum quod in mari duo intelliguntur: scilicet substantia aquarum; et earum dispositio quantum ad salsedinem et commotiones fluctuum. Et quantum ad hoc secundum mare non remanebit, remanebit autem quantum ad primum.

AD TERTIUM dicendum quod ignis ille non aget nisi ut instrumentum providentiae et virtutis divinae. Unde non aget in alia elementa usque ad eorum consumptionem, sed solum usque ad purgationem. Nec oportet quod illud quod efficitur materia ignis, totaliter a specie propria corrumpatur: sicut patet in ferro ignito, quod, a loco ignitionis remotum, ex virtute speciei remanentis ad proprium statum et pristinum redit. Et ita etiam erit de elementis per ignem purgatis.

AD QUARTUM dicendum quod in partibus elementorum non oportet considerari solum quid congruat alicui parti secundum se acceptae: sed etiam quid congruat secundum ordinem ad totum. Dico ergo quod, quamvis aqua esset nobilior, si haberet formam ignis, similiter terra et aer, universum tamen esset imperfectius si tota elementorum materia formam ignis assumeret.

the disturbances of winds and so forth), therefore these elements especially will be changed from the property which they have now.

REPLY OBJ. 2: As Augustine says (*The City of God* 20.16), when it is stated, *and the sea is no more* (Rev 21:1), by the sea we may understand the present world of which he had said previously (*The City of God* 20.13): *the sea gave up its dead*. If, however, the sea be taken literally we must reply that by the sea two things are to be understood, namely, the substance of the waters, and their disposition, as containing salt and as to the movement of the waves. The sea will remain not as to this second, but as to the first.

REPLY OBJ. 3: This fire will not act save as the instrument of God's providence and power; wherefore it will not act on the other elements so as to consume them but only so as to cleanse them. Nor is it necessary for that which becomes the matter of fire to be voided of its proper species entirely, as is clear from red-hot iron, which by virtue of its remaining species returns to its proper and former state as soon as it is taken from the furnace. It will be the same with the elements after they are cleansed by fire.

REPLY OBJ. 4: In the elemental parts we must consider not only what is befitting a part considered in itself, but also what is befitting it in its relation to the whole. I say, then, that although water would be more noble if it had the form of fire, as likewise would earth and air, yet the universe would be more imperfect, if all elemental matter were to assume the form of fire.

Article 6

Whether All the Elements Will Be Cleansed by That Fire?

AD SEXTUM SIC PROCEDITUR. Videtur quod nec omnia elementa per illum ignem purgabuntur. Quia ignis ille, ut iam dictum est, non ascendet nisi quantum ascendit aqua diluvii. Sed aqua diluvii non pervenit usque ad sphaeram ignis. Ergo nec per ultimam purgationem elementum ignis purgabitur.

PRAETEREA, Apoc. 21, dicit Glossa, super illud [v. 1], *vidi caelum novum*, etc.: *immutatio aeris et terrae dubitabile non est quin per ignem fiet. Sed de aqua dubitatur: nam purgationem in seipsa habere creditur*. Ergo ad minus non est certum quod omnia elementa purgentur.

PRAETEREA, locus qui est perpetuae infectionis, nunquam purgatur. Sed in inferno erit perpetua infectio. Cum ergo infernus inter elementa collocetur, videtur quod elementa non totaliter purgentur.

PRAETEREA, paradisus terrestris in terra continetur. Sed ille non purgabitur per ignem: quia etiam nec aquae diluvii illuc ascenderunt, ut Beda dicit, et habetur in Se-

OBJECTION 1: It would seem that neither will all the elements be cleansed by that fire. Because that fire, as stated already (A. 3), will not rise higher than the waters of the deluge. But the waters of the deluge did not reach to the sphere of fire. Therefore, neither will the element of fire be cleansed by the final cleansing.

OBJ. 2: Further, a Gloss on Revelation 21:1: *I saw a new heaven*, says, *there can be no doubt that the transformation of the air and earth will be caused by fire; but it is doubtful about water, since it is believed to have the power of cleansing itself*. Therefore, at least it is uncertain that all the elements will be cleansed.

OBJ. 3: Further, a place where there is an everlasting stain is never cleansed. Now there will always be a stain in hell. Since, then, hell is situated among the elements, it would seem that the elements will not be wholly cleansed.

OBJ. 4: Further, the earthly paradise is situated on the earth. Yet it will not be cleansed by fire, since not even the waters of the deluge reached it, like Bede says as quoted in

cundo *Sententiarum*. Ergo videtur quod non omnia elementa totaliter purgentur.

Sed contra est Glossa supra inducta, quae habetur II Petr. [3, 10], quod *quatuor elementa ignis ille absumet*.

Respondeo dicendum quod quidam dicunt quod ille ignis ascendet usque ad summitatem spatii continentis quatuor elementa, ut sic elementa totaliter purgentur et ab infectione peccati, quo etiam superiores partes elementorum sunt infectae, ut patet per fumum idololatriae superiora inficientis; et etiam a corruptione, quia elementa secundum omnes partes sui corruptibilia sunt.

Sed haec opinio repugnat auctoritati Scripturae: quia II Petr. 3, [5 sqq.] dicitur quod illi *caeli repositi sunt igni* qui fuerunt per aquam purgati. Et Augustinus dicit, XX *de Civ. Dei*, quod *ille mundus qui diluvio periit, igni reservatur*. Constat autem quod aqua diluvii non ascendit usque ad summitatem spatii elementorum, sed solum usque ad *quindecim cubitos super altitudinem montium*.

Et praeterea notum est quod vapores elevati, vel fumi quicumque, non possunt transire per totam sphaeram ignis, ut perveniant ad summitatem eius. Et ita infectio peccati non venit usque ad spatium praedictum.

A corruptibilitate etiam elementa non possunt purgari per subtractionem alicuius quod per ignem possit consumi: sed per ignem poterunt consumi impuritates elementorum, quae ex eorum permixtione proveniunt. Huiusmodi autem impuritates praecipue sunt circa terram usque ad medium aeris interstitium. Unde usque ad illud spatium ignis ultimae conflagrationis elementa purgabit. Tantum enim etiam aquae diluvii ascenderunt: quod probabiliter aestimari potest ex montium altitudine, quos determinata mensura transcenderant.

Primum ergo concedimus.

Ad secundum dicendum quod ratio dubitationis in Glossa exprimitur: quia scilicet *aqua virtutem purgationis in se habere creditur*. Non tamen habet vim purgationis talis qualis futuro statui competit, ut ex dictis patet.

Ad tertium dicendum quod illa purgatio praecipue ad hoc erit ut quidquid est imperfectionis a sanctorum habitatione removeatur. Et ideo in illa purgatione totum quod est foedum ad locum damnatorum congregabitur. Unde infernus non purgabitur: sed ad ipsum deducentur totius mundi purgamenta.

Ad quartum dicendum quod, quamvis peccatum primi hominis in terrestri paradiso sit commissum, non tamen locus ille est locus peccantium, sicut nec caelum empyreum: ex utroque enim loco homo et diabolus statim post peccatum sunt eiecti. Unde locus ille purgatione non indiget.

Sentences II, D. 7 (*Hexaemeron*). Therefore, it would seem that the elements will not all be wholly cleansed.

On the contrary, The Gloss quoted above (A. 5, Obj. 1) on 2 Peter 3:12 declares that *this fire will engulf the four elements.*

I answer that, Some say that the fire in question will rise to the summit of the space containing the four elements: so that the elements would be entirely cleansed both from the stain of sin by which also the higher parts of the elements were infected (as instanced by the smoke of idolatry which stained the higher regions), and again from corruption, since the elements are corruptible in all their parts.

But this opinion is opposed to the authority of Scripture, because it is written that those heavens are *kept in store unto fire* (2 Pet 3:7), which were cleansed by water; and Augustine says (*The City of God* 20.18) that *the same world which perished in the deluge is reserved unto fire*. Now it is clear that the waters of the deluge did not rise to the summit of the space occupied by the elements, but only *fifteen cubits above the mountain tops*.

Moreover, it is known that vapors or any smoke whatever rising from the earth cannot pierce the entire sphere of fire so as to reach its summit; and so the stain of sin did not reach the aforesaid space.

Nor can the elements be cleansed from corruptibility by the removal of something that might be consumed by fire: whereas it will be possible for the impurities of the elements arising from their mingling together to be consumed by fire. And these impurities are chiefly round about the earth as far as the middle of the air: wherefore the fire of the final conflagration will cleanse up to that point, since the waters of the deluge rose to a height which can be approximately calculated from the height of the mountains which they surpassed in a fixed measure.

We therefore grant the first objection.

Reply Obj. 2: The reason for doubt is expressed in the Gloss; namely, because *water is believed to have in itself the power of cleansing*, yet not such a power as will be competent to the future state, as stated above (A. 5; A. 2).

Reply Obj. 3: The purpose of this cleansing will be chiefly to remove all imperfection from the abode of the saints, and consequently in this cleansing all that is foul will be brought together to the place of the damned: so hell will not be cleansed, but all that is purged from the earth will be brought there.

Reply Obj. 4: Although the sin of the first man was committed in the earthly paradise, this is not the place of sinners, as neither is the empyrean heaven: since from both places man and devil were expelled forthwith after their sin. Consequently, that place needs no cleansing.

Article 7

Whether the Fire of the Final Conflagration Is to Follow the Judgment?

AD SEPTIMUM SIC PROCEDITUR. Videtur quod ignis ultimae conflagrationis iudicium debet sequi. Augustinus enim, XX *de Civ. Dei*, hunc ordinem ponit eorum quae in iudicio sunt futura, dicens: *in illo iudicio, vel circa illud iudicium, has res didicimus esse venturas: Eliam Thesbiten, Iudaeorum fidem, Antichristum persecuturum, Christum iudicaturum, mortuorum resurrectionem, bonorum malorumque divisionem, mundi conflagrationem, eiusdemque renovationem.* Ergo conflagratio iudicium sequetur.

PRAETEREA, Augustinus dicit, in eodem libro: *iudicatis impiis et in ignem aeternum missis, figura huius mundi mundanorum ignium conflagratione peribit.* Ergo idem quod prius.

PRAETEREA, Dominus ad iudicandum veniens aliquos vivos reperiet: ut patet ex hoc quod habetur I Thessal. 4, [14 sqq.], ubi ex persona eorum Apostolus dicit: *deinde nos qui vivimus, qui residui sumus in adventu Domini,* etc. Sed hoc non esset si conflagratio mundi praecederet: quia per ignem resolverentur. Ergo ignis ille iudicium sequetur.

PRAETEREA, Dominus dicitur iudicaturus orbem per ignem. Et ideo conflagratio finalis videtur esse executio divini iudicii. Sed executio sequitur iudicium. Ergo ille ignis iudicium sequetur.

SED CONTRA: Est quod dicitur in Psalmo [96, 3]: *ignis ante ipsum praecedet.*

PRAETEREA, resurrectio praecedet iudicium: alias non *videret omnis oculus* Christum iudicantem. Sed mundi conflagratio resurrectionem praecedet. Sancti enim qui resurgent, corpora spiritualia et impassibilia habebunt, et ita non poterunt purgari per ignem: cum tamen in littera dicatur, ex verbis Augustini, quod *per illum ignem purgabitur si quid in aliquibus sit purgandum.* Ergo ille ignis iudicium praecedet.

RESPONDEO dicendum quod illa conflagratio, secundum rei veritatem, quantum ad sui initium iudicium praecedet. Quod ex hinc manifeste colligitur quod mortuorum resurrectio iudicium praecedet. Quod patet ex hoc quod dicitur I Thessal. 4, [14, 16], quod illi etiam qui dormierunt, *rapientur in nubibus in aera obviam Christo ad iudicium venienti.* Simul autem erit resurrectio communis, et corporum sanctorum glorificatio sancti enim resurgentes corpora gloriosa resument, ut patet per illud quod dicitur I Cor. 15, [43], *seminatur in ignobilitate, surget in gloria.* Simul autem cum corpora sanctorum glorificabuntur, etiam tota creatura suo modo renovabitur: ut patet per illud quod dicitur Rom. 8, [21], quod *ipsa*

OBJECTION 1: It would seem that the fire of the final conflagration is to follow the judgment. For Augustine (*The City of God* 20.30) gives the following order of the things to take place at the judgment, saying: *at this judgment we have learned that the following things will occur. Elijah the Thesbite will appear, the Jews will believe, Antichrist will persecute, Christ will judge, the dead will rise again, the good will be separated from the wicked, the world will be set on fire and will be renewed.* Therefore, the burning will follow the judgment.

OBJ. 2: Further, Augustine says (*The City of God*, 20.16): *after the wicked have been judged, and cast into everlasting fire, the figure of this world will perish in the furnace of worldly flames.* Therefore, the same conclusion follows.

OBJ. 3: Further, when the Lord comes to judgment he will find some men living, as appears from the words of 1 Thessalonians 4:16, where the Apostle, speaking in their person, says: *then we who are alive, who remain unto the coming of the Lord.* But it would not be so if the burning of the world were to come first, since they would be destroyed by the fire. Therefore, this fire will follow the judgment.

OBJ. 4: Further, it is said that our Lord will come to judge the earth by fire, and consequently the final conflagration would seem to be the execution of the sentence of divine judgment. Now execution follows judgment. Therefore, that fire will follow the judgment.

ON THE CONTRARY, Psalm 96:3 says: *a fire shall go before him.*

FURTHER, The resurrection will precede the judgment, else every eye would not see Christ judging. Now the burning of the world will precede the resurrection, for the saints who will rise again will have spiritual and impassible bodies, so that it will be impossible for the fire to cleanse them, and yet the text (*Sentences* IV, D. 47) quotes Augustine as saying that *whatever needs cleansing in any way shall be cleansed by that fire* (*The City of God* 20.18). Therefore, that fire will precede the judgment.

I ANSWER THAT, The fire in question will in reality precede the judgment as regards its beginning. This can clearly be gathered from the fact that the resurrection of the dead will precede the judgment, since, according to 1 Thessalonians 4:13–16, those who have slept *shall be taken up in the clouds, into the air, to meet Christ coming to judgment.* Now the general resurrection and the glorification of the bodies of the saints will happen at the same time; for the saints in rising again will assume a glorified body, as evidenced by 1 Corinthians 15:43, *it is sown in dishonor, it shall rise in glory*: and at the same time as the saints' bodies shall be glorified, all creatures shall be renewed, each in its own way, as appears from the statement that *the creature itself shall*

creatura liberabitur a servitute corruptionis in libertatem gloriae filiorum Dei. Cum ergo conflagratio mundi sit dispositio ad renovationem praedictam, ut ex dictis patet, manifeste potest colligi quod illa conflagratio quoad purgationem mundi iudicium praecedet. Sed quoad aliquem actum, qui scilicet est involvere malos, iudicium sequetur.

AD PRIMUM ergo dicendum quod Augustinus non loquitur determinando, sed opinando. Quod patet ex hoc quod sequitur: *quae omnia quidem ventura esse credendum est: sed quibus modis et quo ordine veniant, magis tunc docebit rerum experientia quam nunc ad perfectum hominis intelligentia valeat consequi. Aestimo tamen eo quo a me commemorata sunt ordine esse ventura.* Ergo patet quod haec dixit opinando.

ET SIMILITER dicendum est ad secundum.

AD TERTIUM dicendum quod omnes homines morientur et resurgent. Sed tamen illi dicuntur vivi reperiri qui usque ad tempus conflagrationis vivent in corpore.

AD QUARTUM dicendum quod ille ignis non consequitur sententiam iudicis nisi quoad involutionem malorum. Et quantum ad hoc sequetur iudicium.

be delivered from the servitude of corruption into the liberty of the glory of the children of God (Rom 8:21). Since, then, the burning of the world is a disposition to the aforesaid renewal, as stated above (A. 1, 4); it can clearly be gathered that this burning, so far as it shall cleanse the world, will precede the judgment, but as regards a certain action thereof whereby it will engulf the wicked, it will follow the judgment.

REPLY OBJ. 1: Augustine is speaking not as one who decides the point, but as expressing an opinion. This is clear from his continuing thus: *that all these things are to happen is a matter of faith, but how and in what order we shall learn more then by experience of the things themselves than now by seeking a definite conclusion by arguing about them. I think, however, they will occur in the order I have given.* Hence it is clear that he is speaking as offering his opinion.

THE SAME ANSWER applies to the second objection.

REPLY OBJ. 3: All men shall die and rise again: yet those are said to be found alive who will live in the body until the time of the conflagration.

REPLY OBJ. 4: That fire will not carry out the sentence of the judge except as regards the engulfing of the wicked: in this respect it will follow the judgment.

Article 8

Whether That Fire Will Have Such an Effect on Men as Is Described?

AD OCTAVUM SIC PROCEDITUR. Videtur quod ille ignis non habebit talem effectum in hominibus qualis designatur. Illud enim *consumi* dicitur quod reducitur in nihilum. Sed corpora impiorum non resolventur in nihilum, sed in aeternum conservabuntur, ut aeternam poenam sustineant. Ergo ignis non erit *malis consumptio*, ut in littera dicitur.

SI DICATUR QUOD consumet malorum corpora inquantum ea resolvet in cinerem: contra. Sicut corpora malorum, ita et bonorum in cinerem resolventur: hoc enim est Christi privilegium, ut *caro eius non videat corruptionem.* Ergo etiam bonis tunc repertis erit consumptio.

PRAETEREA, infectio peccati magis abundat in elementis secundum quod veniunt ad compositionem humani corporis, in quo est corruptio fomitis etiam quantum ad bonos, quam in elementis extra corpus humanum existentibus. Sed elementa extra corpus humanum existentia purgabuntur propter peccati infectionem. Ergo multo fortius oportet per ignem purgari elementa in corporibus humanis existentia sive bonorum sive malorum. Et ita oportet utrorumque corpora resolvi.

OBJECTION 1: It would seem that this fire will not have such an effect on men as is described in the text (*Sentences* IV, D. 47). For a thing is said to be *consumed* when it is reduced to naught. Now the bodies of the wicked will not be reduced to naught, but will be kept for eternity, that they may bear an eternal punishment. Therefore, this fire will not *consume the wicked*, as stated in the text.

OBJ. 2: Further, if it be said that it will consume the bodies of the wicked by reducing them to ashes; on the contrary. As the bodies of the wicked, so will those of the good be brought to ashes: for it is the privilege of Christ alone that *his flesh see not corruption.* Therefore, it will consume also the good who will then be found.

OBJ. 3: Further, the stain of sin is more abundant in the elements as combining together to the formation of the human body, wherein is the corruption of the *fomes* even in the good, than in the elements existing outside the human body. Now the elements existing outside the human body will be cleansed on account of the stain of sin. Much more, therefore, will the elements in the human body, whether of the good or of the wicked, need to be cleansed, and consequently the bodies of both will need to be destroyed.

PRAETEREA, quandiu status viae durat, elementa similiter agent in bonos et in malos. Sed adhuc durabit status huius viae in illa conflagratione: quia post statum huius viae non erit mors naturalis, quae tamen per illam conflagrationem causabitur. Ergo ille ignis aequaliter aget in bonos et malos. Et ita videtur quod non sit aliqua discretio inter eos quantum ad effectum illius ignis suscipiendum, sicut in littera ponitur.

PRAETEREA, illa conflagratio quasi in momento perficitur. Sed multi invenientur vivi, in quibus erunt multa purgabilia. Ergo illa conflagratio non sufficiet ad eorum purgationem.

RESPONDEO dicendum quod ignis ille finalis conflagrationis, quantum ad hoc quod iudicium praecedet, aget ut instrumentum divinae iustitiae, et iterum per virtutem naturalem ignis. Quantum ergo pertinet ad virtutem naturalem ipsius, similiter aget in bonos et malos qui vivi reperientur, utrorumque corpora in cinerem resolvendo. Inquantum vero aget ut instrumentum divinae iustitiae, diversimode aget in diversos quantum ad sensum poenae. Mali enim per actionem ignis cruciabuntur. Boni vero in quibus nihil purgandum invenietur, omnino nullum dolorem ex igne sentient, sicut nec pueri senserunt in camino, Dan. 3, [50]: quamvis eorum corpora non serventur integra, sicut puerorum servata fuerunt [vv. 92, 94]. Et hoc divina virtute fieri poterit, ut sine doloris cruciatu resolutionem corporum patiantur. Boni vero in quibus aliquid purgandum reperietur, sentient cruciatum doloris ex illo igne plus vel minus pro meritorum diversitate.

Sed quantum ad actum quem post iudicium ille ignis habebit, in damnatos tantum aget: quia omnes boni habebunt corpora impassibilia.

AD PRIMUM ergo dicendum quod *consumptio* ibi accipitur non pro annihilatione, sed pro resolutione in cinerem.

AD SECUNDUM dicendum quod bonorum corpora, quamvis in cinerem resolventur per ignem, non tamen ex hoc dolorem sentient, sicut nec pueri in fornace existentes. Et quantum ad hoc est dissimile de bonis et malis.

AD TERTIUM dicendum quod elementa in corporibus humanis existentia purgabuntur per ignem etiam in corporibus electorum: sed hoc per divinam virtutem fiet sine cruciatu doloris.

AD QUARTUM dicendum quod ignis ille non aget tantum secundum naturalem elementorum virtutem, sed etiam ut divinae iustitiae instrumentum.

AD QUINTUM dicendum quod tres sunt causae quare subito illi qui vivi reperientur purgari poterunt. Una est quia in eis pauca purganda inveniuntur: cum terroribus et persecutionibus praecedentibus fuerint purgati. Secunda causa est quia, et vivi et voluntarii poenam sustinebunt. Poena autem in hac vita voluntarie suscep-

OBJ. 4: Further, as long as the state of the way lasts, the elements act in like manner on the good and the wicked. Now the state of the way will still endure in that conflagration, since after this state of the way death will not be natural, and yet it will be caused by that fire. Therefore, that fire will act equally on good and wicked; and consequently it does not seem that any distinction is made between them as to their being affected by that fire, as stated in the text.

OBJ. 5: Further, this fire will have done its work in a moment, as it were. Yet there will be many among the living in whom there will be many things to be cleansed. Therefore, that fire will not suffice for their cleansing.

I ANSWER THAT, This fire of the final conflagration, insofar as it will precede the judgment, will act as the instrument of divine justice as well as by the natural virtue of fire. Accordingly, as regards its natural virtue, it will act in like manner on the wicked and good who will be alive, by reducing the bodies of both to ashes. But insofar as it acts as the instrument of divine justice, it will act differently on different people as regards the sense of pain. For the wicked will be tortured by the action of the fire; whereas the good in whom there will be nothing to cleanse will feel no pain at all from the fire, as neither did the boys in the fiery furnace (Dan 3); although their bodies will not be kept whole as were the bodies of the boys: and it will be possible by God's power for their bodies to be destroyed without their suffering pain. But the good in whom matter for cleansing will be found will suffer pain from that fire more or less according to their different merits.

On the other hand, as regards the action which this fire will have after the judgment, it will act on the damned alone, since the good will all have impassible bodies.

REPLY OBJ. 1: *Consumption* there signifies being brought, not to nothing, but to ashes.

REPLY OBJ. 2: Although the bodies of the good will be reduced to ashes by the fire, they will not suffer pain thereby, as neither did the boys in the Babylonian furnace. In this respect a distinction is drawn between the good and the wicked.

REPLY OBJ. 3: The elements that are in human bodies, even in the bodies of the elect, will be cleansed by fire. But this will be done by God's power, without their suffering pain.

REPLY OBJ. 4: This fire will act not only according to the natural power of the element, but also as the instrument of divine justice.

REPLY OBJ. 5: There are three reasons why those who will be found living will be able to be cleansed suddenly. One is because there will be few things in them to be cleansed, since they will be already cleansed by the previous fears and persecutions. The second is because they will suffer pain both while living and of their own will: and pain

ta multo plus purgat quam poena post mortem inflicta: sicut patet in martyribus quod, *si quid purgandum in eis invenitur, passionis falce tollitur*, ut Augustinus dicit; cum tamen poena martyrii brevis fuit in comparatione ad poenam quae in purgatorio sustinetur. Tertia est quia calor ille recuperabit in intensione quantum amittet in temporis abbreviatione.

suffered in this life voluntarily cleanses much more than pain inflicted after death, as in the case of the martyrs, because *if anything needing to be cleansed be found in them, it is cut off by the sickle of suffering*, as Augustine says (*De Unic. Bap.* xiii), although the pain of martyrdom is of short duration in comparison with the pain endured in purgatory. The third is because the heat will gain in intensity what it loses in shortness of time.

Article 9

Whether That Fire Will Engulf the Wicked?

AD NONUM SIC PROCEDITUR. Videtur quod ille ignis non involvet reprobos. Quia Malach. 3, super illud [v. 3], *purgabit filios Levi*, dicit Glossa: *duos ignes legimus futuros: urium quo purgabit electos; et praecedet iudicium; alterum qui reprobos cruciabit*. Sed hic est ignis inferni, qui malos involvet: primus autem est ignis finalis conflagrationis. Ergo ille ignis conflagrationis non erit ille qui malos involvet.

PRAETEREA, ille ignis Deo obsequitur in purgatione mundi. Ergo remunerari deberet, aliis elementis remuneratis: et praecipue cum ignis sit nobilissimum elementorum. Non ergo videtur quod in infernum debeat deiici ad poenam damnatorum.

PRAETEREA, ignis qui malos involvet, erit ignis inferni. Sed ignis ille ab initio mundi praeparatus est damnatis. Unde Matth, 25, [41]: *ite, maledicti, in ignem aeternum, qui paratus est diabolo*. Et Isaiae. 30, [33], *praeparata est ab heri Tophet, a Rege praeparata*, etc: Glossa, *ab heri, idest ab initio; Tophet, idest Vallis Gehennae*. Sed ignis ille finalis conflagrationis non fuit ab initio praeparatus, sed ex concursu mundanorum ignium generabitur. Ergo ille ignis est alius ab igne inferni, qui reprobos involvet.

IN CONTRARIUM: Est quod in Psalmo [96, 3] de illo igne dicitur quod *inflammabit in circuitu inimicos eius*.

PRAETEREA, Dan. 7, [10] dicitur: *fluvius igneus rapidusque egrediebatur a facie eius*: Glossa, *ut peccatores traheret in gehennam*. Loquitur autem auctoritas illa de illo igne de quo nunc est mentio: ut patet per quandam glossam, quae ibi [v. 9] dicit, *ut bonos purget et malos puniat*. Ergo ignis finalis conflagrationis in infernum cum reprobis demergetur.

RESPONDEO dicendum quod tota purgatio mundi et innovatio ad purgationem et innovationem hominis ordinabitur. Et ideo oportet; quod mundi purgatio et innovatio purgationi et innovationi humani generis respondeat. Humani autem generis purgatio quaedam erit quando mali segregabuntur a bonis: unde dicitur

OBJECTION 1: It would seem that that fire will not engulf the wicked. For a Gloss on Malachi 3:3: *he shall purify the sons of Levi*, says, *we read that there will be a twofold fire: one that will cleanse the elect and will precede the judgment, another that will torture the wicked*. Now the latter is the fire of hell that shall engulf the wicked, while the former is the fire of the final conflagration. Therefore, the fire of the final conflagration will not be that which will engulf the wicked.

OBJ. 2: Further, that fire will obey God in the cleansing of the world: therefore, it should receive its reward like the other elements, especially since fire is the most noble of the elements. Therefore, it would seem that it ought not to be cast into hell for the punishment of the damned.

OBJ. 3: Further, the fire that will engulf the wicked will be the fire of hell; and this fire was prepared from the beginning of the world for the damned. Hence it is written in Matthew 25:41: *depart, you cursed, into everlasting fire which was prepared for the devil*. Also Isaiah 30:33: *Tophet is prepared from yesterday, prepared by the king*, etc., on which a Gloss observes: *from yesterday, i.e., from the beginning— Tophet, i.e., the valley of hell*. But this fire of the final conflagration was not prepared from the beginning, but will result from the meeting together of the fires of the world. Therefore, that fire is not the fire of hell which will engulf the wicked.

ON THE CONTRARY, Psalm 96:3 says of this fire that it *shall burn his enemies round about*.

FURTHER, Daniel 7:10 says: *a swift stream of fire issued forth from before him*; and a Gloss adds, *to drag sinners into hell*. Now the passage quoted refers to that fire of which we are now speaking, as appears from a Gloss which observes on the same words: *in order to punish the wicked and cleanse the good*. Therefore, the fire of the final conflagration will be plunged into hell together with the wicked.

I ANSWER THAT, The entire cleansing of the world and the renewal for the purpose of cleansing will be directed to the renewal of man: and consequently the cleansing and renewal of the world must correspond with the cleansing and renewal of mankind. Now mankind will be cleansed in one way by the separation of the wicked from the good, where-

Luc. 3, [17]: *cuius ventilabrum in manu eius, et purgabit aream suam: et congregabit triticum suum*, idest electos, *in horreum suum, paleas autem*, idest reprobos, *comburet igne inextinguibili*. Unde et ita erit de purgatione mundi, quod quidquid erit turpe et foedum, in infernum cum reprobis retrudetur; quidquid vero plulchrum et nobile, conservabitur in superioribus ad gloriam electorum. Et ita etiam erit de illo igne conflagrationis: sicut dicit Basilius, super illud Psalmi [28, 7], *vox Domini intercidentis flammam ignis*. Quia quoad calidum, ustivum, et quantum ad id quod in igne grossum reperietur, descendet ad inferos ad poenam damnatorum: quod vero est ibi subtile et lucidum, remanebit superius ad gloriam electorum.

Ad primum ergo dicendum quod ignis qui purgabit electos ante iudicium, erit idem cum igne conflagrationis mundi, quamvis quidam contrarium dicant: convenit enim ut, cum homo sit. pars mundi, eodem igne purgetur homo et mundus. Dicuntur autem duo ignes qui purgabit hos et cruciabit malos, et quantum ad officium, et aliquo modo ad substantiam: quia non tota substantia ignis purgantis in infernum retrudetur, ut dictum est.

Ad secundum dicendum quod in hoc ille ignis remunerabitur, quod illud quod est grossum in eo, separabitur ab ipso et retrudetur in infernum.

Ad tertium dicendum quod, sicut gloria electorum post iudicium erit maior quam ante, ita et poena reproborum. Et ideo, sicut claritas superiori creaturae addetur ad augmentandum gloriam electorum, ita etiam quidquid est turpe in creaturis retrudetur in infernum ad augmentandam miseriam damnatorum. Et ita igni ab initio praeparato in inferno, non est inconveniens si alter ignis addatur.

fore it is said: *whose fan is in his hand, and he will purge his poor, and will gather the wheat*, i.e., the elect, *into his barn, but the chaff*, i.e., the wicked, *he will burn with unquenchable fire* (Luke 3:17). Hence it will be thus with the cleansing of the world, so that all that is ugly and vile will be cast with the wicked into hell, and all that is beautiful and noble will be taken up above for the glory of the elect: and so too will it be with the fire of that conflagration, as Basil says about Psalm 28:7, *the voice of the Lord divides the flame of fire*, because whatever fire contains of burning heat and gross matter will go down into hell for the punishment of the wicked, and whatever is subtle and full of light will remain above for the glory of the elect.

Reply Obj. 1: The fire that will cleanse the elect before the judgment will be the same as the fire that will burn the world, although some say the contrary. For it is fitting that man, being a part of the world, be cleansed with the same fire as the world. They are, however, described as two fires that will cleanse the good and torture the wicked, both in reference to their respective offices, and somewhat in reference to their substance: since the substance of the cleansing fire will not all be cast into hell, as stated above.

Reply Obj. 2: This fire will be rewarded because whatever it contains of gross matter will be separated from it and cast into hell.

Reply Obj. 3: The punishment of the wicked, even as the glory of the elect, will be greater after the judgment than before. Wherefore, just as charity will be added to the higher creature in order to increase the glory of the elect, so too whatever is vile in creatures will be thrust down into hell in order to add to the misery of the damned. Consequently, it is not unbecoming that another fire be added to the fire of the damned that was prepared from the beginning of the world.

QUESTION 75

THE RESURRECTION

Post hoc considerandum est de circumstantibus et concomitantibus resurrectionem. Quorum prima consideratio est de ipsa resurrectione; secunda, de eius causa; tertia, de eius tempore et modo; quarta, de ipsius termino a quo; quinta, de conditionibus resurgentium.

Circa primum quaeruntur tria.

Primo: utrum resurrectio corporum sit futura.
Secundo: utrum sit omnium generaliter.
Tertio: utrum naturalis vel miraculosa.

In the next place we must consider things connected with and accompanying the resurrection: (1) The resurrection itself; (2) The cause of the resurrection; (3) Its time and manner; (4) Its starting terminus; (5) The condition of those who rise again.

Under the first head there will be three points of inquiry:

(1) Whether there is to be a resurrection of the body?
(2) Whether it is universally of all bodies?
(3) Whether it is natural or miraculous?

Article 1

Whether There Is to Be a Resurrection of the Body?

AD PRIMUM SIC PROCEDITUR. Videtur quod corporum resurrectio non sit futura. Iob 14, [12]: *homo, cum dormierit, non resurget, donec atteratur caelum.* Sed caelum nunquam atteretur: quia *terra,* de qua minus videtur, *in aeternum stat,* ut patet Eccle. 1, [4]. Ergo homo mortuus nunquam resurget.

PRAETEREA, Dominus, Matth. 22, [31–32], probat resurrectionem per auctoritatem illam, *Ego sum Deus Abraham et Deus Isaac et Deus Iacob, quia non est Deus mortuorum, sed viventium.* Sed constat quod, quando verba illa dicebantur, Abraham, Isaac et Iacob non vivebant corpore, sed solum anima. Ergo resurrectio non erit corporum, sed solum animarum.

PRAETEREA, Apostolus, I Cor. 15, [19, 30 sqq.], videtur probare resurrectionem ex remuneratione laborum quos in hac vita sustinent sancti, qui, *si in hac vita tantum confidentes essent, miserabiliores essent omnibus hominibus.* Sed sufficiens remuneratio omnium laborum hominis potest, esse in anima tantum: non enim oportet quod instrumentum simul cum operante remuneretur; corpus autem instrumentum animae est. Unde etiam in purgatorio, ubi animae punientur *pro his quae gesserunt in corpore,* anima sine corpore punitur. Ergo non oportet ponere resurrectionem corporum, sed sufficit ponere resurrectionem animarum: quae est dum transferuntur de morte culpae et miseriae in vitam gratiae et gloriae.

PRAETEREA, ultimum rei est perfectissimum in re: quia per illud attingit finem suum. Sed perfectissimus status animae est ut sit a corpore separata: quia in hoc statu conformior est Deo et angelis; et magis pura, quasi separata ab omni extranea natura. Ergo separatio a cor-

OBJECTION 1: It would seem that there is not to be a resurrection of the body, for Job 14:12 says: *man, when he is fallen asleep, shall not rise again till the heavens be broken.* But the heavens shall never be broken, since the *earth,* to which seemingly this is still less applicable, *stands forever* (Eccl 1:4). Therefore, the dead man will never rise again.

OBJ. 2: Further, our Lord proves the resurrection by quoting the words: *I am the God of Abraham, and the God of Isaac, and the God of Jacob. He is not the God of the dead but of the living* (Matt 22:32). But it is clear that when those words were uttered, Abraham, Isaac, and Jacob lived not in body, but only in the soul. Therefore, there will be no resurrection of bodies but only of souls.

OBJ. 3: Further, the Apostle (1 Cor 15) seemingly proves the resurrection from the reward for labors endured by the saints in this life. For *if they trusted in this life alone, they would be the most unhappy of all men.* Now there can be sufficient reward for labor in the soul alone: since it is not necessary for the instrument to be repaid together with the worker, and the body is the soul's instrument. Wherefore even in purgatory, where souls will be punished *for what they did in the body,* the soul is punished without the body. Therefore, there is no need to hold a resurrection of the body, but it is enough to hold a resurrection of souls, which consists in their being taken from the death of sin and unhappiness to the life of grace and glory.

OBJ. 4: Further, the last state of a thing is the most perfect, since thereby it attains its end. Now the most perfect state of the soul is to be separated from the body, since in that state it is more conformed to God and the angels, and is more pure, as being separated from any extraneous na-

pore est ultimus status eius. Et ita ex hoc statu non redit ad corpus: sicut nec ex viro fit puer.

PRAETEREA, mors corporalis in poenam hominis est inducta pro prima praevaricatione, ut patet Genes. 2, [17]: sicut et mors spiritualis, quae est separatio animae a Deo, est inflicta homini pro peccato mortali. Sed de morte spirituali nunquam redeunt ad vitam post sententiam damnationis acceptam. Ergo nec de morte corporali ad vitam corporalem erit regressus. Et sic resurrectio non erit.

SED CONTRA: Est quod dicitur 19, [25–26]: *scio, quod Redemptor meus vivit, et in novissimo die de terra surrecturus sum, et rursus circumdabor pelle mea*. Ergo resurrectio erit etiam corporum.

PRAETEREA, donum Christi est maius quam peccatum Adae, ut patet Rom. 5, [15 sqq.]. Sed mors per peccatum introducta est [v. 12]: quia, si peccatum non fuisset, mors nulla esset. Ergo per donum Christi a morte reparabitur ad vitam.

PRAETEREA, membra debent esse capiti conformia. Sed caput nostrum vivit, et in aeternum vivet, in corpore et anima: quia *resurgens ex mortuis iam non moritur*, ut patet Rom. 6, [9]. Ergo et homines qui sunt eius membra, vivent in corpore et anima. Et sic oportet carnis resurrectionem esse.

RESPONDEO dicendum quod secundum diversas sententias de ultimo fine hominis diversificatae sunt sententiae ponentium vel negantium resurrectionem. Ultimus enim finis hominis, quem omnes homines naturaliter desiderant, est beatitudo. Quam quidam homini posse provenire in hac vita posuerunt. Unde non cogebantur ponere aliam vitam post istam, in qua homo ultimam sui perfectionem consequeretur. Et sic resurrectionem negabant.

Et hanc opinionem satis probabiliter excludit varietas fortunae, et infirmitas humani corporis, scientiae et virtutis imperfectio, et instabilitas, quibus omnibus beatitudinis perfectio impeditur, ut Augustinus prosequitur in fine *de Civitate Dei*.

Et ideo alii posuerunt aliam vitam esse post hanc, in qua homo tantum secundum animam vivebat post mortem: et hanc vitam ponebant sufficere ad naturale desiderium implendum de beatitudine consequenda. Unde Porphyrius dicebat, ut Augustinus dicit, in libro *de Civ. Dei*, quod *animae, ad hoc quod beata sit, omne corpus fugiendum est*. Unde tales resurrectionem non ponebant.

Huius autem opinionis apud diversos diversa erant falsa fundamenta. Quidam enim haeretici posuerunt omnia corporalia esse a malo principio, spiritualia vero a bono. Et secundum hoc oportebat quod anima summe perfecta non esset nisi a corpore separata, per quod a suo principio distrahitur, cuius participatio ipsam bea-

ture. Therefore, separation from the body is its final state, and consequently it does not return from this state to the body, as neither does a man end in becoming a boy.

OBJ. 5: Further, bodily death is the punishment inflicted on man for his own transgression, as appears from Genesis 2, even as spiritual death, which is the separation of the soul from God, is inflicted on man for mortal sin. Now man never returns to life from spiritual death after receiving the sentence of his damnation. Therefore, neither will there be any return from bodily death to bodily life, and so there will be no resurrection.

ON THE CONTRARY, It is written: *I know that my Redeemer lives, and in the last day I shall rise out of the earth, and I shall be clothed again with my skin* (Job 19:25–26). Therefore, there will be a resurrection of the body.

FURTHER, The gift of Christ is greater than the sin of Adam, as appears from Romans 5:15. Now death was brought in by sin, for if sin had not been, there had been no death. Therefore, by the gift of Christ man will be restored from death to life.

FURTHER, The members should be conformed to the head. Now our Head lives and will live eternally in body and soul, since *Christ, rising again from the dead, dies now no more* (Rom 6:8). Therefore, men who are his members will live in body and soul; and consequently there must be a resurrection of the body.

I ANSWER THAT, According to the various opinions about man's last end, there have been various opinions holding or denying the resurrection. For man's last end, which all men desire naturally, is happiness. Some have held that man is able to attain this end in this life; wherefore they had no need to admit another life after this in which man would be able to attain to his perfection: and so they denied the resurrection.

This opinion is confuted with sufficient probability by the changeableness of fortune, the weakness of the human body, and the imperfection and instability of knowledge and virtue, all of which are hindrances to the perfection of happiness, as Augustine argues at the end of *The City of God* (22.22).

Hence others maintained that after this there is another life wherein, after death, man lives according to the soul only, and they held that such a life sufficed to satisfy the natural desire to obtain happiness: wherefore Porphyrius said, as Augustine states (*The City of God* 22.26): *the soul, to be happy, must avoid all bodies*. Consequently, these did not hold the resurrection.

This opinion was based by various people on various false foundations. For certain heretics asserted that all bodily things are from the evil principle, but that spiritual things are from the good principle: and from this it follows that the soul cannot reach the height of its perfection unless it be separated from the body, since the latter withdraws

tam facit. Et ideo omnes haereticorum sectae quae ponunt a diabolo corporalia esse creata vel formata, negant corporum resurrectionem. Huius autem fundamenti falsitas in Secundi Libri principio ostensa est.

Quidam vero posuerunt totam hominis naturam in anima constare, ita ut anima corpore uteretur sicut instrumento, aut sicut nauta navi. Unde secundum hanc opinionem sequitur quod, sola anima beatificata, homo naturali desiderio beatitudinis non frustraretur. Et sic non oportet ponere resurrectionem. Sed hoc fundamentum sufficienter Philosophus, in II *de Anima*, destruit, ostendens animam corpori sicut formam materiae uniri.

Et sic patet quod, si in hac vita homo non potest esse beatus, necesse est resurrectionem ponere.

AD PRIMUM ergo dicendum quod caelum nunquam atteretur quantum ad substantiam: sed atteretur quantum ad effectum virtutis per quam movet ad generationem et corruptionem inferiorum; ratione cuius dicit Apostolus, I Cor. 7, [31]: *praeterit figura huius mundi.*

AD SECUNDUM dicendum quod anima Abrahae non est, proprie loquendo, ipse Abraham, sed est pars eius: et sic de aliis. Unde vita animae Abrahae non sufficeret ad hoc quod Abraham sit vivens, vel quod Deus Abraham sit Deus viventis: sed exigitur vita totius coniuncti, scilicet animae et corporis. Quae quidem vita, quamvis non esset actu quando verba proponebantur, erat tamen in ordine utriusque partis ad resurrectionem. Unde Dominus per verba illa subtilissime et efficaciter probat resurrectionem.

AD TERTIUM dicendum quod anima non comparatur ad corpus solum ut operans ad instrumentum quo operatur, sed etiam ut forma ad materiam. Unde operatio est coniuncti, et non tantum animae: ut patet per Philosophum, in I *de Anima*. Et quia operanti debetur operis merces, oportet quod ipse homo, compositus ex anima et corpore, operis sui mercedem accipiat. Venialia autem sicut dicuntur peccata quasi dispositiones ad peccandum, non quod simpliciter habeant rationem peccati; ita poena quae eis redditur in purgatorio non est simpliciter retributio, sed magis purgatio quaedam; quae seorsum fit in corpore per mortem et incinerationem, et in anima per purgatorium ignem.

AD QUARTUM dicendum quod, ceteris paribus, perfectior est status animae in corpore quam extra corpus, quia est pars totius compositi, et omnis pars integralis materialis est respectu totius: quamvis sit Deo conformior secundum quid. Tunc enim, simpliciter loquendo, est aliquid maxime Deo conforme quando habet quidquid conditio suae naturae requirit: quia tunc perfectionem divinam maxime imitatur. Unde cor animalis magis est conforme Deo immobili quando movetur, quam

it from its principle, the participation of which makes it happy. Hence all those heretical sects that hold corporeal things to have been created or fashioned by the devil deny the resurrection of the body. The falsehood of this principle has been shown at the beginning of the Second Book.

Others said that the entire nature of man is seated in the soul, so that the soul makes use of the body as an instrument, or as a sailor uses his ship: wherefore according to this opinion, it follows that if happiness is attained by the soul alone, man would not be frustrated in his natural desire for happiness, and so there is no need to hold the resurrection. But the Philosopher sufficiently destroys this foundation (*On the Soul* 2.2), where he shows that the soul is united to the body as form to matter.

Hence it is clear that if man cannot be happy in this life, we must of necessity hold the resurrection.

REPLY OBJ. 1: The heavens will never be broken as to their substance, but as to the effect of their power whereby their movement is the cause of generation and corruption of lower things: for this reason the Apostle says: *the fashion of this world passes away* (1 Cor 7:31).

REPLY OBJ. 2: Abraham's soul, properly speaking, is not Abraham himself, but a part of him (and the same as regards the others). Hence life in Abraham's soul does not suffice to make Abraham a living being, or to make the God of Abraham the God of a living man. But there needs to be life in the whole composite, i.e., the soul and body: and although this life were not actually when these words were uttered, it was in each part as ordained to the resurrection. Wherefore our Lord proves the resurrection with the greatest subtlety and efficacy.

REPLY OBJ. 3: The soul is compared to the body not only as a worker to the instrument with which he works, but also as form to matter: wherefore the work belongs to the composite and not to the soul alone, as the Philosopher shows (*On the Soul* 1.4). And since to the worker is due the reward of the work, man himself, who is composed of soul and body, ought to receive the reward of his work. Now as venial offenses are called sins as being dispositions to sin, and not as having simply and perfectly the character of sin, so the punishment which is awarded to them in purgatory is not a retribution simply, but rather a cleansing, which is wrought separately in the body (by death and by its being reduced to ashes) and in the soul (by the fire of purgatory).

REPLY OBJ. 4: Other things being equal, the state of the soul in the body is more perfect than outside the body, because it is a part of the whole composite, and every integral part is material in comparison to the whole: and though it were conformed to God in one respect, it is not simply. Because, strictly speaking, a thing is more conformed to God when it has all that the condition of its nature requires, since then most of all it imitates the divine perfection. Hence the heart of an animal is more conformed to an

quando quiescit: quia perfectio cordis est in moveri, et eius quies est eius destructio.

AD QUINTUM dicendum quod mors corporalis est introducta per peccatum Adae, quod est morte Christi deletum. Unde poena illa non manet in perpetuum. Sed peccatum quod mortem aeternam per impoenitentiam inducit, ultra non expiabitur. Et ideo mors illa aeterna erit.

immovable God when it is in movement than when it is at rest, because the perfection of the heart is in its movement, and its rest is its destruction.

REPLY OBJ. 5: Bodily death was brought about by Adam's sin, which was blotted out by Christ's death; hence its punishment does not last forever. But mortal sin, which causes everlasting death, through impenitence will not be expiated hereafter. Hence that death will be everlasting.

Article 2

Whether the Resurrection Will Be for All Without Exception?

AD SECUNDUM SIC PROCEDITUR. Videtur quod resurrectio non erit omnium generaliter. In Psalmo [1, 5] enim dicitur: *non resurgent impii in iudicio.* Sed resurrectio non erit hominum nisi tempore iudicii universalis. Ergo impii nullo modo resurgent.

PRAETEREA, Dan. 12, [2] dicitur: *multi de his qui dormiunt in pulvere, evigilabunt.* Sed haec locutio quandam particulationem importat. Ergo non omnes resurgent.

PRAETEREA, per resurrectionem homines conformantur Christo resurgenti: unde I Cor. 15, [20 sqq.] concludit Apostolus quod, si Christus resurrexit, et nos resurgemus. Sed illi soli debent Christo resurgenti conformari qui ipsius *imaginem portaverunt* [v. 49]: quod est solum bonorum. Ergo ipsi soli resurgent.

PRAETEREA, poena non dimittitur nisi ablata culpa. Sed mors corporalis est poena peccati originalis. Ergo, cum non omnibus sit dimissum originale peccatum, non omnes resurgent.

PRAETEREA, sicut per gratiam Christi renascimur, ita per gratiam eius resurgemus. Sed illi qui in maternis uteris moriuntur nunquam poterunt renasci. Ergo nec resurgere poterunt. Et sic non omnes resurgent.

SED CONTRA: Est quod dicitur Ioan. 5, [25, 28]: *omnes qui in monumentis sunt audient vocem Filii Dei,* etc. *qui audierint vivent.* Ergo omnes mortui resurgent.

PRAETEREA, I Cor. 15, [51] dicitur: *omnes quidem resurgemus,* etc.

PRAETEREA, resurrectio ad hoc necessaria est ut resurgentes recipiant pro meritis poenam vel praemium. Sed omnibus debetur vel poena vel praemium: pro merito proprio, sicut, adultis; vel alieno, sicut parvulis. Ergo omnes resurgent.

RESPONDEO dicendum quod ea quorum ratio sumitur ex natura speciei, oportet similiter inveniri in omnibus quae sunt eiusdem speciei. Talis autem est resurrectio: haec enim est eius ratio, ut ex dictis patet, quod

OBJECTION 1: It would seem that the resurrection will not be for all without exception. For it is written: *the wicked shall not rise again in judgment* (Ps 1:5). Now men will not rise again except at the time of the general judgment. Therefore, the wicked shall in no way rise again.

OBJ. 2: Further, it is written: *many of those that sleep in the dust of the earth shall awake* (Dan 12:2). But these words imply a restriction. Therefore, not all will rise again.

OBJ. 3: Further, by the resurrection men are conformed to Christ rising again; wherefore the Apostle argues (1 Cor 15:12) that if Christ rose again, we also shall rise again. Now those alone should be conformed to Christ rising again who have *borne his image*, and this belongs to the good alone. Therefore, they alone shall rise again.

OBJ. 4: Further, punishment is not remitted unless the fault is taken away. Now bodily death is the punishment of original sin. Therefore, as original sin is not forgiven to all, not all will rise again.

OBJ. 5: Further, as we are born again by the grace of Christ, even so shall we rise again by his grace. Now those who die in their mother's womb can never be born again: therefore, neither can they rise again, and consequently not all will rise again.

ON THE CONTRARY, It is said: *all that are in the graves shall hear the voice of the Son of God* (John 5:28), *and they that hear shall live* (John 5:25). Therefore, the dead shall all rise again.

FURTHER, It is written: *we shall all indeed rise again* (1 Cor 15:51).

FURTHER, The resurrection is necessary in order that those who rise again may receive punishment or reward according to their merits. Now either punishment or reward is due to all, either for their own merits, as to adults, or for others', as to children. Therefore, all will rise again.

I ANSWER THAT, Those things, the reason of which comes from the nature of a species, must be found likewise in all the members of that same species. Now such is the resurrection: because the reason thereof, as stated above

anima in perfectione ultima speciei humanae esse non potest a corpore separata. Unde nulla anima in perpetuum remanebit a corpore separata. Et ideo necesse est, sicut unum, ita et omnes resurgere.

AD PRIMUM ergo dicendum quod Psalmus loquitur de spirituali resurrectione, qua impii non resurgent in iudicio discussionis conscientiae, ut Glossa exponit.

Vel loquitur de impiis qui sunt omnino infideles, qui non resurgent ut iudicentur: *iam* enim *iudicati sunt*.

AD SECUNDUM dicendum quod Augustinus exponit *multi*, idest *omnes*. Et hic modus loquendi frequenter invenitur in sacra Scriptura.

Vel particulatio potest intelligi quantum ad pueros damnatos in limbo, qui, quamvis resurgent, non proprie dicuntur evigilare, cum nec sensum poenae nec gloriae habituri sint: vigilia enim est *solutio sensus*.

AD TERTIUM dicendum quod tam boni quam mali conformantur Christo vivendo in ista vita in his quae ad , naturam speciei pertinent: non autem in his quae pertinent ad gratiam. Et ideo omnes ei conformabuntur in reparatione vitae naturalis: non autem in similitudine gloriae, sed soli boni.

AD QUARTUM dicendum quod mortem, quae est poena originalis peccati, qui in originali decesserunt exsolverunt moriendo. Unde, non obstante originali culpa, possunt a morte resurgere: poena enim originalis peccati magis est mori quam morte detineri.

AD QUINTUM dicendum quod renascimur per gratiam Christi nobis datam: sed resurgimus per gratiam Christi qua factum est ut naturam nostram susciperet; quia ex hoc ei in naturalibus conformamur. Unde illi qui in maternis uteris decedunt, quamvis renati non fuerint per susceptionem gratiae, tamen resurgent, propter conformitatem naturae ad ipsum, quam consecuti sunt ad perfectionem humanae speciei pertingentes.

(A. 1), is that the soul cannot have the final perfection of the human species so long as it is separated from the body. Hence no soul will remain forever separated from the body. Therefore, it is necessary for all, as well as for one, to rise again.

REPLY OBJ. 1: As a Gloss expounds these words, they refer to the spiritual resurrection whereby the wicked shall not rise again in the particular judgment.

Or else they refer to the wicked who are altogether unbelievers, who will not rise again to be judged, since *they are already judged* (John 3:18).

REPLY OBJ. 2: Augustine (*The City of God* 20.23) explains *many* as meaning *all*: in fact, this way of speaking is often met with in Sacred Scripture.

Or else the restriction may refer to the children consigned to limbo who, although they shall rise again, are not properly said to awake, since they will have no sense either of pain or of glory, and waking is the *unchaining of the senses*.

REPLY OBJ. 3: All, both good and wicked, are conformed to Christ while living in this life as regards things pertaining to the nature of the species, but not as regards matters pertaining to grace. Hence all will be conformed to him in the restoration of natural life, but not in the likeness of glory, except the good alone.

REPLY OBJ. 4: Those who have died in original sin have, by dying, discharged the obligation of death which is the punishment of original sin. Hence, notwithstanding original sin, they can rise again from death: for the punishment of original sin is to die, rather than to be detained by death.

REPLY OBJ. 5: We are born again by the grace of Christ that is given to us, but we rise again by the grace of Christ whereby it came about that he took our nature, since it is by this that we are conformed to him in natural things. Hence those who die in their mother's womb, although they are not born again by receiving grace, will nevertheless rise again on account of the conformity of their nature with him, which conformity they acquired by attaining to the perfection of the human species.

Article 3

Whether the Resurrection Is Natural?

AD TERTIUM SIC PROCEDITUR. Videtur quod resurrectio sit naturalis. Quia, sicut dicit Damascenus, in III libro, *quod communiter in omnibus inspicitur, naturam characterizat in his quae sub ipso sunt atomis.* Sed resurrectio communiter in omnibus invenitur. Ergo est naturalis.

PRAETEREA, Gregorius dicit, XIV *Moral.*: *qui resurrectionis fidem ex obedientia non tenent, certe hanc ex ratione tenere debuerant. Quid enim quotidie mundus in*

OBJECTION 1: It would seem that the resurrection is natural. For, as the Damascene says (*On the Orthodox Faith* 3.14), *that which is commonly observed in all marks the nature of the individuals contained under it.* Now resurrection applies commonly to all. Therefore, it is natural.

OBJ. 2: Further, Gregory says (*Morals on Job* 14.55): *those who do not hold the resurrection on the principle of obedience ought certainly to hold it on the principle of reason.*

elementis suis nisi resurrectionem nostram imitatur? Et ponit exemplum de luce, quae quasi moriendo oculis subtrahitur, et rursus quasi resurgendo revocatur; et de arbustis, quae viriditatem amittunt, et rursus quasi resurgentia reparantur; et de seminibus, quae putrescentia moriuntur, et rursus germinando quodammodo resurgunt; quod etiam exemplum Apostolus ponit, I Cor. 15, [36 sqq.]. Sed nihil potest ex naturalibus operibus ratione cognosci nisi naturale. Ergo resurrectio erit naturalis.

PRAETEREA, illa quae sunt praeter naturam, non multo tempore manent, quia sunt quasi violenta. Sed vita quae per resurrectionem reparatur in aeternum manebit. Ergo resurrectio erit naturalis.

PRAETEREA, illud ad quod tota naturae expectatio intendit, maxime videtur esse naturale. Sed resurrectio et glorificatio sanctorum est huiusmodi, ut patet Rom. 8, [19 sqq.]. Ergo resurrectio erit naturalis.

PRAETEREA, resurrectio est motus quidam ad perpetuam coniunctionem animae et corporis. Sed motus est naturalis qui terminatur ad quietem naturalem, ut patet V *Physic.* Perpetua autem coniunctio animae et corporis erit naturalis: quia, cum anima sit proprius motor corporis, habet sibi corpus proportionatum et ita in perpetuum est naturaliter vivificabile ab ipsa, sicut ipsa in perpetuum vivit. Ergo resurrectio erit naturalis.

SED CONTRA: A privatione in habitum non erit regressus secundum naturam. Sed mors est privatio vitae. Ergo resurrectio, per quam est reditus de morte ad vitam, non est naturalis.

PRAETEREA, ea quae surit unius speciei, unum habent determinatum modum originis: unde animalia quae generantur ex putrefactione et ex semine nunquam sunt eiusdem speciei, ut dicit Commentator, in VIII *Physic.* Sed naturalis motus quo homo oritur est generatio ex simili in specie: quod non erit in resurrectione. Ergo non est naturalis.

RESPONDEO dicendum quod motus sive actio aliqua se habet ad naturam tripliciter. Est enim aliquis motus sive actio cuius natura nec est principium nec terminus. Et talis motus quandoque est a principio supra naturam, ut patet de glorificatione corporis: quandoque autem a principio alio quocumque, sicut patet de motu violento lapidis sursum, qui terminatur ad quietem violentam. Est etiam alius motus cuius principium et terminus est natura, ut patet in motu lapidis deorsum. Est etiam alius motus cuius terminus est natura, sed non principium: sed quandoque aliquid supra naturam, sicut patet in illuminatione caeci, quia visus naturalis est, sed illuminationis principium est supra naturam; quandoque autem aliquid aliud, ut patet in acceleratione florum vel fructuum per artificium facta. Quod autem principium sit natura et non terminus, esse non potest: quia principia natura-

For what does the world every day but imitate, in its elements, our resurrection? And he offers as examples the light which as it were dies and is withdrawn from our sight and again rises anew, as it were, and is recalled; the shrubs which lose their greenery, and again by a kind of resurrection are renewed; and the seeds which rot and die and then sprout and rise again, as it were: which same example is adduced by the Apostle (1 Cor 15:36). Now from the works of nature nothing can be known save what is natural. Therefore, the resurrection is natural.

OBJ. 3: Further, things that are against nature abide not for long, because they are violent, so to speak. But the life that is restored by the resurrection will last forever. Therefore, the resurrection will be natural.

OBJ. 4: Further, that to which the entire expectation of nature looks forward would seem to be natural. Now such a thing is the resurrection and the glorification of the saints, according to Romans 8:19. Therefore, the resurrection will be natural.

OBJ. 5: Further, the resurrection is a kind of movement towards the everlasting union of soul and body. Now movement is natural if it terminates in a natural rest (*Physics* 5.6); and the everlasting union of soul and body will be natural, for since the soul is the body's proper mover, it has a body proportionate to it: so that the body is likewise forever capable of being quickened by it, even as the soul lives forever. Therefore, the resurrection will be natural.

ON THE CONTRARY, There is no natural return from privation to habit. But death is privation of life. Therefore, the resurrection whereby one returns from death to life is not natural.

FURTHER, Things of the one species have one fixed way of origin: wherefore animals begotten of putrefaction are never of the same species as those begotten of seed, as the Commentator says on *Physics* 8. Now the natural way of man's origin is for him to be begotten of a similar in species: and such is not the case in the resurrection. Therefore, it will not be natural.

I ANSWER THAT, A movement or an action stands related to nature in three ways. For there is a movement or action whereof nature is neither the principle nor the term: and such a movement is sometimes from a principle above nature, as in the case of a glorified body; and sometimes from any other principle whatever: for instance, the violent upward movement of a stone which terminates in a violent rest. Again, there is a movement whereof nature is both principle and term: for instance, the downward movement of a stone. And there is another movement whereof nature is the term, but not the principle, the latter being sometimes something above nature (as in giving sight to a blind man, for sight is natural, but the principle of the sight-giving is above nature), and sometimes something else, as in the forcing of flowers or fruit by artificial process. It is impossible for nature to be the principle and not the term,

lia sunt ad determinatos effectus definita, ultra quos se extendere non possunt.

Operatio ergo vel motus primo modo se habens ad naturam, nullo modo potest dici naturalis: sed vel est miraculosa, si sit a principio supra naturam; vel violenta, si sit ab alio quocumque principio. Operatio autem vel motus secundo modo se habens ad naturam, est simpliciter naturalis. Sed operatio quae tertio modo se habet ad naturam, non potest dici simpliciter naturalis, sed secundum quid, inquantum scilicet perducit ad id quod secundum naturam est: sed vel dicitur miraculosa, vel artificialis aut violenta. *Naturale* enim proprie dicitur *quod secundum naturam est*; secundum autem naturam esse: dicitur habens naturam et quae consequuntur naturam, ut patet in II *Physic.* Unde motus, simpliciter loquendo, non potest dici naturalis nisi eius principium sit natura.

Resurrectionis autem principium natura esse non potest, quamvis ad vitam naturae resurrectio terminetur. Natura enim est *principium motus in eo in quo est*: vel activum, ut patet in motu gravium et levium, et in alterationibus naturalibus animalium; vel passivum, ut patet in generatione simplicium corporum. Passivum autem principium naturalis generationis est potentia passiva naturalis, quae semper habet aliquam potentiam activam sibi respondentem in natura, ut dicitur in IX *Metaphys.* Nec differt, quantum ad hoc, sive respondeat passivo principio activum principium in natura respectu ultimae perfectionis, scilicet formae; sive respectu dispositionis quae est necessitas ad formam ultimam, sicut est in generatione hominis secundum positionem fidei, vel etiam de omnibus aliis secundum opinionem Platonis et Avicennae. Nullum autem principium activum resurrectionis est in natura: neque respectu coniunctionis animae ad corpus; neque respectu dispositionis quae est necessitas ad talem coniunctionem, quia talis dispositio non potest a natura induci nisi determinato modo per viam generationis ex semine. Unde, etsi ponatur esse etiam aliqua potentia passiva ex parte corporis, seu etiam inclinatio quaecumque ad animae coniunctionem, non est talis quod sufficiat ad rationem motus naturalis. Unde resurrectio, simpliciter loquendo, est miraculosa, non naturalis, nisi secundum quid, ut ex dictis patet.

AD PRIMUM ergo dicendum quod Damascenus loquitur de illis quae inveniuntur in omnibus individuis ex principiis naturae creatis. Non enim, si divina operatione omnes homines dealbarentur, vel in uno loco congregarentur, sicut tempore diluvii factum est, propter hoc albedo esset proprietas naturalis hominis, vel esse in tali loco.

AD SECUNDUM dicendum quod ex rebus naturalibus non cognoscitur aliquid ratione demonstrante non naturale. Sed ratione persuadente potest cognosci aliquid su-

because natural principles are appointed to definite effects, beyond which they cannot extend.

Accordingly, the action or movement that is related to nature in the first way can in no way be natural, but is either miraculous if it come from a principle above nature, or violent if from any other principle. The action or movement that is related to nature in the second way is simply natural: but the action that is related to nature in the third way cannot be described as natural simply, but as natural in a restricted sense, insofar, to wit, as it leads to that which is according to nature: but it is called either miraculous, artificial, or violent. For, properly speaking, *natural is that which is according to nature*, and a thing is according to nature if it has that nature and whatever results from that nature (*Physics* 2.1). Consequently, speaking simply, movement cannot be described as natural unless its principle be natural.

Now, nature cannot be the principle of resurrection, although resurrection terminates in the life of nature. For nature is the *principle of movement in that in which it exists*: either the active principle, as in the movement of heavy and light bodies and in the natural alterations of animals; or the passive principle, as in the generation of simple bodies. The passive principle of natural generation is the natural passive potentiality which always has an active principle corresponding to it in nature, according to *Metaphysics* 8.1: nor as to this does it matter whether the active principle in nature correspond to the passive principle in respect of its ultimate perfection, namely, the form; or in respect of a disposition in virtue of which it demands the ultimate form, as in the generation of a man according to the teaching of faith, or in all other generations according to the opinions of Plato and Avicenna. But in nature there is no active principle of the resurrection, neither as regards the union of the soul with the body, nor as regards the disposition which is the demand for that union: since such a disposition cannot be produced by nature, except in a definite way by the process of generation from seed. Wherefore even granted a passive potentiality on the part of the body, or any kind of inclination to its union with the soul, it is not such as to suffice for the conditions of natural movement. Therefore, the resurrection strictly speaking is miraculous and not natural except in a restricted sense, as we have explained.

REPLY OBJ. 1: Damascene is speaking of those things that are found in all individuals and are caused by the principles of nature. For supposing by a divine operation all men to be made white, or to be gathered together in one place, as happened at the time of the deluge, it would not follow that whiteness or existence in some particular place is a natural property of man.

REPLY OBJ. 2: From natural things one does not come by a demonstration of reason to know non-natural things, but by the induction of reason one may know something

pra naturam: quia eorum quae supra naturam sunt, ea quae sunt in natura, aliquam similitudinem repraesentant; sicut unio animae et corporis repraesentat animae unionem ad Deum per gloriam fruitionis, ut Magister dicit. Et simili modo exempla quae Apostolus et Gregorius inducunt, fidei resurrectionis persuasive adminiculantur.

AD TERTIUM dicendum quod illa ratio procedit de operatione illa quae terminatur ad illud quod non est secundum naturam, sed naturae contrarium. Hoc autem non est in resurrectione. Et ideo non est ad propositum.

AD QUARTUM dicendum quod tota operatio naturae est sub operatione divina sicut operatio inferioris artis sub operatione superioris. Unde, sicut omnis operatio inferioris artis expectat aliquem finem ad quem non pervenitur nisi operatione artis superioris inducentis formam vel utentis artificio facto, ita ad ultimum finem ad quem tota expectatio naturae intendit, non potest perveniri opere naturae. Et propter hoc consecutio eius non est naturalis.

AD QUINTUM dicendum quod, quamvis non possit esse motus naturalis qui terminatur ad quietem violentam, tamen potest esse motus non naturalis qui terminatur ad quietem naturalem, ut ex dictis patet.

above nature, since the natural bears a certain resemblance to the supernatural. Thus the union of soul and body resembles the union of the soul with God by the glory of fruition, as the Master says (*Sentences* II, D. 1): and in like manner the examples quoted by the Apostle and Gregory are confirmatory evidences of our faith in the resurrection.

REPLY OBJ. 3: This argument regards an operation which terminates in something that is not natural but contrary to nature. Such is not the resurrection, and hence the argument is not to the point.

REPLY OBJ. 4: The entire operation of nature is subordinate to the divine operation, just as the working of a lower art is subordinate to the working of a higher art. Hence just as all the work of a lower art has in view an end unattainable save by the operation of the higher art that produces the form, or makes use of what has been made by art: so the last end which the whole expectation of nature has in view is unattainable by the operation of nature, and for which reason the attaining thereto is not natural.

REPLY OBJ. 5: Although there can be no natural movement terminating in a violent rest, there can be a nonnatural movement terminating in a natural rest, as explained above.

QUESTION 76

THE CAUSE OF THE RESURRECTION

Deinde considerandum est de causa nostrae resurrectionis.

Circa quod tria quaeruntur.

Primo: utrum resurrectio Christi sit causa nostrae resurrectionis.

Secundo: utrum vox tubae.

Tertio: utrum angeli.

We must next consider the cause of our resurrection.

Under this head there are three points of inquiry:

(1) Whether Christ's resurrection is the cause of our resurrection?

(2) Whether the sound of the trumpet is?

(3) Whether the angels are?

Article 1

Whether the Resurrection of Christ Is the Cause of Our Resurrection?

AD PRIMUM SIC PROCEDITUR. Videtur quod Christi resurrectio non sit causa nostrae resurrectionis. *Posita* enim *causa, ponitur effectus.* Sed, posita resurrectione Christi, non est secuta statim resurrectio aliorum mortuorum. Ergo resurrectio eius non est causa nostrae resurrectionis.

PRAETEREA, effectus non potest esse nisi causa praecesserit. Sed resurrectio mortuorum esset etiam si Christus non resurrexisset: erat enim alius modus possibilis Deo ut homo liberaretur. Ergo resurrectio Christi non est: causa nostrae resurrectionis.

PRAETEREA, idem est factivum unius in tota una specie. Sed resurrectio erit omnibus hominibus communis. Cum ergo resurrectio Christi non sit causa sui ipsius, non erit causa aliarum resurrectionum.

PRAETEREA, in effectu relinquitur aliquid de similitudine causae. Sed resurrectio ad minus quorundam, scilicet malorum, non habet aliquid simile resurrectioni Christi. Ergo resurrectionis illorum non erit causa resurrectio Christi.

SED CONTRA: *Illud quod est primum in quolibet genere, est causa eorum quae sunt post,* ut patet in II *Metaphys.* Sed Christus ratione suae resurrectionis corporalis, dicitur *primitiae dormientium,* I Cor. 15, [20], et *primogenitus mortuorum,* Apoc. 1, [5]. Ergo sua resurrectio est causa resurrectionis aliorum.

PRAETEREA, resurrectio Christi magis convenit cum nostra resurrectione corporali quam cum resurrectione spirituali, quae est per iustificationem. Sed resurrectio Christi est causa iustificationis nostrae: ut patet Rom. 4, [25], *resurrexit propter iustificationem nostram.* Ergo est causa nostrae resurrectionis corporalis.

OBJECTION 1: It would seem that the resurrection of Christ is not the cause of our resurrection. For *given the cause, the effect follows.* Yet given the resurrection of Christ, the resurrection of the other dead did not follow at once. Therefore, his resurrection is not the cause of ours.

OBJ. 2: Further, an effect cannot be unless the cause precede. But the resurrection of the dead could be even if Christ had not risen again: for God could have delivered man in some other way. Therefore, Christ's resurrection is not the cause of ours.

OBJ. 3: Further, the same thing produces the one effect throughout the one same species. Now the resurrection will be common to all men. Since, then, Christ's resurrection is not its own cause, it is not the cause of the resurrection of others.

OBJ. 4: Further, an effect retains some likeness to its cause. But the resurrection at least of some, namely, the wicked, bears no likeness to the resurrection of Christ. Therefore, Christ's resurrection will not be the cause of theirs.

ON THE CONTRARY, *In every genus that which is first is the cause of those that come after it* (*Metaphysics* 2.1). Now Christ, by reason of his bodily resurrection, is called *the first-fruits of them that sleep* (1 Cor 15:20), and *the first-begotten of the dead* (Rev 1:5). Therefore, his resurrection is the cause of the resurrection of others.

FURTHER, Christ's resurrection has more in common with our bodily resurrection than with our spiritual resurrection, which is by justification. But Christ's resurrection is the cause of our justification, as appears from Romans, where it is said that he *rose again for our justification* (4:25). Therefore, Christ's resurrection is the cause of our bodily resurrection.

RESPONDEO dicendum quod Christus ratione humanae naturae dicitur *Dei et hominum mediator*: unde divina dona a Deo in homines mediante Christi humanitate proveniunt. Sicut autem a morte spirituali liberari non possumus nisi per donum gratiae divinitus datum, ita nec a morte corporali nisi per resurrectionem divina virtute factam. Et ideo, sicut Christus primitias gratiae suscepit divinitus et eius gratia est causa nostrae gratiae, quia *de plenitudine eius nos omnes accepimus, gratiam pro gratia*, Ioan. 1, [16]: ita in Christo inchoata est resurrectio, et sua resurrectio causa est nostrae resurrectionis; ut sic Christus inquantum est Deus, sit prima causa nostrae resurrectionis quasi aequivoca; sed inquantum est Deus et homo resurgens, est causa proxima et quasi univoca nostrae resurrectionis.

Causa autem univoca agens producit effectum in similitudine formae suae: unde non solum est causa efficiens, sed exemplaris istius effectus. Hoc autem contingit dupliciter. Quandoque enim ipsa forma per quam attenditur similitudo agentis ad effectum, est directe principium actionis qua producitur ille effectus: sicut calor in igne calefaciente. Quandoque autem illius actionis qua producitur effectus, non est principium primo et per se ipsa forma secundum quam attenditur similitudo, sed principia illius formae: sicut, si homo albus generet hominem album, ipsa albedo generantis non est principium activae generationis, et tamen albedo generantis dicitur causa albedinis generatae, quia principia albedinis in generante sunt principia generativa facientia albedinem in generato.

Et per hunc modum resurrectio Christi est causa nostrae resurrectionis: quia illud quod fecit resurrectionem Christi, qui est causa efficiens univoca nostrae resurrectionis, ad nostram resurrectionem agit, scilicet virtus divinitatis ipsius Christi, quae sibi et Patri communis est. Unde dicitur Rom. 8, [11]: *qui suscitavit Iesum Christum a mortuis, vivificabit mortalia corpora nostra.*

Sed ipsa resurrectio Christi, virtute divinitatis adiunctae, est causa quasi instrumentalis resurrectionis nostrae. Operationes enim divinae agebantur mediante carne Christi quasi quodam organo: sicut ponit exemplum Damascenus, in III libro, de tactu corporali quo mundavit leprosum, Matth. 8, [3].

AD PRIMUM ergo dicendum quod causa sufficiens statim producit effectum suum ad quem immediate ordinatur: non autem effectum ad quem ordinatur mediante alio, quantumcumque sit sufficiens; sicut calor, quantumcumque sit intensus, non statim in primo instanti causat calorem, sed statim incipit movere ad calorem, quia calor est effectus eius mediante motu. Resurrectio autem Christi dicitur causa nostrae resurrectionis, non quia ipsa agat resurrectionem nostram, sed median-

I ANSWER THAT, Christ by reason of his nature is called the *mediator of God and men*: wherefore the divine gifts are bestowed on men by means of Christ's humanity. Now just as we cannot be delivered from spiritual death save by the gift of grace bestowed by God, so neither can we be delivered from bodily death except by resurrection wrought by the divine power. And therefore as Christ, in respect of his human nature, received the first-fruits of grace from above, and his grace is the cause of our grace, because *of his fullness we all have received grace for grace* (John 1:16), so in Christ has our resurrection begun, and his resurrection is the cause of ours. Thus Christ as God is, as it were, the equivocal cause of our resurrection, but as God and man rising again, he is the proximate and, so to say, the univocal cause of our resurrection.

Now a univocal efficient cause produces its effect in likeness to its own form, so that not only is it an efficient, but also an exemplar, cause in relation to that effect. This happens in two ways. For sometimes this very form whereby the agent is likened to its effect is the direct principle of the action by which the effect is produced, as heat in the fire that heats: and sometimes it is not the form in respect of which this likeness is observed that is primarily and directly the principle of that action, but the principles of that form. For instance, if a white man beget a white man, the whiteness of the begetter is not the principle of active generation, and yet the whiteness of the begetter is said to be the cause of the whiteness of the begotten, because the principles of whiteness in the begetter are the generative principles causing whiteness in the begotten.

In this way the resurrection of Christ is the cause of our resurrection, because the same thing that wrought the resurrection of Christ, which is the univocal efficient cause of our resurrection, is the active cause of our resurrection, namely, the power of Christ's divinity which is common to him and the Father. Hence it is written: *he that raised up Jesus Christ from the dead shall quicken also your mortal bodies* (Rom 8:11).

And this very resurrection of Christ by virtue of his indwelling divinity is the quasi-instrumental cause of our resurrection: since the divine operations were wrought by means of Christ's flesh, as though it were a kind of organ; thus the Damascene instances as an example (*On the Orthodox Faith* 3.15) the touch of his body whereby he healed the leper (Matt 8:3).

REPLY OBJ. 1: A sufficient cause produces at once its effect to which it is immediately directed, but not the effect to which it is directed by means of something else, no matter how sufficient it may be: thus heat, however intense it be, does not cause heat at once in the first instant, but it begins at once to set up a movement towards heat, because heat is its effect by means of movement. Now Christ's resurrection is said to be the cause of ours in that it works our resurrection not immediately, but by means of its principle, namely,

te principio suo, scilicet divina virtute, quae nostram resurrectionem faciet ad similitudinem resurrectionis Christi. Virtus autem divina omnia operatur mediante voluntate, quae est propinquissima effectui. Unde non oportet quod statim, resurrectione Christi facta, nostra resurrectio sit secuta: sed tunc sequitur quando voluntas Dei ordinavit.

AD SECUNDUM dicendum quod virtus divina non alligatur aliquibus causis secundis, quin effectus illarum posset immediate, vel aliis causis mediantibus, producere: sicut posset generationem corporum inferiorum causare etiam motu caeli non existente, et tamen, secundum ordinem quem in rebus statuit, motus caeli est causa generationis inferiorum corporum. Similiter etiam, secundum ordinem quem rebus humanis divina providentia praefixit, resurrectio Christi est causa nostrae resurrectionis. Potuit tamen alium ordinem praefigere. Et tunc esset alia causa nostrae resurrectionis, qualem Deus ordinasset.

AD TERTIUM dicendum quod ratio illa procedit quando omnia quae sunt in una specie, habent eundem ordinem ad causam primam illius effectus qui est inducendus in totam illam speciem. Sic autem non est in proposito. Quia humanitas Christi propinquior est divinitati, cuius virtus est prima causa generationis, quam humanitas aliorum. Unde resurrectio Christi causatur a divinitate immediate: sed resurrectio aliorum mediante Christo homine resurgente.

AD QUARTUM dicendum quod resurrectio omnium hominum habebit aliquid de similitudine resurrectionis Christi, quod scilicet pertinet ad vitam naturae, secundum quam omnes Christo fuerunt conformes. Et ideo omnes resurgent in vitam immortalem. Sed in sanctis, qui fuerunt Christo conformes per gratiam, erit conformitas quantum ad ea quae sunt gloriae.

the divine power which will work our resurrection in likeness to the resurrection of Christ. Now God's power works by means of his will, which is nearest to the effect; hence it is not necessary that our resurrection should follow straightway after he has wrought the resurrection of Christ, but that it should happen at the time which God's will has decreed.

REPLY OBJ. 2: God's power is not tied to any particular second causes, but he can produce their effects either immediately or by means of other causes—thus he might work the generation of lower bodies even though there were no movement of the heaven—and yet according to the order which he has established in things, the movement of the heaven is the cause of the generation of the lower bodies. In like manner, according to the order appointed to human things by divine providence, Christ's resurrection is the cause of ours: and yet he could have appointed another order, and then our resurrection would have had another cause ordained by God.

REPLY OBJ. 3: This argument holds when all the things of one species have the same order to the first cause of the effect to be produced in the whole of that species. But it is not so in the case in point, because Christ's humanity is nearer to his divinity, whose power is the first cause of the resurrection, than is the humanity of others. Hence Christ's divinity caused his resurrection immediately, but it causes the resurrection of others by means of Christ as man rising again.

REPLY OBJ. 4: The resurrection of all men will bear some resemblance to Christ's resurrection as regards that which pertains to the life of nature, in respect of which all were conformed to Christ. Hence all will rise again to immortal life; but in the saints who were conformed to Christ by grace, there will be conformity as to things pertaining to glory.

Article 2

Whether the Sound of the Trumpet Will Be the Cause of Our Resurrection?

AD SECUNDUM SIC PROCEDITUR. Videtur quod vox tubae non sit causa nostrae resurrectionis. Dicit enim Damascenus: *crede resurrectionem futuram divina voluntate, virtute et nutu.* Ergo, cum haec sint sufficiens causa resurrectionis nostrae, non oportet ponere causam eius vocem tubae.

PRAETEREA, frustra vox emittitur ad eum qui audire non potest. Sed mortui non habebunt auditum. Ergo non est conveniens quod vox aliqua formetur ad resuscitandum eos.

OBJECTION 1: It would seem that the sound of the trumpet will not be the cause of our resurrection. For the Damascene says (*On the Orthodox Faith* 4): *you must believe that the resurrection will take place by God's will, power, and nod.* Therefore, since these are a sufficient cause of our resurrection, we ought not to assign the sound of the trumpet as a cause of it.

OBJ. 2: Further, it is useless to make sounds to one who cannot hear. But the dead will not have hearing. Therefore, it is unfitting to make a sound to arouse them.

PRAETEREA, si vox aliqua sit causa resurrectionis, hoc non erit nisi sit per virtutem voci divinitus datam: unde super illud Psalmi [67, 34], *dabit voci suae vocem virtutis*, dicit Glossa, *resuscitandi corpora*. Sed ex quo potentia data est alicui, quamvis miraculose detur, tamen actus qui sequitur est naturalis: sicut patet in caeco nato miraculose illuminato, qui postea naturaliter videt. Ergo, si vox aliqua esset causa resurrectionis, resurrectio esset naturalis. Quod falsum est.

SED CONTRA: Est quod dicitur I Thessal. 4, [15]: *ipse Dominus in tuba Dei descendet de caelo, et mortui qui in Christo sunt, resurgent primi*.

PRAETEREA, Ioan. 5, [25, 28] dicitur quod *qui in monumentis sunt audient vocem Filii Dei*, et *qui audierint vivent*. Haec autem vox dicitur tuba, ut in littera patet. Ergo, etc.

RESPONDEO dicendum quod causam effectui Oportet aliquo modo coniungi: quia moveris et motum, faciens et factum, sunt simul, ut patet in VII *Physic*. Christus autem resurgens est causa univoca nostrae resurrectionis. Unde oportet quod in resurrectione corporum communi aliquo signo corporali dato Christus resurgens operetur.

Quod quidem signum, ut quidam dicunt, erit, ad litteram, vox Christi resurrectionem imperantis, sicut imperavit mari et cessavit tempestas, Matth. 8, [26].

Quidam vero dicunt quod hoc signum nihil aliud erit quam ipsa repraesentatio evidens Filii Dei in mundo, de qua dicitur Matth. 24, [27]: *sicut fulgur venit ab oriente ei paret in occidente, sic erit adventus Filii hominis*. Et innituntur auctoritati Gregorii dicentis quod *tubam sonare nihil aliud est quam mundo ut iudicem Filium demonstrare*. Et secundum hoc ipsa apparitio Filii Dei vox eius dicitur: quia ei apparenti obediet tota natura ad corporum humanorum reparationem sicut imperanti; unde *in iussu* venire dicitur I Thessal. 4, [15]. Et sic eius apparitio, inquantum habet vim cuiusdam imperii, vox eius dicitur.

Et haec vox, quaecumque sit, quandoque dicitur clamor, quasi praeconis ad iudicium citantis. Quandoque autem dicitur sonus tubae. Vel propter evidentiam: ut in littera dicitur. Vel propter convenientiam ad usum tubae qui erat in veteri Testamento: tuba enim congregabantur ad concilium, commovebantur ad praelium, et vocabantur ad festum; resurgentes autem congregabuntur ad concilium iudicii, ad praelium quo *orbis terrarum pugnabit contra insensatos*, et ad festum aeternae solemnitatis.

AD PRIMUM ergo dicendum quod Damascenus in verbis illis circa materialem causam: resurrectionis tria tetigit: scilicet voluntatem divinam, quae imperat; vir-

OBJ. 3: Further, if any sound is the cause of the resurrection, this will only be by a power given by God to the sound: wherefore a Gloss on Psalm 67:34, *he will give to his voice the voice of power*, says: *to arouse our bodies*. Now from the moment that a power is given to a thing, though it be given miraculously, the act that ensues is natural, as instanced in the man born blind who, after being restored to sight, saw naturally. Therefore, if a sound be the cause of resurrection, the resurrection would be natural: which is false.

ON THE CONTRARY, It is written: *the Lord himself will come down from heaven with the trumpet of God; and the dead who are in Christ shall rise* (1 Thess 4:15).

FURTHER, It is written that they *who are in the graves shall hear the voice of the Son of God* (John 5:28) and *they that hear shall live* (John 5:25). Now this voice is called the trumpet, as stated in the text (*Sentences* IV, D. 43). Therefore, etc.

I ANSWER THAT, Cause and effect must in some way be united together, since mover and moved, maker and made, are simultaneous (*Physics* 7.2). Now Christ rising again is the univocal cause of our resurrection: wherefore at the resurrection of bodies, Christ must work the resurrection at the giving of some common bodily sign.

According to some, this sign will be literally Christ's voice commanding the resurrection, even as he commanded the sea and the storm ceased (Matt 8:26).

Others say that this sign will be nothing else than the manifest appearance of the Son of God in the world, according to Matthew 24:27: *as lightning comes out of the east, and appears even into the west, so shall also the coming of the Son of Man be*. These rely on the authority of Gregory who says that *the sound of the trumpet is nothing else but the Son appearing to the world as judge*. According to this, the visible presence of the Son of God is called his voice, because as soon as he appears all nature will obey his command in restoring human bodies: hence he is described as coming *with commandment* (1 Thess 4:15). In this way his appearing, insofar as it has the force of a command, is called his voice.

And this voice, whatever it be, is sometimes called a cry as of a herald summoning to judgment (Cf. Mt 25:6); sometimes the sound of a trumpet (Cf. 1 Cor 15:52; 1 Thess 4:15), either on account of its distinctness, as stated in the text (*Sentences* IV, D. 43), or as being in keeping with the use of the trumpet in the Old Testament: for by the trumpet they were summoned to the council, stirred to the battle, and called to the feast; and those who rise again will be summoned to the council of judgment, to the battle in which *the world shall fight against the unwise* (Wis 5:21), and to the feast of everlasting solemnity.

REPLY OBJ. 1: In those words the Damascene touches on three things respecting the material cause of the resurrection: the divine will which commands, the power which

tutem, quae exequitur; et facilitatem exequendi, in hoc quod *nutum* adiunxit, ad similitudinem eorum quae in nobis sunt. Illud enim valde facile est nobis facere quod statim ad dictum nostrum fit: sed multo apparet maior facilitas si, ante verbum prolatum, ad primum signum voluntatis, quod *nutus* dicitur, executio nostrae voluntatis per ministros fiat. Et talis noster nutus est quaedam causa praedictae executionis, inquantum per ipsum inducuntur alii ad nostram voluntatem explendam. Nutus autem divinus, quo fiet resurrectio, nihil aliud est quam signum ab ipso datum, cui tota natura obediet ad resurrectionem mortuorum. Et hoc signum idem est quod *vox tubae*, ut ex dictis patet.

AD SECUNDUM dicendum quod, sicut formae sacramentorum habent virtutem sanctificandi, non ex hoc quod audiuntur, sed ex hoc quod proferuntur, ita illa vox quidquid sit, habebit efficaciam instrumentalem ad resuscitandum, non ex hoc quod sentitur, sed ex hoc quod profertur: sicut etiam vox ex ipsa impulsione aeris excitat dormientem solvendo organum sentiendi, non ex hoc quod cognoscatur; quia iudicium de voce perveniente ad aures sequitur excitationem et non est causa eius.

AD TERTIUM dicendum quod ratio illa procederet si virtus illi voci data esset ens perfectum in natura: quia tunc quod ex ea procederet, virtutem iam naturalem factam principium haberet. Non autem est talis virtus illa: sed qualis supra dicta est esse in formis sacramentorum.

executes, and the ease of execution, when he adds *his nod*, in resemblance to our own affairs. For it is very easy for us to do what is done at once at our word. But the ease is much more evident, if before we say a word, at the first sign of our will (called a *nod*) our servants execute our will at once. And this nod is a kind of cause of that execution, insofar as others are led thereby to accomplish our will. Yet the divine nod, at which the resurrection will take place, is nothing but the sign given by God, which all nature will obey by concurring in the resurrection of the dead. This sign is the same as the *sound of the trumpet*, as explained above.

REPLY OBJ. 2: As the forms of the sacraments have the power to sanctify not through being heard, but through being spoken, so this sound, whatever it be, will have an instrumental efficacy of resuscitation, not through being perceived, but through being uttered. Even so a voice awakens a sleeping person by its very impact on the air striking the organ of sensing, not by the fact that he recognizes it, for the judgment about the voice reaching the ears follows waking, and is not the cause of it.

REPLY OBJ. 3: This argument would proceed if the power given to that sound were a complete being in nature: because then that which would proceed therefrom would have for a principle a power already rendered natural. But this power is not of that kind, but such as we have ascribed above to the forms of the sacraments (*Sentences* IV, D. 1; I, Q. 62, A. 1,4).

Article 3

Whether the Angels Will Do Anything Toward the Resurrection?

AD TERTIUM SIC PROCEDITUR. Videtur quod nullo modo ad resurrectionem angeli operentur. Quia maioris virtutis est ostensiva resurrectio mortuorum quam generatio hominum. Sed quando generantur homines, anima non infunditur corpori mediantibus angelis. Ergo nec resurrectio, quae est iterata coniunctio animae et corporis, fiet ministerio angelorum.

PRAETEREA, si ad aliquos angelos hoc ministerium pertineat, maxime videtur pertinere ad Virtutes, quarum est miracula facere. Sed eis non adscribitur, sed Archangelis, ut patet in littera . Ergo non fiet ministerio angelorum.

SED CONTRA est quod dicitur I Thessal. 4, [15], quod *Dominus in voce Archangeli descendet de caedo, et mortui*

OBJECTION 1: It would seem that the angels will do nothing at all towards the resurrection. For raising the dead shows a greater power than does begetting men. Now when men are begotten, the soul is not infused into the body by means of the angels. Therefore, neither will the resurrection, which is reunion of soul and body, be wrought by the ministry of the angels.

OBJ. 2: Further, if this is to be ascribed to the instrumentality of any angels at all, it would seem especially referable to the Virtues, to whom it belongs to work miracles. Yet it is referred, not to them, but to the Archangels, according to the text (*Sentences* IV, D. 43). Therefore, the resurrection will not be wrought by the ministry of the angels.

ON THE CONTRARY, 1 Thessalonians 4:15 says that *the Lord shall come down from heaven with the voice of an*

resurgent. Ergo resurrectio mortuorum ministerio angelico complebitur.

RESPONDEO dicendum quod, sicut Augustinus dicit, in III de Trin., quod *sicut corpora crassiora et inferiora per subtiliora et potentior a ordine quodam reguntur, ita omnia corpora reguntur a Deo per spiritum vitae rationalem.* Et hoc etiam Gregorius, IV *Dialog.*, tangit. Unde in omnibus quae corporaliter a Deo fiunt, utitur Deus ministerio angelorum. In resurrectione autem est aliquid ad transmutationem corporum pertinens: scilicet collectio cinerum, et eorum praeparatio ad reparationem humani corporis. Unde quantum ad hoc in resurrectione utetur Deus ministerio angelorum. Sed anima, sicut immediate a Deo creata est, ita immediate a Deo corpori iterato unietur, sine aliqua operatione angelorum. Similiter etiam gloriam corporis ipse faciet absque ministerio angelorum, sicut et animam immediate glorificat. Et illud angelorum ministerium dicitur *vox*, secundum unam expositionem, quae tangitur in littera.

AD PRIMUM ergo patet solutio ex dictis.

AD SECUNDUM dicendum quod ministerium istud erit principaliter unius Archangeli, scilicet Michaelis, qui est princeps Ecclesiae, sicut fuit synagogae, sicut, dicitur Dan. 10, [21]. Qui tamen agit ex influentia Virtutum et aliorum superiorum ordinum. Unde quod ipse faciet, superiores ordines quodammodo facient. Similiter inferiores angeli cooperabuntur ei circa resurrectionem singulorum, quorum custodiae deputati fuerunt. Et sic vox illa potest dici *unius* et *plurium angelorum.*

archangel and the dead shall rise again. Therefore, the resurrection of the dead will be accomplished by the angelic ministry.

I ANSWER THAT, According to Augustine (*On the Trinity* 3.4) *just as the grosser and inferior bodies are ruled in a certain order by the more subtle and more powerful bodies, so are all bodies ruled by God through the rational spirit of life*: and Gregory speaks in the same sense (*Dialogues* 4.6). Consequently, in all God's bodily works he employs the ministry of the angels. Now in the resurrection there is something pertaining to the transmutation of the bodies, namely, the gathering together of the mortal remains and the disposal thereof for the restoration of the human body; wherefore in this respect God will employ the ministry of the angels in the resurrection. But the soul, even as it is immediately created by God, so will it be reunited to the body immediately by God without any operation of the angels: and in like manner he himself will glorify the body without the ministry of the angels, just as he immediately glorifies man's soul. This ministry of the angels is called their *voice,* according to one explanation given in the text (*Sentences* IV, D. 43).

THE REPLY to the first objection is evident from what has been said.

REPLY OBJ. 2: This ministry will be exercised chiefly by one Archangel, namely Michael, who is the prince of the Church as he was of the synagogue (Dan 10:13, 21). Yet he will act under the influence of the Virtues and the other higher orders: so that what he shall do, the higher orders will, in a way, do also. In like manner, the lower angels will cooperate with him as to the resurrection of each individual to whose guardianship they were appointed: so that this voice can be ascribed either to *one* or to *many angels.*

THE TIME AND MANNER OF THE RESURRECTION

Deinde considerandum est de tempore et modo resurrectionis.

Circa quod quaeruntur quatuor.

Primo: utrum tempus resurrectionis differatur usque ad finem mundi.

Secundo: utrum tempus illud sit occultum.

Tertio: utrum resurrectio fiet in noctis tempore.

Quarto: utrum fiet subito.

We must now consider the time and manner of the resurrection.

Under this head there are four points of inquiry:

(1) Whether the time of the resurrection should be delayed until the end of the world?

(2) Whether that time is hidden?

(3) Whether the resurrection will occur at night-time?

(4) Whether it will happen suddenly?

Article 1

Whether the Time of Our Resurrection Should Be Delayed Till the End of the World?

AD PRIMUM SIC PROCEDITUR. Videtur quod tempus resurrectionis non oporteat differri usque ad finem mundi, ut omnes simul resurgant. Maior est enim convenientia capitis ad membra quam membrorum ad invicem: sicut causae ad effectus quam effectuum ad invicem. Sed Christus, qui est caput nostrum, non distulit resurrectionem suam usque ad finem mundi ut simul cum omnibus resurgeret. Ergo non oportet quod priorum sanctorum resurrectio usque ad finem mundi differatur, ut simul cum aliis resurgant.

PRAETEREA, resurrectio capitis est causa resurrectionis membrorum. Sed resurrectio quorundam membrorum nobilium, propter vicinitatem ad caput, non est dilata usque ad finem mundi, sed statim resurrectionem Christi secuta est: sicut pie creditur de Beata Virgine et Ioanne Evangelista. Ergo et aliorum resurrectio tanto propinquior erit resurrectioni Christi, quanto per gratiam et meritum magis ei fuerunt conformes.

PRAETEREA, status novi Testamenti est perfectior, et expressius portat imaginem Christi, quam status veteris Testamenti. Sed quidam Patres veteris Testamenti, Christo resurgente, resurrexerunt, sicut dicitur Matth. 27, [52]: quia *multa corpora sanctorum qui dormierant, resurrexerunt.* Ergo videtur quod nec sanctorum novi Testamenti resurrectio differri debeat usque ad finem mundi, ut sit omnium simul.

PRAETEREA, post finem mundi non erit aliquis annorum numerus. Sed post resurrectionem mortuorum adhuc computantur multi anni usque ad resurrectionem aliorum, ut patet Apoc. 20: dicitur enim ibi [4–5]: *vidi*

OBJECTION 1: It would seem that the time of the resurrection ought not to be delayed till the end of the world, so that all may rise together. For there is more conformity between head and members than between one member and another, as there is more between cause and effect than between one effect and another. Now Christ, who is our Head, did not delay his resurrection until the end of the world so as to rise again together with all men. Therefore, there is no need for the resurrection of the early saints to be deferred until the end of the world so that they may rise again together with the others.

OBJ. 2: Further, the resurrection of the Head is the cause of the resurrection of the members. But the resurrection of certain members that desire nobility from their being closely connected with the Head was not delayed till the end of the world, but followed immediately after Christ's resurrection, as is piously believed concerning the Blessed Virgin and John the Evangelist. Therefore, the resurrection of others will be so much nearer Christ's resurrection according as they have been more conformed to him by grace and merit.

OBJ. 3: Further, the state of the New Testament is more perfect, and bears a closer resemblance to Christ, than the state of the Old Testament. Yet some of the fathers of the Old Testament rose again when Christ rose, according to Matthew 27:52: *many of the bodies of the saints that had slept arose.* Therefore, it would seem that the resurrection of the Old Testament saints should not be delayed till the end of the world, so that all may rise together.

OBJ. 4: Further, there will be no numbering of years after the end of the world. Yet after the resurrection of the dead, the years are still reckoned until the resurrection of others, as appears from Revelation 20:4–5. For it is stated

animas decollatorum propter testimonium Iesu et propter verbum Dei; et infra, *et vixerunt et regnaverunt cum Christo mille annis*; et *ceteri mortuorum non vixerunt donec consummentur mille anni.* Ergo resurrectio omnium non differtur usque ad finem mundi, ut sit omnium simul.

Sed contra: Est quod dicitur Iob 14, [12]: *homo, cum dormierit, non resurget donec atteratur caelum, nec evigilabit ut consurgat a somno suo*: et loquitur de somno mortis. Ergo usque ad finem mundi, quando caelum atteretur, resurrectio hominum differetur.

Praeterea, Heb. 11, [39–40] dicitur: *Homines Dei, testimonio fidei probati, non acceperunt repromissionem,* idest plenam animae et corporis beatitudinem, *Deo aliquid aliud pro nobis providente, ne sine nobis consummarentur,* idest perficerentur: Glossa.: *ut in communi gaudio omnium maius fieret gaudium singulorum.* Sed non erit ante resurrectio quam corporum glorificatio: quia *reformabit corpus humilitatis nostrae configuratum corpori claritatis suae,* Philipp. 3, [21]; et *resurrectionis filii erunt sicut angeli in caelo,* ut patet Matth. 22, [30]. Ergo resurrectio differetur usque ad finem mundi, in quo omnes simul resurgent.

Respondeo dicendum quod, sicut Augustinus dicit, in III *de. Trin., divina providentia statuit ut corpora crassiora et inferiora per subtiliora et potentiora quodam ordine regantur.* Et ideo tota materia corporum inferiorum subiacet variationi secundum motum caelestium corporum. Unde esset contra ordinem quem divina providentia in rebus statuit, si materia inferiorum corporum ad statum incorruptionis produceretur, manente motu superiorum corporum. Et quia secundum positionem fidei resurrectio erit in vitam immortalem conformiter Christo, qui *resurgens a mortuis iam non moritur,* ut dicitur Rom. 6, [9]; ideo humanorum corporum resurrectio usque ad finem mundi differtur, in quo motus caeli quiescet. Et propter hoc etiam quidam philosophi, qui posuerunt motum caeli nunquam cessare, posuerunt reditum humanarum animarum ad corpora mortalia, qualia nunc habemus: sive ponerent reditum animae ad idem corpus in fine *magni anni,* ut Empedocles; sive ad aliud, ut Pythagoras posuit *quamlibet animam quodlibet corpus ingredi,* ut dicitur in I *de Anima.*

Ad primum ergo dicendum quod, quamvis caput magis conveniat cum membris convenientia proportionis, quae exigitur ad hoc quod in membra influat, quam membra ad invicem; tamen caput habet causalitatem quandam super membra qua membra carent, et in hoc membra differunt a capite et conveniunt ad invicem. Unde resurrectio Christi est exemplar quoddam nostrae resurrectionis, ex cuius fide spes nobis de nostra resurrec-

there that *I saw the souls of them that were beheaded for the testimony of Jesus, and for the word of God,* and further on: *and they lived and reigned with Christ a thousand years.* And *the rest of the dead lived not till the thousand years were finished.* Therefore, the resurrection of all is not delayed until the end of the world, that all may rise together.

On the contrary, It is written: *man, when he is fallen asleep, shall not rise again till the heavens be broken; he shall neither wake nor rise out of his sleep* (Job 14:12), and it is a question of the sleep of death. Therefore, the resurrection of men will be delayed until the end of the world when the heavens shall be broken.

Further, Hebrews 11:39–40 says: *all these being approved by the testimony of faith received not the promise* (Heb 11:39), i.e., full beatitude of soul and body, since *God has provided something better for us, lest they should be consummated,* i.e., perfected, *without us.* As a Gloss observes, *in order that through all rejoicing each one might rejoice the more.* But the resurrection will not precede the glorification of bodies, because *he will reform the body of our lowness made like to the body of his glory* (Phil 3:21), and *the children of the resurrection will be as the angels in heaven* (Matt 22:30). Therefore, the resurrection will be delayed till the end of the world, when all shall rise together.

I answer that, As Augustine states (*On the Trinity* 3.4), *divine providence decreed that the grosser and lower bodies should be ruled in a certain order by the more subtle and powerful bodies*: wherefore the entire matter of the lower bodies is subject to variation according to the movement of the heavenly bodies. Hence it would be contrary to the order established in things by divine providence if the matter of lower bodies were brought to the state of incorruption so long as there remains movement in the higher bodies. And since, according to the teaching of faith, the resurrection will bring men to immortal life conformably to Christ who, *rising again from the dead, dies now no more* (Rom 6:9), the resurrection of human bodies will be delayed until the end of the world when the heavenly movement will cease. For this reason, too, certain philosophers, who held that the movement of the heavens will never cease, maintained that human souls will return to mortal bodies such as we have now—whether, as Empedocles, they stated that the soul would return to the same body at the end of the *great year,* or that it would return to another body; thus Pythagoras asserted that *any soul will enter any body,* as stated in *On the Soul* 1.3.

Reply Obj. 1: Although the head is more conformed to the members by conformity of proportion (which is requisite in order that it have influence over the members) than one member is to another, yet the head has a certain causality over the members which the members have not; and in this the members differ from the head and agree with one another. Hence Christ's resurrection is an exemplar of ours, and through our faith therein there arises in us the hope of

tione consurgit: non autem resurrectio alicuius membri Christi est causa resurrectionis ceterorum membrorum. Et ideo Christi resurrectio debuit praecedere resurrectionem aliorum, qui omnes simul resurgere debuerunt *in consummatione saeculorum*.

AD SECUNDUM dicendum quod, quamvis inter membra Christi sint quaedam aliis digniora et magis capiti conformia, non tamen pertingunt ad rationem capitis, ut sint causa aliorum. Et ideo ex conformitate ad Christum non debetur eis quod eorum resurrectio praecedat resurrectionem aliorum quasi exemplar exemplatum, sicut dictum est de resurrectione Christi: sed quod aliquibus sit hoc concessum quod eorum resurrectio non sit usque ad communem resurrectionem dilata, est ex speciali gratiae privilegio, non ex debito conformitatis ad Christum.

AD TERTIUM dicendum quod de illa resurrectione sanctorum cum Christo videtur dubitare Hieronymus, in *Sermone de Assumptione*: utrum scilicet, peracto resurrectionis testimonio, iterum mortui sint, ut sic eorum fuerit magis resuscitatio quaedam, sicut Lazari, quam vera resurrectio, qualis erit in fine mundi; an ad immortalem vitam vere resurrexerunt semper in corpore victuri, *in caelum cum Christo ascendentes corporaliter*, ut Glossa dicit, Matth. 27, [52–53]. Et hoc videtur probabilius. Quia ad hoc quod verum testimonium de vera resurrectione Christi proferrent, congruum fuit ut vere resurgerent: sicut Hieronymus ibidem dicit. Nec eorum resurrectio propter ipsos accelerata est: sed propter resurrectionem Christi testificandam. Quod quidem testimonium erat ad fundandam fidem novi Testamenti. Unde decentius factum est per Patres veteris Testamenti quam per eos qui, iam novo Testamento fundato, decesserunt.

Tamen sciendum est quod, etsi de resurrectione eorum in Evangelio mentio fiat ante resurrectionem Christi, tamen, ut per testimonium patet, intelligendum est per anticipationem esse dictum: quod frequenter historiographis accidit. Nulli enim vera resurrectione ante Christum resurrexerunt, eo quod ipse est *primitiae dormientium*, ut dicitur I Cor, 15, [20]: quamvis fuerint aliqui resuscitati ante Christi resurrectionem, ut de Lazaro patet.

AD QUARTUM dicendum quod occasione illorum verborum, ut Augustinus narrat, XX *de Civ. Dei*, quidam haeretici posuerunt primam resurrectionem futuram esse mortuorum ut cum Christo mille annis in terra regnent: unde vocati sunt *Chiliastae*, quasi *Millenarii*. Et ideo Augustinus ibidem ostendit verba illa aliter intelligenda esse: scilicet de resurrectione spirituali, per quam homines a peccatis dono gratiae resurgunt. Secunda autem resurrectio est corporum.

our own resurrection. But the resurrection of one of Christ's members is not the cause of the resurrection of other members, and consequently Christ's resurrection had to precede the resurrection of others who have all to rise again *at the consummation of the world*.

REPLY OBJ. 2: Although among the members some rank higher than others and are more conformed to the Head, they do not attain to the character of headship so as to be the cause of others. Consequently, greater conformity to Christ does not give them a right to rise again before others as though they were exemplar and the others exemplate, as we have said in reference to Christ's resurrection: and if it has been granted to others that their resurrection should not be delayed until the general resurrection, this has been by special privilege of grace, and not as due on account of conformity to Christ.

REPLY OBJ. 3: Jerome, in a sermon on the Assumption (*Epistle to Paula and Eustochium*), seems to be doubtful of this resurrection of the saints with Christ: that is, as to whether they died again, having been witnesses to the resurrection, so that theirs was a resuscitation (as in the case of Lazarus who died again) rather than a resurrection such as will be at the end of the world—or really rose again to immortal life, to live forever in the body, and to ascend bodily into heaven with Christ, as a Gloss says on Matthew 27:52. The latter seems more probable, because, as Jerome says, in order that they might bear true witness to Christ's true resurrection, it was fitting that they should truly rise again. Nor was their resurrection hastened for their sake, but for the sake of bearing witness to Christ's resurrection: and that by bearing witness thereto they might lay the foundation of the faith of the New Testament; wherefore it was more fitting that it should be borne by the fathers of the Old Testament than by those who died after the foundation of the New.

It must, however, be observed that, although the Gospel mentions their resurrection before Christ's, we must take this statement as made in anticipation, as is often the case with writers of history. For none rose again with a true resurrection before Christ, since he is the *first-fruits of them that sleep* (1 Cor 15:20), although some were resuscitated before Christ's resurrection, as in the case of Lazarus.

REPLY OBJ. 4: On account of these words, as Augustine relates (*The City of God* 20.7), certain heretics asserted that there will be a first resurrection of the dead that they may reign with Christ on earth for a thousand years; whence they were called *Chiliasts* or *Millenarians*. Hence Augustine says (*The City of God* 20.7) that these words are to be understood otherwise, namely, of the spiritual resurrection whereby men shall rise again from their sins to the gift of grace: while the second resurrection is of bodies.

Regnum autem *Christi* dicitur Ecclesia, in qua cum Christo non solum martyres, sed etiam alii electi regnant: *ut a parte totum intelligatur.* Vel regnant cum Christo in gloria quantum ad omnes, et fit specialiter mentio de martyribus *quia ipsi praecipue regnant mortui qui usque ad mortem pro veritate certaverunt.*

Millenarius autem non significat aliquem certum numerum, sed designat totum tempus quod nunc agitur, in quo nunc sancti cum Christo regnant . Quia numerus millenarius designat universitatem magis quam centenarius: eo quod centenarius est quadratum denarii; sed millenarius est numerus solidus ex duplici ductu denarii in seipsum surgens, quia decies decem decies mille sunt. Et similiter in Psalmo [104, 8] dicitur: *verbi quod mandavit in mille generationes*, idest *in omnes.*

The reign of Christ denotes the Church wherein not only martyrs but also the other elect reign, *the part denoting the whole;* or they reign with Christ in glory as regards all, and special mention is made of the martyrs, *because they especially reign after death who fought for the truth even unto death.*

The number of a thousand years denotes not a fixed number, but the whole of the present time wherein the saints now reign with Christ, because the number 1,000 designates universality more than the number 100, since 100 is the square of 10, whereas 1,000 is a cube resulting from the multiplication of ten by its square, for 10 X 10 = 100, and 10 X 10 X 10 = 1,000. Similarly, Psalm 104:8 has: *the word which he commanded to a thousand,* i.e., all, *generations.*

Article 2

Whether the Time of Our Resurrection Is Hidden?

Ad secundum sic proceditur. Videtur quod tempus illud non sit occultum. Quia cuius principium est determinatum et scitum, et finis potest determinate sciri: eo quod *omnia mensurantur quadam periodo*, ut dicitur in II *de Generatione.* Sed principium mundi determinate scitur. Ergo et finis ipsius potest determinate sciri. Tunc autem erit tempus resurrectionis et iudicii. Ergo tempus illud non est occultum.

Praeterea, Apoc. 12, [6] dicitur quod *mulier*, per quam Ecclesia significatur, *habet locum paratum a Deo, in quo pascatur diebus mille ducentis sexaginta.* Daniel etiam 12, [11–12] ponitur determinatus numerus dierum, per quos anni significari videntur, secundum illud Ezech. 4, [6], *diem pro anno dedi tibi.* Ergo ex sacra Scriptura potest sciri determinate finis mundi et resurrectionis tempus.

Praeterea, status novi Testamenti praefiguratus fuit in veteri Testamento. Sed scimus determinate tempus in quo vetus Testamentum statum habuit. Ergo et potest sciri tempus determinate in quo novum Testamentum statum habebit. Sed novum Testamentum habebit statum usque ad finem mundi: unde dicitur Matth. 28, [20]: *ecce, ego vobis cum sum usque ad consummationem saeculi.* Ergo potest sciri determinate finis mundi et resurrectionis tempus.

Sed contra: Illud quod est ignoratum ab angelis, est etiam hominibus multo magis occultum: quia ea ad quae homines naturali ratione pertingere possunt, multo limpidius et certius angeli naturali cognitione cognoscunt. Similiter etiam revelationes hominibus non fiunt nisi mediantibus angelis: ut patet per Dionysium, 4 cap. *Cael. Hier.* Sed angeli nesciunt tempus determinate: ut

Objection 1: It would seem that this time is not hidden. Because when we know exactly the beginning of a thing, we can know its end exactly, since *all things are measured by a certain period* (*On Generation and Corruption* 2). Now the beginning of the world is known exactly. Therefore, its end can also be known exactly. But this will be the time of the resurrection and judgment. Therefore, that time is not hidden.

Obj. 2: Further, it is stated that *the woman*, who represents the Church, *had a place prepared by God, in which she is fed one thousand two hundred sixty days* (Rev 12:6). Again, a certain fixed number of days is mentioned, which apparently signify years, according to Ezekiel 4:6: *a day for a year I gave to you.* Therefore, the time of the end of the world and of the resurrection can be known exactly from Sacred Scripture.

Obj. 3: Further, the state of the New Testament was foreshadowed in the Old Testament. Now we know exactly the time wherein the state of the Old Testament endured. Therefore, we can also know exactly the time wherein the state of the New Testament will endure. But the state of the New Testament will last to the end of the world, wherefore it is said: *behold, I am with you to the consummation of the world* (Matt 28:20). Therefore, the time of the end of the world and of the resurrection can be known exactly.

On the contrary, That which is unknown to the angels will be much more unknown to men: because those things to which men attain by natural reason are much more clearly and certainly known to the angels by their natural knowledge. Moreover, revelations are not made to men save by means of the angels, as Dionysius asserts (*On the Heavenly Hierarchies* 4). Now the angels have no exact

patet Matth. 24, [36]: *de die illa et hora nemo scit, neque angeli caelorum*. Ergo illud est hominibus occultum.

PRAETEREA, Apostoli fuerunt magis conscii secretorum Dei quam alii sequentes: quia, ut dicitur Rom. 8, [23], ipsi *primitias Spiritus habuerunt*; Glossa, *tempore prius et ceteris abundantius*. Sed eis de hoc ipso quaerentibus dictum est, Act. 1, [7]: *non est vestrum nosse tempora vel momenta quae posuit Pater in potestate sua*. Ergo multo magis est aliis occultum.

RESPONDEO dicendum quod, sicut Augustinus dicit, in libro *Octoginta trium Quaest.*, *aetas ultima humani generis, quae incipit ab adventu Domini usque ad finem saeculi, quibus generationibus computetur incertum est*: sicut etiam senectus, quae est ultima aetas hominis, non determinatum habet tempus secundum mensuram aliarum, cum quandoque sola *tantum teneat temporis quantum omnes aliae aetates*.

Huius autem ratio est quia determinatus numerus futuri temporis sciri non potest nisi vel per revelationem, vel per naturalem rationem. Tempus autem quod erit usque ad resurrectionem, numerari non potest naturali ratione. Quia simul erit resurrectio et finis motus caeli, ut dictum est. Ex motu autem accipitur numerus omnium quae determinato tempore per naturalem rationem futura praevidentur. Ex motu autem caeli non potest cognosci finis eius: quia, cum sit circularis, ex hoc ipso habet quod secundum naturam suam possit in perpetuum durare. Unde naturali ratione tempus quod erit usque ad resurrectionem, numerari non potest.

Similiter nec per revelationem haberi potest: ideo ut omnes semper sint solliciti et praeparati ad Christo occurrendum. Et propter hoc etiam Apostolis de hoc quaerentibus respondit, Act. 1: *non est vestrum nosse tempora vel momenta quae Pater posuit in sua potestate*; in quo, ut Augustinus dicit, XVIII *de Civ. Dei* 8, *omnium de hac re calculantium digitos resolvit et quiescere iubet*. Quod enim Apostolis quaerentibus noluit indicare, nec aliis revelabit.

Unde omnes illi qui tempus praedictum numerare voluerunt hactenus, falsiloqui sunt inventi.

Quidam enim, ut Augustinus dicit ibidem, dixerunt ab ascensione Domini usque ad ultimum eius adventum quadringentos annos posse compleri; alii quingentos; alii mille. Quorum falsitas patet. Et similiter patebit eorum qui adhuc computare non cessant.

AD PRIMUM ergo dicendum quod eorum quorum finis cognoscitur principio noto, oportet mensuram esse nobis cognitam. Et ideo, cognito principio alicuius rei cuius duratio mensuratur motu caeli, possumus cognoscere eius finem eo quod motus caeli est nobis notus. Sed mensura durationis motus caeli est sola divina di-

knowledge of that time, as appears from Matthew 24:36: *of that day and hour no one knows, nor the angels of heaven*. Therefore, that time is hidden from men.

FURTHER, The apostles were more cognizant of God's secrets than others who followed them, because they had *the first-fruits of the spirit* (Rom 8:23)—*before others in point of time and more abundantly*, as a Gloss observes. And yet when they questioned our Lord about this very matter, he answered them: *it is not for you to know the times or moments which the Father has put in his own power* (Acts 1:7). Much more, therefore, is it hidden from others.

I ANSWER THAT, As Augustine says (*Eighty-three Questions* 58), *as to the last age of the human race, which begins from our Lord's coming and lasts until the end of the world, it is uncertain of how many generations it will consist*: even so old age, which is man's last age, has no fixed time according to the measure of the other ages, since sometimes alone *it lasts as long a time as all the others*.

The reason of this is because the exact length of future time cannot be known except either by revelation or by natural reason: and the time until the resurrection cannot be reckoned by natural reason, because the resurrection and the end of the heavenly movement will be simultaneous, as stated above (A. 1). And all things that are foreseen by natural reason to happen at a fixed time are reckoned by movement: and it is impossible from the movement of the heaven to reckon its end, for since it is circular, it is for this very reason able by its nature to endure forever. Hence the time between this and the resurrection cannot be reckoned by natural reason.

Similarly, it cannot be known by revelation, so that all may be on the watch and ready to meet Christ: and for this reason when the apostles asked him about this, Christ answered: *it is not for you to know the times or moments which the Father has put in his own power* (Acts 1:7), whereby, as Augustine says (*The City of God* 28.53): *he scatters the fingers of all calculators and bids them be still*. For what he refused to tell the apostles, he will not reveal to others.

Therefore, all those who have been misled to reckon the aforesaid time have so far proved to be untruthful;

for some, as Augustine says (*The City of God* 28.53), stated that from our Lord's Ascension to his last coming 400 years would elapse, others 500, others 1,000. The falseness of these calculators is evident, as will likewise be the falseness of those who still do not cease to calculate.

REPLY OBJ. 1: When we know a thing's beginning and also its end, it follows that its measure is known to us: wherefore if we know the beginning of a thing the duration of which is measured by the movement of the heaven, we are able to know its end, since the movement of heaven is known to us. But the measure of the duration of the

spositio, quae est nobis occulta. Et ideo, quantumcumque sciamus principium, finem scire non possumus.

Ad secundum dicendum quod per mille ducentos sexaginta dies, de quibus fit mentio in Apoc. 12, significatur omne tempus in quo Ecclesia durati et non determinatus aliquis numerus annorum. Et hoc ideo quia praedicatio Christi, super quam fundatur Ecclesia, duravit tribus annis cum dimidio, quod tempus fere continet aequalem numerum dierum numero praedicto.

Et similiter etiam numerus eorum qui in Daniele ponuntur, non est referendus ad numerum aliquem annorum qui sunt usque ad finem mundi, vel usque ad praedicationem Antichristi: sed debet referri ad tempus quo praedicabit et quo persecutio eius durabit.

Ad tertium dicendum quod, quamvis status novi Testamenti in generali sit praefiguratus per statum veteris Testamenti, non tamen oportet quod singula respondeant singulis: praecipue cum in Christo omnes figurae veteris Testamenti fuerint completae. Et ideo Augustinus, XVIII *de Civ. Dei*, respondet quibusdam qui volebant accipere numerum persecutionum quas Ecclesia passa est secundum numerum plagarum Aegypti, dicens: *ego per illas res gestas in Aegypto istas persecutiones prophetice significatas esse non arbitror: quamvis ab eis qui hoc putant, exquisite et ingeniose illa singula his singulis comparata videantur, non prophetico spiritu, sed coniectura mentis humanae, quae aliquando ad verum pervenit, aliquando fallitur.*

Et similiter videtur esse de dictis Abbatis Ioachim, qui per tales coniecturas de futuris aliqua vera praedixit, et in aliquibus deceptus fuit.

heavenly movement is God's ordinance alone, which is unknown to us. Therefore, however much we may know its beginning, we are unable to know its end.

Reply Obj. 2: The one thousand two hundred sixty days mentioned in Revelation 12:6 denote all the time during which the Church endures, and not any definite number of years. The reason whereof is because the preaching of Christ, on which the Church is built, lasted three years and a half, which time contains almost an equal number of days as the aforesaid number.

And similarly, the number of days appointed by Daniel does not refer to a number of years to elapse before the end of the world or until the preaching of Antichrist, but to the time of Antichrist's preaching and the duration of his persecution.

Reply Obj. 3: Although the state of the New Testament in general is foreshadowed by the state of the Old Testament it does not follow that individuals correspond to individuals: especially since all the figures of the Old Testament were fulfilled in Christ. Hence Augustine (*The City of God* 28.52) answers certain persons who wished to liken the number of persecutions suffered by the Church to the number of the plagues of Egypt, in these words: *I do not think that the occurrences in Egypt were in their signification prophetic of these persecutions, although those who think so have shown nicety and ingenuity in adapting them severally the one to the other, not indeed by a prophetic spirit, but by the guess-work of the human mind, which sometimes reaches the truth and sometimes not.*

The same remarks would seem applicable to the statements of Abbot Joachim, who by means of such conjectures about the future foretold some things that were true, and in others was deceived.

Article 3

Whether the Resurrection Will Take Place at Night-time?

Ad tertium sic proceditur. Videtur quod resurrectio non erit in noctis tempore. Quia resurrectio non erit *donec atteratur caelum*, ut dicitur Iob 14, [12]. Sed, cessante motu caeli, quod dicitur eius attritio, non erit tempus, neque nox neque dies. Ergo resurrectio non erit in nocte.

Praeterea, finis uniuscuiusque rei debet esse perfectissimus. Sed tunc erit finis temporis: unde in Apoc. [10, 6] dicitur quod *tempus amplius non erit*. Ergo tunc debet esse tempus in sua optima dispositione. Et ita debet esse dies.

Praeterea, qualitas temporis debet respondere his quae geruntur in tempore: unde Ioan. 13, [30] fit mentio de nocte quando Iudas exivit a consortio lucis. Sed tunc erit perfecta manifestatio omnium quae nunc la-

Objection 1: It would seem that the resurrection will not be at night-time. For the resurrection will not be *till the heavens be broken* (Job 14:12). Now when the heavenly movement ceases, which is signified by its breaking, there will be no time, neither night nor day. Therefore, the resurrection will not be at night-time.

Obj. 2: Further, the end of a thing ought to be most perfect. Now the end of time will be then: wherefore it is said that *time shall be no longer* (Rev 10:6). Therefore, time ought to be then in its most perfect disposition, and consequently it should be the daytime.

Obj. 3: Further, the time should be such as to be adapted to what is done therein: wherefore the night is mentioned as being the time when Judas went out from the fellowship of the light. Now, all things that are hidden at

tent; quia, cum venerit Dominus, *illuminabit abscondita tenebrarum et, manifestabit consilia cordium*, ut dicitur I Cor. 4, [5]. Ergo debet esse in die.

Sed contra: Resurrectio Christi est exemplar nostrae resurrectionis. Sed resurrectio Christi fuit in nocte, ut Gregorius dicit, in *Homilia Paschali*. Ergo et nostra resurrectio erit tempore nocturno.

Praeterea, adventus Domini comparatur adventui furis in domum, ut patet Luc. 12, [39–40]. Sed fur in tempore noctis in domum venit. Ergo et Dominus tempore nocturno veniet. Sed veniente ipso fiet resurrectio, ut dictum est. Ergo fiet resurrectio in tempore nocturno.

Respondeo dicendum quod determinata hora temporis qua fiet resurrectio, sciri pro certo non potest, ut patet in littera. Tamen satis probabiliter a quibusdam dicitur quod resurrectio erit quasi in crepuscolo, sole existente in oriente et luna in occidente: quia in tali dispositione sol et luna creduntur esse creata; ut sic eorum circulatio compleatur penitus per reditum ad idem punctum. Unde de Christo dicitur quod tali hora resurrexit.

Ad primum ergo dicendum quod, quando resurrectio erit, non erit tempus, sed finis temporis: quia in eodem instanti in quo cessabit motus caeli, erit resurrectio mortuorum, Et tamen erit situs siderum secundum dispositionem qua se habent nunc in aliqua determinata hora. Et secundum hoc dicitur resurrectio futura tali vel tali hora.

Ad secundum dicendum quod optima dispositio temporis dicitur esse in meridie propter illuminationem solis. Sed tunc *civitas Dei non egebit neque sole neque luna, quia claritas Dei illuminabit eam*, ut dicitur Apoc. [22, 5]. Et ideo quantum ad hoc non refert utrum in die vel in nocte resurrectio fiat.

Ad tertium dicendum quod tempori illi congruit manifestatio quantum ad ea quae tunc gerentur, et occultatio quantum ad determinationem ipsius temporis. Et ideo utrumque congrue fieri potest: ut scilicet sit resurrectio in die vel in nocte.

the present time will then be made most manifest, because when the Lord shall come *he will bring to light the hidden things of darkness, and will make manifest the counsels of the hearts* (1 Cor 4:5). Therefore, it ought to be during the day.

On the contrary, Christ's resurrection is the exemplar of ours. Now Christ's resurrection was at night, as Gregory says in a homily for Easter (XXI in *Evang.*). Therefore, our resurrection will also be at night-time.

Further, The coming of our Lord is compared to the coming of a thief into the house (Luke 12:39–40). But the thief comes to the house at night-time. Therefore, our Lord will also come in the night. Now, when he comes the resurrection will take place, as stated above (Q. 76, A. 2). Therefore, the resurrection will be at night-time.

I answer that, The exact time and hour at which the resurrection will be cannot be known for certain, as stated in the text (*Sentences* IV, D. 43). Nevertheless some assert with sufficient probability that it will be towards the twilight, the moon being in the east and the sun in the west; because the sun and moon are believed to have been created in these positions, and thus their revolutions will be altogether completed by their return to the same point. Wherefore it is said that Christ arose at such an hour.

Reply Obj. 1: When the resurrection occurs, it will not be time but the end of time; because at the very instant that the heavens will cease to move, the dead will rise again. Nevertheless, the stars will be in the same position as they occupy now at any fixed hour: and accordingly it is said that the resurrection will be at this or that hour.

Reply Obj. 2: The most perfect disposition of time is said to be midday, on account of the light given by the sun. But then the *city of God will need neither sun nor moon, because the glory of God will enlighten it* (Rev 22:5). Wherefore in this respect it matters not whether the resurrection be in the day or in the night.

Reply Obj. 3: That time should be adapted to manifestation as regards the things that will happen then, and to secrecy as regards the fixing of the time. Hence either may happen fittingly, namely, that the resurrection be in the day or in the night.

Article 4

Whether the Resurrection Will Happen Suddenly or by Degrees?

Ad quartum sic proceditur. Videtur quod resurrectio non fiet subito, sed successive. Quia Ezech. 37 praenuntiatur resurrectio mortuorum: ubi dicitur [7–8], *accesserunt ossa ad ossa, et vidi, et ecce, super ea nervi et carnes ascenderunt, et extenta est in eis cutis desuper, et spiritum non habebant*. Ergo reparatio corporum prae-

Objection 1: It would seem that the resurrection will not happen suddenly but by degrees. For the resurrection of the dead is foretold where it is written: *the bones came together, bone to its bone; and as I looked, there were sinews on them, and flesh had come upon them, and skin had covered them; but there was no breath in them* (Ezek 37:7–8).

cedet tempore coni unctionem animarum. Et sic resurrectio non erit subita.

PRAETEREA, illud ad quod exiguntur plures actiones se consequentes, non potest subito fieri. Sed ad resurrectionem exiguntur plures actiones se consequentes: scilicet collectio cinerum, reformatio corporis, et infusio animae. Ergo resurrectio non fiet subito.

PRAETEREA, omnis sonus tempore mensuratur. Sed sonus tubae erit causa resurrectionis, ut dictum est. Ergo resurrectio fiet in tempore, et non subito.

PRAETEREA, nullus motus localis potest esse subito, ut dicitur in libro de Sensu et Sensato. Sed ad resurrectionem exigitur aliquis motus localis in collectione cinerum. Ergo non fiet subito.

SED CONTRA: Est quod dicitur I Cor. 15, [51–52]: omnes quidem resurgemus in momento, in ictu oculi. Ergo resurrectio erit subito.

PRAETEREA, virtus infinita subito operatur. Sed, sicut Damascenus dicit: crede resurrectionem futuram divina virtute, de qua constat quod sit infinita. Ergo resurrectio fiet subito.

RESPONDEO dicendum quod in resurrectione aliqua fient ministerio angelorum, et aliqua virtute divina immediate, ut dictum est. Illud ergo quod fiet ministerio angelorum, non erit in instanti, si instans dicat indivisibile temporis: erit tamen instans si instans accipiatur pro tempore imperceptibili. Illud autem quod fiet virtute divina immediate, fiet subito, scilicet in termino temporis quo angelorum opus complebitur: quia virtus superior inferiorem ad perfectionem adducit.

AD PRIMUM ergo dicendum quod Ezechiel loquebatur populo rudi, sicut et Moyses. Unde, sicut Moyses distinxit opera sex dierum per dies, ut rudis populus capere posset, quamvis omnia simul sint facta, secundum Augustinum; ita Ezechiel diversa quae in resurrectione futura sunt expressit, quamvis omnia simul sint futura in instanti.

AD SECUNDUM dicendum quod, quamvis illae operationes sint se invicem consequentes natura, tamen simul sunt tempore: vel quia sunt in eodem instanti; vel una est in instanti ad quod alia terminatur.

AD TERTIUM dicendum quod idem videtur esse dicendum de sono illo et de formis sacramentorum: scilicet quod in ultimo instanti sonus effectum suum habebit.

AD QUARTUM dicendum quod congregatio cinerum, quae sine motu locali esse non potest, fiet ministerio

Therefore, the restoration of the bodies will precede in time their reunion with the souls, and thus the resurrection will not be sudden.

OBJ. 2: Further, a thing does not happen suddenly if it require several actions following one another. Now the resurrection requires several actions following one another: namely, the gathering of the ashes, the refashioning of the body, and the infusion of the soul. Therefore, the resurrection will not be sudden.

OBJ. 3: Further, all sound is measured by time. Now the sound of the trumpet will be the cause of the resurrection, as stated above (Q. 76, A. 2). Therefore, the resurrection will take time and will not happen suddenly.

OBJ. 4: Further, no local movement can be sudden, as stated in On Sense and the Sensed 7. Now the resurrection requires local movement in the gathering of the ashes. Therefore, it will not happen suddenly.

ON THE CONTRARY, 1 Corinthians 15:51–52 says: we shall all indeed rise again in a moment, in the twinkling of an eye. Therefore, the resurrection will be sudden.

FURTHER, Infinite power works suddenly. But the Damascene says (On the Orthodox Faith 4): you shall believe in the resurrection to be wrought by the power of God, and it is evident that this is infinite. Therefore, the resurrection will be sudden.

I ANSWER THAT, At the resurrection something will be done by the ministry of the angels, and something immediately by the power of God, as stated above (1 Cor 15:51–52). Accordingly, that which is done by the ministry of the angels will not be instantaneous, if by instant we mean an indivisible point of time, but it will be instantaneous if by instant we mean an imperceptible time. But that which will be done immediately by God's power will happen suddenly, namely, at the end of the time wherein the work of the angels will be done, because the higher power brings the lower to perfection.

REPLY OBJ. 1: Ezechiel spoke, like Moses, to a rough people, and therefore, just as Moses divided the works of the six days into days in order that the uncultured people might be able to understand, although all things were made together according to Augustine (On the Literal Meaning of Genesis 4), so Ezechiel expressed the various things that will happen in the resurrection, although they will all happen together in an instant.

REPLY OBJ. 2: Although these actions follow one another in nature, they are all together in time: because either they are together in the same instant, or one is in the instant that terminates the other.

REPLY OBJ. 3: The same would seem to apply to that sound as to the forms of the sacraments, namely, that the sound will produce its effect in its last instant.

REPLY OBJ. 4: The gathering of the ashes, which cannot be without local movement, will be done by the ministry of

angelorum. Et ideo erit in tempore, sed imperceptibili, propter facilitatem operandi quae competit angelis.

the angels. Hence it will be in time, though imperceptible, on account of the facility of operation which is competent to the angels.

QUESTION 78

THE STARTING TERMINUS OF THE RESURRECTION

Deinde considerandum est de termino a quo resurrectionis.

Circa quod quaeruntur tria.

Primo: utrum mors sit terminus a quo resurrectionis in omnibus.

Secundo: utrum cineres vel pulveres.

Tertio: utrum illi pulveres habeant naturalem inclinationem ad animam.

We must now consider the starting terminus of the resurrection.

Under this head there are three points of inquiry:

(1) Whether death is the starting terminus of the resurrection in every case?

(2) Whether ashes are, or dust?

(3) Whether this dust has a natural inclination towards the soul?

Article 1

Whether Death Will Be the Starting Terminus of the Resurrection in All Cases?

AD PRIMUM SIC PROCEDITUR. Videtur quod mors non erit terminus a quo resurrectionis in omnibus. Quia quidam non morientur, sed immortalitate *supervestientur*. Dicitur enim in Symbolo quod ipse *venturus est iudicare vivos et mortuos*. Hoc autem non potest intelligi quantum ad tempus iudicii: quia tunc erunt omnes vivi. Ergo oportet quod referatur haec distinctio ad tempus praecedens. Et ita non omnes ante iudicium morientur.

PRAETEREA, naturale et commune desiderium non potest esse vacuum et inane, quin in aliquibus expleatur. Sed secundum Apostolum, II Cor. 5, [4], hoc est commune desiderium, quod *nolumus exspoliari, sed supervestiri*. Ergo aliqui erunt qui nunquam exspoliabuntur corpore per mortem, sed supervestientur gloria resurrectionis.

PRAETEREA, Augustinus, in *Enchirid.*, dicit quod quatuor ultimae petitiones Dominicae orationis ad praesentem vitam pertinent. Quarum una est, *dimitte nobis debita nostra*. Ergo Ecclesia petit in hac vita sibi omnia debita relaxari. Sed Ecclesiae oratio non potest esse cassa, quin exaudiatur: Ioan. 16, [23], *quidquid petieritis Patrem in nomine meo, dabit vobis*. Ergo Ecclesia in aliquo huius vitae tempore omnium debitorum remissionem consequetur. Sed unum de debitis, quo pro peccato primi parentis adstringimur, est quod nascimur in originali peccato. Ergo aliquando hoc Ecclesiae Deus praestabit, quod homines sine originali peccato nascentur. Sed mors est poena originalis peccati. Ergo aliqui homines erunt circa finem mundi qui non morientur. Et sic idem quod prius.

PRAETEREA, via compendiosior est semper sapienti magis eligenda. Sed compendiosior via est quod homines qui invenientur vivi in impassibilitatem resurrectio-

OBJECTION 1: It would seem that death will not be the starting terminus of the resurrection in all cases. Because some shall not die but shall be clothed with immortality: for it is said in the creed that our Lord *will come to judge the living and the dead*. Now this cannot refer to the time of judgment, because then all will be alive. Therefore, this distinction must refer to the previous time, and consequently not all will die before the judgment.

OBJ. 2: Further, a natural and common desire cannot be empty and vain, but is fulfilled in some cases. Now, according to the Apostle, it is a common desire that *we would not be stripped but clothed about* (2 Cor 5:4). Therefore, there will be some who will never be stripped of the body by death, but will be arrayed in the glory of the resurrection.

OBJ. 3: Further, Augustine says (*Handbook on Faith, Hope, and Charity* 115) that the four last petitions of the Lord's prayer refer to the present life. One of them is: *forgive us our debts*. Therefore, the Church prays that all debts may be forgiven her in this life. Now the Church's prayer cannot be void and not granted: *if you ask the Father anything in my name, he will give it to you* (John 16:23). Therefore, at some time of this life the Church will receive the remission of all debts: and one of the debts to which we are bound by the sin of our first parent is that we be born in original sin. Therefore, at some time God will grant to the Church that men be born without original sin. But death is the punishment of original sin. Therefore, at the end of the world there will be some men who will not die: and so the same conclusion follows.

OBJ. 4: Further, the wise man should always choose the shortest way. Now it is shorter for the men who shall be found living to be transferred to the impassibility of the

nis transferantur, quam quod prius moriantur et postea resurgant a morte in immortalitatem. Ergo Deus, qui est summe sapiens, hanc viam eliget in his qui vivi invenientur. Et sic idem quod prius.

SED CONTRA: I Cor. 15, [36]: *quod seminas, non vivificatur nisi prius moriatur*. Et loquitur sub similitudine seminis de resurrectione corporum. Ergo corpora a morte resurgent.

PRAETEREA, I Cor. 15, [22]: *sicut in Adam omnes moriuntur, ita in Christo omnes, vivificabuntur*. Sed in Christo omnes vivificabuntur. Ergo in Adam omnes morientur. Et sic resurrectio omnium erit a morte.

RESPONDEO dicendum quod super hac quaestione varie loquuntur Sancti, ut in littera patet. Tamen haec est securior et communior opinio, quod omnes morientur et a morte resurgent. Et hoc propter tria. Primo, quia magis concordat divinae iustitiae, quae humanam naturam pro peccato primi parentis damnavit, ut omnes qui per actum naturae ab eo originem ducerent, infectionem originalis peccati contraherent, et per consequens mortis debitores essent.

Secundo, quia magis concordat divinae Scripturae, quae omnium futuram resurrectionem praedicit. Resurrectio autem proprie non est nisi *eius quod cecidit et dissolutum est*, ut Damascenus dicit.

Tertio, quia magis concordat ordini naturae, in quo invenimus quod id quod corruptum et vitiatum est, in suam novitatem non reducitur nisi corruptione mediante: sicut acetum non fit vinum nisi aceto corrupto et in humorem vitis transeunte. Unde, cum natura humana in defectum necessitatis moriendi devenerit, non erit reditus ad immortalitatem nisi mediante morte.

Convenit etiam ordini naturae propter aliam rationem. Quia, ut in VIII *Physic*. dicitur, motus caeli est *ut vita quaedam natura existentibus omnibus*: sicut et motus cordis totius corporis vita quaedam est. Unde sicut, cessante motu cordis, omnia membra mortificantur; ita, cessante motu caeli, non potest aliquid vivum remanere illa vita quae ex influentia illius motus conservabatur. Talis autem vita est qua nunc degimus. Unde oportet quod ex hac vita discedant qui post motum caeli quiescentem victuri sunt.

AD PRIMUM ergo dicendum quod distinctio illa mortuorum et vivorum non est referenda ad ipsum iudicii tempus; neque ad totum tempus praeteritum, quia omnes iudicandi aliquo tempore fuerunt vivi et aliquo tempore mortui; sed ad illud tempus determinatum quod immediate iudicium praecedet, quando scilicet iudicii signa incipient apparere.

AD SECUNDUM dicendum quod perfectum desiderium sanctorum non potest esse vanum: sed nihil prohibet desiderium conditionatum eorum vanum esse. Et

resurrection, than for them to die first and afterwards rise again from death to immortality. Therefore, God, who is supremely wise, will choose this way for those who shall be found living.

ON THE CONTRARY, 1 Corinthians 15:36 says: *that which you sow is not quickened unless it die first*, and it is speaking of the resurrection of the body as compared to the seed.

FURTHER, It is written: *as in Adam all die, so also in Christ all shall be made alive* (1 Cor 15:22). Now all shall be made alive in Christ. Therefore, all shall die in Adam: and so all shall rise again from death.

I ANSWER THAT, The saints differ in speaking on this question, as may be seen in the text (*Sentences* IV, D. 43). However, the safer and more common opinion is that all shall die and rise again from death: and this for three reasons. First, because it is more in accord with divine justice, which condemned human nature for the sin of its first parent, that all who by the act of nature derive their origin from him should contract the stain of original sin, and consequently be the debtors of death.

Second, because it is more in agreement with divine Scripture which foretells the resurrection of all; and resurrection is not predicted properly except of that *which has fallen and perished*, as the Damascene says (*On the Orthodox Faith* 4).

Third, because it is more in harmony with the order of nature where we find that what is corrupted and decayed is not renewed except by means of corruption: thus vinegar does not become wine unless the vinegar be corrupted and pass into the juice of the grape. Wherefore, since human nature has incurred the defect of the necessity of death, it cannot return to immortality save by means of death.

It is also in keeping with the order of nature for another reason, because, as it is stated in *Physics* 8.1, the movement of heaven is *as a kind of life to all existing in nature*, just as the movement of the heart is a kind of life of the whole body: wherefore even as all the members become dead on the heart ceasing to move, so when the heavenly movement ceases, nothing can remain living with that life which was sustained by the influence of that movement. Now such is the life by which we live now: and therefore it follows that those who shall live after the movement of the heaven comes to a standstill must depart from this life.

REPLY OBJ. 1: This distinction of the dead and the living does not apply to the time itself of the judgment, nor to the whole preceding time, since all who are to be judged were living at some time, and dead at some time: but it applies to that particular time which shall precede the judgment immediately; that is, when the signs of the judgment shall begin to appear.

REPLY OBJ. 2: The perfect desire of the saints cannot be void; but nothing prevents their conditional desire being void. Such is the desire whereby *we would not be stripped*

tale desiderium est quo *nolumus exspoliari sed supervestiri*: scilicet, si possibile sit. Et hoc desiderium a quibusdam *velleitas* dicitur.

AD TERTIUM dicendum quod hoc est erroneum, dicere quod aliquis sine peccato originali concipiatur, praeter Christum. Quia ille qui sine peccato originali conciperetur, non indigeret redemptione, quae facta est per Christum. Et sic Christus non esset Redemptor omnium.

Nec potest dici quod non hac redemptione indiguerunt quia praestitum fuit eis ut sine peccato conciperentur quia illa gratia facta est parentibus ut in eis vitium naturae sanaretur, quo manente sine originali peccato generare non possent; vel ipsi naturae, quae sanata est. Oportet enim ponere quod quilibet personaliter redemptione Christi indigeat, non solum ratione naturae.

Liberari autem *a malo*, vel *a debito absolvi*, non potest nisi qui debitum incurrit vel in malum deiectus fuit. Et ideo non possent omnes fructum Dominicae orationis in seipsis percipere nisi omnes debitores nascerentur et malo subiecti. Unde *dimissio debitorum*, vel *liberatio a malo*, non potest intelligi quod aliquis sine debito vel immunis a malo nascatur: sed quia, cum debito natus, postea per gratiam Christi liberatur.

Nec etiam sequitur, si potest sine errore poni quod aliqui non moriantur, quod sine originali nascantur, licet mors sit poena peccati originalis. Quia Deus potest ex misericordia relaxare alicui poenam ad quam obligatur ex culpa praeterita: sicut adulteram sine poena dimisit, Ioan. 8, [11]. Et similiter poterit a morte liberare qui reatum mortis contraxerunt cum originali nascendo. Et sic non sequitur: *si non morientur, ergo nascuntur sine originali peccato.*

AD QUARTUM dicendum quod non semper via compendiosior est magis eligenda: sed solum quando est magis vel aequaliter accommoda ad finem consequendum. Et sic non est hic, ut ex dictis patet.

but clothed about, namely, if that be possible: and this desire is called by some a *velleity*.

REPLY OBJ. 3: It is erroneous to say that any one except Christ is conceived without original sin, because those who would be conceived without original sin would not need the redemption which was wrought by Christ, and thus Christ would not be the Redeemer of all men.

Nor can it be said that they needed not this redemption because it was granted to them that they should be conceived without sin. For this grace was vouchsafed either to their parents, that the sin of nature might be healed in them (because so long as that sin remained they were unable to beget without communicating original sin), or to nature itself, which was healed. Now we must allow that every one needs the redemption of Christ personally, and not only by reason of nature.

One cannot be *delivered from an evil* or *absolved from a debt* unless one incur the debt or incur the evil: and consequently all could not reap in themselves the fruit of the Lord's prayer unless all were born debtors and subject to evil. Hence the *forgiveness of debts* or *delivery from evil* cannot be applied to one who is born without a debt or free from evil, but only to one who is born with a debt and is afterwards delivered by the grace of Christ.

Nor does it follow, if it can be asserted without error that some die not, that they are born without original sin, although death is a punishment of original sin; because God can of his mercy remit the punishment which one has incurred by a past fault, as he forgave the adulterous woman without punishment (John 8): and in like manner he can deliver from death those who have contracted the debt of death by being born in original sin. And thus it does not follow that *if they die not, therefore they were born without original sin.*

REPLY OBJ. 4: The shortest way is not always the one to be chosen, but only when it is more or equally adapted for attaining the end. It is not so here, as is clear from what we have said.

Article 2

Whether All Will Rise Again From Ashes?

AD SECUNDUM SIC PROCEDITUR. Videtur quod non omnium resurrectio erit a cineribus. Resurrectio enim Christi est exemplar nostrae resurrectionis. Sed resurrectio eius non fuit a cineribus: quia *caro eius non vidit corruptionem*, ut dicitur in Psalmo [15, 10] et Act. 2, [31]. Ergo resurrectio omnium non erit ex cineribus.

OBJECTION 1: It would seem that all will not rise again from ashes. For Christ's resurrection is the exemplar of ours. Yet his resurrection was not from ashes, for *his flesh saw not corruption*, according to Ps. 15:10 and Acts 2:27–31. Therefore, neither will all rise again from ashes.

PRAETEREA, corpus hominis non semper comburitur. Sed in cineres non potest aliquid resolvi nisi per combustionem. Ergo non omnes a cineribus resurgent.

PRAETEREA, corpus hominis mortui non statim in cinerem redigitur. Sed quidam statim post mortem resurgent, ut in littera dicitur, scilicet illi qui vivi invenientur. Ergo non omnes resurgent a cineribus.

PRAETEREA, terminus a quo respondet termino ad quem. Sed terminus ad quem resurrectionis non est idem in bonis et malis: I Cor. 15, [51], *omnes quidem resurgemus, sed non omnes immutabimur.* Ergo non est idem terminus a quo. Et sic, si mali resurgent a cineribus, boni a cineribus non resurgent.

SED CONTRA: Est quod dicit Haymo: *Omnes in originali peccato natos tenet haec sententia, Terra es et in terram ibis.* Sed omnes qui in communi resurrectione resurgent, fuerunt nati in peccato originali: vel nativitate *ex utero*, vel saltem nativitate *in utero.* Ergo omnes a cineribus resurgent.

PRAETEREA, multa sunt in corpore humano quae non sunt de veritate humanae naturae. Sed omnia illa auferentur. Ergo oportet omnia corpora in cinerem resolvi.

RESPONDEO dicendum quod eisdem rationibus quibus ostensum est omnes a morte resurgere, est etiam ostendendum quod omnes resurgent a Cineribus in communi resurrectione: nisi aliquibus ex speciali privilegio gratiae sit indultum contrarium, sicut et resurrectionis acceleratio.

Scriptura autem sacra, sicut resurrectionem praenuntiat, ita et *corporum reformationem*, Philipp. 3, [21]. Et ideo oportet quod, sicut omnes moriuntur ad hoc quod omnes vere resurgere possint, ita omnium corpora dissolventur ad hoc quod omnium corpora reformari possint. Sicut etiam in poenam hominis mors a divina iustitia est inflicta, ita et corporis resolutio: ut patet Genes. 3, [19]: *terra es et in terram ibis.*

Similiter etiam ordo naturae exigit ut non solum animae et corporis coniunctio solvatur, sed etiam elementorum commixtio: sicut etiam acetum non potest in vini qualitatem reduci nisi prius facta resolutione in materiam praeiacentem. Ipsa etiam elementorum commixtio ex motu caeli causatur et conservatur. Quo cessante, omnia mixta in pura elementa resolventur.

AD PRIMUM ergo dicendum quod resurrectio Christi est exemplar nostrae resurrectionis quoad terminum ad quem: non autem quoad terminum a quo.

AD SECUNDUM dicendum quod *cineres* intelliguntur omnes reliquiae quae remanent, humano corpore resoluto, duplici ratione. Primo, quia communis mos erat

OBJ. 2: Further, the human body is not always burned. Yet a thing cannot be reduced to ashes unless it be burned. Therefore, not all will rise again from ashes.

OBJ. 3: Further, the body of a dead man is not reduced to ashes immediately after death. But some will rise again at once after death, according to the text (*Sentences* IV, D. 43), namely, those who will be found living. Therefore, all will not rise again from ashes.

OBJ. 4: Further, the starting terminus corresponds to the ending terminus. Now the ending terminus of the resurrection is not the same in the good as in the wicked: *we shall all indeed rise again, but we shall not all be changed* (1 Cor 15:51). Therefore, the starting terminus is not the same. And thus, if the wicked rise again from ashes, the good will not rise again from ashes.

ON THE CONTRARY, On Romans 5:10: *for if when we were enemies*, Haymo says, *all who are born in original sin lie under the sentence: "you are earth and into earth shall you go."* Now all who shall rise again at the general resurrection were born in original sin, either at their birth *within the womb* or at least at their birth *from the womb*. Therefore, all will rise again from ashes.

FURTHER, There are many things in the human body that do not truly belong to human nature. But all these will be removed. Therefore, all bodies must be reduced to ashes.

I ANSWER THAT, The same reasons by which we have shown (A. 1) that all rise again from death prove also that at the general resurrection all will rise again from ashes, unless the contrary, such as the hastening of their resurrection, be vouchsafed to certain persons by a special privilege of grace.

For just as Sacred Scripture foretells the resurrection, so does it foretell the *reformation of bodies* (Phil 3:21). And thus it follows that even as all die so that the bodies of all may be able truly to rise again, so will the bodies of all perish that they may be able to be reformed. For just as death was inflicted by divine justice as a punishment on man, so was the decay of the body, as appears from Genesis 3:19: *earth thou art and into earth shalt thou go.*

Moreover, the order of nature requires the dissolution not only of the union of soul and body, but also of the mingling of the elements, even as vinegar cannot be brought back to the quality of wine unless it first be dissolved into the prejacent matter: for the mingling of the elements is both caused and preserved by the movement of the heaven, and when this ceases all mixed bodies will be dissolved into pure elements.

REPLY OBJ. 1: Christ's resurrection is the exemplar of ours as to ending terminus, but not as to the starting terminus.

REPLY OBJ. 2: By *ashes* we mean all the remains that are left after the dissolution of the body for two reasons. First, because it was the common custom in olden times to burn

apud antiquos corpora mortuorum comburere et cineres reservare. Unde inolevit modus loquendi ut ea in quae corpus humanum resolvitur, cineres dicantur. Secundo, propter causam resolutionis, quae est incendium fomitis, quo corpus humanum radicitus est infectum. Unde, ad purgationem huius infectionis, oportet usque ad prima componentia corpus humanum resolvi. Quod autem per incendium resolvitur, dicitur in cineres resolvi. Et ideo ea in quae corpus humanum resolvitur, cineres dicantur.

AD TERTIUM dicendum quod ille ignis qui faciem mundi purgabit, poterit statim corpora eorum qui vivi invenientur usque ad cineres resolvere: sicut et alia mixta resolvet in materiam praeiacentem.

AD QUARTUM dicendum quod motus non accipit speciem a termino a quo, sed a termino ad quem. Et ideo resurrectio sanctorum, quae erit gloriosa, oportet quod differat a resurrectione impiorum, quae non erit gloriosa, penes terminum ad quem: non autem penes terminum a quo. Contingit enim frequenter non esse eundem terminum ad quem, existente eodem termino a quo: sicut de nigredine potest aliquid moveri in albedinem, et in pallorem.

the bodies of the dead, and to keep the ashes, whence it became customary to speak of the remains of a human body as ashes. Second, on account of the cause of dissolution, which is the flame of the *fomes* whereby the human body is radically infected. Hence, in order to be cleansed of this infection, the human body must be dissolved into its primary components: and when a thing is destroyed by fire it is said to be reduced to ashes. Therefore, the name of ashes is given to those things into which the human body is dissolved.

REPLY OBJ. 3: The fire that will cleanse the face of the earth will be able to reduce suddenly to ashes the bodies of those that will be found living, even as it will dissolve other mixed bodies into their prejacent matter.

REPLY OBJ. 4: Movement does not take its species from its starting terminus but from its ending terminus. Hence the resurrection of the saints, which will be glorious, must differ from the resurrection of the wicked, which will not be glorious in respect of the ending terminus, and not in respect of the starting terminus. And it often happens that the ending terminus is not the same, whereas the starting terminus is the same—for instance, a thing may be moved from blackness both to whiteness and to pallor.

Article 3

Whether the Ashes From Which the Human Body Will Be Restored Have Any Natural Inclination Toward the Soul Which Will Be United to Them?

AD TERTIUM SIC PROCEDITUR. Videtur quod pulveres illi ex quibus corpus humanum reparabitur, aliquam habeant inclinationem naturalem ad animam quae eis coniungetur. Si enim nullam inclinationem habent ad animam, eodem modo se habent ad illam animam sicut alii pulveres. Ergo non esset differentia utrum ex illis vel ex aliis pulveribus reficeretur corpus animae coniungendum. Quod falsum est.

PRAETEREA, maior est dependentia corporis ad animam quam animae ad corpus. Sed anima separata a corpore adhuc habet aliquam dependentiam ad corpus: unde *retardatur eius motus in Deum propter appetitum corporis*, ut dicit Augustinus. Ergo multo fortius corpus separatum ab anima adhuc habet naturalem inclinationem ad animam.

PRAETEREA, Iob 20, [11] dicitur: *ossa eius implebuntur vitiis adolescentiae eius, et cum eo in pulvere dormient.* Sed vitia non sunt nisi in anima. Ergo adhuc in illis pulveribus remanebit aliqua naturalis inclinatio ad animam.

SED CONTRA: Corpus humanum potest resolvi ad ipsa elementa, vel in carnes aliorum animalium converti. Sed elementa sunt homogenea: et similiter caro leonis vel alterius animalis. Cum ergo in aliis partibus elementorum vel animalium non sit aliqua inclinatio naturalis

OBJECTION 1: It would seem that the ashes from which the human body will be restored will have a natural inclination towards the soul which will be united to them. For if they had no inclination towards the soul, they would stand in the same relation to that soul as other ashes. Therefore, it would make no difference whether the body that is to be united to that soul were restored from those ashes or from others: and this is false.

OBJ. 2: Further, the body is more dependent on the soul than the soul on the body. Now the soul separated from the body is still somewhat dependent on the body, wherefore *its movement towards God is retarded on account of its desire for the body*, as Augustine says (*On the Literal Meaning of Genesis* 12). Much more, therefore, has the body when separated from the soul a natural inclination towards that soul.

OBJ. 3: Further, it is written: *his bones shall be filled with the vices of his youth, and they shall sleep with him in the dust* (Job 20:11). But vices are only in the soul. Therefore, there will still remain in those ashes a natural inclination towards the soul.

ON THE CONTRARY, The human body can be dissolved into the very elements or changed into the flesh of other animals. But the elements are homogeneous, and so is the flesh of a lion or other animal. Since, then, in the other parts of the elements or animals there is no natural inclination to

ad illam animam, nec in illis partibus in quas conversum est corpus humanum, erit aliqua inclinatio ad animam. Patet per auctoritatem Augustini, in *Enchiridion: corpus humanum, in quamcumque aliorum corporum substantiam, vel in ipsa elementa vertatur; in quorumcumque hominum seu animalium cibum cedat carnemque vertatur; illi animae humanae in puncto temporis redit quae illud prius ut fieret, viveret et cresceret, animavit.*

PRAETEREA, cuilibet inclinationi naturali respondet aliquod agens naturale: alias *natura deficeret in necessariis.* Sed nullo agente naturali possunt praedicti pulveres eidem animae iterato coniungi. Ergo in eis non est aliqua naturalis inclinatio ad praedictam coniunctionem.

RESPONDEO dicendum quod circa hoc est triplex opinio. Quidam dicunt quod corpus humanum nunquam resolvitur usque ad elementa. Et ita semper in cineribus manet aliqua vis addita elementis, quae facit naturalem inclinationem ad eandem animam.

Sed haec positio contrariatur auctoritati Augustini inductae, et sensui, et rationi: quia omnia composita ex contrariis possibile est in ea resolvi ex quibus componuntur.

Et ideo alii dicunt quod illae partes elementorum in quas humanum corpus resolvitur, retinent plus de luce ex hoc quod fuerunt animae humanae coniunctae. Et ex hoc habent quandam inclinationem ad animas.

Sed hoc iterum frivolum est. Quia partes elementorum sunt unius naturae, et aequaliter habent participationem lucis et obscuritatis.

Et ideo aliter dicendum est quod in cineribus illis nulla est inclinatio naturalis ad resurrectionem: sed solum ex ordine divinae providentiae, quo statuit illos cineres iterum animae coniungi. Et ex hoc provenit quod illae partes elementorum iterato coniungentur et non aliae.

UNDE PATET solutio ad primum.

AD SECUNDUM dicendum quod anima separata a corpore manet in eadem natura quam habebat cum corpori esset unita. Quod de corpore non contingit. Et ideo non est simile.

AD TERTIUM dicendum quod verbum illud Iob non est intelligendum quod vitia actu maneant in pulveribus mortuorum: sed secundum ordinem divinae iustitiae, quo sunt deputati cineres illi ad corporis reparationem, quod pro peccatis commissis cruciabitur in aeternum.

that soul, neither will there be an inclination towards the soul in those parts into which the human body has been changed. The first proposition is made evident on the authority of Augustine (*Handbook on Faith, Hope, and Charity* 88): *the human body, although changed into the substance of other bodies or even into the elements, although it has become the food and flesh of any animals whatsoever, even of man, will in an instant return to that soul which first animated it, making it a living and growing man.*

FURTHER, To every natural inclination there corresponds a natural agent: else *nature would fail in necessaries.* Now the aforesaid ashes cannot be reunited to the same soul by any natural agent. Therefore, there is not in them any natural inclination to the aforesaid reunion.

I ANSWER THAT, Opinion is threefold on this point. For some say that the human body is never dissolved into its very elements; and so there always remains in the ashes a certain force besides the elements which gives a natural inclination to the same soul.

But this assertion is in contradiction with the authority of Augustine quoted above, as well as with the senses and reason: since whatever is composed of contraries can be dissolved into its component parts.

Wherefore others say that these parts of the elements into which the human body is dissolved retain more light through having been united to the soul, and for this reason have a natural inclination to human souls.

But this again is nonsensical, since the parts of the elements are of the same nature and have an equal share of light and darkness.

Hence we must say differently that in those ashes there is no natural inclination to resurrection, but only by the ordering of divine providence, which decreed that those ashes should be reunited to the soul: it is on this account that those parts of the elements shall be reunited and not others.

HENCE the reply to the first objection is clear.

REPLY OBJ. 2: The soul separated from the body remains in the same nature that it has when united to the body. It is not so with the body, and consequently the comparison fails.

REPLY OBJ. 3: These words of Job do not mean that the vices actually remain in the ashes of the dead, but that they remain according to the ordering of divine justice, whereby those ashes are destined to the restoration of the body which will suffer eternally for the sins committed.

QUESTION 79

THE CONDITIONS OF THE RESURRECTED, AND FIRST OF THEIR IDENTITY

Consequenter agendum est de conditionibus resurgentium. Ubi prima consideratio erit de his quae communiter ad bonos et malos pertinent; secunda, de his quae tantum ad bonos pertinent; tertia, de his quae spectant tantum ad malos.

Ad bonos autem et malos communiter tria pertinent: scilicet ipsorum identitas, integritas et qualitas. Et primo videndum est de resurgentium identitate; secundo, de corporum integritate; tertio, de ipsorum qualitate.

Circa primum quaeruntur tria,

Primo: utrum idem numero corpus resurget.

Secundo: utrum idem numero homo.

Tertio: utrum oporteat eosdem pulveres ad easdem partes in quibus ante fuerant, reverti.

In the next place we must consider the conditions of those who rise again. Here we shall consider: (1) Those which concern the good and wicked in common; (2) Those which concern the good only; (3) Those which concern only the wicked.

Three things concern the good and wicked in common, namely, their identity, their integrity, and their quality: and we shall inquire (1) About their identity; (2) About their integrity; (3) About their quality.

Under the first head there are three points of inquiry:

(1) Whether the body will rise again the same in number?

(2) Whether it will be the same man in number?

(3) Whether it is necessary that the same ashes should return to the same parts in which they were before?

Article 1

Whether in the Resurrection the Soul Will Be Reunited to the Same Body in Number?

AD PRIMUM SIC PROCEDITUR. Videtur quod non idem corpus numero anima resumat in resurrectione. I Cor. 15, [37]: *non corpus quod futurum est seminas, sed nudum granum.* Sed Apostolus ibi comparat mortem seminationi et resurrectionem pullulationi. Ergo non idem corpus quod per mortem deponitur, in resurrectione resumitur.

PRAETEREA, cuilibet formae aptatur materia secundum suam conditionem; et similiter cuilibet agenti instrumentum. Sed corpus comparatur ad animam sicut materia ad formam, et sicut instrumentum ad agentem. Cum ergo anima in resurrectione non sit eiusdem conditionis sicut modo est, quia vel transfertur totaliter in caelestem vitam, cui inhaesit vivens in mundo, vel deprimitur in brutalem, si brutaliter in hoc mundo vixit; videtur quod non resumet idem corpus, sed vel caeleste vel brutale.

PRAETEREA, corpus humanum usque ad elementa post mortem resolvitur, ut dictum est supra. Sed illae partes elementorum in quas corpus humanum resolutum est, non conveniunt cum humano corpore quod in ea resolutum est nisi in materia prima: quo modo quaelibet aliae partes elementorum cum praedicto corpore conveniunt. Si autem ex aliis partibus elementorum cor-

OBJECTION 1: It would seem that the soul will not be reunited to the same body in number at the resurrection, for *you do not sow the body that shall be, but bare grain* (1 Cor 15:37). Now the Apostle is there comparing death to sowing and resurrection to fructifying. Therefore, the same body that is laid aside in death is not resumed at the resurrection.

OBJ. 2: Further, to every form some matter is adapted according to its condition, and likewise to every agent some instrument. Now the body is compared to the soul as matter to form, and as instrument to agent. Since, then, at the resurrection the soul will not be of the same condition as now (for it will be either entirely borne away to the heavenly life to which it adhered while living in the world, or will be cast down into the life of the brutes if it lived as a brute in this world) it would seem that it will not resume the same body, but either a heavenly or a brutish body.

OBJ. 3: Further, after death, as stated above (Q. 78, A. 3), the human body is dissolved into the elements. Now these elemental parts into which the human body has been dissolved do not agree with the human body dissolved into them except in prime matter, even as any other elemental parts agree with that same body. But if the body were to be formed from those other elemental parts, it would not

123

pus formaretur, non diceretur idem numero. Ergo nec si ex illis partibus reparetur, corpus non erit numero idem.

Praeterea, impossibile est esse idem numero cuius partes essentiales sunt aliae numero. Sed forma mixti, quae est essentialis pars corporis humani sicut forma eius, non poterit eadem numero resumi. Ergo corpus non erit idem numero.

Probatio mediae. Illud enim quod penitus cedit in non-ens, non potest idem numero resumi. Quod patet ex hoc quod non potest esse idem numero cuius est esse diversum: sed esse interruptum, quod est actus entis, est diversus; sicut et quilibet alius actus interruptus. Sed forma mixtionis cedit penitus in non-ens per mortem: cum sit forma corporalis. Et similiter qualitates contrariae, ex quibus fit mixtio. Ergo forma mixtionis non redit eadem numero.

Sed contra: Est quod dicit Iob [19, 26]: *in carne mea videbo Deum salvatorem meum.* Loquitur autem de visione post resurrectionem: quod patet ex hoc quod praecedit [v. 25], *in novissimo die de terra surrecturus sum*: Ergo idem numero corpus resurget.

Praeterea, sicut Damascenus dicit, in IV libro, *resurrectio est eius quod cecidit secunda surrectio.* Sed hoc corpus quod nunc gerimus, per mortem cecidit. Ergo idem numero resurget.

Respondeo dicendum quod circa hanc quaestionem et philosophi erraverunt, et quidam haeretici moderni errant. Quidam enim philosophi posuerunt animas a corpore separatas iterato corporibus coniungi, sed erraverunt in hoc quantum ad duo. Primo quidem, quantum ad modum coniunctionis. Quia quidam ponebant corpori iterum coniungi naturaliter animam separatam per viam generationis. Secundo, quantum ad corpus cui coniungebatur secundo. Quia ponebant quod secunda coniunctio non erat ad idem corpus quod per mortem depositum fuit, sed ad aliud, quandoque quidem idem specie, quandoque autem diversum. Ad diversum quidem, quando anima in corpore existens praeter rationis ordinem vitam duxerat bestialem: unde transibat post mortem de corpore hominis in corpus alterius animalis, cuius moribus vivendo se conformavit, sicut in corpus canis propter luxuriam, in corpus leonis propter rapinam et violentiam, et sic de aliis. Sed in corpus eiusdem speciei, quando anima bene in corpore vivens, post mortem aliqua felicitate perfuncta, post aliqua saecula incipiebat ad corpus velle redire, et sic iterum corpori coniungebatur humano.

Sed haec opinio ex duabus falsis radicibus venit. Quarum prima est, quia dicunt quod anima non coniungitur corpori essentialiter, sicut forma materiae; sed solum accidentaliter, sicut motor mobili, aut sicut homo

be described as the same in number. Therefore, neither will it be the same body in number if it be restored from these parts.

Obj. 4: Further, there cannot be numerical identity where there is numerical distinction of essential parts. Now the form of the mixed body, which is an essential part of the human body as being its form, cannot be resumed in numerical identity. Therefore, the body will not be the same in number.

The minor is proved thus. That which passes away into complete nonentity cannot be resumed in identity. This is clear from the fact that there cannot be identity where there is distinction of existence: and existence, which is the act of a being, is differentiated by being interrupted, as is any interrupted act. Now the form of a mixed body passes away into complete nonentity by death, since it is a bodily form, and so also do the contrary qualities from which the mixture results. Therefore, the form of a mixed body does not return in number.

On the contrary, It is written: *in my flesh I shall see God my Savior* (Job 19:26), where he is speaking of the vision after the resurrection, as appears from the preceding words: *in the last day I shall rise out of the earth* (Job 19:25). Therefore, the same body in number will rise again.

Further, The Damascene says (*On the Orthodox Faith* 4.27): *resurrection is the second rising of that which has fallen.* But the body which we have now fell by death. Therefore, it will rise again the same in number.

I answer that, On this point the philosophers erred and certain modern heretics err. For some of the philosophers allowed that souls separated from bodies are reunited to bodies, yet they erred in this in two ways. First, as to the mode of reunion, for some held the separated soul to be naturally reunited to a body by the way of generation. Second, as to the body to which it was reunited, for they held that this second union was not with the selfsame body that was laid aside in death, but with another, sometimes of the same, sometimes of a different species. Of a different species, when the soul while existing in the body had led a life contrary to the ordering of reason: wherefore it passed after death from the body of a man into the body of some other animal to whose manner of living it had conformed in this life, for instance, into the body of a dog on account of lust, into the body of a lion on account of robbery and violence, and so forth. Into a body of the same species, when the soul had led a good life in the body, and having after death experienced some happiness, after some centuries began to wish to return to the body; and thus it was reunited to a human body.

This opinion arises from two false sources. The first of these is that they said that the soul is not united to the body essentially as form to matter, but only accidentally, as mover to the thing moved, or as a man to his clothes. Hence it was

vestimento. Et ideo ponere poterant quod anima praeexistebat antequam corpori generato infunderetur in generatione naturali; et iterum quod diversis corporibus uniretur. Secunda est, quia ponebant intellectum non differre a sensu nisi accidentaliter: ut si homo diceretur intellectum habere prae aliis animalibus quia in eo propter optimam corporis complexionem vis sensitiva amplius viget. Unde poterant ponere quod anima hominis in corpus animalis bruti transiret: praecipue facta immutatione animae humanae ad effectus brutales. Sed praedictae duae rationes destruuntur a Philosopho in libro *de Anima*. Quibus destructis, patet falsitas praedictae positionis.

Et simili modo destruuntur errores quorundam haereticorum. Quorum quidam in praedictas positiones inciderunt. Quidam autem posuerunt animas iterato coniungi corporibus caelestibus, vel etiam corporibus in modum venti subtilibus: ut Gregorius de quodam Episcopo Constantinopolitano narrat, exponens illud Iob [19, 26], *in carne mea videbo Deum*, etc.

Et praeter hoc, praedicti errores haereticorum destrui possunt ex hoc quod veritati resurrectionis praeiudicant, quam sacra Scriptura profitetur. Non enim resurrectio dici potest nisi anima ad idem corpus redeat: quia resurrectio est *iterata surrectio*; eiusdem autem est surgere et cadere. Unde resurrectio magis respicit corpus, quod post mortem cadit, quam animam, quae post mortem vivit. Et ita, si non est idem corpus quod anima resumit, non dicetur resurrectio, sed magis novi corporis assumptio.

AD PRIMUM ergo dicendum quod similitudo non currit per omnia, sed quantum ad aliquid. In seminatione enim grani granum seminatum et natum non est idem numero, nec eodem modo se habens: cum primo seminatum fuerit absque folliculis, cum quibus nascitur. Corpus autem resurgens erit idem numero, sed alio modo se habens: quia fuit mortale, et surget in immortalitate.

AD SECUNDUM dicendum quod differentia quae est inter animam resurgentis et animam in hoc mundo viventis, non est secundum aliquid essentiale, sed secundum gloriam et miseriam, quae differentiam accidentalem faciunt. Unde non oportet quod aliud corpus numero resurgat, sed alio modo se habens, ut respondeat proportionaliter differentia corporum differentiae animarum.

AD TERTIUM dicendum quod illud quod intelligitur in materia ante formam, remanet in materia post corruptionem: quia, remoto posteriori, adhuc potest remanere prius. Oportet autem, ut Commentator dicit, in I *Physic.* et in libro *de Substantia Orbis*, in materia generabilium et corruptibilium ante formam substantialem intelligere dimensiones non terminatas, secundum quas attendatur divisio materiae, ut diversas formas in diver-

possible for them to maintain that the soul pre-existed before being infused into the body begotten of natural generation, as also that it is united to various bodies. The second is that they held intellect not to differ from sense except accidentally, so that man would be said to surpass other animals in intelligence because the sensitive power is more acute in him on account of the excellence of his bodily complexion; and hence it was possible for them to assert that man's soul passes into the soul of a brute animal, especially when the human soul has been habituated to brutish actions. But these two sources are refuted by the Philosopher (*On the Soul* 2.1), and in consequence of these being refuted, it is clear that the above opinion is false.

In like manner, the errors of certain heretics are refuted. Some of them fell into the aforesaid opinions of the philosophers: while others held that souls are reunited to heavenly bodies, or again to bodies subtle as the wind, as Gregory relates of a certain Bishop of Constantinople, in his exposition of Job 19:26, *in my flesh I shall see God*.

Moreover, these same errors of heretics may be refuted by the fact that they are prejudicial to the truth of resurrection as witnessed to by Sacred Scripture. For we cannot call it resurrection unless the soul return to the same body, since resurrection is a *second rising*, and the same thing rises that falls: wherefore resurrection regards the body, which after death falls, rather than the soul, which after death lives. And consequently if it be not the same body which the soul resumes, it will not be a resurrection, but rather the assumption of a new body.

REPLY OBJ. 1: A comparison does not apply to every particular, but to some. For in the sowing of grain, the grain sown and the grain that is born thereof are neither identical, nor of the same condition, since it was first sown without a husk, yet is born with one: and the body will rise again the same in number, but of a different condition, since it was mortal and will rise in immortality.

REPLY OBJ. 2: The soul rising again and the soul living in this world differ not in essence, but in respect of glory and misery, which is an accidental difference. Hence it follows that the body in rising again differs not in number, but in condition, so that a difference of bodies corresponds proportionally to the difference of souls.

REPLY OBJ. 3: That which is understood as though it were in matter before its form remains in matter after corruption, because when that which comes afterwards is removed that which came before may yet remain. Now, as the Commentator observes on I *Physics* and in *On the Substance of the World*, in the matter of things subject to generation and corruption, we must presuppose undeterminate dimensions by reason of which matter is divisible so as to be

sis partibus recipere possit. Unde et post separationem formae substantialis a materia, adhuc dimensiones illae manent eaedem. Et sic materia sub illis dimensionibus existens, quamcumque formam accipiat, habet maiorem identitatem ad illud quod ex ea generatum fuerat quam aliqua pars aliae materiae sub quacumque forma existens. Et sic eadem materia ad corpus humanum reparandum reducetur quae prius materia eius fuit.

Ad quartum dicendum quod, sicut qualitas simplex non est forma substantialis elementi, sed accidens proprium eius et dispositio per quam materia efficitur propria tali formae; ita forma mixtionis; quae est forma resultans ex qualitatibus simplicibus ad medium venientibus, non est forma substantialis corporis mixti, sed est accidens proprium, et dispositio per quam materia fit necessaria ad formam. Corpus autem humanum praeter hanc formam mixtionis non habet aliam formam substantialem nisi animam rationalem: quia, si haberet aliam formam substantialem priorem, illa daret ei substantiale esse, et sic per eam constitueretur in genere substantiae; unde anima iam adveniret corpori constituto in genere substantiae; et sic comparatio animae ad corpus esset sicut comparatio formarum artificialium ad suas materias, quantum ad hoc quod constituuntur in genere substantiae per suam materiam. Unde coniunctio animae ad corpus esset accidentalis: quod est error antiquorum philosophorum, a Philosopho reprobatus in libro *de Anima*. Sequeretur etiam quod corpus humanum, et singulae partes eius, non aequivoce retinerent priora nomina: quod est contra Philosophum, in II *de Anima*. Unde, cum anima rationalis remaneat, nulla forma corporis humani substantialis cedit penitus in non-ens. Formarum autem accidentalium variatio non facit diversitatem in numero. Unde idem numero resurget: cum materia eadem numero resumatur, ut in praecedenti solutione dictum est.

able to receive various forms in its various parts. Therefore, after the separation of the substantial form from matter, these dimensions still remain the same: and consequently, the matter existing under those dimensions, whatever form it receives, is more identified with that which was generated from it than any other part of matter existing under any form whatever. Thus the matter that will be brought back to restore the human body will be the same as that body's previous matter.

Reply Obj. 4: Even as a simple quality is not the substantial form of an element, but its proper accident, and the disposition whereby its matter is rendered proper to such a form; so the form of a mixed body, which form is a quality resulting from simple qualities reduced to a mean, is not the substantial form of the mixed body, but its proper accident, and the disposition whereby the matter is in need of the form. Now the human body has no substantial form besides this form of the mixed body except the rational soul, for if it had any previous substantial form, this would give it substantial being, and would establish it in the genus of substance: so that the soul would be united to a body already established in the genus of substance, and thus the soul would be compared to the body as artificial forms are to their matter in respect of their being established in the genus of substance by their matter. Hence the union of the soul to the body would be accidental, which is the error of the ancient philosophers refuted by the Philosopher (*On the Soul* 2.2; Cf. I, Q. 76, A. 1.) It would also follow that the human body and each of its parts would not retain their former names in the same sense, which is contrary to the teaching of the Philosopher (*On the Soul* 2.1). Therefore, since the rational soul remains, no substantial form of the human body falls away into complete nonentity. And the variation of accidental forms does not make a difference of identity. Therefore, the selfsame body will rise again, since the same matter in number is resumed as stated in a previous reply (ad 2).

Article 2

Whether It Will Be the Same Man in Number That Shall Rise Again?

Ad secundum sic proceditur. Videtur quod non sit idem numero homo qui resurget. Sicut enim dicit Philosophus, in II *de Generat.*, *quaecumque habent speciem corruptibilem motam, non reiterantur eadem numero.* Sed talis est substantia hominis secundum praesentem statum. Ergo non potest post mutationem mortis reiterari idem numero.

Praeterea, ubi est alia et alia humanitas, non est idem homo numero: unde Socrates et Plato sunt duo homines et non unus homo, quia alia est humanitas utrius-

Objection 1: It would seem that it will not be identically the same man that shall rise again. For, according to the Philosopher (*On Generation and Corruption* 2): *whatsoever things are changed in their corruptible substance are not repeated identically.* Now such is man's substance in his present state. Therefore, after the change wrought by death the same man in number cannot be repeated.

Obj. 2: Further, where there is a distinction of human nature there is not the same identical man: wherefore Socrates and Plato are two men and not one man, since

que. Sed alia est humanitas hominis resurgentis ab ea quam nunc habet. Ergo non est idem homo numero.

Media probari potest dupliciter. Primo, quia humanitas, quae est forma totius, non est forma et substantia, sicut anima, sed est forma tantum. Huiusmodi autem formae cedunt penitus in non-ens: et sic non possunt iterari.

Secundo, quia humanitas resultat ex coniunctione partium. Sed non potest eadem numero coniunctio resumi quae prius fuit, quia iteratio identitati opponitur: iteratio enim numerum importat, identitas autem unitatem, quae se non compatiuntur. In resurrectione autem coniunctio iteratur. Ergo non est eadem coniunctio. Et sic nec eadem humanitas, nec idem homo.

Praeterea, unus homo non est si est plura animalia. Ergo, si non est idem animal, non est unus homo numero. Sed ubi non est idem sensus, non est idem animal: quia animal definitur per sensum primum, scilicet tactum, ut patet in II *de Anima*. Sensus autem; cum non maneant in anima separata, ut quidam dicunt, non possunt idem numero resumi. Ergo in resurrectione non erit homo resurgens idem animal numero. Et sic nec idem homo.

Praeterea, materia statuae principalior est in statua quam materia hominis in homine. quia artificialia tota sunt in genere substantiae ex materia, sed naturalia ex forma, ut patet per Philosophum, II *Physic.*; et Commentator idem dicit in II *de Anima*. Sed, si statua ex eodem aere reficiatur, non est eadem numero. Ergo multo minus, si homo ex eisdem pulveribus reficiatur, non erit idem homo numero.

Sed contra: Est quod dicitur Iob 19, [27]: *quem visurus sum ego ipse et non alius*: et loquitur de visione post resurrectionem [v. 25–26]. Ergo idem homo numero resurget.

Praeterea, Augustinus dicit, VIII *de Trin.*, quod *resurgere nihil est aliud quam reviviscere*. Nisi autem idem homo numero rediret ad vitam qui mortuus est, non diceretur reviviscere. Ergo non resurget. Quod est contra fidem.

Respondeo dicendum quod necessitas ponendi resurrectionem est ex hoc ut homo finem ultimum, propter quem factus est, consequatur, quod in hac vita fieri non potest, nec in vita animae separatae: alias vane esset homo constitutus, si ad finem ad quem factus est, venire non posset. Et quia oportet quod illud idem numero ad finem perveniat quod propter finem est factum, ne in vanum factum esse videatur; oportet quod idem homo numero resurgat. Et hoc quidem fit dum eadem anima eidem numero corpori coniungitur. Alias enim non esset resurrectio, proprie loquendo, nisi idem homo repa-

each has his own distinct human nature. Now the human nature of one who rises again is distinct from that which he has now. Therefore, he is not the same identical man.

The minor can be proved in two ways. First, because human nature, which is the form of the whole, is not both form and substance as the soul is, but is a form only. Now such forms pass away into complete nonentity, and consequently they cannot be restored.

Second, because human nature results from union of parts. Now the same union in number as that which was heretofore cannot be resumed, because repetition is opposed to identity (since repetition implies number, whereas identity implies unity, and these are incompatible with one another.) But resurrection is a repeated union: therefore, the union is not the same, and consequently there is not the same human nature nor the same man.

Obj. 3: Further, one man is not several animals. Therefore, if it is not the same animal, it is not the same identical man. Now where sense is not the same, there is not the same animal, since animal is defined from the primary sense, namely, touch, as is clear from *On the Soul* 2. But sense, as it does not remain in the separated soul (as some maintain), cannot be resumed in identity. Therefore, the man who rises again will not be the same identical animal, and consequently he will not be the same man.

Obj. 4: Further, the matter of a statue ranks higher in the statue than the matter of a man does in man: because artificial things belong to the genus of substance by reason of their matter, but natural things by reason of their form, as appears from the Philosopher (*Physics* 2.1), and again from the Commentator (*On the Soul* 2). But if a statue is remade from the same brass, it will not be the same in number. Therefore, much less will it be identically the same man if he be reformed from the same ashes.

On the contrary, Job 19:27 says: *whom I myself shall see, and not another*, and he is speaking of the vision after the resurrection. Therefore, the same identical man will rise again.

Further, Augustine says (*On the Trinity* 8.5) that *to rise again is nothing else but to live again*. Now unless the same identical man that died should return to life, he would not be said to live again. Therefore, he would not rise again, which is contrary to faith.

I answer that, The necessity of holding the resurrection arises from this—that man may obtain the last end for which he was made; for this cannot be accomplished in this life nor in the life of the separated soul, as stated above (Q. 75, A. 1–2). Otherwise man would have been made in vain, if he were unable to obtain the end for which he was made. And since the end must be obtained by the same thing in number that was made for that end, lest it appear to be made without purpose, it is necessary for the same man in number to rise again; and this is effected by the same soul in number being united to the same body in number. For

raretur. Unde ponere quod idem numero non sit qui resurget, est haereticum, derogans veritati Scripturae, quae resurrectionem praedicat.

Ad primum ergo dicendum quod Philosophus loquitur de iteratione quae fit per motum vel mutationem naturalem. Ostendit enim differentiam circulationis quae est in generatione et corruptione, ad circulationem quae est in motu caeli. Quia caelum per motum localem redit idem numero ad principium motus: quia habet substantiam incorruptibilem motam. Sed generabilia et corruptibilia per generationem redeunt ad idem specie, non ad idem numero: quia ex homine generatur semen, ex quo sanguis, et sic deinceps usquequo perveniatur ad hominem non eundem numero sed specie; et ex igne generatur aer, ex quo aqua, ex aqua terra, ex terra ignis non idem numero sed specie. Unde patet quod ratio inducta, secundum Philosophi intentionem non est ad propositum.

Vel dicendum quod aliorum generabilium et corruptibilium forma non est per se subsistens, ut post compositi corruptionem remanere valeat: sicut est de anima rationali, quae esse quod sibi in corpore acquirit, etiam post corpus retinet, et in participationem illius esse corpus per resurrectionem adducitur; cum non sit aliud esse corporis et aliud animae in homine, alias esset coniunctio animae et corporis accidentalis. Et sic interruptio nulla facta est in esse substantiali hominis, ut non possit idem numero redire homo propter interruptionem essendi: sicut accidit in aliis rebus corruptis, quarum esse omnino interrumpitur, forma non remanente, materia autem sub alio esse remanente.

Sed tamen nec etiam homo per generationem naturalem reiteratur idem numero. Quia corpus generati hominis non fit ex tota materia generantis. Unde est corpus diversum in numero: et per consequens anima, et totus homo.

Ad secundum dicendum quod de humanitate, et qualibet forma totius, est duplex opinio. Quidam enim dicunt quod idem secundum rem est forma totius et forma partis: forma partis, secundum quod perficit materiam; forma autem totius secundum quod ex ea tota ratio speciei consequitur. Et secundum hanc opinionem humanitas secundum rem non est aliud quam anima rationalis. Et sic, cum anima rationalis eadem numero resumatur, eadem numero erit humanitas. Et etiam post mortem manet: quamvis non sub ratione humanitatis, quia ex ea compositum rationem speciei non consequitur.

otherwise there would be no resurrection, properly speaking, if the same man were not reformed. Hence to maintain that he who rises again is not the same man in number is heretical, since it is contrary to the truth of Scripture which proclaims the resurrection.

Reply Obj. 1: The Philosopher is speaking of repetition by movement or natural change. For he shows the difference between the recurrence that occurs in generation and corruption and that which is observed in the movement of the heavens. For the selfsame heaven by local movement returns to the beginning of its movement, since it has a moved incorruptible substance. On the other hand, things subject to generation and corruption return by generation to specific but not numerical identity, because from man blood is engendered, from blood, seed, and so on until a man is begotten, not the same man in number but in species. In like manner, from fire comes air, from air water, from water earth, whence fire is produced, not the same fire in number but in species. Hence it is clear that the argument, so far as the meaning of the Philosopher is concerned, is not to the point.

We may also reply that the form of other things subject to generation and corruption is not subsistent of itself, so as to be able to remain after the corruption of the composite, as it is with the rational soul. For the soul, even after separation from the body, retains the being which accrues to it when in the body, and the body is made to share that being by the resurrection, since the being of the body and the being of the soul in the body are not distinct from one another; otherwise, the union of soul and body would be accidental. Consequently, there has been no interruption in the substantial being of man as would make it impossible for the same man in number to return on account of an interruption in his being, as is the case with other things that are corrupted, the being of which is interrupted altogether since their form does not remain and their matter remains under another being.

Nevertheless, neither does the same man in number recur by natural generation, because the body of the man begotten is not composed of the whole body of his begetter: hence his body is numerically distinct, and consequently his soul and the whole man.

Reply Obj. 2: There are two opinions about humanity and about any form of a whole. For some say that the form of the whole and the form of the part are really one and the same: but that it is called the form of the part inasmuch as it perfects the matter, and the form of the whole inasmuch as the whole specific nature results therefrom. According to this opinion, humanity is really nothing else than the rational soul: and so, since the same rational soul in number is resumed, there will be the same identical humanity, which will remain even after death, although not under the aspect of humanity, because the composite does not derive the specific nature from a separated humanity.

Alia opinio est Avicennae, quae verior videtur: quod forma totius non est forma partis tantum, nec forma aliqua alia praeter formam partis; sed est totum resultans ex compositione formae et materiae, comprehendens in se utrumque; et haec forma partis totius essentia vel quidditas dicitur. Quia ergo in resurrectione idem numero corpus erit et eadem numero anima rationalis, erit de necessitate eadem humanitas.

Ratio autem procedebat ac si humanitas esset quaedam alia forma superveniens formae et materiae. Quod falsum est.

Secunda autem ratio etiam non potest identitatem humanitatis impedire. Quia coniunctio significat actionem vel passionem. Quae quamvis diversa sit, non potest identitatem humanitatis impedire: quia actio et passio ex quibus erat humanitas, non sunt de essentia humanitatis; unde eorum diversitas non inducit diversitatem humanitatis. Constat enim quod generatio et resurrectio non sunt idem motus numero: nec tamen propter hoc identitas resurgentis impeditur. Similiter etiam nec impeditur identitas humanitatis si accipiatur coniunctio pro ipsa relatione. Quia relatio illa non est de essentia humanitatis, sed concomitatur eam: eo quod humanitas non est de illis formis quae sunt compositio et ordo, ut dicitur II *Physic.*, sicut sunt formae artificiatorum; unde, existente alia compositione numero, non est eadem numero forma domus.

Ad tertium dicendum quod ratio illa optime concludit contra illos qui ponunt animam sensibilem et rationalem diversas in homine esse: quia secundum hoc anima sensitiva in homine non esset incorruptibilis, sicut nec in aliis animalibus. Unde in resurrectione non erit eadem anima sensibilis; et per consequens nec idem animal, nec idem homo.

Si autem ponamus quod eadem anima secundum substantiam in homine sit rationalis et sensibilis, nullas in hoc angustias patiemur. Quia animal definitur per sensum qui est anima sensitiva, sicut per formam essentialem; per sensum autem qui est potentia sensitiva, cognoscitur eius definitio sicut per formam accidentalem, *quae maximam partem confert ad cognoscendum quod quid est*, ut in I *de Anima* dicitur. Post mortem ergo manet anima sensibilis, sicut et anima rationalis, secundum substantiam. Sed potentiae sensitivae secundum quosdam non manent. Quae quidem potentiae cum sint accidentales proprietates, earum varietas identitatem animalis totius auferre non potest, nec etiam partium animalis. Nec dicuntur potentiae perfectiones vel actus organorum nisi sicut principia agendi, ut calor in igne.

The other opinion, which seems nearer the truth, is Avicenna's, according to whom the form of the whole is not the form of a part only, nor some other form besides the form of the part, but is the whole resulting from the composition of form and matter, embracing both within itself. This form of the whole is called the essence or quiddity. Since, then, at the resurrection there will be the same body in number, and the same rational soul in number, there will be, of necessity, the same humanity.

The first argument proving that there will be a distinction of humanity was based on the supposition that humanity is some distinct form supervening form and matter; which is false.

The second reason does not disprove the identity of humanity, because union implies action or passion, and though there be a different union, this cannot prevent the identity of humanity because the action and passion from which humanity resulted are not of the essence of humanity, wherefore a distinction on their part does not involve a distinction of humanity: for it is clear that generation and resurrection are not the same movement in number. Yet the identity of the rising man with the begotten man is not hindered for this reason: and in like manner neither is the identity of humanity prevented if we take union for the relation itself: because this relation is not essential to but concomitant with humanity, since humanity is not one of those forms that are composition or order (*Physics* 2.1), as are the forms of things produced by art, so that if there be another distinct composition there is another distinct form of a house.

Reply Obj. 3: This argument affords a very good proof against those who held a distinction between the sensitive and rational souls in man: because in that case the sensitive soul in man would not be incorruptible, as neither is it in other animals; and consequently in the resurrection there would not be the same sensitive soul, and consequently neither the same animal nor the same man.

But if we assert that in man the same soul is by its substance both rational and sensitive, we shall encounter no difficulty in this question, because animal is defined from sense, i.e., the sensitive soul as from its essential form: whereas from sense, i.e., the sensitive power, we know its definition as from an accidental form *that contributes more than another to our knowledge of the quiddity* (*On the Soul* 1.1). Accordingly, after death there remains the sensitive soul, even as the rational soul, according to its substance: whereas the sensitive powers, according to some, do not remain. And since these powers are accidental properties, diversity on their part cannot prevent the identity of the whole animal, not even of the animal's parts: nor are powers to be called perfections or acts of organs unless as principles of action, as heat in fire.

AD QUARTUM dicendum quod statua dupliciter potest considerari: vel secundum quod est substantia quaedam; vel secundum quod est artificiale quoddam. Et quia in genere substantiae ponitur ratione suae materiae, ideo, si consideretur secundum quod est substantia quaedam, est eadem numero statua quae ex eadem materia reparatur. Sed in genere artificialium ponitur secundum quod est forma. Quae accidens quoddam est, et transit, statua destructa. Et sic non redit idem numero: nec statua eadem numero esse potest. Sed forma hominis, scilicet anima, manet post dissolutionem corporis. Et ideo non est similis ratio.

REPLY OBJ. 4: A statue may be considered in two ways: either as a particular substance, or as something artificial. And since it is placed in the genus of substance by reason of its matter, it follows that if we consider it as a particular substance, it is the same statue in number that is remade from the same matter. On the other hand, it is placed in the genus of artificial things inasmuch as it has an accidental form which, if the statue be destroyed, passes away also. Consequently, it does not return identically the same, nor can the statue be identically the same. But man's form, namely, the soul, remains after the body has perished: wherefore the comparison fails.

Article 3

Whether the Ashes of the Human Body Must, by the Resurrection, Return to the Same Parts of the Body That Were Dissolved Into Them?

AD TERTIUM SIC PROCEDITUR. Videtur quod oporteat pulveres humani corporis ad eam partem corporis quae in eis dissoluta est, per resurrectionem redire. Quia secundum Philosophum, in II *de Anima, sicut se habet tota anima ad totum corpus, ita pars animae ad partem corporis, ut visus ad pupillam.* Sed oportet quod post resurrectionem corpus resumatur ab eadem anima. Ergo oportet quod etiam partes corporis resumantur ad eadem membra in quibus eisdem partibus animae perficiantur.

PRAETEREA, diversitas materiae facit diversitatem in numero. Sed, si pulveres non redeant ad easdem partes, singulae partes non reficientur ex eadem materia ex qua prius constabant. Ergo non erunt eaedem numero. Sed si partes sunt diversae, et totum erit diversum: quia partes comparantur ad totum sicut materia ad formam ut patet in II *Physic.* Ergo non erit idem numero homo. Quod est contra veritatem resurrectionis.

PRAETEREA, resurrectio ad hoc ordinatur quod homo operum suorum mercedem accipiat. Sed diversis operibus meritoriis vel demeritoriis diversae partes corporis deserviunt. Ergo oportet quod in resurrectione quaelibet pars ad suum statum redeat, ut pro suo modo praemietur.

SED CONTRA: Artificialia magis dependent ex sua materia quam naturalia. Sed in artificialibus, ad hoc quod idem artificiatum ex eadem materia reparetur, non oportet quod partes reducantur ad eundem situm. Ergo nec in homine oportet.

PRAETEREA, variatio accidentis non facit diversitatem in numero. Sed situs partium est accidens quoddam. Ergo diversitas eius in homine non facit diversitatem; in numero.

OBJECTION 1: It would seem necessary for the ashes of the human body to return by the resurrection to the same parts that were dissolved into them. For, according to the Philosopher, *as the whole soul is to the whole body, so is a part of the soul to a part of the body, as sight to the pupil* (*On the Soul* 2.1). Now it is necessary that after the resurrection the body be resumed by the same soul. Therefore, it is also necessary for the same parts of the body to return to the same limbs in which they were perfected by the same parts of the soul.

OBJ. 2: Further, difference of matter causes difference of number. But if the ashes return not to the same parts, each part will not be remade from the same matter of which it consisted before. Therefore, they will not be the same in number. Now if the parts are different the whole will also be different, since parts are to the whole as matter is to form (*Physics* 2.3). Therefore, it will not be the same man in number; which is contrary to the truth of the resurrection.

OBJ. 3: Further, the resurrection is directed to the end that man may receive the merit of his works. Now different parts of the body are employed in different works, whether of merit or of demerit. Therefore, at the resurrection each part must return to its former state that it may be rewarded in due measure.

ON THE CONTRARY, Artificial things are more dependent on their matter than natural things. Now in artificial things, in order that the same artificial thing be remade from the same matter there is no need for the parts to be brought back to the same position. Neither, therefore, is it necessary in man.

FURTHER, Change of an accident does not cause a change of number. Now the situation of parts is an accident. Therefore, its change in a man does not cause a change of number.

RESPONDEO dicendum quod in hac quaestione differt considerare quid fieri possit sine identitatis praeiudicio, et quid fiet ut congruentia servetur. Quantum ergo ad primum, sciendum est quod in homine possunt accipi diversae partes dupliciter: uno modo, diversae partes totius homogenei, sicut diversae partes carnis, vel diversae partes ossis; alio modo, diversae partes diversarum specierum totius heterogenei, sicut os et caro. Si ergo dicatur quod pars materiae redibit ad aliam partem speciei eiusdem, hoc non faciet nisi varietatem in situ partium. Situs autem partium variatus non variat speciem in totis homogeneis. Et sic, si materia unius partis redeat ad aliam, nullum praeiudicium generabitur identitati totius. Et ita etiam est in exemplo quod ponitur in littera: quia statua non redit eadem numero secundum formam, sed secundum materiam, secundum quam est substantia quaedam; sic autem statua est homogenea, quamvis non secundum formam artificialem.

Si autem dicatur quod materia unius partis redit ad aliam partem alterius speciei, sic de necessitate variatur non solum situs partium, sed etiam identitas earum: ita tamen si tota materia, aut aliquid quod erat de veritate humanae naturae in una, in aliam transferatur; non autem si aliquid quod erat in una parte superfluum, transferatur in aliam. Ablata autem identitate partium aufertur identitas totius, si loquimur de partibus essentialibus: non autem si loquimur de partibus accidentalibus, sicut sunt capilli et ungues, de quibus videtur loqui Augustinus.

Et sic patet qualiter translatio materiae de parte in partem tollit identitatem totius, et qualiter non.

Sed loquendo secundum congruentiam, magis probabile est quod etiam situs partium idem servabitur in resurrectione, praecipue quantum ad partes essentiales et organicas: quamvis forte non quantum ad accidentales, sicut sunt ungues et capilli.

AD PRIMUM ergo dicendum quod obiectio illa procedit de partibus organicis, et non de partibus similibus.

AD SECUNDUM dicendum quod situs diversus partium materiae non facit diversitatem in numero: quamvis eam faciat diversitas materiae;

AD TERTIUM dicendum quod operatio, proprie loquendo, non est partis, sed totius. Unde praemium non debetur parti, sed toti.

I ANSWER THAT, In this question it makes a difference whether we ask what can be done without prejudice to identity, and what will be done for the sake of congruity. As regards the first it must be observed that in man we may speak of parts in two ways: first, as of the various parts of a homogeneous whole, for instance, the various parts of flesh or the various parts of bone; second, as of various parts of various species of a heterogeneous whole, for instance, bone and flesh. Accordingly, if it be said that one part of matter will return to another part of the same species, this causes no change except in the position of the parts: and change of position of parts does not change the species in homogeneous wholes: and so if the matter of one part return to another part, this is in no way prejudicial to the identity of the whole. Thus is it in the example given in the text (*Sentences* IV, D. 44), because a statue, after being remade, is the same in number not as to its form, but as to its matter, in respect of which it is a particular substance, and in this way a statue is homogeneous, although it is not according to its artificial form.

But if it be said that the matter of one part returns to another part of another species, it follows of necessity that there is a change not only in the position of parts, but also in their identity: yet so that the whole matter, or something belonging to the truth of human nature in one is transferred to another, but not if what was superfluous in one part is transferred to another. Now the identity of parts being taken away, the identity of the whole is removed if we speak of essential parts, but not if we speak of accidental parts, such as hair and nails, to which apparently Augustine refers (*The City of God* 22).

It is thus clear how the transference of matter from one part of another destroys the identity, and how it does not.

But speaking of the congruity, it is more probable that even the parts will retain their position at the resurrection, especially as regards the essential and organic parts, although perhaps not as regards the accidental parts, such as nails and hair.

REPLY OBJ. 1: This argument considers organic or heterogeneous parts, but not homogeneous or like parts.

REPLY OBJ. 2: A change in the position of the parts of matter does not cause a change of number, although difference of matter does.

REPLY OBJ. 3: Operation, properly speaking, is not ascribed to the part but to the whole. Hence the reward is due not to the part but to the whole.

QUESTION 80

THE INTEGRITY OF THE BODIES OF THOSE WHO RISE AGAIN

Deinde considerandum est de integritate corporum resurgentium.

Circa quod quaeruntur quinque.

Primo: utrum omnia membra corporis humani in ipso resurgant.

Secundo: utrum capilli et ungues.

Tertio: utrum humores.

Quarto: utrum totum id quod fuit in eo de veritate humanae naturae.

Quinto: utrum quidquid in eo materialiter fuerit.

We must next consider the integrity of the bodies in the resurrection.

Under this head there are five points of inquiry:

(1) Whether all the members of the human body will rise again therein?

(2) Whether the hair and nails will?

(3) Whether the humors will?

(4) Whether whatever the body contained belonging to the truth of human nature will?

(5) Whether whatever it contained materially will?

Article 1

Whether All the Members of the Human Body Will Rise Again?

AD PRIMUM SIC PROCEDITUR. Videtur quod non e omnia membra corporis humani resurgant. Remoto enim fine, frustra reparatur id quod est ad finem. Finis autem cuiuslibet membri est eius actus. Cum ergo nihil frustra sit in operibus divinis; et quorundam membrorum usus post resurrectionem non competat, praecipue genitalium, quia tunc *neque nubent neque nubentur*; videtur quod non omnia membra resurgent.

PRAETEREA, intestina quaedam membra sunt. Sed non resurgent. Plena enim resurgere non possunt: quia immunditias continent. Nec vacua: quia nihil est vacuum in natura. Ergo non omnia membra resurgent.

PRAETEREA, ad hoc corpus resurget ut praemietur de opere quod anima per ipsum gessit. Sed membrum propter furtum amputatum furi qui postea poenitentiam agit et salvatur, non potest in resurrectione remunerari: neque de bono, quia ad hoc non cooperatum est; neque de malo, quia poena membri in poenam hominis redundaret. Ergo non omnia membra resurgent cum homine.

SED CONTRA: Magis pertinent ad veritatem humanae naturae alia membra quam capilli et ungues. Sed capilli et ungues restituentur homini in resurrectione, ut in littera dicitur. Ergo multo fortius alia membra.

PRAETEREA, *Dei perfecta sunt opera*. Sed resurrectio opere divino fiet. Ergo homo reparabitur perfectus in omnibus membris.

OBJECTION 1: It would seem that not all the members of the human body will rise again. For if the end be removed, it is useless to repair the means. Now the end of each member is its act. Since, then, nothing useless is done in the divine works, and since the use of certain members is not fitting to man after the resurrection, especially the use of the genital members, for then *they shall neither marry, nor be married* (Matt 22:30), it would seem that not all the members shall rise again.

OBJ. 2: Further, the entrails are members: and yet they will not rise again. For they can neither rise full, since thus they contain impurities, nor empty, since nothing is empty in nature. Therefore, the members shall not all rise again.

OBJ. 3: Further, the body shall rise again that it may be rewarded for the works which the soul did through it. Now the member of which a thief has been deprived for theft, and who has afterwards done penance and is saved, cannot be rewarded at the resurrection neither for any good deed, since it has not cooperated in any, nor for evil deeds, since the punishment of the member would redound to the punishment of man. Therefore, the members will not all rise again.

ON THE CONTRARY, The other members belong more to the truth of human nature than hair and nails. Yet these will be restored to man at the resurrection according to the text (*Sentences* IV, D.4). Much more, therefore, does this apply to the other members.

FURTHER, *The works of God are perfect* (Deut 32:4). But the resurrection will be the work of God. Therefore, man will be remade perfect in all his members.

RESPONDEO dicendum quod, sicut dicitur in II *de Anima*, anima se habet ad corpus non solum in habitudine formae et finis, sed etiam in habitudine causae efficientis. Est enim comparatio animae ad corpus sicut comparatio artis ad artificiatum, ut dicitur in XIII *de Animalibus*: quidquid autem explicite in artificiato ostenditur, hoc totum implicite et originaliter in ipsa arte continetur. Et similiter quidquid in partibus corporis apparet, totum originaliter et quodammodo implicite in anima continetur. Sicut ergo artis opus non esset perfectum si artificiato aliquid deesset eorum quae ars continet, ita nec homo posset esse perfectus nisi totum quod in anima implicite continetur, exterius in corpore explicaretur: nec etiam corpus animae ad plenum proportionaliter responderet. Cum ergo oporteat in resurrectione corpus hominis esse animae totaliter correspondens, quia non resurget nisi secundum ordinem quem habet ad animam rationalem; oportet etiam hominem perfectum resurgere, utpote qui ad ultimam perfectionem consequendam reparatur: oportet quod omnia membra quae nunc sunt in corpore, in resurrectione hominis reparentur.

AD PRIMUM ergo dicendum quod membra possunt dupliciter considerari in comparatione ad animam: vel secundum habitudinem materiae ad formam, vel secundum habitudinem instrumenti ad agentem; eadem enim est comparatio totius corporis ad totam animam et partium ad partes, ut dicitur in II *de Anima*. Si ergo membrum accipiatur secundum primam comparationem, finis eius non est operatio, sed magis perfectum esse speciei: quod etiam post resurrectionem requiretur. Si autem accipiatur secundum secundam comparationem, sic finis eius est operatio. Nec tamen sequitur quod, quando deficit operatio, frustra sit instrumentum: quia instrumentum non solum servit ad exequendam operationem agentis, sed ad ostendendam virtutem ipsius. Unde oportebit quod virtus potentiarum animae in instrumentis corporeis demonstretur, etsi nunquam in actum prodeant, ut ex hoc commendetur Dei sapientia.

AD SECUNDUM dicendum quod intestina resurgent in corpore, sicut et alia membra. Et plena erunt, non quidem turpibus superfluitatibus, sed nobilibus humiditatibus.

AD TERTIUM dicendum quod actus quibus meremur non sunt, proprie loquendo, manus vel pedis, sed totius hominis: sicut et operatio artis non attribuitur serrae, sed artifici, ut principio. Quamvis ergo membrum quod ante poenitentiam est mutilatum, non sit cooperatum homini in statu illo quo gloriam post meretur, tamen ipse homo meretur ut totum praemietur, qui ex toto quod habet Deo servit.

I ANSWER THAT, As stated in *On the Soul* 2.4, the soul stands in relation to the body not only as its form and end, but also as efficient cause. For the soul is compared to the body as art to the artifact, as the Philosopher says (*On the Generation of Animals* 2.4), and whatever is shown forth explicitly in the artifact is all contained implicitly and originally in the art. In like manner, whatever appears in the parts of the body is all contained originally and, in a way, implicitly in the soul. Thus, just as the work of an art would not be perfect if its product lacked any of the things contained in the art, so neither could man be perfect unless the whole that is contained implicitly in the soul be explicitly unfolded in the body, nor would the body correspond in full proportion to the soul. Since, then, at the resurrection man's body ought to correspond entirely to the soul, for it will not rise again except according to the relation it bears to the rational soul, it follows that man also must rise again perfect, seeing that he is thereby repaired in order that he may obtain his ultimate perfection. Consequently, all the members that are now in man's body must be restored at the resurrection.

REPLY OBJ. 1: The members may be considered in two ways in relation to the soul: either according to the relation of matter to form, or according to the relation of instrument to agent, since the whole body is compared to the whole soul in the same way as one part is to another (*On the Soul* 2.1). If, then, the members be considered in the light of the first relationship, their end is not operation, but rather the perfect being of the species, and this is also required after the resurrection: but if they be considered in the light of the second relationship, then their end is operation. And yet it does not follow that when the operation fails the instrument is useless, because an instrument serves not only to accomplish the operation of the agent, but also to show its virtue. Hence it will be necessary for the virtue of the soul's powers to be shown in their bodily instruments, even though they never proceed to action, so that the wisdom of God be thereby glorified.

REPLY OBJ. 2: The entrails will rise again in the body even as the other members: and they will be filled not with vile superfluities but with noble humors.

REPLY OBJ. 3: The acts whereby we merit are not the acts, properly speaking, of hand or foot but of the whole man; even as the work of art is ascribed not to the instrument but to the craftsman. Therefore, though the member which was cut off before a man's repentance did not cooperate with him in the state wherein he merits glory, yet man himself merits that the whole man may be rewarded who with his whole being serves God.

Article 2

Whether the Hair and Nails Will Rise Again in the Human Body?

Ad secundum sic proceditur. Videtur quod capilli et ungues non resurgent in homine. Sicut enim capilli et ungues ex superfluitatibus cibi generantur, ita urina et sudor et aliae huiusmodi faeces. Sed haec non resurgent cum corpore. Ergo nec capilli et ungues.

Praeterea, inter alias superfluitates quae ex cibo generantur, maxime accedit ad naturae humanae veritatem semen, quod est *superfluum quo indigetur*. Sed semen non resurget in corpore hominis. Ergo multo minus capilli et ungues resurgent.

Praeterea, nihil est perfectum anima rationali quod non sit perfectum anima sensibili. Sed capilli et ungues non sunt perfecti anima sensibili: quia eis, *non sentimus*, ut dicitur in I *de Anima*. Ergo, cum non resurgat corpus humanum nisi propter hoc quod est perfectum ab anima rationali, videtur quod capilli et ungues non resurgent.

Sed contra: Est quod dicitur Luc, 21, [18]: *capillus de capite vestro non peribit*.

Praeterea, capilli et ungues sunt dati in ornamentum homini. Sed corpora hominum, praecipue electorum, debent resurgere cum omni ornatu. Ergo debent resurgere cum capillis.

Respondeo dicendum quod anima se habet ad corpus animatum sicut ars ad artificiatum, et ad partes eius sicut ars ad sua instrumenta: unde et corpus animatum *organicum* dicitur. Ars autem utitur instrumentis quibusdam ad operis intenti executionem, et haec instrumenta sunt de prima intentione artis; utitur etiam aliis instrumentis ad conservationem principalium instrumentorum, et haec sunt de secunda intentione artis; sicut ars militaris utitur gladio ad bellum, et vagina ad gladii conservationem. Ita et in partibus corporis animati quaedam ordinantur ad operationes animae exequendas, sicut cor, hepar, manus et pes; quaedam autem ad conservationem aliarum partium, sicut folia sunt ad cooperimentum fructuum. Ita etiam capilli et ungues sunt in homine ad custodiam aliarum partium. Unde sunt de secunda perfectione corporis humani, quamvis non de prima. Et quia homo resurget in omni perfectione suae naturae, propter hoc oportet quod capilli et ungues resurgant in ipso.

Ad primum ergo dicendum quod illae superfluitates expelluntur a natura, quasi ad nihilum utiles: unde non pertinent ad perfectionem humani corporis. Secus autem est de illis superfluitatibus quas natura sibi retinet ad generationem capillorum et unguium, quibus indiget ad membrorum conservationem.

Objection 1: It would seem that the hair and nails will not rise again in the human body. For just as hair and nails result from the surplus of food, so do urine, sweat and other superfluities or dregs. But these will not rise again with the body. Neither, therefore, will hair and nails.

Obj. 2: Further, of all the superfluities that are produced from food, seed comes nearest to the truth of human nature, since, though *superfluous, it is needed*. Yet seed will not rise again in the human body. Much less, therefore, will hair and nails.

Obj. 3: Further, nothing is perfected by a rational soul that is not perfected by a sensitive soul. But hair and nails are not perfected by a sensitive soul, for *we do not feel with them* (On the Soul 1.5, 3.13). Therefore, since the human body does not rise again except because it is perfected by a rational soul, it would seem that the hair and nails will not rise again.

On the contrary, It is written: *a hair of your head shall not perish* (Luke 21:18).

Further, Hair and nails were given to man as an ornament. Now the bodies of men, especially of the elect, ought to rise again with all their adornment. Therefore, they ought to rise again with hair.

I answer that, The soul is to the animated body as art is to the artifact, and is to the parts of the body as art to its instruments: wherefore an animated body is called an *organic body*. Now art employs certain instruments for the accomplishment of the work intended, and these instruments belong to the primary intention of art: and it also uses other instruments for the safe-keeping of the principal instruments, and these belong to the secondary intention of art: thus the art of warfare employs a sword for fighting, and a sheath for the safe-keeping of the sword. And so among the parts of an animated body, some are directed to the accomplishment of the soul's operations, for instance, the heart, liver, hand, foot; while others are directed to the safe-keeping of the other parts as leaves to cover fruit; and thus hair and nails are in man for the protection of other parts. Consequently, although they do not belong to the primary perfection of the human body, they belong to the secondary perfection: and since man will rise again with all the perfections of his nature, it follows that hair and nails will rise again in him.

Reply Obj. 1: Those superfluities are voided by nature as being useful for nothing. Hence they do not belong to the perfection of the human body. It is not so with the superfluities which nature reserves for the production of hair and nails, which she needs for the protection of the members.

AD SECUNDUM dicendum quod semine non indigetur ad perfectionem individui, sicut capillis: sed solum ad perfectionem speciei.

AD TERTIUM dicendum quod capilli et ungues nutriuntur et augentur: et sic patet quod aliqua operatione participent. Quod non posset esse nisi essent partes aliquo modo ab anima perfectae. Et quia in homine non est nisi una anima, scilicet rationalis, constat quod ab anima rationali perfecta sunt: quamvis non usque ad hoc quod operationem sensus participent; sicut nec ossa, de quibus constat quod resurgent, et sunt de integritate individui.

REPLY OBJ. 2: Seed is not required for the perfection of the individual, as hair and nails are, but only for the protection of the species.

REPLY OBJ. 3: Hair and nails are nourished and grow, and so it is clear that they share in some operation, which would not be possible unless they were parts in some way perfected by the soul. And since in man there is but one soul, namely, the rational soul, it is clear that they are perfected by the rational soul, although not so far as to share in the operation of sense, as neither do bones, and yet it is certain that these will rise again and that they belong to the integrity of the individual.

Article 3

Whether the Humors Will Rise Again in the Body?

AD TERTIUM SIC PROCEDITUR. Videtur quod humores in corpore non resurgent. Quia I Cor. 15, [50] dicitur: *caro et sanguis regnum Dei non possidebunt.* Sed sanguis est principalior humor. Ergo non resurget in beatis, qui regnum Dei possidebunt. Et multo minus in aliis.

PRAETEREA, humores sunt ad restaurationem deperditi. Sed post restaurationem nulla deperditio fiet. Ergo corpus non resurget cum humoribus.

PRAETEREA, illud quod est via generationis in corpore humano, nondum est ab anima rationali perfectum. Sed humores adhuc sunt in via generationis: quia sunt in potentia caro: et os. Ergo nondum sunt perfecti anima rationali. Sed corpus humanum non habet ordinem ad resurrectionem nisi secundum quod est anima rationali perfectum. Ergo humores in eo non resurgent.

SED CONTRA: Quod est de constitutione corporis humani, resurgent in eo. Sed humores sunt huiusmodi: ut patet per Augustinum, qui dicit quod *corpus constat ex membris officialibus, officialia ex consimilibus, consimilia ex humoribus.* Ergo humores resurgent in corpore.

PRAETEREA, resurrectio nostra erit conformis resurrectioni Christi. Sed in Christo resurrexit sanguis: alias nunc vinum non transubstantiaretur in sanguinem eius in Sacramento Altaris. Ergo et in nobis resurget sanguis. Et eadem ratione alii humores.

RESPONDEO dicendum quod quidquid pertinet ad integritatem humanae naturae, in resurgente hoc totum repurget, ratione praedicta. Unde oportet quod illa humiditas corporis resurgat in homine quae ad integritatem eius pertineat.

OBJECTION 1: It would seem that the humors will not rise again in the body. For it is written: *flesh and blood cannot possess the kingdom of God* (1 Cor 15:50). Now blood is the chief humor. Therefore, it will not rise again in the blessed, who will possess the kingdom of God, and much less in others.

OBJ. 2: Further, humors are intended to make up for the waste. Now after the resurrection there will be no waste. Therefore, the body will not rise again with humors.

OBJ. 3: Further, that which is in process of generation in the human body is not yet perfected by the rational soul. Now the humors are still in process of generation because they are potentially flesh and bone. Therefore, they are not yet perfected by the rational soul. Now the human body is not directed to the resurrection except insofar as it is perfected by the rational soul. Therefore, the humors will not rise again.

ON THE CONTRARY, Whatever enters into the constitution of the human body will rise again with it. Now this applies to the humors, as appears from the statement of Augustine (Alcher of Clairvaux, *The Spirit and the Soul* 15) that *the body consists of functional members; the functional members of homogeneous parts; and the homogeneous parts of humors.* Therefore, the humors will rise again in the body.

FURTHER, Our resurrection will be conformed to the resurrection of Christ. Now in Christ's resurrection his blood rose again, else the wine would not now be changed into his blood in the Sacrament of the Altar. Therefore, the blood will rise again in us also, and in like manner the other humors.

I ANSWER THAT, Whatever belongs to the integrity of human nature in those who take part in the resurrection will rise again, as stated above (A. 1–2). Hence whatever humidity of the body belongs to the integrity of human nature must rise again in man.

Est autem in homine triplex humiditas. Quaedam enim humiditas est in recedendo a perfectione huius individui: vel quia est in via corruptionis, et a natura abiicitur, sicut urina, sudor et sanies et huiusmodi; vel quia a natura ordinatur ad conservationem speciei in alio individuo, sive per actum generativae, sicut semen, sive per actum nutritivae, sicut lac. Et nulla talium humiditatum resurget: eo quod non est de perfectione individui resurgentis.

Secunda humiditas est quae nondum pervenit ad ultimam perfectionem quam natura operatur in individuo, sed est ad illam ordinata a natura. Et haec est duplex. Quia quaedam est quae habet aliquam formam determinatam, secundum quam continetur inter partes corporis: sicut sanguis et alii tres humores, quos natura ordinavit ad membra quae ex eis generantur, sed tamen habent aliquas formas determinatas, sicut et aliae partes corporis. Et ideo resurgent cum aliis partibus corporis.

Quaedam vero humiditas est in via transeundi de forma in formam, scilicet de forma humoris in formam membri. Et talis humiditas non resurget. Quia post resurrectionem partes corporis singulae in suis formis stabilientur, ut una in aliam non transeat. Et ideo non resurget illa humiditas quae est in ipso actu transeundi de forma in formam. Haec autem humiditas potest in duplici statu accipi. Vel secundum quod est in principio transmutationis: et sic vocatur *ros*, illa scilicet humiditas quae est in foraminibus parvarum venarum. Vel secundum quod est in progressu transmutationis et incipit iam dealbari: et sic vocatur *cambium*. In neutro autem statu resurget.

Tertium genus humiditatis est quod iam pervenit ad ultimam perfectionem quam natura intendit in corpore individui: quae iam est dealbata et incorporata membris. Et haec vocatur *gluten*. Et, cum sit de substantia membrorum, resurget, sicut alia membra resurgunt.

Ad primum ergo dicendum quod *caro* et *sanguis* in verbis illis Apostoli non accipiuntur pro substantia carnis et sanguinis, sed pro operibus carnis et sanguinis, quae sunt opera peccati, vel opera animalis vitae. Vel, secundum quod dicit Augustinus, in Epistola ad Consentium, *caro et sanguis* accipitur ibi pro corruptione quae nunc dominatur in carne et sanguine. Unde et subditur in verbis Apostoli: *neque corruptio incorruptionem*.

Ad secundum dicendum quod, sicut membra servientia generationi erunt post resurrectionem ad integritatem humanae naturae, non ad operationem quae nunc exercetur per membra illa; ita et humores erunt in corpore, non ad restaurationem deperditi, sed ad integritatem humanae naturae reparandam, et ad virtutis naturalis ostensionem.

Now there is a threefold humidity in man. There is one which occurs as receding from the perfection of the individual—either because it is on the way to corruption, and is voided by nature, for instance, urine, sweat, pus, and so forth—or because it is directed by nature to the preservation of the species in some individual, either by the act of the generative power, as seed, or by the act of the nutritive power, as milk. None of these humidities will rise again, because they do not belong to the perfection of the person rising again.

The second kind of humidity is one that has not yet reached its ultimate perfection which nature achieves in the individual, yet it is directed thereto by nature: and this is of two kinds. For there is one kind that has a definite form and is contained among the parts of the body, for instance, the blood and the other humors which nature has directed to the members that are produced or nourished from it: and yet they have certain definite forms like the other parts of the body, and consequently will rise again with the other parts of the body.

Another kind of humidity is in transition from form to form, namely, from the form of humor to the form of member. Humidities of this kind will not rise again, because after the resurrection each part of the body will be established in its form, so that one will not pass into another. Wherefore this humidity that is actually in transition from one form to another will not rise again. Now this humidity may be considered in a twofold state—either as being at the beginning of its transformation, and thus it is called 'ros', namely the humidity that is found in the cavities of the smaller veins—or as in the course of transformation and already beginning to undergo alteration, and thus it is called 'cambium': but in neither state will it rise again.

The third kind of humidity is that which has already reached its ultimate perfection that nature intends in the body of the individual, and has already undergone transformation and become incorporate with the members. This is called 'gluten', and since it belongs to the members it will rise again just as the members will.

Reply Obj. 1: In these words of the Apostle *flesh* and *blood* do not denote the substance of flesh and blood but deeds of flesh and blood, which are either deeds of sin or the operations of the animal life. Or we may say with Augustine in his letter to Consentius (Ep. cxlvi) that *flesh and blood* here signify the corruption which is now predominant in flesh and blood; wherefore the Apostle's words continue: *neither shall corruption possess incorruption* (1 Cor 15:50).

Reply Obj. 2: Just as the members that serve for generation will be after the resurrection for the integrity of human nature, and not for the operation accomplished now by them, so will the humors be in the body not to make up for waste, but to restore the integrity of human nature and to show forth its natural power.

AD TERTIUM dicendum quod, sicut elementa sunt in via generationis respectu corporum mixtorum, quia sunt eorum materia, non autem ita quod semper sint in transeundo in corpore mixto, ita etiam se habent humores ad membra. Et propter hoc, sicut elementa in partibus universi habent formas determinatas, ratione quarum sunt de perfectione universi, sicut et corpora mixta; ita etiam humores sunt de perfectione corporis humani sicut et aliae partes, quamvis non perveniant ad totam perfectionem, sicut aliae partes; nec elementa habent ita perfectas formas sicut mixta. Sicut autem partes omnes universi a Deo perfectionem consequuntur non aequaliter, sed secundum suum modum unumquodque; ita etiam humores aliquo modo perficiuntur ab anima rationali, non tamen eodem modo sicut partes perfectiores.

REPLY OBJ. 3: Just as the elements are in the course of generation in relation to mixed bodies because they are their matter, yet not so as to be always in transition when in the mixed body, so too are the humors in relation to the members. And for this reason as the elements in the parts of the universe have definite forms, by reason of which they, like mixed bodies, belong to the perfection of the universe, so too the humors belong to the perfection of the human body, just as the other parts do, although they do not reach its entire perfection as the other parts do, and although the elements have not perfect forms as mixed bodies have. But as all the parts of the universe receive their perfection from God not equally, but each one according to its mode, so too the humors are in some way perfected by the rational soul, yet not in the same measure as the more perfect parts.

Article 4

Whether Whatever in the Body Belonged to the Truth of Human Nature Will Rise Again in It?

AD QUARTUM SIC PROCEDITUR. Videtur quod non totum quod fuit in corpore de veritate humanae naturae, resurget in ipso. Quia cibus convertitur in veritatem humanae naturae. Sed aliquando carnes bovis sumuntur in cibum. Si ergo resurget quidquid fuit de veritate humanae naturae, resurget etiam caro bovis: Quod est inconveniens.

PRAETEREA, costa Adae fuit de veritate humanae naturae in ipso, sicut et costa nostra in nobis. Sed costa Adae non resurget in eo, sed in Heva: alias Heva non resurgeret, quae de costa illa formata est. Ergo non resurget in homine quidquid fuit in eo de veritate humanae naturae.

PRAETEREA, non potest esse quod idem in diversis hominibus resurgat. Sed potest esse quod aliquid fuit de veritate humanae naturae in diversis hominibus: sicut si aliquis carnibus humanis vescatur, quae in substantiam eius transeant. Ergo non resurget in aliquo quidquid fuit de veritate humanae naturae in ipso.

SI DICATUR QUOD non quidquid est in carnibus comestis est de veritate humanae naturae, et ita aliquid eorum potest resurgere in primo et aliquid in secundo: contra. De veritate humanae naturae maxime videtur esse illud quod a parentibus trahitur. Sed, si aliquis non comedens nisi carnes humanas filium generet, oportet quod illud quod filius a parente trahit, fuerit de carnibus aliorum hominum, quas pater suus comedit: quia *semen est de superfluo alimenti*, ut Philosophus probat, in libro *de Animalibus*. Ergo illud quod est de veritate humanae

OBJECTION 1: It would seem that what was in the body belonging to the truth of human nature will not all rise again in it. For food is changed into the truth of human nature. Now sometimes the flesh of the ox or of other animals is taken as food. Therefore, if whatever belonged to the truth of human nature will rise again, the flesh of the ox or of other animals will also rise again: which is inadmissible.

OBJ. 2: Further, Adam's rib belonged to the truth of human nature in him, as ours does in us. But Adam's rib will rise again not in Adam but in Eve, else Eve would not rise again at all since she was made from that rib. Therefore, whatever belonged in man to the truth of human nature will not all rise again in him.

OBJ. 3: Further, it is impossible for the same thing from different men to rise again. Yet it is possible for something in different men to belong to the truth of human nature; for instance, if a man were to partake of human flesh which would be changed into his substance. Therefore, there will not rise again in man whatever belonged in him to the truth of human nature.

OBJ. 4: Further, if it be said that not all the flesh partaken of belongs to the truth of human nature and that consequently some of it may possibly rise again in the one man and some in the other: to the contrary. That which is derived from one's parents would especially seem to belong to the truth of human nature. But if one who partook of nothing but human flesh were to beget children, that which his child derives from him must be of the flesh of other men partaken of by his father, since *the seed is from the surplus of food*, as the Philosopher proves (*On the Generation of Ani-*

naturae in puero isto, fuit etiam de veritate humanae naturae in aliis hominibus, quorum carnes pater comedit.

SI DICATUR QUOD illud quod erat de veritate humanae naturae in carnibus hominum comestorum non transit in semen, sed illud quod erat ibi de veritate humanae naturae non existens: contra. Ponatur quod aliquis cibetur solum embryis, in quibus nihil videtur esse quod non sit de veritate humanae naturae, quia totum quod est in eis a parentibus trahitur. Si ergo superfluitas cibi convertitur in semen, oportet quod illud quod fuit de veritate humanae naturae in embryis, quae etiam ad resurrectionem pertinent postquam animam rationalem perceperunt, sit etiam de veritate humanae naturae in puero qui ex tali semine generatur. Et sic, cum non possit idem resurgere in duobus, non poterit in quolibet resurgere quidquid fuit de veritate humanae naturae in ipso.

SED CONTRA: Quidquid fuit de veritate humanae naturae, fuit perfectum anima rationali. Sed ex hoc habet corpus humanum ordinem ad resurrectionem, quia fuit anima rationali perfectum. Ergo quidquid fuit de veritate humanae naturae, resurget in unoquoque.

PRAETEREA, si a corpore hominis subtrahatur aliquid quod est de veritate humanae naturae in ipso, non erit corpus hominis perfectum. Sed omnis imperfectio tolletur in resurrectione: praecipue ab electis, quibus promissum est, Luc. 21, [18], quod *capillus de capite eorum non peribit*. Ergo quidquid fuit de veritate humanae naturae, resurget in homine.

RESPONDEO dicendum quod *unumquodque, sicut se habet ad esse*, ita se habet ad veritatem, ut dicitur in II *Metaphys.*: quia illa res vera est quae est ita ut videtur cognitori secundum actum. Et propter: hoc Avicenna dicit quod *veritas uniuscuiusque rei est proprietas sui esse, quod stabilitum est ei*. Et secundum hoc, aliquid dicetur esse de veritate humanae naturae quia proprie pertinet ad esse humanae naturae. Et hoc est quod participat formam humanae naturae: sicut verum aurum dicitur quod habet veram formam auri, ex qua est proprium esse auri.

Ut ergo videatur quid sit illud quod est de veritate humanae naturae, sciendum est quod circa hoc est triplex opinio. Quidam enim posuerunt quod nihil de novo esse incipit de veritate humanae naturae, sed quidquid ad veritatem humanae naturae pertinet, totum fuit in ipsa institutione humanae naturae de veritate eius; et hoc per seipsum multiplicatur, ut ex eo possit semen decidi a generante, ex quo filius generetur; in quo etiam illa pars decisa multiplicatur, et ad perfectam quantitatem pervenit per augmentum, et sic deinceps; et ita multiplicatum est totum genus humanum. Unde, secundum opinionem hanc, quidquid ex alimento generatur, quamvis videatur

mals 1). Therefore, what belongs to the truth of human nature in that child belonged also to the truth of human nature in other men of whose flesh his father had partaken.

OBJ. 5: Further, if it be said that what was changed into seed was not that which belonged to the truth of human nature in the flesh of the men eaten, but something not belonging to the truth of human nature: to the contrary. Let us suppose that some one is fed entirely on embryos, in which seemingly there is nothing but what belongs to the truth of human nature, since whatever is in them is derived from the parents. If, then, the surplus food be changed into seed, that which belonged to the truth of human nature in the embryos—and after these have received a rational soul, the resurrection applies to them—must belong to the truth of human nature in the child begotten of that seed. And thus, since the same cannot rise again in two subjects, it will be impossible for whatever belonged to the truth of human nature in both to rise again in both of them.

ON THE CONTRARY, Whatever belonged to the truth of human nature was perfected by the rational soul. Now it is through being perfected by the rational soul that the human body is directed to the resurrection. Therefore, whatever belonged to the truth of human nature will rise again in each one.

FURTHER, If anything belonging to the truth of human nature in a man be taken from his body, this will not be the perfect body of a man. Now all imperfection of a man will be removed at the resurrection, especially in the elect, to whom it was promised that *not a hair of their head should perish* (Luke 21:18). Therefore, whatever belonged to the truth of human nature in a man will rise again in him.

I ANSWER THAT, *Everything is related to truth in the same way as to being* (*Metaphysics* 2), because a thing is true when it is as it appears to him who actually knows it. For this reason Avicenna (*Metaphysics* 2) says that *the truth of anything is a property of the being immutably attached thereto*. Accordingly, a thing is said to belong to the truth of human nature because it belongs properly to the being of human nature, and this is what shares the form of human nature, just as true gold is what has the true form of gold whence gold derives its proper being.

In order, therefore, to see what it is that belongs to the truth of human nature, we must observe that there have been three opinions on the question. For some have maintained that nothing begins anew to belong to the truth of human nature, and that whatever belongs to the truth of human nature, all of it belonged to the truth of human nature when this was created; and that this multiplies by itself, so that it is possible for the seed whereof the child is begotten to be detached therefrom by the begetter, and that again the detached part multiplies in the child, so that he reaches perfect quantity by growth, and so on, and that thus was the whole human race multiplied. Therefore, according to this

speciem carnis aut sanguinis habere, non tamen pertinet ad veritatem humanae naturae.

Alii vero dixerunt quod aliquid de novo additur ad veritatem humanae naturae per transmutationem naturalem alimenti in corpus humanum, considerata veritate humanae naturae in specie, ad cuius conservationem ordinatur actus generativae virtutis. Si autem veritas humanae naturae in individuo consideretur, ad cuius conservationem et perfectionem actus nutritivae virtutis ordinatur, non additur aliquid per alimentum quod sit primo de veritate humanae naturae huius individui, sed solum secundario. Ponunt enim quod veritas humanae naturae primo et principaliter consistit in humido radicali, ex quo est prima constitutio humani generis: quod autem convertitur de alimento in veram carnem et sanguinem, non est principaliter de necessitate humanae naturae illius individui, sed secundario; sed potest esse principaliter de veritate humanae naturae alterius individui, quod ex semine illius generatur. Semen enim ponunt esse superfluum alimenti: vel cum admixtione alicuius quod est primo de veritate humanae naturae in generante, ut quidam dicunt; vel sine admixtione eius, ut dicunt alii. Et sic quod est humidum nutrimentale in uno, fit humidum radicale in alio.

Tertia opinio est quod aliquid de novo incipit esse principaliter de veritate humanae naturae etiam in isto individuo. Quia non est distinctio talis in corpore humano ut aliqua pars materialis signata de necessitate per totam vitam remaneat: sed ad hoc indifferenter se habet quaelibet pars signata accepta, quod manet semper quantum ad id quod est speciei in ea, sed potest fluere et refluere quantum ad id quod est materiae in ipsa. Et sic humidum nutrimentale non distinguitur a radicali ex parte principii, ut dicatur radicale quod est ex semine generatum, nutrimentale quod generatur ex cibo: sed magis distinguitur ex termino, quod radicale dicitur quod ad terminum generationis pervenit per actum generativae vel etiam nutritivae virtutis; se nutrimentale, quod nondum pervenit ad hunc terminum; sed est adhuc in via nutriendi.

Et hae tres opiniones in II libro *Sententiarum*, dist. 30, plenius percunctatae et investigatae sunt. Et ideo non debent hic repeti, nisi quantum ad propositum pertinet.

Sciendum est ergo quod secundum has opiniones diversimode ad hanc quaestionem oportet respondere. Prima opinio, per viam multiplicationis quam ponit, potest ponere perfectionem humanae naturae, et quantum ad numerum individuorum et quantum ad debitam quantitatem uniuscuiusque individui, absque eo quod ex alimento generatum est; quod quidem non additur nisi ad resistendum consumptioni quae posset induci

opinion, whatever is produced by nourishment, although it seem to have the appearance of flesh and blood, does not belong to the truth of human nature.

Others held that something new is added to the truth of human nature by the natural transformation of the food into the human body, if we consider the truth of human nature in the species to the preservation of which the act of the generative power is directed: but that if we consider the truth of human nature in the individual, to the preservation and perfection of which the act of the nutritive power is directed, that which is added by food belongs to the truth of the human nature of the individual not primarily but secondarily. For they assert that the truth of human nature, first and foremost, consists in the radical humor, that, namely, which is begotten of the seed of which the human race was originally fashioned: and that what is changed from food into true flesh and blood does not belong principally to the truth of human nature in this particular individual, but secondarily: and that nevertheless this can belong principally to the truth of human nature in another individual who is begotten of the seed of the former. For they assert that seed is the surplus from food, either mingled with something belonging principally to the truth of human nature in the begetter, according to some, or without any such admixture, as others maintain. And thus the nutrimental humor in one becomes the radical humor in another.

The third opinion is that something new begins to belong principally to the truth of human nature even in this individual, because distinction in the human body does not require that any designated material part must remain throughout the whole lifetime; any designated part one may take is indifferent to this, whereas it remains always as regards what belongs to the species in it, although as regards what is material therein it may ebb and flow. And thus the nutrimental humor is not distinct from the radical on the part of its principle (so that it be called radical when begotten of the seed, and nutrimental when produced by the food), but rather on the part of the term, so that it be called radical when it reaches the term of generation by the act of the generative, or even nutritive power, but nutrimental when it has not yet reached this term, but is still on the way to give nourishment.

These three opinions have been more fully exposed and examined in the Second Book (*Sentences* II, D. 30) insofar as the question at issue is concerned.

It must accordingly be observed that this question requires different answers according to these opinions. For the first opinion, on account of its explanation of the process of multiplication, is able to admit perfection of the truth of human nature, both as regards the number of individuals and as regards the due quantity of each individual, without taking into account that which is produced from food; for this is not added except for the purpose of resist-

per actionem caloris naturalis, sicut argento apponitur plumbum ne ex liquefactione consumatur. Unde, cum in resurrectione oporteat naturam humanam in sua perfectione reparari, nec calor naturalis tunc agat ad consumptionem humidi naturalis, nulla necessitas erit quod resurgat aliquid in homine quod ex alimento sit generatum: sed resurget tantum illud quod fuit de veritate humanae naturae individui, et per decisionem et multiplicationem ad praedictam perfectionem pervenit in numero et quantitate.

Secunda autem opinio, quia ponit quod eo quod adgeneratur ex nutrimento, indigetur ad perfectionem quantitatis individui et ad multiplicationem quae fit per generationem, necesse habet ponere aliquid de hoc in quod conversum est alimentum, resurgere: non tamen totum, sed solum quantum indigetur ad perfectam reintegrationem humanae naturae in omnibus suis individuis. Unde ponit haec opinio quod totum illud quod fuit in substantia seminis, resurget in illo homine qui ex illo semine generatus est: quia hoc est principaliter de veritate humanae naturae in ipso. De eo autem quod postea advenit per nutrimentum, tantum resurget in eo quantum est necessarium ad perfectionem quantitatis: et non totum, quia hoc non pertinet aliter ad veritatem humanae naturae nisi quatenus natura indiget eo ad perfectionem quantitatis. Sed quia hoc humidum nutrimentale fluit et refluit, hoc ordine reparabitur quod illud quod primo fuit de substantia corporis hominis, totum reparabitur; et de eo quod secundo et tertio et deinceps advenit, quantum necessarium est ad quantitatem reintegrandam, duplici ratione.

Primo, quia super hoc quod advenit inductum fuit ut illud quod primo erat deperditum repararetur: et ita non ita principaliter pertinet ad veritatem humanae naturae sicut praecedens. Secundo, quia adiunctio humidi extranei ad primum humidum radicale facit quod totum permixtum non ita perfecte participet veritatem speciei sicut primum participabat. Et ponit exemplum Philosophus, in I *de Generat.*, de aqua permixta vino, quae semper virtutem vini debilitat, ita quod in fine ipsum aquosum reddit. Unde, sicut secunda aqua, quamvis assumatur in speciem vini, non tamen ita perfecte speciem vini participat sicut prima quae in vinum assumebatur, ita illud quod de alimento secundo in carnem convertitur, non ita perfecte attingit ad speciem carnis sicut quod primo convertebatur. Et ideo non ita pertinet ad veritatem humanae naturae, nec ad resurrectionem. Sic ergo patet quod haec opinio ponit resurgere totum id quod est de veritate humanae naturae principaliter, non autem totum quod est de veritate humanae naturae secundario.

Tertia autem opinio quantum ad aliquid differt a secunda, et quantum ad aliquid convenit cum ea. Differt

ing the destruction that might result from the action of natural heat, as lead is added to silver lest it be destroyed in melting. Wherefore since at the resurrection human nature ought to be restored to its perfection, nor does the natural heat tend to destroy the natural humor, there will be no need for anything resulting from food to rise again in man, but that alone will rise again which belonged to the truth of the human nature of the individual, and this reaches the aforesaid perfection in number and quantity by being detached and multiplied.

The second opinion, since it maintains that what is produced from food is needed for the perfection of quantity in the individual and for the multiplication that results from generation, must admit that something of this product from food shall rise again: not all, however, but only so much as is required for the perfect restoration of human nature in all its individuals. Hence this opinion asserts that all that was in the substance of the seed will rise again in this man who was begotten of this seed, because this belongs chiefly to the truth of human nature in him: while of that which afterwards he derives from nourishment, only so much will rise again in him as is needed for the perfection of his quantity, and not all, because this does not belong to the perfection of human nature except insofar as nature requires it for the perfection of quantity. Since, however, this nutrimental humor is subject to ebb and flow, the restoration will be effected in this order: what first belonged to the substance of a man's body will all be restored, and of that which was added second, third, and so on, as much as is required to restore quantity; for two reasons.

First, because that which was added was intended to restore what was wasted at first, and thus it does not belong principally to the truth of human nature to the same extent as that which came first. Second, because the addition of extraneous humor to the first radical humors results in the whole mixture not sharing the truth of the specific nature as perfectly as the first did: and the Philosopher instances as an example (*On Generation and Corruption* 1) the mixing of water with wine, which always weakens the strength of the wine, so that in the end the wine becomes watery: so that although the second water be drawn into the species of wine, it does not share the species of wine as perfectly as the first water added to the wine. Even so, that which is second changed from food into flesh does not so perfectly attain to the species of flesh as that which was changed first, and consequently does not belong in the same degree to the truth of human nature nor to the resurrection. Accordingly, it is clear that this opinion maintains that the whole of what belongs to the truth of human nature principally will rise again, but not the whole of what belongs to the truth of human nature secondarily.

The third opinion differs somewhat from the second and in some respects agrees with it. It differs in that it main-

quidem quantum ad hoc, quod ponit totum quod est sub forma carnis et ossis eadem ratione ad veritatem humanae naturae pertinere. Quia non distinguit aliquid materiale signatum permanens in homine toto tempore vitae eius, quod per se pertinet ad veritatem humanae naturae et primo; et aliquid fluens et refluens, quod pertinet ad veritatem humanae naturae solum propter quantitatis perfectionem, non propter primum esse speciei; sicut secunda opinio dicebat. Sed ponit omnes partes quae non sunt praeter intentionem naturae adgeneratae, pertinere ad veritatem humanae naturae quantum ad id quod habent de specie, quia sic manent; non autem quantum ad id quod habent de materia, quia sic fluunt et refluunt indifferenter; ut ita etiam intelligamus contingere in partibus unius hominis sicut contingit in tota multitudine civitatis, quia singuli subtrahuntur a multitudine per mortem, aliis in loco eorum succedentibus; unde partes multitudinis fluunt et refluunt materialiter, sed formaliter manent, quia ad eadem officia et ordines substituuntur alii a quibus priores subtrahebantur, unde respublica una numero remanere dicitur. Et similiter etiam dum, quibusdam partibus fluentibus alia reparantur in eadem figura et in eodem situ, omnes partes fluunt et refluunt secundum materiam sed manent secundum speciem, manet nihilominus homo idem numero.

Sed convenit tertia cum secunda opinione quia ponit quod partes secundo advenientes non ita perfecte attingunt ad veritatem speciei sicut quae primo advenerunt. Et ideo idem quod ponit resurgere in homine secunda opinio, ponit tertia: sed non penitus eadem ratione. Ponit enim totum illud quod ex semine generatum est resurgere, non quia alia ratione pertineat ad veritatem humanae naturae quam hoc quod postea advenit: sed quia perfectius veritatem speciei participat. Quem ordinem ponebat secunda opinio in his quae postea adveniunt ex alimento. In quo etiam haec opinio concordat cum illa.

AD PRIMUM ergo dicendum quod res naturalis non est id quod est ex sua materia, sed ex sua forma. Unde, quamvis illud materiae quod quandoque fuit sub forma carnis bovinae, resurgat in homine sub forma carnis humanae, non sequitur quod resurgat caro bovis, sed caro hominis. Ita enim etiam posset concludi quod resurgeret limus de quo formatum est corpus Adae. Tamen prima opinio concedit hanc rationem.

AD SECUNDUM dicendum quod costa illa non fuit in Adam de perfectione individui, sed ordinata ad multiplicationem speciei. Unde non resurget in Adam, sed in Heva: sicut et semen non resurget in generante, sed in generato.

AD TERTIUM dicendum quod secundum primam opinionem facile est ad hoc respondere. Quia carnes co-

tains that whatever is under the form of flesh and bone all belongs to the truth of human nature, because this opinion does not distinguish as remaining in man during his whole lifetime any designated matter that belongs essentially and primarily to the truth of human nature, besides something ebbing and flowing that belongs to the truth of human nature merely on account of the perfection of quantity, and not on account of the primary being of the species, as the second opinion asserted. But it states that all the parts that are not beside the intention of the nature generated belong to the truth of human nature as regards what they have of the species, since thus they remain; but not as regards what they have of matter, since thus they are indifferent to ebb and flow: so that we are to understand that the same thing happens in the parts of one man as in the whole population of a city, for each individual is cut off from the population by death, while others take their place: wherefore the parts of the people flow back and forth materially, but remain formally, since these others occupy the very same offices and positions from which the former were withdrawn, so that the commonwealth is said to remain the same in number. In like manner, while certain parts are on the ebb and others are being restored to the same shape and position, all the parts flow back and forth as to their matter, but remain as to their species; and nevertheless the same man in number remains.

On the other hand, the third opinion agrees with the second because it holds that the parts which come second do not reach the perfection of the species so perfectly as those which come first: and consequently the third opinion asserts that the same thing rises again in man as the second opinion maintains, but not for quite the same reason. For it holds that the whole of what is produced from the seed will rise again not because it belongs to the truth of human nature otherwise than that which comes after, but because it shares the truth of human nature more perfectly: which same order the second opinion applied to those things that are produced afterwards from food, in which point also these two opinions agree.

REPLY OBJ. 1: A natural thing is what it is not from its matter but from its form; wherefore, although that part of matter which at one time was under the form of bovine flesh rises again in man under the form of human flesh, it does not follow that the flesh of an ox rises again, but the flesh of a man: else one might conclude that the clay from which Adam's body was fashioned shall rise again. The second opinion, however, grants this argument.

REPLY OBJ. 2: That rib did not belong to the perfection of the individual in Adam, but was directed to the multiplication of the species. Hence it will rise again not in Adam but in Eve, just as the seed will rise again, not in the begetter, but in the begotten.

REPLY OBJ. 3: According to the first opinion it is easy to reply to this argument, because the flesh that is eaten never

mestae nunquam sunt de veritate humanae naturae in comedente; fuerunt autem de veritate humanae naturae in eo cuius carnes comeduntur. Et ita resurgent in primo, et non in secundo.

Sed secundum secundam opinionem et tertiam, unusquisque in illo resurget in quo magis accessit ad perfectam participationem virtutis speciei. Et si aequaliter in utroque accesserit, resurget in illo in quo primo fuit; quia in eo primo habuit ordinem ad resurrectionem ex coniunctione ad animam rationalem illius hominis. Et ideo, si in carnibus comestis fuit aliqua superfluitas quae non pertineret ad veritatem humanae naturae in primo, resurgere poterit in secundo. Alias, illud quod pertinebat ad resurrectionem in primo, resurget in eo et non in secundo: sed in loco eius sumeretur vel aliquid de eo quod ex aliis cibis in carnem secundi conversum est; vel, si nullo cibo unquam pastus fuisset nisi carnibus humanis, divina virtute aliunde suppleretur quantum indigeretur ad perfectionem quantitatis; sicut etiam supplet in illis qui ante perfectam aetatem decedunt. Nec per hoc aliquid praeiudicatur identitati in numero: sicut nec praeiudicatur per hoc quod partes secundum materiam fluunt et refluunt.

Ad quartum dicendum quod secundum primam opinionem facile est solvere. Quia ponit quod semen non est ex superfluo alimenti. Unde carnes comestae non transeunt in semen, ex quo puer generatur.

Sed secundum alias duas opiniones, dicendum est quod non est possibile quod totum quod fuit in carnibus comestis in semen convertatur: quia post multam depurationem cibi pervenitur ad decoctionem seminis, quod est superfluitas ultimi cibi. Illud autem quod de carnibus comestis in semen convertitur, pertinet magis ad veritatem humanae naturae in eo quod ex semine nascitur, quam in illo ex cuius carnibus semen est generatum. Et ideo, secundum regulam prius datam, hoc quod in semen conversum est, resurget in eo qui ex semine nascitur; residuum autem materiae resurget in illo ex cuius carnibus comestis semen est generatum.

Ad quintum dicendum quod embrya non pertinent ad resurrectionem ante animationem per animam rationalem. In quo statu iam multum advenit supra substantiam seminis de substantia nutrimenti, qua puer in utero matris nutritur. Et ideo, si aliquis embryis vescatur, et ex superfluo illius cibi generetur aliquis, illud quod erit in substantia seminis, resurget quidem in eo qui ex semine generatur: nisi in illo contineretur aliquid quod fuisset de substantia seminum in illis ex quorum carnibus comestis semen generatum est; quia hoc resurgeret in primo, et non in secundo. Residuum autem carnium comestarum, quod non est conversum in semen, constat quod resurgeret in primo, utrique divina potentia supplente quod deest.

belonged to the truth of human nature in the eater, but it did belong to the truth of human nature in him whose flesh was eaten: and thus it will rise again in the latter but not in the former.

According to the second and third opinions, each one will rise again in that wherein he approached nearest to the perfect participation of the virtue of the species, and if he approached equally in both, he will rise again in that wherein he was first, because in that he first was directed to the resurrection by union with the rational soul of that man. Hence if there were any surplus in the flesh eaten not belonging to the truth of human nature in the first man, it will be possible for it to rise again in the second: otherwise what belonged to the resurrection in the first will rise again in him and not in the second; but in the second its place is taken either by something of that which was the product from other food, or if he never partook of any other food than human flesh, the substitution is made by divine power so far as the perfection of quantity requires, as it does in those who die before the perfect age. Nor does this derogate from numerical identity, as neither does the ebb and flow of parts.

Reply Obj. 4: According to the first opinion this argument is easily answered. For that opinion asserts that the seed is not from the surplus food: so that the flesh eaten is not changed into the seed whereof the child is begotten.

But according to the other two opinions we must reply that it is impossible for the whole of the flesh eaten to be changed into seed, because it is after much separation that the seed is distilled from the food, since seed is the ultimate surplus of food. That part of the eaten flesh which is changed into seed belongs to the truth of human nature in the one born of the seed more than in the one of whose flesh the seed was the product. Hence, according to the rule already laid down (ad 3), whatever was changed into the seed will rise again in the person born of the seed; while the remaining matter will rise again in him of whose flesh the seed was the product.

Reply Obj. 5: The embryo is not concerned with the resurrection before it is animated by a rational soul, in which state much has been added to the seminal substance from the substance of food, since the child is nourished in the mother's womb. Consequently, on the supposition that a man partook of such food, and that some one were begotten of the surplus thereof, that which was in the seminal substance will indeed rise again in the one begotten of that seed; unless it contain something that would have belonged to the seminal substance in those from whose flesh being eaten the seed was produced, for this would rise again in the first but not in the second. The remainder of the eaten flesh, not being changed into seed, will clearly rise again in the first: the divine power supplying deficiencies in both.

Prima autem opinio hac obiectione non arctatur: cum non ponat semen esse ex superfluo alimenti. Sed aliae multae rationes sunt contra eam: ut in II libro, dist. 30, patuit.

The first opinion is not troubled by this objection, since it does not hold the seed to be from the surplus food: but there are many other reasons against it as may be seen in the Second Book.

Article 5

Whether Whatever Was Materially in a Man's Members Will All Rise Again?

Ad quintum sic proceditur. Videtur quod quidquid fuit materialiter in membris hominis, totum resurget. Minus enim videntur pertinere ad resurrectionem capilli quam alia membra. Sed quidquid fuit in capillis, totum resurget, etsi non in capillis, saltem in aliis partibus corporis: ut Augustinus dicit, in littera. Ergo multo fortius quidquid in aliis membris materialiter fuit, totum resurget.

Praeterea, sicut partes carnis secundum speciem perficiuntur ab anima rationali, ita partes secundum materiam. Sed corpus humanum habet ordinem ad resurrectionem ex hoc quod fuit anima rationali perfectum. Ergo non solum partes secundum speciem, sed omnes partes secundum materiam resurgent.

Praeterea, ex parte illa accidit corpori totalitas ex qua parte accidit ei divisio in partes. Sed divisio in partes accidit corpori secundum materiam, cuius dispositio est quantitas, secundum quam dividitur. Ergo et totalitas corporis attenditur secundum partes materiae. Si ergo non omnes partes materiae resurgent, non totum corpus resurget. Quod est inconveniens.

Sed contra: Partes secundum materiam non manent in corpore, sed fluunt et refluunt: ut patet per illud quod dicitur in I *de Generatione*. Si ergo omnes partes secundum materiam resurgent, vel erit corpus resurgentis densissimum; vel erit immoderatae quantitatis.

Praeterea, quidquid est de veritate humanae naturae in uno homine, totum potest esse pars materiae in alio homine qui eius carnibus vescitur. Si ergo omnes partes secundum materiam resurgant in aliquo, sequetur quod resurget in uno id quod est de veritate humanae naturae in alio. Quod est inconveniens.

Respondeo dicendum quod illud quod est in homine materialiter, non habet ordinem ad resurrectionem nisi secundum quod pertinet ad veritatem humanae naturae: quia secundum hoc habet ordinem ad animam rationalem. Illud autem totum quod est in homine materialiter, pertinet quidem ad veritatem humanae naturae quantum ad id quod habet de specie, sed non totum considerata materiae totalitate, quia; tota materia quae fuit in homine a principio vitae usque ad finem, exce-

Objection 1: It would seem that whatever was materially in a man's members will all rise again. For the hair seemingly pertains less to the resurrection than the other members. Yet whatever was in the hair will all rise again, if not in the hair, at least in other parts of the body, as Augustine says (*The City of God* 22) quoted in the text (*Sentences* IV, D. 44). Much more, therefore, whatever was materially in the other members will all rise again.

Obj. 2: Further, just as the parts of the flesh are perfected as to species by the rational soul, so are the parts as to matter. But the human body is directed to the resurrection through being perfected by a rational soul. Therefore, not only the parts of species but also the parts of matter will all rise again.

Obj. 3: Further, the body derives its totality from the same cause as it derives its divisibility into parts. But division into parts belongs to a body in respect of matter, the disposition of which is quantity (in respect of which it is divided). Therefore, totality is ascribed to the body in respect of its parts of matter. If, then, all the parts of matter rise not again, neither will the whole body rise again: which is inadmissible.

On the contrary, The parts of matter do not remain in the body but ebb and flow, as stated in *On Generation and Corruption* I. If, therefore, all the parts of matter, which remain not but ebb and flow, rise again, either the body of one who rises again will be very dense, or it will be immoderate in quantity.

Further, Whatever belongs to the truth of human nature in one man can all be a part of matter in another man, if the latter were to partake of his flesh. Therefore, if all the parts of matter in one man were to rise again, it follows that in one man there will rise again that which belongs to the truth of human nature in another: which is absurd.

I answer that, What is in man materially is not directed to the resurrection except insofar as it belongs to the truth of human nature; because it is in this respect that it bears a relation to the human souls. Now all that is in man materially belongs indeed to the truth of human nature insofar as it has something of the species, but not all if we consider the totality of matter; because all the matter that was in a man from the beginning of his life to the end would surpass the quantity due to his species, as the third opinion

deret quantitatem debitam speciei: ut tertia opinio dicit, quae probabilior inter ceteras mihi videtur. Et ideo totum quod est in homine resurget considerata totalitate speciei, quae attenditur secundum quantitatem, figuram, situm et ordinem partium: non autem resurget totum considerata totalitate materiae.

Secunda autem opinio et prima non utuntur hac distinctione, sed distinguunt inter partes quarum utraque habet speciem et materiam. Conveniunt autem hae duae opiniones in hoc quod utraque dicit quod illud quod est ex semine generatum, totum resurget, etiam totalitate materiae considerata. Differunt autem in hoc quod de eo quod ex alimento generatur, nihil resurgere ponit prima opinio; secunda vero aliquid eius resurgere ponit, et non totum, ut ex dictis patet.

AD PRIMUM ergo dicendum quod, sicut quidquid est in aliis partibus corporis resurget considerata totalitate speciei, non autem considerata totalitate materiae, ita etiam est de capillis. In aliis autem partibus advenit aliquid ex nutrimento quod facit augmentum: et hoc computatur ut alia pars, considerata totalitate speciei, quia obtinet alium locum et situm in corpore, et substat aliis partibus dimensionis. Aliquid autem advenit quod non facit augmentum, sed cedit in restaurationem deperditi nutriendo: et non computatur ut alia pars totius considerati secundum speciem, cum non obtineat alium locum vel situm in corpore quam pars quae defluxit tenebat; quamvis possit alia pars computari considerata totalitate materiae. Et similiter est de capillis. Augustinus ergo loquitur de incisionibus capillorum quae erant partes facientes augmentum. Et ideo oportet quod resurgant: non tamen in quantitate capillorum, ne sit quantitas immoderata; sed in aliis partibus, ut necessarium indicabit divina providentia. Vel loquitur in casu illo quando aliis partibus deficiet. Tunc enim eorum defectus poterit ex superfluitatibus capillorum reparari.

AD SECUNDUM dicendum quod secundum tertiam opinionem eaedem sunt partes secundum speciem, et secundum materiam. Non enim illa distinctione utitur Philosophus, in I *de Generatione* ad distinguendum diversas partes: sed ad ostendendum quod eaedem partes possunt considerari et secundum speciem, quantum ad illud quod esi formae et speciei in ipsis, et secundum materiam, quantum ad illud quod subest formae et speciei. Constat autem quod materia carnis non habet ordinem ad animam rationalem nisi inquantum est sub tali forma. Et ideo ratione eius habet ordinem ad resurrectionem.

Sed prima et secunda opinio, quae ponunt alias esse partes quae sunt secundum speciem et alias quae sunt secundum materiam, dicunt quod anima, quamvis utrasque partes perficiat, tamen perficit partes secun-

states (Cf. A. 4), which opinion seems to me more probable than the others. Wherefore the whole of what is in man will rise again if we speak of the totality of the species which is dependent on quantity, shape, position and order of parts, but the whole will not rise again if we speak of the totality of matter.

The second and first opinions, however, do not make this distinction, but distinguish between parts both of which have the species and matter. But these two opinions agree in that they both state what is produced from the seed will all rise again even if we speak of totality of matter. However, they differ in this: the first opinion maintains that nothing will rise again of that which was engendered from food, whereas the second holds that something, but not all, thereof will rise again, as stated above (A. 4).

REPLY OBJ. 1: Just as all that is in the other parts of the body will rise again if we speak of the totality of the species, but not if we speak of material totality, so is it with the hair. In the other parts something accrues from nourishment which causes growth, and this is reckoned as another part if we speak of totality of species, since it occupies another place and position in the body, and is under other parts of dimension, and there accrues something which does not cause growth, but serves to make up for waste by nourishing. And this is not reckoned as another part of the whole considered in relation to the species, since it does not occupy another place or position in the body than that which was occupied by the part that has passed away; although it may be reckoned another part if we consider the totality of matter. The same applies to the hair. Augustine, however, is speaking of the cutting of hair that was a part causing growth of the body; wherefore it must rise again, not, however, as regards the quantity of hair, lest it should be immoderate, but it will rise again in other parts as deemed expedient by divine providence. Or else he refers to the case when something will be lacking to the other parts, for then it will be possible for this to be supplied from the surplus of hair.

REPLY OBJ. 2: According to the third opinion, parts of species are the same as parts of matter: for the Philosopher does not make this distinction (*On Generation and Corruption* I) in order to distinguish different parts, but in order to show that the same parts may be considered both in respect of species, as to what belongs to the form and species in them, and in respect of matter, as to that which is under the form and species. Now it is clear that the matter of the flesh has no relation to the rational soul except insofar as it is under such a form, and consequently by reason thereof it is directed to the resurrection.

But the first and second opinions, which draw a distinction between parts of species and parts of matter, say that although the rational soul perfects both parts, it does not perfect parts of matter except by means of the parts of spe-

dum materiam mediantibus partibus secundum speciem. Et ideo non habent aequaliter ordinem ad resurrectionem.

AD TERTIUM dicendum quod in materia generabilium et corruptibilium dimensiones interminatas oportet intelligere ante receptionem formae substantialis. Et ideo divisio quae est secundum huiusmodi dimensiones, proprie pertinet ad materiam. Sed quantitas completa et terminata advenit materiae post formam substantialem. Unde divisio quae fit secundum dimensiones terminatas, respicit speciem: praecipue quando ad rationem speciei pertinet determinatus situs partium, sicut est in corpore humano.

cies, wherefore they are not equally directed to the resurrection.

REPLY OBJ. 3: In the matter of things subject to generation and corruption it is necessary to presuppose indefinite dimensions before the reception of the substantial form. Consequently, division which is made according to these dimensions belongs properly to matter. But complete and definite quantity comes to matter after the substantial form; wherefore division that is made in reference to definite quantity regards the species especially when definite position of parts belongs to the essence of the species, as in the human body.

QUESTION 81

THE QUALITY OF THOSE WHO RISE AGAIN

Deinde considerandum est de qualitate resurgentium.

Circa quod quaeruntur quatuor.

Primo: utrum resurgent omnes in aetate iuvenili.

Secundo: utrum in aequali statura.

Tertio: utrum omnes in eodem sexu.

Quarto: utrum in vita animali.

We must now consider the quality of those who rise again.

Under this head there are four points of inquiry:

(1) Whether all will rise again in the youthful age?

(2) Whether they will be of equal stature?

(3) Whether all will be of the same sex?

(4) Whether they will rise again to the animal life?

Article 1

Whether All Will Rise Again of the Same Age?

AD PRIMUM SIC PROCEDITUR. Videtur quod non omnes resurgent in eadem aetate, scilicet iuvenili. Quia Deus resurgentibus, praecipue beatis, nihil subtrahet quod ad perfectionem hominis pertineat. Sed aetas pertinet ad perfectionem hominis: cum senectus sit *venerabilis aetas.* Ergo senes non resurgent in aetate iuvenili.

PRAETEREA, aetas computatur secundum mensuram temporis praeteriti. Sed impossibile est tempus quod fuit praeteritum, non praeteriisse. Ergo impossibile est eos qui maioris aetatis fuerunt, ad aetatem iuvenilem reduci.

PRAETEREA, illud quod magis fuit de veritate humanae naturae in unoquoque, maxime resurget in eo. Sed quanto aliquid primo fuit in homine, tanto videtur magis ad veritatem humanae naturae pertinuisse: quia in fine, propter veritatem speciei debilitatam, comparatur vino aquoso corpus humanum, ut patet per Philosophum, in I *de Generatione.* Ergo, si omnes debent in eadem aetate resurgere, magis decet quod resurgant iri aetate puerili quam iuvenili.

SED CONTRA: Est quod dicitur Ephes. 4, [13]: *donec occurramus omnes in virum perfectum, in mensuram aetatis plenitudinis Christi.* Sed Christus resurrexit in aetate iuvenili, quae circa triginta annos incipit, ut Augustinus dicit. Ergo et alii in aetate iuvenili resurgent.

PRAETEREA, homo in maxima perfectione naturae resurget. Sed natura humana perfectissimum statum habet in aetate iuvenili. Ergo in illa aetate resurgent omnes.

RESPONDEO dicendum quod homo resurget absque omni defectu humanae naturae: quia, sicut Deus humanam naturam absque defectu instituit, ita sine defectu reparabit. Deficit autem humana natura dupliciter: uno

OBJECTION 1: It would seem that all will not rise again of the same, namely, the youthful, age. For God will take nothing pertaining to man's perfection from those who rise again, especially from the blessed. Now age pertains to the perfection of man, since old age is the *age that demands reverence.* Therefore, the old will not rise again of a youthful age.

OBJ. 2: Further, age is reckoned according to the length of past time. Now it is impossible for past time not to have passed. Therefore, it is impossible for those who were of greater age to be brought back to a youthful age.

OBJ. 3: Further, that which belonged most to the truth of human nature in each individual will especially rise again in him. Now the sooner a thing was in man, the more would it seem to have belonged to the truth of human nature, because in the end, through the strength of the species being weakened, the human body is likened to watery wine, according to the Philosopher (*On Generation and Corruption* i). Therefore, if all are to rise again of the same age, it is more fitting that they should rise again in the age of childhood.

ON THE CONTRARY, It is written: *until we all meet unto a perfect man, unto the measure of the age of the fullness of Christ* (Eph 4:13). Now Christ rose again of youthful age, which begins about the age of thirty years, as Augustine says (*The City of God* 22). Therefore, others also will rise again of a youthful age.

FURTHER, Man will rise again at the most perfect stage of nature. Now human nature is at the most perfect stage in the age of youth. Therefore, all will rise again of that age.

I ANSWER THAT, Man will rise again without any defect of human nature, because as God founded human nature without a defect, even so will he restore it without defect. Now human nature has a twofold defect. First, because

modo, quia nondum perfectionem ultimam est consecuta; alio modo, quia iam ab ultima perfectione recessit. Et primo modo deficit in pueris; secundo modo deficit in senibus. Et ideo in utrisque reducetur humana natura per resurrectionem ad statum ultimae perfectionis, qui est in iuvenili aetate, ad quem terminatur motus crementi, et a quo incipit motus decrementi.

Ad primum ergo dicendum quod aetas senectutis habet reverentiam, non propter conditionem corporis, quod in defectu est, sed propter sapientiam animae, quae ibi esse praesumitur ex temporis antiquitate. Unde in electis manebit reverentia senectutis, propter plenitudinem divinae sapientiae quae in eis erit: sed non manebit senectutis defectus.

Ad secundum dicendum quod non loquimur de aetate quantum ad numerum annorum, sed quantum ad statum qui in corpore humano ex annis relinquitur. Unde Adam dicitur in aetate iuvenili formatus propter talem corporis conditionem, quam primo die formationis suae habuit. Et ideo ratio non est ad propositum.

Ad tertium dicendum quod virtus speciei dicitur esse perfectior in puero quam in iuvene quantum ad efficaciam agendi conversionem alimenti aliquo modo: sicut etiam est perfectior in semine quam in homine completo. Sed in iuvenibus est perfectior quantum ad terminum complementi. Unde illud quod maxime ad veritatem naturae pertinuit, ad illam perfectionem reducetur quam habet in aetate iuvenili: non ad illam quam habet in aetate puerili, in qua humores adhuc non pervenerunt ad ultimam digestionem.

it has not yet attained to its ultimate perfection. Second, because it has already gone back from its ultimate perfection. The first defect is found in children, the second in the aged: and consequently in each of these human nature will be brought by the resurrection to the state of its ultimate perfection, which is in the youthful age, at which the movement of growth terminates and from which the movement of decrease begins.

Reply Obj. 1: Old age calls for reverence not on account of the state of the body, which is defective, but on account of the soul's wisdom, which is taken for granted on account of its being advanced in years. Wherefore in the elect there will remain the reverence due to old age, on account of the fullness of divine wisdom which will be in them, but the defect of old age will not be in them.

Reply Obj. 2: We speak of age not as regards the number of years, but as regards the state which the human body acquires from years. Hence Adam is said to have been formed in the youthful age on account of the particular condition of body which he had at the first day of his formation. Thus the argument is not to the point.

Reply Obj. 3: The strength of the species is said to be more perfect in a child than in a young man as regards the ability to transform nourishment in a certain way, even as it is more perfect in the seed than in the mature man. In youth, however, it is more perfect as regards the term of completion. Therefore, that which belonged principally to the truth of human nature will be brought to that perfection which it has in the age of youth, and not to that perfection which it has in the age of a child, in which the humors have not yet reached their ultimate disposition.

Article 2

Whether All Will Rise Again of the Same Stature?

Ad secundum sic proceditur. Videtur quod omnes resurgent eiusdem staturae. Sicut enim homo mensuratur quantitate dimensiva, ita quantitate durationis. Sed quantitas durationis in omnibus reducetur ad eandem mensuram: quia omnes in eadem aetate resurgent. Ergo quantitas dimensionis in omnibus reducetur ad eandem mensuram, ut in eadem statura omnes resurgant.

Praeterea, Philosophus, in II *de Anima*, dicit quod *omnium natura constantium terminus est et ratio magnitudinis et augmenti*. Sed iste terminus non est nisi ex virtute formae, cui debet congruere quantitas, sicut et omnia alia accidentia. Ergo, cum omnes homines habeant eandem formam specificam, in omnibus debet esse secundum materiam eadem quantitatis mensura, nisi sit

Objection 1: It would seem that all will rise again of the same stature. For just as man is measured by dimensive quantity, so is he by the quantity of time. Now the quantity of time will be reduced to the same measure in all, since all will rise again of the same age. Therefore, the dimensive quantity will also be reduced to the same measure in all, so that all will rise again of the same stature.

Obj. 2: Further, the Philosopher says (*On the Soul* 2.4) that *all things in nature have a certain limit and measure of size and growth*. Now this limitation can only arise by virtue of the form, with which the quantity as well as all the other accidents ought to agree. Therefore, since all men have the same specific form, there should be the same measure of quantity in respect of matter in all, unless an error should

error. Sed error naturae corrigetur in resurrectione. Ergo omnes resurgent in eadem statura.

PRAETEREA, quantitatis resurgentis non poterit esse proportionata virtuti naturali quae primo corpus formavit: alias, qui non potuerunt ad maiorem quantitatem perduci virtute naturae, nunquam in maiori quantitate resurgerent; quod falsum est. Ergo oportet quod quantitas illa proportionetur virtuti reparanti corpus humanum per resurrectionem, et materiae de qua reparatur. Sed virtus reparans omnia corpora est eadem numero, scilicet divina virtus: cineres autem omnes, ex quibus reparantur humana corpora, se habent aequaliter ad suscipiendam actionem praedictae virtutis. Ergo ad eandem quantitatem terminabitur resurrectio omnium hominum. Et sic idem quod prius.

SED CONTRA: Quantitas naturalis consequitur naturam uniuscuiusque individui. Sed in resurrectione non variabitur natura individui. Ergo nec quantitas naturalis eius. Sed non est eadem quantitas naturalis omnium hominum. Ergo non omnes resurgent in eadem statura.

PRAETEREA, natura humana reparabitur per resurrectionem ad gloriam vel ad poenam. Sed non erit eadem quantitas gloriae vel poenae in omnibus resurgentibus. Ergo nec eadem quantitas naturae.

RESPONDEO dicendum quod in resurrectione non reparabitur humana natura, solum quantum ad idem specie, sed quantum ad idem numero. Et ideo in resurrectione non solum attendendum est quid competat naturae speciei, sed quid competat naturae individui. Natura autem speciei habet aliquam quantitatem quam nec excedit nec ab ea deficit absque errore: quae tamen quantitas habet aliquos gradus latitudinis, et non est accipienda secundum unam mensuram determinatam. Unumquodque autem individuum in specie humana assequitur, infra terminos illius latitudinis, aliquem gradum quantitatis, quae competit naturae individui; et ad hanc perducitur in termino augmenti, si non fuit aliquis error in opere naturae per quem sit aliquid additum vel subtractum praedictae quantitati. Cuius quidem mensura accipitur secundum proportionem caloris extendentis et humidi extensibilis. Quod non est eiusdem virtutis in omnibus. Et ideo non omnes resurgent in eadem quantitate: sed quilibet resurget in illa quantitate in qua fuisset in termino augmenti, si natura non errasset vel defecisset. Quod autem superest vel deficit in homine, resecabit vel supplebit divina potentia.

AD PRIMUM ergo dicendam quod iam patet ex dictis quod non dicuntur omnes in eadem aetate resurgere quasi omnibus competat eadem quantitas durationis: sed quia idem status perfectionis erit in omnibus. Qui quidem status salvari potest iri magna et in parva quantitate.

occur. But the error of nature will be set right at the resurrection. Therefore, all will rise again of the same stature.

OBJ. 3: Further, it will be impossible for man in rising again to be of a quantity proportionate to the natural power which first formed his body; for otherwise those who could not be brought to a greater quantity by the power of nature will never rise again of a greater quantity, which is false. Therefore, that quantity must be proportionate to the power which will restore the human body by the resurrection, and to the matter from which it is restored. Now the selfsame (that is, the divine) power will restore all bodies; and all the ashes from which the human bodies will be restored are equally disposed to receive the action of that power. Therefore, the resurrection of all men will bring them to the same quantity: and so the same conclusion follows.

ON THE CONTRARY, Natural quantity results from each individual's nature. Now the nature of the individual will not be altered at the resurrection. Therefore, neither will its natural quantity. But all are not of the same natural quantity. Therefore, all will not rise again of the same stature.

FURTHER, Human nature will be restored by resurrection unto glory or unto punishment. But there will not be the same quantity of glory or punishment in all those who rise again. Neither, therefore, will there be the same quantity of stature.

I ANSWER THAT, At the resurrection human nature will be restored not only in the selfsame species but also in the selfsame individual: and consequently we must observe in the resurrection what is requisite not only to the specific but also to the individual nature. Now the specific nature has a certain quantity which it neither exceeds nor fails without error, and yet this quantity has certain degrees of latitude and is not to be attached to one fixed measure; and each individual in the human species aims at some degree of quantity befitting his individual nature within the bounds of that latitude, and reaches it at the end of his growth, if there has been no error in the working of nature resulting in the addition of something to or the subtraction of something from the aforesaid quantity: the measure of which is gauged according to the proportion of heat as expanding, and of humidity as expansive, in point of which all are not of the same power. Therefore, all will not rise again of the same quantity, but each one will rise again of that quantity which would have been his at the end of his growth if nature had not erred or failed: and the divine power will subtract or supply what was excessive or lacking in man.

REPLY OBJ. 1: It has already been explained (A. 1) that all are said to rise again of the same age, not as though the same length of time were befitting to each one, but because the same state of perfection will be in all, which state is indifferent to a great or small quantity.

AD SECUNDUM dicendum quod quantitas huius individui non solum respondet formae speciei, sed etiam naturae individui. Et ideo ratio non sequitur.

AD TERTIUM dicendum quod quantitas resurgentis non proportionatur virtuti reparanti, quia illa non est de natura corporis; neque omnibus secundum illum statum in quo sunt ante resurrectionem; sed naturae quam primo individuum habebat. Tamen, si virtus formativa propter aliquem defectum non poterat perducere ad debitam quantitatem quae competit speciei, divina virtus supplebit in resurrectione defectum: sicut patet de nanis. Et eadem ratio, est de illis qui immoderatae magnitudinis fuerunt, ultra debitum naturae.

REPLY OBJ. 2: The quantity of a particular individual corresponds not only to the form of the species, but also to the nature or matter of the individual: wherefore the conclusion does not follow.

REPLY OBJ. 3: The quantity of the risen person is not proportionate to the power restoring him, for that is not from the nature of the body, nor in all people according to that state in which they exist before the resurrection, but to the nature that the first individual had. Nevertheless, if the formative power on account of some defect was unable to effect the due quantity that is befitting to the species, the divine power will supply the defect at the resurrection, as in dwarfs. And the same goes for those who by immoderate size have exceeded the due bounds of nature.

Article 3

Whether All Will Rise Again of the Male Sex?

AD TERTIUM SIC PROCEDITUR. Videtur quod omnes resurgent in sexu virili. Quia dicitur Ephes: 4, [13] quod *occurremus omnes in virum perfectum.* Ergo non erit nisi sexus virilis ibi.

PRAETEREA, in futuro *omnis praelatio cessabit*, ut dicit Glossa, I Cor. 15, [24]. Sed mulier ordine naturali subdita est viro. Ergo mulieres non resurgent in sexu muliebri, sed virili.

PRAETEREA, illud quod est occasionaliter et praeter intentionem naturae inductum, non resurget: quia in resurrectione omnis error tolletur. Sed sexus muliebris est praeter intentionem naturae inductus ex defectu virtutis formativae in semine, quae non potest perducere materiam conceptus ad perfectionem virilem: unde dicit Philosophus, XVI *de Animal.*, quod *femina est mas occasionatus.* Ergo sexus muliebris non resurget.

SED CONTRA: Est quod dicit Augustinus, XXII *de Civ. Dei: melius sapere videntur qui utrumque sexum resurrecturum esse non dubitant.*

PRAETEREA, Deus reparabit in resurrectione quod in homine fecit in prima conditione. Sed ipse fecit mulierem de costa viri, ut patet Genes. 2, [22]. Ergo ipse sexum femineum in resurrectione reparabit.

RESPONDEO dicendum quod sicut, considerata natura individui, debetur diversa quantitas diversis hominibus, ita, considerata natura individui, debetur diversus sexus diversis hominibus. Et haec etiam diversitas competit perfectioni speciei, cuius diversi gradus implentur per dictam diversitatem sexus vel quantitatis. Et ideo, sicut resurgent homines in diversis staturis, ita in diversis sexibus. Et quamvis sit differentia sexuum, deerit tamen

OBJECTION 1: It would seem that all will rise again of the male sex. For it is written that *we shall all meet unto a perfect man* (Eph 4:13). Therefore, there will be none but the male sex.

OBJ. 2: Further, in the world to come, *all preeminence will cease*, as a Gloss observes on 1 Corinthians 15:24. Now woman is subject to man in the natural order. Therefore, women will rise again not in the female but in the male sex.

OBJ. 3: Further, that which is produced incidentally and beside the intention of nature will not rise again, since all error will be removed at the resurrection. Now the female sex is produced beside the intention of nature through a fault in the formative power of the seed, which is unable to bring the matter of the fetus to the male form. Hence the Philosopher says (*On the Soul* 16, i.e., *On Generation and Corruption* 2) that the female is a *misbegotten male.* Therefore, the female sex will not rise again.

ON THE CONTRARY, Augustine says (*The City of God* 22): *those are wiser, seemingly, who doubt not that both sexes will rise again.*

FURTHER, At the resurrection God will restore man to what he made him at the creation. Now he made woman from the man's rib (Gen 2:22). Therefore, he will also restore the female sex at the resurrection.

I ANSWER THAT, Just as considering the nature of the individual, a different quantity is due to different men, so also, considering the nature of the individual, a different sex is due to different men. Moreover, this same diversity is becoming to the perfection of the species, the different degrees whereof are filled by this very difference of sex and quantity. Wherefore just as men will rise again of various stature, so will they rise again of different sex. And though

confusio mutuae visionis: quia aberit libido incitans ad turpes actus, ex quibus confusio causatur.

AD PRIMUM ergo dicendum quod dicuntur omnes Christo occurrere *in virum perfectum*, non propter sexum virilem, sed propter virtutem animi, quae erit in omnibus et viris et mulieribus.

AD SECUNDUM dicendum quod mulier subditur viro propter imbecillitatem naturae et quantum ad vigorem animi, et quantum ad robur corporis. Sed post resurrectionem non erit differentia in his secundum diversitatem sexuum sed magis secundum diversitatem meritorum. Et ideo ratio non procedit.

AD TERTIUM dicendum quod, quamvis feminae generatio sit praeter intentionem naturae particularis, est tamen de intentione naturae universalis, quae ad perfectionem humanae speciei utrumque sexum requirit. Nec ex sexu erit ibi aliquis defectus, ut ex dictis patet.

there be difference of sex, there will be no shame in seeing one another, since there will no lust to invite them to base deeds, which are the cause of shame.

REPLY OBJ. 1: When it is said that we shall all meet Christ *unto a perfect man*, this refers not to the male sex but to the strength of soul which will be in all, both men and women.

REPLY OBJ. 2: Woman is subject to man on account of the frailty of nature as regards both vigor of soul and strength of body. After the resurrection, however, the difference in those points will be not on account of the difference of sex, but by reason of the difference of merits. Hence the conclusion does not follow.

REPLY OBJ. 3: Although the begetting of a woman is beside the intention of a particular nature, it is in the intention of universal nature, which requires both sexes for the perfection of the human species. Nor will any defect result from sex, as stated above (ad 2).

Article 4

Whether All Will Rise Again to Animal Life so as to Exercise
the Functions of Nutrition and Generation?

AD QUARTUM SIC PROCEDITUR. Videtur quod resurgent in vita animali, ut scilicet utantur actu nutritivae et generativae. Quia resurrectio nostra erit conformis resurrectioni Christi. Sed Christus post resurrectionem legitur comedisse: ut patet Ioan. 21, [12 sqq.] et Luc. 24, [43]. Ergo et homines post resurrectionem comedent. Et eadem ratione generabunt.

PRAETEREA, distinctio sexuum ad generationem ordinatur: et similiter instrumenta quae deserviunt virtuti nutritivae, ordinantur ad comestionem. Sed homo cum omnibus huiusmodi resurget. Ergo utetur actibus virtutis generativae et nutritivae.

PRAETEREA, totus homo beatificatur et secundum animam et secundum corpus. Sed beatitudo sive felicitas, secundum Philosophum, in perfecta operatione consistit. Ergo oportet quod omnes potentiae animae et omnia membra sint in suis actibus in beatis post resurrectionem. Et sic idem quod prius.

PRAETEREA, in beatis post resurrectionem erit perfecta et beata iucunditas. Sed talis iucunditas omnes delectationes includit: quia *beatitudo est status omnium bonorum aggregatione perfectus*; et perfectum est *cui nihil deest*. Cum ergo in actu virtutis generativae et nutritivae sit magna delectatio, videtur quod tales actus ad vitam animalem pertinentes in beatis erunt. Et multo fortius in aliis, qui minus spiritualia corpora habebunt.

OBJECTION 1: It would seem that they will rise again to the animal life, or, in other words, that they will make use of the acts of the nutritive and generative powers. For our resurrection will be conformed to Christ's. But Christ is said to have eaten after his resurrection (John 21; Luke 24). Therefore, after the resurrection men will eat, and in like manner beget.

OBJ. 2: Further, the distinction of sexes is directed to generation; and in like manner the instruments which serve the nutritive power are directed to eating. Now man will rise again with all these. Therefore, he will exercise the acts of the generative and nutritive powers.

OBJ. 3: Further, the whole man will be beatified both in soul and in body. Now beatitude or happiness, according to the Philosopher (*Ethics* 1.7), consists in a perfect operation. Therefore, it must be that all the powers of the soul and all the members should have their respective acts after the resurrection. And so the same conclusion follows as above.

OBJ. 4: Further, after the resurrection there will be perfect joy in the blessed. Now such a joy includes all pleasures, since, according to Boethius, *happiness is a state rendered perfect by the accumulation of all goods* (*Consolation of Philosophy* 3), and the perfect is *that which lacks nothing*. Since, then, there is much pleasure in the act of the generative and nutritive powers, it would seem that such acts belonging to animal life will be in the blessed, and much more in others, who will have less spiritual bodies.

SED CONTRA: Est quod dicitur Matth. 22, [30]: *in resurrectione neque nubent neque nubentur.*

PRAETEREA, generatio ordinatur ad subveniendum defectui qui per mortem accidit, ad multiplicationem humani generis; et comestio ad restaurationem deperditi et ad augmentum quantitatis. Sed in statu resurrectionis iam humanum genus habebit totam multitudinem individuorum a Deo praefinitam: quia usque ad hoc generatio deferetur. Similiter etiam quilibet homo resurget in debita quantitate. Nec erit ultra mors, aut aliqua deperditio fiet a partibus hominis. Ergo frustra esset actus generativae et nutritivae virtutis.

RESPONDEO dicendum quod resurrectio non erit necessaria homini propter primam perfectionem ipsius, quae consistit in integritate eorum quae ad naturam spectant: quia ad hoc homo pervenire potest in statu praesentis vitae per actionem causarum naturalium. Sed necessitas resurrectionis est ad consequendam ultimam perfectionem, quae consistit in perventione ad ultimum finem. Et ideo illae operationes naturales quae ordinantur ad primam perfectionem humanae naturae vel causandam vel conservandam, non erunt in resurrectione. Et huiusmodi sunt actiones animalis vitae in homine, et actiones mutuae in elementis, et motus caeli. Et ideo haec cessabunt in resurrectione. Et quia comedere, bibere et dormire et generare ad animalem vitam pertinent, cum sint ad primam perfectionem naturae ordinata, in resurrectione talia non erunt.

AD PRIMUM ergo dicendum quod illa comestio qua Christus comedit, non fuit necessitatis, quasi cibis indigeret humana natura post resurrectionem: sed fuit potestatis, ut ostenderet se veram naturam humanam resumpsisse, quam prius habuerat in statu illo quando cum discipulis comederat et biberat. Haec autem Ostensio non erit in resurrectione communi: quia omnibus notum erit. Et ideo dicitur dispensative Christus manducasse, eo modo loquendi quo iuristae dicunt, *dispensatio est communis iuris relaxatio*: quia Christus intermisit hoc quod est communiter resurgentium, scilicet non uti cibis, propter causam praedictam. Et propter hoc ratio non sequitur.

AD SECUNDUM dicendum quod differentia sexuum et membrorum varietas erit ad naturae humanae perfectionem reintegrandam et in specie, et in individuo. Unde non sequitur quod sint frustra, quamvis animales operationes desint.

AD TERTIUM dicendum quod praedictae operationes non sunt hominis inquantum est homo, ut etiam Philosophus dicit. Et ideo in eis non consistit beatitudo humani corporis: sed corpus humanum beatificabitur ex redundantia a ratione, a qua homo est homo, inquantum erit ei subditum.

AD QUARTUM dicendum quod delectationes corporales, sicut dicit Philosophus, in VII et X *Ethic.*, sunt

ON THE CONTRARY, Matthew 22:30 says: *in the resurrection they shall neither marry nor be married.*

FURTHER, Generation is directed to supplying the defect resulting from death, and to the multiplication of the human race: and eating is directed to restoring what is lost, and to increasing quantity. But in the state of the resurrection the human race will already have the number of individuals preordained by God, since generation will continue up to that point. In like manner, each man will rise again in due quantity: neither will death be any more, nor any waste affect the parts of man. Therefore, the acts of the generative and nutritive powers would be void of purpose.

I ANSWER THAT, The resurrection will not be necessary to man on account of his primary perfection, which consists in the integrity of those things that belong to his nature, since man can attain to this in his present state of life by the action of natural causes; but the necessity of the resurrection regards the attainment of his ultimate perfection, which consists in his reaching his ultimate end. Consequently, those natural operations which are directed to cause or preserve the primary perfection of human nature will not be in the resurrection: such are the actions of the animal life in man, the action of the elements on one another, and the movement of the heavens; wherefore all these will cease at the resurrection. And since to eat, drink, sleep, and beget pertain to the animal life, being directed to the primary perfection of nature, it follows that they will not be in the resurrection.

REPLY OBJ. 1: When Christ partook of that meal, his eating was an act, not of necessity (as though human nature needed food after the resurrection), but of power, so as to prove that he had resumed the true human nature which he had in that state wherein he ate and drank with his disciples. There will be no need of such proof at the general resurrection, since it will be evident to all. Hence Christ is said to have ate by dispensation in the sense in which lawyers say that a *dispensation is a relaxation of the general law*: because Christ made an exception to that which is common to those who rise again (namely, not to partake of food) for the aforesaid motive. Hence the argument does not follow.

REPLY OBJ. 2: The distinction of sexes and the difference of members will be for the restoration of the perfection of human nature both in the species and in the individual. Hence it does not follow that they are without purpose, although they lack their animal operations.

REPLY OBJ. 3: The aforesaid operations do not belong to man as man, as also the Philosopher states (*Ethics* 10.7), wherefore the happiness of the human body does not consist therein. But the human body will be glorified by an overflow from the reason whereby man is man, inasmuch as the body will be subject to reason.

REPLY OBJ. 4: As the Philosopher says (*Ethics* 7.12, 10.5), the pleasures of the body are *medicinal*, because they

medicinales, quia adhibentur homini ad tollendum fastidium; vel etiam *aegritudines*, inquantum eis homo inordinate delectatur, ac si essent verae delectationes, sicut homo habens infirmum gustum delectatur in quibusdam quae sanis non sunt delectabilia. Et ideo non oportet quod tales: delectationes sint de perfectione beatitudinis, ut Iudaei et Saraceni ponunt, et quidam haeretici posuerunt, qui vocantur Chiliastae. Qui etiam secundum doctrinam Philosophi non videntur sanum habere affectum; solae enim delectationes spirituales, secundum ipsum, sunt simpliciter delectationes, et propter se quaerendae. Et ideo ipsae solae ad beatitudinem requiruntur.

are applied to man for the removal of weariness; or again, they are *unhealthy*, insofar as man indulges in those pleasures inordinately, as though they were real pleasures: just as a man whose taste is vitiated delights in things which are not delightful to the healthy. Consequently, it does not follow that such pleasures as these belong to the perfection of beatitude, as the Jews and Turks maintain, and certain heretics known as the Chiliasts asserted. These, moreover, according to the Philosopher's teaching would seem to have an unhealthy appetite, since according to him none but spiritual pleasures are pleasures simply, and to be sought for their own sake: wherefore these alone are requisite for beatitude.

QUESTION 82

THE IMPASSIBILITY OF THE BLESSED WHO RISE AGAIN

Deinde considerandum est de conditionibus beatorum resurgentium. Et primo, de eorum corporum impassibilitate; secundo, de subtilitate; tertio, de agilitate; quarto, de claritate.

Circa primum, quaeruntur quatuor.

Primo: utrum sancti resurgentes resurgant quoad corpora impassibiles.

Secundo: utrum aequalis impassibilitas omnibus inerit.

Tertio: utrum illa impassibilitas sensum in actu a corporibus gloriosis excludat.

Quarto: utrum sint in eis omnes sensus in actu.

We must now consider the conditions under which the blessed rise again: (1) The impassibility of their bodies; (2) Their subtlety; (3) Their agility; (4) Their clarity.

Under the first head there are four points of inquiry:

(1) Whether the bodies of the saints will be impassible after the resurrection?

(2) Whether all will be equally impassible?

(3) Whether this impassibility excludes actual sensation from the glorified bodies?

(4) Whether in them all the senses are in act?

Article 1

Whether the Bodies of the Saints Will Be Impassible After the Resurrection?

AD PRIMUM SIC PROCEDITUR. Videtur quod corpora sanctorum post resurrectionem non sint impassibilia. Omne enim mortale est passibile. Sed homo post resurrectionem erit *animal rationale mortale*: haec enim est definitio hominis, quae nunquam ab eo separabitur. Ergo corpus erit passibile.

PRAETEREA, omne quod est in potentia ad formam alterius, passibile est ab illo: quia secundum hoc aliquid est passivum ab alio, ut dicitur in I *de Generatione*. Sed corpora sanctorum post resurrectionem erunt in potentia ad aliam formam. Ergo erunt passibilia. Probatio mediae. Quaecumque communicant in materia, unum eorum est in potentia ad formam alterius: materia enim, secundum quod est sub una forma, non amittit potentiam ad aliam formam. Sed corpora sanctorum post resurrectionem communicabunt cum elementis in materia: quia ex eadem materia reparabuntur ex qua nunc sunt. Ergo erunt in potentia ad aliam formam. Et sic erunt passibilia.

PRAETEREA, *contraria nata sunt agere et pati ad invicem*: ut in I *de Generatione*, dicit Philosophus. Sed corpora sanctorum post resurrectionem erunt ex contrariis composita, sicut et nunc sunt. Ergo erunt passibilia.

PRAETEREA, in corpore humano resurget sanguis et alii humores, ut dictum est. Sed ex pugna humorum ad invicem generantur aegritudines et huiusmodi passiones in corpore. Ergo erunt corpora sanctorum post resurrectionem passibilia.

OBJECTION 1: It seems that the bodies of the saints will not be impassible after the resurrection. For everything mortal is passible. But man, after the resurrection, will be *a mortal rational animal*, for such is the definition of man, which will never be dissociated from him. Therefore, the body will be passible.

OBJ. 2: Further, whatever is in potentiality to have the form of another thing is passible in relation to it; for this is what is meant by being passive to another thing (*On Generation and Corruption* I). Now the bodies of the saints will be in potentiality to the form of another thing after the resurrection, since matter, according as it is under one form, does not lose its potentiality to another form. But the bodies of the saints after the resurrection will have matter in common with the elements, because they will be restored out of the same matter of which they are now composed. Therefore, they will be in potentiality to another form, and thus will be passible.

OBJ. 3: Further, according to the Philosopher (*On Generation and Corruption* I), *contraries have a natural inclination to be active and passive towards one another*. Now the bodies of the saints will be composed of contraries after the resurrection, even as now. Therefore, they will be passible.

OBJ. 4: Further, in the human body the blood and humors will rise again, as stated above (Q. 80, A. 3–4). Now, sickness and such passions arise in the body through the antipathy of the humors. Therefore, the bodies of the saints will be passible after the resurrection.

PRAETEREA, magis repugnat perfectioni defectus in actu quam defectus in potentia, Sed passibilitas importat solum defectum in potentia. Cum ergo in corporibus beatorum sint futuri aliqui defectus in actu, sicut cicatrices vulnerum in martyribus, ut in Christo fuerunt; videtur quod nihil deperibit perfectioni eorum si ponantur habere corpora passibilia.

SED CONTRA: Omne passibile est corruptibile: quia *passio magis facta abiicit a substantia*. Sed corpora sanctorum post resurrectionem erunt incorruptibilia, ut dicitur I Cor. 15, [42]: *seminatur in corruptione, resurgent in incorruptione*. Ergo erunt impassibilia.

PRAETEREA, fortius non patitur a debiliori. Sed nullum corpus erit fortius corporibus sanctorum, de quibus dicitur, I Cor. 15, [43]: *seminatur in infirmitate, resurget in virtute*. Ergo erunt impassibilia,

RESPONDEO dicendum quod passio dupliciter dicitur. Uno modo, communiter. Et sic omnis receptio passio dicitur: sive illud quod recipitur sit conveniens recipienti et perfectivum ipsius; sive contrarium et corruptivum. Ab huiusmodi passionis remotione corpora gloriosa impassibilia non dicuntur: cum nihil quod est perfectionis eis sit auferendum.

Alio modo passio dicitur proprie, quam sic definit Damascenus, in II libro: *passio est motus praeter naturam*. Unde immoderatus motus cordis passio eius dicitur: sed moderatus dicitur eius operatio. Cuius ratio est quia omne quod patitur, trahitur ad terminos agentis, quia agens assimilat sibi patiens: et ideo patiens, inquantum huiusmodi, trahitur extra terminos proprios in quibus erat. Sic ergo proprie accipiendo passionem, non erit in corporibus resurgentium sanctorum potentialitas ad passionem. Et ideo impassibilia dicuntur.

Huius autem impassibilitatis ratio a diversis diversimode assignatur. Quidam enim eam attribuunt conditioni elementorum, quae aliter se habebunt tunc in corpore quam modo se habent. Dicunt enim quod elementa remanebunt ibi secundum substantiam, sed qualitates activae et passivae ab elementis auferentur.

Sed hoc non videtur verum. Quia qualitates activae et passivae sunt de perfectione elementorum. Unde, si sine eis repararentur elementa in corpore resurgentis, essent minoris perfectionis quam modo sint. Et praeterea, cum qualitates illae sint propria accidentia elementorum ex forma et materia ipsorum causata, videtur valde absurdum quod causa maneat et effectus tollatur.

Et ideo alii dicunt quod manebunt qualitates, sed non habebunt proprias actiones, divina virtute id faciente ad conservationem humani corporis.

OBJ. 5: Further, actual defect is more inconsistent with perfection than potential defect. But passibility denotes merely potential defect. Since, then, there will be certain actual defects in the bodies of the blessed, such as the scars of the wounds in the martyrs, even as they were in Christ, it would seem that their perfections will not suffer, if we grant their bodies to be passible.

ON THE CONTRARY, Everything passible is corruptible, because *increase of passion results in loss of substance* (Aristotle, *Topics* 6.1). Now the bodies of the saints will be incorruptible after the resurrection, according to 1 Corinthians 15:42, *it is sown in corruption, it shall rise in incorruption*. Therefore, they will be impassible.

FURTHER, The stronger is not passive to the weaker. But no body will be stronger than the bodies of the saints, of which it is written: *it is sown in weakness, it shall rise in power* (1 Cor 15:43). Therefore, they will be impassible.

I ANSWER THAT, We speak of a thing being passive in two ways. First, in a broad sense, and thus every reception is called a passion, whether the thing received be fitting to the receiver and perfect it, or contrary to it and corrupt it. The glorious bodies are not said to be impassible by the removal of this kind of passion, since nothing pertaining to perfection is to be removed from them.

In another way we use the word 'passive' properly, and thus the Damascene defines passion (*On the Orthodox Faith* 2.22) as being *a movement contrary to nature*. Hence an immoderate movement of the heart is called its passion, but a moderate movement is called its operation. The reason of this is that whatever is patient is drawn to the bounds of the agent, since the agent assimilates the patient to itself, so that therefore the patient as such is drawn beyond its own bounds within which it was confined. Accordingly, taking passion in its proper sense, there will be no potentiality to passion in the bodies of the saints after resurrection; wherefore they are said to be impassible.

The reason, however, of this impassibility is assigned differently by different persons. Some ascribe it to the condition of the elements, which will be different then from what it is now. For they say that the elements will remain then as to substance, yet that they will be deprived of their active and passive qualities.

But this does not seem to be true: because the active and passive qualities belong to the perfection of the elements, so that if the elements were restored without them in the body of the man that rises again, they would be less perfect than now. Moreover, since these qualities are the proper accidents of the elements, being caused by their form and matter, it would seem most absurd for the cause to remain and the effect to be removed.

Wherefore others say that the qualities will remain, but deprived of their proper activities, the divine power doing this for the preservation of the human body.

Sed hoc etiam non videtur posse stare. Quia ad mixtionem requiritur actio activarum et passivarum qualitatum: et secundum praedominium unius vel alterius mixta efficiuntur diversae complexionis. Quod oportet ponere in corpore resurgentis: quia erunt ibi carnes et ossa et huiusmodi; partes, quibus omnibus non competit una complexio. Et praeterea, secundum hoc impassibilitas non posset poni dos in eis. Quia non poneret aliquam dispositionem in substantia impassibili, sed solum prohibitionem passionis ab exteriori, scilicet divina virtute, quae etiam posset idem facere de corpore hominis in statu huius vitae.

Et ideo alii dicunt quod in ipso corpore erit aliquid prohibens passionem corporum gloriosorum, scilicet materia quinti corporis, quam ponunt venire in compositionem humani corporis ad conciliandum elementa in harmoniam quandam, per quam possunt esse debita materia animae rationalis; sed tamen in statu huius vitae, propter dominium elementaris naturae, corpus humanum patitur ad similitudinem aliorum elementorum; sed in resurrectione dominabitur natura quinti corporis. Et ideo corpus humanum reddetur impassibile, ad similitudinem corporis caelestis.

Sed hoc non potest stare. Quia corpus quintum non venit materialiter ad compositionem corporis humani, ut in II libro ostensum est. Et praeterea impossibile est dicere quod aliqua virtus naturalis, qualis est virtus corporis caelestis, transferat corpus humanum ad proprietatem gloriae, qualis est impassibilitas corporis gloriosi: cum immutationem corporis humani Apostolus attribuat virtuti Christi; quia *qualis caelestis, tales et caelestes*, I Cor. 15, [48]; et Philipp. 3, [21], *reformabit corpus humilitatis nostrae*, etc. Et praeterea, non potest natura caelestis ita dominari in corpore humano quin natura elementaris remaneat, cui ex essentialibus suis principiis passibilitas inest.

Et ideo aliter dicendum est, quod omnis passio fit per victoriam agentis super patiens: alias non traheret ipsum ad terminos suos. Impossibile est autem quod aliquid dominetur supra patiens nisi inquantum debilitatur dominium formae propriae supra materiam patientis, loquendo de passione quae est contra naturam, de qua nunc loquimur: non enim potest materia subiici uni contrariorum sine hoc quod tollatur dominium alterius super ipsam, vel saltem diminuatur. Corpus autem humanum, et quidquid in eo est, perfecte erit subiectum animae rationali, sicut etiam ipsa perfecte subiecta erit Deo. Et ideo in corpore glorioso non poterit esse ali-

This, however, would seem to be untenable, since the action and passion of the active and passive qualities is necessary for the mixture [of the elements], and according as one or the other preponderates the mixed [bodies] differ in their respective complexions. This must apply to the bodies of those who rise again, for they will contain flesh and bones and like parts, all of which demand different complexions. Moreover, according to this, impassibility could not be one of their gifts because it would not imply a disposition in the impassible substance, but merely an external preventive to passion, namely, the power of God, which might produce the same effect in a human body even in this state of life.

Consequently, others say that in the body itself there will be something preventing the passion of a glorified body, namely, the nature of a fifth or heavenly body, which they maintain enters into the composition of a human body to the effect of blending the elements together in harmony so as to be fitting matter for the rational soul; but that in this state of life, on account of the preponderance of the elemental nature, the human body is passible like other elements, whereas in the resurrection the nature of the fifth body will predominate, so that the human body will be made impassible in likeness to the heavenly body.

But this cannot stand, because the fifth body does not enter materially into the composition of a human body, as was proved above (*Sentences* II, D. 12, Q. 1, A. 1). Moreover, it is absurd to say that a natural power, such as the power of a heavenly body, should endow the human body with a property of glory, such as the impassibility of a glorified body, since the Apostle ascribes to Christ's power the transformation of the human body, because *such as is the heavenly, such also are they that are heavenly* (1 Cor 15:48), and *he will reform the body of our lowness, made like to the body of his glory, according to the operation whereby also he is able to subdue all things unto himself* (Phil 3:21). And again, a heavenly nature cannot exercise such power over the human body as to take from it its elemental nature, which is passible by reason of its essential constituents.

Consequently, we must say otherwise that all passion results from the agent overcoming the patient, else it would not draw it to its own bounds. Now it is impossible for agent to overcome patient except through the weakening of the hold which the form of the patient has over its matter, if we speak of the passion which is against nature, for it is of passion in this sense that we are speaking now. For matter is not subject to one of two contraries except through the cessation (or at least the diminution) of the hold which the other contrary has on it. Now the human body and all that it contains will be perfectly subject to the rational soul, even as the soul will be perfectly subject to God. Wherefore it

qua mutatio contra dispositionem illam qua perficitur ab anima. Et ita corpora illa erunt impassibilia.

AD PRIMUM ergo dicendum quod, secundum Anselmum, *mortale ponitur in definitione hominis a philosophis, qui non crediderunt hominem totum aliquando posse esse immortalem*, quia non viderunt homines nisi secundum huius mortalitatis statum.

Vel potest dici quod, secundum Philosophum, in VII *Metaphys.*, quia differentiae essentiales sunt nobis incognitae, utimur quandoque differentiis accidentalibus ad significandum differentias essentiales, quae sunt accidentalem causae. Unde *mortale* in definitione hominis non ponitur quasi ipsa mortalitas ad essentiam hominis pertineat: sed quia illud quod nunc est causa passibilitatis et mortalitatis secundum praesentem statum, scilicet compositio ex contrariis, est de essentia hominis. Sed tunc non erit causa eius propter victoriam animae super corpus.

AD SECUNDUM dicendum quod duplex est potentia: ligata, et libera. Et hoc non solum est verum de potentia activa, sed etiam passiva: forma enim ligat potentiam materiae, determinando ipsam ad unum, secundum quod dominatur super eam. Et quia in rebus corruptibilibus non perfecte dominatur forma, supra materiam, non perfecte potest ligare ipsam, quin recipiat interdum per aliquam passionem dispositionem contrariam formae. Sed in sanctis post resurrectionem omnino anima dominabitur supra corpus: nec illud dominium aliquo modo poterit auferri, quia ipsa erit immutabiliter Deo subiecta, quod non fuit in statu innocentiae. Et ideo in corporibus illis manet eadem potentia ad formam aliam quae nunc inest, quantum ad substantiam potentiae: sed erit ligata per victoriam animae supra corpus, ut nunquam in actum passionis exire possit.

AD TERTIUM dicendum quod qualitates, elementares sunt instrumenta animae: ut patet, in II *de Anima*, quod calor ignis in corpore humano regulatur in actu nutriendi per virtutem animae. Quando autem agens principale est perfectum, et non est aliquis defectus in instrumento, nulla actio procedit ab instrumento nisi secundum dispositionem principalis agentis. Et ideo in corporibus sanctorum post resurrectionem nulla actio vel passio poterit provenire a qualitatibus elementaribus quae sit contra dispositionem animae, quae intendit conservare corpus.

AD QUARTUM dicendum, secundum Augustinum, in *Epistola ad Consentium*, quod *divina potentia vadet de ista visibili atque tractabili natura corporum, quibusdam manentibus, auferre quas voluerit qualitates.* Unde, sicut ab igne fornacis Chaldaeorum abstulit virtutem comburendi quantum ad aliquid, quia corpora puerorum illaesa servata sunt, sed mansit quantum ad aliquid,

will be impossible for the glorified body to be subject to any change contrary to the disposition whereby it is perfected by the soul; and consequently those bodies will be impassible.

REPLY OBJ. 1: According to Anselm (*Cur Deus Homo* II, 11), *mortal is included in the philosophers' definition of man because they did not believe that the whole man could be ever immortal*, for they had no experience of man otherwise than in this state of mortality.

Or we may say that since, according to the Philosopher (*Metaphysics* 6.12), essential differences are unknown to us, we sometimes employ accidental differences in order to signify essential differences from which the accidental differences result. Hence *mortal* is put in the definition of man not as though mortality were essential to man, but because that which causes passibility and mortality in the present state of life, namely, composition of contraries, is essential to man, but it will not cause it then, on account of the triumph of the soul over the body.

REPLY OBJ. 2: Potentiality is twofold, tied and free: and this is true not only of active but also of passive potentiality. For the form ties the potentiality of matter by determining it to one thing, and it is thus that it overcomes it. And since in corruptible things form does not perfectly overcome matter, it cannot tie it completely so as to prevent it from sometimes receiving a disposition contrary to the form through some passion. But in the saints after the resurrection, the soul will have complete dominion over the body, and it will be altogether impossible for it to lose this dominion because it will be immutably subject to God, which was not the case in the state of innocence. Consequently, those bodies will retain substantially the same potentiality as they have now to another form; yet that potentiality will remain tied by the triumph of the soul over the body, so that it will never be realized by actual passion.

REPLY OBJ. 3: The elemental qualities are the instruments of the soul, as stated in *On the Soul* II, for the heat of fire in an animal's body is directed in the act of nutrition by the soul's power. When, however, the principal agent is perfect, and there is no defect in the instrument, no action proceeds from the instrument except in accordance with the disposition of the principal agent. Consequently, in the bodies of the saints after the resurrection no action or passion will result from the elemental qualities that is contrary to the disposition of the soul, which has the preservation of the body in view.

REPLY OBJ. 4: According to Augustine (*Epistle to Consentius* 146), *the divine power is able to remove whatever qualities he will from this visible and tangible body, other qualities remaining.* Hence, even as in a certain respect he deprived the flames of the Chaldeans' furnace of the power to burn, since the bodies of the boys were preserved without hurt, while in another respect that power remained,

quia ignis ille ligna comburebat, ita auferet ab humoribus passibilitatem, et dimittet naturam. Modus autem quo hoc fiet, dictus est.

AD QUINTUM dicendum quod cicatrices vulnerum non erunt in sanctis, nec in Christo fuerunt, inquantum important aliquem defectum: sed inquantum sunt signa constantissimae virtutis, qua passi sunt pro iustitia et fide, ut ex hoc et ipsis et aliis gaudium crescat. Unde dicit Augustinus, XXII *de Civ. Dei*: *nescio quomodo sic afficimur amore martyrum beatorum ut velimus in illo regno in eorum corporibus videre vulnerum cicatrices quae pro Christi nomine pertulerunt. Et fortasse videbimus. Non enim deformitas in eis, sed dignitas erit; et quaedam, quamvis iri corpore; non corporis, sed virtutis pulchritudo fulgebit. Nec tamen, si aliqua martyribus amputata et ablata sunt membra, sine ipsis membris erunt in resurrectione mortuorum quibus dictum est: capillus de capite vestro non peribit.*

since those flames consumed the wood, so will he remove passibility from the humors while leaving their nature unchanged. It has been explained in the article how this is brought about.

REPLY OBJ. 5: The scars of wounds will not be in the saints, nor were they in Christ, insofar as they imply a defect, but as signs of the most steadfast virtue whereby the saints suffered for the sake of justice and faith: so that this will increase their own and others' joy. Hence Augustine says (*The City of God* xxii, 19): *I do not know how we feel an undescribable love for the blessed martyrs so as to desire to see in that kingdom the scars of the wounds in their bodies, which they bore for Christ's name. Perchance indeed we shall see them, for this will not make them less comely but more glorious. A certain beauty will shine in them, a beauty though in the body, yet not of the body but of virtue. Nevertheless those martyrs who have been maimed and deprived of their limbs will not be without those limbs in the resurrection of the dead, for to them it is said:* "a hair of your head shall not perish" (Luke 21:18).

Article 2

Whether All Will Be Equally Impassible?

AD SECUNDUM SIC PROCEDITUR. Videtur quod impassibilitas in omnibus erit aequalis. Quia I Cor. 15 dicit Glossa quod *aequaliter omnes habent quod pati non possunt*. Sed ex hoc erit in eis quod non possunt pati, quod habent dotem impassibilitatis. Ergo impassibilitas est aequalis in omnibus.

PRAETEREA, negationes non recipiunt magis et minus. Sed impassibilitas est quaedam negatio vel privatio passibilitatis. Ergo non potest esse maior in uno quam in alio.

PRAETEREA, magis album dicitur quod, est nigro impermixtius. Sed nulli corporum sanctorum admiscebitur aliquid de passibilitate. Ergo omnia erunt aequaliter impassibilia.

SED CONTRA: Mento debet respondere praemium proportionaliter. Sed sanctorum quidam fuerunt aliis maioris meriti. Ergo, cum impassibilitas sit quoddam praemium, videtur quod in quibusdam sit maior quam in aliis.

PRAETEREA, impassibilitas dividitur contra dotem claritatis. Sed illa non erit aequalis in omnibus, ut patet I Cor. 15, [41–42]. Ergo nec impassibilitas.

RESPONDEO dicendum quod impassibilitas potest dupliciter considerari: vel secundum se; vel secundum causam suam. Si secundum se consideretur, quia solam negationem vel privationem importat, non suscipit ma-

OBJECTION 1: It would seem that all will be equally impassible. For a Gloss on 1 Corinthians 15:42: *it is sown in corruption*, says that *all have equal immunity from suffering*. Now the gift of impassibility consists in immunity from suffering. Therefore, all will be equally impassible.

OBJ. 2: Further, negations are not subject to be more or less. Now impassibility is a negation or privation of passibility. Therefore, it cannot be greater in one subject than in another.

OBJ. 3: Further, a thing is more white if it have less admixture of black. But there will be no admixture of passibility in any of the saints' bodies. Therefore, they will all be equally impassible.

ON THE CONTRARY, Reward should be proportionate to merit. Now some of the saints were greater in merit than others. Therefore, since impassibility is a reward, it would seem to be greater in some than in others.

FURTHER, Impassibility is condivided with the gift of clarity. Now the latter will not be equal in all, according to 1 Corinthians 15:41. Therefore, neither will impassibility be equal in all.

I ANSWER THAT, Impassibility may be considered in two ways: either in itself or in respect of its cause. If it be considered in itself, since it denotes a mere negation or privation, it is not subject to be more or less, but will be equal

gis et minus, sed erit aequalis in omnibus beatis. Si autem consideretur secundum suam causam, sic erit in uno maior quam in alio. Causa autem eius est dominium animae super corpus. Quod quidem dominium causatur ex hoc quod fruitur Deo immobiliter. Unde in illo qui perfectius fruitur, est maior impassibilitatis causa.

AD PRIMUM ergo dicendum quod Glossa illa loquitur de impassibilitate secundum se, et non secundum causam suam.

AD SECUNDUM dicendum quod, quamvis negationes et privationes secundum se non intendantur nec remittantur, tamen intenduntur et remittuntur ex causis suis: sicut dicitur esse locus magis tenebrosus qui habet plura et maiora obstacula lucis.

AD TERTIUM dicendum quod aliqua non solum intenduntur per recessum a contrario, sed per accessum ad terminum: sicut lux intenditur. Et propterea etiam impassibilitas est maior in uno quod in alio, quamvis in nullo aliquid passibilitatis remaneat.

in all the blessed. On the other hand, if we consider it in relation to its cause, thus it will be greater in one person than in another. Now its cause is the dominion of the soul over the body, and this dominion is caused by the soul's unchangeable enjoyment of God. Consequently, in one who enjoys God more perfectly, there is a greater cause of impassibility.

REPLY OBJ. 1: This Gloss is speaking of impassibility in itself and not in relation to its cause.

REPLY OBJ. 2: Although negations and privations, considered in themselves, are not increased nor diminished, yet they are subject to increase and diminution in relation to their causes. Thus a place is said to be more darkened from having more and greater obstacles to light.

REPLY OBJ. 3: Some things increase not only by receding from their contrary, but also by approach to a term: thus light increases. Consequently, impassibility also is greater in one subject than in another, although there is no passibility remaining in any one.

Article 3

Whether Impassibility Excludes Actual Sensation From Glorified Bodies?

AD TERTIUM SIC PROCEDITUR. Videtur quod impassibilitas sensum in actu a corporibus gloriosis excludat. Quia, sicut dicit Philosophus, in II *de Anima, sentire est quoddam pati.* Corpora autem gloriosa erunt impassibilia. Ergo non sentient in actu.

PRAETEREA, immutatio naturalis praecedit immutationem animalem, sicut esse naturale praecedit esse intentionale. Sed corpora gloriosa ratione impassibilitatis non immutabuntur immutatione naturali. Ergo nec immutatione animali, quae requiritur ad sentiendum.

PRAETEREA, quandocumque fit sensus in actu, cum nova receptione fit novum iudicium. Sed ibi non erit novum iudicium: quia *non erunt ibi cogitationes volubiles.* Ergo non fiet sensus in actu.

PRAETEREA, quando anima est in actu unius potentiae, remittitur actus alterius potentiae. Sed anima summe erit intenta ad actum virtutis intellectivae, qua Deum contemplabitur. Ergo non erit aliquo modo in actu virtutis sensitivae;

SED CONTRA: Est quod dicitur Apoc. 1, [7]: *videbit eum omnis oculus.* Ergo erit ibi sensus in actu.

PRAETEREA, secundum Philosophum, in I *de Anima, animatum ab inanimato distinguitur sensu et mo-*

OBJECTION 1: It would seem that impassibility excludes actual sensation from glorified bodies. For, according to the Philosopher (*On the Soul* 2.11), *sensation is a kind of passion.* But the glorified bodies will be impassible. Therefore, they will not have actual sensation.

OBJ. 2: Further, natural alteration precedes spiritual alteration, just as natural being precedes intentional being. Now glorified bodies, by reason of their impassibility, will not be subject to natural alteration. Therefore, they will not be subject to spiritual alteration, which is requisite for sensation.

OBJ. 3: Further, whenever actual sensation is due to a new perception, there is a new judgment. But in that state there will be no new judgment, because *our thoughts will not then be unchangeable,* as Augustine says (*On the Trinity* 15.16). Therefore, there will be no actual sensation.

OBJ. 4: Further, when the act of one of the soul's powers is intense, the acts of the other powers are remiss. Now the soul will be supremely intent on the act of the contemplative power in contemplating God. Therefore, the soul will have no actual sensation whatever.

ON THE CONTRARY, It is written: *every eye shall see him* (Rev 1:7). Therefore, there will be actual sensation.

FURTHER, According to the Philosopher (*On the Soul* 1.2), *the animate is distinct from the inanimate by sensa-*

tu. Sed ibi erit motus in actu: quia tanquam *scintillae in arundineto discurrent*, Sap. 3, [7]. Ergo et sensus in actu.

RESPONDEO dicendum quod aliquem sensum esse in corporibus beatorum omnes ponunt. Alias corporalis vita sanctorum post resurrectionem assimilantur magis somno quam vigiliae. Quod non competit illi perfectioni: eo quod in somno corpus sensibile non est in ultimo actu vitae; propter quod somnus dicitur *vitae dimidium* in I *Ethic*. Sed in modo sentiendi diversi diversa opinantur.

Quidam enim dicunt quod, quia corpora gloriosa sunt impassibilia, et propter hoc *non receptibilia peregrinae impressionis*, et multo minus quam corpora caelestia, quod non erit ibi sensus in actu per receptionem alicuius speciei a sensibilibus, sed magis extra-mittendo.

Sed hoc non potest esse. Quia in resurrectione natura speciei manebit eadem in homine et omnibus partibus eius. Huiusmodi autem est natura sensus ut sit potentia passiva: ut in II *de Anima* probat Philosophus. Unde, si in resurrectione sancti sentient extra-mittendo et non recipiendo, non esset sensus in eis virtus passiva, sed activa. Et sic non esset eiusdem speciei cum sensu qui nunc est, sed esset aliqua alia virtus eis data: sicut enim materia nunquam fit forma, ita potentia passiva nunquam fit activa.

Et ideo alii dicunt quod sensus in actu fiet per susceptionem, non quidem ab exterioribus sensibilibus, sed per effluxum a superioribus viribus: ut sicut nunc superiores vires accipiunt ab inferioribus, ita e converso tunc inferiores accipient a superioribus.

Sed iste modus receptionis non facit vere sentire. Quia omnis potentia passiva secundum suae speciei rationem determinatur ad aliquid activum speciale: quia potentia, inquantum huiusmodi, habet ordinem ad illud respectu cuius dicitur. Unde, cum proprium activum in sensu exteriori sit res existens extra; animam, et non intentio eius existens in imaginatione vel ratione; si organum sentiendi non moveatur a rebus extra, sed ex imaginatione vel aliis superioribus viribus, non erit vere sentire. Unde non dicimus quod phrenetici et alii mente capti, in quibus propter victoriam imaginativae virtutis fit huiusmodi defluxus specierum ad organa sentiendi, vere sentiant, sed quia videtur eis quod sentiant.

Et ideo dicendum est, cum aliis, quod sensus corporum gloriosorum erit per susceptionem a rebus quae sunt extra animam. Sed sciendum est quod organa sentiendi immutantur a rebus quae sunt extra animam, dupliciter. Uno modo, immutatione naturali: quando scilicet organum disponitur eadem qualitate naturali qua disponitur res extra animam quae agit in ipsum, sicut cum manus fit calida et adusta ex tactu rei calidae, vel

tion and movement. Now there will be actual movement, since they *shall run to and fro like sparks among the reeds* (Wis 3:7). Therefore, there will also be actual sensation.

I ANSWER THAT, All are agreed that there is some sensation in the bodies of the blessed: else the bodily life of the saints after the resurrection would be likened to sleep rather than to vigilance. Now this is not befitting that perfection, because in sleep a sensible body is not in the ultimate act of life, for which reason sleep is described as *half-life*. But there is a difference of opinion as to the mode of sensation.

For some say that the glorified bodies will be impassible, and consequently *not susceptible to impressions from without*, and much less so than the heavenly bodies, because they will have actual sensations not by receiving species from sensibles, but by emission of species.

But this is impossible, since in the resurrection the specific nature will remain the same in man and in all his parts. Now the nature of sense is to be a passive power, as the Philosopher proves (*On the Soul* 2). Wherefore if the saints in the resurrection were to have sensations by emitting and not by receiving species, sense in them would be not a passive but an active power, and thus it would not be the same specifically with sense as it is now, but would be some other power bestowed on them; for just as matter never becomes form, so a passive power never becomes active.

Consequently, others say that the senses will be actualized by receiving species, not indeed from external sensibles, but by an outflow from the higher powers, so that as now the higher powers receive from the lower, so on the contrary the lower powers will then receive from the higher.

But this mode of reception does not result in real sensation, because every passive power, according to its specific nature, is determined to some special active principle, since a power as such bears relation to that with respect to which it is said to be the power. Therefore, since the proper active principle in external sensation is a thing existing outside the soul, and not an intention thereof existing in the imagination or reason, if the organ of sense be not moved by external things, but by the imagination or other higher powers, there will be no true sensation. Hence we do not say that madmen or other witless persons (in whom there is this kind of outflow of species towards the organs of sense, on account of the powerful influence of the imagination) have real sensations, but that it seems to them that they have sensations.

Consequently, we must say with others that sensation in glorified bodies will result from the reception of things outside the soul. It must, however, be observed that the organs of sense are transmuted by things outside the soul in two ways. First, by a natural transmutation, namely, when the organ is disposed by the same natural quality as the thing outside the soul which acts on that organ: for instance, when the hand is heated by touching a hot object,

odorifera ex tactu rei odoriferae. Alio modo, immutatione spirituali: quando recipitur qualitas sensibilis in instrumento secundum esse spirituale, idest species sive intentio qualitatis, et non ipsa qualitas; sicut pupilla recipit speciem albedinis et tamen ipsa non efficitur alba. Prima ergo receptio non causat sensum, per se loquendo: quia *sensus est susceptivus specierum* in materia *praeter materiam*, idest praeter esse materiale quod habebant extra animam, ut dicitur in II *de Anima*. Et haec receptio immutat naturam recipientis: quia recipitur hoc modo qualitas secundum esse suum materiale. Unde ista receptio non erit in corporibus gloriosis: sed secunda, quale per se facit sensum in actu, et non immutat naturam recipientis.

Ad primum ergo dicendum quod iam patet ex dictis quod per hanc passionem quae est in actu sentiendi, quae non est aliud quam receptio praedicta, non trahitur corpus extra naturalem suam qualitatem, sed spiritualiter perficitur. Unde impassibilitas gloriosorum corporum hanc passionem non excludit.

Ad secundum dicendum quod omne passivum recipit actionem agentis secundum suum modum. Si ergo aliquid sit quod natum sit immutari ab activo naturali et spirituali immutatione, immutatio naturalis praecedit immutationem spiritualem, sicut esse naturale praecedit esse intentionale. Si autem natum sit immutari spiritualiter tantum, non oportet quod immutetur naturaliter; sicut de aere, qui non est receptivus coloris secundum esse naturale, sed solum secundum esse spirituale, et ideo hoc solum modo immutatur; sicut e converso corpora inanimata immutantur per qualitates sensibiles solum naturaliter, et non spiritualiter. In corporibus autem gloriosis non poterit esse aliqua immutatio naturalis. Et ideo ibi erit spiritualis immutatio tantum.

Ad tertium dicendum quod, sicut erit nova receptio speciei in organo sentiendi, ita erit novum iudicium sensus communis, non autem novum iudicium intellectus de hoc: sicut fit in eo qui videt aliquid quod prius scivit. Quod autem Augustinus dicit, quod *non erunt ibi cogitationes volubiles*, intelligitur de cogitationibus intellectivae partis. Unde non est ad propositum.

Ad quartum dicendum quod, quando unum duorum est ratio alterius, occupatio animae circa unum non impedit nec remittit occupationem eius circa aliud: sicut medicus, dum videt urinam, non minus potest considerare regulas artis de coloribus urinarum, sed magis. Et quia Deus apprehenditur a sanctis ut ratio omnium quae ab eis agentur vel cognoscentur, ideo occupatio eorum circa sensibilia sentienda, vel quaecumque alia contem-

or becomes fragrant through contact with a fragrant object. Second, by a spiritual transmutation, as when a sensible quality is received in an instrument according to a spiritual mode of being, namely, when the species or the intention of a quality, and not the quality itself, is received: thus the pupil receives the species of whiteness and yet does not itself become white. Accordingly, the first reception does not cause sensation, properly speaking, because *the senses are receptive of species* in matter *but without matter*; that is to say, without the material being which the species had outside the soul (*On the Soul* 2). This reception transmutes the nature of the recipient because in this way the quality is received according to its material being. Consequently, this kind of reception will not be in the glorified bodies, but the second, which of itself causes actual sensation without changing the nature of the recipient, will be.

Reply Obj. 1: As already explained, by this passion that takes place in actual sensation and is no other than the aforesaid reception of species, the body is not drawn away from natural quality, but is perfected by a spiritual change. Wherefore the impassibility of glorified bodies does not exclude this kind of passion.

Reply Obj. 2: Every subject of passion receives the action of the agent according to its mode. Accordingly, if there be a thing that is naturally adapted to be altered by an active principle with a natural and a spiritual alteration, the natural alteration precedes the spiritual alteration, just as natural precedes intentional being. If, however, a thing be naturally adapted to be altered only with a spiritual alteration, it does not follow that it is altered naturally. For instance, the air is not receptive of color according to its natural being, but only according to its spiritual being, wherefore in this way alone is it altered: whereas, on the contrary, inanimate bodies are altered by sensible qualities only naturally and not spiritually. But in the glorified bodies there cannot be any natural alteration, and consequently there will be only spiritual alteration.

Reply Obj. 3: Just as there will be new reception of species in the organs of sensation, so there will be new judgment in the common sense: but there will be no new judgment on the point in the intellect; such is the case with one who sees what he knew before. The saying of Augustine, that *there our thoughts will not be changeable*, refers to the thoughts of the intellectual part: therefore it is not to the point.

Reply Obj. 4: When one of two things is the type of the other, the attention of the soul to the one does not hinder or lessen its attention to the other: thus a physician while looking at urine is not less but more able to bear in mind the rules of his art concerning the colors of urine. And since God is apprehended by the saints as the type of all things that will be done or known by them, their attention to perceiving sensibles, or to contemplating, or doing anything

planda aut agenda, in nullo impediet divinam contemplationem, nec e converso.

Vel dicendum quod ideo una potentia impeditur in actu suo quando alia vehementer operatur, quia una potentia de se non sufficit ad tam intensam operationem nisi ei subveniatur per id quod erat aliis potentiis vel membris influendum a principio vitae. Et quia in sanctis erunt omnes potentiae perfectissimae, una poterit intense operari ita quod ex hoc nullum impedimentum praestabitur actioni alterius potentiae: sicut et in Christo fuit.

else will in no way hinder their contemplation of God, nor conversely.

Or we may say that the reason why one power is hindered in its act when another power is intensely engaged is because one power does not alone suffice for such an intense operation unless it be assisted by receiving from the principle of life the inflow that the other powers or members should receive. And since in the saints all the powers will be most perfect, one will be able to operate intensely without thereby hindering the operation of another power, even as it was with Christ.

Article 4

Whether in the Blessed, After the Resurrection, All the Senses Will Be in Act?

AD QUARTUM SIC PROCEDITUR. Videtur quod non sint ibi omnes sensus in actu. Tactus enim est primus inter omnes alios sensus: ut dicitur in libro *de Anima*. Sed corpora gloriosa carebunt actu sensus tactus: quia sensus tactus fit in actu per immutationem corporis animalis ab aliquo exteriori corpore praedominante in aliqua qualitatum activarum vel passivarum, quarum est tactus discretivus; qualis tunc immutatio esse non poterit. Ergo non. erit ibi omnis sensus in actu.

PRAETEREA, sensus gustus deservit actui virtutis nutritivae. Sed post resurrectionem huiusmodi actus non erit. Ergo frustra esset ibi gustus.

PRAETEREA, post resurrectionem nihil corrumpetur: quia tota creatura vestietur quadam virtute incorruptionis. Sed sensus odoratus in actu suo esse non potest nisi aliqua Corruptione facta: quia odor non sentitur sine aliqua fumali evaporatione, quae in quadam resolutione consistit. Ergo sensus odoratus non erit ibi in suo actu.

PRAETEREA, *auditus deservit disciplinae*: ut dicitur in libro *de Sensu et Sensato*. Sed non erit post resurrectionem beatis necessaria aliqua disciplina per sensibilia: quia divina sapientia replebuntur ex ipsius Dei visione. Ergo non erit ibi auditus.

PRAETEREA, visio fit secundum quod in pupilla recipitur species rei visae. Sed hoc non poterit: esse post resurrectionem in beatis. Ergo non erit ibi visus in actu. Qui tamen est omnium sensuum nobilior.

Probatio mediae. Illud quod est lucidum in actu, non est receptivum speciei visibilis: unde speculum directe positum sub radio solis non repraesentat speciem corporis oppositi. Sed pupilla, sicut et totum corpus, erit claritate dotata. Ergo non recipietur in ea aliqua species colorati corporis.

OBJECTION 1: It would seem that all the senses are not in act there. For touch is the first of all the senses (*On the Soul* 2.2). But the glorified body will lack the actual sense of touch, since the sense of touch becomes actual by the alteration of an animal body by some external body predominating in some one of the active or passive qualities which touch is capable of discerning: and such an alteration will then be impossible. Therefore, all the senses will not be in act there.

OBJ. 2: Further, the sense of taste assists the action of the nutritive power. Now, after the resurrection, there will be no such action, as stated above (Q. 81, A. 4). Therefore, taste would be useless there.

OBJ. 3: Further, nothing will be corrupted after the resurrection because the whole creature will be invested with a certain virtue of incorruption. Now the sense of smell cannot have its act without some corruption having taken place, because smell is not perceived without a volatile evaporation consisting in a certain dissolution. Therefore, the sense of smell is not there in its act.

OBJ. 4: Further, *hearing assists teaching* (*On Sense and the Sensed* 1). But the blessed, after the resurrection, will require no teaching by means of sensible objects, since they will be filled with divine wisdom by the very vision of God. Therefore, hearing will not be there.

OBJ. 5: Further, seeing results from the pupil receiving the species of the thing seen. But after the resurrection this will be impossible in the blessed. Therefore, there will be no actual seeing there, and yet this is the most noble of the senses.

The minor is proved thus: That which is actually lightsome is not receptive of a visible species, and consequently a mirror placed under the sun's rays does not reflect the image of a body opposite to it. Now the pupil, like the whole body, will be endowed with clarity. Therefore, it will not receive the image of a colored body.

Praeterea, secundum perspectivos, omne quod videtur, sub angulo videtur. Sed hoc non competit corporibus gloriosis. Ergo non habebunt sensum visus in actu.

Probatio mediae. Quandocumque aliquid videtur sub angulo, oportet esse aliquam proportionem angulo ad distantiam rei visae: quia quod a remotiori videtur, minus videtur et sub minori angulo. Unde posset esse ita parvus angulus quod nihil de re videretur. Si ergo oculus gloriosus videbit sub angulo, oportet quod videat sub determinata distantia: et ita quod non videat aliquid a remotiori quam modo videmus. Quod videtur valde absurdum. Et sic videtur quod sensus visus actu non erit in corporibus gloriosis.

Sed contra: Potentia coniuncta actui est perfectior quam non coniuncta. Sed natura humana erit in beatis in maxima perfectione. Ergo erunt ibi omnes sensus in suo actu.

Praeterea, vicinius se habent ad animam potentiae sensitivae quam corpus. Sed corpus praemiabitur vel punietur propter merita vel dementa animae. Ergo et omnes sensus praemiabuntur in beatis et punientur in malis secundum delectationem et dolorem vel tristitiam quae in operatione sensus consistunt.

Respondeo dicendum quod circa hoc est duplex opinio: Quidam enim dicunt quod in corporibus gloriosis erunt omnes potentiae sensuum, non tamen erunt in actu nisi duo sensus, scilicet tactus et visus. Nec hoc erit ex defectu sensuum, sed ex defectu medii et obiecti. Nec tamen erunt frustra: quia erunt ad integritatem humanae naturae, et ad commendandam sapientiam Creatoris.

Sed hoc non videtur verum. Quia hoc quod est medium in istis sensibus, est etiam in aliis medium. In visu enim est medium aer, qui etiam est medium in auditu et odoratu: sicut patet in II *de Anima*. Similiter etiam gustus habet medium coniunctum, sicut et tactus: cum gustus sit tactus quidam, ut in eodem libro dicitur. Odor etiam erit ibi, qui est obiectum odoratus: cum Ecclesia cantet quod odor suavissimus erunt corpora sanctorum. Laus etiam vocalis erit in patria: unde Augustinus dicit, super illud Psalmi [149, 6], *exultationes Dei in gutture eorum*, quod *corda et linguae non desinent laudare Deum*. Et idem etiam habetur per Glossam super illud Esdrae 12, [27], *in cantico et cymbalis*, etc.

Et ideo, secundum alios, dicendum quod etiam odoratus et auditus erunt ibi in actu. Sed gustus non erit in actu ita quod immutetur ab aliquo cibo vel potu sumpto, ut patet ex dictis: nisi forte dicatur quod erit gustus in actu per immutationem linguae ab aliqua humiditate adiuncta.

Ad primum ergo dicendum quod qualitates quas tactus percipit, sunt illae ex quibus constituitur animalis corpus. Unde per qualitates tangibiles corpus anima-lis corpus.

Obj. 6: Further, according to the science of perspective, whatever is seen, is seen at an angle. But this does not apply to the glorified bodies. Therefore, they will not have actual sense of sight.

The minor is proved thus. Whenever a thing is seen at an angle, the angle must be proportionate to the distance of the object seen: because what is seen from a greater distance is less seen and at a lesser angle, so that the angle may be so small that nothing is seen of the object. Therefore, if the glorified eye sees at an angle, it follows that it sees things within a certain distance, and that consequently it does not see a thing from a greater distance than we see now: and this would seem very absurd. And thus it would seem that the sense of sight will not be actual in glorified bodies.

On the contrary, A power conjoined to its act is more perfect than one not so conjoined. Now human nature in the blessed will be in its greatest perfection. Therefore, all the senses will be actual there.

Further, The sensitive powers are nearer to the soul than the body is. But the body will be rewarded or punished on account of the merits or demerits of the soul. Therefore, all the senses will, in the blessed, be rewarded, and will, in the wicked, be punished, with regard to pleasure and pain or sorrow, which consist in the operation of the senses.

I answer that, There are two opinions on this question. For some say that in the glorified bodies there will be all the sensitive powers, but that only two senses will be in act, namely, touch and sight; nor will this be owing to defective senses, but from lack of medium and object; and that the senses will not be useless, because they will conduce to the integrity of human nature and will show forth the wisdom of their Creator.

But this is seemingly untrue, because the medium in these senses is the same as in the others. For in the sight the medium is the air, and this is also the medium in hearing and smelling (*On the Soul* 2.7). Again, the taste, like the touch, has the medium in contact, since taste is a kind of touch (*On the Soul* 2.9). Scent also, which is the object of the sense of smell, will be there, since the Church sings that the bodies of the saints will be a most sweet scent. There will also be vocal praise in heaven; hence a Gloss says on Psalm 149:6, *the high praises of God shall be in their mouth*, that *hearts and tongues shall not cease to praise God*. The same is had on the authority of a Gloss on 2 Esdras 12:27, *with singing and with cymbals*.

Hence, according to others, we may say that smelling and hearing will be in act there, but taste will not be in act, in the sense of being affected by the taking of food or drink, as appears from what we have said (Q. 81, A. 4): unless perchance we say that there will be taste in act through the tongue being affected by some neighboring humor.

Reply Obj. 1: The qualities perceived by the touch are those which constitute the animal body. Wherefore the body of an animal has, through its tangible qualities ac-

lis, secundum statum praesentem, natum est immutari immutatione naturali et spirituali ab obiecto tactus. Et ideo tactus dicitur maxime materialis inter alios sensus: quia habet plus de materiali immutatione adiunctum. Non tamen immutatio materialis se habet ad actum sentiendi, qui perficitur spirituali immutatione, nisi per accidens. Et ideo in corporibus gloriosis, a quibus impassibilitas excludit naturalem immutationem, erit immutatio a qualitatibus tangibilibus spiritualis tantum: sicut etiam in corpore Adae fuit, quod nec ignis urere nec gladius scindere potuisset, et tamen horum sensum habuisset.

AD SECUNDUM dicendum quod gustus, secundum quod est sensus alimenti, non erit in actu. Si tamen erit secundum quod est iudicium saporum, hoc esse poterit forte per modum praedictum.

AD TERTIUM dicendum quod quidam posuerunt quod odor nihil aliud est quam quaedam fumalis evaporatio. Sed haec positio non potest esse vera: quod patet ex hoc quod vultures currunt ex odore percepto ad cadaver ex locis remotissimis, nec esset possibile quod evaporatio aliqua pertingeret a cadavere ad tam remota loca, etiam si totum resolveretur in vaporem; et praecipue cum sensibilia in aequali distantia ad quamlibet partem immutent. Unde odor immutat medium quandoque, et instrumentum sentiendi, spirituali immutatione, sine aliqua evaporatione pertingente ad organum. Sed quod aliqua evaporatio requiratur, hoc est quia odor in corporibus est humiditate aspersus: unde oportet resolutionem fieri, ad hoc quod percipiatur.

Sed in corporibus gloriosis erit odor in sua ultima perfectione, nullo modo per humidum suppressus. Unde immutabit spirituali immutatione, sicut odor fumalis evaporationis facit. Et sensus odoratus in sanctis, quia nulla humiditate impedietur, cognoscet non solum excellentias odorum, sicut nunc in nobis contingit, propter nimiam cerebri humiditatem: sed etiam minimas odorum differentias.

AD QUARTUM dicendum quod in patria erit laus vocalis: quamvis quidam aliter dicant, quod sola immutatione spirituali organum auditus immutabitur in beatis. Nec erit propter disciplinam qua scientiam acquirat: sed propter perfectionem sensus et delectationem. Quomodo autem vox ibi formari poterit, dictum est in II libro.

AD QUINTUM dicendum quod intensio luminis non impedit receptionem spiritualem speciei coloris, dummodo maneat in natura diaphani: sicut patet quod, quantumcumque illuminetur aer, potest esse medium in visu; et quanto est magis illuminatus, tanto per ipsum aliquid clarius videtur, nisi sit defectus ex debilitate vi-

cording to the present state of life, a natural aptitude to be affected with a natural and spiritual alteration by the object of touch. For this reason the touch is said to be the most material of the senses, since it has a greater measure of material alteration connected with it. Yet material alteration is only accidentally related to the act of sensation, which is effected by a spiritual alteration. Consequently, the glorified bodies, which by reason of their impassibility are immune from natural alteration, will be subject only to spiritual alteration by tangible qualities. Thus it was with the body of Adam, which could neither be burned by fire nor pierced by sword, although he had the sense of such things.

REPLY OBJ. 2: Taste, insofar as it is the perception of food, will not be in act; but perhaps it will be possible insofar as it is cognizant of flavors in the way mentioned above.

REPLY OBJ. 3: Some have considered odor to be merely a volatile evaporation. But this opinion cannot be true; which is evident from the fact that vultures hasten to a corpse on perceiving the odor from a very great distance, whereas it would be impossible for an evaporation to travel from the corpse to a place so remote, even though the whole corpse were to be dissolved into vapor. This is confirmed by the fact that sensible objects at an equal distance exercise their influence in all directions: so that odor sometimes affects the medium and the instrument of sensation with a spiritual alteration without any evaporation reaching the organ. That some evaporation should be necessary is due to the fact that odor in bodies is mixed with humidity; wherefore it is necessary for dissolution to take place in order for the odor to be perceived.

But in the glorified bodies odor will be in its ultimate perfection, being in no way hampered by humidity: wherefore it will affect the organ with a spiritual alteration, like the odor of a volatile evaporation. Such will be the sense of smell in the saints, because it will not be hindered by any humidity: and it will take cognizance not only of the excellences of odors, as happens with us now on account of the very great humidity of the brain, but also of the minutest differences of odors.

REPLY OBJ. 4: In heaven there will be vocal praise (though indeed some think otherwise), and in the blessed it will affect the organ of hearing by a merely spiritual alteration. Nor will it be for the sake of learning, whereby they may acquire knowledge, but for the sake of the perfection of the sense and for the sake of pleasure. How it is possible for the voice to give sound there, we have already stated (*Sentences* II, D. 2; Q. 2, A. 2).

REPLY OBJ. 5: The intensity of light does not hinder the spiritual reception of the image of color so long as the pupil retains its diaphanous nature; thus it is evident that however much the air be filled with light, it can be the medium of sight, and the more it is illumined, the more clearly are objects seen through it, unless there be a fault through de-

sus. Quod autem in speculo directe opposito radio solis non appareat species corporis oppositi, non est propter hoc quod impediatur receptio: sed propter hoc quod impeditur reverberatio. Oportet enim ad hoc quod forma in speculo appareat, quod fiat quaedam reverberatio ad aliquod corpus obscurum: et ideo plumbum vitro adiungitur in speculo. Hanc autem obscuritatem radius solis repellit: unde non potest apparere species in aliquo speculo. Claritas autem corporis gloriosi non aufert diaphanitatem a pupilla: quia gloria non tollet naturam. Unde magnitudo claritatis in pupilla magis facit ad acumen visus quam ad eius defectum.

AD SEXTUM dicendum quod, quanto sensus est perfectior, tanto ex minori immutatione facta potest obiectum suum percipere. Quanto autem sub minori angulo visus a visibili immutatur, tanto minor immutatio est: et inde est quod visus perfectior magis a remotis aliquid videre potest quam visus debilior, quia quanto a remotiori videtur, sub minori angulo videtur. Et quia visus corporis gloriosi erit perfectissimus, ex parvissima immutatione poterit videre. Unde sub angulo multo minori videre poterit quam modo possit: et per consequens multo magis a remoto.

fective sight. The fact that the image of an object placed in opposition to a mirror directly opposite the sun's rays does not appear therein is not due to the reception being hindered, but to the hindering of reflection: because for an image to appear in a mirror it must be thrown back by an opaque body, for which reason lead is affixed to the glass in a mirror. The sun's ray dispels this opacity so that no image can appear in the mirror. But the clarity of a glorified body does not destroy the diaphanous nature of the pupil, since glory does not destroy nature; and consequently the greatness of clarity in the pupil renders the sight keen rather than defective.

REPLY OBJ. 6: The more perfect the sense, the less does it require to be altered in order to perceive its object. Now the smaller the angle at which the sight is affected by the visible object, the less is the organ altered. Hence it is that a stronger sight can see from a distance more than a weaker sight; because the greater the distance, the smaller the angle at which a thing is seen. And since the sight of a glorified body will be most perfect it will be able to see by the very least alteration [of the organ]; and consequently at a very much smaller angle than now, and therefore from a much greater distance.

QUESTION 83

Deinde considerandum est de subtilitate corporum beatorum.

Circa quod quaeruntur sex.

Primo: utrum subtilitas sit proprietas corporis gloriosi.

Secundo: utrum ratione huius subtilitatis possit esse in eodem loco cum alio non glorioso.

Tertio: utrum per miraculum duo corpora possint simul esse iri eodem loco.

Quarto: utrum corpus gloriosum possit esse cum alio glorioso in eodem loco.

Quinto: utrum corpus gloriosum necessario requirat aequalem sibi locum.

Sexto: utrum corpus gloriosum sit palpabile.

We must now consider the subtlety of the bodies of the blessed.

Under this head there are six points of inquiry:

(1) Whether subtlety is a property of the glorified body?

(2) Whether by reason of this subtlety it can be in the same place with another non-glorified body?

(3) Whether by a miracle two bodies can be in the same place?

(4) Whether a glorified body can be in the same place with another glorified body?

(5) Whether a glorified body necessarily requires a place equal to itself?

(6) Whether a glorified body is palpable?

Article 1

Whether Subtlety Is a Property of the Glorified Body?

AD PRIMUM SIC PROCEDITUR. Videtur quod subtilitas non sit proprietas corporis gloriosi. Proprietas enim gloriae excedit proprietatem naturae sicut claritas gloriae claritatem solis, quae est maxima in natura. Si ergo subtilitas est proprietas corporis gloriosi, videtur quod corpus sit subtilius futurum omni quod est subtile in natura. Et ita erit *ventis aereque subtilius*: quod est haeresis a Gregorio in Constantinopolitana urbe damnata, ut ipse narrat, in XIV libro *Moralium*.

PRAETEREA, sicut caliditas et frigiditas sunt quaedam qualitates simplicium corporum, scilicet elementorum, ita et subtilitas. Sed calor et aliae qualitates elementorum non intendentur in gloriosis corporibus magis quam nunc: immo magis ad medium reducentur. Ergo neque subtilitas in eis erit maior quam nunc sit.

PRAETEREA, subtilitas invenitur in corporibus propter paucitatem materiae: unde corpora quae habent minus de materia sub aequalibus dimensionibus, dicimus magis subtilia, ut ignem aere, et aerem aqua, et aquam terra. Sed tantum de materia erit in corporibus gloriosis quantum nunc est, nec dimensiones erunt maiores, ut ex supra dictis patet. Ergo non erunt magis subtilia quam modo sunt.

SED CONTRA: Est quod dicitur I Cor. 15, [44]: *seminatur corpus animale, resurget corpus spirituale*, idest

OBJECTION 1: It would seem that subtlety is not a property of the glorified body. For the properties of glory surpass the properties of nature, even as the clarity of glory surpasses the clarity of the sun, which is the greatest in nature. Accordingly, if subtlety be a property of the glorified body, it would seem that the glorified body will be more subtle than anything which is subtle in nature, and thus it will be *more subtle than the wind and the air*. And this heresy was condemned by Gregory in the city of Constantinople, as he relates (*Morals on Job* 14.56).

OBJ. 2: Further, as heat and cold are simple qualities of bodies, i.e., of the elements, so is subtlety. But heat and other qualities of the elements will not be intensified in the glorified bodies any more than they are now; in fact, they will be more reduced to the mean. Neither, therefore, will subtlety be in them more than it is now.

OBJ. 3: Further, subtlety is in bodies as a result of scarcity of matter, wherefore bodies that have less matter within equal dimensions are said to be more subtle; as fire in comparison with air, and air as compared with water, and water as compared with earth. But there will be as much matter in the glorified bodies as there is now, nor will their dimensions be greater. Therefore, they will not be more subtle then than now.

ON THE CONTRARY, It is written: *it is sown a corruptible body, it shall rise a spiritual* (1 Cor 15:44), i.e., a spirit-like,

spiritui simile. Sed subtilitas spiritus excedit omnem subtilitatem corporis. Ergo corpora gloriosa erunt subtilissima.

PRAETEREA, corpora quanto sunt subtiliora, tanto nobiliora. Sed corpora gloriosa sunt nobilissima. Ergo erunt subtilissima.

RESPONDEO dicendum quod nomen subtilitatis a virtute penetrandi est assumptum: unde dicitur in II *de Generatione*, quod subtile est *quod est repletivum partibus et partium partibus*. Quod autem aliquod corpus sit penetrativum, contingit ex duobus. Primo, ex parvitate quantitatis: praecipue secundum profunditatem et latitudinem; non autem secundum longitudinem, quia penetratio fit in profundum, unde longitudo penetrationi non obstat. Secundo, ex paucitate materiae: unde rara subtilia dicimus. Et quia in corporibus raris forma praedominatur materiae magis, ideo translatum est nomen subtilitatis ad illa corpora quae optime substant formae, et perficiuntur ab ea completissimo modo: sicut dicimus subtilitatem esse in sole et luna et aliis huiusmodi; sicut etiam aurum vel aliquid huiusmodi potest dici subtile quando perfectissime completur in esse et virtute suae speciei.

Et quia res incorporeae quantitate carent et materia, nomen subtilitatis ad eas transfertur: non solum ratione suae substantiae; sed etiam ratione suae virtutis. Sicut enim subtile dicitur penetrativum quia pertingit usque ad intima rei, ita etiam dicitur aliquis intellectus subtilis quia pertingit ad inspicienda intrinseca principia et proprietates naturales rei latentes. Et similiter dicitur aliquis habere visum subtilem quia aliquod minimum potest visu pertingere. Et similiter est de aliis sensibus.

Et secundum hoc etiam diversi diversimode subtilitatem corporibus gloriosis attribuerunt. Quidam enim haeretici, ut Augustinus narrat, attribuerunt eis subtilitatem secundum modum quo spirituales substantiae subtiles dicuntur, dicentes quod in resurrectione corpus vertetur in spiritum, et ratione huius corpora resurgentium Apostolus *spiritualia* nominat, I Cor. 15, [44,46].

Sed hoc non potest stare. Primo, quia corpus iri spiritum transire non potest: cum non communicent in materia. Quod etiam Boetius ostendit, in libro *de Duabus Naturis*. Secundo quia, si hoc esset possibile, corpore in spiritum converso, non resurgeret homo, qui ex anima et corpore naturaliter constat. Tertio quia, si Apostolus sic intelligeret, sicut nominat *corpora spiritualia*, pari ratione nominaret *corpora animalia* quae in animam sunt conversa. Quod patet esse falsum.

Unde quidam haeretici dixerunt quod corpus in resurrectione remanebit, sed habebit subtilitatem secundum modum rarefactionis, ita quod corpora humana in

body. But the subtlety of a spirit surpasses all bodily subtlety. Therefore, the glorified bodies will be most subtle.

FURTHER, The more subtle a body, is the more exalted it is. But the glorified bodies will be most exalted. Therefore, they will be most subtle.

I ANSWER THAT, Subtlety takes its name from the power to penetrate. Hence it is said in *On Generation and Corruption* II that *a subtle thing fills all the parts and the parts of parts*. Now that a body has the power of penetrating may happen through two causes. First, through smallness of quantity, especially in respect of depth and breadth, but not of length, because penetration regards depth, wherefore length is not an obstacle to penetration. Second, through paucity of matter, wherefore rarity is synonymous with subtlety: and since in rare bodies the form is more predominant over the matter, the term 'subtlety' has been transferred to those bodies which are most perfectly subject to their form, and are most fully perfected thereby: thus we speak of subtlety in the sun and moon and like bodies, just as gold and similar things may be called subtle when they are most perfectly complete in their specific being and power. And since incorporeal things lack quantity and matter, the term 'subtlety' is applied to them not only by reason of their substance, but also on account of their power.

For just as a subtle thing is said to be penetrative, for the reason that it reaches to the inmost part of a thing, so is an intellect said to be subtle because it reaches to the insight of the intrinsic principles and the hidden natural properties of a thing. In like manner, a person is said to have subtle sight because he is able to perceive by sight things of the smallest size: and the same applies to the other senses. Accordingly, people have differed by ascribing subtlety to the glorified bodies in different ways.

For certain heretics, as Augustine relates (*The City of God* 13.22), ascribed to them the subtlety whereby spiritual substances are said to be subtle: and they said that at the resurrection the body will be transformed into a spirit, and that for this reason the Apostle describes as being *spiritual* the bodies of those who rise again (1 Cor 15:44).

But this cannot be maintained. First, because a body cannot be changed into a spirit, since there is no community of matter between them: and Boethius proves this (*On the Person and the Two Natures*). Second, because, if this were possible, and one's body were changed into a spirit, one would not rise again a man, for a man naturally consists of a soul and body. Third, because if this were the Apostle's meaning, just as he speaks of *spiritual bodies*, so would he speak of *natural* [*animale*] *bodies* as being changed into souls [*animam*]: and this is clearly false.

Hence certain heretics said that the body will remain at the resurrection, but that it will be endowed with subtlety by means of rarefaction, so that human bodies in ris-

resurrectione erunt aeri vel vento similia, ut Gregorius narrat, XVI libro *Moralium*.

Sed hoc etiam non potest stare. Quia Dominus post resurrectionem corpus palpabile habuit, ut patet Luc. [24, 39]: quod praecipue subtile credendum est. Et praeterea, corpus humanum cum carnibus et ossibus resurget, sicut corpus Domini, ut dicitur Luc. [ib.], *spiritus carnem et ossa non habet, sicut me videtis habere*. Et Iob 19, [26] dicitur: *in carne mea videbo Deum, Salvatorem meum*. Natura autem carnis et ossis praedictam raritatem non patitur.

Et ideo est assignandus corporibus gloriosis alius modus subtilitatis, ut dicantur subtilia propter completissimam corporis perfectionem. Sed hanc completionem quidam eis attribuunt ratione quintae essentiae, quae eis tunc maxime dominabitur.

Quod esse non potest. Primo, quia nihil de quinta essentia potest venire in compositionem corporis, ut in II libro ostensum est. Secundo quia, dato quod veniret in compositionem corporis humani, non posset intelligi quod dominaretur magis tunc quam nunc supra naturam elementarem, nisi ita quod esset in corporibus humanis plus secundum quantitatem de natura caelesti; et sic corpora humana non essent eiusdem staturae; nisi forte minueretur natura elementaris iri homine, quod repugnat integritati resurgentium. Vel ita quod natura elementaris indueret proprietates naturae caelestis ex eius dominio in corpore. Et sic naturalis virtus esset causa proprietatis gloriosae. Quod absurdum est.

Et ideo alii dicunt quod dicta completio, ex qua corpora humana subtilia dicuntur, erit ex dominio animae glorificatae, quae est forma corporis, super ipsum, ratione cuius corpus gloriosum spirituale dicitur, quasi omnino spiritui subiectum. Prima autem subiectio qua corpus animae subiicitur, est ad participandum esse specificum, prout subiicitur sibi ut materia formae: et deinde subiicitur ei ad alia opera animae, prout anima est motor. Et ita prima ratio spiritualitatis, in corpore est ex subtilitate; et deinde ex agilitate, et aliis proprietatibus corporis gloriosi. Et propter hoc Apostolus in *spiritualitate* tetigit dotem subtilitatis, ut Magistri exponunt. Unde Gregorius dicit, XIV *Moral.*, quod *corpus gloriosum dicitur subtile per effectum spiritualis potentiae*.

ET PER HOC patet solutio ad obiecta, quae procedunt de subtilitate quae est per rarefactionem.

ing again will be like the air or the wind, as Gregory relates (*Morals on Job* 14.56).

But this again cannot be maintained, because our Lord had a palpable body after the Resurrection, as appears from the last chapter of Luke, and we must believe that his body was supremely subtle. Moreover, the human body will rise again with flesh and bones, as did the body of our Lord, according to Luke 24:39, *a spirit has not flesh and bones as you see me to have*, and Job 19:26, *in my flesh I shall see God, my Savior*: and the nature of flesh and bone is incompatible with the aforesaid rarity.

Consequently, another kind of subtlety must be assigned to glorified bodies by saying that they are subtle on account of the most complete perfection of the body. But this completeness is explained by some in relation to the fifth, or heavenly, essence, which will be then predominant in them.

This, however, is impossible, since first of all the fifth essence can in no way enter into the composition of a body, as we have shown above (*Sentences*, D. 12, Q. 1). Second, because granted that it entered into the composition of the human body, it would be impossible to account for its having a greater predominance over the elemental nature then than now, unless either the amount of the heavenly nature in human bodies were increased (thus human bodies would not be of the same stature, unless perhaps elemental matter in man were decreased, which is inconsistent with the integrity of those who rise again)—or unless elemental nature were endowed with the properties of the heavenly nature through the latter's dominion over the body, and in that case a natural power would be the cause of a property of glory, which seems absurd.

Hence others say that the aforesaid completeness by reason of which human bodies are said to be subtle will result from the dominion of the glorified soul (which is the form of the body) over the body, by reason of which dominion the glorified body is said to be spiritual, as being wholly subject to the spirit. The first subjection whereby the body is subject to the soul is to the effect of its participating in its specific being, insofar as it is subject to the soul as matter to form; and second, it is subject to the soul in respect of the other operations of the soul, insofar as the soul is a principle of movement. Consequently, the first reason for spirituality in the body is subtlety, and after that agility and the other properties of a glorified body. Hence the Apostle, as the masters expound, in speaking of *spirituality* indicates subtlety: wherefore Gregory says (*Morals on Job* 14.56) that *the glorified body is said to be subtle as a result of a spiritual power*.

THIS SUFFICES for the replies to the objections which refer to the subtlety of rarefaction.

Article 2

Whether by Reason of This Subtlety a Glorified Body Is Able to Be in the Same Place With Another Body Not Glorified?

AD SECUNDUM SIC PROCEDITUR. Videtur quod ratione huius subtilitatis competat corpori quod sit simul in eodem loco cum alio corpore non glorioso. Quia, ut dicitur Philipp. 3, [21]: *reformabit corpus humilitatis nostrae, configuratum corpori claritatis suae.* Sed corpus Christi potuit simul esse cum alio corpore in eodem loco: ut patet per hoc quod post resurrectionem intravit ad discipulos *ianuis clausis*, ut dicitur Ioan. 20, [19, 26]. Ergo et corpora gloriosa ratione subtilitatis poterunt esse cum aliis corporibus non gloriosis in eodem loco.

PRAETEREA, corpora gloriosa erunt nobiliora omnibus aliis corporibus. Sed quaedam corpora nunc ratione suae nobilitatis possunt esse simul cum aliis corporibus, scilicet radii solares. Ergo multo fortius hoc conveniet corporibus gloriosis.

PRAETEREA, corpus caeleste non potest dividi, ad minus quantum ad substantiam sphaerarum: unde dicitur Iob 37, [18], quod *caeli velut aere solidissimi firmati sunt.* Si ergo corpus gloriosum non potest simul esse cum alio Corpore in eodem loco ratione subtilitatis, nunquam ad caelum empyreum ascendere poterit. Quod est erroneum.

PRAETEREA, corpus quod non potest simul esse cum alio corpore, potest ex alterius obstaculo impediri in motu suo, vel etiam includi. Sed haec non possunt contingere corporibus gloriosis. Ergo possunt simul esse in eodem loco cum aliis corporibus.

PRAETEREA, sicut se habet punctum ad punctum, ita linea ad lineam, et superficies ad superficiem, et corpus ad corpus. Sed duo puncta possunt esse simul, ut patet quando lineae se tangunt; et similiter duae lineae in contactu duarum superficierum; et duae superficies in contactu duorum corporum: quia contigua sunt *quorum ultima sunt simul*, ut patet VI *Physic.* Ergo non est contra naturam corporis quin possit esse simul cum alio corpore in eodem loco. Sed quidquid nobilitatis natura corporis patitur, totum corpori glorioso praestabitur. Ergo corpus gloriosum ex suae subtilitatis proprietate habebit quod possit esse simul cum alio corpore in eodem loco.

SED CONTRA: Est quod Boetius dicit, in libro *de Trinitate*: *in numero differentiam varietas accidentium facit. Nam tres homines neque genere, neque specie, sed suis accidentibus distant. Nam, si vel animo cuncta ab his accidentia separamus, tamen locus est cunctis diversus, quem unum fingere nullo modo possumus.* Ergo, si ponantur duo corpora esse in uno loco, erunt unum corpus numero.

PRAETEREA, corpora gloriosa maiorem convenientiam habebunt cum loco quam spiritus angelici. Sed spi-

OBJECTION 1: It would seem that by reason of this subtlety a body is able to be in the same place with another body not glorified. For, according to Phil. 3:21, *he will reform the body of our lowness made like to the body of his glory.* Now the body of Christ was able to be in the same place with another body, as appears from the fact that after his Resurrection he went in to his disciples, *the doors being shut* (John 20:19, 26). Therefore, the glorified bodies, by reason of their subtlety, will also be able to be in the same place with other bodies not glorified.

OBJ. 2: Further, glorified bodies will be superior to all other bodies. Yet by reason of their superiority certain bodies, namely, the solar rays, are able now to occupy the same place together with other bodies. Much more, therefore, is this befitting glorified bodies.

OBJ. 3: Further, a heavenly body cannot be severed, at least as regards the substance of the spheres: hence it is written that *the heavens are most strong, as if they were of molten brass* (Job 37:18). If, then, the subtlety of a glorified body will not enable it to be in the same place together with another body, it will never be able to ascend to the empyrean, and this is erroneous.

OBJ. 4: Further, a body which is unable to be in the same place with another body can be hindered in its movement or even surrounded by others standing in its way. But this cannot happen to glorified bodies. Therefore, they will be able to be together in the same place with other bodies.

OBJ. 5: Further, as point is to point, so is line to line, surface to surface, and body to body. Now two points can be coincident, as in the case of two lines touching one another, and two lines when two surfaces are in contact with one another, and two surfaces when two bodies touch one another, because *contiguous things are those whose boundaries coincide* (*Physics* 6.6). Therefore, it is not against the nature of a body to be in the same place together with another body. Now whatever excellence is competent to the nature of a body will all be bestowed on the glorified body. Therefore, a glorified body, by reason of its subtlety, will be able to be in the same place together with another body.

ON THE CONTRARY, Boethius says (*On the Trinity* 1): *difference of accidents makes distinction in number. For three men differ not in genus, nor in species, but in their accidents. If we were to remove absolutely every accident from them, still each one has a different place; and it is quite conceivable that they should all occupy the same place.* Therefore, if we suppose two bodies to occupy the same place, there will be but one body numerically.

FURTHER, Glorified bodies will be more suited to being in a place than angelic spirits are. But angelic spirits, as

ritus angelici, ut quidam dicunt, non possent distingui numero nisi essent in diversis locis: et propter hoc ponunt quod necesse est esse eos in loco, et quod ante mundum creari non potuerunt. Ergo multo magis debent dicere quod duo corpora qualiacumque non possunt esse in eodem loco.

RESPONDEO dicendum quod non potest dici quod corpus gloriosum ratione suae subtilitatis habeat quod possit esse cum alio corpore in eodem loco, nisi per subtilitatem auferatur ab eo id per quod prohibetur nunc esse simul cum alio corpore in eodem loco. Dicunt autem quidam quod prohibetur ab hoc in isto statu ratione corpulentiae, per quam habet quod replet locum. Quae, quidem corpulentia ab eo per subtilitatis dotem tolletur.

Sed hoc non potest stare propter duo. Primo, quia corpulentia: quam dos subtilitatis aufert, est ad defectum pertinens: puta aliqua inordinatio materiae non perfecte substantis suae formae. Totum enim quod ad integritatem corporis pertinet, in corpore resurget, tam ex parte formae quam ex parte materiae. Quod autem aliquod corpus sit repletivum loci, hoc habet per illud quod est de integritate naturae eius, et non ex aliquo defectu naturae. Cum enim plenum opponatur vacuo, illud solum non replet locum, quo posito in loco, nihilominus manet vacuus locus. Vacuum autem definitur, in IV *Physic.*, quod *est locus non plenus sensibili corpore.* Dicitur autem aliquod corpus esse sensibile ex materia et forma et naturalibus accidentibus, quae omnia ad integritatem naturae pertinent. Constat etiam quod corpus gloriosum erit sensibile, etiam secundum tactum, ut patet in corpore Domini, Luc. [24, 39]: nec enim deerit materia aut forma, aut naturalia accidentia, scilicet calidum et frigidum et huiusmodi. Unde patet quod corpus gloriosum, non obstante subtilitatis dote, replebit locum. Insania enim videtur dicere quod locus ubi esset corpus gloriosum, esset vacuus.

Secundo ratio eorum praedicta non valet, quia coexistentiam corporis impedire in eodem loco est in plus quam replere locum. Si enim ponamus dimensiones esse separatas sine materia, illae dimensiones non replent locum. Unde quidam ponentes vacuum dixerunt vacuum esse locum in quo sunt huiusmodi dimensiones sine aliquo sensibili corpore. Et tamen istae dimensiones prohibentur ne sint simul cum alio corpore in eodem loco: ut patet per Philosophum, in IV *Physic.* et in III *Metaphys.*, ubi habet pro inconvenienti quod corpus mathematicum, quod nihil est aliud quam dimensiones separatae, sit simul cum alio corpore naturali sensibili. Unde, dato quod subtilitas gloriosi corporis auferret ab eo hoc quod est replere locum, non tamen sequitur quod propter hoc posset esse cum alio corpore in eodem loco: quia, remoto eo quod in minus est, non propter hoc removetur quod in plus est.

some people say, could not be distinguished in number unless they were in different places. And because of this they hold that it is necessary for them to be in a place, and that they could not have been created before the world. Therefore, much more should they say that two bodies, no matter how they exist, cannot be together in the same place.

I ANSWER THAT, It cannot be maintained that a glorified body, by reason of its subtlety, is able to be in the same place with another body, unless the obstacle to its being now in the same place with another body be removed by that subtlety. Some say that in the present state this obstacle is its grossness, by virtue of which it is able to occupy a place; and that this grossness is removed by the gift of subtlety.

But there are two reasons why this cannot be maintained. First, because the grossness which the gift of subtlety removes is a kind of defect, for instance, an inordinateness of matter in not being perfectly subject to its form. For all that pertains to the integrity of the body will rise again in the body, both as regards the matter and as regards the form. And the fact that a body is able to fill a place belongs to it by reason of that which pertains to its integrity, and not on account of any defect of nature. For since fullness is opposed to vacancy, that alone does not fill a place which, being put in a place, nevertheless leaves a place vacant. Now a vacuum is defined by the Philosopher (*Physics* 4.6, 7) as being *a place not filled by a sensible body.* And a body is said to be sensible by reason of its matter, form, and natural accidents, all of which pertain to the integrity of nature. It is also plain that the glorified body will be sensible even to touch, as evidenced by the body of our Lord (Luke 24:39): nor will it lack matter, or form, or natural accidents, namely, heat, cold, and so forth. Hence it is evident that the glorified body, the gift of subtlety notwithstanding, will fill a place: for it would seem madness to say that the place in which there will be a glorified body will be empty.

Second, their aforesaid argument does not avail, because to hinder the coexistence of a body in the same place is more than to fill a place. For if we suppose dimensions separate from matter, those dimensions do not fill a place. Hence some who held the possibility of a vacuum said that a vacuum is a place wherein such dimensions exist apart from a sensible body; and yet those dimensions hinder another body from being together with them in the same place. This is made clear by the Philosopher (*Physics* 4.1, 4.8; *Metaphysics* 2.2), where he considers it impossible for a mathematical body, which is nothing but separate dimensions, to be together with another natural sensible body. Consequently, granted that the subtlety of a glorified body hindered it from filling a place, nevertheless it would not follow that for this reason it is able to be in the same place with another body, since the removal of the lesser does not involve the removal of the greater.

Ergo videtur quod illud quod impedit corpus nostrum nunc ne simul cum alio corpore sit in eodem loco, nullo modo poterit ab eo removeri per dotem subtilitatis. Nihil enim potest prohibere corpus aliquod ne sit simul situatum cum alio corpore in eodem loco, nisi hoc quod in eo requirit diversum situm: nihil enim est impedimentum identitati nisi quod est causa diversitatis. Hanc autem distinctionem situs non requirit aliqua corporis qualitas: quia corpori non debetur aliquis situs ratione suae qualitatis. Unde, remoto a corpore sensibili quod sit calidum aut frigidum, aut grave aut leve, nihilominus in eo remanet necessitas praedictae distinctionis: ut patet per Philosophum, in IV *Physic.*; et etiam per se planum est.

Similiter etiam materia non potest inducere necessitatem praedictae distinctionis: quia materiae non advenit situs nisi mediante quantitate dimensiva. Similiter etiam neque forma situm habet nisi ex materia situm habente. Restat ergo quod necessitas distinctionis duorum corporum in situ causatur a natura quantitatis dimensivae, cui per se convenit situs: cadit enim in. definitione eius, quia quantitas dimensiva est quantitas habens situm. Et inde est quod, remotis omnibus aliis quae sunt in re, distinctionis necessitas invenitur in sola quantitate dimensiva. Si enim accipiatur linea separata, oportet quod, si sint duae lineae vel duae partes unius lineae, quod sint distinctae in situ: alias linea addita lineae non efficeret maius, quod est contra communem animi conceptionem. Et similiter est de superficiebus et corporibus mathematicis. Et quia materiae debetur situs inquantum substat dimensionibus, exinde praedicta necessitas ad materiam situatam derivatur: ut, sicut non est possibile esse duas lineas vel duas partes lineae nisi sint distinctae secundum situm, ita impossibile est esse duas materias vel duas partes materiae nisi sit distinctio situs. Et quia distinctio materiae est principium distinctionis individuorum, inde est quod Boetius dicit, in libro *de Trinitate*, quod *duobus corporibus unum locum fingere nullo modo possumus*, ut hanc saltem accidentium varietatem distinctio individuorum requirat.

Subtilitas autem a corpore glorioso dimensionem non aufert. Unde nullo modo aufert sibi praedictam necessitatem distinctionis situs ab alio corpore. Et ideo corpus gloriosum non habebit ratione suae subtilitatis quod possit esse cum alio corpore. Sed poterit simul cum alio corpore esse ex operatione virtutis divinae. Sicut etiam corpus Petri non habuit ex aliqua proprietate indita quod ad adventionem eius sanarentur infirmi: sed hoc fiebat virtute divina ad aedificationem fidei. Ita faciet virtus divina ut corpus gloriosum possit simul cum alio corpore esse ad perfectionem gloriae.

Accordingly, we must say that the obstacle to our body's being now in the same place with another body can in no way be removed by the gift of subtlety. For nothing can prevent a body from occupying the same place together with another body, except something in it that requires a different place: since nothing is an obstacle to identity save that which is a cause of distinction. Now this distinction of place is not required by any quality of the body, because a body demands a place, not by reason of its quality: wherefore if we remove from a body the fact of its being hot or cold, heavy or light, it still retains the necessity of the aforesaid distinction, as the Philosopher proves (*Physics* 4), and as is self-evident.

In like manner, neither can matter cause the necessity of the aforesaid distinction, because matter does not occupy a place except through its dimensive quantity. Similarly, neither does form occupy a place, unless it have a place through its matter. It remains, therefore, that the necessity for two bodies occupying each a distinct place results from the nature of dimensive quantity, to which a place is essentially befitting. For this forms part of its definition, since dimensive quantity is quantity occupying a place. Hence it is that if we remove all else in a thing from it, the necessity of this distinction is found in its dimensive quantity alone. If the example of a separate line is taken, supposing there to be two such lines, or two parts of one line, they must occupy distinct places, else one line added to another would not make something greater, and this is against common sense. The same applies to surfaces and mathematical bodies. And since matter demands place through being the subject of dimension, the aforesaid necessity results in placed matter, so that just as it is impossible for there to be two lines, or two parts of a line, unless they occupy distinct places, so is it impossible for there to be two matters, or two parts of matter, without there be distinction of place. And since distinction of matter is the principle of the distinction between individuals, it follows that, as Boethius says (*On the Trinity*), *we cannot possibly conceive two bodies occupying one place*, so that this distinction of individuals requires this difference of accidents.

Now subtlety does not deprive the glorified body of its dimension; wherefore it in no way removes from it the aforesaid necessity of occupying a distinct place from another body. Therefore, the subtlety of a glorified body will not enable it to be in the same place together with another body, but it will be possible for it to be together with another body by the operation of the divine power: even as the body of Peter had the power whereby the sick were healed at the passing of Peter's shadow (Acts 5:15) not through any inherent property, but by the power of God for the upbuilding of the faith. Thus will the divine power make it possible for a glorified body to be in the same place together with another body for the perfection of glory.

Ad primum ergo dicendum quod corpus Christi non habuit ex subtilitatis dote quod possit esse simul cum alio corpore in eodem loco: sed hoc factum est virtute divina post resurrectionem, sicut in nativitate. Unde Gregorius, in Homilia, dicit: *illud corpus Domini intravit ad discipulos ianuis clausis quod ad humanos oculos per nativitatem suam clauso exiit utero Virginis.* Unde non oportet quod ratione subtilitatis hoc conveniat corporibus gloriosis.

Ad secundum dicendum quod lumen non est corpus: ut in Prima Parte dictum est. Unde obiectio procedit ex falsis.

Ad tertium dicendum quod corpus gloriosum transibit sphaeras caelorum sine eorum divisione, non ex vi subtilitatis, sed ex divina virtute, quae eis ad nutum in omnibus subveniet.

Ad quartum dicendum quod ex hoc quod Deus eis ad nutum aderit in omnibus quae volunt, sequitur quod non possint includi vel carcerari.

Ad quintum dicendum quod, sicut dicitur in IV *Physic.*, *puncti non convenit esse locum.* Unde, si dicatur esse in loco, hoc non est nisi per accidens, quia corpus cuius est terminus est in loco. Sicut autem totus locus respondet toti corpori, ita terminus loci respondet termino corporis. Contingit autem duorum locorum esse unum terminum: sicut et duas lineas terminari ad unum punctum. Et ideo, quamvis duo corpora non possunt esse nisi in diversis locis, tamen duobus terminis duorum corporum respondet idem terminus duorum locorum. Et secundum hoc dicuntur ultima corporum se contingentium esse simul.

Reply Obj. 1: That Christ's body was able to be together with another body in the same place was not due to its subtlety, but resulted from the power of his divinity after his resurrection, even as in his birth. Hence Gregory says (*Homilies on the Gospels* 26): *the same body went into his disciples when the doors were closed which to human eyes came from the closed womb of the Virgin at his birth.* Therefore, there is no reason why this should be befitting to glorified bodies on account of their subtlety.

Reply Obj. 2: Light is not a body, as we have said above (*Sentences* II, Q. 13, A. 3; I, Q. 67, A. 2): hence the objection proceeds on a false supposition.

Reply Obj. 3: The glorified body will pass through the heavenly spheres without severing them, not by virtue of its subtlety, but by the divine power, which will assist them in all things at will.

Reply Obj. 4: From the fact that God will come to the aid of the blessed at will in whatever they desire, it follows that they cannot be surrounded or imprisoned.

Reply Obj. 5: As stated in *Physics* 4.5, *a point is not in a place*: hence if it be said to be in a place, this is only accidental, because the body of which it is a term is in a place. And just as the whole place corresponds to the whole body, so the term of the place corresponds to the term of the body. But it happens that two places have one term, even as two lines terminate in one point. And consequently though two bodies must be in distinct places, yet the same term of two places corresponds to the two terms of the two bodies. It is in this sense that the bounds of contiguous bodies are said to coincide.

Article 3

Whether It Is Possible, by a Miracle, for Two Bodies to Be in the Same Place?

Ad tertium sic proceditur. Videtur quod nec etiam per miraculum fieri possit quod duo corpora sint in eodem loco. Non enim potest fieri, per miraculum quod duo corpora sint simul duo et unum: quia hoc esset facere contradictoria esse simul. Sed, si ponantur duo corpora esse simul, sequeretur illa duo corpora esse unum. Ergo non est possibile hoc per miraculum fieri.

Probatio mediae. Sint duo corpora in eodem loco, quorum unum dicatur A et aliud B. Aut ergo dimensiones A erunt eaedem cum dimensionibus loci, aut aliae. Si aliae, ergo erunt aliquae dimensiones separatae. Quod non potest poni: quia dimensiones quae sunt inter terminos loci, non sunt in aliquo subiecto nisi sint in corpore locato. Si autem sunt eaedem, ergo eadem ratione dimensiones B erunt eaedem cum dimensionibus loci. Sed *quaecumque uni et eidem sunt eadem, sibi invicem sunt*

Objection 1: It would seem that not even by a miracle is it possible for two bodies to be in the same place. For it is not possible that, by a miracle, two bodies should be at once two and one, since this would imply that contradictions are true at the same time. But if we suppose two bodies to be in the same place, it would follow that those two bodies are one. Therefore, this cannot be done by a miracle.

The minor is proved thus. Suppose two bodies A and B to be in the same place. The dimensions of A will either be the same as the dimensions of the place, or they will differ from them. If they differ, then some of the dimensions will be separate: which is impossible, since the dimensions that are within the bounds of a place are not in a subject unless they be in a placed body. If they be the same, then for the same reason the dimensions of B will be the same as the dimensions of the place. Now *things that are the same with one*

173

eadem. Ergo dimensiones A et B sunt eaedem. Sed duorum corporum non possunt esse eaedem dimensiones: sicut ne eadem albedo. Ergo A et B sunt unum corpus. Et erant duo. Ergo sunt simul unum et duo.

Praeterea, contra *communes animi conceptiones* non potest aliquid miraculose fieri, ut scilicet pars non sit minor toto: quia contraria communibus conceptionibus directe contradictionem includunt. Similiter nec conclusiones geometricae, quae a communibus conceptionibus infallibiliter deducuntur: sicut quod triangulus non habeat, tres angulos aequales duobus rectis. Similiter nec aliquid potest fieri in linea contra definitionem lineae: quia separare definitionem a definito est ponere duo contradictoria esse simul. Sed duo corpora esse in eodem loco est contra conclusiones geometriae, et contra definitionem lineae. Ergo non potest fieri per miraculum.

Probatio mediae. Conclusio est geometriae quod duo circuli non se tangunt nisi in puncto. Si autem duo corpora circularia essent in eodem, duo circuli designati in eis se tangerent secundum totum. Similiter etiam est contra definitionem lineae quod infra: duo puncta sit plus quam una linea recta. Quod contingeret si duo corpora essent in eodem loco: quia infra duo puncta signata in diversis superficiebus loci essent duae lineae rectae duorum corporum locatorum.

Praeterea, hoc non videtur posse fieri per miraculum, quod corpus inclusum in alio corpore non sit, in loco; quia sic haberet locum communem et non proprium, quod non potest esse. Sed hoc sequeretur si duo corpora essent in eodem loco. Ergo non potest fieri per miraculum.

Probatio mediae. Sint duo corpora in eodem loco quorum unum secundum quamlibet dimensionem sit maius alio. Corpus minus erit inclusum in corpore maiore, et locus corporis maioris erit locus eius communis: locum autem proprium non habebit. Quia non erit aliqua superficies corporis actu signata quae contineat ipsum: quod est de ratione loci. Ergo non habebit locum proprium.

Praeterea, locus proportionaliter respondet locato. Sed nunquam potest fieri per miraculum quod idem corpus sit simul in diversis locis, nisi per aliquam conversionem, sicut accidit in Sacramento Altaris. Ergo nullo modo potest fieri per miraculum quod duo corpora sint simul in eodem loco.

Sed contra: Est quod Beata Virgo Filium suum miraculose peperit. Sed in illo partu oportuit duo corpora esse simul in eodem loco: quia corpus pueri exiens *clau-*

and the same thing are the same with one another. Therefore, the dimensions of A and B are the same. But two bodies cannot have identical dimensions, just as they cannot have the same whiteness. Therefore, A and B are one body. But they were two. Therefore, they are at the same time one and two.

Obj. 2: Further, a thing cannot be done miraculously either against *the common principles*—for instance, that the part be not less than the whole; since what is contrary to common principles implies a direct contradiction—or contrary to the conclusions of geometry, which are infallible deductions from common principles—for instance, that the three angles of a triangle should not be equal to two right angles. In like manner, nothing can be done to a line that is contrary to the definition of a line, because to sever the definition from the defined is to make two contradictories true at the same time. Now it is contrary to common principles, both to the conclusions of geometry and to the definition of a line, for two bodies to be in the same place. Therefore, this cannot be done by a miracle.

The minor is proved as follows: It is a conclusion of geometry that two circles touch one another only at a point. Now if two circular bodies were in the same place, the two circles described in them would touch one another as a whole. Similarly, it is contrary to the definition of a line that there be more than one straight line between two points: yet this would be the case were two bodies in the same place, since between two given points in the various surfaces of the place, there would be two straight lines corresponding to the two bodies in that place.

Obj. 3: Further, it would seem impossible that by a miracle a body which is enclosed within another should not be in a place, for then it would have a common and not a proper place, and this is impossible. Yet this would follow if two bodies were in the same place. Therefore, this cannot be done by a miracle.

The minor is proved thus. Supposing two bodies to be in the same place, the one being greater than the other as to every dimension, the lesser body will be enclosed in the greater, and the place occupied by the greater body will be its common place; while it will have no proper place, because no given surface of the body will contain it, and this is essential to place. Therefore, it will not have a proper place.

Obj. 4: Further, place corresponds in proportion to the thing placed. Now it can never happen by a miracle that the same body is at the same time in different places, except by some kind of transformation, as in the Sacrament of the Altar. Therefore, it can in no way happen by a miracle that two bodies be together in the same place.

On the contrary, The Blessed Virgin gave birth to her Son by a miracle. Now in this birth it was necessary for two bodies to be together in the same place, because the

stra pudoris non fregit. Ergo potest miraculose fieri quod duo corpora sint in eodem loco.

PRAETEREA, hoc idem potest ostendi per hoc quod Dominus ad discipulos intravit *clausis ianuis*, Ioan. 20, [19, 26].

RESPONDEO dicendum quod, sicut ex dictis patet, propter hoc necesse est duo corpora in duobus locis esse, quia diversitas materiae requirit distinctionem in situ. Et ideo videmus quod, quando conveniunt duo corpora in unum, destruitur esse distinctum utriusque, et acquiritur utrique simul unum esse distinctum: ut patet in mixtionibus. Non potest ergo esse quod duo corpora remaneant duo et tamen sint simul, nisi utrique conservetur esse distinctum quod prius habebat, secundum quod utrumque erat *ens indivisum in se et divisum ab aliis*. Hoc autem esse distinctum dependet a principiis essentialibus rei sicut a causis proximis, sed a Deo sicut a causa prima. Et quia causa prima potest conservare rem in esse cessantibus causis secundis, ut patet per primam propositionem Libri *de Causis* 2, ergo divina virtute, et ea sola, fieri potest ut accidens sit sine subiecto, ut patet in Sacramento Altaris. Et similiter virtute divina fieri potest, et ea sola, quod corpori remaneat esse distinctum ab alio corpore, quamvis eius materia non sit distincta in situ ab alterius corporis materia. Et sic miraculose fieri potest quod duo corpora sint in eodem loco.

AD PRIMUM ergo dicendum quod ratio illa est sophistica: quia procedit ex suppositione falsi; vel petit principium. Procedit enim ratio illa ac si inter superficies oppositas loci alicuius esset aliqua dimensio propria loco, cui oporteret quod uniretur dimensio corporis locati advenientis. Sic enim sequeretur quod dimensiones duorum corporum locatorum fierent una dimensio, si utraque unum fieret cum dimensione loci. Haec autem positio falsa est: quia secundum hoc, quandocumque corpus acquireret novum locum, oporteret aliquam immutationem fieri in dimensionibus loci vel locati; non enim potest esse quod aliqua duo fiant de novo unum nisi altero eorum immutato. Si autem, ut se rei veritas habet, loco non debentur aliae dimensiones quam dimensiones locati, patet quod ratio nihil probat.

Sed petit principium, quia secundum hoc nihil est aliud dictum quod dimensiones locati sunt eaedem cum dimensionibus loci, nisi quod dimensiones locati continentur infra terminos loci, et secundum eorum mensuram distant termini sicut distarent propriis dimensionibus si eas haberent. Et sic dimensiones duorum corporum esse dimensiones unius loci, nihil est aliud

body of her child when coming forth did not break through *the enclosure of her virginal purity*. Therefore, it is possible for two bodies to be miraculously together in the same place.

FURTHER, This may again be proved from the fact that our Lord went in to his disciples, *the doors being shut* (John 20:19).

I ANSWER THAT, As shown above (A. 2) the reason why two bodies must be in two places is that distinction in matter requires distinction in place. Wherefore we observe that when two bodies merge into one, each loses its distinct being, and one indistinct being accrues to the two combined, as in the case of mixtures. Hence it is impossible for two bodies to remain two and yet be together unless each retain its distinct being which it had hitherto, in so much as each of them was a *being undivided in itself and distinct from others*. Now this distinct being depends on the essential principles of a thing as on its proximate causes, but on God as on the first cause. And since the first cause can preserve a thing in being, though the second causes be done away with, as appears from the first proposition of *On Causes*, therefore by God's power and by that alone it is possible for an accident to be without substance as in the Sacrament of the Altar. Likewise, by the power of God, and by that alone, it is possible for a body to retain its distinct being from that of another body, although its matter be not distinct as to place from the matter of the other body: and thus it is possible by a miracle for two bodies to be together in the same place.

REPLY OBJ. 1: This argument is sophistical because it is based on a false supposition, or begs the question. For it supposes the existence of a dimension proper to the place between two opposite superficies of a place, with which dimension a dimension of the body put in occupation of the place would have to be identified: because it would then follow that the dimensions of two bodies occupying a place would become one dimension, if each of them were identified with the dimension of the place. But this supposition is false, because if it were true, then whenever a body acquires a new place it would follow that a change occurs in the dimensions of the place or of thing placed: since it is impossible for two things to become one anew, except one of them be changed. Whereas if, as is the case in truth, no other dimensions belong to a place than those of the thing occupying the place, it is clear that the argument proves nothing.

But it begs the question, because according to this nothing else has been said but that the dimensions of a thing placed are the same as the dimensions of the place; excepting that the dimensions of the thing placed are contained within the bounds of the place, and that the distance between the bounds of a place is commensurate with the distance between the bounds of the thing placed, just as the

quam duo corpora esse in eodem loco. Quod est principale propositum.

AD SECUNDUM dicendum quod, posito quod duo corpora sint simul in eodem loco per miraculum, non sequitur aliquid neque contra communes animi conceptiones, neque contra definitionem lineae, neque contra conclusiones aliquas geometriae. Sicut enim supra dictum est, quantitas dimensiva in hoc differt ab omnibus aliis accidentibus quod habet specialem rationem individuationis et distinctionis, scilicet ex situ partium, praeter rationem individuationis et distinctionis quae est sibi et omnibus accidentibus communis, scilicet ex materia subiecta. Sic ergo una linea potest intelligi diversa ab alia vel quia est in alio subiecto, quae consideratio non est nisi de linea materiali; vel quia distat in situ ab alia, quae consideratio est etiam de linea mathematica, quae intelligitur praeter materiam.

Si ergo removeatur materia, non potest esse distinctio linearum nisi secundum situm diversum; et similiter nec punctorum nec superficierum, aut quarumcumque dimensionum. Et sic geometria non potest ponere quod una linea addatur alii tanquam distincta ab ea, nisi sit diversa in situ ab ea. Sed, supposita distinctione subiecti sine distinctione situs ex divino miraculo, intelliguntur diversae lineae quae non distant situ, propter diversitatem subiecti; et similiter puncta diversa. Et sic duae lineae designatae in duobus corporibus quae sunt in eodem loco, trahuntur a diversis punctis ad diversa puncta: ut non accipiamus punctum in loco, sed in ipso corpore locato; quia linea non dicitur trahi nisi a puncto quod est terminus eius. Et similiter etiam duo circuli designati in duobus corporibus sphaericis existentibus in eodem loco, quae sunt duo non propter diversitatem situs, alias non possent se tangere secundum totum, sed sunt duo ex diversitate subiectorum, et propter hoc se totaliter tangentes, adhuc manent duo. Sicut etiam circulus signatus in corpore locato sphaerico, tangit secundum totum: alium circulum signatum in corpore locante.

AD TERTIUM dicendum quod Deus posset facere aliquod corpus non esse in loco. Et tamen, illa positione facta, non sequitur quod aliud corpus non sit in loco: quia corpus maius est locus corporis minoris ratione illius superficiei quae designaretur: ex contactu terminorum corporis minoris.

AD QUARTUM dicendum quod unum corpus esse simul localiter in duobus locis non potest fieri per miraculum, corpus enim Christi non est in altari localiter: quamvis miraculose possit fieri quod duo corpora sint in eodem loco. Quia esse in pluribus locis simul repu-

former would be distant by their own dimensions if they had them. Thus that the dimensions of two bodies be the dimensions of one place is nothing else than that two bodies be in the same place, which is the chief question at issue.

REPLY OBJ. 2: Granted that by a miracle two bodies be together in the same place, nothing follows either against common principles, or against the definition of a line, or against any conclusions of geometry. For, as stated above (A. 2), dimensive quantity differs from all other accidents in that it has a special reason of individuality and distinction (namely, on account of the placing of the parts), besides the reason of individuality and distinction which is common to it and all other accidents, arising, that is, from the matter which is its subject. Thus, then, one line may be understood as being distinct from another, either because it is in another subject (in which case we are considering a material line), or because it is placed at a distance from another (in which case we are considering a mathematical line, which is understood apart from matter).

Accordingly, if we remove matter, there can be no distinction between lines save in respect of a different placing: and in like manner neither can there be a distinction of points, nor of superficies, nor of any dimensions whatever. Consequently, geometry cannot suppose one line to be added to another as being distinct therefrom unless it be distinct as to place. But supposing by a divine miracle a distinction of subject without a distinction of place, we can understand a distinction of lines; and these are not distant from one another in place, on account of the distinction of subjects. Again, we can understand a difference of points, and thus different lines described on two bodies that are in the same place are drawn from different points to different points; for the point that we take is not a point fixed in the place, but in the placed body, because a line is not said to be drawn otherwise than from a point which is its term. In like manner, the two circles described in two spherical bodies that occupy the same place are two, not on account of the difference of place, else they could not touch one another as a whole, but on account of the distinction of subjects, and thus while wholly touching one another they still remain two. Even so a circle described by a placed spherical body touches, as a whole, the other circle described by the locating body.

REPLY OBJ. 3: God could make a body not to be in a place; and yet supposing this, it would not follow that a certain body is not in a place, because the greater body is the place of the lesser body by reason of its superficies, which is described by contact with the terms of the lesser body.

REPLY OBJ. 4: It is impossible for one body to be miraculously in two places locally (for Christ's body is not locally on the altar), although it is possible by a miracle for two bodies to be in the same place. Because to be in several places at once is incompatible with the individual, by rea-

gnat individuo ratione eius quod est esse *indivisum in se*: sequeretur enim quod esset distinctum in situ. Sed esse cum alio corpore in eodem loco repugnat ei quantum ad hoc quod est esse *divisum ab alio*. Ratio autem unius perficitur in indivisione, ut patet in IV *Metaphys.*; sed divisio ab aliis est de consequentibus ad rationem unius. Unde quod idem corpus sit localiter simul in diversis locis, includit contradictionem, sicut quod homo careat ratione. Sed duo corpora esse in eodem loco non includit contradictionem, ut ex dictis patet. Et ideo non est simile.

son of its having being *undivided in itself*, for it would follow that it is divided as to place. On the other hand, to be in the same place with another body is incompatible with the individual as *distinct from others*. Now the nature of unity is perfected in indivision (*Metaphysics* 5), whereas distinction from others is a result of the nature of unity. Therefore, that one same body be locally in several places at once implies a contradiction, even as for a man to lack reason, while for two bodies to be in the same place does not imply a contradiction, as explained above. Hence the comparison fails.

Article 4

Whether One Glorified Body Can Be in the Same Place Together With Another Glorified Body?

AD QUARTUM SIC PROCEDITUR. Videtur quod corpus gloriosum possit esse cum alio glorioso in eodem loco. Quia ubi est maior subtilitas, ibi est minor resistentia. Si ergo corpus gloriosum est subtilius quam non gloriosum, minus resistet corpori glorioso. Et ita, si corpus gloriosum poterit esse cum corpore non glorioso in eodem loco, multo fortius cum corpore glorioso.

PRAETEREA, sicut corpus gloriosum est subtilius non glorioso, ita unum gloriosum erit subtilius alio. Si ergo corpus gloriosum poterit esse simul cum non glorioso, et corpus gloriosum magis subtile poterit esse cum glorioso minus subtili.

PRAETEREA, corpus caeli est subtile, et erit tunc glorificatum. Sed corpus alicuius sancti poterit simul esse cum corpore caeli: quia poterunt ad terram descendere et ascendere pro suae libito voluntatis. Ergo duo corpora subtilia vel gloriosa poterunt esse simul.

SED CONTRA: Corpora gloriosa erunt *spiritualia*, idest, spiritibus quantum ad aliquid similia. Sed duo spiritus non possunt esse simul in eodem loco, quamvis spiritus et corpus possint esse in eodem loco: ut in I libro dictum est. Ergo nec duo corpora gloriosa poterunt esse in eodem loco.

PRAETEREA, duorum corporum, simul existentium unum ab alio penetratur. Sed penetrari ab alio corpore est ignobilitatis, quae omnino a corporibus gloriosis aberit. Ergo non poterunt esse duo corpora gloriosa simul.

RESPONDEO dicendum quod corpus gloriosum ratione suae proprietatis non habet quod possit esse cum alio corpore glorioso in eodem loco, sicut nec ut sit simul cum corpore non glorioso. Divina autem virtute fieri posset ut duo corpora gloriosa essent, simul, vel duo non gloriosa, sicut gloriosum et non gloriosum.

OBJECTION 1: It would seem that a glorified body can be in the same place together with another glorified body. For where there is greater subtlety, there is less resistance. If, then, a glorified body is more subtle than a non-glorified body, it will offer less resistance to a glorified body: and so if a glorified body can be in the same place with a non-glorified body, much more can it with a glorified body.

OBJ. 2: Further, even as a glorified body will be more subtle than a non-glorified body, so will one glorified body be more subtle than another. Therefore, if a glorified body can be in the same place with a non-glorified body, a more subtle glorified body can be in the same place with a less subtle glorified body.

OBJ. 3: Further, the body of heaven is subtle, and will then be glorified. Now the glorified body of a saint will be able to be in the same place with the body of heaven, since the saints will be able at will to travel to and from earth. Therefore, two glorified bodies will be able to occupy the same place.

ON THE CONTRARY, The glorified bodies will be *spiritual*, that is, like spirits in a certain respect. Now two spirits cannot be in the same place, although a body and a spirit can be in the same place, as stated above (*Sentences* I, D. 37, Q. 3, A. 3; I, Q. 52, A. 3). Therefore, neither will two glorified bodies be able to be in the same place.

FURTHER, If two bodies occupy the same place, one is penetrated by the other. But to be penetrated is a mark of imperfection, which will be altogether absent from the glorified bodies. Therefore, it will be impossible for two glorified bodies to be in the same place.

I ANSWER THAT, The property of a glorified body does not make it able to be in the same place with another glorified body, nor again to be in the same place with a non-glorified body. But it would be possible by the divine power for two glorified bodies or two non-glorified bodies to be in the same place, even as a glorified body with a non-glorified body.

Sed tamen non est conveniens quod corpus gloriosum sit simul cum alio corpore glorioso; Tum quia in eis servabitur debitus ordo, qui distinctionem requirit. Tum quia unum corpus gloriosum non se opponet alteri. Et sic nunquam duo corpora gloriosa erunt simul.

AD PRIMUM ergo dicendum quod ratio illa procedit ac si corpori glorioso inesset ratione suae subtilitatis quod posset esse simul in eodem loco cum alio corpore. Quod falsum est.

ET SIMILITER dicendum ad secundum.

AD TERTIUM dicendum quod corpus caeli et alia corpora aequivoce dicentur gloriosa, inquantum participabunt aliquid gloriae: et non quod eis conveniant dotes corporum humanorum glorificatorum.

Nevertheless, it is not befitting for a glorified body to be in the same place with another glorified body, both because a becoming order will be observed in them, which demands distinction, and because one glorified body will not be in the way of another. Consequently, two glorified bodies will never be in the same place.

REPLY OBJ. 1: This argument supposes that a glorified body is able by reason of its subtlety to be in the same place with another body: and this is not true.

THE SAME ANSWER applies to the second objection.

REPLY OBJ. 3: The body of heaven and the other bodies will be said equivocally to be glorified insofar as they will have a certain share in glory, and not as though it were becoming for them to have the gifts of glorified human bodies.

Article 5

Whether by Virtue of Its Subtlety a Glorified Body Will No Longer Need to Be in an Equal Place?

AD QUINTUM SIC PROCEDITUR. Videtur quod ex sua subtilitate removeatur a corpore glorificato necessitas existendi in aequali loco. Corpora enim gloriosa erunt conformia corpori Christi: ut patet Philipp. 3, [21]. Sed corpus Christi non coarctatur hac necessitate ut sit in loco aequali: immo continetur totum sub parvis vel magnis dimensionibus hostiae consecratae. Ergo et hoc idem erit in corporibus gloriosis.

PRAETEREA, Philosophus probat, in IV *Physic.*, quod, si duo corpora sunt in eodem loco, sequetur, quod maximum corpus obtineat minimum locum: quia diversae partes eius poterunt esse in eadem parte loci; non enim differt utrum duo corpora vel quotcumque sint in eodem loco. Sed corpus gloriosum erit simul in eodem loco cum alio corpore, ut dicitur communiter. Ergo poterit esse in quovis parvo loco.

PRAETEREA, sicut corpus ratione sui coloris videtur, ita commensuratur loco ratione suae quantitatis. Sed corpus gloriosum ita subiectum erit spiritui quod poterit videri et non videri, et praecipue ab oculo non glorioso, pro suae libito voluntatis: ut in Christo patuit. Ergo ita quantitas subiicietur nutui spiritus quod poterit esse in parvo vel in magno loco, et habere parvam vel magnam quantitatem, ad libitum.

SED CONTRA: Est quod Philosophus dicit, in IV *Physic.*, quod *omne quod est in loco, est in loco aequali sibi.* Sed corpus gloriosum erit in loco. Ergo erit in loco aequali sibi.

PRAETEREA, eaedem sunt dimensiones loci et locati, ut probatur in IV *Physic.* Ergo, si locus esset maior loca-

OBJECTION 1: It would seem that by virtue of its subtlety, a glorified body will no longer need to be in an equal place. For the glorified bodies will be made like to the body of Christ, according to Philippians 3:21. Now Christ's body is not bound by this necessity of being in an equal place: wherefore it is contained whole under the small or great dimensions of a consecrated host. Therefore, the same will be true of the glorified bodies.

OBJ. 2: Further, the Philosopher proves (*Physics* 4.6), that two bodies are not in the same place, because it would follow that the greatest body would occupy the smallest place, since its various parts could be in the same part of the place: for it makes no difference whether two bodies or however many be in the same place. Now a glorified body will be in the same place with another body, as is commonly admitted. Therefore, it will be possible for it to be in any place, however small.

OBJ. 3: Further, even as a body is seen by reason of its color, so is it measured by reason of its quantity. Now the glorified body will be so subject to the spirit that it will be able at will to be seen and not seen, especially by a non-glorified eye, as evidenced in the case of Christ. Therefore, its quantity will be so subject to the spirit's will that it will be able to be in a little or great place, and to have a little or great quantity at will.

ON THE CONTRARY, The Philosopher says (*Physics* iv, text. 30) that *whatever is in a place occupies a place equal to itself.* Now the glorified body will be in a place. Therefore, it will occupy a place equal to itself.

FURTHER, The dimensions of a place and of that which is in that place are the same, as shown in *Physics* IV. There-

to, esset idem maius et minus seipso. Quod est inconveniens.

RESPONDEO dicendum quod corpus non comparatur ad locum nisi mediantibus dimensionibus propriis, secundum quas corpus locatum circumscribitur ex contactu corporis locantis. Unde quod corpus aliquod sit in minori loco quam sit sua quantitas, hoc non potest esse nisi per hoc quod quantitas corporis propria efficitur aliquo modo minor seipsa.

Quod quidem non potest intelligi nisi dupliciter. Uno modo, ex variatione quantitatis circa eandem materiam: ut scilicet materia quae primo subest magnae quantitati, postea subsit parvae. Et hoc quidam posuerunt in corporibus gloriosis, dicentes quod quantitas eorum subest eis ad nutum, ita quod cum voluerint possunt habere magnam quantitatem, et cum voluerint parvam.

Sed hoc non potest esse. Quia nullus motus qui fit secundum aliquid intrinsecum rei, potest esse sine *passione abiiciente a substantia*. Et ideo in corporibus incorruptibilibus, scilicet caelestibus, est solus motus localis, qui non est secundum aliquid instrinsecum. Unde patet quod mutatio quantitatis circa materiam repugnaret impassibilitati corporis gloriosi et incorruptibilitati. Et praeterea, sequeretur quod corpus gloriosum quandoque esset rarius et quandoque spissius: quia, cum nihil dividi possit ab eo de materia sua, quandoque eadem materia esset sub parvis dimensionibus et quandoque sub magnis, et ita rarefieret et densaretur. Quod non potest esse.

Alio modo potest intelligi quod quantitas corporis gloriosi efficiatur minor seipsa per variationem situs: ita scilicet quod partes corporis gloriosi subintrent se invicem, et sic redeat ad quantumcumque parvam quantitatem. Et hoc quidam posuerunt, dicentes quod ratione suae subtilitatis corpus gloriosum habebit quod possit esse simul cum alio corpore non glorioso in eodem loco; et similiter potest una pars esse intra aliam, in tantum quod totum corpus gloriosum poterit intrare per minimum porum unius corporis. Et sic ponunt quod corpus Christi exivit de utero virginali, et intravit *ianuis clausis ad discipulos.*

Sed hoc non potest esse. Tum quia corpus gloriosum non habebit quod sit cum alio corpore simul ratione subtilitatis. Tum quia, etiam si haberet ut esset cum alio corpore, non tamen cum corpore glorioso, ut multi dicunt. Tum quia repugnaret rectae dispositioni corporis humani, quae requirit determinatum situm et distantiam partium. Unde nec per miraculum hoc unquam fiet.

fore, if the place were larger than that which is in the place, the same thing would be greater and smaller than itself, which is absurd.

I ANSWER THAT, A body is not related to place save through the medium of its proper dimensions, in respect of which a located body is confined through contact with the locating body. Hence it is not possible for a body to occupy a place smaller than its quantity, unless its proper quantity be made in some way less than itself: and this can only be understood in two ways.

First, by a variation in quantity in respect of the same matter, so that in fact the matter which at first is subject to a greater quantity is afterwards subject to a lesser. Some have held this to be the case with the glorified bodies, saying that quantity is subject to them at will, so that whenever they want, they are able to have a great quantity, and whenever they like, a small quantity.

But this is impossible, because no movement affecting that which is intrinsic to a thing is possible without *passion to the detriment of its substance*. Hence in incorruptible, i.e., heavenly, bodies, there is only local movement, which is not according to something intrinsic. Thus it is clear that change of quantity in respect of matter would be incompatible with the impassibility and incorruptibility of a glorified body. Moreover, it would follow that a glorified body would be sometimes rarer and sometimes denser, because since it cannot be deprived of any of its matter, sometimes the same matter would be under great dimensions and sometimes under small dimensions, and thus it would be rarefied and densified, which is impossible.

Second, that the quantity of a glorified body become smaller than itself may be understood by a variation of place; namely, so that the parts of a glorified body insinuate themselves into one another, so that it is reduced in quantity, however small it may become. And some have held this to be the case, saying that by reason of its subtlety a glorified body will be able to be in the same place with a nonglorified body: and that in like manner its parts can be one within the other, so much so that a whole glorified body will be able to pass through the minutest opening in another body: and thus they explain how Christ's body came out of the virginal womb; and how it went into *his disciples, the doors being shut.*

But this is impossible; both because the glorified body will not be able, by reason of its subtlety, to be in the same place with another body, and because even if it were able to be in the same place with another body, this would not be possible if the other were a glorified body, as many say; and again because this would be inconsistent with the right disposition of the human body, which requires the parts to be in a certain fixed place and at a certain fixed distance from one another. Wherefore this will never happen, not even by a miracle.

Et ideo dicendum, quod corpus semper erit in loco sibi aequali.

AD PRIMUM ergo dicendum quod corpus Christi in Altaris Sacramento non est localiter, ut dictum est.

AD SECUNDUM dicendum quod probatio Philosophi procedit ex hoc quod una pars eadem ratione subintraret aliam. Sed talis subintratio partium corporis gloriosi in invicem non potest esse, ut dictum est. Et ideo ratio non sequitur.

AD TERTIUM dicendum quod corpus videtur ex hoc quod agit in visum. Quod autem agat in visum vel non agat, nihil variat in ipso corpore. Et ideo non est inconveniens si possit quando, vult videri, et quando vult non videri. Sed esse in loco non est actio aliqua procedens ab eo ratione suae quantitatis, sicut videri ratione sui coloris. Ideo non est simile.

Consequently, we must say that the glorified body will always be in a place equal to itself.

REPLY OBJ. 1: Christ's body is not locally in the Sacrament of the Altar, as stated above.

REPLY OBJ. 2: The Philosopher's argument is that for the same reason one part might permeate another. But this permeation of the parts of a glorified body into one another is impossible, as stated above. Therefore, the argument does not follow.

REPLY OBJ. 3: A body is seen because it acts on the sight: but that it does or does not act on the sight causes no change in the body. Hence it is not unfitting if it can be seen when it will, and not seen when it will. On the other hand, being in a place is not an action proceeding from a body by reason of its quantity, as being seen is by reason of its color. Consequently, the comparison fails.

Article 6

Whether the Glorified Body, by Reason of Its Subtlety, Will Be Impalpable?

AD SEXTUM SIC PROCEDITUR. Videtur quod corpus gloriosum ratione subtilitatis sit impalpabile. Gregorius enim dicit, in *Homilia in octava Paschae*: *corrumpi necesse est quod palpatur*. Sed corpus gloriosum erit incorruptibile. Ergo erit impalpabile.

PRAETEREA, omne quod palpatur, resistit palpanti. Sed quod potest simul esse cum aliquo, non resistit ei. Cum ergo corpus gloriosum possit esse simul cum alio corpore, non erit palpabile.

PRAETEREA, omne corpus palpabile est tangibile. Sed omne tangibile corpus habet qualitates tangibiles excedentes qualitates tangentis. Cum ergo qualitates tangibiles non sint in excessu, sed reductae in maximam aequalitatem in corporibus gloriosis, videtur quod non sint palpabilia.

SED CONTRA: Est quod Dominus cum corpore glorioso resurrexit, et tamen corpus palpabile habuit: ut patet Ioan. 20, *palpate et videte, quia spiritus carnem et ossa non habet*. Ergo et corpora gloriosa erunt palpabilia.

PRAETEREA, haec est haeresis Eutychii Constantinopolitani episcopi, ut Gregorius dicit, in XIV *Moral.*, qui dixit quod *corpus nostrum in resurrectionis gloria erit impalpabile*.

RESPONDEO dicendum quod omne corpus palpabile est tangibile, sed non convertitur. Omne enim corpus est tangibile quod habet qualitates quibus natus est immutari sensus tactus: unde aer, ignis et huiusmodi sunt corpora tangibilia. Sed *palpabile* ulterius addit quod resistat tangenti: unde aer, qui nequaquam resistit transeunti per eum sed est facillimae divisionis, tangibilis quidem est, sed non palpabilis. Sic ergo patet; quod palpabile

OBJECTION 1: It would seem that the glorified body, by reason of its subtlety, is impalpable. For Gregory says (*Homilies on the Gospels* 25): *what is palpable must be corruptible*. But the glorified body is incorruptible. Therefore, it is impalpable.

OBJ. 2: Further, whatever is palpable resists one who handles it. But that which can be in the same place with another does not resist it. Since, then, a glorified body can be in the same place with another body, it will not be palpable.

OBJ. 3: Further, every palpable body is tangible. Now every tangible body has tangible qualities in excess of the qualities of the one touching it. Since, then, in the glorified bodies the tangible qualities are not in excess but are reduced to a supreme degree of equality, it would seem that they are impalpable.

ON THE CONTRARY, Our Lord rose again with a glorified body; and yet his body was palpable, as appears from Luke 24:39: *handle, and see; for a spirit has not flesh and bones*. Therefore, the glorified bodies also will be palpable.

FURTHER, This is the heresy of Eutychius, Bishop of Constantinople, as Gregory states (*Morals on Job* 24): for he said that *in the glory of the resurrection our bodies will be impalpable*.

I ANSWER THAT, Every palpable body is tangible, but not conversely. For every body is tangible that has qualities whereby the sense of touch has a natural aptitude to be affected: wherefore air, fire, and the like are tangible bodies: but a *palpable* body, in addition to this, resists the touch; wherefore the air, which never resists that which passes through it, and is most easily pierced, is tangible indeed, but not palpable. Accordingly, it is clear that a body is said to be

dicitur aliquod corpus ex duobus: scilicet ex qualitatibus tangibilibus; et ex hoc quod resistit tangenti, ut non pertranseatur. Et. quia qualitates tangibiles sunt calidum et frigidum et huiusmodi, quae non inveniuntur nisi in corporibus gravibus et levibus, quae habent contrarietatem ad invicem, ac per hoc surit corruptibilia; ideo corpora caelestia, quae sunt secundum naturam incorruptibilia, sunt sensibilia quidem visu, sed non tangibilia, et sic etiam nec palpabilia. Et hoc est quod Gregorius dicit, quod *corrumpi necesse est omne quod palpatur.*

Corpus ergo gloriosum habet a natura sua qualitates quae sunt natae immutare tactum: sed tamen, quia corpus est omnino subiectum spiritui, in potestate eius est ut secundum eas immutet tactum vel non immutet. Similiter etiam secundum naturam sibi competit ut resistat cuilibet alteri corpori transeunti, ita quod non possit esse cum eo simul in eodem loco: sed miraculose hoc potest divina virtute contingere, ad nutum ipsius, quod sit cum alio corpore in eodem loco; et sic non resistet ei transeunti. Unde secundum naturam suam palpabile est corpus gloriosum: sed ex virtute supernaturali hoc ei competit ut, cum vult, non palpetur a corpore non glorioso. Et ideo Gregorius dicit quod *Dominus palpandam carnem praebuit, quam ianuis clausis introduxit, ut profecto ostenderet post resurrectionem corpus suum esse et eiusdem naturae et alterius gloriae.*

AD PRIMUM ergo dicendum quod incorruptibilitas gloriosi corporis non est ex natura componentium, secundum quam *omne quod palpatur necesse est corrumpi,* ut ex dictis patet. Et ideo ratio non sequitur.

AD SECUNDUM dicendum quod, quamvis aliquo modo possit fieri quod corpus gloriosum sit cum alio corpore in eodem loco, tamen corpus gloriosum habet in potestate sua resistere cuilibet tangenti cum voluerit. Et sic palpari potest.

AD TERTIUM dicendum quod qualitates tangibiles in corporibus gloriosis non erunt reductae ad medium rei secundum aequidistantiam ab extremis acceptum: sed ad medium proportionis, secundum quod optime competit complexioni humanae in singulis partibus. Et ideo tactus illorum corporum est delectabilissimus: quia potentia semper delectatur in convenienti, et tristatur in excessu.

palpable for two reasons: namely, on account of its tangible qualities, and on account of its resisting that which touches it, so as to hinder it from piercing it. And since the tangible qualities are hot and cold and so forth, which are not found save in heavy and light bodies which, through being contrary to one another, are therefore corruptible, it follows that the heavenly bodies, which by their nature are incorruptible, are sensible to the sight but not tangible, and therefore neither are they palpable. This is what Gregory means when he says (*Homilies on the Gospels* 25) that *whatever is palpable must be corruptible.*

Accordingly, the glorified body has by its nature those qualities which have a natural aptitude to affect the touch, and yet since the body is altogether subject to the spirit, it is in its power thereby to affect or not to affect the touch. In like manner, it is competent by its nature to resist any other passing body, so that the latter cannot be in the same place together with it: although, according to its pleasure, it may happen by the divine power that it occupy the same place with another body, and thus offer no resistance to a passing body. Therefore, according to its nature the glorified body is palpable, but it is competent for it to be impalpable to a non-glorified body by a supernatural power. Hence Gregory says (*Homilies on the Gospels* 25) that *our Lord offered his flesh to be handled, which he had brought in through the closed doors, so as to afford a complete proof that after his resurrection his body was unchanged in nature, though changed in glory.*

REPLY OBJ. 1: The incorruptibility of a glorified body does not result from the nature of its component parts; and it is on account of that nature that *whatever is palpable is corruptible,* as stated above. Hence the argument does not follow.

REPLY OBJ. 2: Although in a way it is possible for a glorified body to be in the same place with another body: nevertheless the glorified body has it in its power to resist at will any one touching it, and thus it is palpable.

REPLY OBJ. 3: In the glorified bodies the tangible qualities are not reduced to the real mean that is measured according to equal distance from the extremes, but to the proportionate mean, according as is most becoming to the human complexion in each part. Wherefore the touch of those bodies will be most delightful, because a power always delights in a becoming object, and is grieved by excess.

QUESTION 84

THE AGILITY OF THE BODIES OF THE BLESSED

Deinde considerandum est de agilitate beatorum corporum resurgentium.

Circa quod quaeruntur tria.

Primo: utrum corpora gloriosa sint futura agilia.

Secundo: utrum movebuntur.

Tertio: utrum movebuntur in instanti.

We must now consider the agility of the bodies of the blessed in the resurrection.

Under this head there are three points of inquiry:

(1) Whether the glorified bodies will be agile?

(2) Whether they will move?

(3) Whether they will move instantaneously?

Article 1

Whether the Glorified Bodies Will Be Agile?

AD PRIMUM SIC PROCEDITUR. Videtur quod corpora gloriosa non sint futura agilia. Illud enim quod de se est agile ad motum, non indiget aliquo deferente. Sed corpora glorificata deferentur post resurrectionem *in nubibus obviam Christo in aera*, ab angelis, ut dicit Glossa, I ad Thessal. 4, [17]. Ergo corpora gloriosa non erunt agilia.

PRAETEREA, nullum corpus quod movetur cum labore et poena, potest dici agile. Sed corpora gloriosa hoc modo movebuntur: cum motor eorum, scilicet anima, moveat in contrarium naturae eorum; alias moverentur semper in unam partem. Ergo non erunt agilia.

PRAETEREA, inter omnes operationes animalis, sensus est nobilior et proprior quam motus. Sed non assignatur corporibus gloriosis aliqua proprietas quae perficiat ea ad sentiendum. Ergo nec debet eis attribui agilitas, per quam perficiantur ad motum.

PRAETEREA, natura dat diversis instrumenta dispositionis diversae secundum diversas virtutes ipsorum: unde non eiusdem dispositionis dat instrumenta animali tardo et veloci. Sed Deus multo ordinatius operatur quam natura. Cum ergo corpus gloriosum habeat membra eiusdem dispositionis in figura et quantitate sicut modo, videtur quod non habeat aliam agilitatem quam modo habeat.

SED CONTRA: Est quod dicitur I Cor. 15, [43]: *seminatur in infirmitate, surget in virtute*: Glossa, *idest, mobile et vivum*. Sed mobilitas non potest dicere nisi agilitatem ad motum. Ergo corpora gloriosa erunt agilia.

PRAETEREA, tarditas maxime videtur spiritualitati repugnare. Sed corpora gloriosa erunt *spiritualia*, ut dicitur I Cor. 15, [44]. Ergo erunt agilia.

OBJECTION 1: It would seem that the glorified bodies will not be agile. For that which is agile by itself needs not to be carried in order to move. But the glorified bodies will, after the resurrection, be taken up by the angels *in the clouds to meet Christ, into the air*, according to a Gloss on 1 Thessalonians 4:16. Therefore, the glorified bodies will not be agile.

OBJ. 2: Further, no body that moves with labor and pain can be said to be agile. Yet the glorified bodies will move thus, since the principle of their movement, namely, the soul, moves them counter to their nature, else they would always move in the same direction. Therefore, they are not agile.

OBJ. 3: Further, of all the animal operations sense surpasses movement in nobility and priority. Yet no property is ascribed to glorified bodies as perfecting them in sensation. Therefore, neither should agility be ascribed to them as perfecting them in movement.

OBJ. 4: Further, nature gives different animals instruments of different disposition according to their different powers: hence she does not give instruments of the same disposition to slow as to fleet animals. Now God's works are much more orderly than those of nature. Since, then, the glorified body's members will have the same disposition, shape, and quantity as they now have, it would seem that it will have no agility other than it has now.

ON THE CONTRARY, 1 Corinthians 15:43 says: *it is sown in weakness, it shall rise in power*, that is, according to a Gloss, *mobile and living*. But mobility can only signify agility in movement. Therefore, the glorified bodies will be agile.

FURTHER, Slowness of movement would seem especially inconsistent with the nature of a spirit. But the glorified bodies will be *spiritual* according to 1 Corinthians 15:44. Therefore, they will be agile.

RESPONDEO dicendum quod corpus gloriosum erit omnino subiectum animae glorificatae: non solum ut nihil in eo sit quod resistat voluntati spiritus, quia hoc fuit etiam in corpore Adae; sed etiam ut sit in eo aliqua perfectio effluens ab anima glorificata in corpus, per quam habile redditur ad praedictam subiectionem, quae quidem perfectio *dos* glorificari corporis dicitur. Anima autem coniungitur corpori non solum ut forma, sed etiam ut motor. Utroque autem modo oportet quod corpus gloriosum animae glorificatae sit summe subiectum. Unde, sicut per dotem subtilitatis subiicitur ei totaliter inquantum est forma corporis dans esse specificum, ita per dotem agilitatis subiicitur ei inquantum est motor: ut scilicet sit expeditum et habile ad obediendum spiritui in omnibus motibus et actionibus animae.

Quidam tamen causam istius agilitatis attribuunt quintae essentiae, quae tunc in corporibus gloriosis dominabitur. Sed de hoc frequenter dictum est quod non videtur conveniens. Unde melius est ut attribuatur animae, a qua gloria in corpus emanat.

AD PRIMUM ergo dicendum quod corpora gloriosa dicuntur ferri baiulis angelis, et etiam in nubibus, non quasi eis indigeant: sed ad reverentiam designandam quae corporibus gloriosis et ab angelis et ab omnibus creaturis deferetur.

AD SECUNDUM dicendum quod, quanto virtus animae moventis dominatur magis supra corpus, tanto minor est labor in motu qui etiam fit contra naturam corporis. Unde illi in quibus virtus motiva est fortior, vel qui habent ex exercitio corpus magis habilitatum ad obediendum spiritui moventi, minus laborant in motu. Et quia post resurrectionem anima perfecte dominabitur corpori, tum propter perfectionem propriae virtutis, tum propter habilitatem corporis gloriosi ex redundantia gloriae ab anima in ipsum; non erit aliquis labor in motu sanctorum. Et sic dici poterunt corpora sanctorum agilia.

AD TERTIUM dicendum quod per dotem agilitatis corpus gloriosum redditur habile non solum ad motum localem, sed ad sensum et ad omnes alias animae operationes exequendas.

AD QUARTUM dicendum quod, sicut natura dat velocioribus animalibus instrumenta diversae dispositionis in figura et quantitate, ita Deus dabit corporibus sanctorum aliam dispositionem quam nunc habeant, non quidem in figura et quantitate, sed in proprietate gloriae quae dicitur agilitas.

I ANSWER THAT, The glorified body will be altogether subject to the glorified soul, so that not only will there be nothing in it to resist the will of the spirit, for it was even so in the case of Adam's body, but also from the glorified soul there will flow into the body a certain perfection whereby it will become adapted to that subjection: and this perfection is called the *gift* of the glorified body. Now the soul is united to body not only as its form, but also as its mover; and in both ways the glorified body must be most perfectly subject to the glorified soul. Wherefore even as by the gift of subtlety the body is wholly subject to the soul as its form, whence it derives its specific being, so by the gift of agility it is subject to the soul as its mover, so that it is prompt and apt to obey the spirit in all the movements and actions of the soul.

Some, however, ascribe the cause of this agility to the fifth, i.e., the heavenly essence, which will then be predominant in the glorified bodies. But of this we have frequently observed that it does not seem probable (Q. 82, A. 1; Q. 83, A. 1). Wherefore it is better to ascribe it to the soul, whence glory flows to the body.

REPLY OBJ. 1: Glorified bodies are said to be borne by the angels and also on the clouds not as though they needed them, but in order to signify the reverence which both angels and all creatures will show them.

REPLY OBJ. 2: The more the power of the moving soul dominates over the body, the less is the labor of movement, even though it be counter to the body's nature. Hence those in whom the motive power is stronger, and those who through exercise have the body more adapted to obey the moving spirit, labor less in being moved. And since after the resurrection the soul will perfectly dominate the body, both on account of the perfection of its own power, and on account of the glorified body's aptitude resulting from the outflow of glory which it receives from the soul, there will be no labor in the saints' movements, and thus it may be said that the bodies of the saints' will be agile.

REPLY OBJ. 3: By the gift of agility the glorified body will be rendered apt not only for local movement but also for sensation, and for the execution of all the other operations of the soul.

REPLY OBJ. 4: Even as nature gives to fleeter animals instruments of a different disposition in shape and quantity, so God will give to the bodies of the saints a disposition other than that which they have now, not indeed in shape and quantity, but in that property of glory which is called agility.

Article 2

Whether the Saints Will Never Use Their Agility for the Purpose of Movement?

AD SECUNDUM SIC PROCEDITUR. Videtur quod agilitate sua nunquam utentur ita quod moveantur. Quia secundum Philosophum, *motus est actus imperfecti*. Sed in illis corporibus nulla erit imperfectio. Ergo nec aliquis motus.

PRAETEREA, omnis motus est propter indigentiam: quia omne quod movetur, movetur propter adeptionem alicuius finis. Sed corpora gloriosa non habebunt aliquam indigentiam: quia, ut Augustinus dicit, *ibi erit quidquid voles, non erit quidquid noles*. Ergo non movebuntur.

PRAETEREA, secundum Philosophum, in II *Caeli et Mundi*, quod participat divinam bonitatem sine motu, nobilius participat illam quam quod participat illam cum motu. Sed corpus gloriosum nobilius participat divinam bonitatem quam aliud corpus. Cum ergo quaedam alia corpora omnino sine motu remaneant, sicut corpora caelestia, videtur quod multo fortius corpora humana.

PRAETEREA, Augustinus dicit quod *anima stabilita in Deo, stabiliet et corpus suum consequenter*. Sed anima ita erit in Deo stabilita quod nullo modo ab eo movebitur. Ergo nec in corpore erit aliquis motus ab anima.

PRAETEREA, quanto corpus est nobilius, tanto debetur ei locus nobilior: unde corpus Christi, quod est nobilissimum, habet locum eminentiorem inter cetera loca, ut patet Heb. 7, [26], *excelsior caelis factus*; Glossa, *loco et dignitate*. Et similiter unumquodque corpus gloriosum habebit, eadem ratione, locum sibi convenientem secundum mensuram suae dignitatis. Sed locus conveniens est de pertinentibus ad gloriam. Cum ergo post resurrectionem gloria sanctorum nunquam varietur neque in plus neque in minus, quia tunc erunt omnino in termino; videtur quod corpora eorum nunquam de loco sibi determinato recedent. Et ita non movebuntur.

SED CONTRA est quod dicitur Isaiae 40, [31]: *current et non laborabunt, volabunt et non deficient*; et Sap. 3, [7]: *tanquam scintillae in arundineto discurrent*. Ergo erit aliquis motus corporum gloriosorum.

RESPONDEO dicendum quod corpora gloriosa aliquando moveri necessarium est ponere: quia et ipsum corpus Christi motum est in ascensione; et similiter corpora sanctorum, quae de terra resurgent, ad caelum empyreum ascendent. Sed etiam postquam caelos conscenderint, verisimile est quod aliquando moveantur pro suae libito voluntatis: ut, illud quod habent in virtute actu exercentes, divinam sapientiam commendabi-

OBJECTION 1: It would seem that the saints will never use their agility for the purpose of movement. For, according to the Philosopher (*Physics* 3.2), *movement is the act of the imperfect*. But there will be no imperfection in glorified bodies. Neither, therefore, will there be any movement.

OBJ. 2: Further, all movement is on account of some need, because whatever is in motion is moved for the sake of obtaining some end. But glorified bodies will have no need, since as Augustine says (*De Spiritu et Anima*, lxiii; Cf. Q. 70, A. 2), *whatever you want will be there, and nothing that you do not want*. Therefore, they will not move.

OBJ. 3: Further, according to the Philosopher (*On Heaven and Earth* 2), that which shares the divine goodness without movement shares it more excellently than that which shares it with movement. Now the glorified body shares the divine goodness more excellently than any other body. Since, then, certain bodies, like the heavenly bodies, will remain altogether without movement, it seems that much more will human bodies remain so.

OBJ. 4: Further, Augustine says (*On True Religion* 12) that *the soul, being established in God, will in consequence establish its body*. Now the soul will be so established in God that in no way will it move away from him. Therefore, in the body there will be no movement caused by the soul.

OBJ. 5: Further, the more noble a body is, the more noble a place is due to it: wherefore Christ's body, which is the most exalted of all, has the highest place of all, as is seen in Hebrews 7:26: *made higher than the heavens*, on which the Gloss comments, *in place and dignity*. And again each glorified body will, in like manner, have a place befitting it according to the measure of its dignity. Now a fitting place is one of the conditions pertaining to glory. Since, then, after the resurrection the glory of the saints will never vary, neither by increase nor by decrease, because they will then have reached the final term of all, it would seem that their bodies will never leave the place assigned to them, and consequently will not be moved.

ON THE CONTRARY, Isaiah 40:31 says that *they shall run and not be weary, they shall walk and not faint*; and Wisdom 3:7 says that the just *shall run to and fro like sparks among the reeds*. Therefore, there will be some movement in glorified bodies.

I ANSWER THAT, It is necessary to suppose that the glorified bodies are moved sometimes, since even Christ's body was moved in his ascension, and likewise the bodies of the saints, which will arise from the earth, will ascend to the empyrean. But even after they have climbed the heavens, it is likely that they will sometimes move according as it pleases them; so that by actually putting into practice that which is in their power, they may show forth the excellence

lem ostendant; et ut visus eorum reficiatur pulchritudine creaturarum diversarum, in quibus Dei sapientia eminenter relucebit; sensus enim non potest esse nisi praesentium quamvis magis a longinquo possint sentire corpora gloriosa quam non gloriosa. Nec tamen per motum aliquid deperiet eorum beatitudini, quae consistit in visione Dei, quem ubique praesentem habebunt: sicut et de angelis dicit Gregorius quod *intra Deum currunt quocumque mittantur.*

Ad primum ergo dicendum quod motus localis non variat aliquid eorum quae sunt intranea rei, sed est secundum id quod est extra rem, scilicet locum. Unde illud quod movetur motu locali, est perfectum quantum ad ea quae sunt intra rem, ut dicitur in VIII *Physic.*: quamvis habeat imperfectionem respectu loci, quia, dum est in uno loco est in potentia ad alium locum, quia non potest esse actu in pluribus locis simul; hoc enim solius Dei est. Hic autem defectus non repugnat perfectioni gloriae: sicut nec defectus quod creatura est ex nihilo. Et ideo manebunt defectus huiusmodi in corporibus gloriosis.

Ad secundum dicendum quod aliquis dicitur indigere aliquo simpliciter, et secundum quid. Simpliciter quidem indiget aliquis eo sine quo non potest conservari in esse vel in sua perfectione. Et sic motus in corporibus gloriosis non erit propter aliquam indigentiam: quia ad haec omnia sufficiet eis sua beatitudo. Sed secundum quid indiget quis illo sine quo non potest aliquem finem intentum habere, vel non ita bene, vel tali modo. Et sic motus erit in beatis propter indigentiam: non enim poterunt manifestare virtutem motivam in seipsis experimento nisi moveantur. Huiusmodi enim indigentias nihil prohibet in corporibus gloriosis esse.

Ad tertium dicendum quod ratio illa procederet si corpus gloriosum non posset etiam sine motu participare divinam bonitatem multo altius quam corpora caelestia: quod falsum est. Unde corpora gloriosa non movebuntur ad consequendam perfectam divinae bonitatis participationem, hanc enim habent per gloriam: sed ad demonstrandam virtutem animae. Per motum autem corporum caelestium non posset demonstrari virtus eorum nisi quam habent in movendo corpora inferiora ad generationem et corruptionem: quod non competit illi statui. Et ideo ratio non procedit.

Ad quartum dicendum quod motus localis nihil diminuit de stabilitate ab anima stabilita in Deo: cum non sit secundum aliquid instrinsecum rei, ut dictum est.

Ad quintum quod locus congruus unicuique glorioso corpori deputatus secundum gradum suae dignitatis, pertinet ad praemium accidentale. Non tamen oportet quod diminuatur aliquid de praemio quandocumque est extra locum suum: quia locus ille non pertinet ad

of divine wisdom, and that furthermore their vision may be refreshed by the beauty of the variety of creatures, in which God's wisdom will shine forth with great evidence: for sense can only perceive that which is present, although glorified bodies can perceive from a greater distance than non-glorified bodies. And yet movement will in no way diminish their happiness which consists in seeing God, for he will be everywhere present to them; thus Gregory says of the angels (*Homilies on the Gospels* 34) that *wherever they are sent, their course lies in God.*

Reply Obj. 1: Local movement changes nothing that is intrinsic to a thing, but only that which is without, namely place. Hence that which is moved locally is perfect as to those things which are within (*Physics* 8.7), although it has an imperfection as to place, because while it is in one place, it is in potentiality with regard to another place, since it cannot be in several places at the same time, for this belongs to God alone. But this defect is not inconsistent with the perfection of glory, as neither is the defect whereby a creature is formed from nothing. Hence such defects will remain in glorified bodies.

Reply Obj. 2: A person is said to need a thing in two ways, namely, absolutely and relatively. One needs absolutely that without which one cannot retain one's being or one's perfection: and thus movement in glorified bodies will not be on account of a need, because their happiness will suffice them for all such things. But we need a thing relatively when without it some end we have in view cannot be obtained by us, or not so well, or not in some particular way. It is thus that movement will be in the blessed on account of need, for they will be unable to show forth their motive power practically, unless they be in motion, since nothing prevents a need of this kind being in glorified bodies.

Reply Obj. 3: This argument would proceed if the glorified body were unable even without movement to share the divine goodness much more perfectly than the heavenly bodies, which is untrue. Hence glorified bodies will be moved, not in order to gain a perfect participation in the divine goodness (since they have this through glory), but in order to show the soul's power. On the other hand, the movement of the heavenly bodies could not show their power, except the power they have in moving lower bodies to generation and corruption, which is not becoming to that state. Hence the argument does not prove.

Reply Obj. 4: Local movement takes nothing away from the stability of the soul that is established in God, since it does not affect that which is intrinsic to a thing, as stated above (ad 1).

Reply Obj. 5: The fitting place assigned to each glorified body according to the degree of its dignity belongs to the accidental reward. Nor does it follow that this reward is diminished whenever the body is outside its place; because that place pertains to reward not as actually containing the

praemium secundum quod actu continet corpus locatum, cum nihil influat in corpus gloriosum, sed magis recipiat splendorem ab eo; sed secundum quod est debitus pro meritis. Unde gaudium de tali loco manet etiam ei qui est extra locum illum.

body located therein (since nothing flows therefrom into the glorified body, but rather does it receive splendor therefrom), but as being due to merits. Wherefore, though out of that place, they will still continue to rejoice in it.

Article 3

Whether the Movement of the Saints Will Be Instantaneous?

AD TERTIUM SIC PROCEDITUR. Videtur quod moveantur in instanti. Augustinus enim dicit quod, *ubicumque voluerit spiritus, ibi erit et corpus*. Sed motus voluntatis, secundum quem spiritus vult alicubi esse, est in instanti. Ergo et motus corporis erit in instanti.

PRAETEREA, Philosophus, in IV *Physic.*, probat quod, si fieret motus per vacuum, quod oporteret aliquid moveri in instanti, quia vacuum non resistit aliquo modo mobili, resistit autem plenum, et sic nulla proportio esset motus qui fit in vacuo ad motum qui fit in pleno, in velocitate, cum proportio motuum in velocitate sit secundum proportionem resistentiae quae est in medio; omnium autem duorum motuum qui fiunt in tempore, oportet esse proportionales velocitates, quia omne tempus omni tempori proportionale est. Sed similiter nullum spatium plenum potest resistere corpori glorioso quod potest esse cum alio corpore in eodem loco, quocumque modo fiat: sicut nec vacuum alteri corpori. Ergo, si movetur, in instanti movebitur.

PRAETEREA, virtus animae glorificatae quasi improportionaliter excedit virtutem animae non glorificatae. Sed anima non glorificata movet corpus in tempore. Ergo anima glorificata movet corpus in instanti.

PRAETEREA, omne quod movetur aequaliter cito ad propinquum et distans, movetur in instanti. Sed motus corporis gloriosi est talis: quia ad quantumcumque distans spatium movetur in tempore imperceptibili; unde Augustinus dicit, in *Quaestionibus de Resurrectione*, quod corpus gloriosum *utraque intervalla pari celeritate pertingit, ut radius solis*. Ergo corpus gloriosum movetur in instanti.

PRAETEREA, omne quod movetur, vel movetur in tempore vel in instanti. Sed corpus gloriosum post resurrectionem non movebitur in tempore: quia *tempus iam non erit*, ut dicitur Apoc. 10, [6]. Ergo motus ille, erit in instanti.

SED CONTRA: In motu locali spatium et motus et tempus simul dividuntur, ut demonstrative probatur in

OBJECTION 1: It would seem that movement of the saints will be instantaneous. For Augustine says (*The City of God* 22.30) that *wherever the spirit wishes, there will the body be*. Now the movement of the will, whereby the spirit wishes to be anywhere, is instantaneous. Therefore, the body's movement will be instantaneous.

OBJ. 2: Further, the Philosopher (*Physics* 4.8) proves that there is no movement through a vacuum, because it would follow that something moves instantaneously, since a vacuum offers no resistance whatever to a thing that is in motion, whereas the plenum offers resistance; and so there would be no proportion between the velocity of movement in a vacuum and that of movement in a plenum, since the ratio of movements in point of velocity is as the ratio of the resistance offered by the medium. Now the velocities of any two movements that take place in time must be proportional, since any one space of time is proportional to any other. But in like manner no full place can resist a glorified body, since this can be in the same place with another body, no matter how this may occur; even as neither can a vacuum resist a body. Therefore, if it moves at all, it moves instantaneously.

OBJ. 3: Further, the power of a glorified soul surpasses the power of a non-glorified soul, out of all proportion so to speak. Now the non-glorified soul moves the body in time. Therefore, the glorified soul moves the body instantaneously.

OBJ. 4: Further, whatever is moved equally soon to what is near and what is distant, is moved instantaneously. Now such is the movement of a glorified body, for however distant the space to which it is moved, the time it takes to be moved is imperceptible: wherefore Augustine says (*Questions on the Resurrection, Epistle 102.1*) that the glorified body *reaches equally soon to any distance, like the sun's ray*. Therefore, the glorified body is moved instantaneously.

OBJ. 5: Further, whatever is in motion is moved either in time or in an instant. Now after the resurrection the glorified body will not be moved in time, since *time will not be then*, according to Revelation 10:6. Therefore, this movement will be instantaneous.

ON THE CONTRARY, In local movement, space, movement, and time are equally divisible, as is demonstrated in

VI. *Physic*. Sed spatium quod transit corpus gloriosum per suum motum, est divisibile. Ergo et motus divisibilis, et tempus divisibile. Instans autem non dividitur. Ergo et motus ille non erit in instanti.

PRAETEREA, non potest esse aliquid simul totum in uno loco; et partim in illo, et partim in alio: quia sequeretur quod altera pars esset in duobus locis simul; quod esse non potest. Sed omne quod movetur, partim est in termino a quo, et partim in termino ad quem, ut demonstratum est in 6 *Physic*. Omne autem quod motum est totum est in termino ad quem est motus. Ergo non potest esse quod simul moveatur et motum sit. Sed omne quod movetur in instanti, simul movetur et motum est. Ergo motus localis corporis gloriosi non poterit esse in instanti.

RESPONDEO dicendum quod circa hoc est multiplex opinio. Quidam dicunt quod corpus gloriosum transit de uno loco in alium sine hoc quod pertranseat medium, sicut et voluntas de uno loco transfertur ad alium sine hoc quod pertranseat medium. Et propter hoc potest corporis gloriosi motus esse in instanti, sicut et voluntatis.

Sed hoc non potest stare. Quia corpus gloriosum nunquam perveniet ad nobilitatem naturae spiritualis: sicut nunquam desinit esse corpus. Et praeterea, voluntas, cum dicitur moveri de uno loco in alium, non transfertur essentialiter de loco in locum, quia neutro locorum illorum essentialiter continetur: sed dirigitur in unum locum postquam fuerat directa per intentionem ad alium, et pro tanto dicitur moveri de loco ad locum.

Et ideo alii dicunt quod corpus gloriosum habet de proprietate naturae suae, qua corpus est, quod pertranseat medium, et ita quod moveatur in tempore: sed virtute gloriae, qua habet infinitatem quandam supra naturam, habet quod possit non pertransire medium, et sic in instanti moveri.

Sed hoc non potest esse: quia implicat in se contradictionem. Quod patet sic. Sit aliquod corpus quod moveatur de A in B, et corpus motum sit Z. Constat quod Z, quandiu est totum in A, non movetur. Similiter nec quando est totum in B: quia tunc motum est. Ergo, si aliquando movetur, oportet quod neque sit totum in A neque totum in B. Ergo, quando movetur, vel nusquam est; vel est partim in A et partim in B; vel totum in alio loco medio, puta in C; aut partim in C et partim in A seu in B. Sed non potest poni quod nusquam sit: quia sic esset aliqua quantitas dimensiva non habens situm, quod est impossibile. Neque potest poni quod sit partim in A et partim in B et non sit in medio aliquo modo: quia, cum B sit locus distans ab A, sequeretur in medio interiacente

Physics 6.4. Now the space traversed by a glorified body in motion is divisible. Therefore, both the movement and the time are divisible. But an instant is indivisible. Therefore, this movement will not be instantaneous.

FURTHER, A thing cannot be at the same time wholly in one place and partly in another place, since it would follow that the remaining part is in two places at the same time, which is impossible. But whatever is in motion is partly in a starting terminus and partly in a ending terminus, as is proved in *Physics* 6.6: while whatever has been in motion is wholly in the ending terminus to which the movement is directed; and it is impossible at the same time for it to be moved and to have been moved. Now that which is moved instantaneously is being moved and has been moved at the same time. Therefore, the local movement of a glorified body cannot be instantaneous.

I ANSWER THAT, Opinion is much divided on this point. For some say that a glorified body passes from one place to another without passing through the interval, just as the will passes from one place to another without passing through the interval, and that consequently it is possible for the movement of a glorified body, like that of the will, to be instantaneous.

But this will not hold, because the glorified body will never attain to the dignity of the spiritual nature, just as it will never cease to be a body. Moreover, when the will is said to move from one place to another, it is not essentially transferred from place to place, because in neither place is it contained essentially, but it is directed to one place after being directed by the intention to another: and in this sense it is said to move from one place to another.

Hence others say that it is a property of the nature of a glorified body, since it is a body, to pass through the interval and consequently to be moved in time, but that by the power of glory, which raises it to a certain infinitude above the power of nature, it is possible for it not to pass through the interval, and consequently to be moved instantaneously.

But this is impossible since it implies a contradiction: which is proved as follows. Suppose a body, which we will call Z, to be in motion from A to B. It is clear that Z, as long as it is wholly in A, is not in motion; and in like manner when it is wholly in B, because then the movement is past. Therefore, if it is at any time in motion it must be neither wholly in A nor wholly in B. Therefore, while it is in motion, it is either nowhere, or partly in A and partly in B, or wholly in some other intervening place, say C, or partly in A and C and partly in C and B. But it is impossible for it to be nowhere, for then there would be a dimensive quantity without a place, which is impossible. Nor again is it possible for it to be partly in A and partly in B without being in some way in the intervening space, for since B is a place dis-

quod pars Z quae est in B, non esset continua parti quae est in A.

Ergo restat quod vel sit totum in C; vel partim in eo et partim in alio loco, quod ponetur medium inter C et A, puta D; et sic de aliis. Ergo oportet quod Z non perveniat de A in B nisi prius sit in omnibus mediis: nisi dicatur quod pervenit de A in B et nunquam movetur; quod implicat contradictionem, quia ipsa successio locorum est motus localis. Et eadem ratio est de qualibet mutatione quae habet duos contrarios terminos quorum utrumque est aliquid positive. Secus autem est de illis mutationibus quae habent unum terminum tantum positivum et alteram puram privationem: quia inter affirmationem et negationem seu privationem non est aliqua determinata distantia; unde quod est in negatione potest esse propinquius vel remotius ab affirmatione, vel e converso, ratione alicuius quod causat alterum eorum vel disponit ad ea; et sic, dum id quod movetur est totum sub negatione, mutatur in affirmationem, et e converso. Unde etiam in eis mutans praecedit mutatum esse, ut probatur in VI *Physic*. Nec est simile de motu angeli: quia esse in loco aequivoce dicitur de corpore et angelo. Et sic patet quod nullo modo potest esse quod aliquod corpus perveniat de uno loco ad alium nisi transeat omnia media.

Et ideo alii hoc concedunt, sed tamen dicunt quod corpus gloriosum movetur in instanti. Sed ex hoc sequitur quod corpus gloriosum in eodem instanti sit in duobus locis simul, vel pluribus: scilicet in termino ultimo et in omnibus mediis locis. Quod non potest esse.

Sed ad hoc dicunt quod, quamvis sit idem instans secundum rem, tamen differt ratione: sicut punctus ad quem terminantur diversae lineae. Sed hoc non sufficit. Quia instans mensurat hoc quod est in instanti secundum rem, non secundum hoc quod consideratur. Unde diversa consideratio instantis non facit quod instans possit mensurare illa quae non sunt simul tempore: sicut nec diversa consideratio puncti potest facere quod sub uno puncto loci contineantur quae sunt distantia situ.

Et ideo alii probabilius dicunt quod corpus gloriosum movetur in tempore, sed imperceptibili propter brevitatem. Et quod tamen unum corpus gloriosum potest iri minori tempore idem spatium pertransire quam aliud: quia tempus, quantumcumque parvum accipiatur, est in infinitum divisibile.

Ad primum ergo dicendum quod *illud quod parum deest, quasi nihil deesse videtur*, ut dicitur in II *Physic*. Et ideo dicimus, *statim facio*, quod post modicum tempus fiet. Et per hunc modum loquitur Augustinus, quod *ubicumque erit voluntas, ibi erit statim corpus*.

tant from A, it would follow that in the intervening space the part of Z which is in B is not continuous with the part which is in A.

Therefore, it follows that it is either wholly in C, or partly in C and partly in some other place that intervenes between C and A, say D, and so forth. Therefore, it follows that Z does not pass from A to B unless it is first in all the intervening places: unless we suppose that it passes from A to B without ever being moved, which implies a contradiction, because the very succession of places is local movement. The same applies to any change whatever having two opposite terms, each of which is a positive entity, but not to those changes which have only one positive term, the other being a pure privation. For between affirmation and negation or privation there is no fixed distance; wherefore that which is in the negation may be nearer to or more remote from affirmation (and conversely) by reason of something that causes either of them or disposes thereto, so that while that which is moved is wholly under a negation, it is changed into affirmation, and vice versa. Thus in such things to be changing precedes to be changed, as is proved in *Physics* 6.5. Nor is there any comparison with the movement of an angel, because being in a place is predicated equivocally of a body and an angel. Hence it is clear that it is altogether impossible for a body to pass from one place to another, unless it pass through every interval.

Wherefore others grant this, and yet they maintain that the glorified body is moved instantaneously. But it follows from this that a glorified body is at the same instant in two or more places together, namely, in the ultimate term and in all the intervening places, which is impossible.

To this, however, they reply that although it is the same instant really, it is not the same logically, like a point at which different lines terminate. But this is not enough, because an instant measures the instantaneous according to its reality and not according to our way of considering it. Wherefore an instant through being considered in a different way is not rendered capable of measuring things that are not simultaneous in time, just as a point through being considered in a different way does not make it possible for one point of place to contain things that are locally distant from one another.

Hence others with greater probability hold that a glorified body moves in time, but that this time is so short as to be imperceptible; and that nevertheless one glorified body can pass through the same space in less time than another, because there is no limit to the divisibility of time, no matter how short a space we may take.

Reply Obj. 1: That which is *lacking little is as it were not lacking at all* (*Physics* 2.5); wherefore we say: *I do this immediately*, when it is to be done after a short time. It is in this sense that Augustine speaks when he says that *wheresoever the will shall be, there shall the body be forthwith*.

Vel dicendum quod voluntas nunquam erit inordinata in beatis. Unde nunquam volent corpus suum esse alicubi in aliquo instanti in quo non possit ibi esse. Et sic, quodcumque instans voluntas determinabit, in illo corpus erit in illo loco quem voluntas determinat.

AD SECUNDUM dicendum quod quidam contradixerunt illi propositioni quam Philosophus inducit in parte illa, ut Commentator ibidem dicit: dicentes quod non oportet esse proportionem totius motus ad totum motum secundum proportionem resistentis medii ad aliud medium resistens; sed Oportet quod secundum proportionem mediorum per quae transitur, attendatur proportio retardationum quae accidit in motibus ex resistentia medii. Quilibet enim motus habet determinatum tempus velocitatis et tarditatis ex victoria moventis supra mobile, etiam si nihil resistat ex parte medii: sicut patet in corporibus caelestibus, in quibus non invenitur aliquid quod obstet motui ipsorum, et tamen non moventur in instanti, sed in tempore determinato secundum proportionem potentiae moventis ad mobile. Et ita patet quod, si ponatur aliquid moveri in vacuo, non oportebit quod moveatur in instanti: sed quod nihil addatur tempori quod debetur motui ex proportione praedicta moventis ad mobile, quia motus non retardatur.

Sed haec responsio, ut Commentator dicit ibidem, procedit ex falsa imaginatione qua quis imaginatur quod tarditas quae causatur ex resistentia medii, sit aliqua pars motus addita motui naturali, qui habet quantitatem secundum proportionem moventis ad mobile, sicut una linea additur lineae, ratione cuius accidit iri lineis quod non remanet eadem proportio totius ad totam lineam, quae erat linearum additarum ad invicem: ut sic etiam non sit eadem proportio totius motus ad totum motum sensibilem quae est retardationum contingentium ex resistentia medii.

Quae quidem imaginatio falsa est. Quia quaelibet pars motus habet tantum de velocitate quantum totus motus: non autem quaelibet pars lineae habet tantum de quantitate dimensiva quantum habet tota linea. Unde tarditas vel velocitas addita motui redundat in quamlibet partem eius: quod de lineis non contigit. Et sic tarditas addita motui non facit aliam partem motus, sicut in lineis accidebat quod additum est pars totius lineae.

Et ideo ad intelligendam probationem Philosophi, ut Commentator ibidem exponit, sciendum est quod oportet accipere totum pro uno, scilicet resistentiam mobilis ad virtutem moventem, et resistentiam medii per quod est motus, et cuiuscumque alterius resistentis: ita quod accipiatur quantitas tarditatis totius motus secundum proportionem virtutis moveritis ad mobile resistens quocumque modo, vel ex se vel ex alio extrinseco.

Or we may say that in the blessed there will never be an inordinate will: so that they never will wish their body to be instantaneously where it cannot be, and consequently whatever instant the will shall choose, at that same instant the body will be in whatever place the will shall determine.

REPLY OBJ. 2: Some have contradicted this proposition of the Philosopher's, as the Commentator thereon observes. They say that the ratio of one whole movement to another whole movement is not necessarily as the ratio of one resisting medium to another resisting medium, but that the ratio of the intervening mediums gives us the ratio of retardations attending the movements on account of the resistance of the medium. For every movement has a certain fixed speed, either fast or slow, through the mover overcoming the movable, although there be no resistance on the part of the medium, as evidenced in heavenly bodies, which have nothing to hinder their movement; and yet they do not move instantaneously, but in a fixed time proportionate to the power of the mover in comparison with the movable. Consequently, it is clear that even if we suppose something to move in a vacuum, it does not follow that it moves instantaneously, but that nothing is added to the time which that movement requires in the aforesaid proportion of the mover to the movable, because the movement is not retarded.

But this reply, as the Commentator observes, proceeds from an error in the imagination; for it is imagined that the retardation resulting from the resistance of the medium is a part of movement added to the natural movement, the quantity of which is in proportion to the mover in comparison with the movable, as when one line is added to another: for the proportion of one total to the other is not the same as the proportion of the lines to which an addition has been made. And so there would not be the same proportion between one whole sensible movement and another, as between the retardations resulting from the resistance of the medium.

This is an error of the imagination, because each part of a movement has as much speed as the whole movement: whereas not every part of a line has as much of the dimensive quantity as the whole line has. Hence any retardation or acceleration affecting the movement affects each of its parts, which is not the case with lines: and consequently the retardation that comes to a movement is not another part of the movement, whereas in the case of the lines that which is added is a part of the total line.

Consequently, in order to understand the Philosopher's argument, as the Commentator explains, we must take the whole as being one, that is, we must take not only the resistance of the movable to the moving power, but also the resistance of the medium through which the movement takes place, and again the resistance of anything else, so that we take the amount of retardation in the whole movement as being proportionate to the moving power in comparison

Oportet enim semper quod mobile resistat aliquo modo moventi: cum movens et motum, agens et patiens, inquantum huiusmodi, sint contraria.

Quandoque autem invenitur resistere mobile moventi ex seipso: vel quia habet virtutem inclinantem, ad contrarium motum, sicut patet in motibus violentis; vel saltem quia, habet locum contrarium loco qui est in interitione moventis, cuiusmodi resistentia invenitur etiam corporum caelestium ad suos motores. Quandoque autem mobile resistit virtuti moventis ex alio tantum et non ex seipso; sicut patet in motu naturali gravium et levium. Quia per ipsam formam eorum inclinantur ad motum talem: est enim forma impressio generantis, quod est motor ex parte gravium et levium. Ex parte autem materiae non invehitur aliqua resistentia neque virtutis inclinantis ad contrarium motum, neque contrarii loci: quia locus non debetur materiae nisi secundum quod, sub dimensionibus consistens, perficitur forma naturali. Unde non potest esse resistentia nisi ex parte medii: quae quidem resistentia est motui eorum connaturalis. Quandoque autem resistentia est ex utroque: sicut patet in motibus animalium.

Quando ergo in motu non est resistentia nisi ex parte mobilis, sicut accidit in corporibus caelestibus, tunc tempus motus mensuratur secundum proportionem motoris ad mobile. Et in talibus non procedit ratio Philosophi: quia, remoto omni medio, adhuc manet motus eorum in tempore. Sed in illis motibus in quibus est resistentia ex parte medii tantum, accipitur mensura temporis secundum impedimentum quod est ex medio solum. Unde, si subtrahatur omnino medium, nullum impedimentum remanebit. Et sic vel movebitur in instanti; vel aequali tempore movebitur secundum vacuum spatium et plenum. Quia, dato quod moveatur in tempore per vacuum, illud tempus in aliqua proportione se habebit ad tempus in quo movetur per plenum.

Possibile est autem imaginari aliquod corpus in eadem proportione subtilius corpore quo spatium plenum erat; quo si aliud spatium impleatur aequale, in tam parvo tempore movebitur per illud plenum sicut primo per vacuum: quia, quantum additur ad subtilitatem medii, tantum subtrahitur de quantitate temporis; et quanto est magis subtile, minus resistit. Sed in aliis motibus, in quibus est resistentia ex ipso mobili et ex medio, quantitas temporis est accipienda secundum proportionem moventis potentiae ad resistentiam mobilis et medii simul.

Unde, dato quod totaliter medium subtrahatur vel non impediat, non sequitur quod motus sit in instanti:

with the resisting movable, no matter in what way it resist, whether by itself or by reason of something extrinsic. For the movable must always resist the mover somewhat, since mover and moved, agent and patient, as such, are opposed to one another.

Now sometimes it is to be observed that the moved resists the mover by itself, either because it has a force inclining it to a contrary movement, as appears in violent movements, or at least because it has a place contrary to the place which is in the intention of the mover (and such resistance even heavenly bodies offer their movers.) Sometimes, the movable resists the power of the mover only by reason of something else and not by itself. This is seen in the natural movement of heavy and light things, because by their very form they are inclined to such a movement: for the form is an impression of their generator, which is the mover as regards heavy and light bodies. On the part of matter we find no resistance, neither of a force inclining to a contrary movement nor of a contrary place, since place is not due to matter except insofar as the latter, being circumscribed by its dimensions, is perfected by its natural form. Hence there can be no resistance save on the part of the medium, and this resistance is connatural to their movement. Sometimes again the resistance results from both, as may be seen in the movements of animals.

Accordingly, when in a movement there is no resistance save on the part of the movable, as in the heavenly bodies, the time of the movement is measured according to the proportion of the mover to the movable, and the Philosopher's argument does not apply to these, since if there be no medium at all their movement is still a movement in time. On the other hand, in those movements where there is resistance on the part of the medium only, the measure of time is taken only according to the obstacle on the part of the medium. Thus, if the medium be removed, there will be no longer an obstacle; and so either it will move instantaneously, or it will move in an equal time through a vacuum and through a plenum, because granted that it moves in time through a vacuum, that time will bear some proportion to the time in which it moves through a plenum.

Now it is possible to imagine another body more subtle in the same proportion than the body which filled the space, and then if this body fill some other equal space it will move in as little time through that plenum as it did previously through a vacuum, since by as much as the subtlety of the medium is increased, by so much is the length of time decreased, and the more subtle the medium, the less it resists. But in those other movements where resistance is offered by both the movable and the medium, the quantity of time must be proportionate to the power of the mover as compared with the resistance of both movable and medium together.

Hence, granted that the medium be taken away altogether, or that it cease to hinder, it does not follow that

sed quod tempus motus mensuratur tantum ex resistentia mobilis. Neque erit inconveniens si per idem tempus moveatur per vacuum et per plenum, aliquo subtilissimo corpore imaginato: quia determinata subtilitas medii, quanto est maior, nata est facere tarditatem minorem in motu; unde potest imaginari tanta subtilitas quod erit nata facere minorem tarditatem quam sit illa tarditas quam facit resistentia mobilis; et sic resistentia medii nullam tarditatem adiiciet ad motum.

Patet ergo quod, quamvis medium non resistat corporibus gloriosis, secundum hoc quod possint esse cum alio corpore in eodem loco, nihilominus motus eorum non erit in instanti: quia ipsum corpus mobile resistet virtuti moventi ex hoc ipso quod habet determinatum situm, sicut de corporibus caelestibus dictum est.

AD TERTIUM dicendum quod, quamvis virtus animae glorificatae excedit inaestimabiliter virtutem animae non glorificatae, non tamen excedit in infinitum: quia utraque virtus est finita. Unde non sequitur quod moveatur in instanti.

Si tamen esset simpliciter infinitae virtutis, non sequeretur quod moveretur in instanti, nisi superaretur totaliter resistentia quae est ex parte mobilis. Quamvis autem resistentia qua mobile resistit moventi per contrarietatem quam habet ad talem motum ratione inclinationis ad contrarium motum, possit a movente infinitae virtutis totaliter superari; tamen resistentia quam facit ex contrarietate quam habet ad locum quem intendit motor per motum, non potest totaliter superari, nisi auferatur ab ea esse in tali loco vel in tali situ. Sicut enim album resistit nigro ratione albedinis, et tanto magis quanto albedo magis distat a nigredine; ita corpus resistit alicui loco per hoc quod habet locum oppositum, et tanto est maior resistentia quanto est distantia maior. Non autem potest a corpore removeri quod sit in aliquo loco vel situ nisi auferatur ei sua corporeitas, per quam debetur ei locus vel situs. Unde, quandiu manet in natura corporis, nullo modo potest moveri in instanti, quantacumque sit virtus movens. Corpus autem gloriosum nunquam suam corporeitatem amittet. Unde nunquam in instanti moveri poterit.

AD QUARTUM dicendum quod par celeritas in verbis Augustini est intelligenda quantum ad hoc quod est imperceptibilis excessus unius respectu alterius: sicut et tempus totius motus est imperceptibile.

AD QUINTUM dicendum quod, quamvis post resurrectionem non erit tempus quod est numerus motus caeli, tamen erit tempus consurgens ex numero prioris et posterioris in quolibet motu.

the movement is instantaneous, but that the time is measured according only to the resistance of the movable. Nor will there be any inconsistency if it move in an equal time through a vacuum and through a space filled with the most subtle body imaginable, since the greater the subtlety we ascribe to the medium, the less it is naturally inclined to retard the movement. Wherefore it is possible to imagine so great a subtlety as will naturally retard the movement less than does the resistance of the movable, so that the resistance of the medium will add no retardation to the movement.

It is therefore evident that, although the medium offer no resistance to the glorified bodies insofar as it is possible for them to be in the same place with another body, nevertheless their movement will not be instantaneous, because the movable body itself will resist the motive power from the very fact that it has a determinate place, as we have said in reference to the heavenly bodies.

REPLY OBJ. 3: Although the power of a glorified soul surpasses immeasurably the power of a non-glorified soul, it does not surpass it infinitely, because both powers are finite: hence it does not follow that it causes instantaneous movement.

And even if its power were simply infinite, it would not follow that it causes an instantaneous movement unless the resistance of the movable were overcome altogether. Now, although the resistance of the movable to the mover that results from opposition to such a movement, by reason of its being inclined to a contrary movement, can be altogether overcome by a mover of infinite power, nevertheless the resistance it offers through contrariety towards the place which the mover intends by the movement cannot be overcome altogether except by depriving it of its being in such and such a place or position. For just as white resists black by reason of whiteness, and all the more according as whiteness is the more distant from blackness, so a body resists a certain place through having an opposite place, and its resistance is all the greater according as the distance is greater. Now it is impossible to take away from a body its being in some place or position except one deprive it of its corporeity, by reason of which it requires a place or position: wherefore so long as it retains the nature of a body, it can in no way be moved instantaneously, however greater be the motive power. Now the glorified body will never lose its corporeity, and therefore it will never be possible for it to be moved instantaneously.

REPLY OBJ. 4: In the words of Augustine, the speed is said to be equal because the excess of one over the other is imperceptible, just as the time taken by the whole movement is imperceptible.

REPLY OBJ. 5: Although after the resurrection the time which is the measure of the heaven's movement will be no more, there will nevertheless be time resulting from the before and after in any kind of movement.

QUESTION 85

THE CLARITY OF THE BODIES OF THE BLESSED

Deinde considerandum est de claritate corporum beatorum resurgentium.

Circa quod quaeruntur tria.

Primo: utrum claritas inerit corporibus gloriosis.

Secundo: utrum claritas illa videri poterit ab oculo non glorioso.

Tertio: utrum corpus gloriosum necessario videatur a corpore non glorioso.

We must now consider the clarity of the beatified bodies at the resurrection.

Under this head there are three points of inquiry:

(1) Whether there will be clarity in the glorified bodies?

(2) Whether this clarity will be visible to the non-glorified eye?

(3) Whether a glorified body will of necessity be seen by a non-glorified body?

Article 1

Whether Clarity Is Becoming to the Glorified Body?

Ad primum sic proceditur. Videtur quod corporibus gloriosis claritas non conveniet. Quia, sicut dicit Avicenna, in VI Naturalium, *omne corpus luminosum constat ex partibus perviis.* Sed partes corporis gloriosi non erunt perviae: cum in aliquibus dominetur terra, sicut in carnibus et ossibus. Ergo corpora gloriosa non erunt lucida.

Praeterea, omne corpus lucidum occultat illud quod est post se: unde unum luminare post aliud eclipsatur; flamma etiam ignis prohibet videri quod est post se. Sed corpora gloriosa non occultabunt illud quod intra ea continetur: quia, ut dicit Gregorius, super illud Iob [28, 17], *non adaequabitur ei aurum et vitrum: ibi,* scilicet in caelesti patria, *uniuscuiusque mentem ab alterius oculis membrorum corpulentia non abscondet, patebitque corporalibus oculis ipsa etiam corporalis harmonia.* Ergo corpora illa non erunt lucida.

Praeterea, lux et color contrariam dispositionem requirunt in subiecto: quia *lux est extremitas perspicui in corpore non terminato,* sed *color in corpore terminato,* ut patet in libro *de Sensu et Sensato* 3). Sed corpora gloriosa erunt colorata: quia, ut dicit Augustinus, XXII *de Civ. Dei, pulchritudo corporis est partium convenientia cum quadam coloris suavitate;* pulchritudo autem corporibus glorificatis deesse non poterit. Ergo corpora gloriosa non erunt lucida.

Praeterea, si claritas erit in corporibus gloriosis, oportet quod sit aequalis in omnibus partibus corporis: sicut omnes partes erunt eiusdem impassibilitatis, subtilitatis et agilitatis. Sed hoc non est conveniens: quia una pars habet maiorem dispositionem ad claritatem quam alia, sicut oculi quam manus, et spiritus quam ossa, et

Objection 1: It would seem that clarity is unbecoming to the glorified body. For, according to Avicenna (*Naturalium* 6.2), *every luminous body consists of transparent parts.* But the parts of a glorified body will not be transparent, since in some of them, such as flesh and bones, earth is predominant. Therefore, glorified bodies are not lightsome.

Obj. 2: Further, every lightsome body hides one that is behind it; wherefore one luminary behind another is eclipsed, and a flame of fire prevents one seeing what is behind it. But the glorified bodies will not hide that which is within them, for on Job 28:17: *gold or crystal cannot equal it,* Gregory says, *there,* that is in the heavenly country, *the grossness of the members will not hide one's mind from another's eyes, and the very harmony of the body will be evident to the bodily sight* (*Morals on Job* 18.48). Therefore, those bodies will not be lightsome.

Obj. 3: Further, light and color require a contrary disposition in their subject, since *light is the extreme point of visibility in an indeterminate body; color, in a determinate body* (*On Sense and the Sensed* 3). But glorified bodies will have color, for as Augustine says (*The City of God* 22.3), *the body's beauty is harmony of parts with a certain charm of color*: and it will be impossible for the glorified bodies to lack beauty. Therefore, the glorified bodies will not be lightsome.

Obj. 4: Further, if there be clarity in the glorified bodies, it will need to be equal in all the parts of the body, just as all the parts will be equally impassible, subtle, and agile. But this is not becoming, since one part has a greater disposition to clarity than another, for instance, the eye than the hand, the spirits than the bones, the humors than the

humores quam caro vel nervus. Ergo videtur quod non debeant illa corpora esse lucida.

SED CONTRA: Est quod dicitur Matth. 13, [43]: *fulgebunt iusti sicut sol in regno Patris eorum*; et Sap. 3, [7]: *fulgebunt iusti et tanquam scintillae* etc.

PRAETEREA, I Cor. 15, [43]: *seminatur in ignobilitate, surget in gloria*: quod ad claritatem pertinet, ut patet per praecedentia (v. 41, 42), ubi corporum resurgentium gloriam comparat *claritati stellarum*. Ergo corpora sanctorum resurgent lucida.

RESPONDEO dicendum quod corpora sanctorum fore lucida post resurrectionem ponere oportet propter auctoritatem Scripturae, quae hoc promittit. Sed claritatis huius causam quidam attribuunt quintae essentiae, quae tunc dominabitur in corpore humano. Sed quia hoc est absurdum, ut saepe dictum est, ideo melius est ut dicatur quod claritas illa causabitur ex redundantia gloriae animae in corpus. Quod enim recipitur in aliquo, non recipitur per modum influentis, sed per modum recipientis. Et ita claritas, quae est in anima spiritualis, recipitur in corpore ut corporalis. Et ideo, secundum quod anima erit maioris claritatis secundum maius meritum, ita etiam erit differentia claritatis in corpore: ut patet per Apostolum, I Cor. 15, [v. 41, 42]. Et ita in corpore glorioso cognoscetur gloria animae, sicut in vitro cognoscitur color corporis quod continetur in vase vitreo: ut Gregorius dicit, super illud Iob [28, 17], *non adaequabitur ei aurum vel vitrum*.

AD PRIMUM ergo dicendum quod Avicenna loquitur de illo corpore quod habet ex natura componentium claritatem. Sic autem non habebit corpus gloriosum, sed magis ex merito virtutis.

AD SECUNDUM dicendum quod Gregorius comparat corpora gloriosa auro et vitro: auro, propter claritatem; vitro, propter hoc quod translucebunt. Unde videtur dicendum quod erunt simul pervia et clara. Quod enim aliquod clarum non sit pervium, contingit ex hoc quod claritas corporis causatur ex densitate partium lucidarum: densitas enim repugnat pervietati. Sed tunc causabitur claritas ex alia causa, ut dictum est. Densitas autem corporis gloriosi pervietatem non tollit ab eis: sicut nec densitas vitri a vitro.

Quidam tamen dicunt quod comparantur vitro, non quia sint pervia, sed propter hanc similitudinem quod, sicut aliquid quod in vitro clauditur apparet, ita animae gloria, quae in corpore glorioso claudetur, non latebit. Sed primum melius est: quia magis salvatur dignitas corporis gloriosi; et magis consonat dictis Gregorii.

AD TERTIUM dicendum quod corporis gloria naturam non tollet, sed perficiet. Unde color qui debetur cor-

flesh or nerves. Therefore, it would seem unfitting for those bodies to be lightsome.

ON THE CONTRARY, Matthew 13:43 says that *the just shall shine as the sun in the kingdom of their Father*, and Wisdom 3:7 says that *the just shall shine, and shall run to and fro like sparks among the reeds*.

FURTHER, It is written: *it is sown in dishonor, it shall rise in glory* (1 Cor 15:43), which refers to clarity, as evidenced by the previous context where the glory of the rising bodies is compared *to the clarity of the stars*. Therefore, the bodies of the saints will be lightsome.

I ANSWER THAT, It is necessary to assert that after the resurrection the bodies of the saints will be lightsome, on account of the authority of Scripture which makes this promise. But the cause of this clarity is ascribed by some to the fifth or heavenly essence, which will then predominate in the human body. Since, however, this is absurd, as we have often remarked (Q. 84, A. 1), it is better to say that this clarity will result from the overflow of the soul's glory into the body. For whatever is received into anything is received not according to the mode of the source whence it flows, but according to the mode of the recipient. Wherefore clarity, which in the soul is spiritual, is received into the body as corporeal. And consequently according to the greater clarity of the soul by reason of its greater merit, so too will the body differ in clarity, as the Apostle affirms (1 Cor 15:41). Thus in the glorified body the glory of the soul will be known, even as through a crystal is known the color of a body contained in a crystal vessel; as Gregory says on Job 28:17, *gold or crystal cannot equal it*.

REPLY OBJ. 1: Avicenna is speaking of a body that has clarity through the nature of its component parts. It is not thus but rather by merit of virtue that the glorified body will have clarity.

REPLY OBJ. 2: Gregory compares the glorified body to gold on account of clarity, and to crystal on account of its transparency. Wherefore seemingly we should say that they will be both transparent and lightsome; for that a lightsome body be not transparent is owing to the fact that the clarity of that body results from the density of the lightsome parts, and density is opposed to transparency. Then, however, clarity will result from another cause, as stated above: and the density of the glorified body will not deprive it of transparency, as neither does the density of a crystal deprive crystal.

Some, on the other hand, say that they are compared to crystal not because they are transparent, but on account of this likeness, for as much as that which is enclosed in crystal is visible, so the glory of the soul enclosed in the glorified body will not be hidden. But the first explanation is better, because it safeguards better the dignity of the glorified body, and is more consistent with the words of Gregory.

REPLY OBJ. 3: The glory of the body will not destroy nature, but will perfect it. Therefore, the body will retain

pori ex natura suarum partium, remanebit in eo: sed superaddetur claritas ex gloria animae; sicut etiam videmus corpora colorata ex sui natura solis splendore relucere, vel ex aliqua alia causa extrinseco vel intrinseca.

AD QUARTUM dicendum quod, sicut gloriae claritas redundat ab anima in corpus secundum suum modum et ibi est alio modo quam sit in anima, ita in quamlibet partem corporis redundabit secundum suum modum. Unde non est inconveniens quod diversae partes habeant diversimode claritatem, secundum quod sunt diversimode dispositae ex sui natura ad ipsam. Nec est simile de aliis dotibus corporis, respectu quarum partes corporis non inveniuntur habere diversam dispositionem.

the color due to it by reason of the nature of its component parts, but in addition to this it will have clarity resulting from the soul's glory. Thus we see bodies which have color by their nature aglow with the resplendence of the sun, or from some other cause extrinsic or intrinsic.

REPLY OBJ. 4: Even as the clarity of glory will overflow from the soul into the body according to the mode of the body, and is there otherwise than in the soul, so again it will overflow into each part of the soul according to the mode of that part. Hence it is not unreasonable that the different parts should have clarity in different ways, according as they are differently disposed thereto by their nature. Nor is there any comparison with the other gifts of the body, for the various parts of the body are not differently disposed in their regard.

Article 2

Whether the Clarity of the Glorified Body Is Visible to the Non-glorified Eye?

AD SECUNDUM SIC PROCEDITUR. Videtur quod claritas corporis gloriosi non possit videri ab oculo non glorioso. Oportet enim esse proportionem visibilis ad visum. Sed oculus non glorificatus non est proportionatus ad videndam claritatem gloriae: cum sit alterius generis quam claritas naturae. Ergo corporis gloriosi claritas non videbitur ab oculo non glorioso.

PRAETEREA, claritas corporis gloriosi erit maior quam claritas solis nunc sit: quia etiam claritas solis erit tunc maior quam modo sit, ut dicitur; et multo maior ea erit claritas corporis gloriosi, propter quod sol et totus mundus claritatem maiorem accipiet. Sed oculus non gloriosus non potest inspicere solem in rota propter magnitudinem claritatis. Ergo multo minus poterit inspicere claritatem corporis gloriosi.

PRAETEREA, visibile oppositum oculis videntis necesse est videri, nisi sit laesio aliqua in oculo. Sed claritas corporis gloriosi opposita oculis non gloriosis non necessario videtur ab eis: quod patet de discipulis, qui corpus Domini post resurrectionem viderunt claritatem eius non intuentes. Ergo claritas illa non est visibilis ab oculo non glorioso.

SED CONTRA: Est quod dicit Glossa, Philipp. 3, super illud [v. 21], *configuratum corpori claritatis suae: assimilabimur claritati quam habuit in transfiguratione.* Sed claritas illa visa fuit ab oculis discipulorum non glorificatis. Ergo et claritas corporis glorificari ab oculis non gloriosis visibilis erit.

PRAETEREA, impii videntes gloriam iustorum, ex hoc torquebuntur in iudicio: ut patet per hoc quod di-

OBJECTION 1: It would seem that the clarity of the glorified body is invisible to the non-glorified eye. For the visible object should be proportionate to the sight. But a non-glorified eye is not proportionate to see the clarity of glory, since this differs generically from the clarity of nature. Therefore, the clarity of the glorified body will not be seen by a non-glorified eye.

OBJ. 2: Further, the clarity of the glorified body will be greater than the clarity of the sun is now, since the clarity of the sun also will then be greater than it is now, according to Isaiah 30:26, and the clarity of the glorified body will be much greater still, for which reason the sun and the entire world will receive greater clarity. Now a non-glorified eye is unable to gaze on the very orb of the sun on account of the greatness of its clarity. Therefore, still less will it be able to gaze on the clarity of a glorified body.

OBJ. 3: Further, a visible object that is opposite the eyes of the seer must be seen, unless there be some lesion to the eye. But the clarity of a glorified body that is opposite to non-glorified eyes is not necessarily seen by them: which is evident in the case of the disciples who saw our Lord's body after the resurrection without witnessing its clarity. Therefore, this clarity will be invisible to a non-glorified eye.

ON THE CONTRARY, A Gloss on Philippians 3:21: *made like to the body of his glory*, says, *it will be like the clarity which he had in the Transfiguration.* Now this clarity was seen by the non-glorified eyes of the disciples. Therefore, the clarity of the glorified body will be visible to non-glorified eyes also.

FURTHER, The wicked will be tortured in the judgment by seeing the glory of the just, according to Wisdom 5:2.

citur Sap. 5, [1–2]. Sed non plene viderent gloriam ipsorum nisi claritatem corporum eorum inspicerent. Ergo, etc.

RESPONDEO dicendum quod quidam dixerunt quod claritas corporis gloriosi non potest videri ab oculo non glorioso, nisi forte per miraculum. Sed hoc non potest esse, nisi claritas illa aequivoce diceretur. Quia lux, secundum id quod est, nata est movere visum; et visus, secundum id quod est, natus est percipere lucem; sicut verum se habet ad intellectum, et bonum ad affectum. Unde, si esset aliquis visus qui non posset percipere aliquam lucem omnino, vel ille visus diceretur aequivoce, vel lux illa. Quod non potest in proposito dici: quia sic per hoc quod dicitur gloriosa corpora futura esse lucida, nihil nobis notificaretur; sicut qui dicit canem esse in caelo, nihili notificat ei qui non novit nisi canem qui est animal. Ideo dicendum est quod claritas corporis gloriosi naturaliter ab oculo non glorioso videri potest.

AD PRIMUM ergo dicendum quod gloriae claritas erit alterius generis quam claritas naturae quantum ad causam, sed non quantum ad speciem. Unde, sicut claritas naturae ratione speciei suae est proportionata visui, ita claritas gloriosa.

AD SECUNDUM dicendum quod, sicut corpus gloriosum non potest pati aliquid passione naturae, sed solum passione animae, ita ex proprietate gloriae non aget nisi actione animae. Claritas autem intensa non offendit visum inquantum agit actione animae, sed secundum hoc magis delectat: offendit autem inquantum agit actione naturae, calefaciendo et dissolvendo organum visus, et disgregando spiritus. Et ideo claritas corporis gloriosi, quamvis excedat claritatem solis, tamen de sui natura non offendit visum, sed demulcet. Propter quod claritas illa comparatur claritati iaspidis, Apoc. 21, [11].

AD TERTIUM dicendum quod claritas corporis gloriosi provenit ex merito voluntatis. Et ideo voluntati subdetur, ut secundum eius imperium videatur vel non videatur; et in potestate corporis gloriosi erit ostendere claritatem suam vel occultare. Et haec fuit opinio Praepositini.

But they would not fully see their glory unless they gazed on their clarity. Therefore, etc.

I ANSWER THAT, Some have asserted that the clarity of the glorified body will not be visible to the non-glorified eye, except by a miracle. But this is impossible, unless this clarity were so named equivocally, because light by its essence has a natural tendency to move the sight, and sight by its essence has a natural tendency to perceive light, even as the true is in relation to the intellect, and the good to the appetite. Wherefore if there were a sight altogether incapable of perceiving a light, either this sight is so named equivocally, or else this light is. This cannot be said in the point at issue, because then nothing would be made known to us when we are told that the glorified bodies will be lightsome: even so a person who says that a dog is in the heavens conveys no knowledge to one who knows no other dog than the animal. Hence we must say that the clarity of a glorified body is naturally visible to the non-glorified eye.

REPLY OBJ. 1: The clarity of glory will differ generically from the clarity of nature as to its cause, but not as to its species. Hence just as the clarity of nature is, by reason of its species, proportionate to the sight, so too will the clarity of glory be.

REPLY OBJ. 2: Just as a glorified body is not passible to a passion of nature but only to a passion of the soul, so in virtue of its property of glory it acts only by the action of the soul. Now intense clarity does not disturb the sight insofar as it acts by the action of the soul, for thus it rather gives delight, but it disturbs it insofar as it acts by the action of nature by heating and destroying the organ of sight, and by scattering the spirits asunder. Hence, though the clarity of a glorified body surpasses the clarity of the sun, it does not by its nature disturb the sight but soothes it: wherefore this clarity is compared to the jasper-stone (Rev 21:11).

REPLY OBJ. 3: The clarity of the glorified body results from the merit of the will and therefore will be subject to the will, so as to be seen or not seen according to its command. Therefore, it will be in the power of the glorified body to show forth its clarity or to hide it: and this was the opinion of Praepositivus.

Article 3

Whether a Glorified Body Will Be Necessarily Seen by a Non-glorified Body?

AD TERTIUM SIC PROCEDITUR. Videtur quod corpus gloriosum necessario videatur a corpore non glorioso. Quia corpora gloriosa erunt lucida. Sed corpus lucidum manifestat se et alia. Ergo corpora gloriosa necessario videbuntur.

OBJECTION 1: It would seem that a glorified body will be necessarily seen by a non-glorified body. For the glorified bodies will be lightsome. Now a lightsome body reveals itself and other things. Therefore, the glorified bodies will be seen of necessity.

PRAETEREA, omne corpus quod occultat alia corpora post se existentia, de necessitate visu percipitur, ex hoc ipso quod alia quae sunt post occultantur. Sed corpus gloriosum occultabit a visu alia corpora post se existentia: quia erit corpus coloratum. Ergo et de necessitate videbitur.

PRAETEREA, sicut quantitas est de his quae insunt corpori, ita qualitas, per quam videtur. Sed quantitas non suberit voluntati, ut corpus gloriosum possit esse maioris quantitatis vel minoris. Ergo nec qualitas, per quam visibile est, ut possit non videri.

SED CONTRA: Est quod corpus nostrum glorificabitur in conformitate corporis Christi post resurrectionem. Sed corpus Christi post resurrectionem non necessario videbatur: immo disparuit ab oculis discipulorum in Emmaus, ut dicitur Luc. [24, 31]. Ergo et corpus glorificatum non necessario videbitur.

PRAETEREA, ibi erit summa obedientia corporis ad animam. Ergo corpus poterit videri vel non videri secundum voluntatem animae.

RESPONDEO dicendum quod visibile videtur secundum quod agit in visum. Ex hoc autem quod aliquid agit vel non agit in aliquod extrinsecum, non est aliqua mutatio in ipso. Unde sine mutatione alicuius proprietatis quae sit de perfectione corporis glorificati, potest contingere quod videatur et non videatur. Unde in potestate animae glorificatae erit quod corpus suum videatur vel non videatur, sicut et quaelibet alia actio corporalis in animae potestate erit: alias non esset corpus gloriosum instrumentum summe obediens principali agenti.

AD PRIMUM ergo dicendum quod claritas illa obediet corpori glorioso, ut possit eam ostendere vel occultare.

AD SECUNDUM dicendum quod color corporis non impedit pervietatem ipsius nisi inquantum immutat visum, quia visus non potest immutari simul a duobus eoioribus ut utrumque perfecte inspiciat. Color autem corporis gloriosi erit in potestate animae, ut per ipsum immutet visum vel non immutet. Et ideo erit in potestate eius ut occultet corpus quod est post se, vel non occultet.

AD TERTIUM dicendum quod quantitas est inhaerens ipsi corpori glorioso: neque posset quantitas immutari ad imperium animae sine mutatione intrinseca corporis gloriosi, quae impassibilitati eius repugnaret. Et ideo non est simile de quantitate et visibilitate. Quia etiam qualitas illa per quam est visibile, non potest subtrahi ad imperium animae: sed actio illius qualitatis suspendetur; et sic occultabitur corpus ad imperium animae.

OBJ. 2: Further, every body which hides other bodies that are behind it is necessarily perceived by the sight, from the very fact that the other things behind it are hidden. Now the glorified body will hide other bodies that are behind it from being seen, because it will be a colored body. Therefore, it will be seen of necessity.

OBJ. 3: Further, just as quantity is something in a body, so is the quality whereby a body is seen. Now quantity will not be subject to the will, so that the glorified body be able to be of greater or smaller quantity. Therefore, neither will the quality of visibility be subject to the will, so that a body would be able not to be seen.

ON THE CONTRARY, Our body will be glorified in being made like to the body of Christ after the resurrection. Now after the resurrection Christ's body was not necessarily seen; in fact, it vanished from the sight of the disciples at Emmaus (Luke 24:31). Therefore, neither will the glorified body be necessarily seen.

FURTHER, There the body will be in complete obedience to the will. Therefore, the body will be visible or invisible according to the soul's will.

I ANSWER THAT, A visible object is seen inasmuch as it acts on the sight. Now there is no change in a thing through its acting or not acting on an external object. Wherefore a glorified body may be seen or not seen without any property pertaining to its perfection being changed. Consequently, it will be in the power of a glorified soul for its body to be seen or not seen, even as any other action of the body will be in the soul's power; else the glorified body would not be a perfectly obedient instrument of its principal agent.

REPLY OBJ. 1: This clarity will be obedient to the glorified body so that this will be able to show it or hide it.

REPLY OBJ. 2: A body's color does not prevent its being transparent except insofar as it affects the sight, because the sight cannot be affected by two colors at the same time, so as to perceive them both perfectly. But the color of the glorified body will be completely in the power of the soul, so that it can thereby act or not act on the sight. Hence it will be in its power to hide or not to hide a body that is behind it.

REPLY OBJ. 3: Quantity is inherent to the glorified body itself, nor would it be possible for the quantity to be altered at the soul's bidding without the glorified body suffering some alteration incompatible with its impassibility. Hence there is no comparison between quantity and visibility, because even this quality whereby it is visible cannot be removed at the soul's bidding, but the action of that quality will be suspended, and thus the body will be hidden at the soul's command.

QUESTION 86

THE CONDITION OF THE BODIES OF THE DAMNED

Consequenter considerandum est de conditionibus damnatorum resurgentium.

Circa quod quaeruntur tria.

Primo: utrum corpora damnatorum cum suis deformitatibus resurgant.

Secundo: utrum eorum corpora erunt corruptibilia.

Tertio: utrum erunt impassibilia.

We must next consider the conditions in which the bodies of the damned will rise again.

Under this head there are three points of inquiry:

(1) Whether the bodies of the damned will rise again with their deformities?

(2) Whether their bodies will be corruptible?

(3) Whether they will be impassible?

Article 1

Whether the Bodies of the Damned Will Rise Again With Their Deformities?

AD PRIMUM SIC PROCEDITUR. Videtur quod corpora damnatorum cum suis deformitatibus resurgent. Illud enim quod in poenam peccati inductum est, desinere non debet nisi peccato remisso. Sed membrorum defectus qui accidunt per mutilationem, in poenam peccati inducti sunt; et similiter etiam omnes deformitates corporales. Ergo a damnatis, qui peccatorum remissionem non sunt consecuti, in resurrectione non removebuntur.

PRAETEREA, sicut resurrectio sanctorum erit ad ultimam felicitatem, sic resurrectio impiorum ad ultimam miseriam. Sed sanctis resurgentibus non auferetur aliquid quod ad eorum perfectionem pertinere possit. Ergo nec impiis resurgentibus aliquid auferetur quod ad eorum miseriam pertineat. Huiusmodi autem sunt deformitates. Ergo, etc.

PRAETEREA, sicut ad defectum passibilis corporis pertinet deformitas, ita et tarditas. Sed a corporibus damnatorum resurgentium tarditas non removebitur: quia eorum corpora non erunt agilia. Ergo eadem ratione nec deformitas removebitur.

SED CONTRA: I ad Cor. 15, [52]: *mortui resurgent incorrupti,* Glossa: *mortui, idest peccatores, vel generaliter omnes mortui, resurgent incorrupti, idest, sine aliqua diminutione membrorum.* Ergo mali resurgent sine deformitatibus.

PRAETEREA, in damnatis non erit aliquid quod sensum doloris in eis impediat. Sed aegritudo impedit sensum doloris, inquantum per eam debilitantur organa sentiendi. Et similiter defectus membri impediret ne esset universalis dolor in corpore. Ergo sine istis defectibus damnati resurgent.

OBJECTION 1: It would seem that the bodies of the damned will rise again with their deformities. For that which was appointed as a punishment for sin should not cease except the sin be forgiven. Now the lack of limbs that results from mutilation, as well as all other bodily deformities, are appointed as punishments for sin. Therefore, these deformities will not be taken away from the damned, seeing that they will not have received the forgiveness of their sins.

OBJ. 2: Further, just as the saints will rise again to final happiness, so the wicked will rise again to final unhappiness. Now when the saints rise again, nothing will be taken from them that can pertain to their perfection; therefore, nothing pertaining to the defect or unhappiness of the wicked will be taken from them at the resurrection. But such are their deformities. Therefore, etc.

OBJ. 3: Further, just as deformity is a defect of the passible body, so is slowness of movement. Now slowness of movement will not be taken from the bodies of the damned at the resurrection, since their bodies will not be agile. Therefore, for the same reason neither will their deformity be taken away.

ON THE CONTRARY, It is written: *the dead shall rise again incorruptible* (1 Cor 15:52); where a Gloss says, *the dead, i.e., sinners, or all the dead in general, shall rise again incorruptible, i.e., without the loss of any limbs.* Therefore, the wicked will rise again without their deformities.

FURTHER, There will be nothing in the damned to lessen the sense of pain. But sickness hinders the sense of pain by weakening the organ of sense, and in like manner the lack of a limb would prevent pain from affecting the whole body. Therefore, the damned will rise again without these defects.

RESPONDEO dicendum quod in corpore humano potest esse deformitas dupliciter. Uno modo, ex defectu alicuius membri, sicut mutilatos turpes dicimus: deest enim eis debita proportio partium ad totum. Et de tali deformitate nulli dubium est quod in corporibus damnatorum non erit: quia omnia corpora, tam bonorum quam malorum, integra resurgent.

Alio modo deformitas contingit ex indebita partium dispositione, vel indebita quantitate vel qualitate vel: situ, quae etiam proportionem debitam partium ad totum non patitur. Et de talibus deformitatibus, et similibus defectibus, sicut sunt febres et huiusmodi aegritudines, quae interdum sunt deformitatis causa, Augustinus indeterminatum et sub dubio relinquit in Enchiridio, ut in littera Magister dicit. Sed apud doctores modernos est duplex super hoc opinio.

Quidam enim dicunt quod huiusmodi deformitates et defectus in corporibus damnatorum remanebunt: considerantes eorum damnationem, qua ad summam miseriam deputantur, cui nihil incommoditatis subtrahi debet.

Sed hoc non videtur rationabiliter dici. In reparatione enim corporis resurgentis magis attenditur naturae perfectio quam conditio quae prius fuit: unde et qui infra perfectam aetatem decedunt, in statura iuvenilis aetatis resurgent; Unde et illi qui aliquos defectus naturales in corpore habuerunt, vel deformitates ex eis provenientes, in resurrectione sine illis defectibus vel deformitatibus repararentur nisi peccati meritum impediret: et ita, si aliquis cum defectibus vel deformitatibus resurget, hoc erit ei in poenam. *Modus* autem *poenae est secundum mensuram culpae*. Contingit autem quod aliquis peccator damnandus minoribus peccatis subiectus aliquas deformitates vel defectus habeat quas non habuit aliquis damnandus peccatis gravioribus irretitus. Unde, si ille qui in hac vita deformitates habuit cum eis resurgat, sine quibus constat quod resurget alius gravius puniendus qui eas in hac vita non habuit, modus poenae non responderet quantitati culpae, sed magis videretur aliquis puniri pro poenis quas in hoc mundo passus fuit: quod est absurdum.

Et ideo alii rationabilius dicunt quod Auctor qui naturam condidit, in resurrectione naturam corporis integre reparabit. Unde quidquid defectus vel turpitudinis ex corruptione vel debilitate naturae sive principiorum naturalium in corpore fuit, totum in resurrectione removebitur, sicut febris, lippitudo et similia: defectus autem qui ex naturalibus principiis in humano corpore naturaliter consequuntur, sicut ponderositas, passibilitas et similia, in corporibus damnatorum erunt, quos defectus ab electorum corporibus gloria resurrectionis excludet.

I ANSWER THAT, Deformity in the human body is of two kinds. One arises from the lack of a limb: thus we say that a mutilated person is deformed, because he lacks due proportion of the parts to the whole. Deformities of this kind, without any doubt, will not be in the bodies of the damned, since all bodies of both wicked and good will rise again whole.

Another deformity arises from the undue disposition of the parts, by reason of undue quantity, quality, or place—which deformity is, moreover, incompatible with due proportion of parts to whole. Concerning these deformities and like defects, such as fevers and similar ailments which sometimes result in deformity, Augustine remained undecided and doubtful (*Handbook on Faith, Hope, and Charity* 92) as the Master remarks (*Sentences* IV, D.44). Among modern masters, however, there are two opinions on this point.

For some say that such deformities and defects will remain in the bodies of the damned, because they consider that those who are damned are sentenced to utmost unhappiness from which no affliction should be rebated.

But this would seem unreasonable, for in the restoration of the rising body we look to its natural perfection rather than to its previous condition. Hence those who die under perfect age will rise again in the stature of youth, as stated above (Q. 81, A. 1). Consequently, those who had natural defects in the body, or deformities resulting therefrom, will be restored without those defects or deformities at the resurrection, unless the demerit of sin prevent; and so if a person rise again with such defects and deformities, this will be for his punishment. Now *the mode of punishment is according to the measure of guilt*. But it happens that a certain damned sinner, subject to minor sins, has deformities or defects that someone else who would be damned for more serious sins did not have. Wherefore if he who had deformities in this life should rise again with them, while the other who had them not in this life, and therefore, as is clear, will rise again without them (though deserving of greater punishment), the mode of the punishment would not correspond to the amount of guilt; in fact, it would seem that a man is more punished on account of the pains which he suffered in this world, which is absurd.

Hence others say with more reason that he who fashioned nature will wholly restore the body's nature at the resurrection. Therefore, whatever defect or deformity was in the body through corruption, or weakness of nature or of natural principles (for instance, fever, purblindness, and so forth) will be entirely done away with at the resurrection: whereas those defects in the human body which are the natural result of its natural principles, such as heaviness, passibility, and the like, will be in the bodies of the damned, while they will be removed from the bodies of the elect by the glory of the resurrection.

AD PRIMUM ergo dicendum quod, cum poena in quolibet foro infligatur secundum conditionem illius fori, poenae quae in hac vita temporali infliguntur pro aliquo peccato temporales sunt, et ultra vitae terminum non se extendunt. Et ideo, quamvis peccatum non sit remissum damnatis, non tamen oportet quod easdem poenas ibi sustineant quas in hoc mundo sunt passi: sed divina iustitia requirit ut ibi poenis gravioribus in aeternum crucientur.

AD SECUNDUM dicendum quod non est similis ratio de bonis et malis: eo quod aliquid potest esse pure bonum, non autem pure malum. Unde sanctorum ultima felicitas hoc requirit ut ab omni malo penitus sint immunes: sed ultima malorum miseria non excludit omne bonum; quia *malum, si integrum sit, corrumpit seipsum*, ut Philosophus dicit, in IV *Ethic.* Unde oportet quod miseriae damnatorum substernatur bonum naturae in ipsis: quod est opus Conditoris perfecti, qui ipsam naturam in perfectione suae speciei reparabit.

AD TERTIUM dicendum quod tarditas est de illis defectibus qui naturaliter consequuntur principia humani corporis: non autem deformitas. Et ideo non est similis ratio.

REPLY OBJ. 1: Since in every tribunal punishment is inflicted according to the jurisdiction of the tribunal, the punishments which in this temporal life are inflicted for some particular sin are themselves temporal, and extend not beyond the term of this life. Hence, although the damned are not pardoned their sins, it does not follow that there they will undergo the same punishments as they have in this world: but the divine justice demands that there they shall suffer more severe punishment for eternity.

REPLY OBJ. 2: There is no parity between the good and the wicked, because a thing can be altogether good, but not altogether evil. Hence the final happiness of the saints requires that they should be altogether exempt from all evil; whereas the final unhappiness of the wicked will not exclude all good, because *if a thing be wholly evil it destroys itself*, as the Philosopher says (*Ethics* 4.5). Hence it is necessary for the good of their nature to underlie the unhappiness of the damned, which good is the work of their perfect Creator, who will restore that same nature to the perfection of its species.

REPLY OBJ. 3: Slowness of movement is one of those defects which are the natural result of the principles of the human body; but deformity is not, and consequently the comparison fails.

Article 2

Whether the Bodies of the Damned Will Be Incorruptible?

AD SECUNDUM SIC PROCEDITUR. Videtur quod corpora damnatorum erunt corruptibilia. Omne enim compositum ex contrariis necesse est corrumpi. Sed corpora damnatorum erunt ex contrariis composita, ex quibus etiam nunc componuntur: alias non essent eiusdem speciei, et per consequens nec eadem numero. Ergo erunt corruptibilia.

PRAETEREA, corpora damnatorum si incorruptibilia sunt futura, hoc non erit per naturam: cum sint futura eiusdem naturae cuius et nunc sunt. Nec etiam per gratiam vel gloriam: quia talibus omnino carebunt. Ergo nullo modo erunt incorruptibilia.

PRAETEREA, illis qui sunt in summa miseria subtrahere maximam poenarum videtur inconveniens. Sed maxima poenarum est mors: ut patet per Philosophum, III *Ethic.* Ergo a damnatis, qui sunt in miseria, mors removeri non debet. Ergo eorum corpora corruptibilia erunt.

SED CONTRA: Est quod dicitur Apoc. 9, [6]: *in diebus illis quaerent homines mortem et non invenient eam; desiderabunt mori, et fugiet mors ab eis.*

OBJECTION 1: It would seem that the bodies of the damned will be corruptible. For everything composed of contraries must necessarily be corruptible. Now the bodies of the damned will be composed of the contraries whereof they are composed even now, else they would not be the same, neither specifically nor, in consequence, numerically. Therefore, they will be corruptible.

OBJ. 2: Further, if the bodies of the damned will not be corruptible, this will not be by nature, since they will be of the same nature as now; nor will it be by grace or glory, since they will lack these things altogether. Therefore, they will be corruptible.

OBJ. 3: Further, it would seem inconsistent to withdraw the greatest of punishments from those who are in the highest degree of unhappiness. Now death is the greatest of punishments, as the Philosopher declares (*Ethics* 3.6). Therefore, death should not be withdrawn from the damned, since they are in the highest degree of unhappiness. Therefore, their bodies will be corruptible.

ON THE CONTRARY, It is written: *in those days men shall seek death, and shall not find it, and they shall desire to die, and death shall fly from them* (Rev 9:6).

PRAETEREA, damnati punientur in anima et corpore poena perpetua: Matth. 25, [46], *ibunt hi in supplicium aeternum.* Sed hoc esse non posset si eorum corpora corruptibilia essent. Ergo eorum corpora erunt incorruptibilia.

RESPONDEO dicendum quod, cum in omni motu oporteat esse aliquod principium motus, dupliciter motus aliquis vel mutatio a mobili removetur: uno modo, per hoc quod deest principium motus; alio modo, per hoc quod impeditur principium motus. Corruptio autem mutatio quaedam est. Unde dupliciter potest contingere ut corpus quod ex conditione suorum principiorum corruptibilitatem habet, incorruptibile reddatur. Uno modo, ex hoc quod principium ad corruptionem movens totaliter tollitur. Et hoc modo corpora damnatorum incorruptibilia erunt. Cum enim caelum sit primum alterans per motum suum localem; et alia omnia agentia secunda in virtute ipsius agant, et quasi ab ipso mota; oportet quod, cessante motu caeli, nihil sit agens quod possit corpus per alterationem aliquam transmutare a sua naturali proprietate. Et ideo post resurrectionem, cessante motu caeli, nulla qualitas erit sufficiens ut corpus humanum alterare possit a sua naturali qualitate. Corruptio autem est terminus alterationis, sicut et generatio. Unde corpora damnatorum corrumpi non poterunt. Et hoc deservit divinae iustitiae, ut perpetuo viventes perpetuo puniantur, quod divina iustitia requirit, ut infra dicetur: sicut et nunc corruptibilitas corporum deservit divinae providentiae, per quam ex aliquibus corruptis alia generantur.

Alio modo contingit ex hoc quod principium corruptionis impeditur. Et hoc modo corpus Adae incorruptibile fuit: quia contrariae qualitates in hominis corpore existentes continebantur per gratiam innocentiae ne ad dissolutionem corporis agere possent. Et multo plus continebuntur in corporibus gloriosis, quae erunt omnino subiecta spiritui. Et sia in corporibus beatorum post resurrectionem communem coniungentur duo praedicti modi incorruptibilitatis.

AD PRIMUM ergo dicendum quod contraria ex quibus corpora componuntur, sunt secunda principia ad corruptionem agentia: primum enim agens est motus caelestis, Unde, supposito motu caeli, necesse est ut corpus ex contrariis compositum corrumpatur, nisi sit aliqua causa potior impediens. Sed motu caeli remoto, contraria ex quibus corpus componitur, non sufficiunt ad corruptionem faciendam, etiam secundum naturam, ut patet ex dictis. Cessationem autem motus caeli non cognoverunt philosophi. Unde pro infallibili habebant quod corpus compositum ex contrariis corrumpatur secundum naturam.

FURTHER, The damned will be punished with an everlasting punishment both in soul and body: *these shall go into everlasting punishment* (Matt 25:46). But this would not be possible if their bodies were corruptible. Therefore, their bodies will be incorruptible.

I ANSWER THAT, Since in every movement there must be a principle of movement, movement or change may be withdrawn from a movable in two ways: first, through absence of a principle of movement; second, through an obstacle to the principle of movement. Now corruption is a kind of change: and consequently a body which is corruptible on account of the nature of its principles may be rendered incorruptible in two ways. First, by the total removal of the principle which leads to corruption, and in this way the bodies of the damned will be incorruptible. For since the heaven is the first principle of alteration in virtue of its local movement, and all other secondary agents act in virtue thereof and as though moved thereby, it follows that at the cessation of the heavenly movement there is no longer any agent that can change the body by altering it from its natural property. Wherefore after the resurrection and the cessation of the heavenly movement, there will be no quality capable of altering the human body from its natural quality. Now corruption, like generation, is the term of alteration. Hence the bodies of the damned will be incorruptible, and this will serve the purpose of divine justice, since living forever, they will be punished forever. This is in keeping with the demands of divine justice, as we shall state further on (A. 3), even as now the corruptibility of bodies serves the purpose of divine providence, by which one thing is generated through the corruption of another.

Second, this happens through the principle of corruption being hindered, and in this way the body of Adam was incorruptible, because the conflicting qualities that exist in man's body were withheld by the grace of innocence from conducing to the body's dissolution: and much more will they be withheld in the glorified bodies, which will be wholly subject to the spirit. Thus after the general resurrection the two aforesaid modes of incorruptibility will be united together in the bodies of the blessed.

REPLY OBJ. 1: The contraries of which bodies are composed are conducive to corruption as secondary principles. For the first active principle thereof is the heavenly movement: hence, given the movement of the heaven, it is necessary for a body composed of contraries to be corrupted unless some more powerful cause prevent it: whereas if the heavenly movement be withdrawn, the contraries of which a body is composed do not suffice to cause corruption even in accordance with nature, as explained above. But the philosophers were ignorant of a cessation in the heavenly movement; and consequently they held that a body composed of contraries is, without fail, corrupted in accordance with nature.

Ad secundum dicendum quod incorruptibilitas illa erit per naturam: non quod sit aliquod incorruptionis principium in corporibus damnatorum, sed per defectum primi moventis ad corruptionem.

Ad tertium dicendum quod, quamvis mors sit simpliciter maxima poenarum, secundum quid tamen nihil prohibet mortem esse in poenarum remedium, et per consequens ablationem mortis in poenarum augmentum. *Vivere* enim, ut dicit Philosophus, in IX *Ethic.*, *videtur omnibus delectabile esse, eo quod omnia esse appetunt: non oportet autem, ut ibidem dicitur, accipere malam vitam, neque corruptam, neque quae est in tristitiis.* Sicut ergo vivere simpliciter est delectabile, non autem vita quae est in tristitiis; ita et mors, quae est privatio vitae, simpliciter est poenosa et maxima poenarum, inquantum subtrahit primum bonum, scilicet esse, cum quo omnia alia subtrahuntur; sed inquantum privat malam vitam et quae est in tristitiis, est in remedium poenarum, quas terminat. Et per consequens mortis subtractio est in augmentum poenarum, quas perpetuas facit.

Si autem dicatur mors esse poenalis propter corporalem dolorem quem sentiunt morientes, non est dubium quod, multo maiorem dolorem damnati continue sustinebunt, Unde in perpetua morte esse dicuntur: sicut scriptum est in Psalmo [48, 15]: *mors depascet eos.*

Reply Obj. 2: This incorruptibility will result from nature not as though there were some principle of incorruption in the bodies of the damned, but on account of the cessation of the active principle of corruption, as shown above.

Reply Obj. 3: Although death is simply the greatest of punishments, yet nothing prevents death conducing, in a certain respect, to a cessation of punishments; and consequently the removal of death may contribute to the increase of punishment. For as the Philosopher says (*Ethics* 9.9), *life is pleasant to all, for all desire to be: but we must not apply this to a wicked or corrupt life, nor one passed in sorrow.* Accordingly, just as life is simply pleasant, but not the life that is passed in sorrows, so too death, which is the privation of life, is painful simply, and the greatest of punishments inasmuch as it deprives one of the primary good, namely being, with which other things are withdrawn. But insofar as it deprives one of a wicked life, and of such as is passed in sorrow, it is a remedy for pains, since it puts an end to them. Consequently, the withdrawal of death leads to the increase of punishments by making them everlasting.

If, however, we say that death is penal by reason of the bodily pain which the dying feel, without doubt the damned will continue to feel a far greater pain: wherefore they are said to be in everlasting death, as is written: *death shall feed upon them* (Ps 48:15).

Article 3

Whether the Bodies of the Damned Will Be Impassible?

Ad tertium sic proceditur. Videtur quod futura sint impassibilia. Quia secundum Philosophum, in VI *Topic.*, *omnis passio, magis facta, abiicit a substantia.* Sed *a finito si semper aliquid abiiciatur, necesse est illud tandem consumi*: ut dicitur in I *Physic.* Ergo, si corpora damnatorum erunt passibilia et semper patientur, quandoque deficient et corrumpentur: quod falsum esse ostensum est. Ergo erunt impassibilia.

Praeterea, omne agens assimilat sibi patiens. Si ergo corpora damnatorum patientur ab igne, ignis ea sibi assimilabit. Sed non consumit aliter ignis corpora nisi inquantum ea sibi assimilans resolvit. Ergo, si corpora damnatorum erunt passibilia, ab igne quandoque consumentur. Et sic idem quod prius.

Praeterea, animalia quae in igne sine corruptione dicuntur vivere, ut de salamandra dicitur, ab igne non affliguntur: animal enim dolore corporis non affligitur nisi corpus aliquo modo laedatur. Si ergo corpora damnatorum in igne sine consumptione remanere possunt, sicut et animalia praedicta, ut Augustinus, in libro *de Civ. Dei*,

Objection 1: It would seem that the bodies of the damned will be impassible. For, according to the Philosopher (*Topics* 6), *increase of passion results in loss of substance.* Now *if a finite thing be continually lessened, it must at length be done away with* (*Physics* 1.4). Therefore, if the bodies of the damned will be passible, and will be ever suffering, they will at length be done away with and corrupted: and this has been shown to be false (A. 2). Therefore, they will be impassible.

Obj. 2: Further, every agent likens the patient to itself. If, then, the bodies of the damned are passive to the fire, the fire will liken them to itself. Now fire does not consume bodies except insofar as, in likening them to itself, it disintegrates them. Therefore, if the bodies of the damned will be passible, they will at length be consumed by the fire, and thus the same conclusion follows as before.

Obj. 3: Further, those animals, for instance, the salamander, which are said to remain living in fire without being destroyed, are not distressed by the fire: because an animal is not distressed by bodily pain unless the body in some way is hurt thereby. If, therefore, the bodies of the damned can, like the aforesaid animals, remain in the fire without

dicit, videtur quod nullam afflictionem ibi sustinebunt. Quod non esset nisi eorum corpora impassibilia essent. Ergo, etc.

Praeterea, si corpora damnatorum sunt passibilia, dolor qui ex eorum passione proveniet, ut videtur, superare debet omnem praesentem corporum dolorem: sicut et sanctorum iucunditas superabit omnem praesentem iucunditatem. Sed propter immensitatem doloris quandoque contingit in praesenti statu quod anima a corpore separatur. Ergo multo fortius, si corpora illa futura sunt passibilia, ex immensitate doloris anima a corpore separabitur: et sic corpora corrumpentur. Quod falsum est. Ergo corpora illa erunt impassibilia.

Sed contra: Est quod dicitur I Cor. 15, [52]: *et nos immutabimur*: Glossa, *nos boni tantummodo immutabimur in gloriam immutabilitatis et impassibilitatis*. Ergo non erunt corpora damnatorum impassibilia.

Praeterea, sicut corpus cooperatur animae ad meritum, ita cooperatur ei ad peccatum. Sed propter cooperationem praedictam non solum anima, sed et corpus post resurrectionem praemiabitur. Ergo simili ratione damnatorum corpora punientur. Quod non esset si impassibilia forent. Ergo erunt passibilia.

Respondeo dicendum quod principalis causa quare corpora damnatorum ab igne non consumentur, erit divina iustitia, qua eorum corpora ad poenam perpetuam sunt addicta. Sed divinae iustitiae servit etiam naturalis dispositio ex parte corporis patientis, et ex parte agentium. Quia, cum pati sit recipere quoddam, duplex est modus passionis, secundum quod aliquid in aliquo recipi potest dupliciter. Potest enim aliqua forma recipi in altero aliquo secundum esse naturale materialiter, sicut calor ab igne recipitur in aere. Et secundum hunc modum receptionis est unus modus passionis, qui dicitur passio naturae. Alio modo aliquid recipitur in altero spiritualiter per modum intentionis cuiusdam, sicut similitudo albedinis recipitur in aere et in pupilla: et haec receptio similatur illi receptioni qua anima recipit similitudines rerum. Unde secundum hunc modum receptionis est alius modus passionis, qui vocatur passio animae.

Quia ergo post resurrectionem, motu caeli cessante, non poterit aliquod corpus alterari a sua naturali aequalitate, ut dictum est , nullum corpus pati poterit passione naturae. Unde quantum ad hunc modum passionis corpora damnatorum impassibilia erunt, sicut et incorruptibilia. Sed, cessante motu caeli, adhuc remanebit passio quae est per modum animae: quia et aer a sole illuminabitur, et colorum differentias ad visum deferet. Unde et secundum hunc modum passionis corpora damnatorum passibilia erunt. Et quia in tali passione sensus per-

being corrupted, as Augustine asserts (*The City of God* 21.2, 21.4), it would seem that they will suffer no distress there: which would not be the case unless their bodies were impassible. Therefore, etc.

Obj. 4: Further, if the bodies of the damned be passible, the pain resulting from their suffering seemingly will surpass all present bodily pain, even as the joy of the saints will surpass all present joy. Now in this life it sometimes happens that the soul is severed from the body through excess of pain. Much more, therefore, if those bodies will be passible, the souls will be separate from the bodies through excess of pain, and thus those bodies will be corrupted: which is false. Therefore, those bodies will be impassible.

On the contrary, 1 Corinthians 15:52 says: *and we shall be changed*, and a Gloss says: *we—the good alone—will be changed with the unchangeableness and impassibility of glory*.

Further, Even as the body cooperates with the soul in merit, so does it cooperate in sin. Now on account of the former cooperation not only the soul but also the body will be rewarded after the resurrection. Therefore, in like manner the bodies of the damned will be punished; which would not be the case were they impassible. Therefore, they will be passible.

I answer that, The principal cause of the bodies of the damned not being consumed by fire will be the divine justice by which their bodies will be consigned to everlasting punishment. Now the divine justice is served also by the natural disposition, whether on the part of the passive body or on the part of the active causes; for since passiveness is a kind of receptiveness, there are two kinds of passion, corresponding to two ways in which one thing is receptive of another. For a form may be received into a subject materially according to its natural being, just as the air receives heat from fire materially; and corresponding to this manner of reception there is a kind of passion which we call 'passion of nature.' In another way, one thing is received into another spiritually by way of an intention, just as the likeness of whiteness is received into the air and in the pupil: this reception is like that whereby the soul receives the likeness of things: wherefore corresponding to this mode of reception is another mode of passion, which we call 'passion of the soul.'

Since, therefore, after the resurrection and the cessation of the heavenly movement it will be impossible for a body to be altered by its natural quality, as stated above (A. 2), it will not be possible for any body to be passive with a passion of nature. Consequently, as regards this mode of passion the bodies of the damned will be impassible even as they will be incorruptible. Yet after the heaven has ceased to move, there will still remain the passion which is after the manner of the soul, since the air will both receive light from the sun and will convey the variety of colors to the sight.

ficitur, ideo in corporibus damnatorum sensus poenae erunt, sine mutatione naturalis dispositionis.

Corpora vero gloriosa, etsi recipiant, aliquid et quodammodo patiantur in sentiendo, non tamen passibilia erunt: quia nihil recipient per modum afflictivi vel laesivi, sicut corpora damnatorum, quae ob hoc passibilia dicuntur.

Ad primum ergo dicendum quod Philosophus loquitur de illa passione per quam transmutatur patiens a sua naturali dispositione. Talis autem passio non erit in corporibus damnatorum, ut dictum est.

Ad secundum dicendum quod similitudo agentis est dupliciter in patiente. Uno modo, per modum eundem quo est in agente, sicut est in omnibus agentibus univocis: ut calidum facit calidum, et ignis generat ignem. Alio modo, per modum diversum a modo quo est in agente: sicut est in omnibus agentibus aequivocis. In quibus quandoque contingit quod in agente est forma spiritualiter quae in patiente materialiter recipitur: sicut forma quae est in domo facta per artificem, est materialiter in ipsa, et in mente artificis est spiritualiter. Quandoque vero e converso est materialiter in agente, et recipitur spiritualiter in patiente: sicut albedo materialiter est in pariete, a quo recipitur spiritualiter in pupilla et in medio deferente. Et similiter est in proposito. Quia species quae materialiter est in igne, recipitur spiritualiter in corporibus damnatorum. Et sic ignis sibi assimilabit damnatorum corpora, nec tamen ea consumet.

Ad tertium dicendum quod, secundum Philosophum, in libro de Proprietatibus Elementorum, nullum animal in igne vivere potest. Galienus etiam, in libro de Simplicibus Medicinis, dicit quod nullum corpus est quod tandem ab igne non consumatur, quamvis quaedam corpora sint quae ad horam in igne sine laesione permaneant, ut patet de ebeno. Unde quod inducitur de salamandra, non potest omnino esse simile: quia non posset perseverare finaliter in igne sine corruptione, sicut corpora damnatorum in inferno.

Nec tamen oportet quod, quia corpora damnatorum ab igne inferni per corruptionem aliquam non laeduntur, quod propter hoc ab igne non affligantur. Quia sensibile non solum natum est delectare vel affligere sensum secundum quod agit actione naturae, confortando vel corrumpendo organum; sed etiam secundum quod agit actione spirituali. Quia quando sensibile est in debita proportione ad sentiendum, delectat: e converso autem quando se habet in superabundantia vel defectu. Unde et colores medii et voces consonantes sunt delectabiles: inconsonantes autem offendunt auditum.

Ad quartum dicendum quod dolor non separat animam a corpore secundum quod manet tantum in potentia animae cuius est dolere: sed secundum quod ad passionem animae mutatur corpus a sua naturali dispositione; secundum modum quo videmus quod ex ira

Therefore, in respect of this mode of passion the bodies of the damned will be passible.

But the glorified bodies, although they receive something and are in a manner patient to sensation, will nevertheless not be passible, since they will receive nothing to distress or hurt them, as will the bodies of the damned, which for this reason are said to be passible.

Reply Obj. 1: The Philosopher is speaking of the passion whereby the patient is changed from its natural disposition. But this kind of passion will not be in the bodies of the damned, as stated above.

Reply Obj. 2: The likeness of the agent is in the patient in two ways. First, in the same way as in the agent, and thus it is in all univocal agents, for instance, a thing that is hot makes another thing hot, and fire generates fire. Second, otherwise than in the agent, and thus it is in all equivocal agents. In these it happens sometimes that a form which is in the agent spiritually is received into the patient materially: thus the form of the house built by the craftsman is materially in itself, but spiritually in the mind of the craftsman. On the other hand, sometimes it is in the agent materially but is received into the patient spiritually: thus whiteness is materially on the wall wherein it is received, whereas it is spiritually in the pupil and in the transferring medium. And so it is in the case at issue, because the species which is in the fire materially is received spiritually into the bodies of the damned; thus it is that the fire will assimilate the bodies of the damned to itself, without consuming them withal.

Reply Obj. 3: According to the Philosopher (De Proprietatibus Elementorum), no animal can live in fire. Galen also says that there is no body which at length is not consumed by fire (De Simplicibus Medicinis); although sometimes certain bodies may remain in fire without hurt, such as ebony. The instance of the salamander is not altogether similar, since it cannot remain in the fire without being at last consumed as do the bodies of the damned in hell.

Nor does it follow that because the bodies of the damned suffer no corruption from the fire, they therefore are not tormented by the fire, because the sensible object has a natural aptitude to please or displease the senses not only as regards its natural action of stimulating or injuring the organ, but also as regards its spiritual action: since when the sensible object is duly proportionate to the sense, it pleases, whereas the contrary is the result when it is in excess or defect. Hence subdued colors and harmonious sounds are pleasing, whereas discordant sounds offend the hearing.

Reply Obj. 4: Pain does not sever the soul from the body insofar as it is confined to a power of the soul which feels the pain, but insofar as the passion of the soul leads to the body being changed from its natural disposition. Thus it is that we see that through anger the body becomes heated,

corpus calescit et ex timore frigescit. Sed post resurrectionem corpus non poterit transmutari a sua naturali dispositione, ut ex dictis patet. Unde, quantuscumque sit dolor, animam a corpore non separabit.

and chilled through fear: whereas after the resurrection it will be impossible for the body to be changed from its natural disposition, as stated above (A. 2). Consequently, however great the pain will be, it will not sever the body from the soul.

QUESTION 87

Post hoc agendum est de his quae sequuntur resurrectionem. Quorum prima consideratio est de cognitione quam habebunt resuscitati in iudicio respectu meritorum et demeritorum; secundo de ipso iudicio in generali, tempore et loco in quo erit; tertio, de iudicantibus et iudicatis; quarto, de forma in qua iudex veniet ad iudicandum; quinto, de statu mundi et resurgentium post iudicium.

Circa primum quaeruntur tria.

Primo: utrum cognoscat quilibet homo in iudicio omnia peccata sua.

Secundo: utrum possit quilibet legere conscientiam alterius.

Tertio: utrum omnia merita et demerita uno intuitu quis videre possit.

In the next place we must treat of those things which follow the resurrection. (1) The knowledge which, after rising again, men will have at the judgment concerning merits and demerits; (2) The general judgment itself, as also the time and place at which it will be; (3) Who will judge and who will be judged; (4) The form wherein the judge will come to judge; (5) What will be after the judgment, the state of the world and of those who will have risen again.

Under the first head there are three points of inquiry:

(1) Whether at the judgment every man will know all his sins?

(2) Whether every one will be able to read all that is on another's conscience?

(3) Whether one will be able at one glance to see all merits and demerits?

Article 1

Whether After the Resurrection Every One Will Know What Sins He Has Committed?

AD PRIMUM SIC PROCEDITUR. Videtur quod post resurrectionem non cognoscet quilibet omnia peccata quae fecit. Omne enim quod cognoscimus, vel de novo per sensum accipimus, vel de thesauro memoriae educitur. Sed homines post resurrectionem sua peccata non poterunt sensu percipere: quia iam transierunt; sensu autem est tantum praesentium. Multa etiam peccata a memoria exciderunt peccantis, quae non poterunt de thesauro memoriae educi. Ergo non omnium peccatorum quae fecit resurgens cognitionem habebit.

PRAETEREA, sicut in littera dicitur, *libri conscientiae quidam sunt, in quibus merita singulorum leguntur.* Sed in libris non potest aliquid legi nisi eius nota contineatur in libro. *Notae* autem *quaedam* peccatorum remanent in conscientia, ut patet Rom. 2, [15], in Glossa: quae non videntur aliud esse quam reatus vel macula. Cum ergo multorum peccatorum macula et reatus a inultis sit deletus per gratiam, videtur quod non omnia peccata quae fecit possit aliquis in sua conscientia legere. Et sic idem quod prius.

PRAETEREA, crescente causa, crescit effectus. Sed causa quae facit nos dolere de peccatis quae ad memoriam revocamus, est caritas. Cum ergo in sanctis resurgentibus sit perfecta caritas, maxime de peccatis dole-

OBJECTION 1: It seems that after the resurrection everyone will not be able to know all the sins he has committed. For whatever we know, either we receive it anew through the senses, or we draw it from the treasure house of the memory. Now after the resurrection men will be unable to perceive their sins by means of sense, because they will be things of the past, while sense perceives only the present: and many sins will have escaped the sinner's memory, and he will be unable to recall them from the treasure house of his memory. Therefore, after rising again, one will not be cognizant of all the sins one has committed.

OBJ. 2: Further, it is stated in the text (*Sentences* IV, D. 43), that *there are certain books of the conscience, wherein each one's merits are inscribed.* Now one cannot read a thing in a book, unless it be marked down in the book: and sin leaves *a certain mark* upon the conscience, according to a Gloss of Origen on Romans 2:15: *their conscience bearing witness,* which mark, seemingly, is nothing else than the guilt or stain. Since, then, in many persons the guilt or stain of many sins is blotted out by grace, it would seem that one cannot read in one's conscience all the sins one has committed: and thus the same conclusion follows as before.

OBJ. 3: Further, the greater the cause, the greater the effect. Now the cause which makes us grieve for the sins which we recall to memory is charity. Since, then, charity is perfect in the saints after the resurrection, they will grieve

bunt si ea ad memoriam revocabunt. Quod non potest esse: quia *fugiet ab eis dolor et gemitus*, Apoc. 21 [4]. Ergo propria peccata ad memoriam non revocabunt.

PRAETEREA, sicut se habebunt resurgentes damnati ad bona quae aliquando fecerunt, ita se habebunt resurgentes beati ad peccata quae aliquando commiserunt. Sed resurgentes damnati, ut videtur, cognitionem de bonis quae aliquando fecerunt non habebunt: quia per hoc eorum poena multum alleviaretur. Ergo nec beati habebunt cognitionem peccatorum quae commiserunt.

SED CONTRA est: Quod Augustinus dicit, XX *de Civ. Dei*, quod *quaedam divina vis aderit qua fiet ut cuncta peccata ad memoriam revocentur*.

PRAETEREA, sicut se habet humanum iudicium ad testimonium exterius, ita se habet divinum iudicium ad testimonium conscientiae: ut patet I Reg. 16, [7], *homines vident ea quae parent, Deus autem intuetur cor*. Sed non posset perfecte iudicium humanum esse de aliquo nisi testes de omnibus de quibus iudicandum est, testimonium deponerent. Ergo oportet, cum divinum iudicium sit perfectissimum, quod conscientia teneat omnia de quibus iudicandum est. Sed iudicandum erit de omnibus operibus bonis et malis: II Cor. 5, [10] 5, *omnes adstabimus ante tribunal Christi*, etc. Ergo oportet quod conscientia uniuscuiusque retineat omnia opera quae fecit, sive bona sive mala.

RESPONDEO dicendum quod, sicut dicitur Rom. 2, [15–16], *in illa die cum iudicabit Dominus*, testimonium unicuique sua conscientia reddet, et cogitationes erunt accusantes et defendentes: Et quia oportet quod testis et accusator et defensor in quolibet iudicio habeant eorum notitiam quae in iudicio versantur; in illo autem communi iudicio omnia opera hominum in iudicium venient: oportet quod omnium operum suorum quisque tunc notitiam habeat. Unde conscientiae singulorum erunt quasi quidam libri continentes res gestas, ex quibus iudicium procedet: sicut etiam in iudicio humano registris utuntur. Et isti sunt, libri de quibus, Apoc. 20, [12], dicitur: *libri aperti sunt, et alius liber apertus est qui est vitae; et iudicati sunt mortui ex his quae scripta erant in libris, secundum opera ipsorum*: ut per *libros* qui dicuntur sic *aperti*, ut Augustinus exponit, XX *de Civ. Dei*, *significentur sancti novi et veteris Testamenti*, in quibus Deus ostendit quae mandata fieri iussisset unde, ut Richardus de Sancto Victore dicit, *erunt corda eorum quasi quaedam canonum statuta*; sed per librum vitae, de quo subiungitur, intelliguntur conscientiae singulorum, quae dicuntur singulariter *liber unus*, quia, una virtute divina fiet ut cunctis ad memoriam sua facta revocentur; et haec vis, inquantum ad memoriam homini reducet sua facta, *liber vitae* dicitur. Vel per primos libros conscien-

exceedingly for their sins, if they recall them to memory: yet this is impossible, seeing that according to Revelation 21:4, *sorrow and mourning shall flee away from them*. Therefore, they will not recall their own sins to memory.

OBJ. 4: Further, at the resurrection the damned will be to the good they once did as the blessed to the sins they once committed. Now, seemingly the damned after rising again will have no knowledge of the good they once did, since this would alleviate their pain considerably. Neither, therefore, will the blessed have any knowledge of the sins they had committed.

ON THE CONTRARY, Augustine says (*The City of God* 20) that *a kind of divine energy will come to our aid, so that we shall recall all of our sins to mind*.

FURTHER, As human judgment is to external evidence, so is the divine judgment to the witness of the conscience, according to 1 Samuel 16:7, *man sees those things that appear, but the Lord beholds the heart*. Now man cannot pass a perfect judgment on a matter unless evidence be taken on all the points that need to be judged. Therefore, since the divine judgment is most perfect, it is necessary for the conscience to witness to everything that has to be judged. But all works, both good and evil, will have to be judged: *we must all be manifested before the judgment seat of Christ, that every one may receive the proper things of the body according as he has done, whether it be good or evil* (2 Cor 5:10). Therefore, each one's conscience must retain all the works he has done, whether good or evil.

I ANSWER THAT, According to Romans 2:15–16, *in the day when God shall judge*, each one's conscience will bear witness to him and his thoughts will accuse and defend him. And since in every judicial hearing, the witness, the accuser, and the defendant need to be acquainted with the matter on which judgment has to be pronounced, and since at the general judgment all the works of men will be submitted to judgment, every man ought to be cognizant then of all his works. Wherefore each man's conscience will be as a book containing his deeds on which judgment will be pronounced, even as in the human court of law we make use of records. Of these books it is written in Revelation 20:12: *the books were opened: and another book was opened, which is the book of life; and the dead were judged by those things which were written in the books, according to their works*. According to Augustine's exposition (*The City of God* 20) the *books* (which are here said to be *opened*) *denote the saints of the New and Old Testaments in whom God's commandments are exemplified*. Hence Richard of St. Victor (*On Judiciary Power in the Final and Universal Judgment*) says, *their hearts will be like the code of law*. But the book of life, of which the text goes on to speak, signifies each one's conscience, which is said to be *one* single *book*, because the one divine power will cause all to recall their deeds, and this energy, insofar as it reminds a man of his deeds, is called

tiae intelliguntur; per secundum sententia Iudicis in eius providentia descripta.

AD PRIMUM ergo dicendum quod, quamvis inulta merita et demerita a memoria excidant, tamen nullum eorum erit quod non aliquo modo maneat in suo effectu. Quia merita quae non sunt mortificata, manebunt in praemio quod eis redditur: quae autem mortificata sunt, manent in reatu ingratitudinis, quae augetur ex hoc quod homo post gratiam susceptam peccavit. Similiter etiam demerita quae non sunt per poenitentiam deleta, manent in reatu poenae quae eis debetur: quae autem poenitentia delevit, manent in ipsa poenitentiae memoria, quam simul cum aliis meritis in notitia habebunt. Unde in quolibet homine erit aliquid ex quo possit ad memoriam sua opera revocare. Et tamen, ut Augustinus dicit, principaliter ad hoc *divina vis* operabitur.

AD SECUNDUM dicendum quod iam patet ex dictis quod aliquae notae manent in conscientiis singulorum de operibus a se factis. Nec oportet quod notae istae sint reatus tantum, ut ex dictis patet.

AD TERTIUM dicendum quod, quamvis caritas sit nunc causa dolendi de peccato, tamen sancti in patria erunt ita perfusi gaudio quod dolor in eis locum habere non poterit. Et ideo de peccatis non dolebunt: sed potius gaudebunt de divina misericordia, qua eis peccata sunt relaxata; sicut etiam nunc angeli gaudent de divina iustitia, qua fit ut, deserti a gratia, in peccato ruant illi quos custodiunt, quorum tamen saluti sollicite invigilant.

AD QUARTUM dicendum quod mali cognoscent omnia bona quae fecerunt: et ex hoc non minuetur eorum dolor, sed magis augebitur; quia maximus dolor est multa bona perdidisse. Propter quod dicit Boetius, in II *de Consolat.* quod *summum infortunii genus est fuisse felicem.*

the *book of life.* Or else we may refer the first books to the conscience, and by the second book we may understand the Judge's sentence as expressed in his providence.

REPLY OBJ. 1: Although many merits and demerits will have escaped our memory, yet there will be none of them but will remain somewhat in its effect, because those merits which are not deadened will remain in the reward accorded to them, while those that are deadened remain in the guilt of ingratitude, which is increased through the fact that a man sinned after receiving grace. In like manner, those demerits which are not blotted out by repentance remain in the debt of punishment due to them, while those which have been blotted out by repentance remain in the remembrance of repentance, which they will recall together with their other merits. Hence in each man there will be something whereby he will be able to recollect his deeds. Nevertheless, as Augustine says (*The City of God* 20), the *divine energy* will especially conduce to this.

REPLY OBJ. 2: Each one's conscience will bear certain marks of the deeds done by him; and it does not follow that these marks are the guilt alone, as stated above.

REPLY OBJ. 3: Although charity is now the cause of sorrow for sin, yet the saints in heaven will be so full of joy that they will have no room for sorrow; and so they will not grieve for their sins, but rather will they rejoice in the divine mercy whereby their sins are forgiven them. Even so do the angels rejoice now in the divine justice whereby those whom they guard fall headlong into sin, through being abandoned by grace, and whose salvation nonetheless they eagerly watch over.

REPLY OBJ. 4: The wicked will know all the good they have done, and this will not diminish their pain; indeed, it will increase it, because the greatest sorrow is to have lost many goods: for which reason Boethius says (*Consolation of Philosophy* 2) that *the greatest misfortune is to have been happy.*

Article 2

Whether Every One Will Be Able to Read All That Is in Another's Conscience?

AD SECUNDUM SIC PROCEDITUR. Videtur quod non quilibet possit legere omnia quae sunt in conscientia alterius. Resurgentium enim non erit limpidior cognitio quam nunc sit angelorum, quorum aequalitas resurgentibus promittitur, Matth, 22, [30]. Sed angeli non possunt invicem in suis cordibus videre ea quae dependent a libero arbitrio: unde indigent locutione ad ea invicem innotescenda. Ergo resurgentes non poterunt inspicere ea quae continentur in conscientiis aliorum.

OBJECTION 1: It seems that it will be impossible for every one to read all that is in another's conscience. For the knowledge of those who rise again will not be clearer than that of the angels, equality with whom is promised us after the resurrection (Matt 22:30). Now angels cannot read one another's thoughts in matters dependent on the free-will, wherefore they need to speak in order to notify such things to one another. Therefore, after rising again we shall be unable to read what is contained in another's conscience.

Praeterea, omne quod cognoscitur, vel cognoscitur in se, vel in sua causa, vel in suo effectu. Sed merita vel demerita quae continentur in conscientia alicuius, non poterit alius cognoscere in seipsis: quia solus Deus cordi illabitur et secreta eius intuetur. Similiter nec in causa sua: quia non omnes videbunt Deum, qui solus potest imprimere in affectum, ex quo procedunt merita vel demerita. Similiter etiam nec in effectu: quia multa demerita erunt quorum nullus effectus remanebit, eis totaliter per poenitentiam abolitis. Ergo non omnia quae sunt in conscientia alicuius, poterit quilibet alius cognoscere.

Praeterea, Chrysostomus dicit, in littera: *nunc autem, si recorderis peccatorum tuorum, et frequenter ea in conspectu Dei pronunties et pro eis depreceris, citius illa delebis. Si vero oblivisceris, tunc eorum recordaberis nolens quando publicabuntur, et in conspectu omnium amicorum et inimicorum, sanctorumque angelorum, proferentur.* Ex hoc accipitur quod illa publicatio poena est negligentiae qua homo confessionem praetermittit. Ergo illa peccata de quibus homo confessus est, non publicabuntur aliis.

Praeterea, solatium est alicui si scit se habere multos socios in peccato, et minus inde verecundatur. Si ergo quilibet peccatum alterius cognosceret, cuiuslibet peccatoris erubescentia multum minueretur. Quod non competit. Ergo non omnes omnium peccata cognoscent.

Sed contra: Super illud I Cor. 4, [5], *illuminabit abscondita tenebrarum*, dicit Glossa: *gesta et cogitata bona et mala tunc aperta et nota erunt omnibus.*

Praeterea, omnium bonorum peccata praeterita aequaliter erunt abolita. Sed quorundam sanctorum peccata sciemus: sicut Magdalenae et Petri et David. Ergo pari ratione aliorum electorum peccata scientur. Et multo magis damnatorum.

Respondeo dicendum quod in ultimo et communi iudicio oportet quod divina iustitia omnibus evidenter appareat, quae nunc in plerisque latet. Sententia autem condemnans vel praemians iusta esse non potest nisi secundum merita vel demerita proferatur. Et ideo, sicut oportet quod iudex et assessor iudicis merita causae cognoscant ad hoc quod iustam sententiam proferant, ita oportet, ad hoc quod iusta sententia appareat, quod omnibus sententiam cognoscentibus merita innotescant. Unde quia, sicut cuilibet nota erit sua praemiatio et sua damnatio, ita et omnibus aliis innotescet; oportet quod, sicut quilibet sua merita vel demerita reducet ad memoriam, ita etiam et aliena suae cognitioni subiaceant.

Et haec est probabilior et communior opinio, quamvis contrarium Magister in littera dicat, scilicet quod *peccata quae sunt per poenitentiam deleta*, in iudicio aliis

Obj. 2: Further, whatever is known is known either in itself, or in its cause, or in its effect. Now the merits or demerits contained in a person's conscience cannot be known by another in themselves, because God alone enters the heart and reads its secrets. Neither will it be possible for them to be known in their cause, since all will not see God who alone can act on the will (from which merits and demerits proceed.) Nor again will it be possible to know them from their effect, since there will be many demerits which, through being wholly blotted out by repentance, will leave no effect remaining. Therefore, it will not be possible for every one to know all that is in another's conscience.

Obj. 3: Further, Chrysostom says (*Homilies on Hebrews*), as we have quoted before (*Sentences* IV, D.17): *if you remember your sins now, and frequently confess them before God and beg pardon for them, you will very soon blot them out; but if you forget them, you will then remember them unwillingly when they will be made public, and declared before all your friends and foes, and in the presence of the holy angels.* Hence it follows that this publication will be the punishment of man's neglect in omitting to confess his sins. Therefore, the sins which a man has confessed will not be made known to others.

Obj. 4: Further, it is a relief to know that one has had many associates in sin, so that one is less ashamed thereof. If, therefore, every one were to know the sin of another, each sinner's shame would be much diminished, which is unlikely. Therefore, every one will not know the sins of all.

On the contrary, A Gloss on 1 Corinthians 4:5: *he will bring to light the hidden things of darkness*, says, *deeds and thoughts both good and evil will then be revealed and made known to all.*

Further, The past sins of all the good will be equally blotted out. Yet we know the sins of some saints, for instance, those of Mary Magdalene, Peter, and David. Therefore, in like manner the sins of the other elect will be known, and much more those of the damned.

I answer that, At the last and general judgment the divine justice, which now is in many ways hidden, must appear evidently to all. Now the sentence of one who condemns or rewards cannot be just unless it be delivered according to merits and demerits. Therefore, just as both judge and jury must know the merits of a case in order to deliver a just verdict, so is it necessary, in order that the sentence appear to be just, that all who know the sentence should be acquainted with the merits. Hence, since every one will know of his reward or condemnation, so will every one else know of it, and consequently as each one will recall his own merits or demerits, so will he be cognizant of those of others.

This is the more probable and more common opinion, although the Master (*Sentences* IV, D. 43) says the contrary, namely, that *a man's sins blotted out by repentance* will not

non patefient. Sed ex hoc sequitur quod nec etiam poenitentia de peccatis illis perfecta cognoscetur. In quo multum detraheretur sanctorum gloriae et laudi divinae, quae tam misericorditer sanctos liberavit.

AD PRIMUM ergo dicendum quod omnia merita praecedentia vel demerita facient aliquam quantitatem in gloria vel miseria hominis resurgentis. Et ideo, exterioribus visis, poterunt cuncta in conscientiis videri. Et praecipue divina virtute ad hoc operante, ut sententia Iudicis iusta appareat omnibus.

AD SECUNDUM dicendum quod merita vel demerita poterunt aliis ostendi in suis effectibus, ut ex dictis patet. Vel etiam in seipsis per divinam virtutem: quamvis ad hoc virtus intellectus creati non sufficiat.

AD TERTIUM dicendum quod publicatio peccatorum ad ignominiam peccantis est effectus negligentiae quae committitur in omissione confessionis. Sed quod peccata sanctorum revelantur non poterit eis esse in erubescentiam vel verecundiam, sicut nec Mariae Magdalenae est in confusionem quod peccata sua publice in Ecclesia recitantur: quia verecundia est *timor ingloriationis*, ut Damascenus dicit, qui in beatis esse non poterit. Sed talis publicatio erit eis ad magnam gloriam, propter poenitentiam quam fecerunt: sicut et confessor approbat eum qui magna scelera fortiter confitetur. Dicuntur autem peccata esse deleta, quia Deus non videt ea ad puniendum.

AD QUARTUM dicendum quod ex hoc quod peccator aliorum peccata inspiciet, in nullo sua confusio minuetur, sed magis augebitur, in alieno vituperio suum vituperium magis perpendens. Quod enim ex tali causa confusio minuatur, contingit ex hoc quod verecundia respicit aestimationem hominum, quae ex consuetudine redditur levior. Sed tunc confusio respiciet aestimationem Dei, quae est secundum veritatem de quolibet peccato, sive sit unius tantum sive multorum.

be made known to others at the judgment. But it would follow from this that neither would his repentance for these sins be perfectly known, which would detract considerably from the glory of the saints and the praise due to God for having so mercifully delivered them.

REPLY OBJ. 1: All the preceding merits or demerits will come to a certain amount in the glory or unhappiness of each one rising again. Consequently, through eternal things being seen, all things in their consciences will be visible, especially as the divine power will conduce to this so that the Judge's sentence may appear just to all.

REPLY OBJ. 2: It will be possible for a man's merits or demerits to be made known by their effects as stated above (A. 1), or by the power of God, although the power of the created intellect is not sufficient for this.

REPLY OBJ. 3: The manifestation of his sins to the confusion of the sinner is a result of his neglect in omitting to confess them. But that the sins of the saints be revealed cannot be to their confusion or shame, as neither does it bring confusion to Mary Magdalene that her sins are publicly recalled in the Church, because shame is *fear of disgrace*, as Damascene says (*On the Orthodox Faith* 2), and this will be impossible in the blessed. But this manifestation will bring them great glory on account of the penance they did, even as the confessor commends a man who courageously confesses great crimes. Sins are said to be blotted out because God does not see them for the purpose of punishing them.

REPLY OBJ. 4: The sinner's confusion will not be diminished, but on the contrary increased, through his seeing the sins of others, for in seeing that others are blameworthy he will all the more acknowledge himself to be blamed. For that confusion be diminished by a cause of this kind is owing to the fact that shame regards the esteem of men, who esteem more lightly that which is customary. But then confusion will regard the esteem of God, which weighs every sin according to the truth, whether it be the sin of one man or of many.

Article 3

Whether All Merits and Demerits, One's Own as Well as Those of Others,
Will Be Seen by Anyone at a Single Glance?

AD TERTIUM SIC PROCEDITUR. Videtur quod non omnia merita vel demerita propria et aliena ab aliquo uno intuitu videantur. Ea enim quae singillatim considerantur, non videntur uno intuitu. Sed damnati singillatim considerabunt sua peccata et ea plangent: unde dicunt, Sap. 5, [8]: *quid nobis profuit superbia*, etc. Ergo non omnia videbunt uno intuitu.

OBJECTION 1: It would seem that not all merits and demerits, one's own as well as those of others, will be seen by anyone at a single glance. For things considered singly are not seen at one glance. Now the damned will consider their sins singly and will bewail them, wherefore they say: *what has pride profited us?* (Wis 5:8). Therefore, they will not see them all at a glance.

PRAETEREA, Philosophus dicit, in II *Topic.*, *quod non contingit simul plura intelligere.* Sed merita et demerita propria et aliena non videbuntur nisi intellectu. Ergo non poterunt simul omnia videri.

PRAETEREA, intellectus damnatorum hominum non erit post resurrectionem elevatior quam nunc sit bonorum angelorum quantum ad cognitionem naturalem, qua cognoscunt res per species innatas. Sed tali cognitione angeli non vident plura simul. Ergo nec tunc damnati poterunt omnia facta simul videre.

SED CONTRA: Super illud Iob 8, [22], *induetur confusione*, dicit Glossa: *viso Iudice, mala omnia ante oculos mentis versantur.* Sed Iudicem subito videbunt. Ergo similiter mala quae commiserunt. Et eadem ratione omnia alia.

PRAETEREA, Augustinus, XX *de Civ. Dei*, habet pro inconvenienti quod legatur aliquis liber materialis in iudicio in quo facta singulorum sunt scripta, eo quod nullus valeat aestimare illius libri magnitudinem, vel quanto tempore legi posset. Sed similiter etiam non posset aestimari tempus quantum oporteret ponere ad considerandum omnia merita et demerita sua et aliena ab aliquo homine, si successive diversa videant. Ergo oportet ponere quod omnia simul videat unusquisque.

RESPONDEO dicendum quod circa hoc est duplex opinio. Quidam enim dicunt quod omnia merita et demerita simul aliquis videbit, sua et aliena, in instanti. Quod quidem de beatis facile credi potest: quia omnia in uno videbunt, et sic non est inconveniens quod simul plura videant. Sed de damnatis, quorum intellectus non est elevatus ut possint Deum videre et in eo omnia alia, est magis difficile.

Et ideo alii dicunt quod mali simul omnia videbunt in genere peccata sua, et hoc sufficit ad accusationem illam quae debet esse in iudicio, vel ad absolutionem. Non autem, videbunt omnia simul descendendo ad singula. Sed hoc etiam non videtur consonum dictis Augustini, XX *de Civ. Dei*, qui dicit quod omnia mentis intuitu enumerabuntur: quod autem in genere cognoscitur, non enumeratur.

Unde potest eligi media via: quod singula considerabunt, non tamen in instanti, sed in tempore brevissimo, divina virtute ad hoc adiuvante. Et hoc est quod dicit Augustinus, ibidem, quod *mira celeritate* enumerabuntur. Nec est hoc impossibile: quia in quolibet parvo tempore sunt infinita instantia in potentia.

ET PER HOC patet responsio ad utramque partem.

OBJ. 2: Further, the Philosopher says (*Topics* 2) that *we do not arrive at understanding several things at the same time.* Now merits and demerits, both our own and those of others, will not be visible save to the intellect. Therefore, it will be impossible for them all to be seen at the same time.

OBJ. 3: Further, the intellect of the damned after the resurrection will not be clearer than the intellect of the blessed and of the angels is now as to the natural knowledge whereby they know things by innate species. Now by such knowledge the angels do not see several things at the same time. Therefore, neither will the damned be able then to see all their deeds at the same time.

ON THE CONTRARY, A Gloss on Job 8:22: *they shall be clothed with confusion*, says, *as soon as they shall see the Judge, all their evil deeds will stand before their eyes.* Now they will see the Judge suddenly. Therefore, in like manner will they see the evil they have done, and for the same reason all others.

FURTHER, Augustine (*The City of God* 20) considers it unfitting that at the judgment a material book should be read containing the deeds of each individual written therein, for the reason that it would be impossible to measure the size of such a book, or the time it would take to read. But in like manner it would be impossible to estimate the length of time one would require in order to consider all one's merits and demerits and those of others, if one saw these various things one after the other. Therefore, we must admit that each one sees them all at the same time.

I ANSWER THAT, There are two opinions on this question. For some say that one will see all merits and demerits, both one's own and those of others, at the same time in an instant. This is easily credible with regard to the blessed, since they will see all things in the Word: and consequently it is not unreasonable that they should see several things at the same time. But with regard to the damned, a difficulty presents itself, since their intellect is not raised so that they can see God and all else in him.

Wherefore others say that the wicked will see all their sins and those of others generically at the same time: and this suffices for the accusation or absolution necessary for the judgment; but that they will not see them all down to each single one at the same time. But neither does this seem consonant with the words of Augustine (*The City of God* 20), who says that they will count them all with one glance of the mind; and what is known generically is not counted.

Hence we may choose a middle way, by holding that they will consider each sin not instantaneously, but in a very short time, the divine power coming to their aid. This agrees with the saying of Augustine (*The City of God* 20) that they will be discerned *with wondrous rapidity.* Nor is this impossible, since a space of time, however short, is potentially an infinite number of instants.

THIS SUFFICES for the replies to the objections on either side of the question.

Deinde considerandum est de iudicio generali, tempore et loco in quo fiet.

Circa quod quaeruntur quatuor.

Primo: utrum generale iudicium sit futurum.

Secundo: utrum quantum ad disceptationem

Tertio: utrum fiet tempore ignoto.

Quarto: utrum fiet in valle Iosaphat.

We must next consider the general judgment, as to the time and place at which it will be.

Under this head there are four points of inquiry:

(1) Whether there will be a general judgment?

(2) Whether as regards the debate it will be conducted by word of mouth?

(3) Whether it will take place at an unknown time?

(4) Whether it will take place in the valley of Josaphat?

Article 1

Whether There Will Be a General Judgment?

Ad primum sic proceditur. Videtur quod generale iudicium non sit futurum. Quia, ut dicitur Nahum 1, [9], *non indicabit Deus bis in idipsum.* Sed nunc Deus iudicat de singulis hominum operibus: cum post mortem unicuique poenas vel praemia pro meritis tribuit; et dum etiam quosdam in hac vita pro bonis vel malis operibus praemiat vel punit. Ergo videtur quod non sit aliud iudicium futurum.

Praeterea, in nullo iudicio executio sententiae praecedit iudicium. Sed sententia divini iudicii quoad homines est de adeptione regni vel exclusione a regno, ut patet Matth. 25, [31 sqq.]. Ergo, cum modo aliqui adipiscantur regnum aeternum et quidam excludantur ab ipso perpetuo, videtur quod aliud iudicium non sit futurum.

Praeterea, propter hoc aliqua in iudicium oportet adduci, quia dubium est quid de eis definiendum sit. Sed ante finem mundi determinata est unicuique damnatorum sua damnatio, et cuique sanctorum sua beatitudo. Ergo videtur quod non oporteat aliquod futurum iudicium esse.

Sed contra: Matth. 12, [41] dicitur: *viri Ninivitae surgent in iudicio cum generatione ista, et condemnabunt eam.* Ergo post resurrectionem aliquod iudicium erit.

Praeterea, Ioan. 5, [29] dicitur: *procedent qui bona egerunt in resurrectionem vitae; qui vero mala, in resurrectionem iudicii.* Ergo videtur quod post resurrectionem aliquod iudicium sit futurum.

Respondeo dicendum quod, sicut operatio pertinet ad rerum principium, quo producuntur in esse, ita iudicium pertinet ad terminum, quo res ad suum finem per-

Objection 1: It would seem that there will not be a general judgment. For, according to Nahum 1, *God will not judge the same thing a second time.* But God judges now of man's every work by assigning punishments and rewards to each one after death, and also by rewarding and punishing certain ones in this life for their good or evil deeds. Therefore, it would seem that there will be no other judgment.

Obj. 2: Further, in no judicial inquiry is the sentence carried out before judgment is pronounced. But the sentence of the divine judgment on man regards the acquisition of the kingdom or exclusion from the kingdom (Matt 25: 34, 41). Therefore, since some obtain possession of the kingdom now, and some are excluded from it forever, it would seem that there will be no other judgment.

Obj. 3: Further, the reason why certain things are submitted to judgment is that we may come to a decision about them. Now, before the end of the world each of the damned is awarded his damnation, and each of the blessed his beatitude. Therefore, it seems that there would be no other judgment.

On the contrary, It is written: *the men of Nineveh shall rise in judgment with this generation, and shall condemn it* (Matt 12:41). Therefore, there will be a judgment after the resurrection.

Further, It is written: *they that have done good things shall come forth unto the resurrection of life, but they that have done evil, unto the resurrection of judgment* (John 5:29). Therefore, it would seem that after the resurrection there will be a judgment.

I answer that, Just as operation refers to the beginning wherefrom things receive their being, so judgment belongs to the term wherein they are brought to their end.

ducitur. Distinguitur autem duplex Dei operatio. Una, qua res primitus in esse perduxit, instituens naturam et distinguens ea quae ad completionem ipsius pertinent: a quo quidem opera Deus dicitur *quievisse*, Genes. 2, [2]. Alia eius operatio est qua operatur in gubernatione creaturarum: de qua Ioan. 5, [17]: *pater meus usque modo operatur, et ego operor*. Ita etiam duplex eius iudicium distinguitur, ordine tamen converso. Unum quod respondet operationi gubernationis, quae sine iudicio esse non potest. Per quod quidem iudicium unusquisque singulariter pro suis operibus iudicatur, non solum secundum quod sibi competi, sed secundum quod competit gubernationi universi: unde differtur unius praemiatio pro utilitate aliorum, ut patet Heb. 11, [39, 40], et poenae unius ad profectum alterius cedunt. Unde necesse est ut sit aliquod iudicium universale correspondens ex adverso primae rerum productioni in esse: ut videlicet, sicut tunc omnia processerunt immediate a Deo, ita tunc ultima completio mundo detur, unoquoque accipiente finaliter quod ei debetur secundum seipsum.

Unde in illo iudicio apparebit manifeste divina iustitia quantum ad omnia, quae nunc ex hoc occultantur quod interdum de uno disponitur, ad utilitatem aliorum, aliter quam manifesta opera exigere videantur. Unde etiam et tunc erit universalis separatio bonorum a malis: quia ulterius non erit locus ut mali per bonos vel boni per malos proficiant, propter quem profectum interim commixti inveniuntur boni malis, quoadusque status huius vitae per divinam providentiam gubernatur.

Ad primum ergo dicendum quod quilibet homo et est singularis quaedam persona, et est pars totius generis humani. Unde et duplex ei iudicium debetur. Unum singulare, quod de eo fiet post mortem, quando *recipiet iuxta ea quae in corpore gessit*: quamvis non totaliter, quia non quoad corpus, sed quoad animam tantum. Aliud iudicium debet esse de eo secundum quod est pars totius humani generis: sicut aliquis iudicari dicitur, secundum humanam iustitiam, quando etiam iudicium datur de communitate: cuius ipse est pars. Unde et tunc, quando fiet universale iudicium totius humani generis per universalem separationem bonorum a malis, etiam quilibet per consequens iudicabitur. Nec tamen Deus iudicat *bis in idipsum*: quia non duas poenas pro uno peccato infert; sed poena, quae ante iudicium complete inflicta non fuerat, in ultimo iudicio complebitur, post quod impii cruciabuntur quoad corpus et animam simul.

Ad secundum dicendum quod propria sententia illius generalis; iudicii est universalis separatio bonorum a malis, quae illud iudicium non praecedet. Sed nec etiam quoad particularem sententiam uniuscuiusque plene praecessit iudicii effectus: quia etiam boni am-

Now, we distinguish a twofold operation in God. One is that whereby he first gave things their being, by fashioning their nature and by establishing the distinctions which contribute to the perfection thereof: from this work God is stated *to have rested* (Gen 2:2). His other operation is that whereby he works in governing creatures; and of this it is written: *my Father works until now, and I work* (John 5:17). Hence we distinguish in him a twofold judgment, but in the reverse order. One corresponds to the work of governance, which cannot be without judgment: and by this judgment each one is judged individually according to his works, not only as adapted to himself, but also as adapted to the government of the universe. Hence one man's reward is delayed for the good of others (Heb 11: 13, 39–40), and the punishment of one conduces to the profit of another. Consequently, it is necessary that there should be another, and that a general judgment correspond on the other hand with the first formation of things in being; that is, in order that just as then all things proceeded immediately from God, so at length the world will receive its ultimate complement by each one receiving finally his own personal due.

Hence at this judgment the divine justice will be made manifest in all things, whereas now it remains hidden in the fact that at times some persons are dealt with for the profit of others otherwise than their manifest works would seem to require. For this same reason, there will then be a general separation of the good from the wicked because there will be no further motive for the good to profit by the wicked, or the wicked by the good: for the sake of which profit, the good are meanwhile mingled with the wicked so long as this state of life is governed by divine providence.

Reply Obj. 1: Each man is both an individual person and a part of the whole human race: wherefore a twofold judgment is due to him. One, the particular judgment, is that to which he will be subjected after death, when *he will receive according as he has done in the body* (cf. 2 Cor 5:10), not indeed entirely but only in part, since he will receive not in the body but only in the soul. The other judgment will be passed on him as a part of the human race: thus a man is said to be judged according to human justice even when judgment is pronounced on the community of which he is a part. Hence it follows that each one will be judged at the general judgment of the whole human race by the general separation of the good from the wicked. And yet God will not judge *the same thing a second time*, since he will not inflict two punishments for one sin, and the punishment which before the judgment was not inflicted completely will be completed at the last judgment, after which the wicked will be tormented at the same time in body and soul.

Reply Obj. 2: The sentence proper to this general judgment is the general separation of the good from the wicked, which will not precede this judgment. Yet even now as regards the particular sentence on each individual the judgment does not at once take full effect, since even the good

plius post iudicium praemiabuntur, tum ex gloria corporis adiuncta, tum ex numero sanctorum completo; et mali etiam plus torquebuntur ex adiuncta poena corporis, et impleto in poenis numero damnatorum; quia quanto cum pluribus ardebunt, tanto plus ardebunt.

will receive an increase of reward after the judgment, both from the added glory of the body and from the completion of the number of the saints. The wicked also will receive an increase of torment from the added punishment of the body and from the completion of the number of damned to be punished, because the more numerous those with whom they will burn, the more will they themselves burn.

Ad tertium dicendum quod universale iudicium magis directe respicit universalitatem hominum quam singulos iudicandorum. Quamvis ergo cuilibet homini ante iudicium sit certa notitia de sua damnatione vel praemio, non tamen omnibus omnium damnatio vel praemium innotescet. Unde iudicium necessarium erit.

Reply Obj. 3: The general judgment will regard more directly the generality of men than each individual to be judged, as stated above. Therefore, although before that judgment each one will be certain of his condemnation or reward, he will not be cognizant of the condemnation or reward of everyone else. Hence the necessity of the general judgment.

Article 2

Whether the Judgment Will Take Place by Word of Mouth?

Ad secundum sic proceditur. Videtur quod iudicium illud, quantum ad disceptationem et sententiam, fiet per locutionem vocalem. Quia, ut Augustinus dicit, XX *de Civ. Dei, per quot dies hoc futurum iudicium tendatur, hoc incertum est.* Sed non esset incertum si illa quae in iudicio dicuntur futura, tantum mentaliter complerentur. Ergo iudicium illud vocaliter fiet, et non solum mentaliter.

Praeterea, Gregorius dicit, et habetur in littera: *illi saltem verba iudicis audient qui eius fidem verbo tenuerunt.* Hoc autem non potest intelligi de verbo interiori: quia sic omnes verba Iudicis audient, quia omnibus, bonis et malis, nota erunt omnia facta aliorum. Ergo videtur quod iudicium illud vocaliter peragetur.

Praeterea, Christus secundum formam hominis iudicabit, in qua corporaliter ab omnibus possit videri. Ergo eadem ratione videtur quod corporali voce loquatur, ut ab omnibus audiatur.

Sed contra: Augustinus dicit, XX *de Civ. Dei,* quod *liber vitae,* de quo Apoc. 20, [12], *vis quaedam intelligenda est divina, qua fiet utcuique opera sua vel bona vel mala ad memoriam revocentur, et mentis intuitu mira celeritate cernantur, ut accuset vel excuset scientia conscientiam, atque ita simul et omnes, et singuli iudicentur.* Sed, si vocaliter discuterentur merita singulorum, non possent omnes et singuli iudicari simul. Ergo videtur quod illa discussio non erit vocalis.

Praeterea, sententia proportionaliter debet testimonio respondere. Sed testimonium et accusatio vel excusatio erit mentalis: unde Rom. 2, [15–16], *testimonium illis reddente conscientia ipsorum, et infer se invicem co-*

Objection 1: It would seem that this judgment, as regards the inquiry and sentence, will take place by word of mouth. For, according to Augustine (*The City of God* 20), *it is uncertain how many days this judgment will last.* But it would not be uncertain if the things we are told will take place at the judgment were to be accomplished only in the mind. Therefore, this judgment will take place by word of mouth and not only in the mind.

Obj. 2: Further, Gregory says (*Morals on Job* 26): *those at least will hear the words of the Judge, who have confessed their faith in him by words.* Now this cannot be understood as referring to the inner word, because thus all will hear the Judge's words, since all the deeds of other men will be known to all both good and wicked. Therefore, it seems that this judgment will take place by word of mouth.

Obj. 3: Further, Christ will judge according to his human form, so as to be visible in the body to all. Therefore, in like manner it seems that he will speak with the voice of the body so as to be heard by all.

On the contrary, Augustine says (*The City of God* 20) that the book of life which is mentioned in Revelation 20:12 *is a kind of divine energy enabling each one to remember all his good or evil works, and to discern them with the gaze of the mind, with wondrous rapidity, his knowledge accusing or defending his conscience, so that all and each will be judged at the same moment.* But if each one's merits were discussed by word of mouth, all and each could not be judged at the same moment. Therefore, it would seem that this judgment will not take place by word of mouth.

Further, The sentence should correspond proportionately to the evidence. Now the evidence both of accusation and of defense will be mental, according to Romans 2:15–16, *their conscience bearing witness to them, and*

gitationum accusantium aut etiam defendentium, in die cum iudicabit Deus occulta hominum. Ergo videtur quod illa sententia et totum iudicium mentaliter compleatur.

RESPONDEO dicendum quod quid circa hanc quaestionem sit verum, pro certo definiri non potest. Tamen probabilius aestimatur quod totum illud iudicium, et quoad discussionem, et quoad accusationem malorum et commendationem bonorum, et quoad sententiam de utrisque, mentaliter perficietur. Si enim vocaliter singulorum facta narrarentur, inaestimabilis magnitudo temporis ad hoc exigeretur. Sicut etiam Augustinus dicit, XX *de Civ. Dei: quod si liber, ex cuius scriptura omnes iudicabuntur, ut dicitur Apoc. 20, [12], carnaliter cogitetur, quis eius magnitudinem aut longitudinem valeat aestimare? Aut quanto tempore legi poterit liber in quo scriptae sunt universae vitae universorum?* Non autem minus tempus requiritur ad narrandum ore tenus singulorum facta quam ad legendum, si essent in libro materiali scripta. Unde probabile est quod illa quae dicuntur Matth. 25, [34 sqq.], non vocaliter, sed mentaliter intelligenda sunt esse perficienda.

AD PRIMUM ergo dicendum quod pro tanto dicit Augustinus quod *incertum est per quot dies hoc iudicium tendatur,* quia non est determinatum utrum mentaliter vel vocaliter perficiatur. Si enim vocaliter perficeretur, prolixum tempus ad hoc exigeretur. Si autem mentaliter, in momento fieri poterit.

AD SECUNDUM dicendum quod, etiam si iudicium fiat mentaliter tantum, verbum Gregorii salvari potest. Quia etsi omnibus innotescent sua et aliorum facta, divina virtute hoc faciente, quae in Evangelio locutio dicitur; tamen illi qui fidem habuerunt, quam ex verbis Dei conceperunt, ex ipsis verbis iudicabuntur: quia, ut dicitur Rom, 2, [12], *qui in lege peccaverunt, per legem iudicabuntur.* Unde quodam speciali modo dicetur aliquid his qui fuerunt fideles, quod non dicetur his qui fuerunt infideles.

AD TERTIUM dicendum quod Christus corporaliter apparebit ut ab omnibus Iudex corporaliter cognoscatur: quod quidem subito fieri poterit. Sed locutio, quae tempore mensuratur, requireret immensam temporis prolixitatem, si vocali locutione iudicium perageretur.

their thoughts between themselves accusing or also defending one another in the day when God shall judge the secrets of men. Therefore, seemingly this sentence and the entire judgment will take place mentally.

I ANSWER THAT, It is not possible to come to any certain conclusion about the truth of this question. It is, however, the more probable opinion that the whole of this judgment, whether as regards the inquiry, or as regards the accusation of the wicked and the approval of the good, or again as regards the sentence on both, will take place mentally. For if the deeds of each individual were to be related by word of mouth, this would require an inconceivable length of time. Thus Augustine says (*The City of God* 20) that *if we suppose the book,* from the pages of which all will be judged according to Revelation 20:12, *to be a material book, who will be able to conceive its size and length? or the length of time required for the reading of a book that contains the entire life of every individual?* Nor is less time requisite for telling by word of mouth the deeds of each individual than for reading them if they were written in a material book. Hence, probably we should understand that the details set forth in Matthew 25 will be fulfilled not by word of mouth but mentally.

REPLY OBJ. 1: The reason why Augustine says that *it is uncertain how many days this judgment will last* is precisely because it is not certain whether it will take place mentally or by word of mouth. For if it were to take place by word of mouth, a considerable time would be necessary, but if mentally, it is possible for it to be accomplished in an instant.

REPLY OBJ. 2: Even if the judgment is accomplished solely in the mind, the saying of Gregory stands, since though all will be cognizant of their own and of others' deeds, as a result of the divine energy which the Gospel describes as speech (Matt 25:84), nevertheless those who have had the faith which they received through God's words will be judged from those very words, for it is written: *whosoever have sinned in the law shall be judged by the Law* (Rom 2:12). Hence in a special way something will be said to those who had been believers which will not be said to unbelievers.

REPLY OBJ. 3: Christ will appear in body, so that the Judge may be recognized in the body by all, and it is possible for this to take place suddenly. But speech, which is measured by time, would require an immense length of time if the judgment took place by word of mouth.

Article 3

Whether the Time of the Future Judgment Is Unknown?

Ad tertium sic proceditur. Videtur quod tempus futuri iudicii non sit ignotum. Sicut enim sancti patres expectabant primum adventum, ita nos expectamus secundum. Sed sancti patres sciverunt tempus primi adventus: sicut patet per numerum hebdomadarum qui describitur Dan. 9, [24 sqq.]. Unde et reprehenduntur Iudaei quod tempus adventus Christi non cognoverunt, ut patet Luc. 12, [56]: *hypocritae, faciem caeli et terrae nostis probare: hoc autem tempus quomodo non probatis?* Ergo videtur quod etiam nobis esse debeat determinatum tempus secundi adventus, quo *Deus ad iudicium veniet.*

Praeterea, per signa devenimus in cognitionem signatorum. Sea de futuro iudicio multa signa nobis proponuntur in Scriptura: ut patet Matth. 24, [3 sqq.] et Luc. 21, [7 sqq.] et Marc. 13, [3 sqq.]. Ergo in cognitionem illius temporis possumus pervenire.

Praeterea, Apostolus dicit, I Cor. 10, [11] nos sumus *in quos fines saeculorum devenerunt.* Et I Ioan. 2, [18]: *filioli, novissima hora est,* etc. Cum ergo iam longum tempus transierit ex quo haec dicta sunt, videtur quod saltem nunc scire possumus quod ultimum iudicium sit propinquum.

Praeterea, tempus iudicii non oportet esse occultum nisi propter hoc quod quilibet sollicitus se ad iudicium praeparet, dum determinate tempus ignoret. Sed eadem sollicitudo remaneret etiam si certum esset: quia cuique incertum est tempus suae mortis; et, sicut dicit Augustinus, in *Epistola ad Hesychium, in quo quemque invenerit suus novissimus dies, in hoc eum comprehendet mundi novissimus dies.* Ergo non est necessarium tempus iudicii esse occultum.

Sed contra: Est quod dicitur Marci 13, [32]: *de die illa vel hora nemo scit, nec angeli in caelo nec Filius, nisi Pater.* Dicitur autem Filius nescire, inquantum nos scire non facit.

Praeterea, I Thessal. 5, [2]: *dies Domini sicut fur in nocte, ita veniet.* Ergo videtur, cum adventus furis in nocte sit omnino incertus, quod dies ultimi iudicii sit omnino incertus.

Respondeo dicendum quod Deus per scientiam suam est causa rerum. Utrumque autem creaturis communicat: dum et rebus tribuit virtutem agendi alias res, quarum sunt causae; et quibusdam etiam cognitionem rerum praebet. Sed in utroque aliqua sibi reservat: operatur enim quaedam in quibus nulla creatura ei cooperatur; et similiter cognoscit quaedam quae a nulla pura creatura cognoscuntur. Haec autem nulla alia magis esse debent quam illa quae soli divinae subiacent potestati, in

Objection 1: It would seem that the time of the future judgment is not unknown. For just as the holy fathers looked forward to the first coming, so do we look forward to the second. But the holy fathers knew the time of the first coming, as proved by the number of weeks mentioned in Daniel 9. Hence the Jews are reproached for not knowing the time of Christ's coming: *you hypocrites, you know how to discern the face of the heaven and of the earth, but how is it that you do not discern this time?* (Luke 12:56). Therefore, it would seem that the time of the second coming when *God will come to judgment* should also be certified to us.

Obj. 2: Further, we arrive by means of signs at the knowledge of the things signified. Now many signs of the coming judgment are declared to us in Scripture (Matt 24, Mark 13, Luke 21). Therefore, we can arrive at the knowledge of that time.

Obj. 3: Further, the Apostle says it is on us *that the ends of the world are come* (1 Cor 10:11), and 1 John 2:18 says, *little children, it is the last hour.* Since, then, it is a long time since these things were said, it would seem that now at least we can know that the last judgment is close.

Obj. 4: Further, there is no need for the time of the judgment to be hidden except that each one may be careful to prepare himself for judgment, being in ignorance of the appointed time. Yet the same care would still be necessary even were the time known for certain, because each one is uncertain about the time of his death, of which Augustine says (*Epistle to Hesychius* 199) that *as each one's last day finds him, so will the world's last day find him.* Therefore, there is no necessity for the time of the judgment to be uncertain.

On the contrary, It is written: *of that day or hour no man knows, neither the angels in heaven, nor the Son, but the Father* (Mark 13:32). The Son, however, is said not to know insofar as he does not impart the knowledge to us.

Further, It is written: *the day of the Lord shall so come as a thief in the night* (1 Thess 5:2). Therefore, it appears that as the coming of a thief in the night is altogether uncertain, the day of the last judgment is altogether uncertain.

I answer that, God is the cause of things by his knowledge. Now he communicates both these things to his creatures, since he both endows some with the power of action on others whereof they are the cause, and bestows on some the knowledge of things. But in both cases he reserves something to himself, for he operates certain things wherein no creature cooperates with him, and again he knows certain things which are unknown to any mere creature. Now this should apply to none more than to those

quibus nulla creatura ei cooperatur. Et huiusmodi est finis mundi, in quo erit dies iudicii: non enim per aliquam causam creatam mundus finietur; sicut etiam mundus esse incoepit immediate a Deo: Unde decenter cognitio finis mundi soli Deo reservatur. Et hanc rationem videtur ipse Dominus assignare, Act. 1, [7]: *non est, inquit, vestrum nosse tempora vel momenta quae Pater posuit in sua potestate* quasi diceret, *quae soli potestati eius reservata sunt.*

AD PRIMUM ergo dicendum quod in primo adventu Christus venit occultus: secundum illud Isaiae 45, [15]: *vere tu es Deus absconditus Sanctus Israel, Salvator.* Et ideo, ut a fidelibus cognosci posset, oportuit determinate tempus praedeterminare. Sed in secundo adventu veniet manifeste: ut dicitur in Psalmo [49, 3], *Deus manifeste veniet,* etc. Et ideo circa cognitionem adventus ipsius error esse non poterit. Et propter hoc non est simile.

AD SECUNDUM dicendum quod, sicut dicit Augustinus, in Epistola *de Die Iudicii ad Hesychium,* signa quae in Evangeliis ponuntur, non omnia pertinent ad secundum adventum, qui erit in fine: sed quaedam eorum pertinent ad tempus destructionis Ierusalem, quae iam praeteriit; quaedam vero, et plura eorum, pertinent ad adventum quo quotidie ad Ecclesiam suam venit, eam visitans spiritualiter, prout nos inhabitat per fidem et amorem.

Nec illa quae in Evangeliis vel Epistolis ponuntur ad ultimum adventum spectantia, ad hoc possunt valere ut determinate tempus iudicii possit cognosci. Quia illa pericula quae praenuntiantur, nuntiantia vicinum Christi adventum, etiam a tempore primitivae Ecclesiae fuerunt, quandoque intensius, quandoque remissius: unde et ipsi dies Apostolorum dicti sunt *novissimi dies;* ut patet Act. 2, [16 sqq.], ubi Petrus exponit illud Ioel 2, [28 sqq.], *erit in novissimis diebus* etc., pro tempore illo. Et tamen ex illo tempore tempus plurimum transivit: et quandoque plures, et quandoque pauciores tribulationes in Ecclesia fuerunt. Unde non potest determinari tempus quantum sit futurum, nec de mense nec de anno, nec de centum nec de mille annis, ut Augustinus in eodem libro dicit: etsi credantur in finem huiusmodi pericula magis abundare. Non potest tamen determinari quae sit illa quantitas periculorum quae immediate diem iudicii praecedet, vel Antichristi adventum: cum etiam circa tempora primitivae Ecclesiae fuerint persecutiones aliquae adeo graves, et corruptiones errorum adeo abundarent, quod ab aliquibus tunc vicinus expectaretur vel imminens Antichristi adventus, sicut dicitur in *Ecclesiastica historia,* et in libro Hieronymi *de Viris illustribus.*

AD TERTIUM dicendum quod ex hoc quod dicitur, *novissima hora est,* vel ex similibus locutionibus quae in

things which are subject to the divine power alone, and in which no creature cooperates with him. Such is the end of the world when the day of judgment will come. For the world will come to an end by no created cause, even as it derived its existence immediately from God. Wherefore the knowledge of the end of the world is fittingly reserved to God. Indeed our Lord seems to assign this very reason when he said: *it is not for you to know the times or moments which the Father has put in his own power* (Acts 1:7), as though he were to say, *which are reserved to his power alone.*

REPLY OBJ. 1: At his first coming, Christ came secretly, according to Isaiah 45:15: *verily you are a hidden God, the God of Israel, the Savior.* Hence, that he might be recognized by believers, it was necessary for the time to be fixed beforehand with certainty. On the other hand, at the second coming he will come openly, according to Psalm 49:3, *God shall come manifestly.* Consequently, there can be no error affecting the knowledge of his coming. Hence the comparison fails.

REPLY OBJ. 2: As Augustine says, in his letter to Hesychius concerning the day of judgment (*Epistle to Hesychius* 199), the signs mentioned in the Gospels do not all refer to the second advent which will happen at the end of the world, but some of them belong to the time of the sack of Jerusalem, which is now a thing of the past, while some (in fact many of them) refer to the advent whereby he comes daily to the Church, whom he visits spiritually when he dwells in us by faith and love.

Moreover, the details mentioned in the Gospels and Epistles in connection with the last advent are not sufficient to enable us to determine the time of the judgment, for the trials that are foretold as announcing the proximity of Christ's coming occurred even at the time of the early Church, in a degree sometimes more, sometimes less marked; so that even the days of the apostles were called the *last days* (Acts 2:17) when Peter expounded the saying of Joel 2:28, *it shall come to pass in the last days,* as referring to that time. Yet it was already a long time since then: and sometimes there were more and sometimes fewer afflictions in the Church. Consequently, it is impossible to decide after how long a time it will take place, nor fix the month, year, century, or thousand years, as Augustine says in the same book (*Epistle to Hesychius* 199). And even if we are to believe that at the end these calamities will be more frequent, it is impossible to fix what amount of such calamities will immediately precede the judgment day or the coming of Antichrist, since even at the time of the early Church persecutions were so bitter, and the corruptions of error were so numerous, that some looked forward to the coming of Antichrist as being near or imminent; as related in Eusebius' *History of the Church* 6.7 and in Jerome's book *On Illustrious Men* 52.

REPLY OBJ. 3: The statement, *it is the last hour,* and similar expressions that are to be found in Scripture do not

Scriptura leguntur, non potest aliqua determinata quantitas temporis sciri. Non enim est dictum ad significandum aliquam brevem horam temporis: sed ad significandum novissimum statum mundi, qui est quasi novissima aetas; quae quanto temporis spatio duret, non est definitum, cum etiam nec senio, quod est ultima aetas hominis, sit aliquis certus terminus praefinitus, cum quandoque inveniatur durare quantum omnes praecedentes aetates vel plus; ut dicit Augustinus, in libro *Octoginta trium quaestionum*. Unde etiam Apostolus, II Thessal. 2, [2], excludit falsum intellectum quem quidam ex suis verbis conceperant, ut crederent *diem Domini iam instare*.

AD QUARTUM dicendum quod, etiam supposita mortis incertitudine, dupliciter ad vigilantiam valet incertitudo iudicii. Primo, ad hoc quod ignoratur utrum etiam tantum differatur quantum est hominis vita: ut sic ex duabus partibus incertitudo maiorem diligentiam faciat. Secundo, quantum ad hoc quod homo non gerit solum sollicitudinem de persona sua, sed de familia vel civitate vel regno aut tota Ecclesia, cui non determinatur tempus durationis secundum hominis vitam: et tamen oportet unumquemque horum hoc modo disponi ut dies Domini non inveniat imparatos.

enable us to know the exact length of time. For they are not intended to indicate a short length of time, but to signify the last state of the world, which is the last age of all, and it is not stated definitely how long this will last. Thus neither is fixed duration appointed to old age, which is the last age of man, since sometimes it is seen to last as long as or even longer than all the previous ages, as Augustine remarks (*Eighty-three Questions* 58). Hence also the Apostle (2 Thess 2:2) disclaims the false signification which some had given to his words, by believing that *the day of the Lord was already at hand*.

REPLY OBJ. 4: Notwithstanding the uncertainty of death, the uncertainty of the judgment conduces to watchfulness in two ways. First, as regards the thing ignored, since its delay is equal to the length of man's life, so that on either side uncertainty provokes him to greater care. Second, for the reason that a man is careful not only of his own person, but also of his family, or of his city or kingdom, or of the whole Church, the length of whose duration is not dependent on the length of man's life. And yet each of these ought to be so ordered that the day of the Lord find us not unprepared.

Article 4

Whether the Judgment Will Take Place in the Valley of Josaphat?

AD QUARTUM SIC PROCEDITUR. Videtur quod iudicium non fiet iri valle Iosaphat, aut in loco circumstante. Quia ad minus oportet omnes iudicandos in terra stare; eos autem tantum elevari in nubibus quorum erit iudicare. Sed tota terra promissionis capere non posset multitudinem iudicandorum. Ergo non potest esse quod circa vallem illam sit iudicium.

PRAETEREA, Christo in humanitate datum est iudicium ut iuste iudicet qui iniuste iudicatus est. Sed ipse iniuste iudicatus est in praetorio Pilati, et sententiam iniusti iudicii in Golgotha suscepit. Ergo loca illa magis debent ad iudicium determinari.

PRAETEREA, nubes fiunt ex resolutione vaporum. Sed tunc nulla erit evaporatio vel resolutio. Ergo non poterit esse quod iusti *in nubibus obviam Christo in aera rapiantur*. Et sic oportebit et bonos et malos esse in terra. Et ita locus multo amplior requiretur quam sit vallis illa.

OBJECTION 1: It would seem that the judgment will not take place in the valley of Josaphat or in the surrounding locality. For at least it will be necessary for those to be judged to stand on the ground, and those alone to be raised aloft whose business it will be to judge. But the whole land of promise would not be able to contain the multitude of those who are to be judged. Therefore, it is impossible for the judgment to take place in the neighborhood of that valley.

OBJ. 2: Further, judgment was given to Christ in his humanity that he might judge justly who was unjustly judged. Now, he was unjustly judged in the court of Pilate, and bore the sentence of an unjust judgment on Golgotha. Therefore, these places would be more suitably appointed for the judgment.

OBJ. 3: Further, clouds result from the exhalation of vapors. But then there will be no evaporation or exhalation. Therefore, it will be impossible for the just to be *taken up in the clouds to meet Christ, into the air*: and consequently it will be necessary for both good and wicked to be on the earth, so that a much larger place than this valley will be required.

SED CONTRA: Est quod dicitur Ioel 3, [2]: *congregabo omnes gentes, et educam eas in valle Iosaphat, et disceptabo ibi cum eis.*

PRAETEREA, Act. 1, [11] dicitur: *quemadmodum vidistis eum ascendentem in caelum, ita veniet.* Sed ipse ascendit de monte Oliveti, qui praeeminet valli Iosaphat. Ergo et circa loca illa ad iudicandum veniet.

RESPONDEO dicendum quod qualiter illud iudicium sit futurum, et quomodo homines ad iudicium conveniant, non potest multum per certitudinem sciri. Tamen probabiliter potest colligi ex Scripturis quod circa locum montis Oliveti descendet, sicut et inde ascendit: ut idem esse ostendatur *qui ascendit et qui descendit.*

AD PRIMUM ergo dicendum quod magna multitudo iri parvo spatio comprehendi potest. Sufficit autem ponere quantumcumque spatium circa, locum illum ad capiendum multitudinem iudicandorum, dummodo ab illo spatio Christum videre possint, qui in aere eminens, et maxima claritate refulgens, a longinquo inspici poterit.

AD SECUNDUM dicendum quod, quamvis Christus per hoc quod iniuste iudicatus est iudiciariam potestatem meruit, non tamen iudicabit iri forma infirmitatis, in qua iniuste iudicatus est: sed in forma gloriosa, in qua ad Patrem ascendit. Unde locus ascensionis magis competit iudicio quam locus ubi condemnatus est.

AD TERTIUM dicendum quod *nubes* hic appellantur, ut dicunt quidam, densitates lucis resplendentis a corporibus sanctorum, et non aliquae evaporationes ex terra et aqua.

Vel potest dici quod nubes illae generabuntur divina virtute, ad ostendendum conformitatem in adventu ad iudicium et ascensionem: ut qui ascendit in nube, etiam in nube ad iudicium veniat. Nubes etiam, propter refrigerium, indicat misericordiam iudicantis.

ON THE CONTRARY, It is written: *I will gather together all nations and will bring them down into the valley of Josaphat, and I will plead with them there* (Joel 3:2).

FURTHER, It is written: *this Jesus shall so come as you have seen him going into heaven* (Acts 1:11). Now he ascended into heaven from Mount Olivet, which overlooks the valley of Josaphat. Therefore, he will come to judge in the neighborhood of that place.

I ANSWER THAT, We cannot know with any great certainty the manner in which this judgment will take place, nor how men will gather together to the place of judgment; but it may be gathered from Scripture that in all probability he will descend in the neighborhood of Mount Olivet, even as he ascended from there, so as to show that *he who descends is the same as he who ascended.*

REPLY OBJ. 1: A great multitude can be enclosed in a small space. And all that is required is that in the neighborhood of that locality there be a space, however great, to contain the multitude of those who are to be judged, provided that Christ can be seen there, since being raised in the air, and shining with exceeding glory, he will be visible from a great distance.

REPLY OBJ. 2: Although through being sentenced unjustly Christ merited his judiciary power, he will not judge with the appearance of infirmity wherein he was judged unjustly, but under the appearance of glory wherein he ascended to the Father. Hence the place of his ascension is more suitable to the judgment than the place where he was condemned.

REPLY OBJ. 3: In the opinion of some the name of *clouds* is here given to certain condensations of the light shining from the bodies of the saints, and not to evaporations from earth and water.

Or we may say that those clouds will be produced by divine power in order to show the parallel between his coming to judge and his ascension; so that he who ascended in a cloud may come to judgment in a cloud. For the cloud, on account of its refreshing influence, indicates the mercy of the Judge.

QUESTION 89

THE JUDGES AND THE JUDGED AT THE GENERAL JUDGMENT

Deinde considerandum est de iudicantibus et iudicatis in iudicio generali.

Circa quod quaeruntur octo.

Primo: utrum aliqui homines iudicaturi sint cum Christo.

Secundo: utrum voluntariae paupertati correspondeat iudiciaria potestas.

Tertio: utrum angeli sint etiam iudicaturi.

Quarto: utrum daemones exequaiitur sententiam iudicis.

Quinto: utrum omnes homines in iudicio comparebunt.

Sexto: utrum aliqui boni iudicandi sint.

Septimo: utrum aliqui mali.

Octavo: utrum etiam angeli sint iudicandi.

We must next consider who will judge and who will be judged at the general judgment.

Under this head there are eight points of inquiry:

(1) Whether any men will judge together with Christ?

(2) Whether the judicial power corresponds to voluntary poverty?

(3) Whether the angels also will judge?

(4) Whether the demons will carry out the Judge's sentence on the damned?

(5) Whether all men will come up for judgment?

(6) Whether any of the good will be judged?

(7) Whether any of the wicked will be judged?

(8) Whether the angels also will be judged?

Article 1

Whether Any Men Will Judge Together with Christ?

AD PRIMUM SIC PROCEDITUR. Videtur quod nulli homines iudicabunt cum Christo. Ioan. 5, [22–23]: *Pater omne iudicium dedit Filio ut omnes* etc. Sed honorificentia talis non debetur alicui nisi Christo. Ergo, etc.

PRAETEREA, quicumque iudicat, habet auctoritatem super illud quod iudicat. Sed ea de quibus debet esse futurum iudicium, sicut merita et praemia humana, soli divinae auctoritati subsunt. Ergo nulli competit de his iudicare.

PRAETEREA, iudicium illud non exercebitur vocaliter sed mentaliter, ut probabilius aestimatur. Sed hoc quod cordibus hominum notificentur merita et demerita, quod est quasi accusatio vel commendatio; vel retributio poenae et praemii, quod est quasi sententiae prolatio; sola divina virtute fiet. Ergo nulli alii iudicabunt nisi Christus, qui est Deus.

SED CONTRA: Est quod dicitur Matth. 19, [28]: *sedebitis super sedes iudicantes duodecim tribus Israel.*

PRAETEREA, Isaiae 3, [14]: *Dominus ad iudicium veniet cum senioribus populi sui.* Ergo videtur quod etiam alii iudicabunt cum Christo.

RESPONDEO dicendum quod iudicare multipliciter dicitur. Uno modo, quasi causaliter; ut dicatur illud iudicare unde appareat aliquis iudicandus; et secundum quod aliqui dicuntur iudicare comparatione, inquantum

OBJECTION 1: It would seem that no men will judge with Christ. For it is written: *the Father has given all judgment to the Son, that all men may honor the Son* (John 5:22–23). Therefore, etc.

OBJ. 2: Further, whoever judges has authority over that which he judges. Now those things about which the coming judgment will have to be, such as human merits and demerits, are subject to divine authority alone. Therefore, no one is competent to judge of those things.

OBJ. 3: Further, this judgment will most likely take place not vocally but mentally. Now the publication of merits and demerits in the hearts of all men (which is like an accusation or approval), or the repayment of punishment and reward (which is like the pronouncement of the sentence) will be the work of God alone. Therefore, none but Christ, who is God, will judge.

ON THE CONTRARY, It is written: *you also shall sit on twelve seats judging the twelve tribes of Israel* (Matt 19:28). Therefore, etc.

FURTHER, *The Lord will enter into judgment with the ancients of his people* (Isa 3:14). Therefore, it would seem that others also will judge together with Christ.

I ANSWER THAT, To judge has several significations. First, it is used causally, as it were, when we say it of that which proves that some person ought to be judged. In this sense the expression is used of certain people in compari-

ex comparatione aliorum aliqui iudicandi ostenduntur, sicut patet Matth. 12, [41], *viri Ninivitae surgent in iudicio* etc. Sed sic iudicari in iudicio communiter et bonorum et malorum est.

Alio modo dicitur iudicare quasi interpretative. Interpretamur enim aliquem facere qui facienti consentit. Unde isti qui consentient Christo iudici, eius sententiam approbando, iudicare dicuntur. Et sic iudicare est omnium electorum: unde dicitur Sap. 3, [8]: *iudicabunt sancti nationes.*

Tertio modo dicitur iudicare quasi per similitudinem: quia scilicet similitudinem iudicis habet, inquantum sedet in loco eminenti sicut iudex; sicut assessores dicuntur iudicare. Et secundum hunc modum dicunt quidam quod perfecti viri, quibus iudiciaria potestas promittitur Matth. 19, [27–28], iudicabunt, scilicet per honorabilem consessionem: quia superiores ceteris apparebunt in iudicio, *occurrentes obviam Christo in aera.* Sed istud non videtur sufficere ad promissionem Domini complendam, qua dicitur, *sedebitis iudicantes*: videtur enim iudicium consessioni superaddere.

Et ideo est quartus modus iudicandi, qui perfectis viris conveniet, inquantum in eis continentur decreta divinae iustitiae, ex quibus homines iudicabuntur: sicut si liber in quo continetur lex, iudicare dicatur. Unde Apoc. 20, [12] 2: *iudicium sedit, et libri aperti sunt.* Et per hunc modum hanc iudicationem Richardus de Sancto Victore exponit. Unde dicit: *qui divinae contemplationi assistunt, qui in libro sapientiae quotidie legunt, velut in cordium voluminibus transcribunt quidquid iam perspicua veritatis intelligentia comprehendunt.* Et infra: *quid vero sunt iudicantium corda, divinitus in omnem veritatem edocta, nisi quaedam canonum decreta?*

Sed quia iudicare importat actionem in alium procedentem, ideo, proprie loquendo, iudicare dicitur qui sententiam loquendo in alterum fert. Sed hoc dupliciter contingit. Uno modo, ex propria auctoritate. Et hoc est illius proprie qui habet in alios dominium et potestatem, cuius regimini subduntur qui iudicantur, unde eius est in eos ius ferre. Et sic iudicare est solius Dei. Alio modo, iudicare est sententiam alterius auctoritate latam in aliorum notitiam ducere, quod est sententiam latam pronuntiare. Et hoc modo perfecti viri iudicabunt: quia alios ducent in cognitionem divinae iustitiae, ut sciant quid iuste pro meritis eis debeatur; ut sic ipsa revelatio iustitiae dicatur iudicium. Unde dicit Richardus de Sancto Victore: *iudices coram iudicandi decretorum suorum libros aperire, est ad cordium suorum inspectionem infe-*

son, insofar as some are shown to be deserving of judgment through being compared with others, as is clear from Matthew 12:41: *the men of Nineveh shall rise in judgment with this generation, and shall condemn it.* To rise in judgment thus is common to the good and the wicked.

Second, the expression 'to judge' is used equivalently in a way; for consent to an action is considered equivalent to doing it. Wherefore those who will consent with Christ the Judge, by approving his sentence, will be said to judge. In this sense it will belong to all the elect to judge: wherefore it is written: *the just shall judge nations* (Wis 3:7–8).

Third, a person is said to judge assessorially and by similitude, because he is like the judge in that his seat is raised above the others: and thus assessors are said to judge. Some say that the perfect, to whom judiciary power is promised (Matt 19:28), will judge in this sense, namely, that they will be raised to the dignity of assessors, because they will appear above others at the judgment, and go forth *to meet Christ, into the air.* But this apparently does not suffice for the fulfilment of our Lord's promise: *you shall sit judging* (Matt 19:28), for he would seem to make judging something additional to sitting.

Hence there is a fourth way of judging, which will be competent to perfect men as containing the decrees of divine justice according to which men will be judged: thus a book containing the law might be said to judge, wherefore it is written: [*Judgment took her seat*] *and the books were opened* (Rev 20:12). Richard of St. Victor expounds this judging in this way (*On Judiciary Power in the Final and Universal Judgment*), wherefore he says: *those who persevere in divine contemplation, who read every day the book of wisdom, transcribe, so to speak, in their hearts whatever they grasp by their clear insight of the truth*; and further on: *what else are the hearts of those who judge, divinely instructed in all truth, but a codex of the law?*

Since, however, judging denotes an action exercised on another person, it follows that, properly speaking, he is said to judge who pronounces judgment on another. But this happens in two ways. First, by his own authority: and this belongs to the one who has dominion and power over others, and to whose ruling those who are judged are subject, wherefore it belongs to him to pass judgment on them. In this sense to judge belongs to God alone. Second, to judge is to acquaint others of the sentence delivered by another's authority, that is, to announce the verdict already given. In this way perfect men will judge, because they will lead others to the knowledge of divine justice that these may know what is due to them on account of their merits: so that this very revelation of justice is called judgment. Hence Richard of St. Victor says (*On Judiciary Power in the Final and Uni-*

riorum quorumlibet visum admittere, sensumque suum in his quae ad iudicium pertinent, revelare.

AD PRIMUM ergo dicendum quod obiectio illa procedit de iudicio auctoritatis, quod soli Christo conveniet.

ET SIMILITER dicendum ad secundum.

AD TERTIUM dicendum quod non est inconveniens aliquos sanctorum aliis quaedam revelare: vel per modum illuminationis, sicut superiores angeli inferiores illuminant; vel per modum locutionis, sicut quando inferiores superioribus loquuntur.

versal Judgment) that *for the judges to open the books of their decree in the presence of those who are to be judged signifies that they open their hearts to the gaze of all those who are below them, and that they reveal their knowledge in whatever pertains to the judgment.*

REPLY OBJ. 1: This objection considers the judgment of authority which belongs to Christ alone:

THE SAME ANSWER applies to the second objection.

REPLY OBJ. 3: There is no reason why some of the saints should not reveal certain things to others, either by way of enlightenment, as the higher angels enlighten the lower: or by way of speech, as the lower angels speak to the higher.

Article 2

Whether the Judicial Power Corresponds to Voluntary Poverty?

AD SECUNDUM SIC PROCEDITUR. Videtur quod iudiciaria potestas non correspondeat voluntariae paupertati. Hoc enim solum duodecim Apostolis est promissum, Matth. 19, [28]: *sedebitis super sedes iudicantes*, etc. Cum ergo non omnes voluntarie pauperes sint apostoli, videtur quod non omnibus iudiciaria potestas respondeat.

PRAETEREA, maius est offerre sacrificium Deo de proprio corpore quam de exterioribus rebus. Sed martyres et etiam virgines offerunt de proprio corpore sacrificium Deo: voluntarie autem pauperes de exterioribus rebus. Ergo sublimitas iudiciariae potestatis magis respondet martyribus et virginibus quam voluntarie pauperibus.

PRAETEREA, Ioan. 5, [45]: *est qui accusat vos Moyses, in quo vos speratis*: Glossa quia *voci eius non creditis*. Et Ioan. 12, [48]: *sermo quem locutus sum, ille iudicabit eum in novissimo die*. Ergo ex hoc quod aliquis proponit legem vel verbum exhortationis ad instructionem morum, habet quod indicet contemnentes. Sed hoc est doctorum. Ergo doctoribus magis competit quam pauperibus.

PRAETEREA, Christus ex hoc quod iniuste iudicatus est inquantum homo, meruit ut sit iudex omnium in humana natura: Ioan. 5, [27], *potestatem dedit ei iudicium facere quia Filius hominis est*. Sed qui persecutionem patiuntur propter iustitiam, iniuste iudicantur. Ergo talis potestas magis competit eis quam pauperibus.

PRAETEREA, superior non iudicatur ab inferiori. Sed multi licite divitiis utentes erunt maioris meriti multis

OBJECTION 1: It would seem that the judicial power does not correspond to voluntary poverty. For it was promised to none but the twelve apostles: *you shall sit on twelve seats, judging* (Matt 19:28). Since, then, those who are voluntarily poor are not all apostles, it would seem that the judicial power is not competent to all.

OBJ. 2: Further, to offer sacrifice to God of one's own body is more than to do so of outward things. Now martyrs, and also virgins, offer sacrifice to God of their own body: whereas the voluntarily poor offer sacrifice of outward things. Therefore, the sublimity of the judicial power is more in keeping with martyrs and virgins than with those who are voluntarily poor.

OBJ. 3: Further, John 5:45 says: *there is one that accuses you, Moses, in whom you trust*, upon which the Gloss says, *because you believe not his voice*, and John 12:48 says: *the word that I have spoken shall judge him in the last day*. Therefore, the fact that a man propounds a law or exhorts men by word to lead a good life gives him the right to judge those who scorn his utterances. But this belongs to doctors. Therefore, it is more competent to doctors than to those who are poor voluntarily.

OBJ. 4: Further, Christ, through being judged unjustly, merited as man to be judge of all in his human nature, according to John 5:27: *he has given him power to do judgment, because he is the Son of man*. Now those who suffer persecution for justice's sake are judged unjustly. Therefore, the judicial power is competent to them, rather than to the voluntarily poor.

OBJ. 5: Further, a superior is not judged by his inferior. Now many who will have made lawful use of riches

voluntarie pauperibus. Ergo voluntarie pauperes non iudicabunt ubi alii iudicabuntur.

SED CONTRA: Iob 36, [6]: *non salvat impios, et iudicium pauperibus tribuet.* Ergo pauperum est iudicare.

PRAETEREA, Matth. 19, super illud [v. 28], *vos qui reliquistis omnia* etc., dicit Glossa: *qui reliquerunt omnia et secuti sunt Deum, hi iudices erunt: qui licita habentes recte usi sunt, iudicabuntur.* Et sic idem quod prius.

RESPONDEO dicendum quod paupertati debetur iudiciaria potestas specialiter propter tria. Primo, ratione congruitatis. Quia voluntaria paupertas est eorum qui, omnibus quae mundi sunt contemptis, soli Christo inhaerent. Et ideo non est eis aliquid quod eorum iudicium a iustitia deflectat. Unde idonei ad iudicandum redduntur, quasi veritatem iustitiae prae omnibus diligentes.

Secundo, per modum meriti. Quia humilitati respondet exaltatio pro merito. Inter omnia autem quae hominem in hoc mundo despectum faciunt, praecipuum est paupertas. Unde et pauperibus excellentia iudiciariae potestatis promittitur, ut sic *qui propter Christum se humiliat, exaltetur.*

Tertio, quia paupertas disponit ad praedictum modum iudicandi: Ex hoc enim aliquis sanctorum iudicare dicetur, ut ex dictis patet, quia cor habebit edoctum omni divina veritate, quam aliis potens erit manifestare. In progressu autem ad perfectionem primum quod relinquendum occurrit, sunt exteriores divitiae: quia haec sunt ultimo acquisita; *quod* autem *ultimum est in generatione, est primum in destructione.* Unde et inter beatitudines, quibus est progressus ad perfectionem, prima ponitur paupertas. Et sic paupertati respondet iudiciaria potestas, inquantum est prima dispositio ad potestatem praedictam. Et hinc est quod non quibuscumque pauperibus, etiam voluntarie, repromittitur potestas praedicta: sed illis qui, *relinquentes omnia, sequuntur Christum* secundum perfectionem vitae.

AD PRIMUM ergo dicendum quod, sicut Augustinus dicit, XX *de Civ. Dei: nec, quoniam super duodecim sedes sessuros esse ait, duodecim solos homines cum iudicaturos putare debemus: alioquin, quoniam in locum Iudae proditoris Apostolum Matthiam legimus ordinatum, Paulus, qui plus aliis laboravit, ubi ad iudicandum sedeat non habebit.* Unde *duodenario numero significata est universa iudicantium multitudo, propter duas partes septenarii, scilicet tria et quatuor, quae in se ductae faciunt duodenarium*: duodenarius autem est numerus perfectionis. Vel propter hoc quod consistit in duplici senario, qui est numerus perfectus. Vel quia, ad litteram, duodecim Apostolis loquebatur, in quorum persona hoc omnibus eorum sectatoribus promittebat.

AD SECUNDUM dicendum quod virginitas: et martyrium non ita disponunt ad retinendum in corde decreta

will have greater merit than many of the voluntarily poor. Therefore, the voluntarily poor will not judge where those are to be judged.

ON THE CONTRARY, It is written: *he saves not the wicked, and he gives judgment to the poor* (Job 36:6).

FURTHER, A Gloss on Matthew 19:28: *you who have left all things,* says: *those who left all things and followed God will be the judges; those who made right use of what they had lawfully will be judged.* As so the same as before.

I ANSWER THAT, The judicial power is due especially to poverty on three counts. First, by reason of congruity, since voluntary poverty belongs to those who despise all the things of the world and cleave to Christ alone. Consequently, there is nothing in them to turn away their judgment from justice, so that they are rendered competent to be judges, as loving the truth of justice above all things.

Second, by reason of merit, since exaltation corresponds by way of merit to humility. Now of all the things that make man contemptible in this world, poverty is the chief: and for this reason the excellence of judicial power is promised to the poor, so that *he who humbles himself for Christ's sake shall be exalted.*

Third, because poverty disposes a man to the aforesaid manner of judging. For the reason why one of the saints will be said to judge, as stated above (A. 1), is that he will have the heart instructed in all divine truth, which he will be thus able to make known to others. Now in the advancement to perfection, the first thing that occurs to be renounced is external wealth, because this is the last thing of all to be acquired. And *that which is last in the order of generation is the first in the order of destruction*: wherefore among the beatitudes (whereby we advance to perfection), the first place is given to poverty. Thus judicial power corresponds to poverty, insofar as this is the disposition to the aforesaid perfection. Hence also it is that this same power is not promised to all who are voluntarily poor, but to those who *leave all and follow Christ*, in accordance with the perfection of life.

REPLY OBJ. 1: According to Augustine (*The City of God* 20), *we must not imagine that because he says that they will sit on twelve seats, only twelve men will judge with him: else since we read that Matthias was appointed apostle in the place of the traitor Judas, Paul, who worked more than the rest, will have nowhere to sit as judge.* Hence *the number twelve*, as he states (*The City of God* 20), *signifies the whole multitude of those who will judge, because the two parts of seven, namely, three and four, being multiplied together make twelve.* Moreover, twelve is a perfect number, being the double of six, which is a perfect number. Or, speaking literally, he spoke to the twelve apostles, in whose person he made this promise to all who follow them.

REPLY OBJ. 2: Virginity and martyrdom do not dispose man to retain the precepts of divine justice in his heart

divinae iustitiae sicut paupertas: sicut e contrario exteriores divitiae cx sua sollicitudine *suffocant verbum Dei,* sicut dicitur Luc. 8, [14].

Vel dicendum quod paupertas non solum sufficit ad meritum iudiciariae potestatis: sed quia est prima pars perfectionis, cui respondet iudiciaria potestas. Unde inter ea quae sequuntur ad paupertatem, ad perfectionem spectantia, possunt computari et virginitas et martyrium et omnia perfectionis opera. Non tamen sunt ita principalia sicut paupertas: quia principium est maxima pars rei.

AD TERTIUM dicendum quod ille qui legem proposuit aut exhortatus est ad bonum, iudicabit causaliter loquendo: quia per comparationem ad verba ab ipso proposita alii iudicabuntur. Et ideo non respondet proprie potestas iudiciaria praedicationi vel doctrinae.

Vel dicendum, secundum quosdam, quod tria requiruntur ad iudiciariam potestatem: primo, abdicatio temporalium curarum, ne impediatur animus a sapientiae perfectione; secundo, requiritur habitus continens divinam iustitiam scitam et observatam; tertio, quod illam iustitiam alios docuerint. Et sic doctrina erit complens meritum iudiciariae potestatis.

AD QUARTUM dicendum quod Christus in hoc quod iniuste iudicatus est, *seipsum humiliavit* (*oblatus est* enim *quia voluit*), et meritum humilitatis est iudiciaria exaltatio, qua ei omnia subduntur, ut dicitur Philipp. 3, [21]. Et ideo magis debetur iudiciaria potestas illis qui voluntarie se humiliant bona temporalia abiiciendo, propter quae homines a mundanis honorantur, quam his qui ab aliis humiliantur.

AD QUINTUM dicendum quod inferior non potest iudicare superiorem auctoritate propria: sed tamen auctoritate superioris potest, sicut patet in iudicibus delegatis. Et ideo non est inconveniens si hoc, quasi accidentale praemium pauperibus detur, ut iudicent alios etiam qui sunt excellentioris meriti respectu praemii essentialis.

in the same degree as poverty does: even so, on the other hand, outward riches *choke the word of God* (Luke 8:14) by the cares which they entail.

Or we may reply that poverty does not suffice alone to merit judicial power, but is the fundamental part of that perfection to which the judicial power corresponds. Therefore, among those things regarding perfection which follow after poverty we may reckon both virginity and martyrdom and all the works of perfection: yet they do not rank as high as poverty, since the beginning of a thing is its chief part.

REPLY OBJ. 3: He who propounded the law, or urged men to good, will judge, in the causal sense (Cf. A. 1), because others will be judged in reference to the words he has uttered or propounded. Hence the judicial power does not properly correspond to preaching or teaching.

Or we may reply that, as some say, three things are requisite for the judicial power: first, that one renounce temporal cares, lest the mind be hindered from the contemplation of wisdom; second, that one possess divine justice by way of habit, both as to knowledge and as to observance; third, that one should have taught others this same justice; and this teaching will be the perfection whereby a man merits to have judicial power.

REPLY OBJ. 4: Christ *humbled himself* in that he was judged unjustly; for *he was offered because it was his own will* (Isa 53:7): and by his humility he merited his exaltation to judicial power, since all things are made subject to him (Phil 2:8–9). Hence, judicial power is more due to them who humble themselves of their own will by renouncing temporal goods, on account of which men are honored by worldlings, than to those who are humbled by others.

REPLY OBJ. 5: An inferior cannot judge a superior by his own authority, but he can do so by the authority of a superior, as in the case of a judge-delegate. Hence it is not unfitting that it be granted to the poor as an accidental reward to judge others, even those who have higher merit in respect of the essential reward.

Article 3

Whether the Angels Will Judge?

AD TERTIUM SIC PROCEDITUR. Videtur quod angeli debeant iudicare. Matth. 25, [31]: *cum venerit Filius hominis in maiestate sua et omnes angeli cum eo.* Sed loquitur de adventu ad iudicium. Ergo videtur quod angeli etiam iudicabunt.

PRAETEREA, angelorum ordines nomina sortiuntur ex officio quod exercent. Sed quidam ordo angelorum est ordo Thronorum: quod videtur pertinere ad iudiciariam

OBJECTION 1: It would seem that the angels will judge. For it is written: *when the Son of man shall come in his majesty, and all the angels with him* (Matt 25:31). Now he is speaking of his coming to judgment. Therefore, it would seem that also the angels will judge.

OBJ. 2: Further, the orders of the angels take their names from the offices which they fulfill. Now one of the angelic orders is that of the Thrones, which would seem to

potestatem; thronus enim est sedes iudicis, *solium* regis, *cathedra* doctoris. Ergo aliqui angeli iudicabunt.

PRAETEREA, sanctis post hanc vitam promittitur angelorum aequalitas, Matth. 22, [30]. Si ergo homines hanc habebunt potestatem ut iudicent, multo fortius et angeli.

SED CONTRA: Ioan. 5, [27]: *potestatem dedit ei iudicium facere quia Filius hominis est*. Sed angeli non communicant in humana natura. Ergo nec in iudiciaria potestate.

PRAETEREA, non est eiusdem iudicare et esse iudicis ministrum. Sed angeli erunt in iudicio illo ut ministri: ut dicitur Matth. 13, [41]: *mittet Filius hominis angelos, et colligent de regno eius omnia scandala*. Ergo angeli non iudicabunt.

RESPONDEO dicendum quod assessores iudicis debent iudici esse conformes. Iudicium autem Filio attribuitur quia secundum humanam naturam omnibus apparebit, tam bonis quam malis: quamvis tota Trinitas iudicet per auctoritatem. Et ideo etiam oportet ut assessores iudicis humanam naturam habeant, in qua possint ab omnibus, bonis et malis, videri. Et sic: angelis non competit iudicare. Quamvis angeli etiam aliquo modo possint dici iudicare, scilicet per sententiae approbationem.

AD PRIMUM ergo dicendum quod, sicut ex Glossa ibidem patet, angeli cum Christo venient non ut iudices, sed *ut sint testes humanorum actuum, sub quorum custodia homines bene vel male egerunt*.

AD SECUNDUM dicendum quod nomen Throni attribuitur angelis ratione illius iudicii quod Deus semper exercet, omnia iustissime gubernando, cuius iudicii angeli sunt quodammodo executores et promulgatores. Sed iudicium quod de hominibus per hominem Christum fiet, etiam requirit homines assessores.

AD TERTIUM dicendum quod hominibus promittitur angelorum aequalitas quantum ad praemium essentiale. Nihil tamen prohibet aliquod praemium accidentale exhiberi hominibus quod angelis non dabitur: ut patet de aureola virginum aut martyrum. Et similiter potest dici de iudiciaria potestate.

pertain to the judicial power, since a throne is the judicial bench, a royal *seat*, a professor's *chair* (Cf. St. Isidore *Etymologies* 7.5). Therefore, some of the angels will judge.

OBJ. 3: Further, equality with the angels is promised the saints after this life (Matt 22:30). If, then, men will have this power of judging, much more will the angels have it.

ON THE CONTRARY, It is written: *he has given him power to judgment, because he is the Son of man* (John 5:27). But the angels have not the human nature in common with him. Neither, therefore, do they share with him in the judicial power.

FURTHER, The same person is not judge and judge's minister. Now in this judgment the angels will act as ministers of the Judge, according to Matthew 13:41: *the Son of man shall send his angels and they shall gather out of his kingdom all scandals*. Therefore, the angels will not judge.

I ANSWER THAT, The judge's assessors must be conformed to the judge. Now judgment is ascribed to the Son of man because he will appear to all, both good and wicked, in his human nature, although the whole Trinity will judge by authority. Consequently, the Judge's assessors also ought to have the human nature, so as to be visible to all, both good and wicked. Hence it is not fitting for the angels to judge, although in a certain sense we may say that the angels will judge, namely, by approving the sentence (Cf. A. 1).

REPLY OBJ. 1: As a Gloss on this passage observes, the angels will come with Christ, not to judge, but *as witnesses of men's deeds because it was under their guardianship that men did well or ill*.

REPLY OBJ. 2: The name of Thrones is given to angels in reference to the judgment which God is ever pronouncing, by governing all things with supreme justice: of which judgment angels are in a way the executors and promulgators. On the other hand, the judgment of men by the man Christ will require human assessors.

REPLY OBJ. 3: Equality with angels is promised to men as regards the essential reward. But nothing hinders an accidental reward from being bestowed on men to the exclusion of the angels, as in the case of the virgins' and martyrs' crowns: and the same may be said of the judicial power.

Article 4

Whether the Demons Will Carry Out the Sentence of the Judge on the Damned?

AD QUARTUM SIC PROCEDITUR. Videtur quod post diem iudicii daemones non exequantur sententiam Iudicis in damnatis. Quia secundum Apostolum, I Cor. 15, [24], tunc *evacuabit omnem principatum et potestatem*

OBJECTION 1: It would seem that the demons will not carry out the sentence of the Judge on the damned after the day of judgment. For, according to the Apostle: *he will then bring to naught all principality, and power, and*

et virtutem. Ergo *cessabit omnis praelatio.* Sed exequi iudicis sententiam quandam denotat praelationem. Ergo daemones post diem iudicii non exequentur sententiam iudicis.

PRAETEREA, daemones magis peccaverunt quam homines. Ergo non est iustum quod homines per daemones torqueantur.

PRAETEREA, sicut daemones suggerunt hominibus mala, ita angeli suggerunt bona. Sed praemiare bonos non erit officium angelorum, sed hoc erit ab ipso Deo immediate. Ergo nec punire malos erit officium daemonum.

SED CONTRA est quod homines peccatores se diabolo subdiderunt peccando. Ergo iustum est ut ei subiiciantur in poenis, quasi ab eo puniendi.

RESPONDEO dicendum quod circa hoc tangitur a Magistro in littera duplex opinio: et utraque videtur Dei iustitiae competere. Ex hoc enim quod homo peccat, iuste daemoni subiicitur; sed daemon iniuste ei praeest. Opinio ergo illa quae ponit daemones in futurum, post diem iudicii, hominibus non praeesse in poenis, respicit ordinem divinae iustitiae ex parte daemonum punientium. Contraria vero opinio respicit ordinem divinae iustitiae ex parte hominum punitorum.

Quae autem earum verior sit, certum nobis esse non potest. Verius tamen aestimo quod, sicut ordo servabitur in salvatis quod quidam a quibusdam illuminabuntur et perficientur, eo quod ordines caelestis hierarchiae perpetui erunt; ita servabitur ordo in poenis, ut homines per daemones puniantur; ne totaliter divinus ordo, quo angelos medios inter naturam humanam et divinam constituit, annulletur. Et ideo, sicut hominibus per angelos divinae illuminationes deferuntur, ita etiam daemones sunt executores divinae iustitiae in malos. Nec ob hoc minuitur aliquid de daemonum poena. Quia in hoc etiam quod alios torquent, ipsi torquebuntur: ibi enim miserorum societas miseriam non minuet, sed augebit.

AD PRIMUM ergo dicendum quod praelatio illa quae dicitur evacuanda per Christum in futuro, est accipienda secundum modum praelationis quae est secundum statum huius mundi, in quo et homines hominibus principantur, et angeli hominibus, et angeli angelis, et daemones daemonibus, et daemones hominibus, et hoc totum ad perducendum ad finem vel abducendum a fine. Tunc autem, cum omnia ad finem suum pervenerint, non erit praelatio abducens a fine vel adducens ad finem, sed conservans in fine boni vel mali.

AD SECUNDUM dicendum quod, quamvis meritum daemonum non requirat quod hominibus praeferantur, quia iniuste sibi homines subiecerunt; tamen hoc requi-

virtue (1 Cor 15:24). Therefore, *all supremacy will cease* then. But the carrying out of the Judge's sentence implies some kind of supremacy. Therefore, after the judgment day the demons will not carry out the Judge's sentence.

OBJ. 2: Further, the demons sinned more grievously than men. Therefore, it is not just that men should be tortured by demons.

OBJ. 3: Further, just as the demons suggest evil things to men, so good angels suggest good things. Now it will not be the duty of the good angels to reward the good, but this will be done by God immediately by himself. Therefore, neither will it be the duty of the demons to punish the wicked.

ON THE CONTRARY, Sinners have subjected themselves to the devil by sinning. Therefore, it is just that they should be subjected to him in their punishments, and punished by him as it were.

I ANSWER THAT, The Master in the text of *Sentences* (IV, D. 47), mentions two opinions on this question, both of which seem consistent with divine justice, because it is just for man to be subjected to the devil for having sinned, and yet it is unjust for the demon to be over him. Accordingly, the opinion which holds that after the judgment day the demons will not be placed over men to punish them regards the order of divine justice on the part of the demons punishing; while the contrary opinion regards the order of divine justice on the part of the men punished.

Which of these opinions is nearer the truth we cannot know for certain. Yet I think it truer to say that just as, among the saved, order will be observed so that some will be enlightened and perfected by others (because all the orders of the heavenly hierarchies will continue forever), so, too, will order be observed in punishments, men being punished by demons, lest the divine order, whereby the angels are placed between the human nature and the divine, be entirely set aside. Wherefore, just as the divine illuminations are conveyed to men by the good angels, so too the demons execute the divine justice on the wicked. Nor does this in any way diminish the punishment of the demons, since even in torturing others they are themselves tortured, because then the fellowship of the unhappy will not lessen but will increase unhappiness.

REPLY OBJ. 1: The supremacy which, it is declared, will be brought to naught by Christ in the time to come must be taken in the sense of the supremacy which is in keeping with the state of this world: wherein men are placed over men, angels over men, angels over angels, demons over demons, and demons over men; in every case so as either to lead towards the end or to lead astray from the end. But then, when all things will have attained to that end, there will be no supremacy to lead astray from the end or to lead to it, but only that which maintains in the end, good or evil.

REPLY OBJ. 2: Although the demerit of the demons does not require that they be placed over men, since they made men subject to them unjustly, yet this is required by

rit ordo naturae ipsorum ad naturam humanam. Bona enim naturalia in eis *integra* manent, ut Dionysius dicit, IV *de Divinis Nominibus.*

AD TERTIUM dicendum quod angeli boni non sunt causa principalis praemii electis: quia hoc omnes immediate a Deo percipient. Sed tamen quorundam accidentalium praemiorum angeli hominibus sunt causa: inquantum per superiores angelos inferiores et angeli et homines illuminantur de aliquibus secretis divinorum quae ad substantiam beatitudinis non pertinent. Et similiter etiam principalem poenam damnati percipient immediate a Deo, scilicet exclusionem perpetuam a visione Dei: alias autem poenas sensibiles non est inconveniens hominibus per daemones infligi.

In hoc tamen est differentia, quia meritum exaltat, sed peccatum deprimit. Unde, cum natura angelica sit altior quam humana, quidam propter excellentiam meriti in tantum exaltabuntur quod talis exaltatio excedet altitudinem naturae et praemii in quibusdam angelis, Unde quidam angeli per quosdam homines illuminabuntur. Sed nulli homines peccatores, propter aliquem gradum malitiae, pervenient ad illam eminentiam quae debetur naturae daemonum.

the order of their nature in relation to human nature: since natural goods remain in them *unimpaired*, as Dionysius says (*On the Divine Names* 4).

REPLY OBJ. 3: The good angels are not the cause of the principal reward in the elect, because all receive this immediately from God. Nevertheless, the angels are the cause of certain accidental rewards in men insofar as the higher angels enlighten those beneath them, both angels and men, concerning certain hidden things of God which do not belong to the essence of beatitude. In like manner, the damned will receive their principal punishment immediately from God, namely, the everlasting banishment from the divine vision: but there is no reason why the demons should not torture men with other sensible punishments.

There is, however, this difference: that merit exalts, whereas sin debases. Therefore, since the angelic nature is higher than the human, some on account of the excellence of their merit will be so far exalted as to be raised above the angels both in nature and rewards, so that some angels will be enlightened by some men. On the other hand, no human sinners will, on account of a certain degree of virtue, attain to the eminence that attaches to the nature of the demons.

Article 5

Whether All Men Will Be Present at the Judgment?

AD QUINTUM SIC PROCEDITUR. Videtur quod non omnes homines in iudicio compareant. Quia dicitur Matth. 19, [28]: *sedebitis super sedes iudicantes duodecim tribus Israel.* Sed non omnes homines pertinent ad illas duodecim tribus. Ergo videtur quod non omnes homines compareant.

PRAETEREA, idem videtur per hoc quod dicitur in Psalmo [1, 5]: *non resurgent impii in iudicio.* Sed multi sunt tales. Ergo in iudicio non comparebunt.

PRAETEREA, ad hoc aliquis ad iudicium ducitur ut eius merita discutiantur. Sed quidam sunt qui nulla merita habuerunt: sicut pueri ante perfectam aetatem decedentes. Ergo illos in iudicio comparere non est necesse.

SED CONTRA: Est quod dicitur Act. 10, [42], quod Christus *est constitutus a Deo iudex vivorum et mortuorum.* Sed sub istis differentiis comprehenduntur omnes homines, qualitercumque vivi a mortuis distinguantur. Ergo omnes homines in iudicio comparebunt.

PRAETEREA, Apoc. 1, [7] dicitur: *ecce venit cum nubibus, et videbit eum omnis oculus.* Hoc autem non esset si non omnes homines in iudicio comparerent. Ergo, etc.

RESPONDEO dicendum quod potestas iudiciaria Christo homini collata est in praemium humilitatis

OBJECTION 1: It would seem that men will not all be present at the judgment. For it is written: *you shall sit on twelve seats, judging the twelve tribes of Israel* (Matt 19:28). But all men do not belong to those twelve tribes. Therefore, it would seem that men will not all be present at the judgment.

OBJ. 2: Further, the same apparently is to be gathered from Psalm 1:5: *the wicked shall not rise again in judgment.* But many are such. Therefore, they will not be present at the judgment.

OBJ. 3: Further, a man is brought to judgment that his merits may be discussed. But some there are who have acquired no merits, such as children who died before reaching the perfect age. Therefore, they need not be present at the judgment.

ON THE CONTRARY, It is written that Christ *was appointed by God to be judge of the living and of the dead* (Acts 10:42). Now this division comprises all men, no matter how the living be distinct from the dead. Therefore, all men will be present at the judgment.

FURTHER, It is written: *behold he comes with the clouds, and every eye shall see him* (Rev 1:7). Now this would not be so unless all were present at the judgment. Therefore, etc.

I ANSWER THAT, The judicial power was bestowed on Christ as man in reward for the humility which he showed

quam in passione exhibuit. Ipse autem sua passione; sanguinem pro omnibus fudit quantum ad sufficientiam, licet non in omnibus effectum habuit, propter impedimentum in aliquibus inventum. Et ideo congruum est ut omnes homines in iudicio congregentur ad videndum eius exaltationem in humana natura, secundum quam *constitutus est iudex a Deo vivorum et mortuorum.*

Ad primum ergo dicendum quod, sicut dicit Augustinus, XX *de Civ. Dei: non, quia dictum est, Iudicantes duodecim tribus Israel, tribus Levi, quae tertiadecima est, iudicanda non erit: aut solum illum populum, non etiam gentes ceteras iudicabunt.* Ideo autem per duodecim tribus omnes aliae gentes significatae sunt, quia per Christum in sortem duodecim tribuum omnes gentes sunt vocatae.

Ad secundum dicendum quod hoc quod dicitur, *non resurgent impii in iudicio,* si referatur ad omnes peccatores, sic intelligendum est quod non resurgent ad hoc quod iudicent. Si autem impii dicantur *infideles,* sic intelligendum est quod non resurgent ad hoc quod iudicentur, quia iam *iudicati sunt.* Sed omnes resurgent ut in iudicio compareant ad gloriam iudicis intuendam.

Ad tertium dicendum quod etiam pueri ante perfectam aetatem decedentes in iudicio comparebunt: non autem ut iudicentur, sed ut videant gloriam iudicis.

forth in his passion. Now in his passion he shed his blood for all in point of sufficiency, although through meeting with an obstacle in some, it had not its effect in all. Therefore, it is fitting that all men should assemble at the judgment to see his exaltation in his human nature, in respect of which *he was appointed by God to be judge of the living and of the dead.*

Reply Obj. 1: As Augustine says (*The City of God* 20.5), it does not follow from the saying, "Judging the twelve tribes of Israel," that the tribe of Levi, which is the thirteenth, is not to be judged, or that they will judge that people alone, and not other nations. The reason why all other nations are denoted by the twelve tribes is because they were called by Christ to take the place of the twelve tribes.

Reply Obj. 2: The words, *the wicked shall not rise in judgment,* if referred to all sinners, mean that they will not arise to judge. But if the wicked denote *unbelievers,* the sense is that they will not arise to be judged, because they are *already judged* (John 3:18). All, however, will rise again to assemble at the judgment and witness the glory of the Judge.

Reply Obj. 3: Even children who have died before reaching the perfect age will be present at the judgment, not to be judged, but to see the Judge's glory.

Article 6

Whether the Good Will Be Judged at the Judgment?

Ad sextum sic proceditur. Videtur quod nulli boni in iudicio iudicentur. Quia Ioan. 3, [18] dicitur: *qui credit in eum, non iudicatur.* Sed omnes boni crediderunt in eum. Ergo non iudicabuntur.

Praeterea, illi non sunt beati quibus est incerta sua beatitudo: ex quo Augustinus probat daemones nunquam fuisse beatos. Sed sancti homines nunc sunt beati. Ergo certi sunt de sua beatitudine. Sed quod certum est, non adducitur ad iudicium. Ergo boni non iudicabuntur.

Praeterea, timor beatitudini repugnat. Sed extremum iudicium, quod *tremendum* maxime dicitur, non poterit fieri sine timore eorum qui sunt iudicandi. Unde etiam Gregorius dicit, super illud Iob 41, [16], *cum sublatus fuerit timebunt angeli: consideremus quomodo tunc iniquorum conscientia concutitur, quando etiam iustorum vita turbatur.* Ergo beati non iudicabuntur.

Sed contra: Videtur quod omnes boni iudicentur. Quia dicitur II Cor. 5, [10]: *omnes adstabimus ante tribunal Christi, ut referat unusquisque propria corporis, prout*

Objection 1: It would seem that none of the good will be judged at the judgment. For it is declared that *he that believes in him is not judged* (John 3:18). Now all the good believed in him. Therefore, they will not be judged.

Obj. 2: Further, those who are uncertain of their bliss are not blessed: whence Augustine proves (*On the Literal Meaning of Genesis* 11) that the demons were never blessed. But the saints are now blessed. Therefore, they are certain of their bliss. Now what is certain is not submitted to judgment. Therefore, the good will not be judged.

Obj. 3: Further, fear is incompatible with bliss. But the last judgment, which above all is described as *terrible,* cannot take place without inspiring fear into those who are to be judged. Hence on Job 41:16: *when he shall raise him up, the angels shall fear,* Gregory observes, *consider how the conscience of the wicked will then be troubled when even the just are disturbed about their life* (*Morals on Job* 34). Therefore, the blessed will not be judged.

On the contrary, It would seem that all the good will be judged, since it is written: *we must all be manifested before the judgment seat of Christ, that every one may re-*

gessit sive bonum sive malum. Sed nihil est aliud iudicari. Ergo omnes iudicabuntur.

PRAETEREA, *universale* omnia comprehendit. Sed illud iudicium dicitur *universale*. Ergo omnes iudicabuntur.

RESPONDEO dicendum quod ad iudicium duo pertinent: scilicet discussio meritorum; et retributio praemiorum. Quantum ergo ad receptionem praemiorum, omnes iudicabuntur, etiam boni: in eo quod unusquisque recipiet ex divina sententia praemium merito respondens.

Sed discussio meritorum non fit nisi ubi est quaedam meritorum commixtio bonorum cum malis. Illi autem *qui aedificant supra fundamentum fidei aurum et argentum et lapides pretiosos*, divinis servitiis totaliter insistentes, qui nullam admixtionem notabilem alicuius mali meriti habent, in eis discussio meritorum locum non habet: sicut illi qui, rebus mundi penitus abiectis, *sollicite cogitant solum quae Dei sunt*. Et ideo salvabuntur, sed non iudicabuntur. Illi vero qui *aedificant super fundamentum fidei ligna, foenum, stipulam*, qui adhuc scilicet amant saecularia et *terrenis negotiis implicantur*, ita tamen quod nihil Christo praeponant, sed studeant *peccata eleemosynis expiare*, habent quidem commixtionem bonorum meritorum cum malis, et ideo discussio meritorum in eis locum habet. Unde tales, quantum ad hoc, et iudicabuntur, et tamen salvabuntur.

AD PRIMUM ergo dicendum quod, quia punitio est effectus iustitiae, praemiatio autem misericordiae, ideo magis iudicio, quod est actus iustitiae antonomastice, punitio attribuitur: ut interdum iudicium pro ipsa condemnatione accipiatur. Et sic intelligitur auctoritas inducta, ut per Glossam ibidem patet.

AD SECUNDUM dicendum quod discussio meritorum in electis non erit ad tollendum certitudinem beatitudinis a cordibus ipsorum iudicandorum: sed ut praeeminentia bonorum meritorum ad mala ostendatur omnibus manifeste, et sic Dei iustitia comprobetur.

AD TERTIUM dicendum quod Gregorius loquitur de iustis in carne mortali existentibus. Unde supra praemiserat: *hi qui in corporibus reperiri potuerint, quamvis iam fortes atque perfecti, adhuc, quia in carne sunt positi, non possunt in tanti terroris, turbine nulla formidine concuti.* Unde patet quod terror ille referendus est ad tempus immediate iudicium praecedens, tremendum quidem maxime malis, non autem bonis, quibus nulla erit mali suspicio.

Rationes autem quae sunt ad oppositum, procedunt de iudicio quantum ad retributionem praemiorum.

ceive the proper things of the body, according as he has done, whether it be good or evil (2 Cor 5:10). Now there is nothing else to be judged. Therefore, all will be judged.

FURTHER, The *general* includes all. Now this is called the *general* judgment. Therefore, all will be judged.

I ANSWER THAT, The judgment comprises two things: namely, the discussion of merits and the payment of rewards. As regards the payment of rewards, all will be judged, even the good, since the divine sentence will appoint to each one the reward corresponding to his merit.

But there is no discussion of merits save where good and evil merits are mingled together. Now those *who build on the foundation of faith, gold, silver, and precious stones* (1 Cor 3:12), by devoting themselves wholly to the divine service, and who have no notable admixture of evil merit, are not subjected to a discussion of their merits. Such are those who have entirely renounced the things of the world and *are solicitously thoughtful of the things that are of God*: wherefore they will be saved but will not be judged. Others, however, *build on the foundation of faith, wood, hay, stubble*; they, in fact, love worldly things and *are busy about earthly concerns*, yet so as to prefer nothing to Christ, but strive *to redeem their sins with alms*, and these have an admixture of good with evil merits. Hence they are subjected to a discussion of their merits, and consequently in this account will be judged, and yet they will be saved.

REPLY OBJ. 1: Since punishment is the effect of justice, while reward is the effect of mercy, it follows that punishment is more especially ascribed antonomastically to judgment, which is the act of justice; so that judgment is sometimes used to express condemnation. It is thus that we are to understand the words quoted, as a Gloss on the passage remarks.

REPLY OBJ. 2: The merits of the elect will be discussed not to remove the uncertainty of their beatitude from the hearts of those who are to be judged, but that it may be made manifest to us that their good merits outweigh their evil merits, and thus God's justice be proved.

REPLY OBJ. 3: Gregory is speaking of the just who will still be in mortal flesh, wherefore he had already said: *those who will still be in the body, although already brave and perfect, yet through being still in the flesh must be troubled with fear in the midst of such a whirlwind of terror.* Hence it is clear that this fear refers to the time immediately before the judgment, most terrible indeed to the wicked, but not to the good, who will have no apprehension of evil.

The arguments in the contrary sense consider judgment as regards the payment of rewards.

Article 7

Whether the Wicked Will Be Judged?

AD SEPTIMUM SIC PROCEDITUR. Videtur quod nulli mali iudicabuntur. Sicut enim est certa infidelium damnatio, ita et eorum qui in mortali decedunt. Sed propter damnationis certitudinem dicitur Ioan. 3, [18]: *qui non credit, iam iudicatus est.* Ergo eadem ratione nec alii peccatores iudicabuntur.

PRAETEREA, vox Iudicis est valde terribilis eis qui per iudicium condemnantur. Sed, sicut in littera ex verbis Gregorii habetur, *ad infideles allocutio Iudicis non fiet.* Si ergo fieret ad fideles damnandos, infideles de sua infidelitate commodum reportarent. Quod est absurdum.

SED CONTRA, videtur quod omnes mali sint iudicandi. Quia omnibus malis infligetur poena secundum quantitatem culpae. Sed hoc sine definitione iudicii esse non potest. Ergo omnes mali iudicabuntur.

RESPONDEO dicendum quod iudicium quod est poenarum retributio pro peccatis, omnibus malis competit: iudicium autem quod est discussio meritorum, solum fidelibus. Quia infidelibus non est fidei fundamentum: quo sublato, omnia opera sequentia perfecta rectitudine intentionis carent. Unde non est in eis aliqua permixtio bonorum meritorum ad mala, quae discussionem requirant. Sed fideles, in quibus manet fidei fundamentum, ad minus fidei actum laudabilem habent: quamvis non sit meritorius sine caritate. Tamen, quantum est de se, est ordinatus ad meritum. Et ideo in eis iudicium discussionis locum habet. Unde ipsi fideles, qui fuerunt saltem numero cives Civitatis Dei, iudicabuntur ut cives, in quos sine discussione meritorum sententia mortis non fertur. Sed infideles condemnabuntur, ut hostes, qui consueverunt apud homines absque meritorum audientia exterminari.

AD PRIMUM ergo dicendum quod, quamvis eis qui, in mortali decedunt, pro certo constet de eorum damnatione; quia tamen aliqua quae pertinent ad bene merendum habent annexa, oportet, ad manifestationem divinae iustitiae, ut discussio de eorum meritis fiat, per quam ostendatur eos iuste a sanctorum civitate excludi, cuius esse cives numero exterius videbantur.

AD SECUNDUM dicendum quod allocutio illa, spiritualiter intellecta, secundum hoc non erit aspera fidelibus condemnandis, quod in eis aliqua sibi placentia manifestabit, quae in infidelibus inveniri non possunt, quia *sine fide impossibile est Deo placere,* Heb. ii, [6]. Sed sen-

OBJECTION 1: It would seem that none of the wicked will be judged. For even as damnation is certain in the case of unbelievers, so is it in the case of those who die in mortal sin. Now it is declared because of the certainty of damnation: *he that believes not is already judged* (John 3:18). Therefore, in like manner neither will other sinners be judged.

OBJ. 2: Further, the voice of the Judge is most terrible to those who are condemned by his judgment. Now, according to the text of *Sentences* IV, D. 47, and in the words of Gregory, *the Judge will not address himself to unbelievers* (*Morals on Job* 26). If, therefore, he were to address himself to the believers about to be condemned, the unbelievers would reap a benefit from their unbelief, which is absurd.

ON THE CONTRARY, It would seem that all the wicked are to be judged, because all the wicked will be sentenced to punishment according to the degree of their guilt. But this cannot be done without a judicial pronouncement. Therefore, all the wicked will be judged.

I ANSWER THAT, The judgment as regards the sentencing to punishment for sin concerns all the wicked, whereas the judgment as regards the discussion of merits concerns only believers. For in unbelievers the foundation of faith is lacking, without which all subsequent works are deprived of the perfection of a right intention, so that in them there is no admixture of good and evil works or merits requiring discussion. But believers, in whom the foundation of faith remains, have at least a praiseworthy act of faith, which, though it is not meritorious without charity, yet is in itself directed to merit, and consequently they will be subjected to the discussion of merits. Consequently, believers who were at least counted as citizens of the City of God will be judged as citizens, and sentence of death will not be passed on them without a discussion of their merits; whereas unbelievers will be condemned as foes, who are wont among men to be exterminated without their merits being discussed.

REPLY OBJ. 1: Although it is certain that those who die in mortal sin will be damned, nevertheless, since they have an admixture of certain things connected with meriting well for the manifestation of divine justice, their merits ought to be subjected to discussion, in order to make it clear that they are justly banished from the city of the saints of which they appeared outwardly to be citizens.

REPLY OBJ. 2: Considered under this special aspect, the words addressed to the believers about to be condemned will not be terrible, because they will reveal in them certain things pleasing to them, which it will be impossible to find in unbelievers, since *without faith it is impossible to please*

tentia condemnationis, quae in omnes fertur, omnibus terribilis erit.

Ratio vero in contrarium adducta procedebat de iudicio retributionis.

God (Heb 11:6). But the sentence of condemnation which will be passed on them all will be terrible to all of them.

The argument in the contrary sense considered the judgment of retribution.

Article 8

Whether at the Coming Judgment the Angels Will Be Judged?

AD OCTAVUM SIC PROCEDITUR. Videtur quod angeli in futuro iudicentur. Quia dicitur I Cor. 6, [3]: *nescitis quoniam angelos iudicabimus?* Sed hoc non potest referri ad statum praesentis temporis. Ergo referri debet ad futurum iudicium.

PRAETEREA, Iob 40, [28] dicitur de Behemoth, per quem diabolus intelligitur: *cunctis videntibus praecipitabitur.* Et Marc. 1, [24], exclamavit daemon ad Christum: *venisti ante tempus perdere nos?* Et Glossa dicit ibidem *quod daemones, in terra Dominum cernentes, se continuo iudicandos esse credebant.* Ergo videtur quod eis finale iudicium reservetur.

PRAETEREA, II Petr. 2, [4] dicitur: *Deus angelis peccantibus non pepercit, sed rudentibus inferni detractos in tartarum tradidit cruciandos, in iudicium reservari.* Ergo videtur quod angeli iudicabuntur.

SED CONTRA: Deus *non iudicat bis in idipsum.* Sed mali angeli iam iudicati sunt: unde Ioan. 16, [11], *princeps mundi iam iudicatus est.* Ergo in futuro angeli non iudicabuntur.

PRAETEREA, perfectior est bonitas vel malitia angelorum quam aliquorum hominum in statu viae. Sed quidam homines boni et mali non iudicabuntur. Ergo nec angeli boni vel mali iudicabuntur.

RESPONDEO dicendum quod iudicium discussionis nullo modo habet locum neque in bonis angelis neque in malis: quia neque in bonis potest aliquid mali inveniri, neque in malis aliquid boni ad iudicium pertinens.

Sed si loquamur de iudicio retributionis, sic est distinguenda duplex retributio. Una respondens propriis meritis angelorum. Et haec a principio fuit utrisque facta, dum quidam ad beatitudinem sublimati sunt, quidam vero in miseriam demersi. Alia retributio est quae respondet meritis bonis vel malis per angelos procuratis. Et haec retributio in futuro iudicio fiet : quia boni angeli amplius gaudium habebunt de salute eorum quos ad meritum induxerunt; et mali amplius torquebuntur multiplicata malorum ruina, qui per eos ad mala sunt incitati.

OBJECTION 1: It would seem that the angels will be judged at the coming judgment. For it is written: *know you not that we shall judge angels?* (1 Cor 6:3). But this cannot refer to the state of the present time. Therefore, it should refer to the judgment to come.

OBJ. 2: Further, Job 40:28 says concerning Behemoth, whereby the devil is signified: *in the sight of all he shall be cast down*; and the demon cried out to Christ: *why are you come to destroy us before the time?* (Mark 1:24) for, according to a Gloss, *the demons, seeing our Lord on earth, thought they were to be judged forthwith.* Therefore, it would seem that a final judgment is in store for them.

OBJ. 3: Further, it is written: *God spared not the angels that sinned, but delivered them drawn down by infernal ropes to the lower hell unto torments, to be reserved unto judgment* (2 Pet 2:4). Therefore, it seems that the angels will be judged.

ON THE CONTRARY, Nahum 1:9 says: *God will not judge the same thing a second time.* But the wicked angels are already judged, wherefore it is written: *the prince of this world is already judged* (John 16:11). Therefore, the angels will not be judged in the time to come.

FURTHER, Goodness and wickedness are more perfect in the angels than in men who are wayfarers. Now some men, good and wicked, will not be judged as stated in the text of *Sentences* (IV, D. 47). Therefore, neither will good or wicked angels be judged.

I ANSWER THAT, The judgment of discussion in no way concerns either the good or the wicked angels, since neither is any evil to be found in the good angels, nor is any good liable to judgment to be found in the wicked angels.

But if we speak of the judgment of retribution, we must distinguish a twofold retribution. One corresponds to the angels' personal merits. This was made from the beginning both for those raised to bliss and those plunged into misery. The other corresponds to the merits, good or evil, procured through the angels, and this retribution will be made in the judgment to come, because the good angels will have an increased joy in the salvation of those whom they have prompted to deeds of merit, while the wicked will have an increase of torment through the manifold downfall of those whom they have incited to evil deeds.

Unde, directe loquendo, iudicium nec ex parte iudicantium neque; ex parte iudicandorum erit angelorum, sed hominum. Sed indirecte quodammodo respiciet angelos, inquantum actibus hominum fuerunt commixti.

Ad primum ergo dicendum quod illud verbum Apostoli est intelligendum de iudicio comparationis: quia quidam homines quibusdam angelis superiores invenientur.

Ad secundum dicendum quod ipsi daemones *cunctis videntibus praecipitabuntur*, quia in perpetuum in inferni carcerem detrudentur, ut iam non sit eis liberum egredi extra. Quia hoc eis non concedebatur nisi secundum quod ordinabatur ex divina providentia ad hominum vitam exercendam.

Et similiter dicendum est ad tertium.

Consequently, the judgment will not regard the angels directly neither as judging nor as judged, but only men; but it will regard the angels indirectly somewhat, insofar as they were concerned in men's deeds.

Reply Obj. 1: This saying of the Apostle refers to the judgment of comparison, because certain men will be found to be placed higher than the angels.

Reply Obj. 2: The demons will then *be cast down in the sight of all* because they will be imprisoned forever in the dungeon of hell, so that they will no more be free to go out, since this was permitted to them only insofar as they were directed by divine providence to try the life of man.

The same answer applies to the third objection.

QUESTION 90

THE FORM OF THE JUDGE IN COMING TO THE JUDGMENT

Deinde considerandum est de forma iudicis venientis ad iudicium.

Circa quod quaeruntur tria.

Primo: utrum Christus in forma humanitatis sit iudicaturus.

Secundo: utrum apparebit in forma humanitatis gloriosa.

Tertio: utrum divinitas possit sine gaudio videri.

We must now consider the form of the Judge in coming to the judgment.

Under this head there are three points of inquiry:

(1) Whether Christ will judge under the form of his humanity?

(2) Whether he will appear under the form of his glorified humanity?

(3) Whether his divinity can be seen without joy?

Article 1

Whether Christ Will Judge Under the Form of His Humanity?

AD PRIMUM SIC PROCEDITUR. Videtur quod Christus in forma servi non sit iudicaturus. Iudicium enim auctoritatem requirit in iudicante. Sed auctoritas super vivos et mortuos est in Christo secundum quod est Deus: sic enim est Dominus et Creator omnium. Ergo in forma divinitatis iudicabit.

PRAETEREA, in iudice requiritur potestas invincibilis: unde Eccli. 7, [6]: *noli quaerere fieri iudex, nisi valeas virtute irrumpere iniquitates.* Sed virtus invincibilis convenit Christo secundum quod est Deus. Ergo in forma divinitatis iudicabit.

PRAETEREA, Ioan. 5, [22–23] dicitur: *Pater omne iudicium dedit Filio, ut omnes honorificent Filium sicut honorificant Patrem.* Sed honor aequalis non debetur Patri et Filio secundum humanam naturam. Ergo non iudicabit secundum formam humanam.

PRAETEREA, Dan. 7, [9] dicitur: *aspiciebam donec throni positi sunt, et Antiquus Dierum sedit.* Throni autem iudiciariam potestatem designant; antiquitas autem de Deo dicitur ratione aeternitatis, ut Dionysius dicit, in libro *de Div. Nom.* Ergo iudicare convenit Filio prout est aeternus. Non ergo secundum quod homo.

PRAETEREA, Augustinus dicit, et habetur in littera, quod *per Dei Verbum fit animarum resurrectio, per Verbum factum in carne Filium hominis fit corporum resurrectio.* Sed iudicium illud finale pertinet magis ad animam quam ad carnem. Ergo magis convenit iudicare Christo secundum quod est Deus, quam secundum quod est homo.

SED CONTRA: Ioan. 5, [27] dicitur: *potestatem dedit ei iudicium facere quia Filius hominis est.*

OBJECTION 1: It would seem that Christ will not judge under the form of his humanity. For judgment requires authority in the judge. Now Christ has authority over the living and the dead as God, for thus is he the Lord and Creator of all. Therefore, he will judge under the form of his divinity.

OBJ. 2: Further, invincible power is requisite in a judge; wherefore it is written: *seek not to be made a judge, unless you have strength enough to extirpate iniquities* (Eccl 7:6). Now invincible power belongs to Christ as God. Therefore, he will judge under the form of the divinity.

OBJ. 3: Further, John 5:22–23 says: *the Father has given all judgment to the Son, that all men may honor the Son as they honor the Father.* Now equal honor to that of the Father is not due to the Son in respect of his human nature. Therefore, he will not judge under his human form.

OBJ. 4: Further, it is written: *I beheld till thrones were placed and the Ancient of Days sat* (Dan 7:9). Now the thrones signify judicial power, and God is called the Ancient by reason of his eternity, according to Dionysius (*On the Divine Names* 10). Therefore, it becomes the Son to judge as being eternal; and consequently not as man.

OBJ. 5: Further, Augustine says (*Tractates on John* 19) that *the resurrection of the soul is the work of the Word of God, and the resurrection of the body is the work of the Word made the Son of man in the flesh.* Now that last judgment regards the soul rather than the body. Therefore, it becomes Christ to judge as God rather than as man.

ON THE CONTRARY, It is written: *he has given him power to do judgment, because he is the Son of man* (John 5:27).

Praeterea, Iob [1.7] dicitur: *causa tua quasi impii iudicata est*: Glossa, *a Pilato. Ideo iudicium causamque recipies*: Glossa, *ut iuste iudices*. Sed Christus secundum humanam naturam est iudicatus a Pilato. Ergo secundum humanam naturam iudicabit.

Praeterea, eius est iudicare cuius est legem condere. Sed Christus in humana natura apparens nobis legem Evangelii dedit. Ergo et secundum eandem naturam iudicabit.

Respondeo dicendum quod iudicium aliquod dominium in iudicando requirit: unde Rom. 14, [4], *tu quis es, qui iudicas alienum servum?* Et ideo secundum hoc Christo competit iudicare quod dominium super homines habet, de quibus principaliter erit finale iudicium. Ipse autem est noster Dominus non solum ratione creationis, quia *Dominus ipse est Deus, ipse fecit nos et non ipsi nos*: sed etiam ratione redemptionis, quod ei competit secundum humanam naturam; unde Rom. 14, [9]: *in hoc Christus mortuus est et rexurrexit, ut et vivorum et mortuorum dominetur*. Ad praemium autem vitae aeternae nobis creationis bona non sufficerent, nisi redemptionis beneficium adderetur, propter impedimentum quod naturae creatae supervenit ex peccato primi parentis. Unde, cum finale iudicium ad hoc ordinetur ut aliqui admittantur ad Regnum et aliqui excludantur a Regno, conveniens est ut ipse Christus secundum humanam naturam, cuius redemptionis beneficio ad Regnum admittimur, illi iudicio praesideat. Et hoc est quod dicitur Act. 10, [42], quod *ipse constitutus est a Deo iudex vivorum et mortuorum*. Et quia per redemptionem humani generis non solum homines reparavit, sed universaliter totam creaturam secundum quod tota creatura reparato homine melioratur, ut habetur Coloss. 1, [20], *pacificans per sanguinem crucis eius sive quae in terris sive quae in caelis sunt*; ideo non solum super homines sed super universam creaturam Christus per suam Passionem dominium promeruit et potestatem iudiciariam: Matth. 28, [18], *data est mihi omnis potestas in caelo et in terra*.

Ad primum ergo dicendum quod in Christo secundum divinam naturam est auctoritas dominii respectu universalis creaturae ex iure creationis. Sed in Christo secundum humanam naturam est auctoritas dominii quam promeruit per Passionem: et est quasi auctoritas secundaria et acquisita. Sed prima est naturalis et aeterna.

Ad secundum dicendum quod, quamvis Christus secundum quod homo non habeat a se invincibilem potestatem ex naturali virtute humanae speciei, tamen ex dono divinitatis etiam in humana natura invincibilem habet potestatem, secundum quod *omnia sunt subiecta*

Further, Job 36:17 says: *your cause has been judged as that of the wicked—by Pilate*, according to a Gloss—therefore, *cause and judgment you shall recover—that you may judge justly*, according to the Gloss. Now Christ was judged by Pilate with regard to his human nature. Therefore, he will judge under the human nature.

Further, To him it belongs to judge who made the law. Now Christ gave us the law of the Gospel while appearing in the human nature. Therefore, he will judge under that same nature.

I answer that, Judgment requires a certain authority in the judge. Wherefore it is written: *who are you that judges another man's servant?* (Rom 14:4). Hence it is becoming that Christ should judge in respect of his having authority over men to whom chiefly the last judgment will be directed. Now he is our Lord not only by reason of the Creation, since *the Lord he is God, he made us and not we ourselves* (Ps 99:3), but also by reason of the Redemption which pertains to him in respect of his human nature. Wherefore *to this end Christ died and rose again, that he might be Lord both of the dead and of the living* (Rom 14:9). But the goods of the creation would not suffice us to obtain the reward of eternal life without the addition of the benefit of the Redemption, on account of the obstacle accruing to created nature through the sin of our first parent. Hence, since the last judgment is directed to the admission of some to the kingdom, and the exclusion of others from it, it is becoming that Christ should preside at that judgment under the form of his human nature, since it is by favor of that same nature's redemption that man is admitted to the kingdom. In this sense it is stated that *he was appointed by God to be Judge of the living and of the dead* (Acts 10:42). And as by redeeming mankind he restored not only man but all creatures without exception—inasmuch as all creatures are bettered through man's restoration, according to Colossians 1:20, *making peace through the blood of his cross, both as to things on earth, and the things that are in heaven*, it follows that through his Passion Christ merited lordship and judicial power not over man alone, but over all creatures, according to Matthew 28:18, *all power is given to me, in heaven and in earth*.

Reply Obj. 1: Christ, in respect of his divine nature, has authority of lordship over all creatures by right of creation; but in respect of his human nature he has authority of lordship merited through his Passion. The latter is secondary, so to speak, and acquired, while the former is natural and eternal.

Reply Obj. 2: Although Christ as man has not of himself invincible power resulting from the natural power of the human species, nevertheless there is also in his human nature an invincible power derived from his divinity, whereby *all things are subjected under his feet* (1 Cor 15:25).

pedibus eius, ut dicitur I Cor. 15, [26] et Heb. 2, [8]. Et ideo iudicabit quidem in humana natura, sed ex divinitatis virtute.

AD TERTIUM dicendum quod Christus non suffecisset ad humani generis redemptionem si purus homo fuisset. Et ideo ex hoc ipso quod secundum humanam naturam genus humanum redimere potuit, ac per hoc iudiciariam potestatem consecutus est, manifeste ostenditur quod ipse est Deus, et ita aequaliter honorandus cum Patre, non inquantum homo, sed inquantum Deus.

AD QUARTUM dicendum quod in illa visione Danielis manifeste totus exprimitur ordo iudiciariae potestatis. Quae quidem sicut in prima origine est in ipso Deo, et specialius in Patre, qui est fons totius deitatis. Et ideo primo praemittitur quod *Antiquus Dierum sedit*. Sed a Patre iudiciaria potestas traducta est in Filium, non solum ab aeterno secundum divinam naturam, sed etiam in tempore secundum humanam, in qua eam meruit. Et ideo subiungitur [v. 13–14] in visione praedicta: *ecce, cum nubibus caeli quasi Filius hominis veniebat, et usque ad Antiquum Dierum pervenit: et dedit ei potestatem et honorem et regnum*.

AD QUINTUM dicendum quod Augustinus loquitur per appropriationem quandam: ut videlicet reducat effectus quos Christus in humana natura fecit, ad causas aliquo modo consimiles. Et quia secundum animam sumus ad *imaginem et similitudinem Dei*, secundum carnem autem sumus eiusdem speciei cum homine Christo, ideo ea quae in animabus nostris Christus fecit, divinitati attribuit; quae vero in carne nostra fecit vel facturus est, attribuit carni eius. Quamvis caro eius, inquantum est divinitatis organum, ut dicit Damascenus, habeat etiam effectum in animabus nostris: secundum id quod dicitur Heb. 9, [14], quod *sanguis eius emundavit conscientias nostras ab operibus mortuis*. Et sic etiam *Verbum caro factum est* causa resurrectionis animarum. Unde etiam secundum humanam naturam convenienter est iudex non solum corporalium, sed etiam spiritualium bonorum.

Hence he will indeed judge in his human nature, but by the power of his divinity.

REPLY OBJ. 3: Christ would not have sufficed for the redemption of mankind had he been a mere man. Wherefore from the very fact that he was able as man to redeem mankind, and thereby obtained judicial power, it is evident that he is God, and consequently is to be honored equally with the Father, not as man but as God.

REPLY OBJ. 4: In that vision of Daniel the whole order of the judicial power is clearly expressed. This power is in God himself as its first origin, and more especially in the Father who is the fount of the entire Godhead; wherefore it is stated in the first place that the *Ancient of Days sat*. But the judicial power was transmitted from the Father to the Son, not only from eternity in respect of the divine nature, but also in time in respect of the human nature wherein he merited it. Hence in the aforesaid vision it is further stated: *lo, one like the Son of man came with the clouds of heaven, and he came even to the Ancient of Days: and he gave him power and glory, and a kingdom* (Dan 7:13–14)

REPLY OBJ. 5: Augustine is speaking by a kind of appropriation, so as to trace the effects which Christ wrought in the human nature to causes somewhat similar to them. And since we are made to *the image and likeness of God* in respect of our soul, and are of the same species as the man Christ in respect of our body, he ascribes to divinity the effects wrought by Christ in our souls, and those which he wrought or will work in our bodies he ascribes to his flesh: although his flesh, as being the instrument of his divinity, has also its effect on our souls, as Damascene asserts (*On the Orthodox Faith* 3.15), according to the saying that *his blood has cleansed our conscience from dead works* (Heb 9:14). And thus that *the Word was made flesh* is the cause of the resurrection of souls; wherefore also according to his human nature he is becomingly the Judge not only of bodily but also of spiritual goods.

Article 2

Whether at the Judgment Christ Will Appear in His Glorified Humanity?

AD SECUNDUM SIC PROCEDITUR. Videtur quod Christus in iudicio non apparebit in forma humanitatis gloriosa Ioan. 19, [37]: *videbunt in quem transfixerunt*: Glossa, *quia in ea carne venturus est in qua crucifixus est*. Sed crucifixus est in forma infirma. Ergo in forma infirmitatis apparebit, non in forma gloriosa.

PRAETEREA, Matth. 24, [30] dicitur quod *apparebit signum Filii hominis in caelo*, idest *signum crucis*. Et

OBJECTION 1: It would seem that at the judgment Christ will not appear in his glorified humanity. For a Gloss on John 19:37: *they shall look on him whom they pierced*, says, *because he will come in the flesh wherein he was crucified* (St. Augustine, *Tractates on John* 120). Now he was crucified in the form of weakness. Therefore, he will appear in the form of weakness, and not in the form of glory.

OBJ. 2: Further, it is stated that *the sign of the Son of man shall appear in heaven* (Matt 24:30), namely, *the sign of the*

Chrysostomus dicit quod *veniet in iudicio Christus, non solum vulnerum cicatrices, sed etiam ipsam mortem exprobratissimam ostendens.* Ergo videtur quod non apparebit in forma gloriosa.

Praeterea, secundum hanc formam Christus in iudicio apparebit quae ab omnibus conspici possit. Sed Christus secundum formam humanitatis gloriosam non poterit videri ab omnibus bonis et malis: quia oculus non glorificatus non videtur esse proportionatus ad videndam claritatem gloriosi corporis. Ergo non apparebit in forma gloriosa.

Praeterea, illud quod promittitur iustis in praemium; non conceditur iniustis. Sed videre gloriam humanitatis promittitur iustis in praenium: Ioan. 10, [9], *ingredietur et egredietur et pascua inveniet, idest, refectionem in divinitate et humanitate*: ut Augustinus exponit. Et Isaiae 33, [17]: *regem in decore suo videbunt.* Ergo in iudicio non apparebit omnibus in forma gloriosa.

Praeterea, secundum illam formam Christus iudicabit in qua iudicatus est. Unde super illud Ioan. 5, [21], *sic et Filius quos vult glorificat,* dicit Glossa: *in qua forma iniuste iudicatus est, iuste iudicabit, ut possit ab impiis videri.* Sed iudicatus est in forma infirmitatis. Ergo et in eadem in iudicio apparebit.

Sed contra: Est quod dicitur Luc. 21, [27]: *tunc videbunt Filium, hominis venientem in nube cum potestate magna et maiestate.* Maiestas autem et potestas ad gloriam pertinent. Ergo in forma gloriosa apparebit.

Praeterea, ille qui iudicat, debet eminere illis qui iudicantur. Sed electi, qui iudicabuntur a Christo, corpora gloriosa habebunt. Ergo multo fortius iudex in forma gloriosa apparebit.

Praeterea, sicut iudicari est infirmitatis, ita iudicare est auctoritatis et gloriae. Sed in primo adventu, quo Christus venit ad hoc quod iudicaretur, in forma infirmitatis apparuit. Ergo in secundo adventu, in quo veniet ad hoc quod iudicet, apparebit manifeste in forma gloriosa.

Respondeo dicendum quod Christus dicitur *Dei et hominum mediator* inquantum pro hominibus satisfecit et interpellat apud Patrem; et ea quae sunt Patris hominibus communicat, secundum quod dicitur Ioan. 17, [22], *claritatem quam dedisti mihi, dedi eis.* Secundum hoc autem utrumque convenit ei quod cum utroque communicat extremorum: inquantum enim cum hominibus communicat, vices hominum gerit apud Patrem; inquantum vero cum Patre communicat, dona Patris transmittit ad homines. Quia ergo in primo adventu ad hoc venit ut pro nobis satisfaceret apud Patrem, in forma nostrae infirmitatis apparuit. Quia vero in secundo adventu ad hoc veniet ut iustitiam Patris in homines exequatur, gloriam demonstrare debebit quae inest ei ex

cross, as Chrysostom says, for *Christ, when coming to the judgment, will show not only the scars of his wounds but even his most shameful death* (*Homilies on Matthew*). Therefore, it seems that he will not appear in the form of glory.

Obj. 3: Further, Christ will appear at the judgment under that form which can be gazed upon by all. Now Christ will not be visible to all, good and wicked, under the form of his glorified humanity: because the eye that is not glorified is seemingly unproportionate to see the clarity of a glorified body. Therefore, he will not appear under a glorified form.

Obj. 4: Further, that which is promised as a reward to the righteous is not granted to the unrighteous. Now it is promised as a reward to the righteous that they shall see the glory of his humanity: *he shall go in, and go out, and shall find pastures, i.e., refreshment in his divinity and humanity* (John 10:9), according to the commentary of Augustine and Isaiah 33:17: *his eyes shall see the King in his beauty.* Therefore, he will not appear to all in his glorified form.

Obj. 5: Further, Christ will judge in the form wherein he was judged; hence a Gloss on John 5:21: *so the Son also gives life to whom he will,* says, *he will judge justly in the form wherein he was judged unjustly, that he may be visible to the wicked* (St. Augustine, *Tractates on John* 19). Now he was judged in the form of weakness. Therefore, he will appear in the same form at the judgment.

On the contrary, It is written: *then they shall see the Son of man coming in a cloud with great power and majesty* (Luke 21:27). Now majesty and power pertain to glory. Therefore, he will appear in the form of glory.

Further, He who judges should be more conspicuous than those who are judged. Now the elect who will be judged by Christ will have a glorified body. Much more, therefore, will the Judge appear in a glorified form.

Further, As to be judged pertains to weakness, so to judge pertains to authority and glory. Now at his first coming when Christ came to be judged, he appeared in the form of weakness. Therefore, at the second coming, when he will come to judge, he will appear in the form of glory.

I answer that, Christ is called the *mediator of God and men* (1 Tim 2:5) inasmuch as he satisfies for men and intercedes for them to the Father, and confers on men things which belong to the Father, according to John 17:22: *the glory which you have given me, I have given to them.* Accordingly, then, both these things belong to him in that he communicates with both extremes: for in that he communicates with men, he takes their part with the Father, and in that he communicates with the Father, he bestows the Father's gifts on men. Since, then, at his first coming he came in order to make satisfaction for us to the Father, he came in the form of our weakness. But since at his second coming he will come in order to execute the Father's justice on men, he will have to show forth his glory which is in him by rea-

communione ad Patrem. Et ideo in forma gloriosa apparebit.

AD PRIMUM ergo dicendum quod in eadem carne apparebit, sed non similiter se habente.

AD SECUNDUM dicendum quod signum crucis apparebit in iudicio, non ad indicium tunc exhistentis infirmitatis, sed praeteritae: ut per hoc iustior eorum condemnatio appareat qui tantam misericordiam neglexerunt, et eorum praecipue qui Christum iniuste persecuti sunt. Cicatrices autem quae in eius corpore apparebunt, non pertinebunt ad aliquam infirmitatem, sed erunt indicia maximae virtutis qua Christus per Passionis infirmitatem de hostibus triumphavit. Exprobratissimam etiam mortem ostendet, non sensibiliter eam oculis ingerens, ac si tunc eam pateretur: sed ex his quae apparebunt, scilicet indiciis praeteritae Passionis, homines in recogitationem praeteritae mortis adducet.

AD TERTIUM dicendum quod corpus gloriosum habet in potestate sua ut se demonstret vel non demonstret oculo non glorioso: ut patet ex his quae dicta sunt. Et ideo in forma gloriosa Christus ab omnibus poterit videri.

AD QUARTUM dicendum quod, sicut amici gloria est delectabilis, ita gloria et potestas eius qui odio habetur, maxime contristat. Et ideo, sicut visio gloriae humanitatis Christi erit iustis in praemium, ita inimicis Christi erit in supplicium. Unde Isaiae 26, [11]: *videant et confundantur zelantes populi, et ignis*, scilicet invidiae, *hostes tuos devoret*.

AD QUINTUM dicendum quod forma accipitur ibi pro natura humana, in qua iudicatus est et etiam iudicabit: non autem pro qualitate naturae, quae non erit eadem in iudicante, scilicet infirma, quae in iudicato fuit.

son of his communication with the Father: and therefore he will appear in the form of glory.

REPLY OBJ. 1: He will appear in the same flesh, but not under the same form.

REPLY OBJ. 2: The sign of the cross will appear at the judgment to denote not a present but a past weakness: so as to show how justly those were condemned who scorned so great mercy, especially those who persecuted Christ unjustly. The scars which will appear in his body will not be due to weakness, but will indicate the exceeding power whereby Christ overcame his enemies by his Passion's infirmity. He will also show forth his most shameful death, not by bringing it sensibly before the eye, as though he suffered it there; but by the things which will appear then, namely, the signs of his past Passion, he will recall men to the thought of his past death.

REPLY OBJ. 3: A glorified body has it in its power to show itself or not to show itself to an eye that is not glorified, as stated above (Q. 85, A. 2). Hence Christ will be visible to all in his glorified form.

REPLY OBJ. 4: Even as our friend's glory gives us pleasure, so the glory and power of one we hate is most displeasing to us. Hence as the sight of the glory of Christ's humanity will be a reward to the righteous, so will it be a torment to Christ's enemies: wherefore it is written: *let the envious people see and be confounded and let fire* (i.e., envy) *devour thy enemies* (Isa 26:11).

REPLY OBJ. 5: Form is taken there for human nature wherein he was judged and likewise will judge; but not for a quality of nature, namely, of weakness, which will not be the same in him when judging as when judged (Cf. ad 2).

Article 3

Whether Divinity Can Be Seen by the Wicked Without Joy?

AD TERTIUM SIC PROCEDITUR. Videtur quod divinitas a malis sine gaudio videri possit. Constat enim quod impii manifestissime cognoscent Christum esse Deum. Ergo divinitatem eius videbunt. Et tamen de visione Christi non gaudebunt. Ergo divinitas sine gaudio videri poterit.

PRAETEREA, voluntas impiorum perversa non magis adversatur humanitati Christi quam eius divinitati. Sed hoc quod videbunt gloriam humanitatis, cedet eis in poenam, ut dictum est. Ergo multo fortius, si divinitatem eius viderent, magis contristarentur quam gauderent.

PRAETEREA, ea quae sunt in affectu non de necessitate sequuntur ad ea quae sunt in intellectu: unde Au-

OBJECTION 1: It would seem that divinity can be seen by the wicked without joy. For there can be no doubt that the wicked will know with the greatest certainty that Christ is God. Therefore, they will see his divinity, and yet they will not rejoice in seeing Christ. Therefore, it will be possible to see it without joy.

OBJ. 2: Further, the perverse will of the wicked is not more adverse to Christ's humanity than to his divinity. Now the fact that they will see the glory of his humanity will conduce to their punishment, as stated above (A. 2). Therefore, if they were to see his divinity, there would be much more reason for them to grieve rather than rejoice.

OBJ. 3: Further, the course of the affections is not a necessary sequel to that which is in the intellect: wherefore

gustinus dicit: *praecedit intellectus, et sequitur tardus aut nullus affectus.* Sed visio ad intellectum pertinet, gaudium autem ad affectum. Ergo poterit esse divinitatis visio sine gaudio.

PRAETEREA, *omne quod recipitur in aliquo, recipitur per modum recipientis, et non per modum recepti.* Sed omne quod videtur, quodammodo in vidente recipitur. Ergo, quamvis in se divinitas sit delectabilissima, tamen visa ab iliis qui sunt tristitia absorpti, non delectabit, sed magis contristabit.

PRAETEREA, sicut se habet sensus ad sensibile, ita intellectus ad intelligibile. Sed ita est in sensibus quod *palato non sano poena est panis, qui sano est suavis*, ut dicit Augustinus: et similiter accidit in aliis sensibus. Ergo, cum damnati habeant intellectum indispositum, videtur quod visio lucis increatae magis afferat eis poenam quam gaudium.

SED CONTRA: Est quod dicitur Ioan. 17, [3]: *haec est vita aeterna, ut cognoscant te, verum Deum*; ex quo patet quod essentia beatitudinis in Dei visione consistit. Sed de ratione beatitudinis est gaudium. Ergo divinitas sine gaudio videri non poterit.

PRAETEREA, ipsa essentia divinitatis est essentia veritatis. Sed unicuique est delectabile videre verum: nam *omnes homines natura scire desiderant*, ut dicitur in principio *Metaphys*. 4. Ergo divinitas sine gaudio videri non potest.

PRAETEREA, si aliqua visio non semper est delectabilis, contingit eam quandoque esse tristabilem. Sed visio intellectiva nunquam est contristabilis: quia *delectationi quae est in intelligendo non opponitur aliqua tristitia*, ut dicit Philosophus. Cum ergo divinitas videri non possit nisi per intellectum, videtur quod divinitas sine gaudio videri non possit.

RESPONDEO dicendum quod in quolibet appetibili vel delectabili duo possunt considerari: scilicet id quod appetitur, vel quod est delectabile; et id quod est ratio appetibilitatis vel delectabilitatis in ipso. Sicut autem, secundum Boetium, in libro *de Hebdomadibus*, *id quod est habere aliquid praeterquam quod ipsum est, potest; ipsum vero esse nihil aliud praeter se habet admixtum*: ita id quod est appetibile vel delectabile potest habere aliquid aliud admixtum unde non sit delectabile vel appetibile; sed id quod est ratio delectabilitatis nihil habet admixtum, vel habere potest, propter quod non sit delectabilis vel appetibilis. Res igitur quae sunt delectabiles per participationem bonitatis, quae est ratio appetibilitatis et delectabilitatis, possunt apprehensae non delectare: sed id quod per essentiam suam est bonitas, impossibile est quod eius essentia apprehensa non delectet. Unde, cum Deus essentialiter sit ipsa bonitas, non potest sine gaudio videri.

Augustine says (In Ps 118: conc. 8): *the intellect precedes, the affections follow slowly or not at all.* Now vision regards the intellect, whereas joy regards the affections. Therefore, it will be possible to see the divinity without joy.

OBJ. 4: Further, *whatever is received into a thing is received according to the mode of the receiver and not of the received.* But whatever is seen is, in a way, received into the seer. Therefore, although divinity is in itself supremely enjoyable, nevertheless when seen by those who are plunged in grief, it will give no joy but rather displeasure.

OBJ. 5: Further, as sense is to the sensible object, so is the intellect to the intelligible object. Now in the senses, *to the unhealthy palate bread is painful, to the healthy palate sweet*, as Augustine says (*Confessions* 7), and the same happens with the other senses. Therefore, since the damned have the intellect indisposed, it would seem that the vision of the uncreated light will give them pain rather than joy.

ON THE CONTRARY, It is written: *this is eternal life: that they may know you, the true God* (John 17:3). Wherefore it is clear that the essence of bliss consists in seeing God. Now joy is essential to bliss. Therefore, divinity cannot be seen without joy.

FURTHER, The essence of divinity is the essence of truth. Now it is delightful to every one to see the truth, wherefore *all naturally desire to know*, as stated at the beginning of the *Metaphysics*. Therefore, it is impossible to see divinity without joy.

FURTHER, If a certain vision is not always delightful, it happens sometimes to be painful. But intellective vision is never painful, since *the pleasure we take in objects of understanding has no grief opposed to it*, according to the Philosopher (*Topics* 2). Since, then, divinity cannot be seen save by the intellect, it seems that divinity cannot be seen without joy.

I ANSWER THAT, In every object of appetite or of pleasure two things may be considered: namely, the thing which is desired or which gives pleasure, and the aspect of appetibility or pleasurableness in that thing. Now, according to Boethius (*Hebdomads*), *that which is can have something besides what it is, but "being" itself has no admixture of anything beside itself*. Hence that which is desirable or pleasant can have an admixture of something rendering it undesirable or unpleasant; but the very reason for pleasurableness has not and cannot have anything mixed with it rendering it unpleasant or undesirable. Now it is possible for things that are pleasurable by participation of goodness (which is the reason for appetibility or pleasurableness) not to give pleasure when they are apprehended, but it is impossible for that which is good by its essence not to give pleasure when it is apprehended. Therefore, since God is essentially his own goodness, it is impossible for divinity to be seen without joy.

Ad primum ergo dicendum quod impii manifeste cognoscent Christum esse Deum, non per hoc quod divinitatem eius videant, sed propter manifestissima divinitatis indicia.

Ad secundum dicendum quod divinitatem secundum quod est in se, nullus potest odio habere: sicut nec aliquis potest odio habere ipsam bonitatem. Sed quantum ad aliquos divinitatis effectus dicitur ab aliquibus odio haberi: inquantum scilicet aliquid agit vel praecipit quod est contrarium voluntati. Et ideo visio divinitatis nulli potest esse non delectabilis.

Ad tertium dicendum quod verbum Augustini est intelligendum quando id quod apprehenditur per intellectum praecedentem est bonum per participationem et non per essentiam, sicut sunt omnes creaturae: unde potest in eis esse aliquid quare affectus non moveatur. Similiter etiam in via Deus cognoscitur per effectus, et intellectus non attingit ad ipsam essentiam bonitatis eius. Unde non oportet quod affectus intellectum sequatur, sicut sequeretur si essentiam eius videret, quae est ipsa bonitas.

Ad quartum dicendum quod tristitia non nominat dispositionem, sed magis passionem. Omnis autem passio a contraria causa fortiori superveniente tollitur, et non eam tollit. Et ita tristitia damnatorum tolleretur si Deum per essentiam viderent.

Ad quintum dicendum quod per indispositionem organi tollitur proportio naturalis ipsius organi ad obiectum quod natum est delectare: et propter hoc delectatio impeditur. Sed indispositio quae est in damnatis non tollit naturalem proportionem qua sunt ordinati ad divinam bonitatem: cum imago semper in eis maneat. Et ideo non est simile.

Reply Obj. 1: The wicked will know most clearly that Christ is God, not through seeing his divinity, but on account of the most manifest signs of his divinity.

Reply Obj. 2: No one can hate divinity considered in itself, as neither can one hate goodness itself. But God is said to be hated by certain persons in respect of some of the effects of divinity, insofar as he does or commands something contrary to their will. Therefore, the vision of divinity can be painful to no one.

Reply Obj. 3: The saying of Augustine applies when the thing apprehended previously by the intellect is good by participation and not essentially, such as all creatures are; wherefore there may be something in them by reason of which the affections are not moved. In like manner, God is known by wayfarers through his effects, and their intellect does not attain to the very essence of his goodness. Hence it is not necessary that the affections follow the intellect, as they would if the intellect saw God's essence, which is his goodness.

Reply Obj. 4: Grief denotes not a disposition but a passion. Now every passion is removed if a stronger contrary cause supervene, and does not remove that cause. Accordingly, the grief of the damned would be done away with if they saw God in his essence.

Reply Obj. 5: The indisposition of an organ removes the natural proportion of the organ to the object that has a natural aptitude to please, wherefore the pleasure is hindered. But the indisposition which is in the damned does not remove the natural proportion whereby they are directed to the divine goodness, since its image ever remains in them. Hence the comparison fails.

Question 91

The Quality of the World After the Judgment

Consequenter agendum est de qualitate mundi et resurgentium post iudicium. Ubi triplex consideratio occurrit: prima, de statu et qualitate mundi; secunda, de statu beatorum; tertia, de statu malorum.

Circa primum quaeruntur quinque.
Primo: utrum innovatio mundi sit futura.
Secundo: utrum motus corporum caelestium cessabit.
Tertio: utrum corpora caelestia tunc magis fulgeant.
Quarto: utrum elementa maiorem claritatem recipient.
Quinto: utrum animalia et plantae remanebunt.

We must next discuss the quality which the world and those who rise again will have after the judgment. Here a threefold matter offers itself to our consideration: (1) The state and quality of the world; (2) The state of the blessed; (3) The state of the wicked.

Under the first head there are five points of inquiry:
(1) Whether there will be a renewal of the world?
(2) Whether the movement of the heavenly bodies will cease?
(3) Whether the heavenly bodies will be more brilliant?
(4) Whether the elements will receive an additional clarity?
(5) Whether the animals and plants will remain?

Article 1

Whether the World Will Be Renewed?

Ad primum sic proceditur. Videtur quod mundus nunquam innovabitur. Nihil enim est futurum nisi quod aliquando fuerit secundum speciem: Eccle. 1, [9], *quid est quod fuit? Ipsum quod futurum est.* Sed nunquam mundus aliam dispositionem habuit quam nunc habet, quantum ad partes essentiales et ad genera et ad species. Ergo nunquam innovabitur.

Praeterea, innovatio alteratio quaedam est. Sed impossibile est universum alterari: quia omne alteratum reducitur ad aliquid alterans non alteratum quod tamen secundum locum movetur; quod non est extra universum ponere. Ergo non potest esse quod mundus innovetur.

Praeterea, Gen. 2, [2] dicitur quod *Deus die septimo requievit ab omni opere quod patrarat*: et: exponunt Sancti quod requievit a novis creaturis condendis. Sed in illa prima conditione non fuit alius modus rebus impositus quam ipse quem nunc naturali ordine tenent. Ergo nunquam alium habebunt.

Praeterea, ista rerum dispositio quae nunc inest rebus, naturalis est. Si ergo in aliam dispositionem transmutentur, illa dispositio erit eis innaturalis. Sed illud quod est innaturale et per accidens, non potest esse perpetuum: ut patet in I *Caeli et Mundi.* Ergo etiam illa dispositio novitatis quandoque ab ipsis removebitur. Et ita erit ponere circulationem quandam in mundo, sicut Em-

Objection 1: It would seem that the world will never be renewed. For nothing will be but what was at some time as to its species: *what is it that has been? the same thing that shall be* (Eccl 1:9). Now the world never had any disposition other than it has now as to essential parts, both genera and species. Therefore, it will never be renewed.

Obj. 2: Further, renewal is a kind of alteration. But it is impossible for the universe to be altered, because whatever is altered argues some alterant that is not altered, which nevertheless is a subject of local movement: and it is impossible to place such a thing outside the universe. Therefore, it is impossible for the world to be renewed.

Obj. 3: Further, it is stated that *God rested on the seventh day from all his work which he had done* (Gen 2:2), and holy men explain that he rested from forming new creatures. Now when things were first established, the mode imposed upon them was the same as they have now in the natural order. Therefore, they will never have any other.

Obj. 4: Further, the disposition which things have now is natural to them. Therefore, if they are altered to another disposition, this disposition will be unnatural to them. Now whatever is unnatural and accidental cannot last forever (*De Coelo et Mundo* I). Therefore, this disposition acquired by being renewed will be taken away from them; and thus there will be a cycle of changes in the world, as Empedo-

pedocles et Origenes posuerunt; ut post hunc mundum sit iterum mundus alius, et post illum iterum alius.

PRAETEREA, novitas gloriae in praemium rationali creaturae datur. Sed ubi non est meritum, non potest esse praemium. Cum ergo creaturae insensibiles nil meruerint, videtur quod non innovabuntur.

SED CONTRA: Est quod habetur Isaiae 65, [17]: *ecce, ego creo novos caelos et terram novam, et non erunt in memoria priora.* Et Apoc. 21, [1]: *vidi caelum novum et terram novam: primum enim caelum et prima terra abiit.*

PRAETEREA, habitatio debet habitatori congruere. Sed mundus factus est ut sit habitatio hominis. Sed homo innovabitur. Ergo et mundus innovabitur.

PRAETEREA, *omne animal diligit sibi simile*, Eccli. 13, [19]: ex quo patet quod similitudo est ratio amoris. Sed homo habet aliquam similitudinem cum universo: unde *minor mundus* dicitur. Ergo homo universum diligit naturaliter. Ergo et eius bonum concupiscit. Et ita, ut satisfiat hominis desiderio, debet etiam universum meliorari.

RESPONDEO dicendum quod omnia corporalia propter hominem facta esse creduntur: unde et omnia dicuntur ei *subiecta*. Serviunt autem homini dupliciter: uno modo, ad sustentationem corporalis vitae; alio modo, ad profectum cognitionis divinae, inquantum homo *per ea quae facta sunt invisibilia Dei conspicit*, ut dicitur Rom. I, [20]. Primo ergo ministerio creaturarum homo glorificatus nullo modo indigebit: cum eius corpus omnino incorruptibile sit futurum, divina virtute id faciente per animam, quam immediate glorificat.

Secundo etiam ministerio non indigebit homo quantum ad cognitionem intellectivam: quia tali cognitione Deum sancti videbunt immediate per essentiam. Sed ad hanc visionem essentiae oculus carnis attingere non poterit. Et ideo, ut ei etiam solatium sibi congruens de visione divinitatis praebeatur, inspiciet divinitatem in suis effectibus corporalibus, in quibus manifesta indicia divinae maiestatis apparebunt: et praecipue in carne Christi, et post hoc in corporibus beatorum, et deinceps in omnibus aliis corporibus. Et ideo oportebit ut etiam alia corpora maiorem influentiam a divina bonitate suscipiant: non tamen speciem variantem, sed addentem cuiusdam gloriae perfectionem. Et haec erit mundi innovatio. Unde simul mundus innovabitur et homo glorificabitur.

AD PRIMUM ergo dicendum quod Salomon ibi loquitur de cursu naturalium. Quod patet ex hoc quod subditur, *nihil sub sole novum.* Cum enim sol circulariter moveatur, oportet ea quae solis virtuti subsunt, circulationem aliquam habere, quae consistit in hoc quod illa quae priora fuerunt, iterum redeunt *specie eadem nume-*

cles and Origen (*On First Principles* 2.3) maintained, and after this world there will be another, and after that again another.

OBJ. 5: Further, newness of glory is given to the rational creature as a reward. Now where there is no merit, there can be no reward. Since, then, insensible creatures have merited nothing, it would seem that they will not be renewed.

ON THE CONTRARY, Isaiah 65:17 says: *behold, I create new heavens and a new earth, and the former things shall not be in remembrance,* and Revelation 21:1 says, *I saw a new heaven and a new earth. For the first heaven and the first earth were gone.*

FURTHER, The dwelling should befit the dweller. But the world was made to be man's dwelling. Therefore, it should befit man. Now man will be renewed. Therefore, the world will be likewise.

FURTHER, *Every beast loves its like* (Sir 13:19), wherefore it is evident that likeness is the reason of love. Now man has some likeness to the universe, wherefore he is called *a little world.* Hence man loves the whole world naturally and consequently desires its good. Therefore, that man's desire be satisfied, the universe must also be made better.

I ANSWER THAT, We believe all corporeal things to have been made for man's sake, wherefore all things are stated to be *subject* to him (Ps 8:5, seqq.). Now they serve man in two ways: first, as sustenance to his bodily life; second, as helping him to know God, inasmuch as man *sees the invisible things of God by the things that are made* (Rom 1:20). Accordingly, glorified man will in no way need creatures to render him the first of these services, since his body will be altogether incorruptible, the divine power effecting this through the soul which it will glorify immediately.

Likewise, man will not need the second service as to intellective knowledge, since by that knowledge he will see God immediately in his essence. The carnal eye, however, will be unable to attain to this vision of the essence; wherefore that it may be fittingly comforted in the vision of God, it will see divinity in its corporeal effects, wherein manifest proofs of the divine majesty will appear, primarily in Christ's flesh, and secondarily in the bodies of the blessed, and afterwards in all other bodies. Hence those bodies also will need to receive a greater inflow from the divine goodness than now, not indeed so as to change their species, but so as to add a certain perfection of glory: and such will be the renewal of the world. Wherefore at the one and the same time, the world will be renewed and man will be glorified.

REPLY OBJ. 1: Solomon is speaking there of the natural course. This is evident from his adding: *there is nothing new under the sun.* For, since the movement of the sun follows a circle, those things which are subject to the sun's power must have some kind of circular movement. This consists in the fact that things which were before return *the same*

ro diversa: ut dicitur in fine libri *de Generatione*. Ea vero quae ad statum gloriae pertinent soli non subsunt.

AD SECUNDUM dicendum quod illa ratio procedit de alteratione naturali, quae habet agens naturale, quod ex necessitate naturae agit: non enim potest tale agens variam dispositionem inducere nisi ipsum alio et alio modo se habeat. Sed ea quae divinitus fiunt, procedunt ex libertate voluntatis. Unde sine aliqua immutatione Dei volentis potest nunc haec nunc illa dispositio ab ipso in universo existere. Et sic ista innovatio non reducitur in aliquod principium motum, sed in principium immobile, scilicet Deum.

AD TERTIUM dicendum quod pro tanto dicitur Deus die septimo a novis creaturis condendis cessasse, quia nihil postea factum est quod prius non praecesserit in aliqua similitudine secundum genus vel speciem, vel ad minus sicut in principio seminali, vel etiam sicut in potentia obedientiali. Dico ergo quod novitas mundi futura praecessit quidem in operibus sex dierum in quadam remota similitudine, scilicet in gloria et in gratia angelorum. Praecessit etiam in potentia obedientiae, quae creaturae tunc est indita ad talem novitatem suscipiendam a Deo agente.

AD QUARTUM dicendum quod illa dispositio novitatis non erit naturalis, nec contra naturam: sed erit supra naturam, sicut gratia et gloria sunt supra animae naturam. Et erit a perpetuo agente, quod eam perpetuo conservabit.

AD QUINTUM dicendum quod, quamvis corpora insensibilia non meruerint illam gloriam, proprie loquendo; homo tamen meruit ut illa gloria toti universo conferretur, inquantum hoc cedit in augmentum gloriae hominis; sicut aliquis homo meretur ut ornatioribus vestibus induatur, quem tamen ornatum ipsa vestis nullo modo meretur.

in species but different in the individual (*On Generation and Corruption* 1). But things belonging to the state of glory are not under the sun.

REPLY OBJ. 2: This argument considers natural alteration, which proceeds from a natural agent, which acts from natural necessity. For such an agent cannot produce different dispositions, unless it be itself disposed differently. But things done by God proceed from freedom of will, wherefore it is possible, without any change in God who wills it, for the universe to have at one time one disposition, and another at another time. Thus this renewal will not be reduced to a cause that is moved, but to an immovable principle, namely God.

REPLY OBJ. 3: God is stated to have ceased on the seventh day from forming new creatures, for as much as nothing was made afterwards that was not previously in some likeness either generically, or specifically, or at least as in a seminal principle, or even as in an obediential potentiality. I say, then, that the future renewal of the world preceded in the works of the six days by way of a remote likeness, namely, in the glory and grace of the angels. Moreover, it preceded in the obediential potentiality which was then bestowed on the creature to the effect of its receiving this same renewal by the divine agency.

REPLY OBJ. 4: This disposition of newness will be neither natural nor contrary to nature, but above nature (just as grace and glory are above the nature of the soul): and it will proceed from an everlasting agent which will preserve it forever.

REPLY OBJ. 5: Although, properly speaking, insensible bodies will not have merited this glory, yet man merited that this glory should be bestowed on the whole universe, insofar as this conduces to man's increase of glory. Thus a man merits to be clothed in more splendid robes, which splendor the robes in no way merited themselves.

Article 2

Whether the Movement of the Heavenly Bodies Will Cease?

AD SECUNDUM SIC PROCEDITUR. Videtur quod motus corporum caelestium in illa mundi innovatione non cessabit. Quia Genes. 8, [22] dicitur: *Cunctis diebus terrae frigus et aestus, aestas et hiems, nox et dies, non requiescent*. Sed nox et dies, et hiems et aestas, efficiuntur per motum solis. Ergo nunquam motus solis cessabit.

PRAETEREA, Ierem. 31, [35–36] dicitur: *haec dicit Dominus, qui dat solem in lumine diei, ordinem lunae et stellarum in lumine noctis, qui turbat mare et sonant fluctus eius: Si steterint leges istae coram me, tunc et semen Israel nunquam deficiet, ut non sit gens coram me*

OBJECTION 1: It seems that when the world is thus renewed the movement of the heavenly bodies will not cease. For it is written: *all the days of the earth . . . cold and heat, summer and winter, night and day shall not cease* (Gen 8:22). Now night and day, summer and winter, result from the movement of the sun. Therefore, the movement of the sun will never cease.

OBJ. 2: Further, it is written: *thus says the Lord who gives the sun for the light of the day, the order of the moon and of the stars for the light of the night: who stirs up the sea, and the waves thereof roar . . . If these ordinances shall fail before me . . . then also the seed of Israel shall fail, so as not to be a na-*

cunctis diebus. Sed semen Israel nunquam deficiet, sed in perpetuum permanebit. Ergo leges diei et noctis et fluctuum maris, quae ex motu caeli causantur, in perpetuum erunt. Ergo motus caeli nunquam cessabit.

PRAETEREA, substantia corporum caelestium semper erit. Sed frustra est ponere aliquid nisi ponatur illud propter quod est factum. Corpora autem caelestia ad hoc sunt facta *ut dividant diem et noctem,* et *sint in signa et tempora, dies et annos,* Genes. 1, [14]: quod non possunt facere nisi per motum. Ergo motus eorum semper manebit: alias frustra illa corpora remanerent.

PRAETEREA, in illa mundi innovatione totus mundus meliorabitur. Ergo nulli corpori remanenti auferetur quod est de sui perfectione. Sed motus est de perfectione corporis caelestis: quia, ut dicitur in II *de Caelo et Mundo,* illa corpora participant divinam bonitatem per motum. Ergo motus caeli non cessabit.

PRAETEREA, sol successive illuminat diversas partes mundi secundum quod circulariter movetur. Si ergo motus circularis caeli cesset, sequetur quod in aliqua superficie terrae erit perpetua obscuritas. Quod non convenit illi novitati.

PRAETEREA, si motus caeli cessaret, hoc non esset nisi inquantum motus aliquam imperfectionem in caelo ponit, utpote lassitudinis vel laboris. Quod non potest esse: cum motus ille sit naturalis, et caelestia corpora sint impassibilia; unde in suo motu non fatigantur, ut dicitur in II *Caeli et Mundi.* Ergo motus caeli nunquam cessabit.

PRAETEREA, *frustra est potentia quae non reducitur in actum.* Sed in quocumque situ ponatur corpus caeli, est in potentia ad alium situm. Ergo, nisi reduceretur in actum, illa potentia frustra remaneret, et semper esset imperfecta. Sed non potest reduci in actum nisi per motum localem. Ergo semper movebitur.

PRAETEREA, illud quod se habet indifferenter ad plura, aut utrumque attribuetur ei, aut nullum. Sed sol indifferenter se habet ad hoc quod sit in oriente vel occidente: alias motus eius non esset uniformis per totum, quia ad locum ubi naturalius esset, velocius moveretur. Ergo vel neuter situs attribuetur soli, vel uterque. Sed nec uterque nec neuter potest ei attribui nisi successive: oportet enim, si quiescit, quod in aliquo situ quiescat. Ergo corpus solis in perpetuum movebitur. Et eadem ratione omnia alia corpora caelestia.

PRAETEREA, motus caeli est causa temporis. Si ergo motus caeli deficiat, oportet tempus deficere. Quod si

tion before me forever (Jer 31:35–36). Now the seed of Israel shall never fail, but will remain forever. Therefore, the laws of day and of the sea waves, which result from the heavenly movement, will remain forever. Therefore, the movement of the heaven will never cease.

OBJ. 3: Further, the substance of the heavenly bodies will remain forever. Now it is useless to admit the existence of a thing unless you admit the purpose for which it was made: and the heavenly bodies were made in order *to divide the day and the night* and to be *for signs, and for seasons, and for days and for years* (Gen 1:14). But they cannot do this except by movement. Therefore, their movement will remain forever, else those bodies would remain without a purpose.

OBJ. 4: Further, in this renewal of the world, the whole world will be bettered. Therefore, no body will be deprived of what pertains to its perfection. Now movement belongs to the perfection of a heavenly body, because, as stated in *De Coelo et Mundo* II, those bodies participate of the divine goodness by their movement. Therefore, the movement of the heaven will not cease.

OBJ. 5: Further, the sun successively gives light to the various parts of the world by reason of its circular movement. Therefore, if the circular movement of the heaven ceases, it follows that in some part of the earth's surface there will be perpetual darkness, which is unbecoming to the aforesaid renewal.

OBJ. 6: Further, if the movement were to cease, this could only be because movement causes some imperfection in the heaven, for instance, wear and tear. This is impossible since this movement is natural, and the heavenly bodies are impassible, wherefore they are not worn out by movement (*De Coelo et Mundo* II). Therefore, the movement of the heaven will never cease.

OBJ. 7: Further, *a potentiality is useless if it be not reduced to act.* Now in whatever position the heavenly body is placed, it is in potentiality to another position. Therefore, unless this potentiality be reduced to act, it would remain useless, and would always be imperfect. But it cannot be reduced to act save by local movement. Therefore, it will always be in motion.

OBJ. 8: Further, if a thing is indifferent in relation to more than one alteration, either both are ascribed to it, or neither. Now the sun is indifferent to being in the east or in the west, else its movement would not be uniform throughout, since it would move more rapidly to the place which is more natural to it. Therefore, either neither position is ascribed to the sun, or both. But neither both nor neither can be ascribed to it, except successively by movement; for if it stand still, it must stand in some position. Therefore, the solar body will always be in motion, and in like manner all other heavenly bodies.

OBJ. 9: Further, the movement of the heaven is the cause of time. Therefore, if the movement of the heaven fail,

deficeret, oportet quod deficeret in instanti. Definitio autem instantis est, in VIII *Physic.*, quod *est initium futuri et finis praeteriti*. Et sic post ultimum instans temporis esset tempus. Quod est impossibile. Ergo motus caeli nunquam cessabit.

PRAETEREA, gloria non tollit naturam. Sed motus caeli est ei naturalis. Ergo per gloriam ei non tollitur.

SED CONTRA: Est quod dicitur Apoc. 10. [6], quod angelus qui apparuit *iuravit per viventem in saecula quia tempus amplius non erit*: scilicet postquam septimus angelus tuba cecinerit [v. 7], *qua canente mortui resurgent*, ut dicitur I Cor. 15, [52]. Sed, si non est tempus, non est motus caeli. Ergo motus caeli cessabit.

PRAETEREA, Isaiae 60 [20]: *non occidet ultra sol tuus, et luna tua non minuetur.* Sed occasus solis et diminutio lunae ex motu caeli causatur. Ergo motus caeli quandoque cessabit.

PRAETEREA, ut probatur in II *de Generat.*, *motus caeli est propter continuam generationem in istis inferioribus.* Sed generatio cessabit completo numero electorum. Ergo motus caeli cessabit.

PRAETEREA, omnis motus est propter aliquem finem, ut dicitur in II *Metaphys.* Sed omnis motus qui est propter finem, habito fine quiescet. Ergo vel motus caeli nunquam consequetur finem suum, et sic esset frustra: vel aliquando quiescet.

PRAETEREA, quies est nobilior quam motus: quia secundum hoc quod res sunt immobiles, Deo assimilantur, in quo est summa immobilitas. Sed corporum inferiorum motus terminatur naturaliter ad quietem. Ergo, cum corpora caelestia sint multo nobiliora, eorum motus naturaliter ad quietem terminabitur.

RESPONDEO dicendum quod circa istam quaestionem est triplex positio. Prima est philosophorum, qui dicunt quod motus caeli semper durabit. Sed hoc non est consonum fidei nostrae, quae ponit certum numerum electorum praefinitum a Deo; et sic oportet quod generatio non in perpetuum duret; et, eadem ratione, nec alia quae ad generationem hominum ordinantur, sicut est motus caeli et variationes elementorum.

Alii vero dicunt quod motus caeli cessabit secundum naturam. Sed hoc etiam est falsum. Quia omne corpus quod naturaliter quiescit et naturaliter movetur, habet locum in quo naturaliter quiescit, ad quem naturaliter movetur, et a quo non recedit nisi per violentiam. Nullus autem talis locus potest assignari corpori caelesti: quia non est magis naturalis soli accessus ad punctum orientis quam recessus ab eo. Unde vel motus eius non esset

time must fail: and if this were to fail, it would fail in an instant. Now an instant is defined (*Physics* 8) *the beginning of the future and the end of the past.* Consequently, there would be time after the last instant of time, which is impossible. Therefore, the movement of the heavens will never cease.

OBJECTION 10: Further, glory does not remove nature. But the movement of the heaven is natural. Therefore, it is not deprived thereof by glory.

ON THE CONTRARY, Revelation 10:6 says that the angel who appeared *swore by him that lives forever and ever that time shall be no longer*, namely, after the seventh angel shall have sounded the trumpet, at the sound of which *the dead shall rise again* (1 Cor 15:52). Now if time be not, there is no movement of the heaven. Therefore, the movement of the heaven will cease.

FURTHER: *Your sun shall go down no more, and your moon shall not decrease* (Isa 60:20). Now the setting of the sun and the phases of the moon are caused by the movement of the heavens. Therefore, the heavenly movement will cease at length.

FURTHER, It is shown in *On Generation and Corruption* II that *the movement of the heaven is for the sake of continual generation in this lower world.* But generation will cease when the number of the elect is complete. Therefore, the movement of the heaven will cease.

FURTHER, All movement is for some end (*Metaphysics* 2). But all movement for an end ceases when the end is obtained. Therefore, either the movement of the heaven will never obtain its end, and thus it would be useless, or it will cease at length.

FURTHER, Rest is more noble than movement, because things are more likened to God, who is supremely immovable, by being themselves unmoved. Now the movement of lower bodies terminates naturally in rest. Therefore, since the heavenly bodies are far nobler, their movement terminates naturally in rest.

I ANSWER THAT, There are three opinions touching this question. The first is of the philosophers who assert that the movement of the heaven will last forever. But this is not in keeping with our faith, which holds that the elect are in a certain number preordained by God, so that the begetting of men will not last forever, and for the same reason, neither will other things that are directed to the begetting of men, such as the movement of the heaven and the variations of the elements.

Others say that the movement of the heaven will cease naturally. But this again is false, since every body that is moved naturally has a place in which it rests naturally, to which it is moved naturally, and to which it is not moved except by violence. Now no such place can be assigned to the heavenly body, since it is not more natural to the sun to move towards a point in the east than to move away from it, wherefore either its movement would not be altogether

naturalis totaliter; vel motus eius non terminaretur naturaliter ad quietem.

Unde dicendum est, secundum alios, quod motus caeli cessabit in illa mundi innovatione, non quidem ex aliqua naturali causa, sed divina voluntate faciente. Corpus enim illud sicut et alia in ministerium hominis dupliciter facta sunt, ut prius dictum est. Altero autem horum ministeriorum homo post statum gloriae non indigebit, scilicet secundum quod corpora ei deserviunt ad sustentationem corporalis vitae. Hoc autem modo servit ei corpus caeleste per motum: inquantum per motum caeli multiplicatur genus humanum; et generantur plantae et animalia, quae usui hominum sunt necessaria; et etiam temperies in aere efficitur, conservans sanitatem. Unde, homine glorificato, motus caeli cessabit.

AD PRIMUM ergo dicendum quod verba illa intelliguntur de terra secundum statum istum, in quo potest esse principium generationis et corruptionis plantarum. Quod patet ex hoc quod ibi dicitur, *cunctis diebus terrae sementis ei messis.* Et hoc simpliciter concedendum est, quod, quandiu terra erit sementibus et messibus apta, motus caeli non cessabit.

ET SIMILITER dicendum est ad secundum, quod Dominus loquitur ibi de duratione seminis Israel secundum praesentem statum. Quod patet ex hoc quod dicit, *et semen Israel deficiet ut non sit gens coram me cunctis diebus: vicissitudo enim dierum post illum statum non erit.* Et ideo etiam leges de quibus fecerat mentionem, post istum statum non erunt.

AD TERTIUM dicendum quod finis qui ibi assignatur corporibus caelestibus, est finis proximus: quia est proprius eorum actus. Sed iste actus ulterius ordinatur ad alium finem, scilicet ad ministerium humanum: ut patet per id quod habetur Deut. 4, [19]: *ne forte, oculis elevatis ad caelum, videas solem et lunam et omnia astra caeli, et, errore deceptus, adores ea, quae creavit Dominus Deus, tuus in ministerium cunctis gentibus quae sub caelo sunt.* Et ideo magis debet sumi iudicium de corporibus caelestibus secundum ministerium hominum quam secundum finem in Genesi assignatum. Corpora autem caelestia per alium modum in ministerium hominis glorificati Cedent, sicut prius dictum est. Et ideo non sequitur quod frustra remaneant.

AD QUARTUM dicendum quod motus non est de perfectione corporis caelestis nisi inquantum per hoc est causa generationis in istis inferioribus; et secundum hoc etiam motus ille facit corpus caeleste participare divinam bonitatem per quandam similitudinem causalitatis. Non autem motus est de perfectione substantiae caeli, quae remanebit. Et ideo non sequitur quod, motu

natural, or its movement would not naturally terminate in rest.

Hence we must agree with others who say that the movement of the heaven will cease at this renewal of the world, not indeed by any natural cause, but as a result of the will of God. For the body in question, like other bodies, was made to serve man in the two ways above mentioned (A. 1): and hereafter in the state of glory man will no longer need one of these services, namely, that in respect of which the heavenly bodies serve man for the sustenance of his bodily life. Now in this way the heavenly bodies serve man by their movement, insofar as by the heavenly movement the human race is multiplied, plants and animals needful for man's use generated, and the temperature of the atmosphere rendered conducive to health. Therefore, the movement of the heavenly body will cease as soon as man is glorified.

REPLY OBJ. 1: These words refer to the earth in its present state, when it is able to be the principle of the generation and corruption of plants. This is evident from its being said there: *all the days of the earth, seedtime and harvest.* And it is simply to be granted that as long as the earth is fit for seedtime and harvest, the movement of the heaven will not cease.

THE SAME ANSWER applies to the second objection, that the Lord is speaking there of the duration of the seed of Israel with regard to the present state. This is evident from the words: *then also the seed of Israel shall fail, so as not to be a nation before me forever.* For after this state there will be no succession of days: wherefore the laws also which he had mentioned will cease after this state.

REPLY OBJ. 3: The end which is there assigned to the heavenly bodies is their proximate end, because it is their proper act. But this act is directed further to another end, namely, the service of man, which is shown by the words: *lest perhaps lifting up thy eyes to heaven, you see the sun and the moon and all the stars of heaven, and, being deceived by error, you adore and serve them, which the Lord thy God created for the service of all the nations that are under heaven* (Deut 4:19). Therefore, we should form our judgment of the heavenly bodies from the service of man, rather than from the end assigned to them in Genesis. Moreover, the heavenly bodies, as stated above, will serve glorified man in another way; hence it does not follow that they will remain without a purpose.

REPLY OBJ. 4: Movement does not belong to the perfection of a heavenly body, except insofar as thereby it is the cause of generation and corruption in this lower world: and in that respect also this movement makes the heavenly body participate in the divine goodness by way of a certain likeness of causality. But movement does not belong to the perfection of the substance of the heaven, which sub-

cessante, aliquid de perfectione caeli tollatur secundum quod remanebit.

AD QUINTUM dicendum quod omnia corpora elementorum habebunt in semetipsis quandam gloriae claritatem. Unde quamvis aliqua superficies terrae non illuminetur a sole, nullo tamen modo remanebit ibi obscuritas.

AD SEXTUM dicendum quod Rom. 8, super illud [v. 22], *omnis creatura ingemiscit* etc., dicit Glossa Ambrosii expresse quod *omnia elementa, cum labore explent sua officia: sicut sol et luna non sine labore statuta sibi implent spatia. Quod est causa nostri. Unde quiescent, nobis assumptis.* Labor autem ille, ut credo, non significat aliquam fatigationem vel passionem illis corporibus accidentem ex motu: cum motus ille sit naturalis, nihil habens de violentia adiunctum, ut probatur in I *Caeli et Mundi.* Sed labor ibi intelligitur defectus ab eo ad quod aliquid tendit. Unde, quia motus ille ordinatus est ex divina providentia ad complendum numerum electorum, illo incompleto, nondum assequitur illud ad quod ordinatus est: et ideo similitudinarie dicitur laborare, sicut homo qui non habet quod intendit. Et hic etiam defectus a caelo tolletur, impleto numero electorum.

Vel potest etiam referri ad desiderium futurae innovationis, quam ex divina dispositione expectat.

AD SEPTIMUM dicendum quod in corpore caelesti non est aliqua potentia quae perficiatur per locum, vel quae facta sit propter hunc finem qui est esse in tali loco. Sed hoc modo se habet potentia ab ubi in corpore caelesti, sicut se habet potentia artificis ad hoc quod faciat diversas domus unius modi: quarum si unam faciat, non dicitur frustra potentiam habere. Et similiter, in quocumque situ ponatur corpus caeleste, potentia quae est in ipso ad ubi non remanebit incompleta nec frustra.

AD OCTAVUM dicendum quod, quamvis corpus caeleste secundum suam naturam aequaliter se habeat ad omnem situm qui est ei possibilis, tamen, si comparetur ad ea quae sunt extra ipsum, non aequaliter se habet ad omnes situs, sed secundum unum situm nobilius disponitur respectu quorundam quam secundum alium: sicut quoad nos nobilius disponitur sol in die quam in nocte. Et ideo probabile est, cum tota innovatio mundi ad hominem ordinetur, quod caelum habeat in illa novitate nobilissimum situm qui est possibilis in respectu ad nostram habitabilem.

Vel, secundum quosdam, caelum quiescet in illo situ in quo factum fuit: alias aliqua revolutio caeli remaneret incompleta. Sed ista ratio non videtur conveniens. Quia, cum aliqua revolutio sit in caelo quae non finitur nisi in triginta sex millibus annorum, sequeretur quod tandiu mundus deberet durare. Quod non videtur probabile. Et

stance will remain. Wherefore it does not follow that, when this movement ceases, the substance of the heaven will lose something of its perfection.

REPLY OBJ. 5: All the elemental bodies will have in themselves a certain clarity of glory. Hence, though part of the surface of the earth be not lit up by the sun, there will by no means be any darkness there.

REPLY OBJ. 6: A Gloss of Ambrose on Romans 8:22: *every creature groans,* says explicitly that *all the elements labor to fulfill their offices: thus the sun and moon fill the places appointed to them not without work. This is for our sake, wherefore they will rest when we are taken up to heaven.* This work, in my opinion, does not signify that any stress or passion occurs to these bodies from their movement, since this movement is natural to them and in no way violent, as is proved in *De Coelo et Mundo* i. But work here denotes a defect in relation to the term to which a thing tends. Hence, since this movement is ordained by divine providence to the completion of the number of the elect, it follows that as long as the latter is incomplete, this movement has not reached the term whereto it was ordained: hence it is said metaphorically 'to labor,' as a man who has not what he intends to have. This defect will be removed from the heaven when the number of the elect is complete.

Or it may refer to the desire of the future renewal which it awaits from the divine disposal.

REPLY OBJ. 7: In a heavenly body there is no potentiality that can be perfected by place, or that is made for this end (which is to be in such and such a place). But potentiality to situation in a place is related to a heavenly body as the craftsman's potentiality to construct various houses of one kind: for if he construct one of these, he is not said to have the potentiality uselessly, and in like manner in whatever situation a heavenly body be placed, its potentiality to be in a place will not remain incomplete or without a purpose.

REPLY OBJ. 8: Although a heavenly body, so far as regards its nature, is equally inclined to every situation that it can possibly occupy, nevertheless in comparison with things outside it, it is not equally inclined to every situation: but in respect of one situation it has a more noble disposition in comparison with certain things than in respect of another situation. Thus in our regard the sun has a more noble disposition at daytime than at nighttime. Hence it is probable, since the entire renewal of the world is directed to man, that the heaven will have in this renewal the most noble situation possible in relation to our dwelling there.

Or, according to some, the heaven will rest in that situation wherein it was made, else one of its revolutions would remain incomplete. But this argument seems improbable, for since a revolution of the heaven takes no less than 36,000 years to complete, it would follow that the world must last that length of time, which does not seem prob-

praeterea, secundum hoc posset sciri quando mundus finiri deberet. Probabiliter enim colligitur ab astrologis in quo situ corpora caelestia sunt facta, considerato numero annorum qui computantur ab initio mundi. Et eodem modo posset sciri certus annorum numerus in quo ad dispositionem similem reverteretur. Tempus autem finis mundi ponitur esse ignotum.

AD NONUM dicendum quod tempus quandoque deficiet, motu caeli deficiente, nec illud nunc ultimum erit principium futuri. Dicta enim definitio non datur de nunc nisi secundum quod est continuans partes temporis: non secundum quod est terminans totum tempus.

AD DECIMUM dicendum quod motus caeli non dicitur naturalis quasi sit pars naturae, eo modo quo principia naturae naturalia dicuntur. Nec iterum hoc modo quod habeat principium activum in natura corporis, sed receptivum tantum: principium autem activum eius est in substantia spirituali, ut dicit Commentator, in principio *Caeli et Mundi*. Et ideo non est inconveniens si per novitatem gloriae motus ille tollatur: non enim, eo ablato, natura corporis caelestis variabitur.

Alias rationes concedimus: scilicet duas primas quae sunt ad oppositum, quia debito modo concludunt. Sed quia aliae duae videntur concludere quod motus caeli naturaliter cesset, ideo respondendum est ad eas.

AD PRIMAM ergo earum dicendum quod motus cessat eo habito propter quod est, si illud sequatur motum, et non concomitetur ipsum. Illud autem propter quod est motus caelestis secundum philosophos, concomitatur motum: scilicet imitatio divinae bonitatis in causalitate quam habet super inferiora. Et ideo non oportet quod naturaliter motus ille cesset.

AD SECUNDAM rationem dicendum quod, quamvis immobilitas sit simpliciter nobilior quam motus, tamen motus in eo quod potest per motum consequi aliquam perfectam participationem divinae bonitatis, est nobilior quam quies in illo quod nullo modo per motum posset illam perfectionem consequi. Et ratione hac terra, quae est infimum corporum, est sine motu: quamvis ipse Deus, qui est nobilissimus rerum, sine motu sit, a quo corpora nobiliora moventur. Et inde est etiam quod motus corporum superiorum possent poni secundum viam naturae perpetui, nec unquam ad quietem terminari, quamvis motus inferiorum corporum ad quietem terminetur.

able. Moreover, according to this it would be possible to know when the world will come to an end. For we may conclude with probability from astronomers in what position the heavenly bodies were made, by taking into consideration the number of years that have elapsed since the beginning of the world; and in the same way it would be possible to know the exact number of years it would take them to return to a like position: whereas the time of the world's end is stated to be unknown.

REPLY OBJ. 9: Time will at length cease when the heavenly movement ceases. Yet that last *now* will not be the beginning of the future. For the definition quoted applies to the *now* only as continuous with the parts of time, not as terminating the whole of time.

REPLY OBJ. 10: The movement of the heaven is said to be natural not as though it were part of nature in the same way as we speak of natural principles, but because it has its principle in the nature of a body, not indeed its active but its receptive principle. Its active principle is a spiritual substance, as the Commentator says on *De Coelo et Mundo*; and consequently it is not unreasonable for this movement to be done away with by the renewal of glory, since the nature of the heavenly body will not alter through the cessation of that movement.

We grant the other objections which argue in the contrary sense (namely, the first three) because they conclude in due manner. But since the remaining two seem to conclude that the movement of heaven will cease naturally, we must reply to them.

TO THE FIRST, then, we reply that movement ceases when its purpose is attained, provided this is a sequel to, and does not accompany, the movement. Now the purpose of the heavenly movement, according to philosophers, accompanies that movement, namely, the imitation of the divine goodness in the causality of that movement with respect to this lower world. Hence it does not follow that this movement ceases naturally.

TO THE SECOND we reply that although immobility is simply nobler than movement, yet movement in a subject which thereby can acquire a perfect participation of the divine goodness is nobler than rest in a subject which is altogether unable to acquire that perfection by movement. For this reason the earth, which is the lowest of the elements, is without movement: even though God, who is exalted above all things, is without movement, by whom the more noble bodies are moved. Hence also it is that the movements of the higher bodies might be held to be perpetual, so far as their natural power is concerned, and never to terminate in rest, although the movement of lower bodies terminates in rest.

Article 3

Whether the Brightness of the Heavenly Bodies Will Be Increased at This Renewal?

AD TERTIUM SIC PROCEDITUR. Videtur quod in corporibus caelestibus claritas non augeatur in illa innovatione. Innovatio enim in corporibus superioribus erit per ignem purgantem. Sed ignis purgans nunquam pertingit ad corpora caelestia. Ergo corpora caelestia non innovabuntur per maioris claritatis perceptionem.

PRAETEREA, sicut corpora caelestia per motum sunt causa generationis in istis inferioribus, ita et per lucem. Sed, cessante generatione, cessabit motus, ut dictum est. Ergo similiter cessabit lux caelestium corporum, magis quam augeatur.

PRAETEREA, si, innovato homine, corpora caelestia innoventur, oportet quod, eo deteriorato, fiant deteriorata. Sed hoc non videtur probabile: cum illa corpora sint invariabilia quantum ad eorum substantiam. Ergo nec, innovato homine, innovabuntur.

PRAETEREA, si tunc deteriorata fuerint, oportet quod tantum deteriorata fuerint quantum dicuntur esse melioranda in hominis innovatione. Sed dicitur Isaiae 30, [26] quod *tunc erit lux lunae sicut lux solis*. Ergo et in primo statu ante peccatum luna lucebat quantum nunc lucet sol. Ergo, quandocumque luna erat super terram, faciebat diem sicut nunc sol. Et hoc manifeste apparet esse falsum per id quod dicitur Genes. 1, [16], quod luna facta est *ut praeesset nocti*. Ergo, homine peccante, non sunt caelestia corpora diminuta lumine. Et. ita nec eorum lumen augebitur, ut videtur, in hominis glorificatione.

PRAETEREA, claritas corporum caelestium ordinatur ad usum hominum, sicut et aliae creaturae. Sed post resurrectionem claritas solis non cedet in hominis usum: dicitur enim Isaiae 60, [19]: *non erit tibi amplius sol ad lucendum per diem, nec splendor lunae illuminabit te*; et Apoc. 21, [23]: *civitas illa non eget sole neque luna ut luceant in ea*. Ergo eorum claritas non augebitur.

PRAETEREA, non esset sapiens artifex qui maxima instrumenta faceret ad aliquod modicum artificium construendum. Sed homo est quoddam minimum comparatione caelestium corporum, quae sua ingenti magnitudine quasi incomparabiliter hominis quantitatem excedunt: immo etiam totius terrae, quae se habet ad caelum ut punctum ad sphaeram, ut astrologi dicunt. Cum ergo Deus sit sapientissimus, non videtur quod finis creationis caeli sit homo. Et ita non videtur quod, eo peccante, caelum deterioratum sit; nec, eo glorificato, melioretur.

OBJECTION 1: It would seem that the brightness of the heavenly bodies will not be increased at this renewal. For this renewal as regards the lower bodies will be caused by the cleansing fire. But the cleansing fire will not reach the heavenly bodies. Therefore, the heavenly bodies will not be renewed by receiving an increase of brightness.

OBJ. 2: Further, just as the heavenly bodies are the cause of generation in this lower world by their movement, so are they by their light. But, when generation ceases, movement will cease as stated above (A. 2). Therefore, in like manner the light of the heavenly bodies will cease, rather than increase.

OBJ. 3: Further, if the heavenly bodies will be renewed when man is renewed, it follows that when man deteriorated, they deteriorated likewise. But this does not seem probable, since these bodies are unalterable as to their substance. Therefore, neither will they be renewed when man is renewed.

OBJ. 4: Further, if they deteriorated, then it follows that their deterioration was on a par with the amelioration which, it is said, will accrue to them at man's renewal. Now it is written that *the light of the moon shall be as the light of the sun* (Isa 30:26). Therefore, in the original state before sin the moon shone as much as the sun does now. Therefore, whenever the moon was over the earth, it made it to be day as the sun does now: which is proved manifestly to be false from the statement of Genesis 1:16 that the moon was made *to rule the night*. Therefore, when man sinned, the heavenly bodies were not deprived of their light; and so their light will not be increased, so it seems, when man is glorified.

OBJ. 5: Further, the brightness of the heavenly bodies, like other creatures, is directed to the use of man. Now, after the resurrection, the brightness of the sun will be of no use to man, for Isaiah 60:19 says: *you shall no more have the sun for your light by day; neither shall the brightness of the moon enlighten you*, and Revelation 21:23 says, *the city has no need of the sun, nor of the moon, to shine in it*. Therefore, their brightness will not be increased.

OBJ. 6: Further, a wise craftsman would not make very great instruments for the making of a small work. Now man is a very small thing in comparison with the heavenly bodies, which by their huge bulk surpass the size of man almost beyond comparison: in fact, the size of the whole earth in comparison with the heaven is as a point compared with a sphere, as astronomers say. Since, then, God is most wise, it would seem that man is not the end of the creation of the heavens, and so it is unseemly that the heaven should deteriorate when he sinned, or that it should be bettered when he is glorified.

SED CONTRA: Est quod dicitur Isaiae 30, [26]: *erit lux lunae sicut lux solis, et dux solis septempliciter.*

PRAETEREA, totus mundus innovabitur in melius. Sed caelum est nobilior pars mundi: corporalis. Ergo in melius mutabitur. Sed hoc non potest esse nisi maiori claritate resplendeat. Ergo crescet eius claritas.

PRAETEREA, *omnis creatura quae ingemiscit et parturit, expectat revelationem gloriae futurae filiorum Dei,* ut dicitur Rom. 8, [19, 22]. Sed etiam corpora caelestia sunt huiusmodi, ut ibidem dicit Glossa. Ergo expectant gloriam sanctorum. Sed non expectarent nisi ex hoc eis aliquid accresceret. Ergo claritas eis per hoc accrescet, qua praecipue decorantur.

RESPONDEO dicendum quod ad hoc innovatio mundi ordinatur ut in mundo innovato manifestis indiciis quasi sensibiliter Deus ab homine videatur. Creatura autem praecipue in Dei cognitionem ducit sua specie et decore, quae manifestant sapientiam facientis et gubernantis: unde dicitur Sap. 13, [5]: *a magnitudine speciei cognoscibiliter poterat videri Creator eorum.* Pulchritudo autem Caelestium corporum praecipue consistit in luce: unde Eccli. 43, [10] dicitur: *species caeli gloria stellarum, mundum illuminans in excelsis Dominus.* Et ideo praecipue quantum ad claritatem corpora caelestia meliorabuntur. Quantitas autem et modus meliorationis illi soli cognita est qui erit meliorationis Auctor.

AD PRIMUM ergo dicendum quod ignis purgans non causabit innovationis formam, sed disponet tantum ad eam, purgando a foeditate peccati, et ab impuritate commixtionis, quae in corporibus caelestibus non invenitur. Ideo, quamvis corpora caelestia per ignem non sint purganda, sunt tamen divinitus innovanda.

AD SECUNDUM dicendum quod motus non importat aliquam perfectionem in eo quod movetur secundum quod in se consideratur, cum sit *actus imperfecti*: quamvis possit pertinere ad perfectionem corporis inquantum est causa alicuius. Sed lux pertinet ad perfectionem corporis lucentis etiam in substantia sua considerati. Et ideo, postquam corpus caeleste desinet esse causa generationis, non remanebit motus, sed remanebit claritas eius.

AD TERTIUM dicendum quod super illud Isaiae 30, [26], *erit lux lunae sicut lux solis,* dicit Glossa: *omnia propter hominem facta in eius lapsu peiorata sunt, et sol et luna suo lumine minorata.* Quae quidem minoratio a quibusdam intelligitur secundum realem minorationem luminis. Nec obstat quod corpora caelestia secundum naturam sunt invariabilia: quia illa variatoi facta est a divina virtute.

ON THE CONTRARY, It is written: *the light of the moon shall be as the light of the sun, and the light of the sun shall be sevenfold* (Isa 30:26).

FURTHER, The whole world will be renewed for the better. But the heaven is the more noble part of the corporeal world. Therefore, it will be altered for the better. But this cannot be unless it shine out with greater brightness. Therefore, its brightness will be bettered and will increase.

FURTHER, *Every creature that groans and travails in pain awaits the revelation of the glory of the children of God* (Rom 8:21–22). Now such are the heavenly bodies, as a Gloss says on the same passage. Therefore, they await the glory of the saints. But they would not await it unless they were to gain something by it. Therefore, their brightness will increase thereby, since it is their chief beauty.

I ANSWER THAT, The renewal of the world is directed to the end that after this renewal has taken place, God may become visible to man by signs so manifest as to be perceived by his senses, as it were. Now creatures lead to the knowledge of God chiefly by their comeliness and beauty, which show forth the wisdom of their Maker and Governor; wherefore it is written: *by the greatness of the beauty and of the creature, the Creator of them may be seen, so as to be known thereby* (Wis 13:5). And the beauty of the heavenly bodies consists chiefly in light; wherefore it is written: *the glory of the stars is the beauty of heaven, the Lord enlightens the world on high* (Sir 43:10). Hence the heavenly bodies will be bettered especially as regards their brightness. But the degree and mode of this betterment is only known to him who will be its Maker.

REPLY OBJ. 1: The cleansing fire will not cause the form of the renewal, but will only dispose thereto by cleansing from the vileness of sin and the impurity resulting from the mingling of bodies, and this is not to be found in the heavenly bodies. Hence, although the heavenly bodies are not to be cleansed by fire, they are nevertheless to be divinely renewed.

REPLY OBJ. 2: Movement does not denote perfection in the thing moved, considered in itself, since movement is the *act of that which is imperfect*: although it may pertain to the perfection of a body insofar as the latter is the cause of something. But light belongs to the perfection of a lightsome body, even considered in its substance: and consequently after the heavenly body has ceased to be the cause of generation, its brightness will remain, while its movement will cease.

REPLY OBJ. 3: A Gloss on Isaiah 30:26: *the light of the moon shall be as the light of the sun,* says, *all things made for man's sake deteriorated at his fall, and sun and moon diminished in light.* This diminishment is understood by some to mean a real lessening of light. Nor does it matter that the heavenly bodies are by nature unalterable, because this alteration was brought about by the divine power.

Alii vero probabilius intelligunt, minorationem illam esse dicentes non secundum realem luminis defectum, sed quoad usum hominis, qui non tantum beneficium ex lumine corporum caelestium post peccatum consecutus est quantum ante fuisset: per quem etiam modum dicitur Genes. 3, [17–18]: *maledicta terra in opere tuo, spinas et tribulos germinabit tibi*; quae tamen etiam ante spinas et tribulos germinabat, sed non in hominis poenam.

Nec tamen sequitur, si lux caelestium corporum per essentiam minorata non est homine peccante, quod realiter non sit augenda in eius glorificatione. Quia peccatum hominis non immutavit statum universi: cum etiam homo prius et post animalem vitam habuerat, quae motu et generatione corporalis creaturae indiget. Sed glorificatio hominis statum totius corporalis creaturae immutabit, ut dictum est. Et ideo non est simile.

AD QUARTUM dicendum quod minoratio illa, ut probabilius aestimatur, non fuit secundum substantiam, sed secundum effectum. Unde non sequitur quod luna existens super terram diem fecisset: sed quod tantum commodum ex lumine lunae homo habuisset sicut nunc habet ex lumine solis. Sed post resurrectionem, quando lux lunae augebitur secundum rei veritatem, non erit alicubi nox super terram (sed solum in centro terrae, ubi erit infernus): quia tunc, ut dicitur, luna lucebit quantum lucet nunc sol; sol autem in septuplum quam modo luceat; corpora autem beatorum septies magis sole (quamvis hoc non sit aliqua auctoritate vel ratione probatum).

AD QUINTUM dicendum quod aliquid potest cedere in usum hominis dupliciter. Uno modo, propter necessitatem. Et sic nulla creatura cedet in usum hominis: quia ex Deo plenam sufficientiam habebit. Et hoc significatur in auctoritate Apocalypsis inducta, quae dicit quod civitas illa *non eget sole vel luna*. Alius usus est ad maiorem perfectionem. Et sic homo aliis creaturis utetur: non tamen quasi necessariis ad perveniendum in finem, sicut nunc eis utitur.

AD SEXTUM dicendum quod ratio illa est Rabbi Moysi, qui omninq improbare nititur mundum propter hominem esse factum. Unde hoc quod in veteri Testamento de innovatione mundi legitur, sicut patet in auctoritatibus Isaiae inductis, dicit esse metaphorice dictum: ut, sicut alicui dicitur obtenebrari sol quando in magnam tristitiam incidit, ut nesciat quid faciat, qui etiam modus loquendi consuetus est in Scriptura; ita etiam e contrario dicitur ei sol magis lucere et totus mundus innovari quando ex statu tristitiae, in maximam exultationem convertitur.

Sed hoc dissonat ab auctoritatibus et expositionibus Sanctorum. Unde rationi illi inductae hoc modo respon-

Others, however, with greater probability, take this diminishment to mean not a real lessening of light, but a lessening in reference to man's use; because after sin man did not receive as much benefit from the light of the heavenly bodies as before. In the same sense we read: *cursed is the earth in your work: thorns and thistles shall it bring forth to you* (Gen 3:17–18), although it would have brought forth thorns and thistles before sin, but not as a punishment to man.

Nor does it follow that, supposing the light of the heavenly bodies not to have been lessened essentially through man sinning, it will not really be increased at man's glorification. For man's sin wrought no change upon the state of the universe, since both before and after sin man had an animal life, which needs the movement and generation of a corporeal creature; whereas man's glorification will bring a change upon the state of all corporeal creatures, as stated above (Q. 76, A. 7). Hence there is no comparison.

REPLY OBJ. 4: This diminution, according to the more probable opinion, refers not to the substance but to the effect. Hence it does not follow that the moon while over the earth would have made it to be day, but that man would have derived as much benefit from the light of the moon then as now from the light of the sun. After the resurrection, however, when the light of the moon will be increased in very truth, there will be night nowhere on earth but only in the center of the earth where hell will be, because then, as is said, the moon will shine as brightly as the sun does now; the sun seven times as much as now, and the bodies of the blessed seven times more than the sun, although there be no authority or reason to prove this.

REPLY OBJ. 5: A thing may be useful to man in two ways. First, by reason of necessity, and thus no creature will be useful to man because he will have complete sufficiency from God. This is signified by the words quoted, according to which that *city has no need of the sun* nor *of the moon* (Rev 21:23). Second, on account of a greater perfection, and thus man will make use of other creatures, yet not as needful to him in order to obtain his end, in which way he makes use of them now.

REPLY OBJ. 6: This is the argument of Rabbi Moses who endeavors to prove that the world was by no means made for man's use (*Guide for the Perplexed* 3). Wherefore he maintains that what we read in the Old Testament about the renewal of the world, as instanced by the quotations from Isaiah, is said metaphorically: and that even as the sun is said to be darkened in reference to a person when he encounters a great sorrow so as not to know what to do (which way of speaking is customary to Scripture), so on the other hand the sun is said to shine brighter for a person, and the whole world to be renewed, when he is brought from a state of sorrow to one of very great joy.

But this is not in harmony with the authority and commentaries of holy men. Consequently, we must answer this

dendum est, quod, quamvis corpora caelestia maxime excedant corpus hominis, tamen multo plus excedit anima rationalis corpora caelestia quam ipsa excedant corpus humanum. Unde non est inconveniens si corpora caelestia propter hominem esse facta dicantur: non tamen sicut propter principalem finem, quia principalis finis omnium Deus est.

argument by saying that although the heavenly bodies far surpass the human body, yet the rational soul surpasses the heavenly bodies far more than these surpass the human body. Hence it is not unreasonable to say that the heavenly bodies were made for man's sake; not, however, as though this were the principal end, since the principal end of all things is God.

Article 4

Whether the Elements Will Be Renewed by an Addition of Brightness?

AD QUARTUM SIC PROCEDITUR. Videtur quod elementa non innovabuntur per receptionem alicuius claritatis. Sicut enim lux est qualitas corporis caelestis propria, ita calidum et frigidum, humidum et siccum, sunt qualitates elementorum. Ergo, sicut caelum innovatur per augmentum claritatis, ita debent innovari elementa per augmentum qualitatum activarum et passivarum.

PRAETEREA, rarum et densum sunt propriae qualitates elementorum, quas elementa in illa innovatione non amittent. Sed raritas et densitas elementorum resistere videntur claritati: cum corpus clarum oporteat condensatum esse; unde raritas aeris non videtur quod possit claritatem pati. Et similiter nec densitas terrae, quae pervietatem tollit. Ergo non potest esse quod elementa innoventur per alicuius claritatis additionem.

PRAETEREA, constat quod damnati erunt in terra. Sed ipsi erunt *in tenebris*, non solum interioribus, sed etiam *exterioribus*. Ergo terra non dotabitur claritate in illa innovatione. Et eadem ratione nec alia elementa.

PRAETEREA, multiplicatio claritatis in elementis multiplicat calorem. Si igitur in illa innovatione erit maior claritas elementorum quam nunc sit, erit etiam per consequens maior caliditas. Et sic videtur quod transmutabuntur a suis naturalibus qualitatibus, quae sunt eis secundum certam mensuram. Quod est absurdum.

PRAETEREA, bonum universi, quod consistit in ordine et harmonia, dignius est quam bonum alicuius naturae singularis. Sed, si una creatura efficiatur melior, tollitur bonum universi: quia non remanebit eadem harmonia. Ergo, si corpora elementaria, quae secundum gradum suae naturae quem tenent in universo, claritatis debent esse experta, claritatem recipiant, magis ex hoc deperiet perfectio universi quam accrescet.

SED CONTRA: Est quod dicitur Apoc. 21, [1]: *vidi caelum novum ei terram novam*: Sed caelum innovabitur per maiorem claritatem. Ergo et terra. Et similiter alia elementa.

OBJECTION 1: It would seem that the elements will not be renewed by receiving some kind of brightness. For just as light is a quality proper to a heavenly body, so are hot and cold, wet and dry, qualities proper to the elements. Therefore, as the heaven is renewed by an increase of brightness, so ought the elements to be renewed by an increase of active and passive qualities.

OBJ. 2: Further, rarity and density are qualities of the elements, and the elements will not be deprived of them at this renewal. Now the rarity and density of the elements would seem to be an obstacle to brightness, since a bright body needs to be condensed, for which reason the rarity of the air seems incompatible with brightness, and in like manner does the density of the earth, which is an obstacle to transparency. Therefore, it is impossible for the elements to be renewed by the addition of brightness.

OBJ. 3: Further, it is agreed that the damned will be in the earth. Yet they will be *in darkness* not only internal but also *external*. Therefore, the earth will not be endowed with brightness in this renewal, nor for the same reason will the other elements.

OBJ. 4: Further, increase of brightness in the elements implies an increase of heat. If, therefore, at this renewal the brightness of the elements be greater than it is now, their heat will likewise be greater; and thus it would seem that they will be changed from their natural qualities, which are in them according to a fixed measure: and this is absurd.

OBJ. 5: Further, the good of the universe, which consists in the order and harmony of the parts, is more excellent than the good of any individual creature. But if one creature be bettered, the good of the universe is done away with, since there will no longer be the same harmony. Therefore, if the elemental bodies, which, according to their natural degree in the universe, should be devoid of brightness, were to be endowed with brightness, the perfection of the universe would be diminished thereby rather than increased.

ON THE CONTRARY, It is written: *I saw a new heaven and a new earth* (Rev 21:1). Now the heaven will be renewed by an increase of brightness. Therefore, the earth will also. Likewise, the other elements.

Praeterea, corpora inferiora fuerunt in usum hominis sicut et superiora. Sed creatura corporalis remunerabitur propter ministerium quod homini exhibuit: ut videtur dicere Glossa Rom. 8, [22]. Ergo etiam elementa clarificabuntur, sicut et alia corpora caelestia.

Praeterea, corpus hominis est ex elementis compositum. Ergo partes elementorum quae sunt in corpore hominis, glorificato homine, glorificabuntur per receptionem claritatis. Sed eandem convenit esse dispositionem totius et partis. Ergo et ipsa elementa convenit claritate dotari.

Respondeo dicendum quod, sicut est ordo caelestium spirituum ad spiritus terrenos, scilicet humanos, ita etiam est ordo caelestium corporum ad Corpora terrestria. Cum autem creatura corporalis sit facta propter spiritualem, et per eam regatur, oportet similiter disponi corporalia sicut et spiritualia disponuntur. In illa autem ultima rerum consummatione spiritus inferiores accipient proprietates superiorum spirituum: quia homines *erunt sicut angeli in caelis*, sicut dicitur Matth. 22, [30]. Et hoc erit inquantum ad maximam perfectionem deveniet id secundum quod humanus spiritus cum angelico convenit. Unde etiam similiter, cum corpora inferiora cum caelestibus non communicent nisi in natura lucis et diaphani, ut dicitur in II *de Anima*, oportet corpora inferiora maxime perfici secundum claritatem. Unde omnia elementa claritate quadam vestientur. Non tamen aequaliter, sed secundum suum modum: terra enim, ut dicitur, erit in superficie exteriori pervia sicut vitrum, aqua sicut crystallus, aer ut caelum, ignis ut luminaria caeli.

Ad primum ergo dicendum quod innovatio mundi ordinatur ad hoc quod homo etiam sensu in corporibus quodammodo per manifesta indicia divinitatem videat. Inter sensus autem nostros spiritualior est visus et subtilior. Et ideo quantum ad qualitates visivas, quarum principium est lux, oportet omnia corpora inferiora maxime meliorari. Qualitates autem elementares pertinent ad tactum, qui est maxime materialis: et earum excessus contrarietatis magis est contristativus quam delectativus. Excessus autem lucis erit delectabilis: cum contrarietatem non habeat nisi propter organi debilitatem, quae tunc non erit.

Ad secundum dicendum quod aer non erit clarus sicut radios proiiciens, sed sicut diaphanum illuminatum. Terra vero, quamvis ex natura sua opacitatem habeat propter defectum lucis, tamen ex divina virtute in sui superficie gloria claritatis vestietur, sine praeiudicio densitatis ipsius.

Ad tertium dicendum quod in loco inferni non erit terra glorificata per claritatem: sed loco huius gloriae habebit pars illa terrae spiritus rationales hominum et daemonum, qui quamvis ratione culpae sint infimi, tamen

Further, The lower bodies, like the higher, are for man's use. Now the corporeal creature will be rewarded for its services to man, as a Gloss of Ambrose seems to say on Romans 8:22, *every creature groans*. Therefore, the elements will be glorified as well as the heavenly bodies.

Further, Man's body is composed of the elements. Therefore, the elemental particles that are in man's body will be glorified by the addition of brightness when man is glorified. Now it is fitting that whole and part should have the same disposition. Therefore, it is fitting that the elements themselves should be endowed with brightness.

I answer that, Just as there is a certain order between the heavenly spirits and the earthly or human spirits, so is there an order between heavenly bodies and earthly bodies. Since, then, the corporeal creature was made for the sake of the spiritual and is ruled thereby, it follows that corporeal things are dealt with similarly to spiritual things. Now in this final consummation of things, the lower spirits will receive the properties of the higher spirits, because men *will be as the angels in heaven* (Matt 22:30): and this will be accomplished by conferring the highest degree of perfection on that in which the human spirit agrees with the angelic. Wherefore, in like manner, since the lower bodies do not agree with the heavenly bodies except in the nature of light and transparency (*On the Soul* 2), it follows that the lower bodies are to be perfected chiefly as regards brightness. Hence all the elements will be clothed with a certain brightness, not equally, however, but according to their mode: for it is said that the earth on its outward surface will be as transparent as glass, water as crystal, the air as heaven, fire as the lights of heaven.

Reply Obj. 1: As stated above (A. 1), the renewal of the world is directed to the effect that man even by his senses may, as it were, see divinity by manifest signs. Now the most spiritual and subtle of our senses is the sight. Consequently, all the lower bodies need to be bettered chiefly as regards the visible qualities, the principle of which is light. On the other hand, the elemental qualities regard the touch, which is the most material of the senses, and the excess of their contrariety is more displeasing than pleasant; whereas excess of light will be pleasant, since it has no contrariety, except on account of a weakness in the organ, such as will not be then.

Reply Obj. 2: The air will be bright, not as casting forth rays, but as an enlightened transparency; while the earth, although it is opaque through lack of light, yet by the divine power its surface will be clothed with the glory of brightness without prejudice to its density.

Reply Obj. 3: The earth will not be glorified with brightness in the infernal regions; but instead of this glory, that part of the earth will have the rational spirits of men and demons who, though weak by reason of sin, are never-

ex dignitate naturae sunt qualibet qualitate corporali superiores.

Vel dicendum quod, etiam si sit tota terra glorificata, nihilominus reprobi *in tenebris exterioribus* erunt: quia etiam ignis inferni, qui quantum ad aliquid eis lucebit, quantum ad aliud eis lucere non poterit.

AD QUARTUM dicendum quod claritas illa erit inistis corporibus sicut est in corporibus caelestibus, in quibus caliditatem non causat: quia corpora ista tunc inalterabilia erunt, sicut modo sunt caelestia.

AD QUINTUM dicendum quod non tolletur propter meliorationem elementorum ordo universi. Quia etiam omnes aliae partes meliorabuntur: et sic remanebit eadem harmonia.

theless superior to any corporeal quality by the dignity of their nature.

Or we may say that, though the whole earth be glorified, the wicked will nevertheless be *in exterior darkness*, since even the fire of hell, while shining for them in one respect, will be unable to enlighten them in another.

REPLY OBJ. 4: This brightness will be in these bodies even as it is in the heavenly bodies, in which it causes no heat, because these bodies will then be unalterable, as the heavenly bodies are now.

REPLY OBJ. 5: The order of the universe will not be done away with by the betterment of the elements, because all the other parts will also be bettered, and so the same harmony will remain.

Article 5

Whether the Plants and Animals Will Remain in This Renewal?

AD QUINTUM SIC PROCEDITUR. Videtur quod plantae et alia animalia remaneant in illa innovatione. Elementis enim non debet aliquid subtrahi quod ad eorum ornatum pertinet. Sed animalibus et plantis elementa ornari dicuntur. Ergo non auferentur in illa: innovatione

PRAETEREA, sicut elementa homini: servierunt, ita etiam animalia et plantae et corpora mineralia. Sed elementa propter praedictum ministerium glorificabuntur. Ergo et animalia et plantae et corpora mineralia glorificabuntur.

PRAETEREA, universum remanebit imperfectum si aliquid quod est de perfectione eius auferatur. Sed species: animalium et plantarum et corporum mineralium sunt de perfectione universi. Cum ergo non debeat dici quod mundus in sua innovatione imperfectus remaneat, videtur quod oporteat dicere plantas et alia animalia remanere.

PRAETEREA, animalia et plantae habent nobiliorem formam quam ipsa elementa. Sed mundus in illa finali innovatione in melius mutabitur. Ergo magis debent remanere animalia et plantae quam elementa: cum sint nobiliora.

PRAETEREA, inconveniens est dicere quod naturalis appetitus frustretur. Sed secundum naturalem appetitum animalia et plantae appetunt esse perpetua, etsi non secundum individuum, saltem secundum speciem: et. ad hoc ordinatur eorum generatio continua, ut in II de Generat. dicitur. Ergo inconveniens est dicere quod istae species aliquando deficiant.

SED CONTRA, si plantae et animalia remanebunt, aut omnia aut quaedam. Si omnia, oportebit etiam animalia bruta quae prius fuerunt mortua, resurgere, sicut et homines resurgent. Quod dici non potest: quia, cum forma eorum in nihilum cedat, non potest eadem numero

OBJECTION 1: It would seem that the plants and animals will remain in this renewal. For the elements should be deprived of nothing that belongs to their adornment. Now the elements are said to be adorned by the animals and plants. Therefore, they will not be removed in this renewal.

OBJ. 2: Further, just as the elements served man, so also did animals, plants and mineral bodies. But on account of this service, the elements will be glorified. Therefore, both animals and plants and mineral bodies will be glorified likewise.

OBJ. 3: Further, the universe will remain imperfect if anything belonging to its perfection be removed. Now the species of animals, plants, and mineral bodies belong to the perfection of the universe. Since, then, we must not say that the world will remain imperfect when it is renewed, it seems that we should assert that the plants and animals will remain.

OBJ. 4: Further, animals and plants have a more noble form than the elements. Now the world, at this final renewal, will be changed for the better. Therefore, animals and plants should remain, rather than the elements, since they are nobler.

OBJ. 5: Further, it is unseemly to assert that the natural appetite will be frustrated. But by their natural appetite animals and plants desire to be forever, if indeed not as regards the individual, at least as regards the species: and to this end their continual generation is directed (*On Generation and Corruption* 2). Therefore, it is unseemly to say that these species will at length cease to be.

ON THE CONTRARY, If plants and animals are to remain, either all of them will, or some of them. If all of them, then dumb animals, which had previously died, will have to rise again just as men will rise again. But this cannot be asserted for, since their form comes to nothing, they cannot

resumi. Si autem non omnia, sed quaedam: cum non sit maior ratio de uno quam de alio quod in perpetuum maneat, videtur quod nullum eorum in perpetuum manebit. Sed quidquid remanebit post mundi innovationem, in perpetuum erit, generatione et corruptione cessante. Ergo plantae et animalia penitus post mundi innovationem non erunt.

PRAETEREA, secundum Philosophum, in II *de Generat.*, in animalibus et plantis et huiusmodi corruptibilibus, speciei perpetuitas non conservatur nisi ex continuatione motus caelestis. Sed tunc motus caelestis deficiet. Ergo non poterit perpetuitas in illis speciebus conservari.

PRAETEREA, cessante fine, cessare debet id quod est ad finem. Sed animalia et plantae facta sunt ad animalem vitam hominis sustentandam: unde dicitur Genes. 9, [3]: *sicut olera virentia dedi vobis omnem carnem.* Sed post illam innovationem animalis vita ini homine non erit. Ergo nec plantae nec animalia remanere debent.

RESPONDEO dicendum quod, cum innovatio mundi propter hominem fiat, oportet quod innovationi hominis conformetur. Homo autem innovatus de statu corruptionis in incorruptionem transibit et perpetuae quietis: I Cor. 15, [53], *oportet corruptibile hoc induere incorruptionem.* Et ideo mundus hoc modo innovabitur ut, abiecta omni corruptione, perpetuo maneat in quiete. Unde ad illam innovationem nihil ordinari poterit nisi quod habet ordinem ad incorruptionem. Huiusmodi autem sunt corpora caelestia, elementa et homines. Corpora autem caelestia secundum sui naturam incorruptibilia sunt et secundum totum et secundum partes. Elementa vero sunt corruptibilia quidem secundum partes, sed incorruptibilia secundum totum. Homines vero corrumpuntur et secundum totum et secundum partes: sed hoc ex parte materiae, non ex parte formae, scilicet animae rationalis, quae post corruptionem hominis remanet incorrupta. Animalia vero bruta et plantae et mineralia, et omnia corpora mixta, corrumpuntur et secundum totum et secundum partem, et ex parte materiae, quae formam amittit, et ex parte formae, quae actu non manet. Et sic nullo modo habent ordinem ad incorruptionem. Unde in illa innovatione non manebunt, sed sola ea quae dicta sunt.

AD PRIMUM ergo dicendum quod huiusmodi corpora dicuntur esse ad ornatum elementorum inquantum virtutes activae et passivae generales quae sunt in elementis, ad speciales actiones contrahuntur. Et ideo sunt ad ornatum elementorum in statu actionis et passionis. Sed hic status in elementis non remanebit. Unde nec animalia nec plantas remanere oportet.

resume the same identical form. On the other hand, if not all but some of them remain, since there is no more reason for one of them remaining forever rather than another, it would seem that none of them will. But whatever remains after the world has been renewed will remain forever, generation and corruption being done away with. Therefore, plants and animals will altogether cease after the renewal of the world.

FURTHER, According to the Philosopher (*On Generation and Corruption* 2) the species of animals, plants, and such corruptible things are not perpetuated except by the continuance of the heavenly movement. Now this will cease then. Therefore, it will be impossible for those species to be perpetuated.

FURTHER, If the end cease, those things which are directed to the end should cease. Now animals and plants were made for the upkeep of human life; wherefore it is written: *even as the green herbs have I delivered all flesh to you* (Gen 9:3). Therefore, when man's animal life ceases, animals and plants should cease. But after this renewal animal life will cease in man. Therefore, neither plants nor animals ought to remain.

I ANSWER THAT, Since the renewal of the world will be for man's sake, it follows that it should be conformed to the renewal of man. Now, by being renewed, man will pass from the state of corruption to incorruptibility, and to a state of everlasting rest, wherefore it is written: *this corruptible must put on incorruption* (1 Cor 15:53); and consequently the world will be renewed in such a way as to throw off all corruption and remain forever at rest. Therefore, it will be impossible for anything to be the subject of that renewal, unless it be a subject of incorruption. Now such are the heavenly bodies, the elements, and man. For the heavenly bodies are by their very nature incorruptible both as to their whole and as to their part: the elements are corruptible as to their parts but incorruptible as a whole; while men are corruptible both in whole and in part, but this is on the part of their matter, not on the part of their form (namely, the rational soul) which will remain incorrupt after the corruption of man. On the other hand, dumb animals, plants, and minerals, and all mixed bodies, are corruptible both in their whole and in their parts, both on the part of their matter, which loses its form, and on the part of their form, which does not remain actually; and thus they are in no way subjects of incorruption. Hence they will not remain in this renewal, but those things alone which we have mentioned above.

REPLY OBJ. 1: These bodies are said to adorn the elements inasmuch as the general active and passive forces which are in the elements are applied to specific actions: hence they adorn the elements in their active and passive state. But this state will not remain in the elements: wherefore there is no need for animals or plants to remain.

AD SECUNDUM dicendum quod nec animalia nec plantae nec alia corpora in ministrando homini aliquid meruerunt, cum libertate arbitrii careant, sed pro tanto dicuntur quaedam corpora remunerari, quia homo meruit ut illa innovarentur quae ad innovationem ordinem habent.

Plantae autem et animalia non habent ordinem ad innovationem incorruptionis. Unde ex hoc homo non meruit ut illa innovarentur: quia nullus potest alteri mereri nisi id cuius est capax, nec etiam sibi ipsi. Unde, etiam dato quod animalia bruta mererentur in ministerio hominis, non tamen essent innovanda.

AD TERTIUM dicendum quod, sicut perfectio hominis multipliciter assignatur, est enim perfectio naturae conditae et naturae glorificatae, ita etiam perfectio universi est duplex: una secundum statum huius mutabilitatis; altera secundum statum futurae novitatis. Plantae autem et animalia sunt de perfectione eius secundum statum istum: non autem secundum statum novitatis illius, cum ordinem ad eam non habeant.

AD QUARTUM dicendum quod, quamvis animalia et plantae quantum ad quaedam alia sint nobiliora quam ipsa elementa, tamen quantum ad ordinem incorruptionis elementa sunt nobiliora, ut ex dictis patet.

AD QUINTUM dicendum quod naturalis appetitus ad perpetuitatem quae inest animalibus et plantis, est accipiendus secundum ordinem ad motum caeli, ut scilicet tantum in esse permaneant quantum motus caeli durabit: non enim potest appetitus esse in effectu ut permaneat ultra causam suam. Et ideo si, cessante motu primi mobilis, plantae et animalia non remanent secundum speciem, non sequitur appetitum naturalem frustrari.

REPLY OBJ. 2: Neither animals nor plants nor any other bodies merited anything by their services to man, since they lack free-will. However, certain bodies are said to be rewarded insofar as man merited that those things should be renewed which are adapted to be renewed.

But plants and animals are not adapted to the renewal of incorruption, as stated above. Therefore, for this very reason man did not merit that they should be renewed, since no one can merit for another, or even for himself, that which another or himself is incapable of receiving. Hence, granted even that dumb animals merited by serving man, it would not follow that they are to be renewed.

REPLY OBJ. 3: Just as several kinds of perfection are ascribed to man (for there is the perfection of created nature and the perfection of glorified nature), so also there is a twofold perfection of the universe, one corresponding to this state of changeableness, the other corresponding to the state of a future renewal. Now plants and animals belong to its perfection according to the present state, and not according to the state of this renewal, since they are not capable thereof.

REPLY OBJ. 4: Although animals and plants as to certain other respects are more noble than the elements, the elements are more noble in relation to incorruption, as explained above (Q. 74, A. 1).

REPLY OBJ. 5: The natural desire to be forever that is in animals and plants must be understood in reference to the movement of the heaven, so that they may continue in being as long as the movement of the heaven lasts: since there cannot be an appetite for an effect to last longer than its cause. Therefore, if at the cessation of movement in the first movable body, plants, and animals cease as to their species, it does not follow that the natural appetite is frustrated.

Question 92

The Vision of the Divine Essence in Reference to the Blessed

Consequenter considerandum est de his quae spectant ad beatos post iudicium generale. Et primo, de visione eorum respectu divinae essentiae, in qua eorum beatitudo principaliter consistit; secundo, de eorum beatitudine et eorum mansionibus; tertio, de modo quo se erga damnatos habebunt; quarto, de dotibus ipsorum, quae in beatitudine eorum continentur; quinto, de aureolis, quibus eorum beatitudo perficitur et decoratur.

Circa primum quaeruntur tria.

Primo: utrum sancti videbunt Deum per essentiam.

Secundo: utrum videbunt eum oculo corporali.

Tertio: utrum, videndo eum, videant omnia quae Deus videt.

In the next place we must consider matters concerning the blessed after the general judgment. We shall consider: (1) Their vision of the divine essence, wherein their bliss chiefly consists; (2) Their bliss and their mansions; (3) Their relations with the damned; (4) Their gifts, which are contained in their bliss; (5) The crowns which perfect and adorn their happiness.

Under the first head there are three points of inquiry:

(1) Whether the saints will see God in his essence?

(2) Whether they will see him with the eyes of the body?

(3) Whether, in seeing God, they will see all that God sees?

Article 1

Whether the Human Intellect Can Attain to the Vision of God in His Essence?

Ad primum sic proceditur. Videtur quod intellectus humanus non possit pervenire ad videndum Deum per essentiam. Quia Ioan. 1, [18] dicitur: *Deum nemo vidit unquam.* Et exponit Chrysostomus quod *nec ipsae caelestes essentiae, ipsa dico Cherubim et Seraphim, ipsum ut est nunquam videre potuerunt.* Sed hominibus non promittitur nisi aequalitas angelorum: Matth. 22, [30], *erunt sicut angeli Dei in caelo:* Ergo nec sancti in patria Deum per essentiam videbunt.

Praeterea, Dionysius sic argumentatur in 1 cap. *de Div. Nom.*: cognitio non est nisi exsistentium. Omne autem existens finitum est: cum sit in aliquo genere determinatum. Et sic Deus, cum infinitus sit, est *super omnia exsistentia.* Ergo eius non est cognitio, sed est super cognitionem.

Praeterea, Dionysius, in 1 cap. *de Mystica Theologia,* ostendit quod perfectissimus modus quo intellectus noster Deo coniungi potest, est inquantum coniungitur ei ut ignoto. Sed illud quod est visum per essentiam, non est ignotum. Ergo impossibile est quod intellectus noster per essentiam Deum videat.

Praeterea, Dionysius, in Epistola *ad Caium Monachum,* dicit quod *superpositae Dei tenebrae,* quas abundantiam lucis appellat, *cooperiuntur omni lumini, et absconduntur omni cognitioni: et si aliquis videns Deum intellexit quod vidit, non ipsum vidit, sed aliquid eorum*

Objection 1: It would seem that the human intellect cannot attain to the vision of God in his essence. For it is written: *no man has seen God at any time* (John 1:18); and Chrysostom in his commentary says that *not even the heavenly essences, namely, the Cherubim and Seraphim, have ever been able to see him as he is* (*Homilies on John* 14). Now, only equality with the angels is promised to men: *they shall be as the angels of God in heaven* (Matt 22:30). Therefore, neither will the saints in heaven see God in his essence.

Obj. 2: Further, Dionysius argues thus (*On the Divine Names* 1): knowledge is only of existing things. Now whatever exists is finite, since it is confined to a certain genus: and therefore God, since he is infinite, is *above all existing things.* Therefore, there is no knowledge of him, but he is above all knowledge.

Obj. 3: Further, Dionysius (*Mystical Theology* 1) shows that the most perfect way in which our intellect can be united to God is when it is united to him as to something unknown. Now that which is seen in its essence is not unknown. Therefore, it is impossible for our intellect to see God in his essence.

Obj. 4: Further, Dionysius says (*Epistle to Gaius*) that *the darkness*—for thus he calls the abundance of light—*which screens God is impervious to all illuminations, and hidden from all knowledge: and if anyone in seeing God understood what he saw, he saw not God himself, but one of*

quae sunt eius. Ergo nullus intellectus creatus poterit Deum per essentiam videre.

PRAETEREA, sicut Dionysius dicit, in Epistola *ad Hierotheum: invisibilis quidem Deus est existens propter excedentem claritatem.* Sed claritas eius, sicut excedit intellectum hominis in via, ita excedit intellectum hominis in patria. Ergo, sicut est invisibilis in via, ita erit invisibilis in patria.

PRAETEREA, cum intelligibile sit perfectio intellectus, oportet esse proportionem aliquam inter intelligibile et intellectum, visibile et visum. Sed non est accipere proportionem aliquam inter intellectum nostrum et essentiam divinam: cum in infinitum distent. Ergo intellectus noster non potest pertingere ad essentiam divinam videndam.

PRAETEREA, plus distat Deus ab intellectu nostro quam intelligibile creatum a sensu. Sed sensus nullo modo potest pertingere ad creaturam spiritualem videndam. Ergo nec intellectus noster poterit pertingere ad videndam divinam essentiam.

PRAETEREA, quandocumque intellectus intelligit aliquid in actu, oportet quod informetur per similitudinem intellecti, quae est principium intellectualis operationis in tale obiectum determinatae, sicut calor est principium calefactionis. Si ergo intellectus noster Deum intelligat, oportet quod fiat per aliquam similitudinem informantem ipsum intellectum. Hoc autem non potest esse ipsa divina essentia: quia formae et formati oportet esse unum esse; divina autem essentia ab intellectu nostro differt secundum essentiam et esse. Ergo oportet quod forma qua informatur intellectus noster intelligendo Deum, sit aliqua similitudo impressa a Deo in intellectum nostrum. Sed similitudo illa, cum sit quid creatum, non potest ducere in Dei cognitionem nisi sicut effectus in causam. Ergo impossibile est ut intellectus noster Deum videat nisi per effectum ipsius. Sed visio Dei quae est per effectus, non est visio Dei per essentiam. Ergo intellectus noster non poterit Deum per essentiam videre.

PRAETEREA, divina essentia magis distat ab intellectu nostro quam quicumque angelus vel intelligentia. Sed, sicut dicit Avicenna, in sua *Metaphysica, intelligentiam esse in nostro intellectu non est essentiam intelligentiae esse in intellectu* (quia sic scientia quam de intelligentiis habemus, esset substantia et non accidens): *sed hoc est impressionem intelligentiae esse in nostro intellectu.* Ergo et Deus non est in intellectu nostro, ut intelligatur a nobis, nisi inquantum impressio eius est in intellectu. Sed illa impressio non potest ducere in cognitionem divinae essentiae: quia, cum in infinitum distet a divina essentia, degenerat in aliam speciem; multo amplius quam si species albi degeneraret in speciem nigri. Ergo, sicut ille in cuius visu species albi degenerat in speciem nigri propter indispositionem organi, non dicitur videre album; ita

those things that are his. Therefore, no created intellect will be able to see God in his essence.

OBJ. 5: Further, according to Dionysius (*Epistle to Hierotheus*) *God is invisible on account of his surpassing glory.* Now his glory surpasses the human intellect in heaven even as on the way. Therefore, since he is invisible on the way, so will he be in heaven.

OBJ. 6: Further, since the intelligible object is the perfection of the intellect, there must be proportion between intelligible and intellect, as between the visible object and the sight. But there is no possible proportion between our intellect and the divine essence, since an infinite distance separates them. Therefore, our intellect will be unable to attain to the vision of the divine essence.

OBJ. 7: Further, God is more distant from our intellect than the created intelligible is from our senses. But the senses can in no way attain to the sight of a spiritual creature. Therefore, neither will our intellect be able to attain to the vision of the divine essence.

OBJ. 8: Further, whenever the intellect understands something actually it needs to be informed with the likeness of the object understood, which likeness is the principle of the intellectual operation terminating in that object, even as heat is the principle of heating. Accordingly, if our intellect understands God, this must be by means of some likeness informing the intellect itself. Now this cannot be the very essence of God, since form and thing informed must have one being, while the divine essence differs from our intellect in essence and being. Therefore, the form whereby our intellect is informed in understanding God must be a likeness impressed by God on our intellect. But this likeness, being something created, cannot lead to the knowledge of God except as an effect leads to the knowledge of its cause. Therefore, it is impossible for our intellect to see God except through his effect. But to see God through his effect is not to see him in his essence. Therefore, our intellect will be unable to see God in his essence.

OBJ. 9: Further, the divine essence is more distant from our intellect than any angel or intelligence. Now according to Avicenna (*Metaphysics* 3), *the existence of an intelligence in our intellect does not imply that its essence is in our intellect*, because in that case our knowledge of the intelligence would be a substance and not an accident, *but that its likeness is impressed on our intellect.* Therefore, neither is God in our intellect to be understood by us, except insofar as an impression of him is in our intellect. But this impression cannot lead to the knowledge of the divine essence, for since it is infinitely distant from the divine essence, it degenerates to another image much more than if the image of a white thing were to degenerate to the image of a black thing. Therefore, just as a person in whose sight the image of a white thing degenerates to the image of a black thing,

nec intellectus noster, qui solum per huiusmodi impressionem Deum intelligit, eum per essentiam poterit videre.

PRAETEREA, *in rebus separatis a materia idem est intelligens, et quod intelligitur*: ut patet in III *de Anima*. Sed Deus est maxime a materia separatus. Cum ergo intellectus qui est creatus, non possit ad hoc pertingere ut fiat essentia increata, non poterit esse quod intellectus noster Deum per essentiam videat.

PRAETEREA, omne illud quod videtur per essentiam, de eo scitur quid est. Sed de Deo intellectus noster non potest videre *quid est*, sed solum *quid non est*: sicut dicit Dionysius, et Damascenus. Ergo intellectus noster Deum per essentiam videre non potest.

PRAETEREA, *omne infinitum, inquantum infinitum, est ignotum*. Sed Deus est modis omnibus infinitus. Ergo est omnino ignotus. Ergo per essentiam ab intellectu creato videri non poterit.

PRAETEREA, Augustinus dicit, in libro *de Videndo Deo* 10: *Deus est natura invisibilis*. Sed ea quae insunt Deo per naturam, non possunt aliter se habere. Ergo non potest esse quod per essentiam videatur.

PRAETEREA, omne quod alio modo est et alio modo videtur, non videtur secundum id quod est. Sed Deus alio modo est, et alio modo videtur a sanctis in patria: est enim per modum suum, sed videbitur a sanctis per modum eorum. Ergo non videbitur a sanctis secundum id quod est. Et sic non videbitur per essentiam.

PRAETEREA, illud quod per medium videtur, non videtur per essentiam. Sed Deus in patria videbitur per medium, quod est lumen gloriae: ut patet in Psalmo [35, 10], *in lumine tuo videbimus lumen*. Ergo non videbitur per essentiam.

PRAETEREA, Deus in patria videbitur *facie ad faciem*, ut dicitur I Cor. 13, [12]. Sed hominem quem videmus facie ad faciem, videmus per similitudinem. Ergo Deus in patria videbitur per similitudinem. Et sic non per essentiam.

SED CONTRA: Est quod dicitur I Cor. 13, [12]: *videmus nunc per speculum in aenigmate: tunc autem facie ad faciem*. Sed id quod videtur facie ad faciem, videtur per essentiam. Ergo Deus per essentiam videbitur a sanctis in patria.

PRAETEREA, I Ioan. 3,. [2]: *cum apparuerit, similes ei erimus, et videbimus eum sicuti est*. Ergo videbimus Deum per essentiam.

PRAETEREA, I Cor. 15, super illud [v. 24], *cum tradiderit regnum Deo et Patri*, dicit. Glossa: *ubi*, scilicet in patria, *essentia Patris et Filii et Spiritus Sancti videbitur: quod solum mundis cordibus dabitur, quae est summa beatitudo*. Ergo beati Deum per essentiam videbunt.

on account of an indisposition in the organ, is not said to see a white thing, so neither will our intellect be able to see God in his essence, since it understands God only by means of this impression.

OBJ. 10: Further, *in things devoid of matter that which understands is the same as that which is understood* (*On the Soul* 3). Now God is supremely devoid of matter. Since, then, our intellect, which is created, cannot attain to be an uncreated essence, it is impossible for our intellect to see God in his essence.

OBJ. 11: Further, whatever is seen in its essence is known as to what it is. But our intellect cannot know of God *what he is*, but only *what he is not*, as Dionysius (*On the Heavenly Hierarchies* 2) and Damascene (*On the Orthodox Faith* 1) declare. Therefore, our intellect will be unable to see God in his essence.

OBJ. 12: Further, *every infinite thing, as such, is unknown*. But God is in every way infinite. Therefore, he is altogether unknown. Therefore, it will be impossible for him to be seen in his essence by a created intellect.

OBJ. 13: Further, Augustine says (*On Seeing God* 147): *God is by nature invisible*. Now that which is in God by nature cannot be otherwise. Therefore, it is impossible for him to be seen in his essence.

OBJ. 14: Further, whatever is in one way and is seen in another way is not seen as it is. Now God is one way and will be seen in another way by the saints in heaven: for he is according to his own mode, but will be seen by the saints according to their mode. Therefore, he will not be seen by the saints as he is, and thus will not be seen in his essence.

OBJ. 15: Further, that which is seen through a medium is not seen in its essence. Now God will be seen in heaven through a medium, which is the light of glory, according to Psalm 35:10, *in thy light we shall see light*. Therefore, he will not be seen in his essence.

OBJ. 16: Further, in heaven God will be seen *face to face*, according to 1 Corinthians 13:12. Now when we see a man face to face, we see him through his likeness. Therefore, in heaven God will be seen through his likeness, and consequently not in his essence.

ON THE CONTRARY, It is written: *we see now through a glass in a dark manner, but then face to face* (1 Cor 13:12). Now that which is seen face to face is seen in its essence. Therefore, God will be seen in his essence by the saints in heaven.

FURTHER, It is written: *when he shall appear we shall be like to him, because we shall see him as he is* (1 John 3:2). Therefore, we shall see him in his essence.

FURTHER, A Gloss on 1 Corinthians 15:24: *when he shall have delivered up the kingdom to God and the Father*, says: *where*, i.e., in heaven, *the essence of Father, Son, and Holy Spirit shall be seen: this is given to the clean of heart alone and is the highest bliss*. Therefore, the blessed will see God in his essence.

PRAETEREA, Ioan. 14, [21] dicitur: *si quis diligit me, diligetur d Patre meo, et ego diligam eum et manifestabo ei meipsum.* Sed illud quod manifestatur, essentialiter videtur. Ergo Deus a sanctis in patria essentialiter videbitur.

PRAETEREA, Exod. 33, super illud [v. 20], *non videbit me homo et vivet*, Gregorius improbat opinionem illorum qui dicebant quod *in illa regione beatitudinis Deus in claritate sua conspici potest, sed in natura videri non potest, quia aliud non est eius claritas et eius natura.* Sed natura eius est essentia eius. Ergo videbitur per essentiam suam.

PRAETEREA, sanctarum desiderium non potest omnino frustrari. Sed sanctorum desiderium commune est ut Deum per essentiam videant: ut patet Exod. 33, [18], *ostende mihi gloriam tuam*, et in Psalmo [79, 20], *ostende faciem tuam et salvi erimus*; et Ioan. 14, [8], *ostende nobis Patrem et sufficit nobis.* Ergo sancti per essentiam Deum videbunt.

RESPONDEO dicendum quod, sicut secundum fidem ponimus finem ultimum humanae vitae esse visionem Dei, ita philosophi posuerunt ultimam hominis felicitatem esses intelligere substantias a materia separatas secundum esse. Et ideo circa hanc quaestionem eadem difficultas et diversitas invenitur apud philosophos et apud theologos. Quidam enim philosophi posuerunt quod intellectus noster possibilis nunquam potest ad hoc pervenire ut intelligat substantias separatas: sicut Alpharabius in fine suae *Ethicae.*; quamvis contrarium dixerit in libro *de Intellectu*, ut Commentator refert, in III *de Anima.* Et similiter quidam theologi posuerunt quod intellectus humanus nunquam potest ad hoc pervenire ut Deum per essentiam videat. Et utrosque ad hoc movet distantia inter intellectum nostrum et essentiam divinam, vel alias substantias separatas. Cum enim intellectus in actu sit quodammodo unum cum intelligibili in actu, videtur difficile quod intellectus creatus aliquo modo fiat essentia increata. Unde Chrysostomus dicit: *quomodo creabile videt increabile?* Et maior difficultas in hoc est illis qui ponunt intellectum possibilem esse generabilem et corruptibilem, utpote virtutem a corpore dependentem, non solum respectu visionis divinae, sed respectu visionis quarumcumque substantiarum separatarum.

Sed haec positio omnino stare non potest. Primo, quia repugnat auctoritati Scripturae canonicae: ut Augustinus dicit, in libro *de Videndo Deo.* Secundo quia, cum intelligere sit maxime propria operatio hominis, oportet quod secundum eam assignetur sibi sua beatitudo, cum haec operatio in ipso perfecta fuerit. Cum autem perfectio intelligentis, inquantum huiusmodi, sit ipsum intelligibile; si in perfectissima operatione intellectus homo non perveniat ad videndam essentiam divinam, sed aliquid aliud, oportebit dicere quod aliquid aliud sit beati-

FURTHER, It is written: *he that loves me shall be loved of my Father; and I will love him, and will manifest myself to him* (John 14:21). Now that which is manifested is seen in its essence. Therefore, God will be seen in his essence by the saints in heaven.

FURTHER, Gregory, commenting on Exodus 33:20: *man shall not see me and live*, disapproves of the opinion of those who said that *in this abode of bliss God can be seen in his glory but not in his nature; for his glory differs not from his nature* (Morals on Job 18). But his nature is his essence. Therefore, he will be seen in his essence.

FURTHER, The desire of the saints cannot be altogether frustrated. Now the common desire of the saints is to see God in his essence, according to Exodus 33:13: *show me thy glory*; Psalm 79:20: *show thy face and we shall be saved*; and John 14:8: *show us the Father and it is enough for us.* Therefore, the saints will see God in his essence.

I ANSWER THAT, Even as we hold by faith that the last end of man's life is to see God, so the philosophers maintained that man's ultimate happiness is to understand immaterial substances according to their being. Hence in reference to this question we find that philosophers and theologians encounter the same difficulty and the same difference of opinion. For some philosophers held that our passive intellect can never come to understand separate substances. Thus Alpharabius expresses himself at the end of his *Ethics*, although he says the contrary in his book *On the Intellect*, as the Commentator attests (On the Soul 3). In like manner, certain theologians held that the human intellect can never attain to the vision of God in his essence. On either side, they were moved by the distance which separates our intellect from the divine essence and from separate substances. For since the intellect in act is somewhat one with the intelligible object in act, it would seem difficult to understand how the created intellect is made to be an uncreated essence. Wherefore Chrysostom says (*Homilies on John* 14): *how can the creature see the uncreated?* Those who hold the passive intellect to be the subject of generation and corruption, as being a power dependent on the body, encounter a still greater difficulty not only as regards the vision of God but also as regards the vision of any separate substances.

But this opinion is altogether untenable. First, because it is in contradiction to the authority of canonical scripture, as Augustine declares (*On Seeing God* 147). Second, because, since understanding is an operation most proper to man, it follows that his happiness must be held to consist in that operation when perfected in him. Now since the perfection of an intelligent being as such is the intelligible object, if in the most perfect operation of his intellect man does not attain to the vision of the divine essence, but to something else, we shall be forced to conclude that something other

ficans ipsum hominem quam Deus. Et cum ultima perfectio cuiuslibet sit in coniunctione ad suum principium, sequitur ut aliquid aliud sit principium effectivum hominis quam Deus. Quod est absurdum secundum nos. Et similiter est absurdum apud philosophos qui ponunt animas nostras a substantiis separatis emanare ut in fine eas possimus intelligere. Unde oportet ponere secundum nos, quod intellectus noster quandoque perveniat ad videndam essentiam divinam; et secundum philosophos, quod perveniat ad videndam essentiam substantiarum separatarum.

Quomodo autem hoc possit accidere, restat investigandum. Quidam enim dixerunt, ut Alpharabius et Avempace, quod ex hoc ipso quod intellectus noster intelligit quaecumque intelligibilia, pertingit ad videndam essentiam substantiae separatae. Et ad hoc ostendendum procedunt duobus modis. Quorum primus est quod, sicut natura speciei non diversificatur in diversis individuis nisi secundum quod coniungitur principiis individuantibus, ita forma intellecta hominis non diversificatur apud me et te nisi secundum quod coniungitur diversis formis imaginabilibus.

Et ideo, quando intellectus separat formam intellectam a formis imaginationis, remanet quidditas intellecta, quae est una et eadem apud diversos intelligentes. Et huiusmodi est quidditas substantiae separatae. Et ideo, quando intellectus noster pervenit ad summam abstractionem quidditatis intelligibilis cuiuscumque, intelligit per hoc quidditatem substantiae separatae quae est ei similis. Secundus modus est quia intellectus noster natus est abstrahere quidditatem ab omnibus intelligibilibus habentibus quidditatem. Si ergo quidditas quam abstrahit ab hoc singulari habente quidditatem, sit quidditas non habens quidditatem, intelligendo eam intelliget quidditatem substantiae separatae quae est talis dispositionis: eo quod substantiae separatae sunt quidditates subsistentes non habentes quidditates; quidditas enim simplicis est ipsum simplex, ut Avicenna dicit. Si autem quidditas abstracta ab hoc particulari sensibili sit quidditas habens quidditatem, ergo quidditatem illam intellectus natus est abstrahere. Et ita, cum non sit abire in infinitum, erit devenire ad quidditatem non habentem quidditatem, per quam intelligitur quidditas separata.

Sed iste modus non videtur esse sufficiens. Primo, quia quidditas substantiae materialis quam intellectus abstrahit, non est unius rationis cum quidditatibus substantiarum separatarum. Et ita per hoc quod intellectus noster abstrahit quidditates rerum materialium et cognoscit eas, non sequitur quod cognoscat quidditatem substantiae separatae: et praecipue divinam essentiam, quae maxime est alterius rationis ab omni quidditate creata. Secundo quia, dato quod esset unius rationis,

than God is the object of man's happiness: and since the ultimate perfection of a thing consists in its being united to its principle, it follows that something other than God is the effective principle of man, which is absurd, according to us, and also according to the philosophers who maintain that our souls emanate from the separate substances, so that finally we may be able to understand these substances. Consequently, according to us, it must be asserted that our intellect will at length attain to the vision of the divine essence, and according to the philosophers, that it will attain to the vision of separate substances.

It remains, then, to examine how this may come about. For some, like Alpharabius and Avempace, held that from the very fact that our intellect understands any intelligible objects whatever, it attains to the vision of a separate substance. To prove this they employ two arguments. The first is that just as the specific nature is not diversified in various individuals, except as united to various individuating principles, so the idea understood is not diversified in me and you, except insofar as it is united to various imaginary forms.

Consequently, when the intellect separates the idea understood from the imaginary forms, there remains a quiddity understood, which is one and the same in the various persons understanding it, and such is the quiddity of a separate substance. Hence, when our intellect attains to the supreme abstraction of any intelligible quiddity, it thereby understands the quiddity of the separate substance that is similar to it. The second argument is that our intellect has a natural aptitude to abstract the quiddity from all intelligible objects having a quiddity. If, then, the quiddity which it abstracts from some particular individual be a quiddity without a quiddity, the intellect by understanding it understands the quiddity of the separate substance which has a like disposition, since separate substances are subsisting quiddities without quiddities; for the quiddity of a simple thing is the simple thing itself, as Avicenna says (*Metaphysics* iii). On the other hand, if the quiddity abstracted from this particular sensible be a quiddity that has a quiddity, it follows that the intellect has a natural aptitude to abstract this quiddity, and consequently since we cannot go on indefinitely, we shall come to some quiddity without a quiddity, and this is what we understand by a separate quiddity.

But this reasoning is seemingly inconclusive. First, because the quiddity of the material substance, which the intellect abstracts, is not of the same nature as the quiddity of the separate substances, and consequently from the fact that our intellect abstracts the quiddities of material substances and knows them, it does not follow that it knows the quiddity of a separate substance, especially of the divine essence, which more than any other is of a different nature from any created quiddity. Second, because granted that it

tamen, cognita quidditate rei compositae, non cognosceretur quidditas substantiae separatae nisi secundum genus remotissimum, quod est substantia. Haec autem cognitio est imperfecta, nisi deveniatur ad propria rei: qui enim cognoscit hominem solum inquantum est animal, non cognoscit eum nisi secundum quid et in potentia; et multo minus cognoscit eum si non cognoscat nisi substantiae naturam in ipso. Unde sic cognoscere Deum vel alias substantias separatas non est videre essentiam divinam vel quidditatem substantiae separatae: sed est cognoscere per effectum, et quasi *in speculo*.

Et ideo alius modus intelligendi substantias separatas ponitur ab Avicenna, in sua *Metaphysica*: scilicet quod substantiae separatae intelliguntur a nobis per intentiones suarum quidditatum, quae sunt quaedam earum similitudines, non abstractae ab eis, quia ipsaemet sunt immateriales, sed impressae ab eis in animabus nostris.

Sed hic modus etiam non videtur nobis sufficere ad visionem divinam quam quaerimus. Constat enim quod *omne quod recipitur in aliquo, est in eo per modum recipientis*. Et ideo similitudo divinae essentiae impressa ab ipsa in intellectu nostro, erit per modum nostri intellectus. Modus autem intellectus nostri deficiens est a perfecta receptione divinae similitudinis. Defectus autem perfectae similitudinis potest tot modis accidere quot modis dissimilitudo invenitur. Uno enim modo est deficiens similitudo quando participatur forma secundum eandem rationem speciei, sed non secundum eundem perfectionis modum: sicut est similitudo deficiens eius qui parum habet de albedine, ad illum qui multum habet.

Alio modo adhuc magis deficiens, quando non pervenitur ad eandem rationem speciei, sed tantum ad eandem rationem generis: sicut similitudo inter illum qui habet colorem citrinum, et illum qui habet colorem album. Alio modo adhuc magis deficiens, quando ad rationem eandem generis pertingit, sed solum secundum analogiam: sicut est similitudo albedinis ad hominem in eo quod utrumque est ens. Et hoc modo est deficiens omnis similitudo quae est in creatura recepta respectu divinae essentiae. Ad hoc autem quod visus cognoscat albedinem, oportet quod recipiatur in eo similitudo albedinis secundum rationem suae speciei (quamvis non secundum eundem modum essendi, quia habet alterius modi esse forma in sensu, et in re extra animam): si enim fieret in oculo forma citrini, non diceretur oculus videre albedinem. Et similiter ad hoc quod intellectus intelligat aliquam quidditatem, oportet quod fiat in eo similitudo eiusdem rationis secundum speciem: quamvis forte non sit idem modus essendi utrobique; non enim forma existens in intellectu vel sensu est principium cognitionis secundum modum essendi quem habet utrobique, sed secundum rationem in qua communicat cum re exteriori. Et ita patet quod per nullam similitudinem re-

be of the same nature, nevertheless the knowledge of a composite thing would not lead to the knowledge of a separate substance, except in the point of the most remote genus, namely substance: and such a knowledge is imperfect unless it reach to the properties of a thing. For to know a man only as an animal is to know him only in a restricted sense and potentially: and much less is it to know only the nature of substance in him. Hence to know God thus, or other separate substances, is not to see the essence of God or the quiddity of a separate substance, but to know him in his effect and as *in a mirror*.

For this reason Avicenna in his *Metaphysics* propounds another way of understanding separate substances: namely, that separate substances are understood by us by means of intentions of their quiddities, such intentions being images of their substances; not indeed abstracted therefrom, since they are immaterial, but impressed thereby on our souls.

But this way also seems inadequate to the divine vision which we seek. For it is agreed that *whatever is received into any thing is therein after the mode of the recipient*: and consequently the likeness of the divine essence impressed on our intellect will be according to the mode of our intellect: and the mode of our intellect falls short of a perfect reception of the divine likeness. Now the lack of perfect likeness may occur in as many ways, as unlikeness may occur. For in one way there is a deficient likeness, when the form is participated according to the same specific nature, but not in the same measure of perfection: such is the defective likeness in a subject that has little whiteness in comparison with one that has much.

In another way, the likeness is yet more defective when it does not attain to the same specific nature but only to the same generic nature: such is the likeness of an orange-colored or yellowish object in comparison with a white one. In another way, still more defective is the likeness when it does not attain to the same generic nature, but only to a certain analogy or proportion: such is the likeness of whiteness to man, in that each is a being: and in this way every likeness received into a creature is defective in comparison with the divine essence. Now in order that the sight know whiteness, it is necessary for it to receive the likeness of whiteness according to its specific nature, although not according to the same manner of being, because the form has a manner of being in the sense different from that which it has in the thing outside the soul: for if the form of yellowness were received into the eye, the eye would not be said to see whiteness. In like manner, in order that the intellect understand a quiddity, it is necessary for it to receive its likeness according to the same specific nature, although there may possibly not be the same manner of being on either side: for the form which is in the intellect or sense is not the principle of knowledge according to its manner of being on both sides, but according to its common ratio with the external object.

ceptam in intellectu creato potest Deus intelligi ita quod essentia eius videatur immediate. Unde etiam quidam, ponentes divinam essentiam per hunc modum videri, dixerunt quod ipsa essentia non videbitur, sed quidam, fulgor, quasi radius ipsius. Unde; nec iste modus sufficit ad visionem divinam quam quaerimus.

Et ideo accipiendus est alius modus, quem etiam quidam philosophi posuerunt, scilicet Alexander et Averroes, in III *de Anima*. Cum enim in qualibet cognitione sit necessaria aliqua forma qua res cognoscatur aut videatur, forma ista qua intellectus perficitur ad videndas substantias separatas, non est quidditas quam intellectus abstrahit a rebus compositis, ut dicebat prima opinio; neque aliqua impressio relicta a substantia separata in intellectu nostro, ut dicebat secunda; sed est ipsa substantia separata quae coniungitur intellectui nostro ut forma, ut ipsa sit quod intelligitur et quo intelligitur. Et quidquid sit de aliis substantiis separatis, tamen istum modum oportet nos accipere in visione Dei per essentiam: quia, quacumque alia forma informaretur intellectus noster, non posset per eam duci in essentiam divinam.

Quod quidem non debet intelligi quasi divina essentia sit vera forma intellectus nostri; vel quia ex ea et intellectu nostro efficiatur unum simpliciter, sicut in naturalibus ex forma et materia naturali: sed quia proportio essentiae divinae ad intellectum nostrum est sicut proportio formae ad materiam. Quandocumque enim aliqua duo quorum unum est altero perfectius, recipiuntur in eodem receptibili, proportio unius duorum ad alterum, scilicet magis perfecti ad minus perfectum, est sicut proportio formae ad materiam: sicut lux et color recipiuntur in diaphano, quorum lux se habet ad colorem sicut forma ad materiam. Et ita, cum in anima recipiatur lux intellectiva et ipsa divina essentia inhabitans, licet non per eundem modum, essentia divina se habebit ad intellectum sicut forma ad materiam.

Et quod hoc sufficiat ad hoc quod intellectus per divinam essentiam possit videre ipsam divinam essentiam, hoc modo potest ostendi. Sicut enim ex forma naturali qua aliquid habet esse, et materia efficitur unum ens simpliciter; ita ex forma qua intellectus intelligit, et ipso intellectu, fit unum in intelligendo. In rebus autem naturalibus res per se subsistens non potest esse forma alicuius materiae, si illa res habeat materiam partem sui: quia non potest esse ut materia sit forma alicuius. Sed si illa res per se subsistens sit forma tantum, nihil prohibet eam effici formam alicuius materiae, et fieri quo est ipsius compositi: sicut patet de anima. In intellectu autem oportet accipere ipsum intellectum in potentia quasi materiam, et speciem intelligibilem quasi formam, et intellectus in actu intelligens erit quasi compositum ex

Hence it is clear that by no likeness received in the created intellect can God be understood, so that his essence be seen immediately. And for this reason those who held the divine essence to be seen in this way alone said that the essence itself will not be seen, but a certain brightness, as it were a radiance thereof. Consequently, neither does this way suffice for the divine vision that we seek.

Therefore, we must take the other way, which also certain philosophers held, namely, Alexander and Averroes (*On the Soul* 3). For since in every knowledge some form is required whereby the object is known or seen, this form by which the intellect is perfected so as to see separate substances is neither a quiddity abstracted by the intellect from composite things, as the first opinion maintained, nor an impression left on our intellect by the separate substance, as the second opinion affirmed; but the separate substance itself united to our intellect as its form, so as to be both that which is understood, and that whereby it is understood. And whatever may be the case with other separate substances, we must nevertheless allow this to be our way of seeing God in his essence, because by whatever other form our intellect were informed, it could not be led thereby to the divine essence.

This, however, must not be understood as though the divine essence were in reality the form of our intellect, or as though from its conjunction with our intellect there resulted one being simply, as in natural things from the natural form and matter: but the meaning is that the proportion of the divine essence to our intellect is as the proportion of form to matter. For whenever two things, one of which is the perfection of the other, are received into the same recipient, the proportion of one to the other, namely, of the more perfect to the less perfect, is as the proportion of form to matter: thus light and color are received into a transparent object, light being to color as form to matter. When, therefore, intellectual light is received into the soul together with the indwelling divine essence, though they are not received in the same way, the divine essence will be to the intellect as form to matter.

That this suffices for the intellect to be able to see the divine essence by the divine essence itself may be shown as follows. As from the natural form (whereby a thing has being) and matter, there results one thing simply, so from the form whereby the intellect understands, and the intellect itself, there results one thing intelligibly. Now in natural things a self-subsistent thing cannot be the form of any matter, if that thing has matter as one of its parts, since it is impossible for matter to be the form of a thing. But if this self-subsistent thing be a mere form, nothing hinders it from being the form of some matter and becoming that whereby the composite itself is as instanced in the soul. Now in the intellect we must take the intellect itself in potentiality as matter, and the intelligible species as form; so that the intellect actually understanding will be the com-

utroque. Unde, si sit aliqua res per se subsistens quae non habeat aliquid in se praeter id quod est intelligibile in ipsa, talis res poterit esse forma qua intelligitur. Res autem quaelibet est intelligibilis secundum id quod habet de actu, non secundum id quod habet de potentia, ut patet in IX *Metaphys.*: et huius signum est quod oportet formam intelligibilem abstrahere a materia et ab omnibus proprietatibus materiae. Et ideo, cum divina essentia sit actus putus, poterit esse forma qua intellectus intelligit. Et haec erit visio beatificans. Et ideo Magister dicit quod unio animae ad corpus est quoddam *exemplum beatae unionis qua spiritus unietur Deo.*

AD PRIMUM ergo dicendum quod auctoritas illa potest tripliciter exponi: ut patet per Augustinum, in libro *de Videndo Deo.* Uno modo, ut excludatur visio corporalis, qua nemo vidit vel visurus est Deum in essentia sua. Alio modo, ut excludatur visio intellectualis Dei per essentiam ab his qui in ista mortali carne vivunt. Tertio modo, ut excludatur visio comprehensionis ab intellectu creato. Et sic intelligit Chrysostomus. Unde subdit: *notitiam hic dicit* Evangelista *certissimam considerationem et comprehensionem tantam quantam habet Pater de Filio,* Et hic est Evangelistae intellectus: unde subdit: *Unigenitus qui est,* etc., per comprehensivam visionem volens probare Filium esse Deum.

AD SECUNDUM dicendum quod, sicut Deus excedit omnia existentia quae habent esse determinatum, per essentiam suam infinitam, ita cognitio sua, qua cognoscit, est super omnem cognitionem. Unde quae est proportio cognitionis nostrae ad entia creata, ea est proportio cognitionis divinae ad essentiam suam. Ad cognitionem autem duo concurrunt: scilicet cognoscens, et quo cognoscitur. Visio autem illa qua Deum per essentiam videbimus, est eadem cum visione qua Deus se videt, ex parte eius quo videtur: quia sicut ipse se videt per essentiam suam, ita et nos videbimus. Sed ex parte cognoscentis invehitur diversitas quae est inter intellectum divinum et nostrum. In cognoscendo autem id quod cognoscitur sequitur formam qua cognoscimus, quia per formam lapidis videmus lapidem: sed efficacia in cognoscendo sequitur virtutem cognoscentis, sicut qui habet visum fortem acutius videt. Et ideo in illa visione nos videbimus quod Deus videt, scilicet essentiam suam, sed non ita efficaciter.

AD TERTIUM dicendum quod Dionysius loquitur ibi de cognitione qua Deum in via cognoscimus per aliquam formam creatam, qua intellectus noster formatur ad eum videndum. Sed, sicut dicit Augustinus, *Deus omnem formam intellectus nostri subterfugit*: quia, quamcumque formam intellectus noster concipiat, illa forma non pertingit ad rationem divinae essentiae. Et ideo ipse non potest esse pervius intellectui nostro: sed per

posite, as it were, resulting from both. Hence if there be a self-subsistent thing that has nothing in itself besides that which is intelligible, such a thing can by itself be the form whereby the intellect understands. Now a thing is intelligible in respect of its actuality and not of its potentiality (*Metaphysics* ix): in proof of which an intelligible form needs to be abstracted from matter and from all the properties of matter. Therefore, since the divine essence is pure act, it will be possible for it to be the form whereby the intellect understands: and this will be the beatific vision. Hence the Master says (*Sentences* II, D. 1) that the union of the body with the soul is *an illustration of the blissful union of the spirit with God.*

REPLY OBJ. 1: The words quoted can be explained in three ways, according to Augustine (*On Seeing God* 147). In one way as excluding corporeal vision, whereby no one ever saw or will see God in his essence; second, as excluding intellectual vision of God in his essence from those who dwell in this mortal flesh; third, as excluding the vision of comprehension from a created intellect. It is thus that Chrysostom understands the saying. Hence he adds: *by seeing, the evangelist means a most clear perception, and such a comprehension as the Father has of the Son.* This also is the meaning of the evangelist, since he adds: *the Only-begotten Son who is in the bosom of the Father, he hath declared him*: his intention being to prove the Son to be God from his comprehending God.

REPLY OBJ. 2: Just as God, by his infinite essence, surpasses all existing things which have a determinate being, so his knowledge, whereby he knows, is above all knowledge. Wherefore as our knowledge is to our created essence, so is the divine knowledge to his infinite essence. Now two things contribute to knowledge: namely, the knower and the thing known. Again, the vision whereby we shall see God in his essence is the same whereby God sees himself, as regards that whereby he is seen, because as he sees himself in his essence, so shall we also see him. But as regards the knower there is the difference that is between the divine intellect and ours. Now in the order of knowledge the object known follows the form by which we know, since by the form of a stone we see a stone, whereas the efficacy of knowledge follows the power of the knower: thus he who has stronger sight sees more clearly. Consequently, in that vision we shall see the same thing that God sees, namely, his essence, but not so effectively.

REPLY OBJ. 3: Dionysius is speaking there of the knowledge whereby wayfarers know God by a created form, whereby our intellect is informed so as to see God. But as Augustine says (*On Seeing God* 147), *God evades every form of our intellect*, because whatever form our intellect conceive, that form is out of proportion to the divine essence. Hence he cannot be fathomed by our intellect: but our most perfect knowledge of him as wayfarers is to know that he

hoc eum perfectissime cognoscimus in statu viae quod scimus eum esse super omne id quod intellectus noster concipere potest; et sic ei coniungimur quasi ignoto. Sed in patria idipsum per formam quae est essentia sua videbimus, et coniungemur ei quasi noto.

AD QUARTUM dicendum quod *Deus lux est*, ut dicitur I Ioan. i, [5]. Lumen autem est impressio lucis in aliquo illuminato. Et quia essentia divina est alterius modi quam omnis similitudo ipsius impressa in intellectu, ideo dicit quod *divinae tenebrae cooperiuntur omni lumini*: quia scilicet essentia divina, quam *tenebras* vocat propter claritatis excessum, manet non demonstrata per impressionem intellectus nostri. Et per hoc sequitur quod *abscondatur omni cognitioni*. Et ideo quicumque videntium Deum aliquid mente concipit, hoc non est Deus, sed aliquid divinorum effectuum.

AD QUINTUM dicendum quod claritas Dei, quamvis excedat omnem formam qua nunc intellectus informatur, non tamen excedit ipsam essentiam divinam, quae erit quasi forma intellectus nostri in patria. Et ideo, licet nunc sit invisibilis, tamen tunc erit visibilis.

AD SEXTUM dicendum quod, quamvis finiti ad infinitum non possit esse proportio, quia excessus infiniti supra finitum non est determinatus, potest tamen esse inter ea *proportionalitas*, quae est similitudo proportionum: sicut enim finitum aequatur alicui finito, ita infinito infinitum. Ad hoc autem quod aliquid totaliter cognoscatur, quandoque oportet esse proportionem inter cognoscentem et cognitum: quia porter virtutem cognoscentis adaequari cognoscibilitati rei cognitae; aequalitas autem proportio quaedam est. Sed quandoque cognoscibilitas rei excedit virtutem cognoscentis, sicut cum nos cognoscimus Deum: aut e converso, sicut cum ipse cognoscit creaturas. Et tunc non oportet esse proportionem inter cognoscentem et cognitum, sed *proportionalitatem* tantum: ut scilicet, sicut se habet cognoscens ad cognoscendum, ita se habeat cognoscibile ad hoc quod cognoscatur. Et talis proportionalitas sufficit ad hoc quod infinitum cognoscatur a finito, et e converso.

Vel dicendum quod proportio secundum primam nominis institutionem significat habitudinem quantitatis ad quantitatem secundum aliquem determinatum excessum vel adaequationem: sed ulterius est translatum ad significandum omnem habitudinem cuiuscumque ad aliud. Et per hunc modum dicimus quod materia debet esse proportionata ad formam. Et hoc modo nihil prohibet intellectum nostrum, quamvis sit finitus, dici proportionatum ad videndum essentiam divinam: non tamen ad comprehendendum eam; et hoc propter suam immensitatem.

AD SEPTIMUM dicendum quod duplex est similitudo et distantia. Una secundum convenientiam in natura. Et sic magis distat Deus ab intellectu creato quam in-

is above all that our intellect can conceive, and thus we are united to him as to something unknown. In heaven, however, we shall see him by a form which is his essence, and we shall be united to him as to something known.

REPLY OBJ. 4: *God is light* (John 1:9). Now illumination is the impression of light on an illuminated object. And since the divine essence is of a different mode from any likeness thereof impressed on the intellect, Dionysius says that the *divine darkness is impervious to all illumination*, namely, because the divine essence, which he calls *darkness* on account of its surpassing brightness, remains undemonstrated by the impression on our intellect, and consequently is *hidden from all knowledge*. Therefore, if anyone in seeing God conceives something in his mind, this is not God but one of God's effects.

REPLY OBJ. 5: Although the glory of God surpasses any form by which our intellect is informed now, it does not surpass the divine essence, which will be the form of our intellect in heaven: and therefore although it is invisible now, it will be visible then.

REPLY OBJ. 6: Although there can be no proportion between finite and infinite, since the excess of the infinite over the finite is indeterminate, there can be *proportionality*, or a likeness to proportion, between them: for as a finite thing is equal to some finite thing, so is an infinite thing equal to an infinite thing. Now in order that a thing be known totally, it is sometimes necessary that there be proportion between knower and known, because the power of the knower needs to be adequate to the knowableness of the thing known, and equality is a kind of proportion. Sometimes, however, the knowableness of the thing surpasses the power of the knower, as when we know God, or conversely when he knows creatures: and then there is no need for proportion between knower and known, but only for *proportionality*; namely, so that as the knower is to the knowable object, so is the knowable object to the fact of its being known: and this proportionateness suffices for the infinite to be known by the finite, or conversely.

We may also reply that proportion, according to the strict sense in which it is employed, signifies a ratio of quantity to quantity based on a certain fixed excess or equality; but is further transferred to denote any ratio of any one thing to another; and in this sense we say that matter should be proportionate to its form. In this sense nothing hinders our intellect, although finite, being described as proportionate to the vision of the divine essence; but not to the comprehension thereof, on account of its immensity.

REPLY OBJ. 7: Likeness and distance are twofold. One is according to agreement in nature; and thus God is more distant from the created intellect than the created intelli-

telligibile creatum a sensu. Alia secundum proportionalitatem. Et sic est e converso: quia sensus non est proportionatus ad cognoscendum aliquod immateriale, sed intellectus est proportionata ad cognoscendum quodcumque immateriale. Et haec similitudo requiritur ad cognitionem, non autem prima: quia constat quod intellectus intelligens lapidem non est similis ei in naturali esse. Sicut etiam visus apprehendit mel rubeum et fel rubeum, quamvis non apprehendat mel dulce: fellis enim rubedo magis convenit cum, melle inquantum est visibile, quam dulcedo mellis cum melle.

AD OCTAVUM dicendum quod in visione qua Deus per essentiam videbitur, ipsa divina essentia erit quasi forma intellectus qua intelligit. Nec oportet quod efficiantur unum secundum esse simpliciter: sed solum quod fiant unum quantum pertinet ad actum intelligenda

AD NONUM dicendum quod dictum Avicennae quantum ad hoc non sustinemus: quia ei etiam ab aliis philosophis in hoc contradicitur. Nisi forte velimus dicere quod Avicenna intelligit de cognitione substantiarum separatarum secundum quod cognoscuntur per habitus scientiarum speculativarum, et similitudinibus aliarum rerum. Unde hoc introducit ad ostendendum quod scientia non est in nobis substantia, sed accidens.

Et tamen divina essentia, quamvis plus distet secundum proprietatem naturae suae ab intellectu nostro quam substantia angeli, tamen plus habet de ratione intelligibilitatis: quia est actus purus, cui non admiscetur aliquid de potentia; quod non contingit in aliis substantiis separatis. Nec illa cognitio qua Deum per essentiam videbimus, ex parte eius quod videbitur erit in genere accidentis: sed solum quantum ad actum ipsius intelligentis, qui non erit ipsa substantia intelligentis vel intellecti.

AD DECIMUM dicendum quod substantia separata a materia intelligit se et intelligit alia: et utroque modo potest verificari auctoritas inducta. Cum enim ipsa essentia substantiae separatae sit per seipsam intelligibilis in actu, eo quod est a materia separata, constat quod, quando substantia separata intelligit se, quod omnino est idem intelligens et intellectum: non enim intelligit se per aliquam intentionem abstractam a se, sicut nos intelligimus res materiales. Et hic videtur esse intellectus Philosophi in III de Anima, ut patet per Commentatorem ibidem.

Secundum autem quod intelligit res alias, intellectum in actu fit unum cum intellectu in actu, inquantum forma intellecti fit forma intellectus inquantum est intellectus in actu, non quod sit ipsamet essentia intellectus: ut Avicenna probat, in VI de Naturalibus, quia essentia intellectus manet una sub duabus formis, secundum quod intelligit res duas successive, ad modum quo materia pri-

gible is from the sense. The other is according to proportionality; and thus it is the other way about, for sense is not proportionate to the knowledge of the immaterial, as the intellect is proportionate to the knowledge of any immaterial object whatsoever. It is this likeness and not the former that is requisite for knowledge, for it is clear that the intellect understanding a stone is not like it in its natural being; thus also the sight apprehends red honey and red gall, though it does not apprehend sweet honey, for the redness of gall is more becoming to honey as visible, than the sweetness of honey to honey.

REPLY OBJ. 8: In the vision wherein God will be seen in his essence, the divine essence itself will be the form, as it were, of the intellect, by which it will understand: nor is it necessary for them to become one in being, but only to become one as regards the act of understanding.

REPLY OBJ. 9: We do not uphold the saying of Avicenna as regards the point at issue, for in this other philosophers also disagree with him. Unless, perhaps, we might say that Avicenna refers to the knowledge of separate substances insofar as they are known by the habits of speculative sciences and the likeness of other things. Hence he makes this statement in order to prove that in us knowledge is not a substance but an accident.

Nevertheless, although the divine essence is more distant, as to the property of its nature, from our intellect, than is the substance of an angel, it surpasses it in the point of intelligibility, since it is pure act without any admixture of potentiality, which is not the case with other separate substances. Nor will that knowledge whereby we shall see God in his essence be in the genus of accident as regards that whereby he will be seen, but only as regards the act of the one who understands him, for this act will not be the very substance either of the person understanding or of the thing understood.

REPLY OBJ. 10: A substance that is separate from matter understands both itself and other things; and in both cases the authority quoted can be verified. For since the very essence of a separate substance is of itself intelligible and actual, through being separate from matter, it is clear that when a separate substance understands itself, that which understands and that which is understood are absolutely identical, for it does not understand itself by an intention abstracted from itself, as we understand material objects. And this is apparently the meaning of the Philosopher as indicated by the Commentator (On the Soul 3).

But when it understands other things, the object actually understood becomes one with the intellect in act, insofar as the form of the object understood becomes the form of the intellect inasmuch as the intellect is in act; not that it becomes identified with the essence of the intellect, as Avicenna proves (De Naturalibus vi), because the essence of the intellect remains one under two forms whereby it under-

ma manet una sub diversis formis. Unde etiam Commentator, in III *de Anima*, comparat intellectum possibilem, quantum ad hoc, primae materiae. Et sic nullo modo sequitur quod intellectus noster videns Deum fiat ipsa essentia divina: sed quod ipsa essentia divina comparatur ad ipsum quasi perfectio et forma.

AD UNDECIMUM dicendum quod auctoritates illae, et omnes similes, sunt intelligendae de cognitione qua cognoscimus Deum in via, ratione prius posita.

AD DUODECIMUM dicendum quod infinitum privative dictum est ignotum inquantum huiusmodi: quia dicitur per remotionem complementi, a quo est cognitio rei. Unde infinitum reducitur ad materiam subiectam privationi: ut patet in III *Physicorum*. Sed infinitum negative acceptum dicitur per remotionem materiae terminantis: quia forma etiam quodammodo terminatur per materiam. Unde infinitum hoc modo est maxime de se cognoscibile. Et hoc modo infinitus est Deus.

AD DECIMUMTERTIUM dicendum quod Augustinus loquitur de visione corporali, qua nun quam videbitur. Quod patet ex hoc quod praemittitur: *sicut enim videntur visibilia ista quae nominantur, Deum nemo vidit unquam nec videre potest; et est natura invisibilis, sicut et incorruptibilis*. Sicut autem secundum naturam suam est maxime ens, ita et secundum se est maxime intelligibilis: sed quod a nobis quandoque non intelligatur, est ex defectu nostro. Unde quod videatur postquam visus non fuit a nobis, non est ex mutatione sua, sed nostra.

AD DECIMUMQUARTUM dicendum quod Deus in patria videbitur a sanctis *sicuti est*, si hoc referatur ad modum ipsius visi: videbitur enim a sanctis Deus habere illum modum quem habet. Sed si referatur modus ad ipsum cognoscentem, non videbitur sicuti est: quia non erit tanta efficacia intellectus creati ad videndum quanta est efficacia essentiae divinae ad hoc quod intelligatur.

AD DECIMUMQUINTUM dicendum quod medium in visione corporali et intellectuali invenitur triplex. Primum est medium *sub quo* videtur. Et hoc est quod perficit visum ad videndum in generali, non determinans visum ad aliquod speciale obiectum: sicut se habet lumen corporale ad visum corporalem, et lumen intellectus agentis ad intellectum possibilem. Secundum est medium *quo* videtur. Et hoc est forma visibilis qua determinatur uterque visus ad speciale obiectum: sicut per formam lapidis ad cognoscendum lapidem. Tertium est medium *in quo* videtur. Et hoc est id per cuius inspectionem ducitur visus in aliam rem: sicut inspiciendo speculum ducitur in ea quae in speculo repraesentantur, et videndo imaginem ducitur in imaginatum. Et sic etiam intellectus per cognitionem effectus ducitur in causam, vel e converso.

stands two things in succession, in the same way as prime matter remains one under various forms. Hence also the Commentator (*On the Soul* 3) compares the passive intellect, in this respect, to prime matter. Thus it by no means follows that our intellect in seeing God becomes the very essence of God, but that the latter is compared to it as its perfection or form.

REPLY OBJ. 11: These and all like authorities must be understood to refer to the knowledge whereby we know God on the way, for the reason given above.

REPLY OBJ. 12: The infinite is unknown if we take it in the privative sense, as such, because it indicates removal of completion whence knowledge of a thing is derived. Wherefore the infinite amounts to the same as matter subject to privation, as stated in *Physics* 3. But if we take the infinite in the negative sense, it indicates the absence of limiting matter, since even a form is somewhat limited by its matter. Hence the infinite in this sense is of itself most knowable; and it is in this way that God is infinite.

REPLY OBJ. 13: Augustine is speaking of bodily vision, by which God will never be seen. This is evident from what precedes: *for no man has seen God at any time, nor can any man see him as these things which we call visible are seen: in this way he is by nature invisible even as he is incorruptible*. As, however, he is by nature supremely being, so he is in himself supremely intelligible. But that he be for a time not understood by us is owing to our defect: wherefore that he be seen by us after being unseen is owing to a change not in him, but in us.

REPLY OBJ. 14: In heaven God will be seen by the saints *as he is*, if this be referred to the mode of the object seen, for the saints will see that God has the mode which he has. But if we refer the mode to the knower, he will not be seen as he is, because the created intellect will not have so great an efficacy in seeing as the divine essence has to the effect of being seen.

REPLY OBJ. 15: There is a threefold medium both in bodily and in intellectual vision. The first is the medium *under which* the object is seen, and this is something perfecting the sight so as to see in general, without determining the sight to any particular object. Such is bodily light in relation to bodily vision; and the light of the active intellect in relation to the passive intellect, insofar as this light is a medium. The second is the light *by which* the object is seen, and this is the visible form whereby either sight is determined to a special object, for instance, by the form of a stone to know a stone. The third is the medium *in which* it is seen; and this is something by gazing on which the sight is led to something else: thus by looking in a mirror it is led to see the things reflected in the mirror, and by looking at an image it is led to the thing represented by the image. In this way, too, the intellect, from knowing an effect, is led to the cause, or conversely.

269

In visione igitur patriae non erit tertium medium, ut scilicet Deus per species aliorum cognoscatur, sicut nunc cognoscitur, ratione cuius dicimur nunc videre *in speculo*. Nec erit ibi secundum medium: quia ipsa essentia divina erit qua intellectus noster videbit Deum. Sed erit ibi tantum primum medium, quod elevabit intellectum nostrum ad hoc quod possit coniungi substantiae increatae modo praedicto. Sed ab hoc medio non dicitur cognitio mediata: quia non cadit inter cognoscentem et rem cognitam, sed est illud quod dat cognoscenti vim cognoscendi,

AD DECIMUMSEXTUM dicendum quod creaturae corporales non dicuntur immediate videri nisi quando id quod est in eis coniungibile visui, ei coniungitur. Non sunt autem coniungibiles per essentiam suam, ratione materialitatis. Et ideo tunc immediate videntur quando eorum similitudo intellectui coniungitur. Sed Deus per essentiam suam coniungibilis est intellectui. Unde non immediate videretur nisi essentia sua coniungeretur intellectui. Et haec visio immediata dicitur *visio faciei*.

Et praeterea similitudo rei corporalis recipitur in visu secundum eandem rationem qua est in re, sed non secundum eundem modum essendi: et ideo similitudo illa ducit in illam rem directe.

Non autem potest hoc modo ducere aliqua similitudo intellectum nostrum in Deum, ut ex dictis patet. Et propter hoc non est simile.

Accordingly, in the heavenly vision there will be no third medium, namely, so that God be known by the images of other things, as he is known now, for which reason we are said to see now *in a glass*: nor will there be the second medium, because the essence itself of God will be that whereby our intellect will see God. But there will only be the first medium, which will upraise our intellect so that it will be possible for it to be united to the uncreated substance in the aforesaid manner. Yet this medium will not cause that knowledge to be mediate, because it does not come in between the knower and the thing known, but is that which gives the knower the power to know.

REPLY OBJ. 16: Corporeal creatures are not said to be seen immediately except when that which in them is capable of being brought into conjunction with the sight is in conjunction therewith. Now they are not capable of being in conjunction with the sight of their essence on account of their materiality: hence they are seen immediately when their image is in conjunction with the sight. But God is able to be united to the intellect by his essence: wherefore he would not be seen immediately, unless his essence were united to the intellect: and this vision, which is effected immediately, is called *vision of face*.

Moreover, the likeness of the corporeal object is received into the sight according to the same ratio as it is in the object, although not according to the same mode of being.

Wherefore this likeness leads to the object directly, whereas no likeness can lead our intellect in this way to God, as shown above: and for this reason the comparison fails.

Article 2

Whether After the Resurrection the Saints Will See God with the Eyes of the Body?

AD SECUNDUM SIC PROCEDITUR. Videtur quod sancti post resurrectionem Deum corporalibus oculis videbunt. Oculus enim glorificatus maioris erit virtutis quam aliquis oculus non glorificatus. Sed beatus Iob oculo suo Deum vidit: Iob 42, [5], *auditu auris audivi te: nunc autem oculus meus videt te*. Ergo multo fortius oculus glorificatus per essentiam Deum videre poterit.

PRAETEREA, Iob 19, [26]: *in carne mea videbo Deum, Salvatorem meum*. Ergo videtur quod corporalibus oculis Deus in patria videbitur.

PRAETEREA, Augustinus, XXII *de Civ. Dei*, loquens de visu oculorum glorificatorum, sic dicit: *vis praepollentior erit oculorum illorum, non ut acrius videant quam quidam perhibentur videre serpentes vel aquilae, quantalibet enim acrimonia cernendi eadem animalia vigeant, nihil aliud quam corpora possunt videre: sed ut videant incorporalia*. Quaecumque autem potentia cognoscitiva

OBJECTION 1: It would seem that after the resurrection the saints will see God with the eyes of the body. For the glorified eye has greater power than one that is not glorified. Now the blessed Job saw God with his eyes: *with the hearing of the ear, I have heard you, but now my eye sees you* (Job 42:5). Much more, therefore, will the glorified eye be able to see God in his essence.

OBJ. 2: Further, it is written: *in my flesh I shall see God my Savior* (Job 19:26). Therefore, in heaven God will be seen with the eyes of the body.

OBJ. 3: Further, Augustine, speaking of the sight of the glorified eyes, expresses himself as follows (*The City of God* 22): *a greater power will be in those eyes, not to see more keenly, as certain serpents or eagles are reported to see (for whatever acuteness of vision is possessed by these animals they can see only corporeal things), but to see even incorporeal things*. Now any power that is capable of knowing in-

est incorporalium, potest elevari ad videndum Deum. Ergo oculi gloriosi Deum videre poterunt.

PRAETEREA, quae est differentia corporalium ad incorporalia, eadem est e converso. Sed oculus incorporeus potest corporalia videre. Ergo oculus corporeus potest videre incorporalia. Et sic idem quod prius.

PRAETEREA, Gregorius, in V *Moral.*, super illud Iob 4, [16], *stetit quidam cuius non agnoscebam vultum* etc., sic dicit: *homo, qui, si praeceptum servare voluisset, carne spiritualis futurus fuerat, factus est peccando etiam mente carnalis*. Sed ex hoc quod est mente factus carnalis, ut ibidem dicit, *solum ea cogitat quae ad animum per corporum imagines trahit*. Ergo etiam quando carne spiritualis erit, quod post resurrectionem sanctis promittitur, etiam carne spiritualia videre poterit. Et sic idem quod prius.

PRAETEREA, homo solo Deo potest beatificari. Beatificabitur autem non solum quantum ad animam, sed etiam quantum ad corpus. Ergo non solum intellectu, sed etiam carne Deum videre poterit.

PRAETEREA, sicut Deus est praesens per suam essentiam in intellectu, ita etiam erit praesens in sensu: quia erit *omnia in omnibus*, ut dicitur I Cor. 15, [28]. Sed videbitur ab intellectu ex hoc quod sua essentia ei coniungetur. Ergo poterit videri etiam a sensu.

SED CONTRA: Ambrosius dicit, super Lucam: *nec corporalibus oculis Deus quaeritur, nec circumscribitur visu, nec tactu tenetur*. Ergo nullo corporali sensu Deus videbitur.

PRAETEREA, Hieronymus dicit: *non solum divinitatem Patris, sed nec Filii nec Spiritus Sancti, oculi carnis possunt aspicere: sed oculi nentis, de quibus dicitur, Beati mundo corde.*

PRAETEREA, idem Hieronymus dicit: *res incorporalis corporalibus oculis non videtur*. Sed Deus est maxime incorporeus. Ergo, etc.

PRAETEREA, Augustinus, in libro *de Videndo Deo*: *Deum nemo vidit unquam: vel in hac vita sicuti ipse est; vel in angelorum vita sicut visibilia ista quae corporali visione cernuntur*. Vita autem angelorum dicitur vita beata, in qua resurgentes vivent. Ergo, etc.

PRAETEREA, *secundum hoc homo dicitur factus ad imaginem Dei quod Deum conspicere potest*, ut Augustinus dicit. Sed homo est ad imaginem Dei secundum mentem, non secundum carnem. Ergo mente, et non carne Deum videbit.

RESPONDEO dicendum quod sensu corporali aliquid sentitur dupliciter: uno modo, per se; alio modo, per accidens. Per se quidem sentitur illud quod per se passio-

corporeal things can be upraised to see God. Therefore, the glorified eyes will be able to see God.

OBJ. 4: Further, the disparity of corporeal to incorporeal things is the same as of incorporeal to corporeal. Now the incorporeal eye can see corporeal things. Therefore, the corporeal eye can see the incorporeal: and consequently the same conclusion follows.

OBJ. 5: Further, Gregory, commenting on Job 4:16: *there stood one whose countenance I knew not*, says, *man who, had he been willing to obey the command, would have been spiritual in the flesh, became, by sinning, carnal even in mind* (*Morals on Job* 5). Now through becoming carnal in mind, *he thinks only of those things which he draws to his soul by the images of bodies* (*Morals on Job* 5). Therefore, when he will be spiritual in the flesh (which is promised to the saints after the resurrection), he will be able even in the flesh to see spiritual things. Therefore, the same conclusion follows.

OBJ. 6: Further, man can be beatified by God alone. Now he will be beatified not only in soul but also in body. Therefore, God will be visible not only to his intellect but also to his flesh.

OBJ. 7: Further, even as God is present to the intellect by his essence, so will he be to the senses, because he will be *all in all* (1 Cor 15:28). Now he will be seen by the intellect through the union of his essence therewith. Therefore, he will also be visible to the sense.

ON THE CONTRARY, Ambrose, commenting on Luke 1:2: *there appeared to him an angel*, says, *God is not sought with the eyes of the body, nor surveyed by the sight, nor clasped by the touch*. Therefore, God will by no means be visible to the bodily sense.

FURTHER, Jerome, commenting on Isaiah 6:1: *I saw the Lord sitting*, says, *divinity not only of the Father, but also of the Son and of the Holy Spirit is visible, not to carnal eyes, but only to the eyes of the mind, of which it is said, "Blessed are the pure in heart."*

FURTHER, Jerome says again (as quoted by Augustine, Ep. cxlvii): *an incorporeal thing is invisible to a corporeal eye*. But God is supremely incorporeal. Therefore, etc.

FURTHER, Augustine says (*On Seeing God* 147): *no man has seen God as he is at any time, neither in this life, nor in the angelic life, in the same way as these visible things which are seen with the corporeal sight*. Now the angelic life is the life of the blessed, wherein they will live after the resurrection. Therefore, etc.

FURTHER, According to Augustine (*On the Trinity* 14), *man is said to be made to God's image inasmuch as he is able to see God*. But man is in God's image as regards his mind, and not as regards his flesh. Therefore, he will see God with his mind and not with his flesh.

I ANSWER THAT, A thing is perceptible to the senses of the body in two ways, directly and indirectly. A thing is perceptible directly if it can act directly on the bodily senses.

nem sensui corporali inferre potest. Per se autem potest aliquid passionem inferre aut sensui inquantum est sensus; aut huic sensui inquantum est hic sensus. Quod lutem secundo modo infert per se passionem sensui, dicitur *sensibile proprium*: sicut color respectu visus, et sonus respectu auditus. Quia autem sensus, inquantum est sensus, utitur organo corporali, non potest in eo aliquid recipi nisi corporaliter: cum *omne quod recipitur in aliquo, sit in eo per modum recipientis*. Et ideo omnia sensibilia inferunt passionem sensui, inquantum est sensus, secundum quod habent magnitudinem. Et ideo magnitudo et omnia consequentia, ut motus, quies et numerus et huiusmodi, dicuntur *sensibilia communia, per se tamen*. Per accidens autem sentitur illud quod non infert passionem sensui neque inquantum est sensus neque inquantum est hic sensus, sed coniungitur his quae per se sensui inferunt passionem: sicut *Socrates* et *filius Diaris* et *amicus*, et alia huiusmodi, quae per se cognoscuntur in universali intellectu, in particulari autem virtute cogitativa in homine, aestimativa autem in aliis animalibus. Huiusmodi autem tunc sensus exterior dicitur sentire, quamvis per accidens, quando ex eo quod per se sentitur, vis apprehensiva cuius est illud cognitum per se cognoscere, statim sine dubitatione et discursu apprehendit: sicut videmus aliquem vivere ex hoc quod loquitur. Quando autem aliter se habet, non dicitur illud sensus videre etiam per accidens.

Dico ergo quod Deus nullo modo potest videri visu corporali, aut aliquo alio sensu sentiri, sicut per se visibile, nec hic nec in patria. Quia si a sensu removeatur id quod convenit sensui inquantum est sensus, non erit sensus: et similiter si a visu removeatur illud quod est visus inquantum est visus, non erit visus. Cum ergo sensus, inquantum est sensus, percipiat magnitudinem; et visus, inquantum est talis sensus, percipiat colorem: impossibile est quod visus accipiat aliquid quod non est color nec magnitudo, nisi sensus diceretur aequivoce. Cum ergo: visus et sensus sit futurus idem specie in corpore glorioso, non poterit esse quod divinam essentiam videat sicut visibile per se.

Videbit autem eam sicut visibile per accidens: dum ex parte visus corporalis tantam gloriam Dei inspiciet in corporibus, et praecipue gloriosis, et maxime in corpore Christi; et ex parte alia intellectus tam clare Deum videbit quod in rebus corporaliter visis Deus percipietur, sicut in locutione percipitur vita. Quamvis enim tunc intellectus noster non videat Deum ex creaturis, tamen videbit eum in creaturis corporaliter visis. Et tunc modum quo Deus corporaliter possit videri, ponit Augustinus in fine de Civitate Dei, ut patet eius verba intuenti. Dicit enim sic: *valde credibile est sic nos visuros mundana tunc corpora caeli novi ei terrae novae, ut Deum ubique praesentem et universa corporalia gubernantem clarissima perspicuitate videamus: non sicut nunc invisibilia*

And a thing can act directly either on sense as such or on a particular sense as such. That which acts directly in this second way on a sense is called a 'proper sensible,' for instance, color in relation to the sight, and sound in relation to the hearing. But because sense as such makes use of a bodily organ, nothing can be received therein except corporeally, since *whatever is received into a thing is therein after the mode of the recipient*. Hence all sensibles act on the sense as such, according to their magnitude: and consequently magnitude and all its consequences, such as movement, rest, number, and the like, are called 'common sensibles,' and yet they are direct objects of sense. An indirect object of sense is that which does not act on the sense, neither as sense nor as a particular sense, but is annexed to those things that act on sense directly: for instance, *Socrates*, or *the son of Diares*, or *a friend*, and others like these which are the direct object of the intellect's knowledge in the universal, and in the particular are the object of the cogitative power in man, and of the estimative power in other animals. The external sense is said to perceive things of this kind, although indirectly, when the apprehensive power (whose province it is to know directly this thing known), from that which is sensed directly, apprehends them at once and without any doubt or discourse (thus we see that a person is alive from the fact that he speaks): otherwise the sense is not said to perceive it even indirectly.

I say then that God can in no way be seen with the eyes of the body, or perceived by any of the senses, as that which is seen directly, neither here, nor in heaven: for if that which belongs to sense as such be removed from sense, there will be no sense, and in like manner if that which belongs to sight as sight be removed therefrom, there will be no sight. Accordingly, seeing that sense as sense perceives magnitude, and sight as such a sense perceives color, it is impossible for the sight to perceive that which is neither color nor magnitude, unless we call it a sense equivocally. Since, then, sight and sense will be specifically the same in the glorified body, as in a non-glorified body, it will be impossible for it to see the divine essence as an object of direct vision.

Yet it will see it as an object of indirect vision, because on the one hand the bodily sight will see so great a glory of God in bodies, especially in the glorified bodies and most of all in the body of Christ, and, on the other hand, the intellect will see God so clearly that God will be perceived in things seen with the eye of the body, even as life is perceived in speech. For although our intellect will not then see God from seeing his creatures, yet it will see God in his creatures seen corporeally. This manner of seeing God corporeally is indicated by Augustine (*The City of God* 22), as is clear if we take note of his words, for he says: *it is very credible that we shall so see the mundane bodies of the new heaven and the new earth, as to see most clearly God everywhere present, governing all corporeal things, not as we now see the invisible*

Dei per ea quae facta sunt intellecta conspiciuntur; sed sicut homines, mox ut aspicimus, non credimus vivere, sed videmus.

AD PRIMUM ergo dicendum quod verbum illud Iob intelligitur de oculo spirituali: de quo dicit Apostolus, Ephes: 1, [18]: *illuminatos habere oculos cordis vestri.*

AD SECUNDUM dicendum quod illa auctoritas non intelligitur quod per oculos carnis Deum sumus visuri: sed quia in carne existentes Deum videbimus.

AD TERTIUM dicendum quod Augustinus loquitur inquirendo in verbis illis, et sub conditione. Quod patet ex hoc quod praemittitur: *longe itaque alterius potentiae erunt si per eos videbitur incorporea illa natura*: et postea subdit, *vis itaque* etc.; et postmodum determinat ut dictum est.

AD QUARTUM dicendum quod omnis cognitio fit per aliquam abstractionem a materia. Et ideo, quanto forma corporalis magis abstrahitur a materia, magis est cognitionis principium. Et inde est quod forma in materia existens nullo modo est cognitionis principium; in sensu autem aliquo modo, prout a materia separatur; et in intellectu nostro adhuc melius. Et ideo oculus spiritualis, a quo removetur impedimentum cognitionis, potest videre rem corporalem. Non autem sequitur quod oculus corporalis, in quo deficit vis cognitiva secundum quod participat de materia, possit cognoscere perfecte cognoscibilia quae sunt incorporalia.

AD QUINTUM dicendum quod, quamvis mens, facta carnalis non possit cogitare nisi accepta a sensibus, tamen ea cogitat immaterialiter. Et similiter oportet quod visus illud quod apprehendit, semper apprehendat corporaliter. Unde non potest cognoscere illa quae corporaliter apprehendi non possunt.

AD SEXTUM dicendum quod beatitudo est perfectio hominis inquantum est homo. Et quia homo non habet quod sit homo ex corpore, sed magis ex anima, corpus autem est de essentia hominis inquantum est perfectum per. animam; ideo beatitudo hominis non consistit principaliter nisi in actu animae, et ex ea derivatur ad corpus per quandam redundantiam, sicut patet ex his quae dicta sunt. Quaedam tamen beatitudo corporis nostri erit inquantum Deum videbit in sensibilibus creaturis, et praecipue in corpore Christi.

AD SEPTIMUM dicendum quod intellectus est perceptivus spiritualium, non autem visus corporalis. Et ideo intellectus poterit cognoscere divinam essentiam sibi coniunctam, non autem visus corporalis.

things of God as understood by those that are made, but as when we see men we do not believe but see that they live.

REPLY OBJ. 1: This saying of Job refers to the spiritual eye, of which the Apostle says: *the eyes of your hearts enlightened* (Eph 1:18).

REPLY OBJ. 2: The passage quoted does not mean that we are to see God with the eyes of the flesh, but that in the flesh we shall see God.

REPLY OBJ. 3: In these words Augustine speaks as one inquiring and conditionally. This appears from what he had said before: *therefore, they will have an altogether different power, if they shall see that incorporeal nature*; and then he goes on to say: *accordingly a greater power*, and afterwards he explains himself.

REPLY OBJ. 4: All knowledge results from some kind of abstraction from matter. Wherefore the more a corporeal form is abstracted from matter, the more is it a principle of knowledge. Hence it is that a form existing in matter is in no way a principle of knowledge, while a form existing in the senses is somewhat a principle of knowledge, insofar as it is abstracted from matter, and a form existing in the intellect is still better a principle of knowledge. Therefore, the spiritual eye from which the obstacle to knowledge is removed can see a corporeal object: but it does not follow that the corporeal eye, in which the cognitive power is deficient as participating in matter, be able to know perfectly incorporeal objects of knowledge.

REPLY OBJ. 5: Although the mind that has become carnal cannot think but of things received from the senses, it thinks of them immaterially. In like manner, whatever the sight apprehends it must always apprehend it corporeally: wherefore it cannot know things which cannot be apprehended corporeally.

REPLY OBJ. 6: Beatitude is the perfection of man as man. And since man is man not through his body but through his soul, and the body is essential to man insofar as it is perfected by the soul, it follows that man's beatitude does not consist chiefly otherwise than in an act of the soul, and passes from the soul on to the body by a kind of overflow, as explained above (Q. 85, A. 1). Yet our body will have a certain beatitude from seeing God in sensible creatures: and especially in Christ's body.

REPLY OBJ. 7: The intellect can perceive spiritual things, whereas the eyes of the body cannot: wherefore the intellect will be able to know the divine essence united to it, but the eyes of the body will not.

Article 3

Whether the Saints, Seeing God, See All That God Sees?

AD TERTIUM SIC PROCEDITUR. Videtur quod sancti videntes Deum per essentiam omnia videant quae Deus in seipso videt. Quia, ut dicit Isidorus, in libro *de Summo Bono, angeli in Verbo Dei omnia sciunt antequam fiant.* Sed sancti angelis aequales erunt: ut patet Matth. 22, [30]. Ergo et sancti, videndo Deum, omnia videbunt.

PRAETEREA, Gregorius, in IV *Dialog.*, dicit: *quia illic omnes communi claritate Deum conspiciunt, quid est quod ibi nesciant, ubi scientem omnia sciunt?* Loquitur autem de beatis, qui Deum vident per essentiam. Ergo qui videt Deum per essentiam, omnia cognoscit.

PRAETEREA, sicut dicitur in III *de Anima, intellectus, cum intelligit maxima, magis potest intelligere minima.* Sed maximum intelligibile est Deus. Ergo maxime auget virtutem intellectus in intelligendo. Ergo intellectus eum videris omnia intelligit.

PRAETEREA, intellectus non impeditur ab intelligendo aliquid nisi inquantum id superat ipsum. Sed intellectum Deum videntem nulla creatura superat: quia, ut dicit Gregorius, in II *Dialog., animae videnti Creatorem angusta fit omnis creatura.* Ergo videntes Deum per essentiam omnia cognoscent.

PRAETEREA, omnis potentia passiva quae non est reducta ad rictum, est imperfecta. Sed in intellectu possibili animae humanae est potentia quasi passiva ad cognoscendum omnia: quia intellectus possibilis est *quo est omnia fieri*, ut dicitur in III *de Anima.* Si ergo in illa beatitudine non intelligeret omnia, remaneret imperfectus. Quod est absurdum.

PRAETEREA, quicumque videt speculum, videt ea quae in speculo resultant. Sed in Verbo Dei omnia sicut in speculo resultant: quia ipsum est ratio et similitudo omnium. Ergo sancti, qui vident Verbum per essentiam, vident omnia creata.

PRAETEREA, ut dicitur Proverb. 10, [24], *desiderium suum iustis dabitur.* Sed sancti desiderant omnia scire: quia *omnes homines natura scire desiderant*; nec natura per gloriam aufertur. Ergo dabitur eis a Deo quod omnia cognoscant.

PRAETEREA, ignorantia est quaedam poenalitas praesentis vitae. Sed omnis poenalitas per gloriam a sanctis aufertur. Ergo et omnis ignorantia. Et ita omnia cognoscent.

PRAETEREA, beatitudo sanctorum per prius est in anima quam in corpore. Sed corpora sanctorum formabuntur in gloriam ad similitudinem corporis Christi: ut patet Philipp: 3, [21]. Ergo et animae perficientur ad similitudinem animae Christi. Sed anima Christi in Verbo

OBJECTION 1: It would seem that the saints, seeing God in his essence, see all that God sees in himself. For as Isidore says (*De Summo Bono* 1): *the angels know all things in the Word of God before they happen.* Now the saints will be equal to the angels of God (Matt 22:30). Therefore, the saints also, in seeing God, see all things.

OBJ. 2: Further, Gregory says (*Dialogues* 4): *since all see God there with equal clearness, what do they not know, who know him who knows all things?* and he refers to the blessed who see God in his essence. Therefore, those who see God in his essence know all things.

OBJ. 3: Further, it is stated in *On the Soul* 3.7, that *when an intellect understands the greatest things, it is all the more able to understand the least things.* Now God is the greatest of intelligible things. Therefore, the power of the intellect is greatly increased by understanding him. Therefore, the intellect, seeing him, understands all things.

OBJ. 4: Further, the intellect is not hindered from understanding a thing except by this surpassing it. Now no creature surpasses the intellect that understands God, since, as Gregory says (*Dialogues* 2), *to the soul which sees its Creator all creatures are small.* Therefore, those who see God in his essence know all things.

OBJ. 5: Further, every passive power that is not reduced to act is imperfect. Now the passive intellect of the human soul is a power that is passive, as it were, to the knowledge of all things, since the passive intellect is *in which all are in potentiality* (*On the Soul* 3.18). If, then, in that beatitude it were not to understand all things, it would remain imperfect, which is absurd.

OBJ. 6: Further, whoever sees a mirror sees the things reflected in the mirror. Now all things are reflected in the Word of God as in a mirror, because he is the type and image of all. Therefore, the saints who see the Word in its essence see all created things.

OBJ. 7: Further, Proverbs 10:24 says: *to the just their desire shall be given.* Now the just desire to know all things, since *all men desire naturally to know*, and nature is not done away with by glory. Therefore, God will grant them to know all things.

OBJ. 8: Further, ignorance is one of the penalties of the present life. Now all penalty will be removed from the saints by glory. Therefore, all ignorance will be removed: and consequently they will know all.

OBJ. 9: Further, the beatitude of the saints is in their soul before being in their body. Now the bodies of the saints will be reformed in glory to the likeness of Christ's body (Phil 3:21). Therefore, their souls will be perfected in likeness to the soul of Christ. Now Christ's soul sees all things

omnia videt. Ergo et omnes animae sanctorum videbunt omnia in Verbo.

PRAETEREA, sicut sensus, ita intellectus cognoscit omne illud cuius similitudine informatur. Sed divina essentia expressius indicat quamlibet rem quam aliqua similitudo alia rei. Ergo, cum in illa beata visione essentia divina fiat quasi forma intellectus nostri, videtur quod sancti videntes Deum omnia videant.

PRAETEREA, Commentator dicit, in III *de Anima*, quod *si intellectus agens esset forma intellectus possibilis, intelligeremus omnia*. Sed divina essentia clarius repraesentat omnia quam intellectus agens. Ergo intellectus videns Deum per essentiam omnia cognoscit.

PRAETEREA, propter hoc quod inferiores angeli nunc non omnia cognoscunt, illuminantur de ignotis a superioribus. Sed post diem iudicii angelus non illuminabit angelum: *tunc enim praelatio cessabit*, ut dicit Glossa1,1 Cor. 15, [24]. Ergo inferiores angeli omnia scient. Et eadem ratione omnes alii sancti Deum per essentiam videntes.

SED CONTRA: Sicut dicit Dionysius, in 6 cap. *Cael. Hier.*, angeli superiores inferiores a *nescientia* purgant. Angeli autem inferiores vident essentiam divinam. Ergo angelus videns essentiam divinam potest aliqua nescire. Sed anima non perfectius videbit Deum quam angelus. Ergo animae videntes Deum non oportet quod omnia videant.

PRAETEREA, solus Christus *habet Spiritum non ad mensuram*, ut dicitur Ioan. 3, [34]. Sed Christo inquantum habet Spiritum non ad mensuram, competit quod in Verbo omnia cognoscat: unde ibidem [v. 35] dicitur quod: *Pater, omnia dedit in manu eius*. Ergo nulli alii competit cognoscere omnia in Verbo, nisi Christo.

PRAETEREA, quanto aliquod principium perfectius cognoscitur, tanto plures eius effectus cognoscuntur per ipsum. Sed quidam videntium Deum per essentiam perfectius aliis cognoscent Deum, qui est rerum omnium principium. Ergo quidam aliis plura cognoscent. Et ita non omnes scient omnia.

RESPONDEO dicendum quod Deus, videndo suam essentiam, cognoscit omnia quae sunt vel erunt vel fuerunt: et haec dicitur cognoscere notitia visionis, quia, ad similitudinem visionis corporalis, cognoscit ea quasi praesentia. Cognoscit insuper, videndo suam essentiam, omnia quae potest facere, quamvis nunquam fecerit nec facturus sit: alias non perfecte cognosceret potentiam suam; non enim potest cognosci potentia nisi sciantur potentiae obiecta. Et haec dicitur cognoscere *notitia simplicis intelligentiae*.

Impossibile est autem quod aliquis intellectus creatus cognoscat omnia, videndo divinam essentiam, quae Deus potest facere. Quia quanto aliquod principium per-

in the Word. Therefore, all the souls of the saints will also see all things in the Word.

OBJ. 10: Further, the intellect, like the senses, knows all the things with the image of which it is informed. Now the divine essence shows a thing forth more clearly than any other image thereof. Therefore, since in that blessed vision the divine essence becomes the form, as it were, of our intellect, it would seem that the saints, seeing God, see all.

OBJ. 11: Further, the Commentator says (*On the Soul* 3), that *if the active intellect were the form of the passive intellect, we should understand all things*. Now the divine essence represents all things more clearly than the active intellect. Therefore, the intellect that sees God in his essence knows all things.

OBJ. 12: Further, the lower angels are enlightened by the higher about the things they are ignorant of, for the reason that they know not all things. Now after the day of judgment, one angel will not enlighten another; for then all superiority will cease, as a Gloss observes on 1 Corinthians 15:24: *when he shall have brought to nothing*. Therefore, the lower angels will then know all things, and for the same reason all the other saints who will see God in his essence.

ON THE CONTRARY, Dionysius says (*Hier. Eccles.* vi): the higher angels cleanse the lower angels from *nescience*. Now the lower angels see the divine essence. Therefore, an angel while seeing the divine essence may not know certain things. But the soul will not see God more perfectly than an angel. Therefore, the souls seeing God will not necessarily see all things.

FURTHER, Christ alone *has the spirit not by measure* (John 3:34). Now it becomes Christ, as having the spirit without measure, to know all things in the Word: wherefore it is stated in the same place that *the Father has given all things into his hand* (John 3:35). Therefore, none but Christ is competent to know all things in the Word.

FURTHER, The more perfectly a principle is known, the more of its effects are known thereby. Now some of those who see God in his essence will know God more perfectly than others. Therefore, some will know more things than others, and consequently every one will not know all.

I ANSWER THAT, God, by seeing his essence, knows all things whatsoever that are, shall be, or have been: and he is said to know these things by his 'knowledge of vision', because he knows them as though they were present in likeness to corporeal vision. Moreover, by seeing this essence he knows all that he can do, although he never did it, nor ever will, else he would not know his power perfectly; since a power cannot be known unless its objects be known. And this is called his science, or *knowledge of simple intelligence*.

Now it is impossible for a created intellect, by seeing the divine essence, to know all that God can do, because the more perfectly a principle is known, the more things

fectius cognoscitur, tanto plura sciuntur in illo: sicut in uno demonstrationis principio ille qui est perspicacioris ingenii plures conclusiones videt quam alius, qui est ingenii tardioris. Cum ergo quantitas potentiae divinae attendatur secundum ea in quae potest, si aliquis intellectus videret in divina essentia omnia quae Deus potest facere, eadem esset quantitas perfectionis in intelligendo quae est quantitas divinae potentiae in producendo effectus: et ita comprehenderet divinam essentiam. Quod est impossibile omni creato intellectui.

Illa autem omnia quae Deus scit notitia visionis aliquis intellectus creatus cognoscit in Verbo; scilicet anima Christi. Sed de aliis videntibus divinam essentiam duplex est opinio. Quidam enim dicunt quod omnes videntes Deum per essentiam vident omnia quae Deus videt scientia visionis. Sed hoc repugnat Sanctorum dictis, qui ponunt angelos aliqua ignorare: quos tamen constat, secundum, fidem, omnes Deum per essentiam videre.

Et ideo alii dicunt quod alii a Christo, quamvis videant Deum per essentiam, non tamen omnia vident quae Deus videt, eo quod essentiam divinam non comprehendunt. Non est enim necessarium quod sciens causam sciat omnes eius effectus, nisi causam comprehendat: quod non competit intellectui creato. Et ideo unusquisque videntium Deum per essentiam tanto plura in eius essentia conspicit, quanto clarius divinam essentiam intuetur. Et iride est quod de his potest unus alium instruere. Et sic scientia angelorum et animarum sanctarum potest augeri usque ad diem iudicii: sicut et alia quae ad praemium accidentale pertinent. Sed ulterius non proficiet: quia tunc erit ultimus status rerum. Et in illo statu possibile erit quod omnes omnia cognoscent quae Deus scientia visionis novit.

AD PRIMUM ergo dicendum quod hoc quod dicit Isidorus, quod *angeli sciunt in Verbo omnia antequam fiant*, non potest referri ad ea quae Deus scit scientia simplicis intelligentiae tantum, quia illa nunquam fient: sed referendum est ad ea tantum quae Deus scit scientia visionis. De quibus etiam dicit quod non omnes angeli ea omnia cognoscant, sed forte aliqui. Et illi etiam qui cognoscunt, non perfecte cognoscunt omni. In una enim re est inultas rationes intelligibiles considerare, sicut diversas eius proprietates et habitudines ad res alias; et possibile est quod, eadem re scita a duobus communiter, unus alio plures rationes, percipiat, et has rationes; unus ab alio accipiat. Unde et Dionysius dicit, 4 cap. *de Div. Nom.*, quod *inferiores angeli docentur a superioribus rerum, scibiles rationes*. Et ideo etiam angeli qui omnes creaturas cognoscunt, non oportet quod omnia quae in eis intelligi possunt, percipiant.

are known in it; thus in one principle of demonstration one who is quick of intelligence sees more conclusions than one who is slow of intelligence. Since, then, the extent of the divine power is measured according to what it can do, if an intellect were to see in the divine essence all that God can do, its perfection in understanding would equal in extent the divine power in producing its effects, and thus it would comprehend the divine power, which is impossible for any created intellect to do.

Yet there is a created intellect, namely, the soul of Christ, which knows in the Word all that God knows by the knowledge of vision. But regarding others who see the divine essence there are two opinions. For some say that all who see God in his essence see all that God sees by his knowledge of vision. This, however, is contrary to the sayings of holy men, who hold that angels are ignorant of some things; and yet it is clear that according to faith all the angels see God in his essence.

Wherefore others say that others than Christ, although they see God in his essence, do not see all that God sees because they do not comprehend the divine essence. For it is not necessary that he who knows a cause should know all its effects, unless he comprehend the cause: and this is not in the competency of a created intellect. Consequently, of those who see God in his essence, each one sees in his essence so much the more things according as he sees the divine essence the more clearly: and hence it is that one is able to instruct another concerning these things. Thus the knowledge of the angels and of the souls of the saints can go on increasing until the day of judgment, even as other things pertaining to the accidental reward. But afterwards it will increase no more, because then will be the final state of things, and in that state it is possible that all will know everything that God knows by the knowledge of vision.

REPLY OBJ. 1: The saying of Isidore, that *the angels know in the Word all things before they happen*, cannot refer to those things which God knows only by the knowledge of simple intelligence, because those things will never happen; but it must refer to those things which God knows only by the knowledge of vision. Even of these he does not say that all the angels know them all, but that perhaps some do; and that even those who know do not know all perfectly. For in one and the same thing there are many intelligible aspects to be considered, such as its various properties and relations to other things: and it is possible that while one thing is known in common by two persons, one of them perceives more aspects, and that the one learns these aspects from the other. Hence Dionysius says (*On the Divine Names* 4) that *the lower angels learn from the higher angels the intelligible aspects of things*. Wherefore it does not follow that even the angels who know all creatures are able to see all that can be understood in them.

Ad secundum dicendum quod ex verbo illo Gregorii ostenditur quod in illa beata visione est. sufficientia ad omnia intuenda ex parte divinae essentiae, quae, est medium quo videtur, per quam Deus omnia videt. Sed quod non omnia videantur, est ex defectu intellectus creati, qui divinam essentiam non comprehendit.

Ad tertium dicendum quod intellectus creatus non videt divinam essentiam secundum modum ipsius essentiae, sed secundum modum proprium, qui finitus est. Unde non oportet quod eius efficacia in cognoscendo ex visione praedicta amplietur in infinitum ad omnia cognoscenda.

Ad quartum dicendum quod defectus cognitionis non solum procedit ex excessu cognoscibilis super intellectum, sed etiam ex hoc quod intellectui non coniungitur id quod est ratio cognoscibilis: sicut visus; non videt lapidem quandoque ex hoc quod species lapidis non est ei coniuncta. Quamvis autem intellectui videntis Deum coniungatur ipsa divina essentia, quae est omnium ratio, non tamen coniungitur ei prout est omnium ratio, sed secundum quod est ratio aliquorum: et tanto plurium quanto quisque plenius divinam essentiam intuetur.

Ad quintum dicendum quod, quando potentia passiva est perfectibilis pluribus perfectionibus ordinatis, si perfecta sit sua ultima perfectione, non dicitur imperfecta, etiam si aliquae dispositiones praecedentes ei desint. Omnis autem cognitio qua intellectus creatus perficitur, ordinatur sicut ad finem ad Dei cognitionem. Unde videns Deum per essentiam, etiam si nihil aliud cognosceret, perfectum intellectum haberet. Nec est perfectior ex hoc quod aliquid aliud cum ipso cognoscit, nisi quatenus ipsum plenius videt. Unde Augustinus, in V *Confess.*: *infelix homo qui scit omnia illa*, scilicet creaturas, *te autem nescit. Beatus autem qui te scit, etiam si illa nesciat. Qui vero te et illa novit, non propter illa beatior, sed propter te tantum beatus.*

Ad sextum dicendum quod speculum illud est voluntarium: et, sicut ostendet se cui vult, ita in se ostendet quae vult. Nec est simile de speculo materiali, in cuius potestate non est quod videatur vel non videatur.

Vel dicendum quod in speculo materiali tam res quam speculum videntur sub propria forma: quamvis speculum illud videatur per formam a re acceptam, lapis vero per propriam formam resultantem in re alia, et ideo per quam rationem cognoscitur unum, et aliud. Sed in speculo increato videtur aliquid per formam ipsius speculi, sicut effectus videtur per similitudinem causae et e converso. Et ideo non oportet quod quicumque videt speculum aeternum, videat omnia quae in speculo resul-

Reply Obj. 2: It follows from this saying of Gregory that this blessed vision suffices for the seeing of all things on the part of the divine essence, which is the medium by which one sees, and whereby God sees all things. That all things, however, are not seen is owing to the deficiency of the created intellect, which does not comprehend the divine essence.

Reply Obj. 3: The created intellect sees the divine essence not according to the mode of that same essence, but according to its own mode, which is finite. Hence its efficacy in knowing would need to be infinitely increased by reason of that vision in order for it to know all things.

Reply Obj. 4: Defective knowledge results not only from excess and deficiency of the knowable object in relation to the intellect, but also from the fact that the aspect of knowableness is not united to the intellect: thus sometimes the sight does not see a stone because the image of the stone is not united to it. But even though the divine essence itself, which is the pattern of all things, is joined to the intellect of the one who sees God, it is not joined to it as being the pattern of all things but rather to the extent that it is the pattern of some. And one who beholds the divine essence more fully perceives more of these.

Reply Obj. 5: When a passive power is perceptible by several perfections in order, if it be perfected with its ultimate perfection, it is not said to be imperfect, even though it lack some of the preceding dispositions. Now all knowledge by which the created intellect is perfected is directed to the knowledge of God as its end. Wherefore he who sees God in his essence, even though he know nothing else, would have a perfect intellect: nor is his intellect more perfect through knowing something else besides him, except insofar as it sees him more fully. Hence Augustine says (*Confessions* 5): *unhappy is he who knows all these* (namely, creatures), *and knows not you: but happy whosoever knows you, though he know not these. And whosoever knows both you and them is not the happier for them but for you only.*

Reply Obj. 6: This mirror has a will: and even as he will show himself to whom he will, so will he show in himself whatsoever he will. Nor does the comparison with a material mirror hold, for it is not in its power to be seen or not to be seen.

We may also reply that in a material mirror both object and mirror are seen under their proper image, although the mirror be seen through an image received from the thing itself, whereas the stone is seen through its proper image reflected in some other thing, where the reason for seeing the one is the reason for seeing the other. But in the uncreated mirror a thing is seen through the form of the mirror, just as an effect is seen through the image of its cause and conversely. Consequently, it does not follow that whoever sees

tant. Non enim necesse est quod videns causam videat omnes effectus eius, nisi comprehendat causam.

AD SEPTIMUM dicendum quod sanctorum desiderium quo omnia scire desiderant, implebitur ex hoc solum quod Deum videbunt: sicut desiderium eorum quo omnia bona habere cupiunt, complebitur in hoc quod Deum habebunt. Sicut enim Deus, in hoc quod habet perfectam bonitatem, sufficit affectui, et, eo habito, omnia bona quodammodo habentur; ita eius visio sufficit intellectui: Ioan. 14, [8], *Domine, ostende nobis Patrem, sufficit nobis.*

AD OCTAVUM dicendum quod ignorantia proprie accepta in privationem sonat, et sic poena est: sic enim ignorantia est nescientia aliquorum quae sciri debent, vel quae necesse est scire. Nullius autem horum scientia sanctis deerit in patria.

Quandoque autem ignorantia communiter accipitur pro omni nescientia. Et sic angeli et sancti in patria quaedam ignorabunt: unde Dionysius dicit quod *angeli a nescientia purgantur.* Sic autem ignorantia non est poenalitas sed defectus quidam. Nec est necesse quod omnis talis defectus per gloriam auferatur: sic enim etiam posset dici quod defectus esset in Lino quod non pervenit ad gloriam Petri.

AD NONUM dicendum quod corpus nostrum conformabitur corpori Christi in gloria secundum similitudinem, non secundum aequalitatem: erit enim clarum sicut et corpus Christi, sed non aequaliter. Et similiter, anima nostra habebit gloriam ad similitudinem animae Christi, sed non ad aequalitatem. Et ita habebit scientiam sicut anima Christi: sed non tantam, ut scilicet sciat omnia sicut anima Christi.

AD DECIMUM dicendum quod, quamvis essentia divina sit ratio omnium cognoscibilium, non tamen coniungetur cuilibet intellectui creato secundum quod est ratio omnium. Et ideo ratio non sequitur.

AD UNDECIMUM dicendum quod intellectus agens est forma proportionata intellectui possibili, sicut et potentia materiae est proportionata potentiae agentis naturalis: ut omne quod est in potentia passiva materiae vel intellectus possibilis, sit in potentia activa intellectus agentis vel naturalis agentis. Et ideo, si intellectus agens fiat forma intellectus possibilis, oportet quod intellectus possibilis cognoscat omnia ad quae se extendit virtus intellectus agentis. Divina autem essentia non est forma hoc modo nostro intellectui proportionata. Et ideo non est simile.

AD DUODECIMUM dicendum quod nihil prohibet dicere quod post diem iudicii, quando gloria hominum et angelorum erit penitus consummata, omnes beati scient omnia quae Deus scientia visionis novit: ita tamen quod non omnes omnia videant in essentia divina. Sed ani-

the eternal mirror sees all that is reflected in that mirror: since he who sees the cause does not of necessity see all its effects, unless he comprehend the cause.

REPLY OBJ. 7: The desire of the saints to know all things will be fulfilled by the mere fact of their seeing God: just as their desire to possess all good things will be fulfilled by their possessing God. For, as God suffices the affections in that he has perfect goodness, and by possessing him we possess all goods, as it were, so does the vision of him suffice the intellect: *Lord, show us the Father and it is enough for us* (John 14:8).

REPLY OBJ. 8: Ignorance properly so called denotes a privation, and thus it is a punishment: for in this way ignorance is nescience of things the knowledge of which is a duty or a necessity. Now the saints in heaven will not be ignorant of any of these things.

Sometimes, however, ignorance is taken in a broad sense of any kind of nescience: and thus the angels and saints in heaven will be ignorant of certain things. Hence Dionysius says (*On the Divine Names* 4) that *the angels will be cleansed from their ignorance.* In this sense ignorance is not a penalty but a defect. Nor is it necessary for all such defects to be done away with by glory: for thus we might say that it was a defect in Pope Linus that he did not attain to the glory of Peter.

REPLY OBJ. 9: In glory, our body will be conformed to the body of Christ in likeness, but not in equality, for it will be endowed with clarity even as Christ's body, but not equally. In like manner, our soul will have glory in likeness to the soul of Christ, but not in equality thereto: thus it will have knowledge even as Christ's soul, but not so great, so as to know all as Christ's soul does.

REPLY OBJ. 10: Although the divine essence is the type of all things knowable, it will not be united to each created intellect according as it is the type of all. Hence the objection proves nothing.

REPLY OBJ. 11: The active intellect is a form proportionate to the passive intellect, even as the passive power of matter is proportionate to the power of the natural agent, so that whatsoever is in the passive power of matter or the passive intellect is in the active power of the active intellect or of the natural agent. Consequently, if the active intellect become the form of the passive intellect, the latter must of necessity know all those things to which the power of the active intellect extends. But the divine essence is not a form proportionate to our intellect in this sense. Hence the comparison fails.

REPLY OBJ. 12: Nothing hinders us from saying that after the judgment day, when the glory of men and angels will be consummated once for all, all the blessed will know everything that God knows by the knowledge of vision, yet so that not all will see everything in the divine essence. Christ's

ma Christi ibi plene videbit omnia, sicut et nunc videt: alii autem videbunt ibi plura vel pauciora secundum gradum quo Deum cognoscent. Et sic anima Christi de his quae prae aliis videt in Verbo, omnes alias illuminabit: unde dicitur Apoc. 21, [23] quod *claritas Dei illuminat civitatem beatorum, et lucerna eius est Agnus.* Et similiter alii superiores illuminabunt inferiores: non quidem nova illuminatione, ut scientia inferiorum per hoc augeatur; sed quadam continuatione illuminationis, sicut si intelligatur quod sol quiescens illuminat aerem. Et ideo dicitur Dan. 12, [3] quod *qui ad iustitiam erudiunt plurimos, fulgebunt quasi stellae in perpetuas aeternitates.* Praelatio autem ordinum dicitur cessatura quantum ad ea quae nunc circa nos per eorum ordinata ministeria exercentur: ut patet per Glossam ibidem.

soul, however, will see clearly all things therein, even as it sees them now; while others will see therein a greater or lesser number of things according to the degree of clearness wherewith they will know God: and thus Christ's soul will enlighten all other souls concerning those things which it sees in the Word better than others. Hence it is written: *the glory of God shall enlighten the city of Jerusalem, and the Lamb is the lamp thereof* (Rev 21:23). In like manner, the higher souls will enlighten the lower (not indeed with a new enlightening, so as to increase the knowledge of the lower), but with a kind of continued enlightenment; thus we might understand the sun to enlighten the atmosphere while at a standstill. Wherefore it is written: *they that instruct many to justice shall shine as stars for all eternity* (Dan 12:3). The statement that the superiority of the orders will cease refers to their present ordinate ministry in our regard, as is clear from the same Gloss.

QUESTION 93

THE HAPPINESS OF THE SAINTS AND THEIR MANSIONS

Deinde considerandum est de sanctorum beatitudine et eorum mansionibus.

Circa quod quaeruntur tria.

Primo: utrum sanctorum beatitudo augeatur post iudicium.

Secundo: utrum gradus beatitudinis appellentur mansiones.

Tertio: utrum diversae mansiones distinguantur penes diversos gradus caritatis.

We must next consider the happiness of the saints and their mansions.

Under this head there are three points of inquiry:

(1) Whether the happiness of the saints will increase after the judgment?

(2) Whether the degrees of happiness should be called mansions?

(3) Whether the various mansions differ according to various degrees of charity?

Article 1

Whether the Happiness of the Saints Will Be Greater After the Judgment Than Before?

AD PRIMUM SIC PROCEDITUR. Videtur quod beatitudo sanctorum non sit maior futura post iudicium quam ante. Quanto enim aliquid magis accedit ad similitudinem divinam, tanto perfectius beatitudinem participat. Sed anima a corpore separata Deo similior est quam corpori coniuncta. Ergo maior est eius beatitudo ante corporis resumptionem quam post.

PRAETEREA, virtus unita est magis potens quam multiplicata. Sed anima extra corpus est magis unita quam cum est corpori coniuncta. Ergo virtus est maior ad operandum. Et ita perfectius beatitudinem participat, quae in actu consistit.

PRAETEREA, beatitudo consistit in actu intellectus speculativi. Sed intellectus in suo actu non utitur organo corporali: et sic corpus resumptum non efficiet ut anima perfectius intelligat. Ergo beatitudo animae non erit maior post resurrectionem.

PRAETEREA, infinito non potest esse aliquid maius: et ita infinitum cum aliquo finito non sunt maius quam infinitum ipsum. Sed anima beata ante corporis resumptionem beatitudinem habet de hoc quod gaudet de bono infinito, scilicet Deo: post resurrectionem autem corporis non habebit de alio gaudium, nisi forte de gloria corporis, quae est quoddam bonum finitum. Ergo gaudium eorum post corporis resumptionem non erit maius quam ante.

SED CONTRA: Est quod, Apoc. 6, super illud [v. 9], *vidi subter altare animas interfectorum* etc., dicit Glossa: *modo animae sanctorum sunt existentes sub, idest in mi-*

OBJECTION 1: It would seem that the happiness of the saints will not be greater after the judgment than before. For the nearer a thing approaches to the divine likeness, the more perfectly does it participate in happiness. Now the soul is more like God when separated from the body than when united to it. Therefore, its happiness is greater before being reunited to the body than after.

OBJ. 2: Further, power is more effective when it is united than when divided. Now the soul is more united when separated from the body than when it is joined to the body. Therefore, it has then greater power for operation, and consequently has a more perfect share of happiness, since this consists in action.

OBJ. 3: Further, beatitude consists in an act of the speculative intellect. Now the intellect, in its act, makes no use of a bodily organ; and consequently by being reunited to the body the soul does not become capable of more perfect understanding. Therefore, the soul's happiness is not greater after than before the judgment.

OBJ. 4: Further, nothing can be greater than the infinite, and so the addition of the finite to the infinite does not result in something greater than the infinite by itself. Now the beatified soul before its reunion with the body is rendered happy by rejoicing in the infinite good, namely God; and after the resurrection of the body it will rejoice in nothing else except perhaps the glory of the body, and this is a finite good. Therefore, their joy after the resumption of the body will not be greater than before.

ON THE CONTRARY, A Gloss on Revelation 6:9: *I saw under the altar the souls of them that were slain*, says, *at present the souls of the saints are under the altar, i.e., less ex-*

nori dignitate quam sint futurae. Ergo , maior erit eorum beatitudo post iudicium.

PRAETEREA, sicut bonis beatitudo redditur pro praemio, ita et malis miseria. Sed miseria malorum post resumptionem corporum erit maior quam ante: quia non solum in anima, sed etiam in corpore punientur. Ergo beatitudo sanctorum erit maior post resurrectionem corporum quam ante.

RESPONDEO dicendum quod beatitudinem sanctorum post resurrectionem augeri extensive quidem manifestum est: quia beatitudo tunc erit non solum in anima, sed etiam in corpore. Et etiam ipsius animae beatitudo augebitur extensive: inquantum anima non solum gaudebit de bono proprio, sed etiam de bono corporis.

Potest etiam dici quod etiam beatitudo animae ipsius intensive augebitur. Corpus enim hominis dupliciter potest considerari: uno modo, secundum quod est ab anima perfectibile; alio modo, secundum quod est in eo aliquid repugnans animae in suis operationibus, prout non perfecte corpus per animam perficitur. Secundum autem primam considerationem Corporis, coniunctio ipsius ad animam addit animae aliquam perfectionem. Quia omnis pars imperfecta est, et completur in suo toto: unde et totum se habet ad partem ut forma ad materiam. Unde et anima perfectior est in esse suo naturali cum est in toto, scilicet in homine coniuncta ex anima et corpore, quam cum est per se separata.

Sed unio corporis quantum ad secundarii ipsius considerationem, impedit animae perfectionem: unde dicitur quod *corpus, quod corrumpitur, aggravat animam*, Sap. 9, [15]. Si ergo a corpore removeatur omne illud per quod actioni animae resistit, simpliciter anima erit perfectior in corpore tali existens quam per se separata. Quanto autem aliquid est perfectius in esse, tanto potest perfectius operari. Unde et operatio animae coniunctae tali corpori erit perfectior quam operatio animae separatae. Huiusmodi autem corpus est corpus gloriosum, quod omnino subdetur spiritui. Unde, cum beatitudo in operatione consistat, perfectior erit beatitudo animae post resumptionem corporis quam ante: sicut enim anima separata a corpore corruptibili perfectius potest operari quam ei coniuncta, ita, postquam fuerit coniuncta corpori glorioso, perfectior erit eius operatio quam quando erat separata. Omne autem imperfectum appetit suam perfectionem. Et ideo anima separata naturaliter appetit corporis coniunctionem. Et propter hunc appetitum, ex imperfectione procedentem, eius operatio, qua in Deum fertur, est minus intensa. Et hoc est quod dicit Augustinus, quod *ex appetitu corporis retardatur ne tota intentione pergat in illud summum bonum.*

alted than they will be. Therefore, their happiness will be greater after the resurrection than after their death.

FURTHER, Just as happiness is bestowed on the good as a reward, so is unhappiness awarded to the wicked. But the unhappiness of the wicked after reunion with their bodies will be greater than before, since they will be punished not only in the soul but also in the body. Therefore, the happiness of the saints will be greater after the resurrection of the body than before.

I ANSWER THAT, It is manifest that the happiness of the saints will increase in extent after the resurrection, because their happiness will then be not only in the soul but also in the body. Moreover, the soul's happiness also will increase in extent, seeing that the soul will rejoice not only in its own good, but also in the good of the body.

We may also say that the soul's happiness will increase in intensity. For man's body may be considered in two ways: first, as being dependent on the soul for its completion; second, as containing something that hampers the soul in its operations, through the soul not perfectly completing the body. As regards the first way of considering the body, its union with the soul adds a certain perfection to the soul, since every part is imperfect, and is completed in its whole; wherefore the whole is to the part as form to matter. Consequently, the soul is more perfect in its natural being when it is in the whole—namely, man who results from the union of soul and body—than when it is a separate part.

But as regards the second consideration the union of the body hampers the perfection of the soul, wherefore it is written that *the corruptible body is a load upon the soul* (Wis 9:15). If, then, there be removed from the body all those things wherein it hampers the soul's action, the soul will be simply more perfect while existing in such a body than when separated therefrom. Now the more perfect a thing is in being, the more perfectly is it able to operate: wherefore the operation of the soul united to such a body will be more perfect than the operation of the separated soul. But the glorified body will be a body of this description, being altogether subject to the spirit. Therefore, since beatitude consists in an operation, the soul's happiness after its reunion with the body will be more perfect than before. For just as the soul separated from a corruptible body is able to operate more perfectly than when united thereto, so after it has been united to a glorified body its operation will be more perfect than while it was separated. Now every imperfect thing desires its perfection. Hence the separated soul naturally desires reunion with the body, and on account of this desire which proceeds from the soul's imperfection, its operation whereby it is borne towards God is less intense. This agrees with the saying of Augustine (*On the Literal Meaning of Genesis* 12.35) that *on account of the body's desire, it is held back from tending with all its might to that sovereign good.*

AD PRIMUM ergo dicendum quod anima coniuncta corpori glorioso est magis Deo similis quam ab eo separata, inquantum coniuncta habet esse perfectius: quanto enim est aliquid perfectius, tanto est Deo similius. Sicut etiam cor, cuius vitae perfectio in motu consistit, est Deo similius quando movetur quam quando quiescit, quamvis Deus nunquam moveatur.

AD SECUNDUM dicendum quod virtus quae de sua natura habet quod sit in materia, magis est potens in materia existens quam a materia separata: quamvis, absolute loquendo, virtus a materia separata sit potentior.

AD TERTIUM dicendum quod, quamvis in actu intelligendi anima corpore non utatur, tamen perfectio corporis quodammodo ad perfectionem operationis intellectualis cooperabitur, inquantum ex coniunctione corporis gloriosi anima erit in natura perfectior, et per consequens in operatione efficacior. Et secundum hoc ipsum bonum corporis cooperabitur quasi instrumentaliter ad operationem illam in qua beatitudo consistit: sicut etiam Philosophus ponit, in I *Ethic.*, quod bona exteriora cooperantur instrumentaliter ad felicitatem vitae.

AD QUARTUM dicendum quod, quamvis finitum infinito additum non faciat maius, tamen facit plus: quia finitum et infinitum sunt duo, cum infinitum per se acceptum sit unum. Extensio autem gaudii non recipit maius, sed plus. Unde extensive augetur gaudium secundum quod est de Deo et de gloria corporis, respectu gaudii quod erat de Deo. Gloria etiam corporis operabitur ad gaudii intensionem quod est de Deo, inquantum cooperabitur ad perfectiorem operationem qua anima in Deum feretur: quanto enim operatio conveniens fuerit perfectior, tanto delectatio erit maior, ut patet ex hoc quod dicitur X *Ethicorum.*

REPLY OBJ. 1: The soul united to a glorified body is more like to God than when separated therefrom, insofar as when united it has more perfect being. For the more perfect a thing is, the more it is like to God: even so the heart, the perfection of whose life consists in movement, is more like to God while in movement than while at rest, although God is never moved.

REPLY OBJ. 2: A power which by its own nature is capable of being in matter is more effective when subjected in matter than when separated from matter, although, absolutely speaking, a power separate from matter is more effective.

REPLY OBJ. 3: Although in the act of understanding the soul does not make use of the body, the perfection of the body will somewhat conduce to the perfection of the intellectual operation, insofar as through being united to a glorified body the soul will be more perfect in its nature, and consequently more effective in its operation. Accordingly, the good itself of the body will conduce instrumentally, as it were, to the operation wherein happiness consists: thus the Philosopher asserts (*Ethics* 1.8, 10) that external goods conduce instrumentally to the happiness of life.

REPLY OBJ. 4: Although finite added to infinite does not make a greater thing, it makes more things, since finite and infinite are two things, while infinite taken by itself is one. Now the greater extent of joy regards not a greater thing but more things. Wherefore joy is increased in extent, through referring to God and to the body's glory, in comparison with the joy which referred to God. Moreover, the body's glory will conduce to the intensity of the joy that refers to God, insofar as it will conduce to the more perfect operation whereby the soul tends to God: since the more perfect is a becoming operation, the greater the delight, as stated in *Ethics* 10.8.

Article 2

Whether the Degrees of Beatitude Should Be Called Mansions?

AD SECUNDUM SIC PROCEDITUR. Videtur quod beatitudinis gradus *mansiones* dici non debeant. Beatitudo enim importat rationem praemii. Sed mansio nihil significat quod ad praemium pertineat. Ergo diversi gradus beatitudinis mansiones dici non debent.

PRAETEREA, *mansio* locum significare videtur. Sed locus quo sancti beatificabuntur, non est corporalis, sed spiritualis, scilicet Deus, qui unus est. Ergo non est nisi una mansio, Et ita diversi gradus beatitudinis mansiones dici non debent.

PRAETEREA, sicut in patria, erunt homines diversorum meritorum, ita nunc sunt in purgatorio, et in limbo Patrum fuerunt. Sed in purgatorio et in limbo non

OBJECTION 1: It would seem that the degrees of beatitude should not be called *mansions*. For beatitude implies the notion of a reward: whereas mansion denotes nothing pertaining to a reward. Therefore, the various degrees of beatitude should not be called mansions.

OBJ. 2: Further, *mansion* seemingly denotes a place. Now the place where the saint will be beatified is not corporeal but spiritual, namely, God who is one. Therefore, there is but one mansion: and consequently the various degrees of beatitude should not be called *mansions*.

OBJ. 3: Further, as in heaven there will be men of various merits, so are there now in purgatory, and were in the limbo of the fathers. But various mansions are not distin-

distinguuntur mansiones. Ergo nec in patria mansiones debent distingui.

SED CONTRA: Est quod dicitur Ioan. 14, [2]: *in domo Patris mei mansiones multae sunt*: quod Augustinus exponit de variis dignitatibus praemiorum.

PRAETEREA, in qualibet civitate est ordinata mansionum distinctio. Sed caelestis patria civitati comparatur: ut patet Apoc. 21. Ergo oportet ibi diversas mansiones distinguere, secundum diversos beatitudinis gradus.

RESPONDEO dicendum quod, quia motus localis est prior omnium aliorum motuum, ideo, secundum Philosophum, nomen motus et distantiae, et omnium huiusmodi, derivatum est a motu locali ad omnes alios motus. Finis autem motus localis est locus ad quem cum aliquid pervenerit, ibi manet quiescens et in eo conservatur. Et ideo in quolibet motu ipsam quietationem in fine motus dicimus *collocationem* vel *mansionem*. Et ideo, cum nomen motus derivetur usque ad actum appetitus et voluntatis, ipsa assecutio finis appetitivi motus dicitur mansio aut collocatio in fine. Et ideo diversi modi consequendi finem ultimum diversae mansiones dicuntur: ut sic unitas domus respondeat universitati beatitudinis, quae est ex parte obiecti; et pluralitas mansionum respondeat differentiae quae in beatitudine invenitur ex parte beatorum. Sicut etiam videmus in rebus naturalibus quod est idem locus sursum ad quem tendunt omnia levia, sed unumquodque pertingit propinquius secundum quod est levius; et ita habent diversas mansiones secundum differentiam levitatis.

AD PRIMUM ergo dicendum quod mansio importat rationem finis: et sic per consequens rationem praemii, quod est finis meriti.

AD SECUNDUM dicendum quod, quamvis sit unus locus spiritualis, tamen diversi sunt gradus appropinquandi ad locum illum. Et secundum hoc constituuntur diversae mansiones.

AD TERTIUM dicendum quod illi qui erant in limbo, vel nunc sunt in purgatorio, nondum pervenerunt ad suum finem. Et ideo in purgatorio vel in limbo non distinguuntur mansiones, sed solum in paradiso et in inferno, ubi est finis bonorum et malorum.

guished in purgatory and limbo. Therefore, in like manner neither should they be distinguished in heaven.

ON THE CONTRARY, It is written: *in my Father's house there are many mansions* (John 14:2): and Augustine expounds this in reference to the different degrees of rewards (*Tractates on John* 67).

FURTHER, In every well-ordered city there is a distinction of mansions. Now the heavenly kingdom is compared to a city (Rev 21:2). Therefore, we should distinguish various mansions there, according to the various degrees of beatitude.

I ANSWER THAT, Since local movement precedes all other movements, terms of movement, distance and the like are derived from local movement to all other movements, according to the Philosopher (*Physics* 8.7). Now the end of local movement is a place, and when a thing has arrived at that place it remains there at rest and is maintained therein. Hence in every movement this very rest at the end of the movement is called an *establishment* [*collocatio*] or *mansion*. Therefore, since the term 'movement' is transferred to the actions of the appetite and will, the attainment of the end of an appetitive movement is called a mansion or establishment: so that the unity of a house corresponds to the unity of beatitude, which unity is on the part of the object, and the plurality of mansions corresponds to the differences of beatitude on the part of the blessed: even so we observe in natural things that there is one place above to which all light objects tend, whereas each one reaches it more closely, according as it is lighter, so that they have various mansions corresponding to their various lightness.

REPLY OBJ. 1: Mansion implies the notion of end, and consequently of reward, which is the end of merit.

REPLY OBJ. 2: Though there is one spiritual place, there are different degrees of approaching thereto: and the various mansions correspond to these.

REPLY OBJ. 3: Those who were in limbo or are now in purgatory have not yet attained to their end. Wherefore various mansions are not distinguished in purgatory or limbo, but only in heaven and hell, wherein is the end of the good and of the wicked.

Article 3

Whether the Various Mansions Are Distinguished According to the Various Degrees of Charity?

AD TERTIUM SIC PROCEDITUR. Videtur quod diversae mansiones non distinguantur penes diversos gradus caritatis. Quia Matth. 25, dicitur: *dedit unicuique secundum propriam virtutem*. Propria autem uniuscuiusque

OBJECTION 1: It would seem that the various mansions are not distinguished according to the various degrees of charity. For it is written: *he gave to every one according to his proper virtue* (Matt 25:15). Now the proper virtue of a

virtus est eius vis naturalis. Ergo et dona gratiae et gloriae distribuuntur secundum diversos gradus virtutis naturalis.

Praeterea, in Psalmo [61, 13]. dicitur: *tu reddes unicuique secundum opera sua.* Sed illud quod redditur est beatitudinis mensura. Ergo gradus beatitudinis distinguuntur secundum diversitatem operum, et non secundum diversitatem caritatis.

Praeterea, praemium debetur actui, et non habitui: unde *fortissimi non coronantur, sed agorizantes*, ut patet I *Ethic.*; et II Tim. 2, [5], *non coronabitur nisi qui legitime certaverit.* Sed beatitudo est praemium. Ergo diversi gradus beatitudinis erunt secundum diversos gradus sperum, non secundum diversos gradus caritatis.

Sed contra: Est quod, quanto aliquis erit Deo magis coniunctus, tanto erit beatior. Sed secundum modum caritatis est modus coniunctionis ad Deum. Ergo secundum differentiam caritatis erit et diversitas beatitudinis.

Praeterea, *sicut simpliciter sequitur ad simpliciter, ita magis ad magis.* Sed habere beatitudinem sequitur ad habere caritatem. Ergo et labere maiorem beatitudinem sequitur ad habere maiorem caritatem.

Respondeo dicendum quod principium distinctivum mansionum sive graduum beatitudinis est duplex: scilicet propinquum, et remotum. Propinquum est diversa dispositio quae erit in beatis, ex qua contingit diversitas perfectionis apud omnes in operatione beatitudinis. Sed principium remotum est meritum, quo talem beatitudinem consecuti sunt.

Primo autem modo distinguuntur mansiones secundum caritatem patriae: quae quanto in aliquo erit perfectior, tanto eum reddet capaciorem divinae claritatis, secundum cuius augmentum augebitur perfectio visionis divinae.

Secundo vero modo distinguuntur mansiones secundum caritatem viae. Actus enim noster non habet quod sit meritorius ex ipsa substantia actus, sed solum ex habitu virtutis quo informatur. Vis autem merendi est in omnibus virtutibus ex caritate, quae habet ipsum finem pro obiecto. Et ideo diversitas in merendo tota revertitur ad diversitatem caritatis. Et sic caritas viae distinguet mansiones per modum meriti.

Ad primum ergo dicendum quod virtus ibi non accipitur solum pro naturali capacitate: sed pro naturali capacitate simul cum conatu ad habendam gratiam. Et tunc virtus, hoc modo accepta, erit quasi materialis dispositio ad mensuram gratiae et gloriae suscipiendae: sed caritas est formaliter complens meritum ad gloriam. Et ideo distinctio gradus in gloria accipitur penes gradus caritatis potius quam penes gradus virtutis praedictae.

thing is its natural power. Therefore, the gifts also of grace and glory are distributed according to the different degrees of natural power.

Obj. 2: Further, it is written: *you will render to every man according to his works* (Ps 61:12). Now that which is rendered is the measure of beatitude. Therefore, the degrees of beatitude are distinguished according to the diversity of works, and not according to the diversity of charity.

Obj. 3: Further, reward is due to act and not to habit: hence *it is not the strongest who are crowned but those who engage in the conflict* (Ethics 1.8) and *he shall not be crowned except he strive lawfully* (2 Tim 2:5). Now beatitude is a reward. Therefore, the various degrees of beatitude will be according to the various degrees of works, and not according to the various degrees of charity.

On the contrary, The more one will be united to God, the happier will one be. Now the measure of charity is the measure of one's union with God. Therefore, the diversity of beatitude will be according to the difference of charity.

Further, *As one thing taken simply follows upon another taken simply, so a greater degree of the one follows upon a greater degree of the other*. Now to have beatitude follows from having charity. Therefore, to have greater beatitude follows from having greater charity.

I answer that, The distinctive principle of the mansions or degrees of beatitude is twofold: namely, proximate and remote. The proximate principle is the difference of disposition which will be in the blessed, whence will result the difference of perfection in them in respect to the beatific operation: while the remote principle is the merit by which they have obtained that beatitude.

In the first way, the mansions are distinguished according to the charity of heaven, which, the more perfect it will be in any one, the more will it render him capable of the divine clarity, on the increase of which will depend the increase in perfection of the divine vision.

In the second way, the mansions are distinguished according to the charity of the way. For our actions are meritorious not by the very substance of the action, but only by the habit of virtue with which they are informed. Now every virtue obtains its meritorious efficacy from charity, which has the end itself for its object. Hence the diversity of merit is all traced to the diversity of charity, and thus the charity of the way will distinguish the mansions by way of merit.

Reply Obj. 1: In this passage 'virtue' denotes not the natural ability alone, but the natural ability together with the endeavour to obtain grace. Consequently, virtue in this sense will be a kind of material disposition to the measure of grace and glory that one will receive. But charity is the formal complement of merit in relation to glory, and therefore the distinction of degrees in glory depends on the degrees of charity rather than on the degrees of the aforesaid virtue.

AD SECUNDUM dicendum quod opera non habent quod eis retributio gloriae reddatur nisi inquantum sunt caritate informata. Et ideo secundum diversos caritatis gradus erunt diversi gradus in gloria.

AD TERTIUM dicendum quod, quamvis habitus caritatis, vel cuiuscumque virtutis, non sit meritum, cui debeatur praemium, est tamen principium et tota ratio merendi in actu. Et ideo secundum eius diversitatem praemia distinguuntur. Quamvis etiam ex ipso genere actus possit aliquis gradus in merendo considerari, non quidem respectu praemii essentialis, quod est gaudium de Deo, sed respectu alicuius accidentalis praemii, quod est gaudium de aliquo bono creato.

REPLY OBJ. 2: Works in themselves do not demand the payment of a reward except as informed by charity: and therefore the various degrees of glory will be according to the various degrees of charity.

REPLY OBJ. 3: Although the habit of charity or of any virtue whatever is not a merit to which a reward is due, it is nonetheless the principle and reason of merit in the act: and consequently according to its diversity is the diversity of rewards. This does not prevent our observing a certain degree of merit in the act considered generically, not indeed in relation to the essential reward which is joy in God, but in relation to some accidental reward, which is joy in some created good.

QUESTION 94

THE RELATION OF THE SAINTS TOWARDS THE DAMNED

Deinde considerandum est de modo quo se sancti habebunt erga damnatos.

Circa quod quaeruntur tria.

Primo: utrum sancti poenas damnatorum videant.

Secundo: utrum eis compatiantur.

Tertio: utrum de eorum poenis laetentur.

We must next consider the relations of the saints towards the damned.

Under this head there are three points of inquiry:

(1) Whether the saints see the sufferings of the damned?

(2) Whether they pity them?

(3) Whether they rejoice in their sufferings?

Article 1

Whether the Blessed in Heaven Will See the Sufferings of the Damned?

AD PRIMUM SIC PROCEDITUR. Videtur quod beati qui erunt in patria, non videant poenas damnatorum. Maior enim est distantia damnatorum a beatis quam viatorum. Sed beati semper viatorum facta non vident: unde Isaiae 63, [16], *Abraham nescivit nos*, dicit Glossa: *nesciunt mortui, etiam sancti, quid faciunt vivi, etiam eorum filii.* Ergo multo minus vident poenas damnatorum.

PRAETEREA, perfectio visionis dependet a perfectione visibilis: unde Philosophus dicit, X *Ethic.*, quod *perfectissima sensus operatio est sensus optime dispositi ad pulcherrimum sub sensu iacentium.* Ergo e contrario turpitudo visibilis redundat in imperfectionem visionis: Sed imperfectio nulla erit in beatis. Ergo non videbunt miserias damnatorum, in quibus est summa turpitudo.

SED CONTRA est quod dicitur Isaiae 66, [24]: *egredientur et videbunt cadavera virorum qui praevaricati sunt in me*: Glossa, *electi egredientur, intelligentia vel visione manifesta, ut ad laudem Dei magis accendantur.*

RESPONDEO dicendum quod a beatis nihil subtrahi debet quod ad perfectionem beatitudinis eorum pertineat. Unumquodque autem ex comparatione contrarii magis cognoscitur: quia contraria iuxta se posita magis elucescunt. Et ideo ut beatitudo sanctorum eis magis complaceat, et de ea uberiores gratias Deo agant, datur eis ut poenam impiorum perfecte intueantur.

OBJECTION 1: It would seem that the blessed in heaven will not see the sufferings of the damned. For the damned are more cut off from the blessed than wayfarers. But the blessed do not see the deeds of wayfarers; hence a Gloss on Isaiah 63:16: *Abraham has not known us*, says, *the dead, even the saints, know not what the living, even their own children, are doing* (St. Augustine, *On The Care of the Dead* 8, 15). Much less, therefore, do they see the sufferings of the damned.

OBJ. 2: Further, perfection of vision depends on the perfection of the visible object: wherefore the Philosopher says (*Ethics* 10.4) that *the most perfect operation of the sense of sight is when the sense is most disposed with reference to the most beautiful of the objects which fall under the sight.* Therefore, on the other hand, any deformity in the visible object redounds to the imperfection of the sight. But there will be no imperfection in the blessed. Therefore, they will not see the sufferings of the damned, wherein there is extreme deformity.

ON THE CONTRARY, Isaiah 66:24 says: *they shall go out and see the carcasses of the men that have transgressed against me*, upon which a Gloss says, *the elect will go out by understanding or seeing manifestly, so that they may be urged the more to praise God.*

I ANSWER THAT, Nothing should be denied the blessed that belongs to the perfection of their beatitude. Now everything is known the more for being compared with its contrary, because when contraries are placed beside one another they become more conspicuous. Wherefore in order that the happiness of the saints may be more delightful to them and that they may render more copious thanks to God for it, they are allowed to see perfectly the sufferings of the damned.

AD PRIMUM ergo dicendum quod Glossa illa loquitur de sanctis mortuis secundum impossibilitatem naturae: non enim oportet ut naturali cognitione cognoscant omnia quae erga vivos aguntur. Sed sancti qui sunt in patria omnia clare cognoscunt quae aguntur et apud viatores et apud damnatos. Unde Gregorius dicit, XII lib. *Moral.: de animabus sanctis, sentiendum non est* (hoc scilicet quod Iob dicit, *sive nobiles fuerint filii eius sive ignobiles nesciet* etc.): *quia qui intus habent Dei claritatem, nullo modo credendum est quod sit foris aliquid quod ignorent.*

AD SECUNDUM dicendum quod, quamvis pulchritudo visibilis ad perfectionem faciat visionis, visibilis tamen turpitudo sine visionis infectione esse potest: species enim rerum in anima per quas contraria cognoscuntur, non sunt contrariae. Unde etiam Deus, qui perfectissimam cognitionem habet, omnia pulchra et turpia videt.

REPLY OBJ. 1: This Gloss speaks of what the departed saints are able to do by nature: for it is not necessary that they should know by natural knowledge all that happens to the living. But the saints in heaven know distinctly all that happens both to wayfarers and to the damned. Hence on Job 14:21: *whether his children come to honor or dishonour, he will not know*, Gregory says, *we should not hold this opinion to apply to the souls of the saints, because since they possess the glory of God within them, we cannot believe that external things are unknown to them* (*Morals on Job* 12).

REPLY OBJ. 2: Although the beauty of the thing seen conduces to the perfection of vision, there may be deformity of the thing seen without imperfection of vision: because the images of things whereby the soul knows contraries are not themselves contrary. Wherefore also God, who has most perfect knowledge, sees all things, beautiful and deformed.

Article 2

Whether the Blessed Pity the Unhappiness of the Damned?

AD SECUNDUM SIC PROCEDITUR. Videtur quod beati miseriis damnatorum compatiantur. Compassio enim ex caritate procedit. Sed in beatis erit perfectissima caritas. Ergo maxime miseriis damnatorum compatiuntur.

PRAETEREA, beati nunquam erunt tantum elongati a compassione quantum Deus est. Sed Deus quodammodo miseriis nostris compatitur, unde et *misericors* dicitur: et similiter angeli. Ergo beati compatientur miseriis damnatorum.

SED CONTRA, quicumque alii compatitur, fit miseriae eius quodammodo particeps. Sed beati non possunt esse participes alicuius miseriae. Ergo miseriis damnatorum non compatiuntur.

RESPONDEO dicendum quod misericordia, vel compassio, potest in aliquo inveniri dupliciter: uno modo, per modum passionis; alio modo, per modum electionis. In beatis autem non erit aliqua passio in parte inferiori nisi consequens electionem rationis. Unde non erit in eis compassio vel misericordia nisi secundum electionem rationis. Hoc autem modo ex electione rationis misericordia vel compassio nascitur, prout scilicet aliquis vult malum alterius repelli: unde in illis quae secundum iudicium rationis repelli non volumus, compassionem talem non habemus. Peccatores autem quandiu sunt in hoc mundo, in tali statu sunt quod sine praeiudicio divinae iustitiae possunt in beatitudinem transferri a statu miseriae et peccati. Et ideo beatorum compassio ad eos locum habet: et secundum electionem voluntatis, prout Deus, angeli et beati eis compati dicuntur, eorum salutem volendo; et secundum passionem, sicut compatiun-

OBJECTION 1: It would seem that the blessed pity the unhappiness of the damned. For pity proceeds from charity; and charity will be most perfect in the blessed. Therefore, they will most especially pity the sufferings of the damned.

OBJ. 2: Further, the blessed will never be so far from taking pity as God is. Yet in a sense God has compassion on our afflictions, wherefore he is said to be *merciful*. Therefore, the blessed will pity the miseries of the damned.

ON THE CONTRARY, Whoever pities another shares somewhat in his unhappiness. But the blessed cannot share in any unhappiness. Therefore, they do not pity the afflictions of the damned.

I ANSWER THAT, Mercy or compassion may be in a person in two ways: first, by way of passion; second, by way of choice. In the blessed there will be no passion in the lower powers except as a result of the reason's choice. Hence compassion or mercy will not be in them, except by the choice of reason. Now mercy or compassion comes of the reason's choice when a person wishes another's evil to be dispelled: wherefore in those things which, in accordance with reason, we do not wish to be dispelled, we have no such compassion. But so long as sinners are in this world they are in such a state that without prejudice to the divine justice they can be taken away from a state of unhappiness and sin to a state of happiness. Consequently, it is possible to have compassion on them both by the choice of the will—in which sense God, the angels, and the blessed are said to pity them by desiring their salvation—and by passion, in which way they are pitied by the good men who are in the state of way-

tur eis homines boni in statu viae existentes. Sed in futuro non poterunt transferri a sua miseria. Unde ad eorum miserias non poterit esse compassio secundum electionem rectam. Et ideo beati qui erunt in gloria, nullam compassionem ad damnatos. habebunt.

AD PRIMUM ergo dicendum quod caritas tunc est compassionis principium quando possumus ex caritate velle remotionem miseriae alicuius. Sed sancti ex caritate hoc velle non possunt de damnatis: cum divinae iustitiae repugnet. Unde ratio non sequitur.

AD SECUNDUM dicendum quod Deus dicitur esse misericors inquantum subvenit illis quos secundum ordinem sapientiae et iustitiae suae convenit a miseria liberari: non quod damnatorum misereatur, nisi forte puniendo citra condignum.

farers. But in the future state it will be impossible for them to be taken away from their unhappiness: and consequently it will not be possible to pity their sufferings according to right reason. Therefore, the blessed in glory will have no pity on the damned.

REPLY OBJ. 1: Charity is the principle of pity when it is possible for us out of charity to wish the cessation of a person's unhappiness. But the saints cannot desire this for the damned, since it would be contrary to divine justice. Consequently, the argument does not follow.

REPLY OBJ. 2: God is said to be merciful insofar as he succors those whom it is befitting to be released from their afflictions in accordance with the order of wisdom and justice: not as though he pitied the damned, except perhaps in punishing them less than they deserve.

Article 3

Whether the Blessed Rejoice in the Punishment of the Wicked?

AD TERTIUM SIC PROCEDITUR. Videtur quod beati non laetentur de poenis impiorum; Laetari enim de malo alterius ad odium pertinet. Sed in beatis nullum erit odium. Ergo non laetabuntur de miseriis damnatorum.

PRAETEREA, beati in patria erunt summe Deo conformes. Sed *Deus non delectatur in poenis nostris.* Ergo nec beati delectabuntur in poenis damnatorum.

PRAETEREA, illud quod est vituperabile in viatore, nullo modo cadit in comprehensorem. Sed in homine viatore est maxime vituperabile quod reficiatur aliorum poenis; et maxime commendabile ut de poenis doleat. Ergo beati nullo modo laetantur de poenis damnatorum.

SED CONTRA: Est quod in Psalmo [57, 11] dicitur: *laetabitur iustus cum viderit vindictam.*

PRAETEREA, Isaiae 66, [24]: *erunt usque ad satietatem visionis omni carni.* Satietas autem refectionem mentis designat. Ergo beati gaudebunt de poenis impiorum.

RESPONDEO dicendum quod aliquid potest esse materia gaudii dupliciter. Uno modo, per se: quando scilicet de aliquo gaudetur inquantum huiusmodi. Et sic sancti non laetabuntur de poenis impiorum. Alio modo, per accidens, idest ratione alicuius adiuncti. Et hoc modo sancti de poenis impiorum gaudebunt, considerando in eis ordinem divinae iustitiae et suam liberationem, de qua gaudebunt. Et sic divina iustitia et sua liberatio erunt per se causa gaudii beatorum, sed poenae damnatorum per accidens.

OBJECTION 1: It would seem that the blessed do not rejoice in the punishment of the wicked. For rejoicing in another's evil pertains to hatred. But there will be no hatred in the blessed. Therefore, they will not rejoice in the unhappiness of the damned.

OBJ. 2: Further, the blessed in heaven will be in the highest degree conformed to God. Now *God does not rejoice in our afflictions.* Therefore, neither will the blessed rejoice in the afflictions of the damned.

OBJ. 3: Further, that which is blameworthy in a wayfarer has no place whatever in a comprehensor. Now it is most reprehensible in a wayfarer to take pleasure in the pains of others, and most praiseworthy to grieve for them. Therefore, the blessed in no way rejoice in the punishment of the damned.

ON THE CONTRARY, It is written: *the just shall rejoice when he shall see the revenge* (Ps 57:11).

FURTHER, It is written: *they shall satiate the sight of all flesh* (Isa 56:24). Now satiety denotes refreshment of the mind. Therefore, the blessed will rejoice in the punishment of the wicked.

I ANSWER THAT, A thing may be a matter of rejoicing in two ways. First, directly, when one rejoices in a thing as such: and thus the saints will not rejoice in the punishment of the wicked. Second, indirectly, by reason of something annexed to it: and in this way the saints will rejoice in the punishment of the wicked, by considering therein the order of divine justice and their own deliverance, which will fill them with joy. And thus the divine justice and their own deliverance will be the direct cause of the joy of the blessed: while the punishment of the damned will cause it indirectly.

Ad primum ergo dicendum quod laetari de malo alterius inquantum huiusmodi, pertinet ad odium: non autem laetari de malo alterius ratione alicuius adiuncti. Sic autem aliquis de malo proprio quandoque laetatur: sicut cum quis gaudet de propriis afflictionibus secundum quod prosunt ei ad meritum vitae; Iac. 1, [2], *omne gaudium existimate, fratres mei, cum in tentationes varias incideritis.*

Ad secundum dicendum quod, quamvis Deus non delectetur in poenis inquantum huiusmodi delectatur tamen eis inquantum sunt per suam iustitiam ordinatae.

Ad tertium dicendum quod in viatore non est laudabile quod delectetur de aliorum poenis secundum se: est tamen laudabile si delectetur de eis inquantum habent aliquid annexum. Tamen alia ratio est de viatore et comprehensore. Quia in viatore passiones frequenter insurgunt sine iudicio rationis. Et tamen tales passiones interdum sunt laudabiles, secundum quod bonam dispositionem mentis indicant: sicut patet de verecundia et misericordia et poenitentia de malo. Sed in comprehensoribus non potest esse passio nisi consequens iudicium rationis.

Reply Obj. 1: To rejoice in another's evil as such belongs to hatred, but not to rejoice in another's evil by reason of something annexed to it. Thus a person sometimes rejoices in his own evil, such as when we rejoice in our own afflictions as helping us to merit life: *my brethren, count it all joy when you shall fall into diverse temptations* (Jas 1:2).

Reply Obj. 2: Although God rejoices not in punishments as such, he rejoices in them as being ordered by his justice.

Reply Obj. 3: It is not praiseworthy in a wayfarer to rejoice in another's afflictions as such: yet it is praiseworthy if he rejoice in them as having something annexed. However, it is not the same with a wayfarer as with a comprehensor, because in a wayfarer the passions often forestall the judgment of reason, and yet sometimes such passions are praiseworthy as indicating the good disposition of the mind, like in the case of shame, pity, and repentance for evil: whereas in a comprehensor there can be no passion but such as follows the judgment of reason.

QUESTION 95

THE GIFTS OF THE BLESSED

Deinde considerandum est de dotibus beatorum.
Circa quod quaeruntur quinque.
Primo: utrum beatis sint assignandae aliquae dotes.

Secundo: utrum dos a beatitudine differat.
Tertio: utrum Christo insint dotes.
Quarto: utrum angelis.
Quinto: utrum convenienter assignentur dotes.

We must now consider the gifts of the blessed.
Under which head there are five points of inquiry:
(1) Whether any gifts should be assigned to the blessed?
(2) Whether a gift differs from beatitude?
(3) Whether it is fitting for Christ to have gifts?
(4) Whether this is competent to the angels?
(5) Whether three gifts of the soul are rightly assigned?

Article 1

Whether Any Gifts Should Be Assigned as Dowry to the Blessed?

AD PRIMUM SIC PROCEDITUR. Videtur quod non sint ponendae aliquae dotes in hominibus beatis. Dos enim, secundum iura, datur sponso ad sustinenda onera matrimonii. Sed sancti non gerunt figuram sponsi, sed magis figuram sponsae, inquantum sunt Ecclesiae membra. Ergo eis dotes non dantur.

PRAETEREA, dotes non dantur, secundum iura, a patre sponsi, sed a patre sponsae. Omnia autem dona beatitudinis dantur beatis a Patre Sponsi, scilicet Christi: Iac. 1, [17], *omne datum optimum et omne donum perfectum*, etc. Ergo huiusmodi dona quae beatis dantur, non sunt dotes appellandae.

PRAETEREA, in matrimonio dantur dotes ad facilius toleranda onera matrimonii. Sed in matrimonio spirituali non sunt aliqua onera: maxime secundum statum Ecclesiae triumphantis. Ergo non sunt ibi aliquae dotes assignandae.

PRAETEREA, dotes non dantur nisi, causa matrimonii. Sed matrimonium spirituale contrahitur cum Christo per fidem secundum statum Ecclesiae militantis. Ergo, eadem ratione, si beatis aliquae dotes conveniunt, convenient, etiam sanctis existentibus in via. Sed istis non conveniunt. Ergo nec beatis.

PRAETEREA, dotes ad bona exteriora pertinent, quae dicuntur bona fortunae. Sed praemia beatorum erunt de interioribus bonis. Ergo non debent dotes nominari.

SED CONTRA: Ephes. 5, [32] dicitur: *Sacramentum hoc magnum est: dico autem in Christo et Ecclesia*: ex quo habetur quod spirituale matrimonium per carnale significatur. Sed in carnali matrimonio sponsa dotata tra-

OBJECTION 1: It would seem that no gifts should be assigned as dowry to the blessed. For a dowry is given to the bridegroom for the upkeep of the burdens of marriage, according to law (*Decretals*). But the saints resemble not the bridegroom but the bride, as being members of the Church. Therefore, they receive no dowry.

OBJ. 2: Further, the dowry is given not by the bridegroom's father, but by the father of the bride, according to law (*Decretals*). Now all the beatific gifts are bestowed on the blessed by the father of the bridegroom, who is Christ: *every best gift and every perfect gift is from above coming down from the Father of lights* (Jas 1:17). Therefore, these gifts which are bestowed on the blessed should not be called a dowry.

OBJ. 3: Further, in carnal marriage a dowry is given that the burdens of marriage may be the more easily borne. But in spiritual marriage there are no burdens, especially in the state of the Church Triumphant. Therefore, no dowry should be assigned to that state.

OBJ. 4: Further, a dowry is not given save on the occasion of marriage. But a spiritual marriage is contracted with Christ by faith in the state of the Church Militant. Therefore, if a dowry is befitting the blessed, for the same reason it will be befitting the saints who are wayfarers. But it is not befitting the latter; therefore, neither the blessed.

OBJ. 5: Further, a dowry pertains to external goods, which are called 'goods of fortune': whereas the reward of the blessed will consist of internal goods. Therefore, they should not be called a dowry.

ON THE CONTRARY, It is written: *this is a great sacrament: but I speak in Christ and in the Church* (Eph 5:32). Hence it follows that the spiritual marriage is signified by the carnal marriage. But in a carnal marriage the dowered

ducitur in domum sponsi. Ergo, cum sancti in domum Christi traducantur cum beatificantur, videtur quod aliquibus dotibus dotentur.

PRAETEREA, dotes in matrimonio corporali assignantur ad matrimonii solatium. Sed matrimonium spirituale est delectabilius quam corporale. Ergo ei sunt dotes maxime assignandae.

PRAETEREA, ornamenta sponsarum ad dotem pertinent. Sed sancti ornati in gloriam introducuntur: ut dicitur Isai. 61 [10]: *induit me vestimentis salutis, et quasi sponsam ornatam monilibus suis.* Ergo sancti in patria dotes habent.

RESPONDEO dicendum quod absque dubio beatis, quando in gloriam transferuntur, aliqua dona divinitus dantur ad eorum ornatum: et hi ornatus a magistris dotes sunt nominati. Unde datur quaedam definitio de dote de qua nunc loquimur, talis: *dos est perpetuus ornatus animae et corporis, vitae sufficiens, in aeterna beatitudine iugiter perseverans.* Et sumitur haec descriptio ad similitudinem dotis corporalis, per quam sponsa ornatur et providetur viro unde possit sufficienter sponsam et liberos nutrire, et tamen inamissibiliter dos sponsae conservatur, ut ad eam separato matrimonio revertatur.

Sed de ratione nominis diversi diversimode opinantur. Quidam enim dicunt quod dos non accipitur ex aliqua similitudine ad matrimonium corporale; sed secundum modum loquendi quo omnem perfectionem seu ornatum cuiuscumque hominis *dotem* nominamus; sicut aliquis dicitur esse *dotatus scientia* qui scientia pollet. Et sic Ovidius usus est nomine *dotis,* dicens: *et qua cumque potes dote placere, place.*

Sed istud non videtur usquequaque conveniens. Quia quandocumque aliquod nomen est impositum ad aliquid principaliter significandum, non consuevit ad alia transferri nisi secundum aliquam similitudinem. Unde, cum secundum primam institutionem nominis dos ad matrimonium carnale pertineat, oportet quod in qualibet alia acceptione attendatur aliqua similitudo ad principale significatum.

Et ideo alii dicunt quod secundum hoc similitudo attenditur, quod dos proprie dicitur donum quod in matrimonio corporali datur sponsae ex parte sponsi, quando traducitur in domum sponsi, ad ornatum sponsae pertinens: quod patet ex hoc quod dixit Sichem Iacob et filiis eius, Genes. 34, [12]: *augete dotem et munera postulate*; et Exod. 22, [16]: *si seduxerit quis virginem dormieritque cum ea, dotabit eam et accipiet eam in uxorem.* Unde et ornatus qui a Christo sanctis exhibetur quando traducuntur in domum gloriae, dos nominatur.

Sed hoc manifeste est contra id quod iuristae dicunt, ad quos pertinet de his tractare. Dicunt enim, quod dos

bride is brought to the dwelling of the bridegroom. Therefore, since the saints are brought to Christ's dwelling when they are beatified, it would seem that they are dowered with certain gifts.

FURTHER, A dowry is appointed to carnal marriage for the ease of marriage. But the spiritual marriage is more blissful than the carnal marriage. Therefore, a dowry should be especially assigned thereto.

FURTHER, The adornment of the bride is part of the dowry. Now the saints are adorned when they are taken into glory, according to Isaiah 61:10, *he has clothed me with the garments of salvation as a bride adorned with her jewels.* Therefore, the saints in heaven have a dowry.

I ANSWER THAT, Without doubt, the blessed, when they are brought into glory, are dowered by God with certain gifts for their adornment, and this adornment is called their 'dowry' by the masters. Hence the dowry of which we speak now is defined thus: *the dowry is the everlasting adornment of soul and body adequate to life, lasting forever in eternal bliss.* This description is taken from a likeness to the material dowry, whereby the bride is adorned and the husband provided with an adequate support for his wife and children, and yet the dowry remains inalienable from the bride, so that if the marriage union be severed it reverts to her.

As to the reason of the name there are various opinions. For some say that the name 'dowry' is taken not from a likeness to the corporeal marriage, but according to the manner of speaking whereby any perfection or adornment of any person whatever is called an *endowment*; thus a man who is proficient in knowledge is said to be *endowed with knowledge,* and in this sense Ovid employed the word *endowment*: *by whatever endowment you can please, strive to please* (*The Art of Love* 1.538).

But this does not seem quite fitting, for whenever a term is employed to signify a certain thing principally, it is not usually transferred to another save by reason of some likeness. Wherefore, since by its primary signification a dowry refers to carnal marriage, it follows that in every other application of the term we must observe some kind of likeness to its principal signification.

Consequently, others say that the likeness consists in the fact that in carnal marriage a dowry is properly a gift bestowed by the bridegroom on the bride for her adornment when she is taken to the bridegroom's dwelling: and that this is shown by the words of Sichem to Jacob and his sons: *raise the dowry, and ask gifts* (Gen 34:12), and from Exodus 22:16: *if a man seduce a virgin and lie with her, he shall endow her, and have her to wife.* Hence the adornment bestowed by Christ on the saints, when they are brought into the abode of glory, is called a dowry.

But this is clearly contrary to what jurists say, to whom it belongs to treat of these matters. For they say that a dowry,

proprie est *quaedam datio ex parte mulieris his qui sunt ex parte viri facta pro onere matrimonii quod sustinet vir.* Sed illud quod sponsus dat sponsae, vocatur *donatio propter nuptias.* Et secundum hunc modum accipitur dos III Reg. 9, [16], ubi dicitur quod *Pharao, Rex Aegypti, cepit Gazer, et dedit in dotem filiae suae uxori Salomonis.* Nec contra hoc faciunt auctoritates inductae. Quamvis enim dotes a parente puellae consueverunt assignari, tamen quandoque contingit quod sponsus, vel pater sponsi, assignet dotes vice patris puellae. Quod contingit dupliciter. Vel pro nimio affectu ad sponsam: sicut fuit de Hemor, qui voluit assignare dotem, quam debebat accipere, propter vehementem amorem filii sui ad puellam. Vel hoc fit in poenam sponsi, ut virgini a se corruptae dotem de suo assignet, quam pater puellae debuerat assignare. Et in hoc casu loquitur Moyses in auctoritate inducta.

Et ideo, secundum alios, dicendum est quod dos in matrimonio corporali proprie dicitur quando datur ab his qui sunt ex parte mulieris his qui sunt ex parte viri, ad sustentanda onera matrimonii, ut dictum est.

Sed tunc remanet difficultas, quomodo haec assignatio possit aptari ad propositum: cum ornatus qui sunt in beatitudine, dentur sponsae spirituali a parte sponsi. Quod manifestabitur respondendo ad argumenta.

Ad primum ergo dicendum quod dotes, quamvis assignentur sponso in carnali matrimonio ad usum, tamen proprietas et dominium pertinet ad sponsam: quod patet ex hoc quod, soluto matrimonio, dos remanet sponsae, secundum iura. Et sic etiam in matrimonio spirituali ipsi ornatus qui sponsae spirituali dantur, scilicet Ecclesiae in membris suis, sunt quidem ipsius sponsi, inquantum ad eius gloriam et honorem cedunt, sed sponsae inquantum per eas ornatur.

Ad secundum dicendum quod Pater Sponsi, scilicet Christi, est sola persona Patris: pater autem sponsae est tota Trinitas. Effectus autem in creaturis ad totam Trinitatem pertinent. Unde huiusmodi dotes in spirituali matrimonio, proprie loquendo, magis dantur a patre sponsae quam a Patre Sponsi.

Sed tamen haec collatio, quamvis ab omnibus Personis fiat, singulis Personis potest appropriari per aliquem modum. Personae quidem Patris ut danti: quia in ipso est auctoritas; ei etiam paternitas respectu creaturae appropriatur; ut sic idem sit Pater Sponsi et sponsae. Filio vero appropriatur inquantum propter ipsum et per ipsum dantur. Sed Spiritui Sancto inquantum in ipso et se-

properly speaking, *is a donation on the part of the wife made to those who are on the part of the husband, in view of the marriage burden which the husband has to bear;* while that which the bridegroom gives the bride is called *a donation in view of marriage.* In this sense dowry is taken, when 1 Kings 9:16 says that *Pharoah, the king of Egypt, took Gezer and gave it for a dowry to his daughter, Solomon's wife.* Nor do the authorities quoted prove anything to the contrary. For, although it is customary for a dowry to be given by the maiden's parents, it happens sometimes that the bridegroom or his father gives the dowry instead of the bride's father; and this happens in two ways: either by reason of his very great love for the bride (as in the case of Sichem's father Hemor, who, on account of his son's great love for the maiden, wished to give the dowry which he had a right to receive); or as a punishment on the bridegroom, that he should out of his own possessions give a dowry to the virgin seduced by him, whereas he should have received it from the girl's father. In this sense Moses speaks in the passage quoted above.

Wherefore, in the opinion of others, we should hold that in carnal marriage a dowry, properly speaking, is that which is given by those on the wife's side to those on the husband's side, for the bearing of the marriage burden, as stated above.

Yet the difficulty remains how this signification can be adapted to the case in point, since the heavenly adornments are given to the spiritual spouse by the Father of the Bridegroom. This shall be made clear by replying to the objections.

Reply Obj. 1: Although in carnal marriage the dowry is given to the bridegroom for his use, yet the ownership and control belong to the bride: which is evident by the fact that if the marriage be dissolved, the dowry reverts to the bride, according to law (*Decretals*). Thus also in spiritual marriage, the very adornments bestowed on the spiritual bride, namely, the Church in her members, belong indeed to the Bridegroom insofar as they conduce to his glory and honor, yet to the bride as adorned thereby.

Reply Obj. 2: The Father of the Bridegroom, that is, of Christ, is the Person of the Father alone: while the Father of the bride is the whole Trinity, since that which is effected in creatures belongs to the whole Trinity. Hence in spiritual marriage these endowments, properly speaking, are given by the Father of the bride rather than by the Father of the Bridegroom.

Nevertheless, although this endowment is made by all the Persons, it may be in a manner appropriated to each Person. To the Person of the Father, as endowing, since he possesses authority; also, fatherhood in relation to creatures is also appropriated to him, so that he is Father of both Bridegroom and bride. To the Son it is appropriated inasmuch as it is made for his sake and through him: and to the

cundum ipsum dantur: amor enim est omnis donationis ratio.

AD TERTIUM dicendum quod dotibus per se convenit illud quod per dotes efficitur, scilicet solatium matrimonii: sed per accidens illud quod per eas removetur, scilicet onus matrimonii, quod per dotes alleviatur; sicut gratiae convenit per se facere iustum, sed per accidens quod de impio faciat iustum. Quamvis ergo in matrimonio spirituali non sint aliqua onera, est tamen ibi summa iucunditas. Et ad hanc perficiendam iucunditatem dotes sponsae conferuntur, ut scilicet delectabiliter per eas sponso coniungatur.

AD QUARTUM dicendum quod dotes non consueverunt assignari sponsae quando desponsatur, sed quando in domum sponsi traducitur ut praesentialiter sponsum habeat. Quandiu autem in hac vita sumus, *peregrinamur a Domino*, II Cor. 5, [6]. Et ideo dona quae sanctis in hac vita conferuntur, non dicuntur dotes: sed illa quae conferuntur eis quando transferuntur ad gloriam, in qua Sponso praesentialiter perfruuntur.

AD QUINTUM dicendum quod in spirituali matrimonio interior decor requiritur: ut in Psalmo [4, 14], *omnis gloria eius filiae Regis ab intus*, etc. Sed in matrimonio corporali requiritur decor exterior. Unde non oportet quod dotes huiusmodi assignentur in matrimonio spirituali sicut assignantur in corporali.

Holy Spirit inasmuch as it is made in him and according to him, since love is the reason of all giving.

REPLY OBJ. 3: That which is effected by the dowry belongs to the dowry by its nature, and that is the ease of marriage: while that which the dowry removes, namely, the marriage burden (which is lightened thereby), belongs to it accidentally: thus it belongs to grace by its nature to make a man righteous, but accidentally to make an ungodly man righteous. Accordingly, though there are no burdens in the spiritual marriage, there is the greatest gladness; and, that this gladness may be perfected, the bride is dowered with gifts, so that by their means she may be happily united with the bridegroom.

REPLY OBJ. 4: The dowry is usually settled on the bride not when she is espoused, but when she is taken to the bridegroom's dwelling, so as to be in the presence of the bridegroom, since while we are in the body *we are absent from the Lord* (2 Cor 5:6). Hence the gifts bestowed on the saints in this life are not called a dowry, but those which are bestowed on them when they are received into glory, where the Bridegroom delights them with his presence.

REPLY OBJ. 5: In spiritual marriage inward comeliness is required, wherefore it is written: *all the glory of the king's daughter is within* (Ps 44:14). But in carnal marriage outward comeliness is necessary. Hence there is no need for a dowry of this kind to be appointed in spiritual marriage as in carnal marriage.

Article 2

Whether the Dowry Is the Same as Beatitude?

AD SECUNDUM SIC PROCEDITUR. Videtur quod dos sit idem quod beatitudo. Ut enim ex definitione dotis praedicta patet, dos est *ornatus animae et corporis in aeterna beatitudine iugiter perseverans*. Sed beatitudo est animae quidam ornatus eius. Ergo beatitudo est dos.

PRAETEREA, dos dicitur illud per quod sponsa delectabiliter sponso coniungitur. Sed in spirituali matrimonio beatitudo est huiusmodi. Ergo beatitudo est dos.

PRAETEREA, visio, secundum Augustinum, est tota substantia beatitudinis. Sed *visio* ponitur una de dotibus. Ergo beatitudo est dos.

PRAETEREA, fruitio beatum facit. Fruitio autem est dos. Ergo dos beatum facit. Et sic beatitudo est dos.

PRAETEREA, secundum Boetium, in libro *de Consolatione*, beatitudo est *status omnium bonorum congrega-*

OBJECTION 1: It would seem that the dowry is the same as beatitude. For, as appears from the definition of dowry (A. 1), the dowry is *the everlasting adornment of body and soul in eternal happiness*. Now the happiness of the soul is an adornment thereof. Therefore, beatitude is a dowry.

OBJ. 2: Further, a dowry signifies something whereby the union of bride and bridegroom is rendered delightful. Now such is beatitude in the spiritual marriage. Therefore, beatitude is a dowry.

OBJ. 3: Further, according to Augustine (*Expositions of the Psalms* 92), *vision* is the whole essence of beatitude. Now vision is accounted one of the dowries. Therefore, beatitude is a dowry.

OBJ. 4: Further, fruition gives happiness. Now fruition is a dowry. Therefore, a dowry gives happiness, and thus beatitude is a dowry.

OBJ. 5: Further, according to Boethius (*Consolation of Philosophy* 3), beatitude is *a state made perfect by the aggre-*

tione perfectus. Sed status beatorum perficitur ex dotibus. Ergo dotes sunt beatitudinis partes.

Sed contra: Dos datur sine meritis. Sed beatitudo non datur, sed redditur; Ergo beatitudo non est dos.

Praeterea, beatitudo est una tantum. Dotes vero sunt plures. Ergo beatitudo non est dos.

Praeterea, beatitudo inest homini secundum id quod est potissimum in eo, ut dicitur I *Ethic.* Sed dos etiam in corpore ponitur. Ergo dos et beatitudo non sunt idem.

Respondeo dicendum, quod circa hoc est duplex opinio. Quidam enim dicunt quod beatitudo et dos sunt idem re, sed differunt ratione: quia dos respicit spirituale matrimonium quod est inter Christum et animam, non autem beatitudo. Sed hoc non potest esse, ut videtur: cum beatitudo in operatione consistat; dos autem non sit operatio, sed magis sit qualitas vel dispositio quaedam.

Et ideo, secundum alios, dicendum quod beatitudo et dos etiam realiter differunt: ut beatitudo dicatur ipsa operatio perfecta qua anima beata Deo coniungitur; sed dotes dicuntur habitus vel dispositiones, vel quaecumque aliae qualitates, quae ordinantur ad huiusmodi perfectam operationem; ut sic dotes ordinentur ad beatitudinem magis quam sint in beatitudine ut partes eius.

Ad primum ergo dicendum quod beatitudo, proprie loquendo, non est animae ornatus, sed est aliquid quod ex ornatu animae provenit: cum sit operatio quaedam, ornatus vero dicitur aliquis decor ipsius beati.

Ad secundum dicendum quod beatitudo non ordinatur ad coniunctionem, sed est ipsa coniunctio animae cum Christo, quae est per operationem. Sed dotes sunt dona disponentia ad huiusmodi coniunctionem.

Ad tertium dicendum quod visio dupliciter potest accipi. Uno modo, actualiter, idest pro ipso actu visionis. Et sic visio non est dos, sed est ipsa beatitudo. Alio modo potest accipi habitualiter, idest pro habitu a quo talis operatio elicitur, idest pro ipsa gloriae claritate, qua anima divinitus illustratur ad Deum videndum. Et sic est dos, et principium beatitudinis; non autem est ipsa beatitudo.

Et similiter dicendum ad quartum de fruitione.

Ad quintum dicendum quod beatitudo colligit omnia bona non quasi partes essentiae beatitudinis, sed quasi aliquo modo ad beatitudinem ordinata.

gate of all good things. Now the state of the blessed is perfected by the dowries. Therefore, the dowries are part of beatitude.

On the contrary, The dowries are given without merits: whereas beatitude is not given, but is awarded in return for merits. Therefore, beatitude is not a dowry.

Further, Beatitude is one only, whereas the dowries are several. Therefore, beatitude is not a dowry.

Further, Beatitude is in man according to that which is principal in him (*Ethics* 10.7): whereas a dowry is also appointed to the body. Therefore, dowry and beatitude are not the same.

I answer that, There are two opinions on this question. For some say that beatitude and dowry are the same in reality but differ in aspect: because dowry regards the spiritual marriage between Christ and the soul, whereas beatitude does not. But seemingly this will not stand, since beatitude consists in an operation, whereas a dowry is not an operation, but a quality or disposition.

Therefore, according to others it must be stated that beatitude and dowry differ even in reality, beatitude being the perfect operation itself by which the soul is united to God, while the dowries are habits or dispositions or any other qualities directed to this same perfect operation, so that they are directed to beatitude instead of being in it as parts thereof.

Reply Obj. 1: Beatitude, properly speaking, is not an adornment of the soul, but something resulting from the soul's adornment; since it is an operation, while its adornment is a certain comeliness of the blessed themselves.

Reply Obj. 2: Beatitude is not directed to the union but is the union itself of the soul with Christ. This union is by an operation, whereas the dowries are gifts disposing to this same union.

Reply Obj. 3: Vision may be taken in two ways. First, actually, i.e., for the act itself of vision; and thus vision is not a dowry, but beatitude itself. Second, it may be taken habitually, i.e., for the habit whereby this act is elicited, namely, the clarity of glory, by which the soul is enlightened from above to see God: and thus it is a dowry and the principle of beatitude, but not beatitude itself.

The same answer applies to the fourth objection.

Reply Obj. 5: Beatitude is the sum of all goods not as though they were essential parts of beatitude, but as being in a way directed to beatitude, as stated above.

Article 3

Whether It Is Fitting That Christ Should Receive a Dowry?

AD TERTIUM SIC PROCEDITUR. Videtur quod Christo competat habere dotes. Sancti enim Christo per gloriam conformabuntur: unde dicitur Philipp, 3, [21]: *qui reformabit corpus humilitatis nostrae configuratum corpori claritatis suae.* Ergo Christus etiam dotes habet.

PRAETEREA, in spirituali matrimonio assignantur dotes ad similitudinem matrimonii corporalis. Sed in Christo invenitur quoddam spirituale matrimonium quod est sibi singulare, scilicet duarum naturarum in una persona: secundum quod dicitur natura humana in ipso esse desponsata a Verbo, ut patet ex Glossa super illud Psalmi [18, 6], *in sole posuit tabernaculum* etc.; et Apoc. 21, [3], *ecce tabernaculum Dei cum hominibus.* Ergo et Christo competit habere dotes.

PRAETEREA, ut dicit Augustinus, in libro *de Doctrina Christ.*, Christus, secundum regulam Tyconii, propter unitatem corporis mystici quae est inter caput et membra, nominat se etiam sponsam, et non solum sponsum: ut patet Isaiae 61, [10], *quasi sponsum decoratum corona, et quasi sponsam ornatam monilibus suis.* Cum ergo sponsae debeantur dotes, oportet, ut videtur, in Christo dotes ponere.

PRAETEREA, omnibus membris Ecclesiae debetur dos: cum Ecclesia sit sponsa. Sed Christus est Ecclesiae membrum: ut patet I Cor. 12, [27], *vos estis corpus Christi, et membra de membro*; Glossa, *idest de Christo,* Ergo Christo debentur dotes.

PRAETEREA, Christus habet perfectam visionem, fruitionem et delectationem. Hae autem ponuntur dotes. Ergo Christus habuit dotes.

SED CONTRA: Inter sponsum et sponsam exigitur distinctio personarum. Sed in Christo non est aliquid personaliter distinctum a Filio Dei, qui est sponsus, ut patet Ioan, 3, [29], *qui habet sponsam sponsus est.* Ergo, cum dotes sponsae assignentur, vel pro sponsa, videtur quod Christo non competat habere dotes.

PRAETEREA, non est eiusdem dare dotes et recipere. Sed Christus est qui dat dotes spirituales. Ergo Christo non competit dotes habere.

RESPONDEO dicendum, quod circa hanc difficultatem est duplex opinio. Quidam enim dicunt quod in Christo est triplex unio: una, quae dicitur *consentanea*, qua unitur Deo per connexionem amoris; alia *dignativa*, qua humana natura unitur divinae; tertia, qua ipse Christus unitur Ecclesiae. Dicunt ergo quod secundum duas primas uniones competit Christo habere dotes sub ratione dotis; sed quantum ad tertiam, convenit ei id quod est dos excellentissime, non tamen sub ratione dotis; quia in

OBJECTION 1: It would seem fitting that Christ should receive a dowry. For the saints will be conformed to Christ through glory, according to Phillipians 3:21: *who will reform the body of our lowness made like to the body of his glory.* Therefore, Christ also will have a dowry.

OBJ. 2: Further, in the spiritual marriage a dowry is given in likeness to a carnal marriage. Now there is a spiritual marriage in Christ which is peculiar to him, namely, of the two natures in one Person, in regard to which the human nature in him is said to have been espoused by the Word, as a Gloss has it on Psalm 18:6: *he has set his tabernacle in the sun*, and Revelation 21:3: *behold the tabernacle of God with men.* Therefore, it is fitting that Christ should have a dowry.

OBJ. 3: Further, Augustine says (*De Doctr. Christ.* iii) that Christ, according to the Rule of Tyconius, on account of the unity of the mystic body that exists between the head and its members, calls himself also the Bride and not only the Bridegroom, as may be gathered from Isaiah 61:10: *as a bridegroom decked with a crown, and as a bride adorned with her jewels.* Since, then, a dowry is due to the bride, it would seem that Christ ought to receive a dowry.

OBJ. 4: Further, a dowry is due to all the members of the Church, since the Church is the spouse. But Christ is a member of the Church, according to 1 Corinthians 12:27: *you are the body of Christ, and members of a member*, i.e., of *Christ*, according to a Gloss. Therefore, the dowry is due to Christ.

OBJ. 5: Further, Christ has perfect vision, fruition, and joy. Now these are the dowries. Therefore, Christ has the dowry.

ON THE CONTRARY, A distinction of persons is requisite between the bridegroom and the bride. But in Christ there is nothing personally distinct from the Son of God, who is the Bridegroom, as stated in John 3:29: *he that has the bride is the bridegroom.* Therefore, since the dowry is allotted to the bride or for the bride, it would seem unfitting for Christ to have a dowry.

FURTHER, The same person does not both give and receive a dowry. But it is Christ who gives spiritual dowries. Therefore, it is not fitting that Christ should have a dowry.

I ANSWER THAT, There are two opinions on this point. For some say that there is a threefold union in Christ. One is the union of *concord*, whereby he is united to God in the bond of love; another is the union of *condescension*, whereby the human nature is united to the divine; the third is the union whereby Christ is united to the Church. They say, then, that as regards the first two unions it is fitting for Christ to have the dowries as such, but as regards the third, it is fitting for him to have the dowries in the most excellent

tali coniunctione Christus est ut sponsus, sed Ecclesia ut sponsa; dos autem datur sponsae quantum ad proprietatem et dominium, quamvis detur sponso ad usum.

Sed hoc non videtur esse conveniens. In illa enim coniunctione qua Christus unitur Patri per consensum amoris etiam inquantum est Deus, non dicitur aliquod matrimonium esse: quia non est ibi aliqua subiectio, quam oportet esse sponsae ad sponsum.

Similiter etiam nec in coniunctione humanae naturae ad divinam quae est in unione personae, vel etiam per conformitatem voluntatis, potest esse ratio dotis; propter tria. Primo, quia exigitur conformitas naturae inter sponsum et sponsam in matrimonio illo in quo dantur dotes. Et hoc deficit in coniunctione humanae naturae ad divinam. Secundo, quia exigitur ibi distinctio personarum. Humana autem natura non est personaliter distincta a Verbo. Tertio, quia dos datur quando sponsa de novo introducitur in domum sponsi: et sic videtur ad sponsam pertinere quae de non coniuncta fit coniuncta. Humana autem natura quae est assumpta in unitate personae a Verbo, nunquam fuit quin esset perfecte coniuncta.

Unde, secundum alios, dicendum quod vel omnino non convenit Christo ratio dotis: vel non ita proprie sicut aliis sanctis. Ea tamen quae dotes dicuntur, excellentissime ei conveniunt.

AD PRIMUM ergo dicendum quod conformatio illa est intelligenda secundum id quod est dos, et non secundum rationem dotis quae sit in Christo. Non enim oportet quod illud in quo Christo conformamur, sit eodem modo in nobis et in Christo.

AD SECUNDUM dicendum quod natura humana non proprie dicitur sponsa in coniunctione illa qua Verbo coniungitur: cum non servetur ibi personarum distinctio, quae inter sponsum et sponsam requiritur. Sed quod quandoque desponsata dicatur humana natura secundum quod Verbo coniuncta est, hoc est inquantum habet aliquem actum sponsae: quia scilicet inseparabiliter coniungitur; et quia in illa coniunctione humana natura est Verbo inferior, et per Verbum regitur sicut sponsa per sponsum.

AD TERTIUM dicendum quod hoc quod aliquando dicitur Christus sponsa, non est quia ipse vere sit sponsa: sed inquantum sibi assumit personam sponsae suae, scilicet Ecclesiae, quae est ei spiritualiter coniuncta. Unde nihil prohibet quin per illum modum loquendi posset dici habere dotes: non quod ipse habeat, sed quia Ecclesia habet.

AD QUARTUM dicendum quod nomen Ecclesiae dupliciter accipitur. Quandoque enim nominat tantummodo corpus quod Christo coniungitur sicut capiti. Et sic

degree, considered as to that in which they consist, but not considered as dowries; because in this union Christ is the bridegroom and the Church the bride, and a dowry is given to the bride as regards property and control, although it is given to the bridegroom as to use.

But this does not seem fitting. For in the union of Christ with the Father by the concord of love, even if we consider him as God, there is not said to be a marriage, since it implies no subjection such as is required in the bride towards the bridegroom.

Nor again in the union of the human nature with the divine, whether we consider the personal union or that which regards the conformity of will, can there be a dowry, properly speaking, for three reasons. First, because in a marriage where a dowry is given there should be likeness of nature between bridegroom and bride, and this is lacking in the union of the human nature with the divine. Second, because there is required a distinction of persons, and the human nature is not personally distinct from the Word. Third, because a dowry is given when the bride is first taken to the dwelling of the bridegroom, and thus would seem to belong to the bride, who, from being not united, becomes united; whereas the human nature, which was assumed into the unity of Person by the Word, never was otherwise than perfectly united.

Wherefore in the opinion of others we should say that the notion of dowry is either altogether unbecoming to Christ, or not so properly as to the saints; but that the things which we call dowries befit him in the highest degree.

REPLY OBJ. 1: This conformity must be understood to refer to the thing which is a dowry and not to the notion of a dowry being in Christ: for it is not requisite that the thing in which we are conformed to Christ should be in the same way in Christ and in us.

REPLY OBJ. 2: Human nature is not properly said to be a bride in its union with the Word, since the distinction of persons, which is requisite between bridegroom and bride, is not observed therein. That human nature is sometimes described as being espoused in reference to its union with the Word is because it has a certain act of the bride, in that it is united to the Bridegroom inseparably, and in this union is subject to the Word and ruled by the Word, as the bride by the bridegroom.

REPLY OBJ. 3: If Christ is sometimes spoken of as the Bride, this is not because he is the Bride in very truth, but insofar as he personifies his spouse, namely, the Church, who is united to him spiritually. Hence nothing hinders him, in this way of speaking, from being said to have the dowries, not that he himself is dowered, but the Church.

REPLY OBJ. 4: The term Church is taken in two senses. For sometimes it denotes the body only, which is united to Christ as its Head. In this way alone has the Church the

tantum Ecclesia habet rationem sponsae. Sic vero Christus non est Ecclesiae membrum, sed est caput influens omnibus Ecclesiae membris.

Alio modo accipitur Ecclesia secundum quod nominat caput et membra coniuncta. Et sic Christus dicitur membrum Ecclesiae, inquantum habet officium distinctum ab omnibus aliis, scilicet influere aliis vitam. Quamvis non multum proprie dicatur membrum: quia membrum importat partialitatem quandam; in Christo autem bonum spirituale non est particulatum, sed est totaliter integrum; unde ipse est totum Ecclesiae bonum, nec est aliquid maius ipse et alii quam ipse solus. Sic autem loquendo de Ecclesia, Ecclesia non solum nominat sponsam, sed *sponsum et sponsam*, prout per coniunctionem spiritualem est ex eis unum effectum. Unde, licet Christus aliquo modo dicatur membrum Ecclesiae, nullo tamen modo potest dici membrum sponsae. Et sic ei non convenit ratio dotis.

AD QUINTUM dicendum quod in processu illo est fallacia *accidentis*. Non enim illa Christo conveniunt secundum quod habent rationem dotis.

character of spouse: and in this way Christ is not a member of the Church, but is the Head from which all the members receive.

In another sense, the Church denotes the head and members united together; and thus Christ is said to be a member of the Church, inasmuch as he fulfills an office distinct from all others, by pouring forth life into the other members: although he is not very properly called a member, since a member implies a certain restriction, whereas in Christ spiritual good is not restricted but is absolutely entire, so that he is the entire good of the Church, nor is he together with others anything greater than he is by himself. Speaking of the Church in this sense, the Church denotes not only the bride, but the *bridegroom and bride*, insofar as one thing results from their spiritual union. Consequently, although Christ be called a member of the Church in a certain sense, he can by no means be called a member of the bride; and therefore the idea of a dowry is not becoming to him.

REPLY OBJ. 5: There is here a fallacy of *accident*; for these things are not befitting to Christ if we consider them under the aspect of dowry.

Article 4

Whether the Angels Receive the Dowries?

AD QUARTUM SIC PROCEDITUR. Videtur quod angeli habeant dotes. Quia super illud Cant. 6, [8], *una est columba mea*, dicit Glossa: *una est Ecclesia in hominibus et angelis*. Sed Ecclesia est sponsa, et sic membris Ecclesiae convenit habere dotes. Ergo angeli dotes habent.

PRAETEREA, Luc. 12, super illud [v. 36], *et vos similes hominibus expectantibus dominum suum quando revertatur a nuptiis*, dicit Glossa: *ad nuptias Dominus ivit quando post resurrectionem novus homo angelorum sibi multitudinem copulavit*. Ergo angelorum multitudo est sponsa Christi. Et sic angelis debentur dotes.

PRAETEREA, spirituale matrimonium in spirituali coniunctione consistit. Sed spiritualis coniunctio non est minor inter angelos et Deum quam inter homines beatos et Deum. Ergo, cum. dotes de quibus nunc agimus, ratione spiritualis matrimonii assignentur, videtur quod angelis conveniant dotes.

PRAETEREA, spirituale matrimonium requirit spiritualem sponsum et spiritualem sponsam. Sed Christo, inquantum summus spiritus, magis sunt conformes in natura angeli quam homines. Ergo magis potest esse spirituale matrimonium angelorum ad Christum quam hominum.

OBJECTION 1: It would seem that the angels receive dowries. For a Gloss on Song of Songs 6:8: *one is my dove*, says, *one is the Church among men and angels*. But the Church is the bride, wherefore it is fitting for the members of the Church to have the dowries. Therefore, the angels have the dowries.

OBJ. 2: Further, a Gloss on Luke 12:36: *and you yourselves like to men who wait for their lord, when he shall return from the wedding*, says: *our Lord went to the wedding when after his resurrection the new Man espoused to himself the angelic host*. Therefore, the angelic hosts are the spouse of Christ, and consequently it is fitting that they should have the dowries.

OBJ. 3: Further, the spiritual marriage consists in a spiritual union. Now the spiritual union between the angels and God is no less than between beatified men and God. Since, then, the dowries of which we treat now are assigned by reason of a spiritual marriage, it would seem that they are becoming to the angels.

OBJ. 4: Further, a spiritual marriage demands a spiritual bridegroom and a spiritual bride. Now the angels are by nature more conformed than men to Christ as the supreme spirit. Therefore, a spiritual marriage is more possible between the angels and Christ than between men and Christ.

PRAETEREA, maior convenientia exigitur inter caput et membra quam inter sponsum et sponsam. Sed conformitas quae est inter Christum et angelos sufficit ad hoc quod Christus dicatur *Caput angelorum*. Ergo eadem ratione sufficit ad hoc quod dicatur sponsus respectu eorum.

SED CONTRA: Origenes, super Cantica, distinguit quatuor personas: scilicet *sponsum et sponsam, adolescentulas, et sodales sponsi*. Et dicit quod angeli sunt *sodales sponsi*. Cum ergo dotes non debeantur nisi sponsae, videtur quod angelis dotes non conveniant.

PRAETEREA, Christus desponsavit sibi Ecclesiam per Incarnationem et Passionem: unde figuratur per hoc quod dicitur Exod. 4, [25]: *sponsus sanguinum tu mihi es*. Sed Christus per Passionem et incarnationem non aliter fuit coniunctus angelis quam prius erat. Ergo angeli non pertinent ad Ecclesiam secundum quod Ecclesia dicitur sponsa. Ergo angelis non conveniunt dotes.

RESPONDEO dicendum quod ea quae ad dotes animae pertinent, non est dubium angelis sicut et hominibus convenire. Sed secundum rationem dotis non ita eis sicut hominibus conveniunt: eo quod non ita proprie convenit angelis ratio sponsae sicut hominibus. Exigitur enim inter sponsum et sponsam naturae conformitas, ut sint eiusdem speciei. Hoc autem modo homines cum Christo conveniunt: inquantum naturam humanam assumpsit, per quam assumptionem factus est conformis in natura speciei humanae omnibus hominibus. Angelis autem non est conformis secundum unitatem speciei, neque secundum naturam divinam neque secundum naturam humanam. Et ideo ratio dotis non ita proprie convenit angelis sicut hominibus.

Tamen in his quae metaphorice dicuntur, cum non requiratur similitudo quantum ad omnia, non potest ex aliqua dissimilitudine concludi quod metaphorice aliquid de alio non praedicetur. Et sic ex ratione inducta non potest simpliciter haberi quod angelis dotes non conveniant: sed solum quod non ita proprie sicut hominibus, ratione dissimilitudinis praedictae.

AD PRIMUM ergo dicendum quod, quamvis angeli pertineant ad unitatem Ecclesiae, non tamen sunt membra Ecclesiae secundum quod Ecclesia dicitur sponsa per conformitatem naturae. Et sic non convenit eis proprie habere dotes.

AD SECUNDUM dicendum quod desponsatio illa large accipitur pro unione quae non habet conformitatem naturae in specie. Et sic etiam nihil prohibet, large accipiendo dotes, ponere dotes in angelis.

AD TERTIUM dicendum quod, quamvis in matrimonio spirituali non sit nisi coniunctio spiritualis, tamen illos qui coniunguntur, ad perfectam matrimonii ratio-

OBJ. 5: Further, a greater conformity is required between the head and members than between bridegroom and bride. Now the conformity between Christ and the angels suffices for Christ to be called the *Head of the angels*. Therefore, for the same reason it suffices for him to be called their bridegroom.

ON THE CONTRARY, Origen at the beginning of the prologue to his *Commentary on the Canticles* distinguishes four persons: namely, *the bridegroom, the bride, the young maidens, and the companions of the bridegroom*. He says that the angels are *the companions of the bridegroom*. Since, then, the dowry is due only to the bride, it would seem that the dowries are not becoming to the angels.

FURTHER, Christ espoused the Church by his Incarnation and Passion: wherefore this is foreshadowed in Exodus 4:25: *a bloody spouse you are to me*. Now by his Incarnation and Passion, Christ was not otherwise united to the angels than before. Therefore, the angels do not belong to the Church if we consider the Church as spouse. Therefore, the dowries are not becoming to the angels.

I ANSWER THAT, Without any doubt, whatever pertains to the endowments of the soul is befitting to the angels as it is to men. But considered under the aspect of dowry, they are not as becoming to the angels as to men, because the character of bride is not so properly becoming to the angels as to men. For a conformity of nature is required between bridegroom and bride such that they be of the same species. Now men are in conformity with Christ in this way, since he took human nature, and by so doing became conformed to all men in the specific nature of man. On the other hand, he is not conformed to the angels in unity of species, neither as to his divine nor as to his human nature. Consequently, the notion of dowry is not so properly becoming to angels as to men.

Since, however, in metaphorical expressions it is not necessary to have a likeness in every respect, we must not argue that one thing is not to be said of another metaphorically on account of some lack of likeness; and consequently the argument we have adduced does not prove that the dowries are simply unbecoming to the angels, but only that they are not so properly befitting to angels as to men, on account of the aforesaid lack of likeness.

REPLY OBJ. 1: Although the angels are included in the unity of the Church, they are not members of the Church according to conformity of nature, if we consider the Church as bride: and thus it is not properly fitting for them to have the dowries.

REPLY OBJ. 2: Espousal is taken there in a broad sense for union without conformity of specific nature: and in this sense nothing prevents our saying that the angels have the dowries, taking these in a broad sense.

REPLY OBJ. 3: In the spiritual marriage, although there is no other than a spiritual union, those whose union answers to the idea of a perfect marriage should agree in spe-

nem, oportet in specie naturae convenire. Et propter hoc desponsatio proprie ad angelos non pertinet.

Ad quartum dicendum quod illa conformatio qua angeli conformantur Christo inquantum est Deus, non est talis quae sufficiat ad perfectam matrimonii rationem, cum non sit secundum convenientiam in specie: sed magis adhuc remanet infinita distantia.

Ad quintum dicendum quod nec etiam Christus proprie dicitur caput angelorum, secundum illam rationem qua, caput requirit conformitatem naturae.

Tamen sciendum quod, licet caput et alia membra sint partes individui unius speciei, non tamen si unumquodque per se consideretur, cum alio est eiusdem speciei: manus enim habet aliam speciem partis a capite. Unde, loquendo de membris secundum se, non requiritur inter ea alia convenientia quam proportionis, ut unum ab alio accipiat et unum alii subserviat. Et sic convenientia quae est inter Deum et angelos, magis sufficit ad rationem capitis quam ad rationem sponsi.

cific nature. Hence espousal does not properly befit the angels.

Reply Obj. 4: The conformity between the angels and Christ as God is not such as suffices for the notion of a perfect marriage, since so far are they from agreeing in species that there is still an infinite distance between them.

Reply Obj. 5: Not even is Christ properly called the Head of the angels, if we consider the head as requiring conformity of nature with the members.

We must observe, however, that although the head and the other members are parts of an individual of one species, if we consider each one by itself, it is not of the same species as another member, for a hand is another specific part from the head. Hence, speaking of the members in themselves, the only conformity required among them is one of proportion, so that one receive from another, and one serve another. Consequently, the conformity between God and the angels better suffices for the notion of head rather than for that of bridegroom.

Article 5

Whether Three Dowries of the Soul Are Suitably Assigned?

Ad quintum sic proceditur. Videtur quod inconvenienter ponantur tres esse animae dotes: scilicet *visio*, *dilectio* et *fruitio*. Anima enim coniungitur Deo secundum mentem, in qua est imago Trinitatis secundum memoriam, intelligentiam et voluntatem. Sed dilectio ad voluntatem pertinet, visio ad intelligentiam. Ergo debet aliquid poni quod memoriae respondeat: cum fruitio non pertineat ad memoriam, sed magis ad voluntatem.

Praeterea, dotes beatitudinis dicuntur respondere virtutibus viae quibus Deo coniungimur, quae sunt fides, spes et caritas, quibus est ipse Deus obiectum. Sed dilectio respondet caritati, visio autem fidei. Ergo debet aliquid poni quod pertineret ad spem: cum fruitio magis pertineat ad caritatem.

Praeterea, Deo non fruimur nisi per dilectionem et visionem: illis enim dicimur frui quae diligimus propter se, ut patet per Augustinum, in libro *de Doctrina Christ*. Ergo fruitio non debet poni alia dos a dilectione.

Praeterea, ad perfectionem beatitudinis requiritur comprehensio: I Cor. 9, [24] *sic currite ut comprehendatis*. Ergo deberet adhuc, quarta dos poni.

Praeterea, Anselmus dicit quod haec pertinent ad beatitudinem animae: *sapientia, amicitia, concordia, potestas, honor, securitas, gaudium*. Et sic videntur praedictae dotes inconvenienter assignari.

Objection 1: It would seem unfitting to assign to the soul three dowries: namely, *vision*, *love* and *fruition*. For the soul is united to God according to the mind, wherein is the image of the Trinity in respect of the memory, understanding, and will. Now love regards the will, and vision the understanding. Therefore, there should be something corresponding to the memory, since fruition regards not the memory but the will.

Obj. 2: Further, the beatific dowries are said to correspond to the virtues of the way, which united us to God: and these are faith, hope, and charity, of which God himself is the object. Now love corresponds to charity, and vision to faith. Therefore, there should be something corresponding to hope, since fruition corresponds rather to charity.

Obj. 3: Further, we enjoy God by love and vision only, since we are said to enjoy those things which we love for their own sake, as Augustine says (*De Doctr. Christ.* i, 4). Therefore, fruition should not be reckoned a distinct dowry from love.

Obj. 4: Further, comprehension is required for the perfection of beatitude: *so run that you may comprehend* (1 Cor 9:24). Therefore, we should reckon a fourth dowry.

Obj. 5: Further, Anselm says (*On Likenesses* 48) that the following pertain to the soul's beatitude: *wisdom, friendship, concord, power, honor, security, joy*: and consequently the aforesaid dowries are reckoned unsuitably.

PRAETEREA, Augustinus, in fine *de Civ. Dei* dicit quod Deus *in illa beatitudine sine fine videbitur, sine fastidio amabitur, sine fatigatione laudabitur.* Ergo laus praeassignatis dotibus annumerari debet.

PRAETEREA, Boetius ponit quinque ad beatitudinem pertinentia, in III de Consolat., quae sunt haec: *sufficientia*, quam promittunt divitiae; *iucunditas*, quam promittit voluptas; *celebritas*, quam promittit fama; *securitas*, quam promittit potentia; *reverentia*, quam promittit dignitas. Et sic videtur quod ista potius deberent assignari dotes quam praedicta.

RESPONDEO dicendum quod ab omnibus communiter tres ponuntur animae dotes, diversimode tamen. Quidam enim dicunt quod tres dotes animae sunt *visio, dilectio* et *fruitio*; quidam vero quod sunt *visio, comprehensio* et *fruitio*; quidam vero quod sunt *visio, delectatio* et *comprehensio*. Omnes tamen hae assignationes reducuntur in idem, et eodem modo earum numerus assignatur.

Dictum enim est quod dos est aliquid animae inhaerens per quod ordinatur ad operationem in qua consistit beatitudo. In qua quidem operatione duo requiruntur; scilicet ipsa substantia operationis, quae est visio; et perfectio eius, quae est delectatio; oportet enim beatitudinem esse *operationem perfectam*. Visio autem aliqua est delectabilis dupliciter: uno modo, ex parte obiecti, inquantum id quod videtur est delectabile; alio modo, ex parte visionis, inquantum ipsum videre delectabile est, sicut delectamur in cognoscendo mala, quamvis mala non delectent nos. Et quia operatio illa in qua ultima beatitudo consistit, debet esse perfectissima, ideo requiritur quod visio illa sit utroque modo delectabilis. Ad hoc autem quod ipsa visio sit delectabilis ex parte visionis, requiritur quod sit facta connaturalis videnti per aliquem habitum: sed ad hoc quod sit delectabilis ex parte visibilis, requiruntur duo, scilicet quod ipsum visibile sit conveniens, et quod sit coniunctum.

Sic ergo ad delectabilitatem visionis ex parte sui, requiritur habitus qui visionem eliciat. Et sic est una dos, quae dicitur ab omnibus visio: Sed ex parte visibilis requiruntur duo. Scilicet convenientia, quae est per affectum: et quantum ad hoc ponitur dos a quibusdam *dilectio*, et a quibusdam *fruitio*, secundum quod fruitio ad affectum pertinet; illud enim quod summe diligimus, convenientissimum aestimamus. Requiritur etiam ex parte visibilis coniunctio. Et sic ponitur a quibusdam *comprehensio*, quae nihil est aliud quam in praesentia Deum habere et in seipso tenere: sed secundum alios *fruitio*, prout fruitio est, non spei, sicut est in via, sed iam rei, sicut est in patria.

Et sic dotes tres respondent tribus virtutibus theologicis: scilicet visio fidei; spei vero comprehensio, vel fruitio secundum unam acceptionem; caritati vero delectatio, vel fruitio secundum aliam assignationem. Fruitio

OBJ. 6: Further, Augustine says (*The City of God* 22) that *in that beatitude God will be seen unendingly, loved without wearying, praised untiringly.* Therefore, praise should be added to the aforesaid dowries.

OBJ. 7: Further, Boethius reckons five things pertaining to beatitude (*Consolation of Philosophy* 3) and these are *sufficiency*, which wealth offers, *joy*, which pleasure offers, *celebrity*, which fame offers, *security*, which power offers, *reverence*, which dignity offers. Consequently, it seems that these should be reckoned as dowries rather than the aforesaid.

I ANSWER THAT, All agree in reckoning three dowries of the soul, although in different ways. For some say that the three dowries of the soul are *vision, love,* and *fruition*; others reckon them to be *vision, comprehension,* and *fruition*; others, *vision, delight,* and *comprehension*. However, all these reckonings come to the same, and their number is assigned in the same way.

For it has been said (A. 2) that a dowry is something inherent to the soul, and directing it to the operation in which beatitude consists. Now two things are requisite in this operation: its essence, which is vision, and its perfection, which is delight: since beatitude must be a *perfect operation*. Again, a vision is delightful in two ways: first, on the part of the object, by reason of the thing seen being delightful; second, on the part of the vision, by reason of the seeing itself being delightful, even as we delight in knowing evil things, although the evil things themselves delight us not. And since this operation wherein ultimate beatitude consists must be most perfect, this vision must be delightful in both ways. Now in order that this vision be delightful on the part of the vision, it needs to be made connatural to the seer by means of a habit; while for it to be delightful on the part of the visible object, two things are necessary, namely, that the visible object be suitable, and that it be united to the seer.

Accordingly, for the vision to be delightful on its own part, a habit is required to elicit the vision, and thus we have one dowry, which all call vision. But on the part of the visible object two things are necessary. First, suitableness, which regards the affections—and in this respect some reckon *love* as a dowry, others *fruition* (insofar as fruition regards the affective part) since what we love most we deem most suitable. Second, union is required on the part of the visible object, and thus some reckon *comprehension*, which is nothing else than to have God present and to hold him within ourself; while others reckon *fruition*, not of hope, which is in the way, but of possession which is in heaven.

Thus the three dowries correspond to the three theological virtues: namely, vision to faith, comprehension (or fruition in one sense) to hope, and fruition (or delight according to another reckoning) to charity. For perfect

enim perfecta, qualis in patria habebitur, includit in se delectationem et comprehensionem. Et ideo a quibusdam accipitur pro uno, a quibusdam vero pro alio.

Quidam vero attribuunt has tres dotes tribus animae virtutibus: visionem scilicet rationali; dilectionem concupiscibili; fruitionem vero irascibili, inquantum talis fruitio est per quandam victoriam adepta. Sed hoc non proprie dicitur. Quia irascibilis et concupiscibilis non sunt in parte intellectiva, sed sensitiva: dotes autem animae ponuntur in ipsa mente.

AD PRIMUM ergo dicendum quod memoria et intelligentia non habent nisi unam operationem; vel quia ipsa intelligentia est operatio memoriae; vel, si intelligentia dicatur, esse potentia quaedam, memoria non exit in operationem nisi mediante intelligentia, quia memoriae est notitiam tenere. Unde etiam memoriae et intelligentiae non respondet nisi unus habitus, scilicet notitia. Et ideo utrique respondet tantum una dos, scilicet visio.

AD SECUNDUM dicendum quod fruitio respondet spei, inquantum includit comprehensionem, quae spei succedet. Quod enim speratur, nondum habetur: et ideo spes quodammodo affligit, propter distantiam amati. Et propter hoc in patria non remanet, sed succedet ei comprehensio.

AD TERTIUM dicendum quod fruitio, secundum quod comprehensionem includit, distinguitur a visione et dilectione: alio tamen modo quam dilectio a visione. Dilectio enim et visio diversos habitus nominant, quorum unus pertinet ad intellectum, alter vero ad affectum. Sed comprehensio, vel fruitio secundum quod ponitur pro comprehensione, non importat alium habitum ab illis duobus: sed importat remotionem impedimentorum ex quibus efficiebatur ut non posset mens Deo praesentialiter coniungi. Et hoc quidem fit per hoc quod ipse habitus gloriae animam ab omni defectu liberat: sicut quod facit eam sufficientem ad cognoscendum sine phantasmatibus, et ad praedominandum corpori, et alia huiusmodi, per quae excluduntur impedimenta quibus fit ut nunc *peregrinemur a Domino*.

AD QUARTUM patet responsio ex dictis.

AD QUINTUM dicendum quod proprie dotes sunt immediata principia illius operationis in qua perfecta beatitudo consistit, per quam anima Christo coniungitur. Illa autem quae Anselmus enumerat, non sunt huiusmodi: sed sunt qualitercumque beatitudinem concomitantia vel consequentia, non solum in comparatione ad sponsum, ad quem sola *sapientia* inter enumerata ab eo pertinet, sed etiam in comparatione ad alios; vel, pares, ad quos pertinet *amicitia* quantum ad unionem affectuum, et *concordia* quantum ad consensum in agendis; vel inferiores, ad quos pertinet et potestas, secundum quod a superioribus inferiora disponuntur, et

fruition such as will be had in heaven includes delight and comprehension, for which reason some take it for the one, and some for the other.

Others, however, ascribe these three dowries to the three powers of the soul: namely, vision to the rational, delight to the concupiscible, and fruition to the irascible, seeing that this fruition is acquired by a victory. But this is not said properly, because the irascible and concupiscible powers are not in the intellective but in the sensitive part, whereas the dowries of the soul are assigned to the mind.

REPLY OBJ. 1: Memory and understanding have but one act: either because understanding is itself an act of memory, or—if understanding denote a power—because memory does not proceed to act save through the medium of the understanding, since it belongs to the memory to retain knowledge. Consequently, there is only one habit, namely knowledge, corresponding to memory and understanding: wherefore only one dowry, namely vision, corresponds to both.

REPLY OBJ. 2: Fruition corresponds to hope, insofar as it includes comprehension, which will take the place of hope: since we hope for that which we have not yet; wherefore hope chafes somewhat on account of the distance of the beloved. For this reason it will not remain in heaven, but will be succeeded by comprehension.

REPLY OBJ. 3: Fruition as including comprehension is distinct from vision and love, though in a different way than love is distinguished from vision. For love and vision denote different habits, the one belonging to the intellect, the other to the affective faculty. But comprehension, or fruition as denoting comprehension, does not signify a habit distinct from those two, but the removal of the obstacles which made it impossible for the mind to be united to God by actual vision. This is brought about by the habit of glory freeing the soul from all defects; for instance, by making it capable of knowledge without phantasms, of complete control over the body, and so forth, thus removing the obstacles which result in our *sojourning from the Lord*.

THE REPLY to the fourth objection is clear from what has been said.

REPLY OBJ. 5: Properly speaking, the dowries are the immediate principles of the operation in which perfect beatitude consists and whereby the soul is united to Christ. The things mentioned by Anselm do not answer to this description; but they are such as in any way accompany or follow beatitude, not only in relation to the Bridegroom, to whom *wisdom* alone of the things mentioned by him refers, but also in relation to others. They may be either one's equals, to whom *friendship* refers as regards the union of affections, and *concord* as regards consent in actions, or one's inferiors, to whom *power* refers, so far as inferior things are ordered by superior, and *honor* as regards that which inferi-

honor, secundum id quod ab inferioribus superioribus exhibetur; et etiam per comparationem ad seipsum, ad quod pertinet securitas quantum ad remotionem mali, et *gaudium* quantum ad adeptionem boni.

AD SEXTUM dicendum quod laus, quae ab Augustino ponitur tertium eorum quae in patria erunt, non est dispositio ad beatitudinem, sed magis ad beatitudinem consequens: ex hoc enim ipso quod anima Deo coniungitur, in quo beatitudo consistit, sequitur quod in laudem prorumpat. Unde laus non habet rationem dotis.

AD SEPTIMUM dicendum quod illa quinque quae enumerat Boetius, sunt quaedam beatitudinis conditiones: non autem dispositiones ad beatitudinis actum. Eo quod beatitudo, ratione suae perfectionis, sola et singulariter habet per seipsam quidquid ab hominibus in diversis rebus quaeritur: ut patet etiam per Philosophum, in I et X *Ethic*. Et secundum hoc, Boetius ostendit illa quinque in vera beatitudine esse, quia haec sunt quae ab hominibus in temporali felicitate quaeruntur. Quae vel pertinent ad immunitatem a malo, sicut *securitas*; vel ad consecutionem boni: vel convenientis, sicut *iucunditas*; vel perfecti, sicut *sufficientia*; vel ad manifestationem boni: sicut *celebritas*, inquantum bonum unius est in notitia multorum; et *reverentia*, inquantum illius notitiae vel boni signum aliquod exhibetur; reverentia enim consistit in exhibitione honoris, qui est testimonium virtutis. Unde patet quod ista quinque non debent dici dotes, sed quaedam beatitudinis conditiones.

ors offer to their superiors. Or again [they may accompany or follow beatitude] in relation to oneself: to this *security* refers as regards the removal of evil, and *joy* as regards the attainment of good.

REPLY OBJ. 6: Praise, which Augustine mentions as the third of those things which will obtain in heaven, is not a disposition to beatitude but rather a sequel to beatitude: because from the very fact of the soul's union with God, wherein beatitude consists, it follows that the soul breaks forth into praise. Hence praise has not the necessary conditions of a dowry.

REPLY OBJ. 7: The five things aforesaid mentioned by Boethius are certain conditions of beatitude, but not dispositions to beatitude or to its act, because beatitude by reason of its perfection has of itself alone and undividedly all that men seek in various things, as the Philosopher declares (*Ethics* 1.7, 10.7–8). Accordingly, Boethius shows that these five things to be in perfect beatitude, because they are what men seek in temporal happiness. For they pertain either to immunity from evil, as *security*, or to the attainment either of the suitable good, as *joy*, or of the perfect good, as *sufficiency*, or to the manifestation of good, as *celebrity*, inasmuch as the good of one is made known to others, or as *reverence*, as indicating that good or the knowledge thereof, for reverence is the showing of honor which bears witness to virtue. Hence it is evident that these five should not be called dowries, but conditions of beatitude.

QUESTION 96

THE AUREOLES

Consequenter considerandum est de aureolis. Circa quod quaeruntur tredecim.

Primo: utrum aureola differat a praemio essentiali.

Secundo: utrum differat a fructu.

Tertio: utrum fructus soli virtuti continentiae debeatur.

Quarto: utrum convenienter assignentur tres fructus tribus partibus continentiae.

Quinto: utrum virginibus debeatur aureola.

Sexto: utrum debeatur martyribus.

Septimo: utrum debeatur doctoribus.

Octavo: utrum Christo aureola debeatur.

Nono: utrum angelis.

Decimo: utrum corpori humano debeatur.

Undecimo: utrum convenienter tres aureolae assignentur.

Duodecimo: utrum aureola virginum sit potissima.

Decimotertio: utrum unus alio intensius eandem aureolam habeat.

In the next place we must consider the aureoles. Under this head there are thirteen points of inquiry:

(1) Whether the aureoles differ from the essential reward?

(2) Whether they differ from the fruit?

(3) Whether a fruit is due to the virtue of continence only?

(4) Whether three fruits are fittingly assigned to the three parts of continence?

(5) Whether an aureole is due to virgins?

(6) Whether it is due to martyrs?

(7) Whether it is due to doctors?

(8) Whether it is due to Christ?

(9) Whether to the angels?

(10) Whether it is due to the human body?

(11) Whether three aureoles are fittingly assigned?

(12) Whether the virgin's aureole is the greatest?

(13) Whether one has the same aureole in a higher degree than another?

Article 1

Whether the Aureole Is the Same as the Essential Reward, Which Is Called the Aurea?

AD PRIMUM SIC PROCEDITUR. Videtur quod aureola non sit aliquod aliud praemium a praemio essentiali, quod *aurea* dicitur. Praemium enim essentiale est ipsa beatitudo. Sed beatitudo, secundum Boetium, est *status omnium bonorum aggregatione perfectus*. Ergo praemium essentiale includit omne bonum quod habetur in patria. Et sic aureola includitur in aurea.

PRAETEREA, *magis et minus non diversificant speciem*. Sed illi qui servant consilia et praecepta, magis praemiantur quam illi qui servant praecepta tantum: nec in aliquo praemium eorum videtur differre nisi quod unum est altero maius. Cum ergo aureola nominet praemium quod debetur operibus perfectionis, videtur quod aureola non dicat aliquid distinctum ab aurea.

PRAETEREA, praemium respondet merito. Sed radix totius meriti est caritas. Cum ergo caritati respondeat aureola, videtur quod in patria non erit aliquod praemium ab aurea distinctum.

PRAETEREA, *homines beati assumuntur ad angelorum ordines*, ut dicit Gregorius. Sed in angelis, *licet quae-*

OBJECTION 1: It would seem that the aureole is not distinct from the essential reward, which is called the aurea. For the essential reward is beatitude itself. Now, according to Boethius (*Consolation of Philosophy* 3), beatitude is *a state rendered perfect by the aggregate of all goods*. Therefore, the essential reward includes every good possessed in heaven; so that the aureole is included in the aurea.

OBJ. 2: Further, *more and less do not change a species*. But those who keep the counsels and commandments receive a greater reward than those who keep the commandments only, nor seemingly does their reward differ, except in one reward being greater than another. Since, then, the aureole denotes the reward due to works of perfection it would seem that it does not signify something distinct from the aurea.

OBJ. 3: Further, reward corresponds to merit. Now charity is the root of all merit. Since, then, the aurea corresponds to charity, it would seem that there will be no reward in heaven other than the aurea.

OBJ. 4: Further, *all the blessed are taken into the angelic orders*, as Gregory declares (*Homilies on the Gospels* 34).

dam data sint quibusdam excellenter, nihil tamen ibi possidetur singulariter: omnia enim in Omnibus sunt, non quidem aequaliter, quia alii aliis sublimius possident quae tamen omnes habent, ut etiam Gregorius dicit. Ergo et in beatis non erit aliquod aliud praemium nisi omnium commune. Ergo aureola non est praemium distinctum ab aurea.

PRAETEREA, excellentiori merito excellentius praemium debetur. Si ergo aurea debetur operibus quae sunt in praecepto, aureola vero his quae sunt in consilio, aureola erit perfectior quam aurea. Et ita non deberet deminutive significari. Et sic videtur quod aureola non sit praemium distinctum ab aurea.

SED CONTRA: Exod. 25, super illud [v. 25], *facies alteram coronam aureolam,* dicit Glossa: *ad coronam pertinet canticum novum quod virgines tantum coram Agno concinunt*: ex quo videtur quod aureola sit quaedam corona non omnibus, sed quibusdam specialiter reddita. Aurea autem omnibus beatis redditur. Ergo aureola est aliud quam aurea.

PRAETEREA, pugnae quam sequitur victoria, debetur corona: II Tim. 2, [5], *non coronabitur nisi qui legitime certaverit.* Ergo, ubi est specialis ratio certaminis, ibi debet esse specialis corona. Sed in, aliquibus operibus est specialis ratio certandi. Ergo prae aliis aliquam coronam habere debent. Et hanc dicimus, aureolam.

PRAETEREA, Ecclesia militans descendit a triumphante: ut patet Apoc. 21, [2], *vidi civitatem sanctam* etc. Sed in Ecclesia militante specialia opera habentibus redduntur specialia praemia: sicut victoribus corona, currentibus bravium. Ergo similiter debet esse in Ecclesia triumphante.

RESPONDEO dicendum quod praemium essentiale hominis, quod est eius beatitudo, consistit in perfecta coniunctione animae ad Deum, inquantum eo perfecte fruitur ut viso et amato perfecte. Hoc autem praemium metaphorice *corona* dicitur vel *aurea*: tum ex parte meriti, quod cum quadam pugna agitur, *militia* enim *est vita hominis super terram,* Iob 7, [1]; tum etiam ex parte praemii, per quod homo efficitur quodammodo divinitatis particeps, et per consequens regiae potestatis, Apoc. 5, [10], *fecisti nos Deo nostro regnum et sacerdotes*; corona autem est proprium signum regiae potestatis; Et eadem ratione praemium quod essentiali additur, coronae rationem habet. Significat etiam corona perfectionem quandam, ratione figurae circularis: ut ex hoc etiam perfectioni competat beatorum. Sed quia nihil potest superaddi quin sit eo minus, ideo superadditum praemium *aureola* nominatur.

Huic autem essentiali praemio quod aurea dicitur, aliquid superadditur dupliciter. Uno modo, ex conditione naturae eius qui praemiatur: sicut supra beatitudinem

Now as regards the angels, *though some of them receive certain gifts in a higher degree, nothing is possessed by any of them exclusively, for all gifts are in all of them, though not equally, because some are endowed more highly than others with gifts which, however, they all possess,* as Gregory says (*Homilies on the Gospels* 34). Therefore, as regards the blessed, there will be no reward other than that which is common to all. Therefore, the aureole is not a distinct reward from the aurea.

OBJ. 5: Further, a higher reward is due to higher merit. If, then, the aurea is due to works which are of obligation, and the aureole to works of counsel, the aureole will be more perfect than the aurea, and consequently should not be expressed by a diminutive. Therefore, it would seem that the aureole is not a distinct reward from the aurea.

ON THE CONTRARY, A Gloss on Exodus 25:24–25: *thou shalt make another little golden crown* [*coronam aureolam*], says, *this crown denotes the new hymn which the virgins alone sing in the presence of the Lamb.* Wherefore apparently the aureole is a crown awarded, not to all, but especially to some: whereas the aurea is awarded to all the blessed. Therefore, the aureole is distinct from the aurea.

FURTHER, A crown is due to the fight which is followed by victory: *he is not crowned except he strive lawfully* (2 Tim 2:5). Hence where there is a special kind of conflict, there should be a special crown. Now in certain works there is a special kind of conflict. Therefore, they deserve a special kind of crown, which we call an aureole.

FURTHER, The Church Militant comes down from the Church Triumphant: *I saw the Holy City* (Rev 21:2). Now in the Church Militant, special rewards are given to those who perform special deeds, for instance, a crown to the conqueror, a prize to the runner. Therefore, the same should obtain in the Church Triumphant.

I ANSWER THAT, Man's essential reward, which is his beatitude, consists in the perfect union of the soul with God, inasmuch as it enjoys God perfectly as seen and loved perfectly. Now this reward is called a 'crown,' or 'aurea,' metaphorically, both with reference to merit which is gained by a kind of conflict—since *the life of man upon earth is a warfare* (Job 7:1)—and with reference to the reward whereby in a way man is made a participator of divinity, and consequently endowed with regal power: *thou hast made us to our God a kingdom* (Rev 5:10); for a crown is the proper sign of regal power. In like manner, the accidental reward which is added to the essential has the character of a crown. For a crown signifies some kind of perfection on account of its circular shape, so that for this very reason it is becoming to the perfection of the blessed. Since, however, nothing can be added to the essential but what is less than it, the additional reward is called an 'aureole'.

Now something may be added in two ways to this essential reward which we call the 'aurea'. First, in consequence of a condition attaching to the nature of the one rewarded:

animae gloria corporis adiungitur. Unde et ipsa gloria corporis interdum aureola nominatur: unde super illud Exod. 25, [11], *facies alteram coronam aureolam*, dicit quaedam Glossa quod *in fine aureola superponitur, cum in Scriptura dicatur quod eis sublimior gloria in receptione corporum servetur*. Sic autem nunc de aureola non agitur.

Alio modo ex ratione operis meritorii. Quod quidem rationem meriti habet ex duobus, ex quibus etiam habet bonitatis rationem: scilicet ex radice caritatis, qua refertur in finem ultimum, et sic debetur ei essentiale praemium, scilicet perventio ad finem, quae est aurea; et ex ipso genere actus, quod laudabilitatem quandam habet ex debitis circumstantiis, et ex habitu eliciente, et proximo fine; et sic debetur ei quoddam accidentale praemium, quod aureola dicitur. Et hoc modo de aureola ad praesens intendimus. Et sic dicendum est quod aureola dicit aliquid aureae superadditum: idest, quoddam gaudium de operibus a se factis quae habent rationem victoriae excellentis, quod est aliud gaudium ab eo quo de coniunctione ad Deum gaudetur, quod gaudium aurea dicitur.

Quidam tamen dicunt, quod ipsum praemium commune, quod est aurea, accipit nomen aureolae secundum quod virginibus vel martyribus vel doctoribus redditur, sicut et denarius accipit nomen debiti ex hoc quod alicui debetur, quamvis omnino idem sint debitum et denarius; non tamen ita quod praemium essentiale oporteat esse majus quando aureola dicitur; sed quia excellentiori actui respondet, non quidem secundum meriti intensionem, sed secundum modum merendi; ut quamvis in duobus sit aequalis limpiditas divinae visionis, in uno tamen dicatur aureola, non in altero, inquantum respondet excellentiori merito secundum modum agendi. Sed hoc videtur esse contra intentionem Glossae Exod. 25. Si enim idem esset aurea et aureola; non diceretur aureola aureae superponi. Et praeterea, cum merito respondeat praemium, oportet quod illi excellentiae meriti quae est ex modo agendi, respondeat aliqua excellentia in praemio; et hanc excellentiam vocamus aureolam; unde oportet aureolam ab aurea differre.

AD PRIMUM ergo dicendum quod beatitudo includit in se omnia bona quae sunt necessaria ad perfectam hominis vitam, quae consistit in perfecta hominis operatione. Sed quaedam possunt superaddi, non quasi necessaria ad perfectam operationem ut sine quibus esse non possit: sed quia, his additis, est beatitudo clarior. Unde pertinent ad bene esse beatitudinis, et ad decentiam quandam ipsius. Sicut et felicitas politica ornatur nobili-

thus the glory of the body is added to the beatitude of the soul, wherefore this same glory of the body is sometimes called an aureole. Thus a Gloss of Bede on Exodus 25:25: *thou shalt make another little golden crown*, says that *finally the aureole is added when it is stated in the Scriptures that a higher degree of glory is in store for us when our bodies are resumed*. But it is not in this sense that we speak of an aureole now.

Second, in consequence of the nature of the meritorious act. Now this has the character of merit on two counts, whence also it has the character of good. First, to wit, from its root, which is charity, since it is referred to the last end, and thus there is due to it the essential reward, namely, the attainment of the end, and this is the aurea. Second, from the very genus of the act, which derives a certain praiseworthiness from its due circumstances, from the habit eliciting it, and from its proximate end, and thus is due to it a kind of accidental reward which we call an aureole: and it is in this sense that we regard the aureole now. Accordingly, it must be said that an aureole denotes something added to the aurea, a kind of joy, to wit, in the works one has done, in that they have the character of a signal victory: for this joy is distinct from the joy in being united to God, which is called the aurea.

Some, however, affirm that the common reward, which is the aurea, receives the name of aureole according as it is given to virgins, martyrs, or doctors: even as money receives the name of debt through being due to some one, though the money and the debt are altogether the same. And that nevertheless this does not imply that the essential reward is any greater when it is called an aureole; but that it corresponds to a more excellent act, more excellent not in intensity of merit but in the manner of meriting; so that although two persons may have the divine vision with equal clearness, it is called an aureole in one and not in the other insofar as it corresponds to higher merit as regards the way of meriting. But this would seem contrary to the meaning of the Gloss quoted above. For if aurea and aureole were the same, the aureole would not be described as added to the aurea. Moreover, since reward corresponds to merit, a more excellent reward must correspond to this more excellent way of meriting: and it is this excellence that we call an aureole. Hence it follows that an aureole differs from the aurea.

REPLY OBJ. 1: Beatitude includes all the goods necessary for man's perfect life consisting in his perfect operation. Yet some things can be added, not as being necessary for that perfect operation as though it were impossible without them, but as adding to the glory of beatitude. Hence they regard the well-being of beatitude and a certain fitness thereto. Even so, civic happiness is embellished by nobility and bodily beauty and so forth, and yet it is pos-

tate et corporis pulchritudine et huiusmodi, sine quibus esse potest, ut patet in I *Ethic.* Et hoc modo se habet aureola ad beatitudinem patriae.

AD SECUNDUM dicendum quod ille qui servat consilia et praecepta, semper meretur magis quam ille qui servat praecepta tantum, secundum quod ratio meriti consideratur in operibus ex ipso genere operum: non autem semper secundum quod ratio meriti pensatur ex radice caritatis, cum quandoque ex maiori caritate aliquis servet praecepta tantum quam aliquis praecepta et consilia. Sed ut pluries accidit e converso: quia *probatio dilectionis exhibitio est operis*, ut Gregorius dicit. Non ergo ipsum praemium essentiale magis intensum dicitur aureola, sed id quod praemio essentiali superadditur: indifferenter sive sit maius praemium essentiale habentis aureolam, sive minus, sive aequale praemio essentiali non habentis.

AD TERTIUM dicendum quod caritas est principium merendi, sed actus noster est quasi instrumentum quo meremur. Ad effectum autem consequendum non solum requiritur debita dispositio in primo movente, sed etiam recta dispositio in instrumento, Et ideo in effectu aliquid consequitur ex parte primi principii, quod est principale; et aliquid ex parte instrumenti, quod est secundarium. Unde et in praemio aliquid est ex parte caritatis, scilicet aurea; et aliquid ex genere operationis, scilicet aureola.

AD QUINTUM dicendum quod angeli omnes in eodem genere actus suam beatitudinem meruerunt, scilicet in hoc quod sunt conversi ad Deum: et ideo nullum singulare praemium invenitur in uno quod alius non habeat aliquo modo. Homines autem diversis generibus actuum beatitudinem merentur. Et ideo non est simile.

Tamen illud quod unus videtur specialiter habere inter homines, quodammodo omnes communiter habenti inquantum scilicet per caritatem perfectam unusquisque bonum alterius suum reputat. Non tamen hoc gaudium quo unus alteri congaudet, potest aureola nominari: quia non datur in praemium victoriae eius, sed magis respicit victoriam alienam; corona enim ipsis victoribus redditur, non victoriae congaudentibus.

AD QUINTUM dicendum quod maior est excellentia meriti quae consurgit ex caritate quam illa quae consurgit ex genere actus: sicut finis, ad quem ordinat caritas, *est potior his quae sunt ad finem*, circa quae actus nostri consistunt. Unde et praemium respondens merito ratione caritatis, quantumcumque parvum, est maius, quolibet praemio respondente actui ratione sui generis. Et ideo *aureola* deminutive dicitur respectu *aureae*.

sible without them as stated in *Ethics* 1.8: and thus is the aureole in comparison with the happiness of heaven.

REPLY OBJ. 2: He who keeps the counsels and the commandments always merits more than he who keeps the commandments only, if we gather the notion of merit in works from the very genus of those works; but not always if we gauge the merit from its root, charity: since sometimes a man keeps the commandments alone out of greater charity than one who keeps both commandments and counsels. For the most part, however, the contrary happens, because the *proof of love is in the performance of deeds*, as Gregory says (*Homilies on the Gospels* 30). Wherefore it is not the more excellent essential reward that is called an aureole, but that which is added to the essential reward without reference to the essential reward of the possessor of an aureole being greater, or less than, or equal to the essential reward of one who has no aureole.

REPLY OBJ. 3: Charity is the first principle of merit: but our actions are the instruments, so to speak, whereby we merit. Now in order to obtain an effect, there is requisite not only a due disposition in the first mover, but also a right disposition in the instrument. Hence something principal results in the effect with reference to the first mover, and something secondary with reference to the instrument. Wherefore in the reward also there is something on the part of charity, namely, the aurea, and something on the part of the kind of work, namely, the aureole.

REPLY OBJ. 4: All the angels merited their beatitude by the same kind of act, namely, by turning to God: and consequently no particular reward is found in any one which another has not in some way. But men merit beatitude by different kinds of acts: and so the comparison fails.

Nevertheless among men what one seems to have specially, all have in common in some way, insofar as each one, by charity, deems another's good his own. Yet this joy whereby one shares another's joy cannot be called an aureole because it is not given him as a reward for his victory, but regards more the victory of another: whereas a crown is awarded the victors themselves and not to those who rejoice with them in the victory.

REPLY OBJ. 5: The merit arising from charity is more excellent than that which arises from the kind of action: just as the end to which charity directs us *is more excellent than the things directed to that end*, and with which our actions are concerned. Wherefore the reward corresponding to merit by reason of charity, however little it may be, is greater than any reward corresponding to an action by reason of its genus. Hence *aureole* is used as a diminutive in comparison with *aurea*.

Article 2

Whether the Aureole Differs From the Fruit?

Ad secundum sic proceditur. Videtur quod aureola non differat a fructu. Eidem merito non debentur diversa praemia. Sed eidem merito respondet aureola et *fructus centesimus*, scilicet virginitatis, ut patet in Glossa, Matth. 13, [23]. Ergo aureola est idem, quod fructus.

Praeterea, Augustinus dicit, in libro *de Virginitate*, quod centesimus fructus debetur martyri. Et ideo debetur virgini. Ergo fructus est quoddam praemium commune virginibus et martyribus. Sed eisdem etiam debetur aureola. Ergo aureola est idem quod fructus.

Praeterea, in beatitudine non invenitur nisi duplex praemium: scilicet essentiale; et accidentale, quod essentiali superadditur. Sed praemium essentiali superadditum dictum est esse aureolam: quod patet ex hoc quod, Exod. 25 [25], aureola coronae aureae superponi dicitur. Sed fructus non est praemium essentiale: quia sic deberetur omnibus beatis. Ergo est idem quod aureola.

Sed contra: Quaecumque non sunt eiusdem divisionis, non sunt eiusdem rationis. Sed fructus et aureola non similiter dividuntur: quia aureola dividitur in aureolam virginum, martyrum et doctorum; fructus autem in fructum coniugatorum, viduarum et virginum. Ergo fructus et aureola non sunt idem.

Praeterea, si fructus et aureola essent idem, cuicumque deberetur fructus, deberetur et aureola. Hoc autem patet esse falsum: quia fructus debetur viduitati, non autem aureola. Ergo, etc.

Respondeo dicendum quod ea quae metaphorice dicuntur, possunt varie accipi, secundum adaptationem ad diversas proprietates eius unde fit transumptio. Cum autem fructus proprie in rebus corporalibus dicatur de terra nascentibus, secundum diversas conditiones quae in fructibus corporalibus inveniri possunt, diversimode fructus spiritualiter accipitur. Fructus enim corporalis dulcedo est, quae reficit secundum quod in usum hominis venit; est etiam ultimum ad quod operatio naturae pervenit; est etiam id quod ex agricultura expectatur per seminationem vel quoscumque alios modos.

Quandoque igitur fructus spiritualiter accipitur pro eo quod reficit quasi ultimus finis. Et secundum hanc significationem dicimur *Deo frui*: perfecte quidem in patria; imperfecte autem in via. Et ex hac significatione accipitur *fruitio* quae est dos. Sic autem nunc de fructibus non loquimur.

Quandoque autem sumitur fructus spiritualiter pro eo quod reficit tantum, quamvis non sit ultimus finis. Et sic virtutes fructus dicuntur, inquantum *mentem since-*

Objection 1: It would seem that the aureole does not differ from the fruit. For different rewards are not due to the same merit. Now the aureole and the hundredfold fruit correspond to the same merit, according to a Gloss on Matthew 13:8, *some a hundredfold*. Therefore, the aureole is the same as the fruit.

Obj. 2: Further, Augustine says (*On Virginity* 45) that the hundredfold fruit is due to the martyrs, and also to virgins. Therefore, the fruit is a reward common to virgins and martyrs. But the aureole also is due to them. Therefore, the aureole is the same as the fruit.

Obj. 3: Further, there are only two rewards in beatitude, namely, the essential and the accidental (which is added to the essential.) Now that which is added to the essential reward is called an aureole, as evidenced by the statement that the little crown [*aureola*] is added to the crown (Exod 25:25). But the fruit is not the essential reward, for in that case it would be due to all the blessed. Therefore, it is the same as the aureole.

On the contrary, Things which are not divided in the same way are not of the same nature. Now fruit and aureole are not divided in the same way, since aureole is divided into the aureole of virgins, of martyrs, and of doctors: whereas fruit is divided into the fruit of the married, of widows, and of virgins. Therefore, fruit and aureole are not the same.

Further, If fruit and aureole were the same, the aureole would be due to whomsoever the fruit is due. But this is manifestly untrue, since a fruit is due to widowhood, while an aureole is not. Therefore, etc.

I answer that, Metaphorical expressions can be taken in various ways, according as we find resemblances to the various properties of the thing from which the comparison is taken. Now since fruit, properly speaking, is applied to material things born of the earth, we employ it variously in a spiritual sense, with reference to the various conditions that obtain in material fruits. For the material fruit has sweetness whereby it refreshes so far as it is used by man; again, it is the last thing to which the operation of nature attains; moreover, it is that to which agriculture looks forward as the result of sowing or any other process.

Accordingly, fruit is sometimes taken in a spiritual sense for that which refreshes as being the last end: and according to this signification we are said to *enjoy* [*frui*] *God* perfectly in heaven and imperfectly on the way. From this signification we have *fruition*, which is a dowry: but we are not speaking of fruit in this sense now.

Sometimes fruit signifies spiritually that which refreshes only, though it is not the last end; and thus the virtues are called fruits, inasmuch as *they refresh the mind*

ra dulcedine reficiunt, ut Ambrosius dicit. Et sic accipitur fructus Galat., [22–23]: *fructus autem Spiritus caritas, gaudium*, etc. Sic autem de fructibus nunc etiam non quaeritur.

Potest autem alio modo sumi fructus: spiritualis ad similitudinem corporalis fructus inquantum corporalis fructus est quoddam commodum quod ex labore agriculturae expectatur: ut sic fructus dicatur illud praemium quod homo consequitur ex labore quo in hac vita laborat. Et sic omne praemium quod in futuro habebitur ex nostris laboribus, fructus dicitur. Et sic accipitur fructus Rom. 6, [22]: *habetis fructum vestrum in sanctificationem, finem vero vitam aeternam*. Sic etiam nos nunc de fructu non agimus.

Sed agimus nunc de fructu secundum quod ex semine consurgit: sic enim de fructu Dominus loquitur Matth. 13, [3 sqq.], ubi fructum dividit in tricesimum, sexagesimum et centesimum. Fructus autem secundum hoc potest prodire ex semine, quod vis sementina est efficax ad convertendum humores terrae in suam naturam: et quanto haec virtus est efficacior, et terra ad hoc paratior, tanto fructus sequitur uberior. Spirituale autem semen quod in nobis seminatur est verbum Dei. Unde quanto aliquis magis in spiritualitatem convertitur, a carne recedens, tanto in eo est maior fructus verbi Dei. Secundum hoc igitur fructus differt ab *aurea* et ab aureola, quia aurea consistit in gaudio quod habetur de Deo; aureola vero in gaudio quod habetur de operum perfectione; sed *fructus* in gaudio quod habetur de ipsa dispositione operantis secundum gradum spiritualitatis in quem proficit ex semine verbi Dei.

Quidam distinguunt inter aureolam et fructum dicentes quod aureola debetur pugnanti, secundum illud II Tim. 2, [5], *non coronabitur nisi qui legitime certaverit*; fructus autem laboranti, secundum illud quod dicitur Sap. 3, [15], *bonorum, laborum gloriosus est fructus*. Alii vero dicunt quod aurea respicit conversionem ad Deum; sed aureola et fructus consistunt in his quae sunt ad finem, ita tamen quod fructus principalius respicit voluntatem, aureola autem magis corpus.

Sed, cum in eodem sit labor et pugna et secundum idem; et praemium corporis ex praemio animae dependeat: secundum praedicta non esset differentia inter fructum, auream et aureolam, nisi ratione tantum. Et hoc non potest esse: cum quibusdam assignetur fructus quibus non assignatur aureola.

AD PRIMUM ergo dicendum quod non est inconveniens eidem merito, secundum diversa quae in ipso sunt, diversa praemia respondere. Unde et virginitati respondet aurea, secundum quod propter Deum servatur imperio caritatis; aureola vero secundum quod est quoddam perfectionis opus habens rationem victoriae

with genuine sweetness, as Ambrose says (*On Paradise* 13). In this sense fruit is used in Galatians 6:22: *the fruit of the Spirit is charity, joy*, etc. Nor again is this the sense in which we speak of fruit now; for we have treated of this already.

We may, however, take spiritual fruit in another sense, in likeness to material fruit, inasmuch as material fruit is a profit expected from the labor of husbandry: so that we call fruit that reward which man acquires from his labor in this life: and thus every reward which by our labors we shall acquire for the future life is called a *fruit*. In this sense fruit is taken in Romans 6:22: *you have your fruit unto sanctification, and the end life everlasting*. Yet neither in this sense do we speak of fruit now,

But now we are treating of fruit as being the product of seed: for it is in this sense that our Lord speaks of fruit (Matt 13:23), where he divides fruit into thirtyfold, sixtyfold, and hundredfold. Now fruit is the product of seed insofar as the seed power is capable of transforming the humors of the soil into its own nature; and the more efficient this power, and the better prepared the soil, the more plentiful fruit will result. Now the spiritual seed which is sown in us is the Word of God: wherefore the more a person is transformed into a spiritual nature by withdrawing from carnal things, the greater is the fruit of the Word in him. Accordingly, the fruit of the Word of God differs from the aurea and the aureole, in that the aurea consists in the joy one has in God, and the aureole in the joy one has in the perfection of one's works, whereas the fruit consists in the joy that the worker has in his own disposition as to his degree of spirituality to which he has attained through the seed of God's Word.

Some, however, distinguish between aureole and fruit by saying that the aureole is due to the fighter, according to 2 Timothy 2:5: *he shall not be crowned, except he strive lawfully*; whereas the fruit is due to the laborer, according to Wisdom 3:15: *the fruit of good labors is glorious*. Others again say that the aurea regards conversion to God, while the aureole and the fruit regard things directed to the end; yet so that the fruit principally regards the will, and the aureole the body.

Since, however, labor and strife are in the same subject and about the same matter, and since the body's reward depends on the soul's, these explanations of the difference between fruit, aurea, and aureole would only imply a logical difference: and this cannot be, since fruit is assigned to some to whom no aureole is assigned.

REPLY OBJ. 1: There is nothing incongruous if various rewards correspond to the same merit according to the various things contained therein. Therefore, to virginity corresponds the aurea insofar as virginity is kept for God's sake at the command of charity; the aureole, insofar as virginity is a work of perfection having the character of a signal vic-

excellentis; fructus vero secundum quod per virginitatem homo in quandam spiritualitatem transit; a carnalitate recedens.

AD SECUNDUM dicendum quod fructus secundum propriam acceptionem, prout nunc loquimur, non dicit praemium commune martyrio et virginitati, sed tribus continentiae gradibus. Glossa autem illa quae ponit fructum centesimum martyribus respondere, large accipit fructum, secundum quod quaelibet remuneratio dicitur fructus: ut sic per centesimum fructum remuneratio designetur quae quibuslibet operibus perfectionis debetur.

AD TERTIUM dicendum quod, quamvis aureola sit quoddam accidentale praemium essentiali superadditum, non tamen omne accidentale praemium est aureola: sed praemium de operibus perfectionis, quibus homo maxime Christo conformatur, secundum praedictam victoriam. Unde non est inconveniens quod abstractioni a carnali vita aliquod aliud accidentale praemium debeatur, quod fructus dicitur.

tory; and the fruit, insofar as by virginity a person acquires a certain spirituality by withdrawing from carnal things.

REPLY OBJ. 2: Fruit, according to the proper acceptation as we are speaking of it now, does not denote the reward common to martyrdom and virginity, but that which corresponds to the three degrees of continency. This Gloss which states that the hundredfold fruit corresponds to martyrs takes fruit in a broad sense, according as any reward is called a fruit, the hundredfold fruit thus denoting the reward due to any perfect works whatever.

REPLY OBJ. 3: Although the aureole is an accidental reward added to the essential reward, nevertheless not every accidental reward is an aureole, but only that which is assigned to works of perfection, whereby man is most conformed to Christ in the achievement of a perfect victory. Hence it is not unfitting that another accidental reward, which is called the fruit, be due sometimes to the withdrawal from a carnal life.

Article 3

Whether a Fruit Is Due to the Virtue of Continence Alone?

AD TERTIUM SIC PROCEDITUR. Videtur quod fructus non debeatur soli virtuti continentiae. Quia I Cor. 15, super illud [v. 41], *alia claritas solis* etc., dicit Glossa quod *claritati solis illorum dignitas comparatur qui centesimum fructum habent; lunari autem qui sexagesimum; stellae vero qui tricesimum.* Sed illa diversitas claritatum, secundum intentionem Apostoli, pertinet ad quamcumque beatitudinis differentiam. Ergo diversi fructus non debent respondere soli continentiae.

PRAETEREA, fructus a *fruitione* dicuntur. Sed fruitio pertinet ad praemium essentiale, quod omnibus virtutibus respondet. Ergo, etc.

PRAETEREA, fructus labori debetur: Sap. 3, [15], *bonorum laborum gloriosus est fructus.* Sed maior est labor in fortitudine quam in temperantia vel in continentia. Ergo fructus non respondet soli continentiae.

PRAETEREA, difficilius est modum non excedere in cibis, qui sunt necessarii ad vitam, quam in venereis, sine quibus vita conservari potest. Et sic maior est labor parsimoniae quam continentiae. Ergo parsimoniae magis respondet fructus quam continentiae.

PRAETEREA, fructus refectionem importat. Refectio autem praecipue est in fine. Cum ergo virtutes theologicae finem habeant pro obiecto, scilicet ipsum Deum, videtur quod eis fructus maxime debeat respondere.

OBJECTION 1: It would seem that a fruit is not due to the virtue of continence alone. For a Gloss on 1 Corinthians 15:41: *one is the glory of the sun*, says that *the worth of those who have the hundredfold fruit is compared to the glory of the sun; to the glory of the moon those who have the sixtyfold fruit; and to the stars those who have the thirtyfold fruit.* Now this difference of glory, in the meaning of the Apostle, regards any difference whatever of beatitude. Therefore, the various fruits should correspond to none but the virtue of continence.

OBJ. 2: Further, fruits are so called from *fruition*. But fruition belongs to the essential reward which corresponds to all the virtues. Therefore, etc.

OBJ. 3: Further, fruit is due to labor: *the fruit of good labors is glorious* (Wis 3:15). Now there is greater labor in fortitude than in temperance or continence. Therefore, fruit does not correspond to continence alone.

OBJ. 4: Further, it is more difficult not to exceed the measure in food, which is necessary for life, than in sexual matters, without which life can be sustained: and thus the labor of frugality is greater than that of continence. Therefore, fruit corresponds to frugality rather than to continence.

OBJ. 5: Further, fruit implies delight, and delight regards especially the end. Since, then, the theological virtues have the end for their object, namely, God himself, it would seem that to them especially the fruit should correspond.

SED CONTRA est quod habetur in Glossa Matth. 13, [23], quae fructus assignat virginitati, viduitati et continentiae coniugali, quae sunt continentiae partes.

RESPONDEO dicendum quod fructus est quoddam praemium quod debetur homini ex hoc quod a carnali vita in spiritualem transit. Et ideo illi virtuti praecipue fructus respondet quae hominem praecipue a subiectione carnis liberat. Hoc autem facit continentia: quia per delectationes venereas anima praecipue carni subditur, adeo ut in actu carnali, secundum Hieronymum, *nec Spiritus prophetiae corda tangat prophetarum*; nec *in illa delectatione est possibile aliquid intelligere*, ut Philosophus dicit, in VII *Ethic*. Et ideo continentiae magis respondet fructus quam alii virtuti.

AD PRIMUM ergo dicendum quod Glossa illa accipit fructum large, secundum quod quaelibet remuneratio fructus nominatur.

AD SECUNDUM dicendum quod *fruitio* non sumitur a *fructu* secundum illam similitudinem qua nunc de fructu loquimur.

AD TERTIUM dicendum quod fructus, secundum quod nunc loquimur, non respondet labori ratione fatigationis, sed secundum quod per laborem semina fructificant. Unde et ipsae segetes *labores* dicuntur: inquantum propter eas laboratur, vel labore acquiruntur. Similitudo autem fructus secundum quod oritur ex semine, magis aptatur in continentia quam in fortitudine: quia per passiones fortitudinis homo non subditur carni, sicut per passiones circa quas est continentia.

AD QUARTUM dicendum quod, quamvis delectationes quae surit in cibis, sunt magis necessariae illis quae sunt in venereis, non tamen sunt ita vehementes. Unde per eas anima non ita subditur carni.

AD QUINTUM dicendum quod fructus non sumitur hic secundum quod *frui* dicitur qui reficitur in fine, sed alio modo. Et ideo ratio non sequitur.

ON THE CONTRARY, There is the statement of the Gloss on Matthew 13:23, *the one a hundredfold*, which assigns the fruits to virginity, widowhood, and conjugal continence, which are parts of continence.

I ANSWER THAT, A fruit is a reward due to a person in that he passes from the carnal to the spiritual life. Consequently, a fruit corresponds especially to that virtue which more than any other frees man from subjection to the flesh. Now this is the effect of continence, since it is by sexual pleasures that the soul is especially subject to the flesh; so much so that in the carnal act, according to Jerome (*Epistle to Ageruchia*), *not even the spirit of prophecy touches the heart of the prophet*; nor, as the Philosopher says, *is it possible to understand anything in the midst of that pleasure* (*Ethics* 7.11). Therefore, fruit corresponds to continence rather than to another virtue.

REPLY OBJ. 1: This Gloss takes fruit in a broad sense, according as any reward is called a fruit.

REPLY OBJ. 2: *Fruition* does not take its name from 'fruit' by reason of any comparison with fruit in the sense in which we speak of it now, as evidenced by what has been said.

REPLY OBJ. 3: Fruit, as we speak of it now, corresponds to labor not as resulting in fatigue, but as resulting in the production of fruit. Hence a man calls his crops his *labors* inasmuch as he labored for them, or produced them by his labor. Now the comparison to fruit, as produced from seed, is more adapted to continence than to fortitude, because man is not subjected to the flesh by the passions of fortitude, as he is by the passions with which continence is concerned.

REPLY OBJ. 4: Although the pleasures of the table are more necessary than the pleasures of sex, they are not so strong: wherefore the soul is not so much subjected to the flesh thereby.

REPLY OBJ. 5: Fruit is not taken here in the sense in which *fruition* applies to delight in the end; but in another sense, as stated above (A. 2). Hence the argument proves nothing.

Article 4

Whether Three Fruits Are Fittingly Assigned to the Three Parts of Continence?

AD QUARTUM SIC PROCEDITUR. Videtur quod inconvenienter assignentur tres fructus tribus continentiae partibus. Quia Galat. 5, [22–23] ponuntur duodecim fructus Spiritus, scilicet *gaudium, pax*, etc. Et ideo videtur quod non debeant poni tres tantum.

PRAETEREA, fructus nominat aliquod praemium speciale. Sed praemium quod assignatur virginibus, vi-

OBJECTION 1: It would seem that three fruits are unfittingly assigned to the three parts of continence: because twelve fruits of the Spirit are assigned, *charity, joy, peace*, etc. (Gal 5:22). Therefore, it seems we should reckon only three.

OBJ. 2: Further, fruit denotes a special reward. Now the reward assigned to virgins, widows, and married persons

duis et coniugatis, non est speciale: quia omnes salvandi continentur sub aliquo horum trium; cum nullus salvetur qui continentia careat, et continentia per has tres sufficienter dividatur. Ergo inconvenienter tribus praedictis tres fructus assignantur.

PRAETEREA, sicut viduitas excedit continentiam coniugalem, ita virginitas viduitatem. Sed non similiter excedit sexagenarius tricenarium, et centenarius sexagenarium: neque secundum arithmeticam proportionalitatem, quia sexagenarius excedit tricenarium in triginta, et centenarius sexagenarium in quadraginta; neque etiam secundum proportionalitatem geometricam, quia sexagenarius se habet in dupla proportione ad tricenarium, centenarius vero ad sexagenarium in superbitertia, quia continet totum et duas tertias eius. Ergo inconvenienter aptantur fructus tribus continentiae gradibus.

PRAETEREA, ea quae in sacra Scriptura dicuntur, perpetuitatem habent: Luc. 21:33, *caelum et terra transibunt, verba autem mea non transient*. Sed ea quae ex institutione hominum sunt facta, quotidie possunt mutari. Ergo ex his quae ex institutione hominum sunt, non est accipienda ratio eorum quae in Scriptura dicuntur. Et sic videtur quod inconveniens sit ratio quam Beda assignat de istis fructibus, dicens quod fructus tricesimus debetur coniugatis, quia in repraesentatione quae fit in abaco, triginta significatur per contactum pollicis et indicis secundum suam summitatem; unde ibi quodammodo osculantur se; et sic tricenarius numerus significat coniugatorum oscula. Sexagenarius vero numerus significatur per tactum indicis super medium articulum pollicis: et sic per hoc quod index iacet super pollicem opprimens ipsum, significat oppressionem quam viduae patiuntur in mundo. Cum autem numerando ad centenarium pervenimus, ad dexteram a laeva transimus: unde per centenarium virginitas designatur, quae habet proportionem angelicae dignitatis, qui sunt in dextera, scilicet in gloria, nos autem in sinistra propter imperfectionem praesentis vitae.

RESPONDEO dicendum quod per continentiam, cui fructus respondet, homo in quandam spiritualitatem adducitur, carnalitate abiecta. Et ideo secundum diversum modum spiritualitatis quam continentia facit, diversi fructus distinguuntur. Est enim quaedam spiritualitas necessaria, et quaedam superabundans. Necessaria quidem spiritualitas est in hoc quod rectitudo spiritus ex delectatione carnis non pervertatur: quod fit cum aliquis per rectum ordinem rationis utitur delectationibus carnis. Et haec est spiritualitas coniugatorum. Spiritualitas vero superabundans est per quam homo ab huiusmodi delectationibus carnis, spiritum suffocantibus, omnino se abstrahit. Sed hoc contingit dupliciter. Vel respectu cuiuslibet temporis praeteriti, praesentis et futuri. Et

is not a special reward, because all who are to be saved are comprised under one of these three, since no one is saved who lacks continence, and continence is adequately divided by these three. Therefore, three fruits are unfittingly assigned to the three aforesaid.

OBJ. 3: Further, just as widowhood surpasses conjugal continence, so does virginity surpass widowhood. But the excess of sixtyfold over thirtyfold is not as the excess of a hundredfold over sixtyfold; neither in arithmetical proportion, since sixty exceeds thirty by thirty, and a hundred exceeds sixty by forty; nor in geometrical proportion, since sixty is twice thirty and a hundred surpasses sixty as containing the whole and two-thirds thereof. Therefore, the fruits are unfittingly adapted to the degrees of continence.

OBJ. 4: Further, the statements contained in Sacred Scripture stand for all time: *heaven and earth shall pass away, but my words shall not pass away* (Luke 21:33). But human institutions are liable to change every day. Therefore, human institutions are not to be taken as a criterion of the statements of Sacred Scripture: and it would seem in consequence that the explanation of these fruits given by Bede is unfitting. For he says (*Expositions on the Gospel of Luke* 3.8) that the thirtyfold fruit is assigned to married persons, because in the signs drawn on the abacus the number 30 is denoted by the thumb and index finger touching one another at the tips as though kissing one another: so that the number 30 denotes the embraces of married persons. The number 60 is denoted by the contact of the index finger above the middle joint of the thumb, so that the index finger, by lying over the thumb and weighing on it, signifies the burden which widows have to bear in this world. When, however, in the course of enumeration we come to the number 100 we pass from the left to the right hand, so that the number 100 denotes virginity, which has a share in the angelic excellence; for the angels are on the right hand, i.e., in glory, while we are on the left on account of the imperfection of the present life.

I ANSWER THAT, By continence, to which the fruit corresponds, man is brought to a kind of spiritual nature by withdrawing from carnal things. Consequently, various fruits are distinguished according to the various manners of the spirituality resulting from continence. Now there is a certain spirituality which is necessary, and one which is superabundant. The spirituality that is necessary consists in the rectitude of the spirit not being disturbed by the pleasures of the flesh: and this obtains when one makes use of carnal pleasures according to the order of right reason. This is the spirituality of married persons. Spirituality is superabundant when a man withdraws himself entirely from those carnal pleasures which stifle the spirit. This may be done in two ways: either in respect of all time past, present,

313

haec est spiritualitas virginum. Vel secundum aliquod tempus. Et haec est spiritualitas viduarum.

Servantibus ergo continentiam coniugalem datur fructus trigesimus; vidualem, sexagesimus; virginalem, centesimus; ratione illa quam Beda assignat.

Quamvis possit et alia ratio assignari ex ipsa natura numerorum. Tricenarius enim numerus ex ductu trinarii in denarium surgit. Ternarius enim est *numerus omnis rei*, ut dicitur I *de Caelo et Mundo*, et habet in se perfectionem quandam omnibus communem, scilicet principii, medii et finis. Unde convenienter tricenarius numerus coniugatis assignatur, in quibus supra observationem decalogi, qui per denarium significatur, non additur aliqua perfectio nisi communis, sine qua non potest esse salus. Senarius autem, ex cuius ductu in denarium sexagenarius surgit, habet perfectionem ex partibus: cum constet ex omnibus partibus suis simul aggregatis. Unde convenienter viduitati respondet, in qua invenitur perfecta abstractio a delectationibus carnis quantum ad omnes circumstantias, quae sunt quasi partes virtuosi actus: cum nulla enim persona, et in nullo loco delectationibus carnis viduitas utitur, et sic de aliis circumstantiis. Quod non ierat de continentia coniugali. Sed centenarius convenienter respondet virginitati: quia denarius, ex cuius ductu centenarius surgit, est limes numerorum; et similiter virginitas tenet spiritualitatis limitem, quia ad eam nihil de spiritualitate adiici potest. Habet enim centenarius, inquantum est numerus quadratus, perfectionem ex figura. Figura enim quadrata secundum hoc perfecta est quod ex omni parte aequalitatem habet, utpote habens omnia latera aequalia. Unde competit virginitati, in qua quantum ad omne tempus aequaliter incorruptio invenitur.

AD PRIMUM ergo dicendum quod ibi fructus non accipiuntur hoc modo sicut hic de eis loquimur.

AD SECUNDUM dicendum quod nihil cogit ad ponendum fructum esse praemium non omnibus salvandis conveniens. Non solum enim essentiale praemium commune est omnibus, sed etiam aliquod accidentale: sicut gaudium de operibus illis sine quibus non est salus. Potest tamen dici quod fructus non omnibus conveniunt salvandis: sicut patet de his qui in fine poenitent, et incontinenter vixerunt; eis enim non fructus, sed essentiale praemium tantum debetur.

AD TERTIUM dicendum quod distinctio fructuum magis accipitur secundum species et figuras numerorum quam secundum quantitates ipsorum. Tamen etiam quantum ad quantitatis excessum potest aliqua ratio assignari. Coniugatus enim abstinet tantum a non sua, vidua vero a suo et a non suo: et sic invenitur ibi quaedam ratio dupli, sicut sexagenarius est duplex ad tricenarium.

and future, and this is the spirituality of virgins; or in respect of a particular time, and this is the spirituality of widows.

Accordingly, to those who keep conjugal continence, the thirtyfold fruit is awarded; to those who keep the continence of widows, the sixtyfold fruit; and to those who keep virginal continence, the hundredfold fruit: and this for the reason given by Bede quoted above.

However, another motive may be found in the very nature of the numbers. For 30 is the product of 3 multiplied by 10. Now 3 is *the number of everything*, as stated in *De Coelo et Mundo* I, and contains a certain perfection common to all, namely, of beginning, middle, and end. Wherefore the number 30 is fittingly assigned to married persons, in whom no other perfection is added to the observance of the Decalogue, signified by the number 10, than the common perfection without which there is no salvation. The number six, the multiplication of which by 10 amounts to 60, has perfection from its parts, being the aggregate of all its parts taken together; wherefore it corresponds fittingly to widowhood, in which we find perfect withdrawal from carnal pleasures as to all its circumstances (which are the parts, so to speak, of a virtuous act), since widowhood uses no carnal pleasures in connection with any person, place, or any other circumstance; which was not the case with conjugal continence. The number 100 corresponds fittingly to virginity; because the number 10, of which 100 is a multiple, is the limit of numbers: and in like manner virginity occupies the limit of spirituality, since no further spirituality can be added to it. The number 100 also, being a square number, has perfection from its figure: for a square figure is perfect through being equal on all sides, since all its sides are equal: wherefore it is adapted to virginity, in which incorruption is found equally as to all times.

REPLY OBJ. 1: Fruit is not taken there in the sense in which we are taking it now.

REPLY OBJ. 2: Nothing obliges us to hold that fruit is a reward that is not common to all who will be saved. For not only the essential reward is common to all, but also a certain accidental reward, such as joy in those works without which one cannot be saved. Yet it may be said that the fruits are not becoming to all who will be saved, as is evidently the case with those who repent in the end after leading an incontinent life, for to such no fruit is due, but only the essential reward.

REPLY OBJ. 3: The distinction of the fruits is to be taken according to the species and figures of the numbers rather than according to their quantity. Nevertheless, even if we regard the excess in point of quantity, we may find an explanation. For the married man abstains only from one that is not his, the widow from both hers and not hers, so that in the latter case we find the notion of double, just as 60 is the

Centenarius vero supra sexagenarium addit quadragenarium, qui consurgit ex ductu quaternarii in denarium. Quaternarius autem est primus numerus solidus et cubicus. Et sic convenit talis additio virginitati, quae supra perfectionem viduitatis perpetuam incorruptionem adiungit.

AD QUARTUM dicendum quod, quamvis illa repraesentatio numerorum sit ex humana institutione, tamen fundatur aliquo modo super rerum naturam: inquantum secundum ordinem digitorum et articulorum et contactuum numeri gradatim designantur.

double of 30. Again 100 is 60 plus 40, which latter number is the product of 4 X 10, and the number 4 is the first solid and square number. Thus the addition of this number is fitting to virginity, which adds perpetual incorruption to the perfection of widowhood.

REPLY OBJ. 4: Although these numerical signs are a human institution, they are founded somewhat on the nature of things, insofar as the numbers are denoted in gradation according to the order of the aforesaid joints and contacts.

Article 5

Whether an Aureole Is Due on Account of Virginity?

AD QUINTUM SIC PROCEDITUR. Videtur quod ratione virginitatis non debeatur aureola. Ubi enim est maior difficultas in opere, ibi debetur maius praemium. Sed maiorem difficultatem patiuntur in abstinendo a delectationibus carnis viduae quam virgines: dicit enim Hieronymus quod quanto maior est difficultas ex parte quorundam a voluptatis illecebris abstinere, tanto maius est praemium; et loquitur in commendatione viduarum. Philosophus etiam dicit, in libro *de Animalibus*, quod *iuvenes corruptae magis appetent coitum, propter rememorationem delectationis*. Ergo aureola, quae est maximum praemium, debetur magis viduis quam virginibus.

PRAETEREA, si virginitati deberetur aureola, ubi esset perfectissima virginitas, maxime inveniretur aureola. Sed in Beata Virgine est perfectissima virginitas: unde et *Virgo Virginum* nominatur. Et tamen ei non debetur aureola: quia nullam pugnam sustinuit in continendo, cum corruptione fomitis non fuerit infestata; ergo virginitati aureola non debetur.

PRAETEREA, ei quod non est secundum omne tempus laudabile, non debetur praemium excellens. Sed virginitatem servare non fuisset laudabile in statu innocentiae: cum tunc esset homini praeceptum, *crescite et multiplicamini et replete terram*. Nec etiam tempore legis, cum steriles erant maledictae. Ergo virginitati aureola non debetur.

PRAETEREA, non debetur idem praemium virginitati servatae et virginitati amissae. Sed pro virginitate amissa quandoque debetur aureola: ut si aliqua invita prostituatur a tyranno quia Christum confitetur. Ergo virginitati aureola non debetur.

PRAETEREA, excellens praemium non debetur ei quod inest nobis a natura. Sed virginitas innascitur cuilibet.

OBJECTION 1: It would seem that an aureole is not due on account of virginity. For where there is greater difficulty in the work, a greater reward is due. Now widows have greater difficulty than virgins in abstaining from the works of the flesh. For Jerome says (*Epistle to Ageruchia*) that the greater difficulty certain persons experience in abstaining from the allurements of pleasure, the greater their reward, and he is speaking in praise of widows. Moreover, the Philosopher says (*History of Animals* vii) that *young women who have been deflowered desire sexual intercourse the more for the recollection of the pleasure*. Therefore, the aureole, which is the greatest reward, is due to widows more than to virgins.

OBJ. 2: Further, if an aureole were due to virginity, it would be especially found where there is the most perfect virginity. Now the most perfect virginity is in the Blessed Virgin, wherefore she is called the *Virgin of virgins*: and yet no aureole is due to her because she experienced no conflict in being continent, for she was not infected with the corruption of the *fomes*. Therefore, an aureole is not due to virginity.

OBJ. 3: Further, a special reward is not due to that which has not been at all times praiseworthy. Now it would not have been praiseworthy to observe virginity in the state of innocence, since then was it commanded: *increase and multiply and fill the earth* (Gen 1:28); nor again during the time of the law, since the barren were accursed. Therefore, an aureole is not due to virginity.

OBJ. 4: Further, the same reward is not due to virginity observed and virginity lost. Yet an aureole is sometimes due to lost virginity; for instance, if a maiden be violated unwillingly at the order of a tyrant for confessing Christ. Therefore, an aureole is not due to virginity.

OBJ. 5: Further, a special reward is not due to that which is in us by nature. But virginity is inborn in every man, both

bet homini et bono et malo. Ergo virginitati aureola non debetur.

PRAETEREA, sicut se habet viduitas ad fructum sexagenarium, ita virginitas ad fructum centesimum et ad aureolam. Sed non cuilibet viduae debetur fructus sexagenarius, sed solum viduitatem voventi, ut quidam dicunt. Ergo videtur quod non cuilibet virginitati aureola debeatur, sed solum virginitati ex voto servatae.

PRAETEREA, praemium non respondet necessitati: cum omne meritum in voluntate consistat. Sed quaedam sunt virgines ex necessitate: ut naturaliter frigidi et eunuchi. Ergo virginitati non semper debetur aureola.

SED CONTRA: Est quod habetur Exod. 25, [25], *facies alteram coronam auream*: Glossa. *Ad coronam pertinet canticum novum quod virgines coram Agno concinunt, scilicet qui sequuntur Agnum quocumque ierit.* Ergo praemium quod virginitati debetur, dicitur aureola.

PRAETEREA, Isaiae 56, [4] dicitur, *haec dicit Dominus eunuchis*; et sequitur [V; 5], *dabo eis nomen melius a filiis et filiabus*; Glossa, *propriam gloriam excellentemque significat*. Sed *per eunuchos qui seipsos castraverunt propter regnum caelorum, virgines designantur*. Ergo virginitati debetur aliquod excellens praemium. Et hoc vocatur aureola.

RESPONDEO dicendum quod, ubi est praecellens ratio victoriae, ibi debetur aliqua specialis corona. Unde, cum per virginitatem aliquis singularem quandam victoriam obtineat de carne, contra quam continue bellum geritur, ut patet ad Galat. 5, [17], *spiritus concupiscit adversus carnem* etc., virginitati specialis corona debetur, quae aureola nominatur. Et hoc quidem communiter ab omnibus tenetur. Sed cui virginitati debeatur aureola, non similiter omnes dicunt.

Quidam enim dicunt aureolam actui deberi. Unde illa quae actu virginitatem servat, aureolam habebit, si sit de numero salvandorum. Sed hoc non videtur esse conveniens. Quia secundum hoc illae quae habent voluntatem nubendi et tamen antequam nupserint decedunt, habebunt aureolam.

Unde alii dicunt quod aureola debetur statui et non actui: ut. illae tantum virgines aureolam mereantur quae in statu virginitatis perpetuae servandae per votum se posuerunt. Sed hoc etiam non videtur conveniens. Quia aliquis ex pari voluntate potest servare virginitatem non vovens sicut alius vovens.

Et ideo aliter dici potest quod meritum omne actui virtutis debetur a caritate imperato. Virginitas autem secundum hoc ad genus virtutis pertinet, secundum quod, perpetua incorruptio mentis et corporis sub electione cadit: ut patet ex his quae dicta sunt. Et ideo illis tan-

good and wicked. Therefore, an aureole is not due to virginity.

OBJ. 6: Further, as widowhood is to the sixtyfold fruit, so is virginity to the hundredfold fruit and to the aureole. Now the sixtyfold fruit is not due to every widow, but only, as some say, to one who vows to remain a widow. Therefore, it would seem that neither is the aureole due to any kind of virginity, but only to that which is observed by vow.

OBJ. 7: Further, reward is not given to that which is done of necessity, since all merit depends on the will. But some are virgins of necessity, such as those who are naturally frigid and eunuchs. Therefore, an aureole is not always due to virginity.

ON THE CONTRARY, A Gloss on Exodus 25:25: *thou shalt also make a little golden crown* [*coronam aureolam*] says, *this crown denotes the new hymn which the virgins sing in the presence of the Lamb, those, to wit, who follow the Lamb wheresoever he goes*. Therefore, the reward due to virginity is called an aureole.

FURTHER, Isaiah 56:4 says: *thus says the Lord to the eunuchs*, and the text continues: *I will give to them a name better than sons and daughters* (Isa 56:5). Upon this a Gloss says: *this refers to their peculiar and transcendent glory* (St. Augustine, *On Virginity* 25). Now the eunuchs *who have made themselves eunuchs for the kingdom of heaven* (Matt 19:12) denote virgins. Therefore, it would seem that some special reward is due to virginity, and this is called the aureole.

I ANSWER THAT, Where there is a notable kind of victory, a special crown is due. Wherefore, since by virginity a person wins a signal victory over the flesh, against which a continuous battle is waged (as is clear from Galatians 5:17, *the flesh lusts against the spirit*), a special crown, called the aureole, is due to virginity. This indeed is the common opinion of all; but all are not agreed as to the kind of virginity to which it is due.

For some say that the aureole is due to the act. So that she who actually remains a virgin will have the aureole provided she be of the number of the saved. But this would seem unreasonable, because in this case those who have the will to marry and nevertheless die before marrying would have the aureole.

Hence others hold that the aureole is due to the state and not to the act: so that those virgins alone merit the aureole who by vow have placed themselves in the state of observing perpetual virginity. But this also seems unreasonable, because it is possible to have the same intention of observing virginity without a vow as with a vow.

Hence it may be said otherwise that merit is due to every virtuous act commanded by charity. Now virginity comes under the genus of virtue insofar as perpetual incorruption of mind and body is an object of choice, as appears from what has been said above (*Sentences* IV, D. 33, Q. 3, A. 1–2;

tum virginibus aureola proprie debetur quae propositum habuerunt virginitatem perpetuo conservandi, sive hoc propositum voto firmaverunt sive non (et hoc dico secundum quod aureola proprie accipitur ut praemium quoddam merito redditum): quamvis hoc propositum aliquando fuerit interruptum, integritate tamen carnis manente, dummodo in fine vitae inveniatur; quia virginitas mentis reparari potest, quamvis non virginitas carnis.

Si autem aureolam large accipiamus pro quocumque gaudio quod in patria habebunt super gaudium essentiale, sic etiam incorruptis carne aureola respondebit etiam si propositum non habuerunt perpetuo virginitatem servandi. Non enim est dubium quod de incorruptione corporis gaudebunt: sicut et innocentes de hoc quod immunes a peccato fuerunt, quamvis etiam peccandi opportunitatem non habuerunt, ut patet in pueris baptizatis. Sed haec non est propria acceptio aureolae, sed valde communis.

AD PRIMUM ergo dicendum quod in continendo secundum aliquid maiorem pugnam sustinent virgines, et secundum aliquid viduae, ceteris paribus. Virgines enim concupiscentia inflammat et experiendi desiderium, quod ex quadam quasi curiositate procedit, qua etiam fit ut homo libentius videat quae nunquam vidit; et etiam quandoque in eis concupiscentiam auget aestimatio maioris delectationis quam sit secundum veritatem; et inconsideratio eorum incommodorum quae delectationi huiusmodi adiunguntur. Et quantum ad hoc viduae minorem sustinent pugnam: maiorem autem propter delectationis memoriam. Et in diversis unum alteri praeiudicabit secundum diversas hominis dispositiones: quia quidam magis moventur hoc, quidam illo. Quidquid autem sit de quantitate pugnae, hoc tamen certum est, quod perfectior est victoria virginum quam viduarum. Perfectissimum enim genus victoriae est, et pulcherrimum, hosti nunquam cessisse. Corona autem non debetur pugnae, sed victoriae de pugna.

AD SECUNDUM dicendum quod duplex circa hoc est opinio. Quidam enim dicunt quod Beata Virgo pro virginitatis praemio non habet aureolam, si aureola proprie accipiatur, secundum quod respicit pugnam. Tamen habet aliquid maius aureola, propter perfectissimum propositum virginitatis servandae.

Alii vero dicunt quod aureolam, etiam sub propria ratione aureolae, habet, et excellentissimam. Quamvis enim pugnam non senserit, pugnam tamen carnis aliquam habuit: sed ex vehementia virtutis adeo habuit carnem subditam quod huiusmodi pugna ei insensibilis erat. Sed istud non videtur convenienter dici. Quia, cum Beata Virgo credatur omnino immunis fuisse a fomitis inclinatione propter eius sanctificationem perfectam,

Cf. III, Q. 152, A. 1, 3). Consequently, the aureole is due to those virgins alone who had the purpose of observing perpetual virginity, whether or not they have confirmed this purpose by vow. And I say this to the extent that an aureole is taken in its proper sense as a certain reward rendered for merit, even though this resolution at one time be broken with the integrity of the flesh remaining, as long as it is found at the end of life. For virginity of the mind may be restored, although virginity of the flesh cannot.

If, however, we take the aureole in its broad sense for any joy added to the essential joy of heaven, the aureole will be applicable even to those who are incorrupt in flesh, although they had not the purpose of observing perpetual virginity. For without doubt they will rejoice in the incorruption of their body, even as the innocent will rejoice in having been free from sin, although they had no opportunity of sinning, as in the case of baptized children. But this is not the proper meaning of an aureole, although it is very commonly taken in this sense.

REPLY OBJ. 1: In some respects virgins experience a greater conflict in remaining continent, and in other respects, widows, other things being equal. For virgins are inflamed by concupiscence, and by the desire of experience, which arises from a certain curiosity, as it were, which makes man more willing to see what he has never seen. Sometimes, moreover, this concupiscence is increased by their esteeming the pleasure to be greater than it is in reality, and by their failing to consider the grievances attaching to this pleasure. In these respects, widows experience the lesser conflict, yet theirs is the greater conflict by reason of their recollection of the pleasure. Moreover, in different subjects one motive is stronger than another, according to the various conditions and dispositions of the subject, because some are more susceptible to one, and others to another. However, whatever we may say of the degree of conflict, this is certain—that the virgin's victory is more perfect than the widow's, for the most perfect and most brilliant kind of victory is never to have yielded to the foe: and the crown is due not to the battle, but to the victory gained by the battle.

REPLY OBJ. 2: There are two opinions about this. For some say that the Blessed Virgin has not an aureole in reward of her virginity, if we take aureole in the proper sense as referring to a conflict, but that she has something more than an aureole, on account of her most perfect purpose of observing virginity.

Others say that she has an aureole even in its proper signification, and that a most transcendent one: for though she experienced no conflict, she had a certain conflict of the flesh, but owing to the exceeding strength of her virtue, her flesh was so subdued that she did not feel this conflict. This, however, would seem to be said without reason, for since we believe the Blessed Virgin to have been altogether immune from the inclination of the *fomes* on account of the

non est pium ponere aliquam pugnam a carne fuisse in ea: cum talis pugna non sit nisi a fomitis inclinatione; nec tentatio quae est a carne sine peccato esse possit, ut patet per Glossam II Cor. 12, super illud [v. 7], *datus est mihi stimulus carnis meae* etc.

Unde dicendum est quod aureolam proprie habet, ut in hoc membris aliis Ecclesiae conformetur in quibus virginitas invenitur. Et quamvis non habuit pugnam per tentationem quae est *a carne*, habuit tamen pugnam per tentationem *ab hoste*: qui nec etiam ipsum Christum reveritus fuit, ut patet Matth. 4, [i–ii].

AD TERTIUM dicendum quod virginitati non debetur aureola nisi inquantum addit quandam excellentiam super alios continentiae gradus. Si autem Adam non peccasset, virginitas nullam perfectionem supra continentiam coniugalem habuisset: quia fuissent tunc *honorabiles nuptiae et torus immaculatus*, nulla concupiscentiae foeditate existente. Unde virginitas tunc servata non fuisset: nec ei tunc aureola deberetur. Sed, mutata humanae naturae conditione, virginitas specialem decorem habet. Et ideo ei speciale redditur praemium.

Tempore etiam legis Moysi, quando cultus Dei etiam per carnalem actum propagandus erat, non erat omnino laudabile a commixtione carnis abstinere. Unde nec tali proposito speciale praemium redderetur, nisi ex divino processisset instinctu: ut creditur de Ieremia et Elia, quorum coniugia non leguntur.

AD QUARTUM dicendum quod, si aliqua per violentiam oppressa fuerit, propter hoc non. amittit aureolam, dummodo propositum perpetuo virginitatem servandi inviolabiliter servet, si illi actui nullo modo est consentiens. Nec tamen per hoc virginitatem perdit. Et hoc dico sive pro fide, sive pro quacumque alia causa violenter corrumpatur. Sed si hoc pro fide sustineat, hoc ei erit meritorium, et ad genus martyrii pertinebit. Unde Lucia dixit: *si me invitam violare feceris, castitas mihi duplicabitur ad coronam: non quod habeat duas virginitatis aureolas*; sed quia duplex praemium reportabit, unum pro virginitate custodita, aliud pro iniuria quam passa est. Dato etiam quod taliter oppressa concipiat, nec ex hoc meritum virginitatis perdit. Nec tamen matri Christi aequabitur, in qua fuit cum integritate mentis etiam integritas carnis.

AD QUINTUM dicendum quod virginitas nobis a natura innascitur quantum ad id quod est materiale in virginitate. Sed propositum perpetuae incorruptionis servandae, ex quo virginitas meritum habet, non est innatum, sed ex munere gratiae proveniens.

AD SEXTUM dicendum, quod non cuilibet viduae fructus sexagenarius debetur: sed ei solum quae propositum viduitatis servandae retinet, quamvis etiam votum non emittat; sicut etiam de virginitate dictum est.

perfection of her sanctification, it is wicked to suppose that there was in her any conflict with the flesh, since such conflict is only from the inclination of the *fomes*, nor can temptation from the flesh be without sin, as declared by a Gloss on 2 Corinthians 12:7, *there was given me a sting of my flesh*.

Hence we must say that she has an aureole properly speaking, so as to be conformed in this to those other members of the Church in whom virginity is found: and although she had no conflict by reason of the temptation which is *of the flesh*, she had the temptation which is *of the enemy*, who feared not even Christ (Matt 4).

REPLY OBJ. 3: The aureole is not due to virginity except as adding some excellence to the other degrees of continence. If Adam had not sinned, virginity would have had no perfection over conjugal continence, since in that case *marriage would have been honorable, and the marriage-bed unsullied*, for it would not have been dishonored by lust: hence virginity would not then have been observed, nor would an aureole have been due to it. But the condition of human nature being changed, virginity has a special beauty of its own, and consequently a special reward is assigned to it.

During the time of the Mosaic law, when the worship of God was to be continued by means of the carnal act, it was not altogether praiseworthy to abstain from carnal intercourse: wherefore no special reward would be given for such a purpose unless it came from a divine inspiration, as is believed to have been the case with Jeremiah and Elijah, of whose marriages we do not read.

REPLY OBJ. 4: If a virgin is violated, she does not forfeit the aureole, provided she retain unfailingly the purpose of observing perpetual virginity, and in no way consent to the act. Nor does she forfeit virginity thereby. And this is said whether she be violated for the faith or for any other cause whatever. But if she suffer this for the faith, this will count to her for merit, and will be a kind of martyrdom: wherefore Lucy said: *if you cause me to be violated against my will, my chastity will receive a double crown*; not that she has two aureoles of virginity, but that she will receive a double reward, one for observing virginity, the other for the outrage she has suffered. Even supposing that one thus violated should conceive, she would not for that reason forfeit her virginity: nor would she be equal to Christ's mother, in whom there was integrity of the flesh together with integrity of the mind.

REPLY OBJ. 5: Virginity is inborn in us as to that which is material in virginity: but the purpose of observing perpetual incorruption, whence virginity derives its merit, is not inborn, but comes from the gift of grace.

REPLY OBJ. 6: The sixtyfold fruit is due not to every widow, but only to those who retain the purpose of remaining widows, even though they do not make it the matter of a vow, just as we have said in regard to virginity.

AD SEPTIMUM dicendum quod, si frigidi et eunuchi voluntatem habeant perpetuam incorruptionem servare etiam si facultas esset coeundi, virgines sunt dicendi, et aureolam merentur: *faciunt* enim *de necessitate virtutem.* Si vero voluntatem habeant ducendi coniugem si possent, aureolam non merentur. Unde dicit Augustinus, in libro *de Sancta Virginitate: quibus ipsum virile membrum debilitatur ut generare non possint, ut sunt eunuchi, sufficit, cum Christiani fiunt et Dei praecepta custodiunt, eo tamen proposito sunt ut coniuges, si possent, haberent, coniugatis fidelibus adaequari.*

REPLY OBJ. 7: If frigid persons and eunuchs have the will to observe perpetual incorruption even if they were capable of sexual intercourse, they must be called virgins and merit the aureole: for *they make a virtue of necessity.* If, on the other hand, they have the will to marry if they could, they do not merit the aureole. Hence Augustine says (*On Holy Virginity* xxiv): *For those for whom the male member itself is weakened so that they are not capable of generation, such as eunuchs, when they become Christians and keep the commandments of God though with the resolution that they would have spouses if they could, it is enough for them to be counted equal to the members of the faithful who are married.*

Article 6

Whether an Aureole Is Due to Martyrs?

AD SEXTUM SIC PROCEDITUR. Videtur quod martyribus aureola non debeatur. Aureola enim est praemium quod operibus supererogationis redditur: unde dicit Beda, super illud Exod. 25, [25], *aliam coronam aureolam* etc.: *de eorum praemio potest recte intelligi qui generalia mandata spontanea vitae perfectioris electione transcendunt.* Sed mori pro confessione fidei quandoque est necessitatis, non supererogationis: ut patet ex hoc quod dicitur Rom. 10, [10], *corde creditur ad iustitiam, ore autem confessio fit ad salutem.* Ergo martyrio non semper debetur aureola.

PRAETEREA, secundum Gregorium, *servitia quanto sunt magis libera, tanto sunt magis grata.* Sed martyrium minimum habet de libertate: cum sit poena ab alio violenter inflicta. Ergo martyrio aureola non debetur, quae respondet merito excellenti.

PRAETEREA, martyrium non solum consistit in exteriori passione mortis, sed etiam in interiori voluntate. Unde Bernardus distinguit tria genera martyrum: voluntate, non nec, ut Ioannes; voluntate et nece, ut Stephanus; nece, non voluntate, ut Innocentes. Si ergo martyrio aureola deberetur, magis deberetur martyrio voluntatis quam exteriori martyrio: cum meritum ex voluntate procedat. Hoc autem non ponitur. Ergo martyrio aureola non debetur.

PRAETEREA, afflictio corporis est minor quam afflictio mentis, quae est per interiores dolores et interiores animae passiones. Sed interior etiam afflictio quoddam martyrium est: unde dicit Hieronymus, in *Sermone de Assumptione: recte dixerim, Dei Genitrix Virgo et Martyr fuit, quamvis in pace vitam finierit. Unde: Tuam ipsius animam pertransibit gladius,* scilicet dolor de morte

OBJECTION 1: It would seem that an aureole is not due to martyrs. For an aureole is a reward given for works of supererogation, wherefore Bede, commenting on Exodus 25:25: *thou shalt also make another little golden crown,* says, *this may be rightly referred to the reward of those who by freely choosing a more perfect life go beyond the general commandments.* But to die for confessing the faith is sometimes an obligation, and not a work of supererogation, as appears from Romans 10:10, *with the heart, we believe unto justice, but with the mouth confession is made unto salvation.* Therefore, an aureole is not always due to martyrdom.

OBJ. 2: Further, according to Gregory (*Morals on Job* 9), *the freer the service, the more acceptable it is.* Now martyrdom has a minimum of freedom, since it is a punishment inflicted by another person with force. Therefore, an aureole is not due to martyrdom, since it is accorded to surpassing merit.

OBJ. 3: Further, martyrdom consists not only in suffering death externally, but also in the interior act of the will: wherefore Bernard in a sermon on the Holy Innocents distinguishes three kinds of martyr: in will and not in death, as John; in both will and death, as Stephen; in death and not in will, as the Innocents. Accordingly, if an aureole were due to martyrdom, it would be due to voluntary rather than external martyrdom, since merit proceeds from will. Yet such is not the case. Therefore, an aureole is not due to martyrdom.

OBJ. 4: Further, bodily suffering is less than mental, which consists of internal sorrow and affliction of soul. But internal suffering is also a kind of martyrdom: wherefore Jerome says in a sermon on the Assumption (*Epistle to Paula and Eustochium*): *I should say rightly that the Mother of God was both virgin and martyr, although she ended her days in peace.* Hence, *"Thine own soul a sword*

Filii. Cum ergo interiori dolori aureola non respondeat, nec exteriori respondere debet.

PRAETEREA, ipsa poenitentia martyrium quoddam est: unde dicit Gregorius: *quamvis occasio persecutionis desit, habet tamen et pax nostra martyrium suum: quia, etsi carnis colla ferro non subiicimus, spirituali tamen gladio carnalia desideria in mente trucidamus.* Poenitentiae autem, quae in exterioribus operibus consistit, aureola non debetur. Ergo nec etiam omni exteriori martyrio.

PRAETEREA, illicito operi non debetur aureola. Sed illicitum est sibi ipsi marius iniicere: ut patet per Augustinum, in I lib. *de Civ. Dei.* Et tamen quorundam martyria in Ecclesia celebrata sunt qui sibi manus iniecerunt, tyrannorum rabiem fugientes: ut patet in *Ecclesiastica Historia* de quibusdam mulieribus apud Alexandriam. Ergo non semper martyrio debetur aureola.

PRAETEREA, contingit aliquando aliquem pro fide vulnerari et postmodum aliquo tempore supervivere. Hunc constat martyrem esse. Et tamen ei, ut videtur, aureola non debetur: quia eius pugna non duravit usque ad mortem. Ergo non semper martyrio debetur aureola.

PRAETEREA, quidam magis affliguntur in amissione rerum temporalium quam etiam in propria afflictione: quod patet ex hoc quod multas afflictiones sustinent ad lucra acquirenda. Si ergo eis propter Christum temporalia bona diripiantur, videtur quod sint martyres. Nec tamen eis, ut videtur, debetur aureola. Ergo idem quod prius.

PRAETEREA, martyr videtur esse ille qui pro fide occiditur: unde dicit Isidorus, *martyres graece, testes latine dicuntur: quia propter testimonium Christi passiones sustinuerunt, et usque ad mortem pro veritate certaverunt.* Sed aliquae aliae virtutes sunt fide excellentiores, ut iustitia, caritas et huiusmodi, quae sine gratia esse non possunt: quibus tamen non debetur aureola. Ergo videtur quod nec martyrio aureola debeatur.

PRAETEREA, sicut veritas fidei est a Deo, ita et quaelibet alia veritas, ut dicit Ambrosius: quia *omne verum, a quocumque dicatur, a Spiritu Sancto est.* Ergo, si sustinenti mortem pro veritate, fidei debetur aureola, eadem ratione et sustinentibus mortem pro qualibet alia veritate. Quod tamen non videtur.

PRAETEREA, bonum commune est potius bono particulari. Sed si aliquis pro conservatione reipublicae moriatur in bello iusto, non debetur ei aureola. Ergo etiam si occidatur pro conservatione fidei in seipso. Et sic martyrio aureola non debetur.

hath pierced"—namely, *for her Son's death.* Since, then, no aureole corresponds to interior sorrow, neither should one correspond to outward suffering.

OBJ. 5: Further, penance itself is a kind of martyrdom, wherefore Gregory says (*Homilies on the Gospels* 3): *although persecution has ceased to offer the opportunity, yet the peace we enjoy is not without its martyrdom; since even if we no longer yield the life of the body to the sword, yet do we slay fleshly desires in the soul with the sword of the spirit.* But no aureole is due to penance, which consists in external works. Neither, therefore, is an aureole due to every external martyrdom.

OBJ. 6: Further, an aureole is not due to an unlawful work. Now it is unlawful to lay hands on oneself, as Augustine declares (*The City of God* 1), and yet the Church celebrates the martyrdom of some who laid hands upon themselves in order to escape the fury of tyrants, as in the case of certain women at Antioch (Eusebius, *Ecclesiastical History* 8.24). Therefore, an aureole is not always due to martyrdom.

OBJ. 7: Further, it happens at times that a person is wounded for the faith, and survives for some time. Now it is clear that such a one is a martyr, and yet seemingly an aureole is not due to him, since his conflict did not last until death. Therefore, an aureole is not always due to martyrdom.

OBJ. 8: Further, some suffer more from the loss of temporal goods than from the affliction even of their own body, and this is shown by their bearing many afflictions for the sake of gain. Therefore, if they be despoiled of their temporal goods for Christ's sake, they would seem to be martyrs, and yet an aureole is not apparently due to them. Therefore, the same conclusion follows as before.

OBJ. 9: Further, a martyr would seem to be no other than one who dies for the faith, wherefore Isidore says (*Etymologies* 7): *they are called martyrs in Greek, witnesses in Latin: because they suffered in order to bear witness to Christ, and strove unto death for the truth.* Now there are virtues more excellent than faith, such as justice, charity, and so forth, since these cannot be without grace, and yet no aureole is due to them. Therefore, seemingly, neither is an aureole due to martyrdom.

OBJ. 10: Further, even as the truth of faith is from God, so is all other truth, as Ambrose declares, since *every truth by whomsoever uttered is from the Holy Spirit.* Therefore, if an aureole is due to one who suffers death for the truth of faith, in like manner it is also due to those who suffer death for any other truth: and yet apparently this is not the case.

OBJ. 11: Further, the common good is greater than the good of the individual. Now if a man die in a just war in order to save his country, an aureole is not due to him. Therefore, even though he be put to death in order to keep the faith that is in himself, no aureole is due to him: and consequently the same conclusion follows as above.

PRAETEREA, omne meritum ex libero arbitrio. procedit. Sed quorundam martyria celebrat Ecclesia qui usum liberi arbitrii non habuerunt. Ergo aureolam non meruerunt. Et sic non omnibus martyribus debetur aureola.

SED CONTRA: Augustinus dicit, in libro *de Sancta Virginitate, nemo, quantum puto, ausus fuit praeferre virginitatem martyrio.* Sed virginitati debetur aureola. Ergo et martyrio.

PRAETEREA, corona debetur certanti. Sed in martyrio est specialis difficultas pugnae. Ergo ei debetur specialis aureola.

RESPONDEO dicendum quod, sicut inest quaedam pugna spiritui contra interiores concupiscentias, ita etiam inest homini quaedam pugna contra passiones exterius illatas. Unde, sicut perfectissimae victoriae qua de concupiscentiis carnis triumphatur, scilicet virginitati, debetur specialis corona, quae aureola dicitur; ita etiam perfectissimae victoriae quae habetur de impugnatione exteriori, debetur aureola.

Perfectissima autem victoria de exterioribus passionibus consideratur ex duobus. Primo, ex magnitudine passionis. Inter omnes autem passiones illatas exterius praecipuum locum mors tenet: sicut et in passionibus interioribus praecipuae sunt venereorum concupiscentiae. Et ideo quando quis obtinet victoriam de morte et ordinatis ad mortem, perfectissime vincit. Secundo, perfectio victoriae consideratur ex causa pugnae: quando videlicet pro honestissima causa pugnatur; quae scilicet est ipse Christus.

Et haec duo in martyrio considerantur, quod est mors suscepta propter Christum: *martyrem* enim *non facit poena, sed causa.* Et ideo martyrio aureola debetur, sicut et virginitati.

AD PRIMUM ergo dicendum quod sustinere mortem propter Christum, quantum est de se, est opus supererogationis: non enim quilibet tenetur fidem suam coram persecutore confiteri. Sed in casu est de necessitate salutis: quando scilicet aliquis a persecutore deprehensus de fide sua requiritur, quam confiteri tenetur. Nec tamen sequitur quod aureolam non mereatur. Aureola enim non debetur operi supererogationis inquantum est supererogatio: sed inquantum perfectionem quandam habet. Unde, tali perfectione manente, etiam si non sit supererogatio, aliquis aureolam meretur.

AD SECUNDUM dicendum quod martyrio non debetur aliquod praemium secundum hoc quod ab exteriori infligitur, sed secundum hoc quod voluntarie sustinetur: quia non meremur nisi per ea quae sunt in nobis. Et quanto id quod aliquis sustinet voluntarie est difficilius et magis natum voluntati repugnare, tanto voluntas quae propter Christum illud sustinet, ostenditur firmius fixa in Christo. Et ideo ei excellentius praemium debetur.

OBJ. 12: Further, all merit proceeds from the free will. Yet the Church celebrates the martyrdom of some who had not the use of the free will. Therefore, they did not merit an aureole: and consequently an aureole is not due to all martyrs.

ON THE CONTRARY, Augustine says (*On Holy Virginity* xlvi): *no one, I think, would dare prefer virginity to martyrdom.* Now an aureole is due to virginity, and consequently also to martyrdom.

FURTHER, The crown is due to one who has striven. But in martyrdom the strife presents a special difficulty. Therefore, a special aureole is due thereto.

I ANSWER THAT, Just as in the spirit there is a conflict with the internal concupiscences, so is there in man a conflict with the passion that is inflicted from without. Wherefore, just as a special crown, which we call an aureole, is due to the most perfect victory whereby we triumph over the concupiscences of the flesh, in a word to virginity, so too an aureole is due to the most perfect victory that is won against external assaults.

Now the most perfect victory over passion caused from without is considered from two points of view. First, from the greatness of the passion. Now among all passions inflicted from without, death holds the first place, just as sexual concupiscences are chief among internal passions. Consequently, when a man conquers death and things directed to death, his is a most perfect victory. Second, the perfection of victory is considered from the point of view of the motive of conflict, when, to wit, a man strives for the most honorable cause; which is Christ himself.

Both these things are to be found in martyrdom, which is death suffered for Christ's sake: for *it is not the pain but the cause that makes the martyr,* as Augustine says (*Against Cresconius the Grammarian* 3). Consequently, an aureole is due to martyrdom as well as to virginity.

REPLY OBJ. 1: To suffer death for Christ's sake is, absolutely speaking, a work of supererogation; since every one is not bound to confess his faith in the face of a persecutor: yet in certain cases it is necessary for salvation, namely, when a person is seized by a persecutor and interrogated as to his faith, which he is then bound to confess. Nor does it follow that he does not merit an aureole. For an aureole is due to a work of supererogation, not as such, but as having a certain perfection. Wherefore so long as this perfection remains, even though the supererogation cease, one merits the aureole.

REPLY OBJ. 2: A reward is due to martyrdom not in respect of the exterior infliction, but because it is suffered voluntarily: since we merit only through that which is in us. And the more that which one suffers voluntarily is difficult and naturally repugnant to the will, the more is the will that suffers it for Christ's sake shown to be firmly established in Christ, and consequently a higher reward is due to him.

AD TERTIUM dicendum quod quidam actus sunt qui in ipso actu habent quandam vehementiam delectationis vel difficultatis. Et in talibus actus semper addit ad rationem meriti vel demeriti: secundum quod in actu oportet voluntatem variari ex vehementia actus a statu in quo prius erat. Et ideo, ceteris paribus, actu luxuriam exercens plus peccat quam qui solum in actum consentit: quia in ipso actu voluntas augetur. Similiter et, cum actus martyrii maximam difficultatem habeat, voluntas martyrii non pertingit ad illud meritum quod actui martyrum debetur ratione difficultatis. Quamvis etiam possit pervenire ad alterius praemium considerata radice merendi: quia aliquis ex maiori caritate potest velle sustinere martyrium quam alius sustineat. Unde voluntarie martyr potest mereri sua voluntate praemium essentiale aequale vel maius eo quod martyri debetur. Sed aureola debetur difficultati quae est in ipsa pugna martyrii. Unde aureola voluntarie tantum martyribus non debetur.

AD QUARTUM dicendum quod, sicut delectationes tactus, circa quas est temperantia, praecipuum locum tenent inter omnes delectationes interiores et exteriores, ita dolores tactus omnibus aliis doloribus praeeminent. Et ideo difficultati illi quae accidit in sustinendo dolores tactus, puta qui sunt in verberibus et huiusmodi, debetur aureola, magis quam difficultati sustinendi interiores dolores. Pro quibus tamen non proprie dicitur aliquis martyr, nisi secundum quandam similitudinem. Et hoc modo Hieronymus loquitur.

AD QUINTUM dicendum quod afflictio poenitentiae, proprie loquendo, non est martyrium: quia non consistit in his quae ad mortem inferendam ordinantur; cum ordinetur solum ad carnem domandam, quam mensuram si quis excedat, erit afflictio culpanda. Dicitur tamen propter similitudinem afflictionis martyrium. Quae quidem afflictio excedit martyrii afflictionem diuturnitate: sed exceditur intensione.

AD SEXTUM dicendum quod, secundum Augustinum, in I *de Civ. Dei*, nulli licitum est sibi ipsi manus iniicere quacumque ex causa: nisi forte divino: instinctu fiat, ad exemplum fortitudinis ostendendum, ut mors contemnatur. Illi autem de quibus obiectum est, divino instinctu mortem sibi intulisse creduntur. Et propter hoc eorum martyria Ecclesia celebrat.

AD SEPTIMUM dicendum quod, si aliquis propter fidem vulnus mortale accipiat et supervivat, non est dubium quod aureolam meretur: sicut de beata Caecilia patet, quae triduo supervixit; et de multis martyribus qui in carcere sunt defuncti. Sed etiam si vulnus non mortale accipiat, et tamen exinde mortem incurrat, creditur aureolam mereri: quamvis quidam dicant quod aureolam non meretur si ex incuria vel negligentia propria mor-

REPLY OBJ. 3: There are certain acts which, in their very selves, contain intense pleasure or difficulty: and in such the act always adds to the character of merit or demerit, for as much as in the performance of the act the will, on account of the aforesaid intensity, must undergo an alteration from the state in which it was before. Consequently, other things being equal, one who performs an act of lust sins more than one who merely consents in the act, because in the very act the will is increased. In like manner, since in the act of suffering martyrdom there is a very great difficulty, the will to suffer martyrdom does not reach the degree of merit due to actual martyrdom by reason of its difficulty: although indeed it may possibly attain to a higher reward if we consider the root of merit, since the will of one man to suffer martyrdom may possibly proceed from a greater charity than another man's act of martyrdom. Hence one who is willing to be a martyr may, by his will, merit an essential reward equal to or greater than that which is due to an actual martyr. But the aureole is due to the difficulty inherent to the conflict itself of martyrdom: wherefore it is not due to those who are martyrs only in will.

REPLY OBJ. 4: Just as pleasures of touch, which are the matter of temperance, hold the chief place among all pleasures both internal and external, so pains of touch surpass all other pains. Consequently, an aureole is due to the difficulty of suffering pains of touch, such as from blows and so forth, rather than to the difficulty of bearing internal sufferings (by reason of which, however, one is not properly called a martyr, except by a kind of comparison.) It is in this sense that Jerome speaks.

REPLY OBJ. 5: The sufferings of penance are not a martyrdom properly speaking, because they do not consist in things directed to the causing of death, since they are directed merely to the taming of the flesh: and if any one go beyond this measure, such afflictions will be deserving of blame. However, such afflictions are spoken of as a martyrdom by a kind of comparison. and they surpass the sufferings of martyrdom in duration but not in intensity.

REPLY OBJ. 6: According to Augustine (*The City of God* 1), it is lawful to no one to lay hands on himself for any reason whatever; unless perchance it be done by divine instinct as an example of fortitude that others may despise death. Those to whom the objection refers are believed to have brought death on themselves by divine instinct, and for this reason the Church celebrates their martyrdom.

REPLY OBJ. 7: If any one receive a mortal wound for the faith and survive, without doubt he merits the 'aureole': as instanced in blessed Cecilia who survived for three days, and many martyrs who died in prison. But, even if the wound he receives is not mortal, yet is the occasion of his dying, he is believed to merit the aureole: although some say that he does not merit the aureole if he happen to die through his own carelessness or neglect. For this ne-

tem incurrat. Non enim ista negligentia eum ad mortem perduxisset nisi praesupposita vulnere quod pro fide acceptum est: et ita vulnus propter Christum susceptum est ei prima occasio mortis. Unde propter hoc aureolam non videtur amittere: nisi sit talis negligentia quae culpam mortalem inducat, quae ei et auream aufert et aureolam. Si vero ex mortali vulnere suscepto non moriatur, aliquo casu contingente; vel etiam vulnera non mortalia susceperat, et adhuc carcerem sustinens moriatur; adhuc aureolam meretur. Unde quorundam sanctorum martyria in Ecclesia celebrantur qui in carcere mortui sunt, aliquibus vulneribus longe ante susceptis: sicut patet de Marcello Papa.

Qualitercumque igitur afflictio propter Christum illata usque ad mortem continuatur, sive mors inde sequatur sive non, aliquis martyr efficitur et aureolam meretur. Si vero non continuatur usque ad mortem, non propter hoc aliquis dicetur martyr: sicut patet de Silvestro de quo non solemnizat Ecclesia sicut de martyre, quia in pace vitam finivit, quamvis prius aliquas passiones sustinuerit.

AD OCTAVUM dicendum quod, sicut temperantia non est circa delectationes in pecuniis vel in honoribus et huiusmodi, sed solum in delectationibus tactus, quasi praecipuis; ita etiam fortitudo est circa pericula mortis sicut circa praecipua, ut dicitur in III *Ethic.* Et ideo soli iniuriae quae irrogatur circa corpus proprium, ex qua nata est mors sequi, debetur aureola. Sive igitur aliquis propter Christum res temporales, sive famam, vel quidquid huiusmodi amittat, non efficitur propter hoc proprie martyr, nec meretur aureolam. Nec aliquis potest ordinate res exteriores plus diligere quam proprium corpus. Amor autem inordinatus non coadiuvat ad meritum aureolae. Nec etiam potest dolor de amissione rerum coaequari dolori de corporis occisione, et aliis huiusmodi.

AD NONUM dicendum quod causa sufficiens ad martyrium non solum est confessio fidei, sed quaecumque alia virtus non politica, sed infusa, quae finem habeat Christum. Quolibet enim actu virtutis aliquis testis Christi efficitur: inquantum opera quae in nobis Christus perficit, testimonia bonitatis ipsius sunt. Unde aliquae virgines sunt occisae pro virginitate quam servare volebant, sicut beata Agnes et quaedam aliae, quarum martyria in Ecclesia celebrantur.

AD DECIMUM dicendum quod veritas fidei habet Christum pro fine et pro obiecto. Et ideo confessio ipsius aureolam meretur, si poena addatur, non solum ex parte finis, sed etiam ex parte materiae. Sed confessio cuiuscumque alterius veritatis non est causa sufficiens ad martyrium ratione materiae: sed solum ratione finis, utpote si aliquis vellet prius occidi quam, quodcumque mendacium dicendo, contra ipsum peccare.

glect would not have occasioned his death, except on the supposition of the wound which he received for the faith: and consequently this wound previously received for the faith is the original occasion of his death. Thus he would not seem to lose the aureole for that reason unless his neglect were such as to involve a mortal sin, which would deprive him of both 'aurea' and 'aureole'. If, however, by some chance or other he were not to die of the mortal wound received, or again if the wounds received were not mortal and he were to die while in prison, he would still merit the aureole. Hence the martyrdom of some saints who died in prison, having been wounded long before, is celebrated in the Church, as in the case of Pope Marcellus.

Accordingly, in whatever way suffering for Christ's sake be continued unto death, whether death ensue or not, a man becomes a martyr and merits the aureole. If, however, it be not continued unto death, this is not a reason for calling a person a martyr, as in the case of the blessed Sylvester, whose feast the Church does not solemnize as a martyr's since he ended his days in peace, although previously he had undergone certain sufferings.

REPLY OBJ. 8: Even as temperance is not about pleasures of money, honors, and the like, but only about pleasures of touch as being the principal of all, so fortitude is about dangers of death, as being the greatest of all (*Ethics* 3.6). Consequently, the aureole is due to such injuries only as are inflicted on a person's own body and are of a nature to cause death. Accordingly, whether a person lose his temporalities, or his good name, or anything else of the kind for Christ's sake, he does not for that reason become a martyr, nor merit the aureole. Nor is it possible to love ordinately external things more than one's body, and inordinate love does not help one to merit an aureole: nor again can sorrow for the loss of corporeal things be equal to the sorrow for the slaying of the body and other like things.

REPLY OBJ. 9: The sufficient motive for martyrdom is not only confession of the faith, but any other virtue, not civic but infused, that has Christ for its end. For one becomes a witness of Christ by any virtuous act, inasmuch as the works which Christ perfects in us bear witness to his goodness. Hence some virgins were slain for virginity which they desired to keep, for instance, blessed Agnes and others whose martyrdom is celebrated by the Church.

REPLY OBJ. 10: The truth of faith has Christ for end and object; and therefore the confession thereof, if suffering be added thereto, merits an aureole, not only on the part of the end but also on the part of the matter. But the confession of any other truth is not a sufficient motive for martyrdom by reason of its matter, but only on the part of the end; for instance, if a person were willing to be slain for Christ's sake rather than sin against him by telling any lie whatever.

Ad undecimum dicendum quod etiam bonum increatum excedit omne bonum creatum. Unde quicumque finis creatus, sive sit bonum commune sive privatum, non potest actui tantam bonitatem praestare quantam finis increatus, cum scilicet aliquid propter Deum agitur. Et ideo cum quis propter bonum commune non relatum ad Christum mortem sustinet, aureolam non meretur. Sed si hoc referatur ad Christum, aureolam merebitur et martyr erit: utpote si rempublicam defendat ab hostium impugnatio ne, qui fidem Christi corrumpere moliuntur, et in tali defensione mortem sustineat.

Ad duodecimum dicendum quod quidam dicunt quod Innocentibus occisis pro Christo virtute divina acceleratus est usus rationis: sicut et in Ioanne Baptista dum adhuc esset in materno utero. Et secundum hoc vere martyres fuerunt et actu et voluntate, et aureolam habent.

Sed alii dicunt quod fuerunt martyres actu tantum, et non voluntate: quod videtur sentire Bernardus, distinguens tria genera martyrum, ut dictum est. Et secundum hoc Innocentes, sicut non pertingunt ad perfectam rationem martyrii, sed aliquid martyrii habent ex hoc quod passi sunt pro Christo; ita etiam aureolam, non quidem secundum perfectam rationem, sed secundum aliquam participationem, inquantum scilicet gaudent se in obsequium Christi occisos esse; ut dictum est de pueris baptizatis quod habebunt aliquod gaudium de innocentia et carnis integritate.

Reply Obj. 11: The uncreated good surpasses all created good. Hence any created end, whether it be the common or a private good, cannot confer so great a goodness on an act as can the uncreated end, namely, when an act is done for God's sake. Hence when a person dies for the common good without referring it to Christ, he will not merit the aureole; but if he refer it to Christ, he will merit the aureole and he will be a martyr; for instance, if he defend his country from the attack of an enemy who designs to corrupt the faith of Christ, and suffer death in that defense.

Reply Obj. 12: Some say that the use of reason was by the divine power accelerated in the Innocents slain for Christ's sake, even as in John the Baptist while yet in his mother's womb: and in that case they were truly martyrs in both act and will, and have the aureole.

Others say, however, that they were martyrs in act only and not in will: and this seems to be the opinion of Bernard, who distinguishes three kinds of martyrs, as stated above (Obj. 3). In this case, the Innocents, even as they do not fulfill all the conditions of martyrdom, and yet are martyrs in a sense in that they died for Christ, also have the aureole not in all its perfection, but by a kind of participation, insofar as they rejoice in having. been slain in Christ's service. Thus it was stated above (A. 5) in reference to baptized children, that they will have a certain joy in their innocence and carnal integrity.

Article 7

Whether an Aureole Is Due to Doctors?

Ad septimum sic proceditur. Videtur quod doctoribus aureola; non debeatur. Omne enim praemium quod in futuro habebitur, alicui actui virtutis respondet. Sed praedicare vel docere non est actus alicuius virtutis. Ergo doctrinae vel praedicationi non debetur aureola.

Praeterea, docere et praedicare ex doctrina et studio proveniunt. Sed ea quae praemiantur in futuro, non sunt acquisita per humanum studium: quia naturalibus acquisitis non meremur. Ergo pro doctrina et praedicatione nullus in futuro aureolam promeretur.

Praeterea, exaltatio in futuro respondet humilitati in praesenti: quia *qui se humiliat exaltabitur.* Sed in docendo et in praedicando non est humiliatio: immo magis superbiae occasio; unde Glossa dicit, Matth. 4, [5], quod *diabolus multos decepit honore magisterii inflato*s. Ergo videtur quod praedicationi et doctrinae aureola non debeatur.

Objection 1: It would seem that an aureole is not due to doctors. For every reward to be had in the life to come will correspond to some act of virtue. But preaching or teaching is not the act of a virtue. Therefore, an aureole is not due to teaching or preaching.

Obj. 2: Further, teaching and preaching are the result of studying and being taught. Now the things that are rewarded in the future life are not acquired by a man's study, since we merit not by our natural and acquired gifts. Therefore, no aureole will be merited in the future life for teaching and preaching.

Obj. 3: Further, exaltation in the life to come corresponds to humiliation in the present life, because *he that humbles himself shall be exalted* (Matt 23:12). But there is no humiliation in teaching and preaching; in fact, they are occasions of pride, for a Gloss on Matthew 4:5: *then the devil took him up,* says that *the devil deceives many who are puffed up with the honor of the master's chair.* Therefore, it would seem that an aureole is not due to preaching and teaching.

SED CONTRA: Ephes. 1, super illud [v. 18–19], *ut scia-tis quae sit supereminens* etc., dicit Glossa: *quoddam in-crementum habebunt sancti doctores ultra id quod alii communiter habebunt.* Ergo, etc.

PRAETEREA, Cant. 8, super illud [v, 12], *vinea mea coram me est*, dicit Glossa: *ostendit quid singularis prae-mii doctoribus eius disponit.* Ergo doctores habebunt sin-gulare praemium. Et hoc vocamus aureolam.

RESPONDEO dicendum quod, sicut per martyrium et virginitatem aliquis perfectissimam victoriam obtinet de carae et mundo, ita etiam perfectissima victoria contra diabolum obtinetur quando aliquis non solum diabolo impugnanti non cedit, sed etiam eum expellit, et non so-lum a se, sed etiam ab aliis. Hoc autem fit per praedica-tionem et doctrinam. Et ideo praedicationi et doctrinae aureola debetur, sicut et virginitati et martyrio.

Nec est dicendum, ut quidam dicunt, quod debeatur tantum praelatis, quibus competit ex officio praedicare et docere: sed quibuscumque qui licite hunc actum exer-cent. Praelatis autem non debetur, quamvis habeant offi-cium praedicandi, nisi actu praedicent: quia corona non debetur habitui, sed pugnae actuali; secundum illud II Tim. 2, [5]: *non coronabitur nisi qui legitime certaverit.*

AD PRIMUM ergo dicendum quod praedicare et do-cere sunt actus alicuius virtutis, scilicet misericordiae. Unde et inter spirituales eleemosynas computantur.

AD SECUNDUM dicendum quod, quamvis facultas praedicandi et docendi quandoque ex studio proveniat, tamen usus doctrinae ex voluntate procedit, quae per ca-ritatem informatur a Deo infusam. Et sic actus eius me-ritorius esse potest.

AD TERTIUM dicendum quod exaltatio in hac vita non deminuit alterius vitae praemium nisi ei qui in tali vita *propriam gloriam quaerit.* Qui autem talem exalta-tionem in utilitatem aliorum convertit, ex ea sibi mer-cedem acquirit. Cum autem dicitur quod doctrinae de-betur aureola, intelligendum est: doctrinae quae est de pertinentibus ad salutem, per quam diabolus a cordibus hominum expugnatur sicut quibusdam spiritualibus ar-mis, de quibus dicitur, II Cor. 10, [4]: *arma militiae no-strae non sunt carnalia, sed spiritualia.*

ON THE CONTRARY, A Gloss on Ephesians 1:18–19: *that you may know what is the exceeding greatness*, says, *the holy doctors will have an increase of glory above that which all have in common.* Therefore, etc.

FURTHER, A Gloss on Song of Songs 8:12: *my vineyard is before me*, says, *he describes the peculiar reward which he has prepared for his doctors.* Therefore, doctors will have a peculiar reward: and we call this an aureole.

I ANSWER THAT, Just as by virginity and martyrdom a person wins a most perfect victory over the flesh and the world, so is a most perfect victory gained over the devil, when a person not only refuses to yield to the devil's as-saults, but also drives him out, not from himself alone, but from others also. Now this is done by preaching and teach-ing: wherefore an aureole is due to preaching and teaching, even as to virginity and martyrdom.

Nor can we admit, as some affirm, that it is due to prelates only, who are competent to preach and teach by virtue of their office, but it is due to all whosoever exercise this act lawfully. Nor is it due to prelates, although they have the office of preaching, unless they actually preach, since a crown is due not to the habit, but to the actual strife, accord-ing to 2 Timothy 2:5: *he shall not be crowned, except he strive lawfully.*

REPLY OBJ. 1: Preaching and teaching are acts of a virtue, namely mercy, wherefore they are reckoned among the spiritual almsgiving.

REPLY OBJ. 2: Although ability to preach and teach is sometimes the outcome of study, the practice of teaching comes from the will, which is informed with charity infused by God: and thus its act can be meritorious.

REPLY OBJ. 3: Exaltation in this life does not lessen the reward of the other life, except for him who *seeks his own glory from that exaltation*: whereas he who turns that ex-altation to the profit of others acquires thereby a reward for himself. Still, when it is stated that an aureole is due to teaching, this is to be understood of the teaching of things pertaining to salvation, by which teaching the devil is ex-pelled from men's hearts as by a kind of spiritual weapon, of which it is said: *the weapons of our warfare are not carnal but spiritual* (2 Cor 10:4).

Article 8

Whether an Aureole Is Due to Christ?

AD OCTAVUM SIC PROCEDITUR. Videtur quod Christo aureola debeatur. Debetur enim aureola virgi-nitati et martyrio et doctrinae. Sed in Christo haec tria praecipue fuerunt. Ergo ipsi praecipue aureola competit.

PRAETEREA, omne quod est perfectissimum in re-bus humanis, praecipue Christo est attribuendum. Sed

OBJECTION 1: It would seem that an aureole is due to Christ. For an aureole is due to virginity, martyrdom, and teaching. Now these three were preeminently in Christ. Therefore, an aureole is especially due to him.

OBJ. 2: Further, whatever is most perfect in human things must be especially ascribed to Christ. Now an aure-

praemium aureolae debetur excellentissimis meritis. Ergo et Christo debetur.

PRAETEREA, Cyprianus dicit quod *imaginem Dei virginitas portat*. Virginitatis igitur exemplar in Deo est. Et sic videtur quod Christo, etiam inquantum est Deus, aureola competat.

SED CONTRA: Est quod aureola est gaudium de conformitate ad Christum, ut dicitur. Sed nullus conformatur vel similatur sibi ipsi: ut patet per Philosophum. Ergo Christo aureola non debetur.

PRAETEREA, Christi praemium nunquam est augmentatum. Sed Christus ab instanti suae conceptionis non habuit aureolam: quia tunc nunquam pugnaverat. Ergo nunquam postea aureolam habuit.

RESPONDEO dicendum quod circa hoc est duplex opinio. Quidam dicunt quod in Christo est aureola secundum propriam aureolae rationem: cum in eo pugna inveniatur et victoria, et per consequens corona secundum propriam rationem.

Sed, diligenter considerando, quamvis Christo competat ratio aureae vel coronae, non tamen ei competit ratio aureolae. *Aureola* enim, ex hoc ipso quod deminutive dicitur, importat aliquid quod participative et non secundum sui plenitudinem possidetur. Unde illis competit aureolam habere in quibus est aliqua perfectionis victoriae participatio, secundum imitationem eius in quo perfectae victoriae plena ratio consistit. Et ideo, cum in Christo inveniatur huiusmodi principalis et plena victoriae ratio, per cuius victoriam omnes alii victores constituuntur, ut patet Ioan. 16, [33], *confidite, ego vici mundum*, et Apoc. 5, [5], *ecce, vicit Leo de tribu Iuda*; Christo non competit aureolam habere, sed aliquid unde omnes aureolae originantur. Unde dicitur Apoc. 3, [21]: *qui vicerit, faciam eum sedere in throno meo, sicut ego vici, et sedeo in throno Patris mei*. Unde, secundum alios, dicendum est quod, quamvis id quod est in Christo non habeat rationem aureolae, tamen est excellentius omni aureola.

AD PRIMUM ergo dicendum quod Christus fuit verissime virgo, martyr et doctor. Sed tamen praemium accidentale his respondens in Christo non habet aliquam notabilem quantitatem in comparatione ad magnitudinem essentialis praemii. Unde non habet aureolam sub ratione aureolae.

AD SECUNDUM dicendum quod aureola, quamvis debeatur operi perfectissimo quoad nos, tamen aureola, inquantum deminutive dicitur, significat quandam participationem perfectionis ab aliquo in quo plenarie invenitur. Et secundum hoc ad quandam minorationem pertinet. Et sic in Christo non invenitur, in quo omnis perfectio plenissime invenitur.

AD TERTIUM dicendum quod, quamvis virginitas habeat aliquo modo exemplar in Deo, non tamen habet

ole is due as the reward of most excellent merits. Therefore, it is also due to Christ.

OBJ. 3: Further, Cyprian says (*Of the Clothing of Virgins*) that *virginity bears a likeness to God*. Therefore, the exemplar of virginity is in God. Therefore, it would seem that an aureole is due to Christ, even as God.

ON THE CONTRARY, An aureole is described as joy in being conformed to Christ. Now no one is conformed or likened to himself, as the Philosopher says (*Metaphysics* 9.3). Therefore, an aureole is not due to Christ.

FURTHER, Christ's reward was never increased. Now Christ had no aureole from the moment of his conception, since then he had never fought. Therefore, he never had an aureole afterwards.

I ANSWER THAT, There are two opinions on this point. For some say that Christ has an aureole in its strict sense, seeing that in him there is both conflict and victory, and consequently a crown in its proper acceptation.

But if we consider the question carefully, although the notion of aurea or crown is becoming to Christ, the notion of aureole is not. For from the very fact that *aureole* is a diminutive term, it follows that it denotes something possessed by participation and not in its fullness. Wherefore an aureole is becoming to those who participate in the perfect victory by imitating him in whom the fullness of perfect victory is realized. And therefore, since in Christ the notion of victory is found chiefly and fully, for by his victory others are made victors—as shown by John 16:33: *have confidence, I have overcome the world*, and Revelation 5:5: *behold, the lion of the tribe of Judah has prevailed*—it is not becoming for Christ to have an aureole, but to have something from which all aureoles are derived. Hence it is written: *to him that shall overcome, I will give to sit with me in my throne, as I also have overcome, and am set down in my Father's throne* (Rev 3:21). Therefore, we must say with others that although there is nothing of the nature of an aureole in Christ, there is nevertheless something more excellent than any aureole.

REPLY OBJ. 1: Christ was most truly virgin, martyr, and doctor; yet the corresponding accidental reward in Christ is a negligible quantity in comparison with the greatness of his essential reward. Hence he has not an aureole in its proper sense.

REPLY OBJ. 2: Although the aureole is due to a most perfect work, yet with regard to us, so far as it is a diminutive term, it denotes the participation of a perfection derived from one in whom that perfection is found in its fullness. Accordingly, it implies a certain inferiority, and thus it is not found in Christ, in whom is the fullness of every perfection.

REPLY OBJ. 3: Although in some way virginity has its exemplar in God, that exemplar is not homogeneous. For

exemplar unius rationis. Incorruptio enim Dei, quam virginitas imitatur, non eadem ratione est in Deo et in aliquo virgine.

the incorruption of God which virginity imitates is not in God in the same way as in a virgin.

Article 9

Whether an Aureole Is Due to the Angels?

AD NONUM SIC PROCEDITUR. Videtur quod angelis aureola debeatur. Quia, ut dicit Hieronymus, de virginitate loquens: *in carne praeter carnem vivere potius est vita angelica quam humana.* Et I Cor. 7, [26] dicit Glossa quod *virginitas est portio angelica.* Cum igitur virginitati respondeat aureola, videtur quod angelis debeatur.

PRAETEREA, nobilior est incorruptio spiritus quam in corruptio carnis. Sed in angelis invenitur incorruptio spiritus: quia nunquam peccaverunt: Ergo eis magis debetur aureola quam hominibus incorruptis carne qui alias aliquando peccaverunt.

PRAETEREA, doctrinae debetur aureola. Sed angeli nos docent *purgando, illuminando* et *perficiendo,* ut Dionysius dicit. Ergo eis debetur aureola saltem doctorum.

SED CONTRA: II Tim: 2 [5]: *non coronabitur nisi qui legitime certaverit.* Sed in angelis non est pugna. Ergo eis aureola non debetur.

PRAETEREA, aureola non debetur actui qui per corpus non exercetur: unde amantibus virginitatem, martyrium et doctrinam, si exterius eis haec non insunt, aureola non debetur. Sed angeli sunt incorporei. Ergo aureolam non habent.

RESPONDEO dicendum quod angelis aureola non debetur. Cuius ratio est quia aureola respondet cuidam perfectioni in excellenti merito. Ea vero quae in hominibus ad perfectionem meriti pertinent, angelis sunt connaturalia; vel etiam spectant ad communem eorum statum; aut etiam ad ipsum praemium. Et ideo, ratione eadem qua hominibus aureola debetur, angeli non habent aureolas.

AD PRIMUM ergo dicendum quod virginitas dicitur esse vita angelica, inquantum per gratiam virgines imitantur id quod angeli habeant per naturam. Non enim virtutis est in angelis quod omnino a delectationibus carnis abstinent; cum huiusmodi delectationes in eis esse non possint.

AD SECUNDUM dicendum quod perpetua incorruptio spiritus in angelis praemium essentiale meretur. Est enim de necessitate salutis: cum in eis non possit subsequi reparatio post ruinam.

OBJECTION 1: It would seem that an aureole is due to the angels. For Jerome, speaking of virginity, says: *to live without the flesh while living in the flesh is to live as an angel rather than as a man* (*Epistle to Paula and Eustochium*): and a Gloss on 1 Corinthians 7:26: *for the present necessity,* says that *virginity is the portion of the angels.* Since, then, an aureole corresponds to virginity, it would seem due to the angels.

OBJ. 2: Further, incorruption of the spirit is more excellent than incorruption of the flesh. Now there is incorruption of spirit in the angels, since they never sinned. Therefore, an aureole is due to them rather than to men incorrupt in the flesh who have sinned at some time.

OBJ. 3: Further, an aureole is due to teaching. Now angels teach us by *cleansing, enlightening,* and *perfecting* us, as Dionysius says (*Hier. Eccles.* vi). Therefore, at least the aureole of doctors is due to them.

ON THE CONTRARY, It is written: *he shall not be crowned, except he strive lawfully* (2 Tim 2:5). But there is no conflict in the angels. Therefore, an aureole is not due to them.

FURTHER, An aureole is not due to an act that is not performed through the body: wherefore it is not due to lovers of virginity, martyrdom or teaching, if they do not practice them outwardly. But angels are incorporeal spirits. Therefore, they have no aureole.

I ANSWER THAT, An aureole is not due to the angels. The reason of this is that an aureole, properly speaking, corresponds to some perfection of surpassing merit. Now those things which make for perfect merit in man are connatural to angels, or belong to their state in general, or to their essential reward. Wherefore the angels have not an aureole in the same sense as an aureole is due to men.

REPLY OBJ. 1: Virginity is said to be an angelic life insofar as virgins imitate by grace what angels have by nature. For it is not owing to a virtue that angels abstain altogether from pleasures of the flesh, since they are incapable of such pleasures.

REPLY OBJ. 2: Perpetual incorruption of the spirit in the angels merits their essential reward: because it is necessary for their salvation, since in them recovery is impossible after they have fallen.

AD TERTIUM dicendum quod illi actus secundum quos angeli nos docent, pertinent ad gloriam eorum, et ad communem eorum statum. Unde per huiusmodi actus aureolam non merentur.

REPLY OBJ. 3: The acts whereby the angels teach us belong to their glory and their common state: wherefore they do not merit an aureole thereby.

Article 10

Whether an Aureole Is Also Due to the Body?

AD DECIMUM SIC PROCEDITUR. Videtur quod aureola etiam corpori debeatur. Praemium enim essentiale est potius quam accidentale. Sed dos, quae ad praemium essentiale pertinet, non solum est in anima, sed etiam in corpore. Ergo et aureola, quae pertinet ad praemium accidentale.

PRAETEREA, peccato quod per corpus exercetur, respondet poena in anima et corpore. Ergo et merito quod exercetur per corpus, debetur praemium et in anima et in corpore. Sed meritum aureolae per corpus exercetur. Ergo aureola etiam debetur corpori.

PRAETEREA, in corporibus martyrum apparebit quaedam virtutis pulchritudo in ipsis cicatricibus corporis. Unde Augustinus dicit, XXII *de Civ. Dei*: *nescio quomodo sic afficiamur amore martyrum beatorum ut velimus in illo Regno in eorum corporibus videre vulnerum cicatrices quas pro Christi nomine pertulerunt. Et fortasse videbimus. Non enim erit deformitas in eis, sed dignitas; et quaedam, quamvis in corpore, non corporis, sed virtutis pulchritudo fulgebit.* Ergo videtur quod aureola martyrum etiam in corpore sit. Et eadem ratio est de aliis.

SED CONTRA: Animae quae modo sunt in paradiso, habent aureolas. Nec tamen habent corpora. Ergo proprium subiectum aureolae non est corpus, sed anima.

PRAETEREA, omne meritum est ab anima. Ergo praemium totum in anima esse debet.

RESPONDEO dicendum quod aureola proprie est in mente: est enim gaudium de operibus illis quibus aureola debetur. Sed sicut ex gaudio essentialis praemii, quod est aurea, redundat quidam decor in corpore, qui est gloria corporis, ita ex gaudio aureolae resultat aliquis decor in corpore: ut sic aureola principaliter sit in mente, sed per quandam redundantiam fulgeat etiam in carne.

ET PER HOC patet responsio ad obiecta.

Tamen sciendum est quod decor cicatricum quae in corporibus martyrum apparebunt, non potest dici aureola. Quia aliqui martyres aureolam habebunt in quibus huiusmodi cicatrices non erunt: utpote illi qui sunt submersi, aut famis inedia aut squalore carceris interempti.

OBJECTION 1: It would seem that an aureole is also due to the body. For the essential reward is greater than the accidental. But the dowries which belong to the essential reward are not only in the soul but also in the body. Therefore, there is also an aureole which pertains to the accidental reward.

OBJ. 2: Further, punishment in soul and body corresponds to sin committed through the body. Therefore, a reward both in soul and in body is due to merit gained through the body. But the aureole is merited through works of the body. Therefore, an aureole is also due to the body.

OBJ. 3: Further, a certain fullness of virtue will shine forth in the bodies of martyrs, and will be seen in their bodily scars: wherefore Augustine says (*The City of God* 22): *I do not know how we feel an undescribable love for the blessed martyrs so as to desire to see in that kingdom the scars of the wounds in their bodies, which they bore for Christ's name. Perchance indeed we shall see them, for this will not make them less comely, but more glorious. A certain beauty will shine in them, a beauty, though in the body, yet not of the body but of virtue.* Therefore, it would seem that the martyr's aureole is also in his body; and in like manner the aureoles of others.

ON THE CONTRARY, The souls now in heaven have aureoles; and yet they have no body. Therefore, the proper subject of an aureole is the soul and not the body.

FURTHER, All merit is from the soul. Therefore, the whole reward should be in the soul.

I ANSWER THAT, Properly speaking, the aureole is in the mind: since it is joy in the works to which an aureole is due. But even as from the joy in the essential reward, which is the aurea, there results a certain comeliness in the body, which is the glory of the body, so from the joy in the aureole there results a certain bodily comeliness: so that the aureole is chiefly in the mind, but by a kind of overflow it shines forth in the body.

THIS SUFFICES for the replies to the objections.

It must be observed, however, that the beauty of the scars which will appear in the bodies of the martyrs cannot be called an aureole, since some of the martyrs will have an aureole in which such scars will not appear, for instance, those who were put to death by drowning, starvation, or the squalor of prison.

Article 11

Whether Three Aureoles Are Fittingly Assigned: Those of Virgins, of Martyrs, and of Doctors?

Ad undecimum sic proceditur. Videtur quod inconvenienter designentur tres aureolae, virginum, martyrum et praedicatorum. Aureola enim martyrum respondet virtuti fortitudinis eorum; aureola vero virginum virtuti temperantiae; aureola vero doctorum virtuti prudentiae. Ergo videtur quod debeat esse quarta aureola, quae respondeat virtuti iustitiae.

Praeterea, Exod. 25, [25] dicit Glossa quod *corona aurea additur cum per Evangelium his qui mandata custodiunt, vita aeterna promittitur*: Matth. 19, [17], *si vis ad vitam ingredi, serva mandata. Huic aureola superponitur cum dicitur: si vis perfectus esse, vade et vende omnia quae habes, et da pauperibus.* Ergo paupertati debetur aureola.

Praeterea, per votum obedientiae aliquis se subiicit Deo totaliter. Ergo in voto obedientiae maxima perfectio consistit. Et ita videtur quod ei aureola debeatur.

Praeterea, multa sunt etiam alia supererogationis opera, de quibus homo in futuro speciale gaudium habebit. Ergo multae sunt aliae aureolae praeter istas tres.

Praeterea, sicut aliquis divulgat fidem praedicando et docendo, ita scripta compilando. Ergo et talibus quarta aureola debetur.

Respondeo dicendum quod aureola est quoddam privilegiatum praemium privilegiatae victoriae respondens. Et ideo secundum privilegiatas victorias in tribus pugnis quae cuilibet homini imminent, tres aureolae sumuntur. In pugna enim quae est contra carnem, ille potissimam victoriam obtinet qui a delectabilibus venereis, quae sunt praecipua in hoc genere, omnino abstinet. Et ideo, virginitati aureola debetur. In pugna vero qua contra mundum pugnatur, illa est praecipua cum a mundo persecutionem usque ad mortem sustinemus. Unde et martyribus, qui in ista pugna victoriam obtinent, secunda aureola debetur. In pugna vero qua contra diabolum pugnatur, illa est praecipua victoria cum aliquis hostem non solum a se, sed a cordibus aliorum removet, quod fit per doctrinam et praedicationem. Et ideo doctoribus et praedicatoribus tertia aureola debetur.

Quidam vero distinguunt tres aureolas secundum tres vires animae: ut dicantur tres aureolae respondere potissimis trium virium animae actibus. Potissimus enim actus rationalis est veritatem fidei etiam in aliis diffundere. Et huic actui debetur doctorum aureola. Irascibilis vero actus potissimus est etiam mortem propter Christum superare. Et huic actui debetur aureola marty-

Objection 1: It would seem that the three aureoles of virgins, martyrs, and doctors are unfittingly assigned. For the aureole of martyrs corresponds to their virtue of fortitude, the aureole of virgins to the virtue of temperance, and the aureole of doctors to the virtue of prudence. Therefore, it seems that there should be a fourth aureole corresponding to the virtue of justice.

Obj. 2: Further, a Gloss on Exodus 25:25: *a polished crown*, says that *a golden crown* [*aurea*] *is added when the Gospel promises eternal life to those who keep the commandments*: "*if thou wilt enter into life, keep the commandments*" (Matt 19:17). *To this is added the little golden crown* [*aureola*] *when it is said*: "*if thou wilt be perfect, go and sell all that thou hast, and give to the poor*" (Matt 19:21). Therefore, an aureole is due to poverty.

Obj. 3: Further, a man subjects himself wholly to God by the vow of obedience: wherefore the greatest perfection consists in the vow of obedience. Therefore, it would seem that an aureole is due thereto.

Obj. 4: Further, there are also many other works of supererogation in which one will rejoice in the life to come. Therefore, there are many aureoles besides the aforesaid three.

Obj. 5: Further, just as a man spreads the faith by preaching and teaching, so does he by publishing written works. Therefore, a fourth aureole is due to those who do this.

I answer that, An aureole is an exceptional reward corresponding to an exceptional victory: wherefore the three aureoles are assigned in accordance with the exceptional victories in the three conflicts which beset every man. For in the conflict with the flesh, he above all wins the victory who abstains altogether from sexual pleasures, which are the chief of this kind; and such is a virgin. Therefore, an aureole is due to virginity. In the conflict with the world, the chief victory is to suffer the world's persecution even until death: wherefore the second aureole is due to martyrs, who win the victory in this battle. In the conflict with the devil, the chief victory is to expel the enemy not only from oneself but also from the hearts of others: this is done by teaching and preaching, and consequently the third aureole is due to doctors and preachers.

Some, however, distinguish the three aureoles in accordance with the three powers of the soul, by saying that the three aureoles correspond to the three chief acts of the soul's three highest powers. For the act of the rational power is to publish the truth of faith even to others, and to this act the aureole of doctors is due; the highest act of the irascible power is to overcome even death for Christ's sake, and

rum. Concupiscibilis autem actus potissimus est a delectabilibus maximis penitus abstinere. Et huic debetur aureola virginum.

Alii vero aureolas tres distinguunt secundum ea quibus Christo nobilissime conformamur. Ipse enim mediator fuit inter Patrem et mundum. Fuit ergo doctor, secundum quod veritatem quam a Patre acceperat, mundo manifestavit. Fuit autem martyr, secundum quod a mundo persecutionem sustinuit. Fuit vero virgo, inquantum puritatem in seipso servavit. Et ideo doctores, martyres et virgines ei perfectissime conformantur. Unde talibus debetur aureola.

AD PRIMUM ergo dicendum quod in actu iustitiae non attenditur aliqua pugna, sicut in actibus aliarum virtutum. Nec tamen hoc verum est, quod docere sit actus prudentiae. Immo est potius actus caritatis vel misericordiae, secundum quod ex tali habitu inclinamur ad huiusmodi exercitium; vel etiam sapientiae ut dirigentis.

Vel potest dici, secundum alios, quod iustitia circuit omnes virtutes: et ideo ei specialiter aureola non debetur.

AD SECUNDUM dicendum quod paupertas, quamvis sit opus perfectionis, non tamen tenet summum locum in aliqua spirituali pugna: quia amor temporalium minus impugnat quam concupiscentia carnis, vel persecutio inflicta in corpus proprium. Unde paupertati non debetur aureola. Sed debetur ei iudiciaria potestas, ratione humiliationis, quae consequitur paupertatem. Glossa autem inducta large accipit aureolam pro quolibet praemio quod redditur merito excellenti.

ET SIMILITER dicendum ad tertium et quartum.

AD QUINTUM dicendum quod etiam scribentibus sacram doctrinam debetur aureola. Sed haec non distinguitur ab aureola doctorum: quia scripta componere quidam modus docendi est.

to this act the aureole of martyrs is due; and the highest act of the concupiscible power is to abstain altogether from the greatest carnal pleasures, and to this act the aureole of virgins is due.

Others again, distinguish the three aureoles in accordance with those things whereby we are most signally conformed to Christ, for he was the mediator between the Father and the world. Hence he was a doctor, by manifesting to the world the truth which he had received from the Father; he was a martyr, by suffering the persecution of the world; and he was a virgin, by his personal purity. Wherefore doctors, martyrs and virgins are most perfectly conformed to him: and for this reason an aureole is due to them.

REPLY OBJ. 1: There is no conflict to be observed in the act of justice as in the acts of the other virtues. Nor is it true that to teach is an act of prudence: in fact rather is it an act of charity or mercy—inasmuch as it is by such habits that we are inclined to the practice of such an act; or again of wisdom, as directing it.

We may also reply, with others, that justice embraces all the virtues, wherefore a special aureole is not due to it.

REPLY OBJ. 2: Although poverty is a work of perfection, it does not take the highest place in a spiritual conflict, because the love of temporalities assails a man less than carnal concupiscence or persecution, whereby his own body is broken. Hence an aureole is not due to poverty, but judicial power is due by reason of the humiliation consequent upon poverty. The Gloss quoted takes aureole in the broad sense for any reward given for excellent merit.

THE SAME ANSWER applies to the third and fourth objections.

REPLY OBJ. 5: An aureole is due to those who commit the sacred doctrine to writing: but it is not distinct from the aureole of doctors, since the compiling of writing is a way of teaching.

Article 12

Whether the Virgin's Aureole Is the Greatest of All?

AD DUODECIMUM SIC PROCEDITUR. Videtur quod aureola virginum sit inter alias potissima. Quia Apoc. 14, [4] de virginibus dicitur quod *sequuntur Agnum quocumque ierit*, et quod *nemo alius poterat dicere canticum quod virgines cantabant* [v. 3] Ergo virgines habent excellentiorem aureolam.

PRAETEREA, Cyprianus 1 dicit de virginibus quod sunt *illustrior portio gregis Christi.* Ergo eis maior aureola debetur.

OBJECTION 1: It would seem that the virgin's aureole is the greatest of all. For it is said of virgins that they *follow the Lamb wheresoever he goes* (Rev 14:4), and that *no other man could say the canticle* (Rev 14:3) which the virgins sang. Therefore, virgins have the most excellent aureole.

OBJ. 2: Further, Cyprian (*Of the Clothing of Virgins*) says of virgins that they are *the more illustrious portion of Christ's flock*. Therefore, the greater aureole is due to them.

ITEM, videtur quod potissima sit aureola martyrum. Quia dicit Haymo quod *non omnes virgines coniugatas praecedunt: sed hi specialiter qui in tormento passionis, virginitate insuper custodita, coaequantur martyribus coniugatis.* Ergo martyrium dat virginitati praeeminentiam super alios status. Ergo martyrio potior aureola debetur.

ITEM, videtur quod potissima debeatur doctoribus. Quia Ecclesia militans exemplata est ab Ecclesia triumphante. Sed in Ecclesia militante maximus honor debetur doctoribus: I Tim. 5, [17], *qui bene praesunt presbyteri, duplici honore digni habeantur: maxime autem qui laborant verbo et doctrina.* Ergo in Ecclesia triumphante talibus potior aureola debetur.

RESPONDEO dicendum quod praeeminentia aureolae ad aureolam potest dupliciter attendi. Primo, ex parte pugnae: ut dicatur aureola potior quae fortiori pugnae debetur. Et per hunc modum aureola martyrum aliis aureolis supereminet quodam modo, et aureola virginum alio modo. Pugna enim martyrum est fortior secundum seipsam, et vehementius affligens. Sed pugna carnis est periculosior: inquantum est diuturnior, et magis nobis imminet e vicino. Secundo, ex parte eorum de quibus est pugna. Et sic aureola doctorum inter omnes est potior. Quia huiusmodi pugna versatur circa bona intelligibilia: aliae vero pugnae circa sensibiles passiones.

Sed illa eminentia quae attenditur ex parte pugnae, est aureolae essentialior: quia aureola secundum propriam rationem respicit victoriam et pugnam. Difficultas etiam pugnae quae attenditur ex parte ipsius pugnae, est potior quam illa quae attenditur ex parte nostri inquantum est nobis vicinior. Et ideo, simpliciter loquendo, aureola martyrum inter omnes est potior. Et ideo dicitur Matth. 5, [10], in Glossa, quod in octava beatitudine, quae ad martyres pertinet, scilicet, *beati qui persecutionem patiuntur* etc., omnes aliae perficiuntur. Et propter hoc etiam Ecclesia in connumeratione sanctorum martyres doctoribus et virginibus praeordinat. Sed quantum ad aliquid, nihil prohibet alias aureolas excellentiores esse.

ET PER HOC patet solutio ad obiecta.

OBJ. 3: Again, it would seem that the martyr's aureole is the greatest. For Haymo, commenting on Revelation 14:3: *no man could say the hymn*, says that *virgins do not all take precedence of married folk; but only those who, in addition to the observance of virginity, are by the tortures of their passion on a par with married persons who have suffered martyrdom.* Therefore, martyrdom gives virginity its precedence over other states: and consequently a greater aureole is due to virginity.

OBJ. 4: Again, it would seem that the greatest aureole is due to doctors. For the Church Militant is modelled after the Church Triumphant. Now in the Church Militant the greatest honor is due to doctors: *let the priests that rule well be esteemed worthy of double honor, especially they who labor in the word and doctrine* (1 Tim 5:17). Therefore, a greater aureole is due to them in the Church Triumphant.

I ANSWER THAT, Precedence of one aureole over another may be considered from two standpoints. First, from the point of view of the conflicts, that aureole being considered greater which is due to the more strenuous battle. Looking at it thus, the martyr's aureole takes precedence of the others in one way, and the virgin's in another. For the martyr's battle is more strenuous in itself, and more intensely painful; while the conflict with the flesh is fraught with greater danger, inasmuch as it is more lasting and threatens us at closer quarters. Second, from the point of view of the things about which the battle is fought: and thus the doctor's aureole takes precedence of all others, since this conflict is about intelligible goods, while the other conflicts are about sensible passions.

Nevertheless, the precedence that is considered in view of the conflict is more essential to the aureole; since the aureole, according to its proper character, regards the victory and the battle, and the difficulty of fighting which is viewed from the standpoint of the battle is of greater importance than that which is considered from our standpoint through the conflict being at closer quarters. Therefore, the martyr's aureole is simply the greatest of all: for which reason a Gloss on Matthew 5:10 says that all the other beatitudes are perfected in the eighth, which refers to the martyrs, namely, *blessed are they that suffer persecution.* For this reason, too, the Church in enumerating the saints together places the martyrs before the doctors and virgins. Yet nothing hinders the other aureoles from being more excellent in some particular way.

THIS SUFFICES for the replies to the objections.

Article 13

Whether One Person Has an Aureole More Excellently Than Another Person?

AD DECIMUMTERTIUM SIC PROCEDITUR. Videtur quod unus aureolam virginitatis vel martyrii vel doctoris excellentius alio non habeat. Quia ea quae sunt in termino, non intenduntur et remittuntur. Aureola autem debetur operibus quae sunt in termino perfectionis. Ergo aureola non intenditur neque remittitur.

PRAETEREA, virginitas non suscipit magis et minus: cum importet privationem quandam, et negationes non intendantur nec remittantur. Ergo nec praemium virginitatis, scilicet aureola virginum, intenditur et remittitur.

SED CONTRA, aureola superponitur aureae. Sed aurea est intensior in uno quam in alio. Ergo et aureola.

RESPONDEO dicendum quod, cum meritum sit quodammodo praemii causa, oportet diversificari praemia secundum quod merita diversificantur: aliquid enim intenditur et remittitur per intensionem et remissionem suae causae. Meritum autem aureolae potest esse maius et minus. Unde et aureola potest esse maior et minor.

Sciendum tamen quod meritum aureolae potest intendi dupliciter: uno modo, ex parte radicis; alio modo, ex parte operis. Contingit enim esse aliquos duos quorum unus ex minori caritate maius tormentum martyrii sustinet; vel magis praedicationi instat; aut etiam magis se a delectabilibus carnis elongat. Intensioni ergo meriti quae attenditur penes radicem, non respondet intensio aureolae, sed intensio aureae. Sed intensioni meriti quae est ex genere actus, respondet intensio aureolae. Unde potest esse quod aliquis qui minus in martyrio meretur quantum ad essentiale praemium, habebit pro martyrio maiorem aureolam.

AD PRIMUM ergo dicendum quod merita quibus debentur aureolae, non attingunt ad terminum perfectionis simpliciter, sed secundum speciem: sicut ignis est specie subtilissimum corporum. Unde nihil prohibet unam aureolam alia esse excellentiorem: sicut unus ignis est alio subtilior.

AD SECUNDUM dicendum quod una virginitas potest esse alia maior propter maiorem recessum a virginitatis contrario: ut dicatur in illa esse maior virginitas quae magis occasiones corruptionis vitat. Sic enim privationes intendi possunt: ut cum dicitur homo magis caecus quia magis elongatur a visu.

OBJECTION 1: It would seem that one person has not the aureole either of virginity, or of martyrdom, or of doctors more perfectly than another person. For things which have reached their term are not subject to intension or remission. Now the aureole is due to works which have reached their term of perfection. Therefore, an aureole is not subject to intension or remission.

OBJ. 2: Further, virginity is not subject to being more or less, since it denotes a kind of privation; and privations are not subject to intension or remission. Therefore, neither does the reward of virginity, that is, the virgin's aureole, receive intension or remission.

ON THE CONTRARY, The aureole is added to the aurea. But the aurea is more intense in one than in another. Therefore, the aureole is also.

I ANSWER THAT, Since merit is somewhat the cause of reward, rewards must be diversified according as merits are diversified: for the intension or remission of a thing follows from the intension or remission of its cause. Now the merit of the aureole may be greater or lesser: wherefore the aureole may also be greater or lesser.

We must observe, however, that the merit of an 'aureole' may be intensified in two ways: first, on the part of its cause; second, on the part of the work. For there may happen to be two persons, one of whom, out of lesser charity, suffers greater torments of martyrdom, or is more constant in preaching, or again withdraws himself more from carnal pleasures. Accordingly, intension not of the aureole but of the aurea corresponds to the intension of merit derived from its root; while intension of the aureole corresponds to intension of merit derived from the kind of act. Consequently, it is possible for one who merits less in martyrdom as to his essential reward to receive a greater aureole for his martyrdom.

REPLY OBJ. 1: The merits to which an aureole is due do not reach the term of their perfection simply, but according to their species: even as fire is specifically the most subtle of bodies. Hence nothing hinders one aureole being more excellent than another, even as one fire is more subtle than another.

REPLY OBJ. 2: The virginity of one may be greater than the virginity of another, by reason of a greater withdrawal from that which is contrary to virginity: so that virginity is stated to be greater in one who avoids more the occasions of corruption. For in this way privations may increase, as when a man is said to be more blind if he be removed further from the possession of sight.

QUESTION 97

THE PUNISHMENT OF THE DAMNED

Consequenter considerandum est de pertinentibus ad damnatos post iudicium. Et primo, de poenis damnatorum, et igne quo eorum corpora cruciabuntur; secundo, de his quae pertinent ad eorum affectum et intellectum; tertio, de iustitia et misericordia Dei respectu damnatorum.

Circa primum quaeruntur septem.

Primo: utrum damnati in inferno sola poena ignis affligantur.

Secundo: utrum vermis quo affliguntur sit corporalis.

Tertio: utrum fletus in eis existens sit corporalis.

Quarto: utrum tenebrae eorum sint corporales.

Quinto: utrum ignis quo affliguntur sit corporalis.

Sexto: utrum sit eiusdem speciei cum igne nostro.

Septimo: utrum ignis ille sit sub terra.

In due sequence we must consider those things that concern the damned after the judgment: (1) The punishment of the damned, and the fire by which their bodies will be tormented; (2) Matters relating to their will and intellect; (3) God's justice and mercy in regard to the damned.

Under the first head there are seven points of inquiry:

(1) Whether in hell the damned are tormented with the sole punishment of fire?

(2) Whether the worm by which they are tormented is corporeal?

(3) Whether their weeping is corporeal?

(4) Whether their darkness is material?

(5) Whether the fire whereby they are tormented is corporeal?

(6) Whether it is of the same species as our fire?

(7) Whether this fire is beneath the earth?

Article 1

Whether in Hell the Damned Are Tormented by the Sole Punishment of Fire?

AD PRIMUM SIC PROCEDITUR. Videtur quod damnati in inferno sola poena ignis affligantur. Quia Matth. 25, ubi eorum damnatio exprimitur, fit mentio solum de igne, cum dicitur [v. 41]: *ite, maledicti, in ignem aeternum.*

PRAETEREA, sicut poena purgatorii debetur peccato veniali, ita poena inferni debetur mortali. Sed in purgatorio non dicitur esse, nisi poena ignis: ut patet per hoc quod dicitur I Cor. 3, [13]: *uniuscuiusque opus quale sit, ignis probabit.* Ergo nec in inferno erit nisi poena ignis.

PRAETEREA, poenarum varietas refrigerium praestat: sicut calido cum transfertur ad frigidum. Sed nullum refrigerium est ponere in damnatis. Ergo non erunt diversae poenae, sed sola, poena ignis.

SED CONTRA: Est quod dicitur in Psalmo [10, 7]: *ignis et sulphur et spiritus procellarum pars calicis eorum.*

PRAETEREA, Iob 24, [19]: *transibunt ab aquis nivium ad calorem nimium.*

RESPONDEO dicendum quod, secundum Basilium, in ultima mundi purgatione fiet separatio in elementis, ut quidquid est purum et nobile remaneat superius ad gloriam beatorum; quidquid vero est ignobile et faeculentum in infernum proiiciatur ad poenam damna-

OBJECTION 1: It would seem that in hell the damned are tormented by the sole punishment of fire, because where their condemnation is declared, mention is made of fire only, in the words: *depart from me, you cursed, into everlasting fire* (Matt 25:41).

OBJ. 2: Further, even as the punishment of purgatory is due to venial sin, so is the punishment of hell due to mortal sin. Now no other punishment but that of fire is stated to be in purgatory, as appears from the words: *the fire shall try every man's work, of what sort it is* (1 Cor 3:13). Therefore, neither in hell will there be a punishment other than of fire.

OBJ. 3: Further, variety of punishment affords a respite, as when one passes from heat to cold. But we can admit no respite in the damned. Therefore, there will not be various punishments, but that of fire alone.

ON THE CONTRARY, It is written: *fire and brimstone and storms of winds shall be the portion of their cup* (Ps 10:7).

FURTHER, It is written: *let him pass from the snow waters to excessive heat* (Job 24:19).

I ANSWER THAT, According to Basil (*Hexaemeron*), at the final cleansing of the world there will be a separation of the elements, whatever is pure and noble remaining above for the glory of the blessed, and whatever is ignoble and sordid being cast down for the punishment of the damned: so

torum; ut sicut omnis creatura Dei est beatis materia gaudii, ita damnatis ex omnibus creaturis tormentum accrescat, secundum illud Sap. 5, [21]: *pugnabit cum illo orbis terrae contra insensatos.*

Hoc etiam divinae iustitiae competit: ut sicut, ab uno recedentes per peccatum, in rebus materialibus, quae sunt multa et varia, finem suum constituerent, ita etiam multipliciter et ex multis affligantur.

AD PRIMUM ergo dicendum quod quia ignis est maxime afflictivus, propter hoc quod abundat in virtute activa, ideo nomine ignis omnis afflictio designatur si sit vehemens.

AD SECUNDUM dicendum quod poena purgatorii non est principaliter ad affligendum, sed ad purgandum. Unde per solum ignem fieri debet, qui habet maximam vim purgativam. Sed damnatorum poena non ordinatur ad purgandum. Unde non est simile.

AD TERTIUM dicendum quod damnati transibunt ex vehementissimo calore ad vehementissimum frigus sine hoc quod in eis sit aliquod refrigerium. Quia passio ab exterioribus non erit per transmutationem corporis a sua pristina naturali dispositione, ut contraria passio ad aequalitatem vel temperiem reducendo refrigerium causet, sicut nunc accidit: sed erit per actionem spiritualem, secundum quod sensibilia agunt in sensum prout sentiuntur, imprimendo formas illas secundum esse spirituale in organum, et non secundum esse materiale.

that just as every creature will be to the blessed a matter of joy, so will all the elements conduce to the torture of the damned, according to Wisdom 5:21, *the whole world will fight with him against the unwise.*

This is also becoming to divine justice, that whereas they departed from the one by sin, and placed their end in material things which are many and various, so should they be tormented in many ways and from many sources.

REPLY OBJ. 2: It is because fire is most painful, through its abundance of active force, that the name of fire is given to any torment if it be intense.

REPLY OBJ. 2: The punishment of purgatory is not intended chiefly to torment but to cleanse: wherefore it should be inflicted by fire alone, which is above all possessed of cleansing power. But the punishment of the damned is not directed to their cleansing. Consequently, the comparison fails.

REPLY OBJ. 3: The damned will pass from the most intense heat to the most intense cold without this giving them any respite: because they will suffer from external agencies, not by the transmutation of their body from its original natural disposition, and the contrary passion affording a respite by restoring an equable or moderate temperature, as happens now, but by a spiritual action, in the same way as sensible objects act on the senses being perceived by impressing the organ with their forms according to their spiritual, and not their material, being.

Article 2

Whether the Worm of the Damned Is Corporeal?

AD SECUNDUM SIC PROCEDITUR. Videtur quod vermis quo affliguntur damnati, sit vermis corporalis. Quia caro non potest affligi per vermem spiritualem. Sed caro damnatorum affligetur per vermem: Iudith 16, [21], *dabit ignem et vermes in carnes eorum,* et Eccli. 7, [19], *vindicta carnis impii ignis et vermis.* Ergo vermis ille erit corporalis.

PRAETEREA, Augustinus dicit, XXI *de Civ. Dei: utrumque, idest ignis et vermis, poena erunt carnis.* Et sic idem quod prius.

SED CONTRA est quod Augustinus dicit, XX *de Civ. Dei: in poenis medorum inextinguibilis ignis et vivacissimus vermis ab aliis atque aliis aliter atque aliter est expositus. Alii utrumque ad corpus; alii utrumque ad animam retulerunt; alii proprie ad corpus ignem, tropice ad animam vermem, quod credibilius esse videtur.*

RESPONDEO dicendum quod post diem iudicii in mundo innovato non remanebit aliquod animal, vel ali-

OBJECTION 1: It would seem that the worm by which the damned are tormented is corporeal. For flesh cannot be tormented by a spiritual worm. Now the flesh of the damned will be tormented by a worm: *he will give fire and worms into their flesh* (Jdt 16:21), and: *the vengeance on the flesh of the ungodly is fire and worms* (Sir 7:19). Therefore, that worm will be corporeal.

OBJ. 2: Further, Augustine says (*The City of God* 21.9): *both, namely, fire and worm, will be the punishment of the body.* Therefore, etc.

ON THE CONTRARY, Augustine says (*The City of God* 20.22): *the unquenchable fire and the restless worm in the punishment of the damned are explained in various ways by different persons. Some refer both to the body, some, both to the soul; others refer the fire, in the literal sense, to the body, the worm to the soul metaphorically, and this seems the more probable.*

I ANSWER THAT, After the day of judgment, no animal or mixed body will remain in the renewed world except

quod corpus mixtum (nisi corpus hominis tantum): eo quod non habeat aliquem ordinem ad incorruptionem, nec post illud tempus sit futura generatio et corruptio. Unde vermis qui in damnatis ponitur, non debet intelligi esse materialis, sed spiritualis, qui est conscientiae remorsus; qui dicitur *vermis*, inquantum oritur ex putredine peccati et animam affligit, sicut corporalis vermis ex putredine ortus affligit pungendo.

Ad primum ergo dicendum quod ipsae animae damnatorum dicuntur carnes eorum, pro eo quod carni subiectae fuerunt.

Vel potest dici quod etiam per vermem spiritualem caro affligetur: secundum quod passiones animae redundant in corpus et hic et in futuro.

Ad secundum dicendum quod Augustinus loquitur sub quadam comparatione. Non enim vult simpliciter asserere quod ille vermis sit materialis: sed quod potius esset asserendum ignem et vermem materialiter intelligi quam quod utrumque spiritualiter intelligatur, quia sic damnati nullam poenam corporalem sustinerent; ut patet seriem verborum eius ibidem inspicienti.

only the body of man, because the former are not directed to incorruption, nor after that time will there be generation or corruption. Consequently, the worm ascribed to the damned must be understood to be not of a corporeal but of a spiritual nature: and this is the remorse of conscience, which is called a *worm* because it originates from the corruption of sin, and torments the soul, as a corporeal worm born of corruption torments by gnawing.

Reply Obj. 1: The very souls of the damned are called their flesh for as much as they were subject to the flesh.

Or we may reply that the flesh will be tormented by the spiritual worm, according as the afflictions of the soul overflow into the body, both here and hereafter.

Reply Obj. 2: Augustine speaks by way of comparison. For he does not wish to assert absolutely that this worm is material, but that it is better to say that both are to be understood materially, than that both should be understood only in a spiritual sense: for then the damned would suffer no bodily pain. This is clear to anyone that examines the context of his words in this passage.

Article 3

Whether the Weeping of the Damned Will Be Corporeal?

Ad tertium sic proceditur. Videtur quod fletus qui erit in damnatis, erit corporalis. Quia Luc. 13, [28] dicit quaedam Glossa quod per fletum, quem Dominus reprobis comminatur, potest probari vera corporum resurrectio. Quod non esset si fletus ille tantum esset spiritualis. Ergo, etc.

Praeterea, tristitia quae est in poena, respondet delectationi quae fuit in culpa: secundum illud Apoc. 18, [7]: *quantum glorificavit se et in deliciis fuit, tantum date illi tormentum et luctam*: Sed peccatores in culpa habuerunt delectationem interiorem et exteriorem. Ergo habebunt fletum etiam exteriorem.

Sed contra, fletus corporalis fit per quandam resolutionem lacrimarum. Sed a corporibus damnatorum non potest fieri perpetua resolutio, cum nihil in eis per cibum restauretur: omne enim finitum consumitur si aliquid ab eo continue abstrahatur. Ergo in damnatis non erit corporalis fletus.

Respondeo dicendum quod in fletu corporali duo inveniuntur. Quorum unum est lacrimarum resolutio. Et quantum ad hoc fletus corporalis in damnatis esse non potest. Quia post diem iudicii, quiescente motu primi mobilis, non erit aliqua generatio vel corruptio, vel corporalis alteratio. In lacrimarum autem resolutione oportet esse illius humoris generationem qui per lacrimas

Objection 1: It would seem that the weeping of the damned will be corporeal. For a Gloss on Luke 13:28: *there will be weeping*, says that the weeping with which our Lord threatens the wicked is a proof of the resurrection of the body. But this would not be the case if that weeping were merely spiritual. Therefore, etc.

Obj. 2: Further, the pain of the punishment corresponds to the pleasure of the sin, according to Revelation 18:7: *as much as she has glorified herself and lived in delicacies, so much torment and sorrow give you to her*. Now sinners had internal and external pleasure in their sin. Therefore, they will also have external weeping.

On the contrary, Corporeal weeping results from dissolving into tears. Now there cannot be a continual dissolution from the bodies of the damned, since nothing is restored to them by food; for everything finite is consumed if something be continually taken from it. Therefore, the weeping of the damned will not be corporeal.

I answer that, Two things are to be observed in corporeal weeping. One is the resolution of tears: and as to this corporeal weeping cannot be in the damned, since after the day of judgment, the movement of the first movable being being at an end, there will be neither generation, nor corruption, nor bodily alteration: and in the resolution of tears that humor needs to be generated which is shed forth in the

distillat. Unde quantum ad hoc corporalis fletus in damnatis esse non poterit.

Aliud quod invenitur in corporali fletu, est quaedam commotio et turbatio capitis et oculorum. Et quantum ad hoc fletus in damnatis esse poterit post resurrectionem. Corpora enim damnatorum non solum ex exteriori affligentur: sed etiam ab interiori, secundum quod corpus immutatur ad passionem animae in bonum vel malum. Et quantum ad hoc, fletus carnis resurrectionem indicat; et respondet delectationi culpae, quae fuit in anima et in corpore.

ET PER HOC patet responsio ad obiecta.

shape of tears. Wherefore in this respect it will be impossible for corporeal weeping to be in the damned.

The other thing to be observed in corporeal weeping is a certain commotion and disturbance of the head and eyes, and in this respect weeping will be possible in the damned after the resurrection: for the bodies of the damned will be tormented not only from without, but also from within, according as the body is affected at the instance of the soul's passion towards good or evil. In this sense weeping is a proof of the body's resurrection, and corresponds to the pleasure of sin, experienced by both soul and body.

THIS SUFFICES for the replies to the objections.

Article 4

Whether the Damned Are in Material Darkness?

AD QUARTUM SIC PROCEDITUR. Videtur quod damnati non sint in tenebris corporalibus. Quia, ut dicit Gregorius, in IX lib. *Moral.*, super illud Iob 10, [22], *sempiternus horror inhabitat: quamvis ignis illic ad consolationem non luceat, tamen, ut magis torqueat, ad aliquid lucet: nam sequaces quos secum traxerunt de mundo reprobi, flamma illustrante, visuri sunt.* Ergo non erunt ibi tenebrae corporales.

PRAETEREA, damnati viderit poenam suam: hoc enim est eis ad augmentum poenae. Sed nihil videtur sine lumine. Ergo non sunt ibi tenebrae corporales.

PRAETEREA, damnati ibi habebunt potentiam visivam, post corporum resumptionem. Sed frustra in eis esset nisi aliquid viderent. Ergo, cum nihil videatur nisi in lumine, videtur quod non sint omnino in tenebris.

SED CONTRA: Est quod dicitur Matth. 22, [13]: *ligatis manibus eius et pedibus, proiicite eum in tenebras exteriores.* Super quod dicit Gregorius: *si ignis ille lucem haberet, in tenebras exteriores nequaquam mitti diceretur.*

PRAETEREA, Basilius dicit, super illud Psalmi [28, 7], *vox Domini intercidentis flammam ignis,* quod *virtute Dei separabitur claritas ignis ab eius virtute adustiva: ita quod claritas cedet in gaudium beatorum, et ustivum ignis in tormentum damnatorum.* Ergo damnati habebunt tenebras corporales.

Quaedam vero alia quae ad poenam damnatorum pertinent, determinata sunt supra.

RESPONDEO dicendum quod dispositio inferni erit talis quod maxime miseriae damnatorum competet. Unde secundum hoc sunt ibi lux et tenebra prout maxime spectant ad miseriam damnatorum. Ipsa autem visio secundum se delectabilis est: ut enim dicitur in principio Metaphys., *sensus oculorum est maxime diligibilis, eo*

OBJECTION 1: It would seem that the damned are not in material darkness. For, commenting on Job 10:22: *but everlasting horror dwells,* Gregory says, *although that fire will give no light for comfort, yet, that it may torment the more it does give light for a purpose, for by the light of its flame the wicked will see their followers whom they have drawn thither from the world* (*Morals on Job* 9). Therefore, the darkness there is not material.

OBJ. 2: Further, the damned see their own punishment, for this increases their punishment. But nothing is seen without light. Therefore, there is no material darkness there.

OBJ. 3: Further, there the damned will have the power of sight after being reunited to their bodies. But this power would be useless to them unless they see something. Therefore, since nothing is seen unless it be in the light, it would seem that they are not in absolute darkness.

ON THE CONTRARY, It is written: *bind his hands and his feet, and cast him into the exterior darkness* (Matt 22:13). Commenting on these words, Gregory says (*Morals on Job* 9), *if this fire gave any light, he would by no means be described as cast into exterior darkness.*

FURTHER, Basil says on Psalm 28:7: *the voice of the Lord divides the flame of fire,* that *by God's might the brightness of the fire will be separated from its power of burning, so that its brightness will conduce to the joy of the blessed, and the heat of the flame to the torment of the damned* (Hom. i). Therefore, the damned will be in material darkness.

Other points relating to the punishment of the damned have been decided above (Q. 86).

I ANSWER THAT, The disposition of hell will be such as to be adapted to the utmost unhappiness of the damned. Wherefore accordingly both light and darkness are there, insofar as they are most conducive to the unhappiness of the damned. Now seeing is in itself pleasant, for, as stated in *Metaphysics* 1, *the sense of sight is most esteemed, because*

quod per ipsum plura cognoscimus. Sed per accidens contingit visionem esse, afflictivam, inquantum videmus aliqua nobis nociva, vel nostrae voluntati repugnantia. Et ideo in inferno hoc modo debet esse locus dispositus ad videndum secundum lucem et tenebras, quod nihil perspicue videatur, sed solummodo sub quadam umbrositate videantur ea quae afflictionem cordi ingerere possunt. Unde, simpliciter loquendo, locus est tenebrosus: sed tamen ex divina dispositione est ibi aliquid luminis, quantum sufficit ad videndum illa quae animam torquere possunt. Et ad hoc satisfacit naturalis situs loci: quia in terrae medio, ubi infernus ponitur, non potest esse ignis nisi faeculentus et turbidus et quasi fumosus.

Quidam tamen tenebrarum harum causam assignant ex commassatione corporum damnatorum, quae prae multitudine ita replebunt locum inferni quod nihil ibi de aere manebit. Et sic non erit ibi aliquid de diaphano quod possit esse subiectum lucis et tenebrae, nisi oculi damnatorum, qui erunt obtenebrati.

Et per hoc patet responsio ad obiecta.

thereby many things are known. Yet it happens accidentally that seeing is painful, when we see things that are hurtful to us, or displeasing to our will. Consequently, in hell the place must be so disposed for seeing as regards light and darkness, that nothing be seen clearly, and that only such things be dimly seen as are able to bring anguish to the heart. Wherefore, simply speaking, the place is dark. Yet by divine disposition, there is a certain amount of light, as much as suffices for seeing those things which are capable of tormenting the soul. The natural situation of the place is enough for this, since in the center of the earth, where hell is said to be, fire cannot be otherwise than thick and cloudy, and, as it were, reeky.

Some hold that this darkness is caused by the massing together of the bodies of the damned, which will so fill the place of hell with their numbers that no air will remain, so that there will be no translucid body that can be the subject of light and darkness except the eyes of the damned, which will be darkened utterly.

This suffices for the replies to the objections.

Article 5

Whether the Fire of Hell Will Be Corporeal?

Ad quintum sic proceditur. Videtur quod ignis inferni, quo cruciabuntur corpora damnatorum non sit corporeus. Dicit enim Damascenus, in IV libro, in fine: *tradetur diabolus, et daemones et homo eius,* scilicet Antichristus, *et impii et peccatores, in ignem aeternum, non materialem, qualis est qui apud nos est, sed qualem utique novit Deus.* Sed omne corporeum est materiale. Ergo ignis inferni non erit corporeus.

Praeterea, animae damnatorum a corpore separatae ad ignem inferni deferuntur. Sed Augustinus dicit, XII *super Genesis ad litteram: spiritualem arbitror esse,* locum scilicet ad quem anima defertur post mortem, non corporalem. Ergo ignis ille non est corporeus.

Praeterea, ignis corporeus in modo suae actionis non sequitur modum culpae in eo qui igne crematur, sed magis modum humidi vel sicci: in eodem enim igne corporeo videmus affligi iustum et impium. Sed ignis inferni in modo suae actionis sequitur modum culpae in eo qui punitur: unde dicit Gregorius, in IV *Dialog.: unus quidem est gehennae ignis, sed non uno modo omnes cruciat peccatores: uniuscuiusque enim quantum exigit culpa, tantum sentietur poena.* Ergo non est corporeus.

Sed contra: Est quod dicitur IV *Dialog.: ignem gehennae corporeum esse non ambigo, in quo certum est corpora cruciari.*

Objection 1: It would seem that the fire of hell whereby the bodies of the damned will be tormented will not be corporeal. For Damascene says (*On the Orthodox Faith* 4): *the devil, and demons, and his man,* namely Antichrist, *together with the ungodly and sinners will be cast into everlasting fire, not material fire, such as that which we have, but such as God knows.* Now everything corporeal is material. Therefore, the fire of hell will not be corporeal.

Obj. 2: Further, the souls of the damned, when severed from their bodies, are cast into hell fire. But Augustine says (*On the Literal Meaning of Genesis* 12.32): *in my opinion it is spiritual,* not corporeal, speaking of the place to which the soul is committed after death. Therefore, etc.

Obj. 3: Further, corporeal fire in the mode of its action does not follow the mode of guilt in the person who is burned at the stake: rather does it follow the mode of humid and dry, for in the same corporeal fire we see both good and wicked suffer. But the fire of hell, in its mode of torture or action, follows the mode of guilt in the person punished; wherefore Gregory says (*Dialogues* 4.63): *there is indeed but one hellfire, but it does not torture all sinners equally. For each one will suffer as much pain according as his guilt deserves.* Therefore, this fire will not be corporeal.

On the contrary, Gregory says (*Dialogues* 4.29): *I doubt not that the fire of hell is corporeal, since it is certain that bodies are tortured there.*

PRAETEREA, Sap. 5, [21] dicitur: *pugnabit orbis terrarum contra insensatos.* Sed non totus orbis terrarum contra insensatos pugnaret si solummodo spirituali poena et non corporali punirentur. Ergo punientur igne corporeo.

RESPONDEO dicendum quod de igne inferni multiplex fuit positio. Quidam enim philosophi, ut Avicenna, resurrectionem non credentes, solius animae post mortem poenam esse crediderunt. Et quia eis inconveniens videbatur ut anima, cum sit incorporea, igne corporeo puniretur, negaverunt ignem corporeum esse quo mali punirentur, volentes, quod quidquid dicitur de poena animarum post mortem per aliqua corporalia futura, metaphorice dicatur. Sicut enim bonarum animarum delectatio et iucunditas non erit in aliqua re corporali, sed spirituali tantum, quod erit in consecutione sui finis; ita afflictio malorum spiritualis erit tantum, in hoc scilicet quod tristabuntur de hoc quod separabuntur a fine, cuius inest eis desiderium naturale. Unde, sicut omnia quae de delectatione animarum post mortem dicuntur quae videntur ad delectationem corporalem pertinere, ut quod reficiantur, quod rideant, et huiusmodi, ita etiam quidquid de earum afflictione dicitur quod in corporalem punitionem sonare videtur, per similitudinem debet intelligi, sicut quod in igne ardeant, vel fetoribus affligantur, et cetera huiusmodi. Spiritualis enim delectatio et tristitia, cum sint ignota multitudini, oportet quod per delectationes et tristitias corporales figuraliter manifestentur, ut homines magis moveantur ad desiderium vel timorem.

Sed quia in poena damnatorum non solum erit poena damni, quae respondet aversioni quae fuit in culpa, sed etiam poena sensus, quae respondet conversioni; ideo non sufficit praedictum modum punitionis ponere. Et ideo etiam ipse Avicenna alterum modum superaddit, dicens quod animae malorum post mortem non per corpora, sed per corporum similitudines punientur: sicut in somniis, propter similitudines praedictas in imaginatione existentes, videtur homini quod torqueatur poenis diversis. Et hunc etiam, modum punitionis videtur ponere Augustinus, in XII *super Genesis ad litteram*, sicut ibidem manifeste patet.

Sed hoc videtur inconvenienter dictum esse. Imaginatio enim potentia quaedam est utens organo corporali. Unde non potest esse quod visiones huiusmodi imaginativae fiant in anima separata a corpore, sicut in anima somniantis. Unde etiam Avicenna, ut hoc inconveniens evitaret, dixit quod animae separatae a corpore utebantur quasi pro organo aliqua parte caelestis corporis, cui corpus humanum oportet esse conforme ad hoc quod perficiatur anima rationali, quae est similis motoribus caelestis corporis; in hoc secutus quodammodo opinionem antiquorum philosophorum, qui posuerunt animas redire ad compares stellas.

FURTHER, It is written: *the world shall fight against the unwise* (Wis 5:21). But the whole world would not fight against the unwise if they were punished with a spiritual, and not a corporeal, punishment. Therefore, they will be punished with a corporeal fire.

I ANSWER THAT, There have been many opinions about the fire of hell. For some philosophers, as Avicenna, disbelieving in the resurrection, thought that the soul alone would be punished after death. And as they considered it impossible for the soul, being incorporeal, to be punished with a corporeal fire, they denied that the fire whereby the wicked are punished is corporeal, and pretended that all statements as to souls being punished in future after death by any corporeal means are to be taken metaphorically. For just as the joy and happiness of good souls will not be about any corporeal object, but about something spiritual, namely, the attainment of their end, so will the torment of the wicked be merely spiritual, in that they will be grieved at being separated from their end, the desire for which is in them by nature. Wherefore, just as all descriptions of the soul's delight after death that seem to denote bodily pleasure—for instance, that they are refreshed, that they smile, and so forth—must be taken metaphorically, so also are all such descriptions of the soul's suffering as seem to imply bodily punishment—for instance, that they burn in fire, or suffer from the stench, and so forth. For as spiritual pleasure and pain are unknown to the majority, these things need to be declared under the figure of corporeal pleasures and pains, in order that men may be moved the more to the desire or fear thereof.

Since, however, in the punishment of the damned there will be not only pain of loss corresponding to the aversion that was in their sin, but also pain of sense corresponding to the conversion, it follows that it is not enough to hold the above manner of punishment. For this reason Avicenna himself (*Metaphysics* ix) added another explanation by saying that the souls of the wicked are punished after death, not by bodies but by images of bodies; just as in a dream it seems to a man that he is suffering various pains on account of such images being in his imagination. Even Augustine seems to hold this kind of punishment (*On the Literal Meaning of Genesis* 12.32), as is clear from the text.

But this would seem an unreasonable statement. For the imagination is a power that makes use of a bodily organ: so that it is impossible for such visions of the imagination to occur in the soul separated from the body, as in the soul of the dreamer. Wherefore Avicenna also, that he might avoid this difficulty, said that the soul separated from the body uses as an organ some part of the heavenly body, to which the human body needs to be conformed in order to be perfected by the rational soul, which is like the movers of the heavenly body—thus following somewhat the opinion of certain philosophers of old, who maintained that souls return to the stars that are their compeers.

Sed hoc est omnino absurdum, secundum doctrinam Philosophi. Quia anima utitur determinato organo corporali: sicut ars determinatis instrumentis. Unde non potest transire de corpore in corpus: quod Pythagoras ponit, ut dicitur in I *de Anima*. Qualiter autem ad dictum Augustini sit respondendum, infra dicetur.

Quidquid autem dicatur de igne qui animas separatas cruciat, de igne tamen quo cruciabuntur corpora damnatorum post resurrectionem, oportet dicere quod sit corporeus: quia corpori non potest convenienter adaptari poena nisi sit corporea. Unde Gregorius, in IV *Dialog.*, ex hoc ipso probat ignem inferni esse corporeum, quod reprobi post resurrectionem in eum detruduntur. Augustinus etiam, ut habetur in littera, manifeste confitetur ignem illum quo cruciabuntur corpora, esse corporeum. Et de hoc ad praesens est quaestio. Sed hoc supra dictum est, qualiter animae damnatorum ab igne isto corporeo puniantur.

AD PRIMUM ergo dicendum quod Damascenus, non negat simpliciter illum ignem materialem esse sed quod *non est materialis talis qualis apud nos est*: eo quod quibusdam proprietatibus ab hoc igne distinguitur.

Vel dicendum est quod, quia ignis ille non materialiter alterat corpora, sed quadam spirituali actione agit in ea ad punitionem; ideo dicitur non materialis esse, non quantum ad substantiam, sed quantum ad punitionis effectum in corporibus, et multo amplius in animabus.

AD SECUNDUM dicendum quod dictum Augustini potest hoc modo accipi ut pro tanto dicatur locus ille ad quem animae deferentur post mortem non esse corporeus, quia anima in eo corporaliter non existit, per modum scilicet quo corpora existunt in loco, sed alio modo spirituali, sicut angeli in loco sunt.

Vel dicendum quod Augustinus loquitur opinando, et non determinando: sicut frequenter facit in libro illo.

AD TERTIUM dicendum quod ignis ille erit instrumentum divinae iustitiae punientis. Instrumentum autem non solum agit in virtute propria et per proprium modum, sed etiam in virtute principalis agentis, et secundum quod est regulatum ab eo. Unde, quamvis secundum propriam virtutem non habeat quod aliquos cruciet magis vel minus secundum modum peccati, habet tamen hoc secundum quod eius actio modificatur ex ordine divinae iustitiae. Sicut etiam ignis fornacis modificatur ex industria fabri in sua actione, secundum quod competit ad effectum artis.

But this is absolutely absurd according to the Philosopher's teaching, since the soul uses a definite bodily organ, even as art uses definite instruments, so that it cannot pass from one body to another, as Pythagoras is stated to have maintained (*On the Soul* 1.53). As to the statement of Augustine we shall say below how it is to be answered (ad 2).

However, whatever we may say of the fire that torments the separated souls, we must admit that the fire which will torment the bodies of the damned after the resurrection is corporeal, since one cannot fittingly apply a punishment to a body unless that punishment itself be bodily. Wherefore Gregory (*Dialogues* 4) proves the fire of hell to be corporeal from the very fact that the wicked will be cast thither after the resurrection. Again Augustine, as quoted in the text (*Sentences* IV, D. 44), clearly admits (*The City of God* 21.10) that the fire by which the bodies are tormented is corporeal. And this is the point at issue for the present. We have said elsewhere (Q. 70, A. 3) how the souls of the damned are punished by this corporeal fire.

REPLY OBJ. 1: Damascene does not absolutely deny that this fire is material, but *that it is material as is our fire*, since it differs from ours in some of its properties.

We may also reply that since that fire does not alter bodies as to their matter, but acts on them for their punishment by a kind of spiritual action, it is for this reason that it is stated not to be material, not as regards its substance, but as to its punitive effect on bodies and, still more, on souls.

REPLY OBJ. 2: The assertion of Augustine may be taken in this way, that the place where souls are conveyed after death be described as incorporeal, insofar as the soul is there, not corporeally, i.e., as bodies are in a place, but in some other spiritual way, as angels are in a place.

Or we may reply that Augustine is expressing an opinion without deciding the point, as he often does in those books.

REPLY OBJ. 3: That fire will be the instrument of divine justice inflicting punishment. Now an instrument acts not only by its own power and in its own way, but also by the power of the principal agent, and as directed thereby. Therefore, although fire is not able, of its own power, to torture certain persons more or less, according to the measure of sin, it is able to do so nevertheless insofar as its action is regulated by the ordering of divine justice: even so the fire of the furnace is regulated by the forethought of the smith, according as the effect of his art requires.

Article 6

Whether the Fire of Hell Is of the Same Species as Ours?

AD SEXTUM SIC PROCEDITUR. Videtur quod ignis ille non sit eiusdem speciei cum igne isto corporeo quem videmus. Augustinus enim dicit, et habetur in littera: *ignis aeternus cuiusmodi sit, arbitror neminem scire, nisi cui Spiritus divinus ostendit.* Sed naturam istius ignis omnes, vel fere omnes sciunt. Ergo ignis ille non est eiusdem naturae vel speciei cum isto.

PRAETEREA, Gregorius dicit, XV *Moral.*, exponens illud Iob 20, [26] *devorabit eum ignis qui non succenditur: Ignis corporeus, ut esse valeat, corporeis indiget fomentis: nec valet, nisi succensus, esse; et nisi refotus, subsistere. At contra gehennae ignis, cum sit corporeus et in semetipso reprobos corporaliter exurat, nec studio humano succenditur, nec lignis nutritur; sed, creatus semel, durat inextinguibilis; et succensione non indiget, et ardore non caret.* Ergo non est eiusdem naturae cum igne quem videmus.

PRAETEREA, aeternum et corruptibile non sunt unius rationis: cum nec etiam in genere communicent, secundum Philosophum, in X *Metaphys.* Sed ignis iste est corruptibilis: ille autem aeternus, Matth. 25, [41], *ite, maledicti, in ignem aeternum.* Ergo non est eiusdem speciei.

PRAETEREA, de natura huius ignis qui apud nos est, est ut luceat. Sed ignis inferni non lucet: unde Iob 18, [5]: *nonne lux impii extinguetur?* Ergo non est eiusdem naturae cum isto igne.

SED CONTRA: Secundum Philosophum, in I *Topic.*, *omnis aqua omni aquae est idem specie.* Ergo eadem ratione omnis ignis omni igni est idem specie.

PRAETEREA, Sap. 11, [17] dicitur: *per quae peccat quis, per haec ei torquetur.* Sed homines peccant per res sensibiles huius mundi. Ergo iustum est ut per easdem puniantur.

RESPONDEO dicendum quod ignis, propter hoc quod est maximae virtutis in agendo inter reliqua elementa alia corpora pro materia habet: ut dicitur in IV *Meteor.* Unde et ignis dupliciter invenitur: scilicet in materia propria, prout est in sua sphaera; vel in materia aliena, sive terrestri, ut patet in carbone; sive aerea, ut patet in flamma. Quocumque autem modo ignis inveniatur, semper est idem in specie, quantum ad naturam ignis pertinet: potest autem esse diversitas in specie quantum ad corpora quae sunt materia ignis. Unde flamma et carbo differunt specie; et similiter lignum igneum et ferrum ignitum. Nec differt quantum ad hoc sive ignita sunt per violentiam, ut in ferro apparet; sive ex principio intrinseco naturali, ut accidit in sulphure.

OBJECTION 1: It would seem that this fire is not of the same species as the corporeal fire which we see. For Augustine says (*The City of God* 20.16): *in my opinion no man knows of what kind is the everlasting fire, unless the Spirit of God has revealed it to anyone.* But all or nearly all know the nature of this fire of ours. Therefore, that fire is not of the same species as this.

OBJ. 2: Further, Gregory, commenting on Job 10:26: *a fire that is not kindled shall devour him,* says, *bodily fire needs bodily fuel in order to become fire; neither can it be except by being kindled, nor live unless it be renewed. On the other hand, the fire of hell, since it is a bodily fire, and burns in a bodily way the wicked cast therein, is neither kindled by human endeavor, nor kept alive with fuel, but once created endures unquenchably; at one and the same time it needs no kindling and lacks not heat (Morals on Job 15).* Therefore, it is not of the same nature as the fire that we see.

OBJ. 3: Further, the everlasting and the corruptible differ essentially, since they agree not even in genus, according to the Philosopher (*Metaphysics* 10). But this fire of ours is corruptible, whereas the other is everlasting: *depart from me, you cursed, into everlasting fire* (Matt 25:41). Therefore, they are not of the same nature.

OBJ. 4: Further, it belongs to the nature of this fire of ours to give light. But the fire of hell gives no light, hence Job 18:5 says: *shall not the light of the wicked be extinguished?* Therefore, that fire is not of the same nature as ours.

ON THE CONTRARY, According to the Philosopher (*Topics* 1.6), *every water is of the same species as every other water.* Therefore, in like manner every fire is of the same species as every other fire.

FURTHER, It is written: *by what things a man sins, by the same also he is tormented* (Wis 11:17). Now men sin by the sensible things of this world. Therefore, it is just that they should be punished by those same things.

I ANSWER THAT, As stated in *Meteorology* IV, fire has other bodies for its matter for the reason that, of all the elements, it has the greatest power of action. Hence fire is found under two conditions: in its own matter, as existing in its own sphere, and in a strange matter, whether of earth, as in burning coal, or of air as in the flame. Under whatever conditions, however, fire be found, it is always of the same species so far as the nature of fire is concerned, but there may be a difference of species as to the bodies which are the matter of fire. Wherefore flame and burning coal differ specifically, and likewise burning wood and red-hot iron; nor does it signify, as to this particular point, whether they be kindled by force, as in the case of iron, or by a natural intrinsic principle, as happens with sulphur.

Quod ergo ignis inferni, quantum ad hoc quod habet de natura ignis, sit eiusdem speciei cum igne qui apud nos est, manifestum est. Utrum autem ille ignis sit in propria materia existens, aut, si in aliena, in qua materia sit, nobis ignotum est. Et secundum hoc, potest ab igne qui apud nos est specie differre materialiter consideratus.

Quasdam tamen proprietates differentes habet ab igne isto: ut quod succensione non indiget, nec lignis nutritur. Sed istae differentiae non ostendunt diversitatem in specie quantum ad id quod pertinet ad naturam ignis.

AD PRIMUM ergo dicendum quod Augustinus loquitur quantum ad id quod est materiale in igne illo, non autem quantum ad ignis naturam.

AD SECUNDUM dicendum quod ignis qui apud nos est, lignis nutritur et ab homine succenditur, quia est artificialiter et per violentiam in aliena materia introductus. Sed ignis ille lignis non indiget quibus foveatur: quia vel in propria materia est existens; vel est in materia aliena non per violentiam, sed per naturam a principio intrinseco. Unde non est ab homine succensus sed a Deo, qui naturam illam instituit. Et hoc est quod dicitur Isaiae 30, [33]: *flatus Domini sicut torrens sulphuris succendens eam.*

AD TERTIUM dicendum; quod, sicut corpora damnatorum erunt eiusdem speciei cuius et modo sunt, quamvis nunc sint corruptibilia, tunc autem incorruptibilia, ex ordine divinae iustitiae et propter quietem motus coeli; ita est et de igne inferni, quo corpora illa punientur.

AD QUARTUM dicendum quod lucere non convenit igni secundum quemlibet modum existendi. Quia in propria materia existens non lucet: unde non lucet in propria sphaera, ut philosophi dicunt. Similiter etiam in aliqua materia aliena ignis existens non lucet: sicut cum est in materia opaca terrestri, ut in sulphure. Et similiter etiam quando ex aliquo grosso fumo eius claritas obfuscatur. Unde quod ignis inferni non lucet, non est sufficiens argumentum ad hoc quod non sit eiusdem speciei.

Accordingly, it is clear that the fire of hell is of the same species as the fire we have, so far as the nature of fire is concerned. But whether that fire subsists in its proper matter, or if it subsists in a strange matter (whatever that matter may be), we know not. And in this way it may differ specifically from the fire we have, considered materially.

It has, however, certain properties differing from our fire, for instance, that it needs no kindling, nor is kept alive by fuel. But the differences do not argue a difference of species as regards the nature of the fire.

REPLY OBJ. 1: Augustine is speaking of that fire with regard to its matter, and not with regard to its nature.

REPLY OBJ. 2: This fire of ours is kept alive with fuel and is kindled by man, because it is introduced into a foreign matter by art and force. But that other fire needs no fuel to keep it alive, because either it subsists in its own matter, or is in a foreign matter not by force, but by nature from an intrinsic principle. Wherefore it is kindled not by man but by God, who fashioned its nature. This is the meaning of the words: *the breath of the Lord is as a torrent of brimstone kindling it* (Isa 30:33).

REPLY OBJ. 3: Even as the bodies of the damned will be of the same species as now, although now they are corruptible, whereas then they will be incorruptible both by the ordering of divine justice and on account of the cessation of the heavenly movement, so is it with the fire of hell whereby those bodies will be punished.

REPLY OBJ. 4: To give light does not belong to fire according to any mode of existence, since in its own matter it gives no light: wherefore it does not shine in its own sphere, according to the philosophers. And, in like manner, in certain foreign matters it does not shine, as when it is in an opaque earthly substance, such as sulphur. The same happens also when its brightness is obscured by thick smoke. Wherefore that the fire of hell gives no light is not sufficient proof of its being of a different species.

Article 7

Whether the Fire of Hell Is Beneath the Earth?

AD SEPTIMUM. Videtur quod ignis ille non sit sub terra. Quia Iob 18, [18] de homine damnato dicitur: *et de orbe transferet eum Deus.* Ergo ignis ille quo damnati punientur, non est sub terra, sed est extra orbem.

PRAETEREA, *nullum violentum et per accidens potest esse sempiternum.* Sed ignis ille erit in inferno in sempiternum. Ergo non erit ibi per violentiam, sed naturaliter.

OBJECTION 1: It would seem that this fire is not beneath the earth. For it is said of the damned, *and God shall remove him out of the globe* (Job 18:18). Therefore, the fire whereby the damned will be punished is not beneath the earth, but outside the globe.

OBJ. 2: Further, *nothing violent or accidental can be everlasting.* But this fire will be in hell forever. Therefore, it will be there not by force, but naturally. Now fire cannot be un-

Sed sub terra non potest esse ignis nisi per violentiam. Ergo ignis inferni non est sub terra.

PRAETEREA, in igne inferni omnia corpora damnatorum post diem iudicii cruciabuntur. Sed illa corpora locum replebunt. Ergo, cum futura sit maxima multitudo damnatorum, quia *stultorum infinitus est numerus*, Eccle. 1, [15]; oportet maximum esse spatium in quo ignis ille continetur. Sed inconveniens videtur dicere infra terram esse tantam concavitatem: cum partes terrae naturaliter ferantur ad medium. Ergo ignis ille non erit sub terra.

PRAETEREA, Sap. 11, [17]: *per quae peccat quis, per haec et torquetur*. Sed mali super terram peccaverunt. Ergo ignis eos puniens non debet esse sub terra.

SED CONTRA: Dicitur Isaiae 14, [9]: *infernus subtus conturbatus est in occursum tui*. Ergo ignis inferni sub nobis est.

PRAETEREA, Gregorius, IV *Dialog.*: *quid obstat non video quod infernus esse sub terra credatur.*

PRAETEREA, Ionae 2, super illud [v. 4], *proiecisti me in corde maris*, Glossa interlinearis: *idest, in inferno: pro quo dicitur in Evangelio*, Matth. 12, [40], *in corde terrae: quia, sicut cor est in medio animalis, ita infernus in medio terrae perhibetur esse.*

RESPONDEO dicemdum quod, sicut Augustinus dicit, et habetur in littera, *inqua parte mundi infernus sit, scire neminem arbitror, nisi cui divinus Spiritus revelavit*. Unde Gregorius, in IV *Dialog.*, super hac quaestione interrogatus, respondet: *hac de re temere definire nihil audeo. Nonnulli namque in quadam terrarum parte infernum esse putaverunt: alii vero hunc sub terra esse aestimant*. Et hanc opionem probabiliorem ess ostendit dupliciter. Primo, ex ipsa nominis ratione, sic dicens: *si idcirco infernum dicimus quia inferius iacet quod terra ad caelum est, hoc esse infernus debet ad terram*. Secundo, ex hoc quod dicitur Apoc. 5, [3]: *Nemo poterat, neque in caelo neque in terra neque subtus terram: aperire librum*: ut hoc quod dicitur in caelo, referatur ad angelos; hoc quod dicitur *in terra*, referatur ad homines viventes in corpore; hoc quod dicitur *sub terra*, referatur ad animas existentes in inferno.

Augustinus etiam, in XII *super Genesis ad litteram*, duas rationes tangere videtur quare congruum sit infernum esse sub terra. Una est quoniam defunctorum animae carnis amore peccaverant, hoc eis exhibeatur quod ipsi carni mortuae solet exhiberi, ut scilicet sub terram recondantur. Alia est quod, sicut est gravitas in corporibus, ita tristitia in spiritibus, et laetitia sicut levitas. Unde, sicut secundum corpus, si ponderis sui ordinem teneant, inferiora sunt omnia graviora, ita secundum spiritum inferiora sunt omnia tristiora. Et sic, sicut conveniens locus gaudio electorum est caelum empyreum, ita conveniens locus tristitiae damnatorum est infimum

der the earth save by violence. Therefore, the fire of hell is not beneath the earth.

OBJ. 3: Further, after the day of judgment the bodies of all the damned will be tormented in hell. Now those bodies will fill a place. Consequently, since the multitude of the damned will be exceeding great, for *the number of fools is infinite* (Eccl 1:15), the space containing that fire must also be exceeding great. But it would seem unreasonable to say that there is so great a hollow within the earth, since all the parts of the earth naturally tend to the center. Therefore, that fire will not be beneath the earth.

OBJ. 4: Further, *by what things a man sins, by the same also he is tormented* (Wis 11:17). But the wicked have sinned on the earth. Therefore, the fire that punishes them should not be under the earth.

ON THE CONTRARY, It is written: *hell below was in an uproar to meet you at your coming* (Isa 14:9). Therefore, the fire of hell is beneath us.

FURTHER, Gregory says (*Dialogues* 4): *I see not what hinders us from believing that hell is beneath the earth.*

FURTHER, A Gloss on Jonah 2:4: *you have cast me forth into the heart of the sea*, says, *i.e., into hell*, and in the Gospel the words *in the heart of the earth* (Matt 12:40) have the same sense, for as the heart is in the middle of an animal, so is hell supposed to be in the middle of the earth.

I ANSWER THAT, As Augustine says (*The City of God* 15.16), *I am of the opinion that no one knows in what part of the world hell is situated, unless the Spirit of God has revealed this to some one*. Wherefore Gregory (*Dialogues* 4) having been questioned on this point answers: *about this matter I dare not give a rash decision*. For some have deemed hell to be in some part of the earth's surface; others think it to be beneath the earth. He shows the latter opinion to be the more probable for two reasons. First, from the very meaning of the word. These are his words: *if we call it the "Inferno," the lower place, on this account, that it lies inferiorly, then what earth is to the sky, hell should be to the earth*. Second, from Revelation 5:3: *no man was able, neither in heaven, nor on earth, nor under the earth, to open the book*; where the words *in heaven* refer to the angels, *on earth* to men living in the body, and *under the earth* to souls in hell.

Augustine too (*On the Literal Meaning of Genesis* 12.34) seems to indicate two reasons for the congruity of hell being under the earth. One is that whereas the souls of the departed sinned through love of the flesh, they should be treated as dead flesh is wont to be treated, by being buried beneath the earth. The other is that heaviness is to the body what sorrow is to the spirit, and joy is as lightness. Therefore, just as in reference to the body, all the heavier things are beneath the others, if they be placed in order of gravity, so in reference to the spirit, the lower place is occupied by whatever is more sorrowful; and thus even as the empyrean is a fitting place for the joy of the elect, so the lowest part of

terrae. Neque movere debet quod Augustinus ibidem dicit, quod *inferi sub ferris esse dicuntur vel creduntur.* Quid, ut in libro *Retractationum,* hoc retractans, dicit: *mihi videor docere debuisse magis quod sub terris sunt inferi, quam rationem reddere cur sub terris esse dicuntur sive creduntur.*

Quidam tamen philosophi posuerunt quod locus inferni erit sub orbe terrestri, tamen supra terrae superficiem, ex parte opposita nobis. Et hoc videtur Isidorus sensisse, cum dixit quod *sol et luna in ordine quo creati sunt stabunt, ne impii, in tormentis positi, fruantur luce eorum*: quae ratio nulla esset si infernus infra terram esse dicatur. Qualiter tamen haec verba possint exponi, patuit supra. Pythagoras vero posuit, locum poenarum in sphaera ignis, quam in medio totius orbis esse dixit: ut patet per Philosophum, in II *Caeli et Mundi.* Sed tamen convenientius his quae in Scriptura dicuntur est ut sub terra esse dicatur.

AD PRIMUM ergo dicendum quod verbum illud Iob, *de orbe transferet eum Deus,* intelligendum est de orbe terrarum, idest de hoc mundo. Et hoc modo exponit Gregorius, dicens: *de orbe quippe transfertur, cum superno apparente Iudice, de hoc mundo tollitur, in quo perverse gloriatur.* Nec est intelligendum quod orbis hic accipiatur pro universo, quasi extra totum universum sit locus poenarum.

AD SECUNDUM dicendum quod in loco illo conservatur ignis in aeternum ex ordine divinae iustitiae: quamvis secundum naturam non possit extra suum locum aliquod elementum in aeternum durare, praecipue statu generationis et corruptionis manente in rebus. Ignis autem erit ibi fortissimae caliditatis: quia calor eius erit undique congregatus, propter frigus terrae undique ipsum circumstans.

AD TERTIUM dicendum quod infernus nunquam deficiet in amplitudine quin sufficiat ad damnatorum corpora capienda: infernus enim, Proverb. 30, [15–16], inter tria *insatiabilia* ponitur. Nec est inconveniens quod inter viscera terrae tanta concavitas conservetur divina virtute quae damnatorum omnium corpora possit capere.

AD QUARTUM dicendum quod hoc quod dicitur, *per quae peccat quis, per haec et torquetur,* non est necessarium nisi in principalibus instrumentis peccandi. Quia enim homo in anima peccat et in corpore, in utroque punitur: non autem oportet quod in quo loco quis peccavit, in eodem puniatur; cum alius sit locus qui viatoribus et damnatis debetur.

Vel dicendum quod hoc intelligitur de poenis quibus homo punitur in via: secundum quod quaelibet culpa suam poenam habet annexam, prout *quisque inordinatus animus sibi est poena,* ut dicit Augustinus.

the earth is a fitting place for the sorrow of the damned. Nor does it signify that Augustine says that *hell is stated or believed to be under the earth* (*The City of God* 15.16), because he withdraws this where he says: *It seems that I should have said that hell is beneath the earth, rather than have given the reason why it is stated or believed to be under the earth* (*Retractions* 2.29).

However, some philosophers have maintained that hell is situated beneath the terrestrial orb, but above the surface of the earth, on that part which is opposite to us. This seems to have been the meaning of Isidore when he asserted that *the sun and the moon will stop in the place wherein they were created, lest the wicked should enjoy this light in the midst of their torments.* But this is no argument if we assert that hell is under the earth. We have already stated how these words may be explained (Q. 91, A. 2). Pythagoras held the place of punishment to be in a fiery sphere situated, according to him, in the middle of the whole world, as Aristotle relates (*De Coelo et Mundo* II). It is, however, more in keeping with Scripture to say that it is beneath the earth.

REPLY OBJ. 1: The words of Job, *God shall remove him out of the globe,* refer to the surface of the earth, i.e., from this world. This is how Gregory expounds it (*Morals on Job* 14) where he says: *he is removed from the globe when, at the coming of the heavenly judge, he is taken away from this world wherein he now prides himself in his wickedness.* Nor does globe here signify the universe, as though the place of punishment were outside the whole universe.

REPLY OBJ. 2: Fire continues in that place for all eternity by the ordering of divine justice, although according to its nature an element cannot last forever outside its own place, especially if things were to remain in this state of generation and corruption. The fire there will be of the very greatest heat, because its heat will be all gathered together from all parts, through being surrounded on all sides by the cold of the earth.

REPLY OBJ. 3: Hell will never lack sufficient room to admit the bodies of the damned: since hell is accounted one of the three things that *never are satisfied* (Prov 30:15–16). Nor is it unreasonable that God's power should maintain within the bowels of the earth a hollow great enough to contain all the bodies of the damned.

REPLY OBJ. 4: It does not follow of necessity that *by what things a man sins, by the same also he is tormented,* except as regards the principal instruments of sin: for as much as man has sinned in soul and body, will he be punished in both. But it does not follow that a man will be punished in the very place where he sinned, because the place due to the damned is other from that due to wayfarers.

We may also reply that these words refer to the punishments inflicted on man on the way: according as each sin has its corresponding punishment, since *the inordinate mind is its own punishment,* as Augustine states (*Confessions* 1.12).

QUESTION 98

THE WILL AND INTELLECT OF THE DAMNED

Consequenter considerandum est de pertinentibus ad affectum et intellectum damnatorum.

Circa quod quaeruntur novem.

Primo: utrum damnatorum voluntas sit mala.

Secundo: utrum aliquando poeniteant de malis quae fecerunt.

Tertio: utrum magis vellent non esse quam esse.

Quarto: utrum vellent alios non esse damnatos.

Quinto: utrum impii habeant Deum odio.

Sexto: utrum ipsi demereri possint.

Septimo: utrum possint uti scientia hic acquisita.

Octavo: utrum cogitent aliquando de Deo.

Nono: utrum ipsi videant gloriam beatorum.

We must next consider matters pertaining to the will and intellect of the damned.

Under this head there are nine points of inquiry:

(1) Whether every act of will in the damned is evil?

(2) Whether they ever repent of the evil they have done?

(3) Whether they would rather not be than be?

(4) Whether they would wish others to be damned?

(5) Whether the wicked hate God?

(6) Whether they can demerit?

(7) Whether they can make use of the knowledge acquired in this life?

(8) Whether they ever think of God?

(9) Whether they see the glory of the blessed?

Article 1

Whether Every Act of Will in the Damned Is Evil?

AD PRIMUM SIC PROCEDITUR. Videtur quod non omnis voluntas damnatorum sit mala. Quia, ut dicit Dionysius, 4 cap. *de Div. Nom.*, daemones *bonum et optimum concupiscunt, esse, vivere et intelligere.* Cum ergo damnati homines non sint peioris conditionis quam daemones, videtur quod et ipsi bonam voluntatem habere possint.

PRAETEREA, malum, ut dicit Dionysius, est omnino *involuntarium*. Ergo, si damnati aliquid volunt, illud volunt inquantum est bonum vel apparens bonum. Sed voluntas quae per se ordinatur ad bonum, est bona. Ergo damnati possunt habere voluntatem bonam.

PRAETEREA, aliqui erunt damnati qui in hoc mundo existentes aliquos virtutum habitus secum detulerunt: utpote gentiles qui habuerunt virtutes politicas. Sed ex habitibus virtutum elicitur laudabilis voluntas. Ergo in aliquibus damnatis poterit esse laudabilis voluntas.

SED CONTRA: Obstinata voluntas nunquam potest flecti nisi ad malum. Sed damnati homines erunt obstinati, sicut daemones. Ergo voluntas eorum nunquam poterit esse bona.

PRAETEREA, sicut se habet voluntas beatorum adi bonum, ita se habet voluntas damnatorum ad malum. Sed beati nunquam habent voluntatem malam. Ergo nec damnati aliquam habent voluntatem bonam.

RESPONDEO dicendum quod in damnatis potest duplex voluntas considerari: scilicet voluntas deliberativa;

OBJECTION 1: It would seem that not every act of will in the damned is evil. For, according to Dionysius, the demons *desire the good and the best, namely, to be, to live, to understand* (*On the Divine Names* 4). Since, then, men who are damned are not worse off than the demons, it would seem that they also can have a good will.

OBJ. 2: Further, as Dionysius says (*On the Divine Names* 4), evil is altogether *involuntary*. Therefore, if the damned will anything, they will it as something good or apparently good. Now a will that is directly ordered to good is itself good. Therefore, the damned can have a good will.

OBJ. 3: Further, some will be damned who, while in this world, acquired certain habits of virtue, for instance, heathens who had civic virtues. Now a will elicits praiseworthy acts by reason of virtuous habits. Therefore, there may be praiseworthy acts of the will in some of the damned.

ON THE CONTRARY, An obstinate will can never be inclined except to evil. Now men who are damned will be obstinate even as the demons. Therefore, their wills can in no way be good.

FURTHER, As the will of the damned is in relation to evil, so is the will of the blessed in regard to good. But the blessed never have an evil will. Neither, therefore, have the damned any good will.

I ANSWER THAT, A twofold will may be considered in the damned, namely, the deliberate will and the natural

et voluntas naturalis. Naturalis quidem non est eis ex ipsis, sed ex Auctore naturae, qui in natura hanc inclinationem posuit quae naturalis voluntas dicitur. Unde, cum natura in eis remaneat, secundum hoc bona poterit in eis esse voluntas naturalis:

Sed voluntas deliberativa est eis ex seipsis, secundum quod in potestate eorum est inclinari per affectum ad hoc vel illud. Et talis voluntas est in eis solum mala. Et hoc ideo quia sunt perfecte aversi a fine ultimo rectae voluntatis; nec aliqua voluntas potest esse bona nisi per ordinem ad finem praedictum. Unde etiam, etsi aliquod bonum volunt, non tamen bene volunt illud, ut ex hoc voluntas eorum bona dici possit.

AD PRIMUM ergo dicendum quod verbum Dionysii intelligitur de voluntate naturali, quae est inclinatio naturae in aliquod bonum. Sed tamen ista naturalis inclinatio per eorum malitiam corrumpitur: inquantum hoc bonum quod naturaliter desiderant, sub quibusdam malis circumstantiis appetunt.

AD SECUNDUM dicendum quod malum, inquantum est malum, non movet voluntatem, sed inquantum est aestimatum bonum. Sed hoc ex eorum malitia procedit, quod id quod est malum aestiment ut bonum. Et ideo voluntas eorum mala est.

AD TERTIUM dicendum quod habitus virtutum politicarum non remanent in anima separata: eo quod virtutes illae perficiunt solum in vita civili, quae non erit post hanc vitam. Si tamen remanerent, nunquam in actum exirent, quasi ligatae ex obstinatione mentis.

will. Their natural will is theirs not of themselves, but of the Author of nature, who gave nature this inclination which we call the natural will. Wherefore, since nature remains in them, it follows that the natural will in them can be good.

But their deliberate will is theirs of themselves, inasmuch as it is in their power to be inclined by their affections to this or that. This will is in them always evil: and this because they are completely turned away from the last end of a right will, nor can a will be good except it be directed to that same end. Hence, even though they will some good, they do not will it well so that one be able to call their will good on that account.

REPLY OBJ. 1: The words of Dionysius must be understood of the natural will, which is nature's inclination to some particular good. And yet this natural inclination is corrupted by their wickedness, insofar as this good which they desire naturally is desired by them under certain evil circumstances.

REPLY OBJ. 2: Evil, as evil, does not move the will, but insofar as it is thought to be good. Yet it comes of their wickedness that they esteem that which is evil as though it were good. Hence their will is evil.

REPLY OBJ. 3: The habits of civic virtue do not remain in the separated soul, because those virtues perfect us only in the civic life which will not remain after this life. Even if they remained, they would never come into action, being enchained, as it were, by the obstinacy of the mind.

Article 2

Whether the Damned Repent of the Evil They Have Done?

AD SECUNDUM SIC PROCEDITUR. Videtur quod damnati nunquam poeniteant de malis quae fecerunt. Quia dicit Bernardus, in Cantica, quod damnatus semper vult iniquitatem suam quam fecit. Ergo nunquam de peccato commisso poenitet.

PRAETEREA, velle se non peccasse est bona voluntas. Sed damnati non habebunt bonam voluntatem. Ergo damnati nunquam volent se non peccasse. Et sic idem quod prius.

PRAETEREA, secundum Damascenum, *hoc est hominibus mors quod angelis casus.* Sed angeli voluntas post casum est invertibilis hoc modo, ut non possit recedere ab electione qua prius peccavit. Ergo et damnati non possunt poenitere de peccatis a se commissis.

PRAETEREA, maior erit perversitas damnatorum in inferno quam peccatorum in hoc mundo. Sed aliqui in hoc mundo non poenitent de. peccatis commissis: vel

OBJECTION 1: It would seem that the damned never repent of the evil they have done. For Bernard says on the Song of Songs that the damned consent forever to the evil they have done. Therefore, they never repent of the sins they have committed.

OBJ. 2: Further, to wish one had not sinned is a good will. But the damned will never have a good will. Therefore, the damned will never wish they had not sinned: and thus the same conclusion follows as above.

OBJ. 3: Further, according to Damascene (*On the Orthodox Faith* 2), *death is to man what the fall was to the angels.* But the angel's will is irrevocable after his fall, so that he cannot withdraw from the choice whereby he previously sinned. Therefore, the damned also cannot repent of the sins committed by them.

OBJ. 4: Further, the wickedness of the damned in hell will be greater than that of sinners in the world. Now in this world, some sinners repent not of the sins they have

propter excaecationem mentis, sicut haeretici; vel propter obstinationem, sicut *qui laetantur cum male fecerint, et exultant in rebus pessimis*, ut dicitur Proverb. 2, [14]. Ergo et damnati in inferno de peccatis non poenitebunt.

SED CONTRA: Sap. 5, [3] de damnatis dicitur: *intra se poenitentiam agentes*.

PRAETEREA, Philosophus, in IX *Ethic.*, dicit quod *poenitudine replentur pravi*: mox enim tristantur de hoc in quo prius delectati sunt. Ergo damnati, cum sint maxime pravi, magis poenitent.

RESPONDEO dicendum quod poenitere de aliquo contingit dupliciter: uno modo, per se; et alio modo, per accidens. Per se quidem de peccato poenitet qui peccatum in eo quod est peccatum, abominatur. Per accidens vero, qui illud odit ratione alicuius adiuncti, utpote poenae vel alicuius huiusmodi, Mali igitur non poenitebunt, per se loquendo, de peccatis: quia voluntas malitiae peccati in eis remanet. Poenitebunt autem per accidens: inquantum affligentur de poena quam pro peccato sustinent.

AD PRIMUM ergo dicendum quod damnati iniquitatem volunt, sed poenam refugiunt. Et sic per accidens de iniquitate commissa poenitent.

AD SECUNDUM dicendum quod velle se non peccasse propter turpitudinem iniquitatis, est bona voluntas. Sed hoc non erit in damnatis.

AD TERTIUM dicendum quod sine aliqua aversione voluntatis continget quod damnati de peccatis poeniteant: quia non hoc refugient in peccatis quod prius appetiverunt, sed aliquid aliud, scilicet poenam.

AD QUARTUM dicendum quod homines in hoc mundo, quantumcumque obstinati, per accidens de peccatis suis poenitent si pro eis puniantur: quia, ut dicit Augustinus, in libro *Octoginta trium Quaest.*, *videmus etiam ferocissimas bestias dolore poenarum a maximis voluptatibus abstinere.*

committed, either through blindness of mind, as heretics, or through obstinacy, as those *who are glad when they have done evil, and rejoice in most wicked things* (Prov 2:14). Therefore, etc.

ON THE CONTRARY, It is said of the damned: *repenting within themselves* (Wis. 5:3).

FURTHER, The Philosopher says (*Ethics* 9.4) that *the wicked are full of repentance*; for afterwards they are sorry for that in which previously they took pleasure. Therefore, the damned, being most wicked, repent all the more.

I ANSWER THAT, A person may repent of sin in two ways: in one way directly, in another way indirectly. He repents of a sin directly who hates sin as such: and he repents indirectly who hates it on account of something connected with it, for instance, punishment or something of that kind. Accordingly, the wicked will not repent of their sins directly, because consent in the malice of sin will remain in them; but they will repent indirectly, inasmuch as they will suffer from the punishment inflicted on them for sin.

REPLY OBJ. 1: The damned will wickedness, but shun punishment: and thus indirectly they repent of wickedness committed.

REPLY OBJ. 2: To wish one had not sinned on account of the shamefulness of vice is a good will: but this will not be in the wicked.

REPLY OBJ. 3: It will be possible for the damned to repent of their sins without turning their will away from sin, because in their sins they will not shun what they previously desired, but something else, namely the punishment.

REPLY OBJ. 4: However obstinate men may be in this world, they repent of the sins indirectly if they be punished for them. Thus Augustine says (*83 Questions*, 36): *we see the most savage beasts are deterred from the greatest pleasures by fear of pain.*

Article 3

Whether the Damned by Right and Deliberate Reason Would Wish Not to Be?

AD TERTIUM SIC PROCEDITUR. Videtur quod damnati recta ratione et deliberativa non possint velle se non esse. Augustinus enim dicit, in libro *de Lib. Arbit.*; *considera quantum bonum est esse, quod et beati et miseri volunt*: maius enim est esse et miserum esse, quam omnino non esse.

PRAETEREA, Augustinus ibidem sic arguit. Praeelectio supponit electionem. Sed non esse non est eligibile: cum non habeat apparentiam boni, cum nihil sit. Ergo non esse non potest esse magis appetibile damnatis quam esse.

OBJECTION 1: It would seem impossible for the damned, by right and deliberate reason, to wish not to be. For Augustine says (*On Free Choice of the Will* 3.7): *consider how great a good it is to be; since both the happy and the unhappy will it*; for to be and yet to be unhappy is a greater thing than not to be at all.

OBJ. 2: Further, Augustine argues thus (*On Free Choice of the Will* 3.8): preference supposes election. But not to be is not eligible; since it has not the appearance of good, for it is nothing. Therefore, not to be cannot be more desirable to the damned than to be.

PRAETEREA, maius malum magis est fugiendum. Sed non esse est maximum malum: cum tollat totaliter bonum, eo quod nihil relinquit. Ergo non esse est magis fugiendum quam miserum esse. Et sic idem quod prius.

SED CONTRA: Est quod dicitur Apoc. 9, [6]: *in diebus illis desiderabunt homines mori, et fugiet mors ab eis.*

PRAETEREA, damnatorum miseria omnem huius mundi miseriam excedit. Sed ad vitandam miseriam huius mundi appetibile est aliquibus mori: unde dicitur Eccli. 41, [3–4]: *O mors, quam bonum est iudicium tuum Homini indigenti, et qui minoratur viribus et deficit aetate, et cui de omnibus cura est, et incredibili qui perdit sapientiam!* Ergo multo fortius est damnatis appetibile *non esse* secundum rationem deliberativam.

RESPONDEO dicendum quod non esse potest dupliciter considerari. Uno modo, secundum se. Et sic nullo modo potest esse appetibile: cum non habeat aliquam rationem boni, sed sit pura boni privatio. Alio modo potest considerari inquantum est ablativum poenalis vel miserae vitae. Et sic non esse accipit rationem boni: carere enim malo est quoddam bonum, ut dicit Philosophus, in V *Ethic*. Et per hunc modum melius est damnatis non esse quam miseros esse. Unde Matth. 26, [24]: *bonum erat ei si natus non fuisset homo ille.* Ut Ierem. 20, super illud [v. 14], *maledicta dies in qua natus sum* etc., dicit Glossa Hieronymi: *melius est non esse quam male esse.* Et secundum hoc damnati possunt praeeligere *non esse* secundum deliberativam rationem.

AD PRIMUM ergo dicendum quod verbum Augustini est intelligendum quod non esse per se non est eligibile: sed per accidens, inquantum scilicet est miseriae terminativum. Quod enim dicitur quod esse et vivere ab omnibus appetitur naturaliter, *non oportet hoc accipere quantum ad malam vitam et corruptam, et eam quae est in tristitiis*, ut dicit Philosophus, in IX *Ethicorum*.

AD SECUNDUM dicendum quod non esse non est eligibile per se: sed per accidens tantum, ut dictum est.

AD TERTIUM dicendum quod, licet *non esse* maxime sit malum inquantum privat esse, est tamen valde bonum inquantum privat miseriam, quae est maximum malorum. Et sic *non esse* eligitur.

OBJ. 3: Further, the greater evil is the more to be shunned. Now *not to be* is the greatest evil, since it removes good altogether, so as to leave nothing. Therefore, not to be is more to be shunned than to be unhappy: and thus the same conclusion follows as above.

ON THE CONTRARY, It is written: *in those days men shall desire to die, and death shall fly from them* (Rev 9:6).

FURTHER, The unhappiness of the damned surpasses all unhappiness of this world. Now in order to escape the unhappiness of this world, it is desirable to some to die, wherefore it is written: *O death, your sentence is welcome to the man that is in need and to him whose strength fails; who is in a decrepit age, and that is in care about all things, and to the distrustful that loses wisdom* (Sir 41:3–4). Much more, therefore, is *not to be* desirable to the damned according to their deliberate reason.

I ANSWER THAT, Not to be may be considered in two ways. First, in itself, and thus it can in no way be desirable, since it has no aspect of good, but is pure privation of good. Second, it may be considered as a relief from a painful life or from some unhappiness: and thus not to be takes on the aspect of good, since to lack an evil is a kind of good, as the Philosopher says (*Ethics* 5.1). In this way it is better for the damned not to be than to be unhappy. Hence it is said: *it were better for him if that man had not been born* (Matt 26:24), and, *cursed be the day wherein I was born* (Jer 20:14), where a Gloss of Jerome observes: *it is better not to be than to be evilly.* In this sense the damned can prefer *not to be* according to their deliberate reason.

REPLY OBJ. 1: The saying of Augustine is to be understood in the sense that not to be is eligible not in itself, but accidentally, as putting an end to unhappiness. For when it is stated that to be and to live are desired by all naturally, *we are not to take this as referable to an evil and corrupt life, and a life of unhappiness*, as the Philosopher says (*Ethics* 9.4), but absolutely.

REPLY OBJ. 2: Non-existence is eligible, not in itself, but only accidentally, as stated already.

REPLY OBJ. 3: Although *not to be* is very evil insofar as it removes being, it is very good insofar as it removes unhappiness, which is the greatest of evils, and thus it is preferred *not to be*.

Article 4

Whether in Hell the Damned Would Wish Others Who Are Not Damned To Be Damned?

AD QUARTUM SIC PROCEDITUR. Videtur quod damnati in inferno non vellent alios esse damnatos qui non sunt damnati. Quia Luc. 16, [27–28] dicitur de Divite qui rogabat pro fratribus suis, *ne venirent in locum tormentorum.* Ergo, eadem ratione, et damnati alii non

OBJECTION 1: It would seem that in hell the damned would not wish others were damned who are not damned. For it is said of the rich man that he prayed for his brethren, *lest they should come into the place of torments* (Luke 16:27–28). Therefore, in like manner the other

vellent ad minus carnales suos amicos in inferno damnari.

PRAETEREA, affectiones inordinatae a damnatis non auferuntur. Sed aliqui damnati inordinate aliquos non damnatos dilexerunt. Ergo non vellerit eorum malum, quod est esse damnatos.

PRAETEREA, damnati non desiderant augmentum suae poenae. Sed si plures damnarentur, maior esset eorum poena: sicut etiam multiplicatio beatorum amplificat eorum gaudium. Ergo damnati non vellent salvatos damnari.

SED CONTRA: Est quod Isaiae 14, super illud [v. 9], *surrexerunt de soliis*, dicit Glossa: *solatium est malorum multos socios habere poenarum.*

PRAETEREA, in damnatis maxime regnat invidia. Ergo dolent de felicitate beatorum, et eorum damnationem appetunt.

RESPONDEO dicendum quod, sicut in beatis in patria erit perfectissima caritas, ita in damnatis erit perfectissimum odium. Unde, sicut sancti gaudebunt de omnibus bonis, ita et mali de omnibus bonis dolebunt. Unde et felicitas sanctorum considerata maxime eos affligit: unde dicitur Isaiae 26, [11]: *videant et confundantur zelantes populi, et ignis hostes tuos devoret.* Unde vellent omnes beatos esse damnatos.

AD PRIMUM ergo dicendum quod tanta erit invidia in damnatis quod etiam propinquorum gloriae invidebunt, cum ipsi sint in summa miseria: cum etiam in hac vita hoc accidat, crescente invidia. Sed tamen minus invident propinquis quam aliis; et maior esset eorum poena si omnes propinqui damnarentur et alii salvarentur, quam si aliqui de suis propinquis salvarentur. Et exinde fuit quod Dives petiit fratres suos a damnatione eripi: sciebat enim quod aliqui eriperentur. Maluisset tamen fratres suos cum omnibus aliis damnari.

AD SECUNDUM dicendum quod dilectio quae non fundatur super honestum, facile rescinditur: et praecipue in malis hominibus, ut Philosophus dicit, in VIII *Ethic.* Unde damnati non servabunt amicitiam ad eos quos inordinate dilexerunt. Sed in hoc voluntas eorum remanebit perversa, quod causam inordinatae dilectionis adhuc diligent.

AD TERTIUM dicendum quod, quamvis de damnatorurn multitudine poena singulorum augeatur, tamen tantum superexcrescet odium et invidia quod magis eligerent torqueri magis cum multis quam mirius soli.

damned would not wish at least their friends in the flesh to be damned in hell.

OBJ. 2: Further, the damned are not deprived of their inordinate affections. Now some of the damned loved inordinately some who are not damned. Therefore, they would not desire their evil, i.e., that they should be damned.

OBJ. 3: Further, the damned do not desire the increase of their punishment. Now if more were damned, their punishment would be greater, even as the joy of the blessed is increased by an increase in their number. Therefore, the damned desire not the damnation of those who are saved.

ON THE CONTRARY, A Gloss on Isaiah 14:9: *are risen up from their thrones*, says, *the wicked are comforted by having many companions in their punishment.*

FURTHER, Envy reigns supreme in the damned. Therefore, they grieve for the happiness of the blessed, and desire their damnation.

I ANSWER THAT, Even as in the blessed in heaven there will be most perfect charity, so in the damned there will be the most perfect hate. Wherefore as the saints will rejoice in all goods, so will the damned grieve for all goods. Consequently, the sight of the happiness of the saints will give them very great pain; hence it is written: *let the envious people see and be confounded, and let fire devour your enemies* (Isa 26:11). Therefore, they will wish all the good were damned.

REPLY OBJ. 1: So great will be the envy of the damned that they will envy the glory even of their kindred, since they themselves are supremely unhappy, for this happens even in this life, when envy increases. Nevertheless, they will envy their kindred less than others, and their punishment would be greater if all their kindred were damned and others saved than if some of their kindred were saved. For this reason the rich man prayed that his brethren might be warded from damnation: for he knew that some are guarded therefrom. Yet he would rather that his brethren were damned as well as all the rest.

REPLY OBJ. 2: Love that is not based on virtue is easily voided, especially in evil men, as the Philosopher says (*Ethics* 9.4). Hence the damned will not preserve their friendship for those whom they loved inordinately. Yet the will of them will remain perverse, because they will continue to love the cause of their inordinate loving.

REPLY OBJ. 3: Although an increase in the number of the damned results in an increase of each one's punishment, so much the more will their hatred and envy increase that they will prefer to be more tormented with many, rather than less tormented alone.

Article 5

Whether the Damned Hate God?

AD QUINTUM SIC PROCEDITUR. Videtur quod damnati non habeant Deum odio. Quia, ut dicit Dionysius, 4 cap. de Div. Nom., omnibus diligibile est bonum et pulchrum quod est omnis boni et pulchritudinis causa. Hoc autem est Deus. Ergo Deus a nullo odio haberi potest.

PRAETEREA, nullus potest ipsam bonitatem odio habere: sicut nec ipsam malitiam velle, malum enim est omnino *involuntarium*, ut Dionysius dicit, 4 cap. *de Div. Nom.* Deus autem est bonitas ipsa. Ergo nullus ipsum odio potest habere.

SED CONTRA est quod dicitur in Psalmo [72, 323]: *superbia illorum qui te oderunt ascendit semper.*

RESPONDEO dicendum quod affectus movetur ex bono vel malo apprehenso. Deus autem apprehenditur dupliciter: in se, sicut a beatis, qui eum per essentiam vident; et per effectus, sicut a nobis et damnatis. Ipse igitur in seipso, cum sit per essentiam bonitas, non potest alicui voluntati displicere. Unde quicumque eum per essentiam videret, eum odio habere non posset. Sed effectus eius aliqui sunt voluntati repugnantes, inquantum contrariantur alicui volito. Et secundum hoc aliquis, non in seipso, sed ratione effectuum, Deum odire potest.

Damnati ergo, Deum percipientes in effectu iustitiae qui est poena, eum odio habent, sicut et poenas quas sustinent.

AD PRIMUM ergo dicendum quod verbum Dionysii est intelligendum de appetitu naturali. Qui tamen in damnatis pervertitur per id quod additur ex deliberata voluntate, ut dictum est.

AD SECUNDUM dicendum quod ratio illa procederet si damnati Deum in seipso conspicerent, inquantum est per essentiam bonus.

OBJECTION 1: It would seem that the damned do not hate God. For, according to Dionysius (*On the Divine Names* 4), the beautiful and good that is the cause of all goodness and beauty is beloved of all. But this is God. Therefore, God cannot be the object of anyone's hate.

OBJ. 2: Further, no one can hate goodness itself, as neither can one will badness itself, since evil is altogether *involuntary*, as Dionysius asserts (*On the Divine Names* 4). Now God is goodness itself. Therefore, no one can hate him.

ON THE CONTRARY, It is written: *the pride of them that hate you ascends continually* (Ps 73:23).

I ANSWER THAT, The appetite is moved by good or evil apprehended. Now God is apprehended in two ways: namely, in himself, as by the blessed who see him in his essence; and in his effects, as by us and by the damned. Since, then, he is goodness by his essence, he cannot in himself be displeasing to any will; wherefore whoever sees him in his essence cannot hate him. On the other hand, some of his effects are displeasing to the will insofar as they are opposed to any one: and accordingly a person may hate God not in himself, but by reason of his effects.

Therefore, the damned, perceiving God in his punishment, which is the effect of his justice, hate him, even as they hate the punishment inflicted on them.

REPLY OBJ. 1: The saying of Dionysius refers to the natural appetite. and even this is rendered perverse in the damned, by that which is added thereto by their deliberate will, as stated above (A. 1).

REPLY OBJ. 2: This argument would prove if the damned saw God in himself, as being in his essence.

Article 6

Whether the Damned Demerit?

AD SEXTUM SIC PROCEDITUR. Videtur quod damnati demereantur. Damnati enim habent voluntatem malam, ut dicitur in littera. Sed per malam voluntatem quam hic habuerunt, demeruerunt. Ergo, si ibi non demerentur, ex sua damnatione commodum reportant.

PRAETEREA, damnati sunt eiusdem conditionis cum daemonibus. Sed daemones demerentur post suum casum: unde serpenti qui hominem ad peccandum induxit, est a Deo poena inflicta, ut dicitur Genes. 3, [14–15]. Ergo et damnati demerentur.

PRAETEREA, actus inordinatus ex libertate arbitrii procedens non excusatur quin sit demeritorius etsi ali-

OBJECTION 1: It would seem that the damned demerit. For the damned have an evil will, as stated in the last Distinction of *Sentences* IV. But they demerited by the evil will that they had here. Therefore, if they do not demerit there, their damnation is to their advantage.

OBJ. 2: Further, the damned are on the same footing as the demons. Now the demons demerit after their fall, wherefore God inflicted a punishment on the serpent (Gen 3:14–15). Therefore, the damned also demerit.

OBJ. 3: Further, an inordinate act that proceeds from a deliberate will is not excused from demerit, even though

qua necessitas adsit cuius aliquis sit sibi causa: *ebrius enim meretur duplices maledictiones* si ex ebrietate aliquod aliud peccatum committat, ut dicitur in III *Ethic.* Sed ipsi damnati fuerunt sibi causa propriae obstinationis, per quam quandam necessitatem patiuntur peccandi. Ergo, cum eorum actus inordinatus ex libero arbitrio procedat, non excusantur a demerito.

SED CONTRA: Poena contra culpam dividitur. Sed perversa voluntas in damnatis ex obstinatione procedit, quae est eorum poena. Ergo perversa voluntas in damnatis non est culpa per quam demereantur.

PRAETEREA, post ultimum terminum non relinquitur aliquis motus sive profectus in bonum vel in malum. Sed damnati, maxime post diem iudicii, ad ultimum terminum suae damnationis pervenient: quia tunc *finem habebunt duae civitates,* ut Augustinus dicit. Ergo damnati post diem iudicii perversa voluntate non demerebuntur: quia sic cresceret eorum damnatio.

RESPONDEO dicendum quod de damnatis ante diem iudicii et post distinguendum est. Omnes enim communiter confitentur quod ; post diem iudicii non erit aliquod meritum vel demeritum. Et hoc ideo est quia meritum vel demeritum ordinatur ad aliquod bonum vel malum ulterius consequendum. Post diem, autem iudicii erit ultima consummatio bonorum et malorum, ita quod nihil erit ulterius addendum de bono vel malo. Unde et bona voluntas in beatis non erit meritum, sed praemium; et mala voluntas non erit in damnatis demeritum, sed poena tantum; *operationes* enim *virtutis sunt praecipuae in felicitate, et eorum contrariae sunt praecipuae in miseria,* ut dicitur in I *Ethicorum.*

Sed ante diem iudicii quidam dicunt et beatos mereri, et damnatos demereri. Sed hoc non potest esse respectu praemii essentialis vel poenae principalis: cum quantum ad hoc utrique ad terminum perveniant. Potest tamen hoc esse respectu praemii accidentalis vel poenae secundariae, quae possunt augeri usque ad diem iudicii. Et hoc praecipue in daemonibus vel angelis bonis: quorum officio aliqui trahuntur ad salutem, ex quo bonorum angelorum gaudium crescit; vel ad damnationem, ex quo crescit poena daemonum.

AD PRIMUM ergo dicendum quod hoc est summum incommodum, ad summam malorum pervenisse, ex quo contingit in damnatis quod demereri non possunt. Unde patet quod ex peccato commodum non reportant.

AD SECUNDUM dicendum quod ad damnatorum hominum officium non pertinet alios ad damnationem pertrahere, sicut pertinet ad officium daemonum, ratione cuius demerentur quantum ad secundariam poenam.

there be necessity of which one is oneself the cause: for the *drunken man deserves a double punishment* if he commit a crime through being drunk (*Ethics* 3). Now the damned were themselves the cause of their own obstinacy, owing to which they are under a kind of necessity of sinning. Therefore, since their act proceeds from their free will, they are not excused from demerit.

ON THE CONTRARY, Punishment is contradistinguished from fault. Now the perverse will of the damned proceeds from their obstinacy which is their punishment. Therefore, the perverse will of the damned is not a fault whereby they may demerit.

FURTHER, After reaching the last term there is no further movement or advancement in good or evil. Now the damned, especially after the judgment day, will have reached the last term of their damnation, since then there *will cease to be two cities,* according to Augustine (*Handbook on Faith, Hope, and Charity* 111). Therefore, after the judgment day the damned will not demerit by their perverse will, for if they did, their damnation would be augmented.

I ANSWER THAT, We must draw a distinction between the damned before the judgment day and after. For all are agreed that after the judgment day there will be neither merit nor demerit. The reason for this is because merit or demerit is directed to the attainment of some further good or evil: and after the day of judgment good and evil will have reached their ultimate consummation, so that there will be no further addition to good or evil. Consequently, good will in the blessed will not be a merit but a reward, and evil will in the damned will be not a demerit but a punishment only. For *works of virtue belong especially to the state of happiness and their contraries to the state of unhappiness* (*Ethics* 1.9,10).

On the other hand, some say that before the judgment day, both the good merit and the damned demerit. But this cannot apply to the essential reward or to the principal punishment, since in this respect both have reached the term. Possibly, however, this may apply to the accidental reward or secondary punishment, which are subject to increase until the day of judgment. Especially may this apply to the demons or to the good angels, by whose activities some are drawn to salvation, whereby the joy of the blessed angels is increased, and some to damnation, whereby the punishment of the demons is augmented.

REPLY OBJ. 1: It is in the highest degree unprofitable to have reached the highest degree of evil, the result being that the damned are incapable of demerit. Hence it is clear that they gain no advantage from their sin.

REPLY OBJ. 2: Men who are damned are not occupied in drawing others to damnation, as the demons are, for which reason the latter demerit as regards their secondary punishment.

AD TERTIUM dicendum quod non propter hoc excusantur a demerito quia necessitatem habeant peccandi: sed quia ad summam malorum pervenerunt.

Tamen necessitas peccandi cuius causa sumus, excusat a culpa inquantum est necessitas quaedam: quia omne peccatum oportet esse voluntarium. Sed quod non excuset, hoc est inquantum a voluntate praecedente processit. Et sic totum demeritum sequentis culpae videtur ad primam culpam pertinere.

REPLY OBJ. 3: The reason why they are not excused from demerit is not because they are under the necessity of sinning, but because they have reached the highest of evils.

However, the necessity of sinning of which we are ourselves the cause, insofar as it is a necessity, excuses from sin, because every sin needs to be voluntary; but it does not excuse insofar as it proceeds from a previous act of the will. And so the whole demerit of the subsequent sin would seem to belong to the previous sin.

Article 7

Whether the Damned Can Make Use of the Knowledge They Had in This World?

AD SEPTIMUM SIC PROCEDITUR. Videtur quod damnati non possint uti notitia quam in hoc mundo habuerunt. In consideratione enim scientiae est maxima delectatio. Sed in eis nullam delectationem est ponere. Ergo non possunt uti scientia prius habita secundum aliquam considerationem.

PRAETEREA, damnati sunt in maioribus poenis quam sint aliquae poenae huius mundi. Sed in hoc mundo, dum aliquis est in maximis tormentis constitutus, non potest considerare aliquas intelligibiles conclusiones, abstractus a poenis quas patitur. Ergo multo minus in inferno.

PRAETEREA, damnati sunt subiecti tempori. Sed longitudo temporis est causa oblivionis: ut dicitur in IV *Physic*. Ergo damnati obliviscentur eorum quae hic habuerunt.

SED CONTRA: Est quod Luc. 16, [25] dicitur Diviti damnato: *recordare quia recepisti bona*, etc. Ergo considerabunt ea quae hic sciverunt.

PRAETEREA, species intelligibiles in anima separata remanent, ut supra dictum est. Si igitur eis non uti possent, frustra remanerent in eis.

RESPONDEO dicendum quod, sicut propter perfectam sanctorum beatitudinem nihil erit in eis quod non sit gaudii materia, ita nihil erit in damnatis quod non sit eis materia et causa tristitiae; nec aliquid quod, ad tristitiam possit pertinere, deerit, ut sit eorum miseria consummata. Consideratio ergo aliquorum notorum quantum ad aliquid inducit gaudium: vel ex parte cognoscibilium, inquantum diliguntur; vel ex parte ipsius cognitionis, inquantum est conveniens et perfecta. Potest etiam tristitiae esse ratio: et ex parte cognoscibilium, quae nata sunt contristare; et ex parte ipsius cognitionis, prout eius imperfectio consideratur, utpote cum aliquis

OBJECTION 1: It would seem that the damned are unable to make use of the knowledge they had in this world. For there is very great pleasure in the consideration of knowledge. But we must not admit that they have any pleasure. Therefore, they cannot make use of the knowledge they formerly had by applying their consideration thereto.

OBJ. 2: Further, the damned suffer greater pains than any pains of this world. Now in this world, when one is in very great pain it is impossible to consider any intelligible conclusions through being distracted by the pains that one suffers. Much less, therefore, can one do so in hell.

OBJ. 3: Further, the damned are subject to time. But length of time is the cause of forgetfulness (*Physics* 4.13). Therefore, the damned will forget what they knew here.

ON THE CONTRARY, It is said to the rich man who was damned: *remember that you did receive good things in your lifetime* (Luke 16:25), etc. Therefore, they will consider about the things they knew here.

FURTHER, The intelligible species remain in the separated soul, as stated above (Q. 70, A. 2, ad 3; I, Q. 89, A. 5–6). Therefore, if they could not use them, these would remain in them to no purpose.

I ANSWER THAT, Even as in the saints on account of the perfection of their glory there will be nothing but what is a matter of joy, so there will be nothing in the damned but what is a matter and cause of sorrow; nor will anything that can pertain to sorrow be lacking, so that their unhappiness is consummate. Now the consideration of certain things known brings us joy, in some respect, either on the part of the things known, because we love them, or on the part of the knowledge, because it is fitting and perfect. There may also be a reason for sorrow both on the part of the things known, because they are of a grievous nature, and on the part of the knowledge, if we consider its imperfection; for

considerat se deficere in Cognitione alicuius rei, cuius perfectionem appeteret.

Sic ergo in damnatis erit actualis consideratio eorum quae prius sciverunt, ut materia tristitiae, non autem ut delectationis causa. Considerabunt enim et mala quae gesserunt, ex quibus damnati sunt; et bona dilecta, quae amiserunt; et ex utroque torquebuntur. Similiter etiam torquebuntur de hoc quod considerabunt notitiam quam de rebus speculabilibus habuerunt imperfectam esse, et amisisse summam eius perfectionem, quam poterant adipisci.

AD PRIMUM ergo dicendum quod, quamvis consideratio sit per se delectabilis, tamen ex aliquo accidente potest esse tristitiae causa. Et sic erit in damnatis.

AD SECUNDUM dicendum quod in hoc mundo anima coniungitur corruptibili corpori. Unde per hoc quod corpus affligitur, consideratio animae impeditur. Sed in futuro anima non ita trahetur a corpore: sed, quantumcumque corpus affligatur, tamen anima semper considerabit lucidissime illa quae ei poterunt esse causa maeroris.

AD TERTIUM dicendum quod tempus est causa oblivionis per accidens, inquantum motus, cuius est mensura, est causa transmutationis. Sed post diem iudicii non erit motus caeli; unde nec oblivio esse poterit ex quantacumque diuturnitate. Sed ante diem iudicii anima Separata non mutatur a sua dispositione per motum caeli.

instance, a person may consider his defective knowledge about a certain thing which he would desire to know perfectly.

Accordingly, in the damned there will be actual consideration of the things they knew heretofore as matters of sorrow, but not as a cause of pleasure. For they will consider both the evil they have done, and for which they were damned, and the delightful goods they have lost, and on both counts they will suffer torments. Likewise, they will be tormented with the thought that the knowledge they had of speculative matters was imperfect, and that they missed its highest degree of perfection which they might have acquired.

REPLY OBJ. 1: Although the consideration of knowledge is delightful in itself, it may accidentally be the cause of sorrow, as explained above.

REPLY OBJ. 2: In this world the soul is united to a corruptible body, wherefore the soul's consideration is hindered by the suffering of the body. On the other hand, in the future life the soul will not be so drawn by the body, but however much the body may suffer, the soul will have a most clear view of those things that can be a cause of anguish to it.

REPLY OBJ. 3: Time causes forgetfulness accidentally, insofar as the movement whereof it is the measure is the cause of change. But after the judgment day, there will be no movement of the heavens; wherefore neither will it be possible for forgetfulness to result from any lapse of time however long. Before the judgment day, however, the separated soul is not changed from its disposition by the heavenly movement.

Article 8

Whether the Damned Will Ever Think of God?

AD OCTAVUM SIC PROCEDITUR. Videtur quod aliquando damnati cogitabunt de Deo. Quia non potest haberi odio actu nisi id de quo cogitatur. Sed damnati Deum odio habebunt, ut in littera dicitur. Ergo de Deo aliquando cogitabunt.

PRAETEREA, damnati habebunt remorsum Conscientiae. Sed conscientia patitur remorsum de actis contra Deum. Ergo de Deo aliquando cogitabunt.

SED CONTRA, perfectissima hominis cogitatio est qua cogitat de Deo. Sed damnati erunt in statu imperfectissimo. Ergo de Deo non cogitabunt.

RESPONDEO dicendum quod Deus potest considerari dupliciter. Uno modo, secundum se, et secundum id quod est proprium, scilicet esse totius bonitatis principium. Et sic nullo modo cogitari potest sine delectatione.

OBJECTION 1: It would seem that the damned will sometimes think of God. For one cannot hate a thing actually, except one think about it. Now the damned will hate God, as stated in the last distinction of *Sentences* IV. Therefore, they will think of God sometimes.

OBJ. 2: Further, the damned will have remorse of conscience. But the conscience suffers remorse for deeds done against God. Therefore, they will sometimes think of God.

ON THE CONTRARY, Man's most perfect thoughts are those which are about God: whereas the damned will be in a state of the greatest imperfection. Therefore, they will not think of God.

I ANSWER THAT, One may think of God in two ways. First, in himself and according to that which is proper to him, namely, that he is the fount of all goodness: and thus it is altogether impossible to think of him without delight,

Unde sic nullo modo a damnatis cogitabitur. Alio modo, secundum aliquid quod est ei quasi accidentale in effectibus eius, utpote punire, vel aliquid huiusmodi. Et secundum hoc consideratio de Deo potest tristitiam inducere. Et hoc modo damnati de Deo cogitabunt.

AD PRIMUM ergo dicendum quod damnati non habent Deum odio nisi ratione punitionis, et prohibitionis eius quod malae voluntati eorum consonat. Unde non considerabunt eum nisi ut punitorem et prohibitorem.

ET PER HOC patet etiam solutio ad secundum. Quia conscientia non remordet de peccato nisi inquantum est divino praecepto contraria.

so that the damned will by no means think of him in this way. Second, according to something accidental, as it were, to him in his effects, such as his punishments, and so forth, and in this respect the thought of God can bring sorrow. And in this way the damned will think of God.

REPLY OBJ. 1: The damned do not hate God except because he punishes and forbids what is agreeable to their evil will: and consequently they will think of him only as punishing and forbidding.

THIS SUFFICES for the reply to the second objection, since conscience will not have remorse for sin except as forbidden by the divine commandment.

Article 9

Whether the Damned See the Glory of the Blessed?

AD NONUM SIC PROCEDITUR. Videtur quod damnati gloriam beatorum non videant. Magis enim distat ab eis gloria beatorum quam ea quae in hoc mundo aguntur. Sed ipsi non vident quae circa nos aguntur: unde dicit Gregorius, XII *Moral.*, super illud Iob [14, 21], *sive fuerint nobiles filii eius*, etc.: *sicut hi qui adhuc vivunt, mortuorum animae quo loco habeantur ignorant; ita mortui, qui corporaliter vixerunt, vita in carne positorum qualiter circa eos disponatur, ignorant*. Ergo multo minus possunt videre gloriam beatorum.

PRAETEREA, illud quod conceditur sanctis in hac vita pro magno munere, nunquam concedetur damnatis. Sed Paulo pro magno munere fuit concessum videre vitam illam qua sancti aeternaliter cum Deo vivunt: ut dicitur II Cor. 12, [2], in Glossa. Ergo damnati sanctorum gloriam non videbunt.

SED CONTRA est quod dicitur, Luc. 16, [23], quod Dives, in tormentis positus, *vidit Abraham, et Lazarum in sinu eius.*

RESPONDEO dicendum quod damnati ante diem iudicii vident beatos in gloria, non hoc modo quod gloriam eorum qualis sit cognoscant, sed solum cognoscunt eos esse in gloria quadam inaestimabili. Et ex hoc turbabuntur: tum propter invidiam, dolentes de felicitate eorum; tum propter hoc quod ipsi talem gloriam amiserunt; unde dicitur Sap. 5, [2] de impiis: *videntes turbabuntur timore horribili*. Sed post diem iudicii omnino beatorum visione privabuntur. Nec tamen ex hoc eorum poena minuetur, sed augebitur. Quia memoriam habebunt gloriae beatorum, quam in iudicio videbunt vel ante iudicium: et hoc erit eis in tormentum. Sed ulterius affligentur in hoc quod videbunt se indignos reputari etiam videre gloriam quam sancti merentur habere.

OBJECTION 1: It would seem that the damned do not see the glory of the blessed. For they are more distant from the glory of the blessed than from the happenings of this world. But they do not see what happens in regard to us: hence Gregory commenting on Job 14:21: *whether his children come to honor*, says, *even as those who still live know not in what place are the souls of the dead, so the dead who have lived in the body know not the things which regard the life of those who are in the flesh* (*Morals on Job* 12). Much less, therefore, can they see the glory of the blessed.

OBJ. 2: Further, that which is granted as a great favor to the saints in this life is never granted to the damned. Now it was granted as a great favor to Paul to see the life in which the saints live forever with God (2 Cor 12). Therefore, the damned will not see the glory of the saints.

ON THE CONTRARY, It is stated that the rich man in the midst of his torments *saw Abraham, and Lazarus in his bosom* (Luke 16:23).

I ANSWER THAT, The damned, before the judgment day, will see the blessed in glory, in such a way as to know not what that glory is like, but only that they are in a state of glory that surpasses all thought. This will trouble them, both because they will, through envy, grieve for their happiness, and because they have forfeited that glory. Hence it is written concerning the wicked: *seeing it, they shall be troubled with terrible fear* (Wis 5:2). After the judgment day, however, they will be altogether deprived of seeing the blessed: nor will this lessen their punishment, but will increase it, because they will bear in remembrance the glory of the blessed which they saw at or before the judgment: and this will torment them. Moreover, they will be tormented by finding themselves deemed unworthy even to see the glory which the saints merit to have.

AD PRIMUM ergo dicendum quod ea quae in hac vita aguntur, non ita affligerent damnatos in inferno si viderentur, sicut sanctorum gloria inspecta. Unde non ita ostenduntur damnatis ea quae hic aguntur sicut sanctorum gloria. Quamvis etiam eorum quae hic aguntur, ostendantur eis ea quae in eis tristitiam augere possunt.

AD SECUNDUM dicendum quod Paulus inspexit vitam illam in qua sancti cum Deo vivunt, eam experiendo, et in futurum perfectius sperando. Quod non est de damnatis. Et ideo non est simile.

REPLY OBJ. 1: The happenings of this life would not, if seen, torment the damned in hell as the sight of the glory of the saints; wherefore the things which happen here are not shown to the damned in the same way as the saints' glory; although also of the things that happen here those are shown to them which are capable of causing them sorrow.

REPLY OBJ. 2: Paul looked upon that life wherein the saints live with God by actual experience thereof and by hoping to have it more perfectly in the life to come. Not so the damned; wherefore the comparison fails.

QUESTION 99

GOD'S MERCY AND JUSTICE TOWARDS THE DAMNED

Deinde considerandum est de iustitia et misericordia Dei respectu damnatorum.

Circa quod quaeruntur quinque.

Primo: utrum ex divina iustitia inferatur peccatoribus poena aeterna.

Secundo: utrum per divinam misericordiam omnis poena tam hominum quam daemonum terminetur.

Tertio: utrum saltem poena hominum terminetur.

Quarto; utrum saltem poena Christianorum.

Quinto: utrum illorum qui opera misericordiae fecerunt.

We must next consider God's justice and mercy towards the damned.

Under this head there are five points of inquiry:

(1) Whether by divine justice an eternal punishment is inflicted on sinners?

(2) Whether by God's mercy all punishment both of men and of demons comes to an end?

(3) Whether at least the punishment of men comes to an end?

(4) Whether at least the punishment of Christians has an end?

(5) Whether there is an end to the punishment of those who have performed works of mercy?

Article 1

Whether by Divine Justice an Eternal Punishment Is Inflicted on Sinners?

AD PRIMUM SIC PROCEDITUR. Videtur quod ex divina iustitia non inferatur peccatoribus poena aeterna. Poena enim non debet excedere culpam: Deut. 25, [2], *secundum mensuram delicti erit et plagarum modus*. Sed culpa est temporalis. Ergo poena non debet esse aeterna.

PRAETEREA, duorum peccatorum mortalium unum est altero maius. Ergo unum debet maiori quam alterum poena puniri. Sed nulla poena potest esse maior quam aeterna: cum sit infinita. Ergo non cuilibet peccato mortali debetur poena aeterna. Et si uni non debetur, nulli debetur: cum eorum distantia non sit infinita.

PRAETEREA, a iusto iudice non infertur poena nisi ad correctionem: unde II *Ethic.* dicitur quod *poenae sunt quaedam medicinae*. Sed quod impii in aeternum puniantur, hoc non est ad correctionem eorum: nec aliquorum aliorum, cum tunc non sint aliqui futuri qui per hoc corrigi possint. Ergo secundum divinam iustitiam non infertur pro peccatis poena aeterna.

PRAETEREA, omne quod non est propter se volitum, nullus vult nisi propter aliquam utilitatem. Sed poenae a Deo non sunt propter se volitae: non enim delectatur in poenis. Cum ergo nulla utilitas accidere possit ex perpetuatione poenae, videtur quod perpetuam poenam pro peccato non infert.

OBJECTION 1: It would seem that an eternal punishment is not inflicted on sinners by divine justice. For the punishment should not exceed the fault: *according to the measure of the sin shall the measure also of the stripes be* (Deut 25:2). Now fault is temporal. Therefore, the punishment should not be eternal.

OBJ. 2: Further, of two mortal sins one is greater than the other. Therefore, one should receive a greater punishment than the other. But no punishment is greater than eternal punishment, since it is infinite. Therefore, eternal punishment is not due to every sin; and if it is not due to one, it is due to none, since they are not infinitely distant from one another.

OBJ. 3: Further, a just judge does not punish except in order to correct, wherefore it is stated (*Ethics* 2.3) that *punishments are a kind of medicine*. Now, to punish the wicked eternally does not lead to their correction, nor to that of others, since then there will be no one in future who can be corrected thereby. Therefore, eternal punishment is not inflicted for sins according to divine justice.

OBJ. 4: Further, no one wishes that which is not desirable for its own sake, except on account of some advantage. Now God does not wish punishment for its own sake, for he delights not in punishments. Since, then, no advantage can result from the perpetuity of punishment, it would seem that he ought not to inflict such a punishment for sin.

PRAETEREA, nihil quod est per accidens est perpetuum, ut dicitur in I *Caeli et Mundi*. Sed poena est eorum quae sunt per accidens: cum sit contra naturam. Ergo non potest esse perpetua.

PRAETEREA, iustitia Dei hoc requirere videtur ut peccatores ad nihilum redigantur. Quia propter ingratitudinem debet quis beneficia accepta amittere. Inter cetera autem Dei beneficia est etiam ipsum esse. Unde videtur iustum ut peccator, qui ingratus Deo exstitit, ipsum esse amittat. Sed, si in nihilum redigantur, eorum poena non potest esse perpetua. Ergo non videtur esse consonum divinae iustitiae ut peccatores perpetuo puniantur.

SED CONTRA: Est quod dicitur Matth, 25, [46]: *ibunt hi*, scilicet peccatores, *in supplicium aeternum*.

PRAETEREA, sicut se habet praemium ad meritum, ita poena ad culpam. Sed secundum divinam iustitiam merito temporali debetur praemium aeternum: Ioan. 6, [40], *omnis qui videt Filium et credit in eum, habet vitam aeternam*. Ergo et culpae temporali secundum divinam iustitiam debetur poena aeterna.

PRAETEREA, secundum Philosophum, in V *Ethic.*, poena taxatur secundum dignitatem eius in quem peccatur: unde maiori poena punitur qui percutit alapa principem, quam alium quemcumque. Sed quicumque peccat mortaliter, peccat contra Deum, cuius praecepta transgreditur, et cuius honorem alii impartitur dum in alio finem constituit. Maiestas autem Dei est infinita. Ergo quicumque peccat mortaliter, dignus est infinita poena. Et ita videtur quod iuste pro peccato mortali quis perpetuo puniatur.

RESPONDEO dicendum quod, cum poena duplicem habeat quantitatem, scilicet secundum intensionem acerbitatis, et secundum durationem temporis; quantitas poenae respondet quantitati culpae secundum intensionem acerbitatis, ut secundum quod gravius peccavit, secundum hoc gravior poena ei infligatur; unde Apoc. 18, [7]: *quantum se glorificavit et in deliciis fuit, tantum date ei tormentum et luctum*. Non autem respondet duratio poenae durationi culpae, ut dicit Augustinus, XXI *de Civ. Dei*: non enim adulterium, quod in momento temporis perpetratur, momentanea poena punitur, etiam secundum leges humanas. Sed duratio poenae respicit dispositionem peccantis. Quandoque enim ille qui peccat in aliqua civitate, ex ipso peccato efficitur dignus ut totaliter a societate civitatis repellatur, vel per exilium perpetuum, vel etiam per mortem. Quandoque vero non redditur dignus ut totaliter a civium societate excludatur: et ideo, ut possit esse conveniens membrum civitatis, poena ei prolongatur vel breviatur secundum quod expedit eius curationi, ut in civitate convenienter et pacifice vivere possit.

OBJ. 5: Further, nothing accidental lasts forever (*De Coelo et Mundo* I). But punishment is one of those things that happen accidentally, since it is contrary to nature. Therefore, it cannot be everlasting.

OBJ. 6: Further, the justice of God would seem to require that sinners should be brought to naught: because on account of ingratitude a person deserves to lose all benefits, and among other benefits of God there is being itself. Therefore, it would seem just that the sinner who has been ungrateful to God should lose his being. But if sinners be brought to naught, their punishment cannot be everlasting. Therefore, it would seem out of keeping with divine justice that sinners should be punished forever.

ON THE CONTRARY, It is written: *these*, namely, the wicked, *shall go into everlasting punishment* (Matt 25:46).

FURTHER, As reward is to merit, so is punishment to guilt. Now, according to divine justice, an eternal reward is due to temporal merit: *every one who sees the Son and believes in him has life everlasting* (John 6:40). Therefore, according to divine justice, an everlasting punishment is due to temporal guilt.

FURTHER, According to the Philosopher (*Ethics* 5.5), punishment is taxed according to the dignity of the person sinned against, so that a person who strikes one in authority receives a greater punishment than one who strikes anyone else. Now whoever sins mortally, sins against God, whose commandments he breaks, and whose honor he gives another by placing his end in some one other than God. But God's majesty is infinite. Therefore, whoever sins mortally deserves infinite punishment; and consequently it seems just that for a mortal sin a man should be punished forever.

I ANSWER THAT, Since punishment is measured in two ways, namely, according to the degree of its severity, and according to its length of time, the measure of punishment corresponds to the measure of fault as regards the degree of severity, so that the more grievously a person sins the more grievously is he punished: *as much as she has glorified herself and lived in delicacies, so much torment and sorrow give to her* (Rev 18:7). The duration of the punishment does not, however, correspond with the duration of the fault, as Augustine says (*The City of God* 21.11), for adultery, which is committed in a short space of time, is not punished with a momentary penalty even according to human laws. But the duration of punishment regards the disposition of the sinner: for sometimes a person who commits an offense in a city is rendered by his very offense worthy of being cut off entirely from the fellowship of the citizens, either by perpetual exile or even by death: whereas sometimes he is not rendered worthy of being cut off entirely from the fellowship of the citizens. Hence, in order that he may become a fitting member of the State, his punishment is prolonged or curtailed, according as is expedient for his amendment, so that he may live in the city in a becoming and peaceful manner.

Ita etiam secundum divinam iustitiam aliquis ex peccato redditur dignus penitus a civitatis Dei consortio separari: quod fit per omne peccatum quo quis contra caritatem peccat, quae est vinculum civitatem praedictam uniens. Et ideo pro peccato mortali, quod est contrarium caritati, aliquis, in aeternum a societate sanctorum exclusus, aeternae poenae addicitur: quia, ut Augustinus in libro praedicto dicit, *quod est de civitate ista mortali homines supplicio primae mortis, hoc est de civitate illa immortali homines supplicio secundae mortis auferre.* Quod autem poena quam civitas mundana infligit perpetua non reputatur, hoc est per accidens: vel inquantum homo non perpetuo manet; vel in quantum etiam ipsa civitas deficit. Unde, si homo in perpetuum viveret poena exilii et servitutis, quae per legem humanam inferuntur, in eo perpetuo permanerent. Qui vero hoc modo peccant ut tamen, non reddantur digni totaliter separari a sanctae civitatis consortio, sicut peccantium venialiter, tanto eorum poena erit brevior vel diuturnior, quanto magis vel minus purgabiles erunt, secundum quod eis peccata vel plus vel minus inhaeserunt. Quod in poenis huius mundi et purgatorii secundum divinam iustitiam servatur.

Inveniuntur etiam et aliae rationes a Sanctis assignatae quare iuste pro peccato temporali aliqui poena perpetua puniantur. Una est quia peccaverunt contra bonum aeternum, dum contempserunt aeternam vitam. Et hoc etiam est quod Augustinus in praedicto libro dicit: *factus est malo dignus aeterno, quia hoc in se peremit bonum quod esse posset aeternum.*

Alia ratio est quia homo in suo aeterno peccavit. Unde Gregorius dicit, in IV *Dialog.*: *ad magnam iustitiam iudicantis pertinet ut nunquam careant supplicio qui nunquam voluerunt carere peccato.* Et si obiiciatur quod quidam peccantes mortaliter proponunt vitam suam in melius commutare; et ita, secundum hoc, non essent digni aeterno supplicio, ut videtur: dicendum est, secundum quosdam, quod Gregorius loquitur de voluntate quae manifestatur per opus. Qui enim in peccatum mortale propria voluntate labitur, se ponit in statu a quo erui non potest nisi divinitus. Unde ex hoc ipso quod vult peccare, consequenter vult in peccato manere perpetuo: homo enim est *spiritus vadens*, scilicet in peccatum, *et non rediens* per seipsum. Sicut, si aliquis se iri foveam proiiceret unde exire non posset nisi adiutus, posset dici quod in aeternum ibi manere voluit, quantumcumque aliud cogitaret. Vel potest dici, et melius, quod ex hoc ipso quod mortaliter peccat, finem suum in creatura constituit. Et quia ad finem vitae tota vita ordinatur, ideo ex hoc ipso totam vitam suam ordinat ad illud peccatum; et vellet perpetuo in peccato manere si hoc sibi esset impune. Et hoc est quod Gregorius dicit, in XXXIV lib. *Moral.*, super illud Iob 41, [23], *aestimabit abyssum quasi senescentem: Iniqui ideo cum fine deliquerunt, quia cum*

So too, according to divine justice, sin renders a person worthy to be altogether cut off from the fellowship of God's city, and this is the effect of every sin committed against charity, which is the bond uniting this same city together. Consequently, for mortal sin, which is contrary to charity, a person is expelled forever from the fellowship of the saints and condemned to everlasting punishment, because as Augustine says (*The City of God* xxi, 11), *as men are cut off from this perishable city by the penalty of the first death, so are they excluded from that imperishable city by the punishment of the second death.* That the punishment inflicted by the earthly state is not deemed everlasting is accidental, either because man endures not forever, or because the state itself comes to an end. Thus, if man lived forever, the punishment of exile or slavery, which is pronounced by human law, would remain in him forever. On the other hand, as regards those who sin in such a way as not to deserve to be entirely cut off from the fellowship of the saints, such as those who sin venially, their punishment will be so much the shorter or longer according as they are more or less fit to be cleansed through sin clinging to them more or less: this is observed in the punishments of this world and of purgatory according to divine justice.

We find also other reasons given by the saints why some are justly condemned to everlasting punishment for a temporal sin. One is because they sinned against an eternal good by despising eternal life. This is mentioned by Augustine (*The City of God* 12.12): *he is become worthy of eternal evil who destroyed in himself a good which could be eternal.*

Another reason is because man sinned in his own eternity; wherefore Gregory says (*Dialogues* 4), *it belongs to the great justice of the judge that those should never cease to be punished, who in this life never ceased to desire sin.* And if it be objected that some who sin mortally propose to amend their life at some time, and that these accordingly do not seem to deserve eternal punishment, it must be replied according to some that Gregory speaks of the will that is made manifest by the deed. For he who falls into mortal sin of his own will puts himself in a state whence he cannot be rescued, except God help him: wherefore from the very fact that he is willing to sin, he is willing to remain in sin forever. For man is *a wind that goes*, namely to sin, *and does not return* by his own power (Ps 77:39). Thus, if a man were to throw himself into a pit whence he could not get out without help, one might say that he wished to remain there forever, whatever else he may have thought himself. Another and a better answer is that from the very fact that he commits a mortal sin, he places his end in a creature; and since the whole of life is directed to its end, it follows that for this very reason he directs the whole of his life to that sin, and is willing to remain in sin forever, if he could do so with impunity. This is what Gregory says on Job 41:23, *he shall esteem the deep as growing old: the wicked only put an end*

fine vixerunt. Voluissent quippe sine fine vivere ut sine fine potuissent in suis iniquitatibus permanere: nam magis appetunt peccare quam vivere.

Potest et alia ratio assignari quare poena peccati mortalis sit aeterna: quia per eam contra Deum, qui est infinitus, peccatur. Unde, cum non posset esse infinita poena per intensionem, quia creatura non est capax alicuius qualitatis infinitae; requiritur quod sit saltem duratione infinita.

Est etiam quarta ratio ad hoc idem: quia culpa manet in aeternum; cum culpa non possit remitti sine gratia, quam homo non potest post mortem acquirere. Nec debet poena cessare quandiu culpa manet.

AD PRIMUM ergo dicendum quod poena non debet aequari culpae secundum quantitatem durationis: ut videtur etiam secundum leges humanas accidere.

Vel dicendum, sicut Gregorius solvit, quod, quamvis culpa sit actu temporalis, voluntate tamen est aeterna.

AD SECUNDUM dicendum quod quantitati peccati respondet quantitas poenae secundum intensionem. Et ideo peccatorum mortalium inaequalium erunt poenae inaequales intensione, aequales autem duratione.

AD TERTIUM dicendum quod poenae quae infliguntur his qui a civitatis societate non penitus eiiciuntur, sunt ad correctionem eorum ordinatae: sed illae poenae per quas aliqui totaliter a civitatis societate exterminantur, non sunt ad correctionem eorum. Possunt tamen esse ad correctionem et tranquillitatem aliorum qui in civitate remanent. Et ita damnatio aeterna impiorum est ad correctionem eorum qui nunc sunt in Ecclesia: non enim poenae sunt ad correctionem solum quando infliguntur; sed etiam quando determinantur.

AD QUARTUM dicendum quod impiorum poenae in perpetuum duraturae non erunt omnino ad nihilum utiles. Sunt enim utiles ad duo. Primo, ad hoc quod in eis divina iustitia conservatur: quae est Deo accepta propter seipsam. Unde Gregorius, IV *Dialog.: omnipotens Deus, quia pius est, miserorum cruciatu non pascitur. Quia autem iustus est, ab iniquorum ultione in perpetuum non sedatur.*

Secundo, ad hoc sunt utiles ut de his electi gaudeant, dum in his Dei iustitiam contemplantur, et cum hoc se evasisse cognoscunt. Unde Psalmo [57, 11]: *laetabitur iustus cum viderit vindictam*; et Isaiae 66, [24]: *erunt*, scilicet impii, *usque ad satietatem visionis*, scilicet sanctis, ut Glossa dicit. Et hoc est quod Gregorius dicit, IV *Dialog.: iniqui omnes, aeterno supplicio deputati, sua quidem iniquitate puniuntur: et tamen ad aliquid ardebunt, scilicet ut iusti omnes et in Deo videant gaudia quae perceperunt, et in illis percipiant supplicia quae evaserunt; quatenus tanto magis in aeternum divinae gratiae debitores se*

to sinning because their life came to an end: they would indeed have wished to live forever, that they might continue in sin forever, for they desire rather to sin than to live (*Morals on Job* 34).

Still another reason may be given why the punishment of mortal sin is eternal: because thereby one offends God, who is infinite. Wherefore, since punishment cannot be infinite in intensity, because the creature is incapable of an infinite quality, it must be infinite at least in duration.

And again there is a fourth reason for the same: because guilt remains forever, since it cannot be remitted without grace, and men cannot receive grace after death; nor should punishment cease so long as guilt remains.

REPLY OBJ. 1: Punishment has not to be equal to fault as to the amount of duration, as is seen to be the case also with human laws.

We may also reply with Gregory (*Dialogues* 44) that although sin is temporal in act, it is eternal in will.

REPLY OBJ. 2: The degree of intensity in the punishment corresponds to the degree of gravity in the sin; wherefore mortal sins unequal in gravity will receive a punishment unequal in intensity, but equal in duration.

REPLY OBJ. 3: The punishments inflicted on those who are not altogether expelled from the society of their fellow-citizens are intended for their correction: whereas those punishments whereby certain persons are wholly banished from the society of their fellow-citizens are not intended for their correction, although they may be intended for the correction and tranquillity of the others who remain in the state. Accordingly, the damnation of the wicked is for the correction of those who are now in the Church; for punishments are intended for correction not only when they are being inflicted, but also when they are decreed.

REPLY OBJ. 4: The everlasting punishment of the wicked will not be altogether useless. For they are useful for two purposes. First, because thereby the divine justice is safeguarded, which is acceptable to God for its own sake. Hence Gregory says (*Dialogues* 4): *almighty God on account of his loving kindness delights not in the torments of the unhappy; but on account of his justice, he is forever unappeased by the punishment of the wicked.*

Second, they are useful, because the elect rejoice therein when they see God's justice in them, and realize that they have escaped them. Hence it is written: *the just shall rejoice when he shall see the revenge* (Ps 57:12), and, *they*, namely, the wicked, *shall be a loathsome sight to all flesh* (Isa 66:24), namely, to the saints, as a Gloss says. Gregory expresses himself in the same sense (*Dialogues* 4): *the wicked are all condemned to eternal punishment, and are punished for their own wickedness. Yet they will burn to some purpose, namely, that the just may all both see in God the joys they receive, and perceive in them the torments they have escaped: for which*

esse cognoscant, quanto in aeternum mala puniri conspiciunt, quae eius adiutorio vicerunt.

Ad quintum dicendum quod, quamvis poena per accidens respondeat animae, tamen per se respondet animae culpa infectae. Et quia culpa in perpetuum in ea manebit, ideo et poena perpetua erit.

Ad sextum dicendum quod poena respondet culpae, proprie loquendo, secundum inordinationem quae invenitur in ipsa, et non secundum dignitatem ipsius in quem peccatur: quia sic cuilibet peccato responderet poena infinita intensione. Quamvis ergo ex hoc quod aliquis peccat contra Deum, qui est Auctor essendi, mereatur ipsum esse amittere; considerata tamen ipsius actus inordinatione, non debetur ei amissio esse: quia esse praesupponitur ad meritum et demeritum, nec per inordinationem peccati esse tollitur vel corrumpitur. Et ideo non potest esse debita poena alicuius culpae privatio ipsius esse.

reason they will acknowledge themselves forever the debtors of divine grace the more that they will see how the evils which they overcame by its assistance are punished eternally.

Reply Obj. 5: Although the punishment relates to the soul accidentally, it relates essentially to the soul infected with guilt. And since guilt will remain in the soul forever, its punishment also will be everlasting.

Reply Obj. 6: Punishment corresponds to fault, properly speaking, in respect of the inordinateness in the fault, and not of the dignity in the person offended: for if the latter were the case, a punishment of infinite intensity would correspond to every sin. Accordingly, although a man deserves to lose his being from the fact that he has sinned against God, the author of his being, yet, in view of the inordinateness of the act itself, loss of being is not due to him, since being is presupposed to merit and demerit, nor is being lost or corrupted by the inordinateness of sin: and consequently privation of being cannot be the punishment due to any sin.

Article 2

Whether by God's Mercy All Punishment of the Damned, Both Men and Demons, Comes to an End?

Videtur quod per divinam misericordiam omnis poena terminetur tam hominum quam etiam daemonum: Sap. 11, [24]: *misereris omnium, Domine, quoniam omnia potes.* Sed inter omnia etiam daemones continentur, qui sunt Dei creaturae. Ergo et ipsorum daemonum poena finietur.

Praeterea, Rom. 11, [32]: *conclusit Deus omnia sub peccato ut omnium misereatur.* Sed Deus daemones sub peccato conclusit, idest, sub peccato concludi permisit. Ergo videtur quod etiam daemonum aliquando misereatur.

Praeterea, sicut dicit Anselmus, in libro *Cur Deus homo*: *non est iustum ut Deus creaturam quam fecit ad beatitudinem, omnino perire sinat.* Ergo videtur, cum quaelibet creatura rationalis creata fuerit ad beatitudinem, non esse iustum ut omnino perire permittatur,

Sed contra: Est quod dicitur Matth. 25, [41]: *ite, maledicti, in ignem aeternum, qui paratus est diabolo et angelis eius.* Ergo aeternaliter punientur.

Praeterea, sicut boni angeli effecti sunt beati per conversionem ad Deum, ita mali angeli effecti sunt miseri per aversionem a Deo. Si ergo miseria malorum angelorum finiatur quandoque, et beatitudo bonorum finem habebit. Quod est inconveniens.

Objection 1: It would seem that by God's mercy all punishment of the damned, both men and demons, comes to an end. For it is written: *you have mercy upon all, O Lord, because you can do all things* (Wis 11:24). But among all things the demons also are included, since they are God's creatures. And therefore their punishment will come to an end.

Obj. 2: Further, *God has concluded all in sin, that he may have mercy on all* (Rom 11:32). Now God has concluded the demons under sin, that is to say, he permitted them to be concluded. Therefore, it would seem that he will have mercy even on the demons.

Obj. 3: Further, as Anselm says (*Cur Deus Homo* II), *it is not just that God should permit the utter loss of a creature which he made for happiness.* Therefore, since every rational creature was created for happiness, it would seem unjust for it to be allowed to perish altogether.

On the contrary, It is written: *depart from me, you cursed, into everlasting fire, which is prepared for the devil and his angels* (Matt 25:41). Therefore, they will be punished eternally.

Further, Just as the good angels were made happy through turning to God, so the bad angels were made unhappy through turning away from God. Therefore, if the unhappiness of the wicked angels comes at length to an end, the happiness of the good will also come to an end, which is inadmissible.

RESPONDEO dicendum quod error Origenis fuit, ut Augustinus, XXI *de Civ. Dei*, dicit, quod daemones quandoque per Dei misericordiam liberandi sunt a poenis. Sed iste error est ab Ecclesia reprobatus propter duo. Primo, quia manifeste auctoritati Scripturae repugnat, quae habet, Apoc. 20, [9–10]: *diabolus, qui seducebat eos, missus est in stagnum ignis et sulphuris, ubi bestia et pseudoprophetae cruciabuntur die ac nocte in saecula saeculorum*, per quod in Scriptura significari aeternitas consuevit.

Secundo, quia ex una parte nimis Dei misericordiam extendebat, et ex alia parte nimis eam coarctabat. Eiusdem enim rationis esse videtur bonos angelos in aeterna beatitudine permanere, et malos angelos in aeternum puniri. Unde, sicut ponebat daemones et animas damnatorum quandoque a poena liberandas, ita ponebat angelos et animas beatorum quandoque a beatitudine in huius vitae miserias devolvendas.

AD PRIMUM ergo dicendum quod; Deus, quantum in ipso est, miseretur omnibus: sed quia eius misericordia sapientiae ordine regulatur, inde est quod ad quosdam non se extendit, qui se misericordiae fecerunt indignos, sicut daemones et damnati, qui sunt in malitia obstinati. Tamen potest dici quod etiam in eis misericordia locum habet, inquantum citra condignum puniuntur: non quod a poena totaliter absolvantur.

AD SECUNDUM dicendum quod ibi intelligenda est distributio *pro generibus singulorum*, et non *pro singulis generum*: ut intelligatur auctoritas de hominibus secundum statum viae; quia scilicet et Iudaeorum et gentilium misertus est, sed non omnium gentilium vel omnium Iudaeorum.

AD TERTIUM dicendum quod Anselmus intelligit non esse iustum quantum ad decentiam divinae bonitatis: et loquitur de creatura secundum genus suum. Non enim est conveniens divinae bonitati ut totum unum genus creaturae deficiat a fine propter quod est factum. Unde nec omnes homines, nec omnes angelos damnari convenit. Sed nihil prohibet quin aliqui vel ex hominibus vel ex angelis in aeternum pereant: quia divinae voluntatis intentio impletur in aliis, qui salvantur.

I ANSWER THAT, As Augustine says (*The City of God* 21) Origen erred in maintaining that the demons will at length, through God's mercy, be delivered from their punishment. Now, this error has been condemned by the Church for two reasons. First, because it is clearly contrary to the authority of Sacred Scripture: *the devil who seduced them was cast into the pool of fire and brimstone, where both the beasts and the false prophets shall be tormented day and night forever and ever* (Rev 20:9–10), which is the Scriptural expression for eternity.

Second, because this opinion exaggerated God's mercy in one direction and depreciated it in another. For it would seem equally reasonable for the good angels to remain in eternal happiness, and for the wicked angels to be eternally punished. Therefore, just as he maintained that the demons and the souls of the damned are to be delivered at length from their sufferings, so he maintained that the angels and the souls of the blessed will at length pass from their happy state to the unhappiness of this life.

REPLY OBJ. 1: God, for his own part, has mercy on all. Since, however, his mercy is ruled by the order of his wisdom, the result is that it does not reach to certain people who render themselves unworthy of that mercy, as do the demons and the damned, who are obstinate in wickedness. And yet we may say that even in them his mercy finds a place, insofar as they are punished less than they deserve condignly, but not that they are entirely delivered from punishment.

REPLY OBJ. 2: In the words quoted the distribution [of the predicate] *regards the genera* and not *the individuals*: so that the statement applies to men in the state of wayfarer, inasmuch as he had mercy both on Jews and on Gentiles, but not on every Gentile or every Jew.

REPLY OBJ. 3: Anselm means that it is not just in the sense of becoming God's goodness, and is speaking of the creature generically. For it becomes not the divine goodness that a whole genus of creature fail of the end for which it was made: wherefore it is unbecoming for all men or all angels to be damned. But there is no reason why some men or some angels should not perish forever, because the intention of the divine will is fulfilled in the others who are saved.

Article 3

Whether God's Mercy Suffers at Least Men to Be Punished Eternally?

AD TERTIUM SIC PROCEDITUR. Videtur quod divina misericordia non patiatur saltem homines in aeternum puniri . Genes. 6, [3]: *non permanebit spiritus meus in homine in aeternum, quia caro est*: et accipitur ibi *spiri-*

OBJECTION 1: It would seem that God's mercy does not suffer at least men to be punished eternally. For it is written: *my spirit shall not remain in man forever because he is flesh* (Gen 6:3); where *spirit* denotes indignation, as a Gloss

tus pro indignatione, ut patet per Glossam ibidem. Cum ergo indignatio Dei non sit aliud quam eius poena, non punientur aeternaliter.

PRAETEREA, caritas sanctorum in praesenti hoc facit ut pro inimicis exorent. Sed tunc habebunt perfectiorem caritatem. Ergo tunc orabunt pro inimicis damnatis. Sed orationes eorum esse cassae non poterunt: cum sint maxime Deo acceptae. Ergo precibus sanctorum divina misericordia damnatos quandoque a poena liberabit.

PRAETEREA, hoc quod Deus poenam damnatorum aeternam praedixit, ad prophetiam comminationis pertinet. Sed prophetia comminationis non semper impletur: quod patet per hoc quod dictum est de subversione Ninive, quae non fuit subversa sicut praedictum fuerat per prophetam, qui ex hoc etiam contristatus fuit. Ergo videtur quod multo amplius per divinam misericordiam comminatio poenae aeternae mutabitur in mitiorem sententiam, quando in nullius tristitiam, sed in omnium gaudium cedere poterit.

PRAETEREA, ad hoc facit quod in Psalmo [76, 8] dicitur: *nunquid in aeternum irascetur Deus?* Sed ira Dei est eius punitio. Ergo Deus in aeternum homines non puniet.

PRAETEREA, Isaiae 14, super illud [v. 19], *tu autem proiectus es* etc., dicit Glossa: *si omnes animae aliquando habebunt requiem, tu nunquam*, loquens de diabolo. Ergo videtur quod omnes animae humanae aliquando requiem habebunt de poenis.

SED CONTRA: Est quod dicitur Matth. 25, [46], simul de electis et reprobis: *ibunt hi in supplicium aeternum; iusti autem in vitam aeternam.* Sed inconveniens est ponere quod iustorum vita quandoque finiatur. Ergo inconveniens est ponere quod reproborum supplicium terminetur.

PRAETEREA, sicut dicit Damascenus, *hoc est hominibus mors quod angelis casus.* Sed angeli post casum irreparabiles fuerunt. Ergo et homines post mortem. Et sic reproborum supplicium nunquam terminabitur.

RESPONDEO dicendum quod, sicut Augustinus dicit, XXI *de Civ. Dei*, quidam in hoc ab errore Origenis declinaverunt quod daemones posuerunt in perpetuum puniri, sed omnes homines quandoque liberari a poena, etiam infideles. Sed haec positio omnino est irrationabilis. Sicut enim daemones sunt in malitia obstinati, et ita perpetuo puniendi, ita et animae hominum qui sine caritate decedunt: cum *hoc hominibus sit mors quod angelis casus*, ut Damascenus dicit.

AD PRIMUM ergo dicendum quod verbum illud est intelligendum de homine secundum genus suum: quia ab humano genere quandoque Dei indignatio est remota per Christi adventum. Sed illi qui in hac reconciliatione quae facta est per Christum, noluerunt esse vel perma-

observes. Therefore, since God's indignation is not distinct from his punishment, man will not be punished eternally.

OBJ. 2: Further, the charity of the saints in this life makes them pray for their enemies. Now they will have more perfect charity in that life. Therefore, they will pray then for their enemies who are damned. But the prayers of the saints cannot be in vain, since they are most acceptable to God. Therefore, at the saints' prayers the divine mercy will in time deliver the damned from their punishment.

OBJ. 3: Further, God's foretelling of the punishment of the damned belongs to the prophecy of condemnation. Now the prophecy of condemnation is not always fulfilled: as appears from what was said of the destruction of Nineveh (Jonah 3); and yet it was not destroyed as foretold by the prophet, who also was troubled for that very reason (Jonah 4:1). Therefore, it would seem that much more will the threat of eternal punishment be commuted by God's mercy for a more lenient punishment, when this will be able to give sorrow to none, but joy to all.

OBJ. 4: Further, the words of Ps. 76:8 are to the point, where it is said: *will God then be angry forever?* But God's anger is his punishment. Therefore, God does not punish men eternally.

OBJ. 5: Further, a Gloss on Isaiah 14:19: *but you are cast out*, says, *even though all souls shall have rest at last, you never shall*: and it refers to the devil. Therefore, it would seem that all human souls shall at length have rest from their pains.

ON THE CONTRARY, It is written of the elect conjointly with the damned: *these shall go into everlasting punishment: but the just, into life everlasting* (Matt 25:46). But it is inadmissible that the life of the just will ever have an end. Therefore, it is inadmissible that the punishment of the damned will ever come to an end.

FURTHER, As Damascene says (*On the Orthodox Faith* 2) *death is to men what the fall was to the angels*. Now after their fall the angels could not be restored. Therefore, neither can man after death: and thus the punishment of the damned will have no end.

I ANSWER THAT, As Augustine says (*The City of God* 21.17–18), some evaded the error of Origen by asserting that the demons are punished everlastingly, while holding that all men, even unbelievers, are at length set free from punishment. But this statement is altogether unreasonable. For just as the demons are obstinate in wickedness and therefore have to be punished forever, so too are the souls of men who die without charity, since *death is to men what the fall was to the angels*, as Damascene says.

REPLY OBJ. 1: This saying refers to man generically, because God's indignation was at length removed from the human race by the coming of Christ. But those who were unwilling to be included or to remain in this reconciliation effected by Christ perpetuated the divine anger in them-

nere, in seipsis divinam iram perpetuaverunt: cum non sit nobis aliquis modus reconciliationis concessus nisi per Christum.

Ad secundum dicendum quod, sicut Augustinus dicit, XXI *de Civ. Dei*, et Gregorius, XXXIV *Moral.* et IV *Dialog.*, quod sancti in hac vita ideo pro inimicis exorant, ut convertantur ad Deum: cum adhuc converti possint. Si enim esset nobis notum quod essent praesciti ad mortem, non magis pro eis quam pro daemonibus oraremus. Et quia post hanc vitam decedentibus sine gratia tempus conversionis non erit, nulla pro eis fiet oratio, nec ab Ecclesia militante nec a triumphante. Hic enim pro eis orandum est, ut Apostolus dicit, II Tim. 2, [25–26], *ut det illis Deus poenitentiam, et resipiscant a diaboli laqueis.*

Ad tertium dicendum quod prophetia comminatoria poenae tunc solum immutatur quando variantur merita eius in quem comminatio facta est. Unde Ierem. 18, [7–8]: *repente loquar adversus gentem et adversus regnum, ut eradicem et destruam et disperdam illud. Si poenitentiam egerit gens illa a malo suo, agam et ego poenitentiam super malo quod cogitaveram ei.* Unde, cum damnatorum merita mutari non possint, comminatio poenae semper in eis implebitur. Nihilominus tamen prophetia comminationis semper quantum ad aliquem intellectum impletur. Quia, ut dicit Augustinus, in praedicto libro, *eversa est Ninive quae mala erat, et bona aedificata est, quae non erat: stantibus enim moenibus atque domibus, eversa est civitas in perditis moribus.*

Ad quartum dicendum quod illud verbum Psalmi pertinet ad vasa misericordiae, quae se indignos misericordia non fecerunt: quia in hac vita, quae quaedam ira Dei est propter vitae miserias, vasa misericordiae mutat in melius. Unde sequitur in Psalmo [76, 11]: *haec mutatio dexterae Excelsi.*

Vel dicendum quod hoc intelligitur de misericordia aliquid relaxante, non de misericordia totaliter liberante, si extendatur etiam ad damnatos. Unde non dicit, *continebit ab ira misericordias suas*, sed, *in ira* [v. 10]: quia non totaliter poena tolletur, sed, ipsa poena durante, misericordia operabitur eam diminuendo.

Ad quintum dicendum quod Glossa illa non loquitur simpliciter, sed sub hypothesi impossibilis, ad exaggerandum peccati magnitudinem ipsius diaboli, vel Nabuchodonosor.

selves, since no other way of reconciliation is given to us save that which is through Christ.

Reply Obj. 2: As Augustine (*The City of God* 21.24) and Gregory (*Morals on Job* 34) say, the saints in this life pray for their enemies that they may be converted to God, while it is yet possible for them to be converted. For if we knew that they were foreknown to death, we should no more pray for them than for the demons. And since for those who depart this life without grace there will be no further time for conversion, no prayer will be offered for them, neither by the Church Militant nor by the Church Triumphant. For that which we have to pray for them is, as the Apostle says, that *God may give them repentance to know the truth, and they may recover themselves from the snares of the devil* (2 Tim 2:25–26).

Reply Obj. 3: A punishment threatened prophetically is only then commuted when there is a change in the merits of the person threatened. Hence Jeremiah 18:7 reads: *I will suddenly speak against a nation and against a kingdom, to root out and to pull down and to destroy it. If that nation shall repent of their evil, I also will repent of the evil that I have thought to do to them.* Therefore, since the merits of the damned cannot be changed, the threatened punishment will ever be fulfilled in them. Nevertheless, the prophecy of condemnation is always fulfilled in a certain sense, because as Augustine says (*The City of God* 21.24): *Nineveh has been overthrown, that was evil, and a good Nineveh is built up, that was not: for while the walls and the houses remained standing, the city was overthrown in its wicked ways.*

Reply Obj. 4: These words of the Psalm refer to the vessels of mercy, which have not made themselves unworthy of mercy, because in this life (which may be called God's anger on account of its unhappiness) he changes vessels of mercy into something better. Hence the Psalm continues: *this is the change of the right hand of the most High* (Ps 76:11).

We may also reply that they refer to mercy as granting a relaxation, but not setting free altogether, if it be referred also to the damned. Hence the Psalm does not say: *will he from his anger shut up his mercies?* but *in his anger* (Ps 77:9), because the punishment will not be done away with entirely; but his mercy will have effect by diminishing the punishment while it continues.

Reply Obj. 5: This Gloss is speaking not absolutely, but on an impossible supposition, in order to throw into relief the greatness of the devil's sin, or of Nabuchadnezzar's.

Article 4

Whether the Punishment of Christians Is Brought to an End by the Mercy of God?

Ad quartum sic proceditur. Videtur quod saltem Christianorum poena per divinam misericordiam terminetur. Quia Marc. 16, [16] dicitur: *qui crediderit et baptizatus fuerit, salvus erit*. Sed hoc est omnium Christianorum. Ergo omnes Christiani finaliter salvabuntur.

Praeterea, Ioan. 6, [55] dicitur: *qui manducat meam carnem et bibit, meum sanguinem, habet vitam aeternam*. Sed hoc est communis cibus et potus Christianorum. Ergo omnes Christiani finaliter salvabuntur.

Praeterea, I Cor. 3, [15]: *si cuius opus arserit, detrimentum patietur, ipse autem salvus erit, sic tamen quasi per ignem*: et loquitur de illis in quibus fuit fundamentum fidei Christianae [v. 11–12]. Ergo omnes tales finaliter salvabuntur.

Sed contra: Est quod dicitur I Cor. 6, [9]: *iniqui regnum Dei non possidebunt*. Sed quidam Christiani sunt iniqui. Ergo non omnes Christiani ad Regnum pervenient. Et ita perpetuo punientur.

Praeterea, II Petr. 2, [21] dicitur: *melius erat eis viam veritatis non cognoscere quam post agnitam retroire ab eo quod traditum est illis sancto mandato*. Sed illi qui viam veritatis non cognoverunt, aeternaliter punientur. Ergo et Christiani qui ab agnita retrocesserunt.

Respondeo dicendum quod quidam fuerunt, ut dicit Augustinus, in praedicto libro, qui non omnibus hominibus promiserunt absolutionem a poena aeterna, sed solis Christianis. Et in hoc respectu diversificati sunt. Quidam enim dixerunt quod quicumque sacramenta fidei perceperunt, ab aeterna poena erunt immunes. Sed hoc est, contrarium veritati: quia quidam sacramenta fidei recipiunt et fidem non habent, *sine qua impossibile est placere Deo*, Heb. 11, [6].

Et ideo alii dixerunt quod solum illi ab aeterna poena erunt immunes qui sacramenta fidei sunt consecuti et fidem Catholicam tenuerunt. Sed contra hoc esse videtur quod aliquando aliqui Catholicam fidem tenent et postea resipiscunt: qui non minori poena sunt digni, sed maiori, quia, 11 Petr. 2, [21], *melius erat eis viam veritatis non cognoscere quam post agnitam retroire*. Planum est etiam plus peccare haeresiarchas, qui, de fide Catholica recedentes, novas haereses fingunt, quam illos qui a principio aliquam haeresim sunt secuti.

Et ideo alii dixerunt quod illi soli sunt ab aeterna poena immunes qui in fide Catholica finaliter perseverant, quantumcumque aliis criminibus involvantur.

Objection 1: It would seem that at least the punishment of Christians is brought to an end by the mercy of God. *For he that believes and is baptized shall be saved* (Mark 16:16). Now this applies to every Christian. Therefore, all Christians will at length be saved.

Obj. 2: Further, it is written: *he that eats my body and drinks my blood has eternal life* (John 6:55). Now this is the meat and drink whereof Christians partake in common. Therefore, all Christians will be saved at length.

Obj. 3: Further, *if any man's work burn, he shall suffer loss: but he himself shall be saved, yet so as by fire* (1 Cor 3:15), where it is a question of those who have the foundation of the Christian faith. Therefore, all such persons will be saved in the end.

On the contrary, It is written: *the unjust shall not possess the kingdom of God* (1 Cor 6:9). Now some Christians are unjust. Therefore, Christians will not all come to the kingdom of God, and consequently they will be punished forever.

Further, It is written: *it had been better for them not to have known the way of justice, than after they have known it to turn back from that holy commandment which was delivered to them* (2 Pet 2:21). Now those who know not the way of truth will be punished forever. Therefore, Christians who have turned back after knowing it will also be punished forever.

I answer that, According to Augustine (*The City of God* 21.20–21), there have been some who predicted a delivery from eternal punishment not for all men, but only for Christians, although they stated the matter in different ways. For some said that whoever received the sacraments of faith would be immune from eternal punishment. But this is contrary to the truth, since some receive the sacraments of faith, and yet have not faith, *without which it is impossible to please God* (Heb 11:6).

Wherefore others said that those alone will be exempt from eternal punishment who have received the sacraments of faith, and professed the Catholic faith. But against this it would seem to be that at one time some people profess the Catholic faith, and afterwards abandon it, and these are deserving not of a lesser but of a greater punishment, since according to 2 Peter 2:21: *it had been better for them not to have known the way of justice than, after they have known it, to turn back*. Moreover, it is clear that heresiarchs who renounce the Catholic faith and invent new heresies sin more grievously than those who have conformed to some heresy from the first.

And therefore some have maintained that those alone are exempt from eternal punishment, who persevere to the end in the Catholic faith, however guilty they may have

Sed hoc manifeste contrariatur Scripturae. Quia Iac. 2, [20, 26] dicitur; *fides sine operibus mortua est*; et Matth. 7, [21]: *non omnis qui dicit mihi, Domine, Domine, intrabit in regnum caelorum* et in multis aliis locis Scriptura peccantibus aeternas poenas comminatur.

Unde non omnes finaliter in fide persistentes a poena aeterna erunt immunes, nisi et ab aliis criminibus inveniantur finaliter absoluti.

AD PRIMUM ergo dicendum quod Dominus ibi loquitur de fide formata, *quae per dilectionem operatur*: in qua quicumque decesserit, salvus erit. Sed huic non solum opponitur infidelitatis error, sed quodlibet peccatum mortale.

AD SECUNDUM dicendum quod verbum Domini est intelligendum, non de illis qui tantum sacramentaliter edunt, qui, indigne quandoque sumentes, *iudicium sibi manducant et bibunt*, ut dicitur I Cor. 11, [29]: sed loquitur de manducantibus spiritualiter, qui per caritatem ei incorporantur; quam incorporationem facit sacramentalis comestio si quis digne accedat. Unde, quantum est ex virtute sacramenti, ad vitam aeternam perducit: quamvis aliquis se possit tali fructu privare per peccatum, etiam postquam digne sumpserit.

AD TERTIUM dicendum quod *fundamentum* in verbis Apostoli intelligitur fides formata: supra quam qui peccata venialia aedificaverit, *detrimentum patietur*, quia pro eis punitur a Deo; *ipse tamen salvus erit* finaliter *quasi per ignem*, vel temporalis tribulationis, vel purgatoriae poenae, quae post mortem erit.

been of other crimes. But this is clearly contrary to Sacred Scripture, for James 2:20 says: *faith without works is dead*, and Matthew 7:21 says: *not every one that says to me, "Lord, Lord," shall enter into the kingdom of heaven: but he that does the will of my Father who is in heaven*; and in many other passages Scripture threatens sinners with eternal punishment.

Consequently, those who persevere in the faith unto the end will not all be exempt from eternal punishment, unless in the end they prove to be free from other crimes.

REPLY OBJ. 1: Our Lord speaks there of formed faith *that works by love* (Gal 5:6): wherein whosoever dies shall be saved. But to this faith not only is the error of unbelief opposed, but also any mortal sin whatsoever.

REPLY OBJ. 2: The saying of our Lord refers not to those who partake only sacramentally, and who sometimes by receiving unworthily *eat and drink judgment* (1 Cor 11:29) to themselves, but to those who eat spiritually and are incorporated with him by charity, which incorporation is the effect of the sacramental eating in those who approach worthily. Wherefore, so far as the power of the sacrament is concerned, it brings us to eternal life, although sin may deprive us of that fruit, even after we have received worthily.

REPLY OBJ. 3: In this passage of the Apostle the foundation denotes formed faith, upon which whosoever shall build venial sins *shall suffer loss*, because he will be punished for them by God; yet *he himself shall be saved* in the end *by fire*, either of temporal tribulation, or of the punishment of purgatory, which will be after death.

Article 5

Whether All Those Who Perform Works of Mercy Will Be Punished Eternally?

AD QUINTUM SIC PROCEDITUR. Videtur quod illi omnes qui opera misericordiae faciunt, non punientur aeternaliter: sed solum illi qui opera misericordiae negligunt. Iac. 2, [13]: *iudicium sine misericordia ei qui non fecit misericordiam*. Et Matth. 5, [7]: *beati misericordes: quoniam ipsi misericordiam consequentur*.

PRAETEREA, Matth. 25, [31 sqq.] ponitur disceptatio Domini cum electis et reprobis. Sed illa disceptatio non est nisi de operibus misericordiae. Ergo solum pro operibus misericordiae omissis aliqui aeternaliter punientur. Et sic idem quod prius.

PRAETEREA, Matth. 6, [12] dicitur: *dimitte nobis debita nostra sicut et nos dimittimus debitoribus nostris*: et sequitur [v. 14]: *si enim dimiseritis hominibus* etc. Ergo videtur quod misericordes, qui aliis peccata dimittunt,

OBJECTION 1: It would seem that all who perform works of mercy will not be punished eternally, but only those who neglect those works. For James 2:13 says: *judgment without mercy to him that has not done mercy*, and Matthew 5:7 says: *blessed are the merciful, for they shall obtain mercy*.

OBJ. 2: Further, we find a description of our Lord's discussion with the damned and the elect (Matt 25:35–46). But this discussion is only about works of mercy. Therefore, eternal punishment will be awarded only to such as have omitted to practice works of mercy: and consequently the same conclusion follows as before.

OBJ. 3: Further, it is written: *forgive us our debts, as we also forgive our debtors* (Matt 6:12), and further on: *for if you will forgive men their offenses, your heavenly Father will forgive you also your offenses* (Matt 6:14). Therefore, it

ipsi veniam peccatorum consequentur. Et sic non aeternaliter punientur.

PRAETEREA, I Tim. 4, super illud [v. 8], *pietas ad omnia valet*, dicit Glossa Ambrosii: *omnis summa disciplinae Christianae in misericordia et pietate est: quam aliquis sequens, si lubricum carnis patiatur, sine dubio vapulabit, sed non peribit. Si quis autem solum exercitium corporis habuerit, perennes poenas patietur.* Ergo illi qui insistunt operibus misericordiae, qui peccatis carnalibus detinentur, non in aeternum punientur. Et sic idem quod prius.

SED CONTRA: Est quod dicitur I Cor. 6, [9]: *neque fornicarii neque adulteri regnum Dei possidebunt.* Sed multi qui se exercent in operibus misericordiae, sunt tales. Ergo non omnes misericordes ad regnum aeternum pervenient. Et ita aliqui eorum aeternaliter punientur.

PRAETEREA, Iac. 2, [10] dicitur: *quicumque totam legem servaverit, offendat autem in uno, factus est omnium reus.* Ergo quicumque servat legem quoad opera misericordiae et negligit alia opera, reatum de transgressione legis incurret. Et ita aeternaliter punietur.

RESPONDEO dicendum quod, sicut Augustinus dicit, in libro praedicto, quidam posuerunt non omnes qui Catholicam fidem tenent a poena aeterna esse liberandos, sed solum illos qui operibus misericordiae insistunt, quamvis etiam aliis criminibus sint subiecti. Sed istud non potest stare. Quia sine caritate non potest aliquid Deo esse acceptum; nec sine ea prodest aliquid ad vitam aeternam. Contingit autem aliquos operibus misericordiae insistere qui caritatem non habent. Unde his nihil prodest ad vitam aeternam promerendam, vel ad immunitatem aeternae poenae: ut patet I Cor. 13, [1–3]. Et praecipue hoc apparet absurdum in raptoribus, qui multa rapiunt et tamen aliqua misericorditer largiuntur.

Et ideo dicendum quod quicumque cum peccato mortali decedunt, nec fides nec opera misericordiae eos liberabit a poena aeterna, etiam post quantumcumque spatium temporis.

AD PRIMUM ergo dicendum quod illi misericordiam consequentur qui misericordiam ordinate impendunt. Non autem ordinate misericordiam impendunt qui seipsos in miserendo negligunt: sed magis se impugnant male agendo. Et ideo tales misericordiam penitus absolventem non consequentur: etsi consequantur misericordiam de poenis debitis aliquid relaxantem.

AD SECUNDUM dicendum quod non propter hoc ponitur disceptatio de operibus misericordiae solum quia pro eorum neglectu tantummodo aliqui puniantur aeternaliter: sed quia illi aeterna poena liberabuntur post

would seem that the merciful, who forgive others their offenses, will themselves obtain the forgiveness of their sins, and consequently will not be punished eternally.

OBJ. 4: Further, a Gloss of Ambrose on 1 Timothy 4:8: *godliness is profitable to all things*, says: *the sum total of a Christian's rule of life consists in mercy and godliness. Let a man follow this, and though he should suffer from the inconstancy of the flesh, without doubt he will be scourged, but he will not perish: whereas he who can boast of no other exercise but that of the body will suffer everlasting punishment.* Therefore, those who persevere in works of mercy, though they be shackled with fleshly sins, will not be punished eternally: and thus the same conclusion follows as before.

ON THE CONTRARY, It is written: *neither fornicators nor adulterers shall possess the kingdom of God* (1 Cor 6:9–10). Yet many are such who practice works of mercy. Therefore, the merciful will not all come to the eternal kingdom: and consequently some of them will be punished eternally.

FURTHER, It is written: *whosoever shall keep the whole law, but offend in one point, is become guilty of all* (Jas 2:10). Therefore, whoever keeps the law as regards the works of mercy, and omits other works, is guilty of transgressing the law, and consequently will be punished eternally.

I ANSWER THAT, As Augustine says in the book quoted above (*The City of God* 21.22), some have maintained that not all who have professed the Catholic faith will be freed from eternal punishment, but only those who persevere in works of mercy, although they be guilty of other crimes. But this cannot stand, because without charity nothing can be acceptable to God, nor does anything profit unto eternal life in the absence of charity. Now it happens that certain persons persevere in works of mercy without having charity. Therefore, nothing profits them to the meriting of eternal life or to exemption from eternal punishment, as may be gathered from 1 Corinthians 13:3. Most evident is this in the case of those who lay hands on other people's property, for, after seizing on many things, they nevertheless spend something in works of mercy.

We must therefore conclude that if anyone should die in mortal sin, neither faith nor works of mercy will free him from eternal punishment, not even after any length of time whatever.

REPLY OBJ. 1: Those will obtain mercy who show mercy in an ordinate manner. But those who, while merciful to others, are neglectful of themselves do not show mercy ordinately; rather do they strike at themselves by their evil actions. Wherefore such persons will not obtain the mercy that sets free altogether, even if they obtain that mercy which rebates somewhat their due punishment.

REPLY OBJ. 2: The reason why the discussion refers only to the works of mercy is not because eternal punishment will be inflicted on none but those who omit those works, but because eternal punishment will be remitted to

peccata qui per opera misericordiae sibi veniam impetraverunt, *facientes amicos sibi de mammona iniquitatis.*

AD TERTIUM dicendum quod illud a Domino dicitur his qui petunt sibi debitum relaxari: non illis qui in peccato persistunt. Et ideo soli poenitentes per opera misericordiae consequentur misericordiam iam penitus liberantem.

AD QUARTUM dicendum quod Glossa Ambrosii loquitur de lubrico venialis peccati, a quo aliquis post purgatorias poenas, quas vapulationem dicit, per opera misericordiae absolvetur.

Vel, si loquatur de lubrico mortalis peccati, est intelligendum quantum ad hoc quod, adhuc in vita ista existentes, illi qui ex fragilitate in carnalia peccata incidunt, per opera misericordiae ad poenitentiam disponuntur. Unde talis *non peribit*: idest, disponetur per talia opera ad non pereundum.

those who, after sinning, have obtained forgiveness by their works of mercy, *making unto themselves friends of the mammon of iniquity* (Luke 16:9).

REPLY OBJ. 3: Our Lord said this to those who ask that their debt be forgiven, but not to those who persist in sin. Wherefore the repentant alone will obtain by their works of mercy the forgiveness that sets them free altogether.

REPLY OBJ. 4: The Gloss of Ambrose speaks of the inconstancy that consists in venial sin, from which a man will be freed through the works of mercy after the punishment of purgatory, which he calls a scourging.

Or, if he speaks of the inconstancy of mortal sin, the sense is that those who while yet in this life fall into sins of the flesh through frailty are disposed to repentance by works of mercy. Wherefore such a one *will not perish*, that is to say, he will be disposed by those works not to perish.

Appendix 1

Purgatory

Circa Purgatorium quaeruntur octo.

Primo: utrum sit purgatorium post hanc vitam.

Secundo: utrum sit idem locus quo animae purgantur, et quo damnati puniuntur.

Tertio: utrum poena purgatorii excedat omnem poenam temporalem huius vitae.

Quarto: utrum illa poena sit voluntaria.

Quinto: utrum animae in purgatorio per daemones puniantur.

Sexto: utrum per poenam purgatorii expietur peccatum veniale quoad culpam.

Septimo: utrum ignis purgatorius liberet a reatu poenae.

Octavo: utrum ab illa poena unus liberetur alio citius.

Concerning purgatory, we must ask about eight things:

(1) Whether there is a purgatory after this life.

(2) Whether souls are purified and the damned are punished in the same place.

(3) Whether the suffering of purgatory exceeds all the temporal punishment of this life.

(4) Whether that suffering is voluntary.

(5) Whether souls in purgatory are punished by demons.

(6) Whether venial sin is expiated as to its guilt by the suffering of purgatory.

(7) Whether purgatorial fire delivers from the debt of punishment.

(8) Whether one person is freed from that suffering more quickly than another.

Article 1

Whether There is a Purgatory After This Life?

Ad primum sic proceditur. Videtur quod purgatorium non sit post hanc vitam. Apoc. 14, [13] dicitur: *beati mortui qui in Domino moriuntur. Amodo iam, dicit Spiritus, ut requiescant a laboribus suis.* Ergo his qui in Domino moriuntur non manet aliquis purgatorius labor post hanc vitam. Nec illis qui non in Domino moriuntur: quia illi purgari non possunt. Ergo purgatorium post hanc vitam non est.

Praeterea, sicut se habet caritas ad praemium aeternum, ita peccatum mortale ad supplicium aeternum. Sed decedentes in peccato mortali statim ad supplicium aeternum deportantur. Ergo decedentes in caritate statim ad praemium vadunt. Et ita non manet eis aliquod purgatorium post hanc vitam.

Praeterea, Deus, qui est summe misericors, pronior est ad praemiandum bona quam ad puniendum mala. Sed, sicut illi qui sunt in statu caritatis, faciunt aliqua mala quae non sunt digna supplicio aeterno, ita illi qui sunt in peccato mortali, interdum faciunt aliqua bona ex genere, quae non sunt digna praemio aeterno. Ergo, cum illa bona non praemientur in damnandis post hanc vitam, nec illa mala debent post hanc vitam puniri. Et sic idem quod prius.

Sed contra: II Machab. 12, [46] dicitur: *sancta et salubris est cogitatio pro defunctis exorare ut a peccatis*

Obj. 1: It seems that there is no purgatory after this life. For it says in Revelation 14:13, *blessed are the dead who die in the Lord. From now on the Spirit says that they may rest from their labors.* Therefore, for those who die in the Lord, no purgatorial labor remains after this life; neither for those who do not die in the Lord: for they cannot be purified. Therefore, there is no purgatory after this life.

Obj. 2: Further, charity is related to the eternal reward as mortal sin is to the eternal punishment. But those who die in mortal sin are carried off to eternal punishment immediately. Therefore, those who die in charity go immediately to their reward. And then no purgatory remains to them after this life.

Obj. 3: Further, God, who is consummately merciful, tends more to reward good deeds than to punish bad ones. But just as those who are in the state of charity do commit certain bad deeds that are not deserving of eternal punishment, so too those who are in mortal sin sometimes do things that are good in their genus which are not deserving of the eternal reward. Therefore, since those good deeds are not rewarded in the damned after this life, neither should those bad deeds be punished after this life. And so the same as before.

On the contrary, 2 Maccabees 12:46 says: *it is a holy and wholesome thought to pray for the dead that they might*

solvantur. Sed pro defunctis qui sunt in paradiso, non est orandum: quia illi nullo indigent. Nec iterum pro illis qui sunt in inferno: quia illi a peccatis solvi non possunt. Ergo post hanc vitam sunt aliqui a peccatis nondum absoluti qui solvi possunt. Et tales caritatem habent, sine qua non fit peccatorum remissio: quia *universa delicta operit caritas*, Prov. 10, [12]. Unde ad mortem aeternam non devenient: quia *qui vivit et credit in me, non morietur in aeternum*, Ioan. 11, [26]. Nec ad gloriam inducentur nisi purgati: quia nihil immundum ad illam perveniet, ut patet Apoc. Ergo aliqua purgatio restat post hanc vitam.

Praeterea, Gregorius Nyssenus dicit: *si aliquis Christo amico consentiens in hac vita purgare peccata minus potuerit, post transitum hinc, per purgatorii ignis conflationem expeditur*. Ergo post hanc vitam restat aliqua purgatio.

Respondeo dicendum quod ex illis quae supra determinata sunt, satis potest constare purgatorium esse post hanc vitam. Si enim, per contritionem deleta culpa, non tollitur ex toto reatus poenae; nec etiam semper venialia, dimissis mortalibus, tolluntur; et iustitia Dei hoc exigit ut peccatum per poenam debitam ordinetur: oportet quod ille qui post contritionem de peccato decedit et absolutionem, ante satisfactionem debitam, quod post hanc vitam puniatur.

Et ideo illi qui purgatorium negant, contra divinam iustitiam loquuntur. Et propter hoc erroneum est, et a fide alienum. Unde Gregorius Nyssenus post praedicta verba subiungit: *hoc praedicamus dogma veritatis servantes, et ita credimus*.

Hoc etiam universalis Ecclesia tenet, *pro defunctis exorans ut a peccatis solvantur*: quod non potest nisi de illis qui sunt in purgatorio intelligi. Ecclesiae autem auctoritati quicumque resistit, haeresim incurrit.

Ad primum ergo dicendum quod auctoritas illa loquitur de labore operationis ad merendum, et non de labore passionis ad purgandum.

Ad secundum dicendum quod malum non habet causam perfectam, sed *ex singularibus defectibus contingit*: sed *bonum ex una causa perfecta consurgit*, ut Dionysius dicit. Et ideo quilibet defectus impedit a perfectione boni, sed non quodlibet bonum impedit consummationem aliquam mali: quia nunquam est malum sine aliquo bono. Et ideo peccatum veniale impedit habentem caritatem ne ad perfectum bonum deveniat, scilicet vitam aeternam, quandiu purgatur. Sed peccatum mortale non potest impediri per aliquod bonum adiunctum quominus statim ad ultimum malorum perducat.

Ad tertium dicendum quod ille qui in peccatum mortale incidit, omnia bona ante acta mortificat, et quae in peccato mortali existens facit, mortua sunt: quia ipse, Deum offendens, omnia bona meretur amittere, quae a

be loosed from their sins. But no one needs to pray for the dead who are in paradise, for they lack nothing. Nor again for those who are in hell, for they cannot be released from their sins. Therefore, after this life there are some who can be released from their sins, who have not been yet. And such people have charity, without which the remission of sins does not happen: for *charity covers all sins* (Prov 10:12). Therefore, they do not come to eternal death, for *whoever lives and believes in me shall never die* (John 11:26). Nor will they be admitted into glory unless they are purified, for nothing unclean shall arrive there, as is clear from the book of Revelation. Therefore, some purgatory remains after this life.

Further, Gregory of Nyssa says: *if anyone consenting to Christ as his friend was able to purify his sins less in this life, after his passing from here the fire of purgatory will be enkindled*. Therefore, after this life a certain purgation remains.

I answer that, From the things that have been determined above, it is clear enough that there is a purgatory after this life. For, if after guilt is effaced through contrition, the debt of punishment is not entirely taken away, nor are venial sins always taken away when mortal ones are forgiven, and God's justice requires that sin be ordered by the due punishment, a person who dies after contrition and absolution for sin but before making the due satisfaction must be punished after this life.

And therefore those who deny purgatory are speaking against divine justice. And because of this, it is erroneous and contrary to the faith. Therefore, Gregory of Nyssa adds after the words quoted, *we preach this, preserving the dogma of truth, and so we believe*.

The universal Church also holds this when it prays for the dead that they be released from their sins, which can only be understood about those who are in purgatory. Now anyone who opposes the Church's authority incurs heresy.

Reply Obj. 1: That authority is speaking about the labor of working for meriting and not meriting, and not about the labor of suffering for purification.

Reply Obj. 2: Evil does not have a complete cause, but *comes about from particular defects*, whereas *good arises from one complete cause*, as Dionysius says. And so any defect prevents the perfection of the good, but not any good would prevent some consummation of an evil, for there is never an evil without some good. And therefore venial sin prevents someone who has charity from reaching the perfect good, namely, eternal life, until he is purified. But mortal sin cannot be prevented by having some good attached to it, so that it would lead less directly to the last of evils.

Reply Obj. 3: The person who falls into mortal sin puts to death all his previous good acts, and those that he does while remaining in mortal sin are dead. For he who offends God deserves to lose all the goods that he has from God.

Deo habet. Unde ei qui in peccato mortali decedit, non manet aliquod praemium post hanc vitam: sicut manet aliquando poena ei qui in caritate decedit, quae non semper delet omne malum quod invenit, sed solum hoc quod est sibi contrarium.

Consequently, no reward remains after this life for someone who dies in mortal sin, the way that sometimes punishment remains for one who dies in charity, which does not always blot out every evil that it encounters, but only what is contrary to itself.

Article 2

Whether the Place Where Souls Are Purified is the Same as Where the Damned are Punished?

AD SECUNDUM SIC PROCEDITUR. Videtur quod non sit idem locus quo animae purgantur, et quo damnati puniuntur. Quia poena damnatorum est aeterna: ut dicitur Matth. 25, [46]: *ibunt hi in ignem aeternum.* Sed purgatorius ignis est temporalis: ut supra Magister dixit. Ergo non simul puniuntur hi et illi eodem igne. Et sic oportet loca esse distincta.

PRAETEREA, poena inferni nominatur pluribus nominibus: ut in Psalmo [10, 7], *ignis, sulphur et spiritus procellarum*, etc. Sed poena purgatorii non nisi uno nomine nominatur, scilicet *ignis.* Ergo non eodem igne et eodem loco puniuntur.

PRAETEREA, Hugo de S. Victore dicit: *probabile est quod in his locis puniuntur in quibus commiserunt culpam.* Gregorius etiam, in *Dialogis*, narrat quod Germanus, episcopus Capuanus, Paschasium, qui in balneis purgabatur, invenit. Ergo in loco inferni non purgantur, sed in hoc mundo.

SED CONTRA: Est quod Gregorius dicit, quod, *sicut sub eodem igne aurum rutilat et palea fumat, ita sub eodem igne peccator crematur et electus purgatur.* Ergo idem est ignis purgatorii et inferni. Et sic in eodem loco sunt.

PRAETEREA, sancti patres ante adventum Christi fuerunt in loco digniori quam sit locus in quo nunc purgantur animae post mortem: quia non erat ibi aliqua poena sensibilis. Sed locus ille erat coniunctus inferno, vel idem quod infernus: alias Christus, ad limbum descendens, non diceretur *ad inferos* descendisse. Ergo et purgatorium est in eodem loco, vel iuxta infernum.

RESPONDEO dicendum quod de loco purgatorii non invenitur aliquid expresse determinatum in Scriptura, nec rationes possunt ad hoc efficaces induci. Tamen probabiliter, et secundum quod consonat magis Sanctorum dictis et revelationi factae multis, locus purgatorii est duplex. Unus secundum legem communem. Et sic locus purgatorii est locus inferior inferno coniunctus, ita quod idem ignis sit qui damnatos cruciat in inferno, et qui iustos in purgatorio purgat: quamvis damnati, secundum quod sunt inferiores merito, et loco inferiores ordinandi sint. Alius est locus purgatorii secundum dispensationem. Et sic quandoque in diversis locis aliqui puniti

OBJ. 1: It seems that the place where souls are purified is not the same as where the damned are punished. For the punishment of the damned is eternal, as is clear in Matthew 25:46: *these will go into everlasting fire.* But purgatory is a temporal fire, as the Master said above. Therefore, both cannot be punished together in the same fire, and so it is necessary that there be different places.

OBJ. 2: Further, the punishment of hell is named by many names, as it says in Psalm 11:6: *fire, brimstone, and storms of winds*, etc. But the punishment of purgatory is only named with one name, namely, *fire.* Therefore, they are not punished in the same fire and in the same place.

OBJ. 3: Further, Hugh of St. Victor says: *it is probable they are punished in the places where they incurred guilt.* Gregory also tells in his *Dialogues* that bishop Germanus of Capua found Paschasius being purified in the baths. Therefore, they are not purified in hell, but in this world.

ON THE CONTRARY, Gregory says that *just as in the same fire gold is reddened while chaff turns to smoke, so in the same fire a sinner reduced to ashes while one of the elect is purified.* Therefore, the fire of purgatory and of hell is the same, and thus they are in the same place.

FURTHER, Before the coming of Christ the holy patriarchs were in a worthier place than the place where the souls are purified after death, for there was no sensible pain there. But that place was either the same as hell or attached to it, otherwise Christ would not be said to have descended *into hell* when he descended to limbo. Therefore, purgatory is in the same place as, or connected with, hell.

I ANSWER THAT, Concerning purgatory's location nothing specific is expressly found in Scripture, nor can one offer effective arguments about it. Yet probably, and according to what agrees most with the words of the saints and the revelation made to many, there are two places for purgatory. One is according to the common law. And in this purgatory's location is a lower place, connected with hell, so that it is the same fire that torments the damned in hell and purifies the just in purgatory; although the damned, as lower in merit, are also relegated to a lower place. The other is the place for purgatory by special dispensation; and this is why it is read sometimes that certain people are punished

leguntur: vel ad vivorum instructionem; vel ad mortuorum subventionem, ut viventibus eorum poena innotescens per suffragia Ecclesiae mitigaretur.

Quidam tamen dicunt quod secundum legem communem locus purgatorii est ubi homo peccat. Quod non videtur probabile: quia simul potest homo puniri pro peccatis quae in diversis locis commisit.

Quidam vero dicunt quod puniuntur supra nos secundum legem communem: quia sunt medii inter nos et Deum quantum ad statum. Sed hoc nihil est. Quia non puniuntur pro eo quod supra nos sunt: sed pro eo quod est infimum in eis, scilicet peccatum.

AD PRIMUM ergo dicendum quod ignis purgatorius est aeternus quantum ad substantiam, sed temporalis quantum ad effectum purgationis.

AD SECUNDUM dicendum quod poena inferni est ad affligendum: et ideo nominatur ab omnibus illis quae hic nos affligere consueverunt. Sed poena purgatorii est principaliter ad purgandum reliquias peccati. Et ideo sola poena ignis purgatorio attribuitur: quia ignis habet purgare et consumere.

AD TERTIUM dicendum quod ratio illa procedit secundum dispensationem, et non secundum legem communem.

in different places, whether for the instruction of the living, or for the aid of the dead, so that by making their suffering known to the living, it might be reduced through the Church's intercession.

However, some people say that according to the common law purgatory's place is wherever a man sins. But this does not seem probable, since a man can be punished at the same time for sins that he committed in different places.

But other people say that they are punished above us according to the common law, for they are in a middle place between us and God according to their state. But there is nothing in this, for they are not punished for being above us, but for what is lowest in them, namely, sin.

REPLY OBJ. 1: The fire of purgatory is eternal as to its substance, but temporal as to the effect of purification.

REPLY OBJ. 2: The suffering of hell exists for the sake of affliction, and so it is named from all those things that usually afflict us here. But the suffering of purgatory is chiefly for purifying the traces of sin, and this is why only the suffering of fire is attributed to purgatory, because fire has the capacity to purify and consume.

REPLY OBJ. 3: That argument proceeds according to a special dispensation, and not according to the common law.

Article 3

Whether the Punishment of Purgatory Exceeds All Temporal Suffering of This Life?

AD TERTIUM SIC PROCEDITUR. Videtur quod poena purgatorii non excedat omnem poenam temporalem huius vitae. Quanto enim aliquid est magis passivum, tanto magis affligitur, si *sensum laesionis* habeat. Sed corpus est magis passivum quam anima separata: tum quia habet contrarietatem ad ignem agentem; tum quia habet materiam quae est susceptiva qualitatis agentis, quod de anima non potest dici. Ergo maior est poena quam corpus patitur in hoc mundo, quam poena qua anima purgatur post hanc vitam.

PRAETEREA, poena purgatorii directe ordinatur contra venialia. Sed venialibus, cum sint levissima peccata, levissima poena debetur, si *secundum mensuram delicti sit plagarum modus*. Ergo poena purgatorii est levissima.

PRAETEREA, reatus, cum sit effectus culpae, non intenditur nisi culpa intendatur; Sed in illo cui iam culpa dimissa est, non potest culpa intendi. Ergo in eo cui culpa mortalis dimissa est pro qua non plene satisfecit, reatus non crescit in morte. Sed in hac vita non erat ei reatus respectu gravissimae poenae. Ergo poena quam patietur

OBJ. 1: It seems that the suffering of purgatory does not exceed all the temporal suffering of this life. For the more something is passive, the more it is afflicted if it has *the sensation of injury*. But a body is more susceptible to being acted upon than a separated soul, both because it has a contrariety to the fire acting on it, and because it has matter that is susceptible to a quality acting on it, which cannot be said about a soul. Therefore, the pain that a body suffers in this world is greater than the suffering by which a soul is purified after this life.

OBJ. 2: Further, the suffering of purgatory is directly ordered against venial sin. But venial sins, since they are the lightest of sins, should have the lightest punishment, if *the number of lashes are according to the measure of the offense* (Deut 25:2). Therefore, the suffering of purgatory is very light.

OBJ. 3: Further, liability to punishment, since it is an effect of guilt, is not intensified unless the guilt is intensified. But in someone whose guilt is already forgiven, guilt cannot be intensified. Therefore, when someone has been forgiven for a mortal sin yet has not made full satisfaction for it, his liability to punishment does not grow after he has died. But

post hanc vitam, non erit ei gravior omni poena istius vitae.

SED CONTRA: Est quod Augustinus dicit, in quodam Sermone: *ille ignis purgatorii durior erit quam quidquid in hoc saeculo poenarum qui sentire aut videre aut cogitare quis potest.*

PRAETEREA, quanto poena est universalior, tanto maior. Sed anima separata tota punitur: cum sit simplex. Non autem ita est de corpore. Ergo illa poena quae est animae separatae, est maior omni poena quam corpus patitur.

RESPONDEO dicendum quod in purgatorio erit duplex poena: una damni, inquantum scilicet retardantur a divina visione; alias sensus, secundum quod ab igne corporali punientur; et quantum ad utrumque poena purgatorii minima excedit maximam poenam huius vitae.

Quanto enim aliquid magis desideratur, tanto eius absentia est molestior. Et quia affectus quo desideratur summum bonum, post hanc vitam in animabus sanctis est intensissimus, quia non retardatur affectus mole corporis; et etiam quia terminus fruendi summo bono iam advenisset nisi aliquid impediret; ideo de tardatione maxime dolent.

Similiter etiam, cum dolor non sit laesio, sed *laesionis sensus*, tanto aliquid magis dolet de aliquo laesivo, quanto magis est sensitivum: unde laesiones quae fiunt, in locis maxime sensibilibus, sunt maximum dolorem causantes. Et quia totus sensus corporis est ab anima, ideo, si in ipsam animam aliquod laesivum agat, de necessitate oportet quod maxime affligatur. Quod autem anima ab igne corporali patiatur, hoc ad praesens supponimus: quia de hoc infra, dist. 44, dicetur. Et ideo oportet quod poena purgatorii, quantum ad poenam damni et sensus, excedat omnem poenam istius vitae.

Quidam autem assignant rationem ex hoc quod anima tota punitur, non autem corpus. Sed hoc nihil est. Quia sic poena damnatorum esset minor post resurrectionem quam ante. Quod falsum est.

AD PRIMUM ergo dicendum quod, quamvis anima sit minus passiva quam corpus, tamen est magis cognoscitiva passionis. Et ubi est maior passionis sensus, ibi est maior dolor, etiam si sit minor passio.

AD SECUNDUM dicendum quod acerbitas illius poenae non est tantum ex quantitate peccati, quantum ex dispositione puniti: quia idem peccatum gravius punitur ibi quam hic. Sicut ille qui est melioris complexionis, magis punitur, eisdem plagis impositis, quam alius: et tamen iudex utrique easdem plagas pro eisdem culpis inferens iuste facit.

in this life he was not liable to punishment with respect to the worst punishment. Therefore, the punishment that he will suffer after this life will not be worse than every suffering of this life.

ON THE CONTRARY, Augustine says in one of his sermons: *that fire of purgatory will be harsher than anything one can feel or see or think in this world of punishments.*

FURTHER, The more universal a punishment is, the greater it is. But the whole separated soul is punished, since it is simple; but it is not so with the body. Therefore, that suffering that belongs to the separated soul is greater than every suffering that the body suffers.

I ANSWER THAT, In purgatory there are two punishments: one of loss, namely, inasmuch as souls are held back from the divine vision; the other, of sense, according as they are physically punished by fire. And in both, the least punishment of purgatory exceeds the greatest punishment of this life.

For the more something is desired, the more troubling is its absence. And because the affection by which the highest good is desired in holy souls after this life is the most intense, since the affection is not held back by the weight of the body, and since the enjoyment of the highest good would have been attained by then had nothing impeded it, they suffer extremely from this detainment.

Similarly, because sorrow is not so much due to an injury but to *the sensation of the injury*, the more sensitive someone is, the more he suffers from anything harmful, which is why the injuries that happen in the most sensitive places are the most painful. And since all the sensation of the body is from the soul, for this reason if anything injurious is at work in the soul itself, it necessarily must be most afflicted. Now for the moment we will suppose that the soul suffers from a physical fire (Cf. Q. 70, A. 3; *Sentences* Dist. 44). And therefore the punishment of purgatory in the suffering of loss and of sense exceeds every punishment of this life.

However, some people argue this conclusion from the fact that the whole soul is punished without the body. But there is nothing in this, for then the punishment of the damned would be less after the resurrection than before, which is false.

REPLY OBJ. 1: Although the soul is less susceptible to harm than the body, nevertheless it is more aware of suffering. And where there is greater sense of suffering there is greater pain, even if there is less harm.

REPLY OBJ. 2: The severity of that punishment is not so much from the amount of sin as from the disposition of the one punished, for the same sin is punished more heavily there than here; just as someone who has a finer complexion is punished more than another by the same lashes inflicted, and yet the judge, imposing the same number of lashes on both for the same faults, acts justly.

ET PER HOC etiam patet solutio ad tertium.

THIS SUFFICES for the reply to the third objection.

Article 4

Whether That Suffering is Voluntary?

AD QUARTUM SIC PROCEDITUR. Videtur quod illa poena sit voluntaria. Quia illi qui sunt in purgatorio, rectum cor habent. Sed haec est rectitudo cordis, ut quis voluntatem suam voluntati divinae conformet, ut Augustinus dicit. Ergo, cum Deus velit eos puniri, ipsi illam poenam voluntarie sustinent.

PRAETEREA, omnis sapiens vult illud sine quo non potest pervenire ad finem intentum. Sed illi qui sunt in purgatorio, sciunt se non posse pervenire ad gloriam nisi prius puniantur. Ergo volunt puniri.

SED CONTRA, nullus petit liberari a poena quam voluntarie sustinet. Sed illi qui sunt in purgatorio, petunt liberari: sicut patet per multa quae in *Dialogo* narrantur. Ergo non sustinent illam poenam voluntarie.

RESPONDEO dicendum quod aliquid dicitur voluntarium dupliciter. Uno modo, voluntate absoluta. Et sic nulla poena est voluntaria: quia ex hoc est ratio poenae quod voluntati contrariatur.

Alio modo dicitur aliquid voluntarium voluntate conditionata: sicut ustio est voluntaria propter sanitatem consequendam. Et sic aliqua poena potest esse voluntaria dupliciter. Uno modo quia per poenam aliquod bonum acquirimus: et sic ipsa voluntas assumit poenam aliquam, ut patet in satisfactione. Vel etiam quia ille libenter eam accipit, et non vellet eam non esse: Sicut accidit in martyrio. Alio modo quia, quamvis per poenam nullum bonum nobis accrescat, tamen sine poena ad bonum pervenire non possumus: sicut patet de morte naturali. Et tunc voluntas non assumit poenam, et vellet ab ea liberari, sed eam supportat: et quantum ad hoc voluntaria dicitur. Et sic poena purgatorii est voluntaria.

Quidam autem dicunt quod non est aliquo modo voluntaria: quia sunt ita absorpti poenis quod nesciunt se per poenam purgari, sed putant se esse damnatos. Sed hoc est falsum. Quia, nisi scirent se liberandos, suffragia non peterent: quod frequenter faciunt.

ET PER HOC patet solutio ad obiecta.

OBJ. 1: It seems that that suffering is voluntary. For those who are in purgatory have upright hearts. But this is uprightness of heart, that someone conform his own will to the divine will, as Ambrose says. Therefore, since God wills to punish them, they voluntarily endure that punishment.

OBJ. 2: Further, every wise person wills whatever is necessary for attaining his intended end. But those who are in purgatory know that they cannot attain to glory unless they are first punished. Therefore, they will to be punished.

ON THE CONTRARY, No one begs to be freed from suffering that he willingly endures. But those who are in purgatory beg to be freed, as is clear from many things that are told in the *Dialogues*. Therefore, they do not endure that suffering willingly.

I ANSWER THAT, Something is called voluntary in two ways. In one way, by an absolute will, and then no punishment is voluntary, for by the very nature of punishment it is contrary to the will.

In another way, something is said to be voluntary by a conditional will, as burning is voluntary because of the health that will result; and in this way a punishment can be voluntary in two ways. In one way, because by this punishment we acquire some good, and so the will itself takes on a punishment, as is seen in the case of satisfaction; or also because someone accepts it willingly, and he did not wish it to be, as happens in martyrdom. In the other way, because although no good accrues to us by the punishment, nevertheless we cannot attain the good without the punishment, as is seen in the case of natural death. And then the will does not take on the punishment but wishes to be freed from it; and yet the will endures it, and for this it is said to be 'voluntary.' And this is how the punishment of purgatory is voluntary.

Now some people say that it is not voluntary in any way, for the souls are so absorbed by their sufferings that they do not know they are being purified by them, but they believe themselves to be damned. But this is false: for unless they knew they would be freed, they would not beg for prayers, which they often do.

AND BY THIS the answers to the objections are clear.

Article 5

Whether Souls in Purgatory Are Punished by Demons?

AD QUINTUM SIC PROCEDITUR. Videtur quod animae in purgatorio per daemones puniantur. Quia, sicut infra, dist. 47, dicit Magister, *illos habent tortores in poenis quos habuerunt incentores in culpa*. Sed daemones incitant ad culpam non solum mortalem, sed etiam venialem, quando aliud non possunt. Ergo etiam in purgatorio ipsi animas pro peccatis venialibus torquebunt.

PRAETEREA, purgatio a peccatis competit iustis et in hac vita et post hanc vitam. Sed in hac vita purgantur per poenas a diabolo inflictas: sicut patet de Iob. Ergo etiam post hanc vitam punientur a daemonibus purgandi.

SED CONTRA, iniustum est ut qui de aliquo triumphavit, ei subiiciatur post triumphum. Sed illi qui sunt in purgatorio, de daemonibus triumphaverunt, sine peccato mortali decedentes. Ergo non subiicientur eis puniendi per eos.

RESPONDEO dicendum quod, sicut post diem iudicii divina iustitia succendet ignem quo damnati in perpetuum punientur, ita etiam nunc sola iustitia divina electi post hanc vitam purgantur: non ministerio daemonum, quorum victores exstiterunt; nec ministerio angelorum, qui cives suos non tam vehementer affligerent. Sed tamen possibile est quod eos ad loca poenarum deducant. Et etiam ipsi daemones, qui de poenis hominum laetantur, eos comitantur et assistunt purgandis: tum ut de eorum poenis satientur; tum ut in eorum exitu a corpore aliquid suum ibi reperiant.

In hoc autem saeculo, quando adhuc locus pugnae est, puniuntur homines et a malis angelis, sicut ab hostibus, ut patet de Iob; et a bonis, sicut patet de Iacob, cuius nervus femoris, angelo percutiente, emarcuit. Et hoc etiam expresse Dionysius dicit, in 4 cap. *de Div. Nom.*, quod boni angeli interdum puniunt.

ET PER HOC patet solutio ad obiecta.

OBJ. 1: It seems that the souls in purgatory are punished by the demons. For as the Master says at the end of Distinction 47, *they will have as torturers in their punishments those who were their provokers in sin*. But the demons incite us not only to mortal sin, but also to venial sin, when they cannot do worse. Therefore, they also torture those souls who are in purgatory for venial sins.

OBJ. 2: Further, purification from sins applies to the just both in this life and after this life. But in this life they are purified through the sufferings inflicted by the devil, as is seen in the case of Job. Therefore, those to be purified after this life are also punished by demons.

ON THE CONTRARY, It is unjust that someone who has triumphed over another be subject to him after the triumph. But those who are in purgatory have triumphed over the demons by dying without mortal sin. Therefore, they are not subject to being punished by them.

I ANSWER THAT, Just as after the day of judgment divine justice will set a fire in which the damned will be punished for eternity, so also now the elect are purified after this life only by divine justice, not by the ministry of demons over whom they have arisen as victors, nor by the ministry of angels, for fellow citizens would not afflict their own so forcefully. But nevertheless it is possible that they lead them to places of suffering, and that even the demons themselves, who rejoice in the sufferings of men, accompany them and attend those to be purified, both so that they might be sated by their sufferings, and so that at their departure from the body, they might seize upon something of their own there.

But in this world, while it is still the place of battle, men are punished both by bad angels as enemies, as is seen in Job, and by good ones, as is seen in the case of Jacob, whose femoral nerve withered from the angel's striking it. And Dionysius also says explicitly in *On the Divine Names* 4 that good angels sometimes punish.

AND BY THIS the solutions to the objections are clear.

Article 6

Whether Venial Sin Is Expiated by the Suffering of Purgatory as to Guilt?

AD SEXTUM SIC PROCEDITUR. Videtur quod per poenam purgatorii non expietur peccatum veniale quoad culpam. Quia super illud I Ioan. 5, [16], *est peccatum ad mortem* etc., dicit Glossa: *quod in hac vita non corrigitur, frustra post mortem eius venia postulatur*. Ergo nullum peccatum post hanc vitam quoad culpam dimittitur.

OBJ. 1: It seems that by the punishment of purgatory venial sin is not expiated as to guilt. For commenting on 1 John 5:6: *there is a sin that is mortal*, etc., the interlinear Gloss says: *for what is not corrected in this life, forgiveness is sought in vain after death*. Therefore, no sin is remitted as to its guilt after this life.

PRAETEREA, eiusdem est labi in peccatum, et a peccato liberari. Sed anima post mortem non potest peccare venialiter. Ergo nec a peccato veniali absolvi.

PRAETEREA, Gregorius dicit quod talis in iudicio quisque futurus est, qualis de corpore exivit: quia *lignum ubi ceciderit, ibi erit*, Eccle. 11, [3]. Si ergo aliquis ex hac vita exit cum veniali, in iudicio cum veniali erit. Et ita per purgatorium non expiatur aliquis a culpa veniali.

PRAETEREA, supra dictum est quod culpa actualis non deletur nisi per contritionem. Sed post hanc vitam non erit contritio, quae est actus meritorius: quia tunc non erit meritum neque demeritum, cum, secundum Damascenum: *hoc est hominibus mors quod angelis casus*. Ergo post hanc vitam non dimittitur in purgatorio veniale quoad culpam.

PRAETEREA, veniale non est in nobis nisi ratione fomitis: unde in primo statu Adam venialiter non peccasset, ut in II libro, dist. 21, dictum est. Sed post hanc vitam in purgatorio non erit sensualitas, fomite corrupto, in anima separata: quia fomes dicitur *lex carnis*, Rom, 7, [18 sqq.]. Ergo non erit ibi venialis culpa. Et ita non potest expiari per purgatorium ignem.

SED CONTRA: Est quod Gregorius dicit, in IV *Dialog.*, et Augustinus, de Vera Poenitentia, quod quaedam culpae leves in futuro remittuntur. Nec potest intelligi quoad poenam: quia sic omnes culpae quantumcumque graves, quantum ad reatum poenae per ignem purgatorium expiantur. Ergo venialia quantum ad culpam purgantur per ignem purgatorium.

PRAETEREA, I Cor. 3, [12], per *lignum, fenum* et *stipulam*, ut dictum est, venialia intelliguntur. Sed lignum, fenum et stipula per purgatorium consumuntur. Ergo ipsae veniales culpae post hanc vitam remittuntur.

RESPONDEO dicendum quod quidam dixerunt quod post hanc vitam non dimittitur aliquod peccatum quoad culpam. Et si cum mortali culpa quis decedat, damnatur, et remissionis capax non est. Non autem potest esse quod cum veniali decedat sine mortali: quia ipsa, gratia finalis culpam purgat venialem. Veniale enim peccatum contingit ex hoc quod aliquis, Christum habens in fundamento, nimis aliquod temporale diligit. Qui quidem excessus ex concupiscentiae corruptione contingit. Unde, si gratia omnino concupiscentiae corruptionem vincat, sicut in Beata Virgine fuit, non manet aliquis locus veniali. Et ita, cum in morte omnino diminuatur et annihiletur ista concupiscentia, potentiae animae totaliter gratiae subiicientur, et veniale expellitur.

Sed haec opinio frivola est et in se, et in causa sua. In se quidem, quia dictis Sanctorum et Evangelii adversatur. Quae non possunt exponi de remissione venialium quantum ad poenam, ut Magister in littera dicit: quia sic tam levia quam gravia in futuro dimittuntur; Grego-

OBJ. 2: Further, it is the same faculty that falls into sin and is freed from sin. But the soul cannot sin venially after death. Therefore, neither can it be absolved.

OBJ. 3: Further, Gregory says that everyone will be at the judgment as he left the body; *for where the tree falls, there it will lie* (Eccl 11:3). Therefore, if someone departed this life with venial sin, he will come to the judgment with venial sin, and so no one is expiated from fault by purgatory.

OBJ. 4: Further, it was said above that actual fault is not effaced by anything but contrition. But after this life there will be no contrition, which is a meritorious act, for then there will be neither merit nor demerit, since, according to Damascene, *as the fall was to the angels, so is death to humans*. Therefore, after this life no venial sin is forgiven as to its fault in purgatory.

OBJ. 5: Further, venial sin is only in us by reason of the *fomes*, which is why in the first state of man Adam would not have sinned venially (*Sentences* II, D. 21, Q. 2, A. 3). But after this life in purgatory there will be no sensuality provoked by corrupt *fomes* in the separated soul, for the *fomes* is called *the law of the flesh* (Rom 7:22). Therefore, there will be no venial sin there; and so it cannot be expiated by the fire of purgatory.

ON THE CONTRARY, There is what Gregory says in his *Dialogues* 4, and Augustine says in *On True Repentance*, that certain light faults are forgiven in the future. Nor can this be understood as referring to the punishment, for as to the debt of punishment, every fault, no matter how serious, is expiated by the fire of purgatory. Therefore, venial sins are purified by the fire of purgatory as to their guilt.

FURTHER, By *wood, hay*, and *straw*, venial sins are understood (Cf. 1 Cor 3:12). But wood, hay, and straw are consumed by purgatory. Therefore, venial sins themselves are remitted after this life.

I ANSWER THAT, Some people have said that after this life no sin is remitted as to its fault, and if someone dies with mortal sin, he is damned and has no capacity for forgiveness. But it cannot be that he died with venial sin without mortal sin, for the final grace itself purifies venial fault. For venial sin happens when someone who has Christ as a foundation loves something temporal too much, an excess that indeed happens from the corruption of concupiscence. Hence if grace entirely conquers the corruption of concupiscence, as was the case in the Blessed Virgin, there remains no room for venial sin. And so, since in death that concupiscence is entirely diminished and annihilated, the powers of the soul are completely subjected to grace, and venial sin is expelled.

But this opinion is worthless both in itself and in its cause. In itself, indeed, because it is contrary to the statements of the saints and the Gospel, which cannot be explained about the remission of venial sins as to punishment, as the Master says in the text; for then both light and serious

rius autem leves culpas tantum post hanc vitam remitti perhibet. Nec sufficit quod dicunt, quod hoc dicitur specialiter de levibus, ne putetur nihil grave pro eis nos passuros: quia remissio poenae magis aufert gravitatem poenarum quam ponat.

Quantum ad causam autem frivola apparet, quia defectus corporalis, qualis est in ultimo vitae, non aufert concupiscentiae corruptionem vel diminuit quantum ad radicem, sed quantum ad actum: sicut patet etiam de illis qui graviter infirmantur. Nec iterum tranquillat potentias animae, ut eas gratiae subiiciat: quia tranquillitas potentiarum, et subiectio earum ad gratiam, est quando inferiores vires obediunt superioribus, quae *legi Dei condelectantur*; quod in statu illo esse non potest, cum actus utrarumque impediatur; nisi tranquillitas dicatur privatio pugnae, sicut in dormientibus accidit. Nec tamen propter hoc somnus dicitur concupiscentiam diminuere, aut vires animae tranquillare, aut eas gratiae subdere.

Et praeterea, dato quod concupiscentiam radicaliter diminueret defectus ille et vires animae subderet gratiae, adhuc hoc non sufficeret ad purgationem culpae venialis iam commissae, quamvis sufficeret ad vitationem futurae: quia culpa actualis, etiam venialis, non dimittitur sine actuali contritionis motu, ut supra, dist. 17, dictum est, quantumcumque habitualiter intendatur. Contingit autem quandoque quod aliquis dormiens moritur, in gratia existens, qui cum veniali aliquo obdormivit: et talis non potest actum contritionis habere de veniali ante mortem. Non potest dici, ut dicunt, quod, si non poenituit actu vel proposito, in generali vel speciali, quod sit versum in mortale, propter hoc quod *veniale fit mortale dum placet*: quia non quaelibet placentia venialis facit peccatum mortale, alias omne veniale esset mortale, quia quodlibet veniale placet. Cum sit voluntarium; sed talis placentia quae ad fruitionem spectat, in qua *omnis humana perversitas consistit*, dum *rebus utendis fruimur*, ut Augustinus dicit. Et sic placentia illa quae facit peccatum mortale, est actualis placentia: quia omne peccatum mortale in actu consistit. Potest autem contingere quod aliquis postquam veniale peccatum commisit, nihil actualiter cogitet de peccato vel dimittendo vel tenendo, sed cogitet forte quod triangulus habet tres angulos aequales duobus rectis, et in hac cogitatione obdormiat et moriatur. Unde patet quod haec opinio omnino irrationalis est.

Et ideo cum aliis dicendum quod culpa venialis in eo qui cum gratia decedit, post hanc vitam dimittitur per ignem purgatorium: quia poena illa, aliqualiter voluntaria, virtute gratiae habebit vim expiandi culpam omnem quae simul cum gratia stare potest.

sins would be forgiven in the future. But Gregory holds that light sins alone will be remitted after this life. Nor does it suffice that they say that here specifically light sins are spoken of, lest it be thought that we will suffer nothing serious for them, for the remission of punishment removes more gravity from the punishment than it brings.

Now as to this opinion's cause, its worthlessness is apparent, for bodily defect, such as there is at the end of life, does not remove or diminish the corruption of concupiscence as to its root, but as to its act, as is seen even in those who are extremely weakened. Nor again does it calm the powers of the soul, so that they are subject to grace, for the tranquillity of the powers and their subjection to grace is when the lower powers obey the higher ones that *delight in the law of God* (Rom 7:22); which cannot exist in that state, since the act of either one is impeded; unless tranquillity means the absence of fighting, as also happens in people sleeping. Nor, however, is sleep said to diminish concupiscence because of this, or to calm the powers of the soul, or to subdue them to grace.

And furthermore, if it were granted that that defect would radically diminish concupiscence, and the powers of the soul would be subject to grace, this would still not suffice for the purification of venial sin already committed, although it would suffice for its future avoidance; for actual fault, even venial, is not remitted without an actual movement of contrition, as was said above. Now it sometimes happens that someone dies in his sleep while in a state of grace, who fell asleep with some venial sin; and a person like this cannot have an act of contrition for venial sin before his death. Nor can it be said, as they say, that if he did not repent in act or intention in a general or specific way, it would be turned into mortal sin, because *venial sin becomes mortal when it pleases the one doing it*; for not just any pleasure makes a venial sin mortal (otherwise every venial sin would be mortal, for every venial sin pleases, since it is voluntary); but the kind of pleasure that has to do with the enjoyment *in which every human perversity consists*, when *we enjoy the things that should be used*, as Augustine says. And thus that pleasure that makes a mortal sin is actual pleasure, for every mortal sin consists in an act. However, it can happen that after someone has committed a venial sin, he thinks nothing actually about abandoning the sin or holding to it, but he thinks perhaps that a triangle has three angles equal to two right angles; and in this thought he falls asleep and dies. Therefore, it is clear that this opinion is entirely irrational.

And therefore it should be said with others that venial sin in someone who dies with grace is remitted after this life by the fire of purgatory, for that punishment, which is voluntary in a certain way, will have the power by virtue of grace of expiating every fault that can exist together with grace.

AD PRIMUM ergo dicendum quod Glossa loquitur de peccato mortali.

Vel dicendum quod, quamvis in hac vita non corrigatur in se, corrigitur tamen in merito: quia hic homo meruit ut ibi illa poena sit meritoria sibi.

AD SECUNDUM dicendum quod peccatum veniale contingit ex corruptione fomitis, qui in anima separata in purgatorio existente non erit. Et ideo non poterit peccare venialiter. Sed remissio culpae venialis est ex voluntate gratia informata, quae in purgatorio erit in anima separata. Et ideo non est simile.

AD TERTIUM dicendum quod venialia non variant statum hominis: quia neque tollunt neque deminuunt caritatem, secundum quam mensuratur quantitas gratuitae bonitatis animae. Et ideo per hoc quod venialia dimittuntur vel committuntur, talis manet anima qualis prius.

AD QUARTUM dicendum quod post hanc vitam non potest esse meritum respectu praemii essentialis. Sed respectu alicuius accidentalis potest esse, quandiu manet homo in statu viae aliquo modo. Et ideo in purgatorio potest esse actus meritorius quantum ad remissionem culpae venialis.

AD QUINTUM dicendum quod, quamvis veniale ex pronitate fomitis contingat, tamen culpa in mente consequitur. Et ideo, etiam destructo fomite, culpa adhuc manere potest.

REPLY OBJ. 1: The Gloss is speaking of mortal sin.

Or it could be said that, although it is not corrected in itself in this life, it is, however, corrected in merit, for a man has merited here so that there his suffering may be meritorious to him.

REPLY OBJ. 2: Venial sin happens from the corruption of the *fomes*, which will not exist in a separated soul existing in purgatory. And therefore it could not sin venially, but the remission of venial guilt is from the grace informing it, which will exist in purgatory in a separated soul; and therefore it is not the same.

REPLY OBJ. 3: Venial sins do not change the state of man, for they neither take away nor diminish charity, according as the amount of free goodness of the soul is measured. And therefore when venial sins are remitted, the soul remains as before.

REPLY OBJ. 4: After this life there cannot be merit with regard to the essential reward, but with regard to some extra reward there can be, as long as a person remains in the state of a wayfarer in some way. And therefore in purgatory there can be a meritorious act as to the remission of venial guilt.

REPLY OBJ. 5: Although venial sin happens from the tendency of the *fomes*, nevertheless guilt is contracted in the mind. And therefore, even once the *fomes* are destroyed, guilt still remains.

Article 7

Whether the Fire of Purgatory Delivers From the Debt of Punishment?

AD SEPTIMUM SIC PROCEDITUR. Videtur quod ignis purgatorius non liberet a reatu poenae. Omnis enim purgatio respicit foeditatem. Sed poena non importat aliquam foeditatem. Ergo ignis purgatorius non liberat a poena.

PRAETEREA, contrarium non purgatur nisi per suum contrarium. Sed poena non contrariatur poenae. Ergo per poenam purgatorii non purgatur aliquis a reatu poenae.

PRAETEREA, I Cor. 3, super illud [v. 15], *salvus erit sic tamen* etc., dicit Glossa: *ignis iste est tentatio tribulationis, de qua scriptum est: 'vasa figuli probat fornax'*, etc., Eccli. 27, [6]. Ergo homo expiatur ab omni poena per poenas huius mundi, saltem per mortem, quae est maxima poenarum; et non per purgatorium ignem.

SED CONTRA, poena purgatorii est gravior quam poena quaelibet huius mundi, ut supra dictum est. Sed per poenam satisfactoriam quam aliquis in hac vita su-

OBJ. 1: It would seem that the fire of purgatory does not deliver from the debt of punishment. For every cleansing is in respect of some uncleanness. But punishment does not imply uncleanness. Therefore, the fire of purgatory does not deliver from punishment.

OBJ. 2: Further, a contrary is not cleansed save by its contrary. But punishment is not contrary to punishment. Therefore, one is not cleansed from the debt of punishment by the punishment of purgatory.

OBJ. 3: Further, a gloss on 1 Corinthians 3:15: *He shall be saved, yet so*, says, *this fire is the trial of tribulation of which it is written, "the furnace tries the potter's vessels"* (Cf. Sirach 27:6). Therefore, man expiates every punishment by the pains of this world, at least by death, which is the greatest punishment of all, and not by the fire of purgatory.

ON THE CONTRARY, The pains of purgatory are more grievous than all the pains of this world, as stated above (A. 3). Now the satisfactory punishment which one under-

stinet, expiatur a debito poenae. Ergo multo fortius per poenam purgatorii.

Respondeo dicendum quod quicumque est debitor alicuius, per hoc a debito absolvitur quod debitum solvit. Et quia reatus nihil est aliud quam debitum poenae, per hoc quod aliquis poenam sustinet quam debebat, a reatu absolvitur. Et secundum hoc poena purgatorii a reatu purgat.

Ad primum ergo dicendum quod reatus, quamvis non importet foeditatem quantum in se est, tamen habet ordinem ad foeditatem ex causa sua.

Ad secundum dicendum quod poena, quamvis non contrarietur poenae, tamen contrariatur reatui ad poenam: quia ex hoc manet obligatio ad poenam, quod poenam non sustinuit, quam debebat.

Ad tertium dicendum quod in eisdem verbis sacrae Scripturae latet multiplex intellectus. Unde et ille *ignis* potest intelligi tribulatio praesens, vel poena sequens. Et per utramque venialia purgari possunt. Sed quod mors naturalis ad hoc non sufficiat, supra dictum est.

goes in this life atones for the debt of punishment. Much more, therefore, is this effected by the punishment of purgatory.

I answer that, Whosoever is another's debtor is freed from his indebtedness by paying the debt. And since the obligation incurred by guilt is nothing else than the debt of punishment, a person is freed from that obligation by undergoing the punishment which he owed. Accordingly, the punishment of purgatory cleanses from the debt of punishment.

Reply Obj. 1: Although the debt of punishment does not in itself imply uncleanness, it bears a relation to uncleanness by reason of its cause.

Reply Obj. 2: Although punishment is not contrary to punishment, it is opposed to the debt of punishment, because the obligation to punishment remains from the fact that one has not undergone the punishment that was due.

Reply Obj. 3: Many meanings underlie the same words of Sacred Scripture. Hence this fire may denote both the present tribulation and the punishment to come, and venial sins can be cleansed from both of these. That natural death is not sufficient for this has been stated above.

Article 8

Whether One Person Is Delivered From This Punishment Sooner Than Another?

Ad octavum sic proceditur. Videtur quod ab illa poena unus non liberetur alio citius. Quanto enim gravior est culpa et maior reatus, tanto acerbior poena imponitur in purgatorio. Sed quae est proportio poenae acerbioris ad culpam graviorem, eadem est proportio poenae levioris ad culpam leviorem. Ergo ita cito liberatur unus a poena illa sicut alius.

Praeterea, inaequalibus meritis redduntur aequales retributiones et in caelo et in inferno, quantum ad durationem. Ergo videtur esse similiter in purgatorio.

Sed contra est similitudo Apostoli, qui differentias venialium per *lignum, fenum* et *stipulam* significavit. Sed constat quod lignum diutius manet in igne quam fenum et stipula. Ergo unum peccatum veniale diutius punitur in purgatorio quam aliud.

Respondeo dicendum quod quaedam venialia sunt maioris adhaerentiae quam alia, secundum quod affectus magis ad ea inclinatur et fortius in eis figitur. Et quia ea quae sunt maioris adhaerentiae, tardius purgantur, ideo quidam in purgatorio diutius quam alii torquentur, secundum quod affectus eorum ad venialia fuit magis immersus.

Ad primum ergo dicendum quod acerbitas poenae proprie respondet quantitati culpae: sed diuturnitas re-

Obj. 1: It would seem that one person is not delivered from this punishment sooner than another. For the more grievous the sin, and the greater the debt, the more severely is it punished in purgatory. Now there is the same proportion between severer punishment and graver fault as between lighter punishment and less grievous fault. Therefore, one is delivered from this punishment as soon as another.

Obj. 2: Further, in point of duration unequal merits receive equal retribution both in heaven and in hell. Therefore, seemingly it is the same in purgatory.

On the contrary, There is the comparison of the Apostle, who denotes the differences of venial sins by *wood, hay,* and *stubble.* Now it is clear that wood remains longer in the fire than hay and stubble. Therefore, one venial sin is punished longer in purgatory than another.

I answer that, Some venial sins cling more persistently than others, according as the affections are more inclined to them, and more firmly fixed in them. And since that which clings more persistently is more slowly cleansed, it follows that some are tormented in purgatory longer than others, for as much as their affections were steeped in venial sins.

Reply Obj. 1: Severity of punishment corresponds properly speaking to the amount of guilt: whereas the

spondet radicationi culpae in subiecto. Unde potest contingere quod aliquis diutius moretur qui minus affligitur, et e converso.

AD SECUNDUM dicendum quod peccatum mortale, cui debetur supplicium inferni, et caritas, cui debetur praemium paradisi, post hanc vitam radicantur immobiliter in subiecto. Et ideo quantum ad omnes est eadem diuturnitas utrobique. Secus autem est de peccato veniali, quod in purgatorio punitur, ut ex dictis patet.

length corresponds to the firmness with which sin has taken root in its subject. Hence it may happen that one may be delayed longer who is tormented less, and vice versa.

REPLY OBJ. 2: Mortal sin, which deserves the punishment of hell, and charity, which deserves the reward of heaven, will, after this life, be immovably rooted in their subject. Hence as to all there is the same duration in either case. It is otherwise with venial sin which is punished in purgatory, as stated above (A. 6).

APPENDIX 2

THE PUNISHMENT FOR ORIGINAL SIN

Circa hoc duo quaeruntur.

Primo: utrum peccato originali post mortem debeatur poena sensibilis in illis qui in originali tantum peccato decedunt.

Secundo: utrum aliquem interiorem dolorem sentiant in anima spiritualem qui pro peccato originali tantum puniuntur.

Concerning this we must ask about two things:

(1) Whether a sensible punishment is due to original sin after death among those who die in original sin.

(2) Whether those who are punished for original sin alone feel any interior spiritual sorrow in their souls.

Article 1

Whether a Sensible Punishment Is Due to Original Sin in Itself?

AD PRIMUM SIC PROCEDITUR. Videtur quod peccato originali secundum se debeatur poena sensibilis. Dicit enim Augustinus, *de Fide ad Petrum: firmissime tene, et nullatenus dubites, parvulos qui sine sacramento baptismatis de hoc saeculo transierunt, aeterno supplicio puniendos.* Sed *supplicium* poenam sensibilem nominat. Ergo parvuli, qui pro solo originali punientur, sensibilem poenam sustinebunt.

PRAETEREA, maiori culpae debetur maior poena. Sed originale est maius peccatum quam veniale: quia plus habet de aversione, eo quod gratiam subtrahit, veniale autem gratiam secum compatitur. Et iterum aeterna poena punitur originale: sed veniale temporali. Cum ergo veniali peccato debeatur poena sensibilis, multo amplius originali.

PRAETEREA, gravius puniuntur peccata post hanc vitam quam in vita ista, ubi est misericordiae locus. Sed in hac vita respondet originali poena sensibilis: pueri enim, qui solum originale habent, multas poenas sensibiles sustinent, nec iniuste. Ergo et post hanc vitam poena sensibilis sibi debetur.

PRAETEREA, sicut in peccato actuali est aversio et conversio, ita et in peccato originali aliquid aversioni respondet, scilicet privatio originalis iustitiae; et aliquid conversioni, scilicet concupiscentia. Sed peccato actuali ratione conversionis debetur poena sensibilis. Ergo et originali ratione concupiscentiae.

PRAETEREA, corpora puerorum post resurrectionem aut erunt passibilia, aut impassibilia. Si impassibilia; et nullum corpus humanum potest esse impassibile nisi vel per dotem impassibilitatis, sicut est in beatis, vel

OBJ. 1: It seems that a sensible punishment is due to original sin in itself. For Augustine says, *hold to this unshakeably, and have no doubt that children who pass away from this world without the sacrament of baptism will be punished in eternal suffering (De Fide ad Petrum Diaconum).* But *suffering* means sensible punishment. Therefore, children, who will be punished for original sin alone, will endure a sensible punishment.

OBJ. 2: Further, greater punishment is due to greater fault. But original sin is a greater sin than venial sin, for it contains more turning away from God by the fact that it removes grace, while venial sin can coexist with grace. And again, original sin is punished by eternal punishment, but venial sin by temporal punishment. Therefore, since sensible punishment is due to venial sin, much more is it due to original sin.

OBJ. 3: Further, sins are punished more severely after this life than in this life, where there is room for mercy. But in this life sensible punishment corresponds to original sin, for children who have only original sin endure many sensible sufferings, but not unjustly. Therefore, it is also due sensible suffering after this life.

OBJ. 4: Further, just as in actual sin there is a turning away from God and a turning toward something else, so too in original sin there is something that corresponds to the turning away, namely, the privation of original justice, and something that corresponds to the turning-toward, namely, concupiscence. But a sensible punishment is due to actual sin by reason of the turning-toward. Therefore, it is also owed to original sin by reason of concupiscence.

OBJ. 5: Further, the bodies of children after the resurrection are either possible or impassible. If impassible, since no human body can be impassible except by the gift of impassibility, as it is in the blessed, or by reason of original

ratione originalis iustitiae, sicut in statu innocentiae; ergo corpora puerorum vel habebunt dotem impassibilitatis, et sic gloriosa erunt, et non erit differentia inter pueros baptizatos et non baptizatos, quod est haereticum; vel originalem iustitiam habebunt, et sic originali peccato carebunt, nec pro peccato originali punientur, quod est similiter haereticum. Si autem sint passibilia; omne autem passibile de necessitate patitur activo praesente; ergo, praesentibus corporibus sensibilibus activis, sensibilem poenam patientur.

CONTRA, Augustinus dicit poenam parvulorum, qui originali tantum tenentur, *omnium esse mitissimam.* Sed hoc non esset si sensibili poena torquerentur: quia poena ignis inferni est gravissima. Ergo poenam sensibilem non sustinebunt.

PRAETEREA, acerbitas poenae sensibilis delectationi culpae respondet: Apoc. 18, [7]: *quantum glorificavit, se et in deliciis fuit,* etc. Sed in peccato originali non est aliqua delectatio, sicut nec operatio: delectatio enim operationem consequitur, ut ex X *Ethic.* patet. Ergo peccato originali non debetur poena sensibilis.

RESPONDEO dicendum quod poena debet esse proportionata culpae: ut dicitur Isaiae 27, [8]: *in mensura contra mensuram, cum abiecta fuerit, iudicabit eam.* Defectus autem qui per originem traducitur, rationem culpae habens, non est per subtractionem vel corruptionem alicuius boni quod naturam humanam consequitur ex principiis suis, sed per subtractionem vel corruptionem alicuius quod naturae superadditum erat: nec ista culpa ad hunc hominem pertinet nisi secundum quod talem naturam habet quae hoc bono, quod in eo natum erat esse et possibile conservari, destituta est. Et ideo nulla alia poena sibi debetur nisi privatio illius finis ad quem donum subtractum ordinabat, ad quod per se natura humana attingere non potest. Hoc autem est divina visio. Et ideo carentia huius visionis est propria et sola poena originalis peccati post mortem. Si enim alia poena sensibilis pro peccato originali post mortem infligeretur, puniretur iste non secundum hoc quod culpam habuit: quia poena sensibilis pertinet ad id quod personae proprium est, quia per passionem huius particularis talis poena est. Unde, sicut culpa non fuit per operationem eius, ita nec poena per passionem ipsius esse debet: sed solum per defectum illius ad quod natura de se insufficiens erat. In aliis autem perfectionibus et bonitatibus, quae naturam humanam consequuntur ex suis principiis, nullum detrimentum sustinebunt pro peccato originali damnati.

AD PRIMUM ergo dicendum quod *supplicium* non nominat in auctoritate illa poenam sensibilem, sed solum poenam damni, quae est carentia divinae visionis:

justice, as in the state of innocence: therefore, the bodies of children either will have the gift of impassibility and so they will be glorified, and there will be no difference between baptized and unbaptized children, which is heretical; or else they will have original justice, and then they will be without original sin, nor will they be punished for original sin, which is likewise heretical. But if they are passible, every passible thing necessarily suffers from the presence of anything active; therefore, they will suffer sensible pain from the presence of sensible bodies.

ON THE CONTRARY, Augustine says that the punishment of children who are bound only by original sin *is the slightest of all.* But this would not be the case if they were tormented with sensible punishment, for the punishment of the fires of hell is the most severe. Therefore, they will not endure sensible punishment.

FURTHER, The harshness of sensible punishment corresponds to pleasure in the fault: *as much as she glorified herself and dwelt in pleasures,* etc. (Rev 18:7). But there is no pleasure in original sin, just as there is no operating; for pleasure results from operation, as is evident from *Ethics* 10. Therefore, a sensible punishment is not due to original sin.

I ANSWER THAT, A punishment should be proportionate to guilt, as Isaiah 27:8 says: *in measure against measure, when it has been cast off, then he will judge it.* Now the defect that is contracted by original sin, having the account of guilt, is not by the removal or corruption of any good that human nature obtains by its own principles, but by the removal or corruption of something that was superadded to nature; nor does this guilt belong to this or that man except according as he possesses a nature like this, which is stripped of this good that ought to have been in him by nature and was possible to be preserved. And so no other punishment is owed to him except the privation of that end to which was ordered the gift that was withdrawn, an end that human nature cannot attain by itself. But this is the vision of God. And so the lack of this vision is the sole proper punishment of original sin after death. For if another sensible punishment were inflicted for original sin after death, a person would be punished not only according to his guilt, for sensible punishment pertains to what is proper to the person, since this punishment is through the suffering of this particular one. Therefore, just as his guilt was not through his own operating, so neither should the punishment be through his own suffering, but only by the absence of that for which his nature is insufficient of itself. Now in other perfections and goods that human nature possesses from its principles, the damned will suffer no detriment for original sin.

REPLY OBJ. 1: In the authority cited, *suffering* does not mean sensible punishment, but only the punishment of loss, which is the lack of the divine vision; as also the

sicut etiam nomine *ignis* frequenter in Scriptura quaelibet poena figurari consuevit.

AD SECUNDUM dicendum quod inter omnia peccata minimum est originale, eo quod minimum habet de voluntario: non enim est voluntarium voluntate istius personae, sed voluntate principii naturae tantum. Peccatum autem actuale, et etiam veniale, est voluntarium voluntate eius in quo est. Et ideo minor poena debetur originali quam veniali.

Nec obstat quod originale non compatitur secum gratiam. Privatio enim gratiae non habet rationem culpae, sed poenae, nisi inquantum ex voluntate est. Unde ubi minus est de voluntario, minus est de culpa.

Similiter etiam non obstat quod peccato actuali veniali temporalis poena debetur. Quia hoc est per accidens: inquantum decedens in veniali tantum, gratiam habet, virtute cuius poena purgata est. Si autem veniale peccatum sine gratia, in aliquo esset, perpetuam poenam haberet.

AD TERTIUM dicendum quod non est eadem ratio de poena sensibili ante mortem et post mortem. Quia ante mortem poena sensibilis consequitur virtutem naturae agentis: sive sit poena sensibilis interior, ut febris vel aliquid huiusmodi; sive etiam sensibilis poena exterior, ut ustio sive aliquid huiusmodi. Sed post mortem nihil aget virtute naturae, sed secundum iustitiae divinae ordinem tantum: sive in animam separatam, in quam constat quod ignis naturaliter agere non potest; sive etiam in corpus post resurrectionem, quia tunc omnis actio naturalis cessabit, cessante motu primi mobilis, qui est causa omnis motus et alterationis corporalis.

AD QUARTUM dicendum quod dolor sensibilis respondet delectationi sensibili quae est in conversione actualis peccati. Concupiscentia autem habitualis quae est in originali peccato, delectationem non habet. Et ideo dolor sensibilis non respondet sibi pro poena.

AD QUINTUM dicendum quod corpora puerorum non erunt impassibilia ex defectu potentiae ad patiendum in ipsis, sed ex defectu exterius agentis in ipsa: quia post resurrectionem nullum corpus erit agens in alterum, praecipue ad corruptionem inducendam, per actionem naturae, sed erit actio tantum ad puniendum ex ordine divinae iustitiae. Unde illa corpora poenam non patientur quibus poena sensibilis ex divina iustitia non debetur. Corpora autem sanctorum erunt impassibilia quia deficiet in eis potentia ad patiendum. Et ideo impassibilitas erit in eis dos, non autem in pueris.

word *fire* in Scripture is often used to represent every punishment.

REPLY OBJ. 2: Among all sins, original sin is the least, by the fact that it is the least voluntary. For it is not voluntary by the will of a person, but only by the will of the principle of the nature. Now actual sin, and venial also, is voluntary by the will of the person in whom it exists. And therefore less punishment is due to original sin than to venial sin.

Nor does it matter that original sin cannot coexist with grace. For the lack of grace does not have the account of guilt, but of punishment, except to the extent that it is from the will. Therefore, where there is less of the voluntary, there is less guilt.

Likewise too it does not matter that a temporal punishment is due to actual venial sin. For this is incidental, inasmuch as someone who dies in venial sin alone has grace, by the power of which punishment is purged.

REPLY OBJ. 3: There is no parity between pain of sense before and after death, since before death the pain of sense results from the power of the natural agent, whether the pain of sense be interior, as fever or the like, or exterior, as burning and so forth. Whereas after death nothing will act by natural power, but only according to the order of divine justice, whether the object of such action be the separate soul, on which it is clear that fire cannot act naturally, or the body after resurrection, since then all natural action will cease through the cessation of the first movable, which is the cause of all bodily movement and alteration.

REPLY OBJ. 4: Sensible pain corresponds to sensible pleasure, which is in the conversion of actual sin: whereas habitual concupiscence, which is in original sin, has no pleasure. Hence, sensible pain does not correspond thereto as punishment.

REPLY OBJ. 5: The bodies of children will be impassible not through their being unable in themselves to suffer, but through the lack of an external agent to act upon them: because after the resurrection no body will act on another, least of all so as to induce corruption by the action of nature, but there will only be action to the effect of punishing them by order of the divine justice. Wherefore those bodies to which pain of sense is not due by divine justice will not suffer punishment. On the other hand, the bodies of the saints will be impassible, because they will lack the capability of suffering; hence impassibility in them will be a gift, but not in children.

Article 2

Whether Unbaptized Children Feel Spiritual Affliction in the Soul?

AD SECUNDUM SIC PROCEDITUR. Videtur quod pueri non baptizati afflictionem spiritualem in anima sentiant. Quia, sicut dicit Chrysostomus, in damnatis gravior erit poena quod Dei visione carebunt, quam quod igne inferni cremabuntur. Sed pueri visione divina carebunt. Ergo afflictionem spiritualem ex hoc sentient.

PRAETEREA, carere illo quod quis vult habere, sine afflictione esse non potest. Sed pueri vellent visionem divinam habere: alias voluntas eorum actualiter perversa esset. Ergo, cum ea careant, videtur quod ex hoc afflictionem sentiant.

Si dicatur quod non affliguntur quia sciunt se non culpa propria ea esse privatos: contra. Immunitas a culpa dolorem poenae non minuit, sed auget: non enim, si aliquis non propria culpa exheredatur vel mutilatur, propter hoc minus dolet. Ergo etiam, quamvis pueri non propria culpa tanto bono priventur, ex hoc eorum dolor non tollitur.

PRAETEREA, sicut pueri baptizati se habent ad meritum Christi, ita non baptizati ad demeritum Adae. Sed pueri baptizati ex merito Christi consequuntur praemium vitae aeternae. Ergo et non baptizati dolorem sustinent ex hoc quod per demeritum Adae aeterna vita privantur.

PRAETEREA, absentari a re amata non potest esse sine dolore. Sed pueri naturalem cognitionem de Deo habebunt, et eadem ratione naturaliter eum diligent. Ergo, cum ab eo sint in perpetuum separati, videtur quod hoc sine dolore pati non possint.

CONTRA, Si pueri non baptizati post mortem dolorem interiorem habeant, aut dolebunt de culpa, aut de poena. Si de culpa, cum a culpa illa ulterius emundari non possint, dolor ille erit in desperationem inducens. Sed talis dolor in damnatis est vermis conscientiae. Ergo pueri vermem conscientiae habebunt. Et sic non esset eorum poena *mitissima*, ut in littera dicitur. Si autem de poena dolerent, ergo, cum poena eorum iuste a Deo sit, voluntas eorum divinae iustitiae obviaret. Et sic actualiter deformis esset. Quod non conceditur. Ergo nullum dolorem interiorem sentient.

PRAETEREA, ratio recta non patitur ut aliquis perturbetur de eo quod in ipso non fuit ut vitaretur: propter quod Seneca probat quod *perturbatio in sapientem non cadit*. Sed in pueris est ratio recta nullo actuali pecca-

OBJ. 1: It appears that unbaptized children feel spiritual affliction in the soul, because as Chrysostom says, the punishment of God in that they will be deprived of seeing God will be more painful than their being burned in the fire of hell (*Hom. xxiii in Matth.*). Now these children will be deprived of seeing God. Therefore, they will suffer spiritual affliction thereby.

OBJ. 2: Further, one cannot, without suffering, lack what one wishes to have. But these children would wish to have the divine vision, else their will would be actually perverse. Therefore, since they are deprived of it, seemingly they also suffer.

If it be said that they do not suffer, because they know that through no fault of theirs they are deprived thereof, on the contrary. Freedom from fault does not lessen but increases the pain of punishment: for a man does not grieve less for that he is disinherited or deprived of a limb through no fault of his. Therefore, these children likewise, although deprived of so great a good through no fault of theirs, suffer none the less.

OBJ. 3: Further, as baptized children are in relation to the merit of Christ, so are unbaptized children to the demerit of Adam. But baptized children receive the reward of eternal life by virtue of Christ's merit. Therefore, the unbaptized suffer pain through being deprived of eternal life on account of Adam's demerit.

OBJ. 4: Further, separation from what we love cannot be without pain. But these children will have natural knowledge of God, and for that very reason will love Him naturally. Therefore, since they are separated from Him for ever, seemingly they cannot undergo this separation without pain.

ON THE CONTRARY, If unbaptized children have interior sorrow after death, they will grieve either for their sin or for their punishment. If for their sin, since they cannot be further cleansed from that sin, their sorrow will lead them to despair. Now sorrow of this kind in the damned is the worm of conscience. Therefore, these children will have the worm of conscience, and consequently theirs would not be the *mildest* punishment, as Augustine says it is. If, on the other hand, they grieve for their punishment, it follows, since their punishment is justly inflicted by God, that their will opposes itself to divine justice, and thus would be actually inordinate, which is not to be granted. Therefore, they will feel no sorrow.

FURTHER, Right reason does not allow one to be disturbed on account of what one was unable to avoid; hence Seneca proves that *a wise man is not disturbed*. Now in these children there is right reason deflected by no actual sin.

to obliquata. Ergo non turbabuntur de hoc quod talem poenam sustinent, quam vitare nullo modo potuerunt.

Respondeo dicendum quod circa hoc est triplex opinio. Quidam enim dicunt quod pueri nullum dolorem sustinebunt, quia in eis adeo ratio obtenebrata erit ut non cognoscant se amisisse quod amiserunt. Quod probabile non videtur: ut anima ab onere corporis absoluta ea non cognoscat quae saltem ratione investigari possint, et etiam multo plura.

Et ideo alii dicunt quod in eis est perfecta cognitio eorum quae naturali cognitioni subiacent, et cognoscunt Deum, et se eius visione privatos esse, et ex hoc aliquem dolorem sentient: tamen mitigabitur eorum dolor, inquantum non propria voluntate culpam incurrerunt pro qua damnati sunt. Hoc etiam probabile non videtur. Quia talis dolor parvus esse non potest de tanti boni amissione, et praecipue sine spe recuperationis. Unde poena eorum non esset *mitissima*. Praeterea, omnino eadem ratione qua dolore sensibili et exterius affligente non punientur, etiam dolorem interiorem non sentient. Quia dolor poenae delectationi culpae respondet. Unde, delectatione remota a culpa originali, omnis dolor ab eius poena excluditur.

Et ideo alii dicunt quod cognitionem perfectam habebunt eorum quae naturali cognitioni subiacent, et vita aeterna se privatos esse cognoscent, et causam quare ab ea exclusi sunt, nec tamen ex hoc aliquo modo affligentur. Quod qualiter esse posset, videndum est.

Sciendum ergo quod ex hoc quod caret aliquis eo quod suam proportionem excedit, non affligitur, si sit rectae rationis, sed tantum ex hoc quod caret eo ad quod aliquo modo proportionatus fuit: sicut nullus sapiens homo affligitur de hoc quod non potest volare sicut avis, vel quia non est rex vel imperator, cum sibi non sit debitum; affligeretur autem si privaretur eo ad quod habendum aliquo modo aptitudinem habuit. Dico ergo quod omnis homo usum liberi arbitrii habens proportionatus est ad vitam aeternam consequendam: quia potest se ad gratiam praeparare, per quam vitam aeternam merebitur. Et ideo, si ab hoc deficiant, maximus erit dolor eis, quia amittunt illud quod suum esse possibile fuit. Pueri autem nunquam fuerunt proportionati ad hoc quod vitam aeternam haberent: quia nec eis debebatur ex principii naturae, cum omnem facultatem naturae excedat; nec actus proprios habere potuerunt, quibus tantum bonum consequerentur. Et ideo nihil omnino dolebunt de carentia visionis divinae: immo magis gaudebunt de hoc quod participabunt multum de divina bonitate et perfectionibus naturalibus.

Nec potest dici quod fuerunt proportionati ad vitam aeternam consequendam, quamvis non per actionem suam, tamen per actionem aliorum circa eos, quia

Therefore, they will not be disturbed because they undergo this punishment which they could in no way avoid.

I answer that, On this question there are three opinions. Some say that these children will suffer no pain, because their reason will be so much in the dark that they will not know that they lack what they have lost. It, however, seems improbable that the soul freed from its bodily burden should ignore things which, to say the least, reason is able to explore, and many more besides.

Hence others say that they have perfect knowledge of things subject to natural reason, and know God, and that they are deprived of seeing Him, and that they feel some kind of sorrow on this account, but that their sorrow will be mitigated insofar as it was not by their will that they incurred the sin for which they are condemned. Yet this again would seem improbable, because this sorrow cannot be little for the loss of so great a good, especially without the hope of recovery: wherefore their punishment would not be the *mildest*. Moreover, the very same reason that impugns their being punished with pain of sense, as afflicting them from without, argues against their feeling sorrow within, because the pain of punishment corresponds to the pleasure of sin; wherefore, since original sin is void of pleasure, its punishment is free of all pain.

Consequently others say that they will know perfectly things subject to natural knowledge, and both the fact of their being deprived of eternal life and the reason for this privation, and that nevertheless this knowledge will not cause any sorrow in them. How this may be possible we must explore.

Accordingly, it must be observed that if one is guided by right reason, one does not grieve through being deprived of what is beyond one's power to obtain, but only through lack of that which, in some way, one is capable of obtaining. Thus no wise man grieves for being unable to fly like a bird, or for that he is not a king or an emperor, since these things are not due to him; whereas he would grieve if he lacked that to which he had some kind of claim. I say, then, that every man who has the use of free-will is adapted to obtain eternal life, because he can prepare himself for grace whereby to merit eternal life; so that if he fail in this, his grief will be very great, since he has lost what he was able to possess. But children were never adapted to possess eternal life, since neither was this due to them by virtue of their natural principles, for it surpasses the entire faculty of nature, nor could they perform acts of their own whereby to obtain so great a good. Hence they will in no way grieve for being deprived of the divine vision; nay, rather will they rejoice for that they will have a large share of God's goodness and their own natural perfections.

Nor can it be said that they were adapted to obtain eternal life, not indeed by their own action, but by the actions of others around them, since they could be baptized by others,

potuerunt ab aliis baptizari, sicut et multi pueri eiusdem conditionis baptizati vitam aeternam consecuti sunt. Hoc est enim superexcedentis gratiae ut aliquis sine actu proprio praemietur. Unde defectus talis gratiae non magis tristitiam causat in pueris decedentibus non baptizatis, quam in sapientibus hoc quod eis multae gratiae non fiunt quae aliis similibus factae sunt.

AD PRIMUM ergo dicendum quod in damnatis pro culpa actuali, qui usum liberi arbitrii habuerunt, fuit aptitudo ad vitam aeternam consequendam. Non autem in pueris, ut dictum est. Et ideo non est similis ratio de utrisque.

AD SECUNDUM dicendum quod, quamvis voluntas sit possibilium et impossibilium, ut in III *Ethic.* dicitur, tamen voluntas ordinata et completa non est nisi eorum ad quae quis aliquo modo ordinatus est. Et si in hac voluntate deficiant homines, dolent: non autem si deficiant ab illa voluntate quae impossibilium est. Quae potius *velleitas* quam *voluntas* debet dici: non enim aliquis illud vult simpliciter, sed vellet si possibile foret.

AD TERTIUM dicendum quod ad habendum proprium patrimonium, vel membra corporis sui, quilibet est ordinatus. Et ideo non est mirum si dolet aliquis de eorum amissione, sive pro culpa sua sive aliena eis privetur. Unde patet quod ratio non procedit ex simili.

AD QUARTUM dicendum quod donum Christi excedit peccatum Adae, ut ad Rom. 5, [15 sqq.] dicitur. Unde non oportet quod pueri non baptizati tantum habeant de malo quantum baptizati habent de bono.

AD QUINTUM dicendum quod, quamvis pueri non baptizati sint separati a Deo quantum ad illam coniunctionem quae est per gloriam, non tamen ab eo penitus sunt separati. Immo sibi coniunguntur per participationem naturalium bonorum. Et ita etiam de ipso gaudere poterunt naturali cognitione et dilectione.

like other children of the same condition who have been baptized and obtained eternal life: for this is of superabundant grace that one should be rewarded without any act of one's own. Wherefore the lack of such a grace will not cause sorrow in children who die without baptism any more than the lack of many graces accorded to others of the same condition makes a wise man to grieve.

REPLY OBJ. 1: In those who, having the use of free-will, are damned for actual sin, there was aptitude to obtain eternal life, but not in children, as stated above. Consequently there is no parity between the two.

REPLY OBJ. 2: Although the will may be directed both to the possible and to the impossible as stated in *Ethics* III.5, an ordinate and complete will is only of things which in some way are proportionate to our capability; and we grieve if we fail to obtain this will, but not if we fail in the will that is of impossibilities, and which should be called 'velleity' rather than 'will', for one does not will such things absolutely, but one would if they were possible.

REPLY OBJ. 3: Everyone has a claim to his own inheritance or bodily members, wherefore it is not strange that he should grieve at their loss, whether this be through his own or another's fault: hence it is clear that the argument is not based on a true comparison.

REPLY OBJ. 4: The gift of Christ surpasses the sin of Adam, as stated in Romans 5:15. Hence it does not follow that unbaptized children have as much of evil as the baptized have of good.

REPLY OBJ. 5: Although unbaptized children are separated from God as regards the union of glory, they are not utterly separated from Him: in fact they are united to Him by their share of natural goods, and so will also be able to rejoice in Him by their natural knowledge and love.

Comparative Charts
Supplementum - In IV Sententiis

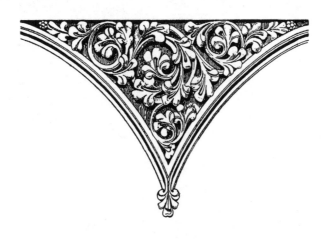

COMPARATIVE CHART

From the *Supplement* to *In IV Sent.* 14–42

Some time after the death of Aquinas, his followers added a "supplement" to the Third Part of the *Summa,* in order to complete its material as per the outline announced ahead of time by the author. The content was taken nearly verbatim from the Fourth Book of the *Sentences* Commentary. In the chart below, the leftmost column lists the questions and articles that make up the *Supplement,* while the right columns indicate the original location of the texts. If the compilers dared not alter the letter of the text, they showed themselves more than willing to move around the pieces, sometimes extensively, to line up in what they considered a more logical sequence.

ST Supplement	*In IV Sent.*		
q. 1, a. 1	d. 17	q. 2	a. 1, qa. 1
q. 1, a. 2	d. 17	q. 2	a. 1, qa. 2
q. 1, a. 3	d. 17	q. 2	a. 1, qa. 3
q. 2, a. 1	d. 17	q. 2	a. 2, qa. 1
q. 2, a. 2	d. 17	q. 2	a. 2, qa. 2
q. 2, a. 3	d. 17	q. 2	a. 2, qa. 3
q. 2, a. 4	d. 17	q. 2	a. 2, qa. 4
q. 2, a. 5	d. 17	q. 2	a. 2, qa. 5
q. 2, a. 6	d. 17	q. 2	a. 2, qa. 6
q. 3, a. 1	d. 17	q. 2	a. 3, qa. 1
q. 3, a. 2	d. 17	q. 2	a. 3, qa. 2
q. 3, a. 3	d. 17	q. 2	a. 3, qa. 3
q. 4, a. 1	d. 17	q. 2	a. 4, qa. 1
q. 4, a. 2	d. 17	q. 2	a. 4, qa. 2
q. 4, a. 3	d. 17	q. 2	a. 4, qa. 3
q. 5, a. 1	d. 17	q. 2	a. 5, qa. 1
q. 5, a. 2	d. 17	q. 2	a. 5, qa. 2
q. 5, a. 3	d. 17	q. 2	a. 5, qa. 3
q. 6, a. 1	d. 17	q. 3	a. 1, qa. 1
q. 6, a. 2	d. 17	q. 3	a. 1, qa. 2
q. 6, a. 3	d. 17	q. 3	a. 1, qa. 3
q. 6, a. 4	d. 21	q. 2	a. 3
q. 6, a. 5	d. 17	q. 3	a. 1, qa. 4
q. 6, a. 6	d. 17	q. 3	a. 1, qa. 5

ST Supplement	In IV Sent.		
q. 7, a. 1	d. 17	q. 3	a. 2, qa. 1
q. 7, a. 2	d. 17	q. 3	a. 2, qa. 2
q. 7, a. 3	d. 17	q. 3	a. 2, qa. 3
q. 8, a. 1	d. 17	q. 3	a. 3, qa. 1
q. 8, a. 2	d. 17	q. 3	a. 3, qa. 2
q. 8, a. 3	d. 17	q. 3	a. 3, qa. 3
q. 8, a. 4	d. 17	q. 3	a. 3, qa. 4
q. 8, a. 5	d. 17	q. 3	a. 3, qa. 5
q. 8, a. 6	d. 20	q. 1	a. 1, qa. 2
q. 8, a. 7	d. 20	q. 1	a. 2, qa. 1
q. 9, a. 1	d. 17	q. 3	a. 4, qa. 1
q. 9, a. 2	d. 17	q. 3	a. 4, qa. 2
q. 9, a. 3	d. 17	q. 3	a. 4, qa. 3
q. 9, a. 4	d. 17	q. 3	a. 4, qa. 4
q. 10, a. 1	d. 17	q. 3	a. 5, qa. 1
q. 10, a. 2	d. 17	q. 3	a. 5, qa. 2
q. 10, a. 3	d. 17	q. 3	a. 5, qa. 3
q. 10, a. 4	d. 17	q. 3	a. 5, qa. 4
q. 10, a. 5	d. 21	q. 2	a. 2
q. 11, a. 1	d. 21	q. 3	a. 1, qa. 1
q. 11, a. 2	d. 21	q. 3	a. 1, qa. 2
q. 11, a. 3	d. 21	q. 3	a. 1, qa. 3
q. 11, a. 4	d. 21	q. 3	a. 2
q. 11, a. 5	d. 21	q. 3	a. 3
q. 12, a. 1	d. 15	q. 1	a. 1, qa. 1
q. 12, a. 2	d. 15	q. 1	a. 1, qa. 2
q. 12, a. 3	d. 15	q. 1	a. 1, qa. 3
q. 13, a. 1	d. 15	q. 1	a. 2
q. 13, a. 2	d. 20	q. 1	a. 2, qa. 3
q. 14, a. 1	d. 15	q. 1	a. 3, qa. 1
q. 14, a. 2	d. 15	q. 1	a. 3, qa. 2
q. 14, a. 3	d. 15	q. 1	a. 3, qa. 3
q. 14, a. 4	d. 15	q. 1	a. 3, qa. 4
q. 14, a. 5	d. 15	q. 1	a. 3, qa. 5
q. 15, a. 1	d. 15	q. 1	a. 4, qa. 1
q. 15, a. 2	d. 15	q. 1	a. 4, qa. 2
q. 15, a. 3	d. 15	q. 1	a. 4, qa. 3
q. 16, a. 1	d. 14	q. 1	a. 3, qa. 2
q. 16, a. 2	d. 14	q. 1	a. 3, qa. 3

ST Supplement	In IV Sent.		
q. 16, a. 3	d. 14	q. 1	a. 3, qa. 4
q. 17, a. 1	d. 18	q. 1	a. 1, qa. 1
q. 17, a. 2	d. 18	q. 1	a. 1, qa. 2
q. 17, a. 3	d. 18	q. 1	a. 1, qa. 3
q. 18, a. 1	d. 18	q. 1	a. 3, qa. 1
q. 18, a. 2	d. 18	q. 1	a. 3, qa. 2
q. 18, a. 3	d. 18	q. 1	a. 3, qa. 3
q. 18, a. 4	d. 18	q. 1	a. 3, qa. 4
q. 19, a. 1	d. 19	q. 1	a. 1, qa. 1
q. 19, a. 2	d. 19	q. 1	a. 1, qa. 2
q. 19, a. 3	d. 19	q. 1	a. 1, qa. 3
q. 19, a. 4	d. 19	q. 1	a. 2, qa. 1
q. 19, a. 5	d. 19	q. 1	a. 2, qa. 2
q. 19, a. 6	d. 19	q. 1	a. 2, qa. 3
q. 20, a. 1	d. 19	q. 1	a. 3, qa. 1
q. 20, a. 2	d. 19	q. 1	a. 3, qa. 2
q. 20, a. 3	d. 19	q. 1	a. 3, qa. 3
q. 21, a. 1	d. 18	q. 2	a. 1, qa. 1
q. 21, a. 2	d. 18	q. 2	a. 1, qa. 2
q. 21, a. 3	d. 18	q. 2	a. 1, qa. 3
q. 21, a. 4	d. 18	q. 2	a. 1, qa. 4
q. 22, a. 1	d. 18	q. 2	a. 2, qa. 1
q. 22, a. 2	d. 18	q. 2	a. 2, qa. 2
q. 22, a. 3	d. 18	q. 2	a. 2, qa. 3
q. 22, a. 4	d. 18	q. 2	a. 3, qa. 1
q. 22, a. 5	d. 18	q. 2	a. 3, qa. 2
q. 22, a. 6	d. 18	q. 2	a. 3, qa. 3
q. 23, a. 1	d. 18	q. 2	a. 4, qa. 1
q. 23, a. 2	d. 18	q. 2	a. 4, qa. 2
q. 23, a. 3	d. 18	q. 2	a. 4, qa. 3
q. 24, a. 1	d. 18	q. 2	a. 5, qa. 1
q. 24, a. 2	d. 18	q. 2	a. 5, qa. 2
q. 24, a. 3	d. 18	q. 2	a. 5, qa. 3
q. 25, a. 1	d. 20	q. 1	a. 3, qa. 1
q. 25, a. 2	d. 20	q. 1	a. 3, qa. 2
q. 25, a. 3	d. 20	q. 1	a. 3, qa. 3
q. 26, a. 1	d. 20	q. 1	a. 4, qa. 1
q. 26, a. 2	d. 20	q. 1	a. 4, qa. 2
q. 26, a. 3	d. 20	q. 1	a. 4, qa. 3

ST Supplement	In IV Sent.		
q. 26, a. 4	d. 20	q. 1	a. 4, qa. 4
q. 27, a. 1	d. 20	q. 1	a. 5, qa. 1
q. 27, a. 2	d. 20	q. 1	a. 5, qa. 2
q. 27, a. 3	d. 20	q. 1	a. 5, qa. 3
q. 27, a. 4	d. 20	q. 1	a. 5, qa. 4
q. 28, a. 1	d. 14	q. 1	a. 5, qa. 1
q. 28, a. 2	d. 14	q. 1	a. 5, qa. 2
q. 28, a. 3	d. 14	q. 1	a. 5, qa. 3
q. 29, a. 1	d. 23	q. 1	a. 1, qa. 1
q. 29, a. 2	d. 23	q. 1	a. 1, qa. 2
q. 29, a. 3	d. 23	q. 1	a. 1, qa. 3
q. 29, a. 4	d. 23	q. 1	a. 3, qa. 1
q. 29, a. 5	d. 23	q. 1	a. 3, qa. 2
q. 29, a. 6	d. 23	q. 1	a. 3, qa. 3
q. 29, a. 7	d. 23	q. 1	a. 4, qa. 1
q. 29, a. 8	d. 23	q. 1	a. 4, qa. 2
q. 29, a. 9	d. 23	q. 1	a. 4, qa. 3
q. 30, a. 1	d. 23	q. 1	a. 2, qa. 1
q. 30, a. 2	d. 23	q. 1	a. 2, qa. 2
q. 30, a. 3	d. 23	q. 1	a. 2, qa. 3
q. 31, a. 1	d. 23	q. 2	a. 1, qa. 1
q. 31, a. 2	d. 23	q. 2	a. 1, qa. 2
q. 31, a. 3	d. 23	q. 2	a. 1, qa. 3
q. 32, a. 1	d. 23	q. 2	a. 2, qa. 1
q. 32, a. 2	d. 23	q. 2	a. 2, qa. 2
q. 32, a. 3	d. 23	q. 2	a. 2, qa. 3
q. 32, a. 4	d. 23	q. 2	a. 2, qa. 4
q. 32, a. 5	d. 23	q. 2	a. 3, qa. 1
q. 32, a. 6	d. 23	q. 2	a. 3, qa. 2
q. 32, a. 7	d. 23	q. 2	a. 3, qa. 3
q. 33, a. 1	d. 23	q. 2	a. 4, qa. 1
q. 33, a. 2	d. 23	q. 2	a. 4, qa. 2
q. 34, a. 1	d. 24	q. 1	a. 1, qa. 1
q. 34, a. 2	d. 24	q. 1	a. 1, qa. 2
q. 34, a. 3	d. 24	q. 1	a. 1, qa. 3
q. 34, a. 4	d. 24	q. 1	a. 1, qa. 4
q. 34, a. 5	d. 24	q. 1	a. 1, qa. 5
q. 35, a. 1	d. 24	q. 1	a. 2, qa. 1
q. 35, a. 2	d. 24	q. 1	a. 2, qa. 2

ST Supplement	In IV Sent.		
q. 35, a. 3	d. 24	q. 1	a. 2, qa. 3
q. 35, a. 4	d. 24	q. 1	a. 2, qa. 4
q. 35, a. 5	d. 24	q. 1	a. 2, qa. 5
q. 36, a. 1	d. 24	q. 1	a. 3, qa. 1
q. 36, a. 2	d. 24	q. 1	a. 3, qa. 2
q. 36, a. 3	d. 24	q. 1	a. 3, qa. 3
q. 36, a. 4	d. 24	q. 1	a. 3, qa. 4
q. 36, a. 5	d. 24	q. 1	a. 3, qa. 5
q. 37, a. 1	d. 24	q. 2	a. 1, qa. 1
q. 37, a. 2	d. 24	q. 2	a. 1, qa. 2
q. 37, a. 3	d. 24	q. 2	a. 1, qa. 3
q. 37, a. 4	d. 24	q. 2	a. 2
q. 37, a. 5	d. 24	q. 2	a. 3
q. 38, a. 1	d. 25	q. 1	a. 1
q. 38, a. 2	d. 25	q. 1	a. 2
q. 39, a. 1	d. 25	q. 2	a. 1, qa. 1
q. 39, a. 2	d. 25	q. 2	a. 1, qa. 2
q. 39, a. 3	d. 25	q. 2	a. 2, qa. 1
q. 39, a. 4	d. 25	q. 2	a. 2, qa. 2
q. 39, a. 5	d. 25	q. 2	a. 2, qa. 3
q. 39, a. 6	d. 25	q. 2	a. 2, qa. 4
q. 40, a. 1	d. 24	q. 3	a. 1, qa. 1
q. 40, a. 2	d. 24	q. 3	a. 1, qa. 2
q. 40, a. 3	d. 24	q. 3	a. 1, qa. 3
q. 40, a. 4	d. 24	q. 3	a. 2, qa. 1
q. 40, a. 5	d. 24	q. 3	a. 2, qa. 2
q. 40, a. 6	d. 24	q. 3	a. 2, qa. 3
q. 40, a. 7	d. 24	q. 3	a. 3
q. 41, a. 1	d. 26	q. 1	a. 1
q. 41, a. 2	d. 26	q. 1	a. 2
q. 41, a. 3	d. 26	q. 1	a. 3
q. 41, a. 4	d. 26	q. 1	a. 4
q. 42, a. 1	d. 26	q. 2	a. 1
q. 42, a. 2	d. 26	q. 2	a. 2
q. 42, a. 3	d. 26	q. 2	a. 3
q. 42, a. 4	d. 26	q. 2	a. 4
q. 43, a. 1	d. 27	q. 2	a. 1
q. 43, a. 2	d. 27	q. 2	a. 2
q. 43, a. 3	d. 27	q. 2	a. 3

ST Supplement	In IV Sent.		
q. 44, a. 1	d. 27	q. 1	a. 1, qa. 1
q. 44, a. 2	d. 27	q. 1	a. 1, qa. 2
q. 44, a. 3	d. 27	q. 1	a. 1, qa. 3
q. 45, a. 1	d. 27	q. 1	a. 2, qa. 1
q. 45, a. 2	d. 27	q. 1	a. 2, qa. 2
q. 45, a. 3	d. 27	q. 1	a. 2, qa. 3
q. 45, a. 4	d. 27	q. 1	a. 2, qa. 4
q. 45, a. 5	d. 28	q. 1	a. 3
q. 46, a. 1	d. 28	q. 1	a. 1
q. 46, a. 2	d. 28	q. 1	a. 2
q. 47, a. 1	d. 29	q. 1	a. 1
q. 47, a. 2	d. 29	q. 1	a. 2
q. 47, a. 3	d. 29	q. 1	a. 3, qa. 1
q. 47, a. 4	d. 29	q. 1	a. 3, qa. 2
q. 47, a. 5	d. 29	q. 1	a. 3, qa. 3
q. 47, a. 6	d. 29	q. 1	a. 4
q. 48, a. 1	d. 28	q. 1	a. 4
q. 48, a. 2	d. 30	q. 1	a. 3
q. 49, a. 1	d. 31	q. 1	a. 1
q. 49, a. 2	d. 31	q. 1	a. 2
q. 49, a. 3	d. 31	q. 1	a. 3
q. 49, a. 4	d. 31	q. 2	a. 1
q. 49, a. 5	d. 31	q. 2	a. 2
q. 49, a. 6	d. 31	q. 2	a. 3
q. 50, a. 1	d. 34	q. 1	a. 1
q. 51, a. 1	d. 30	q. 1	a. 1
q. 51, a. 2	d. 30	q. 1	a. 2
q. 52, a. 1	d. 36	q. 1	a. 1
q. 52, a. 2	d. 36	q. 1	a. 2
q. 52, a. 3	d. 36	q. 1	a. 3
q. 52, a. 4	d. 36	q. 1	a. 4
q. 53, a. 1	d. 38	q. 1	a. 3, qa. 2
q. 53, a. 2	d. 38	q. 1	a. 3, qa. 3
q. 53, a. 3	d. 37	q. 1	a. 1
q. 53, a. 4	d. 37	q. 1	a. 2
q. 54, a. 1	d. 40	q. 1	a. 1
q. 54, a. 2	d. 40	q. 1	a. 2
q. 54, a. 3	d. 40	q. 1	a. 3
q. 54, a. 4	d. 40	q. 1	a. 4

ST Supplement	In IV Sent.		
q. 55, a. 1	d. 41	q. 1	a. 1, qa. 1
q. 55, a. 2	d. 41	q. 1	a. 1, qa. 2
q. 55, a. 3	d. 41	q. 1	a. 1, qa. 3
q. 55, a. 4	d. 41	q. 1	a. 1, qa. 4
q. 55, a. 5	d. 41	q. 1	a. 1, qa. 5
q. 55, a. 6	d. 41	q. 1	a. 2, qa. 1
q. 55, a. 7	d. 41	q. 1	a. 2, qa. 2
q. 55, a. 8	d. 41	q. 1	a. 2, qa. 3
q. 55, a. 9	d. 41	q. 1	a. 5, qa. 1
q. 55, a. 10	d. 41	q. 1	a. 5, qa. 2
q. 55, a. 11	d. 41	q. 1	a. 5, qa. 3
q. 56, a. 1	d. 42	q. 1	a. 1
q. 56, a. 2	d. 42	q. 1	a. 2
q. 56, a. 3	d. 42	q. 1	a. 3, qa. 1
q. 56, a. 4	d. 42	q. 1	a. 3, qa. 2
q. 56, a. 5	d. 42	q. 1	a. 3, qa. 3
q. 57, a. 1	d. 42	q. 2	a. 1
q. 57, a. 2	d. 42	q. 2	a. 2
q. 57, a. 3	d. 42	q. 2	a. 3
q. 58, a. 1	d. 34	q. 1	a. 2
q. 58, a. 2	d. 34	q. 1	a. 3
q. 58, a. 3	d. 34	q. 1	a. 4
q. 58, a. 4	d. 34	q. 1	a. 5
q. 58, a. 5	d. 36	q. 1	a. 5
q. 59, a. 1	d. 39	q. 1	a. 1
q. 59, a. 2	d. 39	q. 1	a. 2
q. 59, a. 3	d. 39	q. 1	a. 3
q. 59, a. 4	d. 39	q. 1	a. 4
q. 59, a. 5	d. 39	q. 1	a. 5
q. 59, a. 6	d. 39	q. 1	a. 6
q. 60, a. 1	d. 37	q. 2	a. 1
q. 60, a. 2	d. 37	q. 2	a. 2
q. 61, a. 1	d. 27	q. 1	a. 3, qa. 1
q. 61, a. 2	d. 27	q. 1	a. 3, qa. 2
q. 61, a. 3	d. 27	q. 1	a. 3, qa. 3
q. 62, a. 1	d. 35	q. 1	a. 1
q. 62, a. 2	d. 35	q. 1	a. 2
q. 62, a. 3	d. 35	q. 1	a. 3
q. 62, a. 4	d. 35	q. 1	a. 4

ST Supplement	In IV Sent.		
q. 62, a. 5	d. 35	q. 1	a. 5
q. 62, a. 6	d. 35	q. 1	a. 6
q. 63, a. 1	d. 42	q. 3	a. 1
q. 63, a. 2	d. 42	q. 3	a. 2
q. 64, a. 1	d. 32	q. 1	a. 1
q. 64, a. 2	d. 32	q. 1	a. 2, qa. 1
q. 64, a. 3	d. 32	q. 1	a. 3
q. 64, a. 4	d. 32	q. 1	a. 4
q. 64, a. 5	d. 32	q. 1	a. 5, qa. 1
q. 64, a. 6	d. 32	q. 1	a. 5, qa. 2
q. 64, a. 7	d. 32	q. 1	a. 5, qa. 3
q. 65, a. 1	d. 33	q. 1	a. 1
q. 65, a. 2	d. 33	q. 1	a. 2
q. 65, a. 3	d. 33	q. 1	a. 3, qa. 1
q. 65, a. 4	d. 33	q. 1	a. 3, qa. 2
q. 65, a. 5	d. 33	q. 1	a. 3, qa. 3
q. 66, a. 1	d. 27	q. 3	a. 1, qa. 1
q. 66, a. 2	d. 27	q. 3	a. 1, qa. 2
q. 66, a. 3	d. 27	q. 3	a. 1, qa. 3
q. 66, a. 4	d. 27	q. 3	a. 2
q. 66, a. 5	d. 27	q. 3	a. 3
q. 67, a. 1	d. 33	q. 2	a. 1
q. 67, a. 2	d. 33	q. 2	a. 2, qa. 1
q. 67, a. 3	d. 33	q. 2	a. 2, qa. 2
q. 67, a. 4	d. 33	q. 2	a. 2, qa. 3
q. 67, a. 5	d. 33	q. 2	a. 2, qa. 4
q. 67, a. 6	d. 33	q. 2	a. 3, qa. 1
q. 67, a. 7	d. 33	q. 2	a. 3, qa. 2
q. 68, a. 1	d. 41	q. 1	a. 3, qa. 1
q. 68, a. 2	d. 41	q. 1	a. 3, qa. 2
q. 68, a. 3	d. 41	q. 1	a. 3, qa. 3
q. 69, a. 1	d. 45	q. 1	a. 1, qa. 1
q. 69, a. 2	d. 45	q. 1	a. 1, qa. 2
q. 69, a. 3	d. 45	q. 1	a. 1, qa. 3
q. 69, a. 4	d. 45	q. 1	a. 2, qa. 1
q. 69, a. 5	d. 45	q. 1	a. 2, qa. 2
q. 69, a. 6	d. 45	q. 1	a. 2, qa. 3
q. 69, a. 7	d. 45	q. 1	a. 3
q. 70, a. 1	d. 44	q. 3	a. 3, qa. 1

ST Supplement	In IV Sent.		
q. 70, a. 2	d. 44	q. 3	a. 3, qa. 2
q. 70, a. 3	d. 44	q. 3	a. 3, qa. 3
q. 71, a. 1	d. 45	q. 2	a. 1, qa. 1
q. 71, a. 2	d. 45	q. 2	a. 1, qa. 2
q. 71, a. 3	d. 45	q. 2	a. 1, qa. 3
q. 71, a. 4	d. 45	q. 2	a. 1, qa. 4
q. 71, a. 5	d. 45	q. 2	a. 2, qa. 1
q. 71, a. 6	d. 45	q. 2	a. 2, qa. 2
q. 71, a. 7	d. 45	q. 2	a. 2, qa. 3
q. 71, a. 8	d. 45	q. 2	a. 2, qa. 4
q. 71, a. 9	d. 45	q. 2	a. 3, qa. 1
q. 71, a. 10	d. 45	q. 2	a. 3, qa. 2
q. 71, a. 11	d. 45	q. 2	a. 3, qa. 3
q. 71, a. 12	d. 45	q. 2	a. 4, qa. 1
q. 71, a. 13	d. 45	q. 2	a. 4, qa. 2
q. 71, a. 14	d. 45	q. 2	a. 4, qa. 3
q. 72, a. 1	d. 45	q. 3	a. 1
q. 72, a. 2	d. 45	q. 3	a. 2
q. 72, a. 3	d. 45	q. 3	a. 3
q. 73, a. 1	d. 48	q. 1	a. 4, qa. 1
q. 73, a. 2	d. 48	q. 1	a. 4, qa. 2
q. 73, a. 3	d. 48	q. 1	a. 4, qa. 3
q. 74, a. 1	d. 47	q. 2	a. 1, qa. 1
q. 74, a. 2	d. 47	q. 2	a. 1, qa. 2
q. 74, a. 3	d. 47	q. 2	a. 1, qa. 3
q. 74, a. 4	d. 47	q. 2	a. 2, qa. 1
q. 74, a. 5	d. 47	q. 2	a. 2, qa. 2
q. 74, a. 6	d. 47	q. 2	a. 2, qa. 3
q. 74, a. 7	d. 47	q. 2	a. 3, qa. 1
q. 74, a. 8	d. 47	q. 2	a. 3, qa. 2
q. 74, a. 9	d. 47	q. 2	a. 3, qa. 3
q. 75, a. 1	d. 43	q. 1	a. 1, qa. 1
q. 75, a. 2	d. 43	q. 1	a. 1, qa. 2
q. 75, a. 3	d. 43	q. 1	a. 1, qa. 3
q. 76, a. 1	d. 43	q. 1	a. 2, qa. 1
q. 76, a. 2	d. 43	q. 1	a. 2, qa. 2
q. 76, a. 3	d. 43	q. 1	a. 2, qa. 3
q. 77, a. 1	d. 43	q. 1	a. 3, qa. 1
q. 77, a. 2	d. 43	q. 1	a. 3, qa. 2

ST Supplement	In IV Sent.		
q. 77, a. 3	d. 43	q. 1	a. 3, qa. 4
q. 77, a. 4	d. 43	q. 1	a. 3, qa. 3
q. 78, a. 1	d. 43	q. 1	a. 4, qa. 1
q. 78, a. 2	d. 43	q. 1	a. 4, qa. 2
q. 78, a. 3	d. 43	q. 1	a. 4, qa. 3
q. 79, a. 1	d. 44	q. 1	a. 1, qa. 1
q. 79, a. 2	d. 44	q. 1	a. 1, qa. 2
q. 79, a. 3	d. 44	q. 1	a. 1, qa. 3
q. 80, a. 1	d. 44	q. 1	a. 2, qa. 1
q. 80, a. 2	d. 44	q. 1	a. 2, qa. 2
q. 80, a. 3	d. 44	q. 1	a. 2, qa. 3
q. 80, a. 4	d. 44	q. 1	a. 2, qa. 4
q. 80, a. 5	d. 44	q. 1	a. 2, qa. 5
q. 81, a. 1	d. 44	q. 1	a. 3, qa. 1
q. 81, a. 2	d. 44	q. 1	a. 3, qa. 2
q. 81, a. 3	d. 44	q. 1	a. 3, qa. 3
q. 81, a. 4	d. 44	q. 1	a. 3, qa. 4
q. 82, a. 1	d. 44	q. 2	a. 1, qa. 1
q. 82, a. 2	d. 44	q. 2	a. 1, qa. 2
q. 82, a. 3	d. 44	q. 2	a. 1, qa. 3
q. 82, a. 4	d. 44	q. 2	a. 1, qa. 4
q. 83, a. 1	d. 44	q. 2	a. 2, qa. 1
q. 83, a. 2	d. 44	q. 2	a. 2, qa. 2
q. 83, a. 3	d. 44	q. 2	a. 2, qa. 3
q. 83, a. 4	d. 44	q. 2	a. 2, qa. 4
q. 83, a. 5	d. 44	q. 2	a. 2, qa. 5
q. 83, a. 6	d. 44	q. 2	a. 2, qa. 6
q. 84, a. 1	d. 44	q. 2	a. 3, qa. 1
q. 84, a. 2	d. 44	q. 2	a. 3, qa. 2
q. 84, a. 3	d. 44	q. 2	a. 3, qa. 3
q. 85, a. 1	d. 44	q. 2	a. 4, qa. 1
q. 85, a. 2	d. 44	q. 2	a. 4, qa. 2
q. 85, a. 3	d. 44	q. 2	a. 4, qa. 3
q. 86, a. 1	d. 44	q. 3	a. 1, qa. 1
q. 86, a. 2	d. 44	q. 3	a. 1, qa. 2
q. 86, a. 3	d. 44	q. 3	a. 1, qa. 3
q. 87, a. 1	d. 43	q. 1	a. 5, qa. 1
q. 87, a. 2	d. 43	q. 1	a. 5, qa. 2
q. 87, a. 3	d. 43	q. 1	a. 5, qa. 3

ST Supplement	In IV Sent.		
q. 88, a. 1	d. 47	q. 1	a. 1, qa. 1
q. 88, a. 2	d. 47	q. 1	a. 1, qa. 2
q. 88, a. 3	d. 47	q. 1	a. 1, qa. 3
q. 88, a. 4	d. 47	q. 1	a. 1, qa. 4
q. 89, a. 1	d. 47	q. 1	a. 2, qa. 1
q. 89, a. 2	d. 47	q. 1	a. 2, qa. 2
q. 89, a. 3	d. 47	q. 1	a. 2, qa. 3
q. 89, a. 4	d. 47	q. 1	a. 2, qa. 4
q. 89, a. 5	d. 47	q. 1	a. 3, qa. 1
q. 89, a. 6	d. 47	q. 1	a. 3, qa. 2
q. 89, a. 7	d. 47	q. 1	a. 3, qa. 3
q. 89, a. 8	d. 47	q. 1	a. 3, qa. 4
q. 90, a. 1	d. 48	q. 1	a. 1
q. 90, a. 2	d. 48	q. 1	a. 2
q. 90, a. 3	d. 48	q. 1	a. 3
q. 91, a. 1	d. 48	q. 2	a. 1
q. 91, a. 2	d. 48	q. 2	a. 2
q. 91, a. 3	d. 48	q. 2	a. 3
q. 91, a. 4	d. 48	q. 2	a. 4
q. 91, a. 5	d. 48	q. 2	a. 5
q. 92, a. 1	d. 49	q. 2	a. 1
q. 92, a. 2	d. 49	q. 2	a. 2
q. 92, a. 3	d. 49	q. 2	a. 5
q. 93, a. 1	d. 49	q. 1	a. 4, qa. 1
q. 93, a. 2	d. 49	q. 1	a. 4, qa. 3
q. 93, a. 3	d. 49	q. 1	a. 4, qa. 4
q. 94, a. 1	d. 50	q. 2	a. 4, qa. 1
q. 94, a. 2	d. 50	q. 2	a. 4, qa. 2
q. 94, a. 3	d. 50	q. 2	a. 4, qa. 3
q. 95, a. 1	d. 49	q. 4	a. 1
q. 95, a. 2	d. 49	q. 4	a. 2
q. 95, a. 3	d. 49	q. 4	a. 3
q. 95, a. 4	d. 49	q. 4	a. 4
q. 95, a. 5	d. 49	q. 4	a. 5, qa. 1
q. 96, a. 1	d. 49	q. 5	a. 1
q. 96, a. 2	d. 49	q. 5	a. 2, qa. 1
q. 96, a. 3	d. 49	q. 5	a. 2, qa. 2
q. 96, a. 4	d. 49	q. 5	a. 2, qa. 3
q. 96, a. 5	d. 49	q. 5	a. 3, qa. 1

ST Supplement	In IV Sent.		
q. 96, a. 6	d. 49	q. 5	a. 3, qa. 2
q. 96, a. 7	d. 49	q. 5	a. 3, qa. 3
q. 96, a. 8	d. 49	q. 5	a. 4, qa. 1
q. 96, a. 9	d. 49	q. 5	a. 4, qa. 2
q. 96, a. 10	d. 49	q. 5	a. 4, qa. 3
q. 96, a. 11	d. 49	q. 5	a. 5, qa. 1
q. 96, a. 12	d. 49	q. 5	a. 5, qa. 2
q. 96, a. 13	d. 49	q. 5	a. 5, qa. 3
q. 97, a. 1	d. 50	q. 2	a. 3, qa. 1
q. 97, a. 2	d. 50	q. 2	a. 3, qa. 2
q. 97, a. 3	d. 50	q. 2	a. 3, qa. 3
q. 97, a. 4	d. 50	q. 2	a. 3, qa. 4
q. 97, a. 5	d. 44	q. 3	a. 2, qa. 1
q. 97, a. 6	d. 44	q. 3	a. 2, qa. 2
q. 97, a. 7	d. 44	q. 3	a. 2, qa. 3
q. 98, a. 1	d. 50	q. 2	a. 1, qa. 1
q. 98, a. 2	d. 50	q. 2	a. 1, qa. 2
q. 98, a. 3	d. 50	q. 2	a. 1, qa. 3
q. 98, a. 4	d. 50	q. 2	a. 1, qa. 4
q. 98, a. 5	d. 50	q. 2	a. 1, qa. 5
q. 98, a. 6	d. 50	q. 2	a. 1, qa. 6
q. 98, a. 7	d. 50	q. 2	a. 2, qa. 1
q. 98, a. 8	d. 50	q. 2	a. 2, qa. 2
q. 98, a. 9	d. 50	q. 2	a. 2, qa. 3
q. 99, a. 1	d. 46	q. 1	a. 3
q. 99, a. 2	d. 46	q. 2	a. 3, qa. 1
q. 99, a. 3	d. 46	q. 2	a. 3, qa. 2
q. 99, a. 4	d. 46	q. 2	a. 3, qa. 3
q. 99, a. 5	d. 46	q. 2	a. 3, qa. 4
De purgatorio, a. 1	d. 21	q. 1	a. 1, qa. 1
De purgatorio, a. 2	d. 21	q. 1	a. 1, qa. 2
De purgatorio, a. 3	d. 21	q. 1	a. 1, qa. 3
De purgatorio, a. 4	d. 21	q. 1	a. 1, qa. 4
De purgatorio, a. 5	d. 21	q. 1	a. 1, qa. 5
De purgatorio, a. 6	d. 21	q. 1	a. 3, qa. 1
De purgatorio, a. 7	d. 21	q. 1	a. 3, qa. 2
De purgatorio, a. 8	d. 21	q. 1	a. 3, qa. 3
De poena orig., a. 1	lib. 2, d. 33	q. 2	a. 1
De poena orig., a. 2	lib. 2, d. 33	q. 2	a. 2

COMPARATIVE CHART

From *In IV Sent.* 14–42 to the *Supplement*

After Aquinas's death, the fourth book of his *Commentary on the Sentences* was utilized by his followers as raw material for a *Supplement* to the unfinished Third Part of the *Summa theologiae*. The *Supplement* makes no more than cosmetic modifications in the text of Aquinas, but radically changes the order in which the text appears, to suit what the compilers viewed as a more logical sequence. The chart below indicates, in the left columns, the texts of Book IV of Thomas's commentary, from distinction 14 through distinction 50, that were taken up into the *Supplement,* and where exactly they landed. If a text is not listed below (e.g., d. 16, or d. 17, q. 1), that is because it was never utilized in the *Supplement*. This occurs when a topic in Book IV has already been treated afresh in the *Summa theologiae.*

In IV Sent.			*ST Supplement*
d. 14	q. 1	a. 3, qa. 2	q. 16, a. 1
		a. 3, qa. 3	q. 16, a. 2
		a. 3, qa. 4	q. 16, a. 3
		a. 5, qa. 1	q. 28, a. 1
		a. 5, qa. 2	q. 28, a. 2
		a. 5, qa. 3	q. 28, a. 3
d. 15	q. 1	a. 1, qa. 1	q. 12, a. 1
		a. 1, qa. 2	q. 12, a. 2
		a. 1, qa. 3	q. 12, a. 3
		a. 2	q. 13, a. 1
		a. 3, qa. 1	q. 14, a. 1
		a. 3, qa. 2	q. 14, a. 2
		a. 3, qa. 3	q. 14, a. 3
		a. 3, qa. 4	q. 14, a. 4
		a. 3, qa. 5	q. 14, a. 5
		a. 4, qa. 1	q. 15, a. 1
		a. 4, qa. 2	q. 15, a. 2
		a. 4, qa. 3	q. 15, a. 3
d. 17	q. 2	a. 1, qa. 1	q. 1, a. 1
		a. 1, qa. 2	q. 1, a. 2
		a. 1, qa. 3	q. 1, a. 3
		a. 2, qa. 1	q. 2, a. 1

In IV Sent.			ST Supplement
		a. 2, qa. 2	q. 2, a. 2
		a. 2, qa. 3	q. 2, a. 3
		a. 2, qa. 4	q. 2, a. 4
		a. 2, qa. 5	q. 2, a. 5
		a. 2, qa. 6	q. 2, a. 6
		a. 3, qa. 1	q. 3, a. 1
		a. 3, qa. 2	q. 3, a. 2
		a. 3, qa. 3	q. 3, a. 3
		a. 4, qa. 1	q. 4, a. 1
		a. 4, qa. 2	q. 4, a. 2
		a. 4, qa. 3	q. 4, a. 3
		a. 5, qa. 1	q. 5, a. 1
		a. 5, qa. 2	q. 5, a. 2
		a. 5, qa. 3	q. 5, a. 3
	q. 3	a. 1, qa. 1	q. 6, a. 1
		a. 1, qa. 2	q. 6, a. 2
		a. 1, qa. 3	q. 6, a. 3
		a. 1, qa. 4	q. 6, a. 5
		a. 1, qa. 5	q. 6, a. 6
		a. 2, qa. 1	q. 7, a. 1
		a. 2, qa. 2	q. 7, a. 2
		a. 2, qa. 3	q. 7, a. 3
		a. 3, qa. 1	q. 8, a. 1
		a. 3, qa. 2	q. 8, a. 2
		a. 3, qa. 3	q. 8, a. 3
		a. 3, qa. 4	q. 8, a. 4
		a. 3, qa. 5	q. 8, a. 5
		a. 4, qa. 1	q. 9, a. 1
		a. 4, qa. 2	q. 9, a. 2
		a. 4, qa. 3	q. 9, a. 3
		a. 4, qa. 4	q. 9, a. 4
		a. 5, qa. 1	q. 10, a. 1
		a. 5, qa. 2	q. 10, a. 2
		a. 5, qa. 3	q. 10, a. 3
		a. 5, qa. 4	q. 10, a. 4
d. 18	q. 1	a. 1, qa. 1	q. 17, a. 1
		a. 1, qa. 2	q. 17, a. 2
		a. 1, qa. 3	q. 17, a. 3
		a. 3, qa. 1	q. 18, a. 1

In IV Sent.			ST Supplement
		a. 3, qa. 2	q. 18, a. 2
		a. 3, qa. 3	q. 18, a. 3
		a. 3, qa. 4	q. 18, a. 4
	q. 2	a. 1, qa. 1	q. 21, a. 1
		a. 1, qa. 2	q. 21, a. 2
		a. 1, qa. 3	q. 21, a. 3
		a. 1, qa. 4	q. 21, a. 4
		a. 2, qa. 1	q. 22, a. 1
		a. 2, qa. 2	q. 22, a. 2
		a. 2, qa. 3	q. 22, a. 3
		a. 3, qa. 1	q. 22, a. 4
		a. 3, qa. 2	q. 22, a. 5
		a. 3, qa. 3	q. 22, a. 6
		a. 4, qa. 1	q. 23, a. 1
		a. 4, qa. 2	q. 23, a. 2
		a. 4, qa. 3	q. 23, a. 3
		a. 5, qa. 1	q. 24, a. 1
		a. 5, qa. 2	q. 24, a. 2
		a. 5, qa. 3	q. 24, a. 3
d. 19	q. 1	a. 1, qa. 1	q. 19, a. 1
		a. 1, qa. 2	q. 19, a. 2
		a. 1, qa. 3	q. 19, a. 3
		a. 2, qa. 1	q. 19, a. 4
		a. 2, qa. 2	q. 19, a. 5
		a. 2, qa. 3	q. 19, a. 6
		a. 3, qa. 1	q. 20, a. 1
		a. 3, qa. 2	q. 20, a. 2
		a. 3, qa. 3	q. 20, a. 3
d. 20		a. 1, qa. 2	q. 8, a. 6
		a. 2, qa. 1	q. 8, a. 7
		a. 2, qa. 3	q. 13, a. 2
		a. 3, qa. 1	q. 25, a. 1
		a. 3, qa. 2	q. 25, a. 2
		a. 3, qa. 3	q. 25, a. 3
		a. 4, qa. 1	q. 26, a. 1
		a. 4, qa. 2	q. 26, a. 2
		a. 4, qa. 3	q. 26, a. 3
		a. 4, qa. 4	q. 26, a. 4
		a. 5, qa. 1	q. 27, a. 1

In IV Sent.			ST Supplement
		a. 5, qa. 2	q. 27, a. 2
		a. 5, qa. 3	q. 27, a. 3
		a. 5, qa. 4	q. 27, a. 4
d. 21	q. 1	a. 1, qa. 1	De purgatorio, a. 1
		a. 1, qa. 2	De purgatorio, a. 2
		a. 1, qa. 3	De purgatorio, a. 3
		a. 1, qa. 4	De purgatorio, a. 4
		a. 1, qa. 5	De purgatorio, a. 5
		a. 3, qa. 1	De purgatorio, a. 6
		a. 3, qa. 2	De purgatorio, a. 7
		a. 3, qa. 3	De purgatorio, a. 8
	q. 2	a. 2	q. 10, a. 5
		a. 3	q. 6, a. 4
	q. 3	a. 1, qa. 1	q. 11, a. 1
		a. 1, qa. 2	q. 11, a. 2
		a. 1, qa. 3	q. 11, a. 3
		a. 2	q. 11, a. 4
		a. 3	q. 11, a. 5
d. 23	q. 1	a. 1, qa. 1	q. 29, a. 1
		a. 1, qa. 2	q. 29, a. 2
		a. 1, qa. 3	q. 29, a. 3
		a. 2, qa. 1	q. 30, a. 1
		a. 2, qa. 2	q. 30, a. 2
		a. 2, qa. 3	q. 30, a. 3
		a. 3, qa. 1	q. 29, a. 4
		a. 3, qa. 2	q. 29, a. 5
		a. 3, qa. 3	q. 29, a. 6
		a. 4, qa. 1	q. 29, a. 7
		a. 4, qa. 2	q. 29, a. 8
		a. 4, qa. 3	q. 29, a. 9
	q. 2	a. 1, qa. 1	q. 31, a. 1
		a. 1, qa. 2	q. 31, a. 2
		a. 1, qa. 3	q. 31, a. 3
		a. 2, qa. 1	q. 32, a. 1
		a. 2, qa. 2	q. 32, a. 2
		a. 2, qa. 3	q. 32, a. 3
		a. 2, qa. 4	q. 32, a. 4
		a. 3, qa. 1	q. 32, a. 5
		a. 3, qa. 2	q. 32, a. 6

In IV Sent.			ST Supplement
		a. 3, qa. 3	q. 32, a. 7
		a. 4, qa. 1	q. 33, a. 1
		a. 4, qa. 2	q. 33, a. 2
d. 24	q. 1	a. 1, qa. 1	q. 34, a. 1
		a. 1, qa. 2	q. 34, a. 2
		a. 1, qa. 3	q. 34, a. 3
		a. 1, qa. 4	q. 34, a. 4
		a. 1, qa. 5	q. 34, a. 5
		a. 2, qa. 1	q. 35, a. 1
		a. 2, qa. 2	q. 35, a. 2
		a. 2, qa. 3	q. 35, a. 3
		a. 2, qa. 4	q. 35, a. 4
		a. 2, qa. 5	q. 35, a. 5
		a. 3, qa. 1	q. 36, a. 1
		a. 3, qa. 2	q. 36, a. 2
		a. 3, qa. 3	q. 36, a. 3
		a. 3, qa. 4	q. 36, a. 4
		a. 3, qa. 5	q. 36, a. 5
	q. 2	a. 1, qa. 1	q. 37, a. 1
		a. 1, qa. 2	q. 37, a. 2
		a. 1, qa. 3	q. 37, a. 3
		a. 2	q. 37, a. 4
		a. 3	q. 37, a. 5
	q. 3	a. 1, qa. 1	q. 40, a. 1
		a. 1, qa. 2	q. 40, a. 2
		a. 1, qa. 3	q. 40, a. 3
		a. 2, qa. 1	q. 40, a. 4
		a. 2, qa. 2	q. 40, a. 5
		a. 2, qa. 3	q. 40, a. 6
		a. 3	q. 40, a. 7
d. 25	q. 1	a. 1	q. 38, a. 1
		a. 2	q. 38, a. 2
	q. 2	a. 1, qa. 1	q. 39, a. 1
		a. 1, qa. 2	q. 39, a. 2
		a. 2, qa. 1	q. 39, a. 3
		a. 2, qa. 2	q. 39, a. 4
		a. 2, qa. 3	q. 39, a. 5
		a. 2, qa. 4	q. 39, a. 6
d. 26	q. 1	a. 1	q. 41, a. 1

In IV Sent.			ST Supplement
		a. 2	q. 41, a. 2
		a. 3	q. 41, a. 3
		a. 4	q. 41, a. 4
	q. 2	a. 1	q. 42, a. 1
		a. 2	q. 42, a. 2
		a. 3	q. 42, a. 3
		a. 4	q. 42, a. 4
d. 27	q. 1	a. 1, qa. 1	q. 44, a. 1
		a. 1, qa. 2	q. 44, a. 2
		a. 1, qa. 3	q. 44, a. 3
		a. 2, qa. 1	q. 45, a. 1
		a. 2, qa. 2	q. 45, a. 2
		a. 2, qa. 3	q. 45, a. 3
		a. 2, qa. 4	q. 45, a. 4
		a. 3, qa. 1	q. 61, a. 1
		a. 3, qa. 2	q. 61, a. 2
		a. 3, qa. 3	q. 61, a. 3
	q. 2	a. 1	q. 43, a. 1
		a. 2	q. 43, a. 2
		a. 3	q. 43, a. 3
	q. 3	a. 1, qa. 1	q. 66, a. 1
		a. 1, qa. 2	q. 66, a. 2
		a. 1, qa. 3	q. 66, a. 3
		a. 2	q. 66, a. 4
		a. 3	q. 66, a. 5
d. 28	q. 1	a. 1	q. 46, a. 1
		a. 2	q. 46, a. 2
		a. 3	q. 45, a. 5
		a. 4	q. 48, a. 1
d. 29	q. 1	a. 1	q. 47, a. 1
		a. 2	q. 47, a. 2
		a. 3, qa. 1	q. 47, a. 3
		a. 3, qa. 2	q. 47, a. 4
		a. 3, qa. 3	q. 47, a. 5
		a. 4	q. 47, a. 6
d. 30	q. 1	a. 1	q. 51, a. 1
		a. 2	q. 51, a. 2
		a. 3	q. 48, a. 2
d. 31	q. 1	a. 1	q. 49, a. 1

	In IV Sent.		ST Supplement
		a. 2	q. 49, a. 2
		a. 3	q. 49, a. 3
	q. 2	a. 1	q. 49, a. 4
		a. 2	q. 49, a. 5
		a. 3	q. 49, a. 6
d. 32	q. 1	a. 1	q. 64, a. 1
		a. 2, qa. 1	q. 64, a. 2
		a. 3	q. 64, a. 3
		a. 4	q. 64, a. 4
		a. 5, qa. 1	q. 64, a. 5
		a. 5, qa. 2	q. 64, a. 6
		a. 5, qa. 3	q. 64, a. 7
d. 33	q. 1	a. 1	q. 65, a. 1
		a. 2	q. 65, a. 2
		a. 3, qa. 1	q. 65, a. 3
		a. 3, qa. 2	q. 65, a. 4
		a. 3, qa. 3	q. 65, a. 5
	q. 2	a. 1	q. 67, a. 1
		a. 2, qa. 1	q. 67, a. 2
		a. 2, qa. 2	q. 67, a. 3
		a. 2, qa. 3	q. 67, a. 4
		a. 2, qa. 4	q. 67, a. 5
		a. 3, qa. 1	q. 67, a. 6
		a. 3, qa. 2	q. 67, a. 7
d. 34	q. 1	a. 1	q. 50, a. 1
		a. 2	q. 58, a. 1
		a. 3	q. 58, a. 2
		a. 4	q. 58, a. 3
		a. 5	q. 58, a. 4
d. 35	q. 1	a. 1	q. 62, a. 1
		a. 2	q. 62, a. 2
		a. 3	q. 62, a. 3
		a. 4	q. 62, a. 4
		a. 5	q. 62, a. 5
		a. 6	q. 62, a. 6
d. 36	q. 1	a. 1	q. 52, a. 1
		a. 2	q. 52, a. 2
		a. 3	q. 52, a. 3
		a. 4	q. 52, a. 4

In IV Sent.			ST Supplement
		a. 5	q. 58, a. 5
d. 37	q. 1	a. 1	q. 53, a. 3
		a. 2	q. 53, a. 4
	q. 2	a. 1	q. 60, a. 1
		a. 2	q. 60, a. 2
d. 38	q. 1	a. 3, qa. 2	q. 53, a. 1
		a. 3, qa. 3	q. 53, a. 2
d. 39	q. 1	a. 1	q. 59, a. 1
		a. 2	q. 59, a. 2
		a. 3	q. 59, a. 3
		a. 4	q. 59, a. 4
		a. 5	q. 59, a. 5
		a. 6	q. 59, a. 6
d. 40	q. 1	a. 1	q. 54, a. 1
		a. 2	q. 54, a. 2
		a. 3	q. 54, a. 3
		a. 4	q. 54, a. 4
d. 41	q. 1	a. 1, qa. 1	q. 55, a. 1
		a. 1, qa. 2	q. 55, a. 2
		a. 1, qa. 3	q. 55, a. 3
		a. 1, qa. 4	q. 55, a. 4
		a. 1, qa. 5	q. 55, a. 5
		a. 2, qa. 1	q. 55, a. 6
		a. 2, qa. 2	q. 55, a. 7
		a. 2, qa. 3	q. 55, a. 8
		a. 3, qa. 1	q. 68, a. 1
		a. 3, qa. 2	q. 68, a. 2
		a. 3, qa. 3	q. 68, a. 3
		a. 5, qa. 1	q. 55, a. 9
		a. 5, qa. 2	q. 55, a. 10
		a. 5, qa. 3	q. 55, a. 11
d. 42	q. 1	a. 1	q. 56, a. 1
		a. 2	q. 56, a. 2
		a. 3, qa. 1	q. 56, a. 3
		a. 3, qa. 2	q. 56, a. 4
		a. 3, qa. 3	q. 56, a. 5
	q. 2	a. 1	q. 57, a. 1
		a. 2	q. 57, a. 2
		a. 3	q. 57, a. 3

	In IV Sent.		ST Supplement
	q. 3	a. 1	q. 63, a. 1
		a. 2	q. 63, a. 2
d. 43	q. 1	a. 1, qa. 1	q. 75, a. 1
		a. 1, qa. 2	q. 75, a. 2
		a. 1, qa. 3	q. 75, a. 3
		a. 2, qa. 1	q. 76, a. 1
		a. 2, qa. 2	q. 76, a. 2
		a. 2, qa. 3	q. 76, a. 3
		a. 3, qa. 1	q. 77, a. 1
		a. 3, qa. 2	q. 77, a. 2
		a. 3, qa. 4	q. 77, a. 3
		a. 3, qa. 3	q. 77, a. 4
		a. 4, qa. 1	q. 78, a. 1
		a. 4, qa. 2	q. 78, a. 2
		a. 4, qa. 3	q. 78, a. 3
		a. 5, qa. 1	q. 87, a. 1
		a. 5, qa. 2	q. 87, a. 2
		a. 5, qa. 3	q. 87, a. 3
d. 44	q. 1	a. 1, qa. 1	q. 79, a. 1
		a. 1, qa. 2	q. 79, a. 2
		a. 1, qa. 3	q. 79, a. 3
		a. 2, qa. 1	q. 80, a. 1
		a. 2, qa. 2	q. 80, a. 2
		a. 2, qa. 3	q. 80, a. 3
		a. 2, qa. 4	q. 80, a. 4
		a. 2, qa. 5	q. 80, a. 5
		a. 3, qa. 1	q. 81, a. 1
		a. 3, qa. 2	q. 81, a. 2
		a. 3, qa. 3	q. 81, a. 3
		a. 3, qa. 4	q. 81, a. 4
	q. 2	a. 1, qa. 1	q. 82, a. 1
		a. 1, qa. 2	q. 82, a. 2
		a. 1, qa. 3	q. 82, a. 3
		a. 1, qa. 4	q. 82, a. 4
		a. 2, qa. 1	q. 83, a. 1
		a. 2, qa. 2	q. 83, a. 2
		a. 2, qa. 3	q. 83, a. 3
		a. 2, qa. 4	q. 83, a. 4
		a. 2, qa. 5	q. 83, a. 5

In IV Sent.			ST Supplement
		a. 2, qa. 6	q. 83, a. 6
		a. 3, qa. 1	q. 84, a. 1
		a. 3, qa. 2	q. 84, a. 2
		a. 3, qa. 3	q. 84, a. 3
		a. 4, qa. 1	q. 85, a. 1
		a. 4, qa. 2	q. 85, a. 2
		a. 4, qa. 3	q. 85, a. 3
	q. 3	a. 1, qa. 1	q. 86, a. 1
		a. 1, qa. 2	q. 86, a. 2
		a. 1, qa. 3	q. 86, a. 3
		a. 2, qa. 1	q. 97, a. 5
		a. 2, qa. 2	q. 97, a. 6
		a. 2, qa. 3	q. 97, a. 7
		a. 3, qa. 1	q. 70, a. 1
		a. 3, qa. 2	q. 70, a. 2
		a. 3, qa. 3	q. 70, a. 3
d. 45	q. 1	a. 1, qa. 1	q. 69, a. 1
		a. 1, qa. 2	q. 69, a. 2
		a. 1, qa. 3	q. 69, a. 3
		a. 2, qa. 1	q. 69, a. 4
		a. 2, qa. 2	q. 69, a. 5
		a. 2, qa. 3	q. 69, a. 6
		a. 3	q. 69, a. 7
	q. 2	a. 1, qa. 1	q. 71, a. 1
		a. 1, qa. 2	q. 71, a. 2
		a. 1, qa. 3	q. 71, a. 3
		a. 1, qa. 4	q. 71, a. 4
		a. 2, qa. 1	q. 71, a. 5
		a. 2, qa. 2	q. 71, a. 6
		a. 2, qa. 3	q. 71, a. 7
		a. 2, qa. 4	q. 71, a. 8
		a. 3, qa. 1	q. 71, a. 9
		a. 3, qa. 2	q. 71, a. 10
		a. 3, qa. 3	q. 71, a. 11
		a. 4, qa. 1	q. 71, a. 12
		a. 4, qa. 2	q. 71, a. 13
		a. 4, qa. 3	q. 71, a. 14
	q. 3	a. 1	q. 72, a. 1
		a. 2	q. 72, a. 2

In IV Sent.			ST Supplement
		a. 3	q. 72, a. 3
d. 46	q. 1	a. 3	q. 99, a. 1
	q. 2	a. 3, qa. 1	q. 99, a. 2
		a. 3, qa. 2	q. 99, a. 3
		a. 3, qa. 3	q. 99, a. 4
		a. 3, qa. 4	q. 99, a. 5
d. 47	q. 1	a. 1, qa. 1	q. 88, a. 1
		a. 1, qa. 2	q. 88, a. 2
		a. 1, qa. 3	q. 88, a. 3
		a. 1, qa. 4	q. 88, a. 4
		a. 2, qa. 1	q. 89, a. 1
		a. 2, qa. 2	q. 89, a. 2
		a. 2, qa. 3	q. 89, a. 3
		a. 2, qa. 4	q. 89, a. 4
		a. 3, qa. 1	q. 89, a. 5
		a. 3, qa. 2	q. 89, a. 6
		a. 3, qa. 3	q. 89, a. 7
		a. 3, qa. 4	q. 89, a. 8
	q. 2	a. 1, qa. 1	q. 74, a. 1
		a. 1, qa. 2	q. 74, a. 2
		a. 1, qa. 3	q. 74, a. 3
		a. 2, qa. 1	q. 74, a. 4
		a. 2, qa. 2	q. 74, a. 5
		a. 2, qa. 3	q. 74, a. 6
		a. 3, qa. 1	q. 74, a. 7
		a. 3, qa. 2	q. 74, a. 8
		a. 3, qa. 3	q. 74, a. 9
d. 48	q. 1	a. 1	q. 90, a. 1
		a. 2	q. 90, a. 2
		a. 3	q. 90, a. 3
		a. 4, qa. 1	q. 73, a. 1
		a. 4, qa. 2	q. 73, a. 2
		a. 4, qa. 3	q. 73, a. 3
	q. 2	a. 1	q. 91, a. 1
		a. 2	q. 91, a. 2
		a. 3	q. 91, a. 3
		a. 4	q. 91, a. 4
		a. 5	q. 91, a. 5
d. 49	q. 1	a. 4, qa. 1	q. 93, a. 1

In IV Sent.			ST Supplement
		a. 4, qa. 3	q. 93, a. 2
		a. 4, qa. 4	q. 93, a. 3
	q. 2	a. 1	q. 92, a. 1
		a. 2	q. 92, a. 2
		a. 5	q. 92, a. 3
	q. 4	a. 1	q. 95, a. 1
		a. 2	q. 95, a. 2
		a. 3	q. 95, a. 3
		a. 4	q. 95, a. 4
		a. 5, qa. 1	q. 95, a. 5
	q. 5	a. 1	q. 96, a. 1
		a. 2, qa. 1	q. 96, a. 2
		a. 2, qa. 2	q. 96, a. 3
		a. 2, qa. 3	q. 96, a. 4
		a. 3, qa. 1	q. 96, a. 5
		a. 3, qa. 2	q. 96, a. 6
		a. 3, qa. 3	q. 96, a. 7
		a. 4, qa. 1	q. 96, a. 8
		a. 4, qa. 2	q. 96, a. 9
		a. 4, qa. 3	q. 96, a. 10
		a. 5, qa. 1	q. 96, a. 11
		a. 5, qa. 2	q. 96, a. 12
		a. 5, qa. 3	q. 96, a. 13
d. 50	q. 2	a. 1, qa. 1	q. 98, a. 1
		a. 1, qa. 2	q. 98, a. 2
		a. 1, qa. 3	q. 98, a. 3
		a. 1, qa. 4	q. 98, a. 4
		a. 1, qa. 5	q. 98, a. 5
		a. 1, qa. 6	q. 98, a. 6
		a. 2, qa. 1	q. 98, a. 7
		a. 2, qa. 2	q. 98, a. 8
		a. 2, qa. 3	q. 98, a. 9
		a. 3, qa. 1	q. 97, a. 1
		a. 3, qa. 2	q. 97, a. 2
		a. 3, qa. 3	q. 97, a. 3
		a. 3, qa. 4	q. 97, a. 4
		a. 4, qa. 1	q. 94, a. 1
		a. 4, qa. 2	q. 94, a. 2
		a. 4, qa. 3	q. 94, a. 3